Canadian Criminology

Canadian Criminology

Perspectives on Crime and Criminality

Margaret A. Jackson and Curt T. Griffiths
Co-editors

Alison Hatch
Research Assistant

School of Criminology
Simon Fraser University

Harcourt Brace Jovanovich, Canada
Toronto Orlando San Diego London Sydney

Canadian Cataloguing in Publication Data

Main entry under title:

Canadian criminology

Includes bibliographical references.
ISBN 0-7747-3128-1

1. Crime - Canada. 2. Criminals - Canada.
I. Jackson, Margaret, 1942-   . II. Griffiths,
Curt T. (Curt Taylor), 1948-

HV6807.C35 1991   364.971   C90-094858-2

Acquisitions Editor: Heather McWhinney
Developmental Editor: Sandra Peltier
Editorial Co-ordinator: Marcel Chiera
Editorial Assistant: Kerry Gibson
Copy Editor: Beverley Endersby
Interior Design: Q.E.D. Design Associates
Cover Illustration: Elizabeth Carefoot
Typesetting and Assembly: Lithocomp Ltd.
Printing and Binding: John Deyell Company

⊖ This book was printed in Canada on acid-free paper.
  2 3 4 5   95 94 93 92

M.A.J.: To John, for sharing his vision
C.T.G.: To my friend and mentor, Rob Balch

Contributors

Bruce Arnold, University of Toronto
Neil Boyd, Simon Fraser University
Christine Boyle, Dalhousie University
Paul Brantingham, Simon Fraser University
Joan Brockman, Simon Fraser University
Brian Burtch, Simon Fraser University
Colin Campbell, University of Windsor
Ian Coneybeer, Simon Fraser University
Raymond Corrado, Simon Fraser University
Dorothy Chunn, Simon Fraser University
John Ekstedt, Simon Fraser University
Thomas Gabor, University of Ottawa
Shelley Gavigan, Osgoode Hall, York University
William Glackman, Simon Fraser University
Robert M. Gordon, Simon Fraser University
Alison Hatch, Simon Fraser University
John Lowman, Simon Fraser University
Robert Menzies, Simon Fraser University
Judith Osborne, Simon Fraser University
Ted Palys, Simon Fraser University
Colin Yerberry, Simon Fraser University

Preface

The past two decades have witnessed a rapid growth of criminology and criminal justice courses at the college and university levels across Canada. Nevertheless, there is still a paucity of materials that can be utilized by instructors and students in the study of Canadian crime and criminality. This situation has resulted in the widespread use of U.S. and British texts that, while providing the basis for comparative study, often function to confuse rather than to enlighten the Canadian student.

Non-Canadian texts do not consider the impact of Canada's historical events, culture, and socio-political influences on crime and criminality in this country. Most importantly, for the focus of criminology, since Canada's law base and governmental structure differ significantly from those of the United States, much of the material presented in U.S. texts is not directly applicable to the Canadian context. *Canadian Criminology* has been designed to capture some of the spirit of the Canadian criminological enterprise and to serve as a foundation for the further exploration of crime and criminality in Canada.

Historically, the multidisciplinary nature of the field of criminology has been reflected in the contributions by scholars from the fields of sociology, political science, geography, psychology, anthropology, and law. The dominant conceptual frameworks and theoretical explanations of criminality have been developed elsewhere—in Italy, France, Great Britain, and the United States. Canadian criminology, however, still in its infancy, has not yet produced major theoretical breakthroughs in the study of crime. However, the contributors to this text share the view that there is a distinct Canadian criminology— that the *context* within which crime and criminality occur and are studied *is* different from that of other jurisdictions. The unique demographic, cultural, historical, and socio-political attributes of Canada contribute to patterns and types of criminality, as well as to the response to it, that are discernibly different from those of other countries. For example, the incidences of certain categories of offences in Canada differ in interesting ways from those in the United States.

The text has been organized into six parts, each designed to reflect a critical dimension in the study of crime and criminality. Part I provides the backdrop for the Canadian criminological enterprise. Part II offers three case examples of the use of the law in defining criminality in Canada relative to issues of morality. Parts III and IV reflect the two major orientations that have been taken in the study of criminal behaviour—those approaches focussing on the individual offender and those considering the role of socio-political factors in "creating" criminality. Part V considers several emerging areas in criminology and emphasizes the attention that is being focussed on these nontraditional areas of inquiry.

• Part I, "The Framework: History, Law, and Policy in Canada," is designed to provide a background against which crime and criminal behaviour in this country can be studied. The introduction identifies several key concepts that are used by criminologists to study crime. Chapter 1 presents a historical overview of crime and criminal justice in Canada. In Chapter 2, the basic tenets of the Canadian criminal law are outlined. This is followed by a discussion of the policy-making process in the area of criminal justice. The final chapter in Part I is a case study of the amendments to the sexual assault laws in Canada and provides an illustration of the relationship between law and policy and the decisions that are involved in the process of law reform.

• In Part II, the issues surrounding the potential and real limits of criminal law and of crime policy in regulating morality in Canadian society are further illustrated by the examination of three areas of Canadian law—drug use, prostitution, and gambling. Gambling, unlike prostitution and drug use, has been dealt with leniently by Canadian law in recent years. Its revenue-generating potential appears to have transformed the government's perception of its potential *harm* to society.

• Part III begins a discussion of what has been the quintessential question in criminology: "What causes people to commit crime?" Tracing the evolution of the discipline, the early theories that focussed on the biological and psychological attributes of offenders are examined. This approach is easily translated into a criminal-justice system response because offenders are viewed as being in some way ill and in need of treatment. These ideas are explored further in Chapter 8, in a consideration of mental disorder and crime. In Chapter 9, we examine a specific offender group: sex offenders. Despite extensive efforts to create effective treatment strategies for sex offenders, to date such interventions have been largely ineffective. There appears to be a need to examine not only the individual offender, but larger societal factors as well.

• Part IV centres on the role played by societal factors in crime and criminality in Canada. Chapter 10 reviews the major sociological approaches and considers what influence critical criminology has had in changing our focus to an even broader level of analysis. Chapters 11 and 12, which address female criminality and crime among indigenous peoples, and a religious sect—the Doukhobors—reveal how criminal behaviour can be studied from a variety of perspectives. The traditional explanations for criminality among women and minority groups used individual pathology as the key variable: the argument that women and minorities were inherently inferior in some way. However, these theories have largely given way to approaches that focus on socio-structural variables such as low socio-economic status and the lack of political and economic power.

• Part V considers the measurement of crime and the patterns of criminality in Canada. Chapter 13 describes the various methods for studying crime and considers the strengths and weaknesses of our techniques for measuring the incidence of crime. Chapter 14 provides an overview of Canadian crime patterns and trends, as well as comparisons with crime in other countries.

• Part VI, the concluding section of the book, focusses on four types of criminality that have, only recently, become the subject of criminological inquiry. The areas covered are the laws that regulate the professional elite, criminal behaviour by corporations, crimes committed by and against the government, and the nature and extent of illegal behaviour among the general public. These chapters illustrate the point that contemporary criminology has not only broadened its focus to include a wide range of criminal behaviour, but also expanded the search for the causes of crime beyond the individual to the study of lawmaking and the criminal justice system itself.

The contributors to this text have attempted to consider the issues surrounding their particular topics in terms of the Canadian context and to highlight critical conceptual and policy-related matters. It is hoped that you will come to see the intricate interrelationships among the theories of criminality that drive criminological study; the various definitions of crime and law derived from these theories and studies; and the varying perceptions, attitudes, and beliefs held about those definitions that ultimately direct the creation of our criminal-justice policy—all of which is necessarily considered within the unique context of Canadian experience. It is important as well to emphasize here a conscious intent on the part of the editors, that is, to ensure that the text does *not* present itself through one perspective only. As its title indicates, this text represents a compendium of perspectives on crime and society. That is a primary strength of the book. Students of criminology should be aware of and attempt to assimilate varying perspectives and ideologies; such diversity reflects the essence of the discipline and the thinking within the field itself.

As the twentieth century comes to a close, Canadian criminology is emerging from the shadows of its European and American influences. It is our hope, as editors of *Canadian Criminology*, that this text will serve as a positive step toward the development of a distinctive Canadian criminology, and will act as a valuable tool for all students interested in studying crime and criminality in Canada.

Margaret A. Jackson
Curt Taylor Griffiths
Burnaby, British Columbia
1991

Acknowledgments

It was Heather McWhinney, acquisitions editor at HBJ, who developed the idea of this text with us and convinced us that the project was worth doing. Heather's enthusiasm and her high professional standards and commitment to excellence combined to ensure that the project would be completed. Sandra Peltier, who served as editor for the text, deserves much credit for assisting us in seeing it through to completion and in helping us over the inevitable "rough" spots with consistent good humour. A grateful acknowledgment must also go to Alison Hatch, who was unfailingly creative and talented in her research assistance with the text. Without her, this text would not have been completed. Additionally, it all would have been for naught had we not acquired the assistance of Donna Robertson, who, at the last minute, under trying conditions, came to our rescue with her most competent and conscientious work. We are indebted to our colleagues who reviewed the manuscript: Richard V. Ericson, Centre of Criminology, University of Toronto; Christopher Murphy, Dalhousie University; Michael Petrunik, University of Ottawa; and John Winterdyk, Mount Royal College and the University of Calgary. Finally, we must acknowledge the significant role played by the students in the School of Criminology, past and present, in providing the stimulus to produce this book.

Publisher's Note to Instructors and Students

This textbook is a key component of your course. If you are the instructor of this course, you undoubtedly considered a number of texts carefully before choosing this as the one that would work best for your students and you. The authors and publishers of this book spent considerable time and money to ensure its high quality, and we appreciate your recognition of this effort and accomplishment.

If you are a student we are confident that this text will help you to meet the objectives of your course. You will also find it helpful after the course is finished as a valuable addition to your personal library.

As well, please do not forget that photocopying copyright work means the authors lose royalties that are rightfully theirs. This loss will discourage them from writing another edition of this text or other books; doing so would simply not be worth their time and effort. If this happens we all lose—students, instructors, authors, and publishers.

Since we want to hear what you think about this book, please be sure to send us the stamped reply card at the end of the text. This will help us to continue publishing high-quality books for your course.

Contents

The Framework: History, Law, and Policy in Canada

The history of Canada is a particularly colourful one, but one that has unfortunately often been subsumed into a North American context and overshadowed by that of the United States. In Part I, we begin to uncover the uniqueness of Canadian national development and explore how it has affected crime, law, and policy.

Frontier justice, the Royal Canadian Mounted Police (RCMP), native peoples, and our ties to Britain—all have left their mark on Canadian society. Indeed, each of these factors continues to affect not only the day-to-day operations of the criminal-justice system, but the very formation of our underlying assumptions about our national character and social and moral values.

Thus, Part I proceeds from a description of the history of crime in Canada (Chapter 1) to a consideration of the major components of the law transformed through that history, and concludes with an examination of the process of policy making, as it is based upon societal change and law reform within the Canadian context (Chapter 3).

The close relationship between criminal law and criminology is explored in Chapter 2. Paraphrasing Durkheim, an early sociologist concerned with explaining criminality, we can say that, in one sense, crime cannot technically exist without criminal law. The chapter highlights some of the issues in this "legal labelling" of criminality, through a discussion of legislation governing specific types of offences, the various courtroom defences, and, of course, the impact that the Canadian Charter of Rights and Freedoms has upon all criminal-justice functioning.

The role that crime policy has, both in establishing certain behaviours as "criminal" and in providing the means by which governments can respond to those behaviours, is discussed in Chapter 3. A critical question to pose here is: Does it make any difference if there is a policy established to deal with crime—that of young offenders, for example—if there are no accompanying effective procedures established or sufficient resources committed to carrying out the objectives of that policy?

Finally, a case study discussing the legislation dealing with sexual assault in Canada brings together a number of ideas considered in Part I. The case study analyzes the development of law reform in relation to sexual assault and the difficulties that arise from the defining of behaviours as criminal acts.

Introduction: The Criminological Enterprise

Curt T. Griffiths

What Is a Crime?

The Criminal Law

From Community Control to State Law: The Centralization of Authority

Defining Crime and Responding to Criminals: Consensus or Conflict?

Toward a Canadian Criminology

While the study of crime and the search for the causes of **criminality** are centuries old, it is only in the past three decades that the field of **criminology** has emerged in Canada. Criminology is a multidisciplinary field, meaning that it draws upon a variety of subject areas, including law, economics, sociology, psychology, anthropology, political science, history, and geography. Criminologists engage in a wide range of activities that centre on the scientific study of crime and the **criminal-justice system**. Some of these activities are listed in Box 1. While it is by no means exhaustive, this list does provide you with some idea of the range of activities of criminologists and the subject matter of the field of criminology.

The multidisciplinary nature of criminology means that crime and criminality are studied from a variety of perspectives: scholars with training in sociology may focus on the societal context within which the **criminal law** is formulated and applied or on explanations of crime that take into account societal factors such as poverty or social class; psychologists in the field of criminology are often involved in exploring causes of crime that focus on the individual offender; criminologists with training in urban geography and planning may study the spatial distribution of crime in urban and rural areas and the role of environmental design in crime prevention.

In Canada, the first centre for the study of criminology was established at the University of Montreal in 1960. The Centre of Criminology at the University of Toronto opened in 1963, the Department of Criminology at the University of Ottawa in 1967, and the Department (now School) of Criminology at Simon Fraser University in 1974.

Since the early 1970s, criminology courses have been developed in many sociology departments at the university level across the country, and departments of criminol-

Box 1   What Do Criminologists Do?

Criminologists:

- study the causes of crime and the various types of criminal activity, i.e., break-and-enter, sexual assault;
- examine official crime statistics and develop alternative methods to measure accurately the nature and extent of crime and patterns of victimization;
- study the law in historical and contemporary contexts, and the factors that influence the enactment (and repeal) of laws;
- develop theories and conceptual frameworks to understand and explain crime, criminality, and the response to individuals and organizations labelled criminal or deviant;
- investigate the processes by which behaviour comes to be defined as criminal and deviant by society and by criminal-justice agencies;

- assess the effectiveness of the law and other measures of social control on criminal and deviant behaviour;
- study the development of criminal-justice policy and the process of program planning and administration;
- assist in the development of criminal law and policy through consultation;
- examine the response of criminal-justice agencies, including the police, criminal courts, and correctional services, to criminal behaviour and the effectiveness of this response in preventing crime, protecting society, and punishing/treating criminal offenders;
- serve as "expert" witnesses in the criminal-trial process;
- study the involvement of particular groups of Canadians, e.g., indigenous peoples, with the criminal law and in the criminal-justice process.

ogy and criminal justice have been created at many two-year colleges. These graduate and undergraduate programs provide the framework for the study of criminology in contrast to "applied" programs, such as those offered as part of police and correctional training and forensic sciences, which are sponsored by the federal and provincial governments.

Criminologists are found in a variety of settings, including the federal, provincial, and territorial governments; colleges and universities; and private research firms and institutes. They fill teaching, research, policy and planning, and administrative positions. Those with undergraduate and graduate degrees in criminology are employed in a variety of positions in the criminal justice system, including policing, probation and parole, social services, and law.

What Is a Crime?

The discipline of criminology is defined by what it studies—crime. In response to the question "What is a crime?" one might correctly say that "a crime is any act that violates the criminal law." And, to the question "What is a criminal?" an appropriate answer would be that "a criminal is anyone who violates the criminal law." Whereas both of these responses are correct in a strict legal sense, there is much more to understanding crime, the criminal law, and the response to criminal offenders in Canadian society.

A good legal definition of **crime** is provided by the Random House dictionary (1968): a crime is "an action or an instance of negligence that is deemed injurious to the public welfare or morals or to the interests of the state and that is legally prohibited." Two critical ingredients of a crime are the commission of an act, *actus reus*, and the mental intent to commit the act, *mens rea*.

In Chapter 2, we will address in considerable detail the various dimensions of crime as it is defined in the **Criminal Code**. At this juncture, it is sufficient to note that a crime occurs when a person (or persons) (a) commits an act, or fails to act when under a legal responsibility to do so; (b) has the intent, or *mens rea*, to commit the act; (c) does not have a legal defence or justification for committing the act; and (d) violates a provision of the criminal law. Of course, the specific factors surrounding an **alleged** crime may not be so straightforward.

The Criminal Law

In discussing the division of law in Canada, Gall (1983) uses the term "domestic or positive law" to describe those statutes that govern "the affairs of all persons within a sovereign, independent nation." The two basic components of **positive law** are **public law**, which involves the public interest, and **private law**, which regulates those areas in which private disputes arise.

Gall (1983, pp. 10–20) identifies four areas of public law:

(1) constitutional law; (2) administrative law; (3) criminal law; and (4) taxation law. Of these four, criminologists are primarily concerned with the criminal law. To give you an idea of where the criminal law fits in the overall system of Canadian law, we have reproduced Gall's diagram depicting the main divisions of law (see Box 2).

Criminologists speak of crimes that are ***mala in se*** (wrong in themselves)—acts that are perceived as so inherently evil as to constitute a violation of "natural law." The act of murder is often mentioned as a *mala in se* crime, although research by anthropologists has revealed that, in many societies, killing another person is not viewed as criminal.

Box 2 The Functions of the Criminal Law

In Canadian society, the criminal law:

1. acts as a mechanism of social control
2. maintains order
3. defines the parameters of acceptable behaviour
4. reduces the risk of personal retaliation, i.e., vigilantism
5. assists in general and specific deterrence
6. serves as a means of punishment
7. criminalizes behaviour
8. protects group interests
9. prevents crime and serves as a deterrent to criminal behaviour.

These are only some of the more obvious functions of the criminal law. The relative importance that one assigns to each function depends, in large measure, upon the particular perspective on the origins and application of the criminal law that is adopted.

Which functions do you feel the criminal law best fulfils and which functions do you feel the criminal law in Canada has difficulty achieving? Can you identify any other functions of the criminal law?

Source: G.L. Gall, (1983), *The Canadian legal system* (p. 22). Toronto: Carswell.

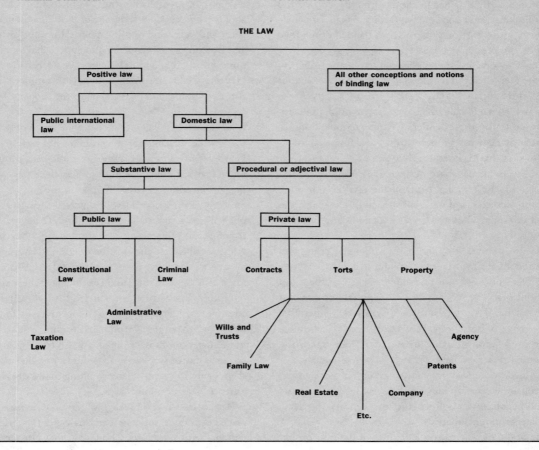

There are also circumstances in our culture where **homicide** is not a crime, such as during a war.

The majority of crimes fall under the category of *mala prohibita* (wrong because prohibited)—acts considered criminal because they violate a criminal statute. As we discuss below, criminologists have expanded their study of the criminal law to include not only specific types of crimes, but the process of lawmaking and enforcement. Why is a certain act considered to be a crime at certain points in history but not in others? The legislated prohibition on the sale and distribution of alcohol, discussed in Chapter 1, is a good example.

One of the main distinctions in law is between criminal law and **civil law**. While certain acts may constitute a violation of both civil and criminal law, and both systems of law involve the imposition of sanctions, there are important differences between the two. When a *crime* is committed, the government assumes the responsibility for prosecuting the alleged offender, and the **criminal courts**, on behalf of the victim and the community, undertake the task of determining the guilt or innocence of the offender. Should the offender be found guilty, the criminal courts impose a **sanction** on the offender, which may involve supervision of him or her in the community or a period of confinement in a correctional facility. Financial penalties may also be part of a **disposition** handed down by a judge in the criminal courts.

In cases involving disputes between two parties, the person who feels wronged by the alleged offender's behaviour brings **suit** in civil court. The wronged party seeks **damages**, which usually involve the payment of monetary compensation by the offender. Divorce actions, disputes over inheritances and property, and breaches of contracts are a few of the more common types of civil actions. It should be noted that some **actions** may involve a violation of both the criminal law and the civil law. In such cases, the victim may proceed with a civil suit against the alleged offender while the government initiates criminal prosecution.

It is also important to distinguish between crime and **deviance**, two categories of behaviour that are often confused. Deviant behaviour encompasses a broad spectrum of actions that may be considered offensive, but may not be against the law. "Deviant" is a term used to describe a wide range of behaviours that depart from social norms or accepted ways of acting in society. There are many behaviours that may be considered deviant, but are not against the law, i.e., eating with your hands in a restaurant, adopting an alternative lifestyle that may involve particular (and peculiar) ways of dressing, or even making inappropriate pronouncements.

One of the more creative depictions of the relationship between crime and deviance has been offered by Hagan (1985). He argues that crime and deviance can be categorized on the basis of the seriousness of the act. There are several measures of seriousness, including (1) the amount of agreement as to the wrongfulness of the act; (2) the severity of the response by society to the act; and (3) the evaluation of the amount of social harm caused by the act.

To illustrate the relationship between crime and deviance, Hagan utilizes a pyramid (see Box 3). At the base of the pyramid are the less serious forms of deviance, which are rarely defined as criminal. These are what Hagan describes as **social diversions** and include such behaviours as individual preferences in dress, language, and lifestyle. At the peak of the pyramid are **consensus crimes**, which are characterized by a high degree of agreement regarding the seriousness of the behaviour and the response to it.

In the middle of the pyramid are what Hagan labels **conflict crimes** and **social deviations**. There is less certainty as to the seriousness of these behaviours and less agreement as to the wrongfulness of the acts; such behaviours generally elicit only a moderate societal response. Conflict crimes, characterized by a high degree of public debate and a lack of societal consensus as to their seriousness, include alcohol and drug offences; the "right-to-life" offences of abortion and euthanasia; public order offences such as mischief and vagrancy, and the political crimes of terrorism and treason. Social deviations include behaviours that are not criminal, but are nevertheless considered disreputable. Hagan includes among these behaviours noncriminal violations of public and financial trust, the subject of Chapter 15.

In Canadian society, there is a wide range of behaviours that, while deviant, are nevertheless not against the law. However, the criminal law is not static and, almost overnight, legislative enactments or judicial decisions can render illegal behaviours that were previously merely deviant. Similarly, the repeal of a law or a judicial decision can render once-illegal activities deviant. Gibbons (1982, p. 9) has attributed this phenomenon to the "elastic boundaries" of crime, noting that "the creation of criminal laws and procedures is a continuing process, as is the decriminalization of some activities resulting from certain laws being expunged."

Criminologists often conduct historical analyses in an attempt to understand: (1) the factors involved in the definition of behaviours as criminal; (2) an increase or decrease in the severity of the criminal law; (3) the response of the criminal justice system; and (4) the factors that influenced the repeal of a criminal law, resulting in the **decriminalization** of certain behaviours.

A key role in criminalizing certain activities is often played by individuals described by Becker (1963) as "moral entrepreneurs"—persons who lead "moral crusades" against

Box 3 Hagan's Pyramid of Deviance

Can you think of examples of behaviour for each level of the pyramid? How might a certain act move from one level of the pyramid to another?

Source: J. Hagan, (1984), *Disreputable pleasures: Crime and deviance in Canada,* 2nd ed. (p.14). Toronto: McGraw-Hill Ryerson.

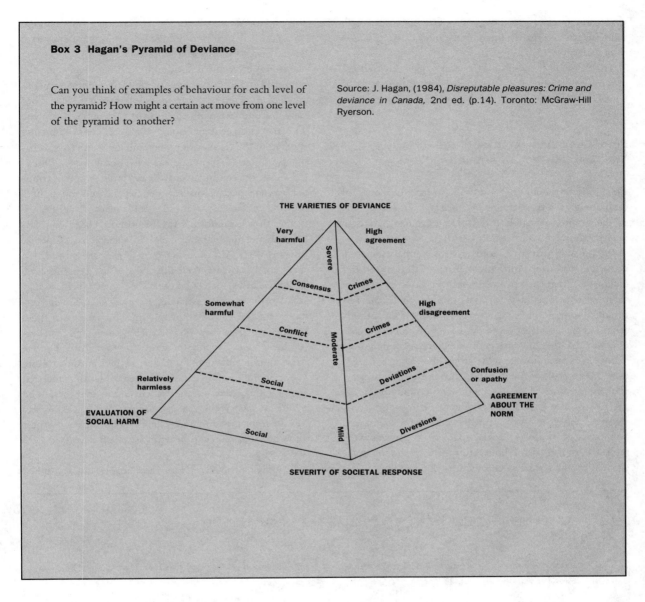

certain groups of people or certain behaviours and bring pressures on legislators to enact criminal statutes. Historically, and recently, moral entrepreneurs have tended to be most active in the area of "victimless" crimes, i.e., drug and alcohol use and prostitution. In Chapter 5, in the discussion of the history of laws against possession or use of some narcotics, we will be introduced to several moral entrepreneurs who had a significant impact on Canadian law and on the response of the criminal justice system. This "legislating of morality" is the subject of Part II of this book.

These shifts in the definition of behaviours as illegal or deviant provide fascinating insights into the dynamic nature of the criminal law. There may be, for example, massive violation of the criminal law and yet the behaviour of the

individuals involved may not be viewed as criminal. A historical example was the massive violation of the prohibition laws against drinking alcoholic beverages by Canadians during and after World War I. An erosion in public support for antidrinking laws, however, ultimately resulted in the repeal of prohibition. By contrast, until recently, driving while impaired by alcohol, while illegal, was not widely viewed as deviant, although changes in attitudes and societal sentiment seem to be altering this view.

A close look at the provisions of the Criminal Code reveals several statutes that are wildly outdated. Del Buono (1985–86, p. 370) has characterized the Criminal Code as "a depository of fossils of social conflicts long since spent" and notes that "to wander through the present *Code* is to stare into the faces of the ghosts of all the social evils thought, at one time, to threaten the very fabric of Canadian society."

The failure of the Criminal Code to remain "up to date" in terms of contemporary attitudes and behaviours is highlighted in Box 4.

From Community Control to State Law: The Centralization of Authority

Obviously, it would not be possible to have criminals (or criminologists) if there was no criminal law. Thus, the study of the origins and applications of the criminal law is of primary concern to criminologists.

In human history, prior to the rise of complex societies, order was maintained through informal social controls. Behaviour was regulated by norms, folkways, and mores, and there were strong in-group pressures to conform. The response to harmful acts generally took the form of personal and group retaliation and was premised on the notion of revenge. Other informal control techniques were gossip, ridicule, and expulsion from the group, the last-named sanction often resulting in the death of the transgressor. A primary attribute of these societies and communities was the lack of any formal agents of control.

As societies evolved and became more complex, however, these informal social control mechanisms were replaced by formal methods of control, including laws, enacted by the state and enforced by designated agencies and officials. Transgressions were no longer responded to on a personal, group, or village basis, but were viewed as harms against society as a whole.

Systems of criminal justice, charged with enforcing the criminal law and responding to offenders, emerged and expanded. As a result, communities and their residents became less and less involved in the process of social control. The increasing centralization of the social control function resulted in the transfer of power and authority to governments and criminal-justice agencies (see Pursley, 1987).

Despite the continued growth and proliferation of criminal laws and criminal-justice agencies and personnel, there is evidence that formal social control methods are less effective than are informal mechanisms in controlling behaviour and maintaining order in society (see Alper & Nichols, 1981). In fact, increasingly it is recognized that there are limits to the effectiveness of the criminal law.

Studies of the deterrent effect of the criminal law suggest the law can serve as a deterrent only when certain conditions are present. First, people must be aware that there are legal sanctions that will be applied if they engage in certain behaviours. Second, there must be certainty of punishment. In fact, certainty of punishment appears to be a more important factor than its severity (see Miller & Anderson, 1986). Third, there is some evidence to suggest that, to be an effective deterrent, the sanction must be applied swiftly when a crime is committed. The issue of deterrence is most often raised in connection with the death penalty debate (see Box 5).

In applying these conditions to Canadian society, it be-

Box 4 Little-known Canadian Laws: Duels, Prize Fights, and Feigned Marriages

Did you know that, in Canada, the Criminal Code defines the following activities as crimes?

- duelling (s. 71)
- engaging in a prize fight (s. 83)
- advertising a reward with no questions asked (s. 143)
- dealing in crime comics (s. 163)
- advertising any means for restoring sexual virility (s. 163)
- possessing a stink bomb (s. 178)
- playing three-card monte or operating a wheel of fortune (s. 206)
- pretending to solemnize a marriage (s. 294)
- procuring a feigned marriage (s. 292)

- selling defective stores to Her Majesty (s. 418)
- pretending to practise witchcraft (s. 365)
- keeping a cock-pit (s. 447)

Many observers have argued that the Criminal Code has not kept up with the changing times, and Parliament has been slow to include sections that sanction activities that may be much more damaging to society. How should decisions be made as to which sections of the Criminal Code are outdated? At what point should a section be repealed? When there is mass violation? When a majority of the general public no longer defines a behaviour as criminal? When politicians decide that a behaviour should no longer be considered criminal?

comes apparent that there may be limitations to the deterrent value of the criminal law. Survey research findings suggest that many Canadians have little or no knowledge about the law and the criminal justice system, and what information citizens do have is gleaned from the mass media and is often distorted or inaccurate (see Daubney, 1988).

Neither is there certainty or swiftness of punishment. Figures produced by the Canadian Centre for Justice Statistics (1988, p. 31) indicate that, in 1987, the clearance (catch) rate for crimes of violence was 75 percent, whereas the clearance rate for property crimes was only 27 percent. Not only do these figures suggest that, at least for property offences, crime does pay, but, more importantly, they indicate that there is no certainty that individuals committing property offences will be caught.

The imposition of punishment if often far from swift.

The Canadian criminal-justice system is premised on an adversarial model that incorporates many elements of **due process**. The response of the system is often slow and deliberate, and months and even years can pass before a determination of guilt or innocence is made and the appeal process exhausted.

Certainly, there remains a great deal that is unknown about the deterrent value of the criminal law, a condition that is reflected in the comment of the Canadian Sentencing Commission (1987, p. 137), following their review of the deterrence literature, that "legal sanctions have an overall deterrent effect which is difficult to evaluate precisely."

The failure of the criminal law to deter people from engaging in criminal behaviour or to protect the public has several consequences, one of which is an increasing fear of crime and feelings of vulnerability among citizens. This

Box 5   The Death Penalty in Canada

Few issues have been debated as emotionally as has the **death penalty**. A gradual decline in executions culminated in the last hanging in Canada, in 1962, and **capital punishment** was officially abolished in 1976. But the debate has continued. Abolitionist arguments include the immorality of state-mandated killing, the risk of executing the innocent, and the fact that the death penalty is imposed disproportionately upon the poor and racial minorities. Retentionists use the just-deserts justification or the retributive, eye-for-an-eye argument. Further, they argue that the homicide rate since the abolition of capital punishment is evidence of the lack of an effective deterrent. Countering this argument is a large body of research that refutes the theory that capital punishment acts as a deterrent.

Isolated attempts to have capital punishment abolished began in 1914 with a series of private members' bills. But it was not until the 1950s that widespread public protests against capital punishment began. The federal cabinet, which reviewed all capital cases, began to increase the number of commutations. The last woman hanged in Canada, Marguerite Pitre, went to her death in 1953. That Wilbert Coffin, who probably was an innocent man, was hanged in 1956 fuelled the controversy (Boyd, 1988). Between 1957 and 1963, the Diefenbaker government commuted 52 of 66 death sentences. Ronald Turpin, convicted of killing a police officer, and Arthur Lucas, also a murderer, were hanged in Toronto's Don Jail in 1962. After the Liberals came to power in 1963, all death sentences were commuted.

Beginning in 1961, a series of amendments gradually reduced the category of capital murder to include only the killing of a prison guard or police officer. In 1976, fourteen years after the hanging of Turpin and Lucas, capital punishment was abolished after a free vote in Parliament, by a margin of six votes. To gain support for the bill, two "compromises" were allowed (Boyd, 1988). The death sentence can be imposed upon conviction of treason, under the **National Defence Act**, and a prison term of 25 years without parole is mandatory for **first-degree murder**.

In the three decades since the last hanging in Canada, the debate between abolitionists and retentionists has rarely subsided. A key point, yet unresolved, is the degree to which the murder rate has changed. While the number of homicides has increased worldwide since the 1960s, many factors cloud our ability to attribute this rise directly to the abolition of capital punishment, in Canada (Boyd, 1988) or in other countries (Archer, & Gartner, 1984).

But the cause-and-effect issue is not the only concern for many. During the 1980s, the Canadian public supported stiffer punishments and increased protection from criminals. Prime Minister Brian Mulroney begrudgingly fulfilled a campaign promise when he permitted a free vote in the House of Commons in June 1987 on the reinstatement of capital punishment. With public-opinion polls showing that a majority of Canadians favoured a return to the noose, a delicate issue for some Members of Parliament was whether they should follow their own consciences or the wishes of their constituents. In the end, the vote was 148 to 127 not to restore the death penalty. While the debate will continue, the federal government has side-stepped this contentious issue for the time being.

consequence may, in turn, lead to situations in which people take the law into their own hands—a form of modern-day **vigilantism**. Box 6 presents a recent Canadian case involving a businessman who had been victimized on several occasions and finally decided to retaliate, with force, against two men who robbed his drugstore.

To counter the long-standing approach of "pass a law, fix the problem," there has been in recent years an increased effort on the part of governments and criminal-justice agencies to involve the general public in the prevention and control of crime. This has resulted in the development of alternative, community-based mechanisms of crime prevention and dispute resolution. Many believe that such mechanisms would be more relevant to the needs of communities and victims, as well as more effective in preventing and deterring criminal behaviour (see Griffiths, 1988).

In recent years, there has been an increased focus on the development of community-based alternatives to the formal justice process, including community accountability panels, mediation boards, and other structures that involve area residents in resolving disputes and problems in the community.

This increased community involvement is evident in the mounting "war" on drugs, as urban residents in the United States and Canada reclaim their neighbourhoods by driving out drug pushers, closing down "crack" houses, and implementing community improvement plans.

In the northern and rural areas of Canada, indigenous peoples are working to create community-based programs and services, many of them premised on customary law or traditional mechanisms of social control, to more effectively address the needs of offenders, residents, and the community. As we will see in Chapter 12, such alternatives may be more effective than the services delivered by nonresident criminal-justice personnel.

Defining Crime and Responding to Criminals: Consensus or Conflict?

In Canada, there are two primary sources of the criminal law: legislation and judicial decisions (see Verdun-Jones, 1989). However, merely denoting the sources of the criminal law tells us very little about the *process* of lawmaking or the factors that influence the creation of the criminal law.

A variety of perspectives have been utilized by scholars studying the phenomenon of crime and the societal response to it. Historically, as we will see in Chapter 7, researchers have focussed on the individual offender and have attempted to determine what factors distinguish criminals from noncriminals. Until the 1960s, little attention was given to the societal context within which crime and the response to it occurred.

The nearly exclusive focus on the criminal offender, par-

Box 6   The Calgary Druggist: Hero or Criminal?

On November 8, 1986, two armed men entered a Calgary drugstore, wearing masks. The store was occupied by the owner, Steven Kesler; his wife, Mary; and their two daughters. One of the robbers, Stephen Flemming, chased Mary Kesler to the rear of the store and ordered her to fill a bag with narcotics. The other robber, Timothy Smith, remained at the front of the store and demanded that Steven Kesler empty the cash register.

After handing over the money, Kesler pulled a shotgun out from under the counter. Smith fled the store but Kesler ran after him, shouting at him to stop. When Smith kept running, Kesler shot him in the back.

Kesler then returned to the store and exchanged gunfire with the remaining robber, wounding him slightly. When Flemming's gun jammed, the robber removed his mask, and Kesler recognized him as the man who had robbed the store seven months earlier. In fact, Kesler had testified against Flemming less than three weeks prior to this robbery attempt. Kesler began to hit Flemming with the shotgun and pursued him as he fled the store, continuing to hit him as he got into his car. At this point, the police arrived and stopped the fight.

Smith succumbed to his injuries several hours later in the hospital, and Kesler was charged with second-degree murder. He pleaded not guilty, even refusing a **plea bargain** that would have reduced the charge to **manslaughter**. At trial, before a jury, Kesler's defence was that he had been afraid for the safety of his family and that he had intended to shoot Smith in the legs, not kill him. The Crown, however, tried to prove that Kesler had been so affected by a series of previous robberies that he had vowed to kill the next person who tried to rob his store. The jury returned with a "not guilty" verdict, apparently believing that Kesler had felt that he and/or his family had been placed in a life-threatening situation.

If you had been a member of the jury, how would you have voted? Why?

ticularly during the early years of criminological research, overshadowed the process by which behaviours and individuals came to be defined as criminal. Over the past two decades, however, attention has increasingly shifted to the process by which laws are formulated and applied and to the activities of legislators, special-interest groups, and criminal-justice decision makers.

Two approaches have been used to explain the processes involved in the definition of crime, the consequences of crime for society, and the etiology (causes) of criminal behaviour: the **consensus** or functionalist **approach** and the **conflict approach**.

Criminologists adopting the consensus/functionalist perspective contend that the criminal law reflects societal consensus and shared values. Conflict theorists contend that the criminal law is formulated and applied by the more economically powerful groups in society to maintain their control and to protect their interests.

To the consensus theorist, law represents the shared values of society; through the application of laws, a society reaffirms the acceptable boundaries of behaviour and maintains social cohesion. To the conflict theorist, power plays a role in the formulation and application of the criminal law; certain groups will be able to enshrine and protect their interests via the criminal law and the system of criminal justice. The "politicization" of the criminal law renders less powerful groups more vulnerable to the law and the criminal justice process.

Box 7 provides a summary of the consensus and conflict approaches to the definition of crime, the consequences of crime for society, and the etiology (cause) of criminal behaviour.

As you will see in Chapter 7, early exploration of the causes of crime centred on individuals convicted of the "traditional" crimes of burglary, larceny, and homicide. Criminal behaviour was viewed as a consequence of a malfunction of the individual offender. Only since the 1960s has the criminal activity of business organizations, government agencies, and professional elites received attention from criminologists.

Utilizing the conflict approach, Canadian and American scholars have documented the role of the economic, social, and political milieus in which the law is created and applied (see Quinney, 1974; Chambliss & Seidman, 1971; Taylor, Walton, & Young, 1973, 1975). Recent years have witnessed an increased amount of research and writing from the conflict perspective in Canada (see McLean, 1986; Ratner & McMullan, 1987; Taylor, 1983).

Scholars conducting research from the conflict perspective ask such questions as:

- Why is it that an individual who robs a 7-Eleven store

for less than $100 often receives a much harsher sentence than does a large company that dumps toxic waste or pollutes the air and causes acid rain?

- Why is it that the "crimes" committed by corporations, such as overpricing goods, illegally disposing of PCBs, or allowing hazardous conditions that kill or injure employees to exist in the work place, are most often dealt with civilly, and involve imposing fines, rather than under the criminal law?

- Why is it that Canadian correctional institutions are populated by large numbers of indigenous peoples (Native Indians, Métis, and Inuit) and by persons with low levels of education and skills, among whom high rates of alcohol and drug abuse, and personal backgrounds involving dysfunctional families frequently occur? Is it that these persons are more criminal than others in society?

- What is the role of pressure groups in influencing the enactment of criminal legislation or in decriminalizing behaviour?

As part of this shift in emphasis to the conflict perspective, scholars have focussed on "nontraditional" types of criminal activity, including crimes committed by professional elites, organizational crime, and political terrorists. The results of these inquiries have indicated that these crimes may do far more damage to individual citizens and to society in general than do the more "traditional" types of crime. These "nontraditional" types of crime, and criminologists' shift of focus to them, are discussed in Part VI of this book.

Rather than viewing the consensus and conflict approaches as polar opposites, it is perhaps useful to view them as at least partially complementary. Research studies have revealed that there are a large number of behaviours, particularly offences against the person, resulting in serious injury, that are considered by the majority of the population to be serious and deserving of severe sanctions.

If survey findings from the United States and other countries are correct and can be generalized from, one would expect to find a considerable degree of consensus among Canadians on the seriousness of a range of specific types of crimes, e.g., robbery and sexual assault. In these instances, the criminal law is reflective of a societal consensus and shared community values. For many other types of behaviour, however, such a consensus does not exist, particularly in a pluralistic society such as Canada's.

The highly vocal and often bitter debates in Canada over the issues of abortion, prostitution, and homosexuality are illustrative of the conflict over the extent to which the criminal law should be invoked (or revoked) to regulate behaviour. This discord creates an environment in which

Box 7 Crime and the Criminal Law: Consensus or Conflict?

Definition of Crime

Consensus or Functionalist Hypothesis

1. Acts are defined as criminal because they offend the moral beliefs of the members of the society.

2. Those who violate the criminal law will be punished according to the prevailing customs of the society.

3. Persons are labeled criminal because their behavior goes beyond the tolerance limits of the community.

4. The lower classes are more likely to be arrested for and convicted of crime because they commit more crimes.

5. As societies become more specialized in the division of labor, more and more laws will become restitutive rather than repressive (penal).

Conflict Hypothesis

1. Acts are defined as criminal because it is in the interests of the ruling class to so define them.

2. Members of the ruling class will be able to violate the laws with impunity, whereas members of the subject classes will be punished.

3. Persons are labeled criminal because it is in the interests of the ruling class to so label them, whether or not the behavior would be tolerated by "the society" at large.

4. The lower classes are more likely to be labeled criminal because the bourgeoisie's control of the state protects themselves from such stigmatization.

5. As capitalist societies industrialize and the gap between the bourgeoisie and the proletariat widens, penal law will expand in an effort to coerce the proletariat into submission.

Consequences of Crime for Society

Consensus or Functionalist Hypothesis

1. Crime establishes the limits of the community's tolerance of deviant behavior and increases moral solidarity among the members of the community.

2. Crime necessitates the expenditure of energy and resources to eradicate it and is thus an economic drain on the society.

3. Crime offends the conscience of everyone in the community, thus creating a tighter bond among them.

4. Crime makes people aware of the interests they have in common.

5. Crime is a real problem that all communities must cope with in order to survive.

Conflict Hypothesis

1. Crime enables the ruling class to create false consciousness among the ruled by making them think their own interests and those of the ruling class are identical.

2. Crime reduces surplus labor by creating employment not only for the criminals but for law enforcers, locksmiths, welfare workers, professors of criminology, and other people who benefit from the existence of crime.

3. Crime diverts the lower classes' attention from the exploitation they experience toward other members of their own class, rather than toward the capitalist or economic system.

4. Defining people as criminal permits greater control of the proletariat.

5. Crime is a reality that exists only as it is created by those in the society whose interests are served by its presence.

Box 7 *(Continued)*

Etiology of Criminal Behavior

Consensus or Functionalist Hypothesis	Conflict Hypothesis
1. Every society has a set of agreed-upon customs (rules, norms, values) that most members internalize. Criminal behavior results from the fact that some members get socialized into criminal behavior.	Criminals and noncriminal behavior stem from people acting in ways that are compatible with their class position. Crime is a reaction to the life conditions of a person's social class.
2. Criminal acts are more frequent among lower classes because the agencies of socialization (especially the family but also the neighborhood, schools, other adult and peer groups) are less likely to work effectively—that is, in ways that lead to the internalization of non-criminal norms and behaviors.	Criminal acts are concentrated in the lower classes because the ruling class can see to it that only acts that grow out of lower-class life are defined as criminal.
3. The lower classes are more likely to be arrested because they commit more crimes.	The lower classes are more likely to be arrested and will then be labeled criminals because the bourgeoisie controls those who manage the law enforcement agencies.
4. Crime is a constant in societies. All societies need and produce crime.	Crime varies from society to society depending on the political and economic structure of society.
5. Socialist and capitalist societies should have the same amounts of crime if they have comparable rates of industrialization and bureaucratization.	Socialist societies should have much lower rates of crime because the less intense class struggle should reduce the forces leading to and the functions of crime.

Source: W. Chambliss, (1976), Functional and conflict theories of crime: The heritage of Emile Durkheim and Karl Marx. In W.J. Chambliss & M. Mankoff (Eds.), *Whose law? What order? A conflict approach to criminology* (pp. 7–9). New York: Wiley.

different interest groups compete with one another in an attempt to have their views adopted as to whether certain behaviours should be either criminalized or decriminalized. In this ongoing "tug-of-war," certain groups will have the power and influence to impact on lawmakers, legislation, and law enforcers. Friedland (1984), for example, has studied the influence of pressure groups on gun control laws in Canada. Mothers Against Drinking Drivers (MADD) is another group that has been very influential in changing both public opinion and laws regarding impaired driving. We will examine this issue in Chapter 3.

Toward a Canadian Criminology

A basic premise of this text is that the historical, social, political, cultural, and geographical attributes of Canada have played a pivotal role in determining both the nature and the extent of criminality, as well as the response to crime. A major objective of this text is to begin the process of defining a Canadian criminology and to distinguish this endeavour from the criminological enterprise in other jurisdictions, most notably the United States.

Following are several key points that can guide an

examination of crime and criminality in Canada and assist in defining, more clearly, a Canadian criminology.

Canada and the United States: The Beaver Meets the Eagle

While there has been a veritable explosion of research and scholarly writing on all aspects of Canadian law, crime and criminality, and the criminal-justice system over the past decade, there is still a considerable amount of work to be done. It is unclear, for example, whether theories of crime developed in other jurisdictions are valid within the Canadian context.

Internationally, the search for the causes of crime continues and, it could be argued, we are no farther along in our quest for an understanding of the reasons why people engage in criminal activity than were the early investigators of decades ago. The factors that precipitate and perpetuate criminal behaviour appear to be as varied as the individuals who become involved in criminal behaviour.

It is often difficult to ascertain—even on an individual level—the relative contribution of rationality and choice in the behaviour and the role played by deterministic factors—biological, psychological, and environmental—that are beyond the individual's control. Conflict theorists would argue, however, that the political systems in Canada and the United States operate in much the same way, with the criminal law serving to criminalize the behaviour of certain groups, while protecting the interests of others.

In both countries, the criminal-justice systems are straining under the weight of record numbers of offenders, increases in crime rates and prison populations, and soaring costs. The criminal-justice systems in both the United States and Canada have been characterized as being marked by an increasing centralization of authority for responding to crime—away from citizens and communities to formal agencies of control. Concurrent with this finding has been that noted by a rising chorus of detractors who have documented the apparent ineffectiveness of the criminal law and its sanctions in preventing and responding to crime.

With the exception of an occasional pause, as a result of changing demographics or wars, crime rates in the two countries continue to climb (the rates of violent crime have accelerated) and the prison populations have mushroomed. Attempts to increase the effectiveness of the criminal-justice system by recruiting citizens into the crime-prevention effort and to supervise offenders on release has proved a difficult task (Rosenbaum, 1987; Duffee, 1984). At the same time, crime victims are seeking more programs and services as well as direct input into the criminal-justice decision-making process (see Rubel, 1986).

It is difficult for both Canadian scholars and practition-

ers to determine the lines of convergence and divergence with our southern neighbours, even though the cultural/ geographical/political context in which the law is formulated and the response to criminality takes place are demonstrably dissimilar. A listing of some of the socio-political, cultural, and geographical differences between the two jurisdictions provides a foundation for understanding crime and criminality in the two countries (see Box 8).

The Historical Context

It is an oft-repeated maxim that we cannot hope to understand the present if we do not understand our past. Canadians have been slow to explore their history, which has hindered the development of an understanding of the evolution of the criminal law, the patterns of crime in early Canada, and the changing response to various types of criminal activity.

This outlook has led to the depiction of Canada as the "peaceable kingdom," particularly in relation to our southern neighbour. Such a characterization has fostered many myths and misconceptions about crime and criminality in Canada. Indeed, as the materials presented throughout this text illustrate, crime and criminality in Canada have distinctive and unique histories, replete with fascinating personalities, unlikely heroes, courageous acts, and shameful behaviour on the part of individuals and groups on both sides of the law.

Dirty Harry and "L.A. Law": Too Much American TV?

There is perhaps no one factor that has hindered the development of Canadian criminology and influenced Canadian's perceptions of crime and criminality as much as the treatment of these subjects by the U.S. media. Canadian research has revealed that the public consistently overestimates both the extent and the seriousness of crime and that they do so in large measure because of the influence of media images. In a survey conducted by Brillon et al. (1984), for example, nearly 75 percent of the respondents stated that violent crimes comprised 30 percent of the offences committed in this country. Police statistics indicate that only about 5.8 percent of the crimes reported to the police involve violence (see Daubney, 1988).

Canadians are bombarded with images of crime, particularly violent crime involving guns, from the United States and, as a result, the distinguishing attributes of crime and criminality in Canada have tended to be obscured (Doob & Roberts, 1982). With a few exceptions (most notably the bank-robbery rate in Montreal, which is several times

Box 8 Canada and the United States: So Close, and Yet So Far Away

While we share the longest unguarded border in the world, Canada and the United States have numerous attributes that distinguish each from the other. These include:

	United States	Canada
Population	243.8 million	25.9 million
Land Area	9 384 658 km^2	9 976 139 km^2
Languages	English	English/French
Visible Minorities	African-Americans/Hispanic	East Indians/Asians/Caribbean
Indigenous Peoples	Native Americans/Alaska Native/Alaska Inuit	Canadian Indian/Métis/Inuit
Government	Executive/Bicameral	Parliamentary/Constitutional Monarchy
Basis of Government	U.S. Constitution/Bill of Rights	Constitution Act/Charter of Rights and Freedoms
Criminal Law	State Criminal Statutes/Federal Criminal Statutes (states have authority to enact criminal codes)	National Criminal Code
Justice Officials	County sheriffs/city and county prosecutors/state judges—all elected	appointment by government
Policing	municipal/county/state/federal	municipal/provincial/federal
Sentencing	indeterminate/determinate (varies from state to state)	indefinite
Corrections	federal/state (jurisdiction determined by code violated)	federal/provincial (jurisdiction determined by length of sentence)

How do you think each of these attributes might influence the nature and extent of crime and the response to criminal behaviour? Can you think of other differences between the two countries that might have an influence?

---

that of many U.S. cities), the per-capita crime rate in Canada is much lower than that of the United States, particularly for violent crimes. While the city of Detroit records a "murder a day" annually, Canadian cities evidence far fewer violent crimes. A major reason for this discrepancy is the pervasiveness of guns in the United States in contrast to the strict gun-control laws in Canada. In Canada, the highest rates of violent crime occur in northern and

rural areas of the country, rather than in urban centres.

The preponderance of U.S. televisions shows depicting the police, lawyers, and courtroom drama has created a situation in which many Canadians know more about the U.S. justice system than about the Canadian system. Certainly, the average Canadian viewer could recite the *Miranda* warning that must be given to all criminal suspects by the police in the United States prior to arrest ("You have the right to remain silent. . . . You have the right to a lawyer. . . . Anything you say can and will be used against you in a court of law. . . .") even though not until the enactment of the Canadian **Charter of Rights and Freedoms** in 1984 was a similar right extended to Canadian suspects.

Canadian viewers of American television are also presented with images of county sheriffs (elected policing officials who have jurisdiction over areas outside of incorporated cities), state troopers and elected city and county district attorneys.

The Demographic Factor

The geography of Canada (a large and diverse land area, sparsely populated) had a major impact on the historical development of the country, the patterns of crime in early days, and the manner in which the criminal law was created and applied. This influence continues to the present day.

The need to secure control over a large land area and to prevent annexation of key parcels by the United States contributed to the development of a strong centralized government and the expansion of the RCMP from a small federal police force charged with guarding federal government buildings to a major policing organization with municipal, provincial, and federal responsibilities.

Today, the demographics of Canada continue to influence crime and criminality. Most Canadians reside in urban areas close to the Canada/U.S. border. However, the majority of indigenous peoples (Native Indian, Métis, and Inuit) live in the rural and northern areas of the country, much of which is accessible only by air or by sea. The northern areas, in particular, experience high rates of Criminal Code offences in comparison with the southern, more urban areas. In 1987, for example, the Yukon had a crime rate of 22 648 per 100 000 and the Northwest Territories a rate of 22 199 per 100 000 as compared with a rate of 13 851 Criminal Code offences in British Columbia, the highest rate among the provinces (Canadian Centre for Justice Statistics, 1988, p. 30).

The violent-crime rate in the Canadian North is even more pronounced: in 1987, the Yukon reported a rate of 3184 violent crime offences per 100 000 population and the Northwest Territories reported a rate of 4410 per 100 000. The violent-crime rate in British Columbia (the highest among the provinces) was 1272 per 100 000 (Canadian Centre for Justice Statistics, 1988, p. 33).

The southern focus of most Canadians has served to render invisible the massive social problems that exist in rural and northern areas of the country and the high rates of conflict with the law experienced by Canada's indigenous peoples. And geography has presented unique challenges in the implementation of the national Criminal Code,

which, at least in principle, is to apply equally to the small fishing village in Nova Scotia, the Inuit settlement near the Arctic Circle, and the high-density urban area.

The Canadian Cultural Mosaic

The cultural mosaic that comprises Canada has played a significant role historically, and recently, in national patterns of crime and response to criminality. In our discussion of the political crime of terrorism in Chapter 17, it is noted that Canada is being used as a staging ground for acts of terrorism by nationalist groups. In the popular press, the United States has often been depicted as a "melting pot" where immigrants from a variety of countries and cultures are absorbed into American culture. Canada, by contrast, has touted itself as a "cultural mosaic," and successive Canadian federal governments have encouraged immigration, particularly from Commonwealth countries.

Canadian society, however, has witnessed a considerable amount of conflict surrounding indigenous and immigrant groups throughout its history. In Chapter 12, we will see the effects of the imposition of the Queen's law on the Indian, Métis, and Inuit peoples as part of the process of colonization. The treatment of the Doukhobor people in British Columbia is an illustration of what happens when provincial and federal governments attempt to enforce the assimilation of the members of a religious minority.

And so, while Canada's cultural diversity has had a significant impact on its history and development, it could be argued that, in the formulation and application of the criminal law, the federal, provincial, and territorial governments have given little consideration to this diversity. Such a view lends support to the conflict perspective and sensitizes us to the importance of social class, socio-economic status, and political power, particularly in majority/minority relations.

The Nature of Crime

In chapters 7 and 10, there are extensive discussions of the search for the causes of crime, a quest that continues to the present. You will see that a variety of biogenetic, psychological, and sociological explanations have been offered by a long line of researchers.

One of the underlying themes of many of these explanations, from ancient times to the present, is the issue of "free will versus determinism"—whether criminal behaviour is the consequence of rational choice by human beings, or whether such behaviour is determined by factors beyond the control of the individual. Of course, scholars adopting the conflict perspective of crime would argue that the exclusive focus on the individual offender obscures the political process by which certain acts and individuals are defined as criminal and that the debate over whether individuals commit crime as a consequence of free will or some deterministic factor is less important.

Several attributes of crime can guide our study in criminology; these attributes provide a backdrop for our discussion throughout the text.

1. Criminality is not inherent in any act; rather, an act must be defined as criminal, and this is generally done through the criminal law.
2. Who and what are criminal change over time, as society changes. Cultural, economic, and socio-political factors influence what acts are defined as criminal at any one time in history.
3. While there is consensus among a large percentage of the population that certain types of behaviour are inherently wrong, there is less agreement on the sanctions that should be imposed on such behaviour. Dissensus is particularly widespread in relation to non-violent offences and those traditionally referred to as "victimless" crimes.
4. Canadian criminal law and the criminal-justice process have tended to focus on certain types of crime and on certain types of offenders (i.e., the more traditional offences of break-and-enter and robbery), to the exclusion of offences committed by corporations and the professional elite.
5. The unique historical, socio-political, and cultural attributes of Canadian society have had a significant impact on the formulation and application of the criminal law, both historically and recently, and provide the basis for the development of a Canadian criminology.

Discussion Question

1. As you continue throughout the text, you should be considering the question posed earlier in the introductory section. That is, why could it be said that crime and criminality are not 'absolute' but rather 'relative'?

References

Alper, B.S., & Nichols, L.T. (1981). *Beyond the courtroom: Programs in community justice and conflict resolution*. Lexington, MA: Lexington.

Archer, D., & Gartner, R. (1984). *Violence and crime in cross-national perspective*. New Haven: Yale University Press.

Becker, H. (1963). *Outsiders: Studies in the sociology of deviance*. New York: Free Press.

Boyd, N. (1988). *The last dance: Murder in Canada*. Scarborough, ON: Prentice-Hall.

Brillon Y., C. Louis-Guérin, and M.-C. Lamarche. (1984). *Attitudes of the Canadian Public Toward Crime Policies*. Montreal: International Centre of Comparative Criminology, University of Montreal.

Canadian Centre for Justice Statistics. (1988). *Canadian crime statistics, 1987*. Ottawa: Supply & Services Canada.

Canadian Sentencing Commission. (1987). *Sentencing reform: A Canadian approach*. Ottawa: Supply & Services Canada.

Chambliss, W. (1976). Functional and conflict theories of crime: The heritage of Emile Durkheim and Karl Marx. In W.J. Chambliss & M. Mankoff (Eds.), *Whose law? What order? A conflict approach to criminology* (pp. 1–28). New York: Wiley.

Chambliss, W., & Seidman, R. (1971). *Law, order and power*. Reading, MA: Addison-Wesley.

Daubney, D. (Chairman). (1988). *Report of the Standing Committee of Justice and Solicitor General on its review of sentencing, conditional release and related aspects of corrections*. Ottawa: Supply & Services Canada.

Del Buono, V.M. (1985–86). Toward a new Criminal Code for Canada. *Criminal Law Quarterly, 28*, 370–89.

Doob, A.N., & Roberts, J.V. (1982). Crime: some views of the Canadian public. Unpublished paper. Toronto: Centre of Criminology, University of Toronto.

Duffee, D.E. (1984). The limits of citizen involvement in correctional programming. *The Prison Journal, 64*, 56–76.

Friedland, M. (1984). *A century of criminal justice: Perspectives on the development of Canadian law*. Toronto: Carswell.

Gall, G.L. (1983). *The Canadian legal system*. Toronto: Carswell.

Gibbons, D.C. (1982). *Society, crime, and criminal behaviour*. Englewood Cliffs, NJ: Prentice-Hall.

Griffiths, C.T. (1988). Community-based corrections for young offenders: Proposal for a "localized" corrections. *International Journal of Comparative and Applied Criminal Justice, 12,* 219–28.

Hagan, J. (1984). *Disreputable pleasures: Crime and deviance in Canada* (2nd ed.). Toronto: McGraw-Hill Ryerson.

Hagan, J. (1985). *Modern criminology: Crime, criminal behavior and its control.* New York: McGraw-Hill.

MacLean, B.D. (1986). *The political economy of crime: Readings for a critical criminology.* Scarborough, ON: Prentice-Hall.

Miller, J.L., & Anderson, A.B. (1986). Updating the deterrence doctrine. *Journal of Criminal Law and Criminology, 77,* 418–38.

Pursley, R.D. (1987). *Introduction to criminal justice* (4th ed.). New York: Macmillan.

Quinney, R. (1974). *Critique of legal order.* Boston: Little, Brown.

Ratner, R.S., & McMullan, J.L. (1987). *State control: Criminal justice politics in Canada.* Vancouver: University of British Columbia Press.

Rosenbaum, D.P. (1987). The theory and research behind neighbourhood watch: Is it a sound fear and crime prevention strategy? *Crime and Delinquency, 33,* 103–34.

Rubel, H.C. (1986). Victim participation in sentencing proceedings. *Criminal Law Quarterly, 28,* 226–50.

Taylor I. (1983). *Crime, capitalism and community: Three essays in socialist criminology.* Toronto: Butterworths.

Taylor, I., Walton, P., & Young, J. (1973). *The new criminology: For a theory of social deviance.* London: Routledge & Kegan Paul.

Taylor, I., Walton, P., & Young, J. (1975). *Critical criminology.* London: Routledge & Kegan Paul.

Verdun-Jones, S.N. (1989). *Canadian criminal law: Issues, cases and questions.* Toronto: HBJ.

1 Historical Legacies in Canadian Criminal Law and Justice

Alison J. Hatch

The boy Allison is of a low craniological type. The skull has a pinched, constricted aspect. The forehead slopes sharply back from the eyebrows. The skull slopes sharply towards the crown from each ear. The back of the skull comes to a sort of truncated mound at the top of the head. Below that there is no cranial development at all. There is almost a perpendicular surface between the crown and the nape of the neck. (Globe and Mail, 1897)

Seventeen-year-old farm hand James Allison, described above, killed his employer's wife, near present-day Cambridge, Ontario. During his trial, the prosecution alleged that Allison shot Emma Orr after she shunned his sexual advances; then, to conceal his crime, he buried her body in the corn patch and told her husband she had run off with a salesman.

John Wilson Murray, the detective who solved the case, was compelled to describe Allison as having the "features of a frog" (1904, p. 197). That Murray considered Allison's peculiar physical characteristics important is an indication of his awareness of the work of European physical anthropologists, such as Cesare Lombroso of Italy, who claimed (1876) that criminals were distinguished by certain physical traits, such as the shape and size of the skull. In fact, Murray noted that Allison's head was very similar to that of a notorious French lust murderer and that he resembled many of the criminals pictured in an authoritative new work by a noted British criminologist (Ellis, 1895). Perhaps it was his observance of these characteristics that led Murray to investigate Allison so tirelessly, even though, at first, the farm hand was not considered a suspect. The evidence Murray accumulated was circumstantial, but Radclive, an infamous executioner, applied for the job even before the jury returned a verdict (Campbell, 1970). James Allison was the first person convicted of murder in Waterloo County, and he was hanged in Berlin (now Kitchener) in February 1898.

As this story illustrates, the Canadian **criminal justice system** has long been influenced by international research and practice. In Chapter 7, we will discuss the theories of crime causation advanced by Lombroso and his contemporaries in the nineteenth century. It was during this time that criminology emerged as a distinct discipline, and any review of criminology in Canada must include some consideration of the influence of these European events. But, in the eighteenth and nineteenth centuries, the ideas of criminologists and penal reformers in England and on the Continent were adapted to fit the unique contingencies of the burgeoning colonies. Thus, the systems that evolved to deal with transported convicts in Australia and outlaws on the American frontier were very different in character, even though they shared common origins.

Similarly, the geographic, economic, political, and cultural attributes of early Canada have served, in large measure, to shape our unique criminal justice system. Canada was initially colonized to serve as a source of natural resources for several European nations. The earliest vestiges of a criminal justice system were, therefore, variants of those in Europe, which were themselves undergoing significant reforms at the time. But direct translation of European practices to this continent proved difficult. The sheer size of Canada and its sequential, westward settlement necessitated a system of **frontier justice**, but that system was governed by a distant authority and administered in vast and remote areas. Initially, prosecutions and the execution of sentence were carried out in Europe; however, by the time the West was opening up, defendants were being taken to the more established parts of Canada for trial. Thus, law enforcement gradually spread west, becoming increasingly sophisticated and professionalized.

The system of crime control that emerged during this time has shaped in many ways our current responses to crime. Many nineteenth-century laws are still in force, but even more significant legacies remain. The most important is the constitutional division of powers agreed to at Confederation that stipulates the jurisdictions of the federal and provincial governments. The power to pass and amend **criminal law** lies exclusively with the federal government, whereas the administration of justice is a provincial responsibility. This division of powers has had a significant impact upon the Canadian crime control system. It also differentiates our system in many significant ways from the U.S. system, which evolved at the same time, but is characterized by greater local autonomy.

How did the crime control function became so centralized with the federal government? Through a consideration of the **British North America Act**, the North-West

Mounted Police, the federal policy toward aboriginal peoples, the **Criminal Code**, and the **War Measures Act**, we will attempt to answer that question; and through an examination of several historical examples, we will consider how the federal/provincial division of powers has affected the criminal justice system. But, first, we will undertake a brief review of the context in which Canadian criminal law and the criminal justice system evolved.

Crime Control in Pre-Confederation Canada

Before Confederation in 1867, there was no criminal justice system, as such, in this country. Each territory had its own laws—albeit derived from a common source—and its own nascent crime control system. The settlement of Canada progressed from the east, pushing the frontier west and, eventually, north. Therefore, at stages during settlement, a relatively sophisticated infrastructure for a justice system existed at one end of the country, while law was being administered by circuit judges in log buildings, if at all, at the other.

The first permanent settlements in the Maritimes were established in the early 1600s, although, since John Cabot's arrival in the 1490s, transient fishermen had been making annual trips to the east coast from Europe. Competition among several nations—England, France, Spain, and Portugal—for territory that would maximize their ability to extract resources for European markets made this period one of instability and warfare. The strong military presence, representing both England and France, performed order maintenance and crime control functions in the area until the late eighteenth century. Only when troops were withdrawn or their force reduced in strength did the local citizenry appoint constables and build jails.

New France as well was first settled in the early 1600s, beginning with Champlain's Habitation at Quebec City in 1608. From the outset, the fur trade dominated life in New France as a series of mercantile groups were granted exclusive right to the natural resources by the French Crown. Those who operated outside the system, for example, the *coureurs de bois*, were considered outlaws (Horwood & Butts, 1984). Bad administration and poor market conditions for beaver pelts in Europe created problems for the colony, and, at its request, King Louis XIV took over the territory as a province of France in 1663. To encourage further settlement, the King attempted to control lawlessness in the area by decreeing, in 1664, that the laws of France would govern the area, assisted by a military presence, and that a system of government modelled after that of France would be created.

The two legal systems, British and French, operated

simultaneously in the areas claimed by each country; but, in Europe and in the New World, the two nations were frequently at war with each other. After the Seven Years' War, however, New France was transferred to the British Crown by the Treaty of Paris (1763) and became known as the colony of Quebec. This treaty marked the end of the military struggle between the two countries, and soon the British system of criminal law and justice was established as the dominant model for Canada.

The last region of the country to be settled (other than the North) was the prairies. The Hudson's Bay Company (HBC) maintained a monopoly there until shortly after Confederation—and in what is now British Columbia, until 1858, when that area became a Crown colony. Collectively, the territory west of Upper Canada (created in 1791 by the division of the colony of Quebec; later to become the province of Ontario) was called "Rupert's Land," for which the HBC had been granted a charter by King Charles II of England in 1670. The HBC had assumed judicial responsibility with its commercial monopoly, although the latter was given greater priority than the former. Among its administrative duties were the adjudication of disputes among its employees and the prosecution of crimes. When the HBC monopoly was suspended, the imposition of British law was made difficult by the absence of anything but the most rudimentary jails and the veritable absence of law enforcement personnel.

Law Enforcement

Public-sponsored, professional law enforcement agencies, as we know them today, did not exist in either Canada or Europe at the time of the settlement of North America. As noted above, the military was most often used to enforce order, before—and sometimes even after— the establishment of civilian law enforcement agencies.[1] Most accounts of this period paint a picture of lawlessness and sectarian violence (Crevel, 1966; Fox, 1971; Raddall, 1971). Organized policing seems to have emerged in the late seventeenth and early eighteenth centuries (Talbot, Jayewardene, & Juliani, 1985; Mitchell, 1965; Fox, 1971), but it was primarily volunteer-based.

A criminal-justice system eventually emerged on the east coast, as the population grew. However, wars between England and France, Indian skirmishes, and the constant battle between the permanent residents and the transient fishermen slowed the progress and resulted in many setbacks. Not until 1730 were taxes levied to finance the building of courthouses and jails, in St. John's; at that time, constables and justices of the peace were appointed to serve on a part-time basis.

The Newfoundland Constabulary, which traces its origins to 1729, claims to be the first organized police force on the continent (Fox, 1971), as does the Halifax Police Department (a constable was first appointed in 1749) (Mitchell, 1965). But, Kelly and Kelly (1976) claim that Canada's first police officer began work in Quebec City, about 1651. Talbot, Jayewardene, and Juliani (1985) note that policing was undergoing major reform in France at that time, but that the nascent system of New France was far more primitive. In eighteenth-century New France, Lachance (1981) believes, many offenders could successfully elude prosecution because there were so few law enforcement personnel to serve a vast area. While the surviving records are fragmentary, there is some evidence that the vast majority of prosecutions were for crimes against the person, most commonly assault. Theft, verbal offences (insult, calumny, defamation), and counterfeiting were also common (Lachance, 1981).

With the advent of British rule, law enforcement changed in New France, both because of the imposition of a new system and because of an apparent increase in crime and public unrest (Talbot, Jayewardene, & Juliani, 1985). The police code of Quebec City had been created with much public input, even allowing for the election of a police commission, but this system was replaced with one patterned after the British model, where justices of the peace were primarily responsible for administering justice.

Reliance upon the military and militias for peace-keeping declined, as the Indians became less of a threat and the hostilities between France and England subsided. In 1833, an inspector of police for Montreal was appointed; in 1838, municipal police forces were established in Montreal and Quebec City, and a rural force was given jurisdiction over the rest of the province.

In Upper Canada, policing evolved slowly, beginning with a volunteer-based night-watch system modelled after that of England. The territory was divided into districts, and the high constables of each municipal district were to appoint citizens to act as unpaid constables. In 1835, Toronto established a permanent, paid police force of six men, to replace the night-watch system (see Rogers, 1984; Boritch & Hagan, 1987), adding to the trend toward the establishment of policing as a full-time profession. With increasing professionalization, the police gradually gained autonomy from local politics (Boritch, 1988).

Before Confederation, the prairie provinces and British Columbia were to have been policed privately, by the Hudson's Bay Company (see Bindon, 1981; Macleod, 1975). However, this duty was not a high priority for the company. Few nonaboriginal inhabitants were not associated with the HBC, and the company did oversee disputes among its employees. In the early nineteenth century, the native population was rarely, if ever, the subject of criminal prosecution by the Euro-Canadians, although that would change. The principal target of HBC efforts to enforce the law during this period were those who traded goods for furs with the "Indians," in violation of the company's monopoly.

When agrarian-based settlements unassociated with the HBC were created in southern Manitoba, arrangements had to be made for law enforcement. Initially, the police force consisted of volunteers assisted by soldiers, but this group was disbanded in 1845. Largely because of the fear of American annexation of the territory, troops were stationed in the area, and they aided in law enforcement, when called upon to do so. When they left, in 1848, a part-time police body of 56 military pensioners was to be paid an annual retainer to operate on a stand-by basis, but this arrangement fell through. It was only after the HBC lost its charter in British Columbia, in 1858, that a police force was created there.[2]

Criminal Law and the Courts

Initially, most Canadian criminal cases were tried in England. When some local authority over such matters was achieved, governors and other local officials appointed by the Crown arbitrated at civil and criminal trials. A major problem with this system was the difficulty of balancing the conflicting priorities of local and absentee landowners, corrupt officials, and honest settlers. The governors rarely had legal training, and they often had no allegiance to the area, as appointments were a matter of patronage and most intended to return to Europe (Parker, 1986). But, gradually, a system of criminal justice, based on European laws but adapted for the unique contingencies of Canada, emerged.

The role of the military in initial efforts to create law and order is evident in the Atlantic provinces. The first court on the continent was apparently established in Newfoundland in 1615, by a captain in the Royal Navy (Fox, 1971). He organized juries in the most frequented harbours and dealt with civil and criminal complaints. He also held a commission from the English Vice-Admiralty for the suppression of piracy (Horwood & Butts, 1984), a serious problem in Europe at the time. In 1634, Charles I of England issued the "First Western Charter," which created the institution of fishing admirals. A fishing admiral was the captain of the first English ship that arrived each spring in any Newfoundland harbour, who was to be governor of that area for the season, charged with preserving the peace (Fox, 1971).

Not until 1750 was it possible to try **capital cases** in Newfoundland. Previously, both trial and execution were held in England. In 1750, the governor of Newfoundland was authorized to hear all criminal cases except those in-

volving treason, but court was held only once per year. When the sentence was death, executions could not be carried out until the British courts had considered the case. One of the first justices was himself murdered, resulting in the hanging of four men and the banishment of five (Fox, 1971).

The court system of New France was modelled after that of France, once French laws had been declared in force in 1663. Judicial bodies were created, such as the provost marshal of Quebec City in 1663 and the royal courts of Trois-Rivières (1665) and Montreal (1693). The Sovereign Council, initially made up of seven members, including the governor and the bishop, acted as a court of appeal for criminal and civil matters heard by these lower courts.

An event of some significance for the criminal justice system of Quebec took place after the takeover by the British. The Quebec Act of 1774 provided that the French **civil law** would apply in the colony of Quebec, but that the statutory and **common law** of England would apply for criminal matters. Before passage of the act, there was much debate about the relative merits of the British and French systems, and Edwards (1984) maintains that the French criminal law came very close to being adopted. However, a key consideration was that judicial torture (see Boyer, 1963a) was still being used to extract confessions under the French system (in six years it would be abolished by Louis XVI [Langbein, 1977]). Friedland (1984) speculates that, if judicial torture had been abolished before the Conquest, French criminal law might have continued in force, as had the civil procedures.[3]

The legal system of Upper Canada was closely modelled after that of England, and the English criminal law, as it stood on September 17, 1792, was deemed to apply in the colony. Only gradually were laws enacted and amended in Canada in anything but lock step with the trends in Britain (see, for example, Backhouse, 1983).

In Upper Canada, lay judges were appointed in each of four judicial districts in 1788 (Wright, 1979). The first justices in the City of York (now Toronto) were sworn in in 1796. They were unpaid and worked only part-time in this capacity. Lay justices of the peace of the eighteenth century performed many functions, including solemnizing marriages and issuing liquor licences. Gradually, however, an independent judiciary emerged, freer of these administrative functions and of ties to government (Craven, 1983). Beginning in 1785, a formal system of legal education had begun (Baker, 1983). In 1794, the Court of King's Bench was created to act as a superior court, to work on a circuit. Minor offences were dealt with locally, as in the Mayor's Court or Police Court of York (Craven, 1983).

In Rupert's Land, a 1786 murder opened the question of whether crimes committed in unorganized territory came under the jurisdiction of the British Crown (Evans, 1968). Rupert's Land was unorganized territory in that the Crown had granted it to some other party to run. Specifically, the issue was whether the HBC had jurisdiction over the criminal behaviour of people not in its employ. The issue was still unresolved when, in 1803, an employee of the company's chief rival, the North West Company, was shot by another trapper during an argument over beaver pelts. A witness relayed the story to the Grand Jury upon his next visit to Montreal, and the accused was summoned to that city to stand trial. Although he did travel to Montreal, he eventually thought better of it and returned to the prairies before the jurisdictional problems could be resolved (Evans, 1968).

The matter of jurisdiction seemed to be clarified that same year with the British Canada Jurisdiction Act of 1803, which granted the courts of Lower Canada authority over crimes committed north and west of the Great Lakes. It would seem, however, that this statute was largely ignored. Indeed, although courts could be established by the governor general of Canada in the territory, this was never done (Macleod, 1975). Instead, in 1815, the HBC issued its own penal code that defined as illegal a restricted range of offences, clearly indicating that the company was interested in enforcing laws only when offences involved threats to their monopoly on the fur trade (Bindon, 1981). The HBC was, at the time, being threatened by both encroaching settlement in what is now Manitoba and rival trading groups, such as the North West Company. Actual crime was said to have been rare, and it was chiefly these jurisdictional disputes that received judicial consideration. However, the lack of any effective police force hampered the enforcement of court judgments, and settlers were enjoined to assist in maintaining order (Macleod, 1975).

In an attempt to resolve some of the problems associated with administering justice from Lower Canada, a new statute was passed, in 1821, that gave the courts of Upper Canada criminal jurisdiction, although provision was made for local justices of the peace to hear less serious cases. Specifically, any case that could result in hanging or transportation was to be tried in Upper Canada. But this law was never applied. The same year, the Hudson's Bay Company merged with the North West Company, thus ending many of the legal difficulties associated with their rivalry (Macleod, 1975).

However, neither group was willing to yield law enforcement and judicial powers to central Canadian courts, because of the expense of transporting defendants and witnesses, and because "court appearances in Canada had produced bizarre and confusing sequences of events that had little to do with the legal requirements of the fur trade" (Bindon, 1981, p. 46). So, the company passed regulations creating a rudimentary justice system that was expanded in 1835. Magistrates were appointed in each of four judicial districts to hear minor civil and criminal matters. A general quarterly court heard more serious cases and appeals. In 1839, the first official with any legal training was appointed to this body.

But, of apparently greater interest to the company was the retention of judicial jurisdiction over the increasing number of traders who were dealing directly with native trappers and hunters (Bindon, 1981) in violation of the HBC monopoly. The principal object of their concern was the so-called whiskey traders, Americans who gave whiskey to the Indians in exchange for furs. The HBC had initially used rum as one instrument of barter (see Foster, 1975) but had found that the intoxicating effect impaired the ability to trap more furs. The company ceased to use liquor about the same time that the whiskey traders began to cross the border, after the American Civil War, in the 1860s. They were independent and little concerned with fostering the symbiotic association between the Indians and the traders (Horwood & Butts, 1984).

In keeping with the HBC penal code, those caught trading liquor with the Indians were fined, and the Indians themselves were obliged to press charges against whiskey traders. As demonstrated by the Sayer trial of 1849, however, the company's ability to enforce judicial judgments was hampered by the lack of effective law enforcement personnel. Sayer, a Métis from the Red River Settlement, was convicted of violating the HBC monopoly, but the presence of an armed and angry mob prevented the execution of sentence. A period of general free trade thus began, and the HBC, in the end, proved powerless to defend its territory, and its monopoly (Macleod, 1975).

In British Columbia, there had also been a slow development of a criminal justice system independent of the HBC. When the British government created the Crown colony of Vancouver Island, it granted the company exclusive jurisdiction, after it agreed to create a system of government and encourage settlement. The Act to Provide for the Administration of Justice in Vancouver's Island (1849) made it clear that a system of criminal justice was to be created. This was made difficult by the fact that extremely few legitimate settlers had been encouraged to share the island with the large population of HBC employees and its aboriginal residents. In 1850, the island's first magistrate resigned because there were no constables to assist him and because all disputes were between the company and its employees. Being himself in the employ of the HBC, he felt it to be a conflict of interest, especially when his first case seemed to involve complicity on the part of the company in the death of three sailors (Watts, 1986). The post was not filled for several years.

Gold was discovered on the mainland in 1857, and when the area became the Crown colony of British Columbia the following year, the HBC monopoly was cancelled and "free trade" began. The English Law Act declared that the laws of England were in force (see Herbert, 1954), and an Englishman, Matthew Baillie Begbie, was appointed as the colony's first judge. He travelled a circuit around the entire colony, following the practice of assize judges who travelled to remote areas so that people could be tried in their community (Williams, 1977, 1986).

Punishment and the Rise of Corrections

For many centuries, in Europe, brutal and public corporal and capital punishments had been the primary responses to all types of crime, both trivial and serious (see, generally, Ives, 1914; Barnes, 1930; Radzinowicz, 1948). This practice was brought to early Canada, where whipping was a common sentence, as were serving time in the stocks,

banishment, and branding. The prison as a place of confinement had yet to emerge in either Canada or Europe, and jails were used for pretrial detention and for those awaiting execution of sentence (Ekstedt & Griffiths, 1988).

As in England, hanging was the punishment for a very wide range of offences, against both property and the person. The date of the first execution in Canada is a matter of some debate. Peter Cartcel may have been the first person tried and hanged for murder, in 1749 in Nova Scotia (Chisholm, 1940). Some feel that the first legally sanctioned hanging took place in 1640, involving a sixteen-year-old girl convicted of theft (Cooper, 1987). The first execution in New France occurred in 1649, also of a young, female thief (Boyer, 1963b). The first hanging in Upper Canada is believed to have taken place in 1792 when Josiah Cutten was convicted of burglary (Anderson, 1973). Children were not exempt from the death penalty. For example, in 1803, a thirteen-year-old boy was hanged in Montreal for stealing a cow (see Box 1.1).

Box 1.1 Capital Punishment in Canada

Dr. William Henry King strongly protested his innocence after receiving the death penalty for murdering his pregnant wife with systematically administered doses of arsenic in 1859. He had written of his wife's impending death to two female patients, asking each to become the next Mrs. King. When one replied in the affirmative, the first Mrs. King became violently ill and, after several weeks of agony, she died (Campbell, 1970).

As the date of his execution grew near, Dr. King confessed and this statement was reprinted in the major newspapers, as was his speech from the gallows, a common practice of the day. The extensive press coverage of capital cases routinely included front-page stories reporting intricate details of the last meal and final visitors, the size and mood of the crowd, and the construction of the gallows. With about 5000 people looking on, Dr. King went to the scaffold in Cobourg, Ontario, at 8:00 a.m. and read a statement.

> After this was finished . . . the executioner came forward and requested the prisoner to kneel down. This functionary's face was covered with a mask so that his features could not be observed. It was said that he came from Toronto. King knelt down on the fatal drop, and the executioner pulled a white cotton cap over his face, and put the noose of the rope around his neck. He then proceeded to tie the hands and legs of the wretched man, and while do-

ing so, King asked the executioner to slacken the rope a little, as it was choking him, which he did. Everything being prepared, the venerable Archdeacon commenced to offer [a prayer] in which King was heard to join by ejaculating the word "Amen!" Before the prayer was quite ended, the Sheriff gave the preconcerted signal; the executioner drew the final bolt, and the unfortunate criminal was launched into eternity. The drop was between five and six feet, and as the culprit fell, an involuntary groan appeared to come from the crowd, who had been all standing with breathless attention, watching the proceedings; and one woman, who was close to the barricade, fainted, which caused a slight excitement in the vicinity of where she was standing. King appeared to expire without a struggle, although his neck was not broken, the noose having slipped round to the back of his head. (*Daily Globe*, 1859, p. 2).

Canada inherited the **death penalty** from Britain and France. In England's "Bloody Code," hundreds of crimes were capital offences (Radzinowicz, 1948). Executions were public spectacles, preceded by dramatic processions from the jail to the gallows. Various degradations were performed upon the corpse, and it was usually left on display. These practices were continued in Canada, where English or French penal law was adopted. Blanchfield (1985) notes

Box 1.1 *(Continued)*

that there were eleven legal methods of execution in New France, including being broken on the wheel, being shot, and having one's head crushed (see also Boyer, 1963b). The nobility were mercifully decapitated. Sixty-seven people were executed before 1763. In 1752, a man named Delisle killed two people during a bungled burglary. For the burglary, he received the death sentence but the murders could not go unpunished, so he "was tied to a scaffold and his bones [were] broken systematically until he was dead (Anderson, 1973, p. 9). Offenders who escaped could be hanged in effigy (Lachance, 1981).

Death was less the punishment than the suffering that preceded and accompanied it. Anderson (1973, p. 10) describes how the cause of death in early hangings was inevitably strangulation: "The hands of the condemned were usually tied behind his or her back with short stretches of cord, but the feet or legs were never secured. The thrashing lower limbs during strangulation were thought to be a further deterrent to the spectators. Hoods or blindfolds were likewise not in vogue for the same reason." Disembowelment and dismemberment could be used for those convicted of treason (see DeSalaberry, 1927). The display of the corpse for several days was routine.

We do not know exactly how many people were hanged in early Canada, as accurate records date only from 1867. It seems, however, that the almost capricious use of hanging in the eighteenth century declined as the eastern and central parts of the country became more socially stable. As in Britain, reprieves and commutations became common. A significant reduction in the number of capital offences beginning in the late eighteenth century has been attributed variously to the influence of the Classical School (see Chapter 7) or to the need for convict labour in the colonies. The trend away from capital offences was echoed in Canada. After Confederation, capital sentences were reviewed by cabinet and could result in a **commutation**, as in the notorious case of Valentine Shortis (Friedland, 1986).

The method of execution was also changing. During the nineteenth and early twentieth centuries, increasing intolerance of the gruesome and degrading aspects of executions was manifested in several ways. In 1833, the practice of leaving the corpse to rot in public was abolished. Hangings gradually became less public, the venue changing from a public place to within the prison walls (but sometimes in view), to inside the prison. At first, black-bordered invitations were sent to all who requested, but eventually

The execution of S. LaCroix in Hull, Quebec, 1902. The executioner, J.R. Radclive, stands behind the condemned man at what is believed to be the last *public* hanging in Canada. (Note the spectators on power poles.)

National Archives of Canada, no. C 14078.

hangings became, as they are today in the United States, very private events.

Death, rather than the ritual tortures of earlier times, became the punishment. Humane methods of execution were sought and the dislocation of the neck came to be preferred to suffocation. Anderson (1973) details the technical advances in gallows designs and knots that led to the modern use of the trapdoor. With the extensive training and practice necessitated by these advances, local sheriffs came to prefer to employ a professional hangman, rather than a local person, for the task.

Two hangmen emerged to take responsibility for most hangings in Canada. They worked without hoods and became quite notorious. J.R. Radclive hanged the first of 132 Canadians in 1890 and became Canada's official hangman by order-in-council in 1892, giving up the profession about 1910. Arthur English, who worked under the trade name of Arthur Ellis, dispatched 549 persons in his 27-year career, replacing Radclive in 1913. The job necessitated extensive travel, and English was able to conceal his profession from his wife for six years, telling her he was a salesman. When she discovered the truth, she left him (O'Brien, 1970). His career ended when a miscalculation resulted in the decapitation of a woman. All subsequent Canadian hangmen went by the name of Mr. Ellis.

The last hanging in Canada took place in Toronto in 1962. **Capital punishment** was abolished in 1976.

Small, local jails were constructed in conjunction with the development of corollary justice institutions, such as law enforcement agencies. The levying of taxes was often the first step to this end. In Upper Canada, for example, legislation encouraging the construction of local and district jails was passed in the late eighteenth century, although in most areas, such construction had low priority (Baehre, 1977) and where jails were built, conditions were deplorable. Early in the nineteenth century, local jails and lock-ups were first used on the prairies (Anderson, 1960). The local jail would eventually become part of a hierarchy of penal institutions designed not just for temporary custody, but for punishment (Kirkpatrick, 1964).

In both England and Canada, a significant reduction in the number of capital offences was evident by the beginning of the eighteenth century (Desaulniers, 1977). This trend has variously been attributed to the influence of **Classical School** thinkers, such as Jeremy Bentham and Cesare Beccaria (see Chapter 7), and to the economic and social transformations that accompanied industrialization and urbanization in Europe. In any event, a dramatic reduction in the number of offenders being executed necessitated the development of alternate techniques of punishment. Several options were tried; however, prison proved to be the most enduring venue for penal servitude.

In the nineteenth century, a hierarchy of prisons developed that consisted of police lockups, jails, and provincial prisons. About mid-century, the reformatory, an institution specifically for young boys, was added to the list, as was the first Canadian penitentiary, at Kingston, which opened in 1835. Borrowing from a U.S. penal model, the penitentiary was a place for penitence, where convicts were confined in cells, were not permitted to speak to each other, and were required to work (Curtis et al., 1985). Ironically, while prisons were viewed as a humane alternative to corporal and capital punishment, the use of severe flogging as a means of discipline was common. A commission of inquiry was convened only a few years after the opening of Kingston to investigate the practices of a particularly brutal warden (Brown, 1849a, 1849b).

To some extent, the building of more and larger penal facilities was linked to public fears about the increase in crime. Whether or not crime was a problem in Canada seems to be a matter of some contention, but there was certainly a time, during the 1830s, when the more established residents began to feel it was (Bellomo, 1972; Beattie, 1977). For example, Backhouse (1983) has charted an increasing concern with violent and sexual offences against women and girls. In addition, concern with immorality, intemperance, illiteracy, and their link with crime, characterized the Victorian period. This concern was fuelled by the waves of immigrants and the general social instability

of the period. Such factors are believed to have led to the push to open Kingston Penitentiary (see Shoom, 1966; Baehre, 1977; Palmer, 1980; Chunn, 1981) and to the creation of institutions for criminal children, including the juvenile court (discussed below).

In summary, by the time of Confederation in 1867, Canada had a criminal justice system that had its roots in Europe, principally in Britain, but that was, to some extent, shaped by the contingencies of the frontier. The military was the first body to maintain law and order, and gradually a volunteer-based system emerged. By this point, British law had been affirmed as the model upon which our legal system would be based. However, over time, the reliance upon Britain declined. A hierarchy of courts developed that gradually reduced the need to refer cases to England, for trial or appeal. With this trend, local politics and priorities began to take precedence over a strict application of British law.[4] However, the tremendous reforms taking place in Europe in the eighteenth and early nineteenth centuries had an impact in Canada as well, manifested in the construction of prisons specifically designed as places of punishment and the rise of a professional police force.

The Centralization of Crime Control

During the time that the Canadian criminal justice system was evolving, so was that of the United States. Both systems were initially based upon the British model and were adapted for use in a frontier country. However, a key feature that distinguishes the Canadian response to crime from that of the Americans, then and today, is the centralization of justice; in the United States, unlike in Canada, justice was treated as a local matter. On the U.S. frontier, **vigilantism**, and the more ephemeral **lynch mob**, were common, first in lieu of organized law enforcement and later in defiance of it (Brown, 1975). Even after formal law enforcement agencies were established, local sentiments played a significant role because those who sought to attain and retain the office of sheriff, prosecutor, or judge had to consider the preferences of the electorate.[5]

This localization of justice remains in the U.S. system today because most criminal law is a matter of state jurisdiction, and there can be significant variation across the country. For example, **capital punishment** is on the books in some states but not in others; and, even in some states where capital punishment is available to the courts, it is not used. Furthermore, some states that use capital punishment permit the execution of murderers who were juveniles at the time of the offence, while others do not (Streib, 1987). Other contentious issues that vary by state include abortion (since 1989), homosexuality, and marijuana use.

In Canada, by contrast, since Confederation, issues such as capital punishment and the definition of what should be against the criminal law are decided by the federal Parliament, and these decisions are applicable across the country. Canadian criminal justice was, and continues to be, far more centralized than its American counterpart. As we shall see, one of the advantages of this arrangement, recognized by politicians of the day, was that perceived threats to national security in the form of rebellions, riots, and political dissent could be easily suppressed, anywhere across the country, by the exercise of the criminal law power (see McNaught, 1975; and Chapter 17). The federal government also established economic policies, the implementation of which was aided by the criminal law power and, more specifically, by a federal police force, the North-West Mounted Police (NWMP).

Much has been written about the role of the NWMP in Canada's West and North. Berton (1982) has credited the NWMP with maintaining order in areas where, apparent-ly, lawlessness prevailed merely a few miles away, south of the border. As Berton writes (1982, p.22), "The Mountie was not part of a popularity contest; he did not have to appear before the electors to justify his conduct. He depended for his authority upon the sure knowledge that no matter what happened to him personally, another man in a scarlet coat would take his place . . . and another and another." The contrast between American and Canadian justice was most evident at border areas, such as during the Klondike gold rush to Yukon (see Box 1.2).

Few today would share this romantic view of the NWMP, as we will see below, but it is apparent that Canadians have been supportive of the unprecedented crime control powers vested in this force. But such power is only an extension of the centralized authority of the federal government in defining and responding to crime. Hagan and Leon (1977) have argued that Canadian opinion has generally favoured the strong, central control exercised by the federal government in the name of law and order,

---

Box 1.2 Miners' Meetings *vs.* The Mounties: American and Canadian Justice on the Yukon Border

In 1895, the NWMP established the most northerly post in Canada, Fort Constantine, near what was to become Dawson City, Yukon. The exact location of the Canada/Alaska border was in dispute at that time, and the area was populated mainly by Americans, prospecting for gold wherever seemed promising, in either country. Before the arrival of the NWMP, law had been administered by a theoretically democratic process called the miners' meeting. Anyone could air a grievance, criminal or civil, and the assembled parties reached a verdict and decided upon the disposition of the case.

The miners' meeting was an example of American frontier justice in that there was much local autonomy and variation. Morrison (1985, p. 13) notes: "The institution of the miners' meeting, although loosely based on U.S. legal precedents, accurately reflected the American ideal of the self-governing community which, unhampered by external controls, felt free to conduct its affairs as it saw fit."

The Canadian government made little effort to intervene in the area for some years, until the imminent gold rush, the boundary dispute with the Americans, and the promise of tax revenues from manning the border combined to stir them to action (Morrison, 1985). In these closing years of the century, there had been some thought about disbanding the NWMP, so to establish a detachment in the North served both to reinforce Canada's sovereignty and to give the force a new frontier to conquer.

Regarding the arrival of the NWMP in Yukon, Morrison (1985, p. 13) notes:

[The] American tradition of frontier self-government was bound to conflict with the Canadian system, which was based upon paternalistic control by a far-off central authority. In British countries the source of authority lies theoretically with the Crown rather than with the "people," especially with the sort of people who found their way to the Yukon at the end of the

A man is about to receive fifteen lashes, the sentence of a miner's court in Sheep Camp (Chilkoot Pass), Alaska, *c.* 1898. Such examples of extrajudicial law enforcement were practically unknown on the Canadian side after the arrival of the North-West Mounted Police.

Provincial Archives of British Columbia, no. HP 18694.

Box 1.2 *(Continued)*

nineteenth century. Even if the miners' meetings had functioned in a fair and rational manner, they were bound in principle to be anathema to the government of Canada.

In an early case involving the disputed ownership of a claim, Inspector Constantine made a ruling unpopular among the miners in that it was not in favour of the party with which the miners' court would have sided. He was able to enforce the judgment with a contingent of well-armed, albeit greatly outnumbered, officers. The lack of resistance from the miners was taken as evidence that British rule was respected and had replaced American-style democratic justice (Morrison, 1985).

The NWMP had barely set up camp when news of the gold rush leaked out in 1897 and the area was immediately besieged with 100 000 hopefuls (Fetherling, 1988). The quickest, and most demanding, route to the gold fields was to climb the Chilcoot Pass, beginning the journey in Alaska and crossing the border into Canada at the foot of the Pass. With activity on both sides of the Canada/Alaska boundary, the differences in law enforcement styles were even more apparent than they had been earlier.

Berton (1981) has painted a picture of stark contrast between the lawless American city of Skagway and the orderly Dawson City. That was certainly the view of the Mounties themselves, as indicated by this passage from the autobiography of Sam Steele, describing Skagway: "At night the crash of bands, shouts of 'murder,' cries for help mingled with the cracked voices of the singers in the variety halls; and the wily 'box-rushers' . . . cheated the tenderfeet" (quoted in Morrison, 1985, p. 35). The police force was apparently controlled by a con man named Soapy Smith, who appointed and paid the officers. When a vigilante group, the epitome of American-style justice, was organized, they were gunned down in public (Berton, 1981; Fetherling, 1988).

Crime and disorder in Dawson City were supposed to have been kept in check by the firm hand of the NWMP. In part, their success in doing so has been attributed to the unorthodox methods employed by the police, which included not enforcing some laws and making up others. For example, prostitutes were permitted to operate in Dawson City as long as they remained in an area called Paradise Alley, and did not work on Sundays. Gambling was also permitted. To prevent these activities would probably have been impossible, so instead, the Mounties regulated them.

But the NWMP served more than a law enforcement function in that their role was order maintenance generally. As an example of extralegal, paternalistic methods used by the NWMP

North-West Mounted Police at the Canadian Customs House at the summit of Chilkoot Pass, Alaska, *c.* 1898.
Glenbow Archives, no. NA-2615-11.

to maintain order among the miners, for their "own good," Morrison (1985, p. 40) describes an order given by Sam Steele that no one could get through the border and enter Canada without enough cash and provisions to last six months. The Department of Justice later declared this measure illegal, but it was undertaken to reduce the number of destitute and starving prospectors, who had to be fed at the expense of the Crown.

The Klondike gold rush dwindled as the more easily accessed gold deposits became scarce. News of another gold strike, in Nome, Alaska, reached Dawson City in 1899, and several thousand people quickly left. The NWMP continued their presence there, as the force had, and retains to the present day jurisdiction in the north of Canada. While many of the accounts of this time are probably exaggerated and romanticized, the contrast between law enforcement in Yukon and Alaska provides a vivid example of the differences between the American and the Canadian approach to criminal justice.

which ultimately facilitated stable economic development on the frontier. While we view our country as the Peaceable Kingdom, as discussed in the Introduction, Wilden (1980) has been one of several to point out that this view is little more than an illusion, an "imaginary Canada," because the government has used repressive means to achieve this order (see also Stewart, 1976; McNaught, 1974; Torrance, 1986). This centralization of control can be traced to the division of powers agreed to at Confederation.

The British North America Act, 1867

The colony of British North America became the Dominion of Canada in 1867 when New Brunswick, Nova Scotia, and Canada (Ontario and Quebec) united. The other provinces joined in later years, beginning with Manitoba in 1870. British Columbia was enticed into the union in 1871 by the promise of a railway that would unite the nation *a mari usque ad mare* (from sea to sea). The railway was also an important component of John A. Macdonald's National Policy, through which he encouraged east/west economic relations rather than the more geographically feasible north/south trade with the United States.

In March 1867, the British Parliament passed the British North America Act (BNAA) permitting Confederation.[6] Among other things, it divided the responsibilities of the federal and provincial governments. Macdonald wanted the criminal law power to lie with the federal government, thereby achieving national uniformity and overcoming what he saw as a "defect" in the U.S. system—that the states have jurisdiction over most crime (Parker, 1981)—promoting inconsistency across the country. Friedland (1984, p. 49) also speculates on the need at the time for a federal criminal law to "[control] political dissent and revolutionary conduct through the laws of treason and sedition," as was eventually done in the case of Louis Riel (discussed below). Friedland (1984) adds that another advantage of federal control was that English criminal law would remain in force in Quebec, consistent with the Quebec Act of 1774. (If given the power to enact criminal law, the Quebec provincial government might have opted to return to the French system.)

In the BNAA, the federal government was given the exclusive power to create criminal law and procedures (s.91[27]), but the provinces were to be responsible for the administration of justice (s.92[14]). This delegation of responsibility was to have significant consequences for the Canadian criminal justice system. If one level of government legislates in an area over which the other has jurisdiction, the law can be declared *ultra vires* and, therefore, null and void. However, if one level of government fails to enact laws in an area under its jurisdiction, the other is powerless to act.

The scope of the criminal law power of the federal government is not precisely clear, and the courts have been required to arbitrate on several issues over the years (Friedland, 1984). But, in 1867, the provincial governments were explicitly given authority over all provincial superior courts of the general jurisdiction, although the federal government appoints and pays the judges. However, the provinces have full jurisdiction over the lower courts, such as the provincial courts that deal with lesser criminal matters. They can also legislate in the areas over which they have constitutional jurisdiction (s. 92[15]), such as education and child welfare. For example, each province has legislation governing motor vehicle infractions by virtue of their responsibility over highways.

Generally, Parliament was given residual authority to effect "peace, order and good government." The federal government had previously assumed jurisdiction over penitentiaries, and this arrangement was retained after Confederation, although it is not explicitly mentioned in the BNAA. The **"two-year rule"** gave the federal government jurisdiction over all offenders sentenced to two years or more in prison (Needham, 1980). This arrangement has remained in effect until the present day, despite much criticism of such factors as the duplication of services (Ekstedt & Griffiths, 1988). In 1875, the federal government created the Supreme Court of Canada as an exercise of its constitutional power. But, in the area of policing, there was some disagreement over which level of government was responsible.

The North-West Mounted Police

At Confederation, policing seemed to be affirmed as a provincial responsibility, by virtue of the provinces' jurisdiction over the administration of justice. But Stenning (1981) notes that the federal government also interpreted the BNAA as placing policing under its jurisdiction. Legislation was almost immediately enacted in Ottawa that would give the federal government policing jurisdiction across the country. The Police of Canada Act was passed in 1868, creating the Dominion Police and giving them Canada-wide jurisdiction. The principal functions of this small force were to guard government buildings and to serve as bodyguards for elected officials. They also assumed security intelligence duties.[7] The same year, the Militia Act was enacted; among other things, it allowed local authorities to call upon Canadian troops to help maintain or restore public order.[8] But the ultimate expression of the federal government's control over policing was the creation of the North-West Mounted Police. Initially given jurisdiction only in the prairies, the force would become the Royal Canadian Mounted Police (RCMP), with national jurisdiction, attained in 1920.

At the time of Confederation, law enforcement services were generally becoming professionalized and centralized, replacing informal, volunteer-based efforts.[9] Large cities had police departments, and unincorporated areas began to be served by large departments that were the forerunners of provincial police agencies such as the Ontario Provincial Police. Thus, the pattern was set for the current system of *municipal* and *provincial* police forces, with a *federal* police agency with jurisdiction over a limited range of criminal matters and to perform security intelligence (see Griffiths & Verdun-Jones, 1989).

But, in the prairie West, by the time of Confederation, there was still no organized system of law enforcement. As discussed above, the HBC was using its employees to enforce its own penal code, but they were not very successful in prosecuting free traders, or, indeed, any offender who was backed by public support. The company was aware that key members of the Dominion government wanted to revoke its charter and remove its monopoly, and to counter such a move, claimed to be setting up a criminal justice system and encouraging settlers when, in reality, it was not. Native fur traders were still the principal inhabitants of the region, but the federal government wanted to encourage settlement, in part to avoid U.S. annexation of the area, and the creation of the NWMP was an important plank in that policy.

The North-West Mounted Police officially came into being in 1873. That statement is possibly the only one over which there is no contention. The motives of Macdonald in creating a federal police force have been hotly debated. On one side, some contend that the force was sent to protect the "Indians" from the Americans and to bring the Queen's justice to a lawless, dangerous territory. On the other side, some see the NWMP as an instrument of federal economic policies and as important in subjugating the aboriginal residents of the area who were no longer needed once the fur trade declined.

Most contemporary accounts assumed the former stance. They painted a picture of a benevolent government seeking to protect the natives from marauding American whiskey traders, triggered into action by the Cypress Hills massacre of 1873, where 36 Assiniboine were killed by wolf hunters from Montana. A resolution passed by the Council of the North-West Territories stated:

persons professing to be American citizens have established themselves in force within the Territory, and they have also proceeded to perpetrate gross outrages upon the native population as well as upon Her

Majesty's Subjects generally, including murders of a most aggravated kind, for which, during the present condition of the Territory, and the absence of all Law and Order there, no redress can be obtained. (quoted in Robertson, 1970, p. 13)

An initial troop of 150 men was supplemented by another 150 the next year, in part because of these fears that American lawlessness was encroaching, making settlement by Euro-Canadians difficult.

The 300 men spent some time training and getting organized in Manitoba, and then they prepared to disperse into detachments across the prairies. In what is now called the Long March, they left Fort Garry (now Winnipeg) in July 1874, following along the U.S. border to the den of the American whiskey traders and the source of most of their concern: Fort Hamilton—located on the Montana/Alberta border (on the Canadian side)—an American fort, protected by artillery and flying a flag styled after the Stars and Stripes. Its nickname best describes its character: Fort Whoop-up. With the exception of women entering for the purposes of prostitution, the natives were not permitted inside the fort. Instead, they pushed their bundles of furs through a hole in the wall and were handed back payment in the form of a rifle or the near-poisonous whiskey that was known as "Whoop-up Bug Juice."[10]

Conditions on the march to Fort Whoop-up were more onerous than anyone expected, and the Mounties were plagued with poor weather, insects, and lack of food. Indians and Métis encountered along the way were told to spread the word that law and order had arrived. At predesignated points, detachments split off to establish posts in several locations around the territory, such as Fort Edmonton. The Whoop-up–bound group dwindled when sick men and horses were left along the way. A Scots-Peigan half-breed named Jerry Potts has been credited with guiding the band to their destination. When they finally arrived at the infamous fort, artillery poised for a hostile takeover, they found the place deserted, save for an old man and a few native women. It was assumed that the Americans had fled in fear.

Such is the stuff of which legends are made, and there have been many accounts of this and other tales of the undaunted Mountie, always getting his man (e.g., Macbeth, 1931; Godsell, 1932; Fetherstonhaugh, 1938; Kelly, 1949; Spettigue, 1955; Young, 1968). The ability of Canada's Mounted Police to maintain law and order on a vast frontier has become legendary, the quintessential Canadian image (Thacker, 1980; Walden, 1982; see Box. 1.3).

More recent accounts of the Mounted Police have presented a revised view, sometimes critical of the force and its creators during this period. At the very least, as Betke (1988) has noted, the NWMP cannot be credited with

Box 1.3 The Squad of One: The Legend of the Mounted Police

Sergeant Blue of the Mounted Police was a so-so kind of guy;
He swore a bit, and he lied a bit, and he boozed a bit on the sly;
But he held the post at Snake Creek Bend for country and home and God,
And he cursed the first and forgot the rest—which wasn't the least bit odd.

Now the life of the North-West Mounted Police breeds an all-round kind of man;
A man who can jug a down-South thug when he rushes the red-eye can;
A man who can pray with a dying man, or break up a range stampede—
Such are the men of the Mounted Police, and such are the men they breed.

The snow lay deep at the Snake Creek post and deep to east and west,
And the sergeant made his ten-league beat and settled down to rest
In his two-by-four that they called a "post" where the flag flew overhead,
And he took a look at his monthly mail, and this is the note he read:

"To Sergeant Blue, of the Mounted Police, at the post of Snake Creek Bend,
From U.S. Marshal of County Blank, greetings to you my friend:
They's a team of toughs give us the slip, though they shot up a couple of blokes,
And we reckon they's hid in Snake Creek Gulch, and posin' as farmer folks.

Colonel Sam Steele with his detachment at Beavermouth, British Columbia, 1885.

Glenbow Archives, NA-194-1.

Box 1.3 *(Continued)*

"They's as full of sin as a barrel of booze, and as quick as a cat with a gun,
So if you happen to hit their trail be first to start the fun;
And send out your strongest squad of men and round them up if you can,
For dead or alive we want them here. Your truly, Jack McMann."

And Sergeant Blue sat back and smiled, "Ho, here is chance of game!
Folks 'round here have been so good that life is getting tame;
I know the lie of Snake Creek Gulch—where I used to set my traps—
I'll blow out there tomorrow, and I'll bring them in—perhaps."

Next morning Sergeant Blue, arrayed in farmer smock and jeans,
In a jumper sleigh he had made himself set out for the evergreens
That grow on the bank of Snake Creek Gulch by a homestead shack he knew,
And a smoke curled up from the chimney-pipe to welcome Sergeant Blue.

"Aha, and that looks good to me," said the Sergeant to the smoke,
"For the lad that owns this homestead shack is East in his wedding-yoke;
There are strangers here, and I'll bet a farm against a horn of booze
That they are the bums that are predestined to dangle in a noose."

So he drove his horse to the shanty door and hollered a loud "Good-day,"
And a couple of men with fighting-irons came out beside the sleigh
And the Sergeant said, "I'm a stranger here and I've driven a weary mile;
If you don't object I'll just sit down by the stove in the shack awhile."

Then the Sergeant sat and smoked and talked of the home he had left down East,

And the cold and the snow, and the price of land, and the life of man and beast,
But all of a sudden he broke it off with, "Neighbors, take a nip?
There's a horn of the best you'll find out there in my jumper, in the grip."

So one of the two went out for it, and as soon as he closed the door
The other one staggered back as he gazed up the nose of a forty-four;
But the Sergeant wasted no words with him, "Now, fellow, you're on the rocks,
And a noise as loud as a mouse from you and they'll take you out in a box."

And he fastened the bracelets to his wrists, and his legs with some binder-thread,
And he took his knife, and he took his gun, and rolled him on to the bed;
And then as number two came in, he said, "If you want to live,
Put up your dukes and behave yourself, or I'll make you into a sieve."

And when he had coupled then each to each and laid them out on the bed,
"It's cold, and I guess we'd better eat before we go," he said.
So he fried some pork and he warmed some beans, and he set out the best he saw,
And they ate thereof, and he paid for it, according to British law.

That night in the post sat Sergeant Blue, with paper and pen in hand,
And this is the word he wrote and signed and mailed to a foreign land;
"To U.S. Marshal of County Blank, greetings I give to you;
My squad has just brought in your men, and the squad was

Sergeant Blue"

Source: Robert J.C. Stead (1919), The squad of one. *Scarlet and Gold* (p. 93). December.

pacifying the prairie settlers as the force predated their arrival. It has been argued that the force symbolized an essentially military presence, representing the federal government and avoiding involvement in local politics (Macleod, 1974). Being a police force, they were able to use the criminal sanction and, in the name of law and order, repress political dissent, control the indigenous population, and maintain sovereignty (Brown & Brown, 1973). Maintenance of order was necessary to encourage settlers to venture west, thereby creating new markets for the manufactured goods of central Canada (Horrall, 1972), consistent with the National Policy (Macleod, 1978). Their role in encouraging the assimilation of minority groups has also been noted (Penner, 1979). But it is their role in the federal policy toward the aboriginal population of the prairies that is perhaps the most controversial.

The NWMP, Federal Policy, and the Aboriginal Peoples

In the traditional, romanticized accounts of the NWMP, their treatment of aboriginal Canadians was benevolent, especially in contrast to the situation in the United States. There, a policy of genocide helped clear the territory for ranchers. Here, it is popularly contended, the police presence on the prairies was, in part, intended to protect natives from exploitation by American whiskey traders. A travelling missionary provides a contemporary account of the situation:

> several whisky mills were vigorously at work, demoralizing and decimating the plains tribes, and this continued right through to the boundary line. Scores of thousands of buffalo robes and hundreds of thousands of wolf and fox skins and most of the best horses the Indians had were taken south into Montana, and the chief article for barter for these was alcohol. In this traffic very many Indians were killed, and also quite a number of white men. Within a few miles of us, that winter of 1873–4, forty-two able-bodied men were the victims among themselves, all slain in drunken rows. These were Blackfeet . . . There was no law but might. Some terrible scenes occurred when whole camps went on the spree, as was frequently the case, shooting, stabbing, killing, freezing, dying.

> Thus these atrocious debauches were continuing all that winter not far from us. Mothers lost their children. These were either frozen to death or devoured by the myriad dogs of the camp. The birth-rate decreased and the poor red man was in a far way towards extinction, just because some men, coming

out of Christian countries, and themselves the evolution of Christian civilization, were now ruled by lust and greed. (McDougall, 1911, pp. 128–9)

In driving out the Americans, the Mounties were seen as saving the natives. They, in return, respected the police and eventually realized that assimilation was in their best interests. The nomadic, hunting lifestyle was abandoned, and the natives remained on reserves and were supervised by agents of the federal government, employees of the Department of Indian Affairs. This peaceful evolution has been attributed to the stabilizing influence of the NWMP. Clearly adopting this view, Jennings (1975, p. 93) stated: "the Indians were given time to understand white laws and came to look on the Mounted Police as their protectors, not their persecutors."

Another view is that economic exploitation was used in Canada in contrast to the genocidal policies south of the border. As long as the fur trade was viable, the native trappers were indispensable. Before the 1821 merger of the Hudson's Bay Company and the North West Company, tremendous competition between the companies meant one tried to surpass the other in what they could offer the natives, and rum was often used in barter for furs. The traditional way of life was lost as the indigenous peoples became dependent upon the trading posts during the nineteenth century.

In the BNAA, section 91.24 had given the federal government exclusive legislative authority over "Indians" and their lands. Ponting (1986) has summarized federal Indian policy of this period as being characterized by paternalistic protection and aimed at conversion to Christianity, settlement on reserves, and agricultural self-sufficiency. The ultimate goal was assimilation: gradually to disenfranchise Indians from their special status and enfranchise them as Canadian citizens. The paternalistic view of Indians as being exploitable and unable to look after themselves had its roots in previous centuries (Tobias, 1983b).

During the years following the creation of the NWMP, the plains Indians experienced tremendous hardships. Near starvation after overhunting had eliminated the buffalo, and many tribes were desperate. They were forced to sign treaties and were becoming dependent upon rations and supplies provided by the federal Indian agents. Many of their traditional survival skills were lost. Disease killed hundreds. But with the increase in population on the prairies, ranching and farming became dominant.

The police were instrumental in the enforcement of the federal policy during this transition period (Tobias, 1983a). Those Indians who resisted assimilation could be prosecuted for breaches of either criminal law or the regulations of the Indian Act. We will read in Chapter 12 of the hunt for and trial of Sinnisiak and Uluksuk, an explicit intention of which was to impress upon the Inuit the certainty of British law (see also Schuh, 1979). There were also many examples of such use of the law on the prairies. For example, in the late 1890s, Almighty Voice, a Cree, was arrested for a regulatory infraction: butchering a cow, without permission of the Indian agent, to feed a sick relative. It has been conjectured that he was afraid he would be hanged for the offence and escaped, fatally shooting one of the NWMP officers sent to recapture him. He lived among his tribe for almost two years while an extensive search was waged, during which time he was a national embarrassment to the force. He was killed by cannon-fire in 1897 when more than 100 heavily armed men cornered him on a bluff (Horwood & Butts, 1987).

Perhaps the most contentious action of the NWMP at this time was their role in the trial and hanging of Louis Riel. In the 1860s, during the lengthy period of negotiation that preceded the takeover of Rupert's Land by Ottawa, the Métis of Manitoba, especially, became worried about their land rights and the preservation of their culture. In the Red River Rebellion of 1869, an armed group seized control of Upper Fort Garry. They proclaimed a provisional government to negotiate the terms of entry into Confederation. Louis Riel emerged as their leader. They instituted a system of government and enacted laws, and with this authority a **court-martial** was convened, and an Irish Protestant, Thomas Scott, found guilty and executed.

At the time of the rebellion, the NWMP had yet to be created, so Canadian and British troops had to be sent from Ontario. Because the journey was a lengthy one, Riel had time to flee to the United States, and many Métis moved west to the less populated North-West Territory. However, Riel was able to gain some concessions from the federal government, and Manitoba entered Confederation with full provincial status, as Canada's fifth province, in 1870. The rebellion exacerbated English-French tensions in central Canada (Owram, 1978) and was an embarrassment to the federal government, leading to speculation that the NWMP had been formed, in part, to forestall, or at least be able to suppress, future political dissent.

Louis Riel was called back from exile in 1884 when it became apparent that the federal government would never consider Métis demands for land rights. By this time, the NWMP had been created and, in response to Métis concerns, the federal government increased police strength in Saskatchewan in anticipation of rebellion (Kelly & Kelly, 1973).

The North-West Rebellion of 1885 began with the re-creation of a provisional government and soon escalated to violence. This time, the federal police presence virtually assured a confrontation. Riel and his men seized a small town north of Saskatoon and met in armed combat a contingent of NWMP officers bolstered by citizen volunteers

Photo 1.1   Frog Lake Cree Indians trading at Fort Pitt on the Saskatchewan River east of Edmonton, 1884. Big Bear, who was jailed in 1885 for his role in the North-West Rebellion, is in the middle.
Royal Canadian Mounted Police Archives, no. 547.

to a strength of 100. Twelve from the police side were killed, as were six of the rebels, including one Indian. The Frog Lake Cree, one of the more militant native groups, headed by Chief Big Bear, had refused to sign a treaty, so the government cut off their rations. The Cree killed ten white men, including two priests and a sub–Indian agent.

The government reaction was swift and severe. A hastily amassed militia was transported over the still-incomplete CPR lines. In less than one month, more than 5000 troops converged on the area, and the defeat of the few hundred rebels was inevitable. The last battle was led by Superintendent Sam Steele of the Mounted Police, near Loon Lake.

Riel was tried for **high treason**, a criminal offence. He tried to use his trial as a forum for the airing of Métis grievances, but this issue was eclipsed by consideration of his mental state. Against Riel's wishes, his lawyer entered a plea of not guilty by reason of insanity (see Chapter 8), but this was not successful and he was hanged in November 1885. Eight Indians were also hanged for murder, and Big Bear was sentenced to three years' imprisonment. A controversy over the hanging of Riel rages to this day.

Before the 1885 rebellion, Jennings (1986) maintains, relations between the NWMP and the native residents of the prairies was generally characterized by mutual respect. This situation was to erode gradually after the establishment of the federal Department of Indian Affairs in the early 1880s and the official policy of total assimilation and segregation on reservations. The goal was to transform the nomadic peoples into farmers, with the receipt of food rations contingent upon attempts made to this end, and upon enrolling one's children in school. The NWMP were called upon

Photo 1.2 Charcoal, shortly before he was hanged on March 16, 1897, at Fort Macleod. The feather headdress and clothes are props to make him appear to be a "wild Indian" for the eastern press. The hat covers the manacles.

Glenbow Archives, no. NA-118-54.

to enforce the latter stipulation, as well as the pass system, started in 1882, whereby "Indians" were not permitted to leave the reserve without a pass from an Indian agent. According to Jennings (1986), the 1885 rebellion merely exacerbated the already-deteriorating relationship between the NWMP and the aboriginal peoples of the area.

But the need for the NWMP to enforce the federal policy of assimilation had declined by the end of the century. In fact, the newly elected Liberal government in Ottawa was considering disbanding the force. Almighty Voice was still on the loose, and when Charcoal, a Blood Indian, killed a member of the NWMP in a situation very similar to that in which Almighty Voice had been involved,[11] Superintendent Sam Steele personally cabled Prime Minister Wilfrid Laurier that Charcoal would be caught.

Charcoal was old and sick, but skilfully evaded capture for almost two months. A reward was offered, and Indians were armed and paid to look for him. An indication of how well under control the native population was by this time was the fact that it was his brothers who finally captured him (Steele had promised them that their sons would be released from jail in return). Charcoal was dying of tuberculosis and had to be carried to the gallows to be hanged, by Radclive the executioner, while sitting in a chair on the trap door, in March 1897 (Horwood & Butts, 1987). At this time, the Klondike Gold Rush had begun, and the NWMP were given a new mandate when they were granted the authority to police the North.

The First Criminal Code (1892)

Another feature of the Canadian legal system that contributes to the centralization of criminal justice is the federal Criminal Code. Before Confederation, as discussed above, British statute and common law were used for criminal prosecutions in each unique part of Canada, including what is now Quebec, after 1763. The laws were generally adopted intact (for example, when Upper Canada introduced the English criminal law as it stood on September 17, 1792), but they were modified over time with judicial **precedent** and legislative amendments. Parker (1981, pp. 259–69) characterizes the laws of that day as "either makeshift, pragmatic laws to solve an immediate problem or, more frequently, . . . lifted from English statutes with few changes in deference to Canadian conditions."

As noted above, John A. Macdonald was very deliberate in his preference for making the criminal law power a matter of federal jurisdiction. One of the stated rationales was national uniformity. With each of the new provinces having its own system of criminal law, what was needed was a unifying force that would clearly draw together the various statutes and common law traditions that had developed in each area. For example, incest was punishable by a severe prison sentence in some provinces but was not even a crime in others (Crouse, 1934, fn 84). Attempts were made shortly after Confederation to consolidate some of the provincial criminal laws into federal statutes (see Crouse, 1934; Mewett, 1967). At this point, the various laws of Canada were to be found scattered about in many different statutes, as was the case in England. There, some laws were written down in statutes (i.e., codified) while other existed at common law.[12]

In England, this system had come under some criticism. English Classical reformers of the eighteenth and nineteenth centuries, such as Jeremy Bentham, advocated the consolidation and codification of the chaos of statutes and unwritten common law precedents. There was much overlap and some contradiction, and the general populace was totally at a loss as to understanding what exactly was against the law. The movement toward codification was most successful in Continental Europe. For example, the French Civil Code (1804) of Napoleon was the forerunner of Quebec's system of civil law today. But it never caught on in England. A legal scholar, Sir James Fitzjames Stephen, brought together all the current laws and precedents in his English Draft Code of 1878, but this was rejected in favour of retaining the *status quo*.

As in England, the major objection to a formal code was that the dynamic and constantly changing common law would be replaced by a static written law that was difficult to amend as social thought evolved and would be subject to tinkering by legislators. In true Canadian style, a compromise was effected. All existing statute law was consolidated, and some common law offences and defences were included, but most of the common law continued to apply to permit the "elasticity which has been so much desired by those who are opposed to codification on general principles" (*Hansard*, 1892, p. 1313). The Criminal Code of 1892, therefore, was a consolidation and simplification of the maze of statutes that existed at the time. Furthermore, many terms were purposely vaguely defined, leaving much room for judicial interpretation (Parker, 1981; see also Friedland, 1984).

Because Canada had inherited British law, and because our first Criminal Code was so heavily based upon Stephen's Draft Code, many offences that found their way into the 1892 Code had their origin in seventeenth century England. But their adoption by Canada's Parliament means that they serve as a reflection of priorities of at least one segment of nineteenth-century society. For example, offences against public order included inciting to mutiny, unlawful drilling (of soldiers), challenging someone to a duel,[13] attending or promoting a prize fight, piracy, possessing a weapon at a public meeting, and pretending to practise witchcraft. But all these laws have remained on the books until this day. In the absence of any direct challenge to their validity or utility, they simply fall into disuse.

Other offences of 1892, since repealed or amended, include seduction of a woman under promise of marriage, carnally knowing idiots, keeping a common bawdy-wigwam, causing bodily harm to servants, attempting to cause bodily injuries by explosive, setting man traps, injuring persons by furious driving, leaving holes in the ice unguarded, selling kidnapped persons into slavery, and abduction of heiresses.[14] In 1892, you could be charged specifically with theft of trees, railway tickets, dogs, pigeons, oysters, fences, election documents, and metal ores. These categories are reflections of items that were considered valuable to Canadians of the time.[15]

The War Measures Act (1914)

Canada of the early twentieth century was significantly affected in many ways by the two world wars. One consequence of the wars that had tremendous impact upon the criminal justice system was that a great deal of power was vested in the federal government, yielded by the provinces to aid in national responses to the exigencies of wartime. During World War I, the federal government passed the War Measures Act (WMA). When the act was invoked, the cabinet was given the power to govern by decree, to give it the freedom to take action quickly, when it perceived the existence of "war, invasion or insurrection, real or apprehended." The Dominion Police had the responsibility of co-ordinating the police and security forces in enforcing the act.

In later years, the WMA would be used to intern members of the Communist Party of Canada (1939), Jehovah's Witnesses (1941–43), Japanese Canadians (1942–49), and Italian Canadians (1939–45). In not all of these cases was national security the primary motivation. After many unsuccessful attempts to prosecute Rocco Perri, a notorious bootlegger reputed to have connections to organized crime, the WMA was used to do what the criminal justice system had been unable to. Hours after Italy entered World War II in 1940, Perri was arrested and interned in Camp Petawawa (Dubro & Rowland, 1987). (As we shall see in Chapter 17, the most controverial use of the WMA was for the perceived domestic crisis of October 1970.)

The Federal/Provincial Split of Jurisdiction

In addition to vesting a great deal of power in a central, federal government, the other significant implication of the BNAA for our current system of crime control was the federal/provincial division of powers. During the first half of this century, in several areas, tension was evident regarding the constitutional division of powers for criminal justice. We will examine three.

First, with the **Juvenile Delinquents Act** of 1908, the federal government abrogated provincial powers over the prosecution of juveniles for provincial offences. Moreover, the federal government became involved to a great extent in child welfare matters, constitutionally a provincial responsibility.

Second, the federal government divested itself of the politically dicey issue of prohibition by passing responsibility for it to the provinces. This created significant variation in practice across the country and left the provincial governments handicapped by the limited enforcement powers constitutionally available to them.

A third example of federal/provincial tension is illustrated in the official response to two political groups. While federal legislation to stop the hate propaganda of fascists and anti-Semites was slow to materialize, provincial governments found themselves unable to pass effective laws that did not intrude into the federal criminal law domain. Conversely, the federal government was quick to outlaw communist groups. When these federal laws were repealed, *ultra vires* provincial laws were sometimes put into effect to fill the void.

Juvenile Delinquents Act (1908)

In the last half of the nineteenth century, individuals who came to be known as "child savers" were very active in lobbying the government to create children's courts, venues where youths could be tried separately from adults, away from stigmatizing publicity. Further, they believed that child offenders should be subject to different types of punishment from that meted out to adults, measures that were thought to be rehabilitative or even prophylactic. The underlying assumptions of the children's court movement were derived directly from the **Positive School** (discussed in Chapter 7) (Brantingham, 1979). Accordingly, sentences were to be chosen not to fit the crime, as Classical reformers would argue, but to fit the offender. **Due process** protections were eclipsed by the desire to do what is best for the child.

By the end of the nineteenth century, the idea of a juvenile court was well supported, and several had been created in other western jurisdictions (Parker, 1967). In Canada, a limited number of correctional institutions, called reformatories, designed to house only juveniles, had appeared beginning in 1858 (Shoom, 1972), followed by Industrial Schools, beginning in 1887 (Morrison, 1974). The child welfare system was also spreading from its origins in Ontario all across the country. The infrastructure for a juvenile justice system awaited the advent of legislation that would give it legitimacy, and would sanction the use of probation as the cornerstone of the juvenile court (Leon, 1977).

Canadian reformers of the late nineteenth century had been successful in encouraging laws permitting separate trials of juveniles, in the federal Criminal Code (see Gagnon, 1984) and in an Ontario child welfare statute. However, being discretionary, these laws were largely disregarded. A significant impediment to effective law reform was the inability of a provincial government to pass a law that could mandate special court procedures for young offenders charged with federal offences, by far the majority. Ironically, however, neither could the federal government pass a law requiring the provincial governments to adopt new court procedures or modify the manner in which they prosecuted offenders charged with violations of provincial laws.

With the Juvenile Delinquents Act (JDA), a unique constitutional arrangement was created. In the United States, the civil *status* of delinquency, and a very old English doctrine called ***parens patriae***, had been used to justify the legal creation of a juvenile court. But, in Canada, the civil status of persons was a provincial responsibility. Feeling that only federal law would be effective (Scott, 1930), the drafters of the JDA elected to create the *offence* of delin-

quency, which included the violation of any existing law (federal, provincial, or municipal) or a variety of "status offences" which the provinces could create (e.g., incorrigibility, vicious conduct, truancy, running away). In sum, being a "delinquent" was declared to be a crime in order to place it squarely under the jurisdiction of the federal government (see Wilson, 1977; Stamm, 1985).

There were other consequences of the division of powers. With the passage of the JDA, the provincial jurisdiction over juveniles who violated provincial laws was abrogated. Moreover, this federal law empowered juvenile court judges to place juvenile delinquents into the care of child protection authorities, even though this was a provincial area of responsibility.

But another constitutional problem remained. Because the provincial governments have responsibility for the administration of justice, the federal government could proclaim the JDA into force only in a jurisdiction that requested it. Although most acknowledged that prevention and rehabilitation were admirable goals where juvenile offenders were concerned, the juvenile court ideal spread very slowly across the country, and very few cities had juvenile courts, especially before World War II (Hatch & Griffiths, 1990). At no point before its repeal in 1984 was the JDA in force nation-wide. Therefore, the national uniformity lauded as a benefit of federal control over criminal law was never to materialize in the case of Canadian juvenile courts, because of the federal/provincial division of powers.

Photo 1.3 Judge Emily Murphy presiding over a juvenile-court session in Edmonton, c. 1920. Judge Murphy wrote under the pseudonym "Janey Canuck" and figured prominently in lobby efforts for laws against narcotics.

Glenbow Archives, no. NC-6-3152.

Enforcing Morality: The Case of Prohibition

In Part II, we will discuss Canadian attempts to regulate and criminalize narcotic drug use, prostitution, and gambling. Here we will examine another effort to use the justice system to enforce moral standards but we will focus upon the contrast between federal and provincial policy on the subject and the constraints placed upon government action by the division of powers in the BNAA.

Whereas today we view alcoholism as a disease, nineteenth-century Canadians saw drunkenness as a moral failing. Alcohol consumption had long been linked to a litany of social problems, chief among them being financial and moral neglect of families, and crime. By the end of the nineteenth century, complete abstinence was advocated, and thousands had signed a temperance pledge. Groups such as the Women's Christian Temperance Union had been an effective lobby force, and the issue became highly politicized. Pursuit of individual temperance evolved into a push for total prohibition of alcohol. In the United States, images of Carry Nation trashing Kansas saloons with a hatchet in the 1890s helped muster the support from the three-quarters of states needed to amend the constitution. In 1920, the 18th Amendment took effect, making illegal the import, manufacture, transportation, or sale of intoxicating liquor. Being a federal law, prohibition in the United States was nation-wide, and it lasted until 1933.

In Canada, however, strong public views existed in support of both sides of the issue, and the federal government was desperately trying to duck decision making. The Dominion Temperance Act of 1878 effectively passed the responsibility for the decision out of federal jurisdiction. It gave local jurisdictions the option to vote "dry" and, in 1901, Prince Edward Island became the first province to do so. Prohibition was a hotly debated issue in most elections, and several referenda were held to gauge the opinion of the electorate. World War I temporarily brought near nation-wide prohibition, created by authority of the War Measures Act on Christmas Eve, 1917. Some areas voted to remain "wet," such as Montreal.[16]

The War Measures Act decree expired on January 1, 1920, and again each province had to decide whether to remain "dry." In B.C., the electorate voted to create government-run liquor stores, thereby quelling the issue. (The president of the B.C. Prohibition Party blamed the result on the newly enfranchised women voters, claiming that they had misunderstood the ballot.) But most provinces voted to continue prohibition, including Nova Scotia (see McGahan, 1988), Ontario, Alberta, Saskatchewan, and Manitoba. In a reverse from the norm, the United States had national uniformity and Canada had interprovincial variation.

Photo 1.4 A parade float from Hillhurst Presbyterian Sunday School in Calgary, c. 1912–16. The sign reads, "Vote to Protect Us: Banish the Bar."

Glenbow Archives, no. NA-1639-2.

In those provinces where prohibition was in force, enforcement was the chief problem. It was hampered not only by corruption and the sheer size of the countryside, but by the fact that several licit sources of hooch existed, and possession, in your home, of a moderate amount for personal use was legal.[17] And there was a large supply of illicit alcohol, available in blind pigs and speakeasies, over the counter in grocery stores, or from the local bootlegger.

Especially in rural areas, moonshine was produced in homemade stills. But the largest sources of alcohol were the breweries and distilleries that were able to use the lack of federal/provincial co-ordination on prohibition policy to their advantage. Ontario and Quebec distilleries and breweries could, with proper documentation from customs officials, load their alcohol onto boats bound for the United States, Cuba, or any of a dozen countries. Many of these shipments made it south, where enforcers of American prohibition would try to intercept them, only rarely successfully.

The American government was not at all pleased. After a low-level Ontario court decision in 1921, it was determined that the provinces could not constitutionally prohibit the export of alcohol to the United States. Federal legislation would be required, and that level of government did not seem inclined to take action. Even the extradition of smugglers to the United States was not allowed by Canada. No doubt the $60 million in tax revenue generated each year by the export of liquor had some bearing on this stance (Dubro & Rowland, 1987). And the owners of distilleries,

ited handsomely
out the tacit ap-
booze from the
crime, already
ed, on both sides
87, p. 352) con-
ment entered a
organized crime
ing Prohibition."
they kept Cana-
of boats that set
rned under cover
e cargo was off-
is, Ontario passed
tion of liquor on
ys declared *ultra*
e provinces juris-
did not constitu-
it. Attempts to
ated by a desire
tance. Neverthe-
stamp out boot-
estricted in their

efforts by the boundaries of their constitutional jurisdiction.

Bootlegging did not die overnight with the repeal of prohibition; rather, it dwindled out over time. When temperance acts were repealed, they were replaced with, for example, the **Liquor Control Act** (1927) of Ontario that granted provincial governments the monopoly on the sale of liquor that they still hold today. Acquisition of liquor was restricted, because there were initially few official outlets, and purchasers had to have a permit. But, alcohol from liquor stores was known to be unadulterated by additives designed to dilute the liquor to maximize profits. In 1930, the federal government finally prohibited the export of alcohol to countries under prohibition.[19]

In the final analysis, there was no decrease in the overall crime rate during prohibition, as was predicted by members of the temperance movement. Watts (1932) tried unsuccessfully to find any correlation between crime rate and the dates during which each province was "dry." One outcome, however, was that prosecutions for alcohol related offences plummeted after prohibition.

Subversion: Communists and Fascists

The hardship of the Great Depression of the 1930s led many to demand political remedies. As Betcherman (1975, p. 3) notes, "in such an atmosphere the 'isms' appealed to many." *Communism* was popular among some intellectuals and students, buoyed by the success of the Russian Revolution of 1917. *Socialism* found expression in the third-party movement on the prairies (Young, 1969) and nascent trade unionism. *Fascism* offered both an extreme alternative to the communism so feared by many and an explanation for the international economic downturn: liberalism and Jews.[20] The government response to communists on the political left and fascists on the extreme political right was inconsistent. Criminal laws were immediately created to come down hard on communists, but response to the criminal behaviour of fascists was delayed until sufficient public pressure had built up, after fascism had become associated with Adolf Hitler. To a lesser extent, the same was true for the Canadian branches of the Ku Klux Klan (see Box 1.4).

In Canada, fascist and Nazi groups began to emerge in the early 1930s. Adrien Arcand, a Quebec journalist, had begun his career as editor of three anti-Semitic newspapers. By 1934, he was so enamoured of fascism that he founded the Parti National Social Chrétien (National Social Christian Party). Like Europe, Canada was experiencing an economic depression and one of his policies, the deportation of Jews, proved moderately popular. He had close ties with the Conservative federal government of R.B. Bennett, having worked as a publicity director in two campaigns (Betch-

Box 1.4 The Canadian Ku Klux Klan: Mob Violence in Canada?

KU KLUX KLAN!
Applications for Membership in the Cranbrook Klan
No. 229 will be received by the undersigned during his two-day stay in Cranbrook, B.C., December 8th and 9th, when Klan No. 229 will be
organized.

APPLICATIONS MUST BE IN WRITING
All applicants must be British subjects, between the
ages of 21 and 40 and must be qualified horsemen
possessing the necessary skill and daring to uphold
the law and order at all costs.

> — H. Moncroft,
> Chief Klansman, Can. Division

(From the *Cranbrook Courier*, quoted in Sher, 1983,
p. 31).

Few Canadians today are aware that the Ku Klux Klan was
once active here, albeit briefly, in the 1920s. The American white-supremacist group, also called the Invisible Empire, is infamous for nocturnal cross burnings, white hoods,
whippings, and lynchings. After a period of dormancy, following its disbandment in the 1870s, the Klan was revived
in the United States during World War I. It became politically very powerful as members were elected to state
and local government, and it is estimated that U.S. membership was between four million and five million by 1925
(Chalmers, 1965).

In Canada, their fanatical ideas found sympathy among
primarily rural individuals who were concerned about urbanization, about the flood of non–Anglo-Saxon immigrants, and about the separate schools of the Roman
Catholics. Concern also spread to Jews, trade unionists, and
communists. The Klan was a secret society: the number
of members was unknown, but it is believed that there were
local chapters all across the country, the first being in Montreal in 1921 (Sher, 1983).

But it was only in Saskatchewan that the Klan was able
to gain any widespread support and achieve some political
influence. There, concern was both with non-British immigrants and with the Roman Catholic French Canadians
who wanted to retain their culture rather than assimilate.
Some anti-Semitism flowed from the association made by
many between Jews and bootlegging (Gray, 1972). Certainly, the American crusaders for prohibition, especially
in the later years, shared many of the Klan's ultra-
conservative values: distrust of urbanism, immigration, and
catholicism (Gusfield, 1963). American organizers arrived

in Saskatchewan in 1926 and, the following year, absconded
with $100 000. But that did not reduce the enthusiasm for
cross burnings. Membership estimates ranged from 10 000
to 50 000 by the end of the decade, and the KKK gained
a certain measure of respectability. A journalist who attacked Klan leaders in the press was prosecuted for **criminal
libel** by the provincial Liberal government. His lawyer,
Emmett Hall, who one day would sit on the Supreme
Court of Canada, was burned in effigy (Stewart, 1976).
While this prosecution was probably undertaken to gain
popularity, Klan support for the Conservative party has been
cited as a key reason for the electoral defeat of the Liberals
in 1929, after 24 years in power.

Support for the Klan waned during the Great Depression of the 1930s. Sher (1983) has attributed this to several
factors. Klaverns (Klan branches) remained localized, and
no national leadership ever emerged to identify one major
enemy to scapegoat. In many cases, the concerns of local
groups were removed by government action. For example,
the reduction in immigration and the passage of laws that
eroded the language rights of French Canadians combined
to make the general public feel less threatened. Provisions
in the Criminal Code permitting the deportation of un-
desirables such as communists were used against immigrants,
often in an effort to reduce welfare costs (Gray, 1966).
Moreover, the dramatic economic downturn seemed to
foster an atmosphere of co-operation, and interethnic conflict abated (Gray, 1966).

As public support for the Klan diminished, so did tolerance for their essentially criminal activities. Rarely had
members of the Canadian Klan been prosecuted for any
of their illegal activities except that, in 1926, three Klan
officers were sent to Kingston Penitentiary for placing a
bomb in St. Mary's Catholic Church in Barrie, Ontario
(Higley, 1984). An early prosecution took place in 1930
in Oakville, Ontario. About 75 gowned and hooded men
had burned a cross on a major street and then had abducted a young Caucasian woman, days before she was to marry
a Native Indian (who, at the time, they erroneously believed was a Negro). Her marriage was perceived as a threat
to the purity of the white race, and she was returned to
her mother.

While the chief of police was fully aware of this incident, even commenting upon the orderly behaviour of the
group, public outcry prompted the provincial attorney
general to prosecute three of the mob. A Hamilton
chiropractor was eventually convicted of wearing a disguise

Criminal Code)
Supreme Court,
rial court judge
e man to three
b's use of illegal

ompan-
as an at-
and, and
ich law,
rcement
ies. The
untry is

the overthrow of the law. Without it there is no security for life or property. Mob law such as is disclosed in this case is a step in that direction, and, like a venomous serpent, whenever its horrid head appears, must be killed, not scotched. (quoted in Montagnes, 1931, p. 268)

In 1933, the charismatic leader J.J. Maloney was jailed for **theft, fraud, vandalism**, and **slander** and that seemed to mark the end of the Klan in Canada (until the early 1980s). In the final analysis, the tactics of the Klan were not compatible with Canadian notions of centralized justice.

o contributed
groups were
wastika Clubs
lian Union of
ansionism and
Canada joined
he provisions
Nazis were in-

anada, but the
975). Arcand's
paganda, and
ress. The libel
ly to the libel
deral govern-
refused to act.
1932 and On-
se of the over-
c government
Code. Being a
der provincial
wspapers, the
ndment were
the Manitoba
il law created,
nction against
ti-defamation

hate propagan-
for publishing
ents, with the
ctant to act.

Moreover, contraventions of existing criminal laws also went unpunished, including riots outside meetings of communist groups and the smashing of windows of Jewish shops (Betcherman, 1975). Referring to the Toronto police, Betcherman (1975, p. 114) notes: "Unquestionably the police regarded communists as a greater threat to law and order than fascists; thus the identification of anti-fascists with communists militated against a genuine effort on the part of the police to contain fascists activities." The RCMP have also been criticized for being sympathetic to fascism, as evidenced by a series of ultra-conservative articles in the *R.C.M.P. Gazette* (Brown & Brown, 1973). Brown and Brown (1973) contend that when, in 1939, the RCMP arrested fascists under the provisions of the War Measures Act, they did so because of the possible threat to national security, and not because of opposition to their ideas.

If the Canadian governments have been tolerant of right-wing extremism, they have had little sympathy for the left. Fear of a communist plot had, in large measure, triggered the violent government reaction to the Winnipeg General Strike of 1919 (see Chapter 17). A mounted contingent of the Royal North-West Mounted Police (as they were known by then) armed with baseball bats and revolvers charged a group of parading strikers, killing two. The leaders of the strike were charged with **seditious conspiracy** (Brown, 1984). The RCMP were also called in to break a strike in Estevan, Saskatchewan, in 1931, where three miners were killed. In 1935, in Corbin, B.C., several women were injured when the police drove a bulldozer through a picket line.

One month after the Winnipeg General Strike, the federal government passed section 98 of the Criminal Code, prohibiting "unlawful associations," and amended the Immigration Act to permit the deportation of British-born immigrants, a move clearly aimed at the leaders of the General Strike. Throughout the 1920s and 1930s, police used these laws to harass union members and break up meetings. Hundreds were deported as suspected communists, without recourse to due process protections. Picketing remained a criminal offence until 1934. The Communist Party was banned under the War Measures Act in 1940. Some communists were briefly interned but released when the USSR entered the war.

In 1936, the newly-elected Liberal government of Mackenzie King fulfilled a promise by repealing section 98. The premier of Quebec, Maurice Duplessis, responded to what he saw as a void by enacting the Act Respecting Communist Propaganda (nicknamed "The Padlock Act") the following year. Provincial authorities could padlock any premises wherein it was suspected that communist literature was being produced or distributed. Newspaper offices and bookstores were often targets, as were the private homes of their employees. Only a small opposition emerged to challenge this essentially popular law, and it stood on the books until 1957 when the Supreme Court of Canada struck it down as being *ultra vires* as an invasion of the federal jurisdiction over criminal law.

Historical Legacies: Summary and Conclusion

A theme evident from this historical discussion is that Canadian criminal justice is highly centralized with the federal government. Initially related to our colonial origins, and the allegiance to a distant power, this centralization was formalized in the constitutional arrangement that gave Ottawa the power to enact criminal law. The considerable regional variations that exist, especially north to south, are difficult to reconcile in a national policy. Indeed, Canadian history has generally been characterized by regional conflicts.

Further, with dubious constitutional jurisdiction, a federal police force was created, first the Dominion Police and later the RCMP. This force has very few parallels in the world. As Rock (1986, p. 143) has noted, the RCMP is "accountable to the [federal] Solicitor General, and that accountability offers a very broad and uncontested entrance into the practical affairs of law and social control in Canada." The result is that the RCMP has often been called upon to exercise the will of the federal government, intervening in what are essentially political matters, rightly falling outside its criminal jurisdiction.

Examples of such intervention include the suppression of the Métis political dissent, strike breaking, harassment of communists, and the illegal tactics used to monitor Que-

bec separatists (discussed in Chapter 17). By constrast, the essentially criminal behaviour of fascist groups was tolerated, and the criminal activities of the Ku Klux Klan were rarely prosecuted. Canadians have been generally supportive of the broad authority granted to their law enforcement agencies, in the name of "peace, order and good government," and to some extent this is why the Ku Klux Klan died out here while remaining so active in the United States.

We have seen that the history of criminal justice in Canada reveals many instances where the federal/provincial division of powers has played a role in defining policy or law. For example, the federal government was successful in passing the responsibility for prohibition onto provincial and municipal shoulders, even though these groups were hampered in enforcement by the powers available to them constitutionally. The federal government also refused to pass effective laws against group libel to permit prosecution of fascists. Attempts made by provincial governments to fill this void were constitutionally tenuous. When federal criminal laws aimed at communist groups were repealed, the Quebec provincial government responded to what it perceived as a void by enacting the padlock law, a statute that was *ultra vires*. Interestingly, the constitutionality of this law was not successfully challenged for two decades. However, the federal government abrogated the provincial power over child welfare and the prosecution of violators of provincial laws when it passed the Juvenile Delinquents Act. It also stepped outside its constitutional jurisdiction to create a federal police force.

The federal-provincial split is still affecting the administration of justice. Attempts by the federal government to initiate a policy package aimed at victims of crime had to be sensitive to "border disputes." Problems were circumvented by vesting much of the responsibility for the victims' initiatives in the police, because of the federal authority over the RCMP (Rock, 1986, p. 143). In the early 1980s, the soliciting provisions in the Criminal Code were essentially struck down by the Supreme Court of Canada, leaving a significant void from the point of view of local officials keen to clear the streets of the burgeoning numbers of prostitutes. In the absence of federal action, in the form of a new law, several municipal governments enacted by-laws to control **soliciting**. These efforts were predictably declared *ultra vires* (see Chapter 4).

An early attempt to replace the Juvenile Delinquents Act was stalled when provincial governments demanded their jurisdiction over the prosecution of provincial offenders and over child welfare be returned (Solicitor General, Canada, 1968). During the nearly two decades of negotiations that followed, the provincial government sought and achieved an expanded role in defining the procedures for the prose-

9). As we shall
ing, an activ-
riminal law.
n the context
ng therapeutic
th a Supreme
r. Henry Mor-
t pressure, the
void by enact-
one or both of
l governments
: of their con-
ttempt to deny
le, was quickly
publicized cases
option for res-
o 1990 that the
ie abortions as
his tactic is to
to avoid the
the provinces

ion of Canadi-
ily been a mul-
s between the
and Protestants
on-British, Eu-
he West, were
as. Ethnic ten-
es of the Cana-

riginal Canadi-
riginals was the
countries seek-
r favours were

bought with desirable European goods, such as blankets. Natives aided exploration, taught survival skills, and were crucial to the fur trade. The French and English each gained the allegiance of different tribes, thereby pitting one against the other in a lengthy series of Indian wars. But once over-hunting and fickle European tastes reduced the importance of the fur trade, natives were forced to sign treaties and were herded onto reserves. The NWMP were used to en-force the federal policy of assimilation through the enforce-ment of both criminal and regulatory offences. The jailing or hanging of high-profile native leaders did much to en-courage the others to acquiesce. With their traditional way of life gone, natives became the victims of paternalistic poli-cies that did little to encourage self-reliance. The contem-porary outcome of this situation is presented in Chapter 12.

This chapter has provided a look into how crime control techniques in Canada, while sharing roots with European and American systems, have a unique background in many respects. Yet, as discussed in the Introduction, Canadian criminologists, until recently, had to rely upon material from other countries in their teaching and research. The whole-sale adoption of theories and research findings from, prin-cipally, American sources was necessitated by the paucity of original Canadian work. Consideration of the differ-ences between our two systems of law and criminal justice was rarely made. But even the Canadian criminological work of today is largely uninformed by a historical per-spective. Material on the history of law and criminal justice in Canada can be found in the literature of such disciplines as history, education, political science, and law, highlight-ing the multidisciplinary nature of criminology. It is hoped that this brief overview of our historical roots will provide added insight into the discussion of specific topics in the remainder of this volume.

of historical influence upon
criminal justice system,

udson's Bay Company's
in Canada? Why was the
d to the law enforcement
tral Canadian courts?

it the rationale used to ex-
/ere dealt with in Canada.
ine of argument.

4. **The federal/provincial split in jurisdiction has created numerous problems in our justice system. Explain why we evolved such a split and whether this is likely to change.**

Notes

1. This has remained a feature of Canadian law enforcement until well into the twentieth century. Senior (1979) has traced the role of British troops in maintaining order in Montreal between 1832 and 1853. Generally, the paramilitary nature of most Canadian police forces today is a legacy of the evolution from military control to civilian law enforcement.

2. For a more detailed history of policing in Canada, see Griffiths and Verdun-Jones (1989).

3. Friedland (1984) outlines several other differences between the two systems. Under the British law, convictions could be gained on circumstantial evidence, and the French did not like the jury system because it required unanimity rather than a majority opinion.

4. This is illustrated by the case of a judge newly arrived from England who questioned the legality of the Court of King's Bench in Upper Canada. While Judge Willis may have been legally correct, the consequences of his decision would have meant chaos in that all decisions rendered by the court would have been nullified. Hett (1973) also notes that the court was operating to the benefit of prominent citizens of the colonial establishment and his criticisms of this practice also contributed to his removal.

5. The election of justice officials has long been considered to be one of the key differences between the American and Canadian systems. See Montagnes (1931).

6. In 1982, with the patriation of the constitution, this statute was renamed the Constitution Act, 1867.

7. Some contend that it was the assassination of D'Arcy McGee in 1868 (see Slattery, 1968) that prompted the creation of the Dominion Police. Security intelligence, albeit in a nascent form, was also made one of the responsibilities of this force because they absorbed the small Western Frontier Constabulary, that had been created in 1864 by John A. Macdonald to control the American-based, Irish republican Fenians. Security intelligence would most appropriately be performed by a federal agency, but the wisdom of having a law enforcement body serve this function was the subject of much debate during the period, leading to the creation of the Canadian Security Intelligence Service (see Chapter 17).

8. This has been used, for example, for penitentiary riots and strike breaking, when there are insufficient numbers of police available. Morton (1970) relates that the Canadian militia was called to the aid of civil power, essentially a police function to meet threats to public order, 48 times between 1867 and 1914.

9. A rural police force had been given jurisdiction over the areas not serviced by the Quebec and Montreal municipal police as early as 1838. The various forces in British Columbia had amalgamated in 1866. In 1871, the system of local constables in Newfoundland was replaced by the centralized Newfoundland Constabulary (Fox, 1971).

The Manitoba Mounted Police were created in 1871. In 1875, John Wilson Murray, the first full-time, salaried constable in Ontario, was appointed as the Detective of the Ontario Department of Justice (Murray, 1904; Campbell, 1970).

10. A popular recipe for "Whoop-up Bug Juice" was: one quart whiskey, one pound of chewing tobacco, a handful of red pepper, one bottle of Jamaican ginger, and one quart of molasses (Kelly and Kelly, 1973, p. 12).

11. Some years previous to this, Charcoal had also slaughtered a steer to feed his family after his treaty rations were cut off. For this he had served one year in jail. Many years later, he became embroiled in a love triangle. According to accepted rules of his tribe, and after much taunting, he killed his wife's lover. Assuming, probably incorrectly, that he would be hanged, he fled. During this pursuit, he killed an officer.

12. This referred to the body of judicial opinion and precedents that had accumulated over the years. Therefore, offences such as public mischief were against the law, because it had traditionally been so, but this was not written down anywhere (this is discussed in more detail in Chapter 2).

13. The laws against duelling were not always popular and so were not always applied. For example, the colourful John Walpole Willis of the Upper Canada Court of King's Bench had the solicitor general tried for murder in 1828, for his role as a second at a fatal duel twelve years earlier (Hett, 1973). His desire to apply the law to the letter was locally unpopular, contributing to his being quickly dismissed.

14. This last offence dates back to 1285. As a result of the input of the Society for the Protection of Women and Young Girls, the Code contained a comprehensive array of offences related to sexual contact with young girls and women, extending the protection of the state to poor girls as well as heiresses. These provisions have largely remained on the books until the reforms of the 1980s discussed in the case study later in this volume.

15. Theft of oysters, cattle, or ore specimens is still illegal today.

16. Consistently, the wets and drys were divided along rural/urban lines, and support for prohibition was least strong in Quebec, especially in Montreal.

17. Alcohol for religious, industrial, artistic, scientific, and medicinal purposes was still permitted. Doctors could issue prescriptions for it and keep a supply on hand to dispense as required. Demand seemed to be greatest around Christmas. In Ontario, a temperance beer of 2.2 percent, and later 4.4 percent alcohol, was legal. Homemade wines were also allowed, with a permit. Because various provinces and areas were dry at different times, a booming mail-order business thrived.

18. Several Canadian bootleggers became notorious. Rocco Perri,

orders, continu-
had left that job.
g of the Ontario
Sun in 1924. At-
were never suc-
e in prison. It was
ar II, that Rocco
put out of busi-
he War Measures
t causes, but their
he federal govern-
due process pro-

the Canada Ex-
the tariff on goods
ariff was raised.
olitical turmoil of
cterized by a belief

that, for the overall good of the nation, civil rights, such as freedom of speech and religion, had to be suspended and the multiparty system eliminated. Social stability was to be the result. The term was coined by Benito Mussolini who came to power in Italy in 1922. He was a fervent anti-communist and espoused economic nationalism. Political opponents were neutralized, strikes outlawed, and the military modernized. Adolf Hitler and his Nazi followers rose to power in Germany in 1933. Hitler's brand of fascism was characterized by extreme anti-Semitism.

21. In each case, the suspected fathers successfully gained a court injunction to stop their former girlfriends from having abortions. Both women eventually did so, however, when higher courts affirmed their rights to self-determination.

22. It is interesting to note that after sixteen years as a federal issue, the 1989 *Webster* decision of the U.S. Supreme court effectively returned to the state governments the authority to legislate in the area of abortion, something state legislators are greeting "with a reserve bordering on clinical depression" (Kinsley, 1989, p. 62).

the old Canadian
-15.
history of a controver-

anadian rape law,
history of Canadian
y of Toronto Press.
n in Upper Canada.

da 1785–1889: The
(Ed.), *Essays in the
oronto: University

ecord of man's inhu-
ith [rprt. 1972].
ment in Upper Cana-
: Centre of Crimi-

towards crime and
4, 11–26.
1896–1899. Toron-
shed 1958].
personal exploration
d & Stewart.
le leaf: Fascist move-
henry & Whiteside.
Canadian prairies,
uthority: Readings on
19). Toronto: Copp

w: Adam Thom and
1839–54. In D.H.
dian law, Vol. I* (pp.
Press.
The penalty is death.

Boritch, H. (1988). Conflict, compromise and administrative convenience: The police organization in nineteenth century Toronto. *Canadian Journal of Law and Society, 3,* 141–74.

Boritch, H., & Hagan, J. (1987). Crime and the changing forms of class control: Policing public order in "Toronto the Good," 1859–1955. *Social Forces, 66,* 307–35.

Boyer, R. (1963a). The question: Judicial torture in New France. *Canadian Journal of Criminology and Corrections, 5,* 284–91.

Boyer, R. (1963b). La peine capitale en Nouvelle-France. *Cité libre, 4,* 13–20.

Brantingham, P.J. (1979). The classical and positive schools of criminology: Two ways of thinking about crime. In F.L. Faust & P.J. Brantingham (Eds.), *Juvenile justice philosophy: Readings, cases and comments,* (2nd ed.) (pp. 36–48). St. Paul: West.

Brown, D.H. (1984). The craftmanship of bias: Sedition and the Winnipeg General Strike trial in 1919. *Manitoba Law Journal, 14*(1), 1–33.

Brown, G. (1849a). *First report of the commissioners appointed to investigate into the conduct, discipline and management of the provincial penitentiary.* Toronto.

Brown, G. (1849b). *Second report of the commissioners appointed to investigate into the conduct, discipline and management of the provincial penitentiary.* Toronto.

Brown, L., & Brown, C. (1973). *An unauthorized history of the R.C.M.P.* Toronto: James Lorimer.

Brown, R.M. (1975). *Strain of violence: Historical studies of American violence and vigilantism.* New York: Oxford University Press.

Campbell, M.F. (1970). *A century of crime: The developments of crime detection methods in Canada.* Toronto: McClelland & Stewart.

Chalmers, D.M. (1965). *Hooded Americanism: The first century of the Ku Klux Klan 1865–1965.* New York: Doubleday.

Chisholm, J. (1940). Our first trial for murder: The King v. Peter Cartcel. *Canadian Bar Review, 18,* 385–89.

Chunn, D. (1981). Good men work hard: Convict labour in Kingston Penitentiary, 1835–1850. *Canadian Criminology Forum, 4,* 13–22.

Cooper, S.D. (1987). The evolution of the federal women's prison. In E. Adelberg & C. Currie (Eds.), *Two few to count: Canadian women in conflict with the law* (pp. 127–44). Vancouver: Press Gang.

Craven, P. (1983). Law and ideology: The Toronto Police Court 1850–80. In D.H. Flaherty (Ed.), *Essays in the history of Canadian law, Vol. II* (pp. 248–307). Toronto: University of Toronto Press.

Crevel, J. (1966). Nécessité d'une police en Gaspésie au 17e siècle. *Revue d'histoire de la Gaspésie, 4*(4), 170–74.

Crouse, G.H. (1934). A critique of Canadian criminal legislation. *Canadian Bar Review, 12*(9), 545–78.

Curtis, D., Graham, A., Kelly, L., & Patterson, A. (1985). *Kingston Penitentiary: The first hundred and fifty years, 1835–1985*. Ottawa: Ministry of Supply & Services.

Daily Globe (1859, June 10). Execution of Dr. King at Cobourg, his confession, 5,000 persons present, p. 3.

DeSalaberry, R. (1927). The first state trial in Lower Canada. *Canadian Bar Review, 5*(7), 467–77.

Desaulniers, C. (1977). Le peine de mort dans législation criminelle de 1760 à 1892. *Revue générale de droit, 8,* 141–84.

Dubro, J. (1985). *Mob rule: Inside the Canadian mafia*. Toronto: Macmillan.

Dubro, J., & Rowland, R.F. (1987). *King of the mob: Rocco Perri and the women who ran his rackets*. Toronto: Viking.

Edwards. J.Ll.L. (1984). The advent of English (not French) criminal law and procedure into Canada—A close call in 1774. *Criminal Law Quarterly, 26*(4), 464–82.

Ekstedt, J., & Griffiths, C.T. (1988). *Corrections in Canada: Policy and practice* (2nd ed.). Toronto: Butterworths.

Ellis, H. (1895). *The criminal* (2nd ed.). London: Walter Scott.

Evans, R.G. (1968). *Murder on the plains*. Calgary: Frontier.

Fetherling, D. (1988). *The gold crusades: A social history of gold rushes, 1849–1929*. Toronto: Macmillan.

Fetherstonhaugh, R.C. (1938). *The Royal Canadian Mounted Police*. New York: Carrick & Evans.

Foster, J.E. (1975). Rupert's Land and the Red River Settlement, 1820–70. In L.G. Thomas (Ed.), *The Prairie West to 1905: A Canadian sourcebook* (pp. 19–72). Toronto: Oxford University Press.

Fox, A. (1971). *The Newfoundland Constabulary*. St. John's: Robinson Blackmore.

Friedland, M. (1984). *A century of criminal justice: Perspectives on the development of Canadian law*. Toronto: Carswell.

Friedland, M. (1986). *The case of Valentine Shortis: A true story of crime and politics in Canada*. Toronto: University of Toronto Press.

Globe and Mail (1897, August 19). Against Allison, the young farm hand believed to be guilty, the murder of Mrs. Orr, p. 4.

Gagnon, D. (1984). *The history of the law for juvenile delinquents*. Ottawa: Ministry of the Solicitor General.

Godsell, P.H. (1932). *They got their man: On patrol with the North West Mounted*. Toronto: Ryerson.

Gray, J. (1966). *The winter years*. Toronto: Macmillan.

Gray, J. (1972). *Booze: The impact of whiskey in the Prairie West*. Toronto: Macmillan.

Griffiths, C.T., & Verdun-Jones, S.N. (1989). *Canadian criminal justice*. Toronto: Butterworths.

Gusfield, J.R. (1963). *Symbolic crusade: Status politics and the American temperance movement*. Chicago: University of Illinois Press.

Hagan, J., & Leon, J. (1977). Philosophy and sociology of crime control: Canadian-American comparisons. *Sociological Inquiry, 47*(3), 181–208.

Hansard (1892). *Official reports of the debates of the House of Commons of the Dominion of Canada*. Second session, seventh Parliament, 34.

Hatch, A.J., & Griffiths, C.T. (1990, February). *The implementation of the Juvenile Delinquents Act in Vancouver: A case of delayed response*. Paper presented at the multidisciplinary workshop concerning children and youth in Canada, University of Manitoba.

Herbert, R.G. (1954). A brief history of the introduction of English law into British Columbia. *University of British Columbia Legal Notes, 2,* 93–101.

Hett, R. (1973). Judge Willis and the Court of King's Bench in Upper Canada. *Ontario History, 65,* 19–30.

Higley, D.D. (1984). *O.P.P.: The history of the Ontario Provincial Police*. Toronto: Queen's Printer.

Horrall, S.W. (1972). Sir John A. Macdonald and the Mounted Police Force for the Northwest Territories. *Canadian Historical Review, 53,* 179–200.

Horwood, H., & Butts, E. (1984). *Pirates and outlaws of Canada, 1610–1932*. Toronto: Doubleday.

Horwood, H., & Butts, E. (1987). *Bandits and privateers: Canada in the age of gunpowder*. Toronto: Doubleday.

Ives, G. (1914). *A history of penal methods: Criminals, witches, lunatics*. London: Hutchinson.

Jennings, J. (1975). Policemen and poachers: Indian relations on the ranching frontier. In A.W. Rasporich & H. Klassen (Eds.), *Frontier Calgary: Town, city and region 1875–1914* (pp. 87–99). Toronto: McClelland & Stewart.

Jennings, J.N. (1986). The North-West Mounted Police and Indian policy after the 1885 Rebellion. In F.L. Barron & J.B. Waldram (Eds.), *1885 and after: Native society in transition* (pp. 225–39). Regina: Canadian Plains Research Centre, University of Regina.

Kelly, N. (1949). *The men of the Mounted*. Toronto: Dent.

Kelly, N., & Kelly, W. (1973). *The Royal Canadian Mounted Police: A century of history, 1873–1973*. Edmonton: Hurtig.

Kelly, W., & Kelly, N. (1976). *Policing in Canada*. Toronto: Macmillan.

Kinsley, M. (1989). The new politics of abortion. *Time,* July 17, p. 62.

Kirkpatrick, A.M. (1964). Jails in historical perspective. *Canadian Journal of Corrections, 6,* 405–18.

Lachance, A. (1981). Women and crime in Canada in the early eighteenth century, 1712–1759. In L.A. Knafla (Ed.), *Crime and criminal justice in Europe and Canada* (pp. 157–97). Waterloo: Wilfrid Laurier University Press.

Langbein, J.H. (1977). *Torture and the law of proof*. Chicago: University of Chicago Press.

Leon, J. (1977). The development of Canadian juvenile justice: A background for reform. *Osgoode Hall Law Journal, 15,* 71–106.

Lombroso, C. (1876). *L'uomo delinquente* [The criminal man]. Translated 1911 by Gina Lombroso-Ferrero. [Rprt. 1972: Montclair, NJ: Patterson Smith].

Macbeth, R.G. (1931). *Policing the plains*. Toronto: Musson.

Macleod, R.C. (1974). The Mounted Police and politics. In H.A. Dempsey (Ed.), *Men in scarlet* (pp. 95–114). Calgary: McClelland & Stewart West.

Macleod, R.C. (1975). The problem of law and order in the Canadian West, 1870–1905. In L.G. Thomas (Ed.), *The Prairie West to 1905: A Canadian sourcebook* (pp. 19–72). Toronto: Oxford University Press.

Macleod, R.C. (1978). Canadianizing the west: The North-West Mounted Police as agents of the National Policy, 1873–1905. In L.H. Thomas (Ed.), *Essays on western history* (pp. 101–10). Edmonton: University of Edmonton Press.

McDougall, J. (1911). *On western trails in the early seventies: Frontier pioneer life in the Canadian North-West*. Toronto: William Briggs.

McGahan, P. (1988). *Crime and policing in Maritime Canada: Chapters from the urban record*. Fredericton: Goose Lane.

McNaught, K. (1974). Violence in Canadian history. In M. Horn &

ory (pp. 376–91).

ian political tradi-
A multidisciplinary
f Toronto Press.
967. *Canadian Bar*

it: A brief history
rterly, 30(4):3–8.
ninals. *North Ameri-*

The case of indus-
rnal of Educational

ted Police and Cana-
ouver: University

Canadian Militia in
Historical Review,

of a Great Detective:
onto: Collins [rprt.

e federal-provincial
ournal of Criminolo-

ic encounters in sport,

ida: The transfer of
w, 2, 7–32.
: The Red River
Prairie Forum, 3(2),

rise of the peniten-

the juvenile court.

Criminal Code. In
Canadian law, Vol.
oronto Press.
. Knafla (Ed.), *Law*
Canadian legal history

it is. In E. Mann &
nada's security service
ng.
n Indians and decoloni-

. Toronto: McClel-

l law from 1750: Vol.
is.
he North-West Mount-
MacEachern.
Ministry of the Solicitor
of crime initiative. Ox-

The development of
Russell (Ed.), *Forging*
. 116–40). Toronto:

er: Early murder trials

of Native accused. *Criminal Law Quarterly, 22,* 74–111.

Scott, W.L. (1930). *Juvenile courts in law and the juvenile courts in action.* Ottawa: Canadian Welfare Council.

Senior, E. (1979). The influence of the British garrison on the development of the Montreal Police, 1832–1853. *Military Affairs, 43,* 63–68.

Sher, J. (1983). *White hoods: Canada's Ku Klux Klan.* Vancouver: New Star.

Shoom, S. (1966). Kingston penitentiary: The early decades. *Canadian Journal of Corrections, 8,* 215–20.

Shoom, S. (1972). The Upper Canada Reformatory, Penetanguishene: The dawn of prison reform in Canada. *Canadian Journal of Criminology and Corrections, 14,* 260–67.

Slattery, T.P. (1968). *The assassination of D'Arcy McGee.* Toronto: Doubleday.

Solicitor General, Canada (1968). *Proceedings of the federal-provincial conference on juvenile delinquency.* Ottawa: Department of the Solicitor General.

Spettigue, D. (1955). *The friendly force.* Toronto: Longmans, Green.

Stamm, M. (1985). Juvenile justice and federalism in the 80s: *Parens patriae,* child advocacy and constitutional constraint in Australia, Canada, and the United States. *Australian-Canadian Studies, 3:* 70–85.

Stenning, P.C. (1981). *Legal status of the police.* Ottawa: Law Reform Commission of Canada.

Stewart, W. (1976). *But not in Canada!* Toronto: Macmillan.

Streib, V.L. (1987). *Death penalty for juveniles.* Bloomington: Indiana University Press.

Talbot, C.K., Jayewardene, C.H.S., & Juliani, T.J. (1985). *Canada's constables: The historical development of policing in Canada.* Ottawa: Crimcare.

Thacker, R. (1980). Canada's Mounted: The evolution of a legend. *Journal of Popular Culture, 14,* 298–312.

Tobias, J.L. (1983a). Canada's subjugation of the Plains Cree, 1879–1885. *Canadian Historical Review, 64,* 519–48.

Tobias, J.L. (1983b). Protection, civilization, assimilation: An outline history of Canada's Indian policy. In J.L. Tobias (Ed.), *As long as the sun shines and the water flows: A reader in Canadian Native studies* (pp. 39–55). Vancouver: University of British Columbia Press.

Torrance, J. (1986). *Public violence in Canada.* Montreal & Kingston: McGill-Queen's University Press.

Walden, K. (1982). *Visions of order: The Canadian Mounties in symbol and myth.* Toronto: Butterworth's.

Watts, A. (1986). *Magistrate-judge: the story of the Provincial Court of British Columbia.* Victoria: Queen's Printer.

Watts, R.E. (1932). The trend of crime in Canada. *Queen's Quarterly, August,* 402–13.

Wilden, T. (1980). *The imaginary Canadian.* Vancouver: Pulp Press.

Williams, D.R. (1977). *The man for a new country.* Sidney, BC: Gray's.

Williams, D.R. (1986). The administration of criminal and civil justice in the mining camps and frontier communities of British Columbia. In L.A. Knafla (Ed.), *Law and justice in a new land: Essays in western Canadian legal history* (pp. 215–31). Toronto: Carswell.

Wilson, L. (1977). Juvenile justice and the criminal law power. *Saskatchewan Law Review, 41:* 251–67.

Wright, J. (1979). The legal system in pioneer days. *Law society of Upper Canada Gazette, 13:*158–60.

Young, D.A. (1968). *The Mounties.* Toronto: Hodder & Stoughton.

Young, W. (1969). *Democracy and discontent.* Toronto: McGraw-Hill Ryerson.

2 The Criminal Law

The relevance of the **criminal law** to **criminology** is not hard to determine, but it is often overlooked. Many texts that focus solely on deviant behaviour and its consequences ignore the fundamental structures and processes that transform that behaviour into "crime" and authorize the imposition of penal **sanctions**. The existence of criminal law is a necessary prerequisite for the existence of **crime, criminality**, and criminals. There can be no crime, in the true sense of the word, without criminal law, and, as Schur (1974) has noted, "crime laws, by definition, create criminals." Accordingly, the purpose of this chapter is to examine Canadian criminal law in order to provide an understanding not only of its fundamental characteristics, but also of its distinctive aspects, which contribute to the uniqueness of Canadian criminology.

The Origins of Canadian Criminal Law

A National *Code*

The majority of Canadian criminal laws can be found in the *Criminal Code*. The fact that Canada has codified its criminal law is distinctive, given its **common-law** antecedents. As a former colony of the United Kingdom, this country inherited the English common-law tradition as opposed to that of codified systems of law prevalent in Europe. The civil law of Quebec, however, has its origins in the French legal system, which, in turn, is based on Roman law.

At the heart of common law is the development of legal rules and principles through the decisions of the courts of the land. They are not laid down in advance by a legislative body. Rather, a court, when confronted with the unique set of facts and circumstances that comprise each individual case, looks to the previous decisions of the courts on similar issues. These are known as **precedents**. The judge will then decide if they apply in this particular case (i.e., whether they are **binding**) and make a decision accordingly. The decision itself becomes part of the common law on this subject, forming a small part of the complex spider's web of common law. The common law grows continuously and changes shape almost imperceptibly. Further, it is recorded not in a single document, code, or legislative enactment, but in the multitude of reported decisions of the courts. In order for the development of the common law to be logical and orderly, the law is fashioned around the concept of *stare decisis*, which means that the courts are organized in a hierarchy (see Figure 2.1) and the essence of the decisions (i.e., the *ratio decidendi*) of the higher courts is binding on the courts beneath in the hierarchy, unless those decisions can be distinguished from the one under consideration on some basis.

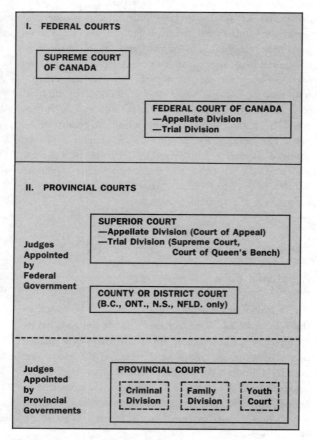

Figure 2.1 The Canadian Criminal Court System

Note: This chart presents a simplified overview of the criminal courts in Canada. The chart does not apply to the Province of Quebec. From C.T. Griffiths & S. Verdun-Jones (Eds.) (1989), *Criminal Justice in Canada* (p. 186). Toronto: Butterworths.

The Criminal Code was enacted in 1892, based in large measure upon the English Draft Code of Sir James Fitzjames Stephen. At that time, the federal government was struggling with the problem of how to unify the criminal law as it existed in the different provinces, which were at quite diverse stages in their legal development. Codification was to provide the answer.

It was, and still is, a legal code of quite a curious nature. Unlike European codes, it is not organized around, and derived from, articulated rational principles, which are adhered to consistently and coherently throughout the body of the code. Rather, it is a body of law that represents a compromise between the common law and a true code. The Criminal Code of Canada is simply a compilation of the criminal law as it existed in its common-law format in 1892, along with subsequent amendments and additions. The principles and concepts guiding the specific enactments, such as the rule of law, *mens rea*, and *actus reus*, are left unstated, but they remain at the heart of Canadian criminal law. Thus, the Criminal Code is simply the common law in a unique Canadian format. The courts still have a fundamental role in the development of the law. The terms of the Criminal Code offer no more than a very general guide. The specifics are developed in the courtrooms across the country, which still search for the *ratio decidendi* of past cases, determine their present applicability, and adhere to the scheme of binding precedent.

When the Criminal Code was first debated in 1892, legislators were reluctant to abandon totally the common-law tradition. The Code defined many offences and their penalties, but a compromise was effected by the preservation of common-law offences and defences in Canada. In other words, the Code was not exhaustive in its catalogue of criminal behaviour. As a result, between 1892 and 1953, successful prosecutions took place for such common-law offences as public mischief, abuse of office in taking fees wrongfully, and conspiracy. It was not until 1955, when the Code underwent a major revision, that all common-law offences except **contempt of court** were abolished in Canada (see s. 9). Those common-law **offences** that were thought worth preserving were specifically enacted into the Criminal Code (e.g., s. 140: public mischief; and s. 465: conspiracy). Common-law **defences**, however, were retained uncodified (see s. 8[3]). Thus, the common law still has a vital role to play in the criminal law of Canada (see Box 2.1).

A *National* Code

Another distinctive aspect of Canadian criminal law is that the Criminal Code issues from the federal government. In other words, it is national in scope. In contrast, in the Unit-

Criminal Code, R.S.C. 1985, c. C-42

841 sections that de-
missions that are ille-
procedures. Various
or amended, but it is
almost a century ago,

y terms that are used
rever it is mentioned
eriod between nine
ock in the forenoon
it" means the victim

by 28 parts. The first
h as jurisdiction. For
h an offence that oc-
place on an airplane.
arious principles, such

These include offences
, offences against the
ting to contracts and
ncy. Each offence has
to state that the com-
therefore against the
nay be defined, but a
example, the discharge
odily harm provisions

ent
gure any person,
ny person, or
detention of any

ir pistol at any per-
n is the one men-
(c), is guilty of an
imprisonment for
years.

This is an **indictable offence**, meaning basically that it is a serious offence that can carry with it a severe penalty. More minor offences are called summary-conviction offences. The penalty for these offences is restricted to a maximum of six months in jail, a $2000 fine, or both. The procedures surrounding the prosecution of these two types of offences are also different.

Many offences are called **mixed** or **hybrid** because the prosecutor may choose, based on the circumstances of the case, to proceed either summarily or by indictment. Sexual assault is such an offence:

> 271. Every one who commits a sexual assault is guilty of
> (a) an indictable offence and is liable to imprisonment for a term not exceeding ten years; or
> (b) an offence punishable on summary conviction.

The Law Reform Commission of Canada has been among the many recommending that Canada start from scratch and write a new code that reflects today's priorities. Archaic sections, such as duelling, are only one reason. The language of the Criminal Code is difficult to understand, there are no guiding principles, and new technology in areas such as telecommunications have created situations for crime that could not even be dreamed of in the nineteenth century. Piracy, for example, is now a term applied to the theft of computer software. Among the changes suggested by the Law Reform Commission in their 1988 document, *Recodifying Criminal Law,* would be the definition of an interest rate over 60 percent per annum as criminal. Child abuse would become a specific offence, as would electronic eavesdropping. Some common-law matters, such as defences, would be codified. The chances of these suggestions being adopted are slim, but the criticisms of the Criminal Code should be addressed by legislators.

the state level; thus,
state boundaries. At
allocated to the fed-
ment, the criminal-
government in order
ncy and uniformity.
he criminal law was

to be a tool to draw the country together. At the same time, it would enhance the power of the central government. Criminal law based on the English common law was to apply across Canada, despite its diverse cultural, geographic, and political makeup.

Thus, under the **Constitution Act, 1867** (formerly the British North America Act), subsection 91(27) bestows upon the federal government jurisdiction over "The Criminal Law, except the Constitution of Courts of Criminal Jurisdiction, but including the Procedure in Criminal Matters."[1] Generally speaking, therefore, the crimes of robbery or sexual assault, for example, will encompass the same forms of behaviour right across the country. When the Supreme Court of Canada renders a decision on a matter of criminal law that arose in one province, it is binding on the courts of all the provinces. The same cannot be said of child-welfare legislation, for example, as that is a matter within provincial jurisdiction.

To state that criminal law and procedure are within the exclusive legislative power of the federal government is to be misleading. While there is no doubt that the Criminal Code, a federal enactment, is the major source of Canadian criminal law, there are numerous other federal and provincial statutes that create criminal and quasi-criminal offences. Under the power granted to them by subsection 92(15) of the Constitution Act, 1867, the provinces may impose penalties for breaches of provincial legislation, such as highway-traffic legislation or liquor-licensing laws. Given that these provincial enactments deal with everyday matters, they probably have a much more immediate impact on our lives than do those governing the more serious criminal offences.

Clearly, it is important to recognize that the term "criminal law" in Canada encompasses different kinds of enactments emanating from different levels of government:

> When one talks about the criminal law of Canada, it is therefore necessary to distinguish between criminal law that arises from section 91(27) and is within the exclusive jurisdiction of the federal government, criminal law that arises from the better enforcement of some other clause in section 91, which is also within the exclusive jurisdiction of the federal government, but which may have certain procedural differences attached to it because of its different basis, and that criminal law which is really the enforcement by way of penal sanction of some clause of section 92 and which is within the exclusive jurisdiction of the provinces. This last is sometimes called quasi-criminal law or provincial penal law, to avoid the confusion of equating it with what is sometimes called "real" criminal law or criminal law "properly so-called." (Mewett, 1988, pp. 2–3)

Finally, there is superimposed over all law, federal and provincial criminal offences included, the overriding legal authority of the **Canadian Charter of Rights and Freedoms** (1982). All legislation and governmental action must conform to the standards set out in the Charter. It must, for example, respect freedom of conscience and religion (s. 2[a]) and freedom of expression (s. 2[b]); it must ensure that the right to life, liberty, and security of the person is not removed except in accordance with the principles of fundamental justice (s. 7), and it must respect each individual's right to equality (s. 15[1]). The Canadian Charter of Rights and Freedoms applies to both federal and provincial levels of government, and thus creates a national standard for Canadian law, regardless of whether it is located in the Criminal Code or other federal or provincial statutes.

The Physical Component of Crime

In this chapter, federal criminal law, found in the Criminal Code and other federal statutes, will be the primary focus of attention. Federal criminal law encompasses the kinds of behaviour that most people would include in the category of criminal. Speaking to this class of criminal law, the following definition was offered by Mr. Justice Rand of the Supreme Court of Canada in 1949 and is still accurate today:

> A crime is an act which the law, with appropriate legal sanctions, forbids; but as prohibitions are not enacted in a vacuum, we can properly look for some evil or injurious or undesirable effect upon the public against which the law is directed. That effect may be in relation to social, economic or political interests; and the legislature has had in mind to suppress the evil or to safeguard the interest threatened....
>
> Is the prohibition then enacted with a view to a public purpose which can support it as being in relation to criminal law? Public peace, order, security, health, morality: these are the ordinary though not exclusive ends served by that law. (*Margarine* case, 1949, pp. 49–51)

In searching for the characteristics that this large family of criminal offences have in common, one must come to the meagre conclusion that each of them consists of a prohibition enforceable by a penal sanction.

There are those who might argue that criminal laws should have a shared relationship to morality; that is, that criminal law and morality should be identical, the former serving to enforce the latter. Prostitution, abortion, gambling, drug use, and consensual homosexual acts are some of the behaviours at the heart of the law-and-morality debate. This issue raises a related one about the source of the criminal law. While it is supposed to constitute a reflection of what our society considers to be abhorrent and worthy of sanction, it is not at all clear that there is general agreement about all the behaviours prohibited by law. As the law now stands in Canada, it is fair to say there is a

crimes against the
⎯d robbery. There
⎯uity outside of this
⎯urthermore, even
⎯siderable room for
⎯ specific incidents
⎯uous.

for a criminal vio-
establish criminal
⎯oubt. The primary
⎯y is that there must
⎯ition of the crimi-
⎯own must establish
⎯e of affairs that was
⎯xample, the crime
⎯he Criminal Code,
⎯ to his or her own
⎯ "fraudulently and
⎯vhether animate or
⎯cribed in subsection
⎯d in three different
⎯lication of force to
⎯) by attempting or
⎯ or gesture; or (3)
⎯egging while openly
⎯weapon. Both theft
⎯t on the part of the
⎯ual harmful conse-
⎯ciety as a whole.
⎯l lexicon, and serves
⎯ariety of behaviour
⎯y speaking, the *actus*
⎯rms of the accused's
⎯lude a failure to act)
⎯nstances. For exam-
⎯entally may not be
⎯ccurrence of certain
⎯death, in which case
⎯accused's actions or
⎯nces.
⎯ presence of an act
⎯iminally responsible.
⎯ alone. Nonetheless,
⎯tself indicates, Cana-
⎯quire proof of some
⎯ can be termed the
⎯responsibility and is
⎯ondary, not in terms
⎯ terms of sequence.

In other words, the *actus reus* must be established first, for, without it, proof of *mens rea* is irrelevant. If a criminal act were not a requirement for criminal responsibility, a guilty state of mind would need to be proved; whereas, while it is not impossible to prove, it certainly is ephemeral. Reliance on *mens rea* would also, as Stephen (1883) indicates, make the criminal law infinitely more uncertain:

> The reasons for imposing this great leading restriction [i.e., the requirement of an act] upon the sphere of criminal law are obvious. If it were not so restricted it would be utterly intolerable; all mankind would be criminals, and most of their lives would be passed in trying and punishing each other for offences which could never be proved.
>
> Criminal law, then, must be confined within narrow limits, and can be applied only to overt acts or omissions capable of being distinctly proved, which acts or omissions inflict definite evils, either on specific persons or on the community at large. (pp. 78–79)

Failing to Act—Is It Criminal?

While criminal responsibility generally depends on the commission of criminally proscribed conduct, an *actus reus* may also consist of a failure to take action, but only where the person in question is under some legal obligation to act in a certain way. This approach follows the position taken by the Indian Law Commissioners (1837, Note M):

> It is, indeed, most highly desirable that men should not merely abstain from doing harm to their neighbours, but should render active services to their neighbours. In general, however, the penal law must content itself with keeping men from doing positive harm, and must leave to public opinion, and to teachers of morality and religion, the office of furnishing men with motives for doing positive good. It is evident that to attempt to punish men by law for not rendering to others all the service which it is their duty to render to others would be preposterous. We must grant impunity to the vast majority of those omissions which a benevolent morality would pronounce reprehensible, and must content ourselves with punishing such omissions only when they are distinguished from the rest by some circumstance which marks them out as peculiarly fit objects of penal legislation.

Accordingly, the Criminal Code provides that a person is criminally negligent who, in omitting to do anything that it is his or her duty to do, "shows wanton or reckless disregard for the lives or safety of other persons" (s. 219). In other words, criminal liability for failing to act exists only where there is a legal duty to act. Such a legal duty exists between spouses, parents and children, and caregivers and their charges (s. 215). Furthermore, there is a legal duty to act where there is a contractual relationship to that effect (s. 217).

One of the most contentious areas in relation to a failure to act arises where a parent or guardian fails to seek medical treatment for a dependent child because of strongly held religious beliefs. For example, in *R. v. Cyrenne, Cyrenne and Cramb* (1981), a child's parents and the family's minister were charged with **criminal negligence** causing death when they removed the child from hospital to forestall her receiving a blood transfusion. As Jehovah's Witnesses, they considered such treatment to be both abhorrent and morally wrong. The trial judge in this case stated that a duty to act existed in this situation under the section of the Criminal Code that stipulates that parents are under an obligation to provide the necessaries of life to their children (s. 215). Accordingly, if the accused, by denying treatment to the child, accelerated her death, then that would support a conviction. The accused were told that, without the transfusion, the child would die, and that, while there could be no guarantee she would not die in any event, transfusion was the only hope of avoiding certain death. In depriving her of that treatment, her parents acted in reckless disregard for her life and safety, judged according to the objective standard of reasonable parents.[3] Nonetheless, the accused were acquitted as the evidence failed to prove beyond a reasonable doubt that this conduct caused the child's death. There was no proof beyond a reasonable doubt that she would have been saved by the transfusion. It was a mere possibility. The parents omitted to act when, in law, they were required to, but the court was not satisfied their conduct (in terms of a failure to act) caused the child's death.

Causes and Consequences

The existence of a causal link between a person's act or omission and the wrongful consequence is, particularly for personal-injury offences such as **culpable homicide** and assault causing bodily harm, an essential component of the *actus reus*. Where the *actus reus* of an offence specifies the occurrence of certain specified consequences, such as death or serious bodily harm, then it must be proved beyond a reasonable doubt that the accused's conduct caused these consequences to occur.

The seriousness of homicide, both for the victim, in terms of the ultimate consequence, and for the perpetrator, in terms of the penal consequences of a conviction, has led to the formulation of a special set of rules found in sections 222 to 228 of the Criminal Code. Some of these have been transcribed from the common law, but others are more unique to Canada. Generally, they address the issue of how much a person should be responsible for in a homicide situation. If the victim is kept alive with the help of medical expertise and technology for several months before he or she eventually expires, should the assailant be responsible for that death? If the victim was terminally ill and destined to die shortly in any event, should that have any bearing on the accused's liability? Or what if the victim succumbs to negligent medical treatment administered after the attack?

Borrowing from English law, the Criminal Code provides that death must occur within a year and a day for an accused person to be criminally liable (s. 227). There is no logic for choosing 366 days as the cut-off point, especially given the advanced state of medical expertise currently in existence for keeping people alive. It does, however, provide some element of closure to the uncertainty of human survival.

While the aggressor's actions must be a contributing, substantial cause of the victim's demise, the criminal law does not insist that it must be the sole cause. Thus, the accused cannot escape liability by pointing to a separate, independent attack on the unfortunate victim's life or person. As long as both injuries are serious and operative at the time of death, both aggressors would be liable for the fatal consequences. Similarly, where the victim was suffering from a pre-existing fatal injury or illness, an accused cannot evade responsibility by arguing that she or he merely accelerated a certain death (s. 226). After all, every killing is an acceleration of the victim's ultimate death.

A good illustration of this principle in practice is *Smithers v. The Queen* (1977). Here, the victim died following a fight outside an ice-hockey arena that was provoked by incidents occurring during a game. Smithers kicked his opponent in the stomach. That kick, or the fear induced by the fight, made him vomit. He choked and died of asphyxiation. Medical evidence presented at trial suggested that Smithers' victim had a malfunctioning epiglottis or windpipe, which caused him to inhale his vomit and choke on it. The argument was made by the defence that Smithers' actions had not been the cause of death. Rather, the victim's own condition had led to his demise. The Supreme Court of Canada rejected this claim, underscoring that as long as the accused's conduct is an operating cause of death outside the *de minimis* range, she or he will be criminally liable. The victim's pre-existing condition and/or weaknesses are irrelevant.

A homicide situation may be complicated, not by pre-existing or simultaneous events, but by intervening events, such as fruitless attempts to save the victim, incompetent

s own actions. In
ikely to occur or
maritan or a trip
ed will remain lia-
s also to situations
elf or herself or to
those actions (s.
appropriate medi-
ample, where a Je-
sion for a stabbing
e consequences of
ase of intervening
is quite specific:

n being a bodi-
ous nature and
he death of that
the immediate
r treatment that

ach to the problem
nent seems to rest
tim has almost re-
he treatment is ad-
e aggressor remains
); if the victim has
ely be liable for the

es the kinds of com-
d by the interaction
v in such situations.
main issue was the
een forcibly ejected
wo employees and
head injuries. The
who were charged
of death was the ac-
ictim, who, having
oved the deceased's
en disconnected him
as keeping his vital
issed this argument,
the accuseds' actions
and that even if the
e an operative cause
xonerated, as long as
rative cause of the
esting about this par-
appeal-court judges
blems posed for the
ology. In law, **death**
exorably linked with

heartbeat and circulation. Those functions can now be performed by sophisticated machinery. As a result, individuals displaying no brain activity, who are kept breathing by virtue of technology, are, in the eyes of the law, alive.

Although it was not found necessary to deal with the definition of death in *Kitching and Adams*, the issue clearly must be dealt with in the near future. It has been addressed by the Law Reform Commission of Canada (1981) as part of its Law and Medicine project. If its recommendations are adopted, Canadian law will shift to a definition of death linked to the cessation of brain functions as well as to heartbeat and circulation. The commission recommended that the following definition be incorporated into law:

> A person is dead when an irreversible cessation of all that person's brain functions has occurred.
>
> The cessation of brain functions can be determined by the prolonged absence of spontaneous cardiac and respiratory functions.
>
> When the determination of the absence of cardiac and respiratory functions is made impossible by the use of artificial means of support, the cessation of the brain functions may be determined by any means recognized by the ordinary standards of current medical practice. (1981, p. 25)

Causation and Constructive Murder

When the criminal law of Canada was first codified in 1892, the common-law doctrine of "**constructive malice**" was adopted. This doctrine acted to transform a **homicide** into **murder**, even in the absence of an intention to kill or cause serious bodily harm, where it occurred as a result of violence committed in the course of a serious criminal offence. This was enacted in what is now subsections 230(a) to (c). In 1947, however, Parliament decided to supplement this with an early version of what is now subsection 230(d). It provided that where, in the course of certain serious criminal offences, a death occurred as a consequence of the use of a weapon, that death would be murder (see Willis, 1951).

Even in that form, this aspect of the constructive murder rule met with significant criticism. Nevertheless, this unique feature of Canadian criminal law was made more pronounced by an amendment enacted in the early 1970s as part of a parliamentary thrust toward "gun control." The section now reads as follows:

> 230. Culpable homicide is murder where a person causes the death of a human being while committing or attempting to commit [the relevant offences are then listed], whether or not the person means to cause death to any human being and

Box 2.2 How to Read a Legal Citation

When lawyers communicate with each other, they use a very specific citation format for cases and statutes. This can be somewhat confusing to the uninitiated. The following are typical case references:

R. v. Tutton and Tutton (1985), 62 C.C.C.(3d) 238 (Ont.Dist.Ct.).

Finestone v. R., [1953] 2 S.C.R. 107, 107 C.C.C. 93, 17 C.R.211.

The information provided includes where to find a copy of the case and in what court it was heard.

The first element is called the *style of cause*. The abbreviation "R. v." stands for *"Regina versus"* and reminds us that all criminal prosecutions are undertaken ostensibly on behalf of the Queen. The other name(s), "Tutton and Tutton" in the first case, are the surnames of the accused. The two may be reversed, as in the second example, if the accused is appealing the decision. If the case involves young offenders or children, initials are used.

Next comes the *year*. A year in parentheses is the year in which the decision was handed down. Accordingly, a comma follows, as in the first example above.

The *volume number* follows. This may be either a number, such as volume 62 in the first example above, or, for reporters that do not use volume numbers, a year printed within square brackets. In the second example above, we know that this case is found in the second volume that was printed in 1953.

The *reporter abbreviation* is the equivalent of the name of the journal. There are dozens of law reporters but, in Canada, those most commonly used in criminal law are:

Canadian Criminal cases   C.C.C., C.C.C.(2d), C.C.C.(3d)

Criminal Reports   CR., C.R.N.S., C.R.(3d)
Dominion Law Reports   D.L.R., D.L.R.(2d), D.L.R.(3d)
Supreme Court Reports   S.C.R.

In addition, there are various regional law reporters that range from *British Columbia Law Reports* (B.C.L.R.) to *Atlantic Provinces Reports* (A.P.R.).

The *series number* is important for those reporters that have, at some point, started with volume number 1 again. For example, *Criminal Reports*, volumes 1 to 50, were followed, in 1967, by the *Criminal Reports New Series*, volumes 1 to 40. In 1978, the *Criminal Reports Third Series* began with volume 1.

The next element is simply the *page number*. In legal citations, only the first page of the case or article is used.

If a case has been reported in more than one place, all the *parallel citations* are usually included. The second case above can be found in at least three reporters. The text of the judgment will the same in all three, but the headnotes summarizing the case will vary.

Finally, the *jurisdiction* and *court* must be listed. The Ontario District Court heard the first case above. Other courts include County Court (Co. Ct.), Court of Appeal (C.A.), Court of Queen's Bench (Q.B.), and the Provincial Court (Prov. Ct.). If the court and jurisdiction can be inferred from the citation, the reference may be omitted. Such is the case for the second example, where it is apparent that the judgment was of the Supreme Court of Canada because it was reported in *Supreme Court Reports*.

---

whether or not he knows that death is likely to be caused to any human being, if

. . .

    (d)   he uses a weapon or has it upon his person
        (i)   during or at the time he commits or attempts to commit the offence, or
        (ii)   during or at the time of his flight after committing or attempting to commit the offence,
      and the death ensues as a consequence.

What this section did was to create an exception to the requirement of a direct causal link between the perpetra-

tor's wrongful act and the death of the victim. There was no longer any requirement that the death must ensue from the use of the weapon, only that it must ensue from the accused having a weapon on her or his person. Thus, the causal link between act and consequence was made extremely tenuous. All that subsection 230(d) required was that there must be a causal connection between the use *or* possession of the weapon and the death. Thus, if, during the course of a bank robbery, a security guard sees that the robber has a gun tucked in his or her belt and so draws and fires his weapon, inadvertently killing a bank customer, then the bank robber would be liable for murder, under the terms of subsection 230(d).

version of this rule
, 1987). Given the
vhich increases the
and sentences that
irearm is used, the
estionable. None-
late in 1987, when
ie majority of the
ning the Canadian
ically section 7 (the
section 11(d) (the

ie Court stated that
of section 230 was
viction for murder
onable doubt as to
own that death was
this was a distinct
prima facie in vio-
of the Charter. In
d come under the
sonable curtailment
that, although the
ently important to
it unduly impaired
Other means were
:e. As a result, sub-
on 230 as a whole,
ough not necessar-
iinal law has been

on should be made
ave been quite in-
y initially followed
erparts, they have,
It has already been
sses on the notion
corollary of this is
i individual's con-
but it must also be
King (1962, p. 749),
: Court of Canada

actus reus unless
liberty to make
her words, there
vhether the ac-
iibited by law.

The law does not hold a person criminally liable for acts stemming from reflex actions, such as a muscle spasm, or for those committed unconsciously, for example, in a state of concussion or while sleepwalking (see Box 2.3). It is not a defence in the traditional sense, since it involves a denial of an essential element of the prosecution's case. The Crown bears the onus of establishing the *actus reus* of the offence, including the voluntariness of the accused's actions. In reality, however, unless the accused presents some cogent evidence pointing to the absence of consciousness, such an argument will not succeed. A further requirement is a total lack of consciousness. Despite the weight of medical opinion, which rejects the contention that the mind is ever completely conscious or unconscious, the criminal law takes an all-or-nothing approach.

There are distinctions drawn between different types of **automatism**, or the performance of unconscious acts. Four categories have been created. This first is *automatism resulting from the voluntary ingestion of intoxicants*. When the consumption of drugs or alcohol is voluntary, criminal offences committed in this state will not be covered by the defence. Only if the accused can show that a **reasonable** person, with the knowledge that the accused had at the time, could not have foreseen that she or he might become impaired by taking the intoxicant will the defence apply. So, for example, where a person did not realize that his driving would be impaired by an anesthetic administered by a dentist, he was found not to be criminally liable for driving while impaired (*R. v. King*, 1962).

The second category is *automatism caused by an apparently normal state such as sleepwalking or hypnosis*. If the evidence supports such a contention, the accused will be found acquitted on the basis of **sane automatism**.

The third category is *automatism caused by an external event*. The typical example is trauma or concussion resulting from a blow to the head as, for example, in *Bleta v. The Queen* (1965). During a fight, Bleta struck his head on the sidewalk and appeared to be dazed. He went on to stab the victim. The Supreme Court recognized that a defence of automatism, resulting in an acquittal, existed in this situation of concussion precipitated by a physical blow.

To this point, the Canadian courts were being fairly faithful to the English decisions on this issue. Starting in 1971, with a relatively low-level Ontario decision, Canadian case law began to develop its own unique characteristics. In *R. v. K.* (1971), the Ontario High Court of Justice extended by analogy **physical-blow automatism** to situations where a person is unconscious as a result of a psychological blow. In this case, a severely depressed unemployed man, upon hearing that his wife intended to leave him, went into an unconscious state as a result of this psychological blow. While in this "dissociative state," he asphyxiated his

Box 2.3 The Sleepwalking Defence

In May 1988, an Ontario Supreme Court jury acquitted a man who had fatally stabbed his mother-in-law on the grounds that he had been sleepwalking at the time. This is the first recorded instance of this defence being successfully used in Canada.

Sleepwalk Case Appeal Unlikely
Thomas Claridge

A Crown appeal is considered unlikely against the acquittal of a Pickering man who fatally stabbed his mother-in-law but was found not guilty because of doubts that he was awake at the time.

An Ontario Supreme Court jury of eight men and four women deliberated about nine hours Thursday before acquitting Kenneth James Parks of second degree murder in the death of Barbara Ann Woods, 41.

The verdict represented the first recorded instance of a Canadian successfully using a somnambulism (sleepwalking) defence in a murder charge.

Mr. Justice David Watt told the jurors they had only two choices—guilty or not guilty—since evidence did not support findings of not guilty by reason of insanity or guilty of manslaughter, a less serious charge.

The jurors were also advised that to find Mr. Parks guilty they must be convinced beyond a reasonable doubt that he was awake and intended to kill.

To reach this conclusion, the jury would have had to accept the Crown's call to reject a defence theory that won unqualified support from five psychiatrists and went unchallenged by a Crown witness.

Any Crown appeal of the acquittal would have to be based on alleged legal errors by Judge Watt, himself a former Crown who, in 2 years on the bench, is considered one of the brightest minds in the Supreme Court.

Although the Parks trial saw two rulings adverse to the Crown—one over admissibility of evidence and one whether the jury should be allowed to consider insanity, Judge Watt's long charge to the jury was accepted by both sides. One lawyer called it "impeccable."

Few facts in the case were in dispute. The jury was told that early last May 24, Mr. Parks drove 23 kilometres from his home to a townhouse in Scarborough. Once there, he attacked Mrs. Woods and her husband Dennis in their bed. He stabbed his mother-in-law five times.

But the five psychiatrists called by the defence said the man's activities and statements to the police that he had fallen asleep at his house and awakened after the killing were consistent with aggressive sleepwalking.

The medical witnesses told the jury they had ruled out all other possible explanations for his conduct.

Source: T. Claridge (1988), Sleepwalk Case appeal unlikely (p. A6). *Globe and Mail*, May 28.

wife but was acquitted of the charge of **manslaughter**.

This decision precipitated some changes in the law regarding the fourth category of automatism, *automatism caused by a "disease of the mind."* The term "disease of the mind" forms part of the definition of insanity (s. 16). This will be discussed in greater detail shortly, but it is important to know that where a person charged with a criminal offence is found to be legally insane at the time of the offence, then he or she will be acquitted, but will nonetheless be confined at the pleasure of the lieutenant governor until such time as he or she is determined to be sane. The same outcome will result for a person who is acquitted on the basis of **insane automatism**. Accordingly, the distinction between *sane* and *insane* automatism is very important in terms of outcome.

The concept of "disease of the mind" is one which continues to cause difficulties. It is a legal, not a medical term, that covers conditions that would not normally be categorized as mental aberrations, such as arteriosclerosis (*R. v. Kemp*, 1956) and psychomotor epilepsy (*Bratty v. A.G. Northern Ireland*, 1963). The key Canadian case on this issue is *Rabey v. The Queen* (1980), in which the classification of dissociative states resulting from a psychological blow was considered. On the question of whether or not a particular state amounts to a "disease of the mind," it was observed that this was a question of law for the judge to determine. This observation underscores the fact noted above that the concept of "disease of the mind" is a legal not a medical determination. Medical experts may be called as witnesses to offer an opinion; however, the judge is not

sease of the mind,"
t forward by the
dered *Rabey* (1977,

wn is between
rom some cause
sed, having its
nal makeup, or
d to a malfunc-
transient effect
factor such as,
ctioning of the
ource primarily
eakness internal
ood or not) may
nts the accused
t transient dis-
tain specific ex-
ncept of disease

aded by the lower
a dissociative state
thin this definition
or a bare majority,
the "psychological
eing an "externally
n a dissociative state
ad recently rejected
of a disease of the
d be one of insane

origins of the psy-
n objective, rather
ermined that "the
f life" that result in
ses. The reasonable
such circumstances
y person who does
ng does so because
which the law will

on in applying the
Court of Canada
new course. This
son (as he then was)
1980, pp. 548–49):

of law, an emo-
cing—should be
matism in some

circumstances and an internal cause in others. . . .

As in all other aspects of the criminal law (except negligence offences) the inquiry is directed to the accused's state of mind. It is his subjective mental condition with which the law is concerned. If he has a brittle skull and sustains a concussion which causes him to run amok, he has a valid defence of automatism. If he has a regular metabolism which induced an unanticipated and violent reaction to a drug, he will not be responsible for his acts. If he is driven into shock and unconsciousness by an emotional blow, and was susceptible to that reaction but has no disease, there is no reason in principle why a plea of automatism should not be available. The fact that other people would not have reacted as he did should not obscure the reality that the external psychological blow did cause a loss of consciousness. A person's subjective reaction, in the absence of any other medical or factual evidence supportive of insanity, should not put him into the category of persons legally insane. Nor am I prepared to accept the proposition, which seems implicit [in the majority's view], that whether an automatic state is an insane reaction or a sane reaction may depend upon the intensity of the shock.

As Mr. Justice Dickson indicates, there was no reason in principle for the Supreme Court to take the approach it did to psychological blow automatism. It was a conclusion dictated more by policy than by principle. Nonetheless, it is an approach that found favour in the Law Reform Commission of Canada's draft Criminal Code, which proposes to codify the defence of automatism as follows: "Everyone is excused from criminal liability for unconscious conduct due to temporary and unforeseeable disturbance of the mind resulting from external factors sufficient to affect an ordinary person similarly" (1982, p. 67). If adopted, this proposal would remove some of the inconsistencies in the defence of automatism noted by Mr. Justice Dickson, but only by making the objective test applicable to all four categories of automatism. Unconscious acts would be excused by the criminal law only in situations deemed appropriate according to the test of the ordinary, or so-called reasonable person. Contrary to established principle, the focus would be not wholly on the physical conduct of the accused and whether it was conscious and voluntary, but on its objective nature.

The Mental Component of Crime

Turning from the physical to the mental component of criminal responsibility, it should be noted at the outset that both must be present contemporaneously for liability to exist. The criminal intent must co-exist with the proscribed conduct. Suppose, for example, the dissolute nephew is planning to kill his wealthy aunt to accelerate receiving his inheritance. He decides to drive to the drugstore to purchase some rat poison with which to achieve his goal. In backing his car out of the driveway, he does not see his aunt, who is kneeling to weed the herbaceous border, and he runs over her, killing her. He clearly has an intention to kill her once he has the rat poison and his conduct does result in her death, but the act and the intention do not coincide. The conduct that resulted in her death was purely accidental and not criminal. If the nephew had seen his aunt kneeling on the driveway and decided to take advantage of the situation, saving himself the unnecessary expense of buying rat poison, then the *mens rea* and *actus reus* would have coincided and the requirements for criminal responsibility would have been fulfilled.

The Subjective Approach to *Mens Rea*

Central to the concept of criminal responsibility in Canada and other common-law countries is the notion of fault or **blameworthiness**. The mental element of criminal responsibility is based upon the philosophy that liability rests upon the free choice of the individual to do something that he or she knows is wrong. Socially dangerous conduct is a necessary- but not a sufficient-condition precedent for criminal responsibility. Proof of a blameworthy state of mind is also required.

Mens rea is a general term that covers intention, knowledge, and recklessness. It carries with it the idea that the person's mind is going with what she or he is doing. Criminal liability thus requires that an accused freely chose to do something, fully appreciating that the act was wrong. The Criminal Code designates this requirement by the use of words such as "means to," "wilfully," "fraudulently," and "knowingly." This fault requirement differs according to the crime. Even if the Code is silent in this regard, however, the courts may nonetheless read in such a requirement. (This point is discussed below where we address strict and absolute liability.)

One question that often puzzles newcomers to the study of criminal law is how the accused's state of mind at the time of the criminal act is established in court. After all, even in this post-1984 era, the state is unable to read the minds of its citizens. Perhaps the most straightforward way to establish state of mind would be to resort to an objective test: what would the ordinary or reasonable person have been thinking, knowing, or intending in such a situation? This approach would, however, be inconsistent with a system based on blameworthiness.

With some exceptions, Canadian criminal law adheres to a subjective standard for *mens rea*. What must be established at a criminal trial is what was going on in the accused's mind at the time of the act. What was the accused actually intending, realizing, or believing at that time? This standard allows the court to take into account individual characteristics of the accused that may have a bearing on his or her state of mind, for example, ignorance, lack of experience, mistake, or superstition. Of course, the court cannot simply depend on what the accused person says about his or her state of mind. Accordingly, in trying to ascertain what was going on in a person's mind, as the subjective approach demands, the court may draw reasonable inferences from that person's words or actions at the time of the act or in the witness box, should the accused choose to give evidence. Perhaps the most common inference that is drawn is that a person intends the natural consequences of his or her actions. The inference cannot simply be based on supposition or implication unsupported by the evidence. Rather, it must rest on facts and circumstances established by evidence that is before the court. Furthermore, the inference can be rebutted by evidence to the contrary.

Mistake of Fact

The defence of **mistake of fact** is perhaps the best illustration of how the subjective approach to criminal responsibility operates. It has also been a source of recent controversy in Canada and in Britain.

Many offences are defined in such a way that they require knowledge or awareness of certain circumstances. For example, one of the requirements of the offence of **perjury** is that the person making a false statement under oath must know that the statement is false (s. 131). Similarly, the offence of **spreading false news** demands that the person publishing the statement must know that it is false (s. 181). Even if the word "knowing" or "knowingly" is not included in the definition of an offence, knowledge of relevant circumstances will be required. For example, one way of committing an assault is by the intentional application of force upon a person without that person's consent (s. 265[1][a]). Knowledge of the presence or absence of consent is an integral part of this offence. An appropriate defence to an assault charge is, therefore, to argue that the "victim" consented to the application of force or that the accused honestly believed that the victim was consenting.

Where knowledge of relevant circumstances is required, the subjective approach to *mens rea* must take into account situations where the accused was mistaken about some aspect(s) of the situation. If the facts, as the accused honestly believed them to be, would not have constituted an offence, then it cannot be maintained that the accused had the neces-

:ample, if a man
ale companion,
to the activity,
f, he cannot be
the absence of

mistake of fact
as it was once
d public debate.
D.P.P. v. Mor-
vas asked to de-
be objectively
ourt in England
rea doctrine by
ef may be suffi-
s that his "vic-
, even if such a
version of the
(1980), another
alleged that he
'as consenting.
irt justices who
of the case, they
.e., that it need
honest.[6] In the
on made several
of fact that are
at has been said

ur system of
n cannot be
ument unless
tarily direct-
ting of some
intention or
act or reck-
st be proved
it may be es-
e of the act
. . . .
on (a) an act
nt. An affir-
nts does not
requirement
also be satis-
arises as to
e extends to
would seem
nt is central
nished only
lation in the

knowledge that consent is withheld, or in a state of recklessness as to whether willingness is present. The intention to commit the act of intercourse, and to commit that act in the absence of consent, are two separate and distinct elements of the offence. . . .

Mistake is a defence, then, where it prevents an accused from having the *mens rea* which the law requires for the very crime with which he is charged. Mistake of fact is more accurately seen as a negation of guilty intention than as the affirmation of a positive defence. It avails an accused who acts innocently, pursuant to a flawed perception of the facts, and nonetheless commits the *actus reus* of an offence. . . .

I am not unaware of the policy considerations advanced in support of the view that if mistake is to afford a defence to a charge of rape it should, at the very least, be one a reasonable man might make in the circumstances. There is justifiable concern over the position of the woman who alleges that she has been subjected to a non-consensual act; fear is expressed that subjective orthodoxy should not enable her assailant to escape accountability by advancing some cock-and-bull story. . . . [But] cases in which mistake can be advanced in answer to a charge of rape must be few in number. People do not normally commit rape per incuriam [through carelessness]. An evidential case must exist to support the plea. . . . By importing a standard external to the accused, there is created an incompatible mix of subjective and objective factors. If an honest lack of knowledge is shown, then the subjective element of the offence is not proved. . . .

The ongoing debate in the courts and learned journals as to whether mistake must be reasonable is conceptually important in the orderly development of the criminal law, but, in my view, practically unimportant, because the accused's statement that he was mistaken is not likely to be believed unless the mistake is, to the jury, reasonable. The jury will be concerned to consider the reasonableness of any grounds found, or asserted to be available, to support the defence of mistake. Although "reasonable grounds" is not a precondition to the availability of a plea of honest belief in consent, those grounds determine the weight to be given the defence. The reasonableness or otherwise of the accused's belief is only evidence for or against the view that the belief was actually held and the intent was therefore lacking. (pp. 486–500)

When the Criminal Code was amended in 1983 to replace rape with sexual assault, Parliament took the opportunity to reinforce *Pappajohn* legislatively:

> 265 (4). Where an accused alleges that he believed that the complainant consented to the conduct that is the subject-matter of the charge, a judge, if satisfied that there is sufficient evidence and that, if believed by the jury, the evidence would constitute a defence, shall instruct the jury, when reviewing all the evidence relating to the determination of the honesty of the accused's belief, to consider the presence or absence of reasonable grounds for that belief.

The issue resurfaced in 1984 in *Sansregret v. The Queen* (1984), where the victim had consented to the sexual intercourse, but the consent had been extorted by threats and fear of bodily harm. The law does not treat such consent as being true consent (e.g., s. 265[3]). The question for the Supreme Court in this instance was to what extent an honest mistake of fact would exculpate an accused in this situation. Repeating the comments of Mr. Justice Dickson in *Pappajohn*, it was stated that the *mens rea* for rape required knowledge regarding consent, or recklessness as to its nature. There was, it was said, an abundance of evidence before the trial court upon which a finding of recklessness could have been made. If the accused had an honest belief that the consent of the victim was not caused by fear or threats, then the defence of mistake of fact would apply. In this instance, however, the Court found that the accused had not merely been reckless as to consent, but had been willfully blind. In other words, he had deliberately closed his eyes to the very real possibility that the woman was not consenting. Where this happens, the law will impute actual knowledge to the accused and his belief in another state of facts will therefore be irrelevant. The honest belief will be ignored (see Manson, 1985).

To conclude on the topic of mistake of fact, it should also be noted that, not only does the law ignore mistakes resulting from willful blindness, it also disregards mistakes that relate merely to the type of offence being committed. Perhaps the most infamous Canadian case on this issue is *R. v. Ladue* (1965), which involved a charge of indecent interference with a dead body contrary to subsection 182(b). The defence offered by the accused was that he did not know that the woman was dead. The court rejected his claim of mistake of fact on the grounds that, although it would be a defence to this charge if the accused did not know that the body was dead and if on the facts, as he believed them, he was acting lawfully and innocently, such a defence was not open to an accused who, believing the person is alive, is attempting to have intercourse with the body. If, as he thought, the woman was alive, he would have been raping her because there was no suggestion that

he thought he had her consent to the act. To be effective, therefore, the mistake of fact must be a totally innocent one.

Before leaving the subject of mistakes, it should be made clear that the criminal law recognizes and excuses honest mistakes **of fact**. It is a fundamental principle of the Canadian legal system that ignorance of the law is no excuse (s. 19). While this rule may be practical from the point of view of the law's efficacy, it is not necessarily realistic, particularly in light of the vast proliferation of the amount of criminal law in the twentieth century. It is even less realistic in a country such as Canada that is made up of aboriginal peoples and ethnic groups largely unaware of the legal concepts protected by Anglo-Canadian criminal law.

Departures from the Subjective Approach to *Mens Rea*

Although the criminal law generally takes a subjective approach to *mens rea*, there are some significant departures from this rule in Canada, three of which will be examined here.

a) Objective *Mens Rea* for Murder
The first relates to certain forms of culpable homicide. Subsection 229(c) of the Code provides that culpable homicide will be classified as murder (as opposed to manslaughter) "where a person, for an unlawful object, does anything that he knows *or ought to know* is likely to cause death, and thereby causes death to a human being, notwithstanding that he desires to effect his object without causing death or bodily harm to any human being" (emphasis added). As the highlighted phrase indicates, it will be no defence to this charge to argue that the accused did not know, or did not believe, that his or her actions would cause death.

The origin of this provision is a section of the English Draft Code upon which the Criminal Code of Canada was based. The English Code commissioners were of the opinion that a person who sets off an explosion to stop a train, and passengers die as a result, would be guilty of murder if that person knew or ought to have known that death was likely.

Liability is imposed for murder in such situations for reasons of policy rather than principle. Indeed, the principle is sacrificed to policy. The most recent Supreme Court of Canada decision to consider this constructive murder rule was *R. v. Vasil* (1981), involving an accused who, while drunk, set fire to a house, killing two children. It was stated that, while the test is objective, and the behaviour of the accused is to be measured by that of the reasonable person, such a test must nonetheless be applied having regard, not to the knowledge a reasonable man would have had

edly made the
~se, arson), but
circumstances.
>t much used,
e same ground
etimes known
> Parker (1987,
rder attracting
 provides that
'specified, seri-
t, robbery, or
irder "whether
ny human be-
ath is likely to
itate the com-
1: (1) he means
overpowering
the breath" of
-and death en-

n his examina-
 predicated on
ie contemplat-
: might lead to
be liability for
ich is question-
-murder rule is
1, and its con-
is questionable
in *Vaillancourt*.
iead of the rule
iaving or using
ng the require-
lity of death, it
istice and the
h are enshrined
:ion of whether
 but the future
omising, unless
; only in situa-
iown that death

pt used in **tort**
by reference to
ierson/medical
er, been grafted
nal responsibil-
 person would

; recognized at

common law where criminal negligence causing death was
a form of manslaughter requiring "a very high degree of
negligence" (*Andrews v. D.P.P.*, 1937, p. 583). In Canada,
criminal negligence is defined in the Code:

> 219 (1). Every one is criminally negligent who
> (a) in doing anything, or
> (b) in omitting to do anything that it is his duty to do,
> shows wanton or reckless disregard for the lives or
> safety of other persons.

This definition applies to both causing bodily harm and
death by criminal negligence (see also ss. 220, 221, and
222[5][b]). The strict wording of the section is objective as it speaks in terms of "showing" wanton or reckless
disregard, rather than "having" such disregard, but the
courts have wavered between interpreting it to mean subjectively tested advertent negligence and interpreting it to
mean objectively tested inadvertent negligence.

For example, the Supreme Court, in *O'Grady v. Sparling*
(1960), in attempting to distinguish a now-repealed Code
offence of criminally negligent driving from a provincial
careless-driving offence, held that the former rested on a
requirement of subjectively tested advertent negligence or
recklessness, rather than objective inadvertence. For the
most part, however, the lower courts ignored this ruling
and used the objective standard of negligence. The Supreme
Court itself seems confused. In *LeBlanc v. The Queen* (1975),
a bush pilot was charged with criminal negligence causing
death. Speaking for the majority, Mr. Justice de Grandpré
defined criminal negligence in specifically objective terms
of showing "a want of ordinary care in circumstances in
which persons of ordinary habits of mind would recognize
that such want of care is not unlikely to imperil human
life" (p. 110). However, he then went on to pay lip-service
to the ruling in *O'Grady* and its requirement of subjective
advertence.

One commentator hypothesizes that the confusion surrounding the *mens rea* requirement for criminal negligence
stems from a misreading of the definition in subsection
202(1). Colvin (1986) suggests that, rather than interpreting
this subsection as a complete definition of criminal negligence, including its *mens rea*, it should be seen as a mere
definition of the conduct involved in criminal negligence.
In other words, the accused's conduct must show wanton
and reckless disregard for the lives or safety of others, but
the accused must also have some form of subjective *mens
rea*, i.e., recklessness or advertent negligence: "Section 202
[now s. 219] must at least circumscribe the conduct which
constitutes criminal negligence. Ordinary principles for the
interpretation of the Code require that unless there is a clear
indication to the contrary, subjective mens rea is to be
implied" (Colvin, 1986, p. 120). The most recent exam-

ple of the courts doing this is the Ontario case *R. v. Tutton and Tutton* (1985), where a subjective standard was adopted for criminal negligence that takes the form of a failure to act as opposed to positive conduct. As Colvin (1986, p. 121) indicates, the basis for this distinction is obscure, but the decision indicates that the strict wording of section 219 did not prevent the Court of Appeal from applying a subjective test of *mens rea*.

Clearly, the transplantation of negligence from the civil to the criminal sphere has not been a total success. Its implications for the subjective approach to *mens rea* are obscure, which has been translated into confused judicial decisions on the issue, with most opting for an objective approach to criminal negligence.

c) Strict and Absolute Liability

As was pointed out at the outset, Canada's criminal law comes from a number of sources. Those that do not originate in the Criminal Code often impose **liability** even in the absence of fault. In other words, all that they require is proof of *actus reus*. Even if the alleged offender did not have intention or knowledge, he or she will be found criminally liable nonetheless. In these situations, it is said that criminal liability is strict or absolute. To distinguish them from traditional criminal law, offences in this category are variously known as **quasi, regulatory, statutory** or **public-welfare** offences. There are a staggering number of them in both federal and provincial legislation. Estimates run in the tens of thousands. Many of our highway-traffic laws, for example, make liability strict, as do antipollution enactments and fishery regulations.

The rationale for not requiring *mens rea* is that intention or knowledge in these areas would be difficult to prove. How would you establish, for example, that a person intended to exceed the speed limit or to catch undersized lobster? In such situations, the protection of the public should be paramount, with those engaged in the activities assuming responsibility for them. For the most part, the penalties for these offences are relatively minor.

The major problem for the courts has been one of determining whether a particular offence is one requiring *mens rea* or one where liability is strict. Offences rarely come with a label attached. Statutes are rarely explicit. The courts therefore had to develop some method for distinguishing those offences that required *mens rea* from those that did not. Although they came up with a number of indicators, such as the subject matter of the offence, the penalties imposed, and the difficulty of law enforcement should *mens rea* be required, the end result was confusion and contradiction between the cases. Perhaps the most widely used test was the one put forward in the English case *Sherras v. DeRutzen* (1895) that absolute responsibility offences cover

acts "not criminal in any real sense" but "which in the public interest are prohibited under a penalty." But this test and others like it offer no guidance as to the precise criteria upon which to decide whether an offence is or is not really criminal.

Another difficulty was that the courts saw themselves as facing a choice between two extremes: full *mens rea* or none at all. There was no middle ground. The Law Reform Commission of Canada (1974) studied **strict liability** and concluded that, in reality, prosecutions were rarely launched in the absence of fault and that strict liability was contrary to the basic principle of no liability without fault. Accordingly, it recommended replacing strict liability with liability based on negligence, with the offender being exonerated upon proof of **due diligence**. In other words, if a person charged with a strict-liability offence could show that she or he had taken all reasonable precautions to prevent the proscribed harm, then she or he should not be convicted. Parliament chose not to act on the commission's recommendations, but, in 1978, the Supreme Court took the initiative.

In *R. v. City of Sault Ste. Marie* (1978), the issue before the Court was whether the city was guilty of causing pollution contrary to the Ontario Water Resources Act when the methods used by the city's garbage contractor discharged pollutants into the river. This involved a determination of whether the offence was one of strict liability or one requiring proof of *mens rea*.

Before coming to any conclusion, the Court engaged in an evaluation of the competing values and policy considerations behind **absolute liability** in public-welfare offences. On the positive side, "absolute liability, it is contended, is the most efficient and effective way of ensuring compliance with minor regulatory legislation and the social ends to be achieved are of such importance as to override the unfortunate by-product of punishing those who may be free of moral turpitude" (*Sault Ste. Marie*, 1978, p. 1311).

The Court, however, was more persuaded by the arguments against absolute liability: that it violates fundamental principles of criminal responsibility and that it rests upon a questionable assumption that it produces a higher standard of care: "If a person is already taking every reasonable precautionary measure, is he likely to take additional measures, knowing that, however much care he takes, it will not serve as a defence in the event of breach?" (p. 1311) The Court chose to ameliorate this perceived injustice in absolute liability by creating a tripartite classification scheme for **criminal offences**: (1) offences that are criminal in the true sense and require proof of *mens rea* by the Crown; (2) offences of strict liability, in which there is no necessity for the Crown to prove the existence of *mens rea*. There is, however, room for the accused to avoid liability by prov-

...hanged in Canada

...clude the Crimi-
...d the Food and
... periodic amend-
...t. The factors that
...groups, represent-
...e a key source of
...e, about capital
...g be ignored by
...dgetary consider-
...nds, such as liber-
...also be addressed.
...w reform follow

...apter 3 details the
...rmulated. This is
...ich a draft is pre-
...y responsible. In
...the Department
...ding in the House
...umbered sequen-
...Those introduced
...-2 to C-200. Pri-
...ntroduce bills, and

...ny interested party
...eading, the Mem-
...of the bill, at this
...these debates may
...pecific clauses that
...nt be approved in
...made up of Mem-
...ills are passed on
...and Legal Affairs.
...s are able to make
...onal organizations
...nts. Using this in-

formation and a clause-by-clause discussion within the committee, amendments are suggested for the bill. These are detailed in a report tabled for the House of Commons, published in *Votes and Proceedings*.

Third reading in the House is usually accompanied by little debate. A vote determines whether the bill will pass. All government bills are successful if they make it this far because government members are required to vote along party lines, regardless of their own opinions. Open votes where members may vote according to their conscience have occurred over capital punishment and may occur over abortion.

After passing third reading, the bill goes to the *Senate* to be read there three times. This is where the matter is to be given a "sober, second thought." Once this largely ceremonial function has been performed, the governor general gives the bill *Royal Assent*, on behalf of the Queen. At this point, the bill is an *act* and it may go into force immediately, or *proclamation* may be delayed. Proclamation dates for all statutes are printed in the *Canada Gazette Part I*.

Once a bill is an act, it receives a chapter number and is printed in the current volume of the *Statutes of Canada*, which are periodically consolidated. The citation to an act tells you where you can find it. For example, the Narcotic Control Act, R.S.C. 1985, c. N-1, can be found in the *1985 Revised Statutes of Canada*, the latest consolidation of Canadian laws, in chapter N-1. Any amendments made to this act in the years between consolidations can be found in the annual *Statutes of Canada*.

Any statute may have associated *regulations* that, unlike laws, which require the debate and approval of legislators, may be created and changed solely within the executive branch. Regulations typically govern purely administrative matters, such as designating salary ranges.

...would be estab-
...le person would
...own as the con-
...asonable mistake
...rally fit into this
...here no *mens rea*
...nce is available,
...respect of which
...lt would follow

proof of the proscribed act. Thus, the terms "strict" and "absolute liability," which were formerly used interchangeably, now refer to two distinct categories of criminal offences.

Although the decision in *Sault Ste. Marie* was creative, it did not answer the fundamental question as to the nature of a public-welfare offence as distinct from a real criminal offence. In this case the charge of causing pollution was designated a public-welfare offence in the absence of any logical or convincing rationale. One might ask why pollution and other socially harmful activities are not considered to be real crime.

Most recently, the third category of offences created by *Sault Ste. Marie* has come under renewed judicial scrutiny in light of the enactment of the Charter. In *Reference re s.94(2) of the B.C. Motor Vehicles Act* (1986), the Court was called upon to assess whether an absolute-liability offence, punishable by a mandatory minimum term of imprisonment, contravened the right to fundamental justice found in section 7 of the Charter. The Court found that absolute liability offends the principles of fundamental justice, which require proof of a guilty mind for criminal liability. Nonetheless, section 7 will only be violated if the absolute-liability offence has the potential of depriving the life, liberty, or security of the person. The section of the provincial legislation under review imposed a mandatory prison term and therefore was in violation of the constitutional guarantee. Although the Charter provides that its terms are subject to reasonable limitations, the Court held that administrative expediency, the main argument in favour of absolute liability, would justify such a limit only in extreme circumstances, none of which existed here. Mr. Justice Lamer offered the following assessment on behalf of the Supreme Court:

> The bottom line of the question to be addressed here is: whether the Government of British Columbia has demonstrated as justifiable that the risk of imprisonment of a few innocent people is, given the desirability of ridding the roads of British Columbia of bad drivers, a reasonable limit in a free and democratic society. That result is to be measured against the offence being one of strict liability open to a defence of due diligence, the success of which does nothing more than let those few who did nothing wrong remain free. . . . I find that this demonstration has not been satisfied, indeed, not in the least. (p. 324)

Defences to Criminal Conduct

There are a number of circumstances that act to justify or excuse criminal behaviour. Some defences—insanity, self-defence, and provocation—have been codified. Others—intoxication, automatism, and necessity—exist by virtue of common law. Mistake of fact and duress have been partially codified.

A great deal could be written on the topic of defences. It is a fascinating and complex area of the law. Given the limited scope of this introductory overview of the criminal law, the following discussion will be generally confined

to highlighting some of the more unusual features of defences as they exist in Canada. Automatism and mistake of fact have already been covered, and insanity, intoxication, necessity, duress, self-defence, and provocation will now be discussed.

Insanity

The outcome of the successful introduction of the **insanity defence** will be discussed in Chapter 8 on mental disorder and crime. Briefly, defendants found not guilty by reason of insanity will be acquitted of the criminal charge but are subject to a judicial order for indeterminate confinement at the pleasure of the lieutenant governor (s. 614). However, this is only possible if the offence for which they were tried was indictable, as opposed to the minor **summary-conviction offences**. It is hoped that during this confinement, the individual will receive mental-health treatment. Periodic reviews are used to assess the need for continued detention.

Those accused who are too mentally ill to participate meaningfully in their defence may be found unfit to stand trial. This relates to their current mental state (see Chapter 8). The insanity defence, however, pertains to their state of mind at the time of the offence. The basic principles involved in the defence of insanity originated in the 1843 opinion of the English House of Lords in the *McNaughtan* case (1843). The defence of insanity goes to the issue of the accused's mental capacity to form the requisite *mens rea*. Accordingly, the **McNaughtan Rule** contains two requirements, both of which must be satisfied: (1) *a disability*: at the time of the offence, the accused must have been suffering from a defect of reason, from a "disease of the mind," as discussed above; (2) *a resulting incapacity*: as a consequence of the disability suffered at the time the offence was committed, the accused did not know the nature and quality of the criminal act or that the act was wrong.

When Canadian criminal law was codified in 1892, this definition of legal insanity was incorporated into what is now section 16, with some significant amendments: (1) the requirement of a defect of reason was removed; (2) "natural imbecility" was added as a qualifying disability; (3) the Canadian provision speaks in terms of the accused failing to appreciate the nature and quality of the act etc., rather than in terms of mere knowledge.

The last-named modification is probably the most important because, unlike the English rule, it requires proof that the accused had more than a bare awareness. Appreciation includes knowledge, but the converse does not hold true. Appreciating is a higher level of the thought process requiring analysis of knowledge or experience. Thus, in 1892, the Canadian Parliament made a deliberate effort to

vond the rather
 (*Cooper v. The*

hwarted by the
strue the terms
" very restric-
 interpretation
nd "appreciat-
erpreted by the
ally wrong as
chwartz v. The
etation will not
 suffering from
s legally wrong
 is in response
lly wrong. Such
 of section 16.
ity disorder, has
 the mind" and
(*Kjeldson v. The*
ity of an act or
nly the physical
 not encompass
ychopaths, who
ty to feel guilt,
eir victims, will
nsanity defence.
y of the act" to
 meaningful in-
preciate will be
physical conse-
nowledge. Read
ity rule may not
row confines of
t have intended.
it is distinctively
lefence may raise
es of the accused.
sing for indefinite
isonment. Given
 guilty by reason
er than she or he
d of the offence,
ght object to the
es it is not the
nsanity a defence

 the criminal-law
cation as a result

of the voluntary ingestion of drugs or alcohol. The key issue here is the degree to which the accused had the capacity to form the requisite *mens rea*. Until the nineteenth century, intoxication was viewed as an aggravating rather than a mitigating factor by the courts. **Aggravating factors** are those that make the crime more serious, such as premeditation, while **mitigating factors** are those that can reduce the defendant's culpability, such as efforts to aid the victim. Even today, when drug and alcohol dependency is viewed by the scientific community as a form of disease, the criminal law sees it more as a character flaw.

The approach taken by Canadian courts adheres fairly closely to that prescribed by the English House of Lords in *D.P.P. v. Beard* (1920) in the form of three basic rules: (1) intoxication that causes an accused to become legally insane will come within the insanity defence; (2) intoxication may negate the existence of the "specific intent essential to constitute the crime" and thus reduce the seriousness of the charge, but only where the accused is charged initially with a crime of specific intent. Intoxication is deemed not to affect the capacity to form the *mens rea* for crimes of general intent; (3) evidence of intoxication falling short of (1) or (2), e.g., drinking for "dutch courage" to commit a robbery, will be ignored by the courts.

The major problem faced by the Canadian courts in applying the *Beard* test is the difficulty in distinguishing crimes of specific intent from crimes of general intent. Like the dichotomy between crimes and public-welfare offences, the distinction between general and specific intent defies rational identification. Mr. Justice Dickson says it best:

> The phrase "specific intent" is not a concept known to psychology. The expression is not contained in the Criminal Code. How a juryman can be expected to recognize such an elusive cerebration in the mind of an accused is obscure. . . . It has been said that such words as "with intent to," "for a fraudulent purpose," "corruptly," "wilfully," "knowingly" and the like, contained in the definition of the charge, identify crimes of specific intent. Why this should be so is not self-evident as there is no specificity to such words as "intentionally" or "knowingly." And it is conceded that the definition of the crime is not exhaustive as a specific intention may sometimes be embodied by implication. . . . All of this suggests that the distinction sought to be made between specific intent and general intent is neither meaningful nor intelligible. (*Leary v. The Queen*, 1978, p. 37)

In this case, rape was held to be a crime of general intent, therefore, drunkenness was no defence.

Necessity

This is a common-law defence that is not at all common and has been infrequently considered by the Canadian courts. With necessity, the accused concedes that a crime has been committed, but argues that he or she was compelled to break the law by external circumstances beyond his/her control, by necessity, and was therefore justified. The application of this defence demands a weighing of harms: the harm averted by committing the criminal offence must be greater than the harm resulting from the crime. This weighing of harms has proved most difficult where the taking of life is involved.

The key case related to this issue is the famous English decision of 1884, *R. v. Dudley and Stephens*, a cannibalism case. Four males were adrift in an open boat, over a thousand miles from land, with virtually no supplies. After eighteen days, the youngest and most feeble, the cabin boy, was sacrificed so that the others could survive on his flesh and blood. They were rescued four days later. At the subsequent trial for the cabin boy's murder, necessity was argued for the defence. The court took a high moral stance and determined that the taking of the life of another in order to preserve one's own could not be justified:

> It is not needful to point out the awful danger of admitting the principle which has been contended for. Who is to be the judge of this sort of necessity? By what measure is the comparative value of lives to be measured? Is it to be strength, or intellect, or what? (p. 287)

As a result, the defence of necessity did not succeed in this case and the accused were convicted of murder, but their sentence was commuted to a mere six months imprisonment.

In Canada, the **necessity defence** is most commonly identified with the offence of procuring a miscarriage or an abortion (s. 287) as a result of the numerous prosecutions of Dr. Henry Morgentaler. Prior to a Supreme Court decision in 1975 involving Dr. Morgentaler, it was not at all clear that the defence of necessity even existed in Canada. Although the Court held that there was no evidence to support the defence in this case, i.e., that he had no alternative but to perform illegal abortions, it did exist nonetheless "to justify non-compliance in urgent situations of clear and imminent peril when compliance with the law is demonstrably impossible" (*Morgentaler v. The Queen*, 1975). In a subsequent prosecution of Dr. Morgentaler in Quebec, the jury was persuaded that the testimony of defence witnesses as to the impossibility of compliance with the therapeutic-abortion provisions of the Code supported the defence of necessity (*R. v. Morgentaler*, 1976).[8]

More recently, the defence of necessity in Canada has been invoked in drug-importation cases. Specifically, ocean-going vessels involved in the transportation of illegal narcotics have been forced by inclement weather to take refuge in Canada, and those involved have been charged with importing contrary to the Narcotics Control Act. In *R. v. Salvador* (1981), the Nova Scotia Supreme Court acknowledged that the defence of necessity covers all cases where noncompliance with the law is excused by an emergency or justified by the pursuit of some greater good. It did not apply to the present case, however, because those involved were committing a crime when the necessitous circumstances arose. In other words, the accused had to come to court with "clean hands." If he or she was engaging in illegal activity when the situation of necessity arose, then the committing of the further crime would not be deemed necessary within the terms of the defence.

This decision was overturned in 1984 by the Supreme Court of Canada in *Perka v. The Queen* (1984), where, again, charges of importation were laid against the crew of a vessel that was forced to seek refuge in Canada because of severe weather. The drugs were being transported from Colombia to Alaska. Addressing the issue of necessity that was raised in the crew's defence, the Court characterized it as an excuse, that conceded the wrongfulness of the act. Nonetheless, the actor did it under circumstances that excused the activity. There was an absence of volition, and therefore they were not really the actions of the accused. The Court also acknowledged that the defence needs to be strictly controlled, and "scrupulously limited" to situations corresponding to its underlying rationale. Accordingly, a test was constructed for determining the applicability of necessity. First, compliance with the law must be "demonstrably impossible" *and* the evil averted must be greater than the harm resulting from the criminal act. In applying this test to the facts before it, the Court determined that, even if the accused were engaging in an illegal activity when it became necessary to commit a further crime, as long as it was not foreseeable and was truly involuntary, then they could benefit from the defence.

Necessity has, as a result of the decision in *Perka*, been placed on a well-articulated footing. Nonetheless, it is expected that it will remain a defence that is rarely invoked, and even more rarely successfully invoked.

Duress or Compulsion

This defence is found partially in section 17 of the Code, but also in the common law, which makes it fairly unusual. In its underlying rationale, it is somewhat similar to the defence of necessity, but it applies not where there is a lack of volition through force of circumstances but where the

1 other words,
·ing compelled
(s).

compulsion by

·er compul-
·odily harm
·e offence is
·e offence if
·l be carried
·a conspiracy
·ject to com-
·y where the
·a or treason,
·l assault, sex-
·ird party or
·assault, forc-
·, assault with
·vated assault,
·or an offence
·nd detention

·atutory defence
·us offences, par-
·No matter how
·o, he or she will
·defence for the
·afters of this sec-
·a caused by the
·osed on the per-
·that the former
·nstances, the law
·hstand them and
·; he succumb to
·law. The second
·l so that it applies
·ion but to com-
·mmediate and so
·escape or to seek

·preme Court of
·which is a good
·e bad law. It arose
·ho was locked in
·a by the other in-
·; trashing his cell.
·ed with malicious
·s defence. Perhaps
·, the Court chose
·eral interpretation
·o be inapplicable

because the threats were not "immediate" and were not uttered by a person who was present in the cell with Carker when the offence was committed. This contrasts with the state of the defence as it existed at common law, prior to codification. There the requirement is that the accused acted solely as the result of threats of death or serious injury to herself or himself, or others, operating on her or his mind at the time of his or her act. The threat must be of immediate or future death or injury. This rule is much more generous.

Although the Court in *Carker (No. 2)* stated that section 17 is an exhaustive definition of the defence as it exists in Canada, less than ten years later, in *R. v. Pacquette* (1976), the Court decided that section 17 applies only to the person who actually committed the offence and not to a person who is merely a party to the offence (see s. 21[2]), or who is merely an aider or abettor of an offence committed by someone else (s. 21[1]). Where duress is claimed as a defence by persons who did not actually commit the alleged offences themselves, e.g., where a person is alleged to have driven the "getaway car" for a bank robbery, then the common law **duress defence** will apply. This version is much less restrictive than its statutory equivalent, and contains no list of exempted offences. To say the least, the current state of the defence of duress or compulsion in Canadian law is confused.

Self-Defence

The terms of this relatively straightforward defence are fully set out in sections 34 to 42 of the Code. The term "self-defence" is somewhat misleading, however, because it applies not only to defence of self but to defence of one's property and to defence of persons under one's protection. The law recognizes that, in such circumstances, what would otherwise be a criminal act is justifiable.

Regarding **self-defence** per se, it is available not only where the accused retaliated against an unprovoked attack, but also in situations where he or she was the initial aggressor. As one would expect, the terms of the defence in the latter situation are much more stringent than those for the former.

Section 34 applies to unprovoked assaults. It has two aspects. First, where the accused does not intend to inflict death or grievous bodily harm, then the court must be satisfied on objective grounds that she or he used no more force than was necessary to defend herself or himself. The second aspect regulates those situations where the accused did intend to inflict death or grievous bodily harm. There the test is whether it was caused under a reasonable apprehension of death or grievous bodily harm and whether the accused believed on reasonable and probable grounds that he or she could not otherwise preserve himself or herself against death or grievous bodily harm. There is no requirement of proportionality of force here, as there is under the first aspect of section 34.

In recent years, the courts in Canada have been confronting an issue which has also arisen in England and Australia: where a person acts in self-defence, but employs excessive force that results in death, is there a compromise solution leading to conviction for manslaughter rather than for murder? In Britain, this question has been answered in the negative, although some states in Australia have adopted such a rule. As a result of a series of decisions from the Supreme Court of Canada, it now seems clear that the compromise defence in situations of excessive use of force does not exist in Canada (*R. v. Gee*, 1982; *R. v. Faid*, 1983; *Brisson v. The Queen*, 1982; and *Reilly v. The Queen*, 1984). If the accused has used excessive force so that the defence provided by section 34 is not available, then, in the absence of any other applicable defence, he or she is liable to be convicted of murder. An alternative defence that may apply in this situation, as well as others, is the partial defence of provocation.

Provocation

A person charged with murder may have the charge reduced to manslaughter if it can be proved that the act was committed "in the heat of passion caused by sudden provocation." This would take the form of "a wrongful act or insult that is of such a nature as to be sufficient to deprive an ordinary person of the power of self-control . . . if the accused acted on it on the sudden and before there was time for his passion to cool" (s. 232[2]).

Provocation is not a general defence—it is available only where a person is charged with murder—nor is it a complete defence—if successfully pleaded it will merely result in a reduction of the severity of the crime charged. It represents an attempt to show some leniency to those individuals who, in the face of extreme provocation, lose their self-control.

The terms of section 232 make it clear that it will not apply simply upon the accused showing that he or she was provoked and acted impulsively, killing the tormentor. The court must be satisfied that wrongful act or insult would have deprived an ordinary person of self-control. The test is objective. It is only after this requirement has been satisfied that the court will look to whether the accused person was so provoked and acted "on the sudden."

The **provocation defence** rests on an objective test because it would otherwise place a premium on having a hair-trigger temper. Nonetheless, until more recent years, the courts interpreted this requirement very strictly, often with harsh results. In *Sampson v. The Queen* (1935), for exam-

ple, a mentally subnormal man, subjected to racial slurs by two boys, killed one of them and pleaded provocation. The trial judge refused to instruct the jury that, *vis-à-vis* provocation, the mental development of the accused should be taken into account. His conduct was to be measured against that of the hypothetical ordinary person of average intelligence. The defence of provocation failed. Sampson was convicted and sentenced to death, an outcome that was confirmed by the Supreme Court of Canada.

During the early 1980s, however, some provincial appellate courts began to move away from such a strict approach, holding that the jury must consider in relation to the objective test the same external pressures of wrongful act or insult as did the accused. In doing so, the court should look beyond the events that immediately triggered the homicide to those that led up to it and may shed more light on the final, triggering insult. For example, in *R. v. Daniels* (1983), the Appeal Court held that, in applying the objective test in section 232 to a woman who killed her husband's lover following a long history of infidelity, beatings, and other indignities, the jury should consider her conduct according to the standard of an ordinary person subjected to the same history of events along with the final insult. That final insult may well be coloured and given meaning only by a consideration of the events that preceded it.

A recent Supreme Court decision, *R. v. Hill* (1986), did not explicitly overrule this more relaxed approach to the objective ordinary-person test in section 232. This case concerned the application of the defence to a young man who killed another man after he had allegedly made homosexual advances. The issue before the Supreme Court was whether the trial judge should have instructed the jury that the ordinary person in this case must be of the same age and sex as the accused, given that this would give real meaning to the final triggering act or insult. In addressing this issue, the Court underscored that the ordinary person under the objective test has a normal temperament and level of self-control and is not unusually excitable, pugnacious, or drunk. Nonetheless, particular characteristics that are not peculiar or idiosyncratic, such as age or gender, can be ascribed to an ordinary person without subverting from the logic of the objective test. However, in the Court's opinion, there was no need for mandatory jury instructions as to the characteristics of the the ordinary person, because the jury, as a matter of good sense, would ascribe to the ordinary person any general characteristics relevant to the provocation in question.

The defence of provocation is undoubtedly complex and tightly circumscribed by the terms of section 232, although the blatant harshness of the narrow objective test is being modified somewhat by the courts.

ng the AIDS virus.
void intimate con-
is transmitting the
after the diagnosis,
ith a woman, who
u think that Frank
e be convicted of
nce under section

ublication of "any
ction 163(1)(a) be
f expression found
Rights and Free-
te? Can subsection
of the Charter as
See R. v. Red Hot

an with a long,
nstrual stress syn-
n wild displays of

anger and violence, usually directed at her husband. On one occasion, however, she assaults her employer. Premenstrual stress syndrome is not a codified defence in Canada, but there is nothing to prevent the courts from recognizing it as such. What do you think?

4. Michael is a four-year-old child. As punishment for perceived wrongdoing on his part, his mother frequently withholds food from him for days at a time. Consequently, he is dangerously underweight. His father chooses to punish his son by caning him on the back and buttocks. Is either parent criminally liable for what might be seen as child abuse? See sections 215, 265, and 43. Where is the dividing line between discipline and abuse?

5. Jenny's common-law husband, Freddy, has beaten her regularly and often severely during their three years of cohabitation. One evening, after he has beaten her and their young child, she waits until he falls asleep, sets fire to the bed, and leaves the house. She is charged with first-degree murder under section 231. Could self-defence or provocation be argued in her defence?

the basic charac-
some of its spe-
as been covered,
n an intellectual
theless, it should
aw is a complex
tute law, judicial
to the particular
2, the overarch-

ing terms of the Canadian Charter of Rights and Freedoms.

Criminologists cannot ignore the role that the criminal law plays in the criminalization process. There is a need to understand not just what the law is and how it operates but also why it takes the form that it does and the social significance this form has. Criminology is, without a doubt, a multidisciplinary enterprise. The legal component is as critical as are the others to a fuller understanding of crime as it exists in Canadian society.

overnment to act on
. These include trade
addition, the federal
sures for the "peace,

ving class of criminal
that does not require

proof of fault (absolute-liability offences) or places a burden on the defendant to prove that he or she acted with due diligence (strict-liability offences).

3. In a recent decision of the Supreme Court of Canada (*R. v. Tutton and Tutton*, 1985) the objective standard of the reasonable parent used in this case was called into question. The Supreme Court found that, like other serious criminal offences, this offence requires

proof of some degree of mental blameworthiness in the form of aware-ness or advertence to the lives or safety of others.

4. In January 1983, the Criminal Code was amended to remove rape as a crime and replace it with three types of sexual assault: simple sexual assault (s. 271); sexual assault with a weapon (s. 272); and ag-gravated sexual assault (s. 273) (S.C. 1980-81-82, c. 125). Sexual assault is a much broader term than its predecessor and is no longer gender specific. For a more detailed discussion, see Osborne (1985).

5. Interestingly, that defence did not succeed in *Morgan* because the accuseds' collective belief that the female victim was consenting was so unreasonable that the triers of fact did not believe that they could have honestly believed it. This may seem to be a contradiction of what was just said, but is, in fact, quite logical: the law, which adheres to a subjective approach, does not demand that a mistake of fact be objectively reasonable. It must merely be honest. The reasonableness of the belief may, however, be relevant for evidentiary purposes, because the more unreasonable a belief is, the more unlikely it is that the jury, or the judge where there is no jury, will be convinced that the accused honestly held the belief. Thus, the *Morgan* decision was consistent with principle, but politically unpopular, particularly among women.

6. Two years before *Pappajohn*, the Supreme Court of Canada created a defence of reasonable mistake of fact for certain types of strict-liability offences. See the discussion below in *R. v. City of Sault Ste. Marie* (1978).

7. Aspects of this rule have already been discussed from the point of view of *actus reus* and causation.

8. In the most recent Morgentaler case (*R. vs. Morgentaler, Smoling and Scott*, 1988), the Supreme Court of Canada struck down the therapeutic-abortion provisions of the Code as they constituted a vio-lation of the woman's right to security of the person. The issue of the necessity of the doctors' actions in violating the law was not con-sidered by the Court.

Discussion Questions

1. What are the advantages and disadvantages of Canada's having a national system of criminal law? Why would the provinces each want a separate code?

2. What role does the concept of fault play in the allocation of criminal responsibility? What form would criminal law take if fault were replaced by the concept of harm?

3. Identify five characteristics of criminal law that are unique to Canada. How do those characteristics affect the trial process itself?

References

Andrews v. D.P.P., [1937] A.C. 576.

Bleta v. The Queen, [1965] 1 C.C.C.1 (S.C.C.).

Bratty v. A.G. Northern Ireland, [1963] A.C. 386.

Brisson v. The Queen (1982), 69 C.C.C.(2d) 97 (S.C.C.).

Colvin, E. (1986). *Principles of criminal law.* Toronto: Carswell.

Cooper v. The Queen (1979), 51 C.C.C.(2d) 129 (S.C.C.).

D.P.P. v. Beard, [1920] A.C. 479.

D.P.P. v. Morgan, [1975] 2 All E.R. 347.

Indian Law Commissioners (1837). *A Penal Code Prepared By The Indian Law Commissioners.*

Kjeldson v. The Queen (1981), 64 C.C.C.(2d) 161 (S.C.C.).

Law Reform Commission of Canada (1974). *The Meaning of guilt—strict liability.* Ottawa: Supply & Services Canada.

Law Reform Commission of Canada (1981). *Criteria for the Determi-nation of Death*, Report No. 15. Ottawa: Supply & Services Canada.

Law Reform Commission of Canada (1982). *The General Part: Liabil-ity and Defences*, Working Paper No. 19. Ottawa: Supply & Ser-vices Canada.

Law Reform Commission of Canada (1988). *Recodifying Criminal Law*, Working Paper No. 31. Ottawa: Law Reform Commission of Canada.

Leary v. The Queen, [1978] 1 S.C.R. 29.

LeBlanc v. The Queen (1975), 29 C.C.C.(2d) 97 (S.C.C.).

Manson, A. (1985). Annotation. 45 C.R. (3d) 194.

Margarine case (1949). *Reference re Section 5(a) of the Dairy Industry Act*, [1949] 1 S.C.R.1.

inal process in Canada.

449, [1976] 1 S.C.R.

w cosmetic for Cana-
4.
) 481 (S.C.C.).
v (3rd ed.). Toronto:

5 (S.C.C.).

86), 48 C.R.(3d) 289.
..).
.C.C.).
1299.
62 C.C.C.(2d) 238

. 149 (N.W.T.C.A.).
273.
.
)
id) 97, [1986] 1 S.C.R.

.

2d) 159 (Man. C.A.).
.A.).

7 C.C.C.(3d) 449.
D.L.R.(3d), 11 N.R.

.S.S.C.).
Л. App. Ct.).
d) 328.
.).
(S.C.C.).

.
3d) 223 (S.C.C.).
Cliffs, NJ: Prentice-Hall.
) 1 (S.C.C.).

) 427 (S.C.C.).
ol. II. New York: Burt

ronto: Carswell.
(3d) 118 (S.C.C.).
r Review, 29, 784–96.

3 Canadian Crime Policy

[To] minimize suffering and to maximize security were natural and proper ends of society and Caesar. But then they became the only ends, somehow, and the only basis of law—a perversion. Inevitably, then, in seeking only them, we found only their opposites: maximum suffering and minimum security. (Miller, 1960, p. 305)

The construction of an acceptable definition of the term "policy" is one of the major difficulties involved in policy studies. Policy making is concerned with competing values and the achievement of social purpose. **Crime policy** seeks to effect compromises between basic social values that are in tension (e.g., liberty, security). In the larger sense, crime policy seeks to address the balance between fairness to the individual and the well-being of society as a whole.

A quick review of the literature will alert the reader to the problems inherent in the definition of policy. It is generally agreed that policy can "be construed as a decision which establishes the *overall direction* which a given organization will take regarding a given issue" (Larsen, 1982, p. 50). Others simply state that "policy is a course of action followed by a set of actors in dealing with a problem" (Gray & Williams, 1980, p. 2). Ekstedt and Griffiths (1988), however, point out that a policy is not merely a decision made by high-level officials that directs other decisions. In a more primary sense, policy is an expression of meaning: "A policy statement in the criminal justice system constitutes a declaration of social value, and it is upon the basis of the declared value that subsequent decisions are shaped" (p. 102).[1]

The problem of policy making in criminal justice has only recently become a subject of concentration for criminologists. While it is true that social and behavioural scientists have maintained a continuing interest in the influence of their research on the decision making of public agencies (e.g., studies that have examined the relationship between urban-renewal strategies and juvenile delinquency), concentration on the specific difficulties inherent in public-policy making has not been of primary concern, especially as it relates to crime policy in Canada. However, there is evidence that the interest in this subject is increasing.

Within the academic community, attention is increasingly being paid to the skills (ways of thinking and acting) involved in the analysis of decision making within government. While decision-making studies are considered an important area of inquiry in their own right, this area of research has been at least partially stimulated by the growing frustration of academics and scholars with the perceived lack of influence that their research has on public-policy decisions. Also, recent developments within the discipline of **criminology** have contributed to the evolution of a more activist stance among some academics engaged in the study of **crime** and its causes. For example, critical criminologists confront the *status quo* as contributing to **criminality** and **deviance** more generally (see, e.g., Chambliss, 1976). All of this has resulted in an increasing desire among scholars, as well as practitioners, to understand the mechanics of decision making within criminal justice and the ways in which policies are influenced and directed. These practitioners include not only the policy makers themselves but the judges and other line-level personnel involved in the enforcement of law or the administration of justice.

Apart from these considerations, other factors have contributed to the requirement for attention to public policy by those interested in problems of social control. Throughout the world, and especially in North America, the social, political, and economic changes emerging since the end of World War II have altered the face of social policy in all areas of public and private life. Policy decisions not only must be made in a context of greater complexity, but within shorter time frames and with an awareness that the conditions associated with the decision may rapidly change.

This growing lack of stability in the environment of policy making has forced changes in the structure of decision making and the support systems associated with it. Public-policy making in areas of critical social awareness has taken on the atmosphere of political "campaigns" with all the attention to the marketing of ideas, the testing of public response, and the selling of policy positions normally associated with an election process. Governments seek to promote policies that can contribute to the common good without resulting in political disruption (Ekstedt & Griffiths, 1988, p. 109–15). Box 3.1 illustrates this process.

In both Canada and the United States, there have been recent examples of this approach to policy making. In the United States, the "Great Society" programs of the 1960s,

including the "War on Poverty," were early attempts to develop public policy in this manner. Many of these programs were intended to prevent or treat crime and delinquency (see Morash, 1982, pp. 8 ff.). The "War on Crime" of the 1970s attempted the reform of the entire **criminal-justice system** in the United States. This initiative resulted in legislation creating the Law Enforcement Assistance Administration, which produced a great number of policy reviews on criminal-justice activity in the United States. No other initiative anywhere else in the world has matched this one for concentration of effort on the assessment of criminal-justice policy in a country or political system.

In Canada, similar activities have taken place, although on a lesser scale. One example is the development of the "peace and security package"[2] that involved a policy review of criminal-justice practice focussing on the management of "dangerous" offenders following the abolition of **capital punishment** in Canada. This initiative emerged as one of a number of policy changes within the framework of the "Just Society" programs implemented by the Liberal government in the late 1960s and early 1970s. As we shall see later in this chapter, the effect of these movements on crime policy in Canada has been considerable, and concentration on the implications of these changes is important to an understanding of crime control in Canada.

In Canada, as elsewhere, this new attention to policy as a subject of study has resulted in a variety of subdisciplines or concentrations under the general heading of "policy studies." Public-policy implementation, policy analysis, organizational politics, policy evaluation, and public-policy making are emphases within the general area of policy studies. Methods and techniques for research and analysis are being developed in all of these areas and have been made to apply to the study of crime policy.

Policy Making for the Public

> Then there came to that place—all this happened in Siberia—a man exiled by the government, a learned man, with books, maps, and all sorts of things like that. So our Man says to the scientist: Do me a favor, please, show me where the true and just land lies and how to get there. The scientist at once opens his books, spreads his maps—looks here, looks there—there's no true and just land anywhere. Everything is right, all the lands are shown—but the true and just land is not there. (Gorki, 1945)

In Canada, crime policy is public policy, and is subject to the same limitations on government action. It is important, therefore, to understand the context and structure of

tice Policy Making in Canada

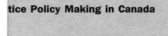

A CRIMINAL JUSTICE POLICY IN CANADA

GESTATION	BIRTH	GROWTH

sted group (response from
n of public-at-large)-critical
established

UCRATIC RESPONSE
    -report
    -control
    -increase
     resources
    -provide legal
     restraints

MEDIA RESPONSE
    -report
    -sensationalize
    -editorialize

POLITICAL RESPONSE
    -reduce
     threat to political
     stability
    -satisfy interests
     of public servants
    -maintain
     equilibrium in
     government
     services (e.g.,
     competition
     among
     "ministries"
     to obtain
     additional
     resources)
    -respond to issue
     through media

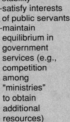

PUBLIC POLICY

EXAMPLE: The government
announces that it will establish a
major initiative to combat
drinking driving. One million
dollars will be committed through
the Ministry of Health and the
Attorney-General. A director will
be appointed to co-ordinate
program development.
[completion of "gestation" period
requires:
1) the interest of bureaucracy
2) continuing (and mounting)
   pressure from groups that
are (or appear to be)
   representatives of the public-
   at-large.
3) continuing attention of the
   media
4) perceived threat to political
   stability]

Provided for the "health" and
continuing development of the
policy (policy pablum)
Establishing procedures for
policy implementation

EDUCATION
(e.g., good school programs
including participation of law
enforcement and other agencies
re: drinking-driving)

LAW
(e.g., increasing civil and criminal
sanctions)

REGULATION
(e.g., "tightening up" on criteria to
obtain a driver's license)

ENFORCEMENT
(e.g., Breath-Analysis testing,
roadside checks, etc.)

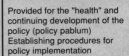

YOND INITIAL RESPONSE   ⟶

order to understand
rges, at least partial-
hniques developing
ly of public policy.
licy, as generally de-
policy is regarded
chieve governmen-
Gray and Williams
olicies are produced
olitical action, it fol-
nsider the relation-
policy." This is the

primary distinction to be made between the study of policy
making in the general sense and the study of public policy.
The study of public policy requires the development of
means by which political behaviour can be observed and
interpreted. Many factors can be identified that are specific
to decision making within a political environment. Not the
least of these is the interaction between politicians and
bureaucrats in setting the parameters for policy making and
policy implementation. In Canadian criminal justice, these
bureaucrats would include persons holding the positions
of Commissioner, Royal Canadian Mounted Police; senior
Crown prosecutor; deputy-ministers of justice (federal and

provincial); municipal police chiefs; directors of corrections (for a discussion of the factors influencing public policy making, see Ekstedt & Griffiths, 1988, Ch. 6). For an example of some of the factors in the context of policy making, see Box 3.1.

Canadian Politics and Crime Control

Every group regarding itself as emancipated is convinced that its predecessors were fearful of reality. It looks upon euphemisms and all the veils of decency with which things were previously draped as obstructions which it, with superior wisdom and praiseworthy courage, will now strip away. Imagination and indirection it identifies with obscurantism; the mediate is an enemy to freedom. One can see this in even a brief lapse of time; how the man of today looks with derision upon the prohibitions of the 1890's and supposes that the violation of them has been without penalty! (Weaver, 1948, p. 26)

In order to appreciate the dynamics of Canadian crime policy, it is important to understand something of Canada's history and political development. For purposes of this chapter, the emphasis will be on those elements of historical development that seem to be the most directly relevant to Canada's position on crime control.

The Canadian Politic

The Canadian system of government is organized on a federal or federated basis, which means that Canada is a union of states (provinces) under a central government. The union of provinces is distinct from the individual governments of those provinces. Consequently, Canada has a federal government responsible for the conditions that govern the union of provinces and the relationship between that union and external governments.

The concept of federalism normally assumes that the central (federal) government will be strong and will exist as a "superior" government in relation to the individual states or provinces. While this is arguably true in Canada, it has been noted that "among the major federal systems of the world, Canada is one of the most decentralized" (Komberg, Mishler, & Clarke, 1982, p. vii). The **British North America Act** (1867), which established the constitutional base for Canada, envisioned a federal system with weak provinces and a strong central government. However, over time, the provinces have evolved a status where, collectively, they enjoy very nearly full partnership with the central government. There are very many factors that

contribute to the way in which the provincial governments and the federal government influence each other or evolve their roles in relation to each other. Significant to the relationship between these two levels of government is the manner in which revenues are gathered and expended. Collectively, provincial spending currently exceeds that of the federal government. Additionally, the provinces enact more legislation, impose more regulations, and employ a considerably larger number of civil servants.

Understanding the division of powers between the two major levels of government in Canada is critical if one wishes to comprehend how crime policy is made and implemented. The British North America Act, now included in the **Constitution Act** (1982), provides the basis for a distribution of power between the central government and the provinces. With regard to criminal-justice matters, the Parliament of Canada has exclusive jurisdiction to make **criminal law**, and the provinces may make laws in relation to the administration of justice. The federal government's power to make criminal law also involves the ability and responsibility to set sanctions in law for offences in violation of the criminal law. Similarly, the Constitution Act provides that the provinces have power to impose punishments by fine, probation, or imprisonment in enforcing any law of the province.

It should, therefore, be evident that, while there is some clarity of distinction between the powers and responsibilities of the two levels of government, their power to make crime policy clearly overlaps in a number of important areas. This means that in order for Canadian crime policy to be effectively made and implemented, some means must be found to provide for conjoint decision making between these two levels of government.

Compounding the negotiations on crime policy in Canada is the requirement for involvement of municipalities as well. A number of changes in recent years have reduced the direct operational involvement of municipalities in the provision of criminal-justice services. In most locations, the lower courts, which used to be administered by the municipalities, are now administered by the provinces. Municipalities are also not as involved in the provision of custodial dispositions for offenders (primarily youth), as was once the case.

However, an important area of crime policy and criminal-justice practice still falls under the administration of municipalities—law enforcement. Municipal police make up 60 percent of all police-force personnel in Canada (Statistics Canada, 1986b). There are federal and provincial police forces in Canada as well, but in the area of policing, the municipal governments play the most significant role in relation to criminal-justice policy.

While it is important to consider the position of munic-

principal negotia-
cy occur between
s. The provincial
(unicipal acts, etc.)
(in the provinces.
e federal govern-
cipalities.

n the distribution
s the existence of
al ethos has been
between Canada's
the English, for a
within the Cana-
c provides the for-
rests of the French
vince, but a special
a level of political
Canada has had a
the provinces to
d to obtain power
l, it has been sug-
wer by the Liberal
has been a signifi-
the central govern-
eneral, but Quebec
1976).
Canadian "politic,"
tween the French
identity, is beyond
, a brief examina-
ight be useful, par-
uence on Canadian

nple, is sometimes
French Canadians
ked a previous in-
d to assimilate the
y governed under
ebec Act provided
d the whole of their
dish **common law**.
atters, the English
asion of the French.
ebec Revenue Act
edule of duties and
of the civil govern-
e.
initiatives accom-
al of French Cana-
dly the question of
nts set in motion a
e establishment of

Canada as a nation in 1867 and onward to the present day. The recent debates resulting in the Meech Lake Accord offer ample evidence of this.[3] The Quebec Act clearly presented a compromise centred in the application of civil and criminal law that was intended to find common ground between the two cultural groups such that some form of administrative government suited to both could be developed.

According to Wade (1964, p. 42), for French Canadians, Confederation is not simply a union of British North American provinces under a central government. It is a "pact or treaty between French and English," guaranteeing to members of each cultural group "an equal right to his own place, language, laws and customs." It seems reasonably clear that, in the minds of French Canadians, the central government is, historically, primarily representative of English interests. Thus, there has been a continuing struggle, reflected in the recent dialogue surrounding the Meech Lake Accord, to create some type of increased power within the governing structure of Quebec to adequately represent French interests. It is not possible to understand public policy, including crime policy, in Canada without an awareness of these historical influences (for further discussion of this subject, see Wade, 1964; Bracq, 1924; McConnell, 1963; Rioux & Martin, 1968; and, Cohen, Smith, & Warwick, 1987).

The emergence of relative parity between the provincial and federal governments of Canada has resulted in the development of specific mechanisms to address national policy issues, particularly where the political responsibilities of the two levels of government overlap. Probably the most important structure for joint decision making between the two levels of government is the institution now known as the federal-provincial conference. The federal-provincial conference is a vehicle enabling the federal government leaders to sit down from time to time with provincial leaders to resolve questions of federal-provincial concern. It is at these conferences that much of the future development of Canada is planned. The federal-provincial conference has, to some extent, replaced the Supreme Court as a vehicle for resolving jurisdictional disputes between the central and regional units of the country. The advent of the Constitution Act, with its **Canadian Charter of Rights and Freedoms**, has, of course, thrust the courts back into the policy making arena in a somewhat different way. However, for purposes of practical administration, including policy making in such areas as criminal justice, the federal-provincial conference is the most important and consistently used device. Since the mid-1970s, there has been approximately one federal-provincial conference each year on criminal-justice matters alone. It is evident from these phenomena that theories of organizational politics, one of the areas of concentration within policy studies, has application to the Canadian politic and helps both to describe and to explain some of the dynamics of crime-policy making within Canadian federalism.

Historical Influences on Canadian Crime Policy

It has become popular to use Packer's (1964) distinction between the **"due process"** and "crime control" models of law enforcement as a way of assessing the emphasis given to crime policy in a country or political system. In particular, these models have been used to describe some of the differences in crime-control policy and practice between Canada and the United States (see, for example, Hagan & Leon, 1978). In this comparison, it is generally assumed that due process is the model of emphasis in the United States, and crime control is the model of emphasis in Canada.

The historical assessment of this difference in emphasis has been based on the proposition that the United States emerged out of a national character that was revolutionary in nature, whereas Canada "evolved" out of forces that were mainly counter-revolutionary (Clark, 1942, p. 190–91).

According to Lipset (1964), three factors are included among the counter-revolutionary forces that influenced Canada's development: (1) the movement of British Loyalists to Canada during and after the American Revolution; (2) the role played by the Church of England and the Roman Catholic church in providing Canada with a set of hierarchical and traditionally rooted control mechanisms; and (3) the threat posed to Canada's frontier expansion by parallel frontier activities in the United States.

Canada is generally assumed to exist within a "conservative mould," thus making it "a country of greater caution, reserve, and restraint" (Naegle 1964, p. 501). It has even been proposed that Canada's conservatism is linked to the nation's two founding peoples. Porter (1967, p. 56) notes that "English and French Canadians are more alike in their conservatism, traditionalism, religiosity, authoritarianism, and elite values than the spokesmen of either group are prepared to admit."

Another common explanation for the difference in crime-control approaches between Canada and the United States has to do with the manner in which each was forced to develop its frontiers. It is proposed that differing conditions of expansion resulted in differing demands for social control (see, e.g., Innis, 1956). Resources in Canada were more difficult to develop than were those in the United States. Canada was vulnerable to attacks from the south, and there were continual threats of American absorption (Clark, 1942). It has been noted that, in the 1870s, the U.S.

government was spending more than $20 million annually fighting the Plains Indians. In 1870, the total Canadian government budget was just over $19 million, and a significant portion of this budget was allocated to the development of essential railway transportation (MacLeod, 1976).

The North-West Mounted Police became an essential part of Sir John A. Macdonald's famous National Policy for Canada, because Canada could not afford to develop the Canadian West through expensive military operations. The mission of the North-West Mounted police was to prevent crime and disorder from developing, as they had done in the United States. To accomplish this end, the North-West Mounted Police "enjoyed powers unparalleled by any other police force in a democratic country" (MacLeod, 1976):

> The NWMP . . . were a radical departure from the British pattern of law enforcement. They were centrally controlled, they had certain military characteristics like the French gendarmes, and . . . they were very much involved in administrative activities and acted in the capacity of such functionaries of the civil law as bailiffs and sheriffs as well. In one very important respect the Mounted Police had powers which exceeded those of European police; they acted as magistrates and passed judgement on criminals as well as apprehending them.

The deployment of an extraordinary police force to effect the safe and orderly development of the Canadian frontier against almost overwhelming political and environmental odds has become symbolic of Canada's "demonstrated willingness to apply coercion in a systematic and concerted way" for the perceived social good (Hagan & Leon, 1978, p. 202). Canadian novelist Margaret Atwood has suggested (1972, p. 171) that "Canada must be the only country in the world where a policeman is used as a national symbol." The symbolism attached to the police role in Canada is a reminder that, for a variety of reasons having to do with the development and evolution of the nation, in Canada social order ideologically precedes individual freedom. Thus, the crime-control model is probably the most accurate of the two models in describing the basis of Canadian crime policy.

The emphasis on crime control in Canada is evidenced throughout its history and in relation to all elements of criminal-justice practice. The events surrounding the Mackenzie Rebellion of 1837; the execution of Louis Riel in 1885; the cases emerging from the Winnipeg General Strike of 1919; the government response to the "Quebec crisis" of 1970—all give evidence of the pattern of "firm action and succeeding lenience which seems to character-

ıdicial tradition"

and practice, this
rence to the for-
dividual rights is
on to the United
d behind in areas
follow American
t of accused per-
emphasized the
n the rights of in-
ty of evidence in
rough the courts,
hen applying the
oms.

nparison with the
erent balance be-
sts. This is not to
e or less just, since
ly encourages or
ss. As Hagan and
is that Canada has
ent to crime con-
mmitment to the
individual rights

at, while Canada
ss than does the
strative guarantees
nages to spend less
n & Leon, 1978).
ppear generally to
y the individual to
that problems of
The primary com-
curb on deviance
dividual creativity)
e ideal of "law and

e this observation:

edom to deviate
inate statuses by
nalization. The
ation and at the
ate likelihood of
hich of these sit-
n empirical than
consequence of
ited to study.

The Problem of Jurisdiction in Canadian Criminal Justice

Law Enforcement

Police services in Canada are provided under several administrative arrangements.[4] Municipalities may have their own police boards and provide their own police forces; municipalities may provide police services under contract with the RCMP; unincorporated areas of a province may receive police services by the RCMP under contract with the province; the RCMP may provide police services in areas of direct responsibility, such as drug-law enforcement; a province may provide a police force under its direct administration, as in Ontario and Quebec; and special police forces may provide services under public or private sponsorship, such as the policing of Canada's ports and the Canadian National or Canadian Pacific Railway police forces.[5]

Prosecutions

The problem of jurisdiction affects prosecutorial services as well as the other service systems within criminal justice. However, in the case of prosecutors, the distinction between federal and provincial jurisdiction is somewhat different. This distinction is based upon the manner in which federal and provincial responsibility for the prosecution of criminal offences is determined. Since prosecutors (Crown counsel, Crown attorneys) act on behalf of the attorney general, it is the authority of the attorney general (federal and provincial) that gives prosecutors their ability to act. It has historically been understood that the prosecution of offences under federal statutes other than the Criminal Code belongs to the federal minister of justice and the attorney general. Prosecutorial responsibility for Criminal Code matters belongs to the provincial attorneys general. There is, on occasion, some confusion as to responsibility for prosecutions as between the minister of justice (attorney general) federally and the attorney general for the province. This has occurred with regard to drug prosecutions or when there has arisen some peculiar problem of jurisdiction or "claim" among federal, provincial, and, possibly, municipal authorities (for a further discussion of problems of prosecutorial jurisdiction, see Stenning, 1986, Ch. 10).

Perhaps the most important organizational difficulty in the prosecutorial area is the relationship between prosecutors and law enforcement. Prosecutors are the "screen" between law-enforcement initiatives of an investigative and evidence-gathering nature and the decision to proceed with a charge. Prosecutorial policy, like law-enforcement policy, can be established without regard to other components of the criminal-justice system. This often results in frustration for law-enforcement agencies as they encounter resistance on the part of prosecutors to proceed with charges that the police feel are legitimate and that have resulted from considerable investigative efforts. The politics involved in the relationship between law enforcement and prosecutors is very important to the understanding of crime control in an area. This relationship becomes part of the "local legal culture."[6] Both law-enforcement and prosecutorial agencies are affected in their planning and decision making by their understanding of the relationship they have with each other.

Courts

The courts, as well, are distributed among the three jurisdictions. The lower courts are primarily administered provincially, although in some areas they remain municipal courts. The areas of law that are addressed by the lower courts include: family law, criminal law, small claims (civil), and traffic. High courts also exist in each province under federal jurisdiction. These include the county courts, supreme courts, and courts of appeal in each province. Finally, there are the federal courts, including the Federal Court of Canada and the Supreme Court of Canada.

The problem of jurisdiction with regard to the courts is not so much its arrangement across the three levels of government (although there are some areas of law, e.g., family law, where the division of responsibilities between the lower and higher courts is confusing and problematic), but is instead found in the unique autonomy maintained by the courts in relation to their administration. The functions of *court administration* can be rationalized across the various levels of the court and levels of political jurisdiction. *Judicial administration*,[7] however, is concerned more with the management of judges in the context of judicial independence (see Deschenes, 1981). Here, the problem of jurisdiction is between the policy-making and implementation powers of the executive arm of government and the case-law function of the judiciary as an independent adjudicating body. In Canada, the provinces with the most firmly established systems of court administration have experienced the most jurisdictional conflict with those responsible for judicial administration. Court administrators are regular civil servants, and judicial administrators are administrative judges. Sometimes the tension between these two "jurisdictions" can be quite severe. For example, in British Columbia, especially in smaller jurisdictions, the responsibility for court scheduling fluctuated in the 1970s between the court administrator and the judicial administrator, with attendant problems of "territoriality" emerging between the two.

Corrections

In the area of Canadian corrections, jurisdictional problems have resulted in the most duplication and waste. Correctional services in Canada are divided between the federal and provincial governments. The problems of jurisdiction, as they affect adult corrections, centre primarily on the administration of the so-called **two-year rule**, the demarcation criterion for determining jurisdictional responsibility in adult corrections. Those offenders receiving a sentence of two years or more are located under federal jurisdiction, and those offenders receiving a sentence of two years less a day, or less, are placed in provincial jurisdiction. Since both the federal and the provincial systems commit the preponderance of their resources to institutional programs (prisons and penitentiaries), it is around the building and maintenance of secure institutions that much jurisdictional conflict occurs. In a single province, there may be both provincial prisons and federal penitentiaries located near each other in the same locale. It is difficult to justify both the duplication and cost associated with such an arrangement and the confusion to the public resulting from the difficulty in understanding where the responsibility for these institutions lies. (For an in-depth discussion of correctional issues in Canada, see Ekstedt & Griffiths, 1988.)

In the juvenile area, the jurisdictional difficulties tend to be found in the relationships between the various provincial departments and ministries responsible for youth services. Even with the passage of the **Young Offenders Act** (1982) to replace the former **Juvenile Delinquents Act** (1929), the difficulty in arranging responsibility for juveniles or young offenders within provincial jurisdiction remains. In the area of juvenile corrections, the phenomenon of the "interministerial committee" has become famous as a means of attempting to co-ordinate the interests of the various jurisdictions involved.

The jurisdictional problem continues with the administration of parole and after-care programs for persons on release from correctional systems. The major conditional release (**parole**) authority in Canada is the National Parole Board, which is federal. However, the supervisory responsibility for federal parolees falls under the administration of the Correctional Service of Canada (federal). Quebec, Ontario, and British Columbia have parole boards responsible for the conditional release of prisoners under provincial jurisdiction. Often, the supervision of federal prisoners released from penitentiaries by the National Parole Board becomes the responsibility of provincial probation agencies because of a lack of federal personnel in an area.

In this case, the jurisdictional confusion can be quite interesting since **probation** is always a responsibility of provincial governments and parole is usually a responsibil-

exceptions noted
n associated with
ition available to
1 may be created
y (provincial pro-
ander the author-
deral corrections

tion are basic to
uthority and con-
and wasteful, not
y, facilities, etc.),
petition between
ical support.
safety of the pub-
petition and stress
for the system's
tion and dysfunc-
as entropy. It has
is a universal law
on move towards
982, p. 21). Juris-
y distracting the
nary purpose. The
ays of arresting or

red axiomatic that
he more it is sub-
It has further been
guishing social sys-
open rather than
ws that the ability
essential to its effi-
. Hagan states that
environment is an
982, p. 19).
an organization or
l must take place
ent. In the case of
ought to be com-
ffensiveness, law-
with an awareness
ontrol, prosecutors
nasis on those types
e most serious, the
dards, and punish-
be in keeping with
, public receptivity
ance of "openness"

minal justice is not
"open" in degrees,

depending upon which part of the system one is discussing. Law-enforcement agencies, the prosecutorial responsibility, judicial independence, the problems of security
within closed institutions—all take on the characteristics
of a "closed" rather than "open" system. Therefore, in
criminal justice, there is constant pressure to limit the interaction with the environment. This not only creates
problems of inefficiency and disorganization, but often, as
previously discussed, places the various components of the
system in competition with each other to maintain favour
and continuing support in spite of the growing "entropy."
The many cases of individuals who have suffered injustice
at the hands of the criminal-justice system are illustrative
of the effect of entropy on the ability of the system to accomplish its purpose.

Policy Making as a Human Process

> It is the nature of common social observances to
> dramatize the role of personality as well. In the
> modern capital, Washington being no doubt the ex-
> treme case, a very large part of all social and other
> intercourse is concerned with who is exercising
> power—who is imposing his or her purposes on
> others. And most social effort consists in seeking
> association with those who are deemed to be power-
> ful. (Galbraith, 1983, p. 43)

There are a number of theoretical perspectives and
models for analysis with regard to the study of public-policy
making that have not been included in this chapter. For
purposes of this text, the most important objective is to
alert the reader to the complexity of factors and potential
problems of analysis involved in understanding crime policy.
However, before addressing some specific problems of
criminal-justice policy in Canada, it is important to spend
some additional time addressing the peculiar "human" factors that influence the policy process.

Policy making is, after all is said and done, an activity
of human beings. Policy development reflects not only the
best and the worst of attempts to apply human knowledge
to the solution of human problems, but also the tendency
of human beings in organizational life to act without regard
to the necessity of policy guidance. Often this tendency
results from the "pragmatic" requirement to act before
policy is made. If there is no policy in place to deal with
a prison riot, for example, then prison officials cannot be
condemned for taking discretionary steps to quell it, by
whatever means they consider necessary.

While it is clear from the literature that opinions vary
as to how policy should be construed, it is, nevertheless,
possible to make a distinction between policy as a type of

decision and other activities that either result from policy or take place in the absence of policy.

Ekstedt and Griffiths (1988, Ch. 6) have suggested that, in the context of organizational life, policy can be understood by concentrating on the location at which the policy is made rather than simply on how it is defined. It is proposed, then, that there are locations of responsibility within any organization that, by definition, exist for the purpose of establishing the directions policy might take. Generally, these are the locations of people holding "management" positions. In government, the ultimate management responsibility for decisions about the way in which the government's power and responsibility will be handled rests with politicians. These politicians interact with the most senior civil servants reporting to them. Ekstedt and Griffiths (1988, pp. 160–64) have called this interaction between politicians and civil servants, the activity of "policy management." In this model, the tasks of management are therefore policy-related; decisions that come out of the management context are thus regarded as policy decisions.

However, in this model, it is pointed out that there is another category of decision making related to policy, but directed toward the *implementation* of policy through the creation of procedures. This activity is described as "executive administration." Procedures act as the means by which policy is implemented. Ideally, in executive administration, decisions cannot be made in the absence of already existing policy, since that would mean that the administrator would be acting without "direction" or "context." But, as we shall shortly see, administrative decisions *are* made in the absence of policy. When this happens, then procedural statements themselves may be interpreted as actually "being policy," since there appears to be no formal policy as the referent. This explains why procedures are often subsequently difficult to change; because they have incorrectly been given policy "weight," they have been defined as *being* the policy.

When using this model, then, it is assumed that policy, not procedure, is the "superior" or directive decision. Therefore, management, rather than administration, is the superior activity. It is assumed that policy gives direction to other decisions, sets out "the way in which judgments can be made between alternative choices" (Ekstedt & Griffiths, 1988, p. 102). Policy declares the underlying value and establishes the overall direction of activities within the organization. Procedures establish the specific means by which the policy can be implemented. But it is important to remember that procedure is not policy.

Using the management model, one can engage in policy studies by determining the decisions made publicly at the management level and then assessing the factors that may have contributed to their development. But, additionally, in policy analysis, one would also examine the procedures that flow from the policy, to see if they have faithfully reflected what was intended for the policy. This is a difficult-enough task at best, when the policy statements are clear and the relationship between the managers and the administrators is straightforward. But, it is often the case that the statements are not clear and the relationship is not straightforward—for a number of reasons: the policy direction may not have been clear; the procedures for the policy may, in fact, distort the policy; procedures may have evolved in the *total absence* of policy. In fact, it is arguable that, in many cases, policy articulation *follows* the development of procedures. This may occur when there is an immediate problem that must be solved. In areas where "crisis management" dominates decision making, it is very often the case that procedures will precede policy. Criminal justice is a type of organization where this occurs.

There appear to be two distinctive types of circumstances under which procedures may be developed in the absence of policy (real-world examples illustrating these two types of circumstances are discussed below, after the general discussion of the types):

1. Procedures may be developed in the absence of policy when a component of the criminal-justice system (law enforcement, courts administration, corrections, etc.) decides to initiate a program change or innovation in response to a crisis or a need for improvement in effectiveness/efficiency. In this category, procedures may be developed for the purpose of keeping an existing program intact in the face of threat of change from the "outside" (e.g., an upper-level management decision to "reorganize" the structure of the system within which the program operates); to meet an immediate crisis (such as a jail break); or to take advantage of the opportunity to gain additional monies if certain changes take place within the program (such as the introduction of a new therapeutic technique in a rehabilitation program for offenders).

2. Procedures may also precede policy when there is a requirement for procedure because of changes in the law, but the law itself does not state what the policy intent actually is. It has been the practice, in recent years, for example, for new legislation to include some kind of preamble or declaration of principle that articulates the policy intent. Often, in the case of federal legislation, this policy intent is something negotiated between the central government and the provinces.

However, when current legislation is amended, or even with new legislation (as just described), attention to the declaration of the policy intent may either be considered not necessary or, for a variety of reasons, be overlooked. While it is possible to think of law as policy, in practice, legislation is a type of procedure used to implement policy

[he policies that
 legislation may
liscussion papers
licy background
 into effect may
nal legislative or
ement of higher
the original legis-
veen the various
ite possible for a
 basis of a legis-
without a clear
ed the legislative

op without articu-
are community-
grams. Consider-
velopment were
'0s. Community-
empt to provide
to the courts that
nders held in se-
eparative" return
programs appear
lopments: (1) an
am experimenta-
roblem with pri-
eration of minor
nsiderable atten-
erceived benefits
s (see also Ekstedt
mmission, 1987).
nterest in the de-
wever, it is argu-
h these programs
 least six to eight
re implemented.
edural confusion
panded and were
ons. For example,
ces, studies, brief-
ken to clarify the
-service order pro-
t was determined
sed and confirmed
al confusion over
ce required (mini-
disposition should
rough probation;
ence is completed.
e development of
resolve, given the

lack of policy. In some cases, these matters had to be tested in court through writs of **habeas corpus** and other challenges to the administrative authority associated with these programs. It has been argued, of course, that the reason for part of the "confusion" was that procedures were developed in a more or less *ad hoc* manner, to serve functions not originally intended, for example, controlling the individual or "net widening." In the absence of clear policy, such unintended results are more likely to occur.

Diversion programs present a similar example but with somewhat broader implications in the criminal-justice system. Again, in the early 1970s, there was considerable interest in reducing court backlogs and making the management of cases through the courts more efficient. There was, concurrently, growing support for the use of nonjudicial strategies for resolving social conflict. Various forms of alternative dispute-resolution schemes began to emerge, and the concept of "diversion" programs began to take shape. In Canada, for the most part, diversion programs were developed by various private-sector agencies, and mechanisms were developed within the criminal-justice system to "divert" some offenders to these programs.

Again, in order to meet what were considered to be operational demands for increased efficiency, and in order to take advantage of available funds for purposes of experimentation, a number of diversion programs were implemented without policy direction. Similar to that of the community-service orders, this situation resulted in some confusion. The absence of policy resulted in court challenges to the validity of certain administrative procedures.[8] Perhaps the most important problem was concern about the perceived "**double jeopardy**" that would apply to an **alleged** offender if such a person were placed in a diversion program and, because of a perceived lack of success in the program, was returned to court to be adjudicated on the original charge. This, in fact, happened, resulting in pressure from the judiciary to reduce or change the use of such programs. It is worth noting that many of these programs were provided by private-sector agencies funded by government grants. A number of these agencies experienced severe operational problems because of the confusion resulting from the absence of policy. As a result, often abrupt and "unexplainable" demands for changes in procedure were made by both the funding agency (government) and the courts.

In the second category, *conditions encouraging the development of procedures in the absence of policy,* i.e., the response to legislation, a number of case examples exist. One example of interest is the development of procedures at the provincial level for the granting of temporary absences from prisons. The legislative base for this had been created federally (the Prisons and Reformatories Act, s. 7). The Prisons and Reformatories Act provides for the temporary release of inmates from secure institutions for specific purposes (home leave, employment, education, emergency medical, etc.). The administrative authority for granting these releases is established in the legislation.

When some of the provinces began to develop community correctional centre (CCC) programs (minimum-security community residences), a means was sought for the release of persons confined in secure institutions to attend these centres. In the absence of any other means provided in legislation, it was decided that the **temporary-absence provision** of the federal law could be used to place persons in these facilities. This was accomplished by authorizing temporary absences "back to back."[9] While this procedure allowed the provincial authorities to meet their objectives in this new program area, considerable debate resulted as to the legitimacy of using the existing legislative provision this way.

Negotiations to resolve this issue were initiated between federal and provincial authorities. A policy decision resulted from these discussions that supported the development of clearer procedures through which inmates could gain access to community correctional centres. It was recommended that direct access be provided either through initial classification *after* sentence or as a direct **disposition** in sentencing (requiring legislative amendment). The procedural difficulties were not resolved, however, until procedural anomalies (in the absence of policy) forced a policy review.

Another recent example in Canadian experience has to do with the change in legislative provisions regarding sexual offences. These changes resulted in a requirement, particularly for provincial authorities, to establish new procedures for dealing with both the victims of sexual assault, including children, and the offenders. The problem was exacerbated because the authority for dealing with these issues is distributed across a number of government ministries in every province, particularly where children and families are involved. The legislative changes forced provincial authorities to develop procedures for dealing with new categories of offensiveness without a clear understanding of the policy intent. Consequently, attempts to resolve these procedural matters became tentative and difficult.[10]

Policy and "Personal" Politics

As Ekstedt and Griffiths (1988, p. 114) point out, one of the influences on public policy is "short-term political need." Very often, the political need is personal and has something to do with the values, beliefs, desire for personal reward, or career aspirations of the individual decision maker. Since, in public-policy making, the individual decision maker is part of the larger political process, the desire to satisfy personal interests is also integrated with the requirement that the entire political organization (party) retain power through the continuing approval of the electorate. Thus, regardless of the extent to which information can be organized "rationally" to assist the decision maker, in public policy, personal/political interests often become the most significant influences on the policy result.

A failure to satisfactorily acknowledge this dynamic in the assessment of Canadian criminal-justice policy will impede the development of an understanding of the reasons why policy decisions are made and the problems that sometimes occur in the implementation of policies.

It is often the case that decisions that are made on the basis of a political need violate the sensitivities of the "professionals" in the bureaucracy who are left with the task of developing the administrative procedures required to implement the policy. As a result, it is sometimes considered *preferable* by the professionals in the bureaucracy that they have the freedom to implement procedure in the absence of policy. Policy established out of political need may be considered potentially distorting of the "real" needs that are being addressed in the delivery of services or in the overall administration of justice.

Thus, we can see that the problem of procedures existing without governing policy is not only a factor associated with the problems of crisis management, but also results from the peculiar problems of providing adequate policy guidance in a "political" environment.

Issues in Canadian Criminal-Justice Practice

It has already been suggested that the environment within which public policy is made has a direct and determining influence on the practices that emerge in the implementation of policy. It is arguable that, of all the recent public-policy initiatives taken in Canada, the patriation of the Constitution of Canada with its Canadian Charter of Rights and Freedoms has had more effect on the relationship between policy and practice, in justice as well as in other areas of public interest, than has any other public or political event. Understanding both the context of Canadian crime policy and the resulting practices requires sensitivity to the implications of the Charter. This can be understood both from the history of its development and the ongoing activity of its interpretation by the courts.

The Canadian Charter of Rights and Freedoms

There were a number of peripheral influences surrounding the entrenchment in the constitution of the Canadian Charter of Rights and Freedoms. Among these was a grow-

World War II.
nt of Japanese
1 the Canadian
ses in Quebec,
oundland, con-
ecting the civil
veloped an in-
the 1960 Cana-
Canadians from
ch as the invo-
Mahon, 1984).
cipitating con-
etween federal
nore significant
can be viewed
uggle over the
ovincial govern-
stitution can be
surrounding this
ntury (Morton,

licy issues were
eralism. Rather
whether a piece
just, controver-
level of govern-
s the legislation.
le foremost and
as been the dis-
ations of public
lisguised as juris-
ed and discussed
ly been demon-

strated in Charter litigation surrounding issues such as Sunday closing, abortion, film censorship, minority language education, etc.

Russell (1982) correctly projected another significant outcome resulting from the Constitution Act and the Canadian Charter of Rights and Freedoms when he stated that one of the principal impacts will be to "judicialize politics and politicize the judiciary." The Charter contains explicit authorization for judicial interpretation and enforcement that has effectively qualified the doctrine of parliamentary supremacy with the parallel concept of constitutional supremacy (the issue here is to determine whether Parliament, as an elected body, or the constitution, as interpreted by the judiciary, is the superior authority in determining social or "public" policy). Russell (1982) suggested that this would create a new and powerful role for the judiciary (particularly the Supreme Court of Canada), one that would explicitly involve them in resolutions concerning Canadian politics and public policy. As Morton (1987) suggests, the courts have begun to carve out a bold and creative constitutional jurisprudence exemplifying the adoption of a noninterpretivist approach to the Charter.[11]

This approach has guided the judiciary in its determinations surrounding a number of areas of public policy. The most significant impact, however, has taken place in the realm of criminal law, law enforcement, and administration, arising from litigation involving the legal rights enumerated in the Charter in sections 7 to 14. A number of Charter cases have been completed that demonstrate the importance of the new role of the judiciary and the effect that their interpretations of the Charter are having in altering the nature or essence of criminal-justice policy and practice in Canada (see Box 3.2).

---

eedoms Cases

984)
persons against un-
his case, the courts
mit the powers of
eral and provincial
reted as guarantee-
e from unreasonable
ion of property and
1al's reasonable ex-

d that, in such cases,
ether the public in-
ent must give way

to the government's interest in intruding on an individual's privacy in order to advance its goals—notably those of law enforcement. The courts ruled that the only way in which such an assessment can be made, without infringing upon the section 8 right, is through a system of prior authorization rather than one of subsequent validation. The purpose of prior authorization is to provide opportunity, prior to the event, for the conflicting interests of the state and the individual to be assessed in a neutral and impartial way by an individual capable of acting in a judicial manner. Failure to obtain prior authorization will result in a presumption of unreasonableness that the party seeking to justify the warrantless search will have to address.

Box 3.2 *(Continued)*

R. v. Noble (1984)

Subsections 10(1)(a) of the **Narcotic Control Act** and 37(1)(a) of the **Food and Drug Act** (both now repealed) authorized the use of writs of assistance that entitled the holder to exercise, without a warrant, statutory powers of search and seizure under the relevant statute. In essence, once an individual was granted a **writ of assistance** by a federal court judge, he or she could perform a warrantless search of a dwelling house at any hour of the day or night, subject only to the reasonable belief that an illegal drug or narcotic was contained within, and irrespective of whether there was any situation of urgency that would make obtaining a warrant impractical.

The Ontario Court of Appeal ruled that searches undertaken under the authority of writs of assistance are unreasonable in their extent and contravene the constitutional rights specified under section 8 of the Charter. Therefore, writs of assistance are deemed to be of no force and effect. The courts ruled that the guarantee against unreasonable search and seizure cannot be narrowly construed and, despite the obstacles confronting law-enforcement officers in the field of drug enforcement, the use and power of warrantless searches, even in cases of emergency, cannot be tolerated or justified under the Charter.

Dubois v. The Queen (1985)

In this case, the defendant confessed to murder at his first trial and was convicted of the offence. The conviction was overturned, however, and a new trial ordered. In the second trial, the Crown sought to use the evidence the accused had given at his first trial. The Supreme Court of Canada ruled that such a use contravened section 13 of the Charter respecting self-incrimination. There it is guaranteed that a witness who gives incriminating evidence has the right not to have that evidence used to incriminate him/her in any other proceedings, except in a prosecution for **perjury** or for the giving of contradictory evidence. The Court adopted a broad interpretation of the section 13 right and stated that the purpose of the section, when viewed in the context of subsection 11(c) (right not to be compelled to give evidence against yourself) and subsection 11(d) (**presumption of innocence**), is to protect individuals from being indirectly compelled to incriminate themselves. The result was that Dubois's confession, despite its validity in the first trial, was deemed inadmissible in the second trial without his direct consent, and a third trial was ordered.

R. v. Therens (1985)

In this case, the Supreme Court of Canada was required to rule on the legitimacy of drinking-and-driving legislation. The crucial factor to be determined was whether an individual who complies with a demand under subsection 235(1) (now s. 254[2]) of the Criminal Code to provide a breath sample is under detention within the meaning of section 10 of the Charter, despite the fact that the person is not under arrest. The Court ruled unanimously that the motorist, in the case before it, was under detention. The significance of this ruling was that the finding allowed the individual the right to retain and instruct counsel, and to be informed of that right prior to being required to submit to the breathalyzer test. Failure to comply with the right specified under section 10 would henceforth render the evidence inadmissible in court. This case effectively overturned its previous ruling in *Chromiac v. The Queen* (1979), which had been applied previously. In that case, the courts adopted a narrow interpretation of the word "detention," disallowing the individual's right to counsel.

Smith v. The Queen (1987)

In this case, the court struck down subsection 5(2) of the Narcotic Control Act, rendering it of no force and effect. This section provided that a minimum sentence of seven years' imprisonment was required for the importation or exportation of narcotics. The courts ruled that this was in violation of section 12 of the Charter, which states that everyone has the right not to be subjected to any **cruel and unusual** treatment or **punishment.** While the state may impose punishment and while a minimum mandatory sentence is not in or of itself cruel and unusual, in this case, subsection 5(2) offended section 12 because inevitably a verdict of guilty would lead to the imposition of a term of imprisonment grossly disproportionate to the offence committed. The court must be able to consider the gravity of offence, the personal characteristics of the offender, and the circumstances of the case in order to determine what range of sentencing would be appropriate to punish, rehabilitate, deter, and/or afford protection to society.

The courts also held that the protection afforded by this section governs the quality of the punishment and is concerned with the effect that the punishment may have on an individual. The criterion that must be applied in order to determine whether a punishment is cruel and unusual is whether the punishment prescribed is so excessive as to

this assessment,
shment is neces-
it is founded on
ether there exist
sed. These stan-
and The Queen

erated for more
in 1970 that he
minal legislation
ention of the in-
punishment, es-
a danger to the
us-offender pro-
ate's record was
courts ruled that
d an opportunity
was not a danger
for an indefinite
cessive and serv-
would be entitled

to remedy under subsection 24(1) of the Charter.

Regina v. Oakes (1986)

The Supreme Court of Canada struck down a "reverse-onus clause" in the Narcotic Control Act, stating that it infringed upon the subsection 11(d) right to be presumed innocent until proven guilty. Under the act, the Crown must prove **beyond a reasonable doubt** that the accused was in possession of a narcotic. Section 8 then requires the accused to prove on the balance of probabilities that she or he was not in possession of a narcotic for the purpose of trafficking. The courts ruled that the purpose of subsection 11(d) is to guarantee the presumption of innocence and to protect the fundamental liberty and human dignity of any person accused by the state of criminal conduct. In light of the gravity of the consequences of conviction, the presumption of innocence is crucial and ensures that, until the state proves an accused's guilt beyond all reasonable doubt, he or she is innocent. This is essential to a society committed to justice and fairness. Therefore, the state must bear the burden of proof, and the reverse-onus clause in section 8 of the Narcotic Control Act is of no force and effect.

nd the numer-
adian criminal-
policy is then
example, a poli-
rney general in
ffice ultimately
ig certain types
ed through the
d to deal with
ve structure.

olicy

f problems and
Canadian crime
ould recall that
on from policy
dian federalism.
tions subsystem
Federated Sys-
wness in estab-
atire corrections

system." The jurisdictional splits within Canadian federalism have been viewed as problematic for years by academics, professionals and practitioners, politicians, and other Canadian commentators (see Ekstedt & Griffiths, 1988, Ch. 10). Operational anomalies, duplications, overlaps, problems in planning, and difficulties in co-operation and co-ordination have become endemic for criminal-justice practice within the organization of Canadian politics. There is no other single factor in the Canadian justice environment that has so much potential to distort the association between policy *intent* at the political or managerial level and policy *implementation* at the administrative level. No issue in Canadian criminal-justice practice can be adequately understood without an awareness of this phenomenon. Recently, the Justice System Report of the 1985 Task Force on Program Review (Neilsen, 1986, pp. 296–7) stated that

the split relates practical difficulties which impede service delivery and efficient administration. Both federal and provincial governments operate programs of imprisonment and programs of community supervision of offenders. Both systems bare the attendant administrative and other overhead costs associated with their service delivery. The two levels of government often end up competing in an unhealthy way for staff, community services and private sector resources.

The following are a few examples of current issues in criminal-justice practice that illustrate the points made above.

Drunk Driving

Drinking-and-driving has exacted an enormous toll on Canadian society for more than 50 years. Impaired driving is purported to be the most frequently committed criminal offence today; yet it is estimated that 95 percent of legally impaired drivers go undetected (Vingilis & Vingilis, 1987). It is estimated that the risk of apprehension in Canada is 1 in 514 impaired trips, or 1 in every 2575 impaired kilometres (Lawson, 1983).

Drinking-and-driving offences and accidents place a considerable burden on enforcement agencies, the legal system, and correctional services. It is difficult to estimate the cost of attempting to regulate impaired driving through the criminal-justice system; however, correctional statistics alone provide some insight. For example, the total provincially sentenced admissions for 1985–86 number 119 629. Seventeen percent of this number were incarcerated for drinking-and-driving or refusing a breathalyzer test (Statistics Canada, 1986a).

Impaired driving is a complex phenomenon involving a variety of physical, psychological, and situational factors. Countermeasures range from public education and legal sanctions to treatment and rehabilitation. Past efforts in the development and evaluation of programs initiated to address this problem have been so fragmented that it is difficult to assess the effectiveness of any of these efforts. For example, Kivikink and associates (1986) found that public-information campaigns have a positive effect, despite any legal sanctions, when individuals believe that impaired driving is a salient issue and when they perceive themselves to be socially and morally responsible. Vingilis and Vingilis (1987) demonstrate that road-side screening devices significantly heighten the probability of detection by police, but suggest that such efforts will not rid the roads of impaired drivers. Boyle (1983) suggests that no single approach deals effectively with the problem and that a combination of approaches will yield the best results. The persistent actions of drinking drivers have created a significant need for information and strategy to better cope with this problem. Donelson (1985, p. 23) summarizes the issue in the following manner: "of primary importance is a detailed and implementable strategic plan, one that combines and integrates action, evaluation and research components.

Commitment, leadership and supportive governments (federal, provincial, and local) are essential prerequisites to the problem. Such approaches, however, represent a process, not a panacea."

Drinking-and-driving is an offence category that clearly demonstrates the problem of creating policy in the absence of information on effective strategies. It also is an example of an obvious "cross-jurisdictional" problem requiring intergovernmental co-ordination. However, cross-jurisdictional responses to the problems created by this offence tend to be organized *procedurally* to satisfy immediate social-control needs without much attention to the governing policy. It is easier, when more than one jurisdiction is involved, to agree on procedure to be used in responding to a problem (road checks, breathalyzer testing, etc.) than to address the policy questions about the cause(s) of the problem and how, if at all, they might be addressed (sale and regulation of liquor, advertising, etc.).

Sexual Assault

In January 1983, the Parliament of Canada proclaimed a new law in which the offences of rape and indecent assault were replaced by a new offence, **sexual assault** (See Case Study for more detail). Prior to this initiative (Bill C-127), a number of studies demonstrated that the criminal-justice response to rape was inherently biased against the victim. Rape was one of the most under-reported crimes and one in which convictions were a relatively rare occurrence (Clark & Lewis, 1977; Brickman, 1979; Kinnen, 1981; and Gibson, Linden, & Johnson, 1980).

The purpose of Bill C-127 was to divest the Criminal Code of sexual discrimination, protect victims from courtroom harassment, and focus attention on the violence of sexual assaults. It was felt that these amendments would encourage reporting, facilitate convictions, and increase the victims' confidence in the criminal-justice system. The issue raised, five years after Bill C-127, is whether or not these goals have been met.

The sexual-assault legislation is a good example of an attempt to establish policy reflected in law and to declare, in the making of law, the policy purposes to be addressed. This issue is discussed at length in the case study that follows this chapter.

Terrorism

Acts of terrorism occur almost daily around the globe (See Chapter 17 for more detail). In 1983, new records were set in total terrorist casualties. Terrorism can no longer be considered as random acts of fanatical violence. It has evolved into a form of warfare used to undermine governments on an international scale (Kerr, 1985).

zation that no
s; the escalat-
t actions; the
virtually any
mical, biolog-
rism an inter-

ology that ter-
orld's terrorist
inate effective
ation technol-
operation and
use these tools

rism is exceed-
on states spon-
lligence; from
ability to assess
normity of the
on is the most
ities.

ternational co-
olombo Com-
he reaction of
e principles on
terrorism must
itutions of the
that it may be
s and freedoms
se. These issues
asideration and
oliticians.

nce today, 1200
d harmful (Soli-
Commission of
ew and distinct
ment, be added
justification for
ition and deter-
ises what Cana-
ue of a right to
il consensus that
onment, a num-
vied at the com-

ectiveness of the
e measure upon
to local govern-
far, it is unclear
em would be.

The commission has suggested that sufficiently large fines and imprisonment should be available in sentencing perpetrators of environmental crime. Wilson (1986) suggests that there are a number of difficulties in applying these traditional sanctions to artificial entities such as corporations. Fine structures will not be adequately sensitive to the wealth of the offender and a wide range of fines that are offender-regarding rather than offence-regarding may be required. Incarceration may prove to be equally problematic, since identifying a responsible actor in a corporation may be exceedingly difficult. Wilson (1986) suggests that innovative strategies such as **divestiture**, revocation of licenses, probation, restitution, and **decriminalization** are alternatives worthy of investigation and consideration.

It has been suggested that legislators and politicians demonstrate concern up to the final decision on a law in Parliament but show a surprising lack of concern with respect to what happens thereafter. Legislators are primarily concerned with formalities; if a bill is properly passed and published, it has become effective, evidence to the contrary usually being ignored.

The above description highlights, again, the problem of relating policy to procedure. Public policy may be made by governments through the legislative process without regard to the procedural implications or the need for effective monitoring of policy implementation. When public policy is made that has an effect on very powerful nongovernment agencies, procedures must be established that are sensitive to the influence these agencies (such as large corporations) have on government. The tensions associated with the desire to act in the public interest while assuring a continuing power base are often quite difficult to resolve.

Victims

During the last decade, there has been a re-emergence of attention to the victim in Canadian criminal justice. A number of factors have influenced this trend, including the women's movement of the 1960s, the American victims' movement, and a general public pressure for the criminal-justice system to respond to a perceived increase in crime and the corresponding likelihood of victimization (Norquay & Weiler, 1981).

It has often been said that the victim is twice victimized; once by the offender and once more by the criminal-justice process. In fact, **secondary injury** is recognized in the literature as the exacerbation of the original victimization resulting from the individual's contact with the criminal-justice system. The result is often a loss of faith in the system and refusal to participate in the criminal-justice process (Hastings, 1983).

The extent of this problem was identified, in part, by

the Canadian Urban Victimization Survey (Solicitor General, 1982), which indicated that more than half of the incidents described to interviewers were never reported to the police. In 1983, the report of the Canadian Federal-Provincial Task Force on Justice for Victims of Crime (Solicitor General, 1983b) made 79 separate recommendations for changes in the criminal-justice response to crime victims. These recommendations included alterations to current practices, greater access and availability of services, and the creation of legislated rights for victims (Bill C-89, which received royal assent on July 21, 1988, deals with rights and responsibilities of victims including matters of evidence, restitution, victim impact, etc.).

It has become increasingly clear that the growing national trend to respond to the plight of victims has created an entirely unique need in Canada for an effective relationship between policy and procedure in criminal-justice practice. For example, evaluative research would assist in determining the effectiveness of services currently available to victims. Recent research has indicated that some implemented programs are not accomplishing their intended goals (Rosenbaum, 1987; Davis, 1987). Of greater importance, perhaps, than these procedural matters, is the question of governing policy. To what extent should the victim influence the adjudication process? Is this trend increasing the danger of confusion between the retributive role of the state and the desire for revenge on the part of the victim? How can the victim be treated fairly while also ensuring fair justice for the accused?

Privatization

Privatization has become a buzzword for the 1980s. The growing trend toward privatization is associated with the desire to curb or reduce the cost of government by placing as many programs as possible in the hands of the private sector. Within the criminal-justice system, the move toward privatization stems from a variety of sources, including public demands for harsher sanctions, soaring costs, diminishing resources, dismal conditions within institutions, the inefficiencies of bureaucracy, and demands for accountability and cost-effectiveness (Robbins, 1986; Camp & Camp, 1985; Elvin, 1985).

The growth of privatization in Canada has raised a number of concerns about the relationship between policy and procedure. The Solicitor General of Canada (1985) has questioned whether any part of the administration of justice is an appropriate market for economic enterprise. Ericson, McMahon, and Evans (1987) warned that, with this trend, the public and private spheres will inevitably become additive rather than complementary, increasing the social-control capacities of both state and nonstate agencies. Other options, such as decarceration, decriminalization, and al-

ternatives to the criminal-justice system, have not been adequately assessed.

Gandy and Hurl (1987) state that privatization and the profit-making goal in corrections may run counter to the co-ordination of an incentive to implement other necessary programs such as education and counselling for criminal-justice clients. Ekstedt and Griffiths (1988) also raise some pertinent issues. For example, what role would private organizations play in quasi-judicial matters involving the legal status of inmates? To what extent would private employers use force, and what legislative safeguards would prisoners have? Would privatization lead to further dispersal of accountability or decrease public scrutiny of the criminal-justice system? Would privatization be cost-effective, and what options would remain if the government became dependent on private agencies and these organizations raised their fees, went bankrupt, or closed because of insufficient profit?

It is readily apparent that social trends, such as privatization, create a number of problems in determining the nature of the relationship between policy and procedure in criminal-justice practice, as well as the selection of a model for decision making that will assure that procedures, once established, will not be in violation of fundamental social precepts.

Establishing the Information Base for Crime Policy in Canada

> A social psychology of human relations which does not take into account these implicit, silently operating mechanisms shaping and misshaping our social perception is in great danger of falling victim to a pseudoempiricism which may be easily bolstered by pseudoverifications. No refined statistical methods will be of any help if the original data upon which our theories are based are already distorted and falsified by misinterpretations operating below the level of our explicit awareness. (Ichheiser, 1970, p. 15)

It has been suggested, in this chapter, that procedures in practice must be informed by policy in order to be consistent and effective over the long term. In turn, policy making requires the support of an information base that most clearly portrays the social needs to be met through public policy. During the last twenty years, there has been considerable energy committed to the development of an information base related to the making of crime policy in Canada. Such an information base, of course, must be organized to accommodate the structure of Canadian federation, which includes federal, provincial, and national interests. There are some information needs peculiar to regions and local interests; some specific to the requirements

me important
vel of govern-
e regarded as
:, however, in
ie policy is not
tion base, even
kers.

vices in Canada
iressed at sever-
al information
:s of structured
icials and direc-
territories. The
il ministries had
gh the informa-
The federal re-
lata that would
rovincial minis-
ion that would
all, it was deter-
iree categories:
:ion.
he Administra-
vincial attorneys
g a national in-
tial information
1978 when the
mation was ap-
ermanent struc-
tion of justice
result of this in-
tistics was estab-
ie gathering and
on in Canada to

ie core programs
ng in the area of
ourts, adult cor-
i program, three
al: caseload data,
of justice service
rce Coordination
81).
 on a small num-
early years, it was
ed and the range
d.[12] The centre's
nt years. For ex-

ample, a number of special projects have been undertaken, including studies on behalf of the heads of corrections for Canada; projects involving the development of comparative information for management within specific jurisdictions; the development of operational and management information systems; and projects that have addressed specific policy issues raised by individual jurisdictions and federal/provincial groups (Martin & Johnston, 1984).

Furthermore, the centre has created the Integration and Analysis Program whose mandate is to provide information gathered by the CCJS in a form that can be used for management and policy-making purposes.

While the CCJS has achieved some success in providing national justice information, it has been suggested that its lack of development past its initial implementation focus has seriously curtailed the potential for creating complete and cohesive justice information that can be used to assist in policy making. Additionally, there is recognition that the CCJS, under the best of circumstances, can contribute only partially to the information base required for policy making:

> It is readily accepted that the agreed upon national elements are a small subset of the information required by each jurisdiction to discharge their management, policy development, and legislative responsibilities. Due to the limited scope and amount of information which will be contained in the core of national statistics it will never meet all the requirements of the jurisdictions for quantitative and qualitative information. (Martin & Johnston, 1984, p.4)

The Effect of Information on Policy and Procedure

Earlier in this chapter, it was suggested that the policy-making process is often not rational and is made in a context that inhibits the decision maker's ability to adequately attend to information, even if it is made available. While this is true, it is nevertheless the case that an increased awareness of the need to have an information base available in policy making has emerged in recent years and is being taken seriously by politicians, bureaucrats, and the judiciary.[13]

Legislative Process

One of the most important areas of national information need is that generated by the legislative process. It is imperative, to Canadian society as a whole, that legislators have the resources necessary to make informed decisions. Information on the history and purpose of current law, and concrete identification of its defects, need to be made available. Cross-jurisdictional and cross-cultural research also proves to be invaluable in determining the most effective solutions to perceived problems. Legislators need to have concise information on the availability and feasibility of means, other than the criminal law, for dealing with social issues. The drafting of legislation needs to be straightforward and intelligible to all Canadians. Therefore, legislators must be informed about how best to communicate the law to the Canadian people.

Other factors that necessarily affect the form and content of legislation are the Canadian Charter of Rights and Freedoms and the constitutional split in jurisdiction between the federal and the provincial governments. The potential impact of these two factors also creates an information need for legislators. Legislators require an awareness and understanding of the effect any proposed legislation will have on the criminal-justice system in Canada as a whole. How will the legislation affect policing, the courts, or corrections? What is the relationship between alternative solutions and the availability of resources? What are the implications of possible legislative initiatives on the political viability of the government making the legislation?

Further, legislators require a means for input from those who must implement policies and those who are otherwise affected by them. Consultation with both the public and professionals operating within the system (e.g., police, judges, lawyers, etc.) not only may provide new information, but is part of the process that helps to assure successful implementation of any legislation made.

Finally, it is also necessary that legislators maintain a global perspective on crime and its treatment. Offences such as drug trafficking and terrorism have both national and international dimensions. Legislators need to be informed, in these instances, about the international impact of the legislation and Canada's obligation to keep faith with its priorities and principles without violating those of other nations.

The extent to which legislation emerges without consideration of these issues or without an information base that can be used to understand the dimensions of the problem being addressed, determines the degree to which difficulties are likely to occur in the relationship between policy and practice.

Cost-Effectiveness in the Implementation of Crime Policy

In recent years, diminishing resources and public demand for cost-effectiveness and accountability have created an important information need for policy makers in the criminal-justice system. There are a number of fundamental issues associated with effectively administering available resources. Decisions must be made about how much of society's resources should be given to addressing problems of crime.

What is the true extent of the financial commitment to crime policy in Canada, and what should it be? What is the comparison between the investment resulting from crime policy and other national expenditures such as health, welfare, and education? Once a determination of the required investment is made, information is needed to allocate resources to specific locations within the criminal-justice system. How are these resources to be distributed among the levels of government responsible for law enforcement and public safety? Finally, informed decisions must be made about how allocated resources should be used to achieve goals within the specific subsystems (i.e., the problem of the relationship between policy and procedure).

Regardless of how politicians make their decisions, as policy makers they are concerned about the results achieved through the investment of taxpayers' dollars. In the criminal-justice system, this is often problematic as performance indicators are not easily identifiable and there is not common agreement about desired results. Nonetheless, there is an increasing requirement that policies be assessed as to their effectiveness and that there be an ability to relate resource allocations to performance measures and the achievement of specific goals and objectives.

In a system where the desired results of program practice are not easily measurable, or even agreed upon, policy makers need to have some other measure of determining what is expected of them. This is particularly true in the area of crime policy. Since the making of crime policy is a political activity, a primary source of information with regard to expectations comes from the electorate. A knowledge of public expectations with regard to crime and its causes is essential if governments are going to have any confidence in their ability to justify their expenditures. An examination of public opinion serves to confirm or refute the level of expectation about results in the implementation of crime policy as well as the various concerns existing in Canadian society that generate the need for crime policy.

Finally, the making of crime policy (through legislation or other means), as well as its implementation, requires effective planning in order to be cost-effective. Therefore, one of the information requirements for cost-effectiveness is the type of information that can assist in developing a consistent and coherent planning base. It is not satisfactory to simply gather information at every point where a decision is required. An information base must exist independent of specific decision-making needs and be available both to signal when the need for decisions occurs and to support the development of alternatives in decision making from which a policy selection can be made.

ious factors in-
nd the methods
ecisions and de-
y, the relation-
efforts that study
structure of the
ed; the formal
l the policies and
deviance are be-
ncreasing atten-
des a disciplined
naking of crime
ated with policy

Societies define crime and formally construct deviance. The peculiar politics and bureaucratic organization of any country or social system also influence the ways in which crime is perceived and the means used to address it. The criminologist must be aware of jurisdictional influence, the nature of the political system, the relative power and determining influence of government bureaucracies, the ability of citizens to participate in the policy process and influence it, the problems of operational agencies in their attempts to implement policy, and the models that might be employed to assess these relationships and effectively comment on them. There seems no doubt that the importance of assessing these factors in an integrated way is now well recognized, and there is a growing effort to increase the expertise and capability of both policy makers and those who evaluate their policy making.

n policy and procedure
pment of community-
have been different if
gram implementation. How
n made? *Could* it have

dministrators (such as
corrections) may actually
guidance.

r of Rights and Freedoms
ial-justice policy and related
ocedures)? Give an

: things of life (ideals,
: of a society have an
held. Therefore, such
gative, as with cruelty.
led two bills that were
: legislation to ensure

the protection of the public against all forms of violent crimes. One bill focussed on the abolition of capital punishment in Canada, and the other was directed toward curbing violent offences and organized crime. Legislative changes to meet these ends included measures providing for increased resources in crime prevention; new sentencing provisions for convicted murderers; more stringent gun-control measures;

special provisions for the control of dangerous offenders; broader powers for police investigation through electronic surveillance and by providing for provincial commissions of inquiry on organized crime; and more effective screening procedures regarding the release of violent offenders and better after-care supervision upon their release (see Möller, 1976, pp. 1–16).

3. The Meech Lake Accord resulted from a meeting of first ministers (the prime minister and provincial premiers) at the federal government's Meech Lake, Quebec, resort on April 30, 1987. A communiqué from this meeting announced agreement in principle on five proposals. In summary, these proposals provide (1) joint control between the federal government and Quebec over immigration to the province; (2) the right of Quebec to have three of nine Supreme Court of Canada judges appointed from Quebec; (3) limitations on federal intrusion in areas of provincial jurisdiction, including the right to opt out, with fiscal compensation, of federal cost-shared programs; (4) recognition of Quebec as a distinct society; and (5) veto power over certain areas of constitutional amendments (certain of these were agreed to apply to all provinces, thus illustrating again the importance of Quebec in "determining" the nature of the power relationship between the central government and the provinces). On June 23, 1987, the Meech Lake Accord underwent a number of revisions and was adopted as a constitutional amendment. This amendment was made subject to ratification hearings in the House of Commons and the provincial legislatures.

A three-year time period was established to allow provincial legislatures the opportunity to ratify the accord. As June 23, 1990 (the deadline) approached, three provinces (Manitoba, Newfoundland, and New Brunswick) had not yet ratified the accord. (Newfoundland had ratified it under a previous administration, but this was subsequently withdrawn.) A highly publicized federal–provincial conference was called in May 1990 to try and obtain the assent of the remaining provinces. While a conditional agreement was reached at that conference, ratification was still required by the provincial legislatures. This, however, was not achieved, and the Meech Lake Accord failed, further delaying any resolution of historical differences between English- and French-Canadians.

4. With the exception of Quebec and Ontario (who have their respective Provincial Police forces), the RCMP provides contracted police services to all provinces and territories. Other than contract services, the RCMP has responsibility for enforcement of federal statutes and executive orders, Canadian police services, and administrative services. Another arm of federal policing is the Canadian Security Intelligence Service (CSIS). The CSIS has authority to conduct security-intelligence investigations and operations on groups or individuals who may, on reasonable grounds, be suspected of constituting a threat to the security of Canada (see Solicitor General, 1988).

5. The Ports Canada Police, through the Canada Ports Corporation, is responsible for policing major ports in Canada; under agreement with the St. Lawrence Seaway Authority, it polices the Champlain and Jacques Cartier bridges in Montreal. The government-owned Canadian National and the privately owned Canadian Pacific Railway companies maintain their own police forces (see Statistics Canada, 1986b).

6. *Local legal culture* is a phrase that refers to the understandings between the various "actors" (judge, prosecutor, defence counsel, police officer, and, possibly, probation officer) to "manage" the administration of justice in an area (usually a court jurisdiction).

7. *Court administration* has been defined as "the administrative component supplied to judges by the executive branch of government." *Judicial administration* includes "all those functions of the judiciary in ordering and expediting the flow of cases through the courts, and

determining the strategic policies of the courts as an independent and self-determining organ of the State" (P.S. Millar & C. Baar (1981). *Judicial Administration in Canada,* Montreal: McGill-Queen's University Press. p. 17).

8. Whitson (1979) discusses *R. v. Lois Jones*. In this case, an initial charge of simple possession of marijuana was revived when the accused failed to complete all the conditions of her diversion contract. The threat of criminal proceedings in order to induce compliance with the diversion agreement was held to be an abuse of process, and the proceedings were stayed. This case went to the Supreme Court of British Columbia, which affirmed the decision of the provincial court judge. Mr. Justice Anderson held that the Crown had bargained away the right to proceed against the alleged offender who assumed certain responsibilities. The trial process became tainted by the threat to resume the proceedings, and this invalidated the revived proceedings. This direction defined the diversion process in the civil or informal sense. The implications of this case were that it confined diversion programs to a civil concept of diversion and that any diversion program that operated under a default provision would run the risk of having any resumed cases declared illegal. It also appeared to affect the number of cases diverted since a backdrop of enforcement no longer existed with this conception of diversion. Also, the need for the development of firm guidelines for the regulation of administration of the diversion process was evident.

9. The maximum length of time a temporary absence can be granted is fifteen days. Technically, the offender should return to the granting institution on or before the fifteenth day. In order to use this mechanism to place persons in CCCs without disrupting their placement every fifteen days, more than one temporary absence would be granted at the outset.

10. For example, in 1987, an interdepartmental committee was established in British Columbia to follow child physical-abuse cases from initial referral to final court disposition. A purpose of this committee is to research procedural matters and recommend policy guidelines.

11. Interpretivism holds that judges should only enforce the "original understanding" of the constitutional language because to do more amounts to illegitimate judicial amendments to the constitution. Noninterpretivism holds that judicial fidelity to the "original understanding" is either impossible (what is it?) or undesirable (results in archaic and unworkable decisions). Noninterpretivism holds that judges must be free to go beyond the original understanding and interpret constitutional rights in light of other factors—the spirit of the constitution, the purpose of the right, contemporary social or economic conditions, etc.

12. A major evaluation of the Canadian Centre for Justice Statistics was completed in September 1988. A draft report with recommendations was submitted to the deputy-ministers responsible for justice programs (federal and provincial) in November 1988. As a result of this review, the Centre has moved into another stage of development within Statistics Canada.

13. Various experiments have been initiated in recent years to improve access to information by the judiciary. For example, the University of British Columbia, in co-operation with I.B.M. Canada, the B.C. and federal governments, private foundations, and the legal profession, designed an experimental project in 1987, entitled "Sentencing Data Base," to provide sentencing information to judges. Another project involving the University of Toronto and Norpark Computer Design Inc. also seeks to develop methods of providing sentencing information. Both of these projects are devising means to give judges information, using computer technology, on an immediate "call" basis while a specific case is being considered.

Canadian literature.

of counter measures
k Force on Drink-
n paper. Toronto:

New York: Mac–

Final results. Paper
sociation of Sexual

tization in perspec-

cing reform: A Cana-
Canada.

ories of crime: The
. In W.J. Chambliss
r? A conflict approach
y.

tional process in Cana-
rson.

57, [1980] 1 S.C.R.
295.

ada: An introductory
ity of Toronto Press.
cive sexuality. Toron–

e vision and the game:
Detselig.
abo Commission. Stras–

search: A systems per-
:on.
es for victims in crisis.

e. Ottawa: Canadian

n Canada: Issues related
by the Traffic Injury
Department of Justice.
13, 48 C.R. (3d) 193,
97.
tions in Canada: Policy
orths.
te prisons. Prison Jour-

7). Punishing for profit:
in corrections. *Cana-*

l discussions on the divi-
federal government and
a.
ton: Houghton Mifflin.
involvement in prison
y, 29, 185–204.
). A situational theory
22, 51–65.

Gorki, M. (1945). *The lower depths and other plays.* New Haven: Yale
University Press.

Gray, V., & Williams, B. (1980). *The organizational politics of criminal
justice.* Lexington, MA: D.C. Heath.

Hagan, J., & Leon, J. (1978). Philosophy and sociology of crime con-
trol: Canadian–American comparisons. In H.M. Johnson (Ed.),
Social system and legal process (pp. 181–208). San Francisco:
Jossey-Bass.

Hastings, R. (1983). *Crime victims.* Working Paper No. 6. Research
and Statistics Section. Policy Planning and Development Branch.
Ottawa: Department of Justice.

Hunter et al. v. Southam Inc. (1984), 14 C.C.C. (3d) 97, 41 C.R. (3d)
97, [1984] 2 S.C.R. 145.

Ichheiser, G. (1970). *Appearances and realities.* San Francisco: Jossey-Bass.

Innis, H.A. (1956). *Essays in Canadian economic history.* Toronto: University of Toronto Press.

Kerr, D. (1985). Coping with terrorism. *Terrorism: An International Journal, 8,* 113–25.

Kinnen, D. (1981). *Report on sexual assault in Canada.* Report to the
Canadian Advisory Council on the Status of Women.

Kivikink, R., Schell, B., Steinke, G. et al. (1986). Study of perceived
drinking-driving behavior change following media campaigns and
police-spot checks in two Canadian cities. *Canadian Journal of
Criminology, 28,* 263–78.

Komberg, A., Mishler, M., & Clarke, H.D. (1982). *Representative
democracy in the Canadian provinces.* Scarborough, ON:
Prentice-Hall.

Larsen, E.N. (1982). *The implications of cybernetics for criminal justice policy:
Juvenile containment as a case history.* Unpublished M.A. thesis.
Department of Criminology, Simon Fraser University, Burnaby,
BC.

Law Reform Commission of Canada. (1985). *Crimes against the environment.* Working Paper No. 44. Ottawa: Information Canada.

Lawson, J.J. (1983). Calculation of chance of arrest for alcohol impairment. Transportation Canada memorandum.

Lipset, S.M. (1964). Canada and the United States—a comparative
view. *Canadian Review of Sociology and Anthropology, 1,* 173–85.

MacLeod, R.C. (1976). *The North-West Mounted Police and law enforcement 1873–1905.* Toronto: University of Toronto Press.

Martin, G., & Johnston, J. (1984, October). Discussion paper on the
future of the Canadian Centre for Justice Statistics. Unpublished
paper. Ottawa: Canadian Centre for Justice Statistics, Justice Information Council.

McConnell, J.G. (1963, May). *Seminar on French Canada.* Proceedings from a seminar: "The French fact," Montreal, Queen
Elizabeth Hotel.

McMahon, M. (1984). The Canadian Charter of Rights and Freedoms:
A study in the creation and use of legal authority. *Canadian Criminology Forum, 6,* 131–50.

McNaught, K. (1975). Political trials and the Canadian political tradition. In M.L. Friedland (Ed.), *Courts and trials: A multi-disciplinary
approach.* Toronto: University of Toronto Press.

Millar, P.S., & Baar, C. (1981). *Judicial administration in Canada.* Montreal: McGill-Queen's University Press, p. 17.

Möller, J. (Ed.). (1976). Peace and security. *Liaison, 2,* 1–16.

Morash, M. (Ed.). (1982). *Implementing criminal justice policies.* Beverly
Hills: Sage.

Morton, F.L. (1987). The political impact of the Canadian Charter of Rights and Freedoms. *Canadian Journal of Political Science, 20,* 31–55.

Morton, F.L. (1984–1985) Charting the Charter—year one: A statistical analysis. *Canadian Human Rights Yearbook,* 237–61.

Naegle, K.D. (1964). Canadian society: Some reflections. In B.R. Blisken, F.E. Jones, K.D. Naegle, & J. Porter (Eds.), *Canadian society* (pp. 1–19). Toronto: Macmillan.

National Project on Resource Coordination for Justice Statistics and Information. (1981). *The future of national justice statistics and information in Canada.* Ottawa: Ministry of Supply & Services.

Neilsen E. (Chair). (1986). *Task force on program review: The justice system.* Ottawa: Ministry of Supply & Services.

Norquay, G., & Weiler, R. (1981). *Services to victims and witnesses of crime in Canada.* Prepared by the Canadian Council on Social Development. Ottawa: Communications Division, Ministry of the Solicitor General.

Packer, H. (1964). Two models of the criminal process. *University of Pennsylvania Law Review, 113,* 1–68.

Prevost, G. (1968). *Crime, justice and society: Commission of Enquiry into the Administration of Justice on Criminal and Penal Matters in Quebec.* Quebec City: Roch Lefébure.

Porter, J. (1967). Canadian character in the twentieth century. *Annals of the American Academy of Political and Social Science, 370,* 48–56.

Re Mitchell and The Queen (1983), 42 O.R. (2d) 481, (sub nom. *Mitchell v. A.G. Ont.)* 35 C.R. (3d) 225 (H.C.).

R. v. Nobel (1984), 42 C.R. (3d) 209, 16 C.C.C. (3d) 146, 48 O.R. (2d) 643 (C.A.).

R. v. Oakes (1986), 24 C.C.C. (3d) 321, 50 C.R. (3d) 1, [1986] 1 S.C.R. 103.

R. v. Therens (1985), 18 C.C.C. (3d) 481, 45 C.R. (3d) 97, [1985] 1 S.C.R. 613, 18 D.L.R.(4th) 655, 38 Alta. L.R. 98.

Rioux, M., & Martin, Y. (Eds.). (1968). *French Canadian society.* Toronto: McClelland & Stewart.

Robbins, I.P. (1986). Privatization of corrections: Defining issues. *Judicature, 69,* 324–31.

Rosenbaum, D. (1987). Coping with victimization: The effects of police intervention on victims' psychological readjustment. *Crime and Delinquency, 33,* 502–19.

Russell, P.H. (1982). The effect of a charter of rights on the policy-making role of Canadian courts. *Canadian Public Administration, 25,* 1–33.

Solicitor General of Canada. (1986). Protecting the environment. *Liaison, 12,* 4–9.

Solicitor General of Canada. (1985). Prisons for profit. *Liaison, 11,* 11–19.

Solicitor General of Canada. (1983a). *The Canadian Federal-Provincial Task Force on Justice for Victims of Crime report.* Ottawa: Communications Division, Programs Branch.

Solicitor General of Canada. (1982). *Programs Branch users report: Preliminary findings of the Canadian Urban Victimization Survey.* Ottawa: Statistics Division.

Smith v. The Queen (1987), 34 C.C.C. (3d) 97, 58 C.R. (3d) 193, [1987] 1 S.C.R. 1045, 15 B.C.L.R. (2d) 273.

Statistics Canada. (1986a). *Adult correctional services in Canada 1985/86.* Canadian Centre for Justice Statistics. Ottawa: Supply & Services Canada.

Statistics Canada. (1986b). *Policing in Canada.* Ottawa: Minister of Supply & Services Canada.

Stenning, Philip C. (1986). *Appearing for the Crown.* Cowansville, PQ: Brown Legal Publications.

Stewart D. (1987). The role of technology in combatting terrorism. *Terrorism: An International Journal, 10,* 211–13.

Thorvaldson, S.A. (1981). Reparation by offenders: How far can we go? In *Selected papers of the Canadian Congress for the Prevention of Crime* (pp. 119–28). Ottawa: Canadian Association for the Prevention of Crime.

Thorvaldson, S.A. (1977). *Issues in sentencing: Toward a provincial response to the proposals of the Law Reform Commission of Canada.* Unpublished paper. B.C. Ministry of Attorney General.

Vingilis, E., & Vingilis, V. (1987). The importance of roadside screening for impaired drivers in Canada. *Canadian Journal of Criminology, 29,* 17–33.

Wade, M. (1964). *The French-Canadian outlook.* Toronto: McClelland & Stewart.

Weaver, R.M. (1948). *Ideas have consequences.* Chicago: University of Chicago Press.

Wilson, J.D. (1986). Re-thinking penalties for corporate environmental offenders: A view of the Law Reform Commission of Canada's sentencing in environmental cases. *McGill Law Journal, 31,* 313–32.

Whitson, D. (1979). *A policy oriented legal analysis of adult pre-trial diversion in the Canadian context.* Unpublished paper. Ottawa: Solicitor General of Canada.

Sexual Assault: A Case Study of Legal Policy Options

While women are significantly underrepresented in the offender population (see Chapter 11), this is not the case with respect to victimization (Solicitor General, 1985). The focus of this case study is on **sexual assault**, the reality and fear[1] of which play a major role in women's experiences of victimization. While researchers gradually add to our knowledge of the phenomenon of sexual assault, and its effects and political significance, legal policy makers continue to confront difficult choices about how the law should respond to this particular method of causing harm to others. This case study describes some of those policy options and invites you to struggle with the issues yourself.

Part I of this text has introduced you to many concepts of **criminology** in the Canadian context. We have seen how theories of crime, research methods, **criminal law**, and **crime policy** have been moulded by Canada's history and governmental structure into a uniquely Canadian perspective; how they have generated certain ways of being with regard to **crime** and criminal justice. The purpose of this case study is to bring together these ideas as they relate to a specific example.

As you read this case study, you should be asking yourself questions that relate back to the other chapters in Part I. For example, what does Chapter 3 suggest might be some of the difficulties in implementation of legal policy developed for sexual assault? What criteria would you use to evaluate the success of these reforms, and how would you go about researching this question? How could the criminal law be further changed in the area of sexual assault legislation if the present reforms prove ineffective?

Thus, the case study attempts to achieve two goals: to have you assimilate the knowledge base established in Part I and apply it to a contemporary social problem, and to serve as a transition to Part II, which will focus on similar specific forms of criminality. These chapters, as well as the case study, will allow you to consider further the foundation upon which this text rests in terms of theory, research, law, and policy. We will begin to see the interrelationship among these specific topic areas. It will become clear, for example, in the next section, that law and policy are not created without reference to society's context.

Sexual Assault: The Context of Reform

Legal decisions about the scope of the law do not have to be made in a vacuum. The literature on rape/sexual assault is quite extensive.[2] The Canadian Urban Victimization Survey, for example, found that, among the people they interviewed, women were seven times as likely as men to have experienced a sexual attack; that young women were most likely to have reported being the victim of a sexual assault; and that, in 41 percent of reported sexual assaults, the women knew their assailants.[3]

Not all women are equally vulnerable. Research on rape in the United States consistently shows black women to be far more vulnerable than white women, as indeed they are with respect to other crimes against the person (see Katz & Mazur, 1979, Ch. 2). Depending on the source of sample selection, prostitutes may constitute a high percentage of rape victims (see Burgess & Holmstrom, 1974, 1976).

The literature goes beyond description to theorizing about the meaning of the social reality. Schwendinger and Schwendinger (1983, Ch. 4) describe some theories as "androcentric." Thus, for instance, victim-precipitation theories tend to explain some rapes as having to do with the behaviour of the victim (see, for example, Amir, 1971). Other, psychoanalytic, theories focus on the offender as being emotionally disturbed (see, for example, Groth, 1979). Feminist theories have tended to focus on structural explanations, viewing rape/sexual assault as an important way in which men contribute to the subordination of women.

Possibly the most significant criminological study in Canada has been *Rape: The Price of Coercive Sexuality* (Clark & Lewis, 1977). On the basis of two empirical studies of the police processing of rape complaints in Toronto and Vancouver, the authors developed the now-familiar "property" analysis of rape. Their findings suggested that the practice of rape indicated the property value of women in that only those women with some property value were offered legal protection. Others were "open territory" victims, for instance, those who were drunk, divorced, or promiscuous. The construction of distinctions between women was also stressed by Edwards (1981). She argued the social reality that was being regulated by the law was not the sexual behaviour of men but that of women, through the formal and informal distinction between chaste and unchaste women.

Feminist analyses provide different ways of thinking about sexual assault. Some feminist theorists see it as a form of violence, not sex, that is "fundamentally different from ordinary sexual activity between men and women because it is characterized by the presence of either real or threatened physical force or violence" (Clark, 1982, p. 12). Others doubt the possibility of consensual heterosexual activity (see Dworkin, 1983, Ch. 3). Indeed, an important theme in feminist work on sexual assault generally has been the emphasis on the need to examine it in the context of the inequality of women and men. The fact that women (and children) are targeted for sexual assault in a world of social and economic inequality means that sexual assault, and the law and legal practice relating to it, have been the subject of intense feminist attention. Possibly the best-known popular discussion can be found in *Against Our Will: Men, Women and Rape* (Brownmiller, 1975). More recently, Gunn and Minch (1988) have argued that "the occurrence of sexual assault can best be understood by viewing it in the context of a patriarchal society, where male aggression is fostered." Feminists have encouraged us to consider the role that gender interests might play in the development of public policy in responses to sexual assault.

Research has also been done on attitudes toward rape. For instance, one Washington study showed that police, judges, and prosecutors tended to believe that rape was caused by sexual frustration, mental illness, or poor judgment by women. In contrast, social services personnel tended to believe that causes lay in the deficiencies of the male socialization process (Feldman-Summers & Palmer, 1980).

The History of the Present Law

Until January 1983, sexual assault was criminalized using the labels "rape" and "indecent assault."[4] There are certain aspects of the offence of rape that deserve attention here because they contribute to an understanding of the significance of the present sexual assault offences.

The old laws (see Box 1) did not present a simplistic picture of protection of the interests of men as a relatively powerful group. Rape and indecent assault were **criminal offences**, and, in so labelling these offences, the law promoted the safety of women. It did not condone men simply forcing sex on any available woman. The law was gender-specific and thus recognized the reality of women's victimization. Only women could be raped. It was recognized that threats and fear of bodily harm and fraud could vitiate consent. The maximum possible sentence for rape was severe—a life sentence. However, many special rules

an Laws Prior to 1983

when he has sexual
who is not his wife,

onsent
ts or fear of bodily

nating her husband,

lse and fraudulent
the nature and qual-

is guilty of an indic-
nprisonment for life.
ommit rape is guilty
s liable to imprison-

er circumstances that
xual intercourse with

a female person
(a)   who is not his wife, and
(b)   who is and who he knows or has good reason
       to believe is feeble-minded, insane, or is an idi-
       ot or imbecile,
is guilty of an indictable offence and is liable to imprisonment for five years.

149.   (1)   Every one who indecently assaults a female per-
             son is guilty of an indictable offence and is
             liable to imprisonment for five years.
       (2)   An accused who is charged with an offence
             under subsection (1) may be convicted if the
             evidence establishes that the accused did any-
             thing to the female person with her consent
             that, but for her consent, would have been an
             indecent assault, if her consent was obtained
             by fraudulent representations as to the nature
             and quality of the act.

lawmakers wished
ial accused persons
ould not be found
the strongest signal
women to physical
. 192). Special rules
d judges to protect
anger of false accu-

a lawyer who is still
w of evidence can
on of the claims of
ssaulted:

studied the be-
women coming
es. Their psychic
ted partly by in-
derangements or
cial environment,
r emotional con-
complexes is that
xual offenses by

influenced by such
uestioned extensively
warned of the danger

of convicting on the uncorroborated testimony of the complainant; and women who complained of rape were unlikely to be believed unless they had resisted to the point
where they bore signs of violence and then immediately
complained to the first available person. It is, therefore, clear
that, prior to 1983, the law contained unusual and startling
protections for males accused of rape.

Reform came in response to pressure generated by concern over these and other factors: rape was significantly
underreported, many complaints were classified as "unfounded" by the police, and there was a low conviction
rate.[6] This led to the passage of the **Criminal Law
Amendment Act**, which contained historic changes to
Canadian law in this area. The old offences of rape, attempted rape, and indecent assault were removed from the
Criminal Code. Three new sexual assault offences were
added to the part of the Code dealing with offences against
the person and reputation. These offences were (i) sexual
assault; (ii) sexual assault with a weapon, threats to a third
party, or with another person; and (iii) aggravated sexual
assault.

There were a number of significant aspects to the new
offences, including the fact that they were gender-neutral
and that the husband's immunity from prosecution for rape
was abolished.[7] Thus, husbands could be charged with
sexual assault. Several important changes were made in the
law of evidence. Judges were no longer permitted to in-

struct juries that it is unsafe to convict without corroboration of the complainant's evidence; new rules were introduced limiting the admission of evidence relating to the sexual history of the complainant; and the "recent complaint" rule, which attached a special significance to the fact that a victim had not made an immediate complaint, was "abrogated". All of these changes were designed to make trials less traumatic for complainants, and thus to encourage reporting. A further protection for complainants was that they could insist that their names or other identifying information not be published by the media. (This and other issues arising out of the new law will be discussed below.)

The new law received a somewhat tentative welcome from commentators. Judith Osborne, in her review of the major areas of change, noted that the "real impact of legislative change depends on how it is interpreted and applied in practice" (1984, p. 63). More critically, Susan Heald expressed doubt about whether "good law" could lead to "good life," that is, a society free of rape, without a fundamental examination of why men rape (1985, p. 117), and why "our sexuality is by tradition and training coercive" (1985, p. 125). Certainly, the new law seemed based on an assumption that there exists an aberrant "violent" version of "normal" sexual activity, rather than on an acceptance of a strong theme in some feminist analysis that "coercion has become integral to male sexuality" (MacKinnon, 1983, p. 646). Other commentators expressed fear that the reforms might interfere with the accused's right to a fair trial (see Doherty, 1984).

Policy Issues and Decision Making under the New Law

While significant changes were made by the legislation, what had essentially been created was a skeleton of a whole new area of law. There were a number of questions that remained. Answers would put flesh on the bare bones of change and give us a much better picture of whether significant change had indeed occurred.

The **criminal justice system** is made up of the decisions of people both inside and outside it. The way it operates in practice depends on the decisions of a wide range of individuals. The system will usually not function at all unless it is triggered by a decision of a victim of sexual assault to report her victimization. The Canadian Urban Victimization Survey revealed that, in the survey year, 62 percent of female sexual assault victims made the decision *not* to report to the police (Solicitor General, 1985, p. 3). There may be individuals who do not even consider reporting because they have not labelled their experience as "sexual as-

sault" or as a crime of any kind.[8] Major policy choices that have to be made by Parliament and by the courts, therefore, relate to steps that should be taken to encourage reporting. Such choices can be seen, for instance, in the law relating to bans on the publication of names of sexual assault victims.

Legislators and judges have to make other significant decisions about the labelling of **deviance**. How much behaviour that *could* be labelled "sexual assault" *should* be so labelled. Examples can be found in the law relating to the meaning of the term *sexual* and the extent to which a person will be seen as a victim of sexual assault where she has been tricked or deceived into engaging in sexual activity.

An ongoing debate of a similar nature relates to whether there should be punishment for "negligent" sexual assault. Should a person who wishes to have sexual contact with another person be required, under threat of punishment, to take reasonable steps to ensure that the other person consents?

Important choices have to be made, too, about the seriousness of different types of sexual assault. Is it less serious, for instance, to assault someone you know than a stranger? The sentencing decisions of judges will reveal a great deal about the "legal" interpretation of women's experiences of victimization.

All of these policy issues can be usefully and intelligently discussed by nonlawyers. What this case study does is focus on the choices of those who are in a position to make their choices particularly influential—victims, legislators, judges, police—people who have an impact on the law of sexual assault.[9]

From this summary, the following issues emerge for further discussion: (1) the publication of identifying information about complainants; (2) the meaning of "sexual"; (3) the meaning of "fraud"; (4) liability for negligent sexual assault; and (5) sentencing for "acquaintance" sexual assault.

The Publication of Identifying Information about Complainants

Jack has been charged with the sexual assault of Sally. He wants Sally's name and description to be published in the newspapers just in case someone will come forward to claim Sally falsely accused him of sexual assault in the past. Sally is afraid and embarrassed and opposes this. Should Sally have a right to insist on nonpublication?

Three sets of decision makers are relevant here. Survivors of sexual assault have to decide whether to proceed to trial on a charge of sexual assault. Legislators have to decide whether to provide any measure of protection for the privacy and security of people who have been sexually assaulted. Judges have to decide whether legislative choices

in the **Canadian**

ned in subsections
ections state that,
makes an applica-
ting that the iden-
published in any

encourage victims
he protection does
ole and willing, or
criminal prosecu-
name of someone
are free to publish
e policy choice to
tual assault victims

ever, was quickly
: argument was that
was an unconstitu-
press as guaranteed
The Charter is the
nust conform to its
ficant guide to, and
ve in Canada. Sub-
lowing fundamental
ef, opinion and ex-
ess and other media

Jay, the judge issued
:wspapers Co. Ltd.
ne ban was ordered,
se went all the way
see *R. v. Canadian*
int it was very clear
ersarial one between
n ban and Canadian
freedom to publish
the case could have
ual assault generally.
en, are women. As a
men's Legal Educa-
to intervene. Inter-
here intervenors are
this case, a feminist
particular issue. The
e arguments of LEAF
Parliament had gone
quiring judges to for-
ne issue was a signifi-
ate is more important
f the press to publish

this information or the security and privacy of sexual assault survivors as well as the need to encourage their co-operation in enforcing the law of sexual assault?

LEAF argued strongly that newspapers had no valid expressive interest in publishing identifying information about victims. They could publish the rest of the information about the trial. Conversely, the publication ban provision facilitated the freedom of expression of women and children as well as protecting their rights to equality and equal rights to liberty and security of the person, also contained in the Charter.

While this analysis was not adopted by the Supreme Court, the result was unanimous. The provision was found to infringe freedom of the press, but its objective in promoting enforcement of the laws of sexual assault was so important that it was saved by section 1 of the Charter, which states that the Charter "guarantees the rights and freedoms set out in it subject only to such reasonable limits prescribed by law as can be demonstrably justified in a free and democratic society." In other words, the Court decided that the legislative policy was an appropriate one in constitutional terms. However, this decision was *not* based on an understanding that when women use the criminal justice system to reveal their victimization they are exercising their constitutional right to freedom of expression. This fact may well be significant when a related constitutional question goes before the court. Does the publication ban provision infringe the rights of accused persons to a fair trial under subsection 11(d) of the Charter? It is likely that a case will come up where a person accused of sexual assault will argue that the publication of the complainant's name might bring forth witnesses helpful to his case and that, therefore, a ban on publication interferes with the fairness of his trial. Perhaps by the time you are reading this, such a case will have been argued or decided.

The Meaning of "Sexual"

Terry has been brought up in such a way that he resents women and views them as inferior. He thinks that they are useful only for sex and for menial tasks in the home or work place. He is a regular user of pornography. He feels particular anger against "career" women whom he thinks emasculate men and steal their jobs. One day, in the street, he see a smartly dressed woman and loses control of himself. He knocks her down and kicks her in the face and legs, shouting, "You bitches are all alike. You want to take over the world." Should this be classified as a sexual assault or as just a plain assault?

While the term "assault" is defined in the Code, "sexual" is not. Its meaning is important since a sexual assault is a more serious offence than is a plain assault. The courts have had to confront this definitional issue, which is a difficult one because, while we may all have a fairly confident intuitive sense of what "sexual" means, that does not mean we can put our feelings into words in a noncircular way. Many judicial attempts to do this boil down in the end to assertions that "sexual" means "sexual."

The Supreme Court of Canada has now given us some guidance on the issue. *R. v. Chase* (1987) was appealed from the New Brunswick Court of Appeal. That court had decided that a man who had grabbed a girl's breasts had committed a plain assault rather than the more serious "sexual" assault. They felt that breasts should not legally be considered sexual. The Supreme Court of Canada disagreed, holding that breasts were indeed sexual. The Court defined a sexual assault as an assault "committed in circumstances of a sexual nature, such that the sexual integrity of the victim is violated" (*Chase*, p. 103). The test is an objective one, that is, what would a reasonable observer consider sexual? All the circumstances are relevant—the part of the body touched; the nature of the contact; the situation, words, and gestures; the intent of the person committing the act. While it is not necessary that the purpose of the act be sexual gratification, the existence of such a motive would be a relevant factor. The court thus recognized that not all sexual assaults are committed for the purpose of sexual gratification.

While this ruling is helpful, questions inevitably still remain about the meaning of "sexual" and thus the scope of this offence. The term "sexual" can be understood in different ways in different contexts. It may be the adjective associated with the noun *sexuality*, relating to sexual activity. Alternatively, it could mean, as it commonly does, *gender*, as in, for example, "sexual discrimination". The expression "sexual harassment" has connotations of both, as could "sexual assault." The decision in *Chase* leaves this open, thus also leaving open the possibility that many instances of domestic violence could be classified as gender = sexual assaults. This issue makes us confront the basic conundrum in our gender-neutral law. Is sexual assault a deviant, *violent* form of sexual activity, or are violence and sex so intermingled in our society that any form of violence against women could conceivably be seen as sexual?

The views of the Supreme Court of Canada on sexual harassment may give us some guidance. In the case of *Janzen and Govereau v. Platy Enterprises Ltd.* (1989), the Court discussed sexual harassment as involving a mixture of sexuality and discrimination on the basis of gender. Dickson C.J., speaking for the Court, said it could be "broadly defined as unwelcome conduct *of a sexual nature* that detrimentally affects the work environment" (*Platy*, p. 64; emphasis added). It was further stated:

> Perpetrators . . . and victims . . . may be either male or female. However, in the present sex stratified labour market, those with the power to harass sexually will predominantly be male and those facing the greatest risk of harassment will tend to be female [*Platy*, p. 65].

> The sexual harassment [in question] fits the definition of sex discrimination offered earlier: practices or attitudes which have the effect of limiting the conditions of employment of, or the employment opportunities available to employees on the basis *of a characteristic related to gender.* (*Platy*, p. 69; emphasis added)

Might such an approach be useful with respect to sexual assault?

The Meaning of Fraud

Jane is promised $100 if she will perform an act of oral sex on Mike. He has no intention of paying and, indeed, has only $10 in his pocket. She provides the sexual service and he refuses to pay. Should he be found guilty of sexual assault?

An issue about the behaviour being labelled as sexual assault that has not yet received much attention is the meaning of "**fraud**." Assault in general means the application of force *without consent*. Normally, there is no consent because of the presence, threat, or fear of force. However, subsection 265(3)(c) of the Code states, as well, that "no consent is obtained where the complainant submits or does not resist by reason of . . . (c) fraud. . . ." Parliament has made a choice to leave to the judiciary the question of what fraud *ought* to mean in this context. The judicial response will tell us whether we have a very wide offence of fraudulent sexual assault or a very narrow one.

The equivalent provision under the old law of rape was very narrow. It stated that only certain types of fraud really counted as fraud in the legal sense, e.g., fraud about the act of sexual intercourse itself or about the fact that the rapist was not the victim's husband. Naturally, there were very few cases of either kind.[10]

The change in the law so that the word "fraud" alone was used simply meant that sexual assault was to be treated in the same way as assault, where the word "fraud" had been used without embellishment in the past. This *could* mean that fraud should be given the same meaning in sexual-assault cases that it had been given historically in assault cases generally, or it could mean that the courts should undertake a fresh examination of the nature of culpability in fraudulently inducing consent to sexual contact. I am inclined to the latter view. Now that the new crimes of sexual assault have been incorporated in the assaults section generally, the courts should ask what kind of behaviour *ought* to be punished in this category.[11] Simple

ault do not pro-
this question.

vhat fraud *should*
ry to ask what it
cover any lie that
esist, sexual con-
luential lies. I do
se. I have lots of
ou. I like poetry,
ou are beautiful.
'presently intend
again tomorrow.
ice, trivial deceits
y on the ignoble
g untruths.

ecide that Parlia-
in the context of
uld not be a self-
an is that it would
t that person had
otherwise would
a serious violation
e minor touching-
of the spectrum of
ge would be that
is uninfluenced by
arious harms: risk
s flowing from the
n circumstances of
e context of a plan
k of control in the
l is simply not the
ave sexual contact
is violation to rela-
it the harm caused
a broad spectrum.

ition by a person she
untrue—he is simply
ot have consented had
ied as sexual assault?

aud" could reason-
Crown counsel in
1987) argued against
ances of conviction
xpansive interpreta-
ocially unacceptable
n adult who lied to
ual intercourse with
ves liable to a charge

The British Columbia Court of Appeal disagreed, failing "to appreciate why, as a matter of policy, we should
restrict fraud." Nevertheless, the Court went on to find
that "Parliament intended" that fraud should be limited to
the nature and quality of the act and the identity of the
offender. The argument of the Crown counsel in *Petrozzi*
finds support in academic literature. In his discussion of the
meaning of fraud, Bryant (1989, p.117) states: "Surely not
every fraud which subjectively causes a complainant to engage in sexual activity is capable of vitiating consent in
law. . . . If the contrary were correct, it would produce
some remarkable results." The following illustration of a
"remarkable" result was included: "if a person gives coun-
terfeit money to a prostitute and engages in sexual activity, can a fraud of this nature constitute a vitiating circumstance?"[12] Bryant concludes that Parliament did not "intend" to create new offences of "obtaining sex by deceit".
If you had to characterize what Parliament intended, what
would you say? Do you think that it would be a good idea
for Parliament to require us to be honest in our sexual relations with others? Do you think it would be a good idea
for the courts to broaden the meaning of fraud somewhat,
to include, for instance, fraudulent denials of infectious-
ness? Or do you think there should be no such crime as
fraudulent sexual assault?

Liability for Negligent Sexual Assault

*John is an affluent heterosexual male living in downtown Van-
couver. He has no criminal record but has been charged with sexual assault. At his trial, he pleaded not guilty, claiming that he
had mistakenly believed the complainant was consenting to sexual
contact with him. He gave evidence that he genuinely believes that,
if he pays for a woman's dinner and afterwards she agrees to come
back to his apartment for "coffee," then she is consenting to have
sexual intercourse.*

*On the occasion in question, Mary had been his guest for din-
ner and later agreed to go to his apartment. She was a secretary
at his firm, and this was their first date. They drank coffee and
listened to some music. They kissed each other a little, and both
were enjoying themselves. Things changed, however, when John
tried to remove Mary's dress. She protested firmly and struggled
with him, but he persisted and succeeded in removing the top part
of her dress and touching her breasts. For some time, Mary had
been trying to stop him without making a scene, but finally she
managed to smack him hard across the face, and he stopped. She
grabbed her purse and ran weeping from the apartment.*

*John was utterly bewildered. He could not understand why Mary
would come to his apartment and kiss him if these were not signals that she wanted sex. Mary has had severe difficulty coming
to terms with the incident. She feels she must have been at fault
in some way and that she does not know whom she can trust any-*

more. She has stopped dating completely as she cannot tell with whom she will be safe.

Do you think that John should be convicted of sexual assault?

An issue that arose before the new law was introduced and that remains today is whether there should be criminal liability for negligent sexual assault. This relates to the situation where the accused honestly thought the victim was consenting to sexual contact but no reasonable, careful, person would have made the same mistake. The Supreme Court of Canada give us its authoritative view in the *Pappajohn* (1980) case. An honest but unreasonable belief in consent was a defence to rape. It remains a defence to sexual assault. This means there is not a legal obligation to take reasonable steps to ensure consent before having sexual contact with someone.[13] Naturally, this has been quite controversial; and the possibility exists that the Court might reconsider its views, although this is unlikely to happen in the near future. Alternatively, Parliament might consider introducing a new offence of negligent sexual assault. The question, therefore, is one that ought to be considered as a possible reform of the present law.

The benefit of the law as it stands is that it avoids the danger of punishing someone who is incapable of taking reasonable care to ascertain consent and thus does not deserve to be punished. The drawback is that individuals who are perfectly capable of taking reasonable care, but do not, also may escape punishment. There are also people who may pose a severe threat to others who are free to engage in harmful behaviour under the *Pappajohn* rule. Some men may have been socialized to have significant and self-interested misconceptions about women's behaviour.[14] Research on convicted rapists has also revealed that there is a type of rapist who uses violence to excite himself and projects the sadistic quality of the experience on to the victim. Cohen *et al.* (1977, pp. 307–8) quote one rapist as saying that "women like to get roughed up, they enjoy a good fight." The authors state that this "belief is maintained even when the victim is literally fighting for her life and the offender has to injure her brutally to force her to submit to intercourse."

Does the present law strike the appropriate balance between the importance of protecting people from sexual assault and the claim that it is unjust to punish an individual who has not consciously considered the possibility of the absence of consent? Should the state classify sexual activity as similar to driving: You can do it, but if you do, you must exercise reasonable care?

Sentencing for "Acquaintance" Sexual Assault

Reread the story of John and Mary (above). Assume that John was convicted in spite of his claim that he believed Mary was consenting. The jury simply did not believe him, since it was such a ridiculous idea. In spite of his conviction, however, John has not rethought his attitudes. He sees nothing wrong in aggressively attempting to have sexual intercourse with women once they have agreed to enter his apartment on a date. As we know, Mary has ongoing problems with the incident and has stopped dating completely. You are the judge who has to sentence John. Your options include an absolute discharge (no criminal record), probation, a fine, and/or imprisonment. What would your sentence be? Give reasons for your decision. Do you think your sentence would be harsher if John and Mary were strangers?

We have seen that important policy choices have to be made at the level of constitutional, legislative, and judicial decision making about guilt. Law reformers also have to consider the appropriateness of the present law. Moreover, even when guilt is determined, important policy decisions remain to be made at the sentencing stage.

Judicial decisions about the appropriate severity of sentences for sexual assault reflect relative views of seriousness, the need for deterrence, and assumptions about harm to victims. A discussion of this nature could focus on many aspects of sentencing, but the issue chosen has been whether judges view sexual assault by an acquaintance, on a date, for example, as somehow less serious than sexual assault by a person unknown to the victim.[15]

The old law of rape had an explicit marital exemption. A husband could not be held criminally liable for the rape of his wife. As we have seen, that exemption was swept away in the sexual-assault reforms.

While there is nothing new in the Code to suggest that the relationship between the victim and the offender is a mitigating or excusing factor, traces of the old idea that a husband has a right to sex with his wife *might* be found in cases suggesting that it is not as bad to sexually assault someone you know as it is to assault a stranger. Could men on dates, for instance, have inherited a weakened (in that it relates to sentencing) but expanded (in that it relates to *any* relationship, not just marriage) form of the old marital exemption?[16]

When the new law came into force, it was reasonable to suppose that this might well be the case. It was clear that a relationship between the victim and the offender was likely to be a mitigating factor (see Boyle, 1984, p. 180). This was in some contrast to the data generated by the Philadelphia Sexual Assault Victim Study (McCahill, Meyer, & Fischman, 1979) that suggested that the victim was most traumatized by being assaulted by a casual acquaintance. Victims suffered from severe feelings of insecurity since it was impossible to tell which acquaintance could be trusted and which could not.[17]

hip as a mitigat-
nce the passage
to research sug-
'crime between
ss serious or not
een victims and
ι, socio-psycho-
quaintance rape
anger rape. One
nile tumescence
k & Malamuth,
at "high sex role
sed to [the story
im reacted more
stereotyping in-
juaintance rape"
ideed, the same
role stereotyping
th rape-myth ac-
women, general
ex beliefs (Check
ınd & Goodstein,
at men who have
red from sexually
kely to "attribute
onships, to accept
bout rape, to feel
onsibility, and to
ession and sexual-
at the very least,
iay be more toler-
n acquaintance,[18]

ionistic about cur-
e case law. It seems
ɔy an acquaintance
ısly as sexual assault
ıas been quoted as
d her attacker had
natter of common
ult less serious than
uver Sun, May 16,
he sentence in the
was two years less
harm.
ı the older case R.
victim had gone to
ıarijuana. The court
ion from the rapist
ittacks them or who
, p. 192).
iite leniently. In one

Ontario case, the assault was on a young woman with
whom the offender, a university student, had been having
a sexual relationship, which was deteriorating. He forced
her to have intercourse, striking her on the face. Watt, J.,
pointing out that the violence was not excessive, imposed
a suspended sentence, with three years' probation, a five-
year firearm prohibition, and a hundred hours of community service (Nadin-Davis & Sproule, 1980, 92.224).

Several marital-rape cases suggest a relatively lenient attitude to nonstranger sexual assault. The sentence was six
months in prison and two years' probation in R. v. H.B.N.
The husband had forced his way into his estranged wife's
trailer and sexually assaulted his wife during a prolonged
struggle. Another husband, in R. v. D.A.B., received a sentence of nine months and one year probation.

Not all cases point in the same direction. In R. v. G.
(1986), in which a husband was sentenced to one year in
prison and two years' probation, Stuart, Terr. Ct. J., said
that it was *not* less serious to assault a friend or spouse.
Rather, the breach of trust involved was an aggravating factor. In the Quebec case R. v. P.T. (1987), the offender
and the victim had spent the evening together. He claimed
that she had aroused him, and this led to the attack. In spite
of this being treated as a mitigating factor, the sentence was
five years' imprisonment. The sentence was also five years
in the B.C. case R. v. H.M.S. The offender met the victim in a bar, and they went to a hotel together. He attacked
her and forced her to have intercourse. A point to note,
however, is that the offender had a substantial criminal
record, including sexual assault.

It should be stressed at this point that it is difficult to
separate out one factor in sentencing. Many factors inter-
mingle. For instance, one Ohio study found that

> blacks who sexually assaulted whites, regardless of the
> offender/victim relationship, received significantly
> harsher penalties than did blacks who sexually assault-
> ed members of their own race. The point is perhaps
> more strongly stated alternatively: blacks who sexu-
> ally assaulted members of their own race received
> significantly more lenient penalties (from an aver-
> age of 12 months if the victim was a stranger to an
> average of 7 months if the victim was an acquain-
> tance) than did blacks who crossed racial lines to
> commit sexual assault. (Walsh, 1987, p. 153)

Conclusion

The above examples should leave you with some sense that
the introduction of the new sexual assault laws was only
a stage in a complex process of policy formation. Decisions

are not arbitrary but influenced by interpretations of the constitution, views on the relative importance of competing goals, legal precedent, perceptions of the harm caused by sexual assault, and views on the legitimate role of the state in punishing antisocial behaviour. All such factors are important, but the overwhelming significance of decisions made about sexual assault lies in its largely gender-specific reality. Thus, the policies underlying the law in this area reveal the extent to which people with power to make *their* choices authoritative wish to use the law to protect women in Canada.

Notes

1. "The Canadian Urban Victimization Survey (CUVS) shows that Canadian women experience a lower frequency of victimization [in general] than men but express greater fear for their personal safety.... In response to the CUVS question, 'How safe do you feel walking alone in your own neighbourhood at night; very safe, relatively safe, somewhat unsafe?' three times as many women responded by saying they felt 'somewhat unsafe' or 'very unsafe'" (Solicitor General, 1985, p. 1).

2. While the focus in this case study is on sexual assault, the literature on rape is relevant in that it is a particular form of sexual assault.

3. "Sexual assault" was defined as rape, attempted rape, molestation, or attempted molestation.

4. For a more detailed account of the legal history of these offences, see Boyle (1984), Ch. 2.

5. Wigmore (1970), p. 736. For an exposé of how Wigmore distorted his authorities, see Bienen (1983), p. 235.

6. For some of the history of the process of law reform, see Kinnon (1981), and Snider (1985).

7. The Honourable Jean Chrétien, then minister of justice, stated that "women are not the chattels of their husbands and sex without the consent of both parties is as unacceptable within marriage as it is outside of marriage" (Canada, House of Commons, 1982).

8. For a study showing considerable difference between legal and social definitions of rape, see Klemmack and Klemmack (1976).

9. Victims are not authoritative, of course, in the same way as other decision makers. "In the case of criminal law, relevant interpretations are made by the police, lawyers, judges and juries. It is, of course, a central argument here that the victims' interpretations are essential too, but they do not have the power—yet—to make their interpretations stick" (Heald, 1985, p. 121). For research on police, see, for example, Clark and Lewis, 1977, and Gunn and Minch, 1988, Ch. 5.

10. For a full discussion of the old fraud cases, see Bryant (1989).

11. This argument was made but rejected by the British Columbia Court of Appeal in *R. v. Pettrozzi* (1987).

12. Byrant (1989, p. 117). Why is this remarkable? The law might well treat the use of superior financial power as vitiating circumstance. Might the sexual contact not be seen, then, as sexual assault, even if the money were real?

13. Of course, the more unreasonable the belief, the less likely it may be that the judge or jury would entertain a reasonable doubt about the honesty of the mistake.

14. One study has tested and found support for the hypothesis that men mistakenly interpret women's friendliness as an indication of sexual interest, whereas women are unlikely to misjudge male intentions (Abbey, 1982). The same study refers to research findings that males are less likely than females to believe that females really meant no when they said no (Abbey, 1982, p. 831).

15. The expression "acquaintance" sexual assault is rather loosely used here. There are no legal distinctions among marital, date, acquaintance, and stranger sexual assault, although criminologists might wish to draw such distinctions for the purposes of their research. If there were a legally significant distinction, then a difficult issue would be how to classify the sexual assault of a prostitute.

16. Russell (1982, chs. 18 & 19) discusses the connection between rape in marriage and date rape.

17. For sources, see Katz and Mazur (1979), p. 230. For a discussion of rape trauma in general, see Koss and Harvey (1987). See also, Ellis, Atkeson, & Calhoun (1981), pp. 263 & 264.

18. For a critique of attitudes current among some Canadian judges, see Marshall (1988), p. 216.

References

Abbey, A. (1982). Sex differences in attributions for friendly behaviour: Do males misperceive females' friendliness? *Journal of Personality and Social Psychology, 42*, pp. 830–838.

Amir, R. (1971). *Patterns in forcible rape.* Chicago: University of Chicago Press.

Bienen, L.B. (1983). A question of credibility: John Henry Wigmore's use of scientific authority in section 924a of the treatise on evidence. *California Western Law Review, 19*, pp. 235–268.

Boyle, C.L.M. (1981). Married women—beyond the pale of the law of rape. *Windsor Yearbook of Access to Justice, 1*, pp. 192–213.

Boyle, C.L.M. (1984). *Sexual assault.* Toronto: Carswell.

Bryant, A.W. (1989). The issue of consent in the crime of sexual as-

tims of crisis. Bowie,

rostitute. In A.W.
health: Target popu-

en, and rape. New

for rape. *Journal of*
–230.
debates (August 4),

le stereotyping and
intance rape. *Journal*
44–356.
ce of coercive sexuali-

ing Committee on
, *Minutes of Proceed-*

pists. In Chappell,
ew York: Columbia

32, c. 125.
ractices in different
e. *International Jour-*

at "spoils" the trial.

f domesticated females.

Oxford: Robertson.
981). An assessment
ormal Psychology, 90,

as viewed by judges,
stice & Behaviour, 7,

ssault in dating/court-
riminal justice system.
n Fraser University,

Plenum.
e dilemma of disclosure,
ty of Manitoba Press.
gy: A critique of the
iinology Forum, 7, pp.

1989]4 W.W.R. 39

he rape victim: A syn-
y.
nada. Ottawa: Cana-
Vomen.
The social definition
.), *Sexual assault*. Lex–

tim: Clinical and com-
1A: Stephen Greene.
ession: A discriminant

analysis of the psychological characteristics of undetected offenders. *Sex Roles, 12*, pp. 981–992.

MacKinnon, C. (1983). Feminism, Marxism, method and the state: Toward feminist jurisprudence. *Signs, 8*, pp. 635–658.

Marshall, P. (1988). Sexual assault, the Charter and sentencing reform. *Criminal Reports (3d), 63*, pp. 216–235.

McCahill, T.W., Meyer, L.C., & Fischman, A.M. (1979), *The aftermath of rape*. Lexington, MA: Lexington.

Nadin-Davis, R.P., & Sproule, C.B. (1980). *Canadian sentencing digest*. Toronto, Calgary, Vancouver: Carswell.

Osborne, J. (1984). Rape law reform: The new cosmetic for Canadian women. *Women and Politics, 4*, pp. 49–64.

R. v. Brown (1983), 34 C.R. (3d), 191 (Alta C.A.).

R. v. Canadian Newspapers Co. Ltd. (1988), 43 C.C.C. (3d) 24 (S.C.C.).

R. v. Chase (1987), 37 C.C.C. (3d) 187 (S.C.C.).

R. v. D.A.B., see Nadin-Davis & Sproule, 1980. (92.236).

R. v. G., (1986), 1 Yr. 106 (Y.T. Terr. Ct.).

R. v. H.B.N., see Nadin-Davis & Sproule, 1980. (92.229).

R. v. H.M.S., see Nadin-Davis & Sproule, 1980. (92.280).

R. v. Pappajohn, [1980] 2 S.C.R. 120.

R. v. P.T. (1987), Hull no. 550-01-000058-86, May 19.

R. v. Pettrozzi (1987), 35 C.C.C. (3d) 528.

Russell, D. (1982). *Rape and marriage*. New York: Macmillan.

Schwendinger, J., & Schwendinger, H. (1983). *Rape and inequality*. Beverly Hills: Sage.

Shotland, R.L., & Goodstein, L. (1983). Just because she doesn't want to doesn't mean it's rape: An experimentally based causal model of the perception of rape in a dating situation. *Social Psychology Quarterly, 46*, pp. 220–232.

Snider, L. (1985). Legal reform and social control: The dangers of abolishing rape. *International Journal of Sociology of Law, 13*, pp. 337–356.

Solicitor General. (1985). *Canadian urban victimization survey bulletin 4: Female victims of crime*. Ottawa: Solicitor General Canada.

Walsh, A. (1987). The sexual stratification hypothesis and sexual assault in light of the changing conceptions of race. *Crimonology, 25*, pp. 153–173.

Wigmore, J.H. (1940). *Evidence in trials at common law* (3rd ed.). Boston: Little, Brown and Co., 924a at 736.

The Legislation of Morality in Canada: What Is the Role of Law?

In Part II, we will see how the criminal law has been used to criminalize certain behaviours. Earlier discussion (in Chapter 1) related the process to the period of prohibition in Canada; our focus shifts now to a consideration of prostitution, drug abuse, and gambling. Nigel Walker (1987, p. 139) describes the term "criminalizing" as "an inelegant but convenient term for the bringing of conduct within the scope of the criminal law." Few of us would have difficulty accepting that there is a need to criminalize certain behaviours, such as murder or personal assault, but when the criminalization process is directed to actions involving "private" behaviour, e.g., prostitution, drug abuse, and gambling, controversy arises. The history of the prohibitions in these areas suggests that we, as a society, have been concerned about the management of moral behaviour of our citizenry.

Now that we have established a framework for studying criminology in Canada, we can begin to address the complex issues surrounding the application of the law. Some of the important questions to ask relate to the maintenance of the balance between public order and private rights. What are the limits of the law? Do we have principles that guide legislators in determining those limits? Are the limits proscribed on the basis of the principles of the moral contract that underlie our society's laws, or are they driven by the public's or legislators' view of what these limits should be? Does it matter if the law set down to control citizens' behaviour is rarely used, or is unenforceable without the public's support?

In Parts II and IV, we will discuss the various theories of crime and criminality that have driven the development of criminal-justice practice; many of the theorists themselves have spoken directly about what the role of the law should be in the prevention, control, and eradication of crime. Two such theorists, Cesare Beccaria and Jeremy Bentham, actually did articulate what they thought should be the limiting principles of the law. For example, one tenet for Beccaria was that no criminal law should be applied to punish behaviour or actions that do not result in harm. Bentham additionally put forward the idea that the criminal law should not be invoked if the harm created by the punishment was greater than the harm that resulted from the offence itself. Another "utilitarian," John Stuart Mill, advanced the notion that the criminal law should not be employed with the intent, of making people act in their own best interests (Walker, 1987, pp. 143–145). Therefore, the law, according to Mill, should not attempt regulation of such behaviours as drinking and gambling.

In contemporary times, more pragmatic rationales have evolved that try to "fix" limits on the criminal law that have no direct bearing on the morality of the citizenry, but rather only on society's smooth functioning and preservation of order. However, this apparently more objective axiom is deceptive in the sense that what constitutes smooth functioning and the preservation of order may well involve the need to control moral behaviour, if the need is so defined by legislators. Therefore, in the recent past, we have had, in Canada, criminal law that prohibited even consensual homosexual activities. Those supporters of the law who tried to escape from the moral quandary associated with the issue asserted that the law was required for the maintenance of order in society.

It is impossible to be value-free in this process of establishing the limits of the law; even the premise that the smooth functioning and preservation of order may not necessarily be the best rationale for determining those limits (Walker, 1987, p. 156). It is thus important to be aware of the values and beliefs that influence the development of the criminal law.

The Law Reform Commission of Canada (1988, p. 1), in its most recent proposed reforms to the Criminal Code, proceeded to write "a comprehensive Code in tune with present values and in keeping with the principle that the strong arm of the law should only be used for 'real' crimes." The process by which these values are determined is thus essential to an understanding of how the law is created and reformed. For instance, the commission determined that there was a national concern over the destruction of the environment and subsequently proposed the creation of a Criminal Code offence (proposed s. 19 [1]) that related to this need for environmental protection. But basing law reform upon perceived public concern implies a consensual view of the process; others have argued that grounding law reform and development on such a premise is illogical and misdirected. Other factors and influences should more appropriately come into play. If we created law based on a strictly "democratic" approach, for example, Canada would at present have capital punishment (see Introduction).

Keep this process of the creation of the law and the determination of the role and limits of the law in mind as you read the next three chapters on prostitution, drug abuse, and gambling. Additionally, when you then continue into parts III and IV, try to determine the relationship between the theories developed about the causes of crime and the role and limits of the criminal law as actually articulated and enforced.

References

Law Reform Commission of Canada (1988). *A new Criminal Code for Canada?* Ottawa: Department of Supply and Services.

Walker, N. (1987). *Crime and criminology.* London: Oxford University Press.

4 Prostitution in Canada

Canada's first laws aimed at prostitutes were imported directly from Britain. There, certain aspects of prostitution related conduct were prohibited by **vagrancy** laws. It was not the act of prostitution itself that was the target of the law, but the nuisance that was created by streetwalkers and "bawdy-house" (brothel) activities. In Canada, as in Britain and the United States, enforcement of these laws was, at most, casual. Indeed, red light areas (referred to as "restricted" or "segregated" districts), where prostitution was openly tolerated by the police, could be found in most North American cities. Nevertheless, Victorian moralists viewed prostitution as one of a series of social evils (including intemperance, illiteracy, juvenile delinquency, and venereal disease) that threatened the fabric of society. From 1903 to 1917 these sentiments came to the fore as part of the "social purity" campaign that washed across North America and Europe. Along with attempts to prohibit alcohol (successful, for a while, in the United States and parts of Canada) concerted efforts were made to extend the scope of prostitution laws and encourage the police to close the brothels operating in the restricted districts. With the waning of the social purity movement after 1920, the sex trade flourished with little public consternation. Not until the mid-1970s did prostitution resurface as a "problem" in Canada. Since then, street prostitution has remained in the limelight as various legal strategies designed to suppress it have proven ineffective.

Our knowledge of the practice of prostitution in Canada was limited until recently by a paucity of research.[1] However, increased academic and government interest was prompted by growing concern about street prostitution in the late 1970s and early 1980s. A trickle of studies turned into a deluge. Feeling compelled to act upon this rising tide of concern, the federal government convened two committees that were charged with, among other things, providing a general picture of the prostitution trade in Canada and recommending reform of social and legal policy relating to it.[2]

In 1981, the Committee on Sexual Offences Against Children and Youth (the Badgley Committee) was appointed "to enquire into the incidence and prevalence in Canada of sexual offences against children and youths and to recommend improvements in laws for the protection of young persons from sexual abuse and exploitation." As part of this package, the committee was also asked to carry out research on youth prostitution (Committee on Sexual Offences Against Children and Youth, 1984, p.3). The result was a review of laws pertaining to youth prostitution (Committee on Sexual Offences, 1984, Ch. 42) and a portrait of prostitutes based on interviews in eight Canadian cities with 145 female and 84 male prostitutes under age twenty (Committee on Sexual Offences Against Children and Youth, Chs. 43-46).

The issue of adult prostitution was left for the Special Committee on Pornography and Prostitution (the Fraser Committee), appointed in 1983. This committee's terms of reference required it to describe pornography and prostitution and the laws regulating them in Canada, to review prostitution law in selected countries around the world, to hold public hearings, to take submissions about problems associated with pornography and prostitution, and to recommend solutions to the various problems identified. As background research for the committee, the federal government sponsored a series of studies on pornography and prostitution.[3]

Given that prostitution (like pornography) was such a politically relevant matter in the early 1980s, a number of other state-sponsored research and information papers were published at the same time.[4] Added to these commentaries were a number of academic works discussing historical[5] and contemporary legal and policy developments in Canada.[6] From these sources, we can gain an understanding of the phenomenon of prostitution in Canada today. But first, some definitional issues require clarification.

Social and Legal Definitions of Prostitution

Although there are numerous ways in which gender power structures in patriarchal societies encourage females (and some males) to barter their sexuality for material advantage, in Canada—as in much of the Western world—the term "prostitute" has generally referred to females who sell brief-encounter sexual services to a variety of men. Thus, while acknowledging the pervasiveness of the material and commercial dimensions of relationships between the sexes—ranging from marriage for pecuniary advantage, to trade of sexual favours for jobs, to men expecting sex in return for the dinners that they buy women, to homeless women exchanging sex for a bottle and a bed—this paper is mainly concerned here with more or less promiscuous and ephemeral sexual services performed for financial reward on an ongoing basis and viewed by the provider as a form of work. Such sexual liaisons are usually devoid of any emotional attachment.[7]

The least ephemeral form of commercial sex is supplied by mistresses or "kept women" (see Salamon, 1984)—women kept, usually by one man or a series of men—and their (probably much less numerous) male equivalents. Some kept women are not much different from "call girls" who service a (mainly) regular group of clients. In contrast are what can be termed "public" prostitutes—those to whom the term "prostitute" is most frequently applied—working for escort agencies and/or in the street prostitution trade. The many "exotic" dancers (or "strippers") who, in some cities, also work as prostitutes,[8] and women working in massage parlours also fit this category. These are "public" prostitutes in the sense that they are generally available to a largely undifferentiated male population; if a man has the money—and meets variable standards of hygiene and appears to be neither a bad trick (see Box 4.1) nor a police decoy—the prostitute will "turn a trick."

Generally, street prostitutes demand the lowest price for their services, although within a given city prices often vary in different prostitution "strolls" (see, for example, Lowman 1986a, pp. 8–10), and they vary among cities. Escorts tend to command higher prices, although, again, prices vary among agencies and geographically. From the customer's point of view, escorts are considerably more expensive than street prostitutes because the agency charges a fee (varying in British Columbia, for example, between $20 and $60) in addition to the payment received by the escort for providing sexual services. The most exclusive prostitutes generally charge the highest prices. It would thus seem, at least in the case of females, that there is an inverse relation between the public visibility of the prostitute and the price that she is able to command.

Prostitution Laws

The earliest criminal prohibition of prostitution in Canada was as a form of vagrancy law. The first provisions proscribing vagrancy in English speaking Canada were contained in the Nova Scotia Act of 1759. Based on British law, the act reflected the view that the activities of prostitutes should be prohibited as part of the general delinquency of the growing ranks of the "idle" or "undeserving" poor.

or Equal Rights)
of the Interna-
stitute and non-
ake changes so-
women.
6'1", 175 lbs.,
, said his name
Nelson and took
. He then drove
e pulled a knife,
money. He took
He drove a small
his.
SAFE SEX: male,
, full beard, 6'2".
blue Mazda with
to use a condom
threatens to use.
did a trannie last
y dangerous.
ssman from Jor-
at——where he
room where he
d wanted to rape

yers who will do
ou guilty just be-
their work. If a

lawyer accepts legal aid and charges you extra, this is illegal for him/her to do. Please report them to us. We have
also had women tell us of being asked for sexual services
on top of the legal aid. This is illegal. If this has happened
to you, report it. Do not put up with any more exploitation by the system. We do keep track of any and all complaints by women. Be choosy about who you get to defend
you; after all it is you who will get the record and do the
time.

We also have access to family lawyers in case you need
one for family disputes or child custody battles.

POWER has access to safe places for women who are trying to get out of battering situations, who need a safe place
to stay for a few days while assessing your personal situation and we sometimes have access to bus tickets etc. just
in case you want/have to leave town.

The Bad Trick Alert is produced by POWER (Prostitutes
and Other Women for Equal Rights) and is endorsed by
other POWER groups across Canada as well as Prostitute's
Rights groups in the U.S.A. and England: U.S. PROS; NO BAD
WOMEN, JUST BAD LAWS; and ECP (the English Collective
of Prostitutes).

To contact POWER call —— after 4:00 p.m. or leave
a number where we can contact you. We provide referral
service to prostitutes and have access to services in the lower
mainland as well as out of province.

Source: Excerpted from "POWER Bad Trick Alert!!", May 23, 1990,
Vancouver, British Columbia.

y imported En-
eet prostitution
er the purview
iseases Acts (see
ada in 1865, but
reasons that are
lapse in 1870
anadian Crimi-
mber of vagran-
eetwalking, and
eries of sections
These provisions
iminal law.
the purview of
arded in Cana-
stitution related
ails of prostitu-

tion; (2) bawdy-house offences; and (3) communicating in
a public place for the purpose of buying or selling sexual
services (see Box 4.2).

Procuring and Living on the Avails

The "**procuring** and **living on the avails**" provisions are
designed to prevent third parties from making any kind of
financial gain from the prostitution of other persons. Subsection 212(1) of the Criminal Code contains eight subsections that prohibit the procuring of persons to become
prostitutes or the enticing of persons to become inmates
of common bawdy-houses. A ninth subsection prohibits
gain arising from the aiding, abetting, or compelling of
another person to engage in prostitution, and a tenth prohibits a person from living "wholly or in part on the avails
of prostitution of another person." Very few individuals

Box 4.2 Laws of the Land: Criminal Code Provisions Pertaining to Prostitution

210. (1) Every one who keeps a common bawdy-house is guilty of an indictable offence and liable to imprisonment for a term not exceeding two years.

(2) Every one who
   (a) is an inmate of a common bawdy-house,
   (b) is found, without lawful excuse, in a common bawdy-house, or
   (c) as owner, landlord, lessor, tenant, occupier, agent or otherwise having charge or control of any place, knowingly permits the place or any part thereof to be let or used for the purposes of a common bawdy-house,
is guilty of an offence punishable on summary conviction.

(3) Where a person is convicted of an offence under subsection (1), the court shall cause a notice of the conviction to be served on the owner, landlord or lessor of the place in respect of which the person convicted or his agent, and the notice shall contain a statement to the effect that it is being served pursuant to this section.

(4) Where a person on whom a notice is served under subsection (3) fails forthwith to exercise any right he may have to determine the tenancy or right of occupation of the person so convicted, and thereafter any person is convicted of an offence under subsection (1) in respect of the same premises, the person on whom the notice was served shall be deemed to have committed an offence under subsection (1) unless he proves that he has taken all reasonable steps to prevent the recurrence of the offence.

211. Every one who knowingly takes, transports, directs, or offers to take, transport, or direct any other person to a common bawdy-house is guilty of an offence punishable on summary conviction.

212. (1) Every one who
   (a) procures, attempts to procure or solicits a person to have illicit sexual intercourse with another person, whether in or out of Canada,
   (b) inveigles or entices a person who is not a prostitute or a person of known immoral character to a common bawdy-house or house of assignation for the purpose of illicit sexual intercourse or prostitution,
   (c) knowingly conceals a person in a common bawdy-house or house of assignation.
   (d) procures or attempts to procure a person to become, whether in or out of Canada, a prostitute,
   (e) procures or attempts to procure a person to leave the usual place of abode of that person in Canada, if that place is not a common bawdy-house, with intent that the person may become an inmate or frequenter of a common bawdy-house, whether in or out of Canada,
   (f) on the arrival of a person in Canada, directs or causes that person to be directed or takes or causes that person to be taken, to a common bawdy-house or house of assignation,
   (g) procures a person to enter or leave Canada, for the purpose of prostitution,
   (h) for the purposes of gain, exercises control, direction or influence over the movements of a person in such a manner as to show that he is aiding, abetting or compelling that person to engage in or carry on prostitution with any person or generally,
   (i) applies or administers to a person or causes that person to take any drug, intoxicating liquor, matter or thing with intent to stupefy or overpower that person in order thereby to enable any person to have illicit sexual intercourse with that person, or
   (j) lives wholly or in part on the avails of prostitution of another person,
is guilty of an indictable offence and liable to imprisonment for a term not exceeding ten years.

(1)(j), every per-
part on the avails
erson who is un-
ars is guilty of an
to imprisonment
fourteen years.
with or is habitu-
ostitute or lives in
in a house of as-
of evidence to the
erson lives on the
purposes of para-
(2).
lace, obtains or at-
leration, the sexu-
is under the age
of an indictable
onment for a term

213. (1) Every person who in a public place or in any place open to public view

(a) stops or attempts to stop any motor vehicle,

(b) impedes the free flow of pedestrian or vehicular traffic or ingress to or egress from premises adjacent to that place, or

(c) stops or attempts to stop any person or in any manner communicates or attempts to communicate with any person

for the purposes of engaging in prostitution or of obtaining the sexual services of a prostitute is guilty of an offence punishable on summary conviction.

(2) In this section, "public place" includes any place to which the public have access as of right or by invitation, express or implied, and any motor vehicle located in a public place or in any place open to public view.

given year (see

the operation of
t. The Criminal
on of "**bawdy-**
ept or occupied,
r the purpose of
ndictable offence
210(1)). This law
such a premises.
n bawdy-house
ties provided for
d the prostitute
ary-conviction
um penalty of six
ng $1000. Since
en charged with
mary-conviction
any part of any
vdy-house, or to
n to such a place.
ng to search war-
199.

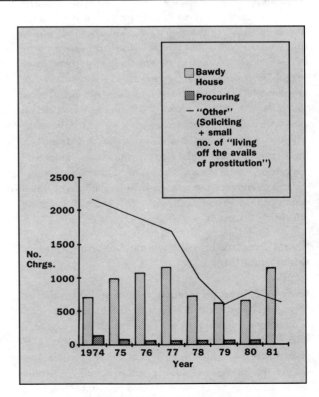

Figure 4.1 Canadian Prostitution Charges, 1974–1981
Source: Statistics Canada Catalogue, pp. 85–205.

The bawdy-house laws contained in the first Canadian Criminal Code (1892) can be traced back to the British Disorderly Houses Act of 1751. Subsequent amendments to these provisions up until 1917 served steadily to increase their ambit (Russel, 1982). Since then, there have been no significant changes. The most important aspect of this legislation is the wide definition of the "places" that come under its purview. Russell mentions one example of a circus tent being defined as a bawdy-house, and another of a 5000-square-foot parking lot being so defined. More commonly, the places involved in prostitution bawdy-house prosecutions since World War II have been the residences of prostitutes (whether owned or rented), "trick pads" (places used solely for servicing customers), and, most frequently, hotel rooms. While a location used only on a one-time basis would not be defined as a bawdy-house, the police are not necessarily required to establish that a place is used more than once by a prostitute or prostitutes to determine that it is used frequently—its "general reputation" may be sufficient to show that it is a place where acts of prostitution occur on an ongoing basis (Russell, 1982).

The combined effect of the bawdy-house and other prostitution laws is that, while prostitution is technically legal in Canada, it is very difficult to envisage how a prostitute could practise the trade without breaking the law. The law is a contradiction in terms (see Box 4.3). It would seem that, in order not to run afoul of this legislation, the prostitute would have to rent a new apartment every time he or she serviced more than two or three customers, or be very diligent in avoiding renting hotel rooms that other prostitutes had also rented! The procuring laws further serve to legally marginalize prostitution dating services (such as escort agencies) and off-street locations (such as massage parlours) that are commonly little more than fronts for prostitution services. Other laws criminalize as "indecent" sex acts occurring in cars. The bawdy-house laws, though difficult to enforce, thus create a socio-legal milieu in which prostitution is systematically censured, and the prostitute effectively outlawed.

Street Prostitution: Vagrancy, Soliciting, and Communicating

Until 1972, street prostitution was controlled by a series of vagrancy statutes that criminalized female prostitutes. **Vagrancy C** (the most recent street prostitution vagrancy offence) treated as a vagrant "any common prostitute or nightwalker . . . found in a public place" who could not, when required, "give a good account of herself." A "common prostitute" (as of 1949) meant a prostitute "available to all and sundry . . . or at least more than one" (Layton, 1979, p.111). Under this law, a prostitute was, by defini-

tion, a female. The law was restricted to the *common* prostitute in order to protect the first time offender from prosecution. In practice, this interpretation meant that police would establish that a woman working the street was a common prostitute by issuing her a warning that she was known to be a prostitute, so that formal charges could be laid should she subsequently reappear on the street.

In 1972, following the postwar repeal of all but a couple of the Canadian vagrancy statutes, Vagrancy C also fell prey to the legislature's scalpel. Criticized on civil libertarian grounds for criminalizing a person's *status* rather than his or her *behaviour*, and on feminist grounds as being sexist because it excluded men from its definition of "prostitute," Vagrancy C was replaced by Criminal Code section 195.1, which read: "Every person who solicits any person in a public place for the purpose of prostitution is guilty of an offence punishable on summary conviction." It was the putative "failure" of this law, and the expansion of street prostitution allegedly created by it, that became the focus of heated public debate and concerted political action across Canada in the late 1970s and 1980s.

From the first point of the use of Section 195.1, the meaning of the term "soliciting" was the subject of much judicial discussion. Could the prostitute,[9] simply by approaching a customer and mentioning a service and a price (the evidence undercover police officers felt was sufficient to lay a charge), be said to solicit? In 1978, an appeal court decision established that a prostitute could not be convicted on these grounds since "soliciting" meant "importuning" or "pressing and persistent" behaviour. As a result, in Vancouver—Canada's third largest city, and the site of some of the most heated debate about street prostitution—the law fell into disuse. Police in other provinces continued successfully to obtain convictions by arguing that a prostitute approaching a number of prospective customers sequentially was being "pressing and persistent." When Vancouver police, in 1980, adopted this interpretation, it too was struck down by a judicial decision (Special Committee on Pornography and Prostitution, 1985, pp. 419–429). At this point, police across the country abandoned enforcement of the street prostitution law.

In 1981 and 1982, a number of communities (Calgary, Montreal, Niagara Falls, and Vancouver) enacted and vigorously enforced municipal by-laws to curtail the street prostitution trade. In 1983, the Supreme Court of Canada ruled that one such by-law lay outside the powers originally vested in them by the **British North America Act** of 1867 because it represented an attempt to legislate criminal law, an area of exclusive federal jurisdiction (Special Committee on Pornography and Prostitution, 1985, p. 446). This decision meant the abandoning of enforcement of equivalent by-laws in other cities.

ition Law

rostitution laws is
cally legal, there is
nning afoul of the
s been about how
ut at other periods
t has been present-
regard lies within
irection. An illus-
een in an example
Williams, director
ntrol for the Brit-
l a three-point plan

e clinic an op-
te arrested and
y, every known

-houses which
eets where they

emises used as
ruary 14, 1939,

ition out onto the
as that it would be
s to meet. This, in
enereal disease.
ign to increase the
ntences for brothel-
ized prostitution to
r effort by spread-
d civilian workers.
the result of police
y those who would
hels:

s of this policy.
because the en-
eir profits in the
ation regarding
latter objection
stances, because
ts have deliber-
icially plausible

propaganda. Frequently well-meaning citizens in their ignorance of the truth unwittingly have given vocal support to a policy which is undermining public health, and by their utterances have facilitated the spread of venereal disease and sealed the doom of many of their fellow citizens.

What is the false propaganda of the bawdy-house interests which have misled so many citizens? It is important that each citizen learn the truth regarding red herrings which have been used in the past and will undoubtedly again be dragged across the public's path by the vested interests of commercialized prostitution. These "red herrings" will be readily recognized; the three principal ones are—that organized and regulated prostitution protects the community from, first, "spreading the professional prostitutes and their diseases throughout the city," second, "endangering the chastity of decent women and young girls by assault and rape," third, "the need for rehabilitation facilities before turning the prostitutes out on the street . . . ."

If these "red herrings" do not deflect public opinion, and law enforcement becomes temporarily an effective reality, bawdy-house interests produce two "plays" for public consumption. These involve utilizing to the fullest extent the nuisance value of the professional prostitute as a follow-up to the "spread" propaganda. Immediately there occurs the "play" of professional prostitutes posing as street walkers and suddenly making themselves a very obvious nuisance on prominent streets. Along with this the exploiters move some of their diseased products to residential districts and often deliberately near the homes of citizens whose cry of "spread" will be loudest and most effective in veering public opinion back to its tragic attitude of tolerance toward re-establishing the disease dispensaries in their former haunts. The public is not cognizant of the fact that effective law enforcement can force landlords and lessors to keep the madames and their diseased wares trundling from house to house until the profits are gone and the patrons give up in their attempt to find the constantly moving madame and her girls. (1941, pp. 365–67)

It was not until December 1985 that new prostitution legislation was enacted, and section 195.1 was replaced by section 213, that created the offence of **"communicating" for the purpose of prostitution.** Research sponsored by the Department of Justice Canada on the effectiveness and general impact of the new version of 195.1 is underway as of this writing. It remains to be seen whether a series of constitutional challenges to this law will be successful; it has already been struck down in Nova Scotia, but is still used extensively elsewhere.

Customers of Youths

On January 1, 1988, following the recommendations of both the Badgley and Fraser committees, an altogether new provision (s. 212(4)) was enacted that makes it an offence to purchase or offer to purchase sexual services from a youth.

Contemporary Law Enforcement Patterns

Contemporary prostitution law enforcement appears to be geared mainly to keeping prostitution out of sight to the extent that, by far, the largest proportion of prostitution charges are laid under the communicating law. In the first two years following the revision of the street prostitution law in 1985, approximately 11 000 charges were laid in Montreal, Toronto, and Vancouver—Canada's three largest cities—and approximately 15 000 in Canada as a whole. It is difficult to establish the exact numbers because, in the Uniform Crime Reporting system used by Statistics Canada, figures for "bawdy-house" and "procuring" charges are recorded separately, whereas those for "living on the avails" and "communicating" are lumped together. Table 4.1 shows the figures for the three categories of offence from 1983 to 1987. As this table indicates, from 1983 to 1985, when no charges were laid under the soliciting law, the remaining handful of charges must have been for living on the avails. Then, in 1986, the first year of enforcement of the communicating law, the number in the category

"other" increases by a factor of more than twenty; it seems safe to assume that only a tiny proportion of these were for living on the avails. Just why the number of procuring charges has risen steadily each year is not clear at this time.

One significant change brought about by the enactment of the communicating law is that customers and prostitutes are equally liable to prosecution; under the original version of s.195.1 (the soliciting law), customers were almost never charged. It remains to be seen how much this attempt to produce formal equality in the written law will be translated into equal law enforcement against prostitutes and their customers on the streets. In Vancouver, during the first two years of prostitution law enforcement, 1648 charges were laid against prostitutes and only 532 against customers, a ratio of about 3 to 1 (Lowman, 1989, p. 195). It remains to be seen from the federally sponsored evaluation of the communicating law (which had not been published at the time of writing) if this ratio holds for other jurisdictions in Canada.

What these statistics generally indicate is that police action against the exploiters of prostitutes in the form of living on the avails and procuring charges is relatively minimal when compared to the effort devoted to the street trade. One powerful indication of the nature of public and police priorities when it comes to different aspects of prostitution is the difference in the response to the enactment of the communicating law in 1985 and the enactment of the law criminalizing the patrons of youths in 1988. We have already seen that the introduction of the communicating law occasioned a substantial police response in terms of the zeal with which they set about the laying of charges; in Vancouver, for example, 760 charges were laid during the first year of its use. For the first few months after the law's enactment, newspapers kept a fairly regular tally of the number of charges laid. During that first year, the communicating law was mentioned no less than 152 times in Vancouver's two main daily newspapers, *The Vancouver Sun* and *The Province* (and a further 169 times the following year). By contrast, during the first year after the enactment of the law criminalizing the customers of youths, only one

Table 4.1   Charges Laid for Bawdy-House, Procuring, and other Types of Prostitution, 1983–1987

Year	Bawdy-House	Procuring	Other	Total
1983	561	151	223	935
1984	675	189	160	1 024
1985	715	236	274	1 225
1986	614	373	6439	7 426
1987	666	530	9243	10 439

Source: Statistics Canada Catalogue, pp. 85–205.

aw was deemed
ns by the same
of this section
ually no public
observations, it
important than
they are youths.

da

nature of prosti-
of the Domin-
c" prostitution,
uropean culture
ul that prostitu-
ct of white con-
), for example,
te that prostitu-
al social organi-
North American
ite contact had
North American
ired little train-
conomy. Prosti-
for many native

Photo 4.1   Cigars and Tobacco store, Dawson City, Yukon, *c.* 1898. This was a "bawdy–cigar store"; the female clerks were prostitutes.

National Archives of Canada, no. PA 13356.

, Calgary, 1911.
d about 50 yards
ver (near present-

Accounts of late nineteenth and early twentieth century prostitution (Brookig, 1976; Boucher, 1985; Gray, 1971; Hansen-Brett, 1986; Keller, 1986; Nilsen, 1980; Rotenberg, 1974) deal mainly with "public" prostitutes. There is little information about the more clandestine aspects of commercial sex, presumably not because it did not exist, but because it remained beyond the scope of law and law enforcement. All these accounts depict the prostitutes of the time as generally poverty-stricken women who had few alternatives to prostitution other than menial low-income domestic positions and agricultural or factory work—that is, if any of these kinds of jobs were available at all (Backhouse, 1985; McLaren, 1986a; Nilsen, 1980; Rotenberg, 1974). In frontier societies, where men often outnumbered women considerably, the incentive to prostitution was presumably amplified.

At the turn of the century and, probably for some time before, the prostitution trade was located in what were referred to as "restricted districts." Certainly, streetwalking occurred (Clark, 1898, pp.131–37), but most of the trade was conducted in bawdy-houses ("disorderly houses" and "houses of ill fame"), including private houses or massage parlours, where anywhere up to five or six women may have worked at any one time. Women working alone were also charged with running bawdy-houses, usually as a result of taking an undercover police officer back to an apartment after meeting him on the street (McLaren, 1986a, p. 151).

According to Gray (1971), the prostitution and liquor trades of early-twentieth-century Canada were intertwined. They were the recurring target of Christian moral reform associations and women's groups (Nilsen, 1980; McLaren, 1986a, 1986c; McLaren & Lowman, 1987), offshoots of those in Britain and the United States. Prostitution was referred to as "the social evil," and a concerted campaign waged against the putative "white slave trade," an international traffic in women (see McLaren, 1986a, 1986c).

Just how successful these campaigns were in bringing about the demise of the restricted districts is difficult to assess. In the United States, it appears that the restricted districts were dispersed by 1920 as a result of the concerted efforts of the social purity movement (Reckless, 1933; Rosen, 1982, pp.28–33). Gray (1971) claims that brothel prostitution in the prairie provinces gave away to a much more decentralized bar and hotel trade after 1920, but he attributes the change to a confluence of forces (such as the economic impact of the Depression and changes in provincial liquor regulation) rather than the singular impact of the vice crusades. Conversely, ongoing research on newspaper reports and archival records suggests that brothel prostitution in Vancouver and Toronto survived these encroachments and formed a major component of the business

through the 1920s and 1930s only to disappear after World War II. This impression is confirmed by the national bawdy-house conviction rate between 1866 and 1966 (Figure 4.2). It is difficult to tell from the national statistics on vagrancy charges how many involved street prostitutes. At the municipal level, the relative number of bawdy-house and street prostitution charges are easier to distinguish. In Toronto, between 1913 and 1937, an average of 182 women were charged annually with vagrancy (excluding the bawdy-house vagrancy statutes), probably most of them prostitutes, while an average of 177 were charged with bawdy-house offences (in contrast, there were only 90 prosecutions for procuring during the 25-year period).

As to styles of prostitution in Canada between 1940 and 1970, very little published research is available. It would seem that the decline in the number of bawdy-house prosecutions after 1940 (Figure 4.2) is a reflection more of a change in the nature of prostitution (the off-street trade became more decentralized after World War II) than of a change in policing practices. Research in Vancouver indicates that street prostitution has always occurred in that city. In the period after 1945, it occasioned little public comment as long as it was confined to traditional zones of permissiveness: Chinatown, skid row, and similar districts. In 1959, there was some media attention, fuelled by fear of organized crime involvement in the trade in "call girls," which the police chief claimed was extensive in the city (see Box 4.4). The main way of contacting these prostitutes was through hotel bellhops and desk clerks or taxi drivers (Lowman, 1989, p. 183). Prostitutes routinely worked in the bars of major downtown and airport hotels, and several cabaret clubs were locally renowned as places to meet prostitutes (Prus and Irini's [1980] ethnography of prostitution in 1970s Toronto describes a similar type of trade). Through the 1950s and 1960s, and into the 1970s, prostitution remained largely out of sight. It was either hidden away in the smoky confines of bars, and hotel lounges, or restricted to the lowest-class residential quarters of the downtown city core. In the 1970s and 1980s, however, street prostitution became a high profile "social problem"; it is said to have increased dramatically after jurisprudence rendered the soliciting law unenforceable.

An examination of the history of prostitution law enforcement in Canada suggests a complex convergence of forces involving shifts in street culture, changing attitudes toward sex, the effects of urban renewal and land-use zoning, patterns of policing, and the power of different social groups to define social problems. In Vancouver, prostitution expanded out of the traditional zones of tolerance well before the demise of the soliciting law in 1978 (Lowman, 1986a; see also Special Committee on Pornography and Prostitution, 1985, pp. 421–29), and in Toronto, the spread

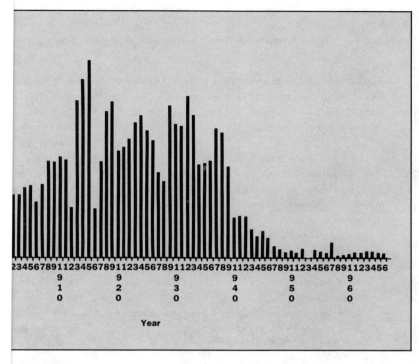

234567891123456789112345678911234567891123456789112345678911123456
9   9   9   9   9   9
1   2   3   4   5   6
0   0   0   0   0   0

Year

ncludes fre-
d all convictions
1966)
1912–1919 Depart-

ment of Trade and Commerce "Statistics of Criminal and Others
Offences," 1920–1966 Dominion Bureau of Statistics Catalogue,
pp. 85–201.

rtially attributable
rlours following
nine boy in 1977.
e is still flourish-
heated public de-

aw

to efforts to sup-
lves in a no-win
fforts have been
it in certain areas,
n. At the turn of
ld probably have
icted districts but
cial purists to do
time thought that
persed it, thereby
ntractable. There
rom both prosti-
ies of scandals oc-
g accusations that

police officers were receiving payoffs from gambling den
and brothel operators (Swan & Richardson, 1986). Public
inquiries prompted by these scandals resulted in the demise
of several police executives. It also seems that fines from
prostitution and gambling formed an important source of
municipal revenue (Keller 1986). Fines resulting from
prostitution convictions were sarcastically referred to as the
"sin tax" in the newspapers of the 1920s.

In the post–World War II period, up to 1972 (when the
prostitution vagrancy law was repealed and the soliciting
law enacted), law enforcement again appears to have been
mostly prophylactic in nature—to keep the prostitute out
of public mind and sight—a pattern that was interrupted
only during periods of police initiated concern that, when
prostitution becomes too invisible, organized crime takes
control of the trade. It was precisely this kind of police initiated concern that led to the closure of Vancouver's sex
trade cabarets in 1975, and it was this, rather than the failure
of the street prostitution law attributed to the 1978 Supreme
Court decision mentioned above, that led to the most
noticeable expansion of street prostitution in that city (Lowman, 1986a). Figure 4.1 shows that the national decline in
the number of charges for soliciting actually began in 1975,
only to accelerate after 1977 to the point where the law
was no longer used after 1981. The most important lesson

Box 4.4 "Trade Brisk in Call Girls": A Police-Inspired Moral Panic

The following article from the front page of the *Vancouver Sun* on January 12, 1959, is an example of political rhetoric used to justify legal action against the off-street prostitution trade.

Trade Brisk in Call Girls
Sun Reveals Taxis Key to Sale of Sex

A lucrative and wide-open call-girl system is flourishing in Vancouver, operating in some of the city's leading hotels and motels, in defiance of token action by police.

Girls can be obtained easily through hotel bell boys, taxi drivers or simply by ringing the dispatchers at certain cab companies.

Some of the girls are employed in ordinary daytime jobs at offices and banks.

The sell their charms at night for the recognized rate of $25 an hour or $100 a night.

One Chinese girl is charging $50 an hour.

12 Reports in Probe

The Vancouver Sun booked 12 senior reporters into downtown Vancouver hotels and motels Saturday night to investigate the extent of the call-girl racket.

The investigation followed the recent arrests of several alleged call-girls and a statement by Prosecutor Roland Bouwman in police court Thursday that Vancouver's call-girl racket was "apparently extensive and lucrative."

Earlier Police Chief George Archer had told a Vancouver police commission meeting he had a "queasy feeling" a big, organized call-girl racket was operating in the city.

The 12 reporters operated in pairs and were booked into hotels under their own names, but with Victoria addresses.

—And What They Found

They found:

- Chief Archer's "queasy feeling" is more than justified.
- Visitors to Vancouver can easily obtain the services of a call-girl within an hour of arrival.
- Two out of three taxi drivers will either deliver a girl themselves or "get in touch with another driver who will get you a girl."
- Some drivers who bring the girls to hotel rooms leave company cards with their car numbers so they can be contacted for future business.
- Some hotel managements turn a blind eye to obvious prostitution.
- Some drivers charge $5 plus cab fare for delivering the girls.
- Lately they have been carefully questioning their clients before bringing girls because, they say, the recent arrests have made business "hot."
- Drivers for one cab company, Diamond Cabs, 1033 Seymour, carry many of the girls, and drivers for other companies often direct customers seeking call-girls to Diamond Cabs.
- Bell boys at some leading hotels have secret telephone numbers they phone for guests who want girls to come to the hotel rooms.
- At least one woman taxi dispatcher is willing to arrange for a girl to be sent to a hotel room, as are male dispatchers at several other companies.

Source: *Vancouver Sun*, January 12, 1959, p.1.

to be learned from this brief sketch of the history of prostitution law enforcement is that the law contains within it the power to be mobilized against prostitution—whether at the behest of the police or some other lobby group able to influence law enforcement activity—no matter where it occurs.

Profiles of Contemporary Prostitutes

In Canada, prostitution is a predominantly female occupation; it is estimated that female street prostitutes outnumber males (including transsexuals and transvestites) by at least three or four to one (Special Committee on Pornography and Prostitution, 1985, p. 371; Crook, 1984, p. 86). Although almost all studies of prostitution in Canada indicate that youth prostitutes (under eighteen years of age) are in the minority (of 720 female prostitutes charged in Vancouver in 1986 and 1987, 13.5 percent were youths, as were 12 percent of the 93 male prostitutes charged), the majority of Canadian street prostitutes interviewed for the Badgley and Fraser committees had "turned out" prior to the age of eighteen (see Figure 4.3).

There are several key differences between the experiences of male and female street prostitutes revealed by the Badgley Committee's research and by Visano's (1987) ethnography of "hustling" (i.e., prostitution by males *dressing as males*) based on interviews with and observation of 33

ed, and they are
ad trick" than are
e are similar to the
d unhappy child-
life, although the
imes different for
oblems sometimes
rowing homosex-
me life was more
zation by family

ed by Canadian
had been thrown
ttee reported that
of the females stat-
e life was of "con-
83–84), 65 percent
at family violence
Lowman, 1984, p.
viewed in the At-
ghting in the fami-
7). Similar findings
the United States

arge proportion of
eir childhood they
rcent of the wom-
's, and roughly 40
ed in Vancouver
embers (the num-
hese surveys is too
—in the case of the
ly as boys to have
had involved "the
victimization, vary-
e been reported in
contradictory find-
which concluded
tion Survey (1984,
ey (1984, Ch. 43)
n other persons to
acts" during their
ttee's data suggests
e youth prostitutes
kely as respondents
have been victims
reats of force" (the
fences that prosti-
eir childhood years
Bagley, 1985).
out the class back-
the weight of evi-

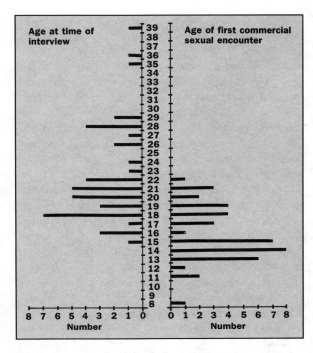

Figure 4.3 Ages of 43 Vancouver Prostitutes at Time of 1984 Interview and at Age of First Commercial Sexual Encounter.
Source: Lowman, 1984, pp. 698–699.

dence suggests that they come mainly, though not entirely, from the lower social strata (see Lowman, 1987, pp. 102–3); one problem with the literature on the subject is that definitions of "social class" are usually not provided.

The "typical" street prostitute enters the trade somewhere between the ages of thirteen and nineteen, and usually after running away from either a state home (group homes, foster homes, etc). or the home of one or both natural parents. They run because they find home life intolerable. None of these factors alone, however, explains why they turn to prostitution. This "choice"—and most of the prostitutes interviewed insist that they made a choice—must be contextualized. Most prostitutes have little education and, by virtue of belonging to the age group with the highest unemployment rate, are only marginally employable. They are not eligible for welfare assistance, until the age of 19 and they have not usually been trained in the skills of independent business. What is attractive about street culture is that it allows the runaway or disaffiliated youth a sense of belonging, a feeling of autonomy, and a means of financial independence. Most importantly, street prostitution provides a means of subsistence. And the fast and substantial money that it does bring to a core group of prostitutes symbolizes much that is cherished in mainstream materialist Western culture.

Because theirs is a culture valuing conspicuous consumption (and in this mirrors mainstream culture) capital is rarely accumulated by these sex-trade workers. Drug use is widespread among prostitutes, although the Badgley Committee noted that it was not as endemic as its authors had expected (Committee on Sexual Offences Against Children and Youth, 1984, p. 1021). When it came to pimping, the committee opined that "while most young females who engaged in prostitution had initially found their way onto the street by themselves, it was the pimps who kept them there" (1984, p. 1060). This argument is not actually supported by any concrete evidence (Lowman, 1987, pp. 107–8). For one thing, it is not particularly clear what the term "pimp" means. Survey research suggests that pimps do turn out some females (for a discussion of the pimp's *modus operandi*, see Lautt, 1984, pp. 47–50), and there is evidence of extensive pimp violence in Canada. But not all prostitutes are "pimped" in the traditional sense. Prostitutes distinguish between "boyfriends" (i.e., lovers) and pimps (who are only sometimes lovers) in a way that the law does not (it is illegal to "live in whole *or in part* on the avails of prostitution of another person"). A boyfriend may well encourage a girlfriend to continue prostituting herself, and in this sense he becomes a "pimp." But many prostitutes who have been pimped sometime in their lives nevertheless insist on distinguishing pimps from other partners, and are critical of a law that effectively makes it impossible for a prostitute to cohabit with anyone (of either sex), pimp or not. Those women who had been pimped had virtually nothing positive to say about the experience. So, it would seem that factors other than the gullibility of prostitutes and their susceptibility to pimps are also responsible for entrenching women in prostitution. In Vancouver, organizers of the local prostitutes' rights group estimate that approximately half of the city's prostitutes work independently. Pimps may well enjoy more control of the trade in other cities (see, for example, Crook, 1984, pp. 74–85).

Profiles of Contemporary Customers

There are three main sources of information on tricks: there is the information reported by prostitutes (Committee on Sexual Offences Against Children and Youth, 1984, pp. 1049–55; Fleischman, 1984, pp. 47–52; Lautt, 1984, pp. 64–70; Lowman, 1984, pp. 211–29); there is information provided by tricks themselves (Crook, 1984, pp. 58–70; Gemme et al., 1984, pp. 133–36); and there is the information about customer's age, occupation, race, and marital status that can now be gleaned from the police records of customers convicted under the new street prostitution

statute (more information will be provided by the Department of Justice Canada's Evaluation of the Communicating Law; see note 6). These various sources indicate that: (a) it is primarily men that buy the services of both male and female street prostitutes and escorts; (b) men of all ages buy sex (men in the 20- to 40-year age group are the most likely to be charged with "communicating"); (c) of 188 men prosecuted in Vancouver for the "communicating" offence, 47 percent were single, separated, or divorced; 53 percent were married or lived in a common law relationship; and (d) men gave a number of different reasons for visiting prostitutes, including (i) sexual problems at home, (ii) loneliness, (iii) curiosity, (iv) desire for sexual acts that a regular partner will not accommodate, (v) an opportunity for discrete homosexual sex, and (vi) a desire for a brief uncomplicated sexual encounter (Gemme et al., 1984, p. 134).

Theories of Prostitution

While there are at least six types of theoretical perspectives on prostitution in the anglophone literature (cf. Lowman, 1988), none of them is peculiarly Canadian. The discussion here focusses on the theoretical perspectives adopted by the Badgley and Fraser committees.

For the most part, the Badgley Committee presents a social-psychological perspective on prostitution. It eschews any kind of structural analysis of the family as a social unit, or of its central role in the relations of production and reproduction. And despite the preponderance of women on the committee, there is virtually no analysis of gender relations generally (Clark, 1986; Brock & Kinsman, 1986; Lowman, 1985b, 1987), or of the male's power to purchase sexual services in particular. Very little is said about the effect of unemployment structures and the marginal position of youth, especially females, in the labour market. While the official overall unemployment rate in Canada between 1978 and 1987 averaged 8.66 percent (*Financial Post*, 1987–88, p. 95), the rate for the under-25 age group was 15.61 percent—and, of course, official rates are generally said to represent the most conservative of possible definitions of "unemployment." In stressing the responsibility of the child prostitute, and by taking the position that such youths "bring upon themselves" (Committee on Sexual Offences Against Children and Youth, 1984, p. 1046) the hazards of street prostitution, the committee effectively individualizes the problems of lumpen youth (Lowman, 1987).

In contrast, while acknowledging the importance of a

raser Committee
ution informed by
elations. This ap-
ortunities, earning
structural factors
ear to be a choice
phy and Prostitu-
vation to become
985, pp. 378–79).
ns are very much
ing to understand
e turn of the cen-
974).

e 1980s

from cities across
incial, and federal
to combat street
ncerned Residents
the movement of
–the most densely
e of the soliciting
980) across Canada
laims were given
ncial government
' laws. The Fraser
tly different ver-
jurisprudence did
ting law, certain
ely abandoned at-
e federal govern-

erful forces, a var-
–the Alliance for
ot, Prostitutes and
R), and The Cana-
stitutes (CORP)—
street prostitution
t control groups.
egal and social re-
t of prostitutes to
n—a state-funded
t the federal level

New Democratic
ade by prostitutes'
the revised street
nservative govern-
chly to uphold the

rights of residents and landowners while continuing to ignore the apparent right of prostitutes to work.

Policy Options

While the history of prostitution in Canada and other countries suggests that it is an activity that is largely impervious
to efforts to suppress it, most political perspectives—in various shades of liberalism, feminism, socialism, and religious
moralism—argue that society should be rid of prostitution.
The moral conservatism of the nineteenth century, still an
influential philosophy today, aspired to eradicate "the social evil" as a form of sin, and worked in concert with
science to oppose commercial sex on medical-
epidemiological grounds. The advocates of a modern secular
disapprobation portray prostitution as either an insidious
source of neighbourhood decay or, at least, a general public nuisance, especially in residential areas. Socialism and
feminism generally call for the long-term elimination of
the prostitution trade because it represents one of the most
extreme forms of commodifying and objectifying women.
Prostitution poses some difficult problems for feminist political action. On the one hand, it is crass sexual exploitation and ought to be eliminated. On the other hand, if
women ought to be allowed to control their own bodies,
they ought to have the right to prostitute themselves. From
this perspective, many sex trade workers argue that prostitution is a form of labour, that sexual commodification is
no different from any other form of human labour sold for
a price, and that any position that criticizes the prostitute's
separation of sex and love is, in fact, an old style moralism
that is not conducive to sexual emancipation (see, generally, Bell, 1987, particularly the papers by Cole, 1987; St.
James, 1987; and Valverde, 1987; also, see Brock, 1985–86).

Many feminists argue for the decriminalization of prostitution; for a Criminal Code without (or with very few)
prostitution laws. They reject "legalization," arguing that
systems of licensing would continue to stigmatize prostitutes and entrench them in the trade (for descriptions of
the various legal models, see Special Committee on Pornography and Prostitution, 1985, pp. 514–22; Shaver, 1985).

Advocates of legalization view it as a more realistic form
of prostitution control than criminalization, and as a pragmatic solution to a trade that is unlikely to go away. One
form of free market conservatism maintains that prostitution should be legalized because the insatiable demand for
it could be harnessed for individual and state profit in a regime that its advocates suggest would facilitate disease control and allow management of the visible aspects of the
prostitution trade (see Block, 1984, writing for the Fraser
Institute, an ultra-conservative think-tank).

Strategies of Intervention: The Badgley and Fraser Committee Recommendations

While one of the Fraser Committee's main tasks was to recommend prostitution law reform, members took the view that the law could play only a minor role in long-term social policy on prostitution. Rather, the state's response should involve policies designed to remove "the economic and social inequalities between men and women and discrimination on the basis of sexual preference" (1985, p. 527) that make prostitution a viable occupational choice for some people. Nevertheless, the committee recommended sweeping changes to prostitution law in order to make it logically and philosophically consistent:

> prostitution cannot be dealt with by the law on a piecemeal basis, but only by carefully linking the provisions on each aspect of prostitution related activity. Moreover, [the recommendations] follow from the Committee's view, that, if prostitution is a reality with which we have to deal for the foreseeable future, then it is preferable that it take place in private, and without the opportunities for exploitation which have been traditionally associated with commercialized prostitution. (1985, p. 547)

If prostitution itself is legal, the law ought to be designed in such a way that prostitutes can conduct their trade legally. Following this logic, and rejecting criminalization as either a workable or a philosophically acceptable option, the committee opted for a blend of **decriminalization** and legalization. It specifically recommended that: (a) bawdy-house laws be changed to allow one or two prostitutes to work out of a private residence; (b) provincial governments be empowered to license small scale prostitution establishments; (c) street prostitution be controlled by a law that would criminalize definable prostitution-related nuisances; and (d) that the "living on the avails" law, because of its paternalistic over-reach, should be revised to apply to coercive or threatening behaviour only.[10] One of the committee members opposed the nuisance law recommended by the majority in favour of a pure decriminalization approach. Decriminalization would require removal of the term "prostitution" from the Criminal Code altogether so that "nuisances" would be defined generically so as to apply to all persons; pimps would be prosecuted under **extortion** laws. Where members of the committee were united was in their belief that the prostitution trade was not likely to leave the street until the law was structured in such a way that it could do so (and even then it would probably not leave the street completely).

In considering youth prostitution, the Badgley Committee was of the opinion that, although juvenile prostitutes were as much victims as offenders, the only way to "help" them was to define them legally as offenders so that they could then be treated as victims. The committee thus recommended criminalizing juvenile prostitutes so that they could be "saved." The Fraser Committee rejected this approach because it did not believe that youths should be criminalized for an activity that is legal for adults, one of the main principles underlying the Canadian **Young Offenders Act** (see Lowman, 1987, for a further critique). Nevertheless, both committees agreed that the customers of youths should be criminalized, a recommendation that the Canadian government acted on in January 1988.

In terms of its broader social policy recommendations, some commentators have criticized the Fraser Committee's version of feminism (Brock, 1985–86). Critics have complained of its failure to specify just what form social and economic initiatives should take (Kanter, 1985), and its failure to consider the full range of political philosophies that are relevant to social policy on prostitution. For instance, there is discussion of conservative, liberal, and liberal-feminist arguments, but no consideration of socialist alternatives, and little recognition of contradictions that may inhere in its recommended synthesis of legalization and decriminalization (Lowman, 1986b). Nevertheless, despite these criticisms, the Fraser Report brings together a wealth of empirical information and an insightful legal analysis to produce a series of forceful policy recommendations and a convincing indictment of the law as it currently stands. The Badgley Committee also presents an informative survey of young prostitutes, but one characterized by an analysis that is overly psychological to the extent that it minimizes the analytic importance of social structures and depoliticizes its policy recommendations (Lowman, 1987).

When it comes to immediate strategies of intervention lying outside the realm of criminal law, neither committee describes in any detail the kind of social services that might be provided for prostitutes or runaways. In this respect, the committees are not much different from any other writer on the subject. Few social services are provided specifically for adult prostitutes—they are probably not particularly interested in "help" anyway, other than financial and medical assistance and, in some cases, substance abuse counselling. The design of social services for youth prostitutes is particularly difficult since "street kids" generally perceive "help" to mean "control"; their main interest is in avoiding people who can exercise control over them. Services for runaways and throwaways vary considerably across different cities and provinces, as do the philosophies of service provision that guide them. The success of different programs is difficult to assess. In some provinces, very few services are provided at all.

Ultimately, none of these programs, because they are

n Law Reform

of different justifi-
on have been ad-
venereal disease,
men, fear of or-
lic nuisances. The
tion itself occurred
urists" campaigned
Criminal Code,
they thought were
stitutes (although,
ercised against the
re were concerted
le," so, too, there
it, not the least of
the main reasons
y of toleration and
This resilience was
ar support for the
morally reprehen-
he man who visit-
ing to what were
en, of course, there
n to "respectable"
. Thus, while there
arters for suppress-
nt reasons to toler-

received little legis-
II, it appears (from
orting in Toronto
y disappeared from
change in the late
to have spread un-
the soliciting law.
es have not neces-
stitution was in the

visions to the Cana-
o prostitution law:
ment of the solicit-
ting law and enact-
; and the enactment
ce to purchase or
person under eigh-
s for the repeal of
f the Royal Com-

mission on the Status of Women (published in 1970), which wanted to see this section struck down because it discriminated against women. Police did not oppose this reform since the soliciting law, by allowing them to charge transvestite prostitutes (who, as males, had been immune from prosecution under Vagrancy C), extended their powers. When the soliciting law was enacted in 1972, it occasioned virtually no commentary in the newspapers of the day. Similarly, the enactment of the section criminalizing the customers of youths in 1988 passed with virtually no media commentary. In contrast, the enactment of the communicating law in 1985 created front page news in virtually every newspaper across Canada and remains newsworthy since it has been the subject of continuing controversy. Much of this controversy concerns the action that legislators should take next. And far from being observers, as they were at the time the soliciting law was enacted, police (through the Canadian Association of Chiefs of Police) have become one of the main lobby groups demanding that the federal government give them the power to "clean up" the streets.

The ongoing debate about prostitution law highlights the political conundrum Canadian legislators still face. By enacting the communicating law, the federal government followed the one strategy that the Badgley and Fraser committees were united against. By enacting this law, the government sought to deal one-sidedly with the public nuisances associated with street prostitution rather than trying to mediate the interests of residents and prostitutes. In all of this, the problems besetting prostitutes and most of the recommendations made by the Fraser Committee to deal with them have been ignored completely. Thus, while Canada's politicians continue to refuse to criminalize prostitution itself (apparently on the grounds that, as Pierre Trudeau once put it, the state has no place in the bedrooms of the nation), they appear equally reluctant to deal with the issue of where prostitution should be located. And therein lies the political conundrum. A police officer interviewed as part of an evaluation of the communicating law had this to say:

> Politicians are afraid to go one way or the other—it could be political suicide. . . . We're not willing to condone prostitution even though it would be easier to do so—it comes down to being a moral question. Right now we are left with the politicians being able to satisfy both sides. You can say,

Box 4.5 *(Continued)*

"I think it should be legalized," and they can say, "Well, yes, it is legal." Somebody else can say, "I think it should not be legalized, I think it should be illegal," and they can say, "Well, yes, that's why we've got these laws to control it." Why should any politician rock the boat and take a hard and fast stand in either direction? (quoted in Lowman, 1989, p. 211)

A Crown attorney in Vancouver offered a similar vision of contemporary realities:

We've been able to turn a blind eye to some of the realities of prostitution. We put blinders on because we have to, given the current structure of the law. No politician is going to stand up and say, "Hey, a red light district is what we need guys." It's just not going to happen, not when that person has to go out and face the church group and get elected. So, we have to find the balance between a variety

of conflicting interests and calls for action. In the final analysis, organizations like ours will always have to keep dancing until some lawmaker is prepared to make a decision that either outlaws prostitution altogether or identifies a location where it can take place. I sure don't see that happening soon. (quoted in Lowman, 1989, p. 211)

If prostitution presents an apparently no-win situation for legislators, it is equally problematic for anyone interested in women's rights. On the one hand, there is the right of the individual woman to control her body, including the provision of sexual services for reward (criminalization of prostitution, but not promiscuity, essentially means that, if women—or men—are going to be promiscuous, they must not be remunerated in the process). On the other hand, the legalization or decriminalization of prostitution might be interpreted as encouraging the sexual commodification and general objectification of women.

pitched at an individual level, is able to contend with structural factors such as unemployment, gender inequalities, and male sexual socialization—all factors that help to generate prostitution. And Canadians are still faced with the immediate problem of prostitution law reform (see Box 4.5).

Government Reactions: More of the Same

Apart from enacting a law against the customers of juvenile prostitutes and increased sentences against pimps who engage youths, the federal government's only reform of prostitution law (against the recommendations of both the Badgley and Fraser committees[11]) has been to revise the street prostitution statute so as to make it easier to enforce. With this legal change, the Canadian government has consolidated its commitment to a policy of backdoor criminalization of prostitution, and entrenched the logical contradiction in the structure of Canadian prostitution law. And it has done so despite public-opinion survey findings that a substantial proportion of Canadians are prepared to tolerate prostitution in private premises (Peat Marwick and Partners, 1984, E-4).

There is a general consensus that the new law has certainly not eradicated the street prostitution trade (Depart-

ment of Justice Canada, 1989). Head counts of street prostitutes in Vancouver from 1982 to 1987 indicate that the number in 1987 was about the same as it was in 1984 —a time when such groups as "Shame the Johns" were picketing prostitutes and lobbying for just this type of legislation. They successfully achieved their legislative goals, but not apparently its desired effect. The very fact that 11 000 charges have been laid in Canada's three largest cities in the first two years of the law's use indicates that there is still plenty of business to prosecute. And, once again, anti–street prostitution activists are demanding that legislators do something to clean up the streets.

It remains to be seen whether the street prostitution law will survive a constitutional challenge. What does seem likely is that, until legislators design laws that describe where prostitutes *can* work, their efforts to eradicate the street prostitution trade will be both discriminatory and futile.

prostitutes are female
What factors appear to
individual's drift into

o equivocate when it
rostitution. Although
legal in Canada, it does
work on an ongoing basis
al prosecution. Should
a criminal offence?
urchase of sexual
e answers "yes" to all of
tion could be offered for
hat would otherwise be
payment involved? If one
uld prostitution be
ould be the goal(s) of

nt enacted a law that
e or offer to purchase
The Badgley Committee
ne step further than this
or young persons to
re the objections to this
of initiatives might be
ocured youths?

written for Green-

adies of prostitution
eries of articles and
entury in Toronto
1898), Vancouver
by Boucher, 1985;
e prairie provinces
nd/or ethnographic
960s (Copeland &
& Irini, 1980), and

ncluded academics,

doctors, judges, lawyers, psychiatrists, social workers, and sundry other professions with backgrounds in parole and policing, but neither committee included a representative of any sex trade. Women outnumbered men on both committees (the Badgley Committee included seven women and four men; the Fraser Committee, four women and three men).

3. Research on prostitution included: a study of newspaper reports on pornography and prostitution (El Komos, 1984); a study of prostitution and venereal disease (Haug & Cini, 1984); three studies of pornography and prostitution law in other countries (Jaywardene, Juliani, & Talbot, 1984; Kiedrowski & Van Dijk, 1984; Sansfaçon, 1984a); a study of U.N. conventions on prostitution (Sansfaçon, 1984b); a survey of public attitudes to prostitution and pornography (Peat Marwick and Partners, 1984); and five regional surveys of prostitution

covering the Atlantic provinces (Crook, 1984), Quebec (Gemme et al., 1984), Ontario (Fleischman, 1984), the prairie provinces (Lautt, 1984), and British Columbia (Lowman, 1984), plus an overview report of the five surveys (Sansfaçon, 1985; also see Special Committee, 1985, Ch. 28).

4. These included several sponsored by the Canadian Advisory Council on the Status of Women (CACSW, 1984; Riddington, 1983; Ruffo, 1983; and Wells, 1983. See also Riddington and Findlay, 1981), 1981) and at least one paper prepared for the Law Reform Commission of Canada (Rounthwaite, 1983).

5. For the history of prostitution laws in Canada, see Backhouse (1985); Layton (1979); McLaren (1986a, 1986c, 1988); McLaren and Lowman (1990); and Russell (1982). On contemporary legal developments and policy options, see Boyle and Noonan (1986); Burstyn (1984); Brock (1984); Brock and Kinsman (1986); Cassels (1985); Kanter (1985); Lowman (1985a, 1986b); McLaren (1986b); Martin (1984); Persky (1985); Shaver (1985); and Sullivan (1986). On male prostitution, see Visano (1987).

6. As if the 501 interviews with prostitutes conducted at the behest of the government by the Badgley and Fraser committees was not enough, another 300 or so interviews will be completed as part of the evaluation of the street prostitution law enacted in 1985. This evaluation—comprising five regional studies (Brannigan, Knafla, & Levy, 1989; Gemme, Payment, & Malenfant, 1989; Graves, 1989; Lowman, 1989; Moyer, 1989) and an overview of their findings (Department of Justice, 1989)—will also provide some general socio-demographic information about the *customers* of prostitutes since several thousand men (but no women that we know of) have now been convicted under the street prostitution law. Unfortunately, only one of these studies (Lowman, 1989) was available at the time of writing.

7. The Canadian *Criminal Code* is not particularly helpful when it comes to definitional issues since it defines a prostitute as "a person of either sex who engages in prostitution" without offering a definition of "prostitution" itself.

8. The coincidence of strip dancing and prostitution varies geographically. In British Columbia, strippers are not usually directly involved in prostitution; in contrast, strippers in parts of Ontario are much more likely to be (cf. Fleischman, 1984). In certain parts of Quebec, "table dancers" are known to turn tricks in the clubs and bars in which they dance.

9. Judicial opinion varied as to whether the soliciting law applied to the activities of customers. The British Columbia Court of Appeal concluded that it did not. But, in Ontario, the conviction of a customer was upheld (Special Committee on Pornography and Prostitution, 1985, p. 420). This difference of opinion mattered little in reality since few attempts were made to prosecute customers.

10. In this respect, the Fraser Committee differed considerably from the Badgley Committee (also called the Committee on Sexual Offences Against Children and Youth), which, in its moral outrage, would have simply strengthened the current "living on the avails" law, especially in cases where the avails were derived from juvenile prostitution; unfortunately, the Badgley Committee did not consider the full implications of its recommendations for adult prostitutes.

11. The Fraser Committee's whole purpose was to argue against this strategy. Similarly, the Badgley Committee (1985, p.1014) argued that "the effects of legislative amendments focussing primarily on the public manifestations of [prostitution] might serve the narrow purpose of 'clearing the streets,' but their enactment would likely achieve little more than having the effect of displacing or diverting most or all of these activities to being performed in out of sight private locations. In the instance of juvenile prostitutes, such a shift in locale would not likely dissuade them from continuing in this line of work, would make their detection by law enforcement authorities more difficult, and would increase the opportunities for their exploitation by pimps."

References

Backhouse, C. (1985). Nineteenth century Canadian prostitution law: Reflection of a discriminatory society. *Social History, 53*, 387–423.

Bagley C. (1985). Child sexual abuse and juvenile prostitution: A comment on the Badgley Report on Sexual Offences against Children and Youth. *Canadian Journal of Public Health, 76*, 65–66.

Bell, L. (Ed.). (1987). *Good girls/bad girls: Sex trade workers and feminists face to face.* Toronto: Women's Press.

Block, W. (1984). Defending the undefendable. Cited in *Highland Echo*. May 24, 1984, p.4.

Boucher, G. (1985). The fallen woman at work: Prostitution in Vancouver, 1890–1920. *The Ascendant Historian, 3*, 130–53.

Boyle, C., & Noonan, S. (1986). Prostitution and pornography: Beyond formal equality. *Dalhousie Law Journal, 10*:(2),225–65.

Brannigan, A., Knafla, L., & Levy C. (1989). *Street prostitution, assessing the impact of the law: Calgary.* Ottawa: Department of Justice Canada.

Brock, D.R. (1984). *Feminist perspectives on prostitution: Addressing the Canadian dilemma..* M.A. diss., Sociology and Anthropology, Carleton University, Ottawa. (1985–86).

Brock, D. (1985–86). From hooker to harlot: Myths of prostitution. *Broadside, 7*(6)8–9.

Brock, D.R., & Kinsman, G. (1986). Patriarchal relations ignored: A critique of the Badgely Report on Sexual Offences against Children and Youths. In J. Lowman, M.A. Jackson, T.S. Palys, & S. Gavigan (Eds.), *Regulating sex: An anthology of commentaries on the Badgley and Fraser reports* (pp. 107–25). Burnaby, BC: School of Criminology, Simon Fraser University.

Brookig, L.W. (1976). Prostitution in Toronto, 1911. In R. Cook & W. Mitchinson (Eds.), *The proper sphere: Women's place in Canadian society* (pp. 241–49). Toronto: Oxford University Press.

Burley, N., & Symanski, R. (1981). Women without: An evolutionary and cross-cultural perspective on prostitution. In R. Symanski (Ed.), *The immoral landscape* (pp. 239–73). Toronto: Butterworths.

Burstyn, V. (1984) Anatomy of a moral panic. *Fuse, Summer*, 29–38.

Canadian Advisory Council on the Status of Women. (1984). Prostitution in Canada. Ottawa.

Cassels, J. (1985). Prostitution and public nuisance: Desperate measures and the limits of civil adjudication. *Canadian Bar Review, 63*, 764–804.

Clark, C.S. (1898). *Of Toronto the Good.* Montreal: Toronto Publishing.

Clark, L. (1986). Boys will be boys: Beyond the Badgley Report, a critical review. In J. Lowman, M.A. Jackson, T.S. Palys, & S.

:ommentaries on the
:r reports. Burnaby,
Jniversity.
nd Youth (1984).
nent of Supply &

ind explosions. In
orkers and feminists
Press.
stitutes. in H. T.
). 261–269). New

provinces. Working
rt No. 12. Ottawa:

ution: Assessing the
artment of Justice

of pornography and
and Prostitution,
tice.
o. Working Papers
No. 10. Ottawa:

M.A., & Payment,
Vorking Papers on
No. 11. Ottawa:

. Street Prostitution:
ra: Department of

t of the law: Halifax.

ork: Signet.
istorical overview
C. Historical Review,

tlemen) of the night
Vorking Papers on
No. 7. Ottawa:

1984). Pornography
rs on Pornography
artment of Justice.
r Report and new
. Osgood Hall Law

86–1914. Ganges,

ohy and prostitution
lands, and Sweden.
ation, Report No.

tution in Vancouver.
iminology, Simon

Provinces. Working
rt No. 9. Ottawa:

ouver: Official and
British Columbia

Layton, M. (1979). The ambiguities of the law or the street walker's dilemma. *Chitty's Law Journal, 27*(4), 109–20.

Lowman, J. (1984) *Vancouver field study of prostitution.* Working Papers on Pornography and Prostitution, Report No. 8. Ottawa: Department of Justice.

Lowman, J. (1985a). From pillar to post. *Policy Options, 6* (8),4–6.

Lowman, J. (1985b). Child saving, legal panaceas, and the individualization of family problems: Some comments on the findings and recommendations of the Badgley Report. *Canadian Journal of Family Law, 4*(4), 508–14.

Lowman, J. (1986a). Street prostitution in Vancouver: Some notes on the genesis of a social problem. *Canadian Journal of Criminology, 28*(1), 1–16.

Lowman, J. (1986b). You can do it, but don't do it here: Some comments on proposals for the reform of Canadian prostitution law. In J. Lowman, M.A. Jackson, T.S. Palys, & S. Gavigan (Eds.), *Regulating sex: An anthology of commentaries on the Badgley and Fraser Reports* (pp.193–213). Burnaby, BC: School of Criminology, Simon Fraser University.

Lowman, J. (1987). Taking young prostitutes seriously. *Canadian Review of Sociology and Anthropology, 24*(1), 99–116.

Lowman, J. (1989). *Street prostitution: Assessing the impact of the law: Vancouver.* Ottawa: Department of Justice.

Lowman, J. (1988). Street Prostitution. In V. Sacco (Ed.), *Deviance: conformity and control in Canadian society.* Toronto: Prentice-Hall.

Martin, D. (1984). Bill C-19, prostitution. *Ottawa Law Review, 16*(2), 400–402.

McLaren, J. (1986a) Chasing the social evil: Moral fervour and the evolution of Canada's laws, 1867–1917. *Canadian Journal of Law and Society, 1*,125–65.

McLaren, J. (1986b). The Fraser Committee. The politics and process of a special committee. In J. Lowman, M.A. Jackson, T.S. Palys, & S. Gavigan (Eds.), *Regulating sex: An anthology of commentaries on the Badgley and Fraser reports* (pp.39–54). Burnaby, BC: School of Criminology, Simon Fraser University.

McLaren, J. (1986c). "White slavers": The reform of Canada's prostitution laws and patterns of enforcement, 1900–1920. Paper presented at the Meeting of the American Society for Legal History, Faculty of Law, University of Toronto, October.

McLaren, J. (1988) The Canadian magistracy and the anti–white slavery campaign, 1900–1920. In W. Pue and B. Wright (Eds.), *Canadian perspectives on law and society* (pp. 328–53.). Ottawa: Carleton University Press.

McLaren, J., & Lowman, J. (1990). Prostitution law and law enforcement, 1892–1920: Unravelling rhetoric and practice. In M. Friedland (Ed.), *Securing compliance: Seven case studies,* Toronto: University of Toronto Press.

Moyer, S., & Carrington, P. (1989). *Street prostitution: Assessing the impact of the law: Toronto.* Ottawa: Department of Justice.

Nilsen, D. (1980). Enforcing Canada's prostitution laws, 1892–1920: Rhetoric and practice. In B. Latham & C. Kess (Eds.), *In her own right: Selected essays on women's history in B.C.* (pp. 205–228). Victoria: Camosun College.

Peat Marwick and Partners. (1984). *A national population study of pornography and prostitution.* Working Papers on Pornography and Prostitution, Report No. 6. Ottawa: Department of Justice.

Persky, S. (1985). Sleepless nights. *This Magazine, 19*(5), 12–17.

Prus, R., & Irini, S. (1980) *Hookers, rounders and desk clerks.* Toronto: Gage.

Reckless, W. (1933). *Vice in Chicago.* Chicago: University of Chicago Press.

Riddington J., & Findlay, B. (1981). Pornography and prostitution.

Vancouver: Vancouver Status of Women.

Riddington, J. (1983). Prostitution law: An international comparison. Ottawa: Canadian Advisory Council on the Status of Women.

Rosen, R. (1982). *The lost sisterhood: Prostitution in America, 1900–1918*. Baltimore: Johns Hopkins University Press.

Rotenberg, L. (1974). The wayward worker: Toronto's prostitute at the turn of the century. In J. Acton, P. Goldsmith, & B. Shepherd (Eds.), *Women at work, Ontario 1850–1930* (pp. 33–69). Toronto: Canadian Women's Educational Press.

Rounthwaite, A. (1983). Issues paper: Prostitution. Ottawa: Law Reform Commission of Canada.

Ruffo, A. (1983). Juvenile prostitution. Ottawa: Canadian Advisory Council on the Status of Women.

Russell, J.S. (1982). The offence of keeping a common bawdy house, in Canadian criminal law. *Ottawa Law Review, 14*, 270–313.

Salamon, A. (1984). *Kept women: Mistresses in the '80s*. London: Orbis.

Sansfaçon, D. (1984a). *Pornography and prostitution in the United States*. Working Papers on Pornography and Prostitution, Report No. 2. Ottawa: Department of Justice.

Sansfaçon, D. (1984b). *Agreements and conventions of the United Nations with respect to pornography and prostitution*. Working Papers on Pornography and Prostitution, Report No. 3. Ottawa: Department of Justice.

Sansfaçon, D. (1985). *Prostitution in Canada: A research review report*. Ottawa: Department of Justice.

Special Committee on Pornography and Prostitution. (1985). *Pornography and prostitution in Canada*. Ottawa: Department of Supply & Services.

Shaver, F. (1985). Prostitution: A critical analysis of three policy approaches. *Canadian Public Policy, 11*(3), 493–503.

St. James, M. (1987). The reclamation of whores. In L. Bell (Ed.), *Good girls/bad girls: Sex trade workers and feminists face to face* (pp. 811–87). Toronto: Women's Press.

Sullivan, T. (1986). The politics of juvenile prostitution. In J. Lowman, M.A. Jackson, T.S. Palys, & S. Gavigan (Eds.), *Regulating sex: An anthology of commentaries on the Badgley and Fraser committees* (pp. 177–91). Burnaby, BC: School of Criminology, Simon Fraser University.

Swan, J., & Richardson. (1986). *A century of service: The Vancouver police 1886–1896*. Vancouver: Vancouver Police Historical Society and Centennial Museum.

Valverde, M. (1987). Too much heat, not enough light. In L. Bell (Ed.), *Good girls/bad girls: Sex trade workers and feminists face to face* (pp. 27–32). Toronto: Women's Press.

Vancouver Sun (1939, February 14). Three-point campaign launched against vice, p.10.

Visano, L. (1987) *This idle trade: The occupational patterns of male prostitution*. Concord, ON: Vita Sana Books.

Walkowitz, J. (1980). *Prostitution in Victorian society: Women, class and the state*. Cambridge: Cambridge University Press.

Weisberg, D.K. (1985). *Children of the night: A study of adolescent prostitution*. Lexington, MA: D.C. Heath.

Wells, D. (1983). *The social history of prostitution in Canada*. Ottawa: Canadian Advisory Council on the Status of Women.

Williams, D.H. (1941). The suppression of commercialized prostitution in the City of Vancouver. *Journal of Social Hygiene, 27*, 364–72.

Winterton, D.L. (1980). The dilemma of our prostitution laws. *Canadian Police Chief, April*, 5–6.

5 Legal and Illegal Drug Use in Canada

For almost 80 years, Canada has been engaged in a policy of selective substance criminalization—first prohibiting opium in 1908, cocaine in 1911, and marijuana in 1923. Over time, other drugs have been added to this schedule of prohibited substances. In 1990, illegal drugs are controlled by two federal statutes, the **Narcotic Control Act** and the **Food and Drug Act**.

Why some drugs are legal and others illegal has never been easy to understand. Tobacco, alcohol, and caffeine are at least as dangerous in terms of individual and collective health as are proscribed substances and yet they are legitimate commodities in the marketplace.

The waters of drug-control policy are further muddied by the involvement of medical and pharmaceutical professionals in determining the nature of the problem, that is, in defining acceptable "medical" drug use. Police, physicians, and pharmacists form a network of control that acts against the use of certain drugs within specific social contexts and for specific purposes. There are a great many drugs available only by prescription. Opiates and their analogues are legitimately used if permitted by a doctor, but criminalized if purchased through other avenues. The law allows the ingestion of opiates for the purpose of relieving intense physical pain, but not for the purpose of providing pleasure for the user. The label of **deviance** created by criminal definition has moral premises that are generally not acknowledged, much less discussed, within our legal and political discourse. This chapter will give an overview of the social and legal issues relevant to the dynamic of drug use and social control within the context of Canadian society.

What Is a Drug?

Our understanding of the word "drug" has been shaped by popular culture. Although alcohol is, in pharmacological terms, a drug, we seldom think of it as such. The media often speak of "alcohol and drugs," setting out a separate category of consciousness alteration for the drinking of fermented fruits and grains and distilled spirits. This method of categorizing represents an ideological rather than a pharmacological position. Those who distribute alcohol and tobacco are contributing, corporate citizens; those who distribute marijuana and other prohibited drugs are, in legal terms, "traffickers" in "narcotics."

An adequate definition of the term "drug" must stress the ability of the substance in question to alter consciousness, even in the instance of relatively small doses. Alcohol, marijuana, tobacco, cocaine, caffeine, opiates, and amphetamines are understandably enough, then, drugs. Substances like sugar and salt are, however, more difficult to categorize. Both, used to any excess, can affect mood and behaviour, and the use of sugar in itself helps, ultimately, to define the physical structure of the human being. We could relabel drugs "poisons," and the classification would be apt enough. But what we see in Canada and elsewhere is the constantly recurring phenomenon of chemical alteration of consciousness. We could label drugs as important "foods" for psychic life, but this would be equally problematic. Drugs, legal and illegal, can bring both pleasure and pain to their users; the experience of use is structured by the pharmacology of the substance, the mental set that one brings to use, the motivations that underlie consumption, and the social setting in which the drug is taken (Weil & Rosen, 1983).

Closely linked to the phenomenon of use are the concepts of physical and psychological dependence. Both legal and illegal drugs vary in terms of their potential for creating physical dependence. Tobacco and heroin seem to pose the most substantial risks for users. Heroin is a very concentrated form of opium, and nicotine makes even more perpetual demands on the body than heroin. Heroin users typically report more difficulty in giving up tobacco than in giving up heroin (Weil & Rosen, 1983; Brecher et al., 1972). At the other end of the continuum of physical dependence, we find inhalants and hallucinogens.

Psychological dependence can occur with any drug, regardless of its specific pharmacological category (Alexander & Hadaway, 1981). The line between psychological and physical dependence is not easily drawn. According to Russell (1971), it is becoming increasingly clear that the usual distinction between physical and psychological dependence is a fine one and that strong dependence may occur in the absence of classical withdrawal symptoms. Psy-

chological processes are mediated by physiological events.

Alexander and Hadaway (1982) have argued that drug dependence and drug addiction are "adaptive" coping strategies that individuals employ in responding to non–drug-related problems. They suggest that stubborn dependence and overwhelming addiction do not develop from exposure to a given drug, but as consequences of a need to develop a coping strategy for the perceived "problems" of social life. This "adaptive orientation" finds no inherent evil in particular drugs, but asks questions about the social and psychological dynamic that propels individuals into dependence and addiction. Alexander and Hadaway see addiction—an overwhelming commitment to a drug as a lifestyle—as a source of individual and collective difficulty. They do not, however, view drug dependence as inherently problematic. Dependence on a given drug is a concern only when it interferes with one's ability to cope with social or physical life.

It is possible to marshal impressive empirical evidence in support of an adaptive understanding of drug dependence and addiction. For example, a significant percentage of American soldiers in Vietnam used heroin while involved in the war effort; but the vast majority discontinued use when they returned home (Alexander & Hadaway, 1981; Brecher et al., 1971). When the soldiers were surrounded by friends and families, and not threatened with death as a matter of daily routine, resort to the pain-killing potential of opiates was much less likely. An experiment with rats (Alexander et al., 1981, pp. 572–776) also found that rodents will self-administer significantly less morphine if placed in a less stressful environment. Rats in cages self-administer morphine to a much greater extent than rats enclosed in a less-confining "Rat Park." There are problems here in generalizing from rats to humans, but the findings are, nonetheless, supportive of an adaptive understanding of drug use. In the language of popular culture, "Drugs don't take people, people take drugs."

One further complication in understanding drug use is introduced when one considers the form in which a drug is taken and its method of ingestion. In the same way that beer presents risks quite different from those of "hard liquor," dilute preparations of a drug carry smaller risks of dependence. At the same time, the way in which a drug is ingested appears crucial. The coca leaf presents quite different risks from freebased cocaine. A drug that is smoked, sniffed, or injected intravenously carries greater risks of dependence than would be expected if the same drug were taken orally (Weil & Rosen, 1983). Legal and illegal drugs cannot be neatly classified, then, in terms of their potential for inflicting individual and social harm. Weil has suggested that the world does not present us with good or bad drugs, but rather with the potential of good or bad rela-

osen, 1985).
s for describ-
:onclude that
ultural terms.
considerable
e general term
ıble extent, a
ɔrical settings.
, the pharma-
ral majority,"
that "drugs"
ities, but they
ite distinctive
al realities.
that the term
ion. Particular
ıch other with
chological and
s. If we fail to
about "drugs"
differences. In
between types
l argue for six
l contraction):
nts, marijuana,

dians are most
:ur in most in-
: day. If coffee
ɪptoms will ap-
l an experiment
no caffeine in
or 300 mg of
ɔrewed coffee);
ɪ in coffee taste.
of their results:

ess alert, less
ıore irritable
when they
d to feel that
ınd they felt
ɪaky as the
when their
vever, these
lly relieved.

ike caffeine and
central nervous
of illegal drugs,

a single illicit gram selling for between $100 and $200. In a single evening, two adults could easily sniff this quantity as a recreational activity. The white powder is typically chopped into fine particles with a razor blade, formed into lines, and sniffed through a paper cylinder, from a glass surface. Paper currency apparently serves as the most popular of cylinders. Cocaine is a refined extract of the coca plant, and "crack" is its most potent form, to date. In many mountainous areas of South America, the coca leaf is chewed to ward off fatigue and is appreciated for its mildly stimulating psychoactive properties. When sniffed in refined form or "freebased," or injected, it is a less stable substance; these forms of coca have attracted a great deal of attention within the past decade and most particularly, within the late 1980s. The socially and physically disastrous consequences of cocaine abuse have been detailed. While most human beings can use cocaine without serious incident, a significant minority become compulsive and self-destructive. Weight loss, anxious paranoia, irritations of the nasal passages, and a discomforting edginess are the most apparent behaviour manifestations of such abuse (Weil & Rosen, 1983).

Amphetamines are synthetic stimulants, first developed in Europe during the 1930s. They are very similar to cocaine in terms of their effects, but are much longer-lasting and more toxic (Weil & Rosen, 1983; Brecher et al., 1972) and hence less attractive. While cocaine's effects normally wear off after about 30 minutes, an amphetamine experience can last for over four hours. Recurrent intravenous injection of amphetamines is a dangerous activity. The "speed freaks" of the late 1960s and early 1970s have now generally disappeared from Canadian and American cities, replaced by a new wave of stimulant abusers, "the coke and crack freaks." The ravages of amphetamine injection were simply overwhelming. As Weil and Rosen (1983) have concluded, the drug subculture itself, realizing the dangers of injecting amphetamines, warned people about it with the phrase "Speed kills."

The legal control of amphetamines in Canada has never been as stringent as the legal control of marijuana, cocaine, or heroin. Amphetamines are "controlled drugs," legitimate items of pharmaceutical commerce. There is no criminal penalty for **possession** of amphetamines, and a maximum term of ten years' imprisonment for those convicted of **trafficking.** In contrast, marijuana, cocaine, and heroin possessors are liable to seven-year terms upon conviction; traffickers in these drugs are liable to maximum sentences of life imprisonment. These disparities are not dictated by an awareness of the inherent dangerousness of the drugs in question; other social forces are at work.

In Japan, amphetamines are the most popular of illegal drugs; about 50 000 offences are detected each year. The offence is amphetamine possession (typically intravenous amphetamine use), and the typical sentence for a first offender is two years' imprisonment (Japan, Ministry of Health & Welfare, 1977). Over 40 percent of all admissions to Japanese jails are for breaches of the Stimulants Control Law. This difference between Japan and Canada illustrates the role of culture in the control of drug abuse. A significant minority of Japanese inject amphetamines in the face of lengthy imprisonment, while few Canadians express interest in a drug that can be legitimately possessed; wars against certain kinds of drug use often appear to produce quite unintended consequences.

Depressants

Alcohol is our most popular depressant. It is a remarkably dangerous drug, and yet it provides pleasurable experiences for most who use it. It is a substance that can create severe and irreversible brain damage and is a major contributing factor in heart disease. The social consequences of alcohol abuse can be disastrous; its effect on health can be seen virtually on any day in any hospital in the country.

We drink alcohol in the form of beers and ciders, wines and spirits. It is distilled alcohol, a relatively recent invention, that is arguably our most troubling form of drink. Weil & Rosen (1983, pp. 61–62) write:

> Brandy was the first distilled liquor made; it was obtained by heating wine and then cooling and condensing vapors in another container. This process increases the alcohol content dramatically: from 12 per cent up to 40 or 50 per cent. The original idea of distillers was to concentrate wine to a smaller volume to make it easier to ship it in barrels overseas. At the end of the voyage the brandy was to be diluted with water back to an alcohol content of 22 per cent. What happened, of course, was that . . . no one waited to add water. Suddenly a new and powerful form of alcohol flooded the world.

Opiates—narcotic painkillers—are the most dreaded of illegal drugs. Heroin is the most potent derivative of opium; it is usually sold as a white powder, converted into liquid form, and then injected. Opiates are remarkably useful drugs for the control of severe pain; they are also powerful depressants. Heroin users will often "nod out"—testimony to the sedative character of the drug. Opiates can also give extreme pleasure to users, a pleasure that is often quickly transformed into a stubborn dependence. The major health problems associated with heroin use are the risk of overdose by uninformed consumers and chronic constipation. In pharmaceutical terms, heroin is a much safer drug than alcohol (Weil & Rosen, 1983; Brecher et al., 1972).

As the most potent painkillers on earth, the opiates oc-

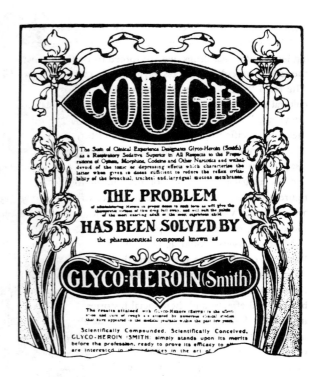

Photo 5.1   Heroin was promoted as a cough suppressant for a few years after its invention. This advertisement appeared in a 1903 medical journal.
Copyright 1903 by the New York Times Company.

cupy a puzzling position in the realm of prohibited drugs. They are prescribed by Canadian doctors; without the approval of the physician, a criminal sanction is attached to possession. Those who seek recreation in relief from pain are the most sought-after of all illegal-drug users. There is a sense in which criminalization of heroin use can be seen as the criminalization of alienation. The heroin user and the heroin trafficker are vilified in popular culture. Former prime minister John Diefenbaker once referred to such drug trafficking as "murder by instalments." Canadian courts have generally suggested that the use and distribution of heroin are to be treated more harshly than other forms of drug use and distribution (MacFarlane, 1979).

Barbiturates, a development of the last century, are also depressants. These are drugs best described, along with sleeping pills, as "downers." They are not very popular as recreational drugs, since they offer a sedative hypnotic effect and little in the way of either euphoria or stimulation. Valium, a tranquillizer with psychoactive properties, is of greater interest, producing a less intense sedative effect. Valium and other "minor" tranquillizers have been aggressively marketed by pharmaceuticals companies and, it has been argued, overprescribed by doctors (Graedon, 1977).

for 9000 Years

eing cultivated
the drug about
ere Greek and

iought to have
it was used as
pean merchants
i, an event that
on and promo-
England.
ine from opium
dle and syringe
phine addiction
of the world.
m in 1906 and
i Act to combat
ie West Coast.
897 and actively

promoted as the latest painkiller—and a replacement for those already addicted to morphine or opium—for several decades before doctors began having doubts about the drug, which was the strongest and most addictive of the opiates.

By 1925, heroin was being tightly restricted by most countries and required a prescription.

Heroin abuse had almost been halted by the end of the Second World War because most of the world's shipping lanes had been so disrupted for so long. Since then, however, illegal use of the drug has mushroomed, partly because Western governments—particularly France and the U.S.—supported regional groups fighting the spread of communism even though they were also involved in trafficking.

Opium dens were declared illegal in Thailand in 1958.

Source: *Vancouver Sun,* May 12, 1989, p. A13.

d diethylamide
38, and found
grams. During
ributed across
The drug has
is, or cocaine.
time and space,
n ten to twelve
arly surprising.
e day after use:
not at all un-

ed as hallucino-
bject of a num-
criminal status
d in the courts,
grounds.[2] The
lucinogen than
so not as long-
the experience
s. While many
ces after initial
tly strong drug

Hallucinogens, also known as psychedelics, have a very low abuse potential, perhaps because, in order to qualify for long-term use, a drug must consistently produce desired psychoactive consequences. Hallucinogens are not consistent in terms of such effects. In addition, individuals who become addicted may develop feelings of increased awareness that are incompatible with the need for escape and withdrawal (McGlothin & Arnold, 1971). Put more simply: an unpredictable drug is unlikely to be a constant companion.

Inhalants

Inhalants and solvents are typically the drugs of the adolescent poor or the powerless. They are generally quite toxic and have a number of potentially unpleasant effects, most particularly nausea and dizziness. In large doses, they can produce hallucinations. Inhalants and solvents are usually taken when other more-desired drugs cannot be obtained.

While it is difficult to speak positively about the sniffing of such substances as gasoline, benzene, and toluene, the dangers of inhaling chemical vapours have been greatly exaggerated. Those who are constantly exposed to such vapours as a condition of their employment would seem to run the greatest risks of physical and mental harm.[3]

There is also a danger that a "get tough" approach to

inhalants and solvents will promote rather than discourage their use. Brecher and Associates (1972, p. 332) write:

> So far as can be determined, gasoline sniffing at the end of the 1960s was neither more nor less popular than at the beginning. The same was true of the sniffing of other readily available organic solvents. Only glue-sniffing was the target of a nationwide campaign (in the United States)—and only glue-sniffing became a popular youth pastime.

Marijuana

Marijuana cannot be easily defined as either a stimulant or a depressant, and it is not really a hallucinogen. It is a substance that, along with hashish, seems to deserve its own category. It is a stimulant in the sense that it increases heart rate, and a depressant in that it ultimately produces a sedative effect. It was first linked to LSD, at least in popular culture, and yet it is not really a hallucinogen or psychedelic. Marijuana's effects are not long-lasting, and, while the drug can alter consciousness substantially, it does not have the force of LSD or its relatives.

As a consequence, marijuana can, for a significant minority of users, become a stubborn source of dependence. Weil & Rosen (1983, p. 119) write:

> In most cases, people begin smoking pot only in special, usually social, situations. At first, because the drug causes such strong effects, they cannot imagine smoking it at other times. With increasing use, however, tolerance develops, and people learn to adapt to being high. Soon they can perform normal activities while under the influence of marijuana. Users may then begin to smoke during the day, perhaps by themselves.

Marijuana is the most popular of illegal drugs; the RCMP estimates that annual retail sales for cannabis exceed $6 billion, in contrast to estimates of about $3 billion for heroin and $2 billion for cocaine (Canada, 1989). The moral legitimacy of marijuana prohibition has been under attack in Canada for almost twenty years. With more than two million users, marijuana sits on the cutting edge between legal and illegal drugs.

The substance is much less toxic than legal drugs such as nicotine or alcohol, but it is not entirely benign. Dependence is a potential problem, and smoking the resinous plant can irritate the respiratory tract and lead to bronchial difficulties. Nonetheless, marijuana's criminal status remains problematic. For more than fifteen years, the majority of young Canadians of high-school age appear to have violated subsection 3(1) of the Narcotic Control Act, mocking the morality of the law (Erickson, 1980). The label

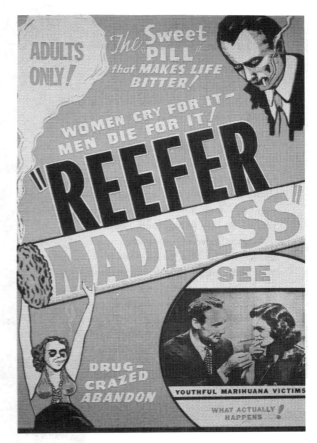

Photo 5.2   The 1936 film *Reefer Madness* warned the youth of America against the dangers of marijuana use: one "puff" could lead to hallucinations, insanity, death.
Copyright © 1982, New Line Cinema Corporation, © 1982, The American Postcard Company Inc.

of deviance is under debate; a substantial community of users undermines, by its very existence, the legitimacy of state authority.

Tobacco

It is very difficult to use tobacco in a responsible manner. Nicotine is a highly addictive drug, and while a few people may be able to limit consumption to one or two cigarettes per day, such behaviour is very much the exception. Lung cancer, emphysema, and coronary-artery disease are inextricably tied to tobacco use. The tobacco industry dispenses the possibility of premature death to its patrons, and most users are not blind to this reality.[4] The smoker celebrates destruction in the sphere of the physical, accelerating the effects of the aging process. Recent empirical research suggests that tobacco use is negatively

educated and
oke (Hadaway

effects of both
ses tobacco for
ng anxiety—as
cost of tobac-
ugh social con-
1610: "Many
t and scattered
ful and beastly
ough his nose,
nking of tobac-
Rosen, 1983).5
more danger-
macy serves to
l dupes" in the

ntrol

rns of drug use
tance criminali-
first occurring
e and manufac-
erchants oper-
coast of British
pers of the day,
nes-Colonist, do
istence of these

th century, the
gun to import
ing of the CPR
ritish Columbia
at members of
re seen as valu-

se and Japanese
on. At first, the
t seen as a sub-
opment was in
vever, the Asiat-
lue and vilified
he century on-
marginal white

907. The Asiatic
Hall in Vancou-
0 000 appeared
n the Far East.

Federal Conservative politicians, sitting in opposition to a Liberal majority in Ottawa, took to the hustings to denounce immigration policies. At the close of the meeting, an angry crowd drifted into the Chinese and Japanese quarters of the city of Vancouver. Chinese and Japanese merchants sustained losses in a hostile night of conflict.

The federal government was developing important relationships with Japan and China and could not ultimately condone such racially directed violence. In fall 1907, the Liberal cabinet dispatched its young deputy minister of labour, Mackenzie King, to Vancouver to settle Japanese claims arising from the riot (initially, Chinese losses were not a concern).[6] In spring 1908, however, King returned to Vancouver to settle Chinese claims for damages.

During the course of his inquiry, King received two claims from opium manufacturers. He was reported to be startled by these businesses and initially called for a licensing of these "Chinese druggists." After receiving a deputation of local Chinese clergymen and affluent Chinese merchants interested in anti-opium legislation, he changed his mind. King told the assembled inquiry on June 3, 1908: "My own opinion is that it should be made impossible to manufacture this drug in any part of the Dominion. We will get some good out of this riot yet" (Boyd, 1984, p. 115). Within two months, Canada, led to the altar by the precocious Mr. King, prohibited the sale and manufacture of smoking-opium.

Substances were first criminalized in Canada as a consequence of a labour crisis. The law would get "some good" out of a racist riot, by criminalizing the drug industry of the race against which the riot was directed. There was no public interest in this legislative initiative. The Chinese opium industry had been in operation for 40 years; the provincial press of that period was not concerned with the practice of opium smoking; provincial and local governments were interested only in taxing the revenues of the businesses involved. Indeed, more opium was sold to whites than to Chinese. Moreover, the white patent-medicine industry continued to dispense opiated tonics, elixirs, and analgesics, without prescription, to Canadians from coast to coast.

Green (1979) has argued that Canadian narcotics law has managed to transform the images of certain drugs. Opium use, once seen as a private indulgence, is now seen as a public evil. At the time of the 1908 enactment, merchants were given six months to sell off their existing stocks, an unthinkable concession in contemporary popular *and* political culture. The line between legal and illegal drug use was not drawn after informed debate about the risks inherent in consciousness-altering substances. Opiated tonics, elixirs, and analgesics were marketed for a decade after the criminalization of smoking-opium. This latter substance was perceived to be categorically separate from alcohol or tobacco, or other opiates, for reasons that seem to flow more from the contradictions of our economic and social history than from informed concerns about public health.

Over the past 70 years, the Canadian public has become very supportive of the criminalization of opiates, cocaine, marijuana, LSD, and a variety of other socially marginal drugs. The temperance movement of the 1920s attempted the prohibition of alcohol, but could not sustain its moral persuasiveness.

A number of important factors have contributed to popular images of drug use. In 1919, the RCMP became the enforcement arm of the Department of Health and began to lobby for greater penalties for those involved with "narcotics," and for increased powers of investigation over potential users and distributors. The force was remarkably successful; whipping was brought into use; longer terms of imprisonment were put in place; legislation also provided for a **"writ of assistance,"** a document giving certain police an extraordinary new power of **search and seizure.** In the pages of *Maclean's,* and in a bold new book, Edmonton juvenile court judge Emily Murphy, known as "Janey Canuck," was trumpeting the virtues of this new ideology. Her book, *The Black Candle* (1922), while amusing or comical by contemporary standards, was compelling to Canadians throughout the 1920s, and beyond. Murphy argued that marijuana could produce insanity, and suggested that cocaine use might lead white women to sleep with black men; her analysis of illegal-drug use is replete with racist insults. She was, in Becker's (1963) terms, a "moral entrepreneur," committed to marketing a political agenda of legal change. Murphy urged severity in the name of decency. And yet, racism was at the core of both Murphy's ideology and police practice. Murphy seemed to fear cultural assimilation at the hands of blacks and Asiatics. She wrote in 1922 (p. 105):

> It behooves the people in Canada and the United States to consider the desirability of these visitors—for they are visitors—and to say whether or not we shall be "at home" to them for the future. A visitor may be polite, patient, persevering . . . but if he carries poisoned lolly-pops in his pocket and feeds them to our children, it might seem wise to put him out. . . .
> In discussing this subject, Major Crehan of British Columbia has pointed out that, whatever their motive, the traffic always comes with the Oriental, and that one would, therefore, be justified in assuming that it was their desire to injure the bright-browed races of the world.

Police practice through the 1920s was similarly focussed on the Chinese user and distributor of illegal drugs. Over 60 percent of all convictions fell upon the Chinese; deportation of drug-trafficking "aliens" was instituted as an adjunct to criminal conviction. In 1923, an amendment to Canada's Immigration Act prohibited any further immigration of Chinese (Canada, 1923).

However, it was not until 1961 that the Canadian government moved with its greatest force against illegal-drug use and distribution. The targets of the criminal **sanction** were no longer the Chinese, but "ordinary" Canadians involved with what were perceived to be death-dealing substances. Fuelled by fears of predatory distributors and convinced of the life-threatening potential of "narcotics" use, the Diefenbaker government, in its new Narcotic Control Act, implemented maximum terms of life imprisonment for traffickers and importers. A proposed amendment to the bill before the House of Commons sought to impose the possibility of **capital punishment** on traffickers and importers. After a lengthy debate, this amendment was defeated.

In the late 1960s—a scant few years after this tough new legislation—a competing interpretion of the morality of illegal-drug use was publicly raised. Middle-class youth flocked to marijuana and to a host of other illegal drugs, calling into question, either implicitly or explicitly, the legitimacy of criminal prohibition.

The Liberal government of Pierre Trudeau, committed to the possibility of a "just society," constructed the Le Dain Commission Inquiry into the Non-medical Use of Drugs. Chaired by law professor Gerald Le Dain, the commission produced critically acclaimed assessments of its subject, bringing out an interim report in 1972, and a final report in 1973. The commission's recommendations, while received with enthusiasm, have never been implemented (see Table 5.1).

However, the government of the day was not entirely silent on the subject of drug control. In 1969, an amendment to the Narcotic Control Act allowed prosecutors to proceed "summarily" in cases of "narcotic" possession; the point of this change in the law seems to have been to indicate that illegal-drug possession was not as serious an offence as had originally been thought.[7] This legislative change, initiated before the completion of the Le Dain Commission reports, was a pragmatic response to increasing numbers of marijuana possessors coming before Canadian criminal courts; the country's jails simply could not accommodate thousands of young marijuana smokers.

In 1972, the federal government introduced absolute and conditional discharges as sentencing options. These new sanctions applied to criminal offences with maximum penalties of less than fourteen years' imprisonment. The discharges allow the accused to tell prospective employers that they have not been convicted of a **criminal offence,**

mmendations for Legal Controls, by Type of Offence and Drug

	Recommended Legal Control						
		Opiates and Cocaine			Strong Hallucinogens (Restricted Drugs)		
	Campbell Minority	Le Dain Majority	Bertrand Minority	Campbell Minority	Le Dain Majority	Bertrand Minority	Campbell Minority
	First offence: A fine of $25. Subsequent offence: a fine of $100.	Maximum penalty: 2 years.	No offence. Confiscation if unjustified possession.	Offence of use for opiates. Move cocaine to FDA.	No imprisonment.	No offence. Confiscation if unjustified possession.	Same as majority.
ld ould l by ıd/or	Same as majority.	No change.	Controlled, legalized sale of opiates to drug-dependent persons.	Same as majority.	No change.	No change.	No change.
illicit ıd ot	Same as majority.	No change.	Same as trafficking.	Same as majority.	No change, except shift of burden of proof.	No change.	No change.
ıd ould d by nd/or	Same as majority.	No change.	Retention and reorganization of criminal penalties.	Same as majority.	No change.	Same as for opiates.	No change.
illicit nd ıot	If not for trafficking, same as simple possession. If for trafficking, same punishment as for trafficking.	No change.		Same as majority.			

ınada. In S. Einstein (Ed.), *The com-*
ew York: Pergamon.

on, and the not-
. The discharges
for the accused,
y the Canadian
charges in about
ssion. While the
ot to change law
l terms, a soften-
ossession of the

nmission and its
ented and helped
e commissioners
l not be cast as a

criminal offence, and, although the Trudeau government would not impose this view, it did commit itself to future reform. Throughout the 1970s, the Liberal government promised future legislative action on cannabis. Finally, in April 1980, the government's Speech from the Throne indicated that a softening of penalties for marijuana use would be set in legislative form. Again, Trudeau and the Liberals of the day did not act on this more formal commitment; both the cabinet, and the Commons itself were apparently divided on the moral validity of such reform. In the late 1980s, cocaine use and abuse have been the subject of much moral hysteria. "Drugs" have re-emerged as a social danger; the **decriminalization** of any illegal drug seems some distance from the Canadian legislative agenda.

Patterns of Drug Use: Aggregate Data

In 1990, the Narcotic Control Act remains very much the same in form as it was in 1961. The kinds of penalties given to both illegal drug users and distributors have changed significantly, however. In 1961, illegal-drug use was a negligible issue, at least in terms of convictions statistics. A small number of offenders was typically imprisoned, if found in possession of cocaine, marijuana, or the opiates. By 1968, however, marijuana convictions were beginning to increase, a fairly direct reflection of increasing rates of use.

The initial response of the Canadian judiciary has been referred to as a "get tough" approach (Erickson, 1980). More than half of all marijuana possessors were jailed, as were virtually all distributors. As the number of Canadians coming before the courts increased, the use of the jail sanction became, as mentioned above, increasingly impractical. There were about 1000 convictions for marijuana possession in 1968, but by the mid-1970s this annual toll had risen to more than 30 000. The imprisonment of more than 30 000 marijuana possessors was neither politically practical nor economically feasible. Noncustodial alternatives emerged as more popular sentencing options: fines, probation, and absolute or conditional discharges.

The users of other illegal drugs benefited indirectly from this change in policy toward marijuana, and from increasing social controversy about the individual and collective dangers contained within "narcotics." As the moral logic of the line between legal and illegal drugs was increasingly assailed in the media and elsewhere, Canadian judges tended to be more reticent in imposing imprisonment on the users of cocaine, LSD, or opiates. Almost 80 percent of heroin possessors were jailed in 1968, but, by the mid-1970s, this figure stood at less than 50 percent, with no apparent increases in heroin use forthcoming. In the past decade, there have been significant decreases in convictions for marijuana possession—drops of about 30 percent per year in 1982 and 1983. These decreases cannot be said to reflect changes in rates of cannabis use within Canada and so point to the likelihood of changes in enforcement strategies by police.[8] It is worth noting, as well, that while the percentage of marijuana users going to jail in the 1980s (about 6 percent of all convicted) is lower than the percentage jailed in the 1960s (over 50 percent), the absolute number of possessors imprisoned has risen substantially over time (from about 500 in 1968 to more than 1500 by the mid-1980s).[9]

Marijuana is a key variable in understanding contemporary patterns of both illegal-drug use and illegal-drug control. Surveys reveal that marijuana is the most popular of illegal drugs in Canada, followed by cocaine and the opiates (Canada, 1984). Less popular but still marketed across the country, are LSD, psilocybin mushrooms, and amphetamines. When we look again to convictions statistics, we find that marijuana is the cornerstone of the drug-control industry, at least in numerical terms. Marijuana convictions (for possession, trafficking, importing, and cultivation) amount to about 25 000 per annum; about 80 percent of these convictions are for possession. In contrast, annual convictions for cocaine offences number about 3000, the opiates about 1000, LSD about 1000, and amphetamines and psilocybin mushrooms much fewer than 1000 each (Canada, 1988).

There are a number of precautions that must be noted in interpreting these statistics. First, as suggested earlier, the numbers generated cannot be said to reflect real rates of use. Survey estimates suggest, in the case of marijuana, that fewer than 1 percent of users are apprehended in any given cross-section of all those in possession. Those who are apprehended are not likely to form a representative cross-section of all those in possession. Those charged are disproportionately younger and poorer, and more likely to be using marijuana in a public setting (Erickson, 1980).

In the instance of cocaine, the opiates, LSD, amphetamines, and psilocybin mushrooms, the discrepancies between real rates of use and convictions statistics are less substantial, at least in absolute terms. Police regard heroin, and more recently, cocaine, as the most dangerous of illegal drugs; the hallucinogens and amphetamines form a kind of middle range of seriousness; and marijuana is seen as the least threatening. Given substantial police interest and energy in a battle against heroin, the opiates remain a politically unpopular choice for those interested in the recreational use of illegal drugs. Convictions statistics for heroin might well more closely reflect real rates of use than do convictions statistics for any other illegal drug.

Even here, however, only a small percentage of all users are caught in the web of the law. The difficulty facing police is one common to all forms of "victimless" crime. Neither party to the transaction—vendor or purchaser—is likely to complain to law enforcers. As a consequence, police must try to infiltrate the underground economy, entering the marketplace as either buyers or sellers, or both. The interested consumer, in turn, must rely on an unregulated market, with a correspondingly unregulated product. As some observers have pointed out, illegal-drug distribution represents the last bastion of a strictly laissez-faire economy in action. In this respect, the drug trade is a not altogether inspiring portrait of free enterprise.

The expansion of illegal drug use that took place in the late 1960s and early 1970s was a social phenomenon with significant prominence. The use of marijuana was, and still is, seen as socially threatening. The line initially drawn between legal and illegal drugs was challenged by the logic of the Le Dain Commission and more directly confronted

oradic dabbling
ther intensified

tantial increases
nt. The erosion
anada's increas-
1950s was fol-
ugh the 1960s.
neration haunt-
lternative reali-
osition, even if

f the "hippies,"
ver of the family
of peace and love
o often became
ity and substance
iopeful idealism.
, always been as-
uana use may cut
nd across a mul-
late 1960s, it was
riant minority, at
rned. It was also
e damaging illegal

of the growth in
)s remains elusive.
new generation?
? The marketing
d West? We must

are generated by
ada. These police
stigation to court-
, charge, province,
l difficulty in the
one of knowing
ics represent real-
l-drug use suggest
ia every year, but
this more directly,
om figures to arrive
Erickson's (1980)
a offender in court
linity, and poverty
marijuana use, but
ition, and sanction)

iat over 90 percent
of 35, and that men
convicted of drug

offences than are women (Canada, 1988). In terms of the variable of provincial jurisdiction, the most significant pattern that emerges is a charge-specific discrepancy; Quebec processes many fewer illegal-drug possession charges per capita than any other province (Canada, 1988).

What our aggregate data tell us, then, is that courtroom statistics represent some kind of melding of a real rate of offence with a control rate, the latter rate reflecting the state's construction of the social importance of a deviant act. Empirical analyses that fail to recognize the parameter of state control in construction of data sets are also inherently flawed. Similarly, however, analyses that fail to recognize the dimensions of deviant behaviour are inherently flawed (Ditton, 1979).

Explaining Illegal Drug Use

Robert Merton's theory of social structure and **anomie** has been quite influential in the sociological study of deviance. In his original formulation, Merton (1938) argued that frustration and thwarted aspiration lead to the search for avenues of escape from a culturally induced intolerable situation. In his discussion of anomie and social structure, Merton was not speaking specifically of illegal-drug use, but of deviance in general. For Merton, deviance could be seen as a normal response to a contradiction in social structure—wealth and prosperity could not be achieved by all members of a developing American society.

According to Merton, anomie is manifested in different adaptive styles: conformity, innovation, ritualism, retreatism, and rebellion. The conformist accepts the goals of the society and endorses the means deemed appropriate by society. There is a sense in which the conformist is unwilling or unable to recognize the contradictions of social structure.

The innovator is an individual who accepts the goals of prosperity and success but not the rules used for the accumulation of such power and prestige. When legitimate avenues appear blocked, the innovator turns to such activities as illegal-drug distribution or prostitution in order to gain a sense of success.

The ritualist is another deviant in Merton's design. The ritualist accepts and lives by the rules of the society, but does not endorse the values of upward mobility and economic dominance. Stephen Pfohl (1985, p. 213) explains:

> Think of the middle-level corporate bureaucrat, government worker, or tenured college professor who really doesn't care about getting further ahead. Such a person may play the game, put in the appropriate time, work the nine-to-five shift. Yet he

or she cares little for advancement, and perhaps desires only to get through the day without making waves and then to go home and get stoned. We all know someone who plays the part without really believing in it.

The realist is a person who neither lives by nor accepts the goals of society. The retreatist is our classic drug abuser, one who has simply retreated from meaningful membership in the social order. Merton labelled the adaptive activities of psychotics, artists, pariahs, outcasts, tramps, chronic drunkards, and drug addicts as representative of retreatism.

Finally, we encounter the rebel, a person who believes in trying to change the dominant values of the society, the "unreasonable man," as George Bernard Shaw called him. The rebel may be a revolutionary in spirit and/or in deed, and may, of course, be male or female. Through the medium of rebellion, some individuals directly address the contradictions of contemporary social structure.

The notion of anomie, or social strain, can be quite helpful in understanding deviant drug use and distribution. The "trafficker" is typically an innovator, working for the cultural values of wealth and prosperity through illegitimate means. The illegal-drug distributor may also be a rebel, seeking to change the prohibitive strategy of substance criminalization by direct defiance. The illegal-drug user may be a ritualist, a retreatist, or a rebel. There is even a sense in which some illegal-drug users can be seen as conformists, supporting both the goals of the dominant society and the means used to achieve those goals. The marijuana user, particularly, may not consider his or her consumption to be deviant in light of the current size of this drug's market.

The anomie perspective is not without its limitations. Merton wrote of social structure with little emphasis on its internal conflicts and little commentary concerning the conflicting nature of human values. In this sense, Merton's analysis is only skeletal, sketching out individuals at odds with dominant culture. Further, while Merton was aware of the structured inequality of social life, he did not turn his energies toward explaining the origins and consequences of political, economic, and social contradictions. "The culturally induced intolerable situation" is not fully explained.

For the learning theorist, the matter of explaining illegal-drug use hinges on positive associations with deviance, such illegal conduct possessing social-psychological roots. Illegal drug use is learned; the individual is reinforced in some important respect; breaking the **criminal law** is seen as more positive than negative. Edwin Sutherland's **"differential association"** theory is perhaps the best known of the social-learning analyses of deviance. Sutherland argued that deviance becomes probable when social forces for deviance exceed social forces for conformity; deviance is accordingly reinforced, at least in a subjective sense.

There is a common-sense truth to **learning theory.** One has to learn to enjoy the experience of drug use itself. Beer is seldom enjoyed on first taste; one learns to associate its bitterness with other physical sensations and comes to enjoy the drink. An individual, in using an illegal drug, also must come to see usage (lawbreaking) as more positive than abstinence (conformity). Andrew Weil (1972) has argued that mental set and social setting are important variables in learning how to use drugs, legal and illegal. The expectations that one has of drugs will often help to shape one's reaction to them, and the social context of use will similarly shape interpretation. The positive "high" of drug use is not released by the trigger of chemistry as much as by the trigger of a positive mental set, influenced by a supportive social setting. It is not surprising, then, that people who drink all day long, or smoke marijuana all day long, do not get the "highs" reached by people who use these drugs in more restricted social circumstances.

The principal limitation of learning theory is that it gives little attention to lawmakers, generally focussing on the psychology of lawbreakers instead. The social origins of law are generally neglected; the lens for the study of criminal justice focusses on those who break laws, not on those who have created the legal form. The study of deviant drug use will always be incomplete if it fails to turn its attention to the moral logic of social control—to the study of law's creation.

In attempting to explain illegal-drug use, we might look, then, to an understanding of law as a power relation, endlessly negotiated in public and private life. The consumption of criminally proscribed substances can be explained by Mertonian anomie, it can be socially learned, or even described as a **labelling** phenomenon. But the phenomenon of deviant drug use is, ultimately, a reflection of the political economy of power relations, the law successfully marketed as a thoughtful response to a century-old problem of drug use and abuse. As Pfohl (1985, p. 383) has concluded:

A long and darkly shrouded history of hierarchical power arrangements has given shape to what we today commonsensically consider normal and what we control against as deviant. By demythologizing and thereby destructuring the oppressive bondage of this common sense, we are able to partially recover our freedom of thought and action.

both medical and
alcohol, tobacco,
eationally; am-
izers may be used
e case of steroids,
ment. Anabolic
tic abilities, their

of legal-drug use
ich a drug's con-
he outset of this
legitimately used
e used to provide
criminal.
issue of appropri-
on pad is a tool of
rug use, and deny-
ed that his or her
oful to the patient.
ically controls the
dical drug use, the
illegal possession.
or dispensing legal
ans. Both pharma-
with pharmaceu-
a wide variety of
ood and behaviour
iticals are, in many
in recourse to ille-
nil promises eleva-
d young housewife
rtisement extolling
ne a similar adver-
ffing cocaine, the
similar kinds of

ological properties
social construction
e seem most con-
out drug-taking that
eatment. When we
g (alcohol, tobacco,
sion that these sub-
character than phar-
ave a fundamentally
. We typically label
e from the category
notwithstanding.

Containing Drug Abuse: Theory and Practice

Police officers cannot respond to illegal-drug use in the way that they can respond to murder, theft, or rape. There are seldom victims to react to here; if it is to be successful, policing must be proactive. The drug-squad member will have to intervene in the underground economy and pay informants to provide information about illegal-drug distributors. Police may offer cash and the promise of non-prosecution to "small time" dealers or users in exchange for courtroom testimony. More frequently, arrests will be a simpler matter. Police will purchase drugs in bars and shopping malls from "street vendors." And, in the case of marijuana, particularly, police may simply react to possession with which they come into contact—individuals smoking in a public setting or possession detected in the course of routine investigation.

The structure of illegal-drug distribution is very similar to that of other forms of commodity distribution. The capital that one has at one's disposal will determine one's level of entry into the market economy. While many distributors are interested only in selling enough to finance personal use, there are others who look to substantial capital gains on investments of $100 000 or more.

To accommodate the distribution of heroin and cocaine, there must be importers willing to risk a substantial prison term for bringing the drugs into the country; neither the opium poppy nor the coca plant can be grown domestically. Marijuana can be grown within Canada, but it is also imported extensively from Mexico, the United States, Jamaica, Thailand, and elsewhere. LSD and amphetamines can be produced in Canadian laboratories; psilocybin mushrooms are also native to Canada. The networks of illegal-drug distribution are structured, then, by climate, geography, and the drug-control practices that operate within particular nation states.

Peter Manning's *The Narc's Game* is an empirical ethnography of drug policing in the United States. Manning (1980, p. 253) writes:

> Policing is a marginal activity with a limited impact on drug markets. It is, on the one hand, a game that occupies some police officers who by and large enjoy the challenge, and on the other hand, from a social point of view, a ceremony that celebrates what the powerful segments of the society consider appropriate levels and kinds of drug use, proper styles of life and occupations, the correct place to live and moral commitment.

Manning found that he came to like many of the narcotics officers with whom he dealt, while becoming increasingly pessimistic about the social value of their work. He argues that there is no inconsistency here, since one can easily adopt the view that the persons one studies are appealing and understandable, while the organizational mandate itself is questionable. Manning's conclusion of his involvement as a participant-observer in drug policing is one that stresses the unintended consequences of present policy. He writes (1980, p. 257):

> The drug laws and drug law enforcement have a number of consequences, most of which are negative and therefore unanticipated by the architects of these laws.... The major drug problems of this country are the excessive use of over-the-counter drugs, tranquilizers, and antibiotics ... and the everyday demons of tobacco and liquor.... We have not seen through the smoke screen of concern about recreational drugs and have not dealt with the problem of controlling the powerful, addictive and destructive, massively ingested everyday drugs.

The United Nations' Division of Narcotic Drugs in Vienna is headquarters for an international attack on illegal substances. The division has a supply-reduction section and a demand-reduction section; these two sections are designed to complement each other. The member states seek to reduce supply through the power of criminal prohibition and to reduce demand through the marketing of diverse educational strategies.

There is a sense, however, in which the power of the criminal law undercuts the strategy of drug education; we lose sight of any real meaning for the term "drugs"; we imprison some substance abusers and tolerate others. A supply-restriction strategy for illegal drugs is ultimately premised on the failure of a demand-restriction strategy, the logic of friendly persuasion yielding to the logic of prohibition.

Nevertheless, the availability of a given drug is a variable of significance. The price of tobacco ensures that it can be used and abused by virtually all members of Canadian society. The price of heroin and its status in criminal law help to ensure that few Canadians will pursue a heroin career. There seems little doubt that supply-restriction strategies can reduce access to certain drugs; the benefits of such approaches must, however, be placed alongside the social and economic costs of control. The unregulated violence of the illicit market is a direct consequence of an arbitrary criminalization of certain psychoactive substances.

Over the past decade, heroin dependents have occasionally turned away from the black market and sought solace in Canada's pharmacies. Again, we face the dual character of the drug, both painkiller and pleasure-giver. A tablet of Dilaudid, a synthetic opiate, will cost a legal user (some-

one with a legitimate prescription) only pennies, but the illicit street price sits at about $50. The opiates and, occasionally, barbituates and amphetamines, are diverted from the pharmacy, becoming valuable commodities within an underground economy. This criminal diversion of licit pharmaceuticals has become a multimillion-dollar business (Stamler, 1984).

There are essentially four kinds of pharmacy crime: prescription forgery, **theft, break-and-enter,** and **robbery.** Increasing awareness of a diversion of licit pharmaceuticals to the illicit market has led some provinces, and the federal government, to embark on policies of pharmacy security. In British Columbia, since 1978, there has been increased vigilance over the possibility of forged prescriptions and improved physical-plant security—the storing of opiates in locked drawers and safes. In the face of this extended security, the province has seen a doubling and then quadrupling of annual robberies of pharmacies (Canada, 1983). Desperate opiate dependents, increasingly unable to forge a prescription, steal, or break-and-enter, have used violence or the threat of violence to obtain desired drugs. Across Canada, in the period 1979–83, the incidence of thefts and break-and-enters against pharmacies increased from 101 to 741 per annum, while that of armed robberies escalated from 74 to 206. There are significant fluctuations among and within provinces, but the general trend is very clear. In the face of increased pharmacy security, we see more violence against Canada's pharmacists. A tightening of physical-plant security and more careful monitoring of prescription forgery appeared to have the consequence of increasing the potential for confrontation between the illegal-drug user and pharmacist.

In certain parts of the United States, pharmacists are taught how to use firearms to ensure that another citizen does not gain access to desired drugs. The assistant director of Canada's Bureau of Dangerous Drugs has noted of this effort that "one objective is to help some pharmacists over the psychological hurdle of actually using firearms and another is to prepare them to deal with the psychology of actually killing a human, should this happen in the event of a robbery" (Wilson, 1984, p. 157).

The premises underlying the logic of this morality seem clear enough: we must stop access to certain drugs, raising the stakes of confrontation to the possible loss of life itself. We are not involved in attempts to persuade and assist opiate dependents to become drug free; we are, rather, in the midst of a war against such potent painkillers; the users of these drugs, if not given legitimacy by a doctor's prescription pad, are to be regarded as our enemies.

The metaphor of war is also to be found within Canadian courts, although here there seems to be some doubt about the social utility of a strategy of increased confron-

ssion, trafficking,
ntially diminished
individuals found
about 30 percent
rlane (1979, pp.
um term for im-
987 declaration of
ment:

ll happy about
scribed for im-
ses coming be-
7, an incredible
ive courts pur-
num sentence,
ing seven years.
um" sentences
ppeal (as would
95 per cent of
bis . . . received
aw.

of the seven-year
as that cannabis or
s deserving of less
some twenty years
ral residue of some
tinues to exert con-
o Supreme Court
accused to twenty
uana, stating, "Drug
affickers profit from
Drug traffickers live
and are thus social
s a pernicious crimi-
ile such rhetoric is
both the effects of
distribution, it does
ibed above by Peter
what the powerful
riate levels and kinds
ccupations, the cor-
ment."

n. For thousands of
experience of cons-
riety of psychoactive
texts, different drugs
fore, have been pro-
of choice—caffeine,

tobacco, and alcohol—have been subject to such controls.

The term "deviant drug use" applies to any possession of illegal drugs and to certain restricted forms of use of legal drugs. The stumbling drunk, for example, can be seen as deviant in Canadian social life; but this designation of deviance is necessarily context-specific—adolescent experimentation with the limits of alcohol consumption can be viewed as an almost normal activity. In Japan, drunken businessmen can be seen with their briefcases, staggering good-naturedly through the night—the label of deviance does not seem to be applied. With legal drugs, then, the line between responsible and irresponsible use is difficult to draw. With illegal drugs, all forms of use are typically considered irresponsible.

The social distribution of illegal-drug use varies by drug and is still very much an open question, some limited survey research notwithstanding. Thio (1983) provides a summary of the findings of several surveys of self-reported illegal-drug use. He concludes that users, when compared to nonusers, are more likely to be male, to be young, and to have parents who use legal drugs such as alcohol, tobacco, or prescription drugs. Moreover, he suggests that, among those who have gone to college, illegal-drug users are more likely to major in social sciences and humanities rather than in the natural sciences. They are more likely to favour liberal politics, to be estranged from religion, and to have a generally permissive and unconventional outlook.

However, dissimilarities in drugs are likely to be reflected in dissimilarities in the patterns and distribution of use. Marijuana, the most popular of illegal substances, probably has a market fundamentally different from that of heroin, amphetamines, and the like. Goode (1984, p. 88) argues that self-report studies support the conclusion that marijuana use is very highly correlated with age (younger persons being more likely to use marijuana) nontraditionality, and "risk-taking." The size of the marijuana-using population is much greater than that of any other group of illegal-drug users, and survey data do indicate widespread use across all socio-economic levels and occupations.

The social distribution of other illegal drugs is more difficult to document, but correlates of usage have been identified in these cases as well. Thio (1983) concludes that, when compared to the users of other illegal drugs, heroin users tend to come from the most socially and economically disadvantaged classes and they tend, on average, to be somewhat older than the consumers of other illicit substances.

While police and courtroom statistics suggest that most illegal-drug users are young, male, and poor, the actual social distribution is unlikely to paint so bleak a picture. The affluent drug user is unlikely to be the subject of surveillance by police (or by social scientists), given his or her secure access to private space in which to use drugs and a measure of social respectability.

The social changes of the late 1960s had the effect of introducing an alternative understanding of drug use to popular culture within North America and to popular culture within most of the industrialized West. Deviant drug use, particularly in the form of marijuana consumption, was dispersed through all levels of society and, in many quarters, rendered socially legitimate.

At the same time, the criminal law itself remains a tool of social organization (albeit a somewhat malleable one), organizing conceptions about "deviant" drug use and lending legitimacy to certain commodities, principally tobacco, caffeine, and alcohol, as acceptable means for the chemical alteration of consciousness.

We live in a society that uses a wide variety of labels to designate disreputable drug use. "Drunk," "doper," "drug fiend," "addict," and "wino," are obvious examples. What remains uncertain, however, is the effect flowing from the application of such labels to those involved in devalued patterns of substance consumption.

The social construction of deviant drug use continues.

In popular culture, we hear that drugs are for people who can't face reality, the meaning of the word "drug" once again failing to encompass alcohol, tobacco, caffeine, and the like.

Our current policies for the management of illegal drugs ignore the very substantial health dangers of such legal drugs as alcohol and tobacco, psychoactive substances that can be empirically correlated, in a significant way, with premature death. This bizarre inversion of public-health priorities and the consequent hysteria over only certain forms of consciousness alteration suggest that we need to reconstruct our social strategies for reducing drug abuse.

The American comedienne Lily Tomlin has suggested that reality is just a crutch for people who can't deal with drugs, inverting the common-sense wisdom set out above. Perhaps there is more to this hyperbole than we want to admit, at least in the context of current drug-control policy. Our fears of strangely altered states of consciousness and of stubborn dependence have been translated into the hostility of the criminal law, pushing us into battle against substances and contradictions that we simply will not trust ourselves to tolerate.

Discussion Questions

1. On what basis has it been determined how a drug is to be labelled an illegal as opposed to a legal drug?

2. What social/political strategies are most likely to have an impact on the abuse of legal and illegal drugs? Discuss.

3. Is it public-health concerns or an unarticulated "morality" that lies behind the "war on drugs"? If it is, indeed, public-health concerns, why have we, as a society, not criminalized cigarette smoking?

Notes

This chapter is adapted from Neil Boyd "Legal and Illegal Drug Use" in V. Sacco (1988) *Deviance*. Scarborough, ON: Prentice-Hall.

1. This is not to say that all drugs are equally dangerous, or equally likely to lead to addiction or dependence. The point here is that evils do not lie in drugs, but in the uses to which they are put.

2. In British Columbia, the legal battle over psilocybin mushrooms has been typically phrased as a problem relevant to legal prohibitions against trespass. The owners of large tracts of land have complained about mushroom pickers combing their fields. This kind of conflict led B.C.'s former attorney general, Allan Williams, to argue that it is the dangers of mushroom consumption and not the problems of trespass that we need to be most concerned with.

3. For a good discussion of the relative nature of the criminal

d Rowland (1979).
eal an awareness on
th consequences of
ɔsen (1983).

ster Wilfrid Laurier,
rence for resolving
ɔuched. "It looks as
gued (cited in Boyd,

accompanies fewer

serious offences than does procedure by indictment. The maximum
penalty for possession of a narcotic, given summary procedure, is one
years' imprisonment; for possession of a narcotic, given procedure by
indictment, the maximum penalty is seven years' imprisonment.

8. At the time of writing, the most recent statistics available from
the Bureau of Dangerous Drugs were *Drug Users and Convictions Statistics*
(Ottawa: Department of National Health and Welfare, 1988).

9. Rod Stamler, chief of the RCMP Drugs Branch, has indicated
that police resources in the 1980s have been oriented more to the
apprehension of marijuana distributors, than to the apprehension of
marijuana possessors (Personal communication, 1985).

es of opiate addiction:
II (Winter), 77–91.
:e addiction: The case
Review, 94, 94–106.
'.F. & Coambs, R.B.
ony housing on oral
logy, Biochemistry and

ociology of deviance.

:otics legislation: The
ɔntext. *Dalhousie Law*

) (1972). *Licit and illicit*

stics: Narcotic, controlled
)epartment of National

ence estimate, 1983.
Canada.

llan.

ɔ: Addiction Research

jury and killing in the
rnal, 17, 507–94.

orter is given 20 years,

c effects of caffeine in
erence associated with
y and Therapeutics, 10,

Englewood Cliffs, NJ:

w York: Avon.
aarcotics control: The
ilty of Law Review, 37,

n, mobility and tobacco
).
: Pharmaceutical Affairs

MacFarlane, B. (1979). *Drug offences in Canada,* Agincourt, ON:
Toronto Law Book.

McGlothin, W.H., & Arnold, D.O. (1971). LSD revisited–a ten year
follow-up of medical LSD use. *Archives of General Psychiatry, 24,*
35–49.

Manning, P. (1980). *The narc's game: Organizational and informational
limits on drug enforcement.* Cambridge, MA: MIT Press.

Merton, R. (1938). Social structure and anomie. *American Sociological
Review, 3* (Oct.), 672–82.

Murphy, E. (1922). *The black candle.* Toronto: Thomas Allen.

Pfohl, S. (1985). *Images of deviance and social control.* New York:
McGraw-Hill.

Robins, L.N. (1975). Alcoholism and labeling theory. In W. R. Gove
(Ed.), *The labeling of deviance* (pp. 21–33). New York: Wiley-
Halstead-Sage.

Russell, M. (1971). Cigarette smoking: Natural history of a dependence
disorder. *British Journal of Medical Psychology, 44* (1), 1–16.

Stamler, R.T. (1984). Enforcement: The Canadian experience. In *The
Canadian symposium on drug diversion.* Ottawa: Department of
National Health & Welfare.

Sutherland, E. (1949). *White collar crime.* New York: Dryden.

Thio, A. (1983). *Deviant behavior* (2nd ed.). Boston: Houghton Mifflin.

Weil, A. (1972). *The natural mind.* Boston: Houghton Mifflin.

Weil, A, & Rosen, W. (1983). *Chocolate to morphine: Understanding
mind active drugs.* Boston: Houghton Mifflin.

Wilson, E.V. (1984). The international response to drug diversion.
In *The Canadian Symposium on Drug Diversion.* Ottawa:
Department of National Health & Welfare.

6 Gambling in Canada

In 1969, an amendment to the **Criminal Code** of Canada opened the way for a significant change in both the type and extent of **gambling** legally permitted in Canada. The most visible example of this change is evident in the growth of lotteries. Before the amendment took effect, legal lotteries were nonexistent. Today, twenty years later, every province and territory in Canada conducts lotteries (in 1984–85, sales were over $1.6 billion) (Beare, Jamieson, & Gilmore, 1988, p. 339).

In Canada, prior to 1970 (when the amendment took effect), the only forms of gambling not formally prohibited by law were: (1) pari-mutuel betting at horse-racing tracks; (2) occasional bingos and raffles for the purpose of charity fundraising; (3) carnival-type games of chance and mixed skill and chance, conducted at annual fairs and exhibitions; and (4) private betting between individuals or within relatively small groups, such as wagers on the outcome of events like the Grey Cup, in private poker games, or in office pools.

Legal lotteries, however, are but one of several forms of legal gambling that have proliferated across Canada since the 1969 amendment. Other forms include large-scale bingos, pull-tab or break-open tickets,[1] raffles, and casinos. Very conservative estimates of the gross revenues indicate that bingos, pull-tabs, raffles, and casinos annually generate approximately $810 million, $305 million, $182 million, and $224 million, respectively.[2] Pari-mutuel betting at horse races, legal in Canada since 1910, annually entails total betting of approximately $1.6 billion (Agriculture Canada, 1986, p. 8).

After providing a working definition of gambling, the history of legal gambling in Canada from 1886 to the present will be traced.[3] Before proceeding, it will be helpful to outline more clearly just what is meant by the term "gambling." Devereaux (1968, p. 53) has defined gambling as "an activity in which the parties involved . . . voluntarily engage to make the transfer of money or something else of value among themselves contingent upon the outcome of some future and uncertain event." This definition contains three elements necessary for an activity to be regarded as gambling: consideration, risk, and prize. *Consideration* is the money or something of value that a participant stands to forfeit in the case of an unsuccessful outcome. *Risk* (or chance) is the element of contingency or uncertainty of outcome. *Prize* is what is awarded or transferred to a participant in the successful outcome of the uncertain event.

Gambling is not to be confused with **gaming**; not all gaming entails gambling. Many recreational games, such as checkers, chess, or backgammon, for example, do not necessarily involve all three of the elements described above. That is, while games may involve chance (or a combination of skill and chance), it is not always the case that consideration (i.e., money or something of value) or prizes are involved. Thus, more precisely, "'gaming' describes the playing of games . . . ; 'gambling' describes the act of wagering on their outcome" (Miers, 1989, np).

A Brief History of Gambling in Canada, 1886–1989

While the decriminalization of drug use and prostitution may have significant public support in some quarters, they still remain matters subject to criminal prosecution. The history of gambling, therefore, represents an important case study in the process of decriminalization in Canada.

In 1886, the Parliament of Canada amalgamated existing English statutes regarding lotteries and games of chance into a general statute. When the Criminal Code of Canada was enacted in 1892, the 1886 legislation was simply incorporated. Under the Criminal Code, in a section originally titled "*Offenses against Religion, Morals and Public Convenience*," keeping common gaming-houses, conducting lotteries, cheating at play, and gambling in public conveyances were prohibited. In 1900, the Code was amended to permit small raffles not exceeding $50 to be conducted at religious and charitable bazaars for the purposes of fundraising (Osborne, 1989). Indeed, from the very early history of the colonization of North America, governments, both imperial and colonial, have looked favourably upon gambling activities such as raffles and lotteries as a way of raising much-needed money for "worthwhile" projects deemed to have general community benefit.

In 1910, after a special committee of the House of Commons had heard extensive testimony demonstrating the importance of horse-racing events to the Canadian horse-breeding industry, Parliament amended the Criminal Code to allow for the introduction of pari-mutuel wagering[4] at duly incorporated racetracks. The testimony presented at the committee hearings argued that betting and wagering on the outcome of racing events was important for stimulating public interest and attendance at race meets (Canada, 1909–10). Further, it was testified, wagering contributed significantly to the purses won by winning horses. In turn, the prospects of such prizes fostered growth in the Canadian horse-breeding industry and contributed to an overall improvement in the quality of horses bred. In a period of history when the horse still played a vital role in commercial and military transport, such considerations weighed heavily in the Special Committee's deliberations. For example, Dr. R.G. Rutherford, veterinary director general and livestock commissioner of Canada, testified that, in the Boer War (1899–1902), the British military had used 800 000 horses and that

> we breed in Canada at the present time a very large number of light legged horses, but there are many, a majority of those horses, useless nondescripts, because insufficient care and attention is being devoted to the selection of proper sires for use on the common mares of the country. If we were to use more thoroughbred blood in this country we would have an infinitely better class of light horses for general use. Not only that, we would be doing our share in furnishing our quota of the horses required for military purposes in the event of the *empire* being engaged in war. That, we are not doing at the present time. (Canada, 1909–10, p. 21; emphasis added)

Today, horse racing and pari-mutuel wagering are conducted under the supervision of the federal government (through Agriculture Canada, Race Track Division) in cooperation with provincial governments (which appoint provincial racing commissions). Thus, pari-mutuel wagering on both thoroughbred and standard-bred horse races is regulated by the two levels of government.

In 1922, the scope of the Criminal Code was broadened to prohibit dice games, shell games, punch boards, and the disposal of goods by chance in which contestants paid money or other valuable consideration. In 1927, three-card monte (see Box 6.1) was added to this list of specifically prohibited games.[5] These prohibitions are still to be found in the current Criminal Code.

In 1925, after strong lobbying efforts by representatives from agricultural fairs and exhibitions, the Criminal Code was once again amended to permit games of chance and games of mixed chance and skill at agricultural fairgrounds during annual fairs. By virtue of this amendment, the prairie

nd is commonly
:n, who find their
ailway trains, fair
iree cards, which
n gamblers' slang
:n the thumb and
lm, and the cards
'ork the trick suc-
, to acquire which
: throwing them,
h he holds in his
he invites bets as

d two aces and a
them in his right
and throws them
ie then asks some
:n may have been
: held in his hand,
be the middle of
ble.
or two confeder-
ietimes come for-
the queen so that
ave been through
. This induces the
hen the "spieler"
1 the victims stake
ith his little finger

dexterously flattens out the corner which his accomplice
has bent up and bends up the corner of an entirely different card. When the cards are next thrown, the victims select
the one with the bent corner, and are deeply chagrined
to discover that it is not the one they believed it to be.

Probably, the king of the monte men was a man known
in sporting circles as "Canada Bill." He was recognized
as a general "all-round confidence operator," and so dis-
trustful were those who knew him of appearances which
he put forth that on the occasion of his funeral, as the coffin
was being lowered into the grave, one of his friends offered
to bet $1,000 to $500 that "Bill was not in the box." The
offer found no takers, for the reason, as one of his acquaintances said, "that he had known Bill to squeeze through
tighter holes than that." It was reported some years before
his death that he had offered one of the Trunk Lines of
Railroad a premium of $25,000 per annum to be allowed
to practice confidence games upon its trains without
molestation, a condition of the offer being that he would
not attempt to victimize any class of passengers except
preachers.

It is to the credit of many of the railroads that they have
issued orders forbidding gambling on any part of their
property, also forbidding their employes [sic] to practice
gambling, either on or off duty.

Source: J.P. Quinn (1912), *Gambling and gambling devices*
(pp. 56–57). Montclair, NJ: Patterson Smith (reprint 1969).

id Alberta have
ties on the mid-
Campbell, 1981).
ce James J. Lay-
vas to note,

wo forms of
:tively as "the
tter consisted
ons greater or
htenment, or
iition of those
games of skill,
ies of chance
lise, food, or
ayer entering
1 a money fee

and then had a chance to win a prize other than
money. In later years, these prizes usually consisted
of a stuffed toy or some novelty item. Gambling
games in which the prize was money were, however,
from an early period in Canadian history a standard
"front end" attraction. (Laycraft, 1978 pp. B1–B2)

In brief, since 1925, Canadian agricultural fairs and
exhibitions have been legally permitted to operate a variety
of gambling games. The willingness of the Canadian Parliament to exempt fairs and exhibitions from the general prohibitions pertaining to gambling can be understood by
looking at the contributions such fairs and exhibitions made
to the economic growth of the community. In addition
to providing an annual festivity, agricultural fairs had the
underlying purpose to promote Canadian agricultural
products and to publicize new technologies that would be

of interest and benefit to farmers and ranchers (Jones, 1983). Handicrafts, arts, and culinary-skill competitions served to celebrate life in the rural communities. Such widely publicized fairs and exhibitions, like the world famous Calgary Stampede, by promoting ranching and farming as a rugged but rewarding way of life, served not only to advertise and promote local agriculture products, but to encourage both new business investment and new residents (Campbell, 1984). Thus, exemptions to the prohibitions against gambling were granted to agricultural fairs for the purposes of assisting the economic viability of the fairs and, in turn, contributing to regional economic growth.

The decade of the 1930s and the Depression saw several attempts by various Canadian politicians to introduce lotteries as a method of generating revenues. During this period, Quebec politicians particularly were in favour of the introduction of lotteries to generate revenues to aid hospitals, education, and the unemployed. For example, in 1933, Montreal City Council passed a resolution calling on the province to lobby Ottawa for a national lottery to be used to benefit the unemployed (Osborne, 1989). Of course, the introduction, in 1930, of the Irish Sweepstakes, and their continued success through the 1930s in generat-

ing funds for Irish hospitals, provided a ready model that Canadian advocates sought to emulate. Proponents of a government-run lottery argued that laws against lotteries, like the prohibition of alcohol after World War I, were ineffective and that significant numbers of Canadians were illegally purchasing Irish Sweepstake tickets. Thus, arguments were made not only that continued prohibition was leading to widespread disrespect for the law in general, but that appreciable amounts of Canadian money were leaving Canada to support Irish hospitals. However, such arguments were to be unsuccessful. When the Royal Commission on Lotteries and Betting, in 1932–33, recommended against the introduction of state lotteries in Great Britain, Canadian resolve against lotteries was reaffirmed.

In 1954, a joint committee of the Senate and House of Commons was convened to hold public hearings on the issues of capital punishment, corporal punishment, and lotteries (Canada, 1956). The subject of this inquiry reflected an increasing perception that there was widespread public support for lotteries and bingos and that they were, more often than not, being conducted in violation of existing law: "policing agencies found it difficult to enforce existing laws in the face of adverse public opinion. This caused

Photo 6.1   Exhibition Grounds, Edmonton, *c.* 1939.
Glenbow Archives, no. ND-3-8210(d).

the absence of
Thus, the com-
and inspection
by provincial
and benevolent
draising lotter-
advocated that
n Canada as the
state to facili-

atives of agen-
Exhibitions, the
unicipal exhibi-
etention in the
ing agricultural
le, the manager
of the Canadian

been grant-
al Code with
uptions were
much need-
ecome an es-
n operations.
Exhibitions,
Edmonton,
estly request
agricultural

ived last year
m games of
total for the
nue has con-
on of our ex-
our plants and
expenses as-
ural phases of
any exhibitions
to operate and
ears, might not
la, 1956, Vol.

a series of private
Commons, seek-
f these bills called
ds for hospitals.
cine in 1966 was
Quebec and the
d ardent support-
or financial com-
Fair and the 1976

Olympic Games, were particularly strident in attempting to convince the federal government of the need for legalized lotteries. Hence, in May 1969, the **Criminal Code Amendment Act** was passed into law. This act was to "allow state lotteries at the option of the federal or provincial governments, the broadening of charity gaming along the lines suggested by the Parliamentary Committee in 1954, [and] the continuation of existing exemptions for gaming at agricultural fairs" (Osborne, 1989, p. 57).

As one commentator has noted, this revision to the Criminal Code "represented a radical departure from the existing law" (Osborne, 1989, p. 57) in that it decriminalized significant forms of gambling, but only if such activities were duly authorized. That is, the revision to the Code fundamentally proposed a "licensing model of decriminalization" where an activity is allowed only under state permit (Skolnick & Dombrink, 1978, p. 200, cited in Osborne, 1989, p. 58). In essence, the **criminal law** in respect to gambling was to be replaced by a system of administrative regulation. Thus, as a result of the amendment, by 1976 every province and territory were conducting state-operated lotteries.

In 1985, another amendment to the Criminal Code gave exclusive control of lotteries and other forms of gambling to the provinces. Additionally, the amendment permitted mechanical devices such as slot machines, illegal in Canada since 1924, to be operated and managed by provincial authorities, and it eliminated the long-standing prohibition against gambling on public conveyances. As a result, the province of British Columbia introduced slot-machine gambling on some government-owned and -operated ferries.

The Introduction of Green-Felt Gambling

In 1967, the operation of the week-long Silver Slipper Saloon casino on the Edmonton Exhibition grounds represented a major turning point in Canada's history with legal gambling. This was the first time that casino-style games played on green-felt tables were legally permitted in Canada. A review of newspaper accounts of the day shows that this casino operated four blackjack games, one roulette table, two crown-and-anchor games, and one over-and-under-seven game. The maximum betting limit was fixed at two dollars (*Edmonton Journal*, July 25, 1967, p. 17). A later newspaper account claimed "the Silver Slipper drew more patrons than it could handle. It was a gambler's paradise where roulette wheels, crown and anchor and black jack ran under a full head of steam" (*Edmonton Journal*, July 6, 1968, p. 24).

The progenitor of the Silver Slipper Casino concept was the general manager of the Edmonton Exhibition. Quota-

Box 6.2 Organized Crime and Gambling in Canada

Whenever the issue of legalized gambling arises, the question "What about the involvement of organized crime?" is inevitably posed.

As Rosecrance (1988, p. 88) has argued, the relationship between organized crime and legal and illegal forms of gambling "is shrouded in misconception, mythology, and misinformation." Rosecrance has stated that an "orthodoxy" regarding organized crime's involvement in gambling has been created and maintained by American police agencies. Contained in the orthodoxy is the firm belief that organized crime derives significant revenues from both legal and illegal gambling operations, which are then used to underwrite other criminal activities. From a methodological perspective, what is problematic for researchers is the difficulty of challenging the orthodoxy independently of police sources of data.

Nonetheless, such an orthodoxy is similarly held by Canadian police agencies. In 1974 and 1979, the Coordinated Law Enforcement Unit (CLEU) of the Ministry of the Attorney General in British Columbia prepared public annual reports that drew extensively on American literature on organized crime. Both reports subscribed to the belief that gambling activity contributed significant amounts to organized-crime coffers. The 1974 report, for example, stated that "most authorities consider gambling the bread and butter activity of organized crime. It is alleged to be a multi-billion dollar industry in the United States where it provides huge profits to invest in drugs and legitimate business" (CLEU, 1974, p. 18).

In brief, the concerns of American police agencies about gambling and organized crime are widely shared by Canadian police authorities. Thus, Canadian police authorities have been prominent in voicing concerns about the increase of legalized gambling in the absence of stringent licensing and regulatory controls. As a consequence, Canadian provinces that have been willing to license greater levels of gambling have implemented extensive gambling-control agencies to oversee and monitor legal gambling operations.

tions printed in the *Edmonton Journal* and attributed to the City of Edmonton's chief Crown prosecutor, himself a member of the grandstand committee of the Edmonton Exhibition Association (EEA), lauded "the whole Silver Slipper idea [as] the brainchild of [the] E.E.A. general manager" (*Edmonton Journal*, July 19, 1969, p. 52). *The Albertan*, in an article titled "Casino Fever Runs High," gives indication that Royal American Shows supplied the casino games and gambling equipment (*The Albertan*, July 4, 1969). With the financial success of Edmonton's Silver Slipper, other agricultural fairs in western Canada soon introduced green-felt casino-style games of chance (Campbell, 1981). By the summer of 1970, the communities of Winnipeg, Brandon, Saskatoon, Regina, Moose Jaw, Edmonton, Calgary, and Lethbridge were operating casinos in conjunction with their annual agricultural fairs.

In early 1975, as a result of criminal-intelligence reports gathered by the Royal Canadian Mounted Police,

the biggest investigative task force ever assembled in Western Canada [was formed]. It was a joint project of the R.C.M.P., local police forces, and the department of national revenue. Its target: Royal American Shows, the carny company that played the major fairs. . . . After it was assembled, the task force decided to aim its investigation at the possible crimes of tax evasion, defrauding of exhibition boards, illegal games, cheating at games, customs offences, drug trafficking, corruption of municipal and fair-board officials, and skimming from casinos. (*Edmonton Sun*, January 7, 1980, p. B6)

In July 1975, the task force raided the midway headquarters of Royal American Shows in Edmonton and seized books, documents, records, and ledgers. Western Canadians were shocked to discover that Royal American Shows had long been suspected of such criminal activities. As subsequent events were to reveal, however, the EEA general manager was closely connected with Royal American Shows, the travelling American carnival midway. In 1977, he was charged with, but later acquitted of, accepting cash payments in return for favourable considerations granted to Royal American Shows. When the furor from the investigation quieted, Royal American Shows had fled back to the United States, and its top corporate officials were charged with fraud, corruption, and weapons offences. Following release on $20 000 bail, these officials refused to appear in Canadian courts. In April 1977, as a result of continued public controversy surrounding Royal American Shows, Albert attorney general James Foster ordered a

yal American
. Justice Lay-
n Shows "had
n of all citizens
be any person
ent, the report

ty of Calgary
cash gifts from
that they were
isfied that no
hermore, Lay-
Edmonton or
val company.
vs was ordered
es after plead-
nan, 1983, p.

mbling

to play a major
nadian exhibi-
g has remained
enon.
n Canadian use
ninent Calgary
rney General's
ino licence for
enue for a chil-
ccessful attempt
al Code, which
tions to manage
ncial licence.
haritable casino
ificant develop-
nbling. Specifi-
organizations in
of casino gam-
gh the late 1970s
tions conducted
ganizations as a
projects. Indeed,
obvious trend in
ve come increas-
anderwrite their

charity gambling
mbia, Manitoba,
enced significant
ed charitable or-
ues through casi-

nos and other forms of gambling such as large-scale bingos and raffles. The significant growth of all forms of charity gambling has forced provincial governments to implement extensive licensing and monitoring systems by which such gambling can be adequately regulated.

Gambling Revenues and the State

In Canada, provinces have created Crown corporations[7] to market and manage lottery sales. Indeed, in Canada, provincial Crown corporations have a monopoly on the sale and distribution of lotteries. In British Columbia, for example, the British Columbia Lottery Corporation has exclusive rights to market and distribute lotteries. The prairie provinces of Alberta, Saskatchewan, and Manitoba, as well as the Yukon and Northwest Territories, are voluntarily joined into the Western Canada Lottery Foundation and co-operate in the marketing and management of lotteries within this western region. In Ontario and Quebec, lotteries are conducted by the Ontario Lottery Corporation and Loto Québec, respectively. The provinces of Nova Scotia, Prince Edward Island, New Brunswick, and Newfoundland are joined in the Atlantic Lottery Corporation. These provincial Crown corporations combined form the Interprovincial Lottery Corporation, a cartel established by the regional lottery operators and through which well-known national lotteries such as Lotto 6/49 and the Provincial are conducted. Each member receives revenues proportionate to the sales within its jurisdiction.

While the situation varies considerably from province to province, revenues generated from the sale of lotteries may either be taken into general revenues or be allocated to a special lottery fund from which disbursements are made in order to fund particular projects. Revenues in Atlantic Canada and Quebec are taken directly into general revenues, whereas, in the western provinces and Ontario, they are largely earmarked for amateur sport, culture, and recreation (Vance, 1986, p. 206). Despite these variations in provincial policies regarding how and to what purposes lottery funds are allocated, Canadian amateur sport, culture, and recreational programs have tended to be the major beneficiaries (Vance, 1986, p. 206).

Conflict and Competition: Splitting the Pot

The recent history of gambling in Canada has not been without conflict. However, unlike earlier years, the conflict has not been a moral one. Rather, it has been (and continues to be) an economic and political conflict over the revenues to be generated through gambling (see Box 6.3). For example, shortly after the Code was amended in

1969, the federal and provincial governments became embroiled in a major struggle over the right to conduct lotteries. Initially, the 1969 amendment legally allowed "the Government of Canada and the Government of a province (by itself or with another province)" (Labrosse, 1985, p. 145) to conduct lotteries. At this time, the federal government had no intention of establishing lottery operations

(Osborne, 1989, p. 64). However, in 1973, aware of the overwhelming success of provincial lotteries, the government of Canada changed its mind and created the Olympic Lottery Corporation of Canada (succeeded, in 1976, by Loto-Canada) to conduct lotteries to raise funds for the 1976 Montreal Olympic Games.

By 1976, all provinces in Canada had successful lotteries

Box 6.3 The Political Economy of Morality and the Law

After the government of Canada had held public hearings in 1909–10 to consider legalizing pari-mutuel gambling on horse races, the Vancouver Board of Trade, in 1913, felt compelled to respond to the growth of horse racing and gambling by dispatching the following letter to the federal minister of justice:

Vancouver Board of Trade
Molsons Building
Vancouver, B.C., Canada

6th October 1913

Honorable C.J. Doherty, K.C.,
Minister of Justice,
Ottawa.

Sir,

I have the honor to report to you that in contravention of the Miller Act regulating horse racing in Canada that Vancouver during this Summer has had continuous racing for ten weeks.

Following these races from the American side are many vicious characters which prey on the community during the course of such races.

The general effect of these races is to depreciate the morals of the community.

The opportunity presented for gambling has been instrumental in destroying the peace of many homes.

The whole business community of our city is aroused at the effrontery of this organization.

The Council of the Board of Trade has instructed me to communicate with you and lay the facts before you.

We anticipate that during the next session of the House [of Commons] relief may be obtained from this ruinous and parasitical organization.

Trusting to hear from you respecting the same at your earliest convenience.

I have the honor to be,
Sir,
Your obedient Servant,

W.A. Blair (signed)

Secretary

In 1987, the Vancouver Board of Trade, established more than 100 years ago to promote and enhance trade and commerce in British Columbia, submitted a report to the provincial attorney general, recommending that the province undertake a cost-benefit analysis of the prospects of introducing commercial casino gambling as a way of stimulating tourism and provincial economic growth. Thus, the relatively recent willingness on the part of the Vancouver Board of Trade to examine seriously the economic potential of gambling represents a radical departure from the moral values reflected some 75 years ago in the letter quoted above.

With the world-wide growth of gambling, both as an important leisure-time activity and as an important source of capital for governments and private-sector companies, has come much more acceptance of the activity. Thus, the seeming willingness of the Vancouver Board of Trade to condone gambling now, after previously vigorously opposing it, indicates a close relationship among morality, law, and economics. In this instance, it is possible to see how economics have led to a weakening of moral opposition to gambling activities and how the appeal of revenues has contributed to the virtual **decriminalization** of gambling in Canada. Thus, as sociologists and criminologists seek to understand criminal laws, it becomes strikingly clear that it is important to examine carefully the social, political, and economic contexts in which laws exist.

of federal in-
e exclusively
iportant elec-
rvative party,
deral involve-
e Progressive
government,
vinces where-
from lottery
t finalized be-
of Commons
Liberals reas-
the provinces,
id introduced
abrosse, 1985;

bject of litiga-
the provinces.
ed, yet another
iservative party
onouring their
Conservative
the provinces
d any claim on
ient resulted in
le that granted
id gambling to
re to make an-
nt as well as to
Winter Olym-

e brought into
d nonprofit or-
rketing and dis-
ers of nonprofit
retailers. Such
provincial lot-
ive distribution
retail sales were
s manner, non-
if lottery opera-
d disbursements
combination of
volunteer retail-
introduction of
d to the gradual
lemise of direct
iprofit organiza-
tions still receive
nues, the loss of
immunity-based
rms of gambling,

such as bingos and casinos, as an alternative source of
revenue.

An area of growing contention exists between provincial lotteries and the Canadian horse-racing industry. Faced
with a relative decline in the amount of money being
wagered at racetracks in Canada, horse-racing interests, including horse owners, breeders, racetrack operators, and
jockeys, have pointed accusing fingers at provincial lotteries. Arguing that the massive advertising campaigns and the
easy accessibility of lottery vendors to customers have
reduced horse racing's market share of disposable income
expended on gambling activities, horse-racing interests have
grown critical of state-operated lotteries.

According to the president of Race Tracks Canada, since
lotteries were legalized in 1970 they have consistently en-
croached on horse-racing revenues. By 1983, he argues,
government-lottery revenues had outstripped wagering on
thoroughbred and standard-bred horse racing. Using British Columbia as an example, he points out that, in 1975,
wagering on horse racing represented 81.74 percent of the
gambling market, and lotteries 5.34 percent. By 1987, those
figures were 17.43 percent and 59.76 percent, respectively. Furthermore, since provincial governments are extensively involved in regulating horse racing, racing interests
argue that their industry cannot compete on an equal footing with government-run lotteries. "Racing," claims the
president of Race Tracks Canada, "is regulated by its competition" (cited in Brunt, 1989, p. A4).

It is apparent that considerable uniformity exists across
the nation in respect to lotteries run by the provinces under
the auspices of the Interprovincial Lottery Corporation.
However, with respect to other forms of licensed gambling,
such as casinos and bingos conducted by charitable organizations, considerable variation between provinces is to be
noted. Formally, it is nonprofit charitable organizations that
are licensed for a provincial fee to conduct charity gambling events. However, once such organizations have been
granted licences, they are obliged to contract with private-
sector business interests that specialize in providing gambling equipment and premises (such as bingo halls or casinos), as well as professional staff (e.g., blackjack dealers) and
management personnel. In some provinces, these companies have become increasingly important industries by virtue of the revenues they generate, the number of people
they employ, and the services they provide to charitable
organizations. Indeed, private-sector companies have actively begun to lobby provincial governments for greater
levels of gambling.

In Canada, unlike Las Vegas or Atlantic City in the
United States, privately owned companies that specialize
in gambling operations have not yet become integrated with
tourist-hospitality industries. Rather, they have tended to

remain at the level of small, but important, independent businesses. However, in some provinces, British Columbia for example, private-sector interests and the government have expressed interest in using casino gambling as a vehicle for diversifying tourism and hospitality industries. That is, in these provinces proponents have called for the introduction of destination resort casinos to cater to affluent tourists. However, were these types of developments to occur, existing laws and policies that direct the majority of gaming revenues to charitable organizations might prove to be incompatible. Accordingly, it is likely that serious political conflict will emerge between charitable organizations and private companies as to who deserves to receive the profits from gambling operations. For example, in British Columbia, the Vancouver Board of Trade, an agency established for the promotion and enhancement of business interests, has declared: "There appears to be no logical reason why the charities and other not-for-profit-organizations should be granted a monopoly on gaming"

(Vancouver Board of Trade, 1987, p. 2). In other words, in the future, as gambling becomes increasingly accepted as a recreational activity, it is likely that private businesses will demand greater incentives in the form of larger shares of gambling-generated revenues. Should such developments take place, provincial governments will be confronted with thorny policy decisions regarding how gambling revenues are to be allocated.[9]

Where gambling has become particularly controversial is in regard to its operations on native reserves. Recently, numerous Indian bands have introduced gambling, in such forms as bingos and casinos, on their reservations. Catering primarily to a non-Indian clientele, gambling operations have been perceived by native leaders to hold the potential for generating large amounts of much-needed capital. Such gambling operations have additionally provided significant numbers of jobs for band members.

Given native sovereignty, which is asserted over tribal lands, as well as the historical autonomy from provincial

---

Box 6.4 Compulsive Gambling: The Extraordinary Saga of Brian Molony

Academic researchers and mental-health specialists in the United States have relatively recently begun to draw attention to the growing incidence of compulsive or pathological gambling. In Canada, however, the problems associated with the increased availability of government-licensed and government-operated gambling have not been seriously addressed (see, for example, Lesieur, 1989). Indeed, unlike the United States, where several state governments have dedicated funds for research into the nature and extent of problem gambling as well as for treatment programs, in Canada authorities remain unaware of—or unconcerned about—the social consequences of problem gambling, particularly among minorities, women, and the relatively poor.

Canada, however, has not remained immune from the negative consequences of problem gambling. In fact, one of the most publicized incidents of excessive gambling yet documented involved Canadian assistant bank manager Brian Molony, who embezzled in excess of $10.2 million from his then-employer, the Canadian Imperial Bank of Commerce.

Molony's saga of compulsive gambling (with bookies, and at Atlantic City casinos), embezzlement, and subsequent arrest and conviction have been vividly documented in the 1987 best-selling biography *Stung: The Incredible Obsession of Brian Molony*, by Gary Ross. Ross's account of Molony's incredible gambling sprees—financed with money stolen from the Toronto branch bank where he

worked—provides a remarkable insight to a "worst-case scenario" of the ravages of compulsive gambling.

Hooked on the action of gambling from childhood, Molony continued to lose to bookies and casinos as an adult; eventually, the highly regarded 26-year-old assistant bank manager was led into twenty months of fraudulent-loan scamming. He was caught and arrested almost by accident by morality-squad officers who had been wire-tapping suspected bookmakers. His banking superiors initially could not believe police reports that Molony had confessed to the largest fraud in Canadian banking history. Ross's biography charts Molony's career as a compulsive gambler and vividly captures the pernicious nature of bookmakers and the complicity of Atlantic City casinos in exploiting Molony's gambling compulsion and accommodating his frauds.

But, while many of Molony's experiences with gambling do clearly typify the behaviours, patterns, and personal problems of compulsive gamblers in general, the celebrated status of Molony's case is quite anomalous. Rather, it is more likely the case that the many men, women, and youths who gamble compulsively on lotteries; at racetracks; and at casinos, bingo halls, and poker clubs—all of which are legal in one or more Canadian provinces—do so in relative anonymity. The devastating problems suffered by compulsive gamblers and their families remain hidden, rarely receiving the public attention focussed on flamboyant cases like that of Molony.

ive refused to
eir gambling
y problematic
ongly to un-
on on native
ges have been
of unlicensed
ports gathered
cies allege that
infiltrate na-
rges have been
nbling is con-
terests and that
es are impera-
prises is to be

res may appear
tended, the is-
mbling activi-
resent a major
reat to native
rs in Canada as
rticularly skep-
heir gambling.
tative threat of

organized crime as little more than a red herring introduced
to usurp their endeavours to attain economic and political
autonomy. Accordingly, the future of native gambling
promises to remain a volatile political issue.

A Recapitulation of Gambling as a Victimless Crime

Beginning with a definition of gambling, this section traced
the history of legal gambling in Canada from 1886 to the
present. Attention was given to the legalization and introduction of such forms of gambling as wagering on horse
racing, lotteries, and casinos. Initial moral arguments against
gambling have given way to political and economic conflicts over gambling revenues. While once prohibited by
criminal law, gambling has been essentially decriminalized
and reconstructed. As we have seen, an understanding of
the social, political, and economic forces that have shaped
(and will continue to shape) the criminal law is crucial. In
short, the removal of criminal prohibitions in respect to
gambling and the apparent move toward a system of control through administrative regulation depicts a noteworthy transformation in criminal law.

---

a vacuum.'' Discuss the
reference to the creation
Canada.

ween the federal
governments over control
e directed the form

contributed to the
ling in Canada.

---

break-open or pull-
umber of perforated
iscovering matching

symbols (e.g., three cherries), indicating an instant win.
2. Figures presented here represent a compilation of data reported
by provincial authorities and cited in Beare, Jamieson, and Gilmore

(1988). It is to be noted that considerable variation exists regarding both the methods used and the precision achieved by provincial authorities in reporting gambling revenues.

3. Extensive illegal gambling, such as bookmaking on sporting events, occurs in Canada. These illegal forms of gambling are tacitly condoned, and even supported, by the mass media who publish odds, point-spreads, statistics, and expert commentaries on the anticipated outcomes of particular sporting events. An analysis of such illegal forms of gambling, however, is beyond the scope of this chapter.

4. Pari-mutuel wagering is a form of gambling in which all bets are pooled. A percentage is subtracted by the operators of the pari-mutuel system. The remaining amount is then distributed to those having wagered correctly on the outcome. Odds are paid on the basis of the amount wagered on a particular outcome in relation to the total amount wagered. For a more thorough explication of pari-mutuel wagering, see Abt, Smith, and Christiansen (1985).

5. Shell games and three-card monte were (and remain even today) scams used by hustlers to dupe suckers out of their hard-earned cash. In the shell game, the sucker was enticed to wager on his or her choice of walnut shell under which a dried pea was located, whereas, in three-card monte, the sucker (or "mark") was invited to try to pick the ace of spades from three face-down playing cards. Both games lend themselves well to sleight-of-hand manipulation and to the inevitable defrauding of innocent and usually willing participants. Punch boards consist of a large sheet of sturdy paper or cardboard that contains numerous perforated holes. For a cash fee, players punch one or more of the perforated holes in the hope of locating a small slip of paper indicating a cash prize. Coin tables, once used at fairs and carnivals, consisted of flat table-like "checker boards," situated low and flat to the ground. Players attempted to toss coins, usually from some distance, onto the checker-board grid in the hope of landing on a square that would award them a cash prize.

6. As Belinda Silberman documents in a report in the *Calgary Herald* of August 27, 1983, Royal American Shows has subsequently had similar law-enforcement problems in Florida, Minnesota, and Wisconsin.

7. A Crown corporation is "an organization with the structure of a private independent enterprise, but which is established by specific acts or pursuant to enabling legislation of a federal or provincial legislature and which usually reports to the legislature through a designated Minister" (McMenemy, 1980, p. 72, cited in Vance, 1986, p. 112).

8. For a detailed discussion of the process by which provinces were granted exclusive jurisdiction over lotteries, see Osborne and Campbell (1988).

9. The province of Manitoba has chosen to eliminate private interests by taking direct government control of all lotteries and charity gambling. Responding to police concerns that private-sector bingos and casino operations had been penetrated by criminal interests, the government opted to take direct control over these enterprises. Thus, the Manitoba Lottery Foundation operates gambling on behalf of charities, appropriates the revenues, and disburses them to eligible community-based nonprofit organizations. In early 1990, the Manitoba Lotteries Foundation opened the Crystal Casino, located in the Hotel Fort Gary in downtown Winnipeg. Revenues from the casino operation are to be directed to the Manitoba Health Services Fund in order to finance medical research. While located in a private-sector hotel, and intended to cater to tourists as well as to local gamblers, the casino operation does not actively engage in such gambling tourist promotions as junkets, complimentary alcoholic beverages, or credit play, nor does it provide live entertainment. In this sense, the government-owned and -operated casino has not become a major vehicle for diversifying tourism and hospitality industries in the province of Manitoba.

References

Abt, V., Smith, J.F., & Christiansen, E.M. (1985). *The Business of risk.* Topeka: University of Kansas Press.

Agriculture Canada, Race Track Division (1986). *Annual review.* Ottawa.

Beare, M.E., Jamieson, H., & Gilmore, A. (1988). *Legalized gaming in Canada.* Ottawa: Solicitor General.

Brunt, S. (1989, March 18). Lotteries seducing gamblers from track. *Globe and Mail,* p. A4.

Canada (1909–10). *House of Commons journals,* Vol. XLV: appendix.

Canada, Joint Committee of the Senate & House of Commons (1956). *Report of the Parliamentary Committee on Capital and Corporal Punishment and Lotteries,* Vols. I & II. Ottawa: Queen's Printer.

Campbell, C.S. (1984). The Stampede: Cowtown's sacred cow. In C.E. Reasons (Ed.), *Stampede City: Power and politics in the West* (pp. 103-22). Toronto: Between the Lines.

Campbell, C.S. (1981). Parasites & paradoxes: Legalized gambling in Alberta, Canada. In W.R. Eadington (Ed.), *The gambling papers.* Reno: University of Nevada.

Casino fever runs high. (1969, July 4). *The Albertan,* p. 5.

Coordinated Law Enforcement Unit (1974). *Initial findings report on organized crime in British Columbia.* Victoria: Ministry of Attorney General.

Coordinated Law Enforcement Unit (1979). *Third findings report on organized crime in British Columbia.* Victoria: Ministry of Attorney General.

Devereaux, E.C. (1968). Gambling in psychological and sociological perspective. *International Encyclopedia of Social Sciences, 6,* 53–62.

Jones, D.C. (1983). *Midways, judges, and smooth-tongued fakirs: Illustrated history of country fairs in the Prairie West.* Saskatoon: Western Producer Prairie.

Labrosse, M. (1985). *The lottery . . . from Jacques Cartier's day to modern times.* Montreal: Stanké.

Laycraft, J.H. (1978). *Royal American Shows Inc. and its activities: Report of a public inquiry.* Edmonton: Queen's Printer.

Lesieur, H. (1989). Pathological gambling in Canada. In C.S. Campbell & J. Lowman (Eds.), *Gambling in Canada: Golden goose or Trojan horse?* (pp. 221–42). Burnaby, BC: School of Criminology, Simon Fraser University.

. Toronto: Wiley.

ming: From the
ented to the West
University.

Canada: Changing
, Faculty of Law,

amendments to
of power between
all Law Journal, 26

cific Grove, CA:

Molony. Toronto:

on ride through

ation of deviance.

Unpublished Ph.D.
pology, Carleton

lation of gaming and
.

Three

Theories of Crime and Criminality: The Individual

The court heard the testimonies of the social worker, the probation officer, and the psychiatrist:

SOCIAL WORKER: His background is problematic, Your Honour. The parents are both unemployed; the father is an alcoholic. The accused himself cannot hold down a steady job, and he has only a grade seven education.

PROBATION OFFICER: Well, he's a repeat B-and-E'er, Your Honour. He was out on parole when he did this last job. Took down an apartment on Davie Street. The problems began when he stole a bike at thirteen and it came to the attention of the police.

PSYCHIATRIST: What we have here, Your Honour, is a young sociopath. He scored high on the MMPI [Minnesota Multiphasic Personality Inventory] for aggression and, in the interview, was caught lying about his past. There is no treatment for his problem. I recommend incarceration.

HER HONOUR (speaking to the convicted offender): This court has dealt with you before. From the information just provided to me, it is understandable why you are before me again, but I don't understand why you began to engage in this criminal activity in the first place.

This scenario highlights a continuing concern of criminology as well as of the criminal-justice system in Canada. How can we determine the actual causes of crime? What kinds of information or procedures do we need to tell us why a person engages in criminal activity? Is it enough to base a theory of crime causation on such factors as the criminal's age, socio-economic status (SES), level of education attained? Is it necessary to also know information about the person's individual characteristics, such as measures of inherent aggression or mental status? Do we need to know additionally about the person's past behaviour and family background? Perhaps information about the individual is not particularly enlightening; it may be the socio-political-economic context of crime that ultimately can provide us with insights into its causes.

As noted in the Introduction, the dominant conceptual frameworks and theoretical explanations in criminology did not originate in Canada, and therefore, for the most part, we will not be discussing Canadian contributions in Chapter 7, which takes a look at individual theories of criminality, or in Chapter 10, which deals with societal explanations of criminality. But it is essential that we become familiar with these traditional ideas in criminology in order to examine their applicability and appropriateness to the Canadian context.

Criminologists themselves are far from unified in their beliefs about crime causation. Many, in fact, feel that it is not an issue worthy of study. Chapters 7 and 10 will delineate the major approaches in criminology that do study the causes of crime, approaches that can be classified according to the level of analysis they employ. As is apparent from Table III.1, these vary from *micro* level, at which differences in individuals are examined, to *macro* level, where broader economic and political trends are studied over time.

A criminologist working at the *biological* level of analysis might study a group of convicted murders to determine if they share certain genetic traits or chromosomal abnormalities. A criminologist with *psychological* training might also study specific individuals, but emphasize the administration of tests to determine various personality characteristics. A criminologist with *sociological* expertise might work at yet another level of analysis and explore crime patterns in neighbourhoods of varying social-class compositions. Such approaches have been criticized by those ciminologists (some of whom borrow from the *historical/economic* methods advocated by Karl Marx) who place an emphasis, instead, on how and why certain behaviours are defined as crime in the first place and how the responses to crime vary historically.

Chapter 7 examines the biological and psychological theories of crime, and Chapter 10 discusses the sociological theories of crime. None of the theories described has been accepted as being totally satisfactory or adequate in its way of explaining the occurrence of crime, but each has something unique to consider about and to contribute to the study of crime.

Table III.1   Levels of Analysis for Criminological Research

	Variables	Units of Analysis
Macro		
Historical /Economic	Political, economic variables (e.g., mode of production, class-based exploitation; ideology)	Country, historical epoch
Sociological	Structural, cultural, situational variables (e.g., neighbourhood, family, socio-economic status; power relations)	Social institutions and groups
Micro		
Psychological /Psychiatric	Personality traits; IQ; mental illness; learning disabilities	Individual
Biological	Chemical imbalances; genetic factors; race; body type/size; autonomic nervous system	Individual; cellular

Why Study Theory? What Does Theory Help Us Do?

If there is no one explanation or theory of crime causation that has been accepted, if it is true that the popularity of individual theories shifts over time, what does this tell us about the value of the theories and the value of studying them? Simply stated: theories provide us with a dimension of knowing and understanding that goes beyond that of mere information. Therefore, we may gather information on a particular type of offence, say child abuse, in terms of its frequency, locale, general nature—and we may also form a profile about a particular offender, for instance, a sexual offender, in terms of his or her attributes, background, past behaviours—but, in order to make meaning of the information, we need some way of organizing it, contextualizing it, according to some agreed-upon criteria. Theories do that for us. In criminology, theories provide us with a way to think about criminal behaviour, to offer a tentative explanation that can then be tested on reality. But, as we will see, there are many theories created and developed that are offered to explain the same phenomena; many different perspectives can be taken on the meaning of essentially the same information.

There is no one true theory waiting to be found that will rightly explain, rendering all the other theories wrongly conceived. Theories are not, in themselves, truth or reality; they are ways of describing reality. There is a danger, then, in confusing theory with reality; when this confusion does occur, theory can be misused. Arguments may be made about the truth or verity of the theory itself, when, in fact, one can argue only about the truth or verity of the information upon which it is based. Theory makes the world "fit" some model or framework. It orders the world so that we can act upon it. At different periods in time, some theories appear more sensible than do others to us; some theories can be acted upon more comfortably than can others. When one theory does prove to be less sensible, does not seem to fit reality as well as does another, then the theory becomes discredited or discarded, often, though, returning in slightly different form at a later time—a "recycling" characteristic that, as we will see, has occurred with regularity. This is yet another reason for the study of earlier theories: to provide us with insights into our contemporary explanations of criminality.

In summary, the validity of a theory (its "truth" empirically demonstrated) is generally evaluated by testing. Criteria are established that can be measured in the real world—applied to an activity, behaviour pattern, etc. Theories are usually discarded when they no longer seem effective in helping us formulate ways of understanding and coping, for example, in creating programs, and law and policy. That is not to say that some explanations do not remain in favour past their proved effectiveness. Many factors—political, economic, social—may influence their continued acceptance. However, when one explanation does fall into disfavour, then another takes its place, because we have a need to order, to categorize, to model, to make sense of what we do not really know. In criminology and the criminal-justice system, we find that one theory dominates for a period of time and then fades.

Theory and Practice

All criminological theories have implications for practice; that is, once you have a theory of crime, you also have a clue to an avenue of prevention and correction that might be effective. Table III.2 illustrates some of the practical implications of the theories advanced, using the four levels of analysis we discussed earlier.

As Table III.2 shows, the translation of theory into policy/practice is not always "straightforward." Thus, we have not yet seen the historical level of analysis, based upon a broader economic interpretation of criminality, actually developed to the point that it can be transformed into reality. The level of analysis rests upon the need for a complete revolution of society; the theory, therefore, appears to have had limited "real-world" application to date, although it does have supporters. The sociological level of analysis has been most successful this century in having its theoretical elements placed into structure and process. Sociologists have focussed on society itself as its level of analysis, and its implications for practice have been carried out in the form of the development of social services intended to improve the social circumstance of man.

The psychological/psychiatric level of analysis has also achieved a measure of success in contemporary times in having practice based upon its theory of criminality: that the individual is responsible for his/her own deviance. The theory, however, has suffered setbacks with the demise of the "medical model" in corrections. Corrections programs using the psychological/psychiatric perspective are no longer as prevalent, since the controversy, in the 1970s, over whether the programs actually "work" and the failure to confirm the programs' effectiveness. Finally, the level of analysis in the biological category is also not currently emphasized. These theories arose originally from the "old chestnuts": the theories of the Lombrosans and Beccarians discussed in Chapter 7. Today, there is occasionally some renewal of interest in the biological level of analysis, such as with IQ and race effects on criminality but, for the most part, the implications for practice are seen to be too unfairly discriminating.

Table III.2   The Application of Theory to Practice

Level of Analysis	Implications for "Crime Problem"	Result
Historical /Economic	Dictates massive restructuring of society; radical law reform; redistribution of wealth	Quite difficult to implement
Sociological	Dictates more socialized society with equal opportunities; social services	As a theory, has more academic support; some attempts to implement, but quite costly
Psychological /Psychiatric	Dictates individual treatment or preventive detention for those thought untreatable (medical model)	Dominant ideology (esp. corrections) for most of century until civil libertarians attacked
Biological	Dictates need to identify offenders and segregate from society	Dominant ideology in nineteenth century: some evidence for revival in recent times

One illustration of how theory translates into practice can be taken, again, from corrections. For example, if the theory that orders correctional practice is based upon the idea of the individual being solely responsible for his or her criminal behaviour—a psychological theory, for instance—the goals and objectives of the corrections program developed in accordance with that theory should reflect that assumption. Thus, we have theories of cognitive and moral development that guide the structuring of many prison education programs. If, instead of a psychological perspective, program developers adhere to a sociological perspective, programming might be directed to improving the conditions in society that influence and encourage criminal behaviour, such as poverty and lack of educational opportunities.

The point is that beliefs in theories are very important considerations to weigh when trying to understand explanations of crime causation. There are wide-ranging studies conducted on just the task of trying to understand how beliefs in theories of crime causation affect responses to criminality. Social psychologists, political scientists, sociologists—and criminologists—are very interested in studying public attitudes and beliefs as well as those of criminal-justice personnel, which is why issues such as capital punishment, abortion, and sentencing are often focussed on in survey studies. It is thought that, if we can gain an understanding of how people/citizens/offenders make meaning, theorize, conceptualize, contextualize, formally structure such phenomena, then we (the government and policy makers) can respond (or not respond) to that understanding.

The way criminality is explained allows one to react formally to it. If homosexuality is thought to represent criminal behaviour, for example, it will be responded to as criminal behaviour. If deterrence to crime holds the greatest priority in sentencing, then programming for rehabilitation of the offender is not likely to gain much support. Similarly, the belief in capital punishment as the ultimate deterrent certainly has obvious implications for correctional programming.

As beliefs in theories of crime causality and prevention shift, however, so, too, will the law and policy and practice emerging from those theories. We will, at many points in this text, see how "government" has used theory/causal attribution to its own advantage, for its own vested interests. If, for example, a theory of criminality that suggests juvenile crime is caused by socio-economic exigencies is held to be credible, then the government can probably argue successfully for more juvenile job-funding projects. As well, if corrections administrators believe that "punishment corrects" is the most appropriate theory upon which to base their operations, it is likely that rehabilitative programming will not be as favourably supported.

Continuing on with the emphasis on individual offenders and theories related to their criminality, Chapter 8 discusses mentally disordered offenders. These offenders have been considered dangerous to the public, although there is no clear evidence to substantiate this stereotyping. They may, in many ways, be seen as victims of the criminal-labelling process, and several areas of this potential for abuse by the criminal-justice system are investigated: insanity, fitness to stand trial, and dangerousness.

Chapter 9 discusses the sexual offender. This offender type, in contrast to that of the mentally disordered offender, has only relatively recently been viewed as a menace to society. Sexual abusers of children, in particular, have elicited the Canadian public's outrage. The incidence, impact, and treatment of these offenders are articulated here.

These last two chapters serve as a "bridge" to Part IV, in which we discuss the search for crime's causes on a societal as opposed to an individual basis. What emerges from chapters 8 and 9 are the difficulties of transforming the "individual" theories' approaches into appropriate and adequate law, programs, and policy to deal with offenders. Therefore, let us begin to trace the study of theories of crime causation/prevention, keeping in mind these introductory remarks. You should be thinking, as you read, of how each of these theories of criminology could translate into criminal-justice law, policy, and practice.

7 Search for the Cause of Crime: Biological and Psychological Perspectives

of Man's

ogy:

Can

eir Effect on

ental

As a discipline, **criminology** began as a micro-level analysis of criminals. Nineteenth-century criminologists and penal reformers shared the optimistic view that the scientific identification of the cause of **crime** would lead to its eradication entirely. This utopian view has largely been abandoned, especially as we came to recognize crime as a more or less normal part of society. The early twentieth century saw the rise of psychiatry and psychology, which, as we shall see in Chapter 8, had a profound influence upon criminology and criminal justice. At about the same time, sociological conceptions of crime causation became popular in academe, but it would not be until the 1960s that such theories had much impact upon policy and law. More recently, critical criminologists have suggested that it is the behaviour of the state as an agent of control that defines individuals and acts as criminal in order to protect the economically powerful groups in society.

In this chapter, we will be examining those theories and explanations of criminality that focus upon the individual. Supporters assume that, if efforts are made to identify features that distinguish criminals from their law-abiding counterparts, then we might be able to determine how best to prevent, control, or eliminate criminal behaviour.

In pursuit of this goal, some early "criminologists" (e.g., anthropologists, doctors, and other professionals interested in searching for the causes of criminality in humankind) suggested that it is necessary to determine physical correlates first, before establishing causes for criminal behaviour in the individual; the size of one's earlobe or forehead could, it was argued, assist in the explication of criminality. In this chapter, we will explore the various nonsociological explanations for criminal behaviour. These explanations can be classified generally into biological and psychological theories. The biological theories hypothesize that the causes of crime lie within human biology, and psychological theories—again, by definition—contend that criminal acts occur as a response to psychological influences—personality influences—within the individual. The sociological theories, which we will examine in Chapter 10, maintain that the social structure of society itself is responsible for criminality.

Most of these theories or explanations, whether non-sociological or sociological, have remained conjectural only; no evidence has been offered to demonstrate convincingly their verity. Indeed, there is no one accepted explanation of criminality today that has met all the standards of social science in terms of validity and applicability. There are, instead, varying definitions and explanations of crime that are closely intertwined with the ways in which the different theories have conceived of the larger societal context.

Before beginning to discuss the biological and psychological theories, we will "set the stage" with a consideration of the early theories of criminal behaviour—the demonic and spiritual explanations.

Demonology: Demons in Control of Man's Evil Ways?

Perhaps the most fascinating attempts to explain "evil" behaviour in man began with demonology. From the perspective of ancient peoples, demons, magic, and spirits worked in mysterious ways in influencing behaviour. Their "presence" allowed for easy explanations of deviant behaviour, since no determination of the individual's role in the acts had to be considered. Thus, the expression "the devil made me do it" saved human beings from having to justify their own actions.

Those who could use magic were held in awe or as suspect, depending on the outcome of their incantations. Magicians or witches could direct spirits or demons through their power, and thus it was possible to hold these individuals responsible as well for the evidenced evil in the world. It is not surprising, therefore, that witch-hunting emerged as a technique for dealing with these creators of evil. Huff (1980) suggests, however, that the exercise of exorcism was triggered not so much by concern for protecting the community from demons as by the desire to make the gods happy, in order that *their* vengeance not be directed at the citizenry. In fact, even human sacrifice might be offered to propitiate the gods. Other techniques were almost as debilitating to the victim as was sacrifice. Trephining, for example, was a method of drilling holes in an individual's skull in order to allow evil spirits to be released: a procedure that was sometimes over-enthusiastically applied.

Punishment for evildoing was almost always directed physically and visibly toward the offender. It was as if the gods had to view the proceedings in order to be satisfied that wrong had been righted. Such punishment also served, of course, to deter others who might consider similar actions. The immersion of an offender in boiling oil as a sanction could provide strong lasting imagery for the rest of the tribal community.

In these ancient times, the determiner of what should be done to appease the gods was often the witch doctor. Rites and rituals were elaborately developed to forestall the gods' revenge upon erring tribes and to ward off evil spirits with the potential to lead individuals astray, which might, in turn, displease the gods. In this way, regulation of behaviour became more formalized, ultimately resulting in articulated codes. The manner in which the individual was conceptualized as being governed by these forces external to himself or herself had a significant impact on the manner in which the rules evolved.

"Justice" was done as much for the gods and/or other supernatural spirits as for the human community. The rites and regulations embodied harsh consequences if broken. In primitive societies, trial by ordeal often meant no trial in the traditional sense of weighing evidence; the ordeal almost inevitably resulted in great physical pain, as did the boiling-oil immersion mentioned above. There was little effort made to distinguish types of deviants from each other or from the general "good citizen" population.

During medieval times, priests took over the role of the witch doctors, in determining which individuals were possessed by the devil and in need of punishment. The church, in controlling the religious life of the community, could set the requirements for forgiveness, create punishments to purge evil from souls, and also benefit from the tithes offered up by the parishioners to maintain the priests in these positions of power (see Box 7.1). After the Protestant Reformation in Europe, threats of hellfire and damnation swept through the countryside, bringing brutal treatment of suspected heretics. The process was often excruciatingly drawn out for those who were "possessed." The public, after all, had to be relieved of the fear that the individual's evil might remain. Foucault (1978, p. 3) offers us a classic description of the public execution of a such a possessed person:

Finally, he was quartered, recounts the *Gazette d'Amsterdam* of 1 April 1757. "This operation was very long, because the horses used were not accustomed to drawing; consequently, instead of four, six were needed; and when that did not suffice, they were forced, in order to cut off the wretch's thighs, to sever the sinews and hack at the joints."

long rejected the
riminal behaviour,
for many in the
rime: The Causes
th (August 1988),
ributed to the ex-
to induce damag-
responded to, lead
It is suggested in
," that the general
n the criminal ac-
:udes, which most
th." It appears that

monic perspective
:heir attack. These
issociated with the
the "radical" right
ve been witness to
t only in their well-
nedia covering their
mpaigns have taken
he Moral Majority

Movement in the 1970s and 1980s exemplified this mindset, with homosexuals and abortionists receiving the brunt of its campaign energy. But it was "old-time religion" at the base of the thrust, with preachers such as Jerry Falwell expounding on the gospel to rid the land of demonically inspired wrong.

There are many difficulties with the demonic perspective as a theory to explain criminal behaviour. The major problem with the explanation is that there is no way to test it; it rests upon beliefs about the order of things and how they are controlled. How could it possibly be determined if Satan or evil spirits are responsible for criminality in individuals? Therefore, as man became less "primitive," such explanations lost favour, but it is true that we still have today whole societies that acknowledge the existence of Satan (e.g., the Iranians), as well as many enclaves within Western society that recognize the influence of evil spirits.

And, finally, it should be said that, while there appears no adequate way we can test whether theories of demonology are "valid," at the outset we claimed that there are no adequate tests for any theory; therefore, demonology should perhaps be allowed to contend on its own merits with other proposed theories of criminality.

of centralizing the
1985, p. 28). But
with forgiveness
ι "eye for an eye"
nonic period into
:rific punishments
rence to the rule

ιght

developed about
iefs in supernatural
Γhe Pythagoreans,
ian traditions, held
form of commu-
onflict with or in
m enter in to pro-
should surrender
)t govern separate-
at spirit, of which
ιought, developed

by the Ionians, emphasized the dichotomy between man and nature, mind and soul. The self was something other than nature and, in fact, viewed the world as a distinct object to be manipulated. These Greek thinkers were precursors of Aristotelian thought and the Western concept of science, which considered that man was in a position of greater control over his own behaviour than was thought true from the Pythagoreans' perspective.

Extensions of these two streams of thinking developed, in the first instance, with the Pythagorean route, into religious beliefs about man's subjective relationship to the gods, a relationship developed through a communal spirit created by symbols and ritual. The Ionians shifted into "scientific" thoughts about man's objective relationship to the world outside himself, a relationship developed through the examination and testing of reality.

The Classical School of Criminology: Choosing Evil?

The emergence of the **Classical School** in Europe around 1700 saw the Ionian "scientific" approach come to dominate. Demons or spirits (which cannot be proved to exist) are not responsible for evil behaviour in mankind. The Classicists argue that an individual is responsible for his or her own behaviour and chooses to do evil or not. Therefore, an individual possesses a "free will" to engage in criminal behaviour. The Classical School, also called the "Liberal" School, provided enlightened thought to the structuring of disorganized eighteenth-century European society. Reform was the intent of the thinkers in this school, and, indeed, their ideas of reform have influenced the development of criminal codes and procedures in more recent times. The Classical School followers were responding to the brutality and harshness of punishment described earlier. They did not feel that religious zealots should be in control of **deviance** management. As long as religion was "mediating" between God and man, man could not assume control of his own destiny.

The abuses of punishment had become rampant by the eighteenth century. There was no certainty about the form of punishment for offences, and the practices themselves were barbaric (Mannheim, 1973). It was the time of the rack and other devices of torture; a time of obsession with the physical abuse of deviants. As Newman (1978) states, nearly 70 percent of the death sentences handed out in eighteenth-century England were for robbery.

Two of the European "reformers," Cesare Beccaria (1738–94) and Jeremy Bentham (1748–1832), were the principal proponents of the Classical School of criminology and are generally acknowledged to be the founders of criminological thought. Beccaria was especially influential through his essays, including one entitled "On Crimes and Punishments" (1764). His writings promoted the utilitarian ideal of justice, that is, the idea that punishment should be proportionate to the crime and should be swiftly dealt with by the community. While man did act with free will, he was also driven by the "pleasure principle," or a hedonism that assumes one weighs actions in order to assure that the greatest pleasure will result (see Box 7.2).

Bentham (see Box 7.3) and Beccaria dismissed punishment handed out to rid evildoers of demons and set down the tenets of "the greatest good for the greatest number," and "let the punishment fit the crime"; deterrence, not revenge, was to be the primary goal of the **criminal-justice system.** Crime came to be considered much more legalistically. Urbanization, migration, and the decline of the extended family (phenomena related to the Industrial Revolution) led to a perception that there was an increasing need for the state to replace local and informal techniques of social control. The Age of Enlightenment (1715–89) offered the promise of Utopia, with citizen-run governments established on the basis that punishment for criminals should be certain, swift, and severe, and barbaric and cruel punishments abolished.

This approach to criminality has been "recycled" in contemporary times. For example, the relatively recent focus in North America on the just-deserts model reflects the

---

Box 7.2 Beccaria: The Utilitarian Aristocrat

Cesare Beccaria was an eighteenth-century philosopher, jurist, and economist who firmly established the principle of utility in the explanation of man's behaviour. Beccaria was born into the Italian aristocracy and received his education under the Jesuits in Parma. He rebelled against the authoritarian instruction of the Jesuits, however, and it was only after he returned to his home in Milan that he developed an interest in philosophy. Two of his friends inspired him to study the social problems of the day— Pietro and Alesandro Verri. Beccaria tended to be lazy and easily dissuaded from concentration, and his two friends stimulated him to industry (Mannheim, 1973, p. 38). As a result of their interest, Beccaria wrote *Dei delitti e delle pene.* The essay outlined his **social-contract theory** of the state: the right to punish criminals is an essential consequence of the nature and scope of the contractual relations of men in society (Mannheim, 1973, pp. 40–41).

Criminals behaved criminally, according to his theory, because the benefits outweighed the drawbacks. Thus, deterrence of criminality must shift the equation to the negative balance. However, Beccaria was strongly opposed to torture or severe punishment because he felt that might only encourage the strong criminal to endure the **sanction** and subsequently be set free to cause more criminality. However, the weak but innocent person might be wrongly subjugated to torture, perhaps even confessing guilt to a crime he did not commit because the sanction was too onerous. Given that man is driven by self-centredness, it is necessary to use punishment, but it needs to be exacting in its application.

ecluse

entury English
inted by human
Mill, Bentham's
: "He had neither
et, even tenor of
spired to exclude
last. . . . He was
or philosophy and
1950, pp. 62–63).
mchair criminol-
real-life examples,
of a very chaotic
conflicting legis-

lation and procedures for dealing with criminals. He tried
to create a method of social control based upon ethical principles. The basic principle was **utilitarianism.** Behaviour
has utility, according to Bentham, if it produces goodness
or happiness or prevents badness or unhappiness. To construct the value of utility of behaviours, Bentham introduced
the pseudo-mathematical **calculus of felicity** (Mannheim,
1973, p. 55). Although his focus was on the individual and
his or her own motivation in engaging in good or bad
behaviour, Bentham should be given credit for being ahead
of his time in advocating a theory of social causation of
crime rather than a limited concept of biological or non-
social causation (Mannheim, 1973, p. 57).

easurements of
The offender
the harm done
ng the pleasure
nishment is ex-
on the offender's
idea in theory,
ult one to trans-
how an amount
pleasure derived
individual com-
of measurement
ppropriate "just

but directed and limited by his own biological and social
parameters.

The implications of the Neoclassical School are enormously different for the criminal-justice system's operation
from those of the Classical School. Instead of punishment
to fit the crime, as the Classicists would advocate, the Neo-
classicists stressed consideration of the mitigating factors
affecting the offender—thus justice is directed to treating
the offender's problems. Therefore, if the criminal is found
to be mentally unstable, he or she is to be partially absolved
of the criminal act and assisted with the problem. The **insanity defence** in law, discussed in Chapter 8, is an example of a Neoclassical type of reform.

sed

-man can choose
ave way in the
School of crimi-
man's culpability
might enter into
rds, there might
hological, phys-
uences, that les-
for his or her
implies that man
self-determining,

The Biological Positivists: Looks Can Be Deceiving

The greatest attack on the Classical conception of crime
and law came from an emerging new school. The
Positivists, as this later group of "criminologists" came to
be labelled, focussed upon the individual criminal and the
search for factors that determined his or her **criminality.**
According to the **Positive School,** the Classicists appeared
to have failed in the attempt to locate the causes of crime,
because crime was still increasing (see boxes 7.4 and 7.5).
"Science" became firmly entrenched as an accepted avenue
to investigating human behaviour. From the view of the

Box 7.4 Table Comparing the Classical and Positive Schools

	Classical School	Positive School
Major Proponents	Beccaria/Bentham	Lombroso/Ferri/Garafalo
Method of Inquiry	Logical/abstract/subjective	Empirical/scientific/objective
Focus of Inquiry	The Act/The Crime	The Actor/The Criminal
View of Crime	Immoral/wrongful act; defined in legalistic terms; crime is transgression against the social contract	Act seen as product of abnormalities; emphasis on the injurious nature of the act; definition need not be legalistic
Crime Causation	Offender has free will and, hence, freely chooses to engage in criminal behaviour; not influenced by external or internal forces; offender morally responsible for his or her actions	Offender behaviour determined by biological, psychological, physiological, sociological factors
The Right to Punish	Based on the theory of social contract and social utility; punishment to serve as deterrence	Protection of society; doctrine of social defence
Nature of Punishment	Punishment not individualized, but to fit the crime; severity equal with the harm done; sanctions determined solely by legislators	Punishment = individualized treatment; goal of treatment = the rehabilitation or curing of the "sick" individual
Role of Judges	Establish guilt or innocence; mechanically apply the legislatively prescribed sanctions; no discretion	Determine treatment need; announce appropriate levels of social defence; discretion
Criminal Policy	Must show respect for the liberty, freedom, and dignity of the offender; protection from abuses by the state	Assessment of the level of dangerousness; need to protect society

Positivists, criminality was not merely the consequence of a rational choice between good and evil. Rather, there were causes of criminality that were beyond the control of the individual. This view came to be known as "**biological determinism**." It is no longer the case for the Positivists that man has the capability to choose between good and evil himself, but that there are other causes beyond man's control that have resulted in his doing evil.

Positivists argued that scientific analysis could yield the true cause of crime, an idea that had important implica-tions for the criminal-justice system. Once the cause was identified, for example, laws and policies could be formu-lated that could help "cure" criminals and possibly prevent or eradicate crime entirely. The nature and severity of a sentence should reflect the individual needs of the offender because each offender, not each offence, is unique. Final-ly, treatment was not viewed as having limits set upon it; anything could be justified (e.g., lobotomies, indeterminate incarceration, etc.), if those in authority thought it might help the individual offender's state.

nd Positivist Schools

ral state. Limita-
however, when
forms the neces-
laws. When man
grees to give up
forms the basis
ainty.

own actions. He
re and minimize
s the pluses and
action to follow.

government must
are maximized
nimized through
mite principle of
mber should take

that advance the
sity, prohibit so-
ficial behaviours.

iple of minimal
le of equality in
procedures at the
e in keeping with

l and specific de-
n punishment. It
pplied to the in-

m over the ages.
yers in the crimi-
rm the Classicists

Positive School

The Organic Society

Man lives in a society that is more than just the sum of its parts. While he himself represents only one of the social units in that society, man owes his total allegiance and duty to it.

Determinism

Man's behaviour is determined by forces that are beyond his control. Free will does not exist. Not only are men not rational, they are probably not hedonistic either.

Societal Protection

Society, in the form of government, protects its citizens from harm. Control of dangerous behaviour requires an assessment of dangerousness by government.

The Medical Model

Crime is a sickness. Thus, criminals are sick people who must be cured. Dangerous people are compelled to act dangerously. The state must be active in seeking out and identifying dangerous behaviour.

The Trial

The purpose of the trial is to attain a scientific analysis of the offender's condition and his future dangerousness. Where incarcerated, the individual will be subject to control and treatment.

Offenders' Rights

The individual has no right to receive a minimum standard of treatment. There is no equality before the law because each individual has his or her own specific needs.

Treatment

Offenders are treated on this individualized basis both for the protection of society and for their own betterment. Treatment is not limited to the offender, however, but extends to his or her relatives and social milieu. Therefore, others may be subjected to treatment with the "justification" of the protection of society.

Positive School Reforms

The Positive School most closely affected the development of the corrections component of the justice system. Such reforms as probation, indeterminate sentences, and dangerous-offender legislation reflect its influence.

Source: Adapted from P.J. Brantingham (1979), The Classical and Positive schools of criminology: Two ways of thinking about crime. In F.L. Faust & P.J. Brantingham (Eds.), *Juvenile justice philosophy: Readings, cases, and comments* (2nd ed.) St. Paul, MN: West Publishing.

Lombroso and the Hootonists

Cesare Lombroso (1835–1901) was the Italian psychiatrist who is traditionally acknowledged as being the person responsible for the major shift in focus from rational evil to fated evil. While a physician in the Italian army, Lombroso had noticed that dishonest soldiers could be distinguished from their law-abiding counterparts by their tattoos. A *post mortem* performed on a notorious criminal revealed certain skeletal characteristics commonly associated with inferior animals. Lombroso spoke of a revelation at this discovery. Armed with a working hypothesis, he collected more data that seemed to confirm this initial observation and, on this basis, he developed the theory of **atavism.** Some men became criminals because of epilepsy, imbecility, or passion; some were merely "criminaloid," occasionally lapsing into crime; some were born criminals. This last group comprised atavistic throwbacks, closer on the evolutionary ladder to the apes, who retained many primal instincts.

Lombroso criticized the Classicists for not being scientific enough. The focus, according to him, should be on the analysis of this "criminal type." If our energies are directed to an exhaustive determination of the criminal type, we should be able to discover enough information to select out and/or control these criminals in society. In this perspective, society itself is viewed conservatively and as not in need of reform. Explanations for deviance and criminality must lie in man, not in the existing social order. This static "accepting" perspective of society is, in fact, what later criminologists criticized most strongly (see Chapter 10). The *status quo* view of crime is held by both the Classical and the Positive schools of criminology. Both adhere to the **consensus approach** to criminality, which proposes that crime violates certain basic societal values that all good citizens agree upon (see Introduction).

Lombroso provides us with titillating exposures of various criminal types in his analysis of man as an inferior being. His efforts, and those of other Positivists who followed, represented the first attempts to apply the scientific method to the study of criminality. In his book, *The Criminal Man* (1911), he made the proposal that some individuals were born to be criminals as a result of congenital, partly pathogenic, factors that impel them to a life of crime. These hapless creatures often had distorted facial features: enlarged ears, receding foreheads, high cheekbones. Other noted defects were character-related: excessive cruelty, lack of morality.

Lombroso's criminal man could be identified by anomalies in the hair and the shape of the head, eyes, eyebrows, nose, ears, skin, teeth, and chin. A man with dark, thick hair; a flat and low forehead; bushy eyebrows; long ears;

pale and wrinkled skin; and a receding chin would be a likely candidate for a criminal career, according to Lombroso. Long arms and short legs, and sloping shoulders, were also indicators, and criminals were thought to be more likely to stammer, squint, smoke, be left-handed, and have tattoos and flat feet. Variations among crime categories were acknowledged. For example, sex offenders were found to have swollen eyelids and lips and were occasionally humpbacked.

Prostitution was equated with criminality for Lombroso. He suggested that, other than prostitution, criminal women participated primarily as passive accomplices in crime or as criminals who kill faithless lovers and husbands, or even their own children. As is discussed in Chapter 11, these women were felt most appropriately left in the home, since that is where they were of most "value."

The obsession with characterizing and categorizing criminals continued in the work of two of Lombroso's students, Enrico Ferri (1856–1929) and Raffaelo Garofalo (1852–1934). Ferri described four types of criminals: born, insane, occasional, passionate. He moved beyond Lombroso's "straight" biological explanations, however, to suggest that political, social, and economic factors played a role in developing criminality in individuals. It is interesting to note that Ferri became a supporter of Mussolini in his later years (Vold, 1979, p. 42).

According to critics, one of the problems of the Positive School is that it lends itself to a support of totalitarian forms of governing. Garofalo similarly supported Mussolini's efforts and was quite proactive in lecturing on the need to eliminate the "unfit." This exercise is only possible if the unfit can be identified, which is, of course, exactly what the classification of criminal types of individuals allows one to do.

Continuing in this "categorizing" tradition, Charles Goring (1870–1919) conducted a study, in 1902, of 3000 English convicts; the study examined their mental and social characteristics and compared them with those of a group of noncriminal men. The twelve-year task was undertaken in an effort to scientifically test the Lombrosian idea that criminals were distinguishable from law-abiding citizens by certain physical characteristics. As a result of his work, published in 1913 in the text, *The English Convict,* Goring is commonly believed to have been the person who delivered the death blow to the notion of the "born criminal."

He compared convicts with hospital patients, college students, and soldiers. College students were found to be "different" from criminals; overall, the criminals weighed less, were shorter, and possessed lower native intelligence than did the comparison groups. But Goring, a English prison physician, rejected Lombroso's idea of visible physical defect: "the preliminary conclusion reached by our inquiry

tistence in fact"
ombroso's ideas
. and question-
of the scientific
himself, which
ierading to-day
ty" (1913, pp.

with little sym-
believed there
s than between
n. Accordingly,
b their offence,
s work is an ex-
alysis, an analy-
Goring applied
relational analy-
s between vari-

ables such as (1) the proportion of individuals in one generation of the general community who are imprisoned from crime; (2) the age of criminals at their first conviction; and (3) the actual and potential fertility of criminals (1913, p. 341). While rejecting Lombroso's "born criminal" idea, Goring concluded nonetheless that "the figures . . . seem markedly to suggest that crime has an hereditary nature" (p. 348). However, this finding may more accurately reflect the fact that the less robust and less intelligent criminals Goring was examining were obviously also less likely to evade capture.

Therefore, in comparing the two approaches, we first see that, while Lombroso may have thought that his theories were derived from the objective interpretation of data, they were actually rooted in the late-nineteenth-century notions of determinism and **Social Darwinism.** Individuals were blamed for their inadequacies, and little attention was paid to the structural roots of behaviour. Goring, although dismissive of Lombroso's ideas, believed as well that environment, social inequalities, and circumstance played little role in criminality. Thus, in retrospect, we can see the similarities between the two researchers: although they themselves felt their views were divergent, both were driven by a focus upon individual traits as the key to understanding the cause of criminal behaviour.

Fascination with the idea of heredity as cause for criminality remained intact in locations other than Europe. An American study by Robert Dugdale (1841–83) traced generations of a family, the Jukes, to uncover an amazing number of related deviants. Dugdale was an investigator for the Prison Association of New York and encountered the Jukes in his role as a field agent for the association. He determined that the Jukes spawned 140 criminals, 50 prostitutes, 60 thieves, 7 murderers, and many other "inferior" citizens. The findings were taken as evidence for inherited criminality. Considerations of environmental factors, such as socio-economic influence on behaviour, were not made. The poverty cycle, with its accompanying limitations on personal health and development, simply was not weighed as a relevant factor in the analysis of criminality.

In 1912, Henry Goddard reported the findings of another study that traced offspring. He followed the lives of the children of a soldier in the American Revolution. The soldier, Martin Kallikak, produced an illegitimate child from a sexual relationship with a young barmaid, who was "feeble-minded." Kallikak left the woman and child to return home and subsequently marry another woman, who was of "normal" intelligence and acceptable family background. Goddard then followed the two streams of offspring that were spawned from Kallikak—with not-surprising results. Through archival records, Goddard found that the barmaid family tree produced feeble-minded offspring as well as significant numbers of "deviants." In the "normal" family tree, there were no apparent defectives. Goddard argued that this supported the heritance argument (see Box 7.6). But, as we see again, the influence of obvious environmental differences in the two women's lives was ignored in the analysis. There were also other methodological problems related to the accuracy of the records he used and his definition of the term "feeble-mindedness."

Another American, Earnest Hooton, conducted a study similar in nature to Goring's in an attempt to refute Goring's dismissal of Lombroso's anthropological arguments. Hooton, a Harvard anthropologist, felt studies such as those done on family trees indicated support for an anthropological element of criminal causation. Over a twelve-year period, Hooton compared 10 000 male criminals with around 4000 noncriminals in terms of a number of physical traits and other demographic variables. On the basis of that study, Hooton argued his conclusions were consistent with those of Goring, but also consistent with Lombroso's more anthropological assessment.

He made an astounding comment about the relationship between physical size and seriousness of offence: the larger the criminal (although criminals were smaller than noncriminals), the more serious his or her offence was likely to be. He also stated that one could predict the type of crime individuals might engage in on the basis of physical build. Thus, small men commit forgery; murderers are tall and heavy. Perhaps his most amusing analysis (but ultimately fairly frightening in its implications for the stereotyping of racial groups) involved the prediction of criminality on the basis of ethnic background. For example, Italians and Teutonics were found by Hooton to engage in first-degree murder far more extensively than were Polish-Americans (see Figure 7.1).

While Hooton's work was met with derision from the sociological community, other proponents continued the Hooton tradition of linking body type to criminality.

Sheldon as the "Inheritance" Heir: Body Types

The focus on inheritance as a causal factor in criminality continued with the work of William Sheldon in the 1950s. He argued from his studies on body classification that personality characteristics are related to certain kinds of behaviour, which are, in turn, related to body type. According to Sheldon, there are basically three body types (termed "somatotypes"): *ectomorphs*, who are thin, worry a lot, and are introverted; *mesomorphs*, who are muscular, extroverted, and aggressive; and *endomorphs*, who are soft and limp, with easygoing ways, yet also extroverted. Sheldon felt that everyone possessed parts of all three types to some degree. These properties were signified through employment of a seven-point scale. To illustrate, a somatotype of 2.0–1.5–6.0 (for the degrees of endomorphy, mesomorphy,

Figure 7.1 First Degree Murder
Rankings—Native Whites—Foreign Parentage
Source: Earnest Albert Hooton (1968), *Crime and the man* (p. 147). New York: Greenwood Press.

e Movement

Canada, begin-

Delinquents

od test for the

identification

(1979) has not-

on of the ideas

the most op-

admit that the

recidivism was

. The idea that

er entertained.

dness became,

hat also seemed

t effective.

sey did not go

ad low intelli-

riminality and

unishment. Us-

lfred Binet in

al age of twelve

of intelligence

oddard (1914)

proportion of

, sometimes up

en prison. As-

ble-mindedness

ection between

sts on military

21) to revise his

ost one-third of

and almost half

years (Zeleny,

and other con-

inued to assume

did members of

1979). Further-

reditary, crimi-

passed to future

ocreation of the

th century, but

ally referred to

le's (1877) study

tabrook in 1916

one of the prin-

ovement. The

Hygiene (1919)

found that more than half (59 percent) of the children in B.C. industrial schools and the detention centre were "mentally abnormal," meaning not that they were mentally ill but that they were morons, imbeciles, backward, or, at best, dull normal. This finding was thought to explain their recidivism:

> British Columbia, like the other provinces of Canada, has apparently proceeded on the basis that the problem of juvenile delinquency was one involving only normal children. This preconception has led to the time honored system of placing offenders on probation or in reformatories with the hope of a successful issue. Failure, instead of success, has frequently been the result after painstaking and conscientious efforts along this line. [After finding that 59 percent of juvenile offenders were mentally abnormal] we would not expect the ordinary parole system or the industrial school to be effective reformatory agencies. . . . We would also be fearful that perchance the industrial school might be hampered in exerting a good influence on their normal charges since they are called upon to deal with a mixed population. (1919, pp. 30–31)

Such children were not generally seen as redeemable, a view contrary to that initially held by juvenile court supporters, and this had three immediate consequences. The first was the increasing reliance upon psychiatrists to aid in dispositional decision making. Such professionals, it was thought, could determine amenability for treatment and generally give guidance to the court about the appropriate course of action. (This is discussed in detail in Chapter 8.) Second, long-term, custodial confinement for "untrainable," feeble-minded children began. Third, because the procreation of the feeble-minded was considered harmful to society, sterilization, especially for girls, was lauded as it permitted their safe release into the community to be engaged as unskilled or domestic labourers (Westman, 1930). (In 1933, the year Adolf Hitler passed a similar law in Germany, the Sterilization Act took effect in British Columbia [McLaren, 1986], following the lead of Alberta [Chapman, 1977]. These were the only provinces to actually legalize the sterilization of institutionalized populations, although 31 U.S. states had eugenics laws.) Eugenics and the custodial confinement of delinquents were but two of the priorities expressed by mental hygienists, who also advocated restrictions on immigration and segregation of the public schools (Sutherland, 1976).

and ectomorphy, respectively) would represent an extreme ectomorph.

Delinquents studied by Sheldon were found to be primarily mesomorphs, lacking in any stable ectomorphy. He termed the type "Dionysian"—these individuals were impulsive, undisciplined, and self-centred. Followup studies comparing delinquents with nondelinquents (matched on a number of demographic variables such as, age, IQ, race, socio-economic level) found delinquents to be significantly more mesomorphic and significantly less ectomorphic than were the nondelinquents, thus confirming Sheldon's earlier findings.

In his later publication, *Atlas of Men* (1954), Sheldon became somewhat more eccentric in his **somatotyping** exercise, designating animal labels for each type. For example, somatotype 5–2–4 was defined as being "the Texas striped under-the-barn kitty. Finest and bushiest-tailed of his family. An ambling, viscerotonic fellow, he grubs for roots and beetles, loves to get fat in the fall and to sleep through the severe weather" (p. 260). Other types similarly defined were termed anteaters, oxen, falcons, great owls, and stingless mosquitoes.

It may have been this trivializing of his "scientific" analysis that led to dismissal of Sheldon's somatotyping techniques by scholars. But, more basically, the Biological Positivists, as they were called, men such as Lombroso, Goring, and Sheldon, had insurmountable difficulties when it came to justifying their arguments. The methodological problems of the studies were in most question. Normally, the samples were small or not appropriately selected; the definitions of what constituted crime and inferiority were not clearly stated. One major difficulty with sample selection, as noted above for Goring's work, was the fact the "criminals" subjected to examination were most often convicted offenders and not *law violators* more generally. Therefore, the larger group is not really being examined.

Additionally, the theorists tended to look at traditional types of crime only, and ignored other forms of criminality. Justice-system functioning, for example, often also generates criminality, e.g., those suspect activities of the police, such as the acceptance of payoffs. Overriding these issues, however, was the point that physical differences between criminals and noncriminals did not take into account the influence of environmental factors, such as socio-economic levels and cultural heritage, upon behaviour. On the basis of these criticisms, the idea of inherited traits is no longer held valid by most contemporary geneticists *or* criminologists.[1] Even with these criticisms, however, Biological Positivism has continued in different forms into contemporary times (see Box 7.7). It proceeds at a higher level of sophistication, perhaps, but still underlying the approaches is the basic premise that there

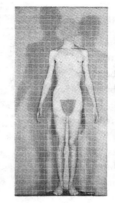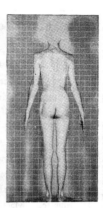

A.

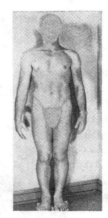

B.

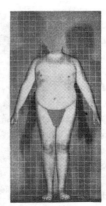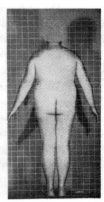

C.

Figure 7.2 Sheldon's Extreme Somatotypes
A. Extreme Ectomorphy
B. Extreme Mesomorphy
C. Extreme Endomorphy

Source: William Sheldon (1940), *The varieties of the human physique: An introduction to constitutional psychology.* New York: Harper & Row [rprt. 1970, Darien, CT: Hafner].

fender Look Like?

by Esses and
sical appearance
n. The question
idea that people
fiable way. The
nation about a
photograph and
ects were asked
round in which
l normality, and
nipulated. Phys-
els: descriptions
rmality and nor-
rent listings, sex-
ls: one present

conviction and five previous convictions. The participants were to address directly the criteria set out for a finding of a dangerous offender (ss. 755–761 of the Canadian Criminal Code).

The subjects perceived the physically unattractive sexual offender as significantly more likely to fulfil the Canadian dangerous-offender criteria than the average-looking and attractive sexual offenders. Their responses were thus consistent with a biased stereotypic perception of criminality, one that has no proven validity in reality. Basically, the subjects were responding in a manner that the biological typologists, such as Lombroso, Sheldon, and Hooton, would suggest is not unreasonable. That is, they were assuming that criminal types are identifiable by physical characteristics.

dual's genetic

Evil vs.

of the genetic-
lity, then one
(or prosocial)
vever, it is also
e rearing con-
ermine if the
socio/psycho-
his confound-
ntical, mono-
(DZ) twins of
ilized egg that
from two eggs
oment of con-
of genes, and
Ellis, 1982).
in studies con-
d that 60 per-
iour patterns,
is shared simi-
leted indicate
r both. Chris-
verall found a
percent corre-
(1983) found

the correlation for delinquent behaviour was higher for MZ twins than for DZ twins, based upon a mail-out questionnaire (with over 50 percent return) sent to twins in grades eight to twelve. Therefore, while it does seem that a great deal of variance can be explained by the genetic factor, further studies must be completed to control for other factors such as differences in experienced parental-treatment patterns between MZ twins and DZ twins (Walters & White, 1989, p. 466).

Adoption studies have used another approach to try to separate the influence of the environment from that of heredity. If children are adopted at birth and do not subsequently know their biological parents, then environmental influence alone can affect behavioural development, if there is no hereditary contribution. It becomes an empirical question as to whether or not the adopted child would display the criminality of the biological parent.

However, the methodology in these studies is difficult to keep "clean," in terms of frequency of contact with biological parents, age at adoption, and placement in similar or different circumstances from biological parents. The largest study was reported by Mednick, Gabrielli, and Hutchings (1984). It was based on all nonfamilial adoptions in Denmark from 1924 to 1947, and included 14 427 male and female adoptees and their biological and adoptive parents. The findings suggest the adoptive-parent criminality does not appear to affect the adoptee's proclivity to crime, but that biological-parent criminality does. However, the socio-economic status (SES) of the adoptive parent turned out to be more highly correlated with adopted-son crime than biological-parent SES. Therefore, once again further research is needed to tease out the genetic influence in the criminality.

More contemporary researchers have attempted to consider the possibility of an interaction between genetic influence and environmental influence in the acting out of criminal behaviour. Rowe and Osgood (1984) did demonstrate in twin data that environmental factors such as social class interacted with genetic factors in a way that resulted in the whole interaction accounting for more of what occurred than each factor taken separately. These authors advocate for further research on interactive effects, which might result in the development of a criminological theory that incorporates a consideration of genetic influences. This idea is contrary to the opinion many sociologists hold as being more appropriate, that is, the dismissal of such ideas as noncredible.

In summary, it appears that genetic influence cannot be said to *directly* affect behaviour.

Crime and the Chromosomes: "Supermales" and Super Evil?

The work of Patricia Jacobs and associates (1965) set the Genetic Positivists in another direction. She and her colleagues found that a large proportion of male inmates in a Scottish prison possessed an extra male chromosome. In human beings, 23 pairs of chromosomes are inherited, one of them determining gender. An X chromosome is inherited for females; and an X and a Y are inherited for males. On occasion, however, as a result of anomalies, a male will receive two Y chromosomes. Jacobs determined that the incidence of occurrence of this anomaly was about 1 in 1000 in the general population, but, in the prisons studied, the frequency was ten to twenty times larger. The "double Ys" were termed "double males" or "supermales." It was hypothesized that these men were abnormally tall, and inclined to violent behaviour.

Later studies did not find this to be a replicable phenomenon in terms of incidence within institutions, and, in fact, a Danish study failed to support the violence hypothesis (Witkin et al., 1976). Double Ys were found to be actually more introverted than normals in that study, although the small number of double Ys discovered in the institutional setting did engage in significantly more criminal behaviour than did matched XY men. It was also clear that the abnormality expressed itself through a lowered intelligence capacity. Therefore, one explanation offered for evidenced criminal behaviour was that these double Ys were not able to attain appropriate educational achievements, a failure that placed them at a disadvantage in society, thus making them more vulnerable to committing deviant behaviour.

This last point about educational deficits as possible causal contributors to criminality raises another consideration discussed in the literature, that is, the connection between low intelligence and criminality. As with the importance in defining what criminality means, we must also be precise with the definition of intelligence. A French psychologist, Alfred Binet, developed an instrument in the 1890s to test what he deemed could reasonably be labelled intelligence in individuals. He carefully created test items that were relevant for different age categories. These were allegedly founded upon reasoning, language comprehension, and judgment making.

Based upon the early administration of Binet's test to offenders and nonoffenders, findings suggested that there is an average difference of about 8 points between the IQ "scores" of offenders and those of the general population (the average for the general population has been determined to be 100 points: Caplan, 1965). Unfortunately, the finding is confounded by the socio-economic status (SES) of the individual being tested. To unconfound the relationship, other researchers have compared the IQs of siblings—offenders and nonoffenders—since the SES among siblings should normally be more consistent than that among nonsiblings (nonsiblings comprised the samples in the early studies). The result of the more controlled matching does reduce the differences in IQ levels between offenders and nonoffenders, but as Wilson and Herrnstein (1984, p. 157) conclude in their review of these studies, IQ is generally more predictive of offending than is social class or cultural background.

There have been many objections to the use of the Binet tests. It has been argued that they are biased against lower socio-economic-level individuals—those who comprise the majority in our penal institutions—that the tests are measuring middle-class expectations; and that they cannot possibly measure, on a point scale, a concept as complex as intelligence. There are other, more qualitative, tests. The Wechsler–Bellevue Scale, for example, attempts to measure other "subcomponents" of intelligence, such as performance. Differences emerge here as well between offenders and nonoffenders, but some of the same criticisms aimed at the Binet results can be levelled against the Wechsler–Bellevue findings. What does seem consistent and agreed upon throughout with both types of tests are differences among different categories of criminals. Thus, in general, rapists, murderers, and assaulters are found to have lower IQs than do forgers, fraud artists, and embezzlers.

In summary, criticisms of methodology in these studies, as in the twins studies and chromosomal studies, again eclipse the possible significance of the results in explaining differences by genetic influence on criminality. The samples are small, and the confoundings of environmental factors

erate, one-time
nurses in their
a criminal, and
d on one of his
d strangulation,
eting. One girl
al attack. Speck
reality of what
he read in the
him to attempt
d an attending
his tattoo.
laimed to have
verified that he

had consumed great quantities of drugs and alcohol that night. Despite this, and substantial evidence of brain damage, his lawyer decided against using the **insanity defence** and adopted the position that Speck had not been at the house that night. In the face of considerable evidence to the contrary, he was found guilty. However, it was noted that Speck shared two physical attributes thought to be indicative of XYY supermales: he was tall and had a bad complexion. It was later proved that he was not an XYY. He was sentenced to the electric chair in June 1967, but the sentence was changed to 400 years in prison after **capital punishment** was effectively abolished by the Supreme Court. In 1978, Richard Speck finally confessed to the crime.

trolled for in
een generally
t attempts to
f the causality

or example,
ible, was ad-
e as an argu-
(see Box 7.8)
a. Speck mur-
s subsequent
ument failed,

ffect on

nal behaviour
the behaviour
cretions (e.g.,
ologists based
where it was
nones resulted
was deemed
ent of sexual
ale hormones
chemical cas-
ive. However,
treatment as a
n incomplete.

The public's concern with such crimes and the apparent lack of other effective therapy programs for sex offenders have sometimes resulted in the use of medical drug treatment, even for juvenile sex offenders (see Chapter 9 for further discussion). It is unfortunate that chemical drug treatment is employed in this manner without having adequate testing completed on its effects. The result, in some cases, is that a treatment regime is imposed, that might, not surprisingly, have implications for the violation of rights of the individual thus "treated."

The effect of other chemical changes on the incidence of types of behaviour has also been studied, for example, the effect of the use of such substances as alcohol and narcotics (see Chapter 5 for further discussion). A causal relationship between their use and criminal behaviour is particularly hard to determine, however, since it is difficult to isolate the chemical effects from either pre-existing physiological states or environmental factors—a difficulty encountered in the research of other Biological Positivists noted earlier. What is clear, though, is that *dependence* on chemical substances can greatly influence the occurrence of criminality, especially for those individuals in the lower socio-economic classes who must generate funds to sustain their addictive habits.

Eating to Become Evil

It has been suggested that what one eats has an impact on behaviour (see Box 7.9). In fact, in a classic case in San Francisco, a man was found not guilty of the murder of the mayor of the city and a city supervisor on that basis.

The accused, Dan White, was known to eat junk food as standard fare and, as a consequence, the jury acquitted him, despite his confession, after he advanced the so-called Twinkie defence. Psychiatrists, serving as expert witnesses in the trial (see Chapter 8 for a discussion of the role of psychiatrists in the court), provided support for this unusual defence, arguing that low blood sugar (hypoglycemia) had influenced the behaviour. The issue of the effect of diet upon criminal behaviour remained highlighted throughout the 1960s, even causing some prison administrators to become concerned about the potential effect of prison diets upon inmates' behaviour (Stasiak, 1982).

Hypoglycemia has been blamed more generally for anti-social behaviours in man. The condition occurs when the body's blood sugar-level falls below that needed to keep the brain functioning properly, with the result that the metabolism slows. Symptoms of hypoglycemia include depression, confusion, and general irritability. Studies have related assaults, murder, and sexual offences to hypoglycemic reactions (Siegel, 1986, p. 154).

Similarly, allergies to foods have been offered as causal factors in criminal behaviour. Interestingly enough, milk, long thought to be health-giving, was at one time believed to be a suspect food substance in the delinquent behaviour of those juveniles who are allergic to milk, in comparison with that of "normal" juveniles. These delinquents were found to drink significantly more milk than nondelinquents (Schauss, 1980). Sociobiologists have also argued that there is a strong link between vitamin deficiency and criminal behaviour, especially with the B-complex vitamins. Vitamin B dependency has been closely associated with hypertension in juveniles (Hippchen, 1976, p. 14).

Neurophysiology is another area of recent interest to sociobiologists. The brain's activities are focussed on through an examination of the electroencephalogram (EEG). The EEG is the measure of an electrical discharge, as it pulses as a "brain wave," through an oscilloscope. The waves are recorded in units called hertz (Hz). At one level of investigation, comparisons are made between criminals and noncriminals, using the same rationale employed by the earlier Biological Positivists: that is, criminals may be differentiated physically from noncriminals.

In 1969, D. Williams reported a study in which 335 violent delinquents were used as subjects to investigate EEG abnormalities. The delinquents were divided into two groups: those classified as "habitual" offenders and those determined to have committed only a single offence. In the first phase of the study, abnormalities were revealed in 65 percent of the habitually aggressive offenders and 24 percent of the single-offence group. The second phase, with tighter controls, was administered on the same group, excluding the mentally retarded, the brain-damaged, and the epileptic. Even with this closer focus, 57 percent of the first group still showed abnormalities; while only 12 percent of the individuals committing one offence only (defined as being legally convicted for one offence) demonstrated abnormalities (Siegel, 1986, p. 156).

The difficulties with interpreting this study, and other studies reporting similar findings, is that, first, there are now extant studies that have found little relationship between EEG and violent behaviour, but more importantly, the research that does find differences can not explain the many nonviolent people who also possess EEG abnormalities.

Box 7.9 Veggies Help Turn Thief into Model Citizen

LONDON—A young glue-sniffer with a string of burglary convictions has been "sentenced" to eat a healthy diet.

As an alternative to being jailed, the 17-year-old has been ordered to give up his favourite junk food and replace it with healthier fare—brown bread, fresh vegetables and fruit.

And within a few weeks, he has turned from a compulsive delinquent into a model citizen.

Instead of stealing money, he is now working, has stopped sniffing glue and is living with his family again after long spells in institutions.

The youth is the trailblazer in a radical scheme in Cumbria in northwest England, where magistrates in juvenile courts—concerned at the failure of conventional deterrents—have agreed to test the theory that anti-social behaviour may be caused by poor diet and poisons in the environment.

The Cumbria venture is one example of how some people fighting juvenile crime—magistrates, probation officers, police—have decided to challenge the skepticism of their critics and put these controversial theories to the test.

But the notion that poor diet can make people violent is viewed with suspicion by the British medical establishment. And research has been impeded by the nation's opposition to experimentation on prisoners.

Source: Nicola Tyrer (1989), *London Daily Telegraph*, May 24.

...erspective

...constitutional,
...tors in trying
... While some
...ted adversely
...uded because
..., definitional
... uncontrolled
...Additionally,
... varied from
...study. Crimi-
...the literature:
...ore specifical-
...tion.
...ver. C. Ray
...rary advocate
...ie topic were
...on in his book

...enetic differ-
...es. Every per-
...ootential, and
...nvironmental
...ider how the
...sential deter-
...s perspective
... of inherited
...hough, place
...mental factors
... environment
...ial's learning
...ervous system
...earning was:

...ient = Behaviour

...nd behaviour
...activated the
...refore, he be-
...id sociopathy
...nemical "pre-
...esult in alco-

...ient is central
...s' perspective

...l

...haeology, and
...search for *the*

criminal type. Psychological Positivists have undertaken the search for a criminal personality. This search, however, instead of being conducted through the measuring of skulls, noses, and other bodily parts and substances, was based on the categorizing and measurement of traits and patterns of thinking. Psychometrists, for example, have long tried to obtain measurable differences between criminals and non-criminals. David Tennenbaum (1977) reviewed the literature in the area of **psychometry** and found no conclusive evidence for the idea that one could determine criminal behaviour on the basis of measured personality traits.

Despite Tennenbaum's findings, the idea that there can be a distinctive criminal personality type has continued to receive support. In 1976, two clinicians, Samuel Yochelson and Stanton Samenow, published the results of a fourteen-year study of 240 criminals housed in a hospital for the criminally insane in Washington, D.C. All ideas of environmental influence on criminality were rejected by the authors, who instead proposed that individual thinking patterns are responsible for criminal actions. Much of their logic is similar to that used by clinicians and criminologists who delineate specific characteristics of behaviour defined as being psychopathic (see Chapter 9). The criminal personality (as is also thought to be true of the psychopath) is unremorseful, manipulative, and genetically determined.

Yochelson and Samenow suggested that the criminal personality emerges at birth and not as a result of familial or environmental influences. In fact, they concluded that individuals with a criminal mind have a deleterious influence on their families *and* on the environment they are in because of their behaviour.

The implications this theory has for the criminal-justice system are primarily in the area of treatment. Yochelson and Samenow did feel that, if these individuals were willing to change their way of thinking and take responsibility for their behaviour through therapeutic intervention, there was hope for change. But, as with the psychopath, significant behaviour change was thought to be unlikely. There were, however, considered to be two other options for such individuals: continuing in a life of criminality or committing suicide.

Cognitive-development theory, a type of psychological theory, also attempts to explain criminal behaviour on the basis of how the mind operates. Again, the underlying assumption is that it is the individual who is the source of "evil." One direction this theory has taken in the past is toward the explanation (similar to that of Yochelson and of Samenow) that criminal thinking is based on deficits in moral-reasoning ability. If the person were able to organize his or her thoughts to be consistent with the moral rule of society, "good" behaviour would result.

Jean Piaget (1896–1980), considered the founder of the moral-development concept, proposed that the orderly development of thinking began at birth and stabilized at around age twelve. During the development, two stages of moral-reasoning development occur: in the first, the child believes all rules are "truth" and interchangeable, and, in the second, the child comes to believe that rules are made by humans.

Lawrence Kohlberg (1969), a psychologist, expanded Piaget's ideas and defined six stages of **moral development** (see Box 7.10). People make judgments differently as they pass through each stage. Applying the concept to criminal thinking has led to the suggestion that perhaps criminals have become arrested at a lower stage of moral development than is true for the rest of the citizenry. If they can be trained or educated to achieve higher stages (again, the treatment orientation of the Positivists surfaces),

the result theoretically would be more moral/law-abiding citizens. In fact, these principles form the basis of many prison education programs in Canada (Duguid, 1979). Further Canadian development of the moral-reasoning/character-development approach can be found in Canadian prison education programs that incorporate the training technique in a life-skills framework (Ross, Fabiano, & Ewles, 1988; Arbuthnot & Gordon, 1988). The idea is essentially that individuals at a high stage of moral development are more likely to make their own decisions and not be influenced by others.

Similar criticism aimed at IQ measurement in relation to criminality can be directed to the use of level of moral development in attempting to explain criminality. Therefore, one of the first questions that must be asked is: who is determining the category boundaries, and what objective meaning can be ascribed to them? For example, why

---

Box 7.10 Kohlberg's Stages of Moral Development

Levels of Moral Development
I. Preconventional Level

At the first level, the child responds to cultural rules and labels of good and bad, right and wrong, but assimilates the labels in terms of the physical consequences of the action (that is, reward, punishment, etc.) or in terms of the physical power of those who articulate the labels. The level has two stages:

Stage 1: The punishment and obedience orientation. Goodness and badness are determined by the physical consequences of action, regardless of the meaning or value of these consequences. Avoidance of punishment and unquestioning deference to power do not occur out of respect for an underlying moral order.

Stage 2: This is the instrumental-relativist orientation. "Right" action serves one's own ends—and, occasionally, the needs of others. Human relations are marketed in a "you scratch my back and I'll scratch yours" way of thinking.

II. Conventional Level

The next level proceeds on the basis that the expectations of significant others, and even the nation, are valuable in considering what is "right" conduct. The individual not only adheres to these expectations, but closely identifies with them and supports them. There are two stages at this level:

Stage 3: The "good boy/nice girl" orientation. Good behaviour is what others want from you and what

pleases them. This results in much conformity and stereotypical imagery. Intention is important in determining goodness or badness.

Stage 4: The "law and order" orientation. Right behaviour is comprised of doing one's duty and showing respect for authority. The existing social order is maintained for its own sake.

III. Postconventional, Autonomous, or Principled Level

There is a concerted effort at this level to articulate moral values and principles that have validity apart from the authority of the individuals or groups who hold these principles and separate from the person's own identification with these groups. This level has two stages as well:

Stage 5: The social-contract legalistic orientation, which has utilitarian implications. Right action is defined in terms of individual rights and standards agreed upon by society. The emphasis is upon the "legal point of view."

Stage 6: The universal-ethical principle orientation. Right action is determined by the decision of the conscience. Principles are abstract and ethical, not concrete rules like the Ten Commandments.

Source: Abstracted from L. Kohlberg (1986). The just community approach to corrections (pp. 57–58). *Journal of Correctional Education* 37 (2).

d not twelve?
legree of reli-
g moral judg-
he importance
stage of moral
oes seem that
g's ideas as in
:he student of
es in assessing
tudying them.
the validity of
levels of moral
e theory's ra-
ce a casual (as
:n the two be-
ngs (Jennings,
more realistic
nt to other fac-
ites a study of
nal variables—
reen sociolog-
iality. In other
r influence be-
: also be con-

Psychological
: that Tennen-
: efforts to de-
ublished *Crime*
heory of crimi-
outgoing per-
criminal than
s). Eysenck felt
bgical training,
:urn, inhibited

to Eysenck, is
litioned to the
he potential to
has considered
l, for example,
criminal act by
l'' condition-
ocess of linking
:iety must pro-
d education, in
rly, to become
irents are obvi-
ick encouraged
ourage bad be-
dure known as
977).

The elements of behaviour-modification training were articulated in detail by behavioural psychologist B.F. Skinner. Skinner's 1953 text, *Science and Human Behavior,* described behaviour as a response to conditioning. According to his theory, it should be possible to eliminate or greatly reduce bad behaviour through reward and punishment. All behaviour is learned, according to this theory and, therefore, theoretically, can be unlearned. Skinner was not as interested in personality types as was Eysenck, since his emphasis was on behaviour alone.

Behaviour therapy became a popular model of "treatment" in penal institutions in the 1970s. This treatment represented a shift away from an emphasis on inherited traits as the cause of crime. According to this theory, behaviour is continually changing in response to the environment. The "behaviourists" argue that criminality is a learned response and does not, therefore, emanate from an inherently evil person.

Social-learning theory is a branch of behaviour theory that takes the behaviour theorists' line of thought farther. Albert Bandura, a social-learning advocate, promoted the idea that individuals come to behave aggressively through a process called "modelling." **Modelling** occurs from simple observation of others' behaviour being rewarded, whether in real life or in the media. It could be described as an abstracted form of classical conditioning, distanced from "first-hand" conditioning of an individual. One example of the application of modelling principles to criminality in recent years is in the area of the effects of the media on behaviour. There has been increasing controversy, for example, over whether violence on TV and in the movies has deleterious modelling effects on youth.

Several explanations have been offered to account for possible behavioural effects of watching media depictions of violence. It has been suggested that modelling may occur in the same manner that other social and cognitive skills are learned, from the role models portrayed on the screen (Siegel, 1986, p. 169). Watching TV violence may increase arousal levels, which, in and of themselves, stimulate aggressive behaviour with no need for a cognitive mediating influence. Or, experiencing the violence vicariously may change basic attitudes and beliefs. If the violence is shown as being socially acceptable, then the viewer becomes sensitized to it and may no longer see it as negative. It may also contribute to the rationalization of violence for those who are already prone to such behaviour. Finally, it has been suggested that violence on television may serve as a disinhibitor. If the viewer sees violence romantically portrayed, or presented in a positive/accepting context, the experience may well serve to reinforce future violence in that individual. Overall, it does appear that *some* people are negatively influenced by watching violence in the visual-media context through types of social-learning processes (Siegel, 1986, p. 169).

While it does seem, at first, that the more contemporary social-learning theorists have finally "escaped" the bonds of the hereditary argument, they, in fact, keep one foot in the door by arguing that individuals may have *predispositions* to deviant behaviour that can become directed and actualized through social-learning processes. And it is, indeed, still the individual who is examined to determine the cause of criminal behaviour.

Summary of Psychological Positivists' Perspective

An evaluation of Psychological Positivism finds observations similar to those offered for the Biological Positivists. First of all, the theories are narrowly defined in that they focus primarily on what has traditionally been considered crime (see Introduction), ignoring a wide variety of victimless crimes, corporate deviance, and political criminality. We must ask the Psychological Positivists, for example, whether an organization is to be considered psychologically predisposed to a life of crime.

The Psychological Positivists' emphasis on the individual (as criminal) results in the development of treatment models. We will explore the **medical model** in more detail in Chapter 8, but generally this means that treatment is offered at every stage of our justice system: pretrial, trial, and posttrial interventions are recommended by experts to assist the *individual's* problem. The Psychological Positivists, however, fail to acknowledge as central the influence of the environment. Even the Behaviourists remained concerned with the individual as primarily responsible for criminality and possibly predisposed to crime.

Failure to consider environmental effects on crime has obvious implications for developing techniques for preventing crime and for social reforms more generally. If it is, indeed, the individual we must be concerned about in determining the causality of criminal behaviour, then levels of unemployment, conditions of poverty, etc., are not conceived of as directly relevant to the problem.

The nature (constitutional/genetic/psychological)-versus-nurture (sociological/environmental) controversy thus has not yet been resolved, but it does appear that some theorists now view the interaction of biological and social factors as central to any understanding of criminal behaviour (e.g., Mednick & Volavka, 1980).

An example of a study examining the **nature/nurture debate** relative to adult behavioural disorders was recently reported by two sociologists at Washington University in St. Louis, Missouri. Holmes and Robins (1989) attempted to tease out causal factors in the noted link between se-

vere punishment in childhood and psychological and behavioural problems in adulthood. They studied 200 adults who were part of a larger survey study: some were diagnosed as depressives, some as alcoholics, and some as having no major psychological problems. In the study, the respondents had to answer a long questionnaire on the severity, fairness, and consistency of discipline their parents provided them between the ages of six and twelve years. Three hypotheses were postulated:

1. harsh discipline in childhood causes adult problems;
2. children may inherit their psychological problems from mentally troubled parents no matter how they are disciplined; and
3. harsh discipline may be a logical parental response to a difficult and aggressive child, one whose adult problems have already begun to show up in childhood (Holmes & Robins, 1989, p. 16).

Their findings suggested that later mental and behavioural disorders may be related to how the child is treated by parents rather than to any inherited traits. Bad behaviour as a child did not necessarily precede adult disorder. Parental practices in disciplining, *not* the inherited bad-temperedness of the parent, contributed most significantly to the behaviour outcome. In the final assessment, however, both variables, nature (heredity) and nurture (environment = parental practices) were found to contribute to the deviant behaviour.

Conclusion

In this chapter we have briefly examined the demonic/biogenetic/psychogenic explanations of criminal behaviour. (See Appendix for table listing these theories/explanations of criminality.) Whether demons enter in to cause the individual to engage in evil behaviour or biological/psychological factors influence such behaviour, the focus has been on the individual as the producer of that criminality, not on society or social milieus or the environment more generally. The meaning such a focus has for the creation of legislative and social policy in the criminal-justice area is significant. Theories placing the individual as the cause of criminality obviously translate in an applied manner to programming and policy directed toward alleviation of individual symptomatology. As we shall see in Chapter 8, psychological theories of criminality have resulted, in the twentieth century, in the creation of the medical model. The concern is for the classification and diagnosis of the offender in order that individualized prevention and treatment programs can assist. The development of the idea of **probation** is a good example of this thinking. As well, we have certain legal defences, such as that of insanity, based

s of criminality,
d into programs
tion of allergic
But both of the

approaches remain grounded, even in the present day, upon the delineation of the individual's problems, whether psychological or biological, rather than of his or her environment.

---

ridual theories of
mselves into actual crime-
For example, what form
take that was based upon
ninality?

iculties that ensue from
"the criminal type" in
e, individual-rights,
oncerns are concerned?

dy type, heredity and
logical factors, in the
d in this chapter, the
redisposed to criminal
theorist with this
ence of environmental
in which many otherwise
uals sometimes appear to

---

nologists" themselves
vidence in Chapter 1
European typologists,

---

nd cognition. *Criminal*

Beccaria (1764). *On crimes and punishments*. Indianapolis: Bobbs-Merrill [rprt. 1963].

Brantingham, P.J. (1979). The classical and positive schools of criminology: Two ways of thinking about crime. In F.L. Faust & P.J. Brantingham (Eds.), *Juvenile justice philosophy: Readings, cases and comments* (2nd ed.) (pp. 36–48). St. Paul: West.

Canadian National Committee for Mental Hygiene (1919). Mental hygiene survey of the Province of British Columbia. *Canadian Journal of Mental Hygiene, 2*, 1–64.

Caplan, N.S. (1965). Intellectual functioning. In H.C. Quay (Ed.), *Juvenile Delinquency* (pp. 100–138). Princeton, NJ: Van Nostrand.

Chapman, T.L. (1977). The early eugenics movement in western Canada. *Alberta History, 25*, 9–17.

d'Orban, R.T., & Dalton, J. (1980). Violent crime and the menstrual cycle. *Psychological Medicine, 10*, 352–59.

Dugdale, R. (1877). *The Jukes: A study in crime, pauperism, and heredity*. New York: Putnam.

Duguid, S. (1979). History and moral education in correctional education. *Canadian Journal of Education, 4*, 81–92.

Ellis, L. (1982). Genetics and criminal behaviour. *Criminology, 20*, 43–66.

Esses, V., & Webster, C.D. (1986). *Physical attractiveness, dangerousness, and the Canadian Criminal Code*. Unpublished manuscript, Clarke Institute of Psychiatry & the University of Toronto.

Estabrook, A.H. (1916). *The Jukes in 1915*. Washington, DC: Carnegie Institute.

Eysenck, H. (1977). *Crime and personality* (3rd ed.). London: Routledge & Kegan Paul.

Faust, F.L., & Brantingham, P.J. (Eds.) (1979). *Juvenile justice philosophy: Readings, cases and comments* (2nd ed.). St. Paul: West.

Foucault, M. (1978). *Discipline and punish: The origins of the prison* (Trans. by A. Sheridan). New York: Pantheon.

Goddard, H.H. (1912). *The Kallikak Family: A study in the heredity of feeblemindedness*. New York: Macmillan.

Goddard, H.H. (1914). *Feeblemindedness: Its causes and consequences*. New York: Macmillan.

Goddard, H.H. (1921). Feeblemindedness and delinquency. *Journal of Psycho-Asthenics, 25*, 168–76.

Goring, C. (1913). *The English convict: A statistical study*. London: HMSO.

Hatch, A.J. (1988). *Theory and praxis in youth justice: Treatment orders and the implementation of the Young Offenders Act*. Unpublished Master's thesis, School of Criminology, Simon Fraser University.

Hippchen, L.J. (1976). Biochemical approaches to offender rehabilitation. *Offender rehabilitation 1* (1), 115–23.

Holmes, S., & Robins, L. (1989). Spare the rod, spoil the child. *Psychology Today*, p. 16.

Hooton, E. (1939). *Crime and the man*. Westport, CT: Greenwood.

Huff, C.R. (1980). Historical explanations of crime. In D. Kelly (Ed.), *Criminal behavior: Readings in criminology* (pp. 155–74). New York: St. Martin's.

Jacobs, P.A., Brunton, M., Melville, M.M., Britain, R.P., & McClement, W.F. (1965). Aggressive behavior, mental subnormality, and the XYY Male. *Nature, 208*, 1351–52.

Jennings, W.S., Kilkenny, R., & Kohlberg, L. (1983). Moral-development theory and practice for youthful and adult offenders. In W.S. Laufer & S.M. Day (Eds.), *Personality theory, moral development, and criminal behavior* (pp. 281–355). Lexington, MA: Lexington.

Kohlberg, L. (1986). The just community approach to corrections. *Journal of Correctional Education, 37*(2), 54–58.

Lombroso, G. (1911). *The criminal man*. Montclair, NJ: Patterson Smith [rprt. 1972].

MacGill, H.G. (1919). The relation of the juvenile court to the community. *Canadian Journal of Mental Hygiene, 1*, 232–6.

McLaren, A. (1986). The creation of a haven for "human thoroughbreds": The sterilization of the feeble-minded in British Columbia. *Canadian Historical Review, 67*, 264–8.

Mannheim, H. (1973). *Pioneers in criminology*. Montclair, NJ: Patterson Smith.

Mednick, S.A., & Volavka, J. (1980). Biology and crime. In N. Morris & M. Tonry (Eds.), *Crime and justice* (pp. 85–158). Chicago: University of Chicago Press.

Mednick, S.A., & Gabrielli Jr., W.F., & Hutchings, B. (1984). Genetic influences in criminal convictions: Evidence from an adoption cohort. *Science, 224*, 891–94.

Morash, M. (1983). An explanation of juvenile delinquency: The integration of moral reasoning, theory and social knowledge. In W.S. Leufer & J.M. Day (Eds.), *Personality theory, moral development, and criminal behavior* (pp. 385–409). Lexington, MA: Lexington.

Mill, J.S. (1950). *On Bentham and Coleridge*. Introduction by F.R. Leavis. New York: Harper & Row.

Newman, G. (1978). *The punishment response*. New York: J.B. Lippincott.

Pfohl, S. (1985). *Images of deviance and social control*. New York: McGraw-Hill.

Piaget, J. (1932). *The moral development of a child*. London: Routledge & Kegan Paul.

Ross, R.R., Fabiano, E.A., & Ewles, C.D. (1988). Reasoning and rehabilitation. *International Journal of Offender Therapy and Comparative Criminology, 32*, 29–35.

Rowe, D.C. (1983). Biometric genetic models of self-reported delinquent behavior: A twin study. *Behavior Genetics, 13*, 473–89.

Rowe, D.C., & Osgood, D.W. (1984). Heredity and sociological theories of delinquency: A reconsideration. *American Sociological Review, 49*, 526–40.

Sutherland, N. (1976). *Children in English Canadian society: Framing the twentieth century consensus*. Toronto: University of Toronto Press.

Schauss, A. (1980). *Diet, crime, and delinquency*. Berkeley, CA: Parker House.

Siegel, L.J. (1986). *Criminology*. St. Paul: West.

Skinner, B.F. (1953). *Science and human behavior*. New York: Macmillan.

Stasiak, E.A. (1982). Nutrition and criminal behaviour. Paper presented at the American Correctional Association Congress, Toronto.

Vold, G.B., & Bernard, T. (1979). *Theoretical criminology* (2nd ed.). New York: Oxford University Press.

Walters, G.D., & White, T.W. (1989). Heredity and crime: bad genes or bad research? *Criminology 27* (3) 455–85.

Westman, A. (1930). Trends in the care of delinquent girls. *Child and Family Welfare, 6*, 33–6.

Wilson, E.O. (1975). *Sociobiology*. Cambridge, MA: Harvard University Press.

Wilson, J.Q., & Herrnstein, R.J. (1985). *Crime and human nature: The definitive study of the causes of crime*. New York: Simon & Schuster.

Witkin, H.A., Mednick, S.A., Schulsinger, F., Bakkestrom, E, Christiansen, K.O., Goodenough, D.R., Hirshhorn, K., Lundsteen, C., Owen, D.R., Philip, J., Rubin, D.B., & Stocking, M. (1976) XYY and XXY men: Criminality and aggression. *Science, 193*, 547–55.

Yochelson, S., & Samenow, S.E. (1976). *The criminal personality*, vols. 1 and 2. New York: Jason Aronson.

Zeleny, L.D. (1933). Feeblemindedness and criminal conduct. *American Journal of Sociology, 38*, 564–76.

planations

	Content of Argument	Cause of Criminality
es	Sin = Crime	Demons, gods spirits, cause evil behaviour
c.	Man is not nature; Man manipulates nature	Man chooses evil
	Man is nature = Cosmos	Conflict with cosmos
	Free will	Man chooses evil
	Humanitarian values	Man is hedonistic
	Biological determinism	The criminal *type* is biologically determined
3	"	
4	"	
	"	
	"	
	"	Goring opposed Lombroso's anthropomorphic explanation, but still thought criminality was biologically determined
3	"	Inheritance of criminal tendencies through family lines
	"	
iry	Support of inheritance theories	Individual inherits criminal traits
	"	Chromosomes cause criminal tendencies
	Psychological determinism	IQ level predicts criminality (Wecheler–Bellevue Scale reduced differences found between offenders and nonoffenders)
	Personality determines proclivity to criminality	Tennenbaum could find no conclusive evidence for predicting criminality on basis of personality traits
	Inherent moral character	Lack of moral development
	"	
	"	Crime caused by criminal mind
	Personality predisposition	Personality determines criminal tendencies (introvert vs. extrovert)
	Behaviour affected by positive and negative reinforcement	
	Behaviour learned	Individuals with predisposition to aggression learn criminality through modelling

8 Mental Disorder and Crime in Canada

In Toronto, an elderly woman is arrested by police for causing a disturbance, after she is caught breaking windows and shouting at passers-by on a busy downtown street corner. Following one week of confinement in a pretrial detention centre, she is remanded to a forensic assessment clinic, diagnosed as a chronic schizophrenic, and referred for a two-month in-patient stay to one of the city's psychiatric hospitals. Outside of Winnipeg, convicted rapists undergo programs of rehabilitative therapy and aversive conditioning while they serve their prison sentences. In the suburbs of Vancouver, a teenager, who has shot to death several members of his immediate family, is found not guilty by reason of insanity and confined indefinitely in a maximum-security institution for the **criminally insane**. In a village in central Quebec, an arsonist is labelled an incurable psychopath by expert court witnesses and sentenced to an indeterminate prison term as a dangerous offender. In small-town New Brunswick, a young man is picked up on a charge of purse snatching, found unfit to stand trial, and spends the next seventeen years of his life as a mental patient.

These five cases represent a vast range of experience in the Canadian response to criminal behaviour, and they involve widely contrasting facets of our **criminal-justice system**. Yet, for all their differences, these scenarios share one important characteristic: their course and outcome are, in some fashion, being shaped by the participation of mental-health professionals. The rise of **forensic psychiatry** and related disciplines such as **forensic psychology**—those branches of each profession that are concerned with legal issues and processes—is one of the most revolutionary hallmarks of present-day Canadian judicial institutions. The influence of psychiatrists and their fellow clinicians is found virtually everywhere in our criminal machinery, from our most global theories about the treatment and control of **criminality**; to the organization of courts, prisons, and related institutions; to the most specific decisions rendered every day by police, judges, probation and parole officers, and other officials working in every part of the country. In our "psychiatric society" (Castel, Castel, & Lovell, 1982), it is hard even to contemplate a facet of the Canadian criminal-justice enterprise that has not been touched in some way by the ideas and practices of mental-health experts.

The study of psychiatry and **criminal law** has, in Canada and elsewhere, matured over the past few decades into a major field of criminological study. Many researchers in Canadian universities and hospitals now devote themselves full-time to studying such topics as the relationship between mental disorder and crime, the role of insanity and related issues in criminal law, and the activities of forensic clinicians in the judicial apparatus. Throughout the world, organizations such as the International Congress of Law and Mental Health, and the American Academy of Psychiatry and the Law, claim hundreds of members. The criminology section in most college libraries now offers an extensive collection of books on forensic psychiatry, and many of these texts present a uniquely Canadian point of view (Menzies, 1989; Savage & McKague, 1987; Schiffer, 1978, 1982; Webster, Menzies, & Jackson, 1982; Weisstub, 1980).

Much of this growth in interest can be attributed to the high profile of mental illness itself, which ranks along with **crime** as one of the most prominent "social problems" in Canadian life. Despite major trends over the past quarter-century toward **deinstitutionalization** (the closing of hospital beds and the discharging of mental patients), more than 25 000 Canadians are still being confined at any given time in both public and private psychiatric institutions. More generally, more than one million people in the country are involved in some form of therapy related to emotional difficulties, and countless others are regularly taking drugs prescribed by physicians for personal problems ranging from insomnia to sexual dysfunction to work-related stress. According to most estimates, about 15 percent of the population develops some form of mental disorder that is serious enough to disrupt their work and personal relationships. Another 20 percent suffer from alcohol or other substance-abuse problems, and 15 percent experience acute levels of depression at some time in their lives (Gallagher, 1987, pp. 2–4; Maris, 1988, pp. 279–80). In a culture that so aggressively emphasizes the importance of personal growth, financial success, and emotional well-being, mental disorder is, for many, a dark and dreaded underside to the Canadian dream, and in some way or another it touches the lives of most of us.

Given its wide reach across so many sectors of the Canadian mosaic, the institution of psychiatry has naturally emerged as one of the major players in the field of **criminology**. Clinical perspectives on crime and mental illness have found a receptive audience among criminologists everywhere, who have been studying the mind of the criminal in various capacities for more than a century (see Chapter 7). Our society is fascinated by ideas about rationality and morality, health and illness, madness and sanity, and so it is not at all surprising that such themes have become embedded in Canadian laws, in the public consciousness, and in the attitudes and actions of our police, court, and prison authorities. Those who break the law are often seen to think in fundamentally different ways from the rest of us, or to be directed by unseen (and sometimes malevolent) mental forces. We are constantly being inundated with media accounts of madmen and madwomen who have wreaked violence and mayhem on the public peace. And, in turn, we read about the apparent powers of psychiatrists to probe the inner reaches of the human mind and to unearth hidden clues to the origins of criminal and other deviant conduct.

But is the commission of a crime really an irrational act? Is there something inherently wrong with the intellect or emotions of those who do wrong? Are criminals different, along some mental or moral dimensions, from people who choose to obey the letter and spirit of the law? More to the point, do people transgress because they are mentally ill? If so, can psychiatrists and other clinical experts provide us with the appropriate diagnostic tools for identifying such people, and with a set of treatments for making them well (and therefore law-abiding)?

The answers to these and other questions vary widely among the many professions and orientations that make up the field of criminology. The vast literature that has grown around the relationship between mental illness and crime—and between psychiatry and law—has represented a variety of theoretical, political, professional, and personal points of view. The field of forensic psychiatry is one of the most contentious in the entire discipline of criminology, with major differences in opinion between those who, respectively, support and oppose the role of mental-health experts in the treatment and control of crime. What is more, forensic medicine is beset by a litany of myths and misconceptions. For these reasons, the participation of psychiatric experts in our courts and prisons has proved to be a fiercely controversial subject, and for many criminologists the entire medico-legal enterprise is very much a double-edged sword.

In what follows, you will be reading about the Canadian system of forensic psychiatry. And, in the course of examining this important cog in our criminal-justice

(and, with luck,
ing debates and
, and about the
:ians in our offi-
iy, you will find
riminology) that
lems of forensic
reen mental dis-
onstantly chang-
id contradictions.
we begin by sur-
king about men-
and a number of
ies a look at the
iatry as a precur-
iethods in medi-
rhat are currently
ninal responsi-
rousness. Finally,
:pth examination
—with the profes-
clinicians at work

ess

d psychiatry must
many competing
ties, and by mem-
racter, and conse-
omenon of crime,
ect of numerous
; own unique per-
, sociological, and
a modern society.
mptions and con-
ly of forensic psy-
o-legal laws and
imp of prevailing
hip between men-
e four viewpoints
model, **labelling**
, and **critical**
is for the develop-
s, for the concrete
inders, and for the
; who work in the
Cockerham, 1981;
; Turner, 1987).

The Medical Model

We begin with the medical model, which, since the nineteenth century, has been the single most prevalent framework for explaining mental illness in all Western societies. Proponents of the medical model (Gibbs, 1972; Gove, 1980; Prins, 1980) assert that mental illness is a disease, a tangible pathology of the brain that is not qualitatively different from physical disorders in other parts of the human body. Spearheaded by spokespersons from the clinical professions, this approach has been the major conceptual justification for the entry of medicine into the realm of emotional disorder. It was not coincidental that the medical model surfaced at the same time that psychiatrists were beginning to receive training in medical schools (Castel, Castel & Lovell, 1982). As well, from the onset, it has been closely linked with the philosophical premises of **Positivism**.

All criminology students are soon acquainted with the Positive School of criminology, with its focus on the individualistic (often biological) causes of crime, its insistence on the fundamental differences between deviant and normal human beings, and its faith in the power of science to establish the causes and cures of such social problems. The medical model applies these same views to the study of mental disorder, and in the process, imparts a variety of deeply rooted understandings that have become engrained over the years into the practice of general and forensic psychiatry alike.

In his classic paper in support of the medical model, David Ausubel (1961) listed the four main tenets that are widely held by those who maintain the authenticity of the medical model:

1. there need not be an overt physical lesion in order for a symptom to qualify as a disease;
2. if psychological problems have an adverse effect on the personality, and if they distort behaviour, they should be regarded as disease;
3. psychological problems, like physical symptoms, should be recognized as disease whether they do or do not affect a person's social adjustment; and
4. there is a fundamental difference between mental illness (a form of sickness) and immoral behaviour (a form of social deviance) (see also Mechanic, 1969).

Medical approaches to mental disorder rest largely on the ability of psychiatrists to diagnose their patients—to classify the many varieties of **psychopathology** into distinct and measurable categories. This process, in turn, depends on the construction of a working definition for **mental disorder** itself, and for this purpose it is generally accepted by clinicians that *"a condition qualifies as a disorder if it causes distress or disability to the person"* (Gallagher, 1987, p. 33). As well, it is necessary to develop a **taxonomy**—a systematic list of symptoms that are identified with various types of disease, which can be consulted and applied consistently by psychiatrists everywhere. The most widely circulated classification system of its kind is the third edition of the *Diagnostic and Statistical Manual of Mental Disorders (DSM-III)*, published by the American Psychiatric Association (APA) in 1980 and revised in 1987 (see Box 8.1). Those disorders appearing in *DSM-III* are established by consulting the membership of the APA, and, over time, their opinions (and with them, the official distinction between normality and disorder) can change. Among the most famous revisions in the definition of "mental illness" has been the long-overdue elimination of homosexuality in 1972.

Box 8.1 reproduces the extensive inventory of mental disorders identified by the *Diagnostic and Statistical Manual*, which provides the basis for the diagnostic methods of most general and forensic psychiatrists practising in Canada. Before proceeding further, here is a brief explanation of the eleven major categories contained in this *DSM-III* taxonomy (see generally Brooks, 1974, Ch. 2; Gallagher, 1987, chs. 4–8; Prins, 1981):

1. *Disorders Usually First Evident in Infancy, Childhood, or Adolescence* include an array of emotional problems that are usually first noticed at a relatively young age, including mental retardation, hyperactivity, anorexia nervosa (the chronic aversion to food), bulimia (binge eating), autism (psychotic withdrawal and the inability to relate with other human beings), and Tourette's disorder (characterized by involuntary facial expressions, vocal tics, and obscene language).

2. *Organic Mental Disorders* result from the actual physical destruction of brain cells, and are typically associated with drug consumption or senility.

3. *Substance-Abuse Disorders* are symptomatic of people whose behaviour is adversely affected by chemical substances.

4. *Schizophrenic Disorders* comprise the most common family of psychoses (that is, mental illnesses so severe as to substantially impair a person's ability to comprehend and cope with reality, and that produce a gross distortion in the perception of surrounding phenomena). Schizophrenia is often accompanied by bizarre and incomprehensible behaviour. Catatonic schizophrenics, for example, tend to vacillate between periods of excessive activity and excitement on the one hand, and stupor,

mutism, and general inhibition of behaviour on the other. The movie *Birdy*, based on the novel by William Wharton, and filmed by the English director Alan Parker, is a captivating portrayal of a psychiatric patient who is afflicted with an acute form of catatonia.

5. *Paranoid Disorders* are "characterized by persecutory or grandiose delusions, and sometimes by hallucinations. The delusions became 'systemic,' a set of beliefs about the paranoid's relation to others" (Gerard, cited in Brooks, 1974, p. 29). Paranoids often perceive threatening conspiracies where none exist, or they view themselves as unrealistically famous or important (to the point of assuming the identity of historical figures like Christ or Napoleon). An interesting, if rare, variety of paranoia is the encapsulated erotic delusion, which consists of a mistaken but overwhelming belief that one is the object of another's romantic affection. A famous Canadian illustration of this disorder is the case of Robert Kieling, the prosperous Saskatchewan farmer who has been repeatedly convicted, imprisoned, and hospitalized over the past decade, as a result of his relentless—and, to the present day, unfulfilled—amorous pursuit of the singer Anne Murray.

6. *Affective Disorders* afflict a person's emotional state, and are also referred to as mood disorders. Their symptoms involve extreme levels of elation or depression that are frequently unrelated to actual events in the individual's life. Cyclothymic or bipolar illness, or manic depression, produces wild swings between frantic hyperactivity at one end, and deep despondency (often with resulting suicidal inclinations) at the other.

7. *Anxiety Disorders* constitute the broad category of emotional problems that, prior to the publication of *DSM-III*, came under the heading of neuroses. These disturbances are uniformly less severe than the class of psychoses (in that a person's capacity to process reality remains generally intact), but they nevertheless can generate some unpleasant emotional and behavioural reactions. Agoraphobia, for example (literally "fear of the marketplace"), is expressed in a patient's inability to step outside his or her home without experiencing acute anxiety, and post-traumatic stress syndrome is a newly recognized disorder often associated with the psychiatric difficulties of many Vietnam veterans in the United States.

8. *Somatoform Disorders* are neuroses that entail an adverse physiological reaction to psychological

al Manual of the American
tegories of Mental Illness and

ric diagnosis lists
nental illness and
ll sample of these
egory. Each item
:ation number:

fancy, childhood,

lation
on
ation

sive

Adolescence

od, or Adolescence

estations

Specific Developmental Disorders
   315.00   Developmental reading disorder
   315.10   Developmental arithmetic disorder
   315.39   Developmental articulation disorder

Organic Mental Disorders

Dementias Arising in the Senium and Presenium
   290.00   Primary degenerative dementia, senile onset

Substance-Induced
   303.00   Alcohol intoxication
   292.83   Barbiturate amnestic disorder
   292.00   Opioid withdrawal
   292.81   Amphetamine delirium
   292.11   Hallucinogen delusional disorder
   305.20   Cannabis intoxication
   292.00   Nicotine withdrawal
   305.90   Caffeine intoxication

Substance Abuse Disorders
   305.00   Alcohol abuse
   303.90   Alcohol dependence (alcoholism)
   305.60   Cocaine abuse
   304.30   Cannabis dependence
   305.10   Tobacco dependence

Schizophrenic Disorders
   295.20   Catatonic schizophrenia
   295.30   Paranoid schizophrenia
   295.90   Undifferentiated schizophrenia

Paranoid Disorders
   297.10   Paranoia
   297.30   Shared paranoid disorder

Psychotic Disorders not Elsewhere Classified
   298.80   Brief reactive psychosis

Affective Disorders
   296.40   Bipolar disorder, manic
   296.30   Major depression, recurrent
   301.13   Cyclothymic disorder

Box 8.1 *(Continued)*

Anxiety Disorders

300.21	Agoraphobia with panic attacks
300.23	Social phobia
300.02	Generalized anxiety disorder
300.30	Obsessive compulsive disorder
309.89	Post-traumatic stress disorder, acute

Somatoform Disorders

300.11	Conversion disorder
307.80	Pyschogenic pain disorder
300.70	Hypochondriasis

Dissociative Disorders

300.12	Psychogenic amnesia
300.13	Psychogenic fugue
300.14	Multiple personality

Psychosexual Disorders

Gender Identity Disorders

302.50	Transsexualism

Paraphilias

302.81	Fetishism
302.30	Transvestism
302.10	Zoophilia
302.20	Pedophilia
302.40	Exhibitionism
302.82	Voyeurism
302.83	Sexual masochism
302.84	Sexual sadism

Other Psychosexual Disorders

302.00	Ego-dystonic homosexuality

Psychosexual Dysfunctions

302.73	Inhibited female orgasm
302.74	Inhibited male orgasm
302.75	Premature ejaculation

Factitious Disorders

300.16	Factitious disorder with psychological symptoms

Disorders of Impulse Control not Elsewhere Classified

312.31	Pathological gambling
312.32	Kleptomania
312.33	Pyromania

Adjustment Disorder

309.23	Work or academic inhibition

Psychological Factors Affecting Physical Condition

Personality Disorders

301.00	Paranoid personality disorder
301.81	Narcissistic personality disorder
301.70	Antisocial personality disorder
301.84	Passive-aggressive personality disorder

Conditions not Attributable to a Mental Condition

V65.20	Malingering
V62.30	Academic problem
V15.81	Noncompliance with medical treatment
V61.10	Marital problem

Source: From the American Psychiatric Association, *Diagnostic and Statistical Manual of Mental Disorders* (3rd ed.). (Washington, D.C.: APA, 1980). Adapted from B.J. Gallagher (1987), *The sociology of mental illness* (2nd ed.) (pp.34–38). Englewood Cliffs, NJ: Prentice–Hall. Used by permission of the American Psychiatric Association.

stress. Conversion reactions can result in the loss of function in various body parts, even to the point of paralysis in the arms and legs. Hypochondriasis is the recurrent experience or complaint of imaginary physical illness.

9. *Dissociative Disorders* include amnesia, fugue states, and multiple personality. In these conditions, entire realms of the memory and experience are apparently walled off from the level of conscious thought. In fugue states, people can exist for years without a trace of identification with the past. In cases of multiple personalities, an entire popula-

bit a single body.
r. Jekyll and Mr.
1 apparently dis-
vo (the "Boston
tz (the "Son of
), criminologists
esults) for a pos-
ive disorders and
nous offences of
oyd, 1988).
general varieties:
e sexual ideas or
ex object) and
number of the
ilia (sexual attrac-
tion to children),
n—can generate
in Canadian law.
of the **Criminal**
up to ten years'
estiality or sexual
r the age of four-
"committing an
esetting" (Crimi-
I 423 [1][f]).
f great interest to
nd particularly to
entation to their
pathological gam-
left), and pyroma-
onsidered to be
criminal offences
sonality disorders
e character traits.
ality disorder (or,
or sociopathy) is
ignosis applied to
with the criminal
rsonalities (or psy-
nal conscience. As
"are basically un-
rings them repeat-
They are incapable
ls, groups, or social
callous, irrespon-
el guilt or to learn
nt" (see Cleckey,
88; Reid, 1978).
ut whether it is an
or simply another
ho engages in re-
haviour (Ennis &

Litwack, 1974; Ingleby, 1981; Pfohl, 1978), the diagnosis of personality disorder has been a major focus of Canadian forensic psychiatry for many decades. Nowhere has this been more apparent than with the special category of sexual psychopathy, where over the years a small number of sexually violent predators such as Saul Betesh and Clifford Olsen have recurrently been the targets of clinical theorizing, legal wrangling, and public fear and loathing.

Labelling Theory

The medical model of mental illness—and, along with it, the Positivistic ideals of clinical theory, the prominent status of psychiatry in the social response to madness, the equation of emotional disorders with crime and other forms of **deviance**, and the use of such diagnostic classification schemes as *DSM-III*—have not gone unchallenged. The first enduring assault on the sanctity of the medical approach to mental disorder came from the labelling theorists (see Chapter 10). With its concentration on the symbolic and socio-cultural aspects of insanity, and on the labelling activities of officials in the psychiatric system, the social-reaction position disputes some of the most deeply held assumptions of the medical model (Conrad & Schneider, 1976; Hawkins & Tiedeman, 1975; Lemert, 1967; Pfohl, 1978; *Psychological Medicine*, 1988; Rosenhan, 1973; Scheff, 1966, 1975). As the sociologist Thomas Scheff has written (1964; see Marshall & Hughes, 1974, pp. 155–56), it turns psychiatric theorizing on its head, by proposing that:

1. the intervention of clinicians is not helpful in a large proportion of cases, as many disorders eventually subside without any mental-health assistance;
2. there are no effective treatments for the large majority of psychiatric disorders;
3. instead of assisting patients, treatment may actually contribute to their problems;
4. since psychiatric involvement is not always benevolent or innocuous, a strict code of legal protections should be adopted to ensure the civil liberties of mental patients; and
5. contrary to conventional wisdom, there is no connection between mental disorder and dangerousness to self or others (see Table 8.1).

In his classic text *Being Mentally Ill*, Scheff (1966) formulated what is still the most sophisticated theory of mental illness in the labelling tradition. Scheff's central idea was that the social reaction to insanity hinges on the existence and violation of what he calls **residual rules**. Unlike the

Table 8.1 The Medical Model Versus Labelling Theory

The Medical Model	Labelling Theory
1. Mental disorder is a form of disease. It does not necessarily require the existence of visible physical abnormalities.	1. Mental disorder is a form of social and cultural maladjustment that reflects society's response to the patient. There is no disease without physical abnormalities.
2. There is a fundamental difference between mental illness (a form of sickness) and immoral behaviour (a form of social deviance).	2. The labelling of mental illness is basically a moral description about a patient's disturbing and undesirable behaviour.
3. The treatment of mental illness is like any other form of medical therapy. It usually helps the patient, but, when it occasionally fails, there is still no adverse effect.	3. The treatment of mental illness, especially when it takes the form of drug therapy, ECT, or psychosurgery, can actually harm the patient and contribute to his or her emotional problems.
4. Psychiatric hospitalization is a benevolent medical procedure, and there should be no obstacles to the commitment of mental patients for their own good.	4. Psychiatric hospitalization is a form of social control, and a strict code of legal procedure is needed to protect patients from arbitrary confinement.
5. Mental illness is inherently a dangerous condition and can often lead to uncontrollable behaviour.	5. The mentally ill are no more violent, nor likely to commit a criminal offence, than anyone else.

Criminal Code—and various other sets of laws, regulations, standards, and norms that govern social life—residual rules do not require confirmation in written, or even verbal form. They are deeply engrained in our culture, and fundamental to our collective sense of normality. Our agreement about them "is so complete that [we] appear to take them for granted" (Scheff, 1966, p. 32). In turn, **residual deviants**—those whom we label as mentally ill—are people whose behaviour consistently breaks these rules, not through criminality or other kinds of obvious wrongdoing, but rather by disrupting our unstated standards for what is normal. When people claim to be famous historical figures, when they talk or dress in a bizarre manner, or when they carry on conversations with invisible beings, they are not doing anything overtly wrong, yet still our most deeply valued notions about rationality and order are being threatened. Consequently, we tend to respond coercively—by locking them up in mental hospitals or by forcing them into unwanted psychiatric treatment—even though their behaviour may be much less harmful than the transgressions of other kinds of deviants.

Labelling theory concentrates on many **stereotypes** (commonly accepted but erroneous beliefs) about mental illness that circulate through society and on the effect of these biases on the practices of those whom we designate to exert authority over the insane. Scheff notes, for example, that stereotypes about insanity are learned at an early age, and that they are continuously reaffirmed by the media and in everyday social interaction. We are conditioned to believe that the mentally disordered are untrustworthy, unpredictable, dangerous, unfit to live on their own, and incapable of earning a living, and that they usually belong in psychiatric institutions (Scheff, 1966, chs. 2, 3; see Conrad & Schneider, 1976; Horwitz, 1982). Others have observed the stereotyping of mental patients by their own families (Horwitz, 1977; *Journal of Social Issues*, 1955), in the diagnostic practices of psychiatrists (Ennis & Litwack, 1974), and through their treatment within the confines of general and forensic institutions (Goffman, 1961; Ryan, 1981).

Labelling theorists contend that such stereotypes also have an effect on the "careers" (Goffman, 1961) of the insane, and on the course of such disorders as paranoic schizophrenia (where the paranoid's fear of a conspiracy may often have more than a little basis in fact: see Lemert, 1967). In his famous study "On Being Sane in Insane Places," for example, David Rosenhan (1973) found that, in psychiatric settings, even "normal" people are vulnerable to the label of mental illness. Rosenhan had eight pseudo patients (researchers with no history of emotional problems) check into various eastern American psychiatric hospitals, complaining of hearing voices. All were immediately admitted as in-patients for periods of up to two months (despite the fact that, apart from their initial complaint, they presented no further symptoms of disorder), and all were eventually released with a diagnosis of "schizophrenia in remission." During their stay, the pseudo patients' everyday activities, such as taking field notes for the research, were regularly noted by staff as symptomatic of their mental illness. Ironically, only the other patients were at all suspicious of their subterfuge.

pproach in its
7; Frank, 1979;
3, 1970, 1971,
r-century, the
nist-psychiatry
mas Szasz. The
nise that men-
lical profession
eople who are
h problems are
different socie-
given society,
l illness. Szasz,
id Cooper and
ween sanity and
logy. Who are
onsidered men-
eople have vio-
human beings
perilously close
d nuclear anni-

e Szasz, society
es onto the in-
imination solely
viour. And this
ughout history,
en invented by
the conduct of
merican South,
e suffering from
h was whipping)
, where a patient
psychiatrist may
r "Ganser's syn-
hiatrists are seen
r witch doctors
rily in the (rather
ag, 1978), using
nedication, elec-
e cases, even the
botomy). Revi-
t expect, that the
n the involuntary
eir involvement
d people actively

writers in the
that there is no
s and crime. The

notion that the insane are somehow predisposed toward
law-breaking and dangerousness, they argue, is a product
of media distortion and public misinformation. Whereas
the occasional case does occur where seriously disturbed
people do commit major crimes, such incidents are rare,
they are not necessarily related to the offender's emotional
problems, and they are unfairly exploited by the press and
politicians to exaggerate the perceived threat posed by the
mentally disordered.

Certainly the criminological research literature overwhelmingly supports this contention. Study after study has
shown that the incidence of crime and violence among
groups of ex–mental patients is generally lower than for
the general population (Mesnikoff & Lauterbach, 1975;
Rabkin, 1979). Similarly, persons discharged from hospitals for the criminally insane in Britain (Walker & McCabe,
1973), the United States (Steadman & Cocozza, 1974;
Thornberry & Jacoby, 1979), and Canada (Quinsey, 1979)
have typically been relatively law-abiding following their
release, with, at most, around a 15 percent rate of violent
recidivism (see, generally, Menzies & Webster, 1989).
High-profile cases of "murder and madness" (Lunde, 1976),
where the mentally disordered run amok and wreak havoc
on the public, are completely unrepresentative of the typical
mental patient, who in his or her entire lifetime will not
once be convicted of a **criminal offence**.

Critical Psychiatry

Critical psychiatry emphasizes the political and economic
aspects of society's response to the mentally ill (Balkan,
Berger & Schmidt, 1980, Ch. 14; Coulter, 1973; Foucault,
1965; Ingleby, 1981; Miller & Rose, 1987; Scull, 1977).
In the tradition of Marxism and other radical analyses of
the capitalist system, advocates of critical psychiatry look
for the causes and consequences of mental illness in the class
structure of modern society. The character of the mental-
health enterprise, they argue, is a mirror image of capitalism itself. The competitive consumerist nature of our market society can literally have the effect of "driving people
crazy." Those who fail the test—who come to occupy the
lower echelons of our social hierarchy—are subject to economic, social, and personal pressures that are largely
unknown to the middle and upper classes. Mental patients,
like prisoners confined in our penal system, are disproportionately drawn from the pool of marginal, homeless, impoverished, and unemployed people who inhabit the inner
cities of Western nations like Canada.

As a consequence, mental hospitals are primarily class institutions. They function to individualize and depoliticize
the emotional problems of society's casualties, by redefin-
ing these problems as the symptoms of disturbed minds in-

stead of the natural product of a disturbing society. Moreover, the mental-hospital complex is an immensely lucrative industry, and reaps vast profits from the plight of its subjects. And psychiatrists are in the business of mind control in the interests of preserving a classist, sexist, and racist *status quo*. Psychiatry, from this critical perspective, is an institution of social regulation, which is used to legitimize and reinforce the ability of elites to confine and control the disadvantaged members of capitalist society.

Like labelling theory and revisionist psychiatry, then, the critical-psychiatry movement offers a progressive alternative to the narrow Positivistic lens of the medical model. These three approaches adopt different perspectives and levels of analysis, but they also overlap in one important way. They all strive to locate mental illness in the wider context of social life, and in the process they encourage us to consider the essential political, ideological, and historical roots of psychiatric disorder and its treatment.

The Historical Origins of Forensic Psychiatry

Since human beings first took up the problem of controlling aberrant behaviour, people have been endlessly concerned with the risky business of distinguishing between deviance and normality. It seems that every organized society has searched widely for answers to some of the most daunting questions that plague our species: What are the origins of ideas and actions that are seen to violate a society's accepted standards of decency and decorum? What is it about such conduct that makes it so intolerable; how is it to be differentiated from behaviour that conforms; and how might it be repressed, or even better, cured? And perhaps most important of all: in coming to terms with the realities of deviance and the engines of its control, what can the inhabitants of any given society learn about the worthiness of their own values, beliefs, and rules for ordering and making sense of the world around them?

In present-day Canada, such complex questions about deviance and social control almost always congregate around the two pivotal themes of **criminality** and mental illness. Yet, it is important to recognize that, in the broader historical context, our current focus on crime and insanity has been a relatively recent development. From the time of the ancient Greeks and Romans through to the Middle Ages, when people misbehaved, their actions were likely to be attributed to the forces of nature or to the interventions of supernatural beings. Their fate was generally entrusted not to professional criminologists and clinicians, but rather to the informal involvement of the entire community (Foucault, 1965; Rosen, 1968).

The "Discovery" of Madness and the Rise of the Asylum

The concept of madness itself did not begin to emerge as a distinct category until the rise of the Industrial Revolution during the seventeenth and eighteenth centuries. Just as there could be no formal conception of crime without a written legal code, so, too, was the significance of insanity dependent on the prior growth of an organized system of social response. And this arrived with the coming of the Age of Enlightenment, with its new-found concentration on rationality as the key to human progress. As the Industrial Revolution gained momentum, political and cultural leaders of the new nation-states came to view insanity as one of the central problems that threatened the social and moral fabric of the new capitalist order. They reacted by setting into motion what Michel Foucault (1965) terms "The Great Confinement." From the 1656 establishment of the Hôpital Général in Paris, madhouses soon became a common sight throughout Europe, and later in North America as well. By the mid-1800s, with the rise of the asylum across the Western world (Rothman, 1971), our contemporary mental-hospital system, emphasizing the segregative confinement of insane people far away from "normal" society, was firmly in place (Balkan, Berger, & Schmidt, 1980; Parry-Jones, 1972; Perrucci, 1974; Scull, 1981).

As these early hospitals began to spring up across the cities and countryside of most industrializing nations, an equally important trend was becoming apparent. The concept of insanity was beginning to assert itself in the realm of criminal law (Walker, 1968). This movement had profound consequences, as jurists became increasingly attentive to the state of the defendant's mind in determining criminal responsibility, and in arriving at an appropriate **disposition** for those who were clearly in the throes of mental illness. From the seventeenth century onward, the massive body of common and statutory law in countries such as Britain and France was marked by recurrent references to intention, motivation, lunacy, idiocy, and related mental states. This, in turn, laid the groundwork for the eventual advance into the criminal courts of experts in the science of mapping the criminal mind: physicians and others who could advise judges on the best method of applying the law to specific cases of mental disorder.

The McNaughtan Case

The English courts were the primary site of this growing convergence between psychiatry and law. A number of controversial and highly publicized **capital cases** during the eighteenth and nineteenth centuries set the stage for

London *Times*

on the grounds
se wave of ou-
ns, the public,
f that this spe-
equivalent of a
could establish
een right and
nit murder (and
impunity. One
o write: "If the
d of justice, by
murderer, it un-
y's subjects from
atisfactory state.
natic at large—
s been invented
his counsel, viz,
n irresistible im-
" For their part,
ng poem (Orm-

glad
rciless mad
es reign
ou omit the

tute controls,

And their murderous charter exists in their souls.
Do they wish to spill blood—they have only to play
A few pranks—get asylum'd a month and a day
Then Heigh! to escape from the mad doctor's keys
And to pistol or stab whomsoever they please.
Now the dog has a human-like wit in creation
He resembles most nearly our own generation
Then if madmen for murder escape with impunity
Why deny a poor dog the same noble immunity
So if a dog or man bit you beware being nettled
For crime is no crime—when the mind is unsettled.

In retrospect, there was scant need for concern. As it happened, Daniel McNaughtan was never again loosed upon the British citizenry. On March 13, 1843, he became the 219th patient of the Criminal Lunatic Asylum operated by Bethlehem Hospital in London (diagnosed as suffering from "monomania"), where he was to spend more than two decades. Soon after his admission to Bethlehem, his case was virtually forgotten by the public. In 1864, he was transferred to the newly-built Broodmoor asylum, where, slightly more than a year later, he died at the age of 52 from "anemia, brain disease and gradual failure of heart's actions." In the words of Henry Rollin: "So ends this strange eventful history which began in 1843 quite literally with a bang, and expired 22 years later with such a pathetic whimper" (Rollin, 1977, p. 99; see Moran, 1981; Smith, 1981; Walker, 1968, Ch. 5; West & Walk, 1977).

r the most in-
iel McNaugh-
e immortalized
try for the fol-
On January 20,
etary to Prime
ndon bobbies),
making his way
cians soon an-
eedy recovery,
lly noticed that
d. The doctors
ering him with
he had less than
his trust in the
d's great misfor-

tune, this was the only medical prognosis that did indeed come to pass.

In the trial that followed, some convincing evidence was offered by McNaughtan's defence lawyer, Alexander Cockburn, along with four medical witnesses, suggesting that the accused had long suffered from delusions of persecution. McNaughtan had been stalking Drummond for some time, believing him to be the apparently not-so-inimitable Sir Robert himself. After being arrested, he had also voiced some ideas about the reigning government, which, while perhaps shared by more than a few Canadians in current times, must nevertheless have sounded bizarre indeed in 1843 London: "The Tories in my native city have compelled me to do this. They follow and persecute me wherever I go, and have entirely destroyed my peace of mind. They followed me to France, into Scotland and all over England. They have accused me of crime of which I am not guilty. In fact, they wish to murder me" (Moran, 1981, p. 10).

McNaughtan's subsequent acquittal on the grounds of insanity brought an immediate public outcry. Although he was sent off to the asylum—where he was to spend to the rest of his life—Britishers, spurred on by the press, were outraged by the thought that an assassin could so readily escape the noose. Letters were sent to the London *Times,* the case was hotly debated in Parliament, and the Queen herself wrote to the prime minister, protesting that "everybody is morally convinced that [the] malefactor [was] perfectly conscious and aware of what [he] did" (quoted in West & Walk, 1977, pp. 9–10). Finally, the task of producing a clear legal doctrine on criminal responsibility was soon put to the fifteen justices of the Queen's Bench.

These judicial peers responded with a fixed definition of insanity that henceforth became the leading guide to judgments about criminal responsibility throughout Western legal systems:

> to establish a defence on the ground of insanity, it must be clearly proved that, at the time of the committing of the act, the party accused was labouring under such a defect of reason, from disease of the mind, as not to know the nature and quality of the act he was doing; or, if he did know it, that he did not know he was doing what was wrong. (West & Walk, 1977, p. 75)

With one stroke, they had: (1) confirmed that all defendants were to be presumed sane until proved otherwise by the Crown; (2) formulated a medical criterion ("disease of the mind") that paved the way for increasing psychiatric participation in these trials; and (3) provided a conservative "knowing right from wrong" test for criminal responsibility, which seemed to exclude an entire class of offenders who might be labouring under irresistible impulse, knowing full well that what they were doing was wrong, yet being unable to restrain themselves. As we will see later in this chapter, these aspects of the test have been the subject of intensive scrutiny and debate for nearly 150 years, and still, with only minor amendments, the **McNaughtan Rule** remains today the criterion for legal insanity in section 16 of our Canadian Criminal Code.

Psychiatry and Criminality

Meanwhile, throughout Europe and North American, the rise of the asylum (Rothman, 1971) had gained full momentum. With the assistance of reformers such as Philippe Pinel in France and the Tuke family in England, madhouses and their medical superintendents were fast becoming the fo-

Photo 8.1 Daniel McNaughtan, *c.* 1856.
Bethlem Royal Hospital Archives.

cal points of society's response to the social problem of insanity. In 1838, Isaac Ray, a New England doctor, published *A Treatise on the Medical Jurisprudence of Insanity*, which was soon the authoritative text in the growing practice of forensic medicine. Writers everywhere were affirming the enormous social importance of mental illness: "I never saw any human being who was of sound mind. I presume the Deity was of sound mind, and He alone" (Haslam, cited in Walker, 1968, p. 89); and its central role in the understanding of crime and other forms of deviance: "There is scarcely any offence against public decorum that has not been frequently the result of mental disease" (Pritchard, cited in Skultans, 1975, p. 7).

A range of new psychiatric disorders were being "discovered" that were seen to hold particular relevance for the causation and control of criminality. Among these was monomania, said to comprise "a morbid perversion of the feelings, affectations, habits, without any hallucination or erroneous conviction impressed upon the understanding; it sometimes co-exists with an apparently unimpaired state of the intellectual faculties" (Pritchard, 1833, p. 14). As the historian Skultans (1975, p. 7) points out, the invention of monomania was a windfall for the emerging psychiatric

icult to detect,
micidal) belief
efore, accord-
an could hope

ch, rather like
efined as "the
moral sense"
hing moral in-
kind of mental
al claim to the
l. For, if crime
in turn, illness
tal defect, then
ement" of vir-
mental health.
ental hygiene"
points for the
twentieth cen-
ull, 1981, Skul-

ife was an end-
ladness was seen
der, and moral
e early peniten-
lossi & Pavarini,
quillity and sta-
othman, 1971).
was an institu-
id public mental
y onward—that
trict regulation.
der to minimize
n of the insane.
itted little con-
s of the outside
vere categorized
nd potential for
oups were phys-
iles were rigidly
be "protected"
rough the use of
ms, and immer-
hey awoke, ate,
and unchanging
were painted in
and the social life
were the precur-
been so graphi-
hospitals in more
ng, 1969; Brandt,
an, 1981).

Canadian Developments

These qualities were also embedded in the growing system of psychiatric and forensic institutions in Canada
(Foulkes, 1961; Smandych, 1982; Smandych & Verdun-
Jones, 1986). As the Canadian criminologists Verdun-Jones
and Smandych (1981) tell us, the asylum-building enterprise was well underway in this country by the middle of
the last century. Our first public mental institution was
opened in Saint John, New Brunswick, in 1835. In Upper
Canada (later Ontario), legislation was passed in 1839 to
permit the building of a new asylum in Toronto. There
was clearly a desperate need for such a facility, for until
then the mentally ill were being held under inhumane conditions that nearly defied description. Their pitiful plight
was recorded by the visiting English reformer J.H. Tuke
in 1845:

> Visited the lunatic asylum. It is one of the most pain-
> ful and distressing places I have ever visited. The
> house was a terribly dark aspect within and without,
> and was intended for a prison. There were, perhaps,
> 70 patients, upon whose faces misery, starvation, and
> suffering were indelibly impressed. The doctor pur-
> sues the exploded system of constantly cupping,
> bleeding, blistering, and purging his patients, giving
> them also the smallest quantity of food, and that of
> the poorest quality. No meat is allowed. Strongly-
> built men were reduced to skeletons, and poor idiots
> were lying on their beds motionless, and as if half-
> dead. Every patient has his or her head shaved. The
> doctor, in response to my questions, boasted that his
> cures are larger than those in any English or con-
> tinental asylum. I left the place sickened with dis-
> gust. (Tuke, 1845, quoted in Verdun-Jones &
> Smandych, 1981, pp. 93–94)

The Toronto Asylum, still in existence today as the
Queen Street Mental Health Centre (although almost completely rebuilt), finally went into operation in January 1850,
and, over the next quarter-century, six more public asylums were built across the province. In Lower Canada (later
Quebec), most institutions were run by religious and private organizations under a contract system of private
management (Smandych, 1982). In British Columbia, an
asylum law was passed by the legislature in 1873, and five
years later patients were moved onto grounds next to the
B.C. Penitentiary in New Westminster (Foulkes, 1961).
Here, as well, these early patients languished under a shameful regime of neglect and physical abuse that was not to
experience much change until the turn of the century, following a scathing report from a 1894 royal commission.
Among their observations:

Equipment such as handcuffs, leather mitts, pinion straps, camisoles and strait jackets were in almost daily use. Torture was applied in addition to strangulations with the "martingale"—the cruel rope halter on the strait jackets. There was the "dip" in which a patient, arms handcuffed behind his back, was plunged head-down into a tub of cold water until he was very nearly drowned. There was "the cage," a box constructed of wooden slats and made only large enough for a human body in which a patient may be confined for many hours. (Royal Commission Report, 1894, quoted in Verdun-Jones & Smandych, 1981, p. 97)

Prior to the twentieth century, only one Canadian institution was founded specifically for the purpose of housing the criminally insane—the Rockwood Asylum near Kingston, Ontario. On the strength of an 1851 law modelled after the British Criminal Lunatics Act of 1800, Rockwood held a large group of insane convicts transferred from the criminal system, along with civilly committed "lunatics dangerous to be at large" and "ordinary lunatics" (kept separate from the others), from 1857 to 1877. But Rockwood was considered an abject failure. After 1877, the criminally insane were shuffled back into the penitentiary system, where, over time, they came to be systematically segregated from other inmates (Verdun-Jones & Smandych, 1981).

Finally, after World War I, the individual provinces began to construct their own facilities for accommodating the "dangerous mentally ill," along with insane convicts, and persons found not guilty by reason of insanity or unfit to stand trial. This process led to the appearance of our many latter-day Canadian institutions for the confinement of the criminally insane, including l'Institut Philippe Pinel in Montreal, Quebec, the Oak Ridge facility in Penetanguishene, Ontario, and the Forensic Institute in Port Coquitlam, British Columbia. It would eventually produce a variety of allied clinics and hospitals, private and public, associated with courts, provincial prisons, and federal penitentiaries, and populated by a host of specially trained psychiatrists, psychologists, social workers, nurses, and other forensic experts. With the advance of the twentieth century, then, several centuries of medico-legal history were culminating in a powerful and enduring relationship between the clinical professions and the criminal-justice system. The modern Canadian institution of forensic psychiatry was solidly in place.

The "Big Three" Issues in Psychiatry and Criminal Law

Today, three issues dominate the field of forensic psychiatry: insanity, fitness to stand trial, and dangerousness.

Insanity and Criminal Responsibility

The **insanity defence** has generally captured the lion's share of attention in the field of forensic psychiatry, because for centuries it has been among the favourite subjects of lawmakers and judges (see Chapter 2), and because it is so often raised in the context of our most lurid and infamous criminal trials. The concept of criminal responsibility has always been crucial to Western systems of law. It rests on the principle that people must not be held accountable for their wrongdoing unless they are of sound mind at the time of their crimes, and that those failing to meet a minimal standard of mental capacity (for example, legal infants, the severely incapacitated, and the insane) must be found not guilty. As we saw earlier in this chapter, the standard for criminal responsibility itself has varied across the centuries, as have the procedures for determining and dealing with the insane within the halls of criminal justice.

This section looks at the nature and operation of the insanity defence in Canada. Like most features of our legal system, Canadian methods for determining and dealing with the concept of criminal responsibility were originally inherited virtually unaltered from the courts of England. From the time of Confederation, provisions for the insanity defence closely mirrored those in "the mother country," until in 1893 the Criminal Code (under the stewardship of Sir James Fitzjames Stephen) finally inscribed the 1843 British McNaughtan Rule into Canadian statutory law. This standard for legal insanity, with a few minor alterations, has survived to the present day in section 16 of the Code:

16 (1) No person shall be convicted of an offence in respect of an act or omission on his part while that person was insane.

(2) For the purposes of this section, a person is insane when the person is in a state of natural imbecility or has disease of the mind to an extent that renders the person incapable of appreciating the nature and quality of an act or omission or of knowing that an act or omission is wrong.

(3) A person who has specific delusions, but is in other respects sane, shall not be acquitted on the ground of insanity unless the delusions caused that person to believe in the existence of a state of things that, if it existed, would have justified or excused the act or omission of that person.

(4) Every one shall, until the contrary is proved, be presumed to be and to have been sane.[1]

Since the enactment of this modified McNaughtan test, a nearly continuous stream of case law has been addressing the many legal ambiguities and conundrums that are related to such questions as: Who may raise the issue before

tural imbecil-
difference be-
are and quality
ity" refer only
ider legal and
'legal wrong"
stances should
oleda-Florez,
bster, & Ben-
1979). These
ence between
have led to a
body of legal
rate, however,
se law, but in-
in particular,
ce in Canada.
own national
termination of
and juries had
al of the great
probably more
fence than has
nderson, 1950;
1963; Verdun-
, many politi-
ercely opposed
ity, largely be-
cal threat who
nt, the success-
event in Cana-
, indeed, who
s of section 16.
instance, only
or murder were
un-Jones, 1979,
d as a more at-
a 25-year mini-
rder in 1976,
in the number
st decade. Still,
ace has been an
ants.
h the dire con-
ason of insanity.
free. They are
nd in the man-
rt judge directs,
of the province
nant Governor
terminate con-
nant-governor's

"pleasure." This does not necessarily mean that he or she finds the task particularly enjoyable (this may or may not be the case), but rather that the defendant will remain in hospital, usually under maximum-security conditions, until the government (in practice, the provincial cabinet) decides otherwise.[3] Small wonder that Canadian defendants are inclined to reject the insanity defence, particularly for minor offences where a criminal conviction would bring, at most, a brief term of imprisonment.

Once sent to hospital under the authority of a WLG, persons found not guilty by reason of insanity are generally subjected to a regimen of psychiatric treatment, with the intention of curing or controlling their mental disorders, and making them safe for release. At one time, in Canada, an insanity disposition was tantamount to a psychiatric life sentence, but, with the advent of new treatments, most criminally insane people today are likely to spend less than ten years in a secure hospital following their acquittal.[4]

A variety of alternative treatments are available to psychiatrists who practise in Canadian forensic institutions. These include: psychotherapy (interpersonal treatment focussing on the establishment of a therapeutic relationship between doctor and patient); psychodrama (another "talking therapy," involving structured role-playing and group acting); **behaviour modification** (the shaping of behaviour, by classical or operant conditioning, applying the principles of **learning theory**); aversive conditioning (the extinction of undesirable thoughts and behaviours— usually related to sex or drugs—through the administration of noxious stimuli such as ammonia or electric shock); alcohol or hallucinogen therapy (the production of inebriation or artificial psychosis); electroconvulsive therapy or ECT (introducing an electrical current to the brain to induce convulsions); and, sometimes in especially violent or psychotic cases, psychosurgery (the destruction or stimulation of brain tissue) (Anand, 1979; Schiffer, 1982, Ch. 4). This wide assortment of potential treatments for the criminally insane reflects the extraordinary diversity of psychiatry itself. Such different therapies range across a wide spectrum of clinical intervention, from the conventional to the experimental, from the interpersonal to the surgical, from the innocuous to the malignant (see Box 8.4).

But, more than any of these, the treatment of the criminally insane in Canada is characterized by the routine reliance on chemotherapy (the ingestion or injection of psychoactive or psychotropic medications). The two most common families of drugs to be found in forensic institutions are the neuroleptics (major tranquillizers, such as chlorpromazine, administered mostly in the treatment of schizophrenia), and the antidepressants (given usually to patients suffering from psychotic mood disorders) (see Schiffer, 1982, Ch. 4). Since the emergence of chemother-

Box 8.3 Knowing Right from Wrong: The Trial of Louis Riel

The most influential political rebellion in Canadian history came to an end on May 14, 1885, with the surrender of Louis David Riel following his ill-fated last stand at Batoche, Saskatchewan. Louis Riel—the dynamic leader of the Métis peoples in the young country's western territories, and historic symbol of francophone rights to the present day—was subsequently charged by the Crown with the capital offence of treason against the Government of Canada. The proceedings opened at 11:00 on the morning of July 20, in the Regina police barracks, before Judge Hugh Richardson and a panel of six jurors. The prosecution's indictment charged Riel "most wickedly, maliciously and traitorously did levy and make war towards our said Lady the Queen . . . and did then maliciously and traitorously attempt and endeavour by force and arms to subvert and destroy the constitution and government of this realm as by law established" (Stanley, 1963, p. 345). Riel's attorney, Fitzpatrick, came to the conclusion that the only possible defence lay in entering a plea of not guilty by reason of insanity. This decision was to set into motion a remarkable "battle of the psychiatric experts" that prefigured much of what ensued in Canadian insanity trials over the course of the next century.

Was Riel insane? It was indisputable that he had twice been an inmate of the Beaufort asylum; that he claimed to experience religious visions and revelations from God; that he had repeatedly incited rebellion, denounced the Pope, and referred to himself as Prophet of the New World (Verdun-Jones, 1979, p. 8). During the trial, the defence summoned two expert witnesses to verify his disturbed state of mind. The first was Dr. Francois Roy of Beauport, who testified that the defendant suffered from megalomania. Such persons, reported Roy, "sometimes give you reasons which would be reasonable if they were not starting from a false idea. They are under a strong impression that they are right and they consider it to be an insult when you try to bring them to reason again. On ordinary questions they may be reasonable and sometimes very clever. In fact, without careful watching, they would lead one to think that they were well. . . . From what I have heard . . . I am ready to say that I believe . . . his mind was unsound." The second defence expert, Dr. Daniel Clark of the Toronto Lunatic Asylum, was somewhat more equivocal: "Assuming that the witnesses have told the truth . . . that the prisoner is not a malingerer . . . there is no other conclusion that any reasonable man could come to . . . than that the man who held these views and did these things must certainly be of insane mind [but] he was quite capable of distinguishing right from wrong, legally speaking. . . . It would take months of examination to be sure" (Osler, 1961, pp. 298–99).

In response, the prosecutor, Robinson, marshalled two physicians who claimed that Riel was perfectly sane, responsible for his actions, and entirely capable of distinguishing between right and wrong. On the basis of a 30-minute interview, Dr. James Wallace of the Hamilton Asylum declared: "I have not discovered any insanity about him— no unsoundness of mind" (Davidson, 1955, p. 194). Dr. Jukes, senior surgeon for the North-West Mounted Police, while cautioning that he was no expert in mental illnesses, advised "that Riel had deliberately pretended to believe more than he really believed in order to influence the metis" (Osler, 1961, p. 299). Moreover, according to Jukes, "there are men who have held very remarkable views with respect to religion and who have been always declared to be insane until they gathered great numbers of followers and become leaders of a new sect, then they became great prophets and great men" (Stanley, 1963, p. 353).

For his part, Riel protested bitterly against his lawyer's efforts to have him declared insane. In addressing the court he maintained: "I cannot abandon my dignity. Here I have to defend myself against the accusation of high treason or I have to consent to the animal life in a asylum" (Davidson, 1955, p. 193). He continued: "While the Crown, with the great talents they have at their service, are trying to show I am guilty . . . my good friends and lawyers, who have been sent here by friends whom I respect—are trying to show that I am insane. . . . I will not be reputed by all men as insane, as a lunatic. . . . I know that through the grace of God I am the founder of Manitoba. What is my insanity about that? My insanity, your Honours, gentlemen of the jury, is that I wish to leave Rome aside, inasmuch as it is the cause of division between Catholics and Protestants. . . . If you take the plea of the defence that I am not responsible for my acts, acquit me completely, since I have been quarreling with an insane and irresponsible Government. If you pronounce in favour of the Crown which contends that I am responsible, acquit me all the same. You are perfectly justified in declaring that having my reason and sound mind, I have acted reasonably and in self-defence, while the Government, my accuser, being irresponsible, and consequently insane, can-

1961, pp. 350,

avidson was to
ore to convince
the Crown had
ur of delibera-
e jury returned
r mercy. Before
last time: "The
that after having
ed a fool.... I
ilfil my mission
being. Should
be executed—I
(Stanley, 1961,
Judge Robin-

sychiatric input.
ns—Jukes, F.X.
arden of King-
undertake yet
A. Macdonald
emonstrate there
ppease his Tory
while weather-
g out of Que-
venient vehicle

for establishing once and for all that Riel was perfectly sane, that he fully merited the ultimate punishment in Canadian law. Indeed, Macdonald had insisted that "he shall hang though every dog in Quebec bark in his favour" (Stanley, 1961, p. 367). In the words of author George Stanley, "It is difficult to look upon this medical commission as anything other than a meaningless political sop" (1961, p. 366). The prime minister's instructions were patently clear: "Your enquiry will be limited to the simple question whether he at the time of your report is a sufficiently reasonable and accountable being to know right from wrong . . . if— whatever illusions he may have—he still knows right from wrong the law should be allowed to take effect." And predictably, the two-day examination resulted in a unanimous finding that Riel was a sane man. Although Valade expressed some initial doubts, even he ultimately concluded that Riel was "sensible and able to distinguish right from wrong" (Davidson, 1955, p. 206).

The denouement was inevitable. On the basis of these medical reports, Macdonald's cabinet—with the compliance even of its francophone members—resolved that no grounds existed for commuting the court's sentence of death. On the morning of November 16, 1985, at the age of 41, Louis David Riel was hanged on the grounds of the Regina barracks. The course of Canadian politics had been forever altered. And in the process the modern practice of forensic psychiatry had, for better or worse, come of age.

Box 8.4 Dr. Strangelove in Canada

From 1943 to 1964, Dr. Ewan Cameron—a Scottish-born American psychiatrist—was director of the Allan Memorial Institute, a prestigious and heavily funded mental-health clinic affiliated with McGill University in Montreal. Dr. Cameron, a renowned behaviourist and one-time president of the American Psychiatric Association, was long considered one of the leading North American practitioners in the field of mental illness and its control. As a behavioural psychiatrist, he had consistently demonstrated little patience with the long-term, open-ended talking therapies being advocated during these years by members of various psychoanalytic schools of clinical practice. Instead, he chose to rely on such physiological treatment methods as lobotomy, electroconvulsive (shock) therapy, insulin-induced comas, LSD injections, and protracted subliminal suggestions through the use of recurrently playing taped messages.

For three and a half years, during the late 1950s and early 1960s, Dr. Cameron accepted a $75 000 grant from a U.S. Central Intelligence Agency front, called the Society for the Investigation of Human Ecology, to conduct experiments in mind control on Canadian psychiatric patients. Without their knowledge, nearly 100 people—who had come to the clinic for treatment of various psychological disorders, ranging from depression to anxiety reaction—were enlisted as subjects of a CIA research project, code-named MKULTRA. They were exposed to brainwashing techniques designed to perfect the Agency's Cold War scientific methods of psychological terror. Dr. Cameron proved himself to be an enthusiastic instrument for the CIA

mission. His subjects were administered massive doses of LSD and other mind-altering drugs. They were "depatterned" through enforced sleep "therapy" sessions that could endure for several weeks at a time. "If they protested his horrifying methods, they were hostile and showed no motivation to get better. If they refused to sit voluntarily and listen to his mind-numbing tapes, he would inject them with curare, a poison that would paralyze them in their chairs" (Drainie, *Globe and Mail*, October 29, 1988, p. C5). Many of Cameron's victims suffered irreparable psychological trauma, memory loss, personality disintegration, and neurological damage. For his part, Dr. Cameron continued to enjoy a lucrative and eminent career until his death in 1967.

In October 1988, nine former patients, including Robert Logie of Vancouver and Val Orlikow of Winnipeg (wife of the former NDP Member of Parliament David Orlikow), received an out-of-court settlement of $907 500 from the CIA. This sum comprised the most extensive monetary damages ever awarded against the U.S. espionage agency. Yet, in relative terms, this was small compensation for the life-long emotional and physical damage inflicted by Dr. Cameron's Orwellian methods, in the name of psychiatric "treatment." As James Thomas, a lawyer representing the Allan Institute patients, remarked: "These people all bear the scars of Dr. Cameron. They went for help and instead they were abused" (*Maclean's*, October 17, 1988, p. 51, see Collins, 1988; Weinstein, 1988).

apy in the 1950s as a generally accepted form of psychiatric treatment, a huge volume of literature has been written about the medical, legal, and ethical implications of distributing drugs to involuntary mental patients. On the one hand, the majority of forensic clinicians argue that psychoactive medication is the most efficient, inexpensive, and benevolent option available for dealing with severe psychiatric illnesses—particularly when crime and violence have been involved—and for ensuring that subjects can eventually return to the community (Klein et al., 1980; Silverstone & Turner, 1974).

In contrast, most critics respond that these drugs are not valid treatments at all. Artificial chemicals such as chlorpromazine, these writers suggest, are employed mainly to control the physical symptoms rather than to resolve the social roots of mental disorder, and, even more troubling,

they can often induce serious side-effects such as seizures, tardive dyskinesia (drug-induced nerve damage), memory loss, and general apathy (Baruch & Treacher, 1978; Coleman, 1984; Schrag, 1978). Civil libertarians point out that the North American pharmaceutical industry is a competitive, multibillion-dollar business, which aggressively promotes its products (see Figure 8.1) and reaps enormous profits from the treatment of people who are being confined in our mental facilities. They also insist that the widespread (and even indiscriminant) reliance on psychoactive medication in Canadian forensic hospitals should be viewed less as treatment than as a form of social control, which, when applied without consent, may well violate a patient's right to humane and adequate medical care (see Anand, 1979; Ericson, 1974; Gordon & Verdun-Jones, 1988; Schiffer, 1982, Ch. 5).

IORE SURMONTIL

and watch her rise and shine tomorrow.

variation. So, consider the advantages of at least 75 mg of Surmontil, once a day:

Tonight, one dose of Surmontil relieves insomnia.[1]

And tomorrow, that same dose continues the therapy ... by relieving *daytime* anxiety.[2]

Without increasing side effects.[1]

Your patients need more than a good night's sleep. And now there's no better way to provide the daytime relief they need. It's as easy as a 75 mg capsule of Surmontil tonight.

rks wonders
's sleep. Now see
r patients' *days*.
r to their best,
s. capsules.*

se enough
be enough for
is of depression.
and mood

RMONTIL 75 mg
(TRIMIPRAMINE)

e days as good as the nights.

RHÔNE·POULENC

*After appropriate maintenance dosage has been established.
For prescribing information, please see page

f depression.

Criminally insane patients also come under the jurisdiction of an **advisory review board** (consisting of three to five members, two of whom must be licensed psychiatrists, and one a lawyer), which is required under section 619 of the Criminal Code to assess the status of all Warrant cases six months after their initial confinement, and once per year thereafter (Schiffer, 1982, Ch. 6; Whitley, 1984). The composition and practices of the boards vary widely across the provinces. Every board, however, has the authority only to *recommend* continued hospitalization or release, based on "whether in its opinion it is in the interest of the public and that of the person . . . to order that he be discharged absolutely or subject to such conditions as the lieutenant-governor may prescribe." The final decision for release always rests with the provincial cabinet, on behalf of the lieutenant-governor. We know very little about the process of decision making by Canadian advisory review boards, since no systematic study of their operations has ever been undertaken. We do know, however, that the boards enjoy broad powers of discretion, and that the final decision about release of the criminally insane (subject to its conforming with standards of procedural fairness and natural justice) is nonreviewable.[5] Some have argued that these current powers are too broad, that Warrant patients should be provided with better legal protection, and the procedures made more open to legal and public observation (see Schiffer, 1982; Whitley, 1984).

As of 1980, a total of 834 Canadians were under the authority of a Lieutenant Governor's Warrant, about three-quarters of whom had been found not guilty by reason of insanity (see Table 8.2). Among people confined under section 16 of the Criminal Code—according to an earlier cross-Canada survey conducted by two researchers at the Oak Ridge facility in Penetanguishene, Ontario (Quinsey & Boyd, 1977)—86 percent had committed crimes against persons and 66 percent were diagnosed as psychotic (with 19 percent personality disordered). The average patient was 36 years old, had only 9 years of education, and had already spent 5 years in hospital at the time of the survey. Media hyperbole and public alarm notwithstanding, criminal-court acquittals on grounds of criminal responsibility do not signal the wholesale release of dangerous lunatics into the community. In reality, section 16 patients are held indefinitely (potentially, for the rest of their lives) in some of the most secure facilities in the country; they are subjected for years to strict regimens of management and treatment (see Quinsey, 1981); and their potential release is governed by a conservative review process whose first priority is to guarantee public protection. What is more, once released, the criminally insane in Canada and elsewhere typically have a lower recidivism rate than do people discharged from prison, and, in most follow-up studies, fewer than 15 percent have committed acts of violence (Quinsey, 1979; Steadman & Cocozza, 1974; Thornberry & Jacoby, 1979; Webster & Menzies, 1987).

Still, there has been much criticism of standards and procedures for determining criminal responsibility, which for years has been levied not just by the standardbearers of public safety, but also by many civil libertarians (Ennis, 1972; Morris, 1982), and those who actively oppose the participation of psychiatrists in the criminal courts (Coleman, 1984; Szasz, 1963; Torrey, 1974). Ferguson (1986, pp. 173–74) has identified a total of fourteen such criticisms (edited slightly down from his original list) that raise

Table 8.2 Frequency and Basis of Lieutenant-Governor's Warrants, By Province

Province	Not Guilty on Account of Insanity	Unfit to Stand Trial	Found Mentally Ill in Prison	Total	Number per 100 000
B.C.	133	6	0	139 (64)	5.5
Alberta	40	3	0	43 (13)	2.2
Sask.	16	9	0	25	2.6
Manitoba	17	3	0	20	1.9
Ontario	—	—	—	310 (200)	3.7
Quebec	186	64	0	250	4.0
N.B.	19	19	2	40	5.8
N.S.	1	0	0	1	0.1
P.E.I.	0	0	0	0	0.0
Nfld.	1	5	0	6	1.0
Canada	—	—	—	834	3.6

Note: Breakdowns of Warrant cases by type were unavailable for Ontario. Bracketed figures represent those living in the community while still under the terms of a WLG.

Source: From *Autonomy, 1* (1980), p.9. Reprinted with permission.

' which are ap-
presented here

:al basis of the

issumption that
act of free will,
inism and other
our.
l nor fair. If the
rder which im-
hould not other
ral deprivation)
e recognized as

c. It encourages
as a helpless vic-
uraging him [or
: crime].
not susceptible
same fashion as
ypes of physical

tric evaluations,
ccused's mental
ritative, reliable,
guesswork.
itrary. Some are
apparent con-

n of the insanity
an unwarranted
t cases.
narrow. It only
ot volitional or
so narrow that
ed persons are

anguage (such as
mind," and "in-
as "capacity to

insanity does not
esponsibility and

ea is too rigid and
e process and the

inity on a balance
and unfair.
der should not be

entitled to usurp the function of judge and jury by offering [a direct] opinion on the ultimate legal issue.

In other parts of the world, the controversy has led to monumental reforms in the criteria for defining legal insanity, and even in the very philosophy of criminal responsibility itself. The United States (which, unlike Canada, has 51 separate jurisdictions, all constantly working on the legal doctrine of criminal justice) is at the forefront of these experiments in psychiatry and law. A number of American alternatives to the McNaughtan test have surfaced over the years. These include:

1. *The Irresistible Impulse Standard:*

Insanity . . . means such a perverted and deranged condition of the mental and moral faculties as to render a person incapable of distinguishing between right and wrong, or unconscious at the time of the nature of the act he is committing, or where, though conscious of it and able to distinguish between right and wrong and know that the act is wrong, yet his will, by which I mean the governing power of his mind, has been otherwise than voluntarily so completely destroyed that his actions are not subject to it, but are beyond his control.[6]

As early as the 1897 *Davis* case, the U.S. Supreme Court had attached a "volitional" condition to the McNaughtan test, by recognizing that people who knew what they were doing, but could not control themselves, should be found legally insane (Brooks, 1974, p. 162). This "control test," involving a consideration of the defendant's will along with the traditional cognitive component contained in McNaughtan, was used for many years in more than half of the American states (Nettler, 1984, p. 30).

2. *The Durham Rule:* The accused is to be found not guilty be reason of insanity "if the unlawful act was the product of mental disease or defect."[7] Also known as the "product test," the 1954 *Durham* decision was handed down by Judge David Bazelon in the Washington, D.C., housebreaking trial of Monte Durham, in order to open up more channels for psychiatric participation in judgments about criminal responsibility, and to increase the numbers of successful insanity pleas. The Court, during a time of unprecedented growth throughout the 1950s in the influence of forensic psychiatrists, reasoned that no person should be convicted of any crime that results from mental illness. This test was viewed by many as far too radical and open-ended, as it placed enormous faith in clinicians to decide which crimes were indeed the product of "illness or defect." As Szasz (1963, p. 131) wrote at the time, "the change from McNaughtan to Durham is . . . a move away from a Rule

of Law toward a Rule of Men." While the number of successful insanity defences did, indeed, increase dramatically
over the next decade in the District of Columbia, the
Durham test never caught on elsewhere, and it was finally
abandoned altogether in 1972 (Quen, 1981).

3. *The American Law Institute (ALI) Test*: In its Model
Penal Code of 1962, the institute suggested that a defendant
should be found criminally insane "if at the time of such
conduct, as a result of mental disease or defect, he lacks
substantial capacity either to appreciate the criminality of
his conduct or to conform his conduct to the requirements
of law." This was offered as a modern compromise between
McNaughtan and *Durham*, which would deal specifically
with an accused person's ability to "appreciate" his or her
"criminality," and at the same time would enclose a
volitional component to the test (namely, "conformity to
the requirements of law"). This American Law Institute
definition found widespread support among courts
throughout the United States and, in 1972, was used to
overturn the *Durham* test in the District of Columbia.[8]
Today the ALI standard is used in about 30 American states,
and in all federal courts (Wexler, 1984).

4. *Guilty But Mentally Ill (GBMI)*: About a quarter of jurisdictions in the United States have now adopted the GMBI
option, where the court has a choice among four possible
judgments in criminal responsibility cases: guilty, not guilty,
not guilty by reason of insanity, or guilty but mentally ill.
The GBMI alternative grants more flexibility to the court
when defendants are emotionally disordered, but not sufficiently ill to permit an acquittal. Its intention is to grant
official recognition to the potential for diminished (or partial) responsibility, instead of relying on the all-or-nothing
selection between sanity and madness. Under this system,
people found both guilty and mentally ill are convicted,
but with recognition of their disorder, which can be a factor in handing down a sentence. The guilty but mentally
ill plea has been roundly criticized over recent years,
because, in such states as Michigan and Illinois, it has failed
to produce its intended reduction in insanity findings, and
because a GBMI finding does not guarantee that mentally
disordered people will, in fact, receive treatment after being
convicted (American Bar Association, 1983; Weiner, 1984).

Finally, there remains the option of expunging the insanity defence totally from criminal law and procedure. This
option has become a very serious point of discussion in the
Canadian criminal-justice system and, like the above alternatives, it has already become reality in several American
court systems. The entire concept of criminal responsibility has everywhere been under assault over recent years,
and the flames of this debate were greatly fuelled in the
United States by the 1982 acquittal of John Hinckley Jr.
following his attempted assassination of Ronald Reagan

(Caplan, 1984; Low, Jeffries, & Bonnie, 1986). The resulting
denunciations of Hinckley's sentence—by politicians, the
media, and the public—rekindled the long-standing myth
that, through their acquittals, insane criminals are escaping
the punishment merited by their deeds. And within five
years of the *Hinckley* decision, the states of Idaho, Montana, and Utah abolished the defence altogether.

In Canada as well, the insanity plea has been broadly
characterized as nothing more than a "glorified **mens rea**
defence" (Ferguson, 1984, p. 294). For all the reasons
reviewed earlier in this section, it is seen by many to rest
on antiquated ideas, vague language, and questionable legal
theory, and (depending on the point of view) to result in
either the premature release of dangerous mad people or
the repudiation of fundamental civil liberties for mentally
disordered offenders.

Yet, despite calls on many fronts—including the judiciary
(*Globe and Mail*, November 14, 1988)—for its abolition,
it is highly likely that some version of the insanity defence
will remain in place here for many years to come. For, instead of promoting a policy of complete abandonment, the
Law Reform Commission of Canada (1982), in its recent
draft legislation, has opted rather for a simple modernization of the test. The commission has offered a choice between an updated version of *McNaughtan* ("Every one is
exempt from criminal liability for his conduct if it is proved
that as a result of disease or defect of the mind he was incapable of appreciating the nature, consequences or un-
lawfulness of such conduct") or a slightly reworded variant
on the American ALI test ("Everyone is exempt from criminal liability for his conduct if it is proved that as a result
of disease or defect of the mind he lacked substantial
capacity either to appreciate the nature, consequences or
moral wrongfulness of such conduct or to conform to the
requirements of the law") (Ferguson, 1984). Still, either
of these reforms would arguably be an improvement over
the current legislation.

Fitness to Stand Trial

The concept of fitness to stand trial dates back to thirteenth-
century Britain (Walker, 1968). Fitness, like many of the
issues involving psychiatric disorder and the law, was originally based on a deceptively simple principle, namely that
persons lacking a minimal mental capacity should not be
forced unfairly to defend themselves before the criminal
courts. As Matthew Hale (1736) wrote in his famous *History of the Pleas of the Crown*: "if a man in his sound memory
commits a capital offence, and before his arraignment he
becomes absolutely mad, he ought not by law to be ar-
raigned during such his phrenzy. . . . and if such person
after his plea, and before his trial, become of non sane

r, 1968, 221).
e was clearly dis-
Unlike criminal
ed to the defen-
d it resulted not
ment of the case
ed.
parently straight-
lways been easi-
nd punishment.
involved the ac-
; among accused
termine whether
r they are utterly
r they are simply
lness in order to
he question was
le to the "peine
efendant failed to
lea, stones would
t, one at a time,
topped breathing
itions, the life ex-
mewhat limited.
1772.
nd other mental-
placed the stones.
l defendants is in
examination by
heir expert opin-
cipation of trained
difficulties persist.
ot even spell out
he stipulation (in
be deemed unfit
rson is not "cap-
see Verdun-Jones,
ine insanity or to
qualify under this
tory standard, our
lusively on British
a few prominent
me general criteria
st-known tests in
ltucky case in Sas-
hether or not the
oceedings";[9] and,
g by the British
"It is prerequisite
e capable of con-
uptive conduct on
ually, linguistically

and communicatively present and able to partake to the best of his natural ability in his full answer and defence of the charge against him."[10]

The Canadian Law Reform Commission conducted its own survey of fitness to stand trial and related issues during the 1970s, which ultimately led to a report to Parliament entitled *Mental Disorder in the Criminal Process* (1976). Following their comprehensive review of law and practices on the subject, the commissioners came to the conclusion that judgments about legal fitness should depend on three related components. They submitted the following standard:

> A person is unfit if, due to mental disorder:
> (1) he does not understand the nature or object of the proceedings against him, or
> (2) he does not understand the personal object of the proceedings, or
> (3) he is unable to communicate with counsel. (1976, p. 44)

Yet, to date, despite various legislative efforts over recent years to overhaul the Criminal Code in general, and the fitness provisions in particular, nothing much has changed. For their part, stranded as they are in such rocky legal terrain, Canadian trial judges have become increasingly reliant on mental-health workers to decide this issue for them. Many criminologists, in this country and elsewhere, have noted the tendency for psychiatrists' recommendations about fitness to be routinely endorsed by the court (Campbell, 1981; Greenland & Rosenblatt, 1972; Jackson, 1978; Menzies, 1989; Steadman, 1973). Judges seldom reverse the opinions of medical experts. In the process, forensic clinicians have come to wield a great deal of power to decide just who is mentally competent to face his or her trial, and who should be sent to hospital.

Critics of the **psychiatric remand** are inclined to stress the dangers of granting such sweeping authority to court psychiatrists (Levy, 1980). For one thing, the vast majority of defendants ordered to hospital for a fitness assessment under a **Warrant of Remand**[11]—sometimes for a period of 30 days or more—are found fully competent, raising questions about the real need for psychiatric participation in these cases, and for the long periods spent by people in confinement prior to their trial (Menzies et al., 1980; Steadman, 1979; Verdun-Jones, 1981). For another, fitness is arguably more a legal than a medical issue, and forensic clinicians may be no more qualified than others to become involved in its diagnosis. In this connection, at least one study (Roesch & Golding, 1980) has found that psychiatrists may not be able to distinguish between incompetency to stand trial, on the one hand, and general psychotic disorder, on the other. Finally, there is the possibility that the fitness

Table 8.3 The Fitness Interview Test

Accused _____

Clinician/rater _____

Date _____

Degree of incapacity

		None	Mild	Moderate	Severe	Total	Unrateable
1.	Understanding of arrest process (How did patient get here?)	1	2	3	4	5	6
2.	Appreciation of charges (What is the charge? Is it serious?)	1	2	3	4	5	6
3.	Understanding of legal process						
	a. Oath?	1	2	3	4	5	6
	b. Plea?	1	2	3	4	5	6
	c. Evidence?	1	2	3	4	5	6
4.	Appraisal of role: key figures						
	a. Defence counsel?	1	2	3	4	5	6
	b. Crown counsel?	1	2	3	4	5	6
	c. Judge?	1	2	3	4	5	6
	d. Defendant?	1	2	3	4	5	6
	e. Police?	1	2	3	4	5	6
	f. Psychiatrist (or other Assessor)?	1	2	3	4	5	6
5.	Capacity to disclose to lawyer pertinent facts surrounding the alleged offence (What happened?)	1	2	3	4	5	6
6.	Quality of relating to lawyer (Can talk to lawyer?)	1	2	3	4	5	6
7.	Appreciation of range and nature of possible penalties (If found guilty, what might happen?)	1	2	3	4	5	6
8.	Planning of legal strategy (Plea bargaining? Ability to follow legal instructions? To disagree with lawyer where appropriate?)	1	2	3	4	5	6
9.	Capacity to challenge prosecution witnesses (If witness lies about you, what to do?)	1	2	3	4	5	6
10.	Capacity to testify relevantly	1	2	3	4	5	6
11.	Global impairment of fitness-legal	1	2	3	4	5	6
12.	Thought disorder	1	2	3	4	5	6
13.	Concentration defect (Seven from 100, etc.)	1	2	3	4	5	6
14.	Intrusion of delusions	1	2	3	4	5	6
15.	Global assessment of psychiatric impairment	1	2	3	4	5	6

Fit _____ Fitness questionable _____ Unfit _____

Source: From R.J. Menzies et al. (1984), The Fitness Interview Test: A semi-structured instrument for assessing competency to stand trial, with a proposal for its implementation (p.162). *Medicine and Law, 3*. Reprinted with permission from *Medicine and Law*.

addressing other
ie more central
/hich are not in
de or provincial
s for ordering a

uestion of what
:d unfit to stand
defendants (like
ane at the time
at the pleasure
As with crimi-
advisory review
h Warrant case,
ive confinement
the accused and
:."[13]

:ason of insanity,
:d to a "**double**
g period of man-
the Lieutenant-
ed to court and
arges. Although
by the Crown,
ing does not al-
persons. In fact,
spitals for longer
m, had they sim-
the court in the
)81). Moreover,
1 their survey of
ts, despite their
ctually confined
IGRI subjects.
>dies some of the
>f indefinite con-
nnar, a nineteen-
in 1964 with al-
>urse. Following
ind trial, Bonnar
:t seventeen years
Box 8.5).
: civil liberties of
vithout even the
s have suggested
Commission, for
>nfinement in its
iclusion that de-
it the pleasure of
1 only "as a last

resort" (1976, p. 43). Under a system of alternative dispo-sitions, unfit defendants could be held in more open set-tings where appropriate, or they could even be released without condition where their charges were not serious and they posed no threat to the community. Moreover, upper limits could be applied to the maximum duration of detention for the unfit, so that people could not be held, for example, beyond a "reasonable" period for re-establishing their competency, or beyond the length of im-prisonment they would suffer if found guilty of the **alleged** crime. Interestingly, various versions of this reform have long since been implemented throughout the United States, following their famous Supreme Court decision in *Jackson v. Indiana*[14] (Roesch & Golding, 1980).

At the level of judicial procedure, critics have also con-centrated on the practice of deciding about fitness before the criminal trial actually occurs. The Law Reform Com-mission, for instance, has proposed that competency hear-ings be postponed where appropriate until after the conclusion of the trial process. Defendants who were acquitted would then go free, without being subjected to any decision about their fitness. This change would pro-vide some measure of protection against unjust confine-ment, since only those persons found guilty of a crime would be vulnerable to being hospitalized as unfit. Although this proposal has received divided support in the legal com-munity (Eaves et al., 1984), and although some have con-demned it as unnecessarily time-consuming and unwieldy (Del Buono, 1975), it has found enthusiastic support elsewhere.

Roesch (1978) has offered a blueprint for integrating post-trial fitness hearings with rapid pretrial fitness screen-ings. Under this system, special panels would conduct brief and efficient assessments before the criminal trial is con-vened. Up to 90 percent of people, Roesch estimates, would be found immediately fit and sent on to face the judge. The remaining 10 percent, whose competency was still in question, would also go to court, but with one of three possible outcomes. Those found innocent at trial would be discharged, since, despite their suspected mental disorder, they have been acquitted of the criminal charge against them. Persons found guilty would go on to a full-scale psychiatric assessment: if fit, they would be sentenced, and if unfit, the verdict would be quashed.

Although these reforms have yet to be implemented, Roesch asserts that this approach would afford protections to mentally disordered defendants while at the same time avoiding an avalanche of new work for Canadian judges and forensic psychiatrists (Roesch, 1978; Roesch & Gold-ing, 1979, 1980). It would also accord with an important

Box 8.5 "At the Pleasure of the Lieutenant-Governor": The Emerson Bonnar Story

On August 15, 1964, Emerson Bonnar was arrested on the streets of Saint John, New Brunswick, for snatching a woman's purse. At the time, Bonnar was a nineteen-year-old mental patient, who, for more than two years, had been receiving psychiatric treatment at the Saint John General Hospital. After taking the purse, he had made no attempt to escape. As his mother, Bessie, later reported: "That woman's purse was never opened. . . . He hung on to it, never tried to get away or nothing. He just stood there and when the police came, they took him off to jail" (*Atlantic Insight,* March 1980, p. 10). This was his first-ever criminal charge.

At his initial appearance in provincial court, Bonnar entered a plea of guilty. He was not represented by a lawyer. His family had not been contacted. Following a week of confinement in the local jail, he was returned to court, to find that a psychiatrist named Robert Gregory had been summoned as an expert witness. Dr. Gregory testified that Bonnar was functioning at a "mentally retarded–moron level." He declared under oath: "I hardly think he would be able to instruct counsel or give a coherent, and logical story which would be acceptable to the court" (Savage, 1980, pp. 4–5). On the basis of the psychiatric evidence, Bonnar was found unfit to stand trial and was ordered to be confined indefinitely, under a Warrant of the Lieutenant-Governor, in a secure mental institution for the criminally insane. He was given no opportunity to respond to the psychiatrist's deposition (*Maclean's,* March 3, 1980, p. 23). The entire hearing lasted about twenty minutes.

Despite the relatively minor nature of the criminal charges, and although he was never clinically assessed to be in any way dangerous, Bonnar was to spend the next seventeen years of his life under involuntary detention— first in the mental institution in Saint John, and after 1972 at the New Brunswick Centricare Hospital in Campbellton. Over the years, he was subjected to insulin shock, electroconvulsive therapy, and many varieties of neuroleptic drugs. On four separate occasions, he was brought to emergency units in an unconscious state, the apparent victim of severe beatings. Daily life in the hospital consisted mainly of endlessly repetitive institutional routines. His principal activity involved sweeping the floors (Verdun-Jones, 1981, p. 367). In his mother's words: "It's a bad place to be. I couldn't survive there one day. Nobody's ever cheerful as far as I can see" (*Atlantic Insight,* March 1980, p. 10).

Finally, in 1980, following the publicization of his case during an episode of the Canadian Broadcasting Corporation television program "Ombudsman," two independent psychiatric evaluations of Bonnar were conducted on behalf of the New Brunswick government and the Canadian Association for the Mentally Retarded. On the basis of these reviews, serious violations of Bonnar's civil rights and outrageous lapses of psychiatric responsibility were uncovered. One of the reports, drafted by Dr. Bruno Cormier, concluded: "At no place do I detect any attempt to determine whether this man would be able to inform a lawyer regarding his defence, could appear in court, knew what a trial was and the consequences that might ensue therefrom. . . . One has the impression that at one stage the medical authorities involved in the treatment of Emerson Bonnar acted somehow as if a diagnosis such as schizophrenia, mental deficiency and dangerosity were criteria to consider someone unfit to stand trial" (Savage, 1980, p. 6). Even more glaring, it was suggested that his current mental difficulties were probably mostly a product of his protracted confinement under conditions of maximum security.

Finally, the province of New Brunswick approved a loosening of the Lieutenant-Governor's Warrant in May 1980, and Bonnar was discharged from the heavy security unit in Campbellton. A year later, the Warrant was vacated altogether. After seventeen years, Emerson Bonnar had gained his freedom. But, in the process, his case had done much to reveal the dangers of the fitness "defence" in Canada, under the auspices of a system where criminal defendants can be involuntarily detained in hospital for life, without benefit of a trail, ostensibly for their own protection. At the time of Bonnar's release, there were more than 800 Canadians being held under Warrants across the country. And according to Dr. Douglas Findley in British Columbia: "There are other cases far more glaring than that of Emerson Bonnar" (*Atlantic Insight,* March 1980, p. 10).

1984 decision by the Quebec Superior Court in the case of Thomas Brigham, the "Mad Bomber" of Montreal, who had killed three French tourists in the Montreal train station with a home-made explosive device. In its judgment, the Court seemed to endorse the general logic of these proposals, by ordering that Brigham could not be confined as mentally unfit unless the Crown first presented the Court with evidence pointing to his guilt.[15]

rnatives of sub-
sions about fit-
ness assessments
e criminologists
h the construc-
ning the fitness
chreiber, 1984;
4). The Fitness
a in an effort to
of standardized
Table 8.3), has
ands of lawyers,
(Roesch, Web-
ed on the prin-
than a clinical
clinical assessors
hiatric expertise
t decisions about

be good reason
ess to stand trial.
d Verdun-Jones
tness "defence"
a protection for
majority of fit-
cessary (as most
l), they are often
wo months and
ite confinement
d mental illness
e charges against
s concluded,

t simply be
oratorium on
easible option
activities, for
for the con-
the provision
mentally dis-
w. (Menzies,

the present day,
h the concept of
e wrestling with
tness defence for

Canadian forensic
years, the predic-

tion of dangerousness is by far the most controversial. The concept of dangerousness can be loosely defined for our purposes as an individual's potential for violent conduct, usually against others, but also in certain contexts against himself or herself (as in the possibility of suicide or self-inflicted injury) (Steadman, 1981). Much forensic work is based on the assumption that clinicians offer a special expertise in forecasting dangerous behaviour, and in equating the relationship between mental illness and violence. This is an especially difficult and contentious task, since psychiatric experts are being asked not just to diagnose their patients, but to look into the future and decide whether and when they might some day engage in criminally assaultive behaviour. Conflict tends to arise when individuals—whether or not they suffer from mental illness—are detained in hospital or prison not because of what they have done, but on the basis of a psychiatrist's (or some other official's) judgment about their predisposition to inflict harm on others. While many authorities claim that this is legitimate forensic work (Hamilton & Freeman, 1982; Held, 1987; Monahan, 1981; Prins, 1986), a great number of observers argue that psychiatrists are no better equipped than laypersons to predict the future, and that when they attempt to do so they are usually wrong (Ennis & Litwack, 1974; Menzies, 1986; Morris & Miller, 1985; Pfohl, 1978; Steadman, 1973; Warren, 1979; Webster & Menzies, 1987).

Whatever the scope of this debate, dangerousness is clearly an influential concept in the Canadian mental-health system, where judgments about involuntary civil commitment, level of institutional security, forms of treatment, and discharge from hospital can reflect a patient's presumed potential for harming himself or herself or others. In our criminal-justice arena, as well, dangerousness is relevant to a range of determinations, including the ordering of psychiatric remands, bail release, the transfer of juveniles to adult court, judicial sentencing, the disposition of special "dangerous" offenders, the level of security in prison, the diversion of prisoners to hospitals or regional psychiatric centres, and the ultimate granting of parole (Menzies, 1986; Shah, 1978). And, for clinicians involved in the crime-control enterprise, the assessment and treatment of dangerousness have evolved into a routine feature of forensic work in pretrial detention centres, forensic assessment units, court clinics, community facilities, private offices, psychiatric institutions, and prisons (Frederick, 1978; Hinton, 1983; Litwack & Schlesinger, 1986; Rennie, 1978; Webster, Dickens, & Addario, 1985).

In one way or another, society has long been concerned with the identification and management of people who are considered a threat to the public peace. In the nineteenth century, such persons included the dangerous classes—the marginal and often homeless urban poor of Europe and North America—who were believed by some to be "thrust back from the customs and laws of civilized life and reduced, by the suffering and privations of poverty, to a state of barbarism" (Buret, 1984, p. 1).

As well, with the rise of Positivism and the Italian **School of Criminal Anthropology**, dangerous individuals came to be viewed as fundamentally (often biologically) distinct from "normal," law-abiding citizens. Dangerousness was considered an enduring feature of the criminal personality, which had to be identified using the scientific tools of criminology, and subjected to long-term (even indefinite) treatment. And the clinical professions soon inherited the lion's share of responsibility for diagnosing and curing dangerous criminals. Largely on the basis of widely held assumptions about the alleged predisposition to violence among the mentally ill, the issue has to this day fallen within the domain of forensic psychiatry.

In the Canadian criminal-justice system, more than 50 percent of pretrial clinical assessments involve the direct investigation of a defendant's dangerousness to others, and, in about one-half of these cases, the psychiatric report concludes that the person is, indeed, dangerous (Menzies, 1989). In this way, psychiatric predictions can have a direct impact on the judge's choice of a criminal disposition. Clinical experts are also involved in the activities of advisory review boards (see above), where the decision to release a forensic in-patient is predicated in part on the question of community safety (Schiffer, 1982; Whitley, 1984). Further, recent legislative amendments have permitted the practice of "gating" by Canadian parole boards, where penitentiary inmates considered dangerous can be denied release on mandatory supervision, and forced to serve the entire term of their sentence (Ratner, 1987).

Nowhere, however, is dangerousness more overtly on display than in the judicial application of Part XXIV of the Canadian Criminal Code. **Dangerous-offender legislation**, as it is usually termed, was passed by Parliament in 1976, as part of an omnibus "peace and security package" (including, among other changes, tighter handgun controls, expanded powers for crime commissions, more rigorous restrictions on the release of prison inmates, and provisions for crime prevention through environmental design). The dangerous-offender section of the package replaced and expanded on the old **dangerous sexual offender** (DSO) law, which had been in effect in Canada since 1948 (Klein, 1976; Marcus, 1971; Price, 1970; Stortini, 1975). It permits the Crown, following a person's conviction for either a **sexual assault** or a violent offence (excluding murder or treason) punishable by a prison term of ten years or more,

to apply for a hearing to determine whether the defendant should be held indefinitely in prison.

In the subsequent hearing, at least two psychiatrists are required to offer their opinions about the subject's dangerousness, specifically whether the offender "constitutes a threat to the life, safety or physical or mental well-being of other persons," or "by his conduct in any sexual matter . . . has shown a failure to control his sexual impulses and a likelihood of his causing injury, pain or other evil to other persons through failure in the future to control his sexual impulses."[16] If the court finds, on a preponderance of evidence, that the person qualifies as a dangerous offender, it can hand down an indeterminate sentence, meaning that he or she remains in prison without a release date, and can be freed only by order of the National Parole Board (which conducts a review three years subsequent to the hearing, and every twelve months thereafter).

Since its passage, this law has been criticized by many observers, who cite the loose procedural and evidentiary standards of the hearing, the punitive severity of indeterminate sentencing itself, and the questionable wisdom of basing decisions on forecasts of dangerousness submitted by forensic psychiatrists (Menzies, 1986; Petrunik, 1983; Price, 1970; Webster, Dickens, & Addario, 1985). There have also been a number of legal challenges focussing on sections 7, 9, and 12 of the **Canadian Charter of Rights and Freedoms** (the rights, respectively, to "life, liberty and security of the person"; to "freedom from arbitrary detention or imprisonment"; and to "protection from cruel and unusual punishment"). To date, these court challenges have been universally unsuccessful (see Gordon & Verdun-Jones, 1988, pp. 853–57). Still, many criminologists continue to reject the need for dangerous-offender legislation in our criminal courts. They are especially troubled by the awesome power of judges to order **preventive detention**, by the role of psychiatrists in helping to send people to prison, and by the potential enlistment of this law even in cases where no overt violence has been involved (see Box 8.6).

What kinds of cases result in dangerous-offender designations? One Canadian team of criminologists (Jakimiec et al., 1986) has reported findings from a general survey of Canadians who were incarcerated under Part XXIV during its first decade of existence (see Table 8.4). All but two of these people are men, and 90 percent are white. Their average age at the time of sentencing was 35 years. As Table 8.4 shows, about half of the country's dangerous offenders come from Ontario, and another quarter from British Columbia. Most have a prior record of imprisonment, and more than 75 percent are sentenced on the basis of **sex**

Mental Disorder and Crime in Canada 225

oyes

s, a former school
f British Columbia,
t justice Raymond
f imprisonment as
now XXIV) of the
t year, Noyes had
ault and nine counts
en different child
er a period of more
his teaching career
ghout the province.
d with young male
victimized. None
on, overt force, or
r criminal record.
nder? Did he merit
ility of spending the
hes that usually, in
ears or less? During
Noyes's guilty plea,
t the defendant was
path—that the chil-
xposed to immense
streets. Altogether,
ourt's schedule over
wn attorney, Barry
nesses in support of
g those giving testi-
irector of the Adult
itlam. Although this
t Noyes, on the basis
report in court that
the Peter Pan Syn-
ty is fixed at an early
is living in a 'Never
, Noyes was "a psy-
ence" and hence it
erience normal feel-
difference between
ur" (*Vancouver Sun*,
ed by testifying that
enormous danger to
He] doesn't have the
sn't have the ability

(*Vancouver Sun*, March 15, 1985, p. A16).

Two subsequent psychiatric witnesses on behalf of the defence, Drs. John Bradford and Roy O'Shaughnessy, fiercely disputed Pos's arm's-length assessment of the defendant. Bradford declared that Noyes was clearly not a psychopath, but merely a "garden-variety pedophile," and he went on to "characterize many of the theories and diagnostic criteria employed by Pos . . . as outdated." Bradford also said he had "'problems' with the ethics of Pos's testimony." For his part, O'Shaughnessy dismissed Pos's diagnosis of psychopathy as "simply absurd." Both defence witnesses agreed that Noyes could be safely supervised under intensive probation conditions, provided that he was maintained on a regular dosage of cyproterone acetate (CPA)—a commonly used libido-inhibiting medication.

Despite these conflicting diagnoses, despite ample testimony concerning the inability of psychiatrists to predict dangerousness, and despite defence arguments that a positive finding would violate sections 9, 15, and 12 of the Canadian Charter of Rights and Freedoms (namely, it would entail arbitrary detention, would infringe equality provisions, and would constitute cruel and unusual punishment), Justice Paris ultimately did determine that Robert Noyes was a dangerous offender as defined by the Criminal Code. In his final written holding for the case, the Justice concluded:

> It is profoundly sad that any person, in particular one with the capabilities of Noyes, should, for some unknown reason, respond to his sexual instincts in this pathetic way. One also feels compassion for his family. However . . . he and people like him cause serious and widespread harm. The bottom line, to borrow a phrase, is whether the protection of the public requires that he be sentenced to an indeterminate term of imprisonment. That solution may seem Draconian to some, but I see no alternative to it. In sum, I find the offender Noyes to be a dangerous offender within the meaning of s. 688 of the Criminal Code (*R. v. Robert Olav Noyes*, 1986, p. 30).

As of this book's publication, Robert Noyes is still in prison.

Table 8.4 Characteristics of Dangerous Offenders in Canada

	Number	Percent
Gender		
Male	48	96
Female	2	4
Race		
White	45	90
Native Indian	3	6
Black	2	4
Province or Territory		
Ontario	29	48
British Columbia	16	27
Alberta	9	15
Nova Scotia	3	5
Saskatchewan	1	2
New Brunswick	1	2
Northwest Territories	1	2
Number of Prior Provincial Imprisonments		
None	9	19
1 to 3	19	40
4 to 8	17	36
9 to 12	1	2
More than 12	1	2
Number of Prior Federal Imprisonments		
None	17	36
1 to 3	25	53
4 to 8	5	11
Type of Offence Leading to DO Finding		
Sexual Offences	39	78
Other Offences vs. Persons	6	12
Property Offences (Arson)	3	6
Possession of Dangerous Weapon	2	4
Maximum Potential Sentence Available without DO Finding		
Less than 10 Years	7	14
10 to 13 Years	5	10
14 to 19 Years	5	10
20 Years or more	6	12
Life	27	54
Actual Length of DO Sentence		
2 Years Less a Day	1	2
10 Years	1	2
14 Years	1	2
Indefinite	47	94

Source: From J. Jakimiec et al. (1986), Dangerous offenders in Canada, 1977–1985. *International Journal of Law and Psychiatry, 9,* 482–486.

offences. Interestingly, the use of Part XXIV has increased steadily since its passage. There were no cases at all in 1977, and three, four, and six, respectively, between 1978 and 1980. The numbers had risen to twelve, nine, and eleven in the 1983–1985 period (the final three years of the study)

(see also Webster, Dickens, & Addario, 1985).

The criminological research literature, in Canada and other countries, seems to give good reason for concern about the role of psychiatrists in dangerous-offender hearings, and in other areas of criminal justice where danger-

l prediction of
psychiatrists are
vho are capable
yet to assemble
s that could do
lonahan, 1981;
ebster & Men-

curate forecast-
an elusive goal
:, most forensic
the prediction
a strong corre-
heir therapeutic
econd, the con-
guous, and has
rt physical vio-
ely the possibil-
: depending on
elled dangerous
sonal-injury as-
base rate (that
tire subpopula-
roups of foren-
y a situational
for psychiatrists
ng the near and
ire especially in-
of about three
of dangerousness
hit (an accurate
are inherently
e seeds of danger
suffer dire con-
pectedly to com-
ean bill of health
ne combinations
1981; Steadman,

gical studies have
y of psychiatric
most influential
of the *Baxstrom*
urt ordered the
New York State
the grounds that
pital beyond the
ice. All of these
ds of psychiatric
ing danger to the
lischarge, these
reatening people

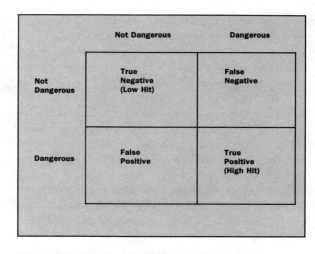

Figure 8.2   The Four Possible Combinations of Decisions and Outcomes in Dangerousness Predictions
Patient's Behaviour During Follow-up
Clinician's Prediction

in the state—turned out to be, at worst, a minor risk indeed. After four years, only 27 of the 927 *Baxstrom* patients had to be returned to secure forensic facilities. In general, the vast majority seemed to have little difficulty in adjusting to more open settings. And only 15 percent of those released to the community subsequently engaged in any kind of violence (Steadman & Cocozza, 1974). Since the time of the *Baxstrom* research, various additional studies, in the United States (Thornberry & Jacoby, 1979), Great Britain (Soothill, Way, & Gibbons, 1980), and Canada (Quinsey, 1979), have confirmed that those patients considered most dangerous by forensic psychiatrists (to the point of apparently requiring maximum-security hospitalization) turn out to be generally innocuous when they are finally returned to the streets.

The actual process of arriving at forensic decisions about future dangerousness would also seem to be fundamentally flawed. The American sociologist Stephen Pfohl conducted an intriguing study of the judgments arrived at by twelve clinical teams at the Lima State Hospital in Ohio (Pfohl, 1978). He observed 130 separate interviews of "criminally insane" in-patients, which were designed to establish whether or not these people were too dangerous to be released to more open psychiatric facilities. Pfohl discovered that the various diagnostic teams (consisting of a psychiatrist, forensic psychologist, and social worker) used very inconsistent standards of dangerousness in their work; that they often arrived at decisions solely on the basis of medical records, before even beginning the face-to-face interviews; that their judgments were based more on intuitive common sense than on professional expertise; that they often ignored or distorted information in order to arrive at a consistent portrayal of subjects' dangerousness; and that, in the process, the rights of patients to a fair hearing were frequently being violated (Pfohl, 1978).

Finally, criminologists have been unable to find any strong correlation between these kinds of clinical predictions, and the subsequent violent or criminal transgressions of forensic patients. In Toronto, one recent research project was designed especially to measure the accuracy of these forecasts with groups of criminal defendants on pretrial remand for clinical assessment (Sepejak et al., 1983; Sepejak, Webster, & Menzies, 1984). Specific predictions of dangerousness were registered at the time of evaluation (1 = no, 2 = low, 3 = medium, 4 = high) by a number of different forensic professionals (including psychiatrists, psychologists, social workers, nurses, and correctional workers) for nearly 600 subjects, whose conduct was then followed up for two years (using hospital and correctional records) and measured on an eleven-point scale of "outcome dangerousness" by independent raters. But the statistical relationship between the predictions and outcome behaviour turned out to be very low. Even for the most successful clinician (one of the psychiatrists), the prediction-outcome correlation was only + 0.27, meaning that he was able to forecast only about 5 percent of the dangerousness displayed by his patients. And even when more sophisticated prediction instruments were used, such as a Dangerous Behaviour Rating Scheme (DBRS) which broke down the prognoses into 22 separate items to be rated on a six-point continuum,[18] the ability to foresee violence was only marginally improved (Menzies, Webster, & Sepejak, 1985). It would seem that Canadian forensic patients, like their counterparts elsewhere, are highly resistant to these various attempts at forensic forecasting.

Yet, these many negative findings notwithstanding, the clinical professions are still daily engaged in the prediction of dangerousness in the service of criminal-justice systems. They continue to do so, because of the number of legal judgments that involve some estimate of how an offender might behave in the future; because of myths about the alleged relationship between mental disorder and violence; and because of widely-held beliefs that psychiatric science might somehow enable us to extend judgments about human beings beyond the limits of the here and now. These assumptions are so engrained that, in places like Texas, the psychiatric prediction of dangerousness has even been a legal requirement for the capital punishment of offenders held on Death Row (Dix, 1981). And however unjustified on the basis of the existing criminological research, it appears inevitable that forensic clinicians will continue to offer their opinions on this difficult issue for many years to come.

The Anatomy of Forensic Psychiatric Assessments

As we have seen, the activities of forensic clinicians have come to play an immensely important role in the Canadian criminal courts. It is estimated that more than 5000 defendants annually receive a pretrial psychiatric assessment in this country (Webster, Menzies, & Jackson, 1982). And, by every account, judges have themselves become increasingly reliant on the advice of medical experts in deciding about cases of suspected mental disorder. Literally from coast to coast, a wide range of forensic services have been developed for the purpose of evaluating fitness, criminal responsibility, dangerousness, and related issues that are relevant to the criminal and psychiatric disposition of accused persons (Akhtar, 1971; Arboleda-Florez, Gupta, & Alcock, 1975; Greenland & Rosenblatt, 1972; Kunjukrishnan, 1979; Schlatter, 1969; Turner, 1980).

This final section of this chapter takes a look at the actual process of forensic assessment in Canada. When the presiding judge orders that a defendant be examined under a Warrant of Remand, that person is typically held in custody until a medical examination can be arranged. The specifics of the procedure vary from one location to another. In some parts of the country, psychiatrists still visit patients in their jail cells or in an interview room set aside in the local court building. More and more, however, special clinics are being established, or sections of existing facilities are set aside, exclusively for the conduct of court-ordered assessments. Particularly in the larger cities, the procedure has become relatively routine. Assessments are often completed in less than a day, and relevant findings can be rapidly sent to judges by means of a dictated court report. Psychiatrists typically make appearances before judges for only the most difficult of cases—where, for example, criminal responsibility or dangerousness is under consideration, or where the testimony is under dispute. Otherwise the clinician remains an outside adviser rather than a direct participant in the trial process.

In order to understand this system in greater detail, we now examine one such Canadian assessment centre. More has been written about the Metropolitan Toronto Forensic Service (METFORS) than about any other forensic clinic in the country (e.g., Butler & Turner, 1980; Levy, 1980; Menzies, 1987a, 1987b; Menzies & Webster, 1989; Menzies, 1989; Mewett, 1981; Tacon, 1979; Turner, 1980; Webster & Menzies, 1987; Webster, Menzies, & Jackson, 1982). METFORS is Canada's purest example of a pretrial psychiatric unit designed for the express purpose of furnishing courts with clinical information about people charged with criminal offences. Opened in 1977, METFORS occupies the fourth and fifth stories of a wing in the Queen

the Ontario
nistered by its
ychiatry. The
it Unit (BAU)
of maximum
for protracted
curity classifi-
arch, line, and
y. In the first
led more than
evaluations of
Menzies, 1989;

prototype for
elp to stream-
nent, while at
ronto criminal
Roy McMur-
ed on the day

for almost
itario, I can
iility of this
often taken
psychiatric]
to provide
iy places in
hese reports
will benefit
process and
vay infringe
irts. (quoted
989, Ch. 1)

t Unit at MET-
of the pretrial
o. At 9:00 a.m.
is are conveyed
the three local
c patients have
court judge fol-
hough about 10
nt, or have been
or the defence.
rred to a secure
iinary interview
orning, they are
oom, where the
ding psychiatrist,
ng correctional
minutes each in

duration. They are relatively open-ended, and they focus
on a range of medical and legal issues that are considered
relevant by the BAU clinical-team members. Following the
examination, patients are returned to the holding cell, fed
a lunch, and transferred later in the afternoon back to their
cell in the local detention centre. Accompanying them is
a letter, which has been dictated by the BAU psychiatrist
and addressed to the presiding criminal-court judge, and
which becomes the single most important product of the
brief assessment.

The Brief Assessment Unit clientele fall into three main
groups. First, about two-thirds of defendants are simply
returned to court as fit to stand trial. People in this largest
category may or may not receive other recommendations
from the BAU psychiatrist concerning their fitness for bail,
general mental condition, need for treatment, dangerousness to self or others, or criminal-court disposition. Second,
around 30 percent are recommended by the clinic for an
extended in-patient assessment under a Warrant of Remand. For a variety of reasons, these patients are seen to
require more extensive scrutiny than can be provided in
the course of a single day, and judges are moved to endorse such recommendations in more than 80 percent of
cases (Menzies, 1989, Ch. 4). Third, a small proportion of
the forensic population (about 5 percent) are considered
sufficiently dangerous *and* mentally disordered to qualify
for immediate involuntary hospitalization under the terms
of the Ontario Mental Health Act. Unless they are facing
extremely serious charges, such persons are usually removed
altogether from the court's jurisdiction, and transferred immediately to the maximum-security units in Penetanguishene, Ontario (for men), or St. Thomas, Ontario (for
women) (see, generally, Webster, Menzies, & Jackson,
1982, Chs. 5, 6; Menzies, 1989, Ch. 1).

What kinds of people are sent to METFORS? A survey
of the first 592 accused persons evaluated in the Brief
Assessment Unit, during the clinic's initial year of operation (Menzies et al., 1978; Webster, Menzies, & Jackson,
1982), revealed that forensic patients—like criminal defendants generally in this country (Ericson & Baranek, 1982)—
are overwhelmingly drawn from the demographic and economic margins of Canadian society. The typical METFORS
patient in this survey was young, unmarried, poor, unemployed, undereducated, and either living alone or homeless. About 90 percent were male. Nearly four out of every
five had a prior criminal conviction, and more than half
had spent time in prison.

However, these forensic subjects were clearly different
from other Canadian defendants on two main dimensions.
First, they were more likely to be violent, with a full 42
percent having been sent to METFORS on the basis of
alleged offences against the person. Second, they reported

a much higher degree of involvement with the mental-health system. About 50 percent of the BAU subjects had previously been confined as psychiatric in-patients. More than half were classified at the highest level of alcohol or other drug abuse, a quarter had at some time attempted to kill themselves, a quarter were diagnosed as psychotic, and another one-third were personality disordered (see Figure 8.3). These people resembled the mainstream of Canada's criminal-trial population in many ways, but, at the same time, their tendency toward violence and their elevated levels of perceived mental disorder made them unique, and appeared to be responsible for their diversion into the forensic assessment system.

How do psychiatrists and other clinicians undertake the process of evaluating the fitness, dangerousness, and related characteristics of criminal defendants? How are their decisions conveyed to the court, and what is the impact of these assessments on the sentences meted out by Canadian judges? How, in general, do forensic clinicians influence the course

of their patients' criminal and mental-health careers? These are some of the central issues in the study of criminal law and mental disorder in Canada. And we are only beginning to unravel the process of psychiatric decision making, and its connection to the broader machinery of criminal justice in this country.

What we have learned about the practices of forensic experts at METFORS and similar Canadian agencies has inspired a fair degree of concern among civil libertarians (Levy, 1980; Mewett 1980; Tacon, 1979; Verdun-Jones, 1981). It appears that the decisions of court psychiatrists do not conform at all to the idealized "black-box" model (Hogarth, 1971) described by some proponents of the medical model (e.g., Dietz, 1977, 1985). Clinicians do not objectively record and digest the words and conduct of their patients, spitting out antiseptic diagnoses that correspond perfectly to the symptoms they have observed. Instead, forensic assessment is a fully human process, and it is subject to the same foibles, biases, and errors that plague the

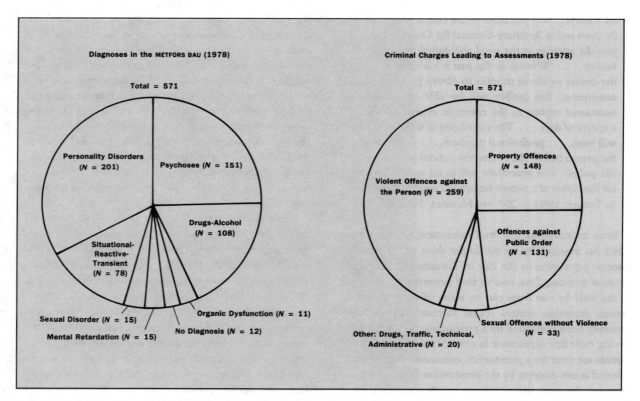

Figure 8.3 Diagnoses and Criminal Offences of Forensic Patients

Diagnoses in the METFORS BAU (1978)
Criminal Charges Leading to Assessments (1978)

Adapted from R.J. Menzies (1989), *Survival of the sanest: order and disorder in a pretrial psychiatric assessment clinic* pp. 256–61). Toronto: University of Toronto Press.

r for that mat-
an beings (see
l, 1978).
g in the MET-
89) identified
ments:

ert to signs
eir patients,
perceived
r or poten-

nited front.
agnosis dur-
cial reports
ferences in
consensual

quiries into
rsons. The
d to their
other moral
ent relation
criminality;
to take the
sult patients
ng or hiding
es;
arching for
assumption
most often

eotypes had
f METFORS
defendants
ethnic, ra-
stereotypes
sessment of
eir ascribed
; see Allen,

lping profes-
prisingly pu-
eir emphasis
not far re-
minal justice
ors; and,
n METFORS
nicians often
inions about
probation,
l. (see Men-

Criminal defendants remanded to *in-patient* clinics are subjected to an even more intensive program of testing and observation. A recent study of the METFORS Inpatient Unit has reported three particularly interesting facets of these long-term forensic assessments. First, almost all of the 123 in-patients in this investigation received an extensive battery of tests from a psychologist or psychometrist, which usually included the Minnesota Multiphasic Personality Inventory (MMPI), Rorschach (Ink-Blot) Test, Wechsler Adult Intelligence Scale (WAIS), and Thematic Apperception Test (TAT), among others. Revealingly, these tests were used to elicit only the negative features of patients' personalities. Positive or encouraging results were virtually nonexistent. In an important sense, patients always failed their examinations, and their responses recurrently became the source of damning profiles that were written up and passed along by attending clinicians. The following example, taken from an actual psychological report, was typical:

> The tests and interview data present a picture of a very depressed individual with strong anti-social and paranoid tendencies. Generally speaking this is a man who harbours a basic fear and distrust of his fellow man. He states that people make him feel "self conscious and paranoid." . . . The defences available to him are primitive ones of displacement and projection. These combined with low impulse control and poor social judgment suggest a potentially explosive personality who is likely to act out his negative feelings towards others particularly under the influence of alcohol. Although motivated to change his hopes and expectations in this area are basically grandiose and unrealistic. . . . The anti-social, immature and hostile elements in this man's personality suggest an individual who is resistant to any meaningful change. This man's prognosis for change is poor. (quoted in Menzies, 1989, Ch. 4)

Second, during their stay at METFORS, the in-patients were under nearly constant supervision from the unit's psychiatric assistants and nursing staff. Like the wards of other mental-health institutions (Goffman, 1961; Horwitz, 1982; Scheff, 1975; Schrag, 1978), the Inpatient Unit was characterized by a closed system of observation, where signs of mental disorder and other deviance were selectively charted in official progress notes, and often made their way into the final psychiatric letters addressed to criminal-court judges.

Third, the forensic social workers participated in assessments by gathering information from family members, friends, employers, and other people in the community who were associated with defendants remanded to the Inpatient Unit. Those closest to the patient could be enlisted to supply information about mental disorder and criminality that was

Box 8.7 A Typical Psychiatric Court Report

23 April 1989

His Honour Judge [   ]
Provincial Court (Criminal Division)
1911 Eglinton Avenue East
Scarborough, Ontario

Your Honour:

Pursuant to your request for mental examination we have completed our brief psychiatric assessment. Phillip R. was examined at the METFORS Brief Assessment Unit on April 23, 1989. I was assisted in the examination by Ms. C.J., psychiatric nurse; and Mr. B.L., correctional officer. Mr. R. is charged with Causing a Disturbance and Assault While Resisting Arrest. I also reviewed the arrest record dated April 18, 1989.

Psychiatric-Legal Opinions

1. Mr. R. shows evidence of a paranoid disturbance in thinking when under the influence of alcohol. He has a history of amphetamine abuse in the past which is well known to induce paranoid thinking in some individuals. In addition he shows some features of depression which relate to the death of his mother two years ago.

2. Mr. R. is fit to stand trial at the present time, despite the psychological disturbance noted above.

3. I would recommend that Your Honour consider remanding Mr. R. for a further inpatient assessment to the METFORS Inpatient Unit. This assessment would allow an opportunity to further evaluate the depth of Mr. R.'s depression and paranoid thinking and whether his pathological suspiciousness relates only to his alcohol abuse or some underlying disorder. This would also allow an opportunity to evaluate Mr. R.'s potential for successful treatment of his alcoholism and the risk of future dangerous behaviour.

Data and Reasoning Basic to Opinions

Mr. R. is a 24-year-old single male. On clinical examination he was oriented to time, place, and person. He was co-operative to questioning and his responses were appropriate and coherent.

Mr. R. showed a blunted affect but at times was markedly tearful. His sadness was most marked when talking about the death of his mother. There was no evidence of any psychotic disturbance in thinking during the interview, but Mr. R. admitted to feeling abnormally suspicious and paranoid when under the influence of alcohol. Mr. R.'s judgment can become grossly impaired under the influence of alcohol. He has some insight into the nature of his alcohol abuse but this is limited.

Mr. R. admits to heavy alcohol abuse on a daily basis. He noted that, when under the influence of alcohol, he feels that people are laughing at him and calling him names. Mr. R. noted that he was experiencing such ideas at the time of the alleged offences of Causing a Disturbance and Assault While Resisting Arrest. Mr. R. dated these experiences back to several years ago when he was abusing amphetamines intravenously. At that time he experienced marked suspiciousness and noted that, since discontinuing amphetamine abuse, he experiences these feelings when under the influence of alcohol.

He understands the nature of the charges against him, the purpose of a criminal justice proceeding, the nature and significance of an oath and can rationally co-operate with counsel. Although he is clearly fit to stand trial, I would recommend that he undergo a further inpatient assessment to identify the depth of his depression and the significance of the paranoid process which he experiences under the influence of alcohol. This is important to accurately assess his potential for response to alcohol treatment and his potential for future dangerous behaviour.

I hope this report is helpful to the Court.
Yours sincerely,

F.Y., Psychiatrist

missing from official records, and they were therefore an important source of data for the METFORS clinicians. They willingly complied with requests for this testimony—which was usually incorporated into the final court reports—for they had often been observers or victims themselves of the patient's criminal or disturbed misconduct:

haviour
as even
owner's
t a fire,
n stores.
e about
ies with
through
ear. She
room is
hurt the
e thinks
d a loud
e kitch-
patient's
that she
n Men-

clinic come
single court
sessment by
8.7). These
o two pages
& Golding,
, and gener-
in question.
what psy-
r the defen-
alization, or
ortant of all,
sequent de-
r Canadian,
of forensic
; Greenland

& Rosenblatt, 1972; Sparks, 1966; Steadman, 1979), the sentencing decisions of Toronto criminal-court judges have consistently complied very closely with the psychiatric recommendations contained in METFORS court reports (Jackson, 1978; Webster, Menzies, & Jackson, 1982). Without any doubt, even though they seldom make personal appearances in the criminal courts, through their letters these clinicians are able to profoundly influence the institutional careers of their patients.

For their part, Canadian judges seem increasingly willing to solicit and endorse the expert opinion of forensic psychiatrists, and, in the process, they are clearly distributing a portion of their sentencing powers to these clinical professionals. As we have seen, the participation of mental-health experts in the courts has become one of the most hotly disputed areas of our criminal-justice system, and many have called for the strict curtailment, or even the total abolition, of METFORS and similar forensic facilities (Levy, 1980; Menzies, 1989; Robitscher, 1980; Torrey, 1974). Their critics have argued that clinicians bring no special expertise to their role as judicial advisers (Boyd, 1980; Ennis & Litwack, 1974), and that medical personnel in any event should feel morally obligated to stay out of the punishment business; however, their supporters maintain that forensic practitioners offer an important service in protecting mentally disordered offenders from criminal **sanctions**, and that they are far better equipped than are judges, prosecutors, lawyers, or any other legal professionals to manage the task of psychiatric assessment (Bonnie & Slobogin, 1980; Prins, 1980). In the coming years, we can expect a continued raging debate in Canadian legal, clinical, and academic circles, along with an avalanche of important court challenges based on the Canadian Charter of Rights and Freedoms—and the final outcome of these ongoing forensic controversies is by no means assured.

erlying the medical-
g mental disorder? How
ves offered by labelling
d critical psychiatry?

ce of the 1843 Daniel
t and status of legal
ts?

3. What are the present criteria for determining criminal responsibility in Canada? What criticisms have been levelled against this country's methods for dealing with the criminally insane? What alternative standards and procedures have been suggested and implemented, here and elsewhere?

4. Discuss the legal consequences of being found unfit to stand trial. Why have civil libertarians been critical of current practices involving mentally incompetent criminal defendants? How might the system be reformed?

Notes

1. The onus in court is therefore on the party raising the defence (usually the accused) to prove the insanity on a balance of probabilities (that is, with more than 50 percent certainty) (see Schiffer, 1978; Verdun-Jones, 1979).

2. The provisions for insanity findings and dispositions are set out in sections 614 and 615 of the Criminal Code of Canada.

3. Criteria for the release of NGRI patients by advisory review boards are described in subsection 619(5)(d) of the Criminal Code.

4. The boards can also recommend, and the lieutenant-governor can order, a "loosening" of the Warrant, so that subjects can be discharged into a less secure hospital or the community, while the LGW powers remain in effect. In April 1980, for example, 64 out of 139 Warrant patients in British Columbia had been discharged out of maximum security conditions.

5. *Re Langley and New Brunswick Board of Review* (1975), 25 C.C.C. (2d) 81 (F.C.A.D.); *Re Abel et al. and Advisory Review Board* (1981), 56 C.C.C. (2d) 153 (Ont. C.A.); and *Re McCann and The Queen* (1980), 58 C.C.C. (2d) 458 (B.C.C.A.). See Whitley (1984).

6. *Davis v. United States* (1897), 165 U.S. 373, 378, 17 S. Ct. 360, 362, 41 L. Ed. 750.

7. *Durham v. U.S.*, 214 F 2d 862 (D.C. Cir 1954).

8. *United States v. Brawner*, 471 F. 2d 969 (1972) (D.C. Cir 1972).

9. *R. v. Woltucky* (1952), 103 C.C.C. 43, 15 C.R. 24, 6 W.W.R. 72 (Sask. C.A.).

10. *R. v. Roberts* (1975), 24 C.C.C. (2d) 539, [1975] 3 W.W.R.

742 (B.C.C.A.).

11. The statutory authority within the Criminal Code (ss. 537, 615, 681, 803) for suspending a trial pending the submission of a psychiatric report.

12. Criminal Code, subsection 615(7).

13. Criminal Code, subsection 617(1)

14. *Jackson v. Indiana* (1972), U.S. 715 (U.S.S.C.).

15. "Court's Ruling on Sanity Lauded," *The Vancouver Sun*, November 13, 1984, p. A15.

16. Criminal Code, sections 752, 753, 755.

17. *Baxstrom v. Herold*, 383 U.S. 107 (1967).

18. The items were: passive-aggressiveness, hostility, anger, rage, emotionality, guilt, capacity for empathy, capacity for change, self-perception as dangerous, control over actions, tolerance, environmental stress, environmental support, likelihood of increased dangerousness under alcohol, likelihood of increased danger under drugs, manipulativeness, accuracy of information, sufficiency of information, and global dangerousness to self in present, to self in future, to others in present, and to others in future.

19. Under the Criminal Code of Canada, subsections 537(1,2), 615(1,2), 681(1,2), or 803(5), or the Ontario Mental Health Act, subsection 14(1,2).

20. Prior to 1982, a clinical psychologist and psychiatric social worker also participated in these brief assessments.

References

Akhtar, S. (1971). Pre-trial evaluation of court referrals. *Canadian Psychiatric Association Journal, 16*, 5–13.

Allen, H. (1987). *Justice unbalanced: Gender, psychiatry and judicial decisions*. Milton Keynes, UK: Open University Press.

American Bar Association (1983). *First tentative draft criminal justice mental health standards*. Washington, DC.

Anand, R. (1979). Involuntary civil commitment in Ontario: The need to curtail the abuses of psychiatry. *Canadian Bar Review, 62*, 250–80.

Anderson, F. (1950). Louis Riel's insanity reconsidered. *Saskatchewan History, 3*, 104–21.

Arboleda-Florez, J. (1978). Insanity defence in Canada. *Canadian*

A two-year
ic Association

se. *American*

itally ill: The
l. In Balkan,
tan: A critical

ed. London:

ls.), *Canadian*
Georgetown,

nental health
for informed

edical reports:
ychiatry, 132,

y insane" and
e wisdom of
, 20, 151–67.
orough, ON:

9). *Methods of*
York: Holt,

ity in America.

system. Boston:

Angleterre et en
oliliques de la

e-arraignment
int. Bulletin of
6, 368–404.
ric presentence
logy, 14, 67–82.
hn W. Hinkley,

ric society. New

s: The forensic
Vest Coast Law
C. March 31.
Mosby.
iglewood Cliffs,

thority, and law.

CIA brainwashing
en Dennys.
dicalization: From

don: Tavistock.
rtin Robertson.
algary: Albertan

inadian Journal of

Criminology and Corrections, 18, 302–18.

Dietz, P.E. (1977). Social discrediting of psychiatry: The protasis of legal disenfranchisement. *American Journal of Psychiatry, 134,* 1356–60.

Dietz, P.E. (1985). Hypothetical criteria for the prediction of individual criminality. In C.D. Webster, M.H. Ben-Aron, & S.J. Hucker (Eds.), *Dangerousness: Probability and prediction, psychiatry and public policy* (pp. 87–102). New York: Cambridge University Press.

Dix, G. (1981). Expert prediction testimony in capital sentencing: Evidentiary and constitutional considerations. *American Criminal Law Review, 19,* 1–48.

Eaves, D., Roesch, R., Glackman, W., & Vallance, S. (1984). Attitudes of the legal profession to the Law Reform Commission recommendations on fitness to stand trial. *Criminal Law Quarterly, 26,* 233–243.

Ennis, B.J. (1972). *Prisoners of psychiatry: Mental patients, psychiatrists, and the law.* New York: Avon/Discus.

Ennis, B.J., & Litwack, T.R. (1974). Psychiatry and the presumption of expertise: Flipping coins in the courtroom. *California Law Review, 62,* 693–752.

Ericson, R.V. (1974). Psychiatrists in prison: On admitting professional tinkers into a tinkers' paradise. *Chitty's Law Journal, 22,* 29–33.

Ericson, R.V., & Baranek, P.M. (1982). *The ordering of justice: A study of accused persons as dependants in the criminal process.* Toronto: University of Toronto Press.

Ferguson, G. (1984). Recent developments in the Canadian law of insanity: Progression, regression or repression? *Medicine and Law, 3,* 287–96.

Ferguson, G. (1986). The insanity defense: Current law and reform options. In A. Carmi (Ed.), *Psychiatry, law and ethics* (pp. 170–181). Berlin: Springer-Verlag.

Foucault, M. (1965). *Madness and civilization: A history of insanity in the age of reason.* New York: Random House.

Foucault, M. (1977). *Discipline and punish: The birth of the prison.* New York: Vintage.

Foulkes, R.G. (1961). British Columbia mental health services: Historical perspective to 1961. *Canadian Medical Association Journal, 85,* 649–55.

Frank, K.P. (1979). *The anti-psychiatry bibliography and resource guide* (2nd ed.). Vancouver: Press Gang.

Frederick, C. (Ed.). (1978). *Dangerous behavior: A problem in law and mental health.* Washington, DC: U.S. Government Printing Office.

Gallagher, B.J. (1987). *The sociology of mental illness* (2nd ed.) Englewood Cliffs, NJ: Prentice-Hall.

Gerard, J.B. (1974). Concepts of mental illness: Statements, critiques, and defenses of the medical model. In A.D. Brooks (Ed.), *Law, psychiatry and the mental health system* (pp. 21–55). Boston: Little, Brown.

Gibbs, J. (1972). Issues in defining deviant behavior. In R.A. Scott & J.D. Douglas (Eds.), *Theoretical perspectives on deviance* (pp. 39–68). New York: Basic.

Globe and Mail. (1988, November 14). Insanity law should be reformed, retired appeal court judge says, p. A1.

Goffman, E. (1961). *Asylums: Essays in the social situation of mental patients and other inmates.* Garden City, NY: Doubleday.

Golding, S.L., Roesch, R., & Schreiber, J. (1984). Assessment and conceptualization of competency to stand trial: preliminary data on the Interdisciplinary Fitness Interview. *Law and Human Behavior, 8,* 321–34.

Gordon, R.M., & Verdun-Jones, S.N. (1988). The trials of mental health law: Recent trends and developments in Canadian mental jurisprudence. *Dalhousie Law Journal, 11,* 833–63.

Gove, W.R. (1980). Labelling and mental illness: a critique. In W.R.

Gove (Ed.), *The labelling of deviance: Evaluating a perspective* (2nd ed.) (pp. 53–110). Beverly Hills: Sage.

Greenland, C., & Rosenblatt, E.M. (1972). Remands for psychiatric examination in Ontario, 1969–70. *Canadian Psychiatric Association Journal, 17,* 387–401.

Hale, M. (1736). *The history of the pleas of the Crown.* London: E.R. Nutt & R. Gosling.

Hamilton, J.R., & Freeman, H. (1982). *Dangerousness: Psychiatric assessment and management.* London: Royal College of Psychiatrists.

Hare, R. (1970). *Psychopathy: Theory and research.* New York: Wiley.

Hawkins, R., & Tiedeman, G. (1975). *The creation of deviance: Interpersonal and organizational determinants.* Columbus, OH: Charles E. Merrill.

Held, H.V. (1987). *Violence prediction: Guidelines for the forensic practitioner.* Springfield, IL: Charles C. Thomas.

Hiday, V.A. (1977). Reformed commitment procedures: An empirical study in the courtroom. *Law and Society Review, 11,* 651–66.

Hinton, J. (Ed.). (1983). *Dangerousness: Problems of assessment and prediction.* London: Allen & Unwin.

Hogarth, J. (1971). *Sentencing as a human process.* Toronto: University of Toronto Press.

Horwitz, A. (1977). Social networks and pathways into psychiatric treatment. *Social Forces, 56,* 86–106.

Horwitz, A. (1982). *The social control of mental illness.* New York: Academic Press.

Hucker, S.J., Webster, C.D., & Ben-Aron, M.H. (Eds.). (1981). *Mental disorder and criminal responsibility.* Toronto: Butterworths.

Ignatieff, M. (1978). *A just measure of pain.* London: Macmillan.

Illich, I. (1976). *Medical nemesis: The expropriation of health.* New York: Random House.

Ingleby, D. (Ed.). (1981). *Critical psychiatry: The politics of mental health.* Harmondsworth, UK: Penguin.

Jackson, M.A. (1978). *An examination of court remands for psychiatric assessment: Factual and theoretical considerations.* Unpublished M.A. thesis, University of Toronto Centre of Criminology.

Jakimiec, J., Porporino, F., Addario, S., & Webster, C.D. (1986). Dangerous offenders in Canada, 1977–1985. *International Journal of Law and Psychiatry, 9,* 479–89.

Journal of Social Issues. (1955). Mental illness in the family. Special issue, *11.*

Klein, D.F., Gittelman, R., Quitkin, F., & Rifkin, A. (1980). *Diagnosis and drug treatment of psychiatric disorders: Adults and children* (2nd ed.). London: Williams & Wilkins.

Klein, J. (1976). The dangerousness of dangerous offender legislation: Forensic folklore revisited. *Canadian Journal of Criminology and Corrections, 18,* 109–23.

Kunjukrishnan, R. (1979). 10 year survey of pretrial examinations in Saskatchewan. *Canadian Journal of Psychiatry, 24,* 683–89.

Laing, R.D. (1965). *The divided self: An existential study in sanity and madness.* Harmondsworth, UK: Penguin.

Laing, R.D. (1972). *Self and others* (2nd ed.). Harmondsworth, UK: Penguin.

Law Reform Commission of Canada. (1976). *Mental disorder in the criminal process.* Report to Parliament. Ottawa: Queen's Printer.

Law Reform Commission of Canada. (1982). *Criminal law, the general part: Liability and defences.* Working Paper No 29. Ottawa: Queen's Printer.

LeBar, F.M. (1973). *Segregative care in an institutional setting: The ethnography of a psychiatric hospital.* New Haven, CT: Human Relations Area Files.

Lemert, E.M. (1967). *Human deviance, social problems and social control.* Englewood Cliffs, NJ: Prentice-Hall.

Levy, H.J. (1980). Mental at gaol. *Criminal Lawyers' Association Newsletter,* 1–7.

Leyton, E. (1986). *Hunting humans: Inside the minds of mass murderers.* Toronto: McClelland & Stewart.

Lindsay, P.S. (1977). Fitness to stand trial: An overview in light of the recommendations of the Law Reform Commission of Canada. *Criminal Law Quarterly, 19,* 303–48.

Litwack, T.R., & Schlesinger, L.B. (1986). Assessing and predicting violence: Research, law and applications. In A. Hess & I. Weiner (Eds.), *Handbook of forensic psychology.* New York: Wiley.

Low, P.W., Jeffries, J.C., & Bonnie, R.J. (1986). *The trial of John W. Hinckley, Jr.: A case study in the insanity defense.* Mineola, NY: Foundation Press.

Lunde, D.T. (1976). *Murder and madness.* San Francisco: San Francisco Book Company.

Maclean's. March, 1980. p. 23.

Marcus, A. (1971). *Nothing is my number: An exploratory study with a group of dangerous sexual offenders in Canada.* Toronto: General.

Maris, R.W. (1988). *Social problems.* Chicago: Dorsey.

Marshall, V., & Hughes, D. (1974). "Nothing else but mad": Canadian legislative trends in the light of models of mental illness and their implication for civil liberties. In J. Haas & B. Shaffir (Eds.), *Decency and deviance* (pp. 146–66). Toronto: McClelland & Stewart.

Maudsley, H. (1879). *The pathology of mind.* London: Macmillan.

McGarry, A.L., Curran, W.J., Lipsitt, P.D., Lelos, D., Schwitzgebel, R.K., & Rosenberg, A.H. (1974). *Competency to stand trial and mental illness.* National Institute of Mental Health. DHEW Publication Number (HSM) 73-9105. Washington, DC: U.S. Government Printing Office.

Mechanic, D. (1969). *Mental health and social policy.* Englewood Cliffs, NJ: Prentice-Hall.

Melossi, D., & Pavarini, M. (1981). *The prison and the factory: Origins of the penitentiary system.* London: Macmillan.

Meloy, J.R. (1988). *The psychopathic mind: Origins, dynamics, and treatment.* Northvale, NJ: Jason Aronson.

Menzies, R.J. (1986). Psychiatry, dangerousness, and legal control. In N. Boyd (Ed.), *The social dimensions of law* (pp. 182–211). Scarborough, ON: Prentice-Hall.

Menzies, R.J. (1987a). Cycles of control: The transcarceral careers of forensic patients. *International Journal of Law and Psychiatry, 10,* 233–49.

Menzies, R.J. (1987b). Psychiatrists in blue: Police apprehension of mental disorder and dangerousness. *Criminology, 25,* 429–53.

Menzies, R.J. (1989). *Survival of the sanest: Order and disorder in a pre-trial psychiatric clinic.* Toronto: University of Toronto Press.

Menzies, R.J., & Webster, C.D. (1989). Mental disorder and violent crime. In M.E. Wolfgang & N.A. Weiner (Eds.), *Pathways to criminal violence* (pp. 109–36). Newbury Park, CA: Sage.

Menzies, R.J., Webster, C.D., Butler, B.T., & Turner, R.E. (1980). The outcome of forensic assessments: A study of remands in six Canadian cities. *Criminal Justice and Behavior, 7,* 471–80.

Menzies, R.J., Webster, C.D., Butler, B.T., Turner, R.E., & Jensen, F.A.S. (1978). *An analysis of the development and process of the Metropolitan Toronto Forensic Service.* Working Paper No. 7. Toronto: METFORS.

Menzies, R.J., Webster, C.D., Roesch, R., Jensen, F.A.S., & Eaves, D. (1984). The Fitness Interview Test: A semi-structured instrument for assessing competency to stand trial, with a proposal for its implementation. *Medicine and Law, 3,* 151–62.

Menzies, R.J., Webster, C.D., & Sepejak, D.S. (1985). The dimensions of dangerousness: Evaluating the accuracy of psychometric predictions of violence among forensic patients. *Law and Human*

ciation of violent
A review of the
5–45.

opolitan Toronto

inations. *Criminal*

sychiatry. Oxford,

itique of the Law
Journal of Law and

ssessment of clinical

ity defense of Daniel

nicago: University

gerousness. In M.
: *An annual review*
f Chicago Press.
ito: McGraw-Hill.
ts predecessors. In
ghton: His trial and
ley Brothers.
ng. Toronto: Long-

lon: Routledge &

ne and institutional-
tice-Hall.
s. *International Jour-*

l construction of psy-

reform and the
sals for the control
iew, 4, 1–61.
n introduction to the
stock.
equivocal relation-
y. *International Jour-*

nental disorder. Lon-

her disorders affecting

onstruction of men-

riminal responsibil-
bster, & M.H. Ben-
nsibility (pp. 1–10).

erousness of mental
tional Journal of Law

ent of the mentally
ebster, & M.H. Ben-
ibility (pp. 137–156).

t of the characteris-

tics and dangerousness of patients held on warrants of the lieutenant-governor. *Crime and/et Justice, 4*, 282–88.

Rabkin, J.G. (1979). Criminal behavior of discharged mental patients: A critical appraisal of the research. *Psychological Bulletin, 86*, 1–27.

Ratner, R.S. (1987). Mandatory supervision and the penal economy. In J. Lowman, R.J. Menzies, & T.S. Palys (Eds.), *Transcarceration: Essays in the sociology of social control* (pp. 291–310). Aldershot, UK: Gower.

Ray, I. (1835). *A treatise on the medical jurisprudence of insanity* (3rd ed.). Boston.

Reid, W.H. (Ed.). (1978). *The psychopath: A comprehensive study of antisocial disorders and behaviours*. New York: Brunner Mazel.

Rennie, Y.F. (1978). *The search for criminal man: A conceptual history of the dangerous offender*. Lexington, MA: Lexington.

Robitscher, J.B. (1980). *The powers of psychiatry*. Boston: Houghton Mifflin.

Roesch, R. (1978). Fitness to stand trial: Some comments on the Canadian Law Reform Commission's proposed procedures. *Canadian Journal of Criminology, 20*, 450–55.

Roesch, R., & Golding, S.L. (1979). Treatment and disposition of defendants found incompetent to stand trial: a review and a proposal. *International Journal of Law and Psychiatry, 2*, 349–70.

Roesch, R., & Golding, S.L. (1980). *Competency to stand trial*. Urbana: University of Illinois Press.

Roesch, R., Webster, C.D., & Eaves, D. (1984). *The Fitness Interview Test: A method for examining fitness to stand trial*. Toronto & Burnaby: University of Toronto Centre of Criminology & Simon Fraser University Criminology Research Centre.

Rollin, H.R. (1977). McNaughtan's madness. In D.J. West & A. Walk (Eds.), *Daniel McNaughtan: His trial and its aftermath.* (pp. 91–99). Ashford, UK: Gaskell.

Rosen, G. (1968). *Madness in society*. Chicago: University of Chicago Press.

Rosenhan, D.L. (1973). On being sane in insane places. *Science, 179*, 250–58.

Rothman, D.J. (1971). *The discovery of the asylum: Social order and disorder in the new republic*. Boston: Little, Brown.

Rothman, D.J. (1980). *Conscience and convenience: The asylum and its alternative in progressive America*. Boston: Little, Brown.

Ryan, T. (1981). *Screw: A guard's view of Bridgewater State Hospital*. Boston: South End.

Savage, H.S. (1980). The relevance of the fitness to stand trial provisions to persons with mental handicap. *Autonomy, 1*, 3–9.

Savage, H.S., & McKague, C. (1987). *Mental health law in Canada*. Toronto: Butterworths.

Scheff, T.J. (1964). Social conditions for rationality: How urban and rural courts deal with the mentally ill. *American Behavioral Scientist, 7*, 21–7.

Scheff, T.J. (1966). *Being mentally ill: A sociological theory*. Chicago: Aldine.

Scheff, T.J. (Ed.). (1975). *Labeling madness*. Englewood Cliffs, NJ: Prentice-Hall.

Schiffer, M.E. (1978). *Mental disorder and the criminal trial process*. Toronto: Butterworths.

Schiffer, M.E. (1982). *Psychiatry behind bars*. Toronto: Butterworths.

Schlatter, E.K. (1969). An empirical study of pre-trial detention and psychiatric illness in the Montreal area—legal, psychiatric and administrative aspects. *McGill Law Journal, 15*, 326–46.

Schrag, P. (1978). *Mind control*. New York: Pantheon.

Scull, A.T. (1977). *Decarceration. Community treatment and the deviant—a radical view*. Englewood Cliffs, NJ: Prentice-Hall.

Scull, A.T. (Ed.). (1981). *Madhouses, mad-doctors and madmen: The social history of psychiatry in the Victorian era*. Philadelphia: University of Pennsylvania Press.

Sepejak, D.S., Menzies, R.J., Webster, C.D., & Jensen, F.A.S. (1983). Clinical predictions of dangerousness: Two-year follow-up of 408 pre-trial forensic cases. *Bulletin of the American Academy of Psychiatry and the Law, 11,* 171–81.

Sepejak, D.S., Webster, C.D., & Menzies, R.J. (1984). The clinical prediction of dangerousness: Getting beyond the basic questions. In D.J. Muller, D.G. Blackman, & A.J. Chapman (Eds.), *Psychology and law: Topics from an international conference* (pp. 113–24). London: Wiley.

Shah, S.A. (1978). Dangerousness: a paradigm for exploring some issues in law and psychology. *American Psychologist, 33,* 224–38.

Silverstone, I., & Turner, P. (1974). *Drug treatment in psychiatry*. London: Routledge & Kegan Paul.

Skultans, V. (1975). *Madness and morals: Ideas on insanity in the nineteenth century*. London: Routledge & Kegan Paul.

Smandych, R.C. (1982). The rise of the asylum in Upper Canada: An application of Scull's "macro-sociological" perspective. *Canadian Criminology Forum, 4,* 142–48.

Smandych, R.C., & Verdun-Jones, S.N. (1986). The emergence of the asylum in 19th century Ontario: a study in the history of segregative control. In N. Boyd (Ed.), *The social dimensions of law* (pp. 166–81). Scarborough, ON: Prentice-Hall.

Smith, R. (1981). *Trial by medicine: Insanity and responsibility in Victorian trials*. Edinburgh: Edinburgh University Press.

Soothill, K.L., Way, C.K., & Gibbons, T.C.N. (1980). Subsequent dangerousness among compulsory hospital patients. *British Journal of Criminology, 20,* 289–95.

Sparks, R. (1966). The decision to remand for medical examination. *British Journal of Criminology, 6,* 6–26.

Stanley, G. (1963). *Louis Riel*. Toronto: Ryerson.

Steadman, H.J. (1973). Some evidence on the inadequacy of the concept and determination of dangerousness in law and psychiatry. *Journal of Psychiatry and Law, 1,* 409–26.

Steadman, H.J. (1979). *Beating a rap? Defendants found incompetent to stand trial*. Chicago: University of Chicago Press.

Steadman, H.J. (1981). Special problems in the prediction of violence among the mentally ill. In J. Hays, T. Roberts, & K. Solway (Eds.), *Violence and the violent individual* (pp. 243–56). New York: SP Medical & Scientific Books.

Steadman, H.J., & Cocozza, J.J. (1974). *Careers of the criminally insane: Excessive social control of deviance*. Lexington, MA: Lexington.

Stone, A.A. (1984). *Law, psychiatry, and morality: Essays and analysis*. Washington, DC: American Psychiatric Association Press.

Stortini, R. (1975). Preventive detention of dangerous sexual offenders. *Criminal Law Quarterly, 17,* 416–39.

Szasz, T.S. (1963). *Law, liberty and psychiatry: An inquiry into the social uses of mental health practices*. New York: Macmillan.

Szasz, T.S. (1970). *Ideology and insanity: Essays on the psychiatric dehumanization of man*. New York: Anchor.

Szasz, T.S. (1971). *The manufacture of madness: A comparative study of the inquisition and the mental health movement*. New York: Dell.

Szasz, T.S. (1977). *Psychiatric slavery*. New York: Free Press.

Tacon, T.A. (1979). A question of privilege: Valid protection or destruction of justice? *Osgoode Hall Law Journal, 17,* 332–54.

Teplin, L.A. (Ed.). (1984). *Mental health and criminal justice*. Beverly Hills: Sage.

Thornberry, T.P., & Jacoby, J.E. (1979). *The criminally insane: A community follow-up of mentally ill offenders*. Chicago: University of Chicago Press.

Torrey, E.F. (1974). *The death of psychiatry*. New York: Penguin.

Turner, B.S. (1987). *Medical power and social knowledge*. Beverly Hills: Sage.

Turner, R.E. (1980). Services note: The development of forensic services at the Metropolitan Toronto Forensic Service. *Canadian Journal of Criminology, 20,* 200–209.

Verdun-Jones, S.N. (1979). The evolution of the defences of insanity and automatism in Canada from 1843 to 1979: A saga of judicial reluctance to sever the umbilical cord to the mother country? *University of British Columbia Law Review, 14,* 1–73.

Verdun-Jones, S.N. (1981). The doctrine of fitness to stand trial in Canada: The forked tongue of social control. *International Journal of Law and Psychiatry, 4,* 363–89.

Verdun-Jones, S.N., & Smandych, R.C. (1981). Catch-22 in the nineteenth century: The evolution of therapeutic confinement for the criminally insane in Canada, 1840–1900. *Criminal Justice History: An International Annual, 2,* 85–108.

Walker, N.D. (1968). *Crime and insanity in England*, Vol. 1. Edinburgh: University of Edinburgh Press.

Walker, N.D., & McCabe, S. (1973). *Crime and insanity in England*, Vol. 2. Edinburgh: University of Edinburgh Press.

Warren, C.A.B. (1979). The social construction of dangerousness. *Urban Life, 8,* 359–84.

Warren, C.A.B. (1982). *The court of last resort: Mental illness and the law*. Chicago: University of Chicago Press.

Webster, C.D., Ben-Aron, M.H., & Hucker, S.J. (1985). *Dangerousness: Probability and prediction, psychiatry and public policy*. New York: Cambridge University Press.

Webster, C.D., Dickens, B.M., & Addario, S.M. (1985). *Constructing dangerousness: Scientific, legal and policy implications*. Toronto: University of Toronto Centre of Criminology.

Webster, C.D., & Menzies, R.J. (1987). The clinical prediction of dangerousness. In D.N. Weisstub (Ed.), *Law and mental health: International perspectives*, Vol. 3. New York: Pergamon.

Webster, C.D., Menzies, R.J. & Jackson, M.A. (1982). *Clinical assessment before trial: Legal issues and mental disorder*. Toronto: Butterworths.

Weiner, B.A. (1984). Interfaces between the mental health and criminal justice system: The legal perspective. In L.A. Teplin (Ed.), *Mental health and criminal justice*. Beverly Hills: Sage.

Weinstein, A. (1988). *A father, a son and the C.I.A.* Toronto: Lorimer.

Weisstub, D.N. (Ed.). (1980). *Law and psychiatry in the Canadian context*. New York: Pergamon.

West, D.J., & Walk, A. (1977). *Daniel McNaughton: His trial and its aftermath*. Ashford, UK: Headley Brothers.

Wexler, D.B. (1984). Incompetency, insanity, and involuntary civil commitment. In L.A. Teplin (Ed.), *Mental health and criminal justice* (pp. 139–54). Beverly Hills: Sage.

Whitley, S. (1984). The lieutenant-governor's advisory boards of review for the supervision of the mentally disordered offender in Canada: A call for change. *International Journal of Law and Psychiatry, 7,* 385–94.

9 The Treatment of Sex Offenders

In recent years, attention has turned from a preoccupation with the offender to a concern for the impact of the crime on the victim. For example, a growing body of literature specifically addresses the short-term effects and long-term consequences of the sexual abuse of children (e.g., Conte, 1988; Briere, 1988; see, generally, Browne & Finkelhor, 1986).

Certainly, the spate of revelations during the late 1980s and early 1990s of child sexual abuse committed by those in a position of trust, such as school teachers and clergymen (e.g., Taylor, 1989), has led to increased public pressure to "do something" with sex offenders. What lies behind this trend? Is there an increase in sexual offending, a change in attitudes about reporting these kinds of crimes, or both? How commonplace are these occurrences? Who are the offenders? What can be done about the problem?

This chapter will offer some insight into those and other related questions. In it, we examine the various indices of the amount of sexual offending, considering their strengths and weaknesses in order to attempt to gain a sense of the magnitude of the problem in Canada. The focus will then shift to the perpetrators of sex offences: who they are and what approaches are available to modify their behaviour. The chapter will end with a review of the effectiveness of treatment for sex offenders.

What Constitutes a "Sex Offence"?

Before considering the magnitude and impact of the problem of sexual offences in Canada, it is necessary to understand what constitutes a **sex offence** under the **Crimi-**

nal Code. If asked to elaborate on what is meant by the term "sex offence," most Canadians would likely refer to the "crimes" of rape and/or child molestation. Sex offences are much more specifically dealt with in the Criminal Code than these colloquial characterizations, however.

We saw in the case study in Part I that the Canadian laws concerning sex offences were substantially amended in 1983, the most significant change being the replacement of the term "rape" with the gender-neutral, multilevel offence of "**sexual assault**" (see Box 9.1).

Box 9.1   Sexual Offences in the Criminal Code

Section	Title	Maximum Penalty	Comments
151	Sexual Interference	10 years	A 1987 amendment that prohibits "sexual touching" with a child under age fourteen
152	Invitation to Sexual Touching	10 years	Prohibits encouraging a child under age fourteen to touch sexually another person, including the accused
153	Sexual Exploitation	5 years	Prohibits conduct described in 151 and 152 by a person in a position of trust or authority toward a young person aged fourteen to eighteen
155	Incest	14 years	Sexual intercourse with a blood relation (parent, child, brother, sister, grandparent, or grandchild)
159	Anal Intercourse	10 years	Does not apply to husband and wife, or consenting parties over age eighteen
173	Indecent Act	6 months	Generally, indecent exposure, but must contain an element of "moral turpitude" as nudity alone is not enough. Subsection (2) specifically forbids exposure of the genitals for a sexual purpose to a child under age fourteen
271	Sexual Assault	10 years	Includes, but is not restricted to, the previous offence of rape
272	Sexual Assault with weapon, with threats to a third party, or causing bodily harm	14 years	
273	Aggravated Sexual Assault	Life	

grouped with-
e. Some of the
relatively "vic-
74), and are not
. Those sections
m was involved
der the revised
lestation involv-
lt in charges un-
nces in Part V
ices of offending
addressed.

te?

iexual

ual offending can
riminal-justice
those who have
eports of sexual
y understand the
e been generated
ppreciate the dis-
nce, and then to
each of the data

the members of a
articular attribute
ers to the rate at
articular attribute
h concept (which
are: (1) unwanted
time in their lives
/ed for the Com-
dren (1984a)—this
ts; (2) 88 "found-
s in the Canadian
in 1987—this is an
iaults.
on of the various
ending, their limi-
in tell us about the

f an offence, they
s, sometimes make
unded" or unlikely
counted as "actu-

al" offences and the numbers of these are reported to Statistics Canada. These numbers are most useful when converted to rates per 100 000 population, to permit comparisons across years.

Figure 9.1 shows the rates of actual sexual offences reported to the police since Statistics Canada began using the Uniform Crime Reporting (UCR) System in 1962. Notice that there is a break in the series between 1982 and 1983 associated with the changes in the Criminal Code at that time. Because of the Criminal Code changes, it is not clear how the sexual crime-rate indices from before 1983 can be compared with those from after that year. Therefore, it is probably best to consider them as separate entities. It is quite clear, however, that there has been a notable rise in the total UCR rate of sexual offences during the period from 1983 to 1987, and that this is almost entirely the result of an increase in the number of founded reports of sexual assault.

There are a number of problems associated with police data that lead researchers to believe they greatly underestimate the actual incidence of sexual offences. For instance, while the process of recording offences is meant to be standardized in accordance with procedures established by Statistics Canada, it is known that there is some variability in the accuracy with which the information is compiled and submitted. In addition, even if the Statistics Canada procedures were followed rigorously, the rules for coding offences will, in some cases, lead to the noncounting of some sexual offences. This discrepancy occurs because many crime incidents involve more than one offence, and the coding rules stipulate that the most serious offence is the one that is to be counted for each victim. For violent offences, the number of offences recorded is equal to the number of victims in the incident. Thus, a sexual assault that took place in conjunction with a more serious offence, such as an attempted murder, would not be counted as a sexual assault.

Undoubtedly, the greatest problem with using police data to estimate the incidence of crime is that a great many offences are never made known to the police (Solicitor General, 1984). This nonreporting phenomenon has long been suspected to be especially great for sex offences (Solicitor General, 1984). Indeed, the 1982 Canadian Urban Victimization Survey (CUVS) revealed that an estimated 62 percent of completed or attempted sexual assaults and molestations were not reported to the police. While it is likely that changing public attitudes are leading to an increase in the reporting of sexual offences, it is also improbable that the reporting rate will ever reach 100 percent. Therefore, UCR statistics will always constitute, to an unknown extent, an underestimate of the true incidence of sexual offences.

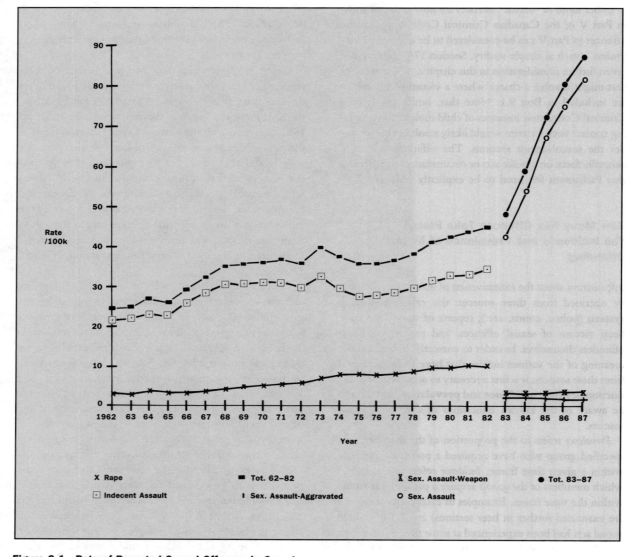

Figure 9.1   Rate of Reported Sexual Offences in Canada 1962–1988

Source: Canadian Centre for Justice Statistics.

Evidence from Victimization Surveys

Victimization surveys appear to offer one of the best possibilities for ascertaining the incidence and prevalence of sexual offending in Canada. Although asking individuals about their experiences of being a victim does turn out to be one of the more useful approaches, there are a number of known methodological difficulties with victimization surveys that limit the accuracy of estimates of the extent of crime that can be developed from them. These problems are discussed in detail in Chapter 13. For the purposes of this chapter, of particular note are the low levels of reporting of sexual assaults to surveyors and the fact that children, often the targets of sexual assaults, are rarely included in victimization-survey samples.

Two victimization surveys are particularly relevant for estimating the extent of sexual offending in Canada. The first was undertaken in early 1982 (Solicitor General, 1983). The CUVS involved more than 61 000 telephone interviews with a random sample of persons over the age of sixteen in seven major population centres of Canada (Greater Vancouver, Edmonton, Winnipeg, Toronto, Montreal, Halifax-Dartmouth, and St. John's). Respondents were asked to provide information about victimization ex-

year 1981. The
r providing es-
sexual assaults.
: for the popu-
drawn. These
s, of 350 sexual
80 per 100 000
:s.

pproximately a
: victim's home
quaintance (9.0
n public places.
41.0 percent of
t 61 percent of
d, in 20 percent
ugh to require

percent of all
he police in ci-
ree of variation
location, rang-
n Montreal to a
ents were asked
rt the incidents.
think the police
negatively about

the Committee
984a, 1984b) in
le ($N = 2008$) of
ly completed and
:en delivered and
oject personnel.

Respondents were asked to provide detailed information on sexual-victimization experiences that they had at any time in their lives. Thus, this survey was explicitly designed to address the issue of the prevalence of sexual victimization.

Unwanted sexual acts had been committed against 53.5 percent of females and 30.6 percent of males. Approximately 1 in 5 females and 1 in 15 males reported being sexually victimized on more than one occasion. Table 9.1 shows the nature of the initial sexual act committed against members of each gender.

Those who had been victims of sexual offences were asked to indicate their age at the time of the first incident. This information was not available for all respondents, but, for those who provided an age, nearly half of females who had experienced physical contact in the form of touching, or an attempted or actual penetration, were under age sixteen. Comparable figures for males were 39.1 percent for touching, and 46.3 percent for attempted or actual assault. For both sexes and both types of contact, a large majority (60 to 75 percent) of the incidents occurred prior to age eighteen. Thus, according to this survey, the bulk of sexual offences involved children and adolescents.

More than half of the incidents took place in the homes of the victims or of the offenders. Most (82.2 percent) of the offenders were known to the victims, with three-fourths being well known.[3] Twenty percent of females and 7 percent of males had been physically injured. Emotional or psychological harm was reported by 24 percent of females and 7 percent of males.

With respect to the reporting of these incidents, the national population survey found that about twice as many females (23.8 percent) as males (11.1 percent) had informed someone else. The likelihood of reporting increased with

ommitted against Males and Females

	Sex of Victims				
s		Females ($N = 1006$)		Total ($N = 2008$)	
02)		Noncumulative		Noncumulative	
ilative %	No.	%	No.	%	
69.4	468	46.5	1163	57.9	
8.9	198	19.7	287	14.3	
5.0	106	10.5	156	7.8	
12.8	236	23.5	364	18.1	
10.6	222	22.1	328	16.3	

als. Two or more sexual acts were com-
and 6.6 percent of male victims.

st Children and Youth (1984), *Sexual*
wa: Supply and Services Canada.

the seriousness of the offence for both sexes, but did not rise above 28.4 percent in any event. The most common reasons given by respondents for not reporting the incidents were that they were too ashamed of what had happened, that they felt it was too personal, and (for females) that they were too afraid of the person who had victimized them.

Given the apparent rise in the incidence of sexual assault as reflected in indices such as the UCR, an issue that is of considerable interest is whether a true increase in offence incidence has been taking place or whether an increased likelihood of reporting accounts for the elevation of the indices. In order to address this issue, the survey results were analyzed to ascertain if there were differing levels of victimization for different age groups of respondents. If the incidence of sexual offending has been increasing over time, it should be reflected in higher prevalence figures for younger as opposed to older respondents. No evidence was found to support the idea that sexual-offence victimization rates have been increasing over time. Similar levels of victimization were found for all ages of adults in the survey, and the overall pattern was the same for all ages, that is, the majority of incidents occurred when the respondents were children or youths. As Quinsey (1986) points out, however, all of the respondents were adults over age eighteen at the time of the survey, so the possibility that incidence rates have been rising in more recent years cannot be ruled out.

These two surveys provide very different views of the occurrence of sexual offending. Recall that the first involved primarily adults (over age sixteen) recalling incidents that had occurred during the previous year, and the second asked adults (over age eighteen) to recall incidents that had taken place at any point in their lives.

From the CUVS, we get a picture of adult women being victimized by strangers in public places. From the Badgley Committee surveys, we can envision children being assaulted by people they know in familiar surroundings.

In other respects, the two surveys have features in common. From both surveys, we are presented with evidence of incidence and prevalence rates that are many orders of magnitude greater than indices based on justice-system sources. Both surveys also offer striking evidence of the low levels of reporting of sexual offences by the victims of these crimes.

Offender Reports

Reports of offence activity from sex offenders provide another perspective on the dimensions of the problem. While no light is shed directly on the overall incidence or prevalence of sexual victimization, information is gained about the extent to which individual offenders engage in victimization incidents.

Groth, Longo, and McFadin (1982) administered a brief questionnaire to two samples of incarcerated sexual offenders, which included 83 rapists and 54 child molesters. The rapists reported an average of 2.8 offences (range 1–20) for which they had been charged, and 5.2 offences (range 0–30) for which they had not been charged. Similarly the child molesters reported a mean of 1.7 offences (range 1–8) that had resulted in charges and 4.7 offences (range 0–30) that had not.

In a study of rapists and child molesters who had volunteered for treatment, Abel, Mittleman, and Becker (1985) obtained reports of large numbers of attempted and completed incidents of rape and child sexual victimization. Because they believed that earlier reports provided by sex offenders about their activities had been greatly underestimated in order to avoid potentially negative consequences, these researchers utilized exhaustive procedures to ensure the confidentiality of their respondents' reports in the hope of obtaining more accurate information. The study subjects were generally relatively young, with most being under 40 years of age.

The 89 rapists reported that they had attempted or completed 744 rapes involving 667 victims, or an average of nearly eight victims per offender.

The 232 child molesters reported, on average, 238 attempts to molest children under age fourteen. Seventy percent of attempts were completed, resulting in an average of 167 molestations involving 76 victims per offender. The real scope of their activities may be better reflected by the group totals of 55 250 attempted and 38 727 completed molestations of 17 585 victims.

It is quite clear from these offender reports that relatively few offenders can have an impact on large numbers of victims. What is missing at this point is an estimate of how many sex offenders there currently are in the population. Such information would be of value not only in providing data on the size of the problem, but for use in planning interventions and responses to it.

Having taken a brief look at the various sources of data relating to the extent of sexual offending and what they tell us, it is apparent that the problem is widespread and much more common than is usually assumed. Thus far, we have been considering the legal classification of behaviour. Now we will turn to issues important in understanding the clinical diagnosis and treatment of this offender group. It should become apparent that the legally defined categories of, for example, "sexual assault" and "incest," have little correspondence with the clinical categorization of sexual offenders.

It has previously been noted that a child molester would

he Criminal Code
ult. However, for
ry important. We
ender typologies.

s the classification
The creation of a
useful for provid-
d to the range of
al of classification
ithin a larger popu-
als who are as simi-
while maintaining
ubgroups. In other
ies sets of individu-
the sets, with the
nt as possible from

pic of sex offenders,
treated in the me-
p (perhaps with, at
"rapists" and "child
ave been determin-
y mixed and heter-
aving a variety of
, the available evi-
more distinct sub-
nly appreciated, but
ion of sex-offender
s constitutes a major
processes underly-

sources in, develop-
offenders might ap-
ation of researchers,
s with doing some-
of these individuals.
tion involves deter-
em," and that is ad-
further complicate
may be required for
tions of the same in-
nding etiology (de-
ur, the most effective
best procedures for
in the community
ler behaviour in that
t there are currently
ilable for any of those
under way.

Early efforts to categorize sex offenders were typified by distinctions based on the presumed underlying psychodynamics of the disorder. More recently, attempts to develop sex-offender typologies have been based on empirical data, and have proceeded through the comparative examination of groups of sex offenders with respect to a wide variety of personal, offence, and victim characteristics. An extensive body of literature (reviewed by Knight, Rosenberg, & Schneider, 1985) has reported on the characteristic differences between various groupings of sex offenders, and, more rarely, between sex offenders and nonoffender populations.

Personal offender characteristics that have been considered include: demographics (age, education, occupational attainment); offence history (sexual and nonsexual); social adjustment (assertiveness, social skills, relationships, history, empathy, etc.); psychological adjustment (personality types, aggressiveness, impulsivity, degree of psychopathology, intelligence, etc.); alcohol and drug use; and sexual-arousal patterns.[4]

Aspects of the offence that have been examined include: the extent of premeditation; time and place of occurrence; nature of sexual acts; degree and nature of violence; involvement of other offenders; and use of alcohol or drugs at the time of the offence.

Finally, victim characteristics that have been considered include: age, gender, and relationship to the offender.

The empirical approach to the development of sex-offender typologies has been particularly well developed at the Massachusetts Treatment Center (MTC) at Bridgewater.

Building on earlier work (Cohen, Seghorn, & Calmas, 1969), researchers at the MTC have continued extensive development of a taxonomic system for rapists (Knight & Prentky, 1987; Prentky, Cohen, & Seghorn, 1985; Prentky, Knight, & Rosenberg, 1988; Rosenberg et al., 1986) and a classification system for child molesters (Knight, 1988).

A Rapist Taxonomy

A recent version of the taxonomy for rapists was presented by Prentky, Knight, and Rosenberg (1988). It provided a means of classifying rapists into eight subtypes (see Figure 9.2).

An initial distinction was made as to the purpose for the offender of the aggressive component of the offence, being either instrumental (necessary for the completion of the offence) or expressive (based on a need to injure the victim). A second distinction was made within each of the foregoing subtypes as to the meaning of the sexuality involved in the offence. In those cases where instrumental

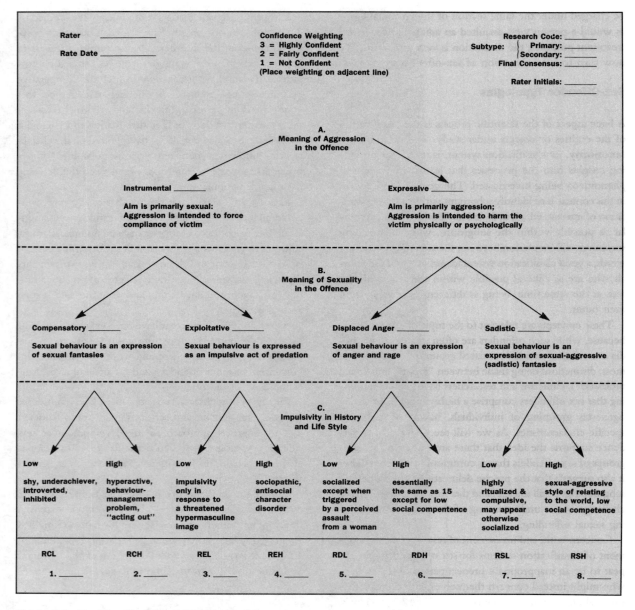

Figure 9.2 Decision Tree For Subtyping Rapists

Source: R.A. Prentky, R.A. Knight, & R. Rosenberg (1988), Validation analyses on a taxonomic system for rapists: Disconfirmation and reconceptualization, in R.A. Prentky & V.L. Quinsey (Eds.). *Human sexual aggression: Current perspectives* (p. 23). Annals of the New York Academy of Sciences, *528*.

aggression was employed, a distinction was made between compensatory sexuality (based on deviant sexual fantasies) and exploitative sexuality (a relatively spontaneous predatory act). In cases of expressive aggression, a differentiation at the second level is made between displaced anger, where the victim is seen primarily as a surrogate for another hated individual or group, and sadistic aggression, with the behaviour rooted in sadistic fantasy. The final distinction, made at the third level within each of the four previously constituted subgroups, was related to the degree of impulsivity. An impulsive versus nonimpulsive lifestyle was expected to be useful in discriminating groups of rapists.

l alterations to the
e tested in subse-
d to be necessary
ulsivity so that it
l history of the
ld be seen to have
ge of the offender.
versus expressive-
lable historical in-

omy involved data
rentky, Knight, &
vas completed on
lid not always sup-
omy for rapists. It
dimensions of the
e aggression, sexu-
ation, and lifestyle
istinction based on
victim, after which

categorizations relating to the meaning of the aggression and the victim to the offender would be made. An additional discriminating variable, social competence, also emerged as a potentially important factor in making distinctions among types of rapists.

Classifying Child Molesters

The current status of the MTC classification system for child molesters has been presented by Knight (1988). The development of this system is a particularly instructive example of the interplay of rational and empirical approaches to the development of a typological system. Beginning with what was originally a typology generated from within a psychodynamic framework, the researchers proceeded through a number of rationally guided stages of empirical data analysis to arrive at what currently appears to be a relatively reliable and valid method of classifying child molesters. The classification system is described in Box 9.2.

Classifications based on this model will now be used in

:em for Child Molesters

rizing an offender on
mensional combina-
der is fixated on chil-
of social competence
rmed "normal" adult

o one of six subtypes.
n those offenders who
with children (that is,
nt of time in close
th low contact (those
th children outside of

next differentiation is
and the nature of the
ype is chosen in those
npted to establish an
ith a child, with com-
ensitivity to the needs
cally did not involve
issistic type is assigned
r's own needs are pre-
een mainly aimed at
he offender.

For *low contact* offenders, those who have had little contact with children beyond occasions of assault, the next level of differentiation concerns the amount of physical damage inflicted on the victim. *Low injury* includes cases with no physical damage and only acts such as shoving, holding, slapping, threats, etc. These offenders are further subdivided on the basis of the meaning of the aggression into *exploitative* (aggression is instrumental to gain compliance) and *muted sadistic* (including features of eroticized aggression) types.

High injury involves all cases where the victim is physically injured as a result of hitting, punching, choking, etc. Again, the next level of discrimination involves the meaning of the aggression to the offender, either *nonsadistic*, where the violence resulted during noneroticized anger or as an "accident" as a result of clumsiness or ineptitude, or *sadistic*, where the violence is a component of sexual arousal for the offender.

Source: From R.A. Knight (1988), A taxonomic analysis of child molesters. In R.A. Prentky & V.L. Quinsey (Eds.), *Human sexual aggression: Current perspectives* (p. 18). New York: Annals of the New York Academy of Sciences, *528*.

attempts to further understand the development of deviance and to predict offender **recidivism** and response to treatment.

Offence Crossover

Many attempts to understand the differences and similarities between and among sex offenders begin with categorizations based on offence types, for example, child molesters, rapists, and incest offenders. An assumption is made that offenders are essentially consistent with respect to the type of offence committed, and, indeed, it has been shown that most pedophiles who are reapprehended have reoffended with victims of similar sex and age (Revitch & Weiss, 1962). However, more recent evidence presents difficulties for offence-based typologies, as it indicates that the situation is not as simple as has been assumed.

Abel and associates (1988) have published information about the offence patterns of 561 men seen in out-patient clinics. The investigators conducted extensive interviews with the offenders. The offenders were given unusually strong guarantees of confidentiality, including government certification of the immunity of their records from **subpoena**. During the interviews, the participants were explicitly questioned about sex-offence activity outside the range of that identified by their primary diagnosis. Care was taken to obtain as accurate as possible counts of prior offences of every type as a result of these extraordinary procedures, startling results emerged.

Of those participating in the study, only 10.4 percent had engaged in only one type of deviant activity. Two diagnostic categories were appropriate for 19.9 percent, three for 20.6 percent, four for 11.5 percent, and the remaining 37.6 percent could be diagnosed as fitting from five to ten diagnostic categories.

Although not a criminal offence, one diagnostic category, transsexualism, contained 52 percent of single-diagnosis individuals, the highest percentage for any category. The other categories contained fewer than 30 percent of individuals having that category as their sole classification.

Two examples of the pattern of offence involvement will serve to demonstrate the meaning of these data. The study included 224 individuals with a primary diagnosis of heterosexual nonincestuous pedophilia, the usual stereotype categorization of a "child molester." Thirty-five percent of those individuals had also been involved in homosexual pedophilia, 29 percent in exhibitionism, 25 percent in adult rape, and 14 percent in voyeurism. Among the 126 individuals diagnosed as rapists, 44 percent had engaged in nonincestuous heterosexual pedophilia, 28 percent in exhibitionism, 24 percent in heterosexual incest, and 14 percent in homosexual nonincest pedophilia.

These findings clearly present a challenge to those attempting to create taxonomies based on offence characteristics.

Treatment of Sex Offenders

In this section, we will consider various approaches to modifying the behaviour of sex offenders. In many instances, more than one of the methods to be described are used simultaneously or sequentially within the framework of a treatment program. A first step in most treatment efforts involves diagnosis of the specific nature of an individual's disorder (Bradford, 1988a). The focus is most often upon the individual's deficiencies, rather than those of his or her surrounding social context.

Diagnosis

Normally a psychodiagnosis includes a psychological history and psychometric testing. The latter often includes the use of instruments that assess intelligence and various aspects of personality style and functioning.

For sex offenders, an obvious focus of historical analysis is on the individual's sexual development and experiences. Additional psychometric devices to explore sexually related attitudes and behaviours are also often employed. Because it is common to find social and assertiveness deficits in sex offenders, devices to explore these domains are frequently used.

While most psychodiagnostic procedures consider physiological issues to the extent needed to exclude physical causes of mental disorder, in the case of sex offenders, additional physiological assessments are usually appropriate. These include testing to determine the levels of free testosterone in the blood, luteinizing hormone (LH), follicle-stimulating hormone (FSH), prolactin, and progesterone.

Another psychophysiological technique, the penile plethysmograph, is frequently used to assess the specific pattern of sexual deviance of a particular individual.

Phallometry

The penile plethysmograph (PPG) consists of sensors that are attached to the genitalia of the individual being assessed that continuously measure the degree of sexual arousal. One of the more common sensors consists of a very thin rubber tube filled with indium–gallium. This tube is positioned around the phallus, and a very weak electric current is passed through the indium–gallium solution. Changes in the conductivity of the tube as a result of varying degrees of erection are measured electronically and recorded for later analysis.

l with a varie-
nt and degree
ated as still im-
ensions varied
nd the degree

nonarousal to
deviance pat-
een shown to
s of offenders.
Murphy et al.,
ing conducted
ridual diagnos-
most clinicians
other sources

the PPG is the
suppress their
sessment. This,
id with respect
an individual.
t there may be
sed to alert cli-
(Freund, Wat-

een used with
d (1985, 1988a,
rosurgery, cas-
urosurgery and
st being a very
nd the second
ne means to an
nal treatments.
s often used in
trates offer evi-
in preventing

treatments are
icing the levels
osterone) in the
tosterone have
our (Bradford,

tration for the
y Freund (1980)
ation recidivism

rates in the range of 1.1 percent to 7.3 percent, compared with precastration rates of 50.0 percent to 84.0 percent, are reported. This body or research has been methodologically criticized by Heim and Hursch (1979) and Heim (1981) who identified flaws in the way recidivism rates were calculated and cast some doubt on the utility of castration as a means to prevent further sexual offending. Taking those criticisms into account, however, it still appears that castration is effective to some degree in the reduction of recidivism in sexual offenders.

Antiandrogens

Two drugs have been widely used in the treatment of sex offenders: medroxyprogesterone acetate (MPA; Depo-Provera) and cyproterone acetate (CPA). Both of these drugs reduce male testosterone levels through somewhat different physiological processes. Both also produce a range of side-effects, some of which are somewhat negative, such as gynecomastia (breast enlargement), loss of body hair, weight gain, and drowsiness (Bradford, 1988b).

These drugs do appear to be somewhat effective in reducing aggressive sexual drives and accompanying fantasies (Berlin, 1983; Bradford, 1988b). The main problem with their use is the quick return of the male hormone system to normal levels upon their discontinuance. Given the somewhat unpleasant side-effects, dropout rates from antiandrogen treatment programs are relatively high (Quinsey & Marshall, 1983).

Psychological Methods

Aversion Therapy

This approach is based on **behaviour-modification** principles of associating aversive stimuli with the occurrence of unwanted behaviours. In practice, evidence of arousal to deviant sexual stimuli, such as audiotaped descriptions or slides, results in the administration of an aversive stimulus, most often an extremely noxious odour or electric shock.

Covert Sensitization

This is a cognitive form of aversion therapy whereby deviant sexual arousal is associated with an aversive stimulus in the offender's mind. The offender is taught to develop an extremely detailed fantasy of the most negative imaginable consequences that might result from his sexual offending. Being brutally raped by other inmates in prison or having one's children victimized at school because of their father's crime are typical examples (Marshall & Barbaree, 1988). These fantasies are then brought to mind by the offender at the onset of any sexually deviant thinking.

Masturbatory Satiation

This technique is taught to the offender and is intended to reduce his arousal to inappropriate sexual stimuli while increasing arousal to appropriate sexual objects. The process involves masturbating for such extended periods of time that considerable discomfort and pain results. During this experience, the offender is to engage continuously in his particular repertoire of deviant sexual fantasies. The offender is sometimes instructed to verbalize the details of his fantasies aloud with a tape-recorder present, in order to monitor compliance with the technique. During the period of time leading up to ejaculation, the offender is to engage in appropriate sexual fantasy. The rationale for this procedure is based on cognitive behaviour-therapy principles of associating aversive consequences with mental representations of undesirable behaviours and positive consequences with desirable behaviours.

Facilitation of Appropriate Sexual Behaviour

Because of ignorance arising from impoverished socialization and other circumstances, many offenders are very poorly informed about normal sexual activity. In order to alleviate this problem, many programs include sex-education and human-sexuality components.

Group Therapy

One of the most common approaches to the treatment of sex offenders is broadly labelled "group therapy." This technique involves the exchange, often in a confrontational atmosphere, of information between group members about their personal backgrounds and sexual-offending histories. Most clinicians believe that a necessary first step in beginning the process of behaviour change is the admission of responsibility for the offence. Many offenders engage in cognitive distortions surrounding their offending, believing, for instance, that the victim was partly or completely responsible for the occurrence of the incident, or that sexual experience is a healthy educational component of a child's life. A confrontative group experience may be an effective means of breaking down an offender's resistance to accepting full responsibility for his deviant behaviour.

Social Skills and Assertiveness

Many offenders are found to be unskilled in conducting normal social relations with appropriate peers. Many are also deficient in assertiveness and are unable to get needs met appropriately. Behavioural training programs for both of these problems are often components of comprehensive sex-offender treatment programs.

Relapse Prevention

A major focus in most treatment programs is the training of the offender in techniques that will preclude a relapse after leaving the program (Pithers et al., 1988). These techniques, which offer one of the most promising approaches at the present time for the treatment of sex offenders, are based on similar approaches to the treatment of addictions (Marlatt, 1982).

In most sex-offender treatment programs, a major emphasis is placed on helping the offender to understand his deviance and develop means for avoiding a future reoffence. One of the most comprehensive systems for accomplishing this is relapse prevention. This approach was originally developed by Marlatt (1982) for the treatment of substance abuse. It was later modified by Pithers and associates (1983) for application to sex offending. A key aspect of the relapse prevention model is its relationship to current understanding of the precursors of the commission of sex crimes.

The Crime Cycle.   A fairly common sequence of events leading up to the commission of a sexual offence has been identified. The process often starts with an alteration in the offender's affective state, that is, "feeling moody" or "brooding." Following that, there are often fantasies of committing a deviant act. The fantasies are then made more concrete through the use of pornographic materials and concomitant masturbation. Next, the offender begins to develop cognitive distortions related to the act, such as rationalizations that minimize the negative effects of actually carrying it out, and ascribing characteristics to potential victims that make commission of the offence more acceptable. Passively working out a plan to carry out a specific offence than follows, again, frequently while engaging in masturbation.

This process continues, with the planning becoming more and more specific, until an actual offence is committed. It is notable that the offender usually believes that the early phases of this process are "harmless" and rarely appreciates that a dangerous sequence of events has begun. It is also worth noting that a similar, but perhaps more "unconscious," process has been found in conjunction with what offenders describe as "spontaneous" offences (Burgess et al., 1978; Marshall, Abel, & Quinsey, 1981; Pithers et al., 1988).

The Relapse-Prevention Model.   Relapse prevention focusses on helping the offender understand and intervene in the crime-cycle sequence in order to avoid a recurrence of an offence, or a "relapse." The components of the relapse process, as addressed by the relapse-prevention approach, are shown in Box 9.3.

Treatment Effectiveness

The overriding question with respect to the treatment methods described above is, "Do they work?" Evidence

n has been in-
time, the sim-
lers appears to
: sound overly
e available evi-
nder treatment

tion, after hav-
nders for more
essment of the
social problem
e, the offender
re no reliable
e are no effec-
able predictors

Furby, Weinrott, and Blackshaw (1989) conducted a review of the earlier studies of sex-offender recidivism in an effort to assess the effectiveness of the treatments provided. They included studies with a range of types of offenders and treatment approaches. Recidivism was defined in terms of the recommission of a sex offence that was recorded in official records. As discussed above, this is a very conservative index of sex offending but it is clearly the one that is most relevant to issues of treatment effectiveness.

After a consideration of criteria for methodological adequacy, Furby, Weinrott, and Blackshaw (1989) described the outcomes of 42 methodologically sound studies. The result of their efforts was summarized simply: "we can at least say with confidence that there is no evidence that treatment effectively reduces sex offense recidivism" (1989, p. 25). They qualified their judgment by noting that the studies

odel

the offender un-
sequence in order
a "relapse." The
addressed by the
n in the figure

naintaining absti-
as actually offend-
self-control and
essfully avoid fu-

er a high-risk sit-
his sense of con-
he offender is able
s sense of control
n enhanced. If he
ice, "lapses" into
d self-esteem are

ultimately results
tion effect." This
en the offender's
abstainer and his
results in a growth
ctive and failure-
age in subsequent
ents of the relapse-

prevention program are directed at counteracting the build-up of "abstinence-violation effect."

Another feature of the relapse process is the occurrence of "apparently irrelevant decisions." These are decisions made by the offender that, at the time, do not appear to have any relevance to the likelihood of a subsequent lapse or relapse. The concept is well illustrated by an example from another context (Marlatt & Gordon, 1985). A currently abstinent compulsive gambler from Seattle was vacationing in Los Angeles. While driving home, he decided he would like to see Lake Tahoe, because its waters had been described to him as "amazingly blue." Later he "found himself" in downtown Reno, needing to go into a casino to get change for a parking meter. He later claimed that he was unable to resist such powerful external circumstances and relapsed into gambling.

Clearly, a sex offender who places himself in the midst of a tempting high-risk opportunity will be very likely to reoffend. A central focus of relapse prevention is teaching the offender to recognize "apparently irrelevant decisions" and take steps to avoid their consequences.

One of the main points made within the relapse-prevention approach is that there is no "after relapse prevention." Relapse prevention is conceptualized as an approach to living that the offender will have to undertake for a lifetime.

Box 9.3 *(Continued)*

A Cognitive-Behavioural Model of the Relapse Process

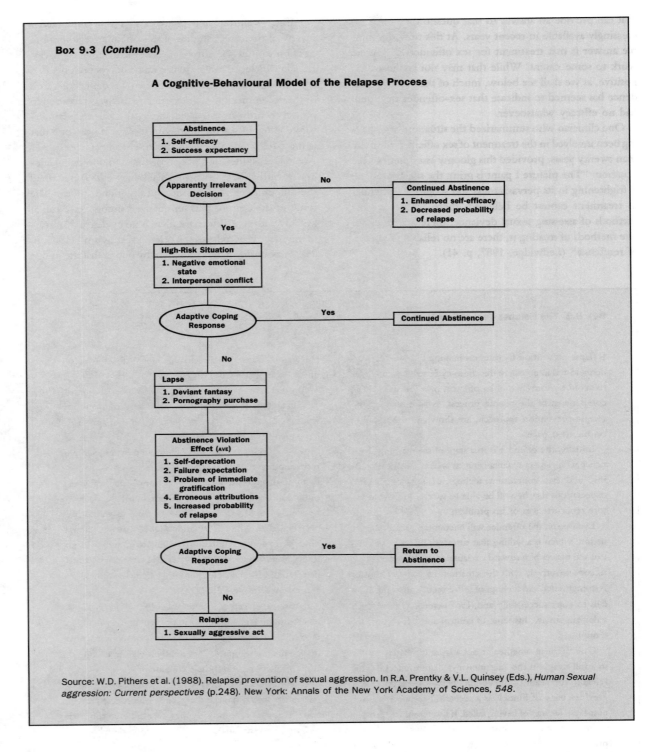

Source: W.D. Pithers et al. (1988). Relapse prevention of sexual aggression. In R.A. Prentky & V.L. Quinsey (Eds.), *Human Sexual aggression: Current perspectives* (p.248). New York: Annals of the New York Academy of Sciences, *548*.

reviewed had been using the treatment methods that were in common use in somewhat earlier times, and that newer methods might prove more effective.

As we have seen, the newer methods of treatment can be collectively characterized as cognitive-behavioural approaches, which are directed toward increasing personal and interpersonal competence, modifying distorted thinking patterns, and altering or reducing deviant sexual fixations.

nave the long-
; the effective-
rams, the data

es for inmates
:havioural pro-
'ears previous-
on a matched
:eption of the
roup of child
rate of 6.2 per-
:tched controls.
lata on 64 par-
an out-patient
iton, Ontario,
: treatment had
d an overall re-
ated group had

one of the most
ng many of the
h a specific fo-
mics leading to

rams have been
: United States.
new that infor-
'ailable or very

itment Program
elapse rate (de-
if 4 percent for
e than one year
., 1988).
tate Hospital by
)84) is seen as a
n, both in terms
remely rigorous

After post-release at risk periods of slightly over a year, those who had been treated had a rearrest rate of 8 percent in comparison with 20 percent and 21 percent in each of two control groups, one which had volunteered for treatment but for whom space was unavailable and one comprised of those refusing treatment (Marques et al., 1989).

About all that seems clear at this point is that there are no outstandingly successful "cures" available to sexual offenders. The most promising approaches appear to be those that predicate their interventions on the assumption that what they have to offer are tools for managing a disorder that will, in most cases, persist throughout the individual's life.

Concluding Comment

Perhaps, as for no other offender group, the **medical model** (discussed in Chapter 8) still has a significant impact upon the criminal-justice system's response to sexual offenders. These offenders are generally viewed as "sick," and their behaviour is thought to be determined by physiological or psychological factors that appear to be beyond their control. While the types of theories described in chapters 7 and 8 have lost favour since the 1970s, it remains the commonly held opinion that incarceration of sex offenders, without provision of treatment, not only is inhumane, but will, in all likelihood, result in the release of an offender who will reoffend. But ultimately, it may be that the "individual" theories upon which the various treatment programs herein discussed have been based are not alone adequate to the task. Even with this type of offender, we may need to consider societal influences to a larger extent than we do currently: the effects of socio-economic, cultural, and historical factors that have shaped our collective attitudes and beliefs about such behaviour.

With that observation, we now move to Part III and a discussion of the sociological explanations of criminality.

different data sources
ence of sexual offending in

2. Why would it make any difference if the medical and legal exercises in the classification process of sexual offenders collapsed into one?

3. The most disturbing issue in sexual-offender treatment processes lies in the question of their effectiveness. If it is true that there appears to be no truly effective treatment process yet evolved for sexual offenders, how should the criminal-justice system "deal" with such individuals?

Notes

1. There were too few sexual assaults of males to make reliable estimates of the characteristics of such incidents.

2. This group is commonly referred to as the "Badgley Committee" after the committee chair, Robin F. Badgley.

3. Information about the locations of incidents and identities of assailants was obtained by the Badgley Committee from a national survey of incidents reported to the police.

4. Sex offenders appear to be almost exclusively male, although there has been some work done on female sex offenders (see Mathews, Matthews, & Speltz, 1988).

References

Abel, G.G., Becker, J.V., Cunningham-Rathner, J., Mittelman, M., & Rouleau, J.L. (1988). Multiple paraphilic diagnoses among sex offenders. *Bulletin of the American Academy of Psychiatry and Law, 16*(2), 153–68.

Abel, G.G., Mittleman, M.S., & Becker, J.V. (1985). Sexual offenders: Results of assessment and recommendations for treatment. In J.S. Ben-Aron, S.J. Hucker, & C.D. Webster (Eds.), *Clinical criminology: The assessment and treatment of criminal behavior* (pp. 191–206). Toronto: M & M Graphics.

Berlin, F. (1983). Sex offenders: A biomedical perspective and status report on biomedical treatment. In J. Greer & I. Stuart (Eds.), *The sexual aggressor: Current perspectives on treatment* (pp. 83–123). New York: Van Nostrand Reinhold.

Bradford, J.M.W. (1985). Organic treatments for the male sex offender. *Behavioral Sciences and the Law, 3*(4), 355–75.

Bradford, J.M.W. (1988a). Treatment of sexual offenders. *Hospital and Community Psychiatry, 39*, 152–54.

Bradford, J.M.W. (1988b). Organic treatment for the male sexual offender. In R.A. Prentky & V.L. Quinsey (Eds.), *Human sexual aggression: Current perspectives.* Annals of the New York Academy of Sciences, *528*, 193–202.

Briere, J. (1988). The long-term clinical correlates of childhood sexual victimization. In R.A. Prentky & V.L. Quinsey (Eds.), *Human sexual aggression: Current perspectives.* Annals of the New York Academy of Sciences, *528*, 327–34.

Browne, A., & Finkelhor, D. (1986). Impact of child sexual abuse: A review of the research. *Psychological Bulletin, 99*(1), 66–77.

Burgess, A.W., Groth, A.N., Holmstrom, L.L., & Sgroi, S.M. (1978). *Sexual assault of children and adolescents.* Lexington, MA: D.C. Heath.

Cohen, M.L., Seghorn, T., & Calmas, W. (1969). Sociometric study of sex offenders. *Journal of Abnormal Psychology, 74*, 249–55.

Committee on Sexual Offences against Children. (1984a). *Sexual offences against children.* Vol. 1. Ottawa: Supply & Services Canada.

Committee on Sexual Offences against Children. (1984b). *Sexual offences against children.* Vol. 2. Ottawa: Supply & Services Canada.

Conte, J.R. (1988). The effects of sexual abuse on based treatment program for sex offenders. Paper presented at the Conference on the Assessment and Treatment of Sex Offenders, Kingston, Ontario.

Davidson, P.R. (1984). Outcome data for a penitentiary. *Psychiatrica Scandinavica, 63*(Suppl. No. 287), 1–38.

Freund, K. (1980). Therapeutic sex drive reduction. Acta of pedophilia. *Journal of Consulting and Clinical Psychology, 57*(1), 100–105.

Freund, K., & Blanchard, R. (1989). Phallometric diagnosis feigning in the phallometric test. *Behavior Research and Therapy, 26*(2), 105–12.

Freund, K., Watson, R., & Rienzo, D. (1988). Signs of offender recidivism: A review. *Psychological Bulletin, 105*, 3–30.

Furby, L., Weinrott, M.R., & Blackshaw, L. (1989). Sex offender recidivism: A review. *Psychological Bulletin, 105*, 3–30.

Groth, A.N., Longo, R.E., & McFadin, J.B. (1982). Undetected recidivism among rapists and child molesters. *Crime and Delinquency, 28*(3), 450–58.

ffenders. *Archives*

offenders: Treat-
recent European
304.
nolesters. In R.A.
aggression: Current
of Sciences, *528*,

al components in
Criminal Justice and

85). Classification
validation. In A.
rch handbook (pp.

iances: Some ob-
37–43.
ntrol program for
Stuart (Ed.), *Ad-*
ioral medicine (pp.

ntion. New York:

m for sex offenders.
al Health.
M.H. (1989). *The*
eport to the Legis-
California Depart-

1). The assessment
n-Jones & A. Kelt-
52). Burnaby, BC:
r University.
tpatient treatment
.L. Quinsey (Eds.),
nnals of the New

D. (1986). Sexual
ferences for age of
rnal of Behavioural

Female sex offenders:
ety Press.
lanagan, B. (1986).
groups of sexual
ology and Behavioral

apse be prevented?
tment Program for
prevention with sex
rd Press.
Beal, L.S., & Buell,
aggression. In R.A.
l aggression: Current
ty of Sciences, *528*,

arlatt, G.A. (1983).
self-control model
J.G. Greer & I.R.
spectives on treatment
einhold.
985). Development

of a rational taxonomy for the classification of sexual offenders: Rapists. *Bulletin of the American Academy of Psychiatry and Law*, *13*, 39–70.

Prentky, R.A., Knight, R.A., & Rosenberg, R. (1988). Validation analyses on a taxonomic system for rapists: Disconfirmation and reconceptualization. In R.A. Prentky & V.L. Quinsey (Eds.), *Human sexual aggression: Current perspectives*. Annals of the New York Academy of Sciences, *528*, 21–40.

Quinsey, V.L. (1986). Men who have sex with children. In D.N. Weisstub (Ed.), *Law and mental health: International perspectives*. Vol. 2 (pp.140–72). New York: Pergamon.

Quinsey, V.L., & Marshall, W.E. (1983). Procedures for reducing inappropriate sexual arousal: An evaluative review. In J. Greer & I. Stuart (Eds.), *The sexual aggressor: Current perspectives on treatment* (pp. 267–89). New York: Van Nostrand Reinhold.

Revitch, E., & Weiss, R. (1962). The pedophiliac offender. *Diseases of the Nervous System*, *23*, 73–78.

Rosenberg, R., Knight, R.A., Prentky, R.A., & Lee, A. (1988). Validating the components of a taxonomic system for rapists: A path analytic approach. *Bulletin of the American Academy of Psychiatry and Law*. *16*(2), 169–186.

Solicitor General Canada. (1983). *Victims of Crime*. Canadian Urban Victimization Survey, Bulletin No. 1. Ottawa: Minister of the Solicitor General.

Solicitor General Canada. (1984). *Reported and unreported crimes*. Canadian Urban Victimization Survey, Bulletin No. 2. Ottawa: Ministry of the Solicitor General.

Taylor, G.W. (1989, July 17). Sins of the flesh. *Maclean's*, pp. 10–12.

Theories of Crime and Criminality: The Society

The major criticisms of the individual approaches to explaining crime have been noted in Part III; many of those criticisms are made by sociologists. After our consideration of the two case exemplars, the mentally disordered offender and the sexual offender, it is now time, in Part IV, to turn to a consideration of the sociological explanations of criminality. Many of the explanations move beyond the consensus rationale implicit in the nonsociological arguments, and take a more macro-level view of the dynamics involved in criminality. One final comment should be made before proceeding: the differences in explanations of causality of criminal behaviour between the nonsociological, or individual, theories and the sociological, or societal-system, theories do not necessarily mean we must discard the one perspective for the other.

It is true that we have referred to some theorists who feel theories based upon an interaction of the two approaches might be most accurate in "fitting a model" to reality, and, as we said at the beginning of Chapter 7, theories are not truth themselves. There is a place for both kinds of theories—"kinds of people" theories and "kinds of social structure" theories. The people theories have meanings for the structure theories, and the converse is true as well. According to Cohen (1966), for example, psychological theories are concerned with identifying variables and processes involved in the motivation of criminal behaviour—and conformity. Sociological theory, in contrast, "is concerned with identifying variables and process in the larger social system that in turn shape those that are involved in motivation, and that determine their distribution within the system" (Cohen, 1966, pp. 46–47, cited in Bottomley, 1979, p. 51). Therefore, we are not rejecting all the theories presented in Part III to move on to the more "correct" sociological perspective.

Chapter 10 opens with a consideration of contemporary theories of crime causation that focus on the society as integral to explanations of criminality and gives an analysis of a select number of criminological theories in terms of their elements, underlying assumptions, and implications for the explanation of crime. We are provided with comparison of the theories, as well, that permits the student to consider which theory might possess the best "fit" in explaining the various types of Canadian crime.

With Chapter 11, we enter into a discussion of female criminality and how it compares with male criminality. The trends and patterns appear to indicate that females engage in offences similar to those of men, but with strikingly different rates of occurrence. Violent crime is a rarity and is often family-directed, when it does occur. Explanations for female criminality also differ from the traditional theories presented in chapters 7 and 10. Gender-based explanations explore the contribution of socialization processes and patriarchy in the creation of deviance.

In Chapter 12, we view the world of minorities as one in which concerns arise about disparities in the treatment and processing of minorities in the Canadian criminal-justice system. Again, as with the female offender, there is empirical evidence to substantiate the concern. Additional questions, however, emerge with the treatment of different cultural minorities in the nation. We must confront the disturbing issue surrounding the customary law vs. traditional law debate. Are we to have one law for all citizens, thus creating injustice in the nonrecognition of different cultural mores and sanctions; or do we create a different kind of injustice by acknowledging the validity of aboriginal and other ethnic-group sanctioning over that of our own Criminal Code authority—an authority derived from our European traditions of justice?

10 Search for the Cause of Crime: Sociological Perspectives

Brian E. Burtch and Bruce L. Arnold

Criminological Theories:
Sociological Perspectives

Overview: Determining the Breadth of
Criminological Theory

This chapter, and the two chapters following it, focus on how social structure and processes impact upon human criminal behaviour. We will see that it is not the individual alone to whom cause of criminal behaviour is attributable, but the individual's relationship with social institutions and processes—those that, in turn, influence the definition and development of criminal behaviour.

This chapter introduces eight key approaches to sociological theory in **criminology.** They are depicted in Box 10.1, together with brief references to key concepts and exemplars (influential writers) associated with each approach. In familiarizing yourself with these approaches, give special attention to some central debates in criminological theory and appreciate the differences between particular approaches. It is important to note that, given limitations of space, the following discussion is quite condensed, and reference could be made to more detailed approaches to these sociological theories (e.g., Vold & Bernard, 1986).

In addition, as noted in the Introduction, a continuum with the polarities of *consensus* and *conflict* is useful for a consideration of theories of **crime** and control. Therefore, each of the theoretical perspectives can be understood as viewing **criminality** or **deviance** with an emphasis on (1) crime as a deviation from generally accepted rules and values (consensus) or (2) criminalization and **criminal law** as a reflection of numerous forms of conflict between competing groups, in order to secure the advantages of more powerful interest groups or classes (conflict).

The consensus–conflict debate can be traced to the time of Socrates, and has remained a controversial issue for criminological theory and social science in general. Indeed,

Box 10.1   Selected Sociological Disciplines in Criminological Theory

Theory	Key Concepts	Exemplars
1. Anomie	social regulation; ends and means	Emile Durkheim Robert K. Merton
2. Differential Association	definitions favourable to crime	Edwin Sutherland
3. Opportunity Theory	opportunity structures	Cloward & Ohlin
4. Control Theory	social bonds, constraints	T. Hirschi
5. Power-Control	structural explanations versus individualistic, or psychological explanations	J. Hagan
6. Subcultural Theory	focal concerns	W. Miller, A. Cohen
7. Labelling	social reaction	H. Becker, E. Lemert
8. Marxist/neo-Marxist	class conflict; political economy of crime	K. Marx, W. Bonger, Ian Taylor et al.
9. Critical, non-Marxist theory	power, discipline; social ordering	Michel Foucault Richard Ericson & Patricia Baranek

the nature of justice and equality in democratic societies is at the heart of the fragile relationship between the need for social order and the need to protect individual rights and liberties. This chapter offers a discussion of theoretical approaches, using the variables of class and power to illuminate the value of each sociological perspective for criminological theory.

Criminological Theories: Sociological Perspectives

The complexities of criminal phenomena and long-standing controversies over the nature of criminal law and social control undermine the possibility of positing a single theory of crime. In this section, eight broad categories of criminological theory are reviewed to outline how crime has been addressed and to set out some of the limits of each approach to crime and its control.

Anomie Theories

Emile Durkheim, a prominent, nineteenth-century sociologist, argued that, far from being a pathological event, crime served to reinforce the common sentiments essential to the survival of any society. In this respect, crime was a normal and indispensable aspect of any social formation.

Among his many contributions to sociology and social science generally, Durkheim's discussion of **anomie** is central to much of the subsequent writing on crime and deviance. Durkheim began by outlining the shortcomings of theories that were too abstract (metaphysics) or too empirical and descriptive (history), or that looked for causes of behaviour primarily within individuals (psychology) (Durkheim, 1951). Instead, Durkheim advocated a deductive, scientific study of *social structures* and their importance for social thought and behaviour.

His general proposition was that, as the force of the **collective conscience** weakened, rates of crime, suicide, and other behaviours increased. Durkheim presumed that a healthy social order was characterized by a general value consensus, and therefore would have comparatively low rates of anomic—or normless, unregulated—behaviours, including excessive rates of crime. Durkheim therefore maintained that crime and punishment were natural societal responses to maintaining a normative social and moral order. He strongly advocated that such propositions be empirically measured and tested. His works tended to confirm his premise that empirical methods were crucial in testing abstract propositions and theories, and his argument about the force of the collective conscience remains vital today in explanations of crime.

One difficulty with this theoretical approach to crime is that Durkheim begs the question of why crime is so vital in reinforcing social sentiments and the collective conscience. It is possible that other forces are as effective, or more effective, in preserving this collective conscience. A second point is that Durkheim does not allow for societies in which crime is far less common than in others. A modern example of this is Clinard's (1978) study of crime patterns in Switzerland, entitled *Cites with Little Crime*. Using Swiss crime statistics, Clinard found that rates for criminal homicide and robbery were low in comparison to those of the United States and several other European countries. Clinard (1978, p. 147) notes: "On the whole, ordinary crime presents a far less acute problem than it does in other highly urbanized, affluent countries, and to this extent it may be said to represent an exception to the general pattern of close relationship between crime problems and high degrees of development, urbanization, and affluence." While a number of factors might contribute to this comparatively low rate of "ordinary crime" in Switzerland—low rates of crime among youths and foreign workers, lack of slum areas in the cities, and firearms control, among others—Clinard noted that **white-collar crime** was apparently quite extensive in Switzerland.

Durkheim is often categorized as a *consensus* theorist. He did not, however, overlook the importance of class relations in nineteenth-century societies or the impact of class relations upon the social order. He suggested that, as the division of labour increased in complexity, there would be times of pathological class relations, which he classified as "the forced division of labour." Although Durkheim did not apply this classification directly to criminality, his logic can be extended to argue that, as class relations become more conflict-oriented and anomic, crime rates should increase, with corresponding increases in punishments for criminals. This extension would suggest that increasing crime rates can be linked structurally with the larger social formations, rather than reflecting personal immorality.

Durkheim's theoretical contributions and his insistence upon empirical tests of theoretical propositions remain influential in the social sciences. His focus on macro-social influences on social relations is particularly important in conceptualizing crime and control. Unfortunately, Durkheim did not demonstrate that the ultimate cause of anomie was located in external, cultural forces, which he thought comprised the collective conscience. Furthermore, the tautology of using crime as an indicator of general anomie, as well as its consequence, has led criminologists to reconsider the origins of anomie and reasons why social regulation varies across time and place, particularly with respect to class structures and power structures (see Box 10.2).

Box 10.2 Robert Merton and Anomie Theory

One of the most influential formulations of anomie theory was written by Robert K. Merton. Like Durkheim, Merton was concerned with aggregate (or group) phenomena. Merton's theoretical framework was broader, however, since it could be applied to the study of drug abuse, crime, and other forms of deviance in a more specific manner than Durkheim had provided.

In his widely cited 1938 article "Social Structure and Anomie," Merton provided an elaborate account of how anomic conditions could be linked with crime and other forms of deviance. One of the major insights Merton provided was the ways in which a *cultural emphasis* on goals such as economic success, material possessions, and so forth did not correspond with the *institutionalized means* for realizing them (Merton, 1957, p. 133). The gap between these culturally prescribed ends and the actual means to realize them produced strain, and this strain, in turn, could produce a variety of innovative, deviant responses. Merton classified these responses as retreatism, conformity, innovation, rebellion, and ritualism:

Merton also developed a system of classification of why those who are subject to such pressures tend toward deviance, without engaging in certain forms of deviance. This conformity served to stabilize socio-cultural systems. Conformity could be explained by exposure, acceptance, relative accessibility to the goal, the degree of discrepancy

Box 10.2 (Continued)

(between the end and the means), the degree of anomie, and the rates of deviant behaviour stated above (see Merton, 1957, p. 175).

Merton's account of these variations illustrated that the structure of legitimate opportunity, whether by conformity to norms or deviance, varied by social characteristics, including social class. Unfortunately, while he asserted a relationship between social class and crime, he did not explain why class distinctions emerged, or how they were maintained. Merton was thus primarily concerned more with developing a descriptive typology of the range of variations of deviance than with empirically testing his theory of anomie.

Modes of Adaptation	Culture Goals	Institutionalized Means
Conformity	+	+
Innovation	+	−
Ritualism	−	+
Retreatism	−	−
Rebellion	±	±

Note: (+) signifies "acceptance," (−) signifies "rejection," and (±) signifies "rejection of prevailing values and substitution of new values."

Edwin Sutherland and Differential Association

Other criminologists have been concerned with understanding how criminal activity is rationalized by those engaged in crime. Edwin Sutherland (1949, p. 234) formulated the concept of **differential association:** "criminal behavior is learned in association with those who define such behavior favorably and in isolation from those who define it unfavorably, and . . . a person in an appropriate situation engages in such criminal behavior if, and only if, the weight of favorable definitions exceeds the weight of the unfavorable definitions."

The concept of differential association could be applied to a variety of criminal activities, including gang activity, organized crime, assault, and homicide, to list a few possibilities. In *White Collar Crime* (1949), Sutherland applied this concept in his research on illegal practices, using a sample of 70 American corporations (see Chapter 15 for further discussion). He concluded that the process of differential association applied to these illegal practices. White-collar offenders conducted their deviant activities using an ideology that justified illegal practices as "good business," and viewed government regulation of their business practices with contempt.

Opportunity Theory

Opportunity theory builds on the explanation of social pathology arising from deregulation of social life, adding that crime could be linked with illegitimate opportunity structures. Cloward and Ohlin's *Delinquency and Opportu-*

nity (1960) developed a theory that bridges the work on delinquent subcultures, on the one hand, and anomie theory, on the other. Cloward and Ohlin contended that American delinquents frequently committed offences to gain status or goods denied them by the American structure of economic and social opportunities. The overriding emphasis on material success meant that many people would be blocked in their (legitimate) desires for success. Thus, delinquent behaviour needed to be understood as an expression of blocked opportunities more so than of immorality or personal pathology. The prescription for reducing such delinquency was to eliminate or reduce structural obstacles in the economy, the educational system, access to resources and goods, and so forth.

Cloward and Ohlin (1960) were also concerned with the relative availability of illegitimate means in some neighbourhoods. They concluded that "illegal opportunity structures tend to emerge only when there are stable patterns of accommodation between the adult carriers of conventional and of deviant values" (p. 158). They hypothesized that alienated adolescents could avail themselves of existing criminal structures that would protect them, provide a source of income, and avoid many of the problems associated with what Cloward and Ohlin described as the "vagaries of private entrepreneurship" (p. 158).

Control Theories

The importance of bonds in the creation of delinquency and in criminal careers generally is fairly widely appreciated within criminology and arguably in commonsensical explanations of crime. **Control theory** is oriented by the hypothesis that an individual's bonds are crucial in whether or not that individual becomes delinquent or criminal. These bonds include one's family or origin (the family a person is raised in), school, work, community ties, friendships, and church affiliation.

Hirschi (1969, Preface) portrayed the delinquent as someone who is "relatively free of the intimate attachments, the aspirations and the moral beliefs that bind most people to a life within the law." The control (or bond) theory builds on elements of anomie theory, particularly in the sense that conditions of deregulation may produce egoism or anomie within a particular social order (Hirschi, 1969, p. 3). The key elements of Hirschi's control theory emerge from the strength or weakness of the bond to what Hirschi terms "conventional society." These elements included attachment (of the individual to others), commitment, involvement with conventional activities (which limits the person's opportunity for delinquent or deviant involvement), and belief—that is, to what extent the individual's belief system corresponds to a common, or consensual value system (Hirschi, 1969, Ch. 2).

More recently, Nicole Hahn Rafter (1985, pp. 137–41) incorporated control theory in explaining why black women in the United States were more likely to have high crime rates than were white women, for some offences. Rafter suggests that black women are more likely to experience disruption in their conventional bonds with families, churches, and with stable employment. Thus, "often single, moving northward, fending for themselves with few resources, they had greater reason to engage in crime than

all but immigrant white women" (Rafter, 1985, p. 140). She cautions, however, that control theory is not *in itself* an adequate explanation of differing patterns in arrest and incarceration rates, as it omits the crucial variable of responses by criminal-justice officials in processing accused persons.

Subcultural Theories

Walter Miller (1958) stipulated that the focal concerns of members of the American working-class included violence. Working-class life was portrayed as a distinctive lifestyle that differed from middle-class behaviour and beliefs. Toughness, violence, masculinity were focal concerns of working-class males.

There are several difficulties with this **subcultural theory.** First, there is an emphasis on male, working-class youth, with little mention of girls or women. Second, this equation of working-class culture with violence is questionable, considering the ubiquitous nature of crime in many societies. Assault, for example, is not peculiar to any particular class, and it has been argued that violence against spouses is fairly evenly distributed throughout the social classes. Third, the focus on publicly visible crimes, such as prostitution and street violence, obscures other crimes, such as environmental crimes, unsafe working conditions, and political corruption.

There is also a failure to account for delinquency in non–working class neighbourhoods. Even if middle-class delinquency differs in character from the delinquency represented in Miller's approach, there has been consider-

---

Box 10.3 Hagan and McCarthy's Power-Control Theory

Recent theoretical work in Canada has been undertaken to integrate the central issues of conflict and consensus, and to link macro-level and micro-level explanations of criminality. Drawing from the Marxist tradition and Hirschi's theory of control, Hagan and his associates (1979, 1985, 1987) have put forth empirically based theoretical propositions concerning the causes of delinquency. Their concern is to illustrate and explain how and why common delinquency varies in relation to social class and gender within and outside the home.

Initially, Hagan, Simpson, and Gillis (1979) were exploring the gender-class relationship and delinquency. Their findings supported the theoretical assertion that women are

more likely to be controlled through informal processes, whereas men tended to be controlled through more formal processes, such as incarceration.

In order to extend this relationship between gender and control mechanisms, Hagan, Simpson, and Gillis (1985) located this variance within the context of social class. Specifically, they sought to integrate the theoretical concepts of control and power in their analysis of common delinquency. By examining the central focus of Bonger's (1916) Marxist propositions, Hagan, Simpson, and Gillis confirmed Bonger's proposition that the lower one's class position, the less effect gender had on delinquency. The presence of power and the relative absence of control were

Box 10.3 *(Continued)*

influential in specifying and regulating the gender-delinquency relationship.

This theoretical proposition was further tested, and confirmed, in specific socio-historical contexts through an examination of the effects of drastically increased male unemployment, during the Great Depression in Canada (McCarthy & Hagan, 1987). They conclude that

> neither national origin, referral practices, legislative changes, nor changes in social services, can account for the observed variation in delinquency distribution by gender, or provide more information about the nature of this relationship. This is not to say that changes in these variables did not influence the absolute amount of reported juvenile delinquency. However, they appear to explain less of the variation in these data than might previously have been assumed. In any case, the concordance of the data presented with the predictions of power control theory, together with the other variables' failure to account for the changing gender-delinquency relationship, support a fundamental prediction derived from power-control theory; namely, that males were affected more than females by the increased presence of fathers in homes during the Great Depression. (1987, p. 165).

More recent work has been undertaken to explore gender differences within the workplace, and thereby complement their earlier studies of household power and control. Their basic premise is that "positions of power in the workplace are translated into power relations in the household and that the latter, in turn, influence the gender-determined control of adolescents, their preferences for risk-taking, and the patterning of gender and delinquency" (McCarthy & Hagan, 1988, p. 812). This statement represents a theoretical and empirical challenge to patriarchal views of familial control. Specifically, more egalitarian families (where mothers and fathers have relatively high authority positions in the workplace) should witness daughters having tastes for risk and deviance similar to their brothers'. This extended version of **power-control theory** is empirically verified by the Canadian-based research by Hagan and his colleagues.

Subsequent research by Singer and Levine (1988) extends these power-control studies, suggesting that relations of *affiliation* as well as parental authority are influential in delinquent behaviour, and its relationship with gender. Using a sample of American youths and their parents (560 households responded, comprising 79.4 percent of parents), telephone interviews were conducted in addition to questionnaires completed in public and private schools. Singer and Levine (1988, p. 640) concluded, in part:

> What appears to shape the relationship among class, gender, and delinquency is the effect of peers, particularly as reflected in our measure of group risk-taking. In unbalanced households, both boys and girls are less willing to take negative group risks, and therefore, their rate of delinquency is substantially lower.

able research that suggests that middle-class delinquency is commonplace (Vaz, 1967, pp. 132–33). Another consideration is that Miller's motif of working-class culture as a milieu that promotes delinquency is largely descriptive, but fails to account for *why* delinquency emerges so prominently—or *appears* to emerge—in neighbourhoods that are primarily working-class in their composition. As discussed earlier, careful descriptions and measures of criminal activity are not sufficient for theory development, but need to address *why* crime occurs and *how* it develops and is controlled.

The subcultural perspective was further developed by Albert Cohen in *Delinquent Boys* (1955). Cohen contested the assumptions that delinquency emerged from a biological pre-disposition, or that delinquency was something invented, or "contrived" by the delinquent. Rather, independent of biological or psychological factors, children *learn* to become delinquent through contact with delinquent subcultures, and especially the delinquent gang. Cohen defined subcultures in this way: "every society is internally differentiated into numerous sub-groups, each with ways of thinking and doing that are in some respects peculiarly its own, that one can acquire only by participating in these sub-groups, and that one can scarcely help acquiring if he is a full-fledged participant" (1955, p. 12).

Cohen described the delinquent gang as quintessentially working class, and characterized by nonutilitarian (irrational), malicious, and negativistic behaviour. He continued to ascribe "short-run hedonism" to the gang, a mixture of impulsiveness and impatience that reflected the gang's class origins: "short-run hedonism is not characteristic of delinquent groups alone. On the contrary, it is common throughout the social class from which delinquents characteristically come" (Cohen, 1955, p. 30).

The Labelling Perspective

The heritage of criminology includes a focus on the criminal offender. There has however been a redirection of criminological activity that examines the *process* by which laws are made, and whose interests are served by criminal law. In this sense, it becomes important to ask why certain laws come into existence, and how these laws are actually enforced. **Labelling theory** (or, the labelling perspective) corresponds to this interest in the wider context of criminalization as a process. Deviance, including crime, is thus reconceptualized as a social category that is created. Becker's (1963, p. 9) *Outsiders* establishes this point:

> *social groups create deviance by making the rules whose infraction constitutes deviance,* and by applying those rules to particular people and labeling them as outsiders. From this point of view, deviance is *not* a quality of the act the person commits, but rather a consequence of the application by others of rules and sanctions to an "offender." The deviant is one to whom that negative label has successfully been applied; deviant behavior is behavior that people so label. (emphasis in original)

Lemert (1967) formulated the concepts of **primary deviance** and **secondary deviance.** Primary deviance can arise from a variety of social factors, as well as biological or psychological factors. While the origins of primary deviance may be quite diverse, secondary deviance involves a redefinition of self-image following social reaction from other people, including criminal-justice officials. Under this condition of secondary deviance, then, criminal behaviour stems from social reaction, rather than from the polygenetic factors characteristic of primary deviance.

Labelling theory thus emphasizes that the criminal label is created through a process of interaction. Crime is not inherent in acts, and similar actions can receive dramatically different sanctions. For example, the excuse of "command responsibility" for war crimes was upheld in the prosecution of William Calley, an American lieutenant, following the killing of civilians in Vietnam. In the wake of World War II, however, the defence of command responsibility was not accepted in the trails, and this doctrine resulted

in the execution of Japanese generals (Steiner, 1985).

A key criticism of labelling theory arises from its preoccupation with the interactive process—how individuals or groups negotiate the deviant label—without attending to wider issues, such as economic forces that shape the criminal law, or sanctions in general. Another criticism is that labelling theory tends to favour the underdog, but to downplay his or her power in contesting the deviant label.

There have also been serious criticisms of labelling theory for its lack of empirical evidence of its assumptions. For example, a number of researchers have concluded that secondary deviance is not as applicable to many situations (drug addiction, mental retardation, alcoholism) as some labelling theorists imply (see Petrunik, 1980, pp. 223–24).

Marxist and Neo-Marxist Theory

The development of Marxist approaches to crime has been hindered in North America through research restrictions (see Arnold, 1984). Vold and Bernard (1986, p. 314), referring to criminological research in the United States, also speak of political influences on the conduct of criminological research:

> the major sources of funding for criminological research are the federal and private foundations that are or have been associated with large corporate enterprises. These funding sources tend to focus criminological research onto individuals and their immediate social environments, and away from research into the broader political-economic contexts of crime. It would be unrealistic to expect any group to fund studies that would tend to undermine their most important interests.

There seems to be a general sense that Marxism is profoundly irrelevant to liberal-democratic political systems. This dismissal of **Marxist theory** and theories that have been developed within a Marxist framework (neo-Marxism) contrasts sharply with the continuing prominence of Karl Marx's thought in political and social theory, and in practice: specifically, Marx remains one of the most widely cited philosophers in the humanities and social sciences, and his theory of socialism has been very influential worldwide, even in countries that are not conventionally described as socialist.

Within criminology, there have been a number of criticisms of Marxist theorizing about crime (see Inciardi, 1980). These include the weak empirical base underlying much of this theorizing, a reluctance to address the totalitarian potential (or actuality) in socialist countries, and the simplistic reduction of criminal behaviour to class forces and the mode of production. Marxists have countered by developing a more sophisticated approach to crime, which does not reduce criminal behaviour so directly to political and economic forces (see MacLean, 1986; Beirne & Quinney, 1982). It is also noteworthy that there is an ongoing debate among Marxist writers. This has, for example, included criticisms of archival research and use of statistics in formulating a Marxist approach to legislation, including **vagrancy** legislation (see the exchange between Adler, 1989, and Chambliss, 1989). Notwithstanding these criticisms, there is a considerable body of criminological research attesting to the impact of *class* differentials in patterns of arrest, prosecution, conviction, and incarceration within the criminal process.

Wilhelm Bonger, a Dutch criminologist, formulated many of the key applications of Marxist theory to crime. Bonger, a professor at the University of Amsterdam, sought to explain how crime emerged from social and economic conditions. Bonger was concerned not only with working-class crime, but also with criminal activities of the bourgeoisie. Taylor, Walton, and Young (1973, p. 223) observe that

> the criminal thought, which runs through the bulk of Bonger's analysis of crime, is seen as the product of the tendency in industrial capitalism to create "egoism" rather than "altruism" in the structure of social life. It is apparent that the notion performs two different functions for Bonger, in that he is able to argue, at different points, that, first, "the criminal thought" is engendered by the conditions of misery forced on sections of the working class under capitalism and that, second, it is also the product of the greed encouraged when capitalism thrives.

Taylor, Walton, and Young (1973, p. 223) add that this approach allows Bonger to address the difficult question of the relationship between "general economic conditions and the propensity to economic crime."

Bonger provided several categories of crime—economic crimes, sexual crimes, crimes from vengeance (and other motives), political crimes, and pathological crimes—and linked these crimes with the wider influence of the developing capitalist mode of production and a culture of egoism. Taylor, Walton, and Young (1973, p. 226) observe that

> "egoism" constitutes a favourable climate for the commission of criminal acts, and this, for Bonger, is an indication that an environment in which men's social instincts are encouraged has been replaced by one which confers legitimacy on asocial or "immoral" acts of deviance. The commission of these acts . . . has a demoralizing effect on the whole of the body politic.

Bonger theorized that *self-interest* (egoism) was the key trait of humans in capitalist societies. Living in a class-divided society, in which individual competitiveness is encouraged and rewarded, weakened the human trait of *altruism,* or mutual support. Bonger added that the coercive power in capitalist societies is mirrored in the criminal law, inasmuch as the interests of a dominant class are served through punishment of acts that threaten the position of the dominant class.

Bonger contended that law in a class-divided society reflected the interests of the dominant class, in contrast to rival philosophies of the **penal law** serving the interests of the commonwealth. As such, Bonger's approach coincides with a Marxist instrumentalist perspective, in which the state legislated and enforced laws to protect the interests of the bourgeoisie. In a passage from *Conditions* (1972, p. 146), Bonger outlines this coincidence of state power with bourgeois interests:

> In every society which is divided into a ruling class and a class ruled, penal law has been principally constituted according to the will of the former. . . . In the existing penal code, hardly an act is punished if it does not injure the interests of the dominant classes as well as the other, and if the law touching it protects only the interests of the other.

Barlow (1987, p. 61) notes three criticisms of Bonger's approach to crime and criminal law. First, Bonger's focus on economic conditions and crime is too broadly applied in explaining the origins of crime, even touching on "psychic disturbance and degeneracy." Second, Bonger's use of arrest statistics reflects the actions of officials, more so than criminal activity in general. Finally, the key variable of egoism is not measured, but is inferred from the presence of crime.

In 1973, the landmark work of three British criminologists—Ian Taylor, Paul Walton, and Jock Young—established a clear break from the correctionalist and Positivist tradition in criminology. In *The New Criminology* (1973), the authors provided a powerful critique of conventional paradigms of crime and correction, including the focus on individual pathology and the ways in which criminals were thought to be impelled into crime by biological, personality, or social factors.

A key point in *The New Criminology* was that existing paradigms, with few exceptions, ignored links between crime and political economy. Accordingly, Taylor, Walton, and Young advocated the development of a new, **critical criminology** that would seriously examine the nature of power in class societies, the political nature of the criminal sanction, and strategies of achieving social justice that went well beyond the reformist limits of liberal criminology. Taylor, Walton, and Young (1973, p. 279) argued for "a political economy of criminal action" that incorporates social-reaction (labelling) theory and "a politically informed social psychology of these ongoing social dynamics."

While their critique of Positivist criminology was strong, this particular work did not in itself provide a comprehensive, alternative framework for mainstream criminology. In particular, despite their claim that their approach constructed "formal elements of a theory" that would be more adequate to criminology (Taylor, Walton, & Young, 1973, p. 279), it has been argued that the new criminology lacked a solid empirical basis as well as other, formal elements of theory. Taylor, Walton, and Young—and other critical criminologists—did however produce a variety of works that were more empirically based and served to articulate the connections among political structures, ideology, and criminalization (e.g., Taylor, 1981). Critical criminology has developed internationally, with contributions from Canada, England, France, Italy, and the United States, among others.

Unlike earlier theories of crime (which assumed that crime emerged from biological or psychological factors), Marxist criminology places great emphasis on the nature of the state, particularly within capitalist economies. This emphasis is understandable since the state enjoys a monopoly on the use of legitimate force in modern societies (Weber, cited in Cotterrell, 1984, p. 50), and directs the activities of police forces and the military in repressing crime and some forms of dissent. Unlike those who espouse more liberal theories of the state, Marxist theorists generally agree that the state serves to conceal the exploitative nature of economic and social relations. This concealment is achieved through a considerable degree of repressive force, including police deployment and incarceration (see Poulantzas, 1982), and largely through ideological beliefs that become widely adopted. The value of private property, and of individual liability and guilt for criminal activity, are two examples of ideological beliefs.

Marxist criminology has been faulted for its tendency toward determinism; for example, the equation of criminalization with the working class, and the asymmetrical nature of law enforcement. Chambliss (1988) counters that Marxist theory is "widely misunderstood" in the Western world. Speaking directly to oversimplified versions of Marxism, Chambliss notes:

> Critics often depict Marxist theory as one that invokes a simplistic economic determinism, that is, as a theory that reduces everything to economic conditions and economic motivations. Reading Marx

---

Box 10.4 Left Realism and Marxist Criminology

The critical approach to crime and crime control has emerged from Marxist and neo-Marxist traditions. Currently, there have been several works that are often grouped as expressions of **Left Realism**. Jock Young (1979) articulated the groundwork of the Left Realist approach, counterposing the realist approach with Left Idealism. For Young, *Left Idealism* was a force that emerged from marginalized, politicized groups in the late 1970s and through the 1980s. These groups—Black power, the prisoners' rights movement, women's liberation, radical student politics, and others—drew strength from a radicalized version of social-contract theory: that is, while assuming that individuals were fundamentally rational and creative, individual freedom is undermined by social-control apparatuses (Young, 1979, p. 13). Young contends that, for Left Idealists, *real crime* is perpetrated by powerful individuals, even as poorer criminals are punished for (relatively) minor offences. Moreover, crime by working-class people against other working-class people is minimized in Left Idealism, while emphasis is shifted to how crimes by the powerful are unexposed and unpunished by the control apparatuses (see Young, 1979, p. 15).

Left Reformism, as depicted by Young (1979, p. 18), has a different approach to control apparatuses. Rather than seeing them as fundamentally coercive, a "single control apparatus" (Young, 1979, p. 14), Left Reformists distinguish between control apparatuses, such as the police, the courts, and legislators. Crime is seen as natural, and neither crime nor the need for punishment of some offenders will disappear with the establishment of a socialist order. Young (1979, p. 19) adds that "crime is the universal enemy which unites all sections of the population."

Young (1979) identified several flaws with the Left Idealist approach. In assuming that crime was fundamentally an expression of class conflicts, the Left Idealist approach could not account for crimes that emerged within classes, for example, crimes against the person. Young is not wholly comfortable with either the realist or idealist positions. Young does not agree with the Left Idealist notion that formal equality and legal rights are a sham and undermine

Box 10.4 *(Continued)*

a truly socialist movement. Using the prison as one example, he argues that formal equality in the use of the penal sanction would (a) reduce the size of the prison population, (b) reconstitute its population (such that a higher proportion of middle-class and upper-class offenders would be incarcerated, with fewer "petty offenders" held in prison), and (c) redress the lack of formal rights of prisoners, as those rights became entrenched in the prison setting (see Young, 1979, p. 26).

In a more recent discussion, Kinsey, Lea, and Young (1986, pp. 164–65) criticize the Left Idealist model for its analysis of the police as a monolithic agent of the state. Furthermore, public demands for improved policing are seen by Left Idealists as media manipulation; in contrast,

Kinsey, Lea, and Young (1986, pp. 214–15) note that there is a need to take crime seriously, and to accept that governments need to intervene in the crime problem, especially at a local (e.g., municipal) level. They conclude by linking public interest with the police force:

> the police are necessary and . . . a minimum level of coercion is an inevitable feature of social order. Nonetheless we have not argued for more police— with greater public confidence and greater respect for the public, we could cope with less. We do not want to extend the role of the police, but to restrict it. We are not anti-police, just totally against undemocratic forms of policing.

and those who have developed the tradition, it is obvious that this depiction is a gross distortion. The bedrock of Marxist methodology is the *dialectic*. The dialectic sees people responding to, effecting, and changing the constraints and resources that exist. As such, it gives people a central place in shaping and directing their own lives and creating their social structure . . . not a paradox; it is the starting point of the theory that people inherit a particular social structure but react to and change it. (1988, pp. 281–82; italics added)

As with labelling theory, some have criticized Marxist criminology for its failure to link abstractions with careful, empirical measurements (Inciardi, 1980). Hagan (1985, pp. 224–26) notes that Marxist formulations of crime and class tend to be "difficult, if not impossible" to test, and the development of a Marxist theory of crime is hindered by its inability to accurately predict to what extent the criminal law is autonomous from class interests.

Another criticism is that Marx did not discuss *crime* in great detail (see Vold & Bernard, 1986, p. 302), and that his writings suggested that criminals were, in some respects, unlikely to support the class struggle. Furthermore, the Marxist perspective, with its focus on political and economic creation of criminogenic conditions and class-biased law enforcement, disregards personality and biological variables that help to explain the often unpredictable nature of crime.

Thus, critical criminology provides a strong argument for an appreciation of class structures, historical accounts

of criminalization, the role of property as a source of struggle, and the interests served by the differential use of criminal sanctions. According to some critics, however, it does not address the necessity of criminal law—or the legitimacy that may underlie some applications of criminal law— in a satisfactory manner. As indicated above, it also does not account for why some individuals engage in deviant conduct—ranging from addiction to homicide, property crimes, and so forth—while others are not involved in crime or, if they are involved, are so at a different level of intensity or seriousness.

Crime and Power: Non-Marxist, Critical Theories

Other criminological theorists have developed approaches to understanding crime that do not fit conveniently into the categories chosen for this chapter. This section provides a brief review of some of these theorists, and how their work can be distinguished from other approaches.

The nature of power and knowledge is central to the prolific work of Michel Foucault, the late, influential French scholar whose work spanned questions of knowledge, the development of medicine, treatment of the insane and, in *Discipline and Punish* (1979), the complex question of micro-technologies of power. In *Discipline and Punish,* Foucault contended that the modern edifice of crime surveillance, prosecution, and punishment was not designed to eliminate or reduce crime. Rather, crime was useful in consolidating the power of the state and interests served by the state. The prison was but one institution designed to exercise these micro-technologies. Other institutions included the workplace, schools, and places of religious instruction.

The spectacular and bloody punishments of the scaffold, drawing and quartering, and other measures had been largely replaced by more far-reaching forms of monitoring and control. It was not enough to exact suffering from the criminal subject, for the extension of power required a more ubiquitous network of surveillance technologies and knowledge systems that would ensure "normalized repression" of individuals. It is notable that Foucault does not develop his theoretical approach within such conventional approaches as Marxism or liberalism, but views power as a subject in its own right, that is, not properly tied to the precepts of these traditions.

Foucault thus provides a dramatic approach to understanding crime and power, an approach that does not build directly from the anomie, subcultural or control paradigms. While influenced by Marxist and neo-Marxist tenets, Foucault's work is set beyond the traditional focus on class and economy, as power is applied in a more ubiquitous manner throughout societies (see Lowman, Menzies, & Palys, 1987). One criticism of Foucault's work is that it is not well-linked with specific, testable propositions, and is not readily applied to empirical research other than documentary accounts and macro-historical work. His outline of the importance of structures is graphic and innovative, but does not meet the more stringent requirements of a scientific explanation of crime and social control.

There has also been a resurgence of interest in the state and its control of deviance and crime. This represents a major shift away from Positivist criminology (with its focus on individuals and criminogenic conditions), as the very nature of state power is addressed. Much of the work wi-

thin this approach rests solidly on principles of political economy, although others such as Ericson and Baranek (1982), and Ericson, Baranek, and Chan (1987) take a critical, inductive approach to the growth in state powers, without adopting a Marxist or neo-Marxist perspective. The state and its agents serve to reproduce various ideologies and, in so doing, to maintain key aspects of social order, including acceptance of legal and political authority, and dominant images of deviance and respectability. Therefore, the range of possible solutions and alternative explanations is limited through these influential structures of policing, the courts, and the media, among others. Ericson (1987) has further argued that reform in criminal justice tends not to undermine or challenge political authority, but to reinforce its legitimacy. In this respect, he departs from a liberal approach that sees values in many reformist efforts (see for example, Fattah, 1987).

Conclusion

Criminological theory encompasses a great range of assumptions and methods of research. At one extreme, criminological theory has focussed on characteristics of the offender, especially with respect to physiological, genetic, and personality differences (as discussed in Chapter 7). An underlying premise is that the criminal or delinquent is measurably different from the noncriminal or nondelinquent. At another extreme, individual characteristics of offenders are not the subject of inquiry, as crime and deviance are seen as the results of major economic and political forces. In the centre of these approaches is the still-dominant, liberal approach that focusses on opportunity structures and the need for criminal-justice reforms (for a discussion of the dominance of liberal reformism, see Ratner, 1985).

A point that is repeated throughout this chapter is that

Box 10.5 Bill Moyers Interviewing Northrop Frye

MOYERS: I remember something you said in a sermon delivered on the one hundred and fiftieth anniversary of the founding of Victoria College here. You said, "I seldom hear people talking about systems with any confidence now. The world today is in so deeply revolutionary a state that all systems, whatever they're called, are equally on the defensive, trying to prevent further change." Do you still hold to that?

FRYE: Oh, I think so, yes. Doctrinaire Marxism will not work anywhere in the world—not because it's Marxism,

but because it's doctrinaire. I don't think anything doctrinaire will work anywhere.

MOYERS: And by "doctrinaire," you mean—?

FRYE: I mean a simplified deductive pattern that carries out policies from major premises about ideology—

MOYERS:—instead of from the experience of the real world

FRYE: Yes.

Source: From Bill Moyers (1989), *A World of Ideas* (p. 501). Toronto: Doubleday.

none of these theoretical approaches has been established to the exclusion of other, competing explanations. This is partly because of the complexity of crime and criminal justice, and also because measurement and proof are frequently not accomplished, and in some attempts, measurement and proof are not undertaken at all. This gap between the *assertion* of a causal relationship between variables and the *demonstration* of such relationships is often very broad, and students of criminology should be cautious in weighing the merits of particular theoretical approaches.

Overview: Determining the Breadth of Criminological Theory

The development of criminology as a scientific discipline is rooted in the premise of scientific rigour in the definition, prediction, and measurement of criminal behaviour. This scientific approach thus extends beyond the *definition* of crime as an action that violates the criminal law. Rather, a central concern is with *explaining* crime in terms of its origins, its nature, prediction of future patterns of crime and crime control, and treatment or control of crime. This chapter ends with an overview of the various meanings of scientific theory, especially as this concept has been applied to criminology.

It is important to remember that criminological theory, as we have seen, is quite diverse, and that this chapter has provided a selective account of differing approaches in criminology. The approaches discussed were presented thematically, and illustrated with reference to some key works within each of the approaches. We will now review some key elements of theory in social science, as introduced in Chapter 7, with specific reference to criminology, in order to consider how to determine the verity of such theories.

Science and Social Science

As stated earlier, scientific theory refers to an *explanation of events that is testable*. In science, it is commonplace for various competing theories to be considered in explaining particular phenomena. As such, theoretical work is comparative, and is best grounded in factual and counterfactual inquiry.

All scientific enterprises are primarily interested in both describing and explaining phenomena in a logical and systematic manner. Criminology is generally concerned with the pursuit of scientific knowledge of the causes and consequences of various forms of deviant and criminal behaviour, and with the implications of formal and informal social control of crime and deviance. Criminological the-

ory begins with two basic assumptions. First, that there are variations related to social characteristics of organizations, groups, and individuals. Second, notwithstanding such variations, that there are also constant patterns of normal and deviant ideas and behaviour. In other words, criminological theory attempts to describe and explain the range and distribution of similarities and differences related to criminality. Nevertheless, in order to appreciate the contributions (and limitations) of criminological theory, the problematic relationship between the scientific goals of explanation and description requires clarification.

Description is concerned with collecting and organizing empirical information, based on experience, observation, or experimentation. For example, a researcher might be interested in finding the percentage of prison inmates who have completed high school. It is quite another thing then to postulate that low educational attainment causes crime. This would be the realm of explanatory research. *Explanation,* therefore, involves the construction of abstract statements in demonstrating a causal or functional relationship between variables. Various techniques have been developed that facilitate the objective and systematic study of social phenomena. These include making sure that the individuals we choose to study are typical or representative, and that our variables are accurately and precisely measured. This can aid in the avoidance of errors that commonly plague our everyday observations, such as inaccurate or selective observation, overgeneralization, and bias (Babbie, 1983, pp. 10–16).

The task of theory construction in the criminological enterprise is to construct abstract statements, or propositions, that accurately generalize from empirical or descriptive data. This process of theory construction allows us to make valid and reliable general statements about empirical relationships related to criminality and social control. Theories can be constructed after systematic observation that permits us to see empirical generalizations. This is called *inductive,* or grounded, theory construction (Glaser & Strauss, 1967). More commonly, criminological research seeks to test or verify theories that have been developed deductively. *Deductive* theory construction begins with predictions about a social phenomenon based upon some logical reasoning. Therefore, theory construction can be inductive, deductive, or a combination of both modes of logic, and its aim is to construct valid and reliable general statements about empirical relations associated with criminality and social control.

The important point worth repeating, however, is that there is no single theory that can adequately explain all aspects of criminality. Lacking the precision of the physical sciences such as chemistry and physics, theory construction in criminology requires that we attempt to develop more satisfactory *estimations* of some of the more prominent relationships in the origins of criminality and the implications of social control. In order to reduce errors, which are inherent in abstract and empirical endeavours, theorists tend to emphasize either abstraction or description of the social relationships contributing to crime. Therefore, various theoretical endeavours are best evaluated and understood as being developed along a conceptual continuum. At each end of the continuum, conceptual extremes (or opposites) are found. Nevertheless, most theoretical perspectives are best viewed in terms of *the emphasis* on a particular variable or set of variables. This approach is set out in Figure 10.1.

Criminologists have several analytic tools at their disposal for theory construction. These tools serve to develop the association between more accurate descriptions of criminal phenomena and control, and more sophisticated explanations of the origins and nature of such phenomena. *Concepts* serve as the building blocks of all theoretical work. Concepts are mental constructs that serve to organize and draw imaginary boundaries around aspects of the empirical world (e.g., power). As discussed above, some aspects are more abstract than others, and therefore serve a different purpose than more concrete variables. Concrete variables (e.g., criminal record) can be operationalized, for purposes of measurement, in the study of particular questions or issues of interest to criminologists.

To illustrate how theories are constructed and tested, consider the hypothesis that criminal law, in contemporary, class-based societies, is applied to the disadvantage of working-class people. The association of these two variables, class and criminalization, is fundamental to much of the theorizing about crime, and has generated great controversy over its usefulness in explaining the criminal sanction and the meaning of its application.

Causes of crime, therefore, are seen in terms of criminalizing certain behaviours that are characteristic of one group or class of individuals. Criminality, is seen as a political process, and not as inherently criminal. This class-conflict perspective begins with the concept of *power*, which serves as a focal point for understanding criminal and non-criminal relations. It therefore represents a challenge to the assumption of a general, social consensus about morality and punishment. That is, the perspective that emphasizes discrimination in law enforcement and criminal sanctions challenges the consensual perspective in two fundamental respects: first, this conflict perspective challenges the assumption that law emerges from a shared morality that is common to all (or most) citizens in a particular society; and second, it questions the application of the criminal **sanction**, especially the assumption that extralegal variables such as race, gender, and social class are not influential in ex

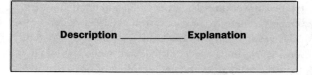

Figure 10.1   Explanation and Description

plaining particular dispositions in criminal justice.

A starting point for scholarship on the class-and-crime controversy is a definition of class and a definition of crime (see Introduction and Chapter 7) that is specific enough to allow their measurement. For research, we need to know: Who is a criminal? Who is a member of the working class? But these categories are quite complex, since the variable of social class may encompass income, prestige, wealth, and geographical location of individuals (see Grabb & Lambert, 1982) and criminologists refer to vastly different phenomena when they speak of criminality (Chunn & Gavigan, 1988). At a descriptive level, class can be used as a marker of social and economic status for an individual, or for a larger grouping, such as a family, clan, or neighbourhood or community. Class is thus a comparative term, used to locate people within a hierarchy of income, status, and power.

For some, the creation of social classes is seen as a natural phenomenon, a reflection of natural differences between individuals with respect to motivation, talent, and ability. Other contest this assumption, arguing that these supposed natural differences are, in fact, ascribed to groupings in order to promote the economic, cultural, and social superiority of other groupings (for a discussion of this history, with respect to scientific appraisals of race, see Gould, 1981). Some interpret class as a phenomenon that is explained by the development of capitalist social relations of production. Social class is, in practice, usually measured by such variables as income, occupation, neighbourhood, and educational attainment.

Crime is likewise not established as a single definition. As discussed in Chapter 2, it is commonplace to refer to crime as an offence that is prohibited by the criminal law of a particular country. But this approach has been viewed as too simplistic because we need to explain why particular behaviours are prohibited through criminal law, while other behaviours are either not criminalized or, if formally criminalized, ignored or selectively prosecuted. As has been discussed in Chapter 5, the criminalization of certain forms of drug use—for example, possession or trafficking in cannabis or cocaine—and not of other forms of drug use, most notably alcoholic beverages, is one case-in-point (see Boyd, 1986). In addition, we must consider disparities in sentencing practices and the question of why some crimes become typified as working-class crimes while other offences, e.g., business crimes, are commonly treated outside of the criminal law, and often with less severe sanctions (Goff & Reasons, 1978). In its classic formulation, while law ideally is applied equally to everyone, regardless of one's station in life, the reality has been that criminal law (and other forms of law) are not so evenly applied. It has been argued that, in *relative* terms, "the rich get rich, while the poor get prison," and that prison populations in Canada, from jails to federal penitentiaries, are largely composed of disadvantaged, relatively powerless individuals from the poorest sections of society (Culhane, 1985; Gosselin, 1982). Despite these problems in the conceptualization of "crime," most criminological researchers measure criminality as official involvement with the criminal-justice system, such as arrest, conviction, or admission to prison.

These critical questions have been developed by criminological theorists. The premise that criminal law serves the interests of a particular class is central to some of the early writings on crime. For example, Wilhelm Bonger distinguished between the *formal* definition of crime[1] and *material* aspects of the conception of crime. Bonger argued that the creation of criminal law stemmed from a conflict between emerging classes over ownership of the means of production and property relations generally. He cautioned that, while penal law in class-divided societies is "principally constituted" in keeping with the will of a ruling class, most criminal-law penalties are directed "against acts that are prejudicial to the interests of *both classes equally* (for example, homicide, rape, etc.)" (Bonger, 1972, p. 130). Nevertheless, Bonger insisted that criminal law rarely punishes any act unless it interferes with the interests of the ruling class. Foremost in his writings is an appreciation of how *economic conditions* deserved a far more significant status in explaining the etiology (origins) of crime: specifically, poverty, brutalizing working conditions, the subordinate economic position of women, and the opposing interests of workers and capitalists contribute to a weakening of "social feelings," such that community and altruism are eclipsed by isolation, domination, and jealousy (see Bonger, 1972, pp. 144–45).

Others have contested this premise of class-based creation and enforcement of law. Historically, criminal law has frequently been portrayed as a public creation, a necessary force in addressing the predatory behaviours of some citizens. This involves seeing that justice is served through punishment or treatment, as well as providing a means of *general deterrence* for others tempted to engage in crime. Sociologists such as Emile Durkheim argued that designations of deviance were inevitable for the survival of social systems. In its ideal form, criminal justice is class-blind: that is, offences are dealt with equally, regardless of one's class.

It is thus in the public interest to preserve the criminal sanction. Crime control is not monopolized by—or need not be monopolized by—a particular class. Crime appears throughout all social strata, and is best understood, perhaps, as a moral failing on the part of individuals. This individualized explanation of criminality is arguably the dominant ideology of the origins of crime, an ideology that corresponds with a cultural emphasis on individualism more so than on the collectivity, and free will more so than determinism.

This framework for understanding crime is inseparable from the long-standing controversy over whether crime is freely chosen or, as Durkheim argued, whether social action is generally determined by factors *external* to the will of the individual. Conservative thinking on crime emphasizes the will of individuals as a force independent from larger forces or pressures to engage in criminal activity. Thus, individuals freely choose to engage in crime. Conversely, even if particular categories of individuals may be tempted into crime, this temptation does not usually amount to a form of compulsion. As van den Haag (1975, p. 109) states, "causation of one's choice of behavior does not deprive it of its character as free choice or relieve the actor of responsibility for it—unless the causation is compulsion, external or internal."

Crime, responsibility, and punishment thus become fused in the free choices of the individual. The individual initiates the crime, is properly held responsible for the criminal act (with only a few exceptions), and merits punishment for personal misconduct. This reduction of criminal activity to personal choice has considerable appeal, given the doctrine of free will and the tendency to attribute success or failings to personal initiative or vice. This individualistic perspective treats structural pressures to commit crimes as incidental, or as irrelevant. Others argue that certain individuals are at a much greater risk of prosecution and punishment. In its classic formulation, while law ideally is applied equally to everyone, regardless of one's station in life, the reality has been that criminal law (and other forms of law) are not so evenly applied. In the nineteenth century, the French novelist Anatole France remarked: "The majestic equality of the law . . . forbids rich and poor alike to sleep under bridges, to beg in the streets, and to steal bread" (quoted in Cotterrell, 1984, p. 124).

Discussion Questions

1. Outline how the variable of social class might be used in explaining delinquency; for example, illicit-drug use or break-and-enter. What approaches would you expect a Marxist criminologist to take; what approaches would a control theorist take?

2. Contrast the anomie perspective (e.g., Merton, Durkheim) and the labelling perspective (Becker, Lemert) with respect to the origins of crime, and appropriate methods of intervention (or nonintervention) for deviants.

3. Review the key elements of theory construction, particularly the distinction between description and explanation. What is the value of a criminological approach that is essentially descriptive? What are its limitations?

4. How does the research of Hagan and his associates on power-control theory add to our understanding of criminal behaviour?

Note

1. Bonger defined the *formal* conception of crime as follows: "A crime is an act committed within a group of persons that form a social unit, and whose author is punished by the group (or a part of it) as such, or by organs designated for this purpose, and this by a penalty whose nature is considered to be more severe than that of moral disapprobation" (see Bonger, 1972, p. 29).

References

Adler, J. (1989). Rejoinder to Chambliss. *Criminology, 27*(2), 229–50.

Arnold, B.L. (1984). Criminal justice education in British Columbia: A political perspective. *Canadian Criminology Forum, 7*(1), 21–40.

Barlow, H. D. (1987). *Introduction to criminology* (4th ed.). Boston: Little, Brown.

Becker, H. (1963). *Outsiders: Studies in the sociology of deviance*. New York: Free Press.

Beirne, P., & Quinney, R. (Eds.). (1982). *Marxism and law*. New York: Wiley.

Bonger, W. (1972). In S. Sylvester Jr. (Ed.), *The heritage of modern criminology* (pp. 128–48). Cambridge, MA: Schenkman.

Boyd, N. (1986). Law and social control, law as social control. In N. Boyd (Ed.), *The social dimensions of law* (pp. 126–44). Scarborough, ON: Prentice-Hall.

Chambliss, W.J. (1988). *Exploring criminology*. New York: Macmillan.

Chambliss, W.J. (1989). On trashing Marxist criminology. *Criminology, 27*(2), 231–38.

Chunn, D., & Gavigan, S. (1988). Social control: Analytical tool or analytical quagmire?" *Contemporary Crises, 12*, 107–24.

Clinard, M. (1978). *Cities with little crime*. Cambridge: Cambridge University Press [reprt. 1985].

Cloward, R.A., & Ohlin, L.E. (1960). *Delinquency and opportunity: A theory of delinquent gangs*. New York: Free Press.

Cohen, A.K. (1955). *Delinquent boys: The culture of the gang*. New York: Free Press [reprt. 1964].

Cotterrell, R. (1984). *The Sociology of law: An introduction*. Toronto: Butterworths.

Culhane, C. (1985). *Still barred from prison*. Montreal: Black Rose.

Durkheim, Emile. 1951. *Suicide: A study in sociology* [Translated by John Spaulding & George Simpson]. New York: Free Press.

Ericson, R. (1987). The state and criminal justice reform. In R.S. Ratner & J.L. McMullan (Eds.), *State control: Criminal justice politics in Canada* (pp. 21–37). Vancouver: University of British Columbia Press.

Ericson, R.V., & Baranek, P.M. (1982). *The ordering of justice: The accused as dependant in criminal justice*. Toronto: University of Toronto Press.

Ericson, R.V., Baranek, P.M., & Chan, J.B.L. (1987). *Visualizing deviance: A study of news organizations*. Toronto: University of Toronto Press.

Fattah, E. (1987). Ideological biases in the evaluation of criminal justice reform. In R.S. Ratner & J.L. McMullan (Eds.), *State control: Criminal justice politics in Canada* (pp. 69–82). Vancouver: University of British Columbia Press.

Foucault, M. (1979). *Discipline and punish: The birth of the prison*. New York: Vintage.

Glaser, B., & Strauss, A. (1967). *The discovery of grounded theory*. Chicago: Aldine.

Gould, S.J. (1981). *The mismeasure of man*. New York: W.W. Norton.

Goff, I., & Reasons, C. (1978). *Corporate crime in Canada*. Scarborough, ON; Prentice-Hall.

Gosselin, L. (1982). *Prisons in Canada*. Montreal: Black Rose.

Grabb, E., & Lambert, R. (1982). The subjective meanings of social class among Canadians. *Canadian Journal of Sociology, 7*(3), 297–308.

Hagan, J. (1985). *Modern criminology: Crime, criminal behavior, and its control*. New York: McGraw-Hill.

Hagan, J., Simpson, J.H., & Gillis, A.R. (1979). The sexual stratification of social control: A gender-based perspective on crime and delinquency. *British Journal of Sociology, 30*(1), 25–38.

Hagan, J., Gillis, A.R., & Simpson, J.H. (1985). The class structure of gender and delinquency: Toward a power-control theory of common delinquent behavior. *American Journal of Sociology, 90*(6), 1151–78.

Hagan, J. Simpson, J., & Gillis, A.R. (1987). Class in the household: A power-control theory of gender and delinquency. *American Journal of Sociology, 92*(4), 788–816.

Hirschi, T. (1969). *Causes of delinquency*. Berkeley: University of California Press.

Inciardi, J. (Ed.). (1980). *Radical criminology: The coming crises*. Beverly Hills: Sage.

Kinsey, R., Lea, J., & Young, J. (1986). *Losing the fight against crime*. London: Basil Blackwell.

Lemert, E. (1967). *Human deviance, social problems, and social control*. Englewood Cliffs, NJ: Prentice-Hall.

Lowman, J., Menzies, R., & Palys, T. (Eds.). (1987). *Transcarceration: Essays in the sociology of social control*. London: Gower.

MacLean, B. (Ed.). (1986). *The political economy of crime*. Toronto: Prentice-Hall.

Mandel, M. (1985). "Relative autonomy" and the criminal justice system. In R.S. Ratner & J.L. McMullan (Eds.), *State control: Criminal justice statistics in Canada* (pp. 149–64). Vancouver: University of British Columbia Press.

McCarthy, B., & Hagan, J. (1987). Gender, delinquency and the Great Depression: A test for power-control theory. *Canadian Review of Sociology and Anthropology, 24*(2), 153–77.

Miller, W. (1958). Lower-class culture as a generating milieu of gang delinquency. *Journal of Social Issues, 15*, 5–19.

Petrunik, M. (1980). The rise and fall of "labelling theory": The construction and deconstruction of a sociological strawman. *Canadian Journal of Sociology, 5*(3), 213–34.

Poulantzas, N. (1982). Law. In P. Beirne & R. Quinney (Eds.). *Marxism and law* (pp. 185–95). New York: Wiley.

Rafter, N.H. (1985). *Partial justice: Women in state prisons, 1800–1935*. Boston: Northeastern University Press.

Ratner, R.S. (1985). Inside the liberal boot: The criminological enterprise in Canada. In T. Fleming (Ed.), *The new criminologies in Canada* (pp. 13–26). Toronto: Oxford University Press.

Singer, S., & Levine, M. (1988). Power-control theory, gender, and delinquency: A partial replication with additional evidence on the effects of peers. *Criminology, 26*(4), 627–47.

Steiner, K. (1985). War crimes and command responsibility: From the Bataan Death March to the My Lai Massacre. *Pacific Affairs, 5*(2), 293–98.

Sutherland, E. (1949). *White collar crime*. New York: Dryden.

Taylor, I. (1981). *Law and order: Arguments for socialism*. London: Macmillan.

Taylor, I., Walton, P., & Young, J. (1973). *The new criminology: For a social theory of deviance*. London: Routledge & Kegan Paul.

van den Haag, E. (1975). *Punishing criminals: Concerning a very old and painful question*. New York: Basic.

Vaz, E.W. (1967). Juvenile delinquency in the middle-class youth culture. In E.W. Vaz (Ed.), *Middle-class juvenile delinquency* (pp. 131–42). New York: Harper & Row.

Vold, G.B., & Bernard, T.J. (1986). *Theoretical criminology* (3rd ed.). New York: Oxford University Press.

Young, J. (1979). Left idealism, reformism and beyond: From new criminology to Marxism. In National Deviancy Conference/Conference of Socialist Economists [Editorial Collective], *Capitalism and the rule of law: From deviancy theory to Marxism* (pp. 11–18). London: Hutchinson.

Dorothy E. Chunn and
Shelley A.M. Gavigan

11 Women and Crime in Canada

Who Are Canada's Women Criminals?

Why Do Women Commit Crime?

Women, Criminal Law, and Criminal Justice

What Should Be Done about Canada's Women Criminals?

Historically, criminologists, criminal-justice practitioners, and political decision makers were virtually silent on the subject of women's **criminality**. Moreover, the sporadic attention that was directed at the adult female offender typically focussed on the most sensational cases involving serious violence or sexual immorality. Since the late 1960s, however, a veritable explosion of research and writing about women and **crime** has occurred. Although the bulk of the new literature is about female offenders in other locales (Adler, 1975; Allen, 1987a, 1987b; Carlen & Worrall, 1987; Daly & Chesney-Lind, 1988; Eaton, 1986; Edwards, 1984, 1985; Heidensohn, 1985; Morris, 1987; Naffine, 1987; Simon, 1975; Smart, 1976), Canadians are also engaged in a reappraisal and reconceptualization of women's criminality, as is evident from government reports (Canada, 1969, 1970, 1977a, 1977b, 1984, 1985) and other research (Adams, 1978; Adelberg, 1985; Adelberg & Currie, 1987; Bertrand, 1979; Boyle et al., 1985; Gavigan, 1983, 1988; Hagan, Simpson, & Gillis, 1979; Johnson, 1986; Langelier-Biron & Collette-Carriere, 1983; Lowman et al., 1987; National Association of Women and the Law [NAWL], 1987).

In Canada, as elsewhere, feminists have initiated and carried out much of this contemporary work. Indeed, their collective writing and research constitute an explicit critique of traditional, male-dominated **criminology** for a failure to include women in the analysis of crime. At the same time, the picture of the female offender emerging from the recent literature is by no means a uniform or homogeneous one. While they have broken with tradition, feminists themselves express extremely divergent views about how to interpret women's criminality and what to do about it. Moreover, many nonfeminist analysts continue to embrace and utilize conventional criminological perspectives on women and crime.

Not surprisingly, the very contradictory findings and conclusions that characterize the contemporary literature on adult female offenders have sparked intense debate that centres on four major questions relating to women and crime. The first, and most basic issue—determining who women offenders are—is also an extremely contentious one. Thus, discussions of female criminality reveal a decided lack of consensus about what official crime statistics and data from other sources, such as self-report and victimization surveys, tell us. Arguments erupt over exactly how much crime women commit, whether they specialize in certain sex-specific offences, and if they are perpetrating dramatically more crime now than ever before.

Explaining why women commit criminal offences is a second question that evokes diverse responses from commentators. All perspectives on female criminality must try to make sense of and account for the fact that women commit so little crime, but different theories offer competing explanations. The dominant theories, past and present, point to bio- and psychogenetic traits, which presumably characterize women's fundamental nature, as both the cause and inhibitor of female criminality. Other explanations focus on the supposedly unique social-psychological processes experienced by girls. And, since the 1960s, the women's liberation movement has stimulated the development of sociological perspectives that relate female criminality either to women's structural inequality or to their growing equality with men in society.

A third disputed issue in the contemporary literature about female offenders pertains to **criminal law** and its administration. Debate centres on the question of whether women receive more lenient treatment than do men. Some commentators maintain that they do because our primarily male lawmakers and law-enforcers are guided by paternalism and chivalry toward women. However, many feminists insist the opposite is true because criminal law and criminal justice reflect a male perspective and therefore cannot be applied to women without discriminating against them. Still other feminists argue that criminal law is not a direct instrument of male benevolence toward or dominance over women but, rather, a mechanism that operates indirectly to help perpetuate women's subordinate position in Canadian society.

Finally, since every theory has different implications for policy, the question of how Canada's women offenders ought to be handled inevitably generates conflicting responses. Most explanations of female criminality support reform policies of two general types: those aimed at changing the offender through individual or social intervention, and, more recently, those directed at reforming the criminal law and the administration of justice. However, some feminist perspectives suggest that only a total transformation of the structures and institutions that perpetuate women's unequal status in Canadian society, and hence their criminality, will solve the problem of the female offender.

In summary, then, this chapter addresses four controversial questions: What are the statistical facts about female offenders in Canada? Why do women commit crimes? How do the law and the criminal-justice apparatus respond to female offenders? What policies are considered appropriate for reducing and possibly eliminating criminality among Canadian women?

Who Are Canada's Women Criminals?

We can construct a reasonably comprehensive profile of female offenders in Canada using information of two general types: official crime statistics and unofficial statistical data from such sources as self-report and victimization surveys. These data tell us not only who the typical female offender is but also what differences exist among women and between women and men who engage in crime.

The Official Portrait: Crime Statistics

The "Average" Female Offender
In Canada, national police statistics are the major source of information about offenders who come to official attention each year (see Chapter 14). However, researchers also gain access to important supplementary data compiled by criminal-justice, mental-health, and welfare agencies in specific cities or provinces. Collectively, these statistics give us a picture of how many charges the police file against women annually, what kinds of offences they are accused of committing, and, to a lesser extent, who the recidivists are (Adams, 1978; Adelberg, 1985; Canada, 1938, 1969 1970, 1977a, 1977b; Giffen, 1965, 1976; Johnson, 1986). The first and most striking impression conveyed by official data is that only a small minority of Canadian women engage in crime. In 1987, for example, police departments across the country laid 747 063 criminal charges against adults, but female accused accounted for only 14.3 percent of them (Statistics Canada, 1988).

Second, official statistics reveal that women are primarily perpetrators of "street" crime—offences against the person, property, and morality—as opposed to white-collar, corporate, organized, or political crime. Moreover, they are concentrated in certain categories of less serious offences. As Figure 11.1 illustrates, in 1987 almost 60 percent of Canada's adult female accused faced charges for three types of nonviolent offence—petty theft, **fraud**, and provincial statute violations. The minor nature of most female criminality becomes even clearer when we discover that 86 percent of women charged with theft of goods valued at $1000 and under were arrested for shoplifting, and 76 percent of those charged with breaches of provincial laws were arrested for offences under liquor statutes, such as appearing drunk in a public place (Statistics Canada, 1988; see also Adams, 1978; Adelberg, 1985, p. 10).

Nonetheless, Figure 11.1 also tells us that Canadian women do commit violent crimes. Indeed, assault was the fourth most frequent charge faced by a female accused during 1987. At the same time, we should note that 63 percent of those charges involved the least serious category of level-one, or common, assault. Moreover, women who perpetrate the gravest acts of violence against the person or property are an extremely rare phenomenon. In 1987, homicide, attempted murder, and robbery accounted for only 0.6 percent of the 106 604 charges against adult women (Statistics Canada, 1988).

Notwithstanding the data above, some commentators cite statistics that suggest a dramatic leap in the amount of female-perpetrated crime, particularly violent offences, from the 1960s onward. For example, the author of an addendum to the *Report on the Female Offender* (Canada, 1977a, p.68) noted with alarm that, between 1964 and 1973, the total number of women charged with **Criminal Code** offences rose 115 percent. Furthermore, during the same period, police charges against women for assault, **robbery**,

and **break-and-enter** jumped 206, 200, and 255 percent, respectively (see also Adams, 1978). However, critics are quick to point out that these percentages are misleading because they artificially inflate the actual crime increase (Giffen, 1976; Johnson, 1986). Thus, a 600 percent leap in the number of women charged with **first-degree murder** between 1976 and 1984 seems less ominous when we learn that, in real terms, that represents an increase from two to fourteen offenders (Johnson, 1986, p. 8).

One way to place such statistical ups and downs in perspective is to look at crime *rates*, which are calculated on the basis of population, and do not rely on absolute numbers and percentages. Several studies concur that, while recorded female crime has increased steadily since the 1950s in Canada, women still account for a very small proportion of all police charges each year (Adams, 1978; Canada, 1969, 1970; Giffen, 1965, 1976; Johnson, 1986, 1987). More importantly, as Table 11.1 reveals (see also Adams, 1978, pp.20–24; Johnson, 1986, p.6), a historical look at crime rates demonstrates conclusively that women are not committing dramatically more serious violent crime than they have in the past. Between 1975 and 1984, nonsexual assault accounted for the largest rate increase (+21.3 per 100 000 population) in female-perpetrated violent crimes against the person and property. During the same period, however, the rates for first-degree murder, sexual offences, and robbery rose only slightly, and those for **second-degree murder, manslaughter, infanticide,** and **attempted murder** either stayed the same or declined. Clearly, it was the jump in the rates for economic and liquor-related offences by women that contributed most to the overall rise in the female crime rate over the decade. Thus, the increased rates for shoplifting (+64.5), in particular, as well as fraud (+37.9), impaired driving (+38.6), and liquor violations (+28.5), exceeded those for violent offences.

Unfortunately, although official statistics tell us how many charges police lay against adult women annually in Canada and what the criminal charges are, they do not provide information about **recidivism**; that is, how many women are charged more than once. However, fragmentary evidence available from other sources indicates that many women are not repeat offenders. Even a good proportion of those who are sentenced to prison in a given year do not have extensive criminal records. For example, 37 percent of the 338 women admitted to the Vanier Centre in Ontario during 1970–71 (Lambert & Madden, 1975, p.12) and a third of the 154 inmates in the federal Prison for Women in Kingston at the end of 1974 (Canada, 1977a, pp. 12–13) had no previous convictions. Moreover, a follow-up study of the Vanier Centre women upon release showed that only 37 percent were reconvicted during a

Theft $1000 and under	26.5%
Provincial Statutes	23.4%
Fraud	9.3%
Assault	7.3%
Municipal By-Laws	5.4%
Prostitution	4.6%
Federal Statutes (Drugs)	4.5%
Bail Violations	3.7%
Break-and-Enter	1.5%
Possession of Stolen Goods	1.5%

1. **Women over age eighteen.**
2. **Total charges against adult women = 106 604.**

Figure 11.1 The Ten Most Common Offences for which Canadian Women Were Charged, 1987 (as percentage of total charges laid against women)

Source: Statistics Canada (1988). *Canadian crime statistics, 1987* (Table 2). Ottawa: Minister of Supply and Services.

Table 11.1 Change in Charging Rates for Selected Offences by Women, 1975 to 1984[1]

Offence Categories	Rate of Change
Murder—Capital/1st Degree	0.1
Murder—Noncapital/2nd Degree	−0.2
Manslaughter	0.0
Infanticide	—
Attempted Murder/Wounding	−1.4
Rape/Other Sexual Offences	1.0
Assault	21.3
Robbery	0.6
Break-and-Enter	5.3
Theft over $200	9.8
Theft under $200	3.3
Shoplifting	64.5
Motor-Vehicle Theft	0.1
Fraud	37.9
Prostitution	−16.5
Impaired Driving	38.6
Federal Statute Drugs	−6.9
Provincial Liquor Acts	28.5
Other Criminal Code[2]	33.1
TOTAL	218.9

[1]Rates per 100 000 female population.
[2]Includes possession of stolen goods, gaming and betting, offensive weapons, arson, bail violations, disturbing the peace, kidnapping, obstructing public peace officer, willful damage.

Source: H. Johnson (1986), *Women and crime in Canada* (Table 1.5). Ottawa: Solicitor General of Canada.

two-year period (Lambert & Madden, 1975, p. 3).

At the same time, more recent evidence seems to indicate that female recidivism may be increasing. For example, 50 percent of the 8000 women sentenced to provincial and territorial institutions in 1985 had served at least one previous jail term (Johnson, 1987, p. 34). Similarly, the number of federal women inmates who have served a previous federal term of incarceration is also on the rise (Johnson, 1987, pp. 36–37). However, we must use these statistics with caution since they necessarily exclude women who were not caught and/or charged for every offence.

Like data on recidivism, information about characteristics of female offenders, such as age, marital status, social class, and race/ethnicity, is not collected in any systematic manner, but the available evidence tells us that the typical woman facing formal criminal charges in Canada is young, single, poor, and white. Although women of all ages are charged with crimes, the average age of female accused has dropped historically (Canada, 1969, p.474; Giffen, 1976, p. 94; Tepperman, 1977, p.216) and a majority are now under age 25. With respect to marital status, most women facing criminal charges are not involved in a marriage or common-law relationship, although many are mothers with dependent children who may well be in the care of others (Adelberg, 1985; Adelberg & Currie, 1987; Benson, 1973; Johnson, 1986; Misch et al., 1982).

The poverty of many female accused is directly linked to their lack of formal education and job skills. Unable to be self-supporting, they often live alone in extremely poor conditions, reliant on government welfare payments and/or support from friends, relatives, and charitable organizations. Those who are married tend to be housewives and/or employees in low-paid domestic and clerical occupations, dependent upon a male breadwinner (Adelberg, 1985; Canada, 1970; Chunn & Menzies, 1989; Johnson, 1986; Lambert & Madden, 1975; Misch et al., 1982; Tepperman, 1977). For example, the Ontario recidivism study cited above revealed that a majority of the women committed to Vanier Centre during 1970–71 had less than a grade-ten education; about one-fifth had completed any special job-related training; and only 32 percent were engaged in paid employment at the time of their arrest (Lambert & Madden, 1975, p.13). Similarly, a mere 37 percent of the women incarcerated in provincial institutions during the national one-day survey of Misch et al. a decade later had previously held a paying job (1982, p.8). Other research has revealed that more than one-third of the women convicted for indictable offences in 1967 (Canada, 1970) and 44 percent of women convicted of **homicide** between 1961 and 1983 (Silverman & Kennedy, 1987, p. 6) were full-time housewives.

Differences among Women Offenders

To this point, the discussion has focussed on what official statistics tell us about the typical adult female offender. However, we also need to be aware of differences both among women themselves and between male and female accused. With respect to women offenders as a group, it is apparent that age and marital status vary in relation to offence and type of sentence. Studies reveal, for example, that women who commit homicide are older on average than other female offenders and that, with the exception of those who commit infanticide, they are more likely to be married or cohabiting, probably because they are older (Silverman & Kennedy, 1987, p. 4; see also Rosenblatt & Greenland, 1974). Similarly, women incarcerated in provincial institutions are younger and more apt to be single than are their counterparts in the federal penitentiary (Misch et al., 1982, pp. 3–6; Benson, 1973, p. 42; Lambert & Madden, 1975, p. 12; Johnson, 1986).

The greatest divisions among female accused are related to race/ethnicity. Thus, although non-native women do comprise the majority of those women charged with criminal offences, native women are grossly overrepresented in official crime statistics relative to their numbers in the general population (Adelberg, 1985; Bienvenue & Latif, 1974; Gavigan, 1987; Hagan, 1985; Johnson, 1986, 1987; LaPrairie, 1984, 1987; Misch et al., 1982). With respect to specific offences, native female accused are also proportionately much more likely to be charged with alcohol-related violations than are their nonaboriginal counterparts, and they comprise the overwhelming majority of those incarcerated for liquor offences (Canada, 1970, p.380; Misch et al., 1982; Birkenmeyer & Jolly, 1981). However, one study revealed that, over a ten-year period, nonaboriginal women were eight times as likely as were their native counterparts to be admitted to the federal correctional system for non–alcohol-related drug offences (Johnson, 1986, p. 65).

Native women are also disproportionately charged with and convicted of violent crimes. The one-day survey of Misch et al. (1982, p. 14) revealed that native women in provincial institutions were more than twice as likely as were non-native women to be incarcerated for violent offences, and Johnson (1986, p. 68) found that 68 percent of native, as opposed to 31 percent of non-native, women admitted to the federal correctional system over a ten-year period (1975–84) had been convicted of violent crimes.

The scant available evidence also indicates that native female offenders have a higher recidivism rate than do non-native women (Lambert & Madden, 1975, p. 16) and are more likely to be reincarcerated (Johnson, 1986, p. 71). Seemingly, native women offenders are younger, more likely to be unmarried with dependants, and even more economically marginal than are non-native women (Dubec, 1982; Birkenmeyer & Jolly, 1981). Furthermore, native women are the least educated (Dubee, 1982) and self-supporting of all female offenders (Birkenmeyer & Jolly, 1981).

Differences between Male and Female Offenders

Official statistics reveal that men and women engage in the same range of "street" crime, but that there is a sizable gender gap. Indeed, although the male-female ratio has narrowed over time, women are still charged with far fewer offences than are men. Thus, the number of women among every 100 adults facing police charges for any offence rose from 9 in 1965 to 11 in 1975, to 14 in 1987, but, during 1987 the male-female charge ratio was still 6:1 (Adams, 1978, p. 5; Statistics Canada, 1988). Moveover, it is quite possible that the apparent increase in numbers of women offenders over the past two decades is reflective more of changes in victim reporting and police charging behaviours than of changes in female criminality.

If we compare men and women over time with respect to specific criminal charges, the size of the gender gap varies considerably, depending on the offence. For example, Table 11.2 reveals (see also Adams, 1978, p. 28) that the male-female ratio for minor theft was the lowest for any Criminal Code offence both in 1966 and in 1987. During the same period, the gender ratios for major theft and fraud narrowed considerably, but men were still more than five times as likely as were women to be charged with theft over $1000 in 1987. The same is true of ratios for traditional "male" offences, such as break-and-enter and automobile theft, where, despite a closing of the gender gap, men continued to predominate.

Women in general also commit fewer and less serious crimes of violence against persons and property than do men. Even though the male-female ratio for violent interpersonal offences has dropped—from 21:1 in 1968 to 15:1 in 1972 (Adams, 1978, p. 28), to 9:1 in 1987—the increased rate of violent offending by women has not brought their proportionate contribution to crimes against the person anywhere near parity with that of men. The latter, for example, remain responsible for virtually all sexual assault, being 71.5 times as likely as their female counterparts to be so charged in 1987 (Statistics Canada, 1988). At the same time, Table 11.2 tells us that men charged with homicide, attempted murder, and nonsexual assault have continued to outstrip women charged with those crimes. Similarly, with

Table 11.2 Number of Charges and Ratio of Male-to-Female Charges for Selected Criminal Code Offences in Canada, 1966 and 1987[1]

Offence	Number of Charges		Male-to-Female Ratio	
	1966	1987	1966	1987
Murder[2]	184	533	6.1:1	6.2:1
Manslaughter	27	55	2.0:1	5.1:1
Attempted Murder	107	709	10.9:1	6.9:1
Assault[3]	20 136	70 872	16.1:1	8.2:1
Robbery	2 160	6 115	26.7:1	11.1:1
Theft under[4]	20 049	85 751	3.5:1	2.0:1
Theft over[4]	8 441	5 804	9.5:1	5.4:1
Fraud	10 126	37 088	7.9:1	2.7:1
Possn. Stolen Goods	3 913	13 438	14.4:1	7.5:1
Car Theft	6 535	9 383	49.2:1	17.2:1
Break-and-Enter	13 038	38 681	48.9:1	22.4:1
Prostitution	1 981	10 278	0.3:1	1.1:1
Gaming and Betting	2 953	1 670	16.9:1	8.1:1
Offensive Weapons	2 340	8 224	29.0:1	13.1:1

[1]In 1966, men and women over age sixteen; in 1987, men and women eighteen and older.
[2]In 1966, capital and noncapital murder; in 1987, first- and second-degree murder.
[3]Excludes sexual assault.
[4]In 1966, theft $50 and under, and theft over $50; in 1987, theft $1000 and under, and theft over $1000.

Sources: M. Benson (1968), *Adult female offenders: An examination of the nature of their offences, the criminal process and service patterns* (Table 2) (p. 12). Toronto: Elizabeth Fry Society; and Statistics Canada (1988), *Canadian crime statistics, 1987*. Ottawa: Minister of Supply and Services.

respect to robbery, the male–female ratio for 1987 was still 11.1:1, notwithstanding the more than 50 percent decrease from the 1966 equivalent. However, we should also note that at least one study (Bienvenue & Latif, 1974) found native women were twice as likely as were native men to be charged with violent offences.

Men and women also differ markedly with respect to the victims of their interpersonal violence—at least so far as homicide is representative of such crime. As we can see in Table 11.3, women most often kill immediate family members—children and husbands—or other relatives, as opposed to friends, acquaintances, and strangers. Thus, between 1975 and 1983, domestic intimates comprised 63.4 percent of the victims of female-perpetrated homicide, a pattern confirmed by other studies (Greenland, 1988; Rosenblatt & Greenland, 1974; Silverman & Kennedy, 1987, pp. 5–6). In contrast, fewer than 30 percent of the victims of male-perpetrated homicide during the same period were relatives, and men were twice as likely as were women to kill someone during the commission of another criminal act.

When we turn to the existing official data on age, marital status, education, and employment, female and male accused are generally similar. However, while differences are rarely statistically significant, they do exist. For example, the average woman offender has become younger over time, but she is still older than her male counterpart (Adams, 1978, p. 43). Similarly, while most male and female accused are single, the latter are much more likely to have dependent children. That said, we should also note that, with the exception of infanticide, women who kill are much more likely to be living in a marriage or common-law relationship than men who commit homicide (Johnson, 1986, p. 16; Silverman & Kennedy, 1987, p. 10).

In addition, female offenders are more economically disadvantaged overall than are their male counterparts. For example, one study of men and women accused who were sent for forensic assessment in Toronto during 1978 found 75 percent of the former and 95 percent of the latter had been unemployed at the time of their arrest (Chunn & Menzies, 1989). When we consider race/ethnicity, the disparity remains, with native and non-native women being less economically independent than their respective male equivalents. At the same time, non-native female offenders seem to be materially better off than either native men or native women who face criminal charges (Birkenmeyer & Jolly, 1981; Hagan, 1985; Johnson, 1986, 1987; LaPrairie, 1984, 1987).

The "Unofficial" Portrait: Self-Report and Victimization Surveys

Although official statistics are an important source of data, they cannot provide us with a complete picture of crime and criminals in any jurisdiction, including Canada. Otto Pollak (1961) was among the first analysts to challenge their accuracy in relation to women with his assertion that much female criminality was masked, and women actually committed many more offences than showed up in police statistics. Thus, he believed, some women were literally getting away with murder because they used undetectable methods (e.g., poison) while, in other cases involving theft or assault, victims declined to report them. The severe critique of official statistics that subsequently emerged demonstrated how they were socially constructed by those who detected, reported, and reacted to crime. These revelations then stimulated the development of new measurement techniques, particularly self-report and victimization surveys, aimed at discovering how much crime and how many criminals remained "hidden" (see Chapter 13).

Have these new data-collection methods revealed anything about Canada's female offenders that official statistics do not? Very few Canadian crime surveys have been

Table 11.3 Homicide[1] Suspects by Sex and Relationship to Victim, 1975-1983

	Male Suspect	Percent	Female Suspect	Percent
Domestic[2]	1309	28.2	442	63.4
Nondomestic[3]	2464	53.0	190	27.3
Nondomestic[4] (Criminal)	871	18.8	65	9.3
TOTAL	4644	100.0	697	100.0

[1]Includes murder, manslaughter, infanticide.
[2]Includes immediate family, extended family, step relative, inlaw relations, foster relations, common-law relations.
[3]Includes social and business relationships, close friends, casual acquaintances, and strangers.
[4]Includes homicide committed during a criminal act where a relationship other than a domestic one existed.

Source: Statistics Canada. H. Johnson, (1986). *Women and crime in Canada* (Table 1.10) (p. 17) Ottawa: Solicitor General of Canada.

Box 11.1 Murders at Home Most in 10 Years, Statscan Reports

More than half of Canada's 642 murders last year were committed in the victim's home—the highest number in the past 10 years, Statistics Canada said yesterday.

And in 80 per cent of the solved cases, the victim knew the killer.

People murdered in their homes included 68 per cent of the female homicide victims and 45 per cent of the male victims.

A total of 183 murders involved family members: 78 women were killed by their husbands, 33 men were killed by their wives, 41 children were killed by their parents, 15 parents were killed by their children, and 16 people were killed by siblings.

The number of men killed by wives was the highest since Statscan began compiling murder statistics in 1961.

Men accounted for almost two-thirds of homicide victims and more than 85 per cent of the homicide suspects arrested by police.

Source: Canadian Press, *Globe and Mail*, October 7, 1988, p. A4.

conducted thus far, and we now know that these information-gathering techniques have their own limitations. Nonetheless, both the self-report (Biron, 1981; Gomme, 1984; Hagan, Simpson, & Gillis, 1979; Tepperman, 1977; West, 1984) and victimization (Canada, 1983–88) studies that have been carried out show that, like their male counterparts, women perpetrate a considerable number of crimes that are undetected and/or unreported. Indeed, while these "unofficial" data replicate the gender ratios of police statistics with respect to adult offenders (Johnson, 1986), some self-report surveys of youth showed that the gap between male and female respondents who admitted to delinquencies was considerably smaller than that indicated in official data for all categories of offence. For example, one survey found that the overall male-female ratio in a sample of adolescent respondents was only 1.3:1 (Gomme, 1984).

Thus, some self-report and victimization studies contradict the picture, painted by official statistics, that a number of offences are virtually sex-specific. While survey data indicate that, in general, female offenders commit fewer and less serious crimes than do their male counterparts, they also reveal that both groups are involved more frequently in certain criminal activities than official statistics show. For example, self-reports tell us that young men commit proportionately as much or even more sexual "**deviance**" and shoplifting than do young women (Morris, 1987). The latter, on the other hand, engage in breaking-and-entering, automobile theft, and alcohol-related offences to a greater extent than official crime data indicate (Gomme, 1984).

Similarly, the Canadian Urban Victimization Survey (CUVS) (Canada, 1983–88) confirmed that women commit very serious crimes but, at the same time, did not uncover a huge amount of hidden female violence. Only 5 percent of an estimated 321 200 robbery and assault incidents were committed by women acting alone or with other women, while another 4 percent involved groups of men and women (Johnson, 1986, pp. 23–24).

Almost two-thirds of those assaulted or robbed by women were acquaintances or relatives, whereas the reverse was true of those victimized by men (Johnson, 1986, p. 31). However, most victims of the women who committed these nonlethal violent acts were other women or girls. This is a very interesting finding because, as we know from official homicide statistics, when women commit lethal violence, the majority of their victims are men (Silverman & Kennedy, 1987).

Analysis of the CUVS data revealed a second noteworthy pattern. Victims reported proportionately fewer violent women than men to the police, despite the fact that attacks carried out by the former caused more injury. Thus, victims contacted the authorities in 29 percent of assault

and robbery incidents involving lone female offenders, as opposed to 33 percent of those with lone male perpetrators. However, when multiple female and multiple male perpetrators were involved, the respective reporting percentages were 47 and 41, and when men and women were in groups, victims reported them 58 percent of the time (Johnson, 1986, p. 31).

Overall, despite the lack of comprehensive statistical information about female offenders in Canada, the existing data do provide us with a reasonably clear picture of those women who are charged with criminal offences and a preliminary outline of the ones who are not detected or reported. We turn now to a consideration of why women commit crime.

Why Do Women Commit Crime?

All theories of female offending must address and try to account for the fact that women perpetrate so much less crime than men. In short, they have to explain why women are seemingly more conformist than men. As previous discussion revealed, the gender gap that has characterized official rates of crime over time is replicated in the findings of contemporary self-report and victimization surveys. Until recently, however, few criminologists have been interested in this question. Thus, none of the major criminological theories (see chapters 7 and 10) can provide a completely satisfactory account of female delinquency, and some can offer no explanation at all (Gavigan, 1983; Heidensohn, 1985; Naffine, 1987; Smart, 1976). Nevertheless, despite researchers' general lack of interest in the female offender, some criminologists have formulated theories of women's criminality that fit into three broad types of explanation: bio- and psychogenetic, social-psychological, and sociological.

Bio- and Psychogenetic Explanations: Natural Differences

Historically and recently, the dominant theories about the female offender have been what might be called individual-pathology theories, that is, they point to biological and/or psychological characteristics that predispose her to commit crime. All such explanations are also premised on the general assumption that, because there are fundamental and natural differences between women and men, we cannot apply the same criminological theory to both male and female offenders. Consequently, sex-specific explanations must be developed.

The nineteenth-century physician Cesare Lombroso was the first criminologist to attempt a detailed analysis of women and crime. After studying 26 skulls and 5 skeletons of prostitutes, he and his colleague Enrico Ferrero wrote *The Female Offender* (1900, pp. 2–3), in which they offered bio-genetic arguments to account for the fact that female offenders were a tiny minority. They concluded that, on the one hand, women were less intelligent, and therefore more passive, than men, which predisposed them toward conformity. Yet, at the same time, women shared many traits with children, including a "deficient" moral sense, and possessed a strong sexual instinct that, if unchecked (see Box 11.2), could lead to criminal behaviour (1900, p. 151).

However, most women were conformists because the fulfilment of their maternal role and repression of their sexuality acted to control any deviant tendencies. Therefore, the few who did commit crimes were going against type. They were really "pseudo-male" women:

> when piety and maternal sentiments are wanting, and in their place are strong passions and intensely erotic tendencies, much muscular strength and a superior intelligence for the conception and execution of evil, it is clear that the innocuous semi-criminal present in the normal woman must be transformed into a born criminal more terrible than any man. (1900, p. 151)

Lombroso's work is noteworthy because it incorporates the contradictory images of women and female sexuality that had emerged in criminal law and medical practice throughout the nineteenth century: chaste/unchaste, good/bad, madonna/whore. For example, much criminal legislation enacted at this time was based on the assumption that women are sexually passive and require protection from sexually aggressive male predators, yet the enforcement of such laws frequently reflected a view of female victims as seductresses (Edwards, 1981, pp.49–50). Similarly, the growing influence of medical concepts of sexuality during the nineteenth century increasingly meant that "as law breakers women were rarely, if ever, recognized as criminals. . . . Instead, the female law breaker was defined as 'sick', and the origin of her sickness was located in her gynaecology" (Edwards, 1981, p. 74).

Although Lombroso's particular ideas about the female (and male) offender (see Chapter 7) were soon out of fashion, his legacy lived on. Throughout this century, theorists have continued the search for physiological causes of women's criminality. Otto Pollak was one of the most famous successors to Lombroso and Ferrero. More than 50 years after the latter published their work on the female offender, Pollak wrote *The Criminality of Women* (1961) in which he discussed the relationship between what he termed the "generative phases" of women and crime. Menstruation, pregnancy, and menopause, Pollak concluded, were all danger times for women because hormonal changes made them more prone to commit delinquent acts.

Despite Pollak's failure to provide any substantial evidence for his hypothesis, subsequent researchers have conducted numerous studies in an attempt to establish a significant relationship between the menstrual cycle and

Box 11.2 Lombroso's Influence in Canada

The assumption of Lombroso and Ferrero that women would naturally fall into deviant behaviour if they were not well supervised is illustrated in the following excerpt from the 1922 Report of the Toronto Family Court (1923, p.18):

> In the case of girl delinquents, almost without exception, it is inherited tendencies that are responsible for the girl's first mis-step. After the appetite has been created, it requires patient and careful handling to divert their thoughts and energy into other channels.
>
> A girl of fifteen, brought up in a home where there was frequent drinking and also immorality, and the family often dependent upon relief, took a position with the father's careless consent in the home of a widower with grown sons. The attention of a welfare worker was attracted to the fact that the man was taking the girl to movies and dance halls. It was reported, the case brought to Court, and only because of lack of sufficient evidence it was dismissed, the man being warned, the father reprimanded, and the daughter allowed to go home. Shortly afterwards the girl was accused of stealing a piece of jewellery. This was her first attempt to get what she could not afford to buy, but like most girls she craved pretty things and they often take other, and more fatal, means of getting them. The girl was brought to Court, found guilty and placed on probation to the Court.

crime. In 1961, Katharina Dalton claimed to have discovered such a link. She studied a sample of female inmates and concluded that almost 60 percent of them had committed their offences either during the sixteen-day period of hormonal disturbance before and after menstruating or during the menstrual period itself (Campbell, 1981, p. 46). Dalton's work, which is ongoing, laid the basis for the currently influential theory of female criminality known as **premenstrual syndrome** (PMS), or premenstrual tension (PMT), **theory**.

Notwithstanding the continuities with Lombroso and Ferrero's research, *The Criminality of Women* reflected the move away from an emphasis on absolute biological determinism in explaining female criminality and toward a more psychogenetic perspective. Unlike most criminologists, Pollak (1961, pp. 8–10) believed that women actually commit a great deal of crime, but the "real" extent of their criminal involvement is "hidden" or "masked." Why? According to Pollak, it is because women are manipulative by nature. While this deviousness is rooted in biology—especially the ability to feign interest and enjoyment in sex—Pollak also emphasized that deceit is a "socially prescribed form of behaviour" for women in Western culture (1961, p. 111). Thus, women become practised at doing what they are naturally predisposed to do, that is, use deception and manipulation to achieve their objectives.

Consequently, in Pollak's view, those who engage in crime are able to conceal most of their illegal activity, specifically through the cunning abuse of the "natural" female role. For example, as mothers, women generally have unquestioned access to children and possibilities for infanticide and physical abuse. As caregivers, they administer to the sick and gain opportunities to commit homicide using undetectable methods such as poisoning. Or, as behind-the-scenes instigators, women may trade on their sexual desirability and feminine wiles to persuade men to perpetrate crimes—and pay the penalty if they are caught (Pollak, 1961; see also Campbell, 1981, p. 53; Smart, 1976, p. 47).

More recently, the assumption that women and men have inherently different characters has formed the basis for what might be called the **functional-equivalence thesis** of crime. Proponents argue that women and men are equally likely to be deviant, but they engage for the most part in sex-specific forms of deviance which reflect their respective natures. The former are emotional, altruistic, and passive; the latter, rational, instrumental, and aggressive. Thus, since women are predisposed to turn in on themselves, female deviance most often takes the form of mental illness, and because men are outward-directed by nature, male deviance generally manifests itself as crime (see Box 11.3). From this perspective, then, women who do engage in criminal behaviour are double deviants—both mad and bad (Smart, 1976, Ch. 6; Smith, 1975).

Box 11.3 Personality Disorder Cited in Women Who Steal at Work

Revenge, not greed, is what motivates many women to defraud their employers, says University of B.C. forensic psychologist Peggy Koopman.

Although the problem often goes unrecognized, such women suffer from an identifiable psychological problem called a borderline personality disorder, she says.

Women suffering from this disorder have "extremely needy personalities," says Koopman. They are often overachievers who knock themselves out to impress their employers, she says.

But no matter how much recognition they get for their hard work, "the employer can't give them enough praise," she says. As a result, "they respond with this inner infantile rage," Koopman says.

Since these women have often worked themselves into positions of power and trust, it is relatively easy for them to exact revenge by stealing from the company, she says.

They feel their actions are justified because they haven't received a return on their emotional investment, she says.

For reasons that aren't yet clear, women suffering from the disorder develop intense feelings of insecurity in childhood, she says. "Way back, there was a fear of abandonment, of lack of love and nurturing."

As a result, says Koopman, they try to deal with life on an intellectual level, constantly trying to "fight off their fears and anxieties by becoming perfect."

Men can also suffer from borderline personality disorders, she says, but they are more apt to resort to violence as a means of venting their anxiety and anger.

Source: Joanne Blain, *Vancouver Sun*, October 8, 1988, p.B6.

Despite their past and present popularity, bio- and psychogenetic explanations of female offending have been severely critiqued (Campbell, 1981; Gavigan, 1983; Heidensohn, 1985; Morris, 1987; Smart, 1976). First of all, the classic studies of the female offender outlined above are methodologically suspect. Lombroso and Ferrero based their conclusions entirely on an examination of incarcerated women, making no attempt to analyze a comparable control group in the general population. Pollak provided no empirical evidence whatsoever for his assertions, relying completely on myths and folklore about women.

Critics also maintain that no amount of research, even methodologically sound research, can provide convincing support for bio- and psychogenetic theories of female offending. There are always too many negative cases. Taking the attempts to link women's crime and the so-called generative phases as typical of such studies, for example, how do we account for the fact that the majority of women do not commit criminal offences? After all, most women are pregnant at some point in their lives, and all women experience menstruation and menopause.

Finally, and most importantly, critics reject the assumptions underlying bio- and psychogenetic theories of women's criminality. All such explanations are based on a stimulus-response model of behaviour—specifically, the belief that the female offender is inherently flawed and that some individual deficiency, whether it be raging hormones or a personality disorder, propels her to commit crime. Thus, women who perpetrate offences are depicted as automatons with no control over their actions; irrational, pathetic creatures at the mercy of internal forces.

Such a theoretical model may well explain animal behaviour but is problematic when applied to human beings because it ignores the fact that people have a subjective side. Individuals do not simply react to stimuli. Rather, they interpret the world around them, and their behaviour reflects that ongoing interpretation of social reality. Certainly, a growing body of literature based on interviews with female offenders seems to support this view (Adelberg & Currie, 1987; Carlen, 1985; Heidensohn, 1985; Walford, 1983).

Moreover, as some critics point out, explanations of male deviance have long emphasized the importance of external factors—cultural and structural. Consequently, individual-pathology theories of criminal men co-exist with many social-psychological and sociological explanations, all of which accord male offenders a certain degree of rationality and control (Heidensohn, 1985; Naffine, 1987). Over the past 30 years, this realization has inspired some researchers to abandon the "pathology" model of the female offender and to develop similar theories about women who commit crime.

Social-Psychological Explanations: Socialization Differences

Several influential social-psychological theories of female offending that shift the emphasis from nature to nurture have emerged since the 1960s. All are based on the assumption that the observable difference in the amount and types of crime perpetrated by women *vis-à-vis* men stems from cultural rather than innate factors. The particular focus of social-psychological explanations is how femininity and masculinity are produced through sex-specific socialization, especially within the family, that is, how girls and boys *learn* to assume their respective, culturally mandated gender roles. Ultimately, then, such theories argue that it is differential socialization practices, not individual pathology, which accounts for the gender gap in criminal statistics.

In attempting to explain the impact of social-psychological factors on female criminality, some researchers found themselves updating or reformulating existing explanations of male deviance. For example, **role theory** became very important in modern studies of women and crime. As originally conceived in the 1940s, the basic premise of this perspective was that mothers employ differential socialization to prepare sons and daughters for their future roles in a nuclear family unit characterized by a sexual division of labour. Boys will become family breadwinners working for pay in the public realm, and girls will become homemakers acting as unpaid caregivers and housekeepers in the private sphere. Therefore, the former must learn to be assertive, tough and risk-taking, and the latter to be passive, dependent, and cautious (Campbell, 1981, pp. 57–64; Naffine, 1987, pp. 43–47; see Box 11.4).

Clearly, such differential socialization has implications for behaviour. As the Canadian criminologist Marie Andrée Bertrand observed in an article describing her early research on female offending (1969, p. 74),

> while our culture condones and even expects a certain amount of acting out and aggressive behaviour in young boys, it is less tolerant of the foibles of young girls. Physical strength, shrewdness in business matters, for instance, are very compatible with our "ideal types" of the "normal" adult male, while such attributes—oftentimes necessary for the performance of recurrent crimes—are not usually associated with femininity because society does not want women trained or practised in such matters.

In short, all the qualities associated with maleness are the same ones demanded of the criminal. Crime, then, is symbolically masculine, and boys who engage in it are asserting their masculinity. At the same time, the qualities

Box 11.4 The Canadian Committee on Corrections (1969)

Differences between women offenders and men offenders can hardly be discussed adequately without relating them to differences in male and female roles in society generally. The lower **incidence** of crimes involving violence may, to some degree, represent constitutional differences between male and female in terms of physical strength, but appears likely to be still more closely related to differences in social roles and expectations. Directly aggressive behaviour is more characteristic of the male, while the female tends to express aggression in more indirect ways.

expressive of femininity make crime unsuitable for girls. Therefore, feminine women do not commit crime; they conform. Hence, criminal women must be poorly socialized or "masculinized" women (Campbell, 1981, pp. 57–64; Naffine, 1987, pp. 43–47).

Another influential social-psychological explanation of male deviance that has been reformulated and applied to women is Hirschi's **social–control theory** (see Chapter 7). Although he initially focussed on the general question of why most people are conformists, in the end, Hirschi dropped his female cases and confined himself to a discussion of the conforming male. In 1979, three Canadian sociologists (Hagan, Simpson, & Gillis, 1979; see also West, 1984) attempted to even the balance with "a gender-based perspective on crime and delinquency."

Their basic thesis, supported by data from interviews with over 600 Ontario high-school students, was that social control is sex-specific and linked to the public/private split. Generally, men are "ascripted to the public arena" where they are visible and therefore subject to formal forms of control such as the criminal law and **criminal-justice system**. In contrast, women are identified with the private realm, which makes them "less available for the public ascription of criminal and delinquent statuses" and more subject to informal controls within the family (1979, pp. 25–27).

As the primary socializers of children, mothers are the main instruments of these informal familial controls, which are applied more to daughters than sons. Why? Hagan, Simpson, & Gillis (1979) suggest that, if girls are to acquire the characteristics of the female gender role—passivity, compliance, and dependence—they must be protected. Similarly, boys can learn the requirements of the male gender role—aggressiveness, independence, and assertiveness—only if they are given a certain amount of freedom. As a result, most young women are "oversocialized" or "overcontrolled"; their activities outside the family are more stringently monitored than are those of young men; and they commit much less delinquency and crime than do their male peers. Delinquent girls, then, are those

who have not been contained by informal controls.

Another influential contemporary social-psychological perspective on women and crime is a feminist version of Lawrence Kohlberg's **moral–development theory**. On the basis of empirical research, Kohlberg identified six stages of cognitive development and concluded that girls were arrested at a lower stage of moral maturity than were boys since girls failed to progress beyond the third level. Thus, although women become sensitive to the needs of particular others, they do not acquire the concern for abstract, impersonal, and universal rights, which characterizes the final stage of maturity (Daly, 1989, p. 3; Naffine, 1987, pp. 115–16.)

In *In a Different Voice* (1982), Carol Gilligan, a former student of Kohlberg, challenged his conclusion that women generally operate at a lower level of moral development than do men. After all, if that were so, they would surely commit more crime than men. Gilligan then proceeded to argue that what Kohlberg had demonstrated was not the inferiority of women's moral reasoning but, rather, the masculinist bias of his theory, and of psychology as a discipline. He failed to realize that moral orientation is gender-linked. Thus, although there are two distinct moral "voices," Kohlberg's scheme recorded only one (1982, pp. 1–19).

According to Gilligan, the female moral "voice," which she calls an "ethic of responsibility," is a concrete morality that centres on care and relationships. In contrast, the male moral "voice," dubbed an "ethic of rights," is an abstract morality focussed on justice and rules. These opposing moral orientations stem from the very different experiences of girls who understand at a young age that they are like their mothers and of boys who realize that they are not, and can never be, like their mothers. Therefore, girls learn about connection and maintaining relationships, and boys about separation and respecting individual rights, and their respective moral imperatives reflect this differential socialization. Ultimately, because women are more nurturing and altruistic than are men, they are less inclined to hurt others or be deviant, as is evidenced by criminal statistics.

Although bio- and psychogenetic explanations remain

dominant among criminologists, the attempts to apply refor-mulated social-psychological theories of male deviance to female offending have been widely influential, particular-ly Gilligan's work. However, these revisionist explanations have also been the subject of much criticism (Campbell, 1981; Daly, 1989; Morris, 1987; Naffine, 1987; Smart, 1976). First, there are problems of evidence and method. For example, the results of empirical research on **role theory** and female offending are inconclusive. In no small part, this seems to reflect "conceptual imprecision": researchers cannot agree about how to define masculinity and femininity; what tests to use; nor who should be test-ed (Naffine, 1987, p. 61).

Similarly, the results from tests of **social–control theory** and female conformity are far from clear-cut. Thus, studies showing the greater social "bonding" of girls than boys have yet to unequivocally link this to either femininity or con-formity. Moreover, cumulative evidence indicating that girls with the weakest social bonds are neither stereotypically male nor stereotypically female also contradicts the picture of the undersocialized, undercontrolled female delinquent painted by Hagan, Simpson, and Gillis (Naffine, 1987, pp. 74–75).

However, probably the sharpest methodological criti-cism has been levelled at Carol Gilligan. The primary research that confirmed her theory of a distinct female moral "voice" is a set of interviews with 29 women between the ages of 15 and 33 about the ethical problem raised by the decision to abort a pregnancy and about how they would resolve several hypothetical moral dilemmas (Gilligan, 1982, pp. 71–72). But, since there is no parallel study of men's responses to similar problems, how do we know that men may not, in some circumstances, also embrace "the ethic of responsibility" (Daly, 1989)? Even more significantly, Gilligan's study provides no evidence that children follow sex-specific moral-development paths.

The other major critique directed at social-psychological theories of female offending is focussed on the two basic assumptions that underpin such explanations: namely, that differential socialization into distinct gender roles explains the greater conformity of women *vis-à-vis* men; and that the public and private spheres are completely separate. With respect to the former, many commentators do acknowledge that explanations of female criminality that focus on the social differentiation of gender roles represented a genuine break with bio- and psychogenetic theories.

At the same time, as Smart (1976) points out, such ex-planations suffer from two serious shortcomings. First, the discussion of sex-specific roles is divorced from any expla-nation of the historical, economic, and cultural factors that originally produced the sexual division of labour and wom-en's socially inferior status. Thus, social-psychological the-

ories of female deviance do not strongly combat "the prevailing belief that gender differences are 'natural' . . . [or] biologically determined" (1976, p. 69). Second, by concentrating on why women conform, differential so-cialization perspectives neglect the motivation of the not-inconsequential number who engage in crime. The very concept of poor or unsuccessful socialization that **role** and **social–control** theories offer as an explanation of female deviance suggests that women are passive objects rather than rational, intelligent architects of their actions. Moreover, it implies the existence of "a pathology existing within the individual which requires treatment" and thus reinforces a basic assumption of bio- and psychogenetic explanations of women's criminality (Smart, 1976).

Carol Gilligan has also been assailed for coming "dan-gerously close to the traditional view of the sexes—that men think and women feel" (Naffine, 1987, p. 118). Her dis-cussion of women's moral development seems to suggest that they have a "natural" inclination to be compassionate and caring. Furthermore, in contrast to other social-psychological theorists, Gilligan implies that "women have something men do not": their moral orientation is not only different but possibly even superior (Daly, 1989, p. 3). Thus, some critics say that she has simply turned Kohlberg's the-ory upside down, thereby romanticizing women rather than men.

The other basic assumption that characterizes social-psychological theories of female deviance—that there is a clear division between the public and private realms along gender lines—has been strongly denounced by feminists (Chunn & Gavigan, 1988; Daly & Chesney-Lind, 1988; Heidensohn, 1985; Smart, 1984). The notion of "separate spheres" is more ideological than real, they say, and demon-strably inadequate as an explanation of why women com-mit less crime than men. For one thing, the private realm is not a "haven" from state intervention; it has always been structured by legislation governing both intrafamilial and state-family relations, including criminal laws. Furthermore, the argument that women are primarily subject to infor-mal, familial controls, and men to public, formal ones, breaks down in the face of the evidence that shows that many women straddle both spheres (and always have).

Eventually, some researchers who were dissatisfied with social-psychological theories of female deviance began to think about developing more macro-level sociological per-spectives.

Sociological Explanations: Structural Differences

Macro-level sociological theories of female offending have emerged over the past two decades within the general context of second-wave feminism. Whether feminist or not, they all focus on the relationship between women's structural position in society and women's crime. Frieda Adler was one of the first criminologists to argue that there was a causal link between the two. Her book, *Sisters in Crime* (1975; see also Simon, 1975), presented what is now known as the **women's liberation thesis** of crime.

Adler's perspective essentially places role theory in a structural context. Her basic argument is that women's liberation leads to increases in the amount and types of female criminality. During the 1960s, she says, feminist movements in Western, industrialized countries fuelled a transformation of women's unequal status relative to that of men. On the positive side, women gained formal equality and legal rights, which gave them parity with men in ev-

ery area of social life, but particularly within the occupational structure.

As this trend toward equality unfolded, however, women also began to catch up to men in negative ways. Thus, according to Adler, the down side of women's liberation is the "new female criminal" who, having abandoned her traditional sex role and become more assertive, aggressive, and "masculine," is fast overtaking her male counterpart in both the amount and type of crime being committed. As Adler puts it (1975, p. 15), "like her legitimate based sister, the female criminal knows too much to pretend, or return to her former role as a second-rate criminal confined to 'feminine' crimes such as shoplifting and prostitution." Thus, the "liberated female crook" is perpetrating dramatically more "street crime," particularly serious, vio-

---

Box 11.5 Women Turning to Violent Crime: More Than Ever Before Being Jailed for Slayings, Robbery, Assault

More female offenders than ever before are being incarcerated for manslaughter, armed robbery, wounding and assault, corrections officials say.

Some say this new breed of female offender is a sign of the times and officials fear the violent woman boom in the United States in the last 10 years could be heading our way.

According to information recently compiled by the Justice Department, the number of female criminals is growing at a faster rate than males.

Over the last decade, the number of women charged has grown to 12 percent from nine percent of accused. The number of violent crimes among women in the same period rose also, to 9.5 percent from eight percent.

At the Portage Correctional Centre for Women, 13 of the 35 women incarcerated there last week were in for violent crimes. Twelve women were incarcerated for break and enters, shoplifting and other property crimes.

Last winter, the growth in the number of female offenders was felt in Portage for the first time as the number of women behind bars swelled to 55. Portage has a capacity for about 35 to 40 women.

"It was chaotic," says Wayne Bott, assistant superintendent of the Portage la Prairie centre. "In the six years I have been here, I've never seen it that high."

Bott said there has been a surge in the past few years in the number of women incarcerated for violent crimes.

"We've seen a drastic increase in our institution," he said. "We have women in here from sexual assault caus-

ing bodily harm, armed robbery to murder."

"At one time to have a woman in here for manslaughter was a rarity. . ."

Psychologists such as Dr. Lawrence Breen, associate professor at the University of Manitoba, said the increase in violent female offenders comes with changing sexual roles.

As women strive to become equal with men, he said they glean the bad characteristics with the good.

"Women are adopting the unfortunate characteristics identified with males and therefore we have an increasing involvement with women in crime," Breen said.

Although violent crimes among women are on the increase, Breen said they are nowhere near the instances among men.

"Women have a long way to go to catch up to males," he said.

"But then I don't care if I was stabbed by a 115-pound female or a 250-pound male, I'd still be dead."

Hans Schneider, Manitoba's Corrections Commissioner, said he is surprised there hasn't been a more significant increase in the incidence of female violence. "Women have become less sheltered," he said.

"They lead less sheltered lives and are less sheltered from their own compulsions. It's obvious the opportunity has become greater for crime."

Source: Catherine Clark, *Winnipeg Free Press*, June 23, 1983, pp. 1,4.

lent offences, than ever before (see Box 11.5). At the same time, women are taking advantage of their "vocational liberation" and upward mobility in the workplace to engage in white-collar crime (1975, p. 167).

As evidence, Adler (1975, pp. 16–18) cited data from case studies and from the FBI Uniform Crime Reports between 1960 and 1972, which showed dramatic percentage increases in the number of women arrested for robbery, embezzlement, larceny, and burglary compared with increases in the number of male arrests. However, subsequent research on the liberation thesis is contradictory. On the one hand, some analyses apparently support Adler's hypothesis. For example, a Canadian time-series study (a statistical analysis of a particular phenomenon over time to determine any variation or change) (Fox & Hartnagel, 1979) linked changes in women's structural position in society from the early 1930s to the late 1960s—specifically, their growing participation in extrafamilial roles—with increases in female conviction rates for property crime. Similarly, a recent analysis of convicted women robbers in Quebec revealed no significant differences with their male counterparts (Girouard, 1988).

In contrast, Adler has many critics, particularly among feminists, who argue convincingly that the women's liberation thesis of crime is refuted by reality (Box & Hale, 1983; Gavigan, 1983; Heidensohn, 1985; Morris, 1987; Naffine, 1987; Smart, 1979). First, they point out that most contemporary women, including offenders, have not abandoned the stereotypical, female sex role and become "competitive, masculine and aggressive" (Naffine, 1987, p. 93). Adler's contention that women's liberation is now the motive for female criminality simply does not stand up to empirical examination. On the contrary, the existing research indicates that, far from being feminists, women who commit crime today are very similar to their predecessors—perhaps even "more conservative and traditional in their attitudes toward women" than comparable nonoffenders (Widom, 1981, p. 38; see also Adelberg & Currie, 1987; Bertrand, 1969; Box, 1983; Carlen, 1985; Heidensohn, 1985; Walford, 1983). Indeed, one study found that girls with feminist attitudes were less likely to engage in delinquent acts (Morris, 1987, p. 71).

Second, critics reject Adler's assertion that women have "made it." Despite the feminist movement, the majority of women have not achieved true (e.g., substantive) equality with men in any sphere, including the criminal one. They remain in a position of structural inequality. Thus, most contemporary female offenders continue to engage in the same types of petty, nonviolent "street crime" that they always have. As statistics reveal, they are not committing noticeably more of the traditional "masculine" crimes against the person and property, particularly those involving serious violence. And, they are certainly not perpetrating proportionately more offences such as embezzlement, which are tied to upward mobility in the occupational structure (Heidensohn, 1985; Naffine, 1987; Smart, 1979). For example, in contrast to the earlier Canadian study (Fox & Hartnagel, 1979), which supported Adler's thesis, Box and Hale (1983) concluded on the basis of a similar British investigation that women's offending from the early 1950s to the late 1970s was more reflective of their "economic marginalisation" than greater employment opportunities.

Furthermore, women's criminal activity has not skyrocketed since the 1960s, as Adler would have us believe. Her use of percentages to compare changes in the amount of crime committed by women and men is very misleading because the base numbers for female offenders are much smaller, making increases or decreases appear dramatically greater than they really are. Moreover, if we look at male and female crime rates over the past 30 years in various Western countries, we discover that women offenders are far from achieving parity with their male counterparts (Box & Hale, 1983; Heidensohn, 1985; Johnson, 1986, 1987; Smart, 1979).

But if the "liberated female crook" is a myth, how do Adler's critics account for the real increase in women's offending since the 1960s, also revealed by official statistics? A number have argued that recorded crime tells us more about the decision making of enforcement agents than about the amount of criminal activity. Although the feminist movement has not produced a new breed of woman offender, then, perhaps it has changed "the consciousness and perceptions of the police, social workers, magistrates, judges and others, who may well interpret female behaviour in the light of the belief that women are becoming more 'liberated'" (Smart, 1979, p. 57). Thus, changes in the number of women charged, convicted, or incarcerated since the 1960s could stem more from a new attitude among enforcement personnel—"if it's equality they want, we'll see that they get it" (Chesney-Lind, 1980, pp. 14–15)—than from a rise in the actual amount of female criminality.

It is hardly surprising that feminists take especially strong exception to Adler's equation of women's liberation and increased criminality. At the same time, their analyses of criminal law have tended to focus more on women as victims than offenders (Boyle et al., 1985; Daly & Chesney-Lind, 1988). Nonetheless, a few feminist writers have begun the task of developing alternate explanations of female offending, all of which point to women's structural subordination in society as the root of both their criminality and their conformity. In short, the powerlessness of women is strongly linked to the way they act (Adelberg & Currie, 1987; Hanmer & Maynard, 1987; Heidensohn, 1985; Hutter & Williams, 1981; Lahey, 1989; Naffine, 1987; Smart, 1976; Smart & Smart, 1978).

These recent examples of the **feminist perspective** can be divided into two general types, according to how they explain the structural subordination of women. The first has many similarities with the **conflict approach** (see Introduction). It points to **patriarchy**, or male domination, which is based on men's control over women's sexuality and reproduction, as the source of female oppression throughout history. Thus, adherents argue that women as a group have always been, and continue to be, controlled through patriarchal structures, including law, that men as a group create and operate in their own interests. In short, men have power and they act to maintain it (Hanmer & Maynard, 1987; Heidensohn, 1985; Lahey, 1989).

Although only a minority of women ever face criminal charges, then, all women are subject to controls (Hutter & Williams, 1981, Ch. 1). Indeed, according to some feminists, men control women primarily through means other than criminalization. Perhaps the most important one is fear. The constant threat, and frequently the reality, of

male violence in the form of either sexual harassment (see Box 11.6) or sexual and physical assault intimidates most women into silent conformity. They realize from a very early age the price of questioning their inferior status (Hanmer & Maynard, 1987; Kasinsky, 1978).

Nonetheless, some women do challenge the patriarchal *status quo* by behaving in ways that are not consistent with their position of structural subordination. For the most part, they attack male dominance indirectly by expressing dissatisfaction with aspects of their own lives such as the lack of opportunity or the sexual and physical abuse inflicted upon them by men. The common response is a medical one that treats the woman as the problem and tries to modify her behaviour. Thus, the causes of that behaviour are ignored, and women's concerns trivialized (Hanmer & Maynard, 1987, Ch. 8; Smart, 1976, Ch. 6; Smart & Smart, 1978, Ch. 3).

Psychiatrists play a particularly prominent part in controlling women. While the latter have no greater propensity toward mental illness than do men, they are much likelier to receive a psychiatric label. If a woman is defined

---

Box 11.6 Survey Reports SFU Rife with Sexual Harassment

Fifty-three per cent of the respondents to a campus-wide survey of female students at Simon Fraser University reported being sexually harassed in educational settings on campus, an SFU ad hoc committee on sexual harassment says.

The results were even higher with graduate students, with 61 per cent complaining of some form of sexual harassment.

In a 26-page submission to university president William Saywell, the committee recommends that SFU hire a sexual harassment complaint officer, draw up a sexual harassment policy and open an office to deal with the large number of complaints on campus.

The committee, which had representatives from student, faculty, staff and administration, said the lack of any policy has meant years of undocumented harassment cases on campus, leaving women with the feeling they have nowhere to go if they are being victimized.

"We're not saying that no one can ever smile or wink at anyone again," committee chairman Rev. Barbara Blakely said Thursday. "It's when the advance is unwanted, when there's an element of force, then it's harassment."

The survey, conducted through a four-page questionnaire filled out by students, found the most common form

of harassment was discriminatory remarks, with 33 per cent of the 444 respondents complaining they had such an experience in a classroom setting.

Eleven per cent said they had experienced "advances suggesting sexual intimacy." Four per cent said they had been sexually assaulted. Two women reported they had been abducted, while two reported they had suffered physical injury as a result of refusing sexual contact.

Undergraduate students said that most often another student was bothering them, while graduate students said the harassment came mostly from faculty.

Some students said they had been threatened with lower marks or other reprisals for not complying with requests for sexual intimacy.

Yet in the whole survey, only 10 women said they had reported what happened to them to some university authority.

SFU president Saywell said today the committee's recommendations would provide a very major input into the university's development of a policy on sexual harassment.

Source: Kim Dolan, *Vancouver Sun*, February 20, 1987, p.A3.

as "sick," her perceptions of reality are no longer valid. A doctor can then prescribe treatments that will re-establish compliance with a code of behaviour consistent with her inferior status. Resistance to treatment simply elicits more radical modes of psychiatric control, including long-term hospitalization, electroconvulsive therapy, and leucotomy (Hanmer & Maynard, 1987, Ch. 8; Smart, 1976, Ch. 6; Smart & Smart, 1978, Ch. 3).

In general, criminalization is the control mechanism reserved for the few women who are not constrained by fear and medicalization, that is, those who directly attack male power. Historically, men have frequently used criminal law against women who attempt to assert control over their own reproduction and sexuality. Thus, women who make autonomous decisions about their bodies with respect to contraception, abortion, or selling sex have been, and still are in many cases, subject to criminal **sanction** (Lahey, 1989, pp. 104–7). Similarly, female victims of male power who fight back are often prosecuted as criminals. For example, as later discussion will reveal, many women who kill their spouses after long-time physical and mental abuse find themselves being further victimized by a criminal-justice system that represents male interests (Browne, 1987).

In *Women, Crime and Criminology* (1976), her classic critique of traditional theories, Carol Smart laid the foundations for a second type of structural feminist perspective on female offending, upon which other researchers have subsequently expanded (Carlen, 1987; Daly & Chesney-Lind, 1988; Gavigan, 1983, 1988; Greenwood, 1981; Gregory, 1986). This emergent perspective, which has some parallels with developments in contemporary **critical legal studies** (Bottomley, Gibson, & Meteyard, 1987), is based on several assumptions that distinguish it from the conflict-control perspective discussed above. First, Smart and her successors argue that it is impossible to construct a monocausal, universally applicable, and trans-historical theory of female criminality or of women's subordination more generally. Explanations of both must be historically and culturally specific (Chunn & Gavigan, 1988; Gavigan, 1983; Greenwood, 1981; Smart, 1976, Ch. 7).

In short, **patriarchy** has assumed different forms over time, and these are related to distinct types of state and of law. Today, for example, most Canadian women continue to occupy an inferior status despite the fact that they are formally equal to men in law. At the same time, however, their position is hardly the same as that of their counterparts a century ago when women were nonpersons with few legal rights (Bacchi, 1983; see also Brophy & Smart, 1985, Ch. 1).

Furthermore, even countries that are generally similar have unique aspects that must be considered in any analysis of women's inequality. Contemporary Canada and England are both liberal democracies, yet they do not have identical types of state and legal institutions. The former is a two-level state where the federal government has complete power to enact criminal law but the provinces can implement quasi-criminal statutes (e.g., welfare, traffic, liquor) and, moreover, are responsible for the administration of the courts (see Chapter 2). The latter is a unitary state where only the national government can implement criminal law and oversee the courts. Thus, Canadian and English legal institutions may quite likely help perpetuate women's structured inequality in somewhat different ways.

Feminists who emphasize the importance of historical and cultural specificity make another assumption that differentiates them from their conflict-control counterparts. While in agreement that the "particular condition of women requires a specific form of analysis" (Greenwood, 1981, p. 76), they also maintain that gender, considered in isolation from factors of social class and race/ethnicity, cannot provide a complete explanation of female criminality and women's inequality. Thus, a structural feminist analysis of either must look at the interaction and relative importance of social class, gender, and race/ethnicity, as well as the images and ideologies associated with them (Carlen, 1987; Daly & Chesney-Lind, 1988; Eaton, 1986; Edwards, 1985; Gavigan, 1983, 1988).

In contrast to conflict-control feminists, then, Smart and her successors argue that men and women do not constitute homogeneous and opposing groups. Thus, although gender divisions are important, the similarities between women and men as well as the differences among women and among men must be addressed to explain criminality. For example, research indicates that the male and female offenders who make up official criminal statistics have much in common. They are typically marginal individuals who have failed the tests of "normality" in a given society at a particular time.

Thus, in liberal democracies such as England, Canada, and the United States, "normal" people are those who make the requisite class, gender, and/or racial/ethnic "deals" (Carlen, 1987). That is, they meet middle-class, white standards. Those least able to do so are the "triple failures"—poor, nonwhite women and, second, poor, nonwhite men. It is hardly surprising, then, that they are so markedly overrepresented in criminal statistics (Greenwood, 1981, p. 81; Johnson, 1986, 1987).

Nonetheless, as we know, women commit far less crime than do men. However, in contrast to conflict-control feminists, Smart and her successors argue that the primary reason for this is linked to the sexual division of labour, which designates women as caregivers and helpmates and men as providers within a nuclear-family unit (Smart, 1984). As a result, women are both economically and psychologically dependent upon men. Moreover, women's inequality is perpetuated not only inside the family but also outside, in the workplace, where many work at so-called pink-ghetto jobs, often part-time, for much less pay than men in comparable positions.

At the same time, millions of women actively pursue and willingly enter into a dependency relationship (e.g., marriage) without thinking of it as such. Thus, they may recognize their structured inequality *vis-à-vis* men only when such relationships break down (Smart, 1984). Perhaps, then, for some women who do not have a male provider, or have little chance of finding one, crime becomes a rational option. Indeed, the increase in women's property crime over the last two decades could well be linked to what has been called the "feminization of poverty" (Box & Hale, 1983; Gregory, 1986). For example, the liberalization of Canadian divorce law in the 1960s was followed, during the 1970s, by provincial family-law reforms that

granted wives formal legal equality with their husbands. However, since most women remained economically unequal to men, the soaring divorce rate has produced a huge rise in the number of single-parent families, the majority of whom are female-headed. Clearly, shoplifting, welfare fraud, and prostitution (see Box 11.7) are rational acts from the perspective of economically marginal women who want to feed their children and keep their families together (Baxter, 1988).

Overall, despite their trenchant critiques of traditional criminological theories, feminists have yet to provide any systematic alternative explanations of female criminality. However, they have convincingly responded to those who argue that theories of crime do not need to focus on gender because women criminals constitute such a tiny number (Daly & Chesney-Lind, 1988, p. 131). We turn now to a consideration of what happens to the women who do face criminal charges.

Box 11.7 Racism Thriving in Nova Scotia, Welfare Recipients Tell Conference

When Halifax single mother Terry Garrison could not feed her family of four on social assistance, she became a prostitute.

When that didn't work, she turned to forging cheques and spent 20 days in jail. Two of her children were placed in foster homes.

"This is not living," she said, choking back tears as she told her story to a convention of social workers yesterday. "This is just existing in a trap. I keep hoping for a way out so I don't have to lie, cheat and steal."

Ms Garrison's story was one of several painful tales told by welfare recipients and low-income workers at a conference sponsored by the federal Department of Health and Welfare and the City of Halifax.

While the social workers are debating new ways of dealing with the growing numbers of people relying on public assistance, the recipients are talking about survival. They believe that social assistance payments are woefully inadequate and that the rest of society looks down on them.

Suzanne Murray said she had to borrow clothes from friends and relatives to attend the conference because she cannot afford to both buy clothing and support her five children on $1023 she gets each month in public assistance.

"I'm not on welfare to take advantage of the system," she said. "I'm just not qualified to get a position that will pay me enough to support my children and meet their basic needs. . . . It's very humiliating to have to tell people I'm on welfare. In a rich country like this, things like this just shouldn't be."

Linda Randolph, a black single mother of two children, said black children are victims of racism in a Nova Scotia that leaves them without any role models.

"They look at the labor force and there is little visibility of blacks. Those they see working are cleaners . . . racism is alive and well in Nova Scotia. It may be covert but it is there," said Ms Randolph, who has a university degree but works at a low-paying job without pension or other benefits.

Another black woman, Liona Crawley, told the meeting that while politicians boast that Halifax's unemployment rate has fallen to 7 per cent, "in black communities we have 75 to 80 per cent unemployment. Racism is rampant."

Peter Harrington, head of a welfare rights group in Halifax, argued that the welfare system must be dismantled and reformed.

"We have people in this province living in extreme hell, without enough food in the fridge to feed their children," he said. "This conference has to take the system and rip it up . . . and rebuild it."

Source: Kevin Cox, *Globe and Mail*, October 4, 1988, p. A10.

Women, Criminal Law, and Criminal Justice

The debate about why a relatively small number of women engage in crime is linked to another dispute in the literature about whether criminal law and the administration of criminal justice are gender-based, and thus discriminatory. Although the question of legal bias with respect to the poor and/or racial/ethnic minorities has long concerned researchers, only very recently did they begin to focus on the issue of whether female offenders are treated more leniently or more severely than are their male counterparts. Nonetheless, a substantial literature on gender bias and criminal justice now exists in which three major positions on this question are advanced: the chivalry-paternalism thesis; the double-standard thesis; and the law-as-ideology thesis.

The Chivalry-Paternalism Thesis

Otto Pollak (1961; see also Moulds, 1980) was among the first criminologists to argue that the female offender is treated more leniently than her male equivalent because she benefits from the operation of chivalry. Men, he concluded, are naturally inclined to be protective or paternalistic toward women. Consequently, male lawmakers and enforcers, as well as men victimized by women, are all supposedly loath to invoke the criminal law against female offenders. Thus, the latter are much more likely than men to be processed informally, outside the justice system, when they commit crimes. This chivalrous attitude is ultimately reflected in the statistics, which reveal that women are reported to and charged by police much less often than are men. Furthermore, when female offenders are brought before the courts, they are convicted less often and receive lighter sentences vis-à-vis their male counterparts, particularly with respect to incarceration.

Looking at Canada, we immediately discover a problem: the compilation of comprehensive national court data ceased in 1968 and the subsequent collection of information on criminal convictions and sentences for all provinces except Alberta and Quebec continued only until 1972. Nonetheless, the available crime statistics can easily be cited in support of the thesis that women are treated more leniently than are men at all stages of the criminal-justice process. As previous discussion indicated, for example, the Canadian Urban Victimization Survey (Canada, 1983–88) revealed that, in cases involving nonlethal violence, specifically assault and robbery, victims reported to police less often when the perpetrator was a woman. Moreover, an examination of specific reasons for not reporting an incident to the police shows that victims of female offenders were more likely than victims of male perpetrators to say

that they wished to protect the offender and/or that it was a personal matter (Johnson, 1986, p. 32).

Similarly, some studies of both young and adult offenders indicate that the police and the courts have traditionally been more disposed toward informal treatment of girls and women than of boys and men, an inclination which partly explains the sizable gender gap in official delinquency and crime statistics (Canada, 1969, pp. 390–91; Chunn, 1990; Hatch & Faith, 1990). And, available data on conviction shows that female accused are less likely than are male accused to be convicted of violent offences, particularly those against property. Over the five-year period between 1968 and 1972, for example, 75 percent of all women, compared with 90 percent of all men, charged with violent property offences were convicted (Canada, 1977b, pp. 13–15).

With respect to sentencing, male offenders have historically received harsher dispositions on average than have their female counterparts (Canada, 1969, p. 396). Thus, while the corporal punishment of convicted women was abandoned by 1850 (Cooper, 1987), the penalty was still being applied to men in the late 1960s (Canada, 1969, pp. 207–8). Today, despite the lack of comprehensive annual statistics on the operation of Canadian courts, the existing data indicate that women are still subject to less severe sentences overall than are men, being much more likely to avoid incarceration. For example, over a twelve-year period beginning in 1960, an increasing proportion of female, as opposed to male, offenders convicted of indictable offences received fines so that, by 1972, one of every two women, compared with one of every three men, was fined (Boyle et al., 1985, pp. 128–9). Another study of the years between 1968 and 1972 showed a similar pattern of apparent leniency: 85 percent of women, compared to 58 percent of men, convicted of indictable offences received a noncustodial disposition (Adams, 1978, pp. 28–33; see also Canada, 1977b, pp. 16–22).

Available data reveal a continuation of the same sentencing trend through the 1970s and 1980s. Statistics on convictions in selected judicial districts for 1978, 1979, and 1980, compiled by the Canadian Centre for Justice Statistics, show that more than 80 percent of women convicted under the Criminal Code or federal statutes over the three-year period were given a noninstitutional **disposition**. Specifically, one of every two convicted women was fined, and one out of three was placed on probation (Boyle et al., 1985, p. 129). Moreover, as Table 11.4 tells us, a growing proportion of all probation admissions in Canada are women. Whereas, in 1978–79, they comprised 14 percent of total admissions, by 1987–88, women accounted for 18 percent.

Turning to the total correctional institutional population over time, we find further evidence of apparent lenien-

Table 11.4 Number of Admissions[1] to Probation, Provincial Custody, and Federal Custody, and Percent[2] Female, 1978–79 to 1987–88

	Probation Total No.	% Female	Provincial Custody Total No.	% Female	Federal Custody Total No.	% Female
1978/79	48 293	14	82 084	6	4866	3
1979/80	50 394	13	93 644	5	4602	2
1980/81	54 511	14	103 788	6	4787	2
1981/82	66 245	16	112 458	6		
1982/83	65 550	16	131 291	6	4080	2
1983/84	63 567	17	129 748	6	4059	2
1984/85	62 986	17	123 771	6	3956	2
1985/86	54 838	17	119 299	7	4076	3
1986/87	52 749	17	116 269	6	3741	2
1987/88	53 521	18	117 374	7	3988	2

[1]Figures for custodial admissions exclude transfers, lock-ups, and remanded prisoners.
[2]Percentage figures are rounded.

Source: Statistics Canada, *Adult correctional services in Canada*. Ottawa: Canadian Centre for Justice Statistics, for the years 1980–81, 1985–86, and 1987–88; Canada Year Book (1985), Table 20.12.

cy in the sentencing of female offenders. During the period from 1960 to 1972, the percentage of prison terms handed down to women dropped sharply from 21.9 to 11.5 percent of all sentences imposed on female offenders, but the percentage of convicted men sentenced to prison declined only slightly, from 36 percent to 32 percent (Boyle et al., 1985, pp. 128–29). When we differentiate between provincial and federal sentences, data for the years between 1968 and 1972 reveal that only 13 percent of convicted women, compared with 36 percent of convicted men, ended up in provincial institutions, while 1 and 6 percent, respectively, served penitentiary terms (Adams, 1978, pp. 28–33). Since the early 1970s, the male-female ratio for inmates admitted to Canadian jails and penitentiaries has narrowed (Adams, 1978, p. 41; Canada, 1969, p. 391). However, as Table 11.4 reveals (see also Adams, 1978, p. 41; Johnson, 1986, p. 40), this trend has not led to a dramatic increase in the proportion of inmates who are women. They consistently made up 6 or 7 percent of provincial admissions and about 2 percent of the total penitentiary population between 1978–79 and 1987–88.

Moreover, when we compare *rates* of incarceration under federal sentence per 100 000 male and female population, the differences between men and women become even sharper. Data for the period between 1975 and 1984 reveal that the women's rate showed almost no change during those years, while the men's rate rose from 37.4 to 47.0 per 100 000 over the decade. Stated another way: the rate of incarceration under federal sentence, which was already 40 times greater for men than women in 1975, had be-

come 50 times greater by 1984 (Johnson, 1986, p. 42).

So far as release from custody is concerned, the scanty information available suggests that women prisoners are more likely than men to be granted temporary absences (TAs). For example, between July 1976 and September 1980, female inmates at the Prison for Women in Kingston received 7497 group and single TAs, while the totals accorded their counterparts in the nine male maximum-security penitentiaries for the same period ranged from a low of 190 to a high of 1523 (Canada, 1981). Women also serve less time than men because the former are more likely to be released on parole and the latter under mandatory supervision (Statistics Canada, 1979). One study commissioned by the federal Ministry of the Solicitor General found that female prisoners under federal sentence who became eligible for **parole** between 1980 and 1983 had a 50 percent greater chance of receiving a full parole than did male prisoners during the same period (Hann & Harman, 1986). If only first-time penitentiary inmates are considered, the parole release rate was 64 percent for women, as opposed to 47 percent for men. Similarly, women had higher release rates than men for all offence categories except robbery and break-and-enter (Hann & Harman, 1986).

Proponents of the **chivalry-paternalism thesis** also point to the emergence and utilization of certain sex-specific offences and criminal defences that have resulted in reduced sentences for women, particularly in cases involving serious violence. For example, the special offence of infanticide in the Criminal Code stipulates that the maximum sentence for women who kill their infant children by reason of post-partum depression is five years' imprisonment. This is very lenient relative to the maximum sentences for first- and second-degree murder or manslaughter faced by men who kill babies. Moreover, in practice, women charged with infanticide are often acquitted and serve no sentence at all (see Box 11.8). One study of women who were prosecuted in nineteenth-century Ontario revealed that the accused was more likely to go free than be convicted, even when she admitted guilt (Backhouse, 1984).

A contemporary analysis of child abuse and neglect (CAN) deaths in Ontario between 1973 and 1982 found a similar pattern. Of eleven women charged with infanticide, only two received a penal disposition, and neither was sentenced to more than two years' imprisonment (Greenland, 1988). Moreover, a comparison of the 37 women and 32 men who were prosecuted for CAN deaths suggested that, overall, the former faced less serious charges, were more likely to receive a nonpenal disposition, and received shorter prison terms when convicted of homicide and manslaughter than did the latter.

Very recently, sex-specific or status defences such as premenstrual syndrome (PMS) and the battered-wife syndrome (BWS) have also been used to the advantage of female defendants. Although Canadian law does not yet recognize PMS as a cause of diminished responsibility, defence counsel in a number of cases have pointed to the "syndrome" as the chief reason for their clients' criminal behaviour, and some judges have given direct consideration to PMS in the sentencing of female offenders. The 1987 case of *R. v. Edwards* (unreported) set a precedent for the use of premenstrual syndrome as a mitigating factor in the disposition of women who commit violent crimes (see Box 11.9). However, a PMS plea appears to have indirectly influenced judicial decision making in some earlier Canadian cases. For example, although he did not accept PMS as a disease, an Alberta provincial court judge acquitted a Calgary woman charged with shoplifting in 1984 because she was "irrational" and not capable of forming the intent to commit a criminal act (Fennell, 1984).

Recently, in the precedent-setting case of *Regina v. Lavallee* (unreported; see also Comack, 1988), a Canadian trial court accepted the "battered wife syndrome" as a means of establishing self-defence. After enduring long-time abuse from her common-law husband, Angelique Lavallee killed him after he handed her a loaded rifle and dared her to shoot at him. Although charged with second-degree murder, Lavallee was ultimately acquitted following a trial where her lawyer used psychiatric evidence to reveal how the BWS applied to his client, and the judge referred to the syndrome in his charge to the jury. Subsequently, the Manitoba Court of Appeal, with one Justice dissenting, overturned the verdict and ordered a new trial (*R. v. Lavallee*, 1988), but the Supreme Court of Canada later unanimously upheld the acquittal of Lavallee. This judgment clearly enhanced the legitimacy of BWS as a sex-specific criminal defence in Canada.

Assuming that the chivalry-paternalism thesis is correct, what accounts for the seeming leniency toward women *vis-à-vis* their male counterparts. First of all, the widespread assumption that female offenders are "sick" or pathological individuals acting on irrational impulses may work to their advantage; that is, they are viewed as "double

---

Box 11.8 *Regina v. Smith* (1976), Cummings, D.C.J., Newfoundland:

Reviewing the evidence of this very sad case I find an atmosphere of unreality that would not preclude an irrational act by the accused without consideration of consequences. She contended throughout that she did not know she was pregnant and her contention is supported to an extent by the fact the members of her family did not know and certainly took no steps to prepare her for the birth of the child. She was only 17 years of age and had just come through the traumatic experience of an unassisted child birth. Her little brother shared the bed with her at the time. When the mother pulled down the bed clothes and revealed a bed full of blood and the body of the baby, the accused irrationally denied she had had a baby. She maintained throughout her sole purpose in putting her hand over the baby's face was to prevent it from crying and if she did tell Mrs. Pardy she put her hand over the throat, which she denies, she still stated the purpose was to prevent the baby from crying.

Considering all the evidence against the background of a disturbed mind, I have a reasonable doubt the act of the accused in causing the death of her child was willful. I therefore dismiss the charge of infanticide.

I have considered the included offence of concealing the dead body of a child under [then] s.227. I am satisfied there is insufficient evidence to substantiate that offence.

The accused is acquitted and the case dismissed. (p. 232)

Box 11.9 Women's Syndrome Brings Leniency

LONDON, Ont.—A woman who stabbed her husband in the back last year while suffering from premenstrual syndrome was placed on probation Monday because she couldn't get proper treatment in a correctional institution.

District Court Judge Joseph Winter suspended sentencing Marsali Edwards, 29, for three years.

"For what I am about to do, I am of course going to be severely criticized," Judge Winter said before passing sentence.

But he warned that his decision should not be viewed as a license for other women to repeat Edwards' actions.

Winter also ordered her to report regularly to a probation officer and to undergo treatment by a "competent, appropriate, knowledgeable medical practitioner other than a psychiatrist."

The case establishes a precedent in Canadian law for the use of premenstrual syndrome as a mitigating factor in sentencing people charged with violent crime.

The disorder, which experts say affects 20 to 40 per cent of women, has been blamed for a wide range of symptoms, including hostility, anxiety and depression to food cravings, acne and changes in hair texture.

It has been used in a few cases in the United States to win acquittals.

Source: Canadian Press, *Vancouver Sun*, February 10, 1987, p. B7.

---

deviants"—both mad and bad—a perception strongly related to the nature of much female criminality. For example, women shoplifters are frequently depicted as PMS-propelled kleptomaniacs. Similarly, women who kill their children are often deemed to be mentally ill because it seems inconceivable that a "normal" mother would commit such an act (Rosenblatt & Greenland, 1974; Silverman & Kennedy, 1987; see also Allen, 1987a, 1987b). Thus, although legally guilty of a crime, they are found not morally culpable and the result is less severe treatment than a comparable male offender would receive (see Box 11.10).

A second factor which may lead to lenient treatment of women accused is the common perception of them as either helpless victims or unwilling accomplices of men. Over the past few years, for example, some women who killed their spouses after suffering long-time physical abuse have been acquitted or given noncustodial sentences, even when the homicide was not a response to an actual assault by the man. Similarly, when men and women commit crimes together, the former are generally viewed as the planners and implementers and the latter as passive, even reluctant, participants who are therefore less accountable for their actions.

The Double-Standard Thesis

Not everyone is convinced by the chivalry-paternalism thesis. Indeed, many feminists argue that exactly the opposite is true. Both in the past and at the present time, they maintain, those who enact and enforce the criminal law are predominantly men. Thus, criminal law and its administration must necessarily reflect and support the interests of men, thereby contributing directly to the ongoing subordination of women (Lahey, 1985, 1989). Inevitably, then, female offenders are subjected to sexist and discriminatory treatment relative to the treatment given their male counterparts (Chesney-Lind, 1986; NAWL, 1987).

Like the advocates of the chivalry thesis, Canadian proponents of the **double-standard thesis** rely on the available, and demonstrably incomplete, statistical data to support their position that women offenders are treated more harshly than are men. They begin by emphasizing how these data reveal a clear increase in the female conviction rate over time (Adams, 1978; Canada, 1969, pp. 472–74) so that, by the late 1960s, women were no less likely to be convicted than were their male counterparts. For example, during a five-year period from 1968 to 1972, the overall rate for both men and women was 88 percent (Canada, 1977b, p. 13). Moreover, the ratio of men to women convicted of the more serious indictable offences, which ranged from 13:1 to 17:1 during the 1950s, dropped markedly to 7:1 by 1966 and to 5:1 by 1977 (Adams, 1978, p. 26; Canada, 1969, p. 389); Canada, 1977a, p. 15).

Proponents of the double-standard thesis also point out that, while infanticide carries a lesser penalty than murder, mothers who kill their babies are not automatically handled under section 233. The Crown makes the final decision about what the charge will be in such cases (Boyle et al., 1985). More importantly, women accused generally face less serious charges and have shorter criminal histories than do men. Therefore, the statistics showing that convicted female offenders are more likely than males to receive a noncustodial disposition or, if incarcerated, to be released on full parole, do not reflect chivalry-paternalism toward the former but, rather, legal differences with respect to seriousness of offence and prior record (Adams, 1978, pp. 28–33; Boyle et al., 1985; Johnson, 1986). Although there is little Canadian data about convicted women offenders who are not incarcerated, we can see these legal differences by examining the available statistical information on men and women under federal sentence.

In relation to major offences, for example, a greater proportion of men than women are serving prison terms for the most serious crimes of violence. Women, however, are much more likely than are men to enter prison for violations of federal drug statutes. Thus, over a ten-year period from 1975 to 1984, violent crimes, including robbery, accounted for 44 percent of male and 37 percent of female admissions under federal sentence, but women were

---

Box 11.10 "I Wanted My Baby to Live," Killer-Mom Tells Court

SAINT JOHN N.B.—"I just feel bad that the baby hasn't had a chance in life," a sobbing Darlene Evelyn Alexander said as she was sentenced Friday to two years in prison for manslaughter in the death of her three-month-old baby.

"I was crying. I wanted my baby to be living . . . . "

With those words, the tiny 23-year-old woman from Bonny River, N.B., lost her family and freedom, but ended years of abuse by her husband.

Her common-law husband, Merton Walsh, told Court of Queen's Bench he couldn't remember how many times he had spit on her and slapped her.

"Whatever happened, happened as a result of frustrations, fear and anger," Justice Turney Jones said in a courtroom crowded with Alexander's tearful neighbours and social workers.

But the sentence had to "reflect society's revulsion at the loss of human life."

Jones also sentenced Alexander to two years' probation to help her get support and psychiatric treatment.

Last December, Alexander, who was seven-months pregnant with her third child, pleaded guilty to manslaughter. Her infant son, Jay, had died next to her in a car bed from a skull fracture after she threw a glass baby bottle at him last June.

She said she had been scared the baby's crying would wake Walsh and cause him to beat their two-year-old son. At the time they were staying at Walsh's mother's home on Grand Manan where he was starting a new job.

Sentencing was delayed to allow Alexander to give birth.

"It's one of the most tragic cases we'll ever see," said defence lawyer David Lutz. "This is a woman virtually destroyed."

Alexander gave up her new baby, a boy, for adoption earlier this month and Walsh has custody of the other son.

The woman and her former husband took the stand Friday because Lutz and Crown prosecutor Randy DiPaolo wanted the judge to hear their versions of what happened.

In a shaky voice, Alexander told the court how frightened she was of her husband on the morning she killed her baby. A woman who sheltered her after she was charged gave her a defiant thumbs-up sign from the front row.

"I was afraid of him; he made the room echo," Alexander said, describing the sounds Walsh made when he used to spank their older son until he stopped crying.

She said that during their relationship, Walsh pushed her, spit at her and shoved her around, especially after drinking binges. Once he broke their car window with a chainsaw when she refused to give him the car keys, and then he threw the saw at her.

During her pregnancy with Jay, she said Walsh only let her go to the doctor once and made her lug water to their home. A week after the baby was born, she said he forced her to have sex with him.

"I told him I was too sore," she said, crying.

"I thought I loved him. He didn't love me, he just wanted me to look after the house. He pushed me under the counter when I wouldn't go get water."

After one beating, she tried to call a shelter for battered women but Walsh "tore the phone out of the wall," she told the court.

Walsh, grinning ruefully at one point, told the court he admitted "some of the bad stuff. But we had good times, too."

He said he loved his children and helped Alexander with housework, doing quite a bit of cooking and often walking their eldest son to sleep late at night.

He said he probably called her a "fat, lazy bitch" on occasion and admitted telling her "stop laying around, it's time to get up" a couple of days after she came home with baby Jay.

Source: Canadian Press, *Vancouver Sun*, February 25, 1989, p. B16.

Table 11.5   Aggregate Sentence Length of Male and Female Inmates Under Federal Sentence[1], 1975 to 1984

Length of Aggregate Sentence	1975 M	%	F	%	1984 M	%	F	%	1975–1984 TOTALS M	%	F	%
Less than 2 years	472	12.3	5	5.6	710	13.5	13	13.1	5 395	12.7	97	9.3
2 to less than 3 years	1315	34.3	30	33.7	1725	32.7	21	21.2	13 735	32.5	500	20.7
3 to less than 5 years	1097	28.6	26	29.2	1611	30.6	33	33.3	12 807	30.3	357	34.2
5 to less than 10 years	620	16.2	19	21.3	852	15.8	17	17.2	6 738	15.9	188	18.0
10 to less than 20 years	172	4.5	4	4.5	177	3.4	1	1.0	1 667	5.9	27	2.6
20 years to life or indefinite	158	4.1	5	5.6	210	4.0	14	14.1	1 968	4.7	76	7.3
TOTAL	3834	100%	89	100%	5263	100%	99	100%	42 388	100%	1045	100%

[1]Includes admissions to federal institutions and transfers to provincial institutions; excludes readmissions for straight revocation of parole and mandatory supervision.

A federal sentence under two years reflects a recalculation of sentence after day-parole revocation or being unlawfully at large.

Source: H. Johnson (1986), *Women and crime in Canada* (Table 4.11). Ottawa: Solicitor General of Canada.

more than three times as likely as men to be admitted for drug convictions (Johnson, 1986). Criminal history, not leniency toward women, also seems to explain the greater number of men sentenced to federal prison terms. During the same decade, almost three-quarters of women, compared with 55 percent of men, admitted to the penitentiary system had no previous federal committals (Johnson, 1986).

We should note, too, that, despite the fact that a greater proportion of women than men serving federal sentences have been convicted of nonviolent offences and have no prior penitentiary committals, there are no marked differences in aggregate sentence length. As Table 11.5 reveals, between 1975 and 1984, the majority or 63 percent of both male and female inmates were admitted to the federal system with sentences of between two and five years. At the same time, we can see that women began to receive longer prison terms over this period. Thus, the proportion of female admissions with sentences of two to five years dropped from almost two-thirds to just over one-half of the total, while those with sentences of twenty years to life increased from 6 to 14 percent over the decade. Indeed, by 1985, there were 49 Canadian women serving minimum 20-year terms (Johnson, 1987, p. 36). Similarly, women serving federal terms of less than two years rose from 6 to 13 percent of the total between 1975 and 1984, suggesting that they were increasingly subject to revocation of parole (see Box 11.11) and mandatory supervision.

The longer sentences being meted out to convicted female offenders seem to be directly related to changes in their offence patterns and criminal histories. For example, between 1975 and 1984, female admissions to the penitentiary system for crimes of violence increased from 30 to 42 percent of the total, while those for violations of federal drug statutes declined from 37 to 18 percent (Johnson, 1986). During the same period, the proportion of female admissions with no prior federal sentence dropped from 79 percent in 1975 to 65 percent in 1984. Statistics, then, do not bear out the contention that women offenders receive more lenient treatment than their male counterparts.

On the contrary, according to advocates of the double-standard thesis, criminal law and its enforcement inevitably disadvantage female offenders. Historically, for example, women were charged with certain offences far more often than were men. Thus, under the **Juvenile Delinquents Act**, young women were proportionately much more likely than male juveniles to be charged with and convicted of noncriminal, **status offences**, such as truancy, "incorrigibility," and "sexual immorality" (Geller, 1987). One study (Chunn, 1990) of the Toronto Juvenile and Family Court between 1920 and 1940 showed that status offences accounted for at least 40 percent of the charges resulting in formal delinquency hearings for girls but less than 20 percent of those leading to court appearances by boys each year. Another analysis (Matters, 1984, pp. 269–70) of the 600 admissions to the Provincial Industrial Home for Girls in Vancouver from 1914 to 1937 revealed that 88 percent had been convicted of status offences, 2.6 percent of serious criminal offences, and 9.4 percent of minor theft charges.

Similarly, until the 1980s all the procuring offences, except **living on the avails of the prostitution** of another person, were sex-specific, referring explicitly to "female" persons (Boyle & Noonan, 1986, p. 228; see also Backhouse, 1985; Boyle et al., 1985). In addition, before its repeal in 1972, many women were charged and convicted under the "**Vagrancy C**" section of the Criminal Code, which stipulated that only women could be common prostitutes or nightwalkers (Boyle & Noonan, 1986, p. 229); see also Chapter 4 in this volume). For example, a study of criminal cases in York Judicial District, including Toronto, for 1966 (Benson, 1968, p. 18) revealed that the Vagrancy C offence accounted for 38 percent of all Criminal Code charges against adult women. Moreover, 26 percent of the women convicted for "Vagrancy C" received jail terms, which meant that, with respect to dispositions meted out for all Criminal Code offences, a higher percentage of women than men received custodial sentences.

Proponents of the double-standard thesis also suggest that women are more liable to criminal prosecution for certain activities related to birthing and reproduction than men. For example, in the case of *Sullivan et al.* (unreported), several Victoria midwives were convicted of **criminal negligence** causing the death of an infant while it was still in the birth canal. In the 1988 appeal, the B.C. Supreme Court overturned the original conviction but found the

defendants guilty of another charge—criminal negligence causing bodily harm to the mother. A further appeal will soon be argued before the Supreme Court of Canada. But, even if the midwives are ultimately exonerated, it is important to note that there are no reported Canadian cases where doctors have faced criminal charges for injury or negligence with respect to babies that have not yet left the mother's body.

Certain quasi-criminal offences also discriminate against women. Thus, except in Ontario, provincial welfare legislation still incorporates the "man in the house" rule, which is based on the assumption that, if a woman lives with a man, he must be supporting her and she is not entitled to claim welfare benefits. As a result, women are prosecuted for fraud, sometimes under the Criminal Code, while men in the reverse situation are not.

For example, in *Regina v. Thurrott* (1974), an Ontario case that preceded the 1987 law reform, a woman with three children applied for and received welfare benefits without disclosing that she had a common-law husband. Moreover, she continued to collect social-assistance payments after her spouse obtained employment. As a result, Mrs. Thurrott was convicted of welfare fraud in the amount of $1700 and sentenced to five months in jail. The sen-

Box 11.11 Sentence in 1975 Killing Wrong, High Court Rules

OTTAWA—Janice Gamble of Vancouver, one of the first people in Canada to be handed a mandatory 25-year sentence for first-degree murder, was wrongly sentenced and should be eligible for parole immediately, the Supreme Court of Canada ruled today.

In a 3–2 decision, the court ruled that Gamble was sentenced under the wrong provision of the Criminal Code at a time when the law was newly modified by Parliament with the abolition of capital punishment in 1976.

The decision does not overturn the conviction. But the sentence that made Gamble ineligible for parole for 25 years—until the year 2001—was ruled to violate her constitutionally guaranteed right to fundamental justice.

Gamble was convicted in the slaying of Calgary detective Allan Harrison, who was gunned down in a shootout with four suspects after a credit-union robbery in Calgary in March 1975.

Two of the accused—Gamble and William Nichols—were at first charged with murder punishable by death. But after the abolition of capital punishment in July 1976, they

were tried for the new offence of first-degree murder, punishable by life in prison with no possibility of parole for 25 years.

Gamble was 22 in 1976 when she and Nichols, then 27 and from White Rock, were jointly charged with the shooting of 40-year-old Harrison.

The killing started a bizarre 44-hour hostage-taking and siege in a Calgary home. Gamble's husband, John Frederick Gamble, 23, of Vancouver died during the siege from a self-inflicted over-dose of the drug methadone.

During the trial, about 55 witnesses were called and 145 exhibits entered into evidence.

Janice Gamble went to court in 1985 to challenge the sentence, claiming she would have been eligible for parole after 10 years if she had been sentenced to a prison term under the old law.

Source: Canadian Press, *Vancouver Sun*, December 8, 1988, p. A2.

tence of incarceration was upheld on appeal, although the judge varied it from a definite to an indeterminate term not to exceed five months.

Advocates of the double-standard thesis also argue that, even when criminal law is premised on the concept of formal legal equality, women experience discrimination *vis-à-vis* men. Thus, the reformulation of the prostitution offences in gender-neutral terms has apparently not ended the differential treatment of men and women by the police and courts. On the one hand, the police may be charging more men under the new laws. As Table 11.2 showed us, the male-female ratio with respect to police charges for all prostitution-related offences in 1987 was 1.1:1. However, the category "Other Prostitution Offences" does not distinguish between those charged with pimping (historically male) and those charged with soliciting (historically female). Moreover, the traditional reluctance of the police and courts to prosecute the predominantly male clients of street prostitutes remains despite the fact that, in theory, customers do not enjoy immunity from **criminal liability** under the current law (Boyle & Noonan, 1986, pp. 240–44). Perhaps more importantly, it is not at all clear that men and women are now being convicted of prostitution-related offences at the same rate. (For a further discussion of prostitution, see Chapter 4.)

Similarly, female accused are less able than are their male counterparts to utilize certain criminal defences that are presumably gender-neutral. For example, the **self-defence** provision of the Criminal Code (see Chapter 2) obviously operates to the disadvantage of women because of the provisions on excessive force and imminent threat, both of which assume adversaries of similar size and strength. Thus, when a woman uses a knife or a gun against an unarmed man, particularly in cases where a battered wife kills her spouse, she is often unable to successfully plead self-defence. Only three days after a BWS plea helped Angelique Lavallee gain an acquittal on charges of murdering her common-law spouse, Verna Mae Leach was convicted of aggravated assault in the near-fatal stabbing of her common-law partner and sentenced to two years imprisonment despite a plea of self-defence. During an argument, after Leach's partner slapped her, pinned her against a door, and began choking her, she had picked up a paring knife from a nearby kitchen table and stabbed him twice in the heart and arm. Emergency surgery saved his life, but the jury rejected Leach's self-defence argument because she used "excessive force" in defending herself (Comack, 1988, p. 8).

Self-defence is even more difficult to use in cases where the woman kills an abusive spouse who is not actually threatening her at the time. In the case of *R. v. Whynot* (1983), the Nova Scotia Supreme Court overturned the acquittal of Jane Stafford in the shooting of her common-law husband and ordered a new trial on the grounds that the trial judge incorrectly directed the jury that the defence of self-defence was available. The Court ruled that, although Billy Stafford had threatened to injure or kill her son on the evening in question, the victim was drunk and asleep at the time he was shot and therefore posed no imminent threat to anybody. Prevented from raising self-defence at the retrial, Jane Stafford pleaded guilty to manslaughter and was sentenced to six months in prison. While agreeing with the prosecutor that Billy Stafford had been a man "on the outer fringe of a definition of humanity" who subjected his wife to severe physical and sexual abuse, Justice Merlin Nunn emphasized that the accused had committed "a cold, calculating and brutal act" by shooting a sleeping man and that other women in the same situation had to realize that "you can't go out and shoot your husband" (*Vancouver Sun*, February 15, 1984, p. A12).

Even if women and men are convicted at about the same rate and receive sentences in keeping with offence and prior record, gender-neutral dispositions do not have gender-neutral effects. For example, female offenders are generally less able to pay fines than are their male counterparts. Therefore, women end up in jail for default at a proportionately higher rate than men. Thus, approximately 29 percent of all admissions, compared with about 34 percent of female admissions, to provincial jails in Canada are for fine default (Statistics Canada, 1989; Johnson, 1987, p.34). Similarly, in terms of **fine-option programs**, women with children are frequently unable to fulfil their service or other responsibilities because they cannot find and/or afford daycare.

Overall, imprisonment is almost certainly a harsher sanction for women than for men. Because they are so few, incarcerated women do not have access to the same range of programs and resources as do male inmates (Adelberg, 1985; Adelberg & Currie, 1987; Berzins & Cooper, 1982; Boyle et al., 1985; Misch et al., 1982; NAWL, 1987). Moreover, the Prison for Women in Kingston is the only federal penitentiary for female offenders, so inmates cannot move from maximum-security to minimum-security institutions prior to release in the same way that male prisoners can. In addition, female inmates have special needs that cannot be met by a system based on formal equality. For example, they are often farther away than male prisoners from friends, family, and other support networks, particularly women serving a federal sentence at the Kingston facility. Many female inmates are also single mothers who cannot keep their children with them in prison. Separation often means that these women lose not only contact with but also custody of their children (MacLeod, 1986).

Box 11.12 "'I Will Not Make Him a Scapegoat,' Judge Says"

Inwood Gets 30 Days for Assault

Saying he refused to make Kirby Inwood "a scapegoat for all battered women," a provincial court judge yesterday sentenced the Toronto advertising executive to 30 days in jail and three years of probation for assaulting his baby and Russian wife, Tatyana Sidorova.

In an extremely brief judgment Judge Gordon Hachborn said that he had "sadly formed the impression during this proceeding that I was observing the functioning of a sick mind and a twisted personality."

The sentence ended a hugely publicized 23-day proceeding that ultimately put on trial the entire issue of wife battering and how it is dealt with by the system.

In his sentence yesterday, Judge Hachborn also ordered Mr. Inwood to take psychiatric treatment for alcoholism and for his chronic violent tendencies toward women. But he rejected Crown counsel Glen Orr's suggestion of a substantial prison term to show that "mean and vicious cowards" like Mr. Inwood cannot beat women with impunity.

"I will not make him a scapegoat for all battered women," the judge said. Neither was it open to him, he said, to sentence Mr. Inwood for assaulting at least five other women who testified to their ordeals this week.

Judge Hachborn said he could only take into account Mr. Inwood's conviction on charges of assault causing bodily harm to Ms Sidorova and of common assault against the couple's son, Misha, who was then a year old. The 30-day jail sentence related only to the assault on Misha—"a helpless, defenceless infant who was terrified by what was going on around him," the judge said, while the probation term and psychiatric treatment order related to both assault convictions.

The assaults took place Sept. 13, 1987, just nine days after Ms Sidorova and Misha arrived in Canada in a blaze of publicity stoked by Mr. Inwood's massive public campaign to force the Soviet Government to grant them exit visas.

Ms. Sidorova testified that she was punched, kicked, choked and thrown out of their house, and that Misha was dropped twice, spanked harshly and doused with cold water.

Mr. Inwood was expressionless yesterday as he was led away to serve his sentence. Ms Sidorova, meanwhile, struggled to suppress her anger toward Mr. Inwood and violent men in general.

"I think everybody is the loser," she told reporters. I am the loser, my son is the loser, and Kirby the loser.

"Somebody must protect women," she said beseechingly. "Women must defend themselves and not always be victims."

Source: Kirk Makin, *Globe and Mail*, September 21, 1988, pp. A1–2.

Assuming that female offenders are treated more severely than are males, why does such discrimination exist? One of the major sources of this double standard of justice is the pronounced tendency among lawmakers and enforcers to sexualize women's offences, no matter what they do, but not men's. Clearly, deviant sexual behaviour—that is, sex outside a heterosexual marriage—has always been considered more reprehensible in the former (Barnhorst, 1978; Boyle et al., 1985; Chunn, 1990; Matters, 1984). Thus, self-report studies reveal that young men are actually more sexually active than are female youths, yet, as was discussed earlier, girls and women have consistently been penalized more heavily for "promiscuity" and prostitution offences. Moreover, if a man and a woman each commit both a property offence and a sexual offence, the woman is much more likely to be prosecuted for the sexual offence (Geller, 1987, pp. 114–15; see also Boyle & Noonan, 1986; Lowman et al., 1987).

The double standard of justice also arises because criminal law and its administration reflect male-centred perspectives on reality that are presented as universal. However, women's experience of the world is different from that of men. Therefore, conceptions of reality based on men's experience cannot be gender-neutral (Lahey, 1989; NAWL, 1987). That is why the present trend toward gender-neutrality in criminal law and its administration continues to leave women in a disadvantaged position. For example, as Boyle has observed (NAWL, 1987, p. 109), the Criminal Code section on self-defence seems to be "an explicit direction *not* to attempt to view the facts from the perspective of an abused woman . . . a direction to divorce the incident from its context." For those who make and enforce law, the legal subject is still a rational man.

The Law-As-Ideology Thesis

Despite the persuasive arguments on both sides, however, the existing literature does not yield any conclusive findings about the issue of gender bias and criminal justice. For example, American researchers have produced a spate of quantitative studies that fail to demonstrate any evidence of across-the-board chivalry toward or discrimination against women offenders (Chesney-Lind, 1986; Daly & Chesney-Lind, 1988). While there is virtually no Canadian empirical research on this question, a few statistical analyses seem to support the same conclusion; namely, that sometimes criminal law and the criminal-justice system apparently favour women *vis-à-vis* men, and sometimes not (Adams, 1978; Hatch & Faith, 1990; Johnson, 1986).

The conflicting results of such studies prompted some feminists to suggest that researchers concerned with the chivalry-severity debate have been asking the wrong question. Since no blanket legal privileging or repression of women can seemingly be demonstrated, perhaps criminal law and its administration do not operate *directly* for or against the interests of any individual or group in liberal-democratic states such as Canada (Bottomley, Gibson & Meteyard, 1987; Gavigan, 1988). If criminal law is an instrument of male power, for example, why are so many more men than women arrested (Daly & Chesney-Lind, 1988, p. 116)? Even the most powerful people in Canada and other Western democracies—affluent, white men— are still subject to the law and, occasionally, to criminal prosecution.

At the same time, criminal law and its administration clearly do help sustain and reproduce unequal power relations between rich and poor, men and women, whites and nonwhites in our society. But how does this happen if there is no overt, systemic legal discrimination based on social class, gender, and race/ethnicity? Recently, a number of feminist authors have articulated what we might call the **law-as-ideology thesis** (Daly, 1987a, 1987b; Eaton, 1986; Edwards, 1985; Gavigan, 1988; Smart, 1985). It is not necessary, they argue, to demonstrate that law always reflects and operates directly in the interests of men to prove that the legal system helps maintain and reproduce gender inequality. In countries like Canada, England, and the United States, criminal law and criminal justice incorporate and are mediated by ideologies—stereotypical assumptions and beliefs about social reality that are taken for granted because they seem to be "natural." Although few lawmakers and enforcers are intentionally lenient or harsh toward partic-

ular categories of offender, then, they are all influenced to a greater or lesser extent by ideologies and thus contribute *indirectly* to the reproduction of class, gender, and racial/ethnic inequalities.

Moreover, the findings from several contemporary research studies have convinced some feminists that the impact of **familial ideology** on those who enact and administer criminal law is a major reason for disparities in the processing of defendants facing similar criminal charges. This ideology pervades all our institutions, including law, and rests on the core belief that the nuclear family is the basic unit in society, "sacred, timeless and . . . natural" (Gavigan, 1988, p. 293). In short, the only appropriate form of family is one organized around a heterosexual, monogamous marriage relationship, and the sexual division of labour.

This conception of the family incorporates two assumptions about the acceptable relations between women and men, adults and children. First, "normal" women and men marry, have children, and carry out sex-specific duties and responsibilities related to their "natural" roles within the nuclear family: the husband/father as the primary breadwinner/provider and protector of his dependents; the wife/mother as the primary caregiver/homemaker and socializing agent. Second, "normal" parents prevent their children from behaving like adults, and they are particularly careful to guard the sexual purity of daughters (Smart, 1976, 1985; Smart & Smart, 1978).

The pervasiveness of familial ideology is evidenced by the fact that only a small minority of the population in Canada, the United States, Britain, and other Western nations actually lives in the ideal-type nuclear unit where the wife/mother is a full-time homemaker, yet many people continue to view that as the "normal" family. For example, in 1987, a mere 7 percent of the Canadian and American population fitted the "norm," but in a *Newsweek* poll the following year, 19 percent of respondents said "children, no job," and 25 percent "children, part-time job," would be the most interesting and satisfying lifestyle for them. Moreover, 84 percent said they did not expect to be separated or divorced in their lives (January 4, 1988, pp. 46–47), notwithstanding the high rate of family breakdown and the increasing number of one-parent families since the 1960s (Mossman & MacLean, 1986).

Indeed, the feminist conceptualization of law as ideology seems particularly relevant today because, despite the trend toward gender-neutral criminal laws, discrepancies in the processing of accused persons remain. Why is this so? Seemingly, those who enforce the law and administer justice continue to be influenced by the assumptions incorporated in familial ideology. A number of contemporary studies have revealed that police, probation officers, judges, and other criminal-justice agents handle offenders who are members of a "normal" family (or have the potential to be) more leniently than those who are not (Daly, 1987a, 1987b; Eaton, 1986; Edwards, 1985; Mitra, 1987; Smart, 1985; see Box 11.13).

What this body of research demonstrates, then, is how the decision making of most legal agents in our society reflects and reinforces the dominant ideology of "the family." Individuals who are in the same or similar circumstances seem to receive equal treatment, regardless of class, gender, or racial/ethnic differences. In other words, familial ideology operates to the advantage of those who conform to what are essentially white, middle-class standards and to the detriment of those who do not (Daly, 1987a, 1987b; Eaton, 1986). Consequently, male and female offenders will not always be handled differently, and same-sex defendants will not inevitably have identical case outcomes.

A recent Canadian study of psychiatric decision making about a cohort of male and female defendants remanded for pretrial or presentence assessment replicated the findings of research done elsewhere (Chunn & Menzies, 1989; Menzies, Chunn, & Webster, forthcoming). As Table 11.6 reveals, there were no significant gender differences in either the clinical depictions of the subjects or the recommendations to the court about disposition. Thus, the psychiatrists were not significantly more likely to diagnose women as mentally ill and therefore less accountable for their crimes than were men, nor were they noticeably more reluctant to recommend a custodial disposition for female, as opposed to male, defendants.

In attempting to explain why the clinicians were relatively harsh in their assessments of both men and women, the researchers concluded that the two groups of defendants were very much alike. For the most part, they were individuals living on society's fringe who had consistently flouted all the "norms" governing sexuality and gender roles associated with "the family" and were deemed to have little potential for change. Thus, few of the male and female accused were, or had the prospect of being, part of a stable nuclear family unit, and the psychiatrists judged them accordingly.

However, proponents of the law-as-ideology thesis also emphasize that male and female defendants rarely are in the same circumstances, either legal or extralegal (Eaton,

---

Box 11.13 "Woman Acquitted in Stabbing Death of Abusive Husband"

A Vancouver woman who was abused for years by her husband was acquitted of manslaughter Friday after a provincial court judge ruled she acted in self-defence when she fatally stabbed the man.

Calling the incident "a very tragic case," Judge Erik Bendrodt dismissed the charge against Catherine Dewilde, 39, saying he accepted evidence that while being choked by her husband Peter, 41, Dewilde reached for the only thing she could find to defend herself—a steak knife.

The incident occurred Dec. 8 at the Greenbrier Apartment Hotel, at 1392 Robson. The husband died of a single stab wound to the chest.

Dewilde told Crown prosecutor Elaine Ferbey that she stayed with her husband "because even though we had difficult times and he was violent and things got worse as time went on, I believed things could get better. He did, too. I never dreamed it would go this far."

She said her late husband was an unaffectionate father to their three-year-old son Christopher: "He didn't take care of his needs. He didn't make an effort."

Defence lawyer Harry Rankin depicted the dead man as a professional academic "who was, to put it simply, a total failure" at providing for his family.

Family friend Andre Arp, called as a Crown witness, agreed with Rankin that the unemployed Dewilde often took out his frustration not only by abusing his wife, but also his son.

Arp told the court the couple was bickering most of the day prior to the stabbing as he helped them hunt for an apartment. He said Catherine called him at home around 11 p.m. that night complaining that she and her husband were having "a bad argument."

After the second or third call, during which Catherine said her husband had shoved her against a wall, Arp said: "I knew he'd become violent and I said I'd come right over. But when I arrived, the door was locked and I could hear Christopher crying. . . ."

Arp said he heard Catherine cry out: "Don't, don't Peter!"

About to break down the door at that point, Arp said it suddenly opened and he saw Peter slump to the floor.

Source: Joanne MacDonald, *Vancouver Sun*, March 21, 1987, p. C19.

Table 11.6 Psychiatric Recommendations in Court Letters about Female and Male Suspects[1] in the Metropolitan Toronto Forensic Service, Brief Assessment Unit

| | Subject | | | | Row Total | |
| | Male | | Female | | | |
	No.	%	No.	%	No.	%
No recommendation	11	19.3	12	21.1	23	20.2
Through Courts	9	15.8	6	10.5	15	13.2
Probation/Treatment	7	12.3	5	8.8	12	10.5
Probation/No Treatment	5	8.8	2	3.5	7	6.1
Prison/Treatment	5	8.8	4	7.0	9	7.9
Prison/No Treatment	3	5.3	4	7.0	7	6.1
Further Psych. Assmnt.	15	26.3	17	29.8	32	28.1
Inpatient Treatment	1	1.8	7	12.3	8	7.0
Release	1	1.8	0	—	1	.9
Column Total	57	50.0	57	50.0	114	100.0

[1]Female subjects represent all women assessed in 1978; male subjects are a random sample of all men assessed in 1978.

Source: Derived from R.J. Menzies, D.E. Chunn, & C.D. Webster, Female follies: The forensic psychiatric assessment of women defendants, *International Journal of Psychiatry and Law*, (15(1): forthcoming).

1986). For example, if sexual offences are involved, familial ideology produces a double standard of justice; acting as a mitigating factor for a male accused and an aggravating circumstance for a female accused. One study of incest appeals in England (Mitra, 1987) revealed that the judges almost always reduced a man's sentence when the victim and/or the wife did not conform to their "normal" familial roles. Thus, if the daughter was a nonvirgin, the appeal court seemed to view her as "a willing partner" who had "forfeited the right to parental protection" because of her sexual promiscuity and virtually ignore "the father's breach of trust" (Mitra, 1987, pp. 136–37). Similarly, in appeal cases where there had been a breakdown of sexual relations between the spouses, the judges apparently considered the husband/father less culpable for turning to his daughter, because they reduced his sentence over 80 percent of the time (Mitra, 1987, p. 145).

In contrast, another English study of how magistrates responded to prostitution (Smart, 1985) found that assumptions about the family made them most unsympathetic toward women who worked the streets. While they differed in their specific perceptions of the problem, all the magistrates—female as well as male—discussed prostitution "in a context which idealised marriage or monogamous relationships." They believed that the only legitimate expression of female sexuality occurs within such relationships. Thus, by selling sex to strangers, prostitute women are "quite beyond the pale"; threats to the very foundation of society—the family—who must be subject to some

type of "coercive intervention" by the state (1985, p. 54).

The impact of familial ideology on legal decision makers leads to differential treatment of same-sex defendants as well. Statistics tell us that native men and women are grossly overrepresented in the criminal-justice system relative to their non-native counterparts, and this seems to be related to their greater inability to abide by the "norms" associated with the white, middle-class, nuclear family. So far as native women are concerned, for example, we know that they are the most marginal people in our society (LaPrairie, 1984) and therefore the least able to comply with the demands of familial ideology. Moreover, many native women (and men) operate with a different cultural conception of family that is not tied to monogamous, heterosexual marriage. Thus, in 1980, almost one-third of native women, as opposed to one-quarter of non-native women, were without an income. Similarly, the 1981 census showed that single-parent families were twice as common and the incidence of birth outside marriage four to five times the national average among native Indians, compared with non-native people (Johnson, 1987, pp. 39–40).

It is hardly surprising, then, that native women are overrepresented at all stages of the criminal-justice system relative to their non-native peers. Their disproportionate presence is particularly obvious in prison. For example, the one-day survey of Misch et al. (1982, p. 12) revealed that 25 percent of all female inmates in provincial and territorial institutions across Canada were native women, although Inuit, Indian, and Métis people comprise only about 3 percent of the Canadian population. Moreover, the over-representation varied from province to province, being greatest in Alberta, Saskatchewan, Manitoba, and Ontario where native women constituted 29, 77, 71, and 17 percent of female offenders, respectively (Misch et al., 1982; see also Johnson, 1987, p. 41). It is also significant that a much greater proportion of native, as opposed to non-native, female inmates end up in prison because they are unable to pay fines (Johnson, 1987, p. 41; Misch et al., 1982, p. 15). Indeed, one survey at the Pine Grove Correctional Centre in Saskatchewan during June 1986 revealed that 45 percent of female inmates, most of whom were native, had defaulted on fine payments (Canada, 1988, p. 221).

As Table 11.7 reveals, the proportion of all female offenders serving federal sentences who were native ranged from 14 to 19 percent between 1980 and 1984. Moreover, native women were more likely than their non-native counterparts to be incarcerated at the Prison for Women in Kingston as opposed to provincial institutions closer to home. Indeed, over the five-year period, three-quarters of native women under federal jurisdiction were from the Pacific and prairie regions yet anywhere from 60 to 70 percent of them were sent to the Kingston facility. Clearly, although imprisonment is difficult for all female offenders, the "isolation from family and community resulting from incarceration is particularly marked for native women" (Johnson, 1986, p. 71).

However, although social class and race/ethnicity are crucial factors that, to a certain extent, determine whether an individual is able to abide by the "norms" embodied in familial ideology, men and women who could conform but do not will most likely incur a severe response from criminal-justice agents. Thus, it may not be enough for a woman offender to be white and middle class if she unrepentently flouts gender norms. We can see this very clearly if we examine the treatment of female offenders

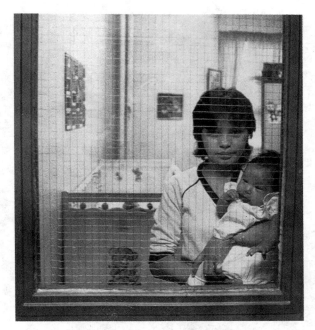

Photo 11.1   Native women are disproportionately represented in prisons and correctional institutions in Canada.

Canapress Photo Service.

convicted and sentenced for political crimes (Gavigan, 1987, p. 56).

For example, consider the legal response to the women members of Direct Action—Juliet Belmas and Ann Hansen. Together with three male colleagues, they committed a series of illegal acts in support of moral and political causes from 1981 to their arrest in 1983. The crimes included arson against a number of video stores that stocked pornographic films; the bombing of a B.C. Hydro substation that the group linked to environmental destruction;

Table 11.7   Race/Ethnicity of Women Serving Federal Sentences, 1980 to 1984[1]

| | Non-native | | Native | | Other/ Not stated | | Total No. |
	No.	%	No.	%	No.	%	
1980	152	73.8	31	15.0	23	11.2	206
1981	144	76.6	31	16.5	13	6.9	188
1982	159	81.1	27	13.8	10	5.1	196
1983	162	76.0	40	18.8	11	5.2	213
1984	172	76.1	40	17.7	14	6.2	226

[1]Includes federal inmates in both the Prison for Women and provincial institutions.

Source: H. Johnson (1986), *Women and crime in Canada* (Table 5.10). Ottawa: Solicitor General of Canada.

Photo 11.2 What They Got.

Anne Hansen: Sentenced to life imprisonment after being found guilty of conspiracy to rob an armoured-car guard. Terms of up to twelve years to run concurrently after being convicted of or admitting to a number of other offences, including the B.C. Hydro and Litton bombings, arson at Red Hot Video, unlawful possession

of explosives and weapons, auto theft, and possession of stolen property.
Juliet Belmas: Sentenced to a total of twenty years after admitting to the Litton bombing, robbery, conspiracy, possession of weapons and explosives, attempted arson, auto theft, and possession of stolen property.

Source: (captions) *Vancouver Sun* (June 9, 1984) p. A10; (photos) Canapress Photo Service.

and the bombing of a Toronto factory that produced parts for American weapons systems (see also Chapter 17 for a discussion of the Squamish Five.)

Familial ideology seems to have been an important factor in the disposition of Hansen and Belmas. Before trial, the women published a letter justifying their actions and rejecting the depiction of Direct Action as a terrorist group: "For centuries the authorities have reacted violently to womyn [sic] who resisted: they used to brand us as 'witches' and burn us, now they label us 'terrorists' and will try to bury us in their cement tombs" (*Vancouver Sun*, June 5, 1984, p. A-1).

The "unfeminine" militancy of the defendants seemed to influence the trial judge as much as the seriousness of the charges against them. Although Juliet Belmas later expressed remorse for her actions, Justice Toy exhibited no leniency toward the female defendants *vis-à-vis* their male counterparts. Indeed, he described Hansen as "a menace—a real threat to our Canadian way of life" and

imposed the most severe disposition on her: life imprisonment. Similarly, he expressed a "longstanding scepticism" about incarcerated people who "set about convincing others that they have been rehabilitated," said that Belmas's youth was not a mitigating circumstance and sentenced her to a total of twenty years in prison (*R. v. Belmas, Hansen and Taylor*, 1986, p. 157).

Ultimately, however, the influence of familial ideology on legal decision makers worked in favour of Juliet Belmas. On appeal, the Court upheld the life sentence of an unrepentant Hansen, but reduced that of Belmas to fifteen years. The Justices concluded that the latter, who was "only 18 years old at the beginning of these events," had been "influenced by Miss Hansen." However, they were apparently convinced that Belmas was restored to "normal" womanhood because she "renounced the path she had taken and abandoned her former views." The Court agreed with the warden of the Prison for Women who said that the "committed urban terrorist" was now "a friendly, motivated [and conventional] young woman" (1986, pp. 156–57).

Clearly, the question of how the criminal law and criminal-justice system respond to female offenders relative to their male counterparts cannot be answered definitively without more research. Thus, the debate continues. We turn now to examine a similar debate about what policies are most appropriate for dealing with female offenders.

What Should Be Done about Canada's Women Criminals?

Whether the link is explicitly acknowledged or not, all correctional policies are based on particular theories or explanations of the "crime problem." Thus, there have been and continue to be quite divergent proposals and programs relating to the female offender in Canada. However, most strategies for coping with female criminality fit into three categories: those that focus on individual reclamation and reform; those that emphasize the need to change the criminal law and enforcement; and those that suggest that fundamental structural inequalities—racial, gender, and social class—must be removed or reduced before women's criminality can be adequately addressed.

Changing the Offender: Individual and Social Reform

Given their dominance, it is not surprising that the traditional bio- and psychogenetic theories of women's criminality have exerted the strongest influence on policies and programs directed at the female offender in Canada. As earlier discussion revealed, such explanations are premised on the assumptions that criminals are fundamentally different from noncriminals, and women from men. At the same time, social-psychological explanations of the female offender also suggest that women and men are different because they are socialized to play sex-specific roles within the family. Thus, although one type of theory emphasizes nature and the other nurture, both can lead to an emphasis on similar policies (Canada, 1938; 1969; 1970; 1977a).

If women are motivated to commit crime by innate physiological and psychological factors or defective socialization, the solutions to female criminality must necessarily be individualized and, frequently, paternalistic or protectionist ones aimed at the transformation of the offender herself. To that end, both historically and in the present context, women who have committed crimes are most likely to experience two general types of state intervention that are often interrelated. On the one hand, policies based on

medical, psychiatric, and psychological interventions attempt to correct the problematic characteristics of the female offender that generate criminal behaviour, such as mental and emotional instability, drug and alcohol dependency. On the other hand, social interventions emphasize the pathological aspects of the offender's environment that propel her toward deviance, particularly bad or nonexistent family relationships (Ross & Fabiano, 1986).

For much of this century, the correctional response to female offenders was segregation on an indeterminate sentence so that individualized treatment could be carried out. Sometimes that included sterilization of young women who had been institutionalized for "sexual immorality" (McLaren, 1986; see also Matters, 1984). However, most of the time, institutional programs were geared toward the resocialization of delinquent women. Female inmates received instruction and training aimed at transforming them into "good" mothers, wives, and housekeepers (Canada, 1938; Matters, 1984).

Today, we find that many programs aimed at female offenders are still premised on stereotypical assumptions about women (see Box 11.14). For example, that their criminality is the result of a basic irrationality and impulsiveness or a lack of "femininity." However, now therapy and **behaviour modification** have been added to the treatment arsenal for the resocialization of the deviant. Indeed, the psychotherapies are "the most popular treatment programs for female offenders, both adolescent and adult," inside and outside institutions (Ross & Fabiano, 1986, p. 13).

At present, many convicted female offenders who do not go to prison are placed in community-based therapeutic programs. Often, these programs are run by private agencies on contract with the federal and/or provincial ministries of corrections. Many of the programs also target one particular type of offender or offence. For example, both the Elizabeth Fry Societies and the Salvation Army have developed special counselling programs for women shoplifters that are based on the assumption that "emotional factors have contributed to their anti-social behavior." Thus, therapy is necessary to deal with "the underlying problems that have led to shoplifting" (Liaison, 1988, p. 4; see Box 11.15).

As far as female inmates are concerned, correctional planners and administrators have long emphasized therapy as a crucial factor in rehabilitation. During the 1960s, they began to promote the creation of so-called "therapeutic communities" in custodial facilities. The stimulus for many such programs was a belief that a reduction of staff–inmate and intra–inmate conflict would facilitate the rehabilitation of individual inmates (Ross & Fabiano, 1986, p. 16). To that end, correctional personnel promoted "open staff–resident communication, frank discussions about personal

Box 11.14 The View of the Ouimet Committee (1969) on Female Offenders

Examination of the kinds of offences most frequently committed by women has revealed a number of factors which require to be taken into account in planning for the woman offender. Additional factors have been drawn to our attention by a number of experienced correctional workers and which appear also in literature concerning the woman offender; these also deserve examination.

One such factor is the particular importance for the woman offender of personal appearance, clothing, and physical surroundings. This is perhaps only an aspect of the more general principle that human beings have a marked tendency to respond with the type of behaviour which others appear to expect of them. Thus, good personal grooming and reasonably pleasant physical surroundings are important in enhancing a feeling of self-respect in both men and women. The difference appears to lie in the fact that they seem to be of somewhat more central importance to the woman, who tends more typically to use clothing and personal surroundings as a significant expression of her personality. Thus, any correctional institution for either short-term or long-term custody, or any program which is part of an

endeavour to change the attitudes and behaviour of women offenders for the better, must pay special attention to these things.

A second factor which has been drawn to our attention is an apparent tendency of women offenders to need and use specialized medical, psychiatric and social treatment resources in higher proportion than is true of the same number from an undifferentiated group of men offenders. This may simply be an aspect of the marked difference in numbers between men and women offenders proportionate to the general population. That is, since fewer women out of the total population are sentenced by the courts than is true of men, the sentenced group may represent overall a more socially aberrant and emotionally disturbed group than do the sentenced men. Also, the difference may reflect a general difference in attitude towards the use of such treatment resources as between women and men in the general community.

Source: *Canadian Committee on Corrections* (1969), *Report* (p. 398). Ottawa: Queen's Printer.

and group goals, and a high level of resident participation in decision-making" (Lambert & Madden, 1975, p. 4). In Canada, the "therapeutic milieu" established at the Vanier Centre was one of the most extensive of these programs for women offenders.

More recently, the **Women In Conflict With the Law Program** established by the federal Solicitor General reflected the new correctional philosophy of self-help (WICL, 1986). Thus, women who were, or might have been, in conflict with the law, particularly native and rural women, were provided with the opportunities and support to help themselves. Priority was given to programs which emphasized the creation of community-based services for native and rural women, the treatment and prevention of substance abuse, the provision of opportunities for the development of life, and employment-related skills and training.

Despite the emphasis on choice, however, the available programs continue to focus on the individual woman and her problems and needs. Moreover, most of the training is still related to what are perceived as women's activities—hair dressing, waiting on tables, and so on—and the emphasis remains on the adaptation of self to social constraints.

Changing the Criminal Law and Its Administration

As we know, some explanations of women's criminality emphatically reject the notion that the offender is defective. These theories thus imply that the problem lies outside the individual woman and her immediate environment with the lawmakers and enforcers; that is, the male-dominated legal structures that sexualize female deviance and contain a built-in bias against women. Consequently, it is necessary to focus on legal initiatives as a means of attacking female criminality. Specifically, criminal law and criminal-justice reforms must be implemented to establish equality between men and women offenders (Boyle et al., 1985; Canada, 1969, 1970, 1987; Lahey, 1989; NAWL, 1987).

However, there are two distinct views on how this objective can be accomplished. The first, which was expressed by both feminists and nonfeminists in the early 1970s, stresses the realignment of criminal law and its administration to effect gender neutrality and **formal legal equality** for women *vis-à-vis* men. Thus, the elimination of status

Box 11.15 A Voyage of Discovery

In 1982, 59 957 charges were laid against women for violations of the Criminal Code. Of these, 64 percent were laid for shoplifting and fraud.

Since counselling has proven to be an effective method of reducing recidivism among this type of offender, last fall, Solicitor General Canada sponsored a two-day workshop that was co-ordinated by the Elizabeth Fry Society to help E. Fry agencies across Canada to develop a specific counselling program for women who shoplift.

As a result of this initiative, the Peel-Halton branch has developed the *Stop-lifter* program to address some of the emotional needs of these women. "The program deals with the underlying problems that have led to the shoplifting," says Susan Koswan, Public Relations Co-ordinator for the branch. "The women learn about assertiveness, dealing positively with their anger and understanding themselves in the context of society. By addressing these issues," she says, "the underlying problems are ameliorated and the shoplifting ceases."

The group meets once a week for 12 sessions, each session dealing with a different topic, some of which are often repressed or denied in the average woman's life. "Un-

resolved grief and depression are subjects that many people don't want to deal with or don't understand," says Koswan. "Some don't have the support network to discuss their feelings. Talking about these subjects has been bred out of many of them." There is a session on self-esteem because many women have been raised to play a submissive role and don't realize their own strengths and possibilities, she says. Other topics include self-awareness, women's place in society, effective communication, anger, stress management and assertiveness.

Stop-lifter is designed to offer direction and support to females who have been apprehended for shoplifting. The program aims to develop skills, through positive group experiences and individual counselling, to deal with problems in a more responsible manner. Groups are composed of eight to 12 participants having similar life situations, problems and ages. Sessions focus on developing and maintaining socially responsible behaviour by examining feelings and attitudes and exploring alternate responses.

Source: *Liaison*, March 4, 1988, (pp. 4–7).

---

offences and sex-specific provisions of the Criminal Code, such as the **soliciting** clause, was proposed and, in many instances, has occurred. Today, the push for gender-neutral law continues with calls for the abolition of sex-specific offences like infanticide, the complete **decriminalization** of prostitution, and the reformulation of the self-defence provision to make it equally applicable to men and women.

Similarly, reformers have argued that changes must be implemented at every stage of the justice system to achieve equal enforcement of criminal law. They advocate the adoption of policies aimed at recruiting more women police, prosecutors, judges, and corrections personnel. With respect to offenders, reformers promote equal access to legal-aid programs and an emphasis on community-based sentences for both men and women (Canada, 1987). Most offenders do not merit or require incarceration, and women, in particular, commit trivial, nonviolent property and morality offences. To prevent imprisonment of men and women for default, day-fine programs must also be implemented.

At the same time, women and men who are incarcerat-

ed must receive equal treatment. One of the ongoing proposals since the 1938 Archambault Commission has been to close the Prison for Women in Kingston. While the Archambault Commission was more concerned about the isolation and "contamination" of female inmates than with equality, the 1977 Report of the Parliamentary Sub-Committee on the Penitentiary System stated bluntly that the prison represented "outright discrimination" against women and was "obsolete in every respect" (P4W, 1988, p.15). Three years later, a group of female personnel in the criminal-justice system formed a group called Justice for Women that filed a complaint with the Canadian Human Rights Commission alleging sexual discrimination by the Correctional Service of Canada in its treatment of women sentenced to the penitentiary (Berzins & Hayes, 1987).

To date, the Prison for Women has not been phased out (see Box 11.16). However, the growing pressure for reform since the late 1960s has generated some changes. A 1974 federal-provincial agreement for exchange of services makes it possible for some women sentenced to more than two years in prison to serve their time in provincial institutions closer to their communities rather than in the Kingston facility. Indeed, by 1988, approximately half of all federal inmates were housed in provincial jails across the country. Moreover, when the provinces build new custodial facilities, they usually include accommodation for female inmates under federal sentence. For example, the Provincial Correctional Centre for Women, presently under construction in British Columbia, will have 50 beds for women serving penitentiary terms.

However, simply transferring women to provincial institutions is hardly a panacea. These jails generally have even fewer programs and resources than the Prison for Women, and the agreement between Ottawa and the provinces does not include Ontario. Similarly, relying on complaints to human-rights bodies will not produce the intended outcome. For example, the Canadian Human Rights Commission finally handed down a ruling that upheld nine of eleven charges made by Justice for Women, but left it up

to them to negotiate remedial action with the Correctional Service of Canada. As a result, "cosmetic changes" were made at the Prison for Women that did not address the fundamental issues like "distances from home for inmates, security classification and segregation facilities" (Berzins & Hayes, 1987, p. 175).[1]

The disappointing result of such initiatives has convinced some feminists that the implementation of **formal legal equality** is not enough because most female offenders are in a substantively different position from their male counterparts. Therefore, criminal law based on the principle of gender-neutrality will still produce different, and inequitable outcomes for women *vis-à-vis* men. Thus, the law and its administration must be reorganized to guarantee **result equality** for women and men. Such an approach would entail the adoption of a type of affirmative action with respect to both criminal law and criminal justice.

For example, some reformers, including feminists, ad-

Box 11.16 Women in Prison

Discrimination against women in federal prisons in an issue now under the microscope of a federal study, which was appointed in April by Correctional Services of Canada commissioner Ole Ingstrup.

It won't be the first study critical of conditions for women.

In 1938, just four years after the [Kingston] prison opened, a royal commission recommended it be closed so women could be kept in regional facilities.

The same recommendation has been made 15 times in government and private sector studies, most recently last year by the Parliamentary justice committee and the Canadian Bar Association.

"There's a lot of women here who are cynical about commissions," says Cherel (Cherry) Platts of Toronto, an armed robbery convict and member of the prisoners' committee.

But there's an unusual amount of optimism among prisoners and prisoner rights groups that this commission will be different.

That's because the federal government's female offender program is in violation of the Charter of Rights' equality section, according to Bonnie Diamond [Executive Director of Canadian Association of Elizabeth Fry Societies].

There's one case charging discrimination now before the courts filed by one current P4W inmate and a former prisoner.

Another major suit will be filed against Ottawa this fall charging discrimination against a number of inmates. The suit is being initiated by the Toronto-based Legal Education Action Fund.

Diamond said the legal case will give the government a strong incentive to follow the recommendations of the latest report.

The study group, made up of members of the government and private sector groups such as Elizabeth Fry, will present its findings to Ingstrup on Dec. 15.

Diamond, a member of the panel, says the objective is not just to outline discrimination. That would be redundant.

Instead, it will be seeking solutions that could include far greater integration of women inmates into their communities.

Diamond said the provinces have consistently shown no ability to develop suitable programs for long-term female prisoners.

The panel travelled across Canada in June and July to meet various groups and individuals involved in prison reform and met twice with the P4W prisoners' committee.

Source: *Vancouver Sun*, August 5, 1987, p. B3.

vocate incorporating PMS and BWS as women's (i.e., status) defences. With tongue in cheek, Boyle (1985) has even called for the adoption of a contempt-of-women provision in the criminal law. The rationale for such reforms is that women cannot possibly receive equal treatment before the law and they must therefore use stop-gap measures to even things up. Nonfeminists who support these legal initiatives argue on the basis that PMS and BWS are identifiable medical conditions that, therefore, must be taken into account by the criminal law.

Similarly, to attain sentencing equality between men and women, the greater economic deprivation of the latter needs to be considered. In assessing fines, for example, judges have to realize that fine-option programs are often more problematic for women with children than for male offenders because the former lack access to the child care that would free them to work off their debt. And, as previous discussion revealed, although only a relatively small number of women are incarcerated, it is not enough to simply provide the same resources and facilities available to men, which are less than adequate in any event.

Female inmates have special needs that must be accommodated. For example, many incarcerated women are mothers who face long-term separation from and perhaps permanent loss of their children, yet very few institutions have programs for maintaining parent-child contact on a regular basis (MacLeod, 1986). Those that do usually house women who are serving shorter sentences. Thus, at the minimum-security Twin Maples in British Columbia and at Portage LaPrairie in Manitoba, women who are pregnant when they go to jail are allowed to keep their babies with them in prison while they are infants (Maintaining the Bond, 1988, p. 18; see also MacLeod, 1986).

Unfortunately, the Twin Maples institution is being phased out. Moreover, maintaining contact with older children is often impossible for female inmates (Misch et al., 1982). To date, one of the only programs for women under federal sentence was a pilot project launched in 1987 by the Solicitor General of Canada at Maison Tanguay, the Montreal correctional facility. Incarcerated mothers were allowed to live with their preschool children two days a week in a house trailer on the prison grounds (Maintaining the Bond, 1988, p. 15).

Changing the System: Transforming Existing Structures

Although they support legal reforms that focus on **result equality**, many feminists who link female criminality to the structural inequality of women in our society also argue that only a radical transformation of the *status quo* can ultimately solve those problems. Some maintain that women can never obtain justice from a legal system created by, and inevitably serving the interests of men. The way for women to avoid injustice, then, is to create a separate legal system administered by women who operate on the basis of a feminist perspective.

Other feminists argue that it is not enough to simply focus on the gender inequities in criminal law and the administration of justice. On the contrary, both female offenders and women generally must be analyzed in relation to the operation of all the institutions in our society. Thus, we must identify and eliminate the structural sources of women's subordination—which are class and racial/ethnic as well as gender-based—to solve the problem of female criminality. That, of course, would entail a compete reordering of Canadian society.

Discussion Questions

1. What are the major gaps in and/or problems with the existing information about the types and incidence of women's crime?

2. If, as Adler argues, the "women's liberation thesis" of crime is a feminist theory, why do most feminists reject it?

3. Identify the major differences between feminist and nonfeminist explanations of women's crime and explain the enduring popularity of the latter.

4. The "double-standard thesis" of criminal law and its
   administration can be viewed as the mirror image of the
   "chivalry-paternalism thesis." Discuss.

Note

1. At the time of publication of this text, plans were being
implemented to close the Kingston Penitentiary for Women.

References

Adams, S. (1978). *The female offender: A statistical perspective*. Ottawa: Solicitor General of Canada.

Adelberg, E. (1985). *A forgotten minority: Women in conflict with the law*. Ottawa: Canadian Association of Elizabeth Fry Societies.

Adelberg, E., & Currie, C. (Eds.). (1987). *Too few to count: Canadian Women in conflict with the law*. Vancouver, BC: Press Gang.

Adler, F. (1975). *Sisters in crime: The rise of the new female criminal*. New York: McGraw-Hill.

Allen, H. (1987a). *Justice unbalanced: Gender, psychiatry and judicial decisions*. Milton Keynes, UK: Open University Press.

Allen, H. (1987b). Rendering them harmless: The professional portrayal of women charged with serious violent crimes. In P. Carlen & A. Worrall (Eds.), *Gender, crime and justice* (pp. 81–94). Milton Keynes, UK: Open University Press.

Bacchi, C. (1983). *Liberation deferred?* Toronto: University of Toronto Press.

Backhouse, C.B. (1984). Desperate women and compassionate courts: Infanticide in nineteenth-century Canada. *University of Toronto Law Journal, 34*, 447–78.

Backhouse, C.B. (1985). Nineteenth-century Canadian prostitution law: Reflection of a discriminatory society. *Histoire social/Social History, 18*, 387–423.

Barnhorst, S. (1978). Female delinquency and the role of women. *Canadian Journal of Family Law, 1*, 254–73.

Baxter, S. (1988). *No way to live: Poor women speak out*. Vancouver, BC: New Star.

Benson, M. (1968). *Adult female offenders: An examination of the nature of their offences, the criminal process and service patterns*. Toronto: Elizabeth Society.

Benson, M. (1973). *The Elizabeth Fry Society, Toronto: Clients, contact patterns and agency services*. Toronto: Elizabeth Fry Society.

Bertrand, M.-A. (1969). Self-image and delinquency: A contribution to the study of female criminality and women's image. *Acta Criminologica, 2*, 71–144.

Bertrand, M.-A. (1979). *La femme et le crime*. Montreal: L'Aurore.

Berzins, L., & Cooper, S. (1982). The political economy of correctional planning for women: The case of the bankrupt bureaucracy. *Canadian Journal of Criminology, 24*, 399–416.

Berzins, L., & Hayes, B. (1987). The diaries of two change agents. In E. Adelberg & C. Currie (Eds.), *Too few to count: Canadian women in conflict with the law* (pp. 163–79). Vancouver, BC: Press Gang.

Bienvenue, R., & Latif, A.H. (1974). Arrests, dispositions and recidivism: A comparison of Indians and Whites. *Canadian Journal of Criminology and Corrections, 16*, 105–16.

Birkenmeyer, A.C., & Jolly, S. (1981). *The native inmate in Ontario*. Toronto: Ontario Ministry of Correctional Services & the Ontario Native Council on Justice.

Biron, L. (1981). An overview of self-reported delinquency in a sample of girls in the Montreal area. In A. Morris & L. Gelsthorpe (Eds.), *Women and crime* (pp. 1–18). Cambridge, UK: Institute of Criminology.

Bottomley, A., Gibson, S., & Meteyard, B. (1987). Dworkin? Which Dworkin? Taking feminism seriously. *Journal of Law and Society, 14*, 47–60.

Box, S. (1983). *Power, crime and mystification*. London: Tavistock.

Box, S., & Hale, C. (1983). Liberation and female criminality in England and Wales. *British Journal of Criminology, 23*, 35–49.

Boyle, C., & Noonan, S. (1986). Prostitution and pornography: Beyond formal equality. *Dalhousie Law Journal, 10*, 225–65.

Boyle, C., Bertrand, M.-A., Lacerte-Lamontagne, C., & Shamai, R. (1985). *A feminist review of criminal law*. Ottawa: Minister of Supply & Services Canada.

Brophy, J., & Smart, C. (1985). *Women in law: Explorations in law, family and sexuality*. London: Routledge & Kegan Paul.

Browne, A. (1987). *When battered women kill*. New York: Free Press.

Campbell, A. (1981). *Girl delinquents*. Oxford: Basil Blackwell.

Canada. (1938). *Report of the Royal Commission to Investigate the Penal System of Canada* (Chair: J. Archambault). Ottawa: King's Printer.

Canada. (1969). *Report of the Canadian Committee on Corrections* (Chair: R. Ouimet). Ottawa: Queen's Printer.

Canada. (1970). *Report of the Royal Commission on the Status of Women* (Chair: F. Bird). Ottawa: Supply & Services Canada.

Canada. (1977a). *Report of the National Advisory Committee on the Female Offender* (Chair: D. Clark). Ottawa: Solicitor General of Canada.

Canada. (1977b). *Report of the National Advisory Committee on the Female Offender: The female offender—selected statistics*. Ottawa: Solicitor General of Canada.

Canada. (1981). *Solicitor General's study of conditional release: Report of the Working Group*. Ottawa: Supply & Services Canada.

Canada. (1983–88). *The Canadian Urban Victimization Survey* (Bulletins 1–10). Ottawa: Programs Branch, Research and Statistics Group, Solicitor General of Canada.

Canada. (1984). *Report of the Committee on Sexual Offences against Children and Youths* (Chair: R. Badgely). Ottawa: Supply & Services Canada.

Canada. (1985). *Report of the Special Committee on Pornography and Prostitution* (Chair: J. Fraser). Ottawa: Supply & Services Canada.

Canada. (1987). *Sentencing reform: A Canadian approach; Report of the Canadian Sentencing Commission*. Ottawa: Supply & Services Canada.

Canada. (1988). *Report of the Standing Committee on Justice and Solicitor General on its review of sentencing, conditional release and related aspects of corrections* (Chair: D. Daubney). Ottawa: Supply & Services Canada.

Carlen, P. (1985). *Criminal women: Autobiographical accounts*. Cambridge, UK: Polity Press.

Carlen, P. (1987). Out of custody, into care: Dimensions and deconstructions of the state's regulation of twenty-two young working class women. In P. Carlen & A. Worrall (Eds.), *Gender, crime and justice* (pp. 126–60). Milton Keynes, UK: Open University Press.

Carlen, P., & Worrall, A. (Eds.). (1987). *Gender, crime and justice*. Milton Keynes, UK: Open University Press.

Chesney-Lind, M. (1986). Women and crime: The female offender. *Signs: Journal of Women in Culture and Society, 12*, 78–96.

Chesney-Lind, M. (1980). Re-discovering Lilith: Misogyny and the new female criminal. In C.T. Griffiths & M. Nance (Eds.), *The female offender: Selected papers from an international symposium* (pp. 1–35). Burnaby, BC: Criminology Research Centre, Simon Fraser University.

Chunn, D.E. (1990). Boys will be men, girls will be mothers: The legal regulation of childhood in Toronto and Vancouver. *Sociological Studies of Childhood Development, 3*, 87–110.

Chunn, D.E., & Gavigan, S.A.M. (1988). Social control: Analytical tool or analytical quagmire? *Contemporary Crises, 12*, 107–24.

Chunn, D.E., & Menzies, R.J. (1989). *Female follies: The forensic assessment of women defendants*. West Coast Law and Society Group Symposium, Vancouver, BC, March 31.

Comack, E. (1988). Justice for battered women? *Canadian Dimension, 22*, 8–11.

Cooper, S. (1987). The evolution of the federal women's prison. In E. Adelberg & C. Currie (Eds.), *Too few to count: Canadian women in conflict with the law* (pp. 127–44). Vancouver, BC: Press Gang.

Daly, K. (1987a). Discrimination in the criminal courts: Family, gender and the problem of equal treatment. *Social Forces, 66*, 152–75.

Daly, K. (1987b). Structure and practice of familial-based justice in a criminal court. *Law and Society Review, 21*, 267–90.

Daly, K. (1989). Criminal justice ideologies and practices in different voices: Some feminist questions about justice. *International Journal of the Sociology of Law, 17*, 1–18.

Daly, K., & Chesney-Lind, M. (1988). Feminism and criminology. *Justice Quarterly, 5*, 101–43.

Dubec, B. (1982). *Native women and the criminal justice system: An increasing minority*. Thunder Bay: Ontario Native Women's Association.

Eaton, M. (1986). *Justice for women? Family court and social control*. Milton Keynes, UK: Open University Press.

Edwards, S. (1981). *Female sexuality and the law*. Oxford: Martin Robertson.

Edwards, S. (1984). *Women on trial*. Manchester, UK: Manchester University Press.

Edwards, S. (1985). *Gender, sex and the law*. London: Croom Helm.

Fennel, T. (1984). Premenstrual shoplifting. *Alberta Report, II* (28 May), 30.

Fox, J., & Hartnagel, T. (1979). Changing social roles and female crime in Canada. *Canadian Review of Sociology and Anthropology, 16*, 96–104.

Gavigan, S.A.M. (1988). Law, gender and ideology. In A. Bayefsky (Ed.), *Legal theory meets legal practice* (pp. 283–95). Edmonton: Academic.

Gavigan, S.A.M. (1987). Women's crime: New perspectives and old theories. In E. Adelberg & C. Currie (Eds.), *Too few to count: Canadian women in conflict with the law* (pp. 47–66). Vancouver, BC: Press Gang.

Gavigan, S.A.M. (1983). Women's crime and feminist critiques. *Canadian Criminology Forum, 6*(1), 75–90.

Geller, G. (1987). Young women in conflict with the law. In E. Adelberg & C. Currie (Eds.), *Too few to count: Canadian women in conflict with the law* (pp. 113–26). Vancouver, BC: Press Gang.

Giffen, P.J. (1965). Rates of crime and delinquency. In W.T. McGrath (Ed.), *Crime and its treatment in Canada* (pp. 59–90). Toronto: Macmillan.

Giffen, P.J. (1976). Official rates of crime and delinquency. In W.T. McGrath (Ed.), *Crime and its treatment in Canada* (Rev.ed.) (pp. 66–110). Toronto: Macmillan.

Gilligan, C. (1982). *In a different voice*. Cambridge, MA: Harvard University Press.

Girouard, D. (1988). Les femmes incarcerées pour vol qualifié, au Québec, en 1985: Importance de leur rôle. *Canadian Journal of Criminology, 30*, 121–34.

Gomme, I.M. (1984). Rates, types and patterns of male and female delinquency in an Ontario county. *Canadian Journal of Criminology, 26*, 313–23.

Greenland, C. (1988). *Preventing CAN deaths: An international study of deaths due to child abuse and neglect*. London: Tavistock.

Greenwood, V. (1981). The myths of female crime. In A. Morris & L. Gelsthorpe (Eds.), *Women and crime* (pp. 73–87). Cambridge, UK: Institute of Criminology.

Gregory, J. (1986). Sex, class and crime: Towards a non-sexist criminology. In B.D. Maclean (Ed.), *The political economy of crime: Readings for a critical criminology* (pp. 317–35). Scarborough, ON: Prentice-Hall.

Hagan, J. (1985). Toward a structural theory of crime, race and gender: The Canadian case. *Crime and Delinquency, 31*, 129–46.

Hagan, J., Simpson, J., & Gillis, A.R. (1979). The sexual stratification of social control. *British Journal of Sociology, 30*, 25–38.

Hanmer, J., & Maynard, M. (Eds.). (1987). *Women, violence and social control*. Atlantic Highlands, NJ: Humanities Press International.

Hann, R., & Harman, W. (1986). *Full parole release: An historical descriptive analysis*. Ottawa: Solicitor General of Canada.

Hatch, A., & Faith, K. (1990). The female offender in Canada: A statistical profile. *Canadian Journal of Women and the Law, 3*, 432–56.

Heidensohn, F. (1985). *Women and crime*. Basingstoke, UK: Macmillan.

Hutter, B., & Williams, G. (1981). *Controlling women*. London: Croom Helm.

Johnson, H. (1986). *Women and crime in Canada*. Ottawa: Solicitor General of Canada.

Johnson, H. (1987). Getting the facts straight. In E. Adelberg & C. Currie (Eds.), *Too few to count: Canadian women in conflict with the law* (pp. 23–46). Vancouver, BC: Press Gang.

Kasinsky, R.G. (1978). Rape: The social control of women. In W.K. Greenaway & S.L. Brickey (Eds.), *Law and social control in Canada* (pp. 59–69). Scarborough, ON: Prentice-Hall.

Lahey, K. (1985). Until women themselves have told all there is to tell. *Osgoode Hall Law Journal, 23,* 519–41.

Lahey, K. (1989). Celebration and struggle: Feminism and law. In A.R. Miles & G. Finn (Eds.), *Feminism: From pressure to politics* (pp. 99–122). Montreal: Black Rose.

Lambert, L.R., & Madden, P.G. (1975). *The adult female offender before-during-after incarceration: Summary, conclusions and recommendations.* Vanier Research Centre Report No. 3. Toronto: Ontario Ministry of Correctional Services.

Langelier-Biron, L., & Collette-Carriere, R. (Eds.). (1983). Les femmes et la justice penale, Special issue. *Criminologie, 16*(2).

LaPrairie, C.P. (1984). Selected criminal justice and socio-demographic data on native women. *Canadian Journal of Criminology, 26,* 161–69.

LaPrairie, C. (1987). Native women and crime in Canada: A theoretical model. In E. Adelberg & C. Currie (Eds.). *Too few to count: Canadian women in conflict with the law* (pp. 103–12). Vancouver, BC: Press Gang.

Lombroso, C., & Ferrero, E. (1900). *The female offender.* New York: D. Appleton.

Lowman, J., Jackson, M.A., Palys, T., & Gavigan, S.A.M. (Eds.). (1987). *Regulating sex: An anthology of commentaries on the findings and recommendations of the Badgely and Fraser reports.* Burnaby, BC: School of Criminology, Simon Fraser University.

McLaren, A. (1986). The creation of a haven for "human thorough-breds": The sterilization of the feeble-minded and the mentally ill in British Columbia. *Canadian Historical Review, 67,* 127–50.

MacLeod, L. (1986). *Sentenced to separation: An exploration of the needs and problems of mothers who are offenders and their children.* Ottawa: Solicitor General of Canada.

Maintaining the bond. (1988). *Liaison, 14*(3), 15–18.

Matters, I. (1984). Sinners or sinned against?: Historical aspects of female juvenile delinquency in British Columbia. In B.K. Latham & R.J. Pazdro (Eds.), *Not just pin money: Selected essays on the history of women's work in British Columbia* (pp. 265–77). Victoria, BC: Camosun College.

Menzies, R.J., Chunn, D.E., & Webster, C.D. Female follies: The forensic psychiatric assessment of women defendants. *International Journal of Psychiatry and Law* 15(1): forthcoming).

Misch, C. et al. (1982). *National survey concerning female inmates in Provincial and Territorial institutions.* Ottawa: Canadian Association of Elizabeth Fry Societies.

Mitra, C.L. (1987). Judicial discourse in father–daughter incest appeal cases. *International Journal of the Sociology of Law, 15,* 121–48.

Morris, A. (1987). *Women, crime and criminal justice.* Oxford: Basil Blackwell.

Mossman, M.J., & MacLean, M. (1986). Family law and social welfare: Toward a new equality. *Canadian Journal of Family Law, 5,* 79–110.

Moulds, E.F. (1980). Chivalry and paternalism: Disparities of treatment in the criminal justice system. In S.K. Datesman & F.R. Scarpitti (Eds.), *Women, crime and justice* (pp. 277–99). New York: Oxford University Press.

Naffine, N. (1987). *Female crime: The construction of women in criminology.* Sydney: Allen & Unwin.

National Association of Women and the Law [NAWL]. (1987). *Women and criminal justice: Workshop proceedings.* Ottawa.

Pollak, O. (1961). *The criminality of women.* Philadelphia: University of Pennsylvania Press.

P4W: Looking for answers to 50-year old problems. (1988). *Liaison, 14*(4), 15–17.

R. v. Belmas, Hansen and Taylor (1986), 27 C.C.C.(3d) 155.

R. v. Lavallee (1988), 44 C.C.C.(3d) 113 (Man.C.A.).

R. v. Smith (1976), 32 C.C.C.(2d) 224.

R. v. Sullivan et al. (1988), 43 C.C.C.(3d) 65 (B.C.S.C.).

R. v. Thurrott (1974), 5 C.C.C.(2d) 129.

R. v. Whynot (1983), 9 C.C.C.(3d) 449 (N.S.S.C., A.D.).

Rosenblatt, E., & Greenland, C. (1974). Female crimes of violence. *Canadian Journal of Criminology and Corrections, 16,* 173–80.

Ross, R.R., & Fabiano, E.A. (1986). *Female offenders: Correctional afterthoughts.* Jefferson, NC: McFarland.

Silverman, R.A., & Kennedy, L.W. (1987). *The female perpetrator of homicide in Canada.* Edmonton: Centre for Criminological Research, University of Alberta.

Simon, R.J. (1975). *Women and crime.* Lexington, MA: Lexington Books.

Smart, C. (1985). Legal subjects and sexual objects: Ideology, law and female sexuality. In J. Brophy & C. Smart (Eds.), *Women in law: Explorations in law, family and sexuality* (pp. 50–70). London: Routledge & Kegan Paul.

Smart, C. (1976). *Women, crime and criminology: A feminist critique.* London: Routledge & Kegan Paul.

Smart, C. (1979). The new female criminal: Reality or myth? *British Journal of Criminology, 19,* 50–59.

Smart, C. (1984). *The ties that bind.* London: Routledge & Kegan Paul.

Smart, C., & Smart, B. (Eds.). (1978). *Women, sexuality and social control.* London: Routledge & Kegan Paul.

Smith, D. (1975). The statistics on mental illness: What they will not tell us about women and why. In D.E. Smith & S.J. David (Eds.), *Women look at psychiatry* (pp. 73–119). Vancouver, BC: Press Gang.

Statistics Canada. (1979). *Correctional institutions statistics, 1976.* Ottawa: Minister of Industry, Trade and Commerce.

Statistics Canada. (1988). *Canadian crime statistics, 1987.* Ottawa: Minister of Supply and Services.

Statistics Canada. (1989). *Adult correctional Services in Canada, 1987–88.* Ottawa: Minister of Supply and Services.

Tepperman, L. (1977). *Crime control.* Toronto: McGraw-Hill Ryerson.

Toronto Family Court. (1923). *Annual report, 1922* (p. 18) Toronto.

A voyage of discovery. (1988). *Liaison, 14*(3), 4–7.

Walford, B. (1983). *Lifers: The stories of eleven women serving life sentences for murder.* Montreal: Eden.

West, G. (1984). *Young offenders and the state.* Toronto: Butterworths.

Widom, C.S. (1981). Perspectives of female criminality: A critical examination of assumptions. In A. Morris & L. Gelsthorpe (Eds.), *Women and crime* (pp. 33–48). Cambridge, UK: Institute of Criminology.

WICL: A look at the past, a plan for the future. (1986). *Liaison, 12*(9), 18–23.

12 Minorities, Crime, and the Law

J. Colin Yerbury and Curt T. Griffiths

Some Important Definitions

Canadian Indigenous Peoples and the Law

The "Sons of Freedom" Doukhobors and the Canadian State: The Laws of God versus the Laws of the State

Summary and Conclusions

In the Introduction, it was noted that one of the major considerations in studying **crime** and **criminality** in Canada is recognizing that Canada is a multicultural society with myriad cultural and ethnic groups. In this chapter, we explore the issues surrounding minorities and the law, focussing on the patterns of crime and the nature and extent of contact with the legal system of two groups: Canada's indigenous people and the Doukhobors. Both are characterized by a lack of political, social and, in some cases, legal and economic *power*. In this, these minority groups share much with women, the topic of Chapter 11. We will see that the application of a national **Criminal Code** to indigenous peoples, and to religious sects, historically and in contemporary times, has often been characterized by discrimination and conflict. There remain many unanswered questions about crime among minorities and how to effectively administer justice in a country as geographically and ethnically diverse as Canada.

Some Important Definitions

At the outset of our discussion, it is important to define a number of terms that are widely, albeit often incorrectly, used. First, what is a minority? Dictionaries generally define a minority as "a racial, religious, political, national or other group regarded as being different from the larger group of which it is a part." For purposes of our discussion, we will use the term *minority group* to refer to one whose members are relegated to a subordinate position in society and thus experience lack of prestige, privilege, and power. As a result, the minority group members may be subjected to a wide range of discriminatory treatment by societal institutions, including schools, the employment sector, and the law.

Race has been used in a variety of ways—to categorize linguistic groupings (Aryan, English-speaking), to categorize religious groupings (Moslem, Hindu, Jewish), to denote a national grouping (Portuguese, Italian, German), and to categorize mystical, quasi-scientific groupings (Teutonic). The definition of race has largely been a societal definition. A scientific definition, however, would require us to be able to isolate the physical or biologically transmitted characteristics of a group and to show how their differentiating factors influence their behaviour and way of life. For example, the adherents of **biological determinism** discussed in Chapter 7 might seek to show how members of certain racial groups displayed greater propensities for criminal behaviour. This is not possible, nor of interest to most social scientists. As a matter of fact, *race* has become a "four-letter word" to serious researchers.

Many groups referred to as "racial" by laymen are what social scientists define as *ethnic*. Most scientists have rejected the notion that human behavioural traits are transmitted genetically; rather, such traits are acquired through learning during the socialization and education process in a society. *Culture,* rather than biological makeup, is the primary determinant of behaviour, and an ethnic group is identifiable by its distinctive cultural characteristics. Ethnicity, then, suggests the existence of a distinct culture or subculture within which group members feel themselves bound together by common ties that are recognized by other members of the society. Nationality, language, religion, and tribal identity are ethnic categories that can be used to distinguish groups.

Ethnic groups are inherently *ethnocentric*. Members of the group look upon their cultural characteristics such as religious values, sexual behaviours, eating and drinking habits, political conceptions, economic structures, laws, and customs and other cultural elements as natural, correct, and superior to those of other ethnic groups: the cultural characteristics of other groups are considered bizarre, inferior, strange, and, perhaps, immoral.

Prejudice is a manifestation of ethnocentrism. This is an aversive or hostile attitude toward an individual because he or she belongs to a particular group and is assumed to share the objectionable qualities ascribed to the group. This is often called stereotyping. **Discrimination,** however, is the acting out of prejudice. Prejudice is an attitude; discrimination is behaviour.

When one ethnic group has political power, that group's views are reflected in criminal law; so, laws and the administration of justice can be ethnocentric, even discriminatory. In our discussion, we will see that Canadian indigenous peoples and religious minorities have been subjected to prejudiced and discriminatory laws.

Further, we will see that members of some minority groups are involved with the **criminal justice system** to a greater extent than are members of the dominant Euro-Canadian society, both historically and in contemporary times. This involvement is manifested in three ways:

1. Behaviours accepted in one culture may clash with the standards and laws of the dominant culture. For example, laws were passed criminalizing opium use (see Chapter 5); and, existing laws against arson were used to prosecute Sons of Freedom Doukhobors (see below).

2. Rebellion against dominant authority or political dissent can be responded to as a crime. This was the case with Louis Riel, discussed in Chapter 1.[1] The selling of cigarettes on some Native Indian reserves is interpreted variously as a crime or as a legitimate expression of native sovereignty.

3. The high rate of conventional crime, such as assault and theft, can be seen as a consequence of a disadvantaged position in Canadian society and the treatment of minority group members by successive generations of Euro-Canadians.

When minority groups such as Canada's indigenous peoples and the Freedomite Doukhobors are perceived to have problems or are acknowledged to be problems by Euro-Canadian society, these problems are inevitably ascribed to the inherent characteristics of the minority group, rather than to defects in the larger social system. For example, Canadians often attribute the high school dropout rate of indigenous students, their chronic poverty, and their overrepresentation in correctional institutions to deficiencies inherent in native persons themselves.

And, in the following discussion, we will see that, while Canada's indigenous people have made initial attempts to develop their own community-based justice services such as police forces, the strong, centralized government in Canada and the national Criminal Code have mitigated the potential effectiveness of such initiatives in reducing native conflict with the law. In fact, it could be argued that, despite Canada's self-identification as a multicultural society, this diversity has not extended into the legal realm, and that such a label eschews the socio-structural disparities that exist between the dominant Euro-Canadian majority and indigenous, religious, and immigrant groups, which, in turn, increases their likelihood of conflict with the law and involvement in the legal system.

Canadian Indigenous Peoples and the Law

In the following discussion, we will consider the socio-structural position of indigenous peoples in Canadian society, including the relations between Euro-Canadians and indigenous peoples and the plight of indigenous communities, as well as the nature and extent of indigenous contact with and conflict with the **criminal law**.[2]

Indigenous peoples in Canada are distinguished by their cultural and linguistic attributes as well as by their legal status. Status Indians are indigenous people who are registered under the federal *Indian Act*. Non-Status Indians are those who identify themselves as indigenous people but who are not registered under the *Indian Act*. Métis are the descendants of mixed Indian and European ancestry, while Inuit are a distinct cultural group who reside primarily in the Northwest Territories, Labrador, and in Arctic Quebec. In Figure 12.1, the major groups of indigenous people in Canada and Alaska are presented.

Indigenous peoples comprise approximately 2 percent of the total Canadian population and are distributed, albeit unevenly, across the country. Figure 12.2 illustrates the percentage of indigenous people in each province/territory. It is apparent that, in the northern territories, indigenous peoples comprise the greatest proportion of the population.

Statistics from the 1981 Census of Canada indicate that these groups are distributed as follows: Status Indians (59.9 percent); Métis (20.0 percent); non-Status Indians (15.3 percent); and Inuit (5.2 percent). In the following discussion, we often use the term "indigenous peoples" to include all of these groups, but we do make reference to specific groups where the distinction is significant. A discussion of these groups is hindered by the lack of published materials. Statistical information is collected in a systematic manner only on Status or registered Indians. In 1987, there were 415 898 Status Indians in Canada.

There is considerable diversity among the 573 recognized Indian bands in Canada in terms of their culture, social, and political organizations, and in the attributes of individual Indian communities. The majority of the Indian bands in Canada—nearly 65 percent of the registered Indian population—are situated in rural and remote areas of the country, compared to 25 percent of the national population. The remoteness is a key factor in Indian involvement with the law and the delivery of justice services to Indian people.

The majority of registered Indians live on reserves, although the growth rate for off-reserve registered Indians is higher than the on-reserve growth rate. In recent years, an increasingly larger number of Indians has migrated to urban areas of the country and the proportion of off-reserve Indians has increased in all regions.

Explaining Indigenous Criminality

In the published literature, there are a number of perspectives that have been developed in an attempt to explain crime among indigenous peoples and their involvement in the criminal-justice system (May, 1982). These approaches are not mutually exclusive and, as we will see in the following discussion, they are closely connected with the process and consequences of colonization.

The five dominant explanations for indigenous crime are as follows:

1. *Adjustment/acculturation:* Criminality and conflict with the law are consequences of colonization and the difficulty that indigenous peoples have in relating to the dominant society and its institutions.

2. *Social disorganization:* Crime among indigenous peoples is the result of conflict between the indigenous culture and that of the dominant Euro-Canadian society. This results in a breakdown of community and leadership structures and the internal mechanisms of social control that traditionally served to maintain order and prevent crime.

3. *Traditional social organization:* Crime among indigenous peoples is an extension of traditional cultural behaviour. The patterns of crime and deviance vary across cultural groups, based on the types of behaviours encouraged by the group. Such behaviours may conflict with the dominant, non-indigenous law and legal systems.

4. *Overt and covert discrimination:* Indigenous peoples are more visible to agents of the criminal-justice system, such as the police, and, once detected, are more likely to become involved in the criminal-justice process. Once in the criminal-justice system, indigenous peoples have less ability to "escape" from conviction and incarceration. The likelihood of discrimination is increased when an alien system of law and justice are imposed on a colonized people and when criminal-justice practitioners have little or no understanding of the culture and lifeways of indigenous peoples.

5. *Indigenous peoples as victims of socio-structural deprivation:* The likelihood of conflict with the criminal law and involvement in the criminal-justice process is increased by the pervasive socio-structural deprivation and economic and psychological dependency of indigenous peoples.

In the following discussion, we will consider the various dimensions of these explanations.

Indigenous Peoples in Canadian Society

The law and the criminal-justice system are only two of several primary societal institutions (others being health care, education, etc.). We must first consider the larger societal context within which Canada's indigenous population lives

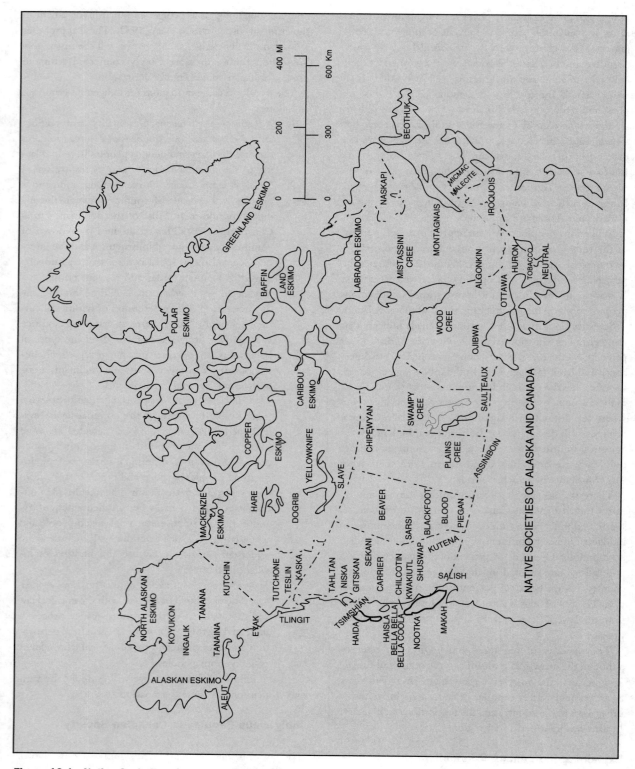

Figure 12.1   Native Societies of Alaska and Canada

Source: J.A. Price (1978). *Native studies: American and Canadian Indians* (p. vii). Toronto: McGraw-Hill Ryerson.

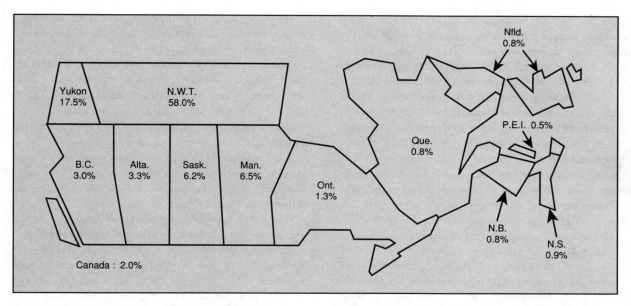

Figure 12.2 Native People as a Percentage of the Total Population, Canada, Provinces and Territories, 1981*

*Native people are a small proportion of Canada's total population. The 491 460 individuals who identified themselves as native people in the 1981 Census made up just 2 percent of the total population. However, they were not evenly distributed across the country. In the Northwest Territories they were the major-ity—nearly 60 percent of all residents—and about 20 percent of Yukon inhabitants were native people. Among the provinces, Manitoba and Saskatchewan had the highest proportions of native people—more than 6 percent. Around 3 percent of the residents of Alberta and British Columbia claimed native ancestry. East of Manitoba, about 1 person in 100 was identified as native.

Source: Statistics Canada. 1984. *Canada's Native People*. Ottawa: Minister of Supply and Services, n.p.

before narrowing our focus to contact and conflict with the law. If Canada's indigenous peoples are in conflict with the law and with the criminal-justice system, it is highly likely that they will also be expecting conflict in other areas, be they economic, educational, or cultural.

We must, therefore, not lose sight of the larger structural factors that may be related to the nature and extent of crime among indigenous peoples and that contribute to high rates of violent crime, alcohol and solvent abuse, domestic violence, and property offences that are present among indigenous bands and communities in many jurisdictions across the country.

Many observers argue that the subordinate political and economic position of indigenous peoples in Canada is a consequence of the colonization by Europeans and by Canadian government policies that have exerted control over virtually every aspect of indigenous life. As we saw in Chapter 1, the indigenous population was exploited by early entrepreneurs to extract resources, principally furs, for European markets. As settlement, and therefore agriculture, moved from east to west, Indians were forced out, gradually being contained in nonviable reserves, reliant upon government support to survive. The federal Indian

Act enshrined in law a paternalistic policy that denied them any legal, political, or economic autonomy or self-determination.

A major consequence of this subordinate, minority status is the "victimization" of indigenous people, which is evidenced by pervasive poverty, high rates of unemployment and reliance upon public assistance, low levels of education, high death rates from accidents and violence, and increasing rates of family and community breakdown. Particularly vulnerable are youth, aged 15 to 24, who are most susceptible to violent and accidental death, suicide, and alcohol and solvent abuse (Griffiths, Yerbury & Weafer, 1987; Siggner, 1979). An example of the consequences of the socio-structural condition of indigenous peoples is provided in Figure 12.3, which compares the suicide rate of Status Indians with the Canadian suicide rate.

Throughout Canada's Arctic, there are high rates of violent and property-related offences, widespread alcohol and drug abuse, an increasing incidence of suicide and family breakdown, and other symptoms of community and cultural disintegration. Sociological and anthropological studies have documented the decline of Inuit from a proud, independent, and self-determinant people to wards of the

Canadian state (see Irwin, 1988; Mayes, 1982).

While there is a paucity of published material on the socio-economic condition of non-Status Indians, Métis, and Inuit, data on registered Indians presented by Siggner (1986) and Lithwick, Schiff, & Vernon (1986) indicate that:

—in 1984, 47 percent of Indian housing was in poor physical condition, 36 percent was overcrowded, and 38 percent lacked running water and/or indoor plumbing;

—in 1981, the unemployment rate for Indians was two and one-half times that for the Canadian workforce; twice as many members of the experienced Indian labour force did not work in 1980, as compared to the non-Indian experienced labour force;

—in 1980, the average annual income for Indians was 60 percent that of the general Canadian population; one-fourth of the Indians had no income;

—in 1981, 19 percent of Indians had completed some post-secondary education, compared with 36 percent of the total Canadian population; in 1978–79 and 1982–83, nearly one-half of the Indian students in the fourteen-to-fifteen age range were in grade levels below those appropriate for their ages.

These data indicate that on-reserve Indians fare far worse in terms of "social conditions" than do their off-reserve counterparts, although the socio-economic disparities between Indians and non-Indians extend to urban areas of the country. In Winnipeg, Clatworthy (1980) found that the unemployment rate among Indians was four times higher than that for non-Indians, while household income for Indians was about one-half that of the total population. Among the Indian population, there was a high percentage of single-parent families, and Indian youth and women experienced particular hardships. Similar findings have been reported in Edmonton (see Native Counselling Services of Alberta and Native Affairs Secretariat, 1985).

There does appear to have been some improvement in the socio-structural position of some indigenous peoples over the past three decades. In a recent study of registered Indians, Indian and Northern Affairs Canada (1988) reported:

—the mortality rate per 1000 had declined from 10.5 in 1955 to 5.3 in 1986;

—the infant mortality rate per 1000 had declined from 80.2 in 1960 to 16.5 in 1986;

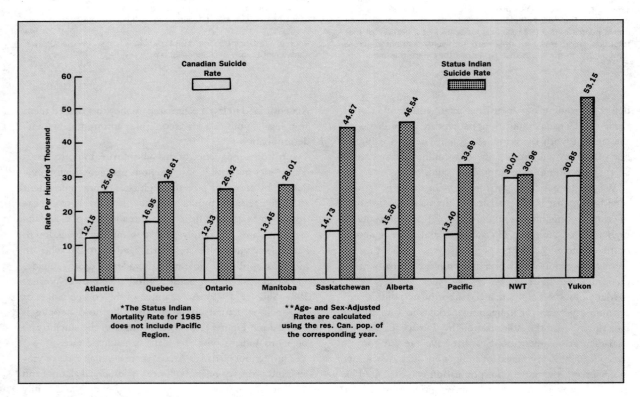

Figure 12.3 Regional Age- and Sex-Adjusted Suicide Rates, Canadian and Status Indian, 1982 to 1985 Average

Sources: Statistics Can. Cat. 84-206; Medical Services Branch Statistics.

—the number of Indian children who are in grade twelve or thirteen after consecutive years of schooling has increased from 3.4 percent in 1980–61 to 33.9 percent in 1985–86;

—the number of Indians enrolled in university has increased from 50 in 1960–61 to 5800 in 1985–86;

—since 1977, there has been a steady decline in the number of children in the care of child-welfare authorities;

—during the period 1963–86, the percentage of houses with running water increased from under 14 percent to 75 percent.

This report also provides some evidence of the increasing involvement of indigenous peoples in assuming control over key institutions in their communities and in self-government:

—the number of band operated schools has increased from 53 in 1975–76 to 243 in 1986–87;

—in 1971, status Indians administered 20 percent of Department of Indian Affairs and Northern Development program expenditures, a figure that had risen to 64.1 percent in 1986–87.

Such figures should be viewed with caution, however, as they relate only to Status Indians on an aggregate level. There are wide disparities between Status Indians across the country, and there is no systematic information gathered on non-Status, Métis, and Inuit peoples. Further, even among Status Indians, there are signs of continuing dependency. Over the period 1981–82 to 1986–87, the number of dependants on social assistance steadily increased, and total social assistance expenditures to Status Indians increased twofold from 1973 to 1986.

There are also concerns about the relations between indigenous peoples and nonindigenous Canadians, particularly in terms of the stereotyping of indigenous people as "lazy drunks." There are several excellent studies that examine patterns of interaction between "whites" and indigenous peoples at the community level including one by Niels Braroe (1975). More recently, the sensitivities surrounding white-indigenous relationships have been highlighted by the publicity and inquiry into the death of a young Indian woman, Helen Osborne, in the northern Manitoba community of The Pas (see Box 12.1).

Indigenous Peoples and the Euro-Canadians: Colonization and Conflict

The relationships between the federal government of Canada and indigenous peoples, both historically and recently, are best understood from a majority/minority or colonial perspective (see Havemann, 1989; Kellough, 1980; Morrison, 1986; Ponting, 1986). For purposes of our discussion, *colonialism* is defined as a set of processes whereby the resources and destiny of a satellite region are controlled by an imperial, metropolitan region.

In Canada, colonization has been an intentional, long-term process and has involved replacing the traditional, self-determinant lifestyle of indigenous people with a dependent and subordinate status. Historically, the whalers, missionaries, fur traders, and government officials have been the primary agents of change in the westernization process (Coates, 1985; Crowe, 1974; Swiderski, 1985).

In the Canadian North and in other areas of the country, coerced resettlement was used by the federal government to establish sovereignty over indigenous peoples. This involved moving people from their traditional camps and villages to newly created, "artificial" communities, ostensibly for humanitarian and administrative reasons. These settlements were based on Euro-Canadian notions of community: streets rather than the traditional Indian and Inuit cluster groups of families, and single-family housing units that did not accommodate the traditional extended-family arrangement of the indigenous people.

The traditional hunting-and-gathering, subsistence lifestyle was gradually replaced by one based on a wage economy. The consequence of this process was the transformation of the social, cultural, and political life of the residents. The experience of the Grassy Narrows reserve, as documented by Shkilnyk (1984), illustrates the consequence of these processes for an indigenous community.

Over time, the indigenous culture was increasingly displaced, and many Indian and Inuit communities were swept into resignation and feelings of hopelessness. The introduction of Euro-Canadian culture resulted in rapid and overwhelming change in the culture of Indians and Inuit. This, in turn, created widespread culture shock and **anomie** on both the community and individual levels.

One of the major consequences of the colonization and the attendant government policies has been the destruction of indigenous communities and of the very foundations of indigenous culture and traditions. The high rates of death and conflict with the law are, in many instances, a manifestation of this loss of community. In the preface to the book *A Poison Stronger than Love* (Shkilnyk, 1984) Kai T. Erikson used the term "collective trauma" to describe the destruction of indigenous communities:

the community no longer exists as an effective source of support and . . . an important part of their world has disappeared without even so much as a sound. As people begin to emerge hesitantly from the protective shells into which they had reflexively shrunk at the time of the assault, they learn that they are isolated and alone, living in a kind of social wasteland with no one to turn to. They have lost both the

Box 12.1 Conspiracy of Silence: The Death of Helen Osborne

Helen Betty Osborne wanted to be one of the fewer than 5 percent of indigenous peoples in Canada to complete high school. To accomplish this, she had to leave her family on the Norway House reserve and live during the school year in The Pas, Manitoba. It was during her third year, in 1971, that, while walking alone, she was forced into a car by four local boys, driven to a remote area, and stabbed more than 50 times with a screwdriver, including one blow that went 5.5 centimetres into her brain. She was nineteen years old.

Her naked body could have lain there for months or years but she was discovered the next day by a young boy chasing rabbits. Positive identification of her body could not be made visually, and only with fingerprints was she determined to be treaty Indian 848. The condition of her body led authorities to believe that a frenzied killer was on the loose.

While the case baffled the local RCMP for a while, it soon became apparent that several local kids were responsible: Lee Cogan, 17; Jim Houghton, 23; Norman Manger, 25; and, Dwayne Johnston, 18. Cogan, whose alcoholism was already apparent, was bragging all over town about the murder. His father's Chrysler had been used in the abduction. And he and Betty attended the same high school. Over the years he confessed to perhaps dozens of people, including the local sheriff, but no one came forward with that information. In fact, it was felt that perhaps the majority of people in the town knew about the boys' involvement in the murder.

But the police were not able to lay charges until 1987, sixteen years later. Meanwhile, Cogan's health had deteriorated as a result of his alcoholism, and his wife had left him after years of physical abuse. Manger had continued his life as a vagrant, and years of drug and alcohol abuse had taken their toll. Johnston had continued his association with motorcycle gangs and, after some initial trouble with the law and with his long-time girlfriend, he had married and was employed in Revelstoke, B.C. Houghton had fared the best and was living with his wife and two children in Lethbridge.

By 1987, no new evidence had surfaced, but the police were able to gain the co-operation of one of the participants. After a charge of **first-degree murder** was laid against Cogan, he exchanged his testimony against the others for total immunity. Johnston and Houghton went on trial in November 1987, but only Johnston was convicted.

We may never know exactly what happened that night, but Cogan's version of the story was that the four had been drinking heavily and Johnston had lured Betty into the car to force her to have sex. While she violently fought off his advances, the car drove to the weekend cabin of Jim Houghton's parents and, because of her screams, eventually to an even remoter place. There, Johnston dragged her, now nearly naked, out of the car and began beating her against the rear trunk. At some point, he returned to the car and retrieved a screwdriver from under the seat. Houghton got out of the car, but for some reason did not assist Betty, even though he was much bigger than Johnston. Perhaps it was because she was already unconscious, or perhaps, as the prosecution alleged, he helped. One or both of the men dragged her body into the bush and left her there to bleed to death. They then drove back to town and attended a local dance.

Many have been critical of the police's inability to lay charges for sixteen years and the fact that only one of the four was convicted. Much attention has also focussed on the residents of The Pas and why they kept quiet about the affair for so long. Discrimination has often been cited to explain all these facts.

Lisa Priest, in her 1990 book *Conspiracy of Silence*, paints a picture of The Pas as a town that experienced tremendous social disorganization after the building of a mill brought an influx of people, money, and the related social problems. Alcohol abuse was common to many of the key participants and their families, including Betty Osborne. However, Priest feels that the nearly 200 police officers that worked on the case off and on for sixteen years were guilty only of lack of leadership and inexperience in an investigation of this complexity. In fact, several officers systematically tried to unnerve the killers by sending them vodka and orange juices ("Screwdrivers") when they were drinking in public or with anonymous Christmas gifts of green-handled screwdrivers. It was not new evidence that triggered the prosecution but the assignment of an officer to the case full-time.

Testimony presented to the Manitoba Aboriginal Justice Inquiry revealed that, among others, the sheriff in The Pas had been told of Betty Osborne's murder by one of the alleged participants. Despite the new evidence that emerged during the hearings and the calls for a new criminal investigation into the case, the Attorney General of Manitoba decided that a reopening of the case was not warranted.

physical and spiritual health that comes from being in communion with kinsmen and neighbors who can be counted on to care. (p. xvi)

The imposition of Euro-Canadian culture also had an impact on the traditional Indian and Inuit systems of social control. Morse (1983) identifies four possible outcomes when the legal system of a dominant, colonizing government comes into contact with the traditional system of social control of an indigenous minority:

1. *total avoidance:* the two systems of law function separately, with neither assuming jurisdiction over the other;
2. *co-operation:* the two systems of law function side by side, with clearly defined jurisdictional boundaries;
3. *incorporation:* one society dominates the other to the extent that certain elements of the other's law that do not fundamentally conflict with its own are adopted; and
4. *rejection:* there is outright rejection of the indigenous legal system by the dominant group, in this case Euro-Canadian society.

Historically, the position of the Canadian federal government in relation to indigenous peoples can be characterized as one of "total rejection." Keon-Cohen (1982, pp. 191–92) notes that, while American Indian tribes in the United States have enjoyed a unique constitutional position that provides them with legal sovereignty over the administration of criminal justice on reservations, the Canadian government has traditionally resisted attempts by indigenous peoples to assume jurisdiction in this area: "tribal governments and justice systems based on inherent powers have not, to date, developed in Canada.... Canadian natives, like their [Australian] Aboriginal counterparts, and unlike their American Indian brethren, are thus totally subject to, and processed by the Anglo-Canadian legal system, as compared to separate tribal justice systems." The reluctance of the federal government in Canada to encourage or recognize the development of "autonomous" or separate indigenous justice systems continues to the present, although in recent years several indigenous-controlled police forces and court-worker and social service programs have been created (see Griffiths & Verdun-Jones, 1989).

A major dimension of the involvement of indigenous peoples in crime and with the Canadian legal system is the conflict between the traditional Indian and Inuit "law" and Euro-Canadian laws. The basic principles of each system of laws are outlined in Box 12.2.

There are key distinctions between the Euro-Canadian and Indian/Inuit concepts of crime. As was noted in Chapter 2, the general components of a criminal offence in Euro-Canadian law are *actus reus* and *mens rea:* in order for a criminal offence to have occurred, there must have been a prohibited act and a guilty mind. Such is not the case within traditional Indian and Inuit culture. To the Inuit, for example, an offence is completely subjective and situational: the *actus reus* may have occurred in conjunction with the *mens rea,* yet the act may be considered a "nonoffence" by Indian or Inuit standards if:

—the act occurred, such as theft, and the offender intended to return the property or pay restitution at a later date;

—the act occurred, and the offender apologizes to the victim;

—the act occurred, and it was done for prestige gathering; or

—the act was attempted, such as a break-and-enter, with the intent to steal an item that was then not taken, and the actor did not complete the act as intended; therefore, nothing wrong was done.

Box 12.2 illustrates that Indian and Inuit customary law relied heavily upon consensus. Law was closely intertwined with the natural environment, and personal offences were viewed as transgressions against the individual rather than the community. **Sanctions** were on an individual-to-individual basis, rather than emanating from the collective. This system of dispute resolution, in which a primary objective was the restoration of order in the community, was in stark contrast to the adversarial Euro-Canadian system of law, which places an emphasis on deterrence and punishment, and the notion that the response to offensive behaviour should come from the collective or from those in positions of authority acting on behalf of the collective.

Indigenous Peoples and the Law: A Historical View

The whalers, missionaries, and fur traders who had initial contact with the indigenous peoples brought with them Euro-Canadian concepts of law and justice. The Hudson's Bay Company, with its monopoly over the fur trade, imposed Euro-Canadian laws in order to maintain order and insure a steady flow of commerce. The officials in charge of the Hudson's Bay Company trading posts acted in the roles of police officer, prosecutor, and judge (Morrison, 1985). As we saw in Chapter 1, once settlement of the prairies began, the criminal justice system was used to isolate the Indians on reserves and enforce dependence upon the federal government.

With the westward pattern of settlement, Indians were pushed out of their homelands to somewhat marginal land reserves. In the Arctic, the Inuit had remained largely isolated from Western culture, until the beginning of the

Box 12.2 Comparison of Legal Concepts: Euro-Canadian and Traditional Native Indian/Inuit

Euro-Canadian Laws	Traditional Native Indian/Inuit Laws
Laws formulated by elected representatives	Laws formulated by the community through tradition and consensus
Laws tied to man-made economy and therefore complex and numerous	Laws tied to the natural environment; only a few universally condemned actions in Native Indian/Inuit customary law
Protestant Ethic and Christianity the moral foundation of the law	Traditional Native Indian/Inuit religions the foundation of Native Indian/Inuit codes of behaviour
Personal offences seen as transgressions against the state as represented by the monarch	Personal offences seen as transgressions against the victim and his or her family; community involved only when the public peace is threatened
Law administered by representatives of the state in the form of officially recognized or operated social institutions	Law usually administered by the offended party, i.e., the family, clan or the tribe, through a process of mediation or negotiation
Force and punishment used as methods of social control	Arbitration and ostracism usual peace-keeping methods
Individualistic basis for society, and the use of the law to protect private property	Communal basis for society; no legal protection for private property; land held in trust by an individual and protected by the group

Source: C. Jefferson (1983), *Conquest by law: A betrayal of justice in Canada* (p. 283). Burnaby: Northern Justice Society Resource Centre, Simon Fraser University.

twentieth century. Even today, as Figure 12.2 illustrates, there are very few people who claim Indian ancestry living in the Atlantic provinces, while indigenous peoples constitute a majority of the population in the Northwest Territories and almost 20 percent in the Yukon.

The North-West Mounted Police (NWMP) had first ventured north in the late nineteenth century, and became well established in the Yukon during the Klondike gold rush (see Chapter 1). The maintainance of Canadian sovereignty, in the face of a dispute over the Alaska/Canada border, occupied much of their attention until the discovery of gold in Alaska ended the massive migration into the Yukon. It was during the early 1900s that the first attempts to enforce the Queen's law on the indigenous peoples of the Canadian North occurred, and this provides us with an illustration of the conflict between the indigenous and Euro-Canadian culture and legal systems as well as the policy

of rejection of the indigenous culture by the federal government in its attempt to colonize indigenous people and establish sovereignty over the vast areas of the North and West.

Early patrols of the NWMP often visited the Inuit and Indian communities of the Northwest Territories to "show the flag" and assist the government in establishing sovereignty over more remote areas of the country. Among the duties of the police were census taking, surveying, the collection of taxes from the fur traders and whalers, acting as customs officers, and enforcing the peace between indigenous peoples and Euro-Canadians. Company officers also acted in the role of police magistrates and justices of the peace.

In Box 12.3 the case of Sinnisiak and Uluksuk, the first two Inuit charged under the Queen's law, is presented. This case illustrates the events that took place when Euro-

Photo 12.1 The trial of an Inuit at Port Harris, Quebec, 1935. The man standing with his back to the camera is probably translating.

Royal Canadian Mounted Police Archives, no. 2367.

Canadian law came into contact with and was imposed on indigenous peoples. (The case has been documented by R.G. Moyles in the book *British Law and Arctic Men* [1990].)

Patterns of Indigenous Crime

Our consideration of the nature and extent of crime among indigenous peoples is hindered by a lack of published research. Official statistics generally include only Status or registered Indians, and there are few data on the crime patterns of Métis, Inuit, and non-Status Indians. Still unexplained are the data from the Uniform Crime Reporting System (Canadian Centre for Justice Statistics, 1989, (p. 30) that reveal that the Northwest Territories (22 199 Criminal Code offences per 100 000 population) is second only to the Yukon Territory (22 648 per 100 000) in the number of Criminal Code offences per 100 000 population. In 1987, the rate of violent crime in the Northwest Territories (4410 per 100 000 population) and the rate of property offences (9841 per 100 000 population) were the highest reported rates in the country. It is noted in Chapter 14 that the same pattern is found in other Arctic countries. Given the high concentration of indigenous peoples in the territories, it is difficult to examine crime in the North without a consideration of crime by indigenous peoples.

Despite these rough indicators, there have been very few empirical studies on crime among indigenous youth, adults, women, and the elderly, or their involvement in the criminal-justice system. Neither do we have a clear understanding of the crime patterns in the various jurisdictions —"northern" and "southern," rural, and urban—across the country.[3]

As a consequence of this, we are able to present only a general overview of the patterns of indigenous crime in Canada, with the *caveat* that there are wide variations across the country, between rural and urban areas, and across the different cultural and linguistic groups. From the materials that have been produced, we can distil the following attributes of indigenous crime:

—indigenous peoples tend to commit less serious crimes than do their nonindigenous counterparts, with the exception that, in many jurisdictions, indigenous peoples are involved in a large number of violent crimes against persons (see discussion in Chapter 11 of violent crime and native women);

—the socio-economic condition of indigenous peoples plays a significant role in their involvement in criminal behaviour;

—alcohol use is present in a high percentage (up to 90 percent in some jurisdictions) of crimes committed by indigenous peoples;

—in comparison with their nonindigenous counterparts, indigenous offenders were first identified by the criminal-justice system at an earlier age;

—in many jurisdictions, indigenous youth evidence rates of arrest are up to three times that of their nonindigenous counterparts.

An illustration of the types of crimes committed by Canada's indigenous peoples is presented in Box 12.4 from data compiled from the Correctional Service of Canada for the period 1974 to 1983 (in Lithwick Rothman Schiff Associates, Ltd. 1986, p. 175).

Further insights into criminality among indigenous peoples are provided by the findings of a longitudinal study of Indian offenders in the province of Manitoba conducted by McCaskill (1985). Several of the results are presented in Box 12.4.

Indigenous Peoples in the Criminal-Justice System

There has also been increasing concern about the extensive involvement of Inuit peoples in the criminal-justice system and, in particular, the conflict experienced by Inuit with the Euro-Canadian systems of law and justice. To date, there have been no comprehensive, cross-national studies of indigenous peoples in the Canadian criminal-justice system. From the research that has been conducted to date,

Box 12.3 British Law and Arctic Men: The Case of Sinnisiak and Uluksuk

In a landmark case in 1917, two Inuit men from the Coppermine area of the Northwest Territories became the first Inuit charged under the King's law for the alleged murder of two Oblate priests. The Inuit, Sinnisiak and Uluksuk, were pursued for nearly two years by officers of the Royal North-West Mounted Police, lead by Inspector Denny La Nauze. The Inuit were brought to Edmonton, Alberta, for trial before judge and jury.

Sinnisiak and Uluksuk were found "not guilty" by the jury in Edmonton, but were subsequently retried in Calgary before the same judge and another jury, and found guilty. In his charge to the jury in the second trial, and in response to arguments by the defence counsel that the two men had little knowledge of the law and had acted on the basis of their traditional lifeways, the presiding judge, Chief Justice Horace Harvey (quoted in Moyles, 1990, pp. 70–80), stated: "They have a right to have their case considered fairly, and fully and honestly; but on the other hand they owe a corresponding duty . . . the laws are the same for all; they are all equal before our laws, and what would be an offence for one would be an offence for all."

Convicted of murder, they were given the mandatory sentence of death. But, prior to passing sentence, the judge had secured a promise of clemency from Ottawa, and the death sentence was commuted by the governor general. Justice Harvey (Moyles, 1990, p. 81) asked of the translator: "Patsy, you might tell them when they get back home, if they do, they must let their people know that if any of them kill any person they will have to suffer death. They

know now what our law is."

The pair served less than two years in a minimum-security-detention police guardroom at Fort Resolution on Great Slave Lake. Upon their release they were again admonished to spread the word of the Canadian law.

The first Inuit to be hanged was Alikomiak, tried by an all-white jury in 1924 for killing two police officers. His trial took place in the North, so the Inuit could witness the dispensing of Canadian justice (Moyles, 1990).

In the following years, there were additional cases in which Indians and Inuit were charged and brought to trial under the King's law (Schuh, 1979). The principle established through these cases was that the Canadian criminal law applied to all Canadians, including indigenous peoples.

While the trial case of Sinnisiak and Uluksuk took place three-quarters of a century ago, many of the issues that were raised during the two trials remain today. Should the Canadian Criminal Code apply equally in Burnaby, B.C.; Buffalo Narrows, Saskatchewan; Povungnituk, Quebec; and Pond Inlet, Northwest Territories? Is "justice" imperilled when indigenous peoples do not understand either that their actions may be against the law or the proceedings of the criminal courts in which they are tried? Should the culture and traditions of indigenous peoples be considered by criminal-justice personnel, including the police and the presiding judge, when deciding whether to charge an indigenous person with a crime or when determining the guilt or innocence and passing sentence?

however, we can make the following *general* statements:

—while indigenous peoples tend, on average, to commit less serious crimes than do their nonindigenous counterparts, they are more frequently arrested, found guilty, and incarcerated;

—indigenous peoples, both adults and youths, are overrepresented (in proportion to their representation in the general population) in arrest statistics, court conviction statistics, and correctional institution populations in many areas of the country;

—indigenous peoples comprise about 7 percent of the total federal inmate population; in provincial institutions, they often constitute 60 to 70 percent of the inmate population;

—on average, the sentences received by indigenous peoples were shorter than those given to nonindigenous

peoples, accounting for their overrepresentation in provincial corrections-institutions populations;

—in many jurisdictions, indigenous youth are overrepresented in arrest statistics, in youth court systems, in detention facilities, and in child care systems;

—indigenous women are overrepresented in the criminal-justice system in many jurisdictions, particularly in the Prairie provinces, where, in 1982, indigenous women constituted up to 40 percent of the admissions to provincial correctional facilities in Alberta and more than 70 percent in the Northwest Territories, Yukon, and Manitoba (see also Chapter 11).

More specifically, Hylton (1980) found, in Saskatchewan, that male Status Indians were 37 times more likely to be incarcerated, while Métis and non-Status Indians were 12 times more likely to be confined than were non-Indians.

Compared to their non-Indian counterparts, Indian women were 118 times more likely to be incarcerated, and Métis and non-Status Indian women 25 times more likely to be incarcerated than non-Indian women.

During the period 1985–90, several events forced Canadians to face the possibility of discrimination and prejudice in the administration of justice for indigenous peoples. These include the case of Donald Marshall, a Nova Scotia Micmac Indian (see Box 12.5); the shooting of Indian leader J.J. Harper by police in Winnipeg in 1987 (see Box 12.6); and the inquiry into the 1977 killing of Helen Osborne in The Pas, Manitoba.

The circumstances surrounding the shooting of J.J. Harper by a Winnipeg police officer (see Box 12.6) and the inquiry into the murder of Helen Osborne were examined as part of the work of the Manitoba Aboriginal Justice Inquiry, co-chaired by Mr. Justice A.C. Hamilton and Judge Murray Sinclair of the Provincial Court of Manitoba. This inquiry was perhaps the highest-profile examination of the issues surrounding indigenous peoples and the law, and involved extensive hearings in Indian communities throughout Manitoba as well as submissions and testimony from criminal justice personnel, Indian leaders, and community residents.

Box 12.4 The McCaskill Study of Indian Crime Patterns

This investigation involved comparison of data gathered from correctional-institution inmate files and parole files and interviews with individuals in Indian organizations and communities and social service and criminal-justice agencies in 1970, and again in 1984. The findings of this study provide valuable insights into Indian criminality.

In comparing the socio-economic and offence profiles of inmates in 1970 with those in 1984, McCaskill found that the backgrounds of Indian inmates and parolees in 1970 and 1984 were characterized by serious social and personal disorganization, including family instability, alcohol abuse, and low levels of education and skill development.

1. Comparison of Background Characteristics of Native Offenders

Variable	1970	1984
Native Status		
(% of Status Indians)	high	high
Age		
(% over 35 years of age)	very low	high
Family Size		
(% with over 6 siblings)	high	high
Marital Status		
(% single)	high	high
Level of Education		
(% with some high-school experience)	very low	low
Level of Skill	very low	moderate
Employment Record	poor	fair
Degree of Alcohol Problem	very high	very high
Degree of Urbanization at Birth		
(% born in urban areas)		
Degree of Urbanization at		
Time of Admission		
(% living in urban areas)	moderate	high

The following system was used to rank the samples:
under 20% of sample	very low
20% to 30% of sample	low
40% to 59% of sample	moderate
60% to 79% of sample	high
80% or more of the sample	very high

Box 12.4 *(Continued)*

2. Comparison of Types of Crime Committed by Native Offenders

Type of Crime	1970		1984	
	Number	%	Number	%
Murder	4	1.8	20	8.6
Attempted Murder	—	—	2	.9
Manslaughter	14	6.3	33	14.2
Rape	3	1.8	11	4.7
Other Sex Crimes	3	1.8	6	2.6
Wounding	2	1.3	—	—
Assault	36	16.4	6	12.1
Robbery	40	17.9	49	21.1
Offensive Weapon	5	2.2	5	2.2
Break-and-Enter	49	21.9	31	13.7
Theft over $200	31	13.8	10	4.3
Theft under $200	—	—	2	.9
Possession of Stolen Goods	2	1.3	2	.9
Fraud	6	2.9	2	.9
Criminal Negligence	1	.4	—	—
Other	9	4.0	5	2.2
Arson-Theft	2	.9	1	.4
B.E.T.—Assault	2	1.3	10	4.3
Alcohol Related	3	1.8	1	.4
Driving Non-Alcohol	3	1.8	1	.4
Auto Theft	6	2.7	—	—
B.E.T.—Robbery	1	.4	6	2.6
Mischief	1	.4	2	.9
Willful Damage	1	.4	—	—
Prison Breach	—	—	1	.4
Narcotics	—	—	3	1.3
Total	224	100.0	209	100.0

While the police are the "front line" and point of first contact between indigenous peoples and the criminal-justice system, the relationships between police and Canadian Indians and Inuit in rural and urban areas are often characterized by mutual hostility and distrust. This situation increases the likelihood of conflict between the two groups and may be a contributory factor in the high arrest rates experienced by indigenous peoples in many areas of the country.

In a study of police-Indian relations in the Prairie provinces of Alberta, Saskatchewan, and Manitoba, Donald Loree (1985) surveyed regular RCMP members as well as Indian Special Constables. Loree found that nearly 43 percent of the regular members described the general state of Indian–non-Indian relations in their detachment area as "fair," while almost 34 percent defined them as "good" and only 3.7 percent as "very good." According to the regular members interviewed by Loree, the greatest areas of difficulty in policing Indian communities were "differences in cultural values and outlook on life," "problems linked to high unemployment," and "dealing with young people."

Two of the more significant findings from the Loree (1985) study are: (1) for regular members, alcohol-related incidents are the most common context within which police officers come into official contact with Indian people and (2) a primary determinant of the quality of Indian-police relations appears to be the age, experience, and personal policing style of the individual police officer.

Police officers' knowledge of the communities and people they are policing is also important, although Loree (1985) found that a significant proportion of the officers he interviewed described themselves as having only a "fair" level of general knowledge about Indians. And, as impor-

Box 12.4 *(Continued)*

3. Comparison of Categories of Crimes Committed by Native and Non-Native Offenders in 1983 and 1984

Crime Category	Federal Correctional Institutions*				Provincial Correctional Institutions**			
	Native		Non-Native		Native		Non-Native	
	No.	%	No.	%	No.	%	No.	%
Crimes against Persons	93	46.5	82	19.7	314	15.6	121	5.7
Crimes against Property	86	43.0	237	56.18	602	30.2	665	31.5
Sex Offences	9	4.5	16	3.8	27	1.3	46	2.2
Narcotics Offences	—	—	31	7.4	21	1.0	131	6.2
White-Collar Offences (Fraud)	—	—	20	4.8	28	1.4	104	5.0
Driving Offences	—	—	—	—	162	8.1	328	15.5
Alcohol-Related Driving Offences	—	—	—	—	366	18.2	501	23.7
Liquor Control Act	—	—	—	—	183	9.1	47	2.2
Other	12	6.0	31	7.5	308	15.1	168	8.0
Total	200	100.0	417	100.0	2011	100.0	2111	100.0

* Data from *Native Population Profile Report*, Analysis and Information Services, Correctional Service Canada, Ottawa, April, 1984
** Data from Adult Corrections Directorate, Department of Community Services and Corrections, Province of Manitoba, Winnipeg, 1984.

In 1970, the majority of offences were for either theft or assault, were unpremeditated, and involved alcohol. In 1984, the Indian inmates in the study had committed a larger number of crimes of violence and sexual assaults and there had been a corresponding decrease in property-related offences. Table 3 (above) reveals that Indian offenders in federal and provincial correctional institutions had committed more crimes against persons than had their non-Indian counterparts.

McCaskill's study also revealed significant increases in crimes committed by Indian offenders in urban areas, with a corresponding decrease in the crime rate in Indian communities in rural areas of the province. In those rural communities in which there had been a decrease in the crime rate over the fourteen-year period, several discernible changes had occurred, including the emergence of strong leadership in the community, an increase in community awareness and participation in crime control and crime prevention initiatives, and a resurgence of traditional, indigenous methods of social control.

Source: All tables McCaskill (1985), Tables 2.3, 3.1, 3.2.

tantly, most of the knowledge the officers did have had been acquired after they had arrived in the community. A high percentage of the officers surveyed felt that the police-Indians relations could be improved through an increased emphasis on police-community relations and more active involvement of officers in sports and social activities in the community.

Conflict between indigenous peoples and agents of the Canadian criminal-justice system may also be precipitated by a lack of knowledge on the part of Indians and Inuit peoples about the law and the legal system. Many observers have argued that indigenous peoples in rural, urban, and northern areas of the country have only a cursory understanding of the law, their legal rights, and the criminal-justice process and that this contributes to the high rates of arrest, guilty pleas, and confinement. In a study of police-Indian relations in the Yukon, for example, Parnell (1979) found that nearly 90 percent of the Indians interviewed stated that they required more information about the law, and 55 percent desired information on their legal rights.

Conflict between indigenous peoples and the police may also occur in urban areas. In a study of police officers in

Box 12.5 Justice Denied: The Case of Donald Marshall

Shortly before midnight on May 28, 1971, Donald Marshall, Jr., a seventeen-year-old Micmac, and Sandy Seale, a seventeen-year-old black, met by chance and were walking through Wentworth Park in Sydney, Nova Scotia, when they met two other men, Roy Ebsary, 59, a former ship's cook; and James (Jimmy) MacNeil, 25, an unemployed labourer.

Following a brief conversation, Marshall and/or Seale tried to "panhandle" Ebsary and MacNeil. That simple request triggered a deadly overreaction in the drunken and dangerous Ebsary. "This is for you, black man," Ebsary said, and stabbed Seale in the stomach. He then lunged at Marshall, cutting him on the arm. Marshall's wound was superficial; Seale died less than a day later.

This following is an excerpt from the Royal Commission on the Donald Marshall, Jr., Prosecution: Digest of Findings and Recommendations (Hickman, 1989, pp. 2–3; see also Harris [1986]):

> The Commissioners have found that Seale was not killed during the course of a robbery or attempted robbery. Seale, who came from a strict family and was expected home before his midnight curfew, had enough money to catch a bus home. We heard no evidence during our hearings that he had ever been involved in any criminal activity. Although Marshall had had a few brushes with the law, they were of a minor nature that did not involve theft. Roy Ebsary, on the other hand, had a reputation for violence and unpredictable behaviour, and had previously been convicted on a weapons charge involving a knife.
>
> In our view, Seale and Marshall, who barely knew one another, would not have the time or the inclination to plan a robbery in the few moments between their accidental meeting and the stabbing. According to the evidence we heard, they didn't even initiate the fateful conversation with MacNeil and Ebsary that ended in the stabbing.
>
> The four Sydney police officers who initially responded to the report of the stabbing—Constables Leo Mroz, Howard Dean, Richard Walsh and Martin MacDonald—did not do a professional job. . . . We found their conduct entirely inadequate, incompetent and unprofessional.
>
> The same can be said of the subsequent police investigation directed by the then Sergeant of

Detectives John MacIntyre. MacIntyre very quickly decided that Marshall had stabbed Seale in the course of an argument, even though there was no evidence to support such a conclusion. MacIntyre discounted Marshall's version of events partly because he considered Marshall a troublemaker and partly because, in our view, he shared what was a general sense in Sydney's White community at the time that Indians were not "worth" as much as Whites.

Regardless of the reasons for his conclusion, MacIntyre's investigation seemed designed to seek out only evidence to support his theory about the killing and to discount all evidence that challenged it.

Largely because of the untrue statements MacIntyre had obtained, Donald Marshall, Jr., was charged on June 4, 1971, with murdering Sandy Seale.

The commission went on to censure the Crown attorney and Marshall's defence counsel for failing to discharge their professional obligations, and the judge for several legal

Donald Marshall and his lawyer emerge from the Nova Scotia Court of Appeal in 1983.
Canapress Photo Service.

Box 12.5 (Continued)

errors. Ten days after Marshall was convicted, Jimmy Mac-Neil came forward to accuse Ebsary of the murder. However, this information was not given to Marshall during his unsuccessful appeal. Other evidence came to light over the years but was also ignored.

Not until 1982 was the case reopened, after Marshall learned that Ebsary had admitted the crime. At the request of Marshall's new lawyer, the RCMP conducted an investigation. Although they uncovered the evidence that verified Marshall's innocence, during their questioning of him they solicited a statement that the murder had occurred during a robbery attempt. The commission believed that this statement was not voluntary in that the police had pres-sured Marshall, a man wrongly imprisoned at this point for eleven years, into verifying Ebsary's version of events. While the Nova Scotia Court of Appeal quashed Marshall's conviction, the Court made, in the words of the commission (1989, p. 7) a "serious and fundamental error" by blaming Marshall for his misfortunes. Believing that he had been involved in a robbery, the Court concluded that Marshall had perjured himself in the first instance by claiming that he and Seale had been only panhandling.

The conclusion was given great weight by those called upon to determine the amount of financial compensation due Donald Marshall because of his eleven years of imprisonment.

Regina in the 1970s, Hylton and his colleagues found that a large percentage of the officers viewed Indians as "lazy" and as "drunks." Perhaps no one event, however, has served to focus attention on police-Indian relations in urban centres more than the death of Indian leader J.J. Harper in Winnipeg in winter 1987.

Concerns have also been voiced that indigenous peoples in the Canadian North, many of whom do not speak English, have little understanding of the principles of Cana-dian law and the functioning of the adversarial system of criminal justice. This may also be true of indigenous peoples in other remote areas of the country.

While police officers are posted to northern communities, judicial services are provided via the circuit court, which has been the subject of increasing attention (and criticism) in recent years. Circuit court parties—comprised of a provincial or territorial court judge, court clerk, defence lawyer, and Crown counsel—travel to communities (gener-

---

Box 12.6 The Death of J.J. Harper

On the night of March 8, 1988, Constable Robert Cross of the Winnipeg Police Department stopped Mr. J.J. Harper on a Winnipeg street for suspicion of auto theft. During Constable Cross's exchange with Mr. Harper, a scuffle ensued and Mr. Harper was shot by Constable Cross's revolver. A police investigation, completed within 48 hours of the shooting, concluded that there had been no wrongdoing on the part of Constable Cross and that the weapon had discharged accidentally during the struggle.

The incident ignited a strong response, and charges of police racism were levelled by Indian leaders in Manitoba and across the country. The incident was one of the primary reasons for the creation of the Manitoba Aboriginal Justice Inquiry by the provincial government.

The inquiry's extensive hearings into the incident revealed a large number of irregularities surrounding the case, including: (1) officers attending the scene had altered the notes in their notebooks from the time of the incident to the time of the hearing; (2) critical evidence at the scene had been destroyed; (3) Constable Cross's weapon had not been fingerprinted; and (4) a full investigation of the shooting had not been conducted by the police department.

Among the more disturbing findings of the inquiry was that officers in the police department had made racial jokes at the police station in the hours following the shooting. And an instructor at the police training program testified that new officers often made racial remarks about Indian people.

(For more detailed materials on the Harper shooting, see the Report of the Manitoba Aboriginal Justice Inquiry [1990], available from the Attorney General of Manitoba.)

ally, by air) on a regular basis to hold court.

While many communities are served monthly, others are visited every three months, or more infrequently if there are no cases to be heard or if the weather prevents a scheduled visit. The most extensive circuit-court systems are in the Northwest Territories, where Territorial and Supreme Court justices travel on 6 circuits to the 62 communities, and in northern Quebec, where the circuit criminal courts cover the James Bay and Ungava Bay regions.

Indigenous organizations and communities have argued that many of the defendants who appear before the circuit courts do not understand the adversarial proceedings of the court nor the legal terminology that is used. A major dilemma that often confronts the sentencing judge is whether to impose a **disposition** that results in the removal of the indigenous offender to a correctional facility many miles from the community or to utilize community-based programs and services. Further, it is argued that the dispositions available under the Criminal Code do not address the unique needs of the specific community, offenders, and victims.

Government-Sponsored and Indigenous-Controlled Initiatives to Reduce Conflict with the Law

The conflict with the law experienced by indigenous peoples and their extensive involvement in the criminal-justice system has placed pressure on the federal, provincial, and territorial governments to develop policies and implement programs to address these problems.

A close examination of the response of the federal government provides key insights into how the dominant majority has approached the task of addressing indigenous crime and conflict with the law. The basis of government initiatives was the National Conference on Native Peoples and the Criminal Justice System, held in Edmonton in 1975. This conference was attended by federal, provincial, and territorial, as well as Indian and Inuit leaders, and was the first attempt to identify and discuss the major areas of conflict that indigenous peoples experienced with the law.

A major recommendation of the conference participants was that programs and services for indigenous peoples in conflict with the law be developed and that indigenous communities become more extensively involved in the design and delivery of justice services. During the years following the conference, a number of program initiatives were undertaken, including the deployment of Indian Special Constables who assist regular RCMP officers in policing indigenous communities and reserves (a program that is now being phased out), and the creation of native court-worker programs to provide assistance to indigenous

offenders during the court process (Griffiths & Yerbury, 1984; Hathaway, 1986).

Despite the proliferation of government-sponsored programs and services, there has not been, in the two decades since the 1975 Edmonton conference, a significant decrease in the numbers of indigenous persons in conflict with the law and, in most areas of the country, the rates of arrest, conviction, and incarceration are higher than they were prior to the conference. Many observers have argued that the failure of government-sponsored initiatives to reduce indigenous conflict with the law is the result of the failure to address the causal factors related to indigenous crime, including the socio-structural position of indigenous peoples in Canadian society.

Critics such as Havemann (1989) also point to the reluctance of the federal government to encourage the development of "autonomous" or separate justice systems for indigenous peoples, and contend that the federal government has pursued a policy of "indigenization," whereby indigenous people are recruited to fill such positions as Special Constable and court-worker, within the criminal-justice system, and that such policies insure that the federal government retains power over indigenous peoples.

Despite the preference of the federal government for developing programs and services for indigenous peoples within the framework of established criminal-justice and social service delivery systems, many bands and communities have taken the initiative to create autonomous, community-based programs. There are several indigenous-controlled police forces operating in Canada, including the Amerindian Police Force in Quebec, the Dakota-Ojibway Tribal Council Police in Manitoba, and several reserve-based police forces in Alberta.

There has been an increased involvement of Indian and Inuit communities in developing community-based alternatives to the formal justice system and, in many instances, these alternative programs and services incorporate customary law and traditional methods of social control. In the province of Quebec and in the Northwest Territories, for example, "traditional" Inuit adoption, whereby an Inuit mother may "give" a child to a member of the extended family or to another community resident for upbringing, has been recognized in provincial law. In many Inuit and Indian communities, elders are playing an increasingly larger and more influential role in addressing problems relating to youth and adult crime.

There are other examples of community-based initiatives designed to address crime problems and conflict with the criminal-justice system. Often these initiatives occur in conjunction with the revitalization of the community— the assertion of independence and individual and community confidence to confront and resolve problems. One of the more widely publicized "success" stories was the transformation of the Alkali Lake Indian Band in British Columbia from nearly 100 percent alcoholic to over 95 percent abstinent.

Such initiatives have an opportunity to work where government policies and programs have failed. There is an emerging consensus that indigenous communities must play the primary role in addressing problems of crime, and that they should be given the necessary resources and jurisdictional authority to do so. For it is the indigenous communities that can best identify the problems and needs of the people and mobilize community-based resources to address them.

The failure of the Canadian federal government to give indigenous peoples the legal sovereignty and jurisdiction over the administration of justice, however, means that the development of community-based, indigenous-controlled programs and services will continue to be uneven. And, even with increased autonomy of reserve-based peoples, this leaves large numbers of non-Status, Métis, and Inuit peoples, as well as Status Indians residing off reserves, who will continue to come into contact (and conflict) with the criminal-justice system.

The "Sons of Freedom" Doukhobors and the Canadian State: The Laws of God versus the Laws of the State

Our second exercise of relating criminality to minorities is taken from a category of minority group we can label "religious sect."[4] The "Sons of Freedom," a small radical group of Doukhobors, are well known to government authorities for their bombing, burning, nude parades of protest, and hunger strikes. Unfortunately, explanations for such extreme behaviour have been simplistic and have not explained the Doukhobor pattern of life and "Sons of Freedom" criminality and deviance. Some writers have portrayed the Doukhobors as zealots raised at the breast of ignorance, hatred, and madness, and as bent and twisted, moulded and conditioned to fit into their warped society

of crime and mass paranoia (Holt, 1964, p. 288). Such interpretations, however, do little to explain conflict between the "Sons of Freedom" and the Canadian government and its legal system (see Box 12.7). It is clearly not possible to discuss fully in this chapter the complexities of the relationships within the Doukhobor sect and with the various levels of Canadian government and the general population or the "host" majority. Nevertheless, when you have completed the section, you should have a better understanding of the Doukhobor sect and the sometimes violent action of its zealot wing, as well as the resultant governmental intervention and public resentment of the sect.

The Doukhobors, and particularly the Sons of Freedom, have demonstrated a capacity to defend themselves against both "enforced assimilation" and "individual assimilation" through noncompliance with legislative requirements and through revitalization processes. Under severe social-structural conditions and politico-economic stress, a religious minority's beliefs and rituals generally tend to become concerned with achieving a significant improvement in the immediate conditions of collective life or in the prospects for a better afterlife, or both. Revivalist subsects such as the Sons of Freedom are ultra-conservative, and generally that places the onus of their problems and distress back onto their individual members: disciples are urged to adopt a pure life without smoking, drinking, lying, fornicating, and so forth, in order to attain a new identity, free from sin and ready for the promise of eternal life. Extremist revitalization processes involve purification rituals of burning material possessions. Such actions serve as a mechanism for temporarily increasing group unity. The disciples have to work together communally to rebuild and to restore their community, and for a time there are no problems of group membership defections. Conservation of the religious *status quo* is, thus, achieved in the struggle *against* assimilation.

The Doukhobors and their Sectarian Lives: A Historical Overview

The Doukhobors' social movement emerged in the mid-eighteenth century. A group of dissident Russian peasants

---

Box 12.7 Doukhobors Will Need a Constant Watching

Doukhobors will need a constant watching until schools and contact with other settlers will transform them and make them think in the same way as an ordinary man does (Department of the Interior, 1907, 10).

It is useless and silly for me to proceed further until the crazy people are put in the mental asylum, and criminals locked up in the penitentiary (Judge Harry J. Sullivan, January 7, 1948).

renounced the Russian Orthodox Church, and formed a sect called the "People of God" (Woodcock & Avakumovic, 1977, p. 19). During a much earlier phase of their movement, they were called "Ikonobortsi," or ikon wrestlers, because of their rejection of the Russian Orthodox Church's ritual of using ikons (religious paintings) in their worship. Rather than bowing to a wooden ikon, members of the sect assumed the ritual of bowing to each other to formally recognize the Spirit of God, which was believed to dwell within each of them. In an effort to identify the sect as heretics, in 1785, Archbishop Amvrosii Serebrennikov referred to this dissident group as "Doukho-bortsi," meaning spirit wrestlers. The archbishop intended this as a derogatory label suggesting that the sect was struggling against the Holy Spirit. The Doukhobors adopted the label by changing its connotation so that it was interpreted: "We are Spirit Wrestlers because we wrestle with and for the Spirit of God" (Union of Spiritual Communities of Christ (USCC), n.d., p. 3). In other words, the sect would struggle for a better life by using the spiritual power of love, rather than any form of violence or coercion.

Over time, this social movement was to incorporate other changes and self-inspired customs into its belief system that would distinguish it as an exclusive sect (see Box 12.8). The Doukhobors abandoned most features of the Russian Orthodox Church such as the liturgy, ikons, fasts, festivals, churches, sacraments, the priesthood, and baptism. Heaven and hell were incorporated into their belief system as states of mind: because of this belief, the Doukhobor bury their dead without ceremonial rituals. Marriages were also regarded as mutual consent between individuals, not contracts imposed by church and state (Woodcock & Avakumovic, 1977, p. 19; Stoochnoff, 1961, p. 30). Finally, their rejection of the Bible as an ultimate source of inspiration sets them off from most Christian sectarian movements. The Doukhobors' unwritten theology and history is referred to as the "Living Book." In other words, they make use of an oral scripture in place of the rejected Bible. This practice contains an idea of progressive revelation and strong utopian and millenarian elements (Woodcock & Avakumovic, 1977, p. 26; Whitworth, 1979, p. 210). Their only other symbols of the basic elements of existence and faith are the loaf of bread, the container of salt, and the jug of water, which are always present on a table in the middle of their meeting-halls.

The denial of the right of the state or any external authority to dictate Doukhobor behaviour comes from their central belief in the eminence of God and the presence within each man of the Christ Spirit. This belief has perhaps engendered most of their conflict with the state and the monolithic church in Russia, and later with the Canadian state. Under the leadership of Peter Vasilievitch Verigin,

"Peter the Lordly," the Doukhobors refused to take an oath of allegiance to the Tsar, since their allegiance was to God alone. In 1895, they were asked to burn all of their weapons as a symbolic act of renouncing the taking of human life (see Popoff, 1975, pp. 76–77). As they considered human beings as vessels for devine essence, to kill another human was to kill Christ.

This move toward radical introversionism, in which a sect isolates itself from the external world by developing agrarian communal societies and by practising endogamy (marriage within the group), led the tsarist government to view these activities as open resistance (Woodcock & Avakumovic, 1977, p. 90). The introversionist activities of the Doukhobors were met with harsh oppression by the state and church authorities, and the Doukhobors were subjected to violent persecutions: stories of these persecutions have been retold from generation to generation, and reinforced by Doukhobor encounters with various Canadian governments. Open resistance to governmental demands had, thus, become a tradition before their emigration from Russia, although there was no hint of the more bizarre eccentricities among the sect membership before their arrival in Canada.

The Canadian Doukhobors and the Canadian State

As a religious and ethnic minority, the Doukhobors entered Canada without persecution and with substantive privileges before the law (Hawthorn, 1955, pp. 15–16). There were two special concessions, which had been accorded to other minority groups in the country long before the sect emigrated to Canada. First, the Militia Act of Canada exempted from service "Quakers, Mennonites, or Tunkers, and every inhabitant of Canada of any religious denomination, otherwise subject to military service, who from the doctrine of his religion, is averse to bearing arms." This was completely compatible with Doukhobor ideas of nonviolence and pacifism. Second, in the late 1870s, the Dominion Land Act had been amended to include the Hamlet Clause to aid the settlement of Mennonites. The Hamlet Clause allowed a number of homestead settlers, embracing at least twenty families, to settle together in a hamlet or village with a view to greater convenience in the establishment of schools and churches, and for the attainment of similar social advantages. The clause originally required that the homestead settlers cultivate or make improvements on each separate quarter-section entered as a homestead. In May 1898, the act was amended to allow for improvements proportional to the total land grant rather than in proportion to each quarter-section. These earlier practical and political gestures would appear on the sur-

Box 12.8 Doukhobors Are Similar to Anabaptist Christians

The Doukhobors are similar to Anabaptist Christians such as the Hutterites, Mennonites, and Amish in that they regard the state as evil, official churches as corrupt, and war as intolerable, but there is still a significant principal doctrinal difference. The Hutterites, for example, practise a continuous and daily surrender of self to the will of God in communal life. The individual "will" must be broken, and this is achieved through intensive indoctrination. Humble-ness, submissiveness, and obedience are necessary in a system governed by divine order: male over female, older over younger, and parent over child. Individual eccentric or confrontational behaviour is absent. Faced with "host majority" discriminatory behaviour and restrictive land legislation by the Prairie provinces, the Hutterites merely avoided involvement with the larger society.

face to facilitate the ideal Doukhobor agrarian communal society in the vacant Dominion Lands in Manitoba and the North West Territories of Canada (P.C. 2747), but there were conflicts with law and government, among themselves, and with rival land-seekers and neighbours soon after their settlement in two reserves near Yorkton, in the territory of Assiniboia, and on one reserve in Saskatchewan Territory, near Prince Albert.

Most conflicts between the Doukhobors and government have occurred over land and its laws of registration and ownership and over Canadian citizenship and its privileges and obligations. Seemingly unknown to the Doukhobors, it was eventually necessary for each of them to take oaths of allegiance to the Crown in order to secure full title to their land. It is relatively certain that Canadian officials had not pointed out such a requirement to the Doukhobor delegates during the negotiations of 1898. Oaths of allegiance had earlier been grounds for contention with the tsarist authorities. From the beginning of 1901, the Commissioner of Crown Lands began to exert increasing pressure on the Doukhobors to register individually for quarter-sections. Notices were eventually posted threatening that any lands not entered by May 1, 1902, would be open to any homesteader who wished to settle on them (Woodcock & Avakumovic, 1977, p. 171). Political pressure had been exerted on the government by rival land-seekers and ranchers and by local merchants and labour leaders, who viewed the Doukhobors as having unfair advantages over them. Most of the Prince Albert colonists did comply with the order and registered individually for their lands, but in the two colonies near Yorkton only a few registered while under severe ostracism by their brethren (Woodcock & Avakumovic, 1977, p. 173). It was not possible for the government to fulfil its threat of withdrawing land from the Doukhobors since more than 4000 individuals would have been left homeless on the prairies. The land issue was to remain simmering under the surface for a few more years,

although this issue and others served to factionalize the Canadian Doukhobors.

Between the time of their arrival and 1902, about one-third of the Doukhobors had abandoned their form of "communism" and had moved toward individualism, especially at Prince Albert. Only the North Colony near Yorkton remained devoted to the ideals of a communistic religious brotherhood, but with variations. This pronounced shift toward individualism can serve to demarcate the beginning of the Independent Doukhobors. The Independents quickly moved toward assimilation into Canadian society, and it was the Independents who later formally renounced Verigin's leadership in 1939 (see below).

The conflicts between the Doukhobors and government over land registration, citizenship requirements, registration of vital statistics, taxation, the general hostility encountered by the sect from the public and government officials, and the sectarian movement from religious communism toward individualism engendered the formation of a radical subsect expressing an extreme assertion of Doukhobor ideals. During the 1899–1902 period, the Canadian Doukhobors were having problems with leadership, since Verigin remained exiled in Siberia until 1902. This allowed other eccentric individuals to interpret Verigin's rare communications puritanically, to articulate Doukhobor dissatisfaction, and to form a subsect. Between June 1900 and the early months of 1901, a group of discontent zealots, some of whom eventually called themselves the "Sons of God," produced a series of statements and petitions expressing total disapproval of Canadian laws and the Canadian government (Woodcock & Avakumovic, 1977, p. 177). Specifically, they were concerned with the requirements under the Hamlet Clause, and wished for provisions similar to Indian lands. Other Canadian laws that they disapproved of dealt with the registration of marriages, births, and deaths. In retrospect, if the government had made compromises at this time rather than later, the "Sons of God" might never have gained prominence. The participants of this movement later became the leaders of the violently disposed chiliasts—the "Sons of Freedom."

The relations between the Doukhobors and their Canadian neighbours were further fractured by other peculiar practices of the "Sons of God." Interpreting Verigin's messages, they determined that, to be members of the "Sons of God," people had to give freedom to all creation. All domesticated animals were given emancipation by the zealots, and everything made of leather or animal skins was ritually burnt. Men and women were hitched to wagons and farm equipment to replace draft animals. Needless to say, the arrival in a prairie town of a team of a dozen men and women hitched to a wagon astounded their Canadian neighbours, who were further perplexed by a mass pilgrimage through the Doukhobor communities and other parts of Saskatchewan and Manitoba. Verigin had talked about a land near the sun where fruit would grow "raised by an abundance of solar heat" (Wright, 1940, p. 189). In July 1902, the "Sons of God" had asked Dominion Land Officials to transfer them to the fruit-growing areas of British Columbia or Southern Ontario, but they received no response. By October, the zealous had gathered more than a thousand men, women, and children into a millenarian type pilgrimage to find the promised land and to meet Christ. This strange assemblage of barefooted, singing pilgrims, foraging for seed pods of wild rose bushes, leaves, grass, and almost anything of vegetable nature, contrasted with everyday prairie life and provided political opportunity for the opposition Conservative party as well as sensationalistic fuel for the Canadian press (Wright, 1940, pp. 194–97; Woodcock & Avakumovic, 1977, pp. 178–81). While the women and children were stopped at Yorkton, 600 male marchers reached Minnedosa, Manitoba, on November 6, 1902. By then, their millenarian enthusiasm had waned through exhaustion and bitter weather. Very few resisted the immigration officials' efforts to send them back to Assiniboia, and those who did were carried on a special train by the police. The only other form of resistance was a brief hunger strike by women and children, a type of protest that was to repeat itself.

Verigin was released from his Siberian exile in autumn 1902, and arrived in Canada on December 18, 1902. One of his more immediate concerns upon his arrival in the colonies was to re-establish unity among the Canadian Doukhobors by drawing all the disputing factions under the aegis of his influence. Another problem requiring immediate attention was the formalities concerning land registration. He was made aware of the requirements of the Dominion Land Act, and he determined that registration was a mere formality as long as his followers did not regard land as individual property, but as communally owned. Only a few

dissidents refused to register their quarter-sections. At the time, it appeared that Verigin had united the Doukhobors, but less than six months after his arrival the dissidents were beginning to evangelize and to resist what they perceived as Verigin's concessions to the corrupt external society (Wright, 1940, pp. 213–15; Woodcock & Avakumovic, 1977, pp. 193–94).

This group calling themselves *Svobodniki,* or "Freedomites" (labelled "Sons of Freedom" by western Canadians), began wandering through the communities, preaching resistance to the temptations of the external world. Confused by Verigin's concessions, they evolved the theory that Verigin's actions were an attempt to deceive the Canadian government. Through perversion of reasoning, they conjured the idea that he meant his followers should understand the opposite of his public statements and that they should continue to act in the radical spirit of his sermons for his approval. Their radical preaching was largely ignored by the busy farmers until the Freedomites began to evangelize, during May 1903, in the nude "in the manner of the first man Adam and Eve, to show nature to humanity" (Woodcock & Avakumovic, 1977, p. 194).

The nude parades and the prison sentence served to create a strong nucleus for the Sons of Freedom subsect for several reasons. The radical zealots were now convinced that Verigin was no longer the Christ, since he had denounced their behaviour. They vowed to owe allegiance to him no longer, nor to any other leader. They were convinced, too, that the Community Doukhobors were moving away from the true faith through following Verigin and through secularization. The immigrants were adopting Canadian farming methods by purchasing satanic farm machinery. Metal implements were evil since, in the mines, people were tortured to obtain ore. On their release, some of the zealots attempted to set fire to a threshing machine to force the non–Sons of Freedom back to the pure and holy life. Verigin insisted on prosecuting them for arson, and six men received three years' imprisonment. Again, destruction was used as an agent of purification and renunciation. While the zealots had doubted government before, their experience of both physical punishment and confinement for demonstrating their freedom from worldly influences served to solidify their view of the external world. In addition, their incarceration allowed them to identify with Christ and his disciples who had also been persecuted. The zealots were placed in the coveted position of being **martyrs**, and they knew that future protest parades would result in widespread publicity and imprisonment or martyrdom—a tool that is used effectively by their descendants (Zubek & Solberg, 1952, pp. 67–68; Woodcock & Avakumovic, 1977, p. 197).

The movement of the Independents was more threatening to Verigin's community organization than that of the Freedomites. From 1902 until 1906, the movement had grown to about 849 individuals, or about 10 percent of the Canadian Doukhobors. The Veriginites numbered about 7852 in 1906 (Woodcock & Avakumovic, 1977, p. 198). Most of the dissidents were expelled from the colonies to take up homesteads outside of the Doukhobor reserves. The Independents retained the Doukhobor religion, but rejected the communistic organization. Others submitted to the leadership of Verigin and to the community. Under Verigin, the community, which became known as the "Christian Community of Universal Brotherhood" (CCUB), was highly centralized and successful by 1907; however, the question of the oath of allegiance was to become an issue.

In autumn 1906, the newly appointed minister of the interior, Frank Oliver, ordered that Doukhobor land registrations were to be dealt with as ordinary homesteads. This required that improvements had to be made on every quarter-section, including the construction of a dwelling. It was difficult for the Doukhobors to comply since they were already living in communal villages in the centre of their land reserves. Verigin advised that no sectarian should sign for lands independently.

Faced with the resultant "Doukhobor problem," Oliver appointed a commission to tour the colonies to ascertain which sectarians had followed the Homestead Act regulations, and to report those who had not. The commission was also to encourage Doukhobors to sign independently, and, during 1907, the Independents numbered more than a thousand. By June, over half the land entered by the Doukhobors between 1902 and 1905 was confiscated. The government made available about 258 880 acres of choice farm lands to the general public, which resulted in the greatest land rush in Prairie history (Department of the Interior, 1907, pp. 7–8; Zubek & Solberg, 1952, p. 71; Woodcock & Avakumovic, 1977, p. 222). Some 122 880 acres of land were reserved by the government for the Community Doukhobors, but this did not provide sufficient pastures or the capacity for agricultural expansion. The Community Doukhobors were, thus, dispirited and disheartened, and this situation encouraged the revival of the radical sectarians.

The "Sons of Freedom" became active during the summer of 1907. A party of about 70, dressed in long blue gowns and straw hats, began a pilgrimage, passing through Yorkton and Winnipeg to Fort William on Lake Superior. They rented a former vicarage. Following various nude parades, nineteen of the Freedomites were arrested and sentenced to six months' imprisonment. Through jurisdictional disputes between the Dominion government and the provinces of Ontario and Saskatchewan, the zealots were returned via various prisons to their villages (Woodcock

& Avakumovic, 1977, p. 223).

During the year of the Freedomites' absence, Verigin attempted to restore the community's prosperity. He set up a brick factory near Yorkton in summer 1907, and, in 1908, he mortgaged some 8800 acres of land in British Columbia (see Blakemore, 1912). Within a month of this purchase, Doukhobor parties had begun to prepare the land for the settlement of the second Community of Doukhobors. The Community people who eventually moved to British Columbia included most of the Sons of Freedom, and it is in British Columbia that the "Sons of Freedom" movement grew and became dedicated to the conservative ideals of Doukhoborism.

The Second Community and the Sons of Freedom

Economically, the B.C. group (which became incorporated as the Christian Community of Universal Brotherhood Ltd.) prospered, but there were soon problems with the provincial government and the general public. The Doukhobors had been opposed to any form of education other than that given to their children through the "Living Book" and the practical instruction necessary for agricultural work and crafts in their communitarian way of life. A few of the prominent sectarians were literate and acted as mediators between the community and government officials. While Verigin extolled the value of literacy to his followers from Russia, in Canada, he had taken the more orthodox view that "the letter killeth." In British Columbia, children were required to attend school. In 1911 and 1912, two schools were constructed for Doukhobor children, and were a success, but all the children were withdrawn after four Doukhobor men were suddenly arrested and sentenced to three months' imprisonment in the Nelson Gaol for failing to register a death (Woodcock & Avakumovic, 1977, p. 245).

The Community decided on mass refusal to comply with registration laws regarding births, deaths, and marriages, and with compulsory secular education, which they regarded as immoral. After two years of a series of commissions, negotiations, and threats and counterthreats, including a threat of Adamite demonstrations by 6000 orthodox Community Doukhobors, the first specifically anti-Doukhobor legislation in Canada was passed by the British Columbia government in 1914. The Community Regulation Act repeated the obligations to provide vital statistics and to send children to school, but included a clause allowing distraint on Community possessions for the offences of its members. The Doukhobors did not send their children to school during the winter of 1914–15, and the government decided on legal action against the Community. Before the provisions of the act were enforced, a compromise was reached: Doukhobor children were not to be subjected to para-military exercises or religious education. The compromise solution lasted for seven years, until 1922, although only about two-thirds of the children of school age attended school about half the time (Woodcock & Avakumovic, 1977, p. 251; Johnson, 1963, pp. 528–41).

Over the course of the World War I years, the Community had prospered significantly, which fostered the resentment and hostility of outsiders, especially returning soldiers who objected to conscientious objectors making money. The provincial government responded by depriving the sect of the right to vote in provincial elections in 1919, and government officials aroused public feelings through speeches dealing with the Doukhobor's non-cooperation in providing contributions to the Patriotic Fund.

The Community's situation began to deteriorate sharply in 1921 because of crop failures and the lack of employment. Growing discontent among the sectarians and public pressures led Verigin to make dramatic threats that the Community might as well kill all the old people and children, throw their bodies into the Columbia, sell their lands to pay off debts, and wander off to preach the gospel of Christ (Woodcock & Avakumovic, 1977, p. 254). Gestures aimed at arousing public attention began to increase from 1921 onward. In 1922, Doukhobor parents began to withdraw their children from schools, which resulted in government fines. Following the seizure of Community property in lieu of fines in 1923, a school was burnt to the ground. This first act of arson in British Columbia was followed by the burning of eight more schools in the Brilliant school district. All burnings coincided with the attempt of the police to seize Community property for payment of fines.

The radical "Sons of Freedom" were probably the arsonists, since Verigin's house and other Community property were burnt: certainly Verigin attributed these activities to the "Nudes," Anarchists," and "Outlaws" who were discontented with him. In October 1924, the railroad car in which Verigin was riding was blown up. Verigin and eight other travellers, including a provincial member of the legislature, were killed. While the "Sons of Freedom" were suspects, their guilt has never been proved, but from this incident onward the Sons of Freedom frequently used explosives.

Krestova, "the Place of the Cross," became the centre of Sons of Freedom activity. Led by various temporary eccentric individuals, such as Louis Popoff, the self-proclaimed Tsar of Heaven who sometimes paraded in a white robe with a crown of oranges on his head, members of the new Community engaged themselves in discussions concerning the state of the world and their role as spiritual saviours.

The more fanatical members became the most resistant to the evils of the non-Doukhobor materialistic world. The increased use of dynamite and fire to rid the world of concessions to materialism, as well as the nude demonstrations, compelled the federal government to implement punitive action for the first time since the seizure of land in 1907. In 1931, the Criminal Code was amended to provide a mandatory penalty of three years' imprisonment for nudity in a public place, which is severe, considering that the maximum penalty for an intentionally indecent act was six months' imprisonment. The length of sentence did not serve as a deterrent. By May 1932, 745 men, women, and children were confined within an improvised detention camp at Nelson for nudity. More than 600 adults were sentenced to three years' imprisonment on Piers Island in Haro Strait, and 365 children were placed either in orphanages or in industrial schools for delinquent children (Johnson, 1963, p. 534). Many of these children later returned to their communities to become the more extreme "Freedomites" of the post–World War II period.

Universal resistance to the Selective Services and Mobilization program of 1943 was one of the last unified acts of the Doukhobors. The program, which included almost complete industrial military regimentation to direct individuals to jobs, was not explained beforehand to the Doukhobors, and public relations were handled clumsily (Hawthorn, 1955, pp. 53–58; Woodcock & Avakumovic, 1977, p. 321). The Honorary Chairman of the USCC, John J. Verigin, the grandson of Peter the Purger, stage-managed a large gathering of 3500 Doukhobors at Brilliant during December 1943 in protest against the selective-service program. As a result the federal government exerted little pressure to enforce regulations.

The Sons of Freedom marked this occasion by burning down the jam factory once owned by the Community. This was followed by other demonstrations and burnings. Within months, Sons of Freedom zealots were evangelizing throughout the communities and collecting registration and ration cards and bibles to burn ritually. Nude parades in Nelson and Vancouver's Stanley Park resulted in sixteen arrests. The attorney general of B.C. added whipping as punishment for those convicted of disrobing in public (Woodcock & Avakumovic, 1977, p. 322). These Sons of Freedom activities were the beginning of a new and more intense era of direct action, lasting until 1962–63.

While the selective-service and mobilization program may appear, on the surface, to have motivated the zealots to renewed action, the underlying causes are much more complicated. The benefits of wartime employment and the resultant individual prosperity are two factors that require consideration. The standard of living of the Doukhobors increased substantially over the war years, especially since

Photo 12.2 The burning of ration books by the Sons of Freedom, Gilpin, British Columbia, c. 1940.

Provincial Archives of British Columbia, no. HP 47281.

workers no longer had to turn their wages in to a central fund. The tendency toward compromise with the values of the individualistic and materialistic Euro-Canadian society and toward assimilation by both USCC and Sons of Freedom members were perceived by the zealots as leading their brethren toward becoming "slaves of corruption" (Woodcock & Avakumovic, 1977, p. 322). The prolonged campaign of nude parades, arson, and bombings were largely directed against those Doukhobors who were buying back Community lands from the government and establishing themselves as independent farmers. There is no evidence of an organized terrorist conspiracy against the state or the Doukhobor community, although it has been suggested by Tarasoff (1982, pp. 136, 214–15) that the RCMP and non-Doukhobor zealots may have engaged in clandestine activities in an attempt to discredit and disrupt the Community Doukhobors. This deserves further consideration.

The actions of the Sons of Freedom can be divided into two classes. The first involved mass protests that often included hundreds of people who paraded nude or burnt their own homes or cars. The second involved terrorist acts or "black work" by gangs of young men. Their burning and dynamiting were generally unplanned, unlike an organized and enduring terrorist conspiracy. The erratic actions of the Sons of Freedom, the waves of protest activities and mass emotion, and the periods of calm lack logical structures, for these various activities were never directed by formal leaders (Woodcock & Avakumovic, 1977, pp. 322–31;

Zubek & Solberg, 1952, pp. 207–8). The figures who rose to pre-eminence among the zealots served as spokesmen rather than leaders since the zealots had earlier vowed never to bestow total allegiance to any leader. Some radical zealots were even too eccentric to be accepted by the Sons of Freedom. Louis Popoff was never generally accepted as a leader. He was arrested in spring 1944 for appearing in Nelson, wearing only a crown of oranges. He died shortly after in prison (Woodcock & Avakumovic, 1977, p. 323). Other prophets emerged during the early 1940s, but had little impact (Yerbury, 1984, pp. 47–70).

Stefan Sorokin is perhaps the only spokesman who briefly united the Sons of Freedom during the decade after World War II. Sorokin, a non-Doukhobor, had shifted his allegiance from the Russian Orthodox Church to the Plymouth Brethren, from the Brethren to the Lutherans, and then to the Seventh Day Adventists before visiting the Independent Doukhobors in Saskatchewan during March 1949. Over a period of several months, he learnt Doukhobor psalms and rituals before joining the Doukhobors in British Columbia. The arrival of a Russian-speaking stranger with long hair and a long black beard, carrying a self-designed harp, seemed a godsend to the Freedomites who were under the influence of John Lebedoff, a Freedomite who established the Spiritual Community of Christ in 1946, and awaiting a mass exodus to either Turkey or the Soviet Union.

Provoked by Verigin's criticism of this scheme, a party

of zealots dragged Verigin out of his bed and burnt his house in April 1950. The arrest of the zealots was a signal to the Krestova population to burn their houses—an event that Sorokin witnessed soon after his arrival. More than 400 Sons of Freedom were arrested and eventually incarcerated. Sorokin's remonstrations against Freedomite "black work" were not heeded at first. However, his community and committee efforts eventually brought both government and sectarian confidence in him (*Iskra*, 1950). Through his influence and the overcrowded conditions of prison and the cost of confinement, the authorities released 395 arsonists, who were persuaded by Sorokin to sign pledges to refrain from further acts of violence and to conform to Canadian law (Expanded Kootenay Committee on Intergroup Relations [EKCIR], 1982, Vol. 2, p. 43; Woodcock & Avakumovic, 1977, pp. 330–31; Zubek & Solberg, 1952, pp. 230–31). Most Sons of Freedom accepted Sorokin as their spokesman, although some continued to set a few fires in an attempt to discredit Sorokin with the authorities. Those who resisted Sorokin were mainly the radical followers of John Lebedoff. Sorokin had Lebedoff ousted from Krestova for instigating burning and dynamiting, and this doubtlessly encouraged Lebedoff Freedomite resistance and retaliation (EKCIR, 1982, Vol. 2, p.59). Sorokin's followers became known as the "Christian Community and Brotherhood of Reformed Doukhobors (CCBRD)," and this subsect has remained relatively passive.

Power and material gain soon became important to Sorokin. The migration scheme was used to his advantage. His followers were urged to put aside their savings for resettlement in an unoccupied part of British Columbia, near Kamloops. When this scheme failed (it became an election issue), a migration to Uruguay was proposed. Sorokin left Canada with more than $90 000. Although it was reported that the money was returned, Sorokin settled in Montevideo in 1953 to live in relative prosperity, returning to Canada for brief periods of residence over the years (Tarasoff 1982, pp. 174–75). Free from his influence and restraints, the Sons of Freedom burnt more houses in 1953 than in any previous year (Woodcock & Avakumovic, 1977, p. 331).

During the years of Sorokin's influence, a research project was initiated by the Liberal-Conservative coalition government (1950) to investigate the Doukhobor situation. The Doukhobor Research Committee was led by Harry Hawthorn, head of the Department of Sociology and Anthropology at the University of British Columbia. The committee published its report in 1952 and made a number of recommendations that were later implemented. The report recommended the recognition of Doukhobor marriages and legislative revisions to prevent misunderstandings and difficulties for the registration of Doukhobor deaths

and births in British Columbia (Hawthorn, 1955, pp. 189–97). The repeal of other discriminatory legislation was also called for. In 1952, the Doukhobors constituted the sole minority group excluded from the provincial franchise. Exclusion from provincial registration as a voter meant disqualification from the Dominion and municipal franchise and from election of school trustees. Changes in the Canadian Criminal Code applying to the penalty of three years' incarceration for parading in the nude were also suggested. The committee felt that the public should not have to accept Sons of Freedom nudity with complaisance. The problem was to provide punishment that was a deterrent, but would not create martyrs. A shorter sentence and a fine or both were proposed. The committee proposed that other offences, such as the destruction of private and public property by bombing or arson, should receive more rigorous prosecution. Since the Doukhobors had exemption from military service, it was also proposed that Sons of Freedom guilty of violence should be denied eligibility for future exemption in the event of future mobilization.

Other recommendations suggested various programs directed at providing improved social-assistance and public-health services and at rehabilitating Doukhobor lands. The committee also recommended that a commission on Doukhobor affairs be appointed to co-ordinate the services of "all levels of government as they relate to the Doukhobors, and to give leadership in new approaches toward promoting better relations between the group and other Canadian people" (Hawthorn, 1955, pp. 217–18). Action on these constructive and humane recommendations was, however, interrupted by political and revitalizing events in 1953.

The failure of the plan of emigration to Uruguay and subsequent general disillusionment motivated the Sons of Freedom to revive the idea of "migration through the prisons." Reconciliation to the radicals meant paying the price of assimilation, and they were not prepared to do so. Throughout the summer of 1953, a rash of fires set by zealots left the people of Krestova homeless. Early in September, the homeless Sons of Freedom began a millenarian-type pilgrimage into the Slocan Valley to establish a tent village at Perry's Siding. The political climate of British Columbia had changed by 1953, and a new Social Credit government had been elected on hard-line issues. The attorney general ordered that all of the inhabitants be arrested for contributing to juvenile delinquency by parading in the nude. In an operation clearly planned in advance, 148 adults were loaded on a train for Vancouver to receive a mass sentence to the customary three years' imprisonment. The operation lasted less than three days.

This set the stage for the government to invoke the Children's Protection Act and to apply "forced assimilation."

All zealot children who had not entered school during the fall of 1953 were sought by the police. One hundred and four truant children were taken from their families to be placed in a TB sanatorium at New Denver (Cameron, 1976, pp. 17–22; Johnson, 1963, pp. 528–41; Maloff, 1957, p. 32). They became wards of the provincial government in an institution that resembled a small concentration camp. Over a period of six years, Sons of Freedom communities and households were subjected to periodic police raids in search of children. Before the institution closed its doors in 1959, a total of 170 zealot children passed through its doors, some of whom became recruits to the terrorists.

During the period of calculated coercion and the arbitrary use of compulsion on the part of the Social Credit government, the sons of Freedom became obsessed with the idea of martyrdom. Passive resistance, stripping, and refusal to comply with the requests of authorities were mixed with arson and burnings that were no longer directed solely toward the Doukhobors and their communities. The patterns of purification and renunciation included railway lines, power poles, government buildings, and ferries. The whole period of intense agitation was also accompanied by a new scheme of migration to the Soviet Union (Tarasoff, 1969, p. 20). The Canadian government agreed to assist the Sons of Freedom, but the Soviet Union never consented. The Community Doukhobors at this time were investigating the option of buying back Community lands, which the Freedomites viewed as a compromise with a corrupt and evil government. In an extreme act of purification, zealots turned against the Community Doukhobors and destroyed the village of Ooteshenie in 1961, at the beginning of the most dramatic, and the last, of their major campaigns against the external world and dissidents.

By the end of 1961, more than 106 bombings and burnings had occurred; and, in 1962, there were an estimated 274 depredations, including 259 bombings and burnings. The actual destruction costs and police, court, and prison costs totalled almost $3 million in 1962. The Special D Squad of the Royal Canadian Mounted Police was formed in August of that year to deal with the "Doukhobor problem." Special D (For "Depredation") Section consisted of a select force of ten officers, most of whom spoke Russian. It was their task to assemble evidence against the Sons of Freedom. The number of Royal Canadian Mounted Police in the Kootenays consisted of 200 men out of 700 under contract to the B.C. government, and additional emergency squads were formed from detachment members flown into the area from throughout Canada to make mass arrests (Woodcock & Avakumovic, 1977, p. 350; Holt, 1964, p. 8).

Sixty-nine alleged terrorists were arrested in the early months of 1962, to be charged with conspiracy. Documen-

Photo 12.3 Visiting day at the New Denver Institution for the Sons of Freedom children, 1954.
Provincial Archives of British Columbia, no. HP 47354.

tary evidence, later assembled in a document exhibit entitled "Arch-Criminals and Arch-Conspirators," accused the Freedomites with conspiracy, between April 1, 1955, and March 22, 1962, "to commit an indictable offence; to wit, to do acts of violence in order to intimidate the Parliament of Canada, contrary to the form of statute in such case made and provided" (Holt, 1964, p. 250). Other charges included (1) conspiracy to intimidate the Legislature of British Columbia, (2) conspiracy to commit arson, and (3) conspiracy "to place explosive substances in various places with intent to damage property" (Holt, 1964, p. 250). In a trial that lasted 38 days, almost 500 documents (most of which were public statements that cannot be termed conspiratorial) and 98 witnesses, whose testimony filled 3370 pages of court transcript, were presented by the Crown in what has been termed a ludicrous fiasco of a trial (Woodcock & Avakumovic, 1977, p. 352). The Crown's case rested on the confessions provided by two convicted Freedomites, which implicated members of their fraternal council. The two later withdrew their confessions in court, claiming that these had been made under duress. The grand conspiracy fantasy of the prosecution and provincial government was dismissed in August 1962. This fiasco cost an estimated $100 000. Some of those arrested were acquitted on the other charges since their repudiated confessions were the only evidence against them, and stay of proceedings were entered for others because of flimsy evidence. Those Freedomites who had been involved in the destruction of Ooteshenie and other terrorist activities were sentenced to twelve years. Because of the high value placed on martyrdom by the Freedomites, as well as governmental blundering, some of those sentenced may not have been guilty of the relevant crimes (Woodcock & Avakumovic, 1977, p. 351).

The trial of the Fraternal Council served only to intensify the revitalizing process of the Sons of Freedom and to foster nihilistic radical outbursts. In June 1962, the people of Krestova were seized once again with the idea of a millenarian migration. Almost 300 homes were burnt in preparation for the final departure. The opening of Mountain Prison near Agassiz for 104 previously convicted Sons of Freedom became an irresistible attraction to the homeless people of Krestova. Led by a large assemblage of women, the Sons of Freedom abandoned the ruins of Krestova

and passed through the various Doukhobor communities to assemble a following of about 1200 pilgrims by the time they reached Hope in the Fraser Valley. A large number of Freedomites eventually settled on land near Mountain Prison, and, in 1967, 400 still remained (Woodcock & Avakumovic, 1977, p. 354).

This mass pilgrimage marked the end of an era for the Sons of Freedom. Since then there have been few mass nude parades and dynamitings (Woodcock & Avakumovic, 1977, p. 355). Over the course of the last fifteen years, most house and community-centre burnings have been directed toward the Community Doukhobors; these activities are, nevertheless, symptoms of potentially violent depredations, mostly orchestrated by Gilpin Freedomites.

Following the 1977 burning of the USCC community centre in Grand Forks and several community homes in 1978, the USCC honorary chairman, Verigin, was arrested and charged with four counts of conspiracy to commit arson. The prosecution's case was based on the testimony of

Photo 12.4   Sons of Freedom delegation at parliament buildings in Victoria, British Columbia, 1954.

Provincial Archives of British Columbia, no. HP 47355.

admitted lawbreakers who were Verigin's bitterest enemies; none of them were arrested (Woodcock, 1979, p. 5; *Castlegar News*, 1979). In September 1979, Verigin was found not guilty on three charges, while a stay of proceedings was entered on the fourth; a witness for the prosecution could not be found. The witnesses now admit that their testimony was "a vile bare-faced lie, simply a fabrication" (EKCIR, 1983, Vol. 2, p. 86).

In recent years, several hundred Sons of Freedom have demonstrated over the refusal of the Parole Board of Canada to grant **parole** to an arsonist and over the presence of Simma Holt as a Parole Board member. Holt's notions about the Sons of Freedom as a "huge crime syndicate" and "a backwoods Mafia-like organization" and her proposal that there should have been special laws enacted against this minority suggest that objectivity required of a Parole Board member is lacking. Her presence may feed the resentment of the sect and encourage the martyr complex. Only through condemning and challenging worldly values, morality, and state systems can a sect preserve its identity and solidarity. Any generation of hostility and persecution could revitalize the Sons of Freedom conviction that they are living witness to the truth. Without an "optimal level" of persecution on the part of the host majority, the Sons of Freedom will probably succumb to the inevitability of assimilation into the Veriginite Community (Whitworth, 1979, p. 225).

Summary and Conclusions

The Sons of Freedom have demonstrated a capacity during their history to defend themselves against both "enforced assimilation" and "individual assimilation" through noncompliance with the laws and regulations of the host majority and through the revitalization process. While oppressive and discriminatory legislation was enacted against the Doukhobors, there were also a number of conciliatory gestures to aid Doukhobor communities. Political opportunism and the unfounded fear of an organized terrorist conspiracy were the prime reasons for the enactment of retrogressive legislation at a time when government may have found it advantageous not to interfere with revitalization processes. Divisive tendencies were evident throughout Doukhobor history, and retrogressive legislation may have functioned to hold temporarily many Doukhobors to the Veriginite Community of the Sons of Freedom movement rather than moving toward the government's goal of "individual" assimilation. Doukhobor revitalization was profoundly passive and introversionist. Political intervention and coercion fostered and perpetuated nihilistic radical outbursts by the "Sons of Freedom."

The aspiration of the Doukhobor people is to preserve their own unique cultural, religious, and philosophical heritage, which is a legitimate aspiration for any minority in Canadian society (EKCIR, 1983, Vol. 2, pp. 12–13). As governments now profess to support individualism and the protection of individual rights, they should demonstrate their commitment to the dictates of cultural pluralism and ethnic diversity, and should not interfere in the Doukhobor people's struggle to attain a peaceful, productive lifestyle as part of Canada's multicultural society (Union of Spiritual Communities of Christ [USCC], 1981, p. 14).

In recent times in Canada, we have experienced expanding numbers of ethnic and racial groups, both as a result of the growth of resident members of these groups as well as through immigration processes. Therefore, we as a society have greater opportunity to come into contact with different cultural perspectives, differing orders of being. Whether based solely on physical attributes, such as skin colour, or cognitive attributes, such as differently held opinions on social, moral, or personal issues, the consequent differences have at times been viewed as deviant from our acceptable norms—occasionally even being defined as criminal. Both prejudice and discrimination have historically disadvantaged such groups of individuals—politically, economically, and socially. When these beliefs and actions become structured into our law and policies, it should be of concern to a country whose government has been explicitly based upon multicultural concepts of justice.

For example, section 15 of the **Charter of Rights and Freedoms** gives deliberate instruction regarding the disallowance of discrimination on the basis of different categories of persons, such as racial, sexual, or religious. As well, the Charter reinforces the concept of multiculturalism within its mandate.

We return, therefore, as we must throughout this text, to the question of who is in the position of defining what is unacceptable behaviour in a multicultural society. The degree to which a lack of understanding and lack of tolerance exist for differing cultural mores and behaviour may well be the measure of the reality of the multicultural ideal. While we do not approve of the burning of others' property, the display of public nudity, or the common assault upon spouses, as sometimes appears to be condoned by particular minority groups, a wide range of beliefs and behaviours exists that really does not threaten our consensual moral contract. In fact, such differences might strengthen and deepen the maturity and growth of the nation.

Discussion Questions

1. Are you aware of the indigenous people who reside in your area? What is the nature and extent of your contact with indigenous people?

2. What would you suggest are the two or three components of "aboriginal" culture that would come into conflict with Western culture, relative to matters in the criminal-justice system in Canada?

3. In relation to aboriginal people and the Doukhobors, how do you think the special claims made by them influence the criminal justice response to them? In what categories of claims would this be most relevant, e.g., in land ownership, language, and/or religious issues?

4. The Sons of Freedom have not become "assimilated" into Canadian society. The group led a relatively passive existence until actions on the part of the Canadian government appeared to promote radical response. What other means could have been employed by the government to deal with the perceived threat of the Doukhobors?

5. Do you think that the beliefs of groups such as the Sons of Freedom can/should be accommodated within Canadian society? If no, why not? If yes, how would such an accommodation be undertaken?

Notes

1. This was also true of the activities of labour unions. See Chapter 17 on political crime for a further discussion of the criminalization of political dissent.

2. The authors would like to acknowledge the assistance of Allan L. Patenaude in compiling the materials for the section on indigenous peoples and the law.

3. Perhaps the most extensive collection of materials on indigenous peoples and the law and criminal-justice system is the Northern Justice Society Resource Centre, located in the School of Criminology at Simon Fraser University. The Resource Centre contains research reports, policy papers and program descriptions from Canada, as well as materials from Alaska and the lower 48 states, Australia, Greenland, and Scandinavia.

4. The article "The 'Sons of Freedom Doukhobors' and the Canadian State" is reprinted with permission from *Canadian Ethnic Studies*.

References

Blakemore, Robert. (1912). *Report of the Royal Commission on matters relating to the sect of Doukhobors in the province of British Columbia*. Victoria, BC: Government of British Columbia.

Braroe, N.W. (1975). *Indian and White: Self-image and interaction in a Canadian plains community*. Stanford, CA; Stanford University Press.

Cameron, R. (1976). Children of protest. *Weekend Magazine*, pp. 16–25.

Canada. Indian and Northern Affairs. (1988). *Basic departmental data*. Ottawa: Evaluation Directorate, Indian and Northern Affairs Canada.

Canadian Centre for Justice Statistics. (1989). *Adult correctional services in Canada, 1987–88*. Ottawa: Supply and Services Canada.

Castlegar News. (1979, October 10). Pulpit and pew.

Clatworthy, S.J. (1980). *The demographic composition and economic circumstances of Winnipeg's native population*. Winnipeg: Institute of Urban Studies, University of Winnipeg.

Coates, K. (1985). *Canada's colonies: A history of the Yukon and Northwest territories*. Toronto: Lorimer.

Crowe, K.J. (1974). *A history of the aboriginal peoples of northern Canada*. Montreal: Arctic Institute of North America.

Department of the Interior. (1907). *Reports and maps relating to lands held under homestead entry by Doukhobors and the disposition of same*. Ottawa: Government Printing Bureau.

Griffiths, C.T., & Yerbury, J.C. (1984). Native Indians and criminal justice policy: The case of native policing. *Canadian Journal of Criminology, 26*, 147–160.

Griffiths, C.T., Yerbury, J.C., & Weafer, L.F. (1987). Canada's natives: Victims of socio-structural deprivation? *Human Organization, 46*, 277–82.

Griffiths, C.T., & Verdun-Jones, S.N. (1989). *Canadian criminal justice*. Toronto: Butterworths.

Harris, M. (1986). *Justice denied: The law versus Donald Marshall*. Toronto: Macmillan.

Hathaway, J.C. (1986). Native Canadians and the criminal justice system: A critical examination of the native courtworker program. *Saskatchewan Law Review, 49*, 210–37.

Havemann, P. (1989). Law, state, and Canada's indigenous people: Pacification by coercion and consent. In T.C. Caputo, M. Kenney, C.E. Reasons, & A. Brannigan (Eds.), *Law and society: A critical perspective* (pp. 54–74). Toronto: HBJ.

Hawthorn, Harry B. (1955). *The Doukhobors of British Columbia*. Vancouver: J.M. Dent & Sons.

Hickman, Chief Justice T. Alexander (Chair). (1989). *Royal commission on the Donald Marshall, Jr., prosecution: Digest of findings and recommendations*. Halifax: Royal Commission on the Donald Marshall, Jr., Prosecution, Province of Nova Scotia.

Holt, Simma. (1964). *Terror in the name of God*. Toronto: McClelland & Stewart.

Hylton, J.H. (1980). *Admissions to Saskatchewan correctional centres: Projections to 1993*. Regina: Prairie Justice Research Consortium, University of Regina.

Irwin, C. (1988). *Lords of the Arctic: Wards of the state*. Ottawa: Health & Welfare Canada.

Iskra (1950, December 8). An appeal for peace.

Johnson, F. Henry. (1963). The Doukhobors of British Columbia. *Queen's Quarterly, 70*, 528–41.

Kellough, G. (1980). From colonialism to imperialism: The experience of Canadian Indians. In J. Harp & J.R. Hofley (Eds.), *Structured inequality in Canada* (pp. 343–77). Scarborough, ON: Prentice-Hall.

Keon-Cohen, B.S. (1982). Native justice in Australia, Canada and the U.S.A.: A comparative analysis. *Canadian Legal Aid Bulletin, 5*, 187–250.

Lithwick, N.H., M. Schiff, and E. Vernon. (1986). An overview of registered Indian conditions in Canada. Ottawa: Indian and Northern Affairs Canada.

Loree, D. (1985). Policing native communities. Ottawa: Canadian Police College.

Maloff, Peter. (1957). *In quest of a solution (Three reports on Doukhobor problem)*. Vancouver: Hall Printing.

May, Phillip A. (1982). Contemporary crime and the American Indian: A survey and analysis of the literature. *Plains Anthropologist, 27*, 225–38.

Mayes, R. (1982). Contemporary Inuit society. *Musk-Ox, 30*, 36–74.

McCaskill, D. (1985). *Patterns of criminality and correction among native offenders in Manitoba: A longitudinal analysis*. Ottawa: Correctional Planning Branch, Solicitor General of Canada.

Morrison, W.R. (1985). *Showing the flag: The Mounted Police and Canadian sovereignty in the North, 1884–1925*. Vancouver: University of British Columbia Press.

Morrison, W.R. (1986). Canadian sovereignty and Inuit of the central and eastern Arctic. *Etudes Inuit Studies, 10*, 245–59.

Morse, B.W. (1983). Indigenous law and state legal systems: Conflict and compatibility. In H.E. Finkler (Ed.), *Proceedings of the XIth International Congress of Anthropological and Ethnological Sciences: Commission of Folk Law and Legal Pluralism* (pp. 381–402). Ottawa: Indian & Northern Affairs.

Moyles, R.G. (1990). *British law and Arctic men*. Burnaby, BC: The Northern Justice Society, Simon Fraser University.

Native Counselling Services and Native Affairs Secretariat. (1985). *Demographic characteristics of natives in Edmonton*. Edmonton.

Parnell, T. (1979). *We mean no harm—Yukon Indian–Police relations: A preliminary study of attitudes*. Burnaby, BC: The Northern Justice Society, Simon Fraser University.

Ponting, J.R. (1986). *Arduous journey: Canadian Indians and decolonization*. Toronto: McClelland & Stewart.

Popoff, Eli. (1975). *Tanya*. Grand Forks: Mir Publication Society.

Priest, L. (1990). *Conspiracy of silence* (2nd ed.). Toronto: McClelland & Stewart.

Schuh, C. (1979). Justice on the Northern frontier: Early murder trials of Native accused. *Criminal Law Quarterly, 22*, 74–111.

Shkilnyk, A. M. (1984). *A poison stronger than love: The destruction of an Ojibway community*. New Haven: Yale University Press.

Siggner, A.J. (1979). *An overview of demographic, social and economic conditions among Canada's registered Indian population*. Ottawa: Indian & Inuit Affairs Program.

Siggner, A.J. (1986). The socio-demographic conditions of registered Indians in Canada. *Canadian Social Trends, Winter*, 2–9.

Stoochnoff, J.P. (1961). *Doukhobors as they are*. Toronto: Ryerson Press.

Swiderski, A. (1985). *Images of an Inuit community: Cape Dorset, N.W.T.* Unpublished M.A. thesis. Edmonton: University of Alberta.

Tarasoff, Koozma J. (1969). *Pictorial history of the Doukhobors.* Saskatoon: Modern Press.

Tarasoff, Koozma, J. (1982). *Plakun Trava: The Doukhobor.* Grand Forks: Mir Publications Society.

Union of Spirtual Communities of Christ. "People's Committee for Justice and Human Rights News Release." September 20, 1982.

Whitworth, John. (1979). The Doukhobors, the Hutterites and the Canadian state. *Acts of the International Conference on the Sociology of Religion, Venice: Religion et Politique,* pp. 207–228.

Woodcock, G. (1979, September 28–Octiber 4). "Victim of RCMP Conspiracy." *Vancouver Free Press.*

Woodcock, G., & Avakumovic, I. (1977). *The Doukhobors.* Toronto: McClelland & Stewart.

Wright, J.F.C. (1940). *Slava Bohu.* Toronto: Farrar & Rinehart.

Yerbury, J.C. (1984). The "Sons of Freedom" Doukhobors and the Canadian State. *Canadian Ethnic Studies,* pp. 47–70.

Zubek, J.P., & Solberg, P.A. (1952). *Doukhobors at war.* Toronto: Ryerson Press.

Five

Crime Statistics and Patterns of Crime: How to Make Meaning

The relationship between theories of crime, whether biological, psychological, or sociological, and research on crime is one of interdependence. If research is theory-bound, then its methods and analysis of findings will be driven by the underlying assumptions of the theory upon which it is based. For criminology, a primary interest lies in the determination of how much and what kinds of crime exist. Using that kind of data, not only can we attempt to see which theory appears to explain the data "best," but, more pragmatically, we can employ such information to evaluate crime policies and programming; assist criminal-justice decision making; and, more generally, provide legislators with quantifiable indicators of criminality to aid them in the creation of criminal law and legislation.

In Chapter 13, we will investigate the importance of research methods in criminology. How can we "accurately" measure criminal behaviour? How do we obtain data; make sense of crime statistics; determine and predict criminal trends in offences? We must have measurement of crime, and, one hopes, employ valid methods to obtain that measurement. It should become clear that theories underlying our research and the tools we use greatly influence the questions we ask, as well as the answers and interpretations we find.

For example, if a criminologist wishes to determine the rate of occurrence of a certain offence in the community, one method might be to use self-report data—to ask the public directly. Another way might be to look at official police statistics for the number of charges laid over a certain time period. These two approaches might produce quite different figures or, interestingly, if the same results emerge, they could be interpreted rather differently by academics from different disciplinary or ideological orientations.

In Chapter 14, we see the images of Canadian crime through statistics. A fascinating array of figures and tables illustrate our "brand" of criminality. For instance, we discover, to our surprise, that some parts of Canada have higher rates of robbery than do some parts of the United States, although we do appear to be a safer society when it comes to crime rates more generally. We are also given other comparative snapshots that place Canada in an international context.

13 Interpreting Criminal-Justice System Records of Crime[1]

John Lowman and T.S. Palys

In much social science, "observation" has been conceived of as a matter of collecting "facts," and "theory" has been construed as a separate, largely abstract exercise designed to make sense of the relationships among the facts. But it turns out that this distinction is artificial, for observation is unavoidably theoretical in nature.

In **criminology**, the theoretical nature of observation is perhaps most vividly expressed in the concept around which the discipline originally found its *raison d'être*—namely, **crime** itself. Certainly, any consideration of what causes crime, who is victimized by it, what its general social impacts are, and what should be done about it will require some understanding of what "crime" is and how it is distributed (in terms of where, when, and how much of it occurs). Until recently, most of our information about what crime is came from **criminal-justice system** records of crime (particularly police-produced crime statistics). Such records are still the most lengthy time-series crime data available to us, having been collected in parts of Europe and North America since the early nineteenth century. Thus, Ferdinand (1967), for example, is able to describe crime data for a 100-year period in Boston. But what do these numbers mean? What factors influence their compilation? What relationship do they bear to "crime"? Not surprisingly, authors adopting different philosophies of social science and different political positions have marshalled evidence for very different interpretations of crime statistics. Interpretations range from the traditional perspective (dominating anglophone criminology up to 1960), which suggests that police-produced crime statistics provide a relatively accurate, albeit incomplete, index of the amount of crime (i.e., although there is a large "dark figure," crime statistics represent an unbiased sample of the total), to a "controlological" perspective, which suggests that crime statistics can be interpreted only as an index of the activities of controllers and that crime takes on meaning only through these activities.

To capture the issues at stake here, Brantingham and Brantingham (1984) use the analogy of a weigh-scale to describe the debate about the measurement accuracy of crime statistics. One image of the inaccuracy of statistics is captured by the image of a weigh-scale that is mis-set in such a way that it erroneously shows people to weigh 20 kilograms less than they really do. Although the readings from this scale would not show us a person's real weight, the knowledge that the error is constant would nonetheless allow us to validly compare the *relative* heaviness of different people, or changes in the weights of particular people over time. The question, of course, is whether different police jurisdictions are equally erroneous in their measurement of crime, as indicated in the weigh-scale analogy. Another possibility is that the degree of error varies from jurisdiction to jurisdiction (i.e., from weigh-scale to weigh-scale and from time to time), such that measures taken in different jurisdictions, or at different times in the same jurisdiction, are not at all comparable. Other possibilities are that the scales do not actually measure "weight" at all, or if they do, they systematically weigh certain groups of people, whereas other groups do not make it onto the scale at all.

Although our discussion here will focus on debates about the interpretation of crime data produced by police, we also refer to the implications of self-report studies and victimization surveys for this debate. The discussion focusses on criminology in England and the United States as well as Canada because the issues raised in these other contexts have set much of the agenda for Canadian criminology and are still relevant to it (be it anglophone or francophone). For the most part, this discussion relates to crimes known to the police (although, where appropriate, references are made to the differences in crimes discovered, crimes reported, crimes recorded, and crimes cleared).[2]

For organizational and descriptive purposes, we identify four main genres of crime-statistic interpretation (and indicate here the main schools of criminological thought that adopt them—see chapters 7 and 10 for a discussion of theories based upon these schools of thought):

1. A **prima facie** or **realist interpretation** (adopted by **positivist, instrumentalist,** and **technicist** approaches), which views crime statistics as a fairly accurate index of crime. Crime is conceived as a discrete type of behaviour, and the criminal and non-criminal as being somehow fundamentally different.

2. A **social-constructionist** or **institutionalist interpretation** (advanced in **labelling** perspectives, the **sociology of deviance, ethnomethodology, symbolic interactionist,** and **controlological** perspectives), which suggests that crime statistics tell us more about the persons and institutions constructing them (e.g., the police and courts) than about "crime" and "criminals."

3. **Structural interpretations** (offered by various types of **Marxist, feminist,** and **pluralist–conflict** perspectives), which suggest that crime statistics tell us more about power structures and ideological forces (first, in terms of what falls under criminal law, and second, in terms of police practices) than they do about the social distribution of misconduct.

4. An **integrationist interpretation** (taken generally by a variety of authors with an eclectic bent, and by **left realists** in particular), which synthesizes various elements of the other three perspectives by suggesting that a variety of forces (including both offender and controller activity and the social-political context in which laws are enacted) influence crime rates and that the relative importance of each must be decided empirically.

The chapter describes the points and counterpoints of the debate through which these perspectives have emerged.

Prima Facie Interpretations

The problematic status of the representativeness of crime statistics has been expressed throughout the history of their use (e.g., see Bottomley & Coleman, 1981, Ch. 1). As long ago as 1842, Quetelet conveyed the same doubt that has subsequently plagued criminology—the measurement accuracy of official crime statistics leaves all analyses based on them suspect. But, lacking data to the contrary, crime analysts of the nineteenth and early twentieth centuries have mostly proceeded as if official crime statistics reliably indexed amounts of crime, and many researchers still continue to do so. In this respect, they have taken a *prima facie* interpretation of criminal-justice system records of crime.

A *prima facie* interpretation assumes that crime categories correspond to discrete behaviour types. This literal interpretation follows a positivistic epistemological imperative, separating facts from values—crime categories are part of an observational language, not a theoretical one. The hallmark of positivist criminology was its analytic separation of "crime" and "justice" (cf. Matza, 1964, 1969). Criminal behaviour was explained in terms of either the biological or the psychological attributes of the individual, or the immediate social environment (family or neighbourhood) from which the criminal came. Conceived of this way, the task of criminology was to isolate the characteristics that set the criminal apart from the noncriminal. Crime statistics were treated as a fairly straightforward index of "crime," albeit one that was incomplete by virtue of excluding a "dark figure" of those offences that remained undetected, unreported, or unrecorded (e.g., see Skogan, 1976). Although the extent of this dark figure remained unknown, crime statistics were thought to provide an accurate portrayal of the spatial and social distribution of crime, i.e., they were considered to be an unbiased sample of the total.

Construed in this empirically pragmatic way, problems of crime rate interpretation occur mainly in comparative or aggregate analyses, because reporting systems are often imperfectly developed and subject to change. Jurisdictional variations in recording practices, such as inconsistencies in the way crimes are classified, would make comparative analyses difficult. Nonetheless, within the *prima facie* view, crime rates are problematic only to the extent that the technical systems generating them are imperfect. It was the visualization of the problem in this way that led to the gradual adoption of Uniform Crime Reporting (UCR) systems such as those in Britain, Canada, and the United States (and many other countries) in an effort to enhance interjurisdictional reliability in the way crime statistics are gathered and recorded. In Canada, a Uniform Crime Reporting Survey was adopted for a five-year trial period in 1962, and permanently in 1967.[3]

There can be no doubt that, without a uniform crime-reporting system, there are considerable interjurisdictional variations in the way that crime is recorded. But, even where uniform recording systems are in place, there can be considerable differences in what gets recorded as crime. Perhaps the most striking example of the influence of crime-recording practices on crime rates is provided by Farrington and Dowds (1985) in a study of the differences in officially recorded crime rates in Leicestershire, Nottinghamshire, and Staffordshire. Nottinghamshire had gained a reputation for having one of the highest crime rates in England, with about twice the rate of those in several neighbouring counties. A victimization survey (victimization surveys are described below) revealed that Nottinghamshire did, indeed, have a higher crime rate than did the other two counties, but only by about one-third to one-quarter of the difference suggested by official crime statistics. By studying the crime-recording practices of police in the three counties, Farrington and Dowds offer convincing evidence to suggest that the difference is largely explained by police crime-recording practices.

Just as changes in recording practices may influence interjurisdictional differences in crime rates geographically and temporally, so they can influence crime rates within a jurisdiction through time. Three examples of such effects are

provided by McCleary, Neinstedt, and Erven (1982) in a study of U.S. police departments. Their first example reveals how burglary rates dropped sharply in one city as a result of differences in the way that crimes were "unfounded"[4] and through the reduction of double-counting problems. In another example, they show how the crime-recording policies of two different police chiefs resulted in the production of quite different crime rates. A third example shows how civilian dispatchers, when working alone, were more likely to dispatch an officer in response to a call for service than they were during a period when their work was overseen by a police sergeant (the sergeant, using his knowledge of the day-to-day contingencies of street policing, would screen out more calls as not being worth responding to than would civilian dispatchers). The reduction in responses to calls for service resulted in fewer crime records being made. Some authors have concluded that changes of police crime recording practices over time are so substantial that comparison of temporal trends in police-recorded crime rates is almost impossible (see, for example, Bottomley & Coleman, 1981, p. 81).

A somewhat different argument about the effects of police activity on crime statistics concerns the effect of police numbers and expenditures on how much crime gets recorded. Carr-Hill and Stern (1979), again in a study of English crime recording, argue that the size of the funds available to police forces play an important and independent role in the determination of both offence and clearance rates.[5] Lynn McDonald (1969), in examining national data for Canada, argued that increases in police numbers produce more crime by producing more crime reports. Similar arguments are made by Chan and Ericson (1981) and MacLean (1986), who suggest that, as police numbers increase, there is a tendency to produce more crime-occurrence reports. Whether the increase in crime rates occurs because police classify more trivial events as crimes, or whether the change is driven by public crime-reporting patterns (or both) is unclear. But if this relationship between police numbers and recorded crime holds for various periods in the twentieth century, one is left wondering why the same phenomenon did not occur in the latter part of the nineteenth century in England, when the number of police was gradually increasing, but crime rates decreased (cf. Brantingham and Brantingham, 1984, p. 179).

Aside from the issue of the way that police-force size and police expenditures influence crime rates, there are, as we have seen, all sorts of examples in the criminological literature of the way in which technical inconsistencies in crime defining and recording methods can have a profound impact on temporal and interjurisdictional variations in crime rates. These would seem to suggest that, at a minimum, an analysis using official crime statistics ought to be mindful of these effects. But the debate that we are going to describe goes far beyond these technical issues about recording practices to suggest that the problems involved in interpreting criminal-justice records of crime are theoretical in nature. Before we examine the character of these arguments, let us consider some of the alternatives to police records of crime (self-report studies and victimization surveys) and what they might tell us.[6] What we will find here is that, if official crime statistics are difficult to interpret, alternative measures of crime are no less so.

Questions Raised by Self-Report Studies of Delinquency[7]

The **constructionist critique** of official statistics dates back at least as early as Sophie Robison's (1937) *Can Delinquency Be Measured?*, a critique of Shaw and McKay's **Ecological** studies of delinquency. In her view, the data presented in that study "definitely indicate that for the field of delinquency, index-making is not at present feasible" (p. 209). This conclusion followed from her observation that "delinquency and non-delinquency are not mutually exclusive. The label 'delinquent' depends on many subjective factors in the observer and the observed" (p. 195). Although this statement seems to have become a ubiquitous sociological axiom, its subsequent adherents do not always recognize its pedigree. Concern over what crime statistics signify was accentuated in the 1950s and 1960s when alternatives to police-agency counts of crime, in the form of self-report studies and victimization surveys, were developed.

Self-report studies involve asking samples of persons, usually juveniles, to report in a confidential questionnaire or interview setting, the "crimes" (or other "delinquencies") they have committed. When compared to official police data, they have been interpreted as suggesting that official crime statistics are socially biased to the extent that they overrepresent the infractions of lower-class persons (e.g., Gold, 1966; Short & Nye, 1957). But the results of different studies are actually contradictory on this score. Short and Nye's (1957) study *did* confirm some findings evident in official statistics: for example, males did commit more delinquent acts than did females in almost every delinquency category. Gold (1966) suggests that official records exaggerate differences in delinquency: "About five times more lowest than highest status boys appear in the official records; if records were complete and unselective, we estimate that the ratio would be closer to 1.5:1" (p. 44).

Subsequent self-report studies of delinquency have been equivocal in their findings.[8] Box (1981, pp. 65-84) offers an extensive review of 40 self-report studies. Of these, he suggests that 24 discover "no difference" in levels of delin-

quency between middle-class and lower-class youths, while 16 argue that lower-class youths are more delinquent than are their middle-class peers (p. 76). Such studies are also open to a range of criticisms, three of which Box (pp. 165-75) extensively reviews, which question: (a) the validity of self-report measures in terms of the honesty of responses; (b) the relevance and comparability of items used in self-report studies as compared with behaviour officially designated as delinquent (many of the studies sought responses for behaviour that would normally be classified as "deviant" at worst rather than delinquent); and (c) the representativeness of samples of juveniles reporting.[9]

Box's overall assessment of the findings of self-report studies lead him to conclude that

> official statistics showing more delinquency amongst lower class adolescents are not supported by evidence revealed from self-reported delinquency studies, and since the latter are more reasonably valid than the former, we should be very skeptical of those who continue to argue that delinquency is located at the bottom of the stratification system. (1981, p. 80)

Other authors reviewing a range of self-report studies concur with Box's (1981) conclusion. Tittle, Villemez, and Smith (1978), for example, similarly argue that the distribution of delinquency contained in official statistics does not represent its "real" social distribution.

At the same time, the conclusions of Box (1981) and Tittle and associates (1978) do *not* represent a consensus in the literature. Clelland and Carter (1980) reassessed the evidence and pronounced Tittle and associates' analysis faulty. Elliott and Ageton (1980) criticized numerous studies for their inclusion of mostly trivial and nonserious types of behaviour as indices of delinquency. After developing a self-report scale with 47 items reflecting "more serious offences," they were led to conclude that "class differences in total offences are significant and, while they are not large, they are in the traditionally expected direction, with lower class youth reporting higher frequencies" (1980, p. 103). Although Box (1981) was aware of the problem of the overloading of self-report studies with trivial "offences," he cited other studies that indicated no class differences in the more serious offences. Nonetheless, Elliott and Ageton's (1980) findings cannot simply be dismissed and, at the very least, serve to temper Box's conclusion. But, like Gold (1966), they suggest that the differences are not nearly as great as the ones suggested by official statistics. If these conclusions are correct, they suggest that criminal-justice system records about offenders exaggerate lower-class delinquency and underestimate the incidence of delinquency in other social classes. Unfortunately, self-report studies have rarely been administered to adults.

What Do Victimization Surveys Tell Us about the Distribution of "Crime"?

Victimization surveys ask samples of people for information about crimes that have been committed against them during a specific time period prior to the point at which the survey is conducted. Such surveys deal variously with the characteristics of the offender, reasons for reporting or not reporting crimes to the police, fear of crime, perceptions of crime problems, and attitudes to the police—all of which can then be compared to the basic socio-demographic characteristics (age, gender, marital status, "race," family income, etc.) of the respondents. But they do not necessarily give equal emphasis to all these issues. MacLean, in his critical analysis of victimization research (1989a, pp. 79–94), identifies three generations of victimization surveys: the first were designed to gauge the extent of unrecorded crime and refine technical instruments; the second placed more emphasis on the characteristics of the persons victimized (thus developing the notion of victim-precipitated crime); and the third, in the form of the local crime survey (e.g., Jones, MacLean, and Young, 1986), while providing information about these other phenomena, also aim to understand how the formal process through which crime is defined organizes certain of the layperson's experiences into legalistic categories. The purpose of the local crime survey is to make victimization research work toward certain political ends rather than simply describing the characteristics of crime victims.

The development of victimization surveys was given its main impetus by the U.S. President's Commission on Law Enforcement and the Administration of Justice in the mid-1960s. Since then, a variety of city-based studies and a series of national crime-panel studies have been conducted in the United States. Victim surveys have also been conducted in Canada, Scandinavia, England, Switzerland, Germany, India, and Tasmania (Box, 1981, p. 62) and many more since then. A cross-national survey has just been published, utilizing the same research instrument in some twenty countries (Van Dijk, Mayhew, & Killies, 1990). A brief description of the 1982 Canadian Urban Victimization study involving 61 000 respondents in seven cities[10] is provided in Chapter 14. Local crime surveys have focussed on much smaller areas—i.e., they are *intra*-jurisdictional—than has been the case with state-sponsored national and city-wide surveys, which are usually *inter*jurisdictional in scope. And although local crime survey researchers have been interested in examining levels of crime victimization, they also show a particular interest in public perceptions of policing, the relationship between police and public definitions of crime, and attitudes about what policing priorities ought to be.

While there are reasons to believe victimization surveys underreport crime in certain ways (e.g., see Box, 1981, p. 62)—certainly they can detect crimes only in instances where the victim is aware of being victimized—there are also reasons to think that, in other ways, they may over-represent crime in a geographic sense by, for example, recording crimes committed against respondents in jurisdictions other than where they live, and in a temporal sense by "telescoping" past events (for a short discussion of the difficulties involved in interpreting victimization surveys, see Brantingham & Brantingham [1984, pp. 69–81]; for more extensive discussions, see O'Brien, 1985; Skogan, 1981; and Sparks, 1982). Nevertheless, even when over-reporting possibilities are taken into consideration, victimization surveys have consistently uncovered a much greater amount of crime than have official crime statistics (but with a considerable variation in underreporting, depending on the type of crime category in question); i.e., they give credence to the idea that there is a substantial "dark figure" of crime. In Chicago, for example, one of the first victimization surveys estimated that official police records cover only one-quarter of the total volume of *serious* crime (Box, 1981, pp. 61–62; see also Skogan, 1976). Sparks (1976) estimated from a survey conducted in three London boroughs that only one in eleven of all types of crimes were actually reported to the police. In Chapter 14, Paul Brantingham provides the equivalent comparison of Canadian Urban Victimization Survey and Uniform Crime Report rates, which again reveal a substantial number of incidents that could have been defined as crimes, but were not reported to the police.

Nonetheless, in some important respects, victimization surveys in North America and Europe *do* reveal patterns similar to those shown by the Uniform Crime Reports. For example, several gross trends seem to be very much the same in both sources: males are more likely to be victimized than are females; in terms of age, the highest rates of victimization are for males 15 to 25 years of age; and people living in "nonmetropolitan" areas are not victimized to the same extent as are people in metropolitan areas.

In terms of temporal trends, victimization surveys have offered only limited possibilities for comparison with official crime statistics (in Canada there have been two national surveys,[11] and in Britain three[12]). The American National Crime Survey (NCS), however, allows a comparison with UCRs from 1975 to the present. When we examine specific types of crime for which reasonable comparisons can be made, we find that trends in levels of certain crimes look very different in NCS as compared to UCR data. The U.S. Uniform Crime Reports indicate that the rate of almost all types of crimes (as measured by incident rate per capita)

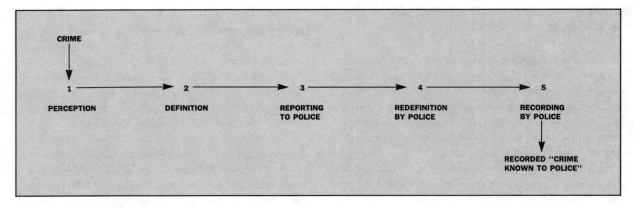

Figure 13.1A. Processes Involved in the Construction of Police Statistics of "Crimes Known"

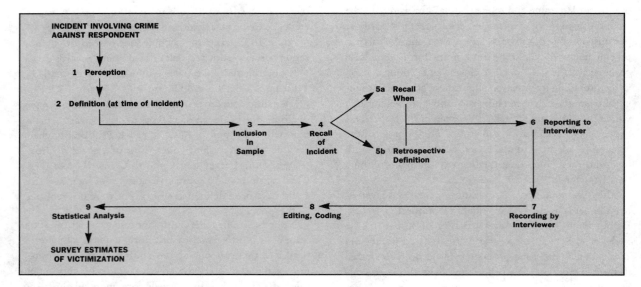

Figure 13.1B. Processes Involved in the Construction of Survey Estimates of Criminal Victimization
Source: R.F. Sparks (1982), *Research on victims of crime: Accomplishments, issues and new directions*, Rockville, MD: U.S. Department of Health and Social Services. (A: p.14; B: p.66).

during this period rose considerably (from 1975 to 1982, for example, the violent crime rate increased by 26 percent while the property crime rate increased by 21 percent, and there have been further increases since then). For the period 1975 to 1988, NCS rates, in contrast, as measured by the percentage of households victimized, suggest that crime has gone down—by −23 percent overall; by −32 percent in the case of personal theft without contact; household burglary by −30 percent; rape, robbery, and assault by −17 percent; and motor-vehicle theft by −12 percent (U.S. Department of Justice, 1989).[13] But before the read-

er jumps to any conclusions from these seemingly stunning U.S. statistics, it still may be that the declining rates we see in the NCS rates are an artifact of the method of compiling them—if the number of households has risen sharply during the period of the comparison, it may be that it is the use of this denominator to construct victimization rates that is responsible for producing the statistical trend that we see. Also, these household data do not include multiple victimizations of the same household, thereby underestimating the potential victimization rate. Nevertheless, it should be noted that the same downward trends are apparent, but not nearly as sharp (with the exception of personal larceny, which has gone down dramatically), if the denominator used is number of *personal* as opposed to *household* victimizations. When this denominator is used, most categories of personal victimization showed a slight increase from 1973 to 1980, and then a small decrease from roughly 1981 to 1988 (U.S. Department of Justice, 1988). Still, this is a very different picture from the one provided by U.S. UCR rates. The debate on the cause of these differences is likely to continue for some time yet.[14]

No matter how we interpret victimization survey data, it seems reasonable to conclude that victimization surveys have confirmed that police-produced crime statistics underrepresent crime as it is perceived by victims. But do they underrepresent this perceived crime in a spatially unbiased way? Of particular interest in this respect is the comparison of victimization survey and Uniform Crime Reports at both *inter-* and *intra*jurisdictional levels.

It turns out that the evidence on this score is mixed. Nelson (1979), for example, compared the relationship between U.S. Uniform Crime Reports and National Crime Survey results for 26 cities and found fairly high city-by-city **zero-order correlations** in the case of motor-vehicle theft and robbery (0.91 and 0.81, respectively); somewhat less in the case of burglary (0.69), and less again in the case of robbery without a weapon (0.56); virtually none in the case of simple assault (0.05) and rape (0.04); and a negative correlation in the case of aggravated assault (−0.36). Similar findings based upon alternative analyses have been produced by several other researchers (for a review, see Gove, Hughes, & Geerken, 1985, p. 478). For certain kinds of crime, notably motor vehicle theft and robbery, there is a high degree of correspondence between NCS and UCR rates at an intercity level. For other kinds of crime, there is not.

Bottomley and Pease (1986, p. 21) note that, in England, National Surveys show wide variations in crime and rates at which crimes were reported to the police, implying that, to some extent, the rates at which members of the public report crimes to the police may contribute to area differences in crime rates that show up in official statistics. In a study of three London boroughs, Sparks and his colleagues found that police crime-recording practices differed in important ways, and they concluded that "police statistics present different patterns of crime in the three areas from those which emerge from our survey estimates" (Sparks, Genn, & Dodd, 1977, p. 157). They found that Brixton and Kensington had approximately the same overall crime rate according to the victim survey, but that the officially recorded crime rate for Brixton was about three-fifths what it was for Kensington. Nevertheless, in certain respects, victim surveys reveal similar geographic patterns as UCRs. A

recent victimization survey examining ten Canadian provinces (Sacco & Johnson, 1990, p. 21) indicates that "rates of both personal and household crime tend to increase from eastern to western regions of the country." A similar east–west gradient occurs in Canadian UCRs (see Ch. 14).

When it comes to intrajurisdictional crime rates, *victimization surveys generally have established that crime victimization is extremely spatially concentrated*. The problem, however, is that, when it comes to detailed spatial comparisons between Uniform Crime Report and victim survey rates, victimization surveys have not been particularly helpful—the costs of producing survey samples large enough to allow such detailed spatial comparisons are simply too prohibitive to be undertaken. Thus, the question remains, even though victimization surveys reveal a substantial "dark figure" of crime, do Uniform Crime Reports represent an accurate portrayal of geographic crime-rate variations *within* police jurisdictions? Most of the debate about this issue has revolved around an entirely different kind of research[15]—that which examines the actual activities of police in discovering and processing crime. It was the initial phase of this research, together with the findings of early self-report studies, that gave the institutionalist perspective much of its impetus.

Social-Constructionist or Institutionalist Perspectives on Crime Statistics

The essence of the institutionalist perspective is that the inaccuracies of police-produced crime statistics result from the ways in which control personnel select certain kinds of individuals (according to age, "race," gender, and social status) as eligible for criminal labelling. In sum, writers taking this position have argued that the problem of interpreting crime statistics is not just a *technical* problem but a *theoretical* one as well. Biderman and Reiss (1967) classified the antagonists thus:

> The contending arguments were fundamentally between what we can loosely term "realist" as opposed to "institutionalist" emphases. The former represented the virtues of completeness with which data represented the "real crime that takes place." The institutionalist perspective emphasized that crime could have valid meaning only in terms of the organized, legitimate social response to it. (p. 2)

Several types of institutionalist or social-constructionist approaches can be identified. A **controlological** position (Ditton, 1979) asserts that crime rates are independent of "criminal" behaviour to the extent that they are exclusively the product of control activity and, in that sense (i.e., as indicators of control), are unbiased. Symbolic interactionist and ethnomethodological perspectives also focus on the social context in which the crime labelling process unfolds. From these perspectives, the social construction of the meaning of the term "crime" makes the statistical component of bias (i.e., systematic error) irrelevant. Nonetheless, there is a sense in which some constructionist perspectives do invoke a concept of bias, and that is by demonstrating the effect of such factors as race, social class, and gender on the application of the criminal label. Consistent with this perspective, research attention was focussed increasingly on the day-to-day activities of control personnel, particularly the police.

Studies of Police Behaviour

One of the first studies of police encounters with juveniles suggested that social status was as important a criterion as the behaviour of the juveniles in the police decision to arrest and signify a juvenile as delinquent (e.g., Werthman & Piliavin, 1967).

The theoretical implications of such findings were developed by Kitsuse and Cicourel, who warn against viewing bias in official statistics simply as a technical or instrumental problem. Rather, they assert, the problem concerns differentials in the definition of deviant behaviour: "the theoretical conception which guides us is that the *rates of deviant behaviour* are produced by *the actions taken by persons in the social system* which define, classify and record certain behaviours as deviant" (1963, p. 135).

Similarly, Donald Black makes rates of criminal behaviour an end rather than a means of study, advocating a position that "treats the crime rate as itself a social fact, an empirical phenomenon with its own existential integrity . . . from this standpoint crime statistics are not evaluated as inaccurate or unreliable. They are an aspect of social organization and cannot, sociologically, be wrong" (1970, p. 734).

From these perspectives, the concerns of the deviance theorist include not only how different forms of behaviour come to the attention of the criminal-justice system, but also (and sometimes only) how individuals manifesting such behaviours are organizationally processed to produce rates of crime.

The Ethnomethodological Critique of *Prima Facie* Interpretations

In *The Social Organization of Juvenile Justice*, Cicourel (1968) takes an ethnomethodological stance to question the scientific "fact" of delinquency. His study purports to show how the "problem of delinquency" is generated by the every-day activities of professionals and laymen in contact with juveniles. From this perspective, the decision making activities that produce the social problem called "delinquency" are important because they reveal how mechanisms of social control operate and how "social order" is reproduced (1968, p. vii). Thus, the study of delinquents tells us as much about the articulation of notions of legality and justice as it does about adolescent behaviour. Furthermore, "the interaction of legal and non-legal rules implies that what is considered deviant by some members of the community (including the police) is not always obvious to the suspect or his supporters, and that what ends up being called justice is negotiable within the boundary conditions of established organizations" (Cicourel, 1968, p. 22).

Cicourel directs his attention to "theories of delinquency employed by police, court and probation officers when deciding the existence of delinquency." It is a study of the "background expectancies" of the officials who channel juveniles in and out of the justice system. The major thrust of the argument is that legal categories, such as "delinquent," do not correspond to the positivistic-type system where the category represents some actual object. Rather, Cicourel argues, these categories are given meaning through social interaction: "persons involved in deciding matters of legality and justice carry with them a stock of knowledge about social types they encounter in different situations in the community, and their social actions reflect conceptions of what is normal, strange, acceptable, safe, likely, usual etc." (1968, p. 45). In the process, the justice system selectively assembles certain kinds of juveniles to be labelled as delinquent:

> My observations suggest police and probation perspectives follow community typifications in organizing the city into areas where they expect to receive the most difficulty from deviant or difficult elements, to areas where little trouble is expected, and where more care should be taken dealing with the populace because of socio-economic and political influence. The partition of the city into areas of more or less anticipated crimes provides both police and probation officers with additional typifications about what to expect when patrolling or making calls in the areas. Thus the officer's preconstituted typifications and stock of knowledge at hand leads him to prejudge much of what he encounters, which an independent observer does not always "see." Thus particular ecological settings, populated by persons with "known" styles of dress and physical appearance, provide the officer with quick inferences about "what is going on" although not based on factual-type material he must describe sooner or later in oral or written form. (Cicourel, 1968, p. 67)

This description is very much akin to Sacks's (1972, pp. 281–86) discussion of what he calls *incongruity procedures* whereby police devote systematic attention to individuals who "look out of place" in particular ecological settings: the black in a white neighbourhood, the juvenile on the street late at night, the woman standing for long periods on a street corner, etc.

Part of Cicourel's empirical research attempts to examine the extent to which official records revealed or did not reveal the **incidence** and form of middle-/upper-class delinquency as compared with that of lower-income groups. In the study of middle-class Chicago suburb, he found a fairly high incidence of delinquency, much higher than suggested by the official statistics (1968, pp. 32–33). In one comparison of two unidentified cities, he also notes the influence of police organizational procedures on differences in the overall rates of **deviance** in the two cities, and in the same city at different times.

Cicourel uses these findings to indicate the "indexical" nature of the label "delinquent" and to show how rates of delinquency are officially produced; each instance of invoking the label requires decisions that transform a truncated behavioural description of "what happened" in a particular incident into some precoded, but almost never unidimensional, category that enables police to invoke legal language. This invocation is often more a reflection of a junvenile's status or demeanour than of his/her behaviour. The construction of official statistics may consequently be seen to employ improvised or *ad hoc* procedures for obtaining, labelling, and presenting their information. Such procedures produce technical errors that may be controlled. But, more problematically, these procedures are integral procedures for arriving at and interpreting the end product, and cannot, in Cicourel's view, be corrected by statistical estimates of error.

Limitations of the Ethnomethodological Critique

Cicourel's study shows that delinquency is not a discrete behaviour. But how much is this the case with other crime categories? Is adult crime "assembled" in the same way? The central problem that the critique raises concerns the *meaning* of law. Following an ethnomethodological program, Cicourel shows how the common-sense rules of everyday life dictate the interaction between police and public in deciding who the delinquents are. But such a view ignores the way more widely pervasive ideological beliefs mould this process. Indeed, ethnomethodology has been criticized in general for failing to incorporate an understanding of ideology (e.g., Beng-Huat Chua, 1977; Freund & Abrams, 1976), an issue to which we will return later when

we discuss structural perspectives on official crime data.

Ethnomethodology leaves the impression that meaning is constructed solely through the process of immediate social interactions, and has thus been suggested as offering an unwarranted and highly relative pluralism with an inadequate grasp of the relation between knowledge and social structure (e.g., Taylor, Walton, & Young, 1973, pp. 193–208). Young takes the position that it is only in atypical situations that the idiosyncratic values and ideologies of particular social-control agencies assume *paramount* importance (1975, p. 87). Thus, however dubious the traditional "positivistic" acceptance of criminal statistics, their wholesale rejection would be equally cavalier.

Hindess (1973) highlights the unstated problem of *classification by fiat* this way:

> With respect to which categories do these difficulties arise? What proportion of cases must be decided in this fashion: 0.01 percent, 5 percent, 95 percent? If it is the last then the final tabulation is obviously worthless; if the first, then classification by fiat may be ignored as a source of error in the tabulation in question. (p.18)

The result of this neglect, Hindess suggests, is that ethnomethodology has demonstrated only the incompleteness of any set of categories and instructions. But this is not the end of the story when it comes to police practices and crime rates. In a rather different (but nevertheless related) sense, David Matza has suggested that methods by which police discover offences that *have* occurred lead to the most important systematic bias in police statistics.

Further Elements of the Institutionalist Critique: "Incidental" Versus "Methodical" Suspicion

Matza (1969) suggests that the major source of systematic bias in charge statistics arises from the method of suspicion routinely utilized by the police when investigating crimes (1969, pp. 180–95). However important the promise of protection by civil rights, the most important way in which a citizen's rights are protected is evident in the expectation that, under ordinary circumstances, he or she will remain above police suspicion (1969, p. 182). To fall under suspicion, most members of society would have to go out of their way. But, conspicuously, this is not the case for certain groups. To illustrate this assertion, Matza draws a distinction between "incidental" and "methodical" suspicion.

Most people are subject to police attention only under special circumstances, particularly traffic offences. In these cases, the method of suspicion is incidental. It is suspicion that flows from a citizen's apparent dereliction of legal duty (1969, pp. 183–84). But this, Matza asserts, is not the usual method of suspicion used by police in their routine criminal investigations. "*Methodical* suspicion," he suggests, is the customary mode that leads to the most profound source of systematic bias in official crime statistics. This method of suspicion employs police knowledge of known criminals to expedite their apprehension and the subsequent clearing of citizens' complaints. Rather than a specific incident evoking it, suspicion arises from being "known to the police" ("known" in the sense that a particular identity or resemblance produces attention). Matza terms this "bureaucratic suspicion," because it arises from the police need to account (both to higher officialdom and to the public) for their activity. The method is "outgoing" in that it seeks a regular suspect who, it is hoped, can be persuaded to admit having committed any one or a whole series of other uncleared offences (i.e., to have other charges "taken into consideration" when he is sentenced). The advantage of an offender taking charges into consideration from the point of view of the police is that it boosts their "clear-up" rate. The advantage for the accused is that he or she will not be liable to be charged in future for offences already committed, and that the sentences for these other offences will run concurrently with the sentence he or she is about to receive. The use of methodical suspicion is common, Matza suggests, in burglary and larceny investigations in an attempt to produce better clear-up rates, or in drugs and other vice areas in the form of stop-and-search tactics, but only the stopping and searching of people who "look" suspicious. In this sense, the method of suspicion continuously sustains criminal and delinquent identity.

Of course, the primary issue in relation to Matza's speculations about the role of incidental versus methodical suspicion in the process of identifying criminals is ultimately an empirical one: Is methodical suspicion really the primary method by which police identify criminals? But before examining the literature that tries to answer this question, a description of one further development in the institutionalist perspective is in order. This "controlological" position is one that suggests that a "pure" institutionalist position should rule out any conception of bias altogether.

"Controlology:" From Crime Rates to Control Rates

Kitsuse and Cicourel broke through an important theoretical barrier by suggesting that official statistics be treated as independent rather than dependent variables. But is their focus on the production of crime statistics really meant to suggest that crime rates bear no relationship to offender be-

haviour? In *Controlology*, Jason Ditton (1979) unequivocally argues the affirmative by contending that official crime rates can *never* be interpreted as indexing the "real" distribution of criminal behaviour, and that the notion that there is a "real" amount of crime is itself untenable. Ditton's argument, which purports to provide an integrated theoretical base for a reformulation of labelling theory, is based on Edwin Lemert's belief that "older sociology . . . tended to rest heavily upon the idea that deviance leads to social control. I have come to believe the reverse idea, i.e., social control leads to deviance, is equally tenable, and the potentially richer premise for studying deviance in modern society" (1967, p. v).

Ditton makes this "potentially richer premise" the *raison d'être* of criminology. Accordingly, he advances the neologism "controlology" to replace "criminology" stylistically and analytically. While Lemert viewed the argument that control leads to deviance as "equally tenable" as the reverse proposition, Ditton treats it as the *only* tenable position, at least in terms of providing an adequate base for a coherent labelling theory (1979, p. 9). He treats control as operating independently of crime, and of crime as being dependent on control.

Following Bottomley and Coleman (1976), Ditton argues that most of the proponents of the labelling perspective have followed an "instrumentalist" conception of official statistics by unwittingly reproducing the same image of bias conjured up by traditional theorists by virtue of giving credence to the concept of a "dark figure of crime" (in the conclusion of this paper we offer a somewhat different perspective by suggesting that several different conceptions of bias—some of which are *not* statistical—have characterized this literature). It is this statistical image of bias that Ditton wants to lay to rest.

In its place, Ditton registers what he calls a "qualified" theoretical "atheism," suggesting that the "dark figure" is not merely unknowable, but nonexistent: "the atheist position holds that *everything* can be known about 'crime' from official statistical collations of the constitutive reactions to and of it" (p. 23). This "juristic" view holds that a given crime is not validly known to have taken place until a court finds someone guilty of that offence (Biderman & Reiss, 1967, p. 2); "'criminal activity' is the activity of calling activities crimes" (Ditton, 1979, p. 23). Following Kitsuse and Cicourel's (1963, pp. 247–48) recommendation that official statistics can be used only to analyze those that they were collected *by*, not those they were collected *of*, Ditton argues: "the construction of statistics is such that no acceptable deductions can be made about the 'motives' or 'intentions' of the accused from them. . . . The central implication of these conceptual observations is that variations in the official crime-rates are allowable as evidence of 'control-waves' but never of 'crime-waves,'" (1979, p. 24).

Problems with Controlology

From the controlological perspective, crime is not an activity engaged in by an offender, but one formulated in court by others. In rejecting the instrumentalist interpretation of crime rates as corresponding to some real amount of crime, Ditton simply inverts the *prima facie* interpretation to suggest that crime rates measure real amounts of control. But problematic in this formula is the implication that police control of the citizenry is achieved only through the use of criminal sanctions—there is no sense of Ericson's (1981) suggestion that the use of criminal procedure may often be the last resort in a policeman's effort to restore "law and order" and that police often achieve "order" without having to invoke the formal criminal-law process. We can learn very little about this form of police control by examining criminal statistics.

Most problematic of all in Ditton's *Controlology* (1979) is its empirical foundation—a study of petty pilferage from a bakery. One wonders in what sense a parallel can be drawn between the control personnel of the bakery—mostly the bakery management (and only infrequently security personnel) who perform many other occupational functions as well as control—and the police, whose *primary* occupational task is control. Additionally, much police work is generated by calls for action from the public (a very important point that we return to in a more general sense below). In Ditton's bakery, however, the one employee report to the management about illegal activity was ignored, and the "explanation" of "control waves" against pilfering is located elsewhere. The question becomes how much control practices in the bakery can be generalized to the police. Ditton does address this difference, but only to explain it away. What he terms "fantasy" rises in crime rates (i.e., when more crimes originally committed are discovered) are suggested as arising when certain kinds of crime are brought to public attention by control authorities and other "moral entrepreneurs." But differences in public reporting are completely and conveniently ignored, with the exception of a passing reference as to how police-community public-relations campaigns may increase public reporting (Ditton, 1979, p. 13); otherwise, differential rates of public reporting are glossed over as an ideological construction. But, for other authors, the role of the public in discovering crimes and identifying criminals becomes central to the issue of interpreting crime statistics.

Proactive and Reactive Police Work: Problems with the Conflation of Methods of Suspicion and Methods of Detection

The American studies appearing in the 1960s that stressed the effects of operational stereotypes and the working philosophies of police officers significantly changed the image of bias inherent in crime statistics. But, as various authors have pointed out, most of the early evidence on the exercise of police discretion came from studies of police work where interactions with "offenders" are *initiated by the police* (Bottomley & Coleman, 1981, pp. 53–54), i.e., in *proactive* police work. The studies of Briar and Piliavin (1964), Skolnick (1966), and Werthman and Piliavin (1967) involved police interactions with juveniles or enforcement of legislation concerning vice and narcotics, areas that reflect the maximum extent of police discretionary practices. But, as Reiss and Bordua (1967) pointed out when they drew the distinction between proactive and reactive law-enforcement modes, the greatest proportion of police work is *reactive* to citizen complaints, especially that dealing with indictable crimes. The contribution of reactive policing is variously given as 73 percent and 83 percent in two different jurisdictions studied by McCabe and Sutcliffe (1978); 80 percent (Mawby, 1979); and 70 percent (Bottomley & Coleman, 1981).

Bottomley and Coleman argue that observations of police discretion in proactive situations were uncritically generalized to the rest of police work: "In the majority of reported crimes, therefore, we need to examine the role of other parties involved before being able to describe the kind of bias likely to be found" (1981, p. 54).

Like Mawby (1979, pp. 18–22), Bottomley and Coleman suggest that Matza's speculations about the bias produced by the preponderance of methodical over incidental suspicion conflates methods of suspicion with methods of detection and unjustifiably downplays the role of the public in reporting crime:[16] "there seems little doubt that methodical suspicion pervades the investigation of crime by the police and it certainly pervades the documents we have examined. . . . The problem is that Matza glides rather too smoothly from his discussion of types of suspicion into a discussion of methods of detection" (Bottomley & Coleman, 1981, p. 114).

Importantly, Matza misses the large component of cases in which the police are provided with a suspect, making the method of police suspicion irrelevant. Bottomley and Coleman point out that in no more than four out of ten cases in their study sample was there any real possibility of the various kinds of police initiative being responsible for the identification of suspects (1981, p. 117). They extend this criticism to Sacks's discussion of "incongruity proce-dures" (1972, pp. 281–86). While Bottomley and Cole-man do not question the idea that police use incongruity procedures, they do question its importance in generating arrest statistics. They conclude that Sacks's speculations are gratuitous in lieu of a consideration of the proportion of arrest statistics generated in this way (Bottomley & Cole-man, 1981, p. 104). Significantly, Sacks's examples—prostitution, gambling and numbers rackets, drugs and drunkenness—are all, to a large extent, policed proactive-ly. These examples once again miss the significance of public reporting and identification of suspects.

In a U.S. study, Greenwood, Chaiken, and Petersilia (1977) make a point similar to that made by Werthman and Piliavin (1967) in their discussion of police work with juveniles. While it may well be the case that officers inter-acting with juveniles in the San Francisco Bay area pro-ceed by what Matza termed methodical suspicion, it is dangerous to generalize from this to other police work.

The question now becomes what implications these qualifications to Matza's speculative formula have for the interpretation of crime patterns.

Policing and the Geography of Intrajurisdictional Crimes Rates

In his *Policing the City* (1979), and a later article entitled "Police Practices and Crime Rates" (1981), Rob Mawby tackles head-on the effect of police practices on the intra-jurisdictional geographic distribution of crime. In address-ing the question as to how much geographic variations in crime rates reflect different law-enforcement practices, Mawby offers an unequivocal conclusion:

> I anticipated that such an exercise would reveal that area differences in offence and offender rates were to a large extent due to different policing styles, and the differential involvement of the police, in con-trasting areas of the city. In fact I found no such thing. An area analysis of policing patterns revealed that there was little or no evidence that differential polic-ing affected the relative offender rates of contrast-ing residential areas. Similarly, although there was some suggestion that offence rates may have been affected by the extent of police presence, the dis-tinctions found were between residential and other areas, rather than between different types of residen-tial area (p. 2).

Mawby (1979) draws this conclusion from an analysis of four elements of the criminal labelling process: the discov-ery and reporting of crime, the detection process, police recording practices, and the handling of identified offenders.

Furthermore, as well as considering spatial differentiation in terms of official statistics on indictable crimes, other meas-ures of deviance were included in the Sheffield study to see how well they reproduced areal differentiations appear-ing in official police statistics. As well as including police measures of nonindictable crime (excluding traffic offences), Mawby considered crimes handled by agencies other than the police, notably the Post Office, which kept records of television licence evasion and telephone-kiosk vandalism (1981, p. 140). He also developed alternative data collec-tion methods, including a self-report study (which covered only three of nine sample areas—but more on the issue of representativeness later). From these analyses, Mawby con-cluded that area differences were evident no matter what statistics were used, and that geographic variations in crime rates could not be dismissed simply as an artifact of police practices: "the most striking conclusion . . . is that the role of the police in the discovery of crime in these residential areas is minimal, and that variation between areas does not fit the amplification hypothesis"; and further, "it . . . appears that whether we consider offence or offender data, all reported offences, all detected offences, or only police detections, there is no evidence to suggest (let alone demon-strate) that police involvement in any way creates differ-ences in crime rates between different residential areas" (1979, pp. 98, 125).

This is an enormously important finding, if it is correct, in that it reasserts the credibility of a *prima facie* interpreta-tion of crime statistics. It also serves to discredit the am-plification of deviance hypothesis (cf. Wilkins, 1964) at the core of labelling theory (which suggests that police prac-tices and the criminal labelling process might help to en-trench, and thus amplify, crime). Closer scrutiny of Mawby's work, however, suggests that he does not actually employ a methodology that is capable of testing the am-plification of deviance hypothesis in all its guises (an issue that we take up below). There are also several reasons to think that his conclusions about the more direct effects of police practices on crime rates are too one-sided:

1. Mawby actually *does* provide evidence of a police impact on crime rates. He offers a variety of exam-ples of a police impact, particularly in terms of "vic-timless" crime. For example, the amount of recorded drug use is directly related to extent and types of police activity (1979, pp. 160) and evidence is given for a relationship between enforcement and offence rates for under-age drinking, and also of a sexual bias (1979, pp. 135–36). Police involvement in rates of family violence is similarly important. There was a clear and statistically significant difference in the proportion of offences cleared by "tics" (offences "taken-into-consideration") in different offender

rate areas, with a higher rate of this type of "indirect clearing" of offences in the high-rate areas. But there was only a slight indication that offenders from high-rate areas each committed a greater number of offences than those from low-rate areas (pp. 109–10). It thus appeared to Mawby that the police were more likely to attempt to "clear their books" when they faced offenders from "disreputable" areas. Also, offences cleared by "tics" constitute a fairly important proportion of the total clearance rate. In this way, the contribution of the high-rate areas to the total proportion of cleared offences may be greatly exaggerated; 40 percent of the cleared crimes in Mawby's sample were accounted for by charges taken-into-consideration (1979, p. 109), while 28 percent of Bottomley and Coleman's sample could be accounted for in the same way (1981, p. 139). As Bottomley and Coleman put it: "there seems to us to be some reason to regard many of these as the result of the application of methodical suspicion . . . there seems little doubt that such methods have a critical impact on clear-up rates, and, more important, many serve to bloat the records of established offenders" (1981, p. 130).

But Mawby does not seem to include "indirect clearing" as a form of methodical suspicion thus allowing him to dispose of Matza's arguments perhaps too easily. These findings do show that indirect clearing may contribute to the definition of a criminal underclass.

While the Sheffield study is largely confined to residential areas, Mawby suggests that police proactivity may be more common in the city centre and commercial and industrial areas (1981, p. 145): "official offence rates in these areas may be magnified somewhat by the greater proportion of crimes there which are discovered directly by the police." The term "magnified" is the important one here, for it represents what seems to be a much more realistic understanding of the potential effects of police practice; while crime rates are not totally an artifact of police discretion, they may partly be, with the extent of this bias depending upon the kind of crime and the type of area in which it is committed.

2. Mawby concentrates on nine "contrasting residential areas" in Sheffield. But just how "contrasting" are these? It turns out that eight can be classified as "working class" (1981, p. 186). While these areas were chosen specifically because of their variation in crime rate, the differences between areas containing different social classes is largely ignored. Certainly one area is characterized as containing a higher

social class, but on what grounds could this area sample be considered to be representative in a wider sense? We are left with the possibility that the role of the police in distinguishing between rates in working-class areas is minimal, but may be significant if we compared areas of different social class. While Mawby does acknowledge this problem, it does not alter his conclusions. This is curious because many labelling theorists suggest that social class is one of the most poignant indicators of the differential operation of police discretion. Mawby does not really provide a way of testing this hypothesis.

3. In the American studies that Mawby uses as a reactive springboard for his own findings, race is one of the most important variables in hypothetical statements about the operation of police discretion. One wonders how representative a city Sheffield is, particularly of Mawby's nine areas, which do not seem to contain much of a racial mix. Mawby thus provides no means of testing hypotheses about the relationship between race and the operation of police discretion. This limitation does not seem to temper his conclusions.

Taken together, these observations suggest that Mawby's dismissal of the direct influence of police practices on crime rates is rather too confident.[17] Despite these various reservations, however, Mawby's work *does* serve as an important corrective to the excesses of a one-sided institutionalist perspective on crime statistics. As he put it: "the finding that area differences in one study cannot be 'explained away' suggests that differences elsewhere should be considered on a multi-dimensional level rather than being skeptically written off as due to policing practices" (1981, p.183).

For the reasons outlined above, the effect of policing practices on crime rates should not be skeptically written off either.

Police Practices and the Amplification-of-Deviance Hypothesis

Mawby's methodology is not appropriate for an assessment of the amplification-of-deviance hypothesis for two reasons. First, he misses the potential importance of informal labelling processes in generating criminal behaviour (while police discretionary practices and use of incongruity procedures may not be important in identifying criminals, they may play an important part in defining certain social groups as "deviant" by helping to reproduce that identity). In other words, an examination of police detection practices in producing suspects does not provide a full measure of the police impact on crime rates. Even if the process of methodical suspicion does not produce many adjudicated offenders, it may play an important part in the definition of subcultural groups, particularly those whose self-identity comes to be reinforced by engagement in illegal activity (see, for example, Gill, 1977). What Mawby does not consider in his rejection of the amplification hypothesis, is the indirect effect of police practices in producing deviant identity, although it should be acknowledged that this is a very difficult issue to examine empirically.

Second, Mawby does not consider the possibility that the effect of policing on residential crime rates occurred before the time that his study was conducted. The amplification of deviance literature suggests that the criminal labelling process can act as an ongoing and self-fulfilling prophecy. To study patterns of crime incidence and criminal residence in Sheffield at one particular time may provide only a partial answer to the effect of policing. Remember that the amplification hypothesis posits an actual increase in crime as a response to the mobilization of the criminal labelling process. It may be that differential policing was responsible for amplification of crime in the high–crime rate residential areas, and that what Mawby is describing now is the result of this process. The effect of policing on the pattern of crime incidence or offender residence may have occurred during the period of development of certain residential areas or at some time more recently. The point of invoking a self-fulfilling prophecy is that, at some time, high rates in certain areas may reflect policing, and then become real through the amplification process. Mawby fails to consider this possibility by virtue of dislocating the pattern of crime from its historical context. Having realized this, one is left with an amplification hypothesis that is quite consistent with Mawby's findings. In response to this criticism, Mawby (1989) has pointed out that another component of the Sheffield study (Bottoms & Xanthos, 1981) did provide a historical perspective by examining local-authority housing policies and tenant selection/choices and, in the case of Sheffield, concluded that "the housing department seemed a more influential agency than the police" in the genesis of a criminal area. This does not negate the point, however, that the methodology Mawby employed did not include an examination of past police practices in Sheffield, and that what happened in Sheffield may be quite different from what happened in other cities in Britain and elsewhere (Lowman, 1991).

Police Influence on Public Definitions of Crime and Crime Reporting

While consideration of reporting agents other than the police is essential to the problem of whether crime statistics represent crime rates or control rates, it is also essential to recognize the power of the police in moulding the "definitions of the situation" of other reporting agents. Thus, if we examine Ericson's (1981) observational study of patrol police, we see them portrayed as having an important influence on the way that members of the public define events as crimes. It is precisely this kind of relationship that third-generation victimization surveys—the local crime surveys carried out under the banner of British left realism (see Chapter 10)—attempt to understand by examining the correspondence between public and police definitions of crime (see particularly, Jones, MacLean, & Young, 1986; and MacLean, 1989a). As MacLean (1989b, p. 15) notes in discussing the purposes of local crime surveys:

> A criminology which uses crime statistics as its empirical basis will only be valid to the extent that definitional difference between the police and the public are quite similar. If they are not similar, the further the gap between the rate of crime as publicly defined and the apparent rate of crime as officially defined the less applicable such a criminology will be.

Furthermore, left realists have posited a different kind of amplification-of-deviance formula in the process of examining the interaction between members of the public who report crime and police who respond to their complaints. One issue here is whether different types of policing policy affect the way that members of the public define "crimes" and the rate at which they report them to the police. In this vein, Left Realists have speculated that a deviancy amplification spiral in British inner-city neighbourhoods has been initiated by the development of military or fire-brigade policing, a new policing style that does not provide a general service to the community, but responds only when some crisis occurs (in very much the same way that a fire department does when called to put out fires). They suggest that this military policing style has alienated inner-city residents from the police, thereby restricting the flow of information about crime from the public to the police, which in turn undermines the power of the police to do anything about crime, which in turn results in increases in crime and a further loss of confidence in the police, thereby further restricting the information flow to them, and so on (Kinsey, Lea, & Young, 1986; Lea & Young, 1984).

These kinds of issues lie beyond the type of cross-sectional analysis presented by Mawby. But then so do a variety of other considerations that have to be taken into account in understanding "crime" rates, and these, moreover, are not dealt with by the institutionalist perspective on crime statistics either (although they are dealt with, in one way or another, by left realism). They involve the social, historical, economic, and political context in which police agencies operate and from which criminal law emerges.

Official Crime Statistics, Social Structure, and Political Ideology

The constructionist perspective suggests that official crime statistics do not necessarily represent the "real" distribution of crime and delinquency, but rather depend on the operation of social control organizations in dealing with such actions. This critique shows that official statistics are social constructions and that administrative guidelines and conceptual categories used to produce and process crime and delinquency statistics are by no means unambiguous or definitive. But does that view incorporate all the analytic elements necessary to understand criminal-justice-system records of crime? In a paper entitled "The Critique of Official Statistics," Miles and Irvine (1979) suggest that it does not.

In Miles and Irvine's view, the instrumentalist reading of statistics as objective facts was, in the institutionalist rendition, replaced by a perspective treating them solely as subjective judgments reflecting individual and organizational decisions. Looked at this way, society is an environment in which individuals are free to create their own realities and practices—they have replaced a view of crime statistics as a "neutral snapshot" with one that treats them as a patchwork aggregation of "impressionistic sketches of individuals" (p. 117). This is not to suggest, according to Miles and Irvine, that no consideration has been made of social structure and ideology in the institutionalist position. They note that Cicourel refers to organizational processes in shaping statistics, and these certainly provide a link to wider social ideologies (p. 118). Ericson's (1981, 1982) discussion of the organizational and societal contexts of police work provides similar links. But even in these formulas, certain features of the process of creating the statistics remain beyond the margins of the analysis—the "commonsense" notions of police officers and their "recipe rules" of action are not analyzed in the context of wider social and economic organization. Nor do these accounts consider the way that certain kinds of organizations developed in the first place (p. 118). Stated briefly: there are too many givens.

The institutionalists (Miles and Irvine use the term "phenomenologists") offer a pluralist model of society that does not probe sufficiently the structure of individual subjective experience in terms of wider systems of meaning as they are influenced by social class, gender, "race," and ethnicity. The state institutions that produce statistics are taken for granted in the interactionist program, rather than being viewed also as social products that historically unfold:

> The structures and social relations of these institutions, and the formal categories of statistics they produce, are just as much a product of human interests and conflicts as are the different interpretations of these formal categories by their officials. Official statistics are, therefore, not just a social product, but a particular product whose form and content are structured by much more than individual and organizational practices. (Miles & Irvine, 1979, p. 119)

The point of their argument is that the state is not a technical and neutral arbiter of statistics, but is selective in its choice of statistics for publication. A critical analysis of the state is thus needed to understand how its economic and political functions are embedded in the production of official statistics: "Behind the veil of neutrality, official statistics thus form part of the process of maintaining and reproducing the dominant ideologies of capitalist societies" (1979, p. 126). In addition to this, the legislature is highly selective in the type of rule infractions it designates as "criminal." There is a considerable political advantage in distinguishing "suite" infractions and "street" infractions, and in referring only to the latter as "crime" (see Goff & Reasons, 1978). Furthermore, official crime statistics rarely contain details about anything other than "street" crime. The exclusion from Uniform Crime Reports of white-collar, government, corporate, and environmental crime thus partly fulfils the ideological function of making the crime problem the "street" crime problem. And, even when corporate and white-collar activity is included under the criminal law, it is often virtually ignored by policing authorities. Thus, one finds very few prosecutions in Canada under anti-combines legislation. Similarly, other forms of legislation controlling company behaviour are often policed only sporadically and, when prosecutions are initiated, penalties are minimal. In British Columbia, for example, pollution law violators of one kind and another (including some municipal governments) receive what amount to token penalties, if they are charged at all, even when shown to be chronic reoffenders (Brown & Rankin, 1990). And despite several efforts by the *Vancouver Sun* to get them, the B.C. Environment ministry refuses to release the names of corporations or institutions said to be in "significant non-compliance" with the Waste Management Act (*Vancouver Sun* May 2, 1990, p. A15). Only recently do we find North American police departments establishing "white-collar crime" squads (see Part VI for further discussion).

There are signs that "upper-echelon" crime may be

widespread. Before 1980, one rarely read about prosecutions of insider traders. Since then, major insider-trading scandals have rocked almost every stock market in the world. And, if upper-echelon crime is thought to be relatively innocuous, a growing literature in criminology has drawn attention to the extensiveness of "corporate violence." Monahan, Novaco, and Geis (1979, p. 118) define corporate violence as "behaviour producing an unreasonable risk of physical harm to customers, employees or other persons as a result of decision making by corporate executives or culpable negligence on their part." The point is that this kind of behaviour is not limited to such well-known cases as the decision not to recall a certain model of the Ford Pinto when it was found to have an explosive gasoline tank, or the massive medical damage done by the dispensing of 4.5 million Dalkon Shields (see Hills, 1987). Ellis (1987), for example, estimates that the corporate violence rate in Canada is 28 times greater than the "street violence" rate, and the death rate more than 6 times greater than the "street death" rate (see Chapter 16). Although the magnitude of these differences and the definitions used are open to debate, they certainly bring home the particularities of law and law enforcement efforts and the one-sidedness of the information that is included in Uniform Crime Reports.

A variety of theoretical perspectives adopt this sort of view of crime statistics. What Turk (1979) describes as "non-partisan conflict analysis" (a Weberian perspective on power and law) seeks to understand the distinctive social stratification of crime as a reflection of the power structures that allow the differential definition of some types of rule-breaking as crimes but control others through the use of civil law instead (e.g., Turk, 1969). One of the ways that groups in power seek to reproduce the political *status quo* is through the selective criminalization of the activities of subordinate groups. Various kinds of Marxist analyses (and particularly "instrumental" Marxism) view the law as an instrument for reproducing class relations in terms of both the way it is defined and the manner in which it is enforced (although it should be noted that different varieties of neo-Marxism have quite different perspectives on law and the state—cf. Collins, 1984; see Chapter 10). Feminist analysts have also been concerned with the way power structures are implicated in criminal justice. Here the main concern is with how male power over women is expressed in criminal law, how it shapes police practices in relation to female crime, and how it shapes the response of the criminal-justice system more generally to the female crime victim (although, as with Marxian analyses, it should be noted that different varieties of feminism have quite different perspectives on law and the state—see Chapter 11).

What nonpartisan conflict and instrumental Marxist per-

spectives share is the view that crime rates are explicable mainly in terms of differential definitions of rule-breaking rather than differences in the rule-breaking propensities of different social strata. What distinguishes rule-breakers from conformers becomes secondary or unimportant. Similarly, in much Marxist analysis in criminology, street crime becomes unimportant as the main task becomes an exposé of the "calculated cupidity" of the powerful. It is against this tendency that **left realism** has emerged in Britain and, with it, as we have already seen with reference to the development of local crime surveys, a reorientation of the debate on the interpretation of crime statistics.

For left realism, "street crime" once again assumes a central place. Indeed, it does so by suggesting the focus on definitions of crime and the crimes of the powerful that was taken in much Marxian analysis in criminology in the 1970s—Lea and Young (1984) refer to this as **"left idealism"**—became too one-sided. In particular, left realists have argued, it minimized the very real plight of the crime victim and provided little by way of direction for the development of progressive crime policies (Lea & Young, 1984; Kinsey, Lea & Young, 1986). What is particularly interesting about left realism from the point of view of the present discussion is that it takes an explicitly integrationist approach to the problem of understanding police-produced crime statistics.

An Integrationist Approach

Although the above perspectives seem clear enough in what it is that distinguishes them, it would seem that there is no single "truth" when it comes to what crimes rates mean. And, although we have provided all sorts of examples in the foregoing discussion of the way that criminal statistics reflect the processes by which they are produced, it would seem erroneous to assume that they reflect only these processes. Definitional issues are obviously important no matter how one looks at it (crime categories do not fall like rain, they are socially produced), but police do not have *carte blanche* in terms of what they can classify as a crime. Even if there is disagreement about exactly what constitutes a "burglary" or an "assault," broad legal parameters generally set limits to the sort of behaviour that can be inserted into these pigeonholes.

It is also worth remembering that, from a phenomenological point of view, many of the persons involved in crime understand that what they are doing violates rules (whether they agree with the designation of the activity as "criminal" is another matter) and consequently try to avoid apprehension. Thus, the burglar usually enters an empty house to avoid discovery, just as the international drug smuggler conceals his or her wares. And while such an observation still leaves all sorts of questions about why one thing should be called "theft" and another "profit," or why cannabis is illegal but nicotine is not, there still is a specifiable (but probably unknowable) quantity of marijuana smuggled into Canada in any given year, just as a certain number of cigarettes are sold. To this end, it would seem that crime rates *can* be and *are* influenced by changes in the incidence of the behaviour that is susceptible to being defined as "crime." It is, for example, difficult to conceive of how one might explain the kinds of *seasonal variations* in crime rates that are described by Harries (1980, pp. 106–12), for example, as being purely an artifact of the practices of crime controllers or recorders even if other temporal trends can be explained this way. Similarly, it would seem that other crime rate differentials, be they spatial or temporal, can also be affected by the activities that crime records are about just as they can be affected by the activities of the recorders. The extent to which any crime rate differential is produced by the one or the other must ultimately remain an empirical question; it cannot be decided ahead of time theoretically. This still leaves the possibility that control factors are far more important than criminal behaviour in producing crime rates in certain instances, vice versa in others. The most reasonable perspective on crime rate interpretation would thus appear to follow the dimensions of the model proposed by Jock Young for left realism (noting that one would not necessarily have to be a leftist or a realist to agree with it):

> The most crucial dimension of deviance is that it is a product of action and reaction, of actors and reactors, of behaviour and of rules. . . . Each part of this dyad is vital to realism. . . . The crime rate . . . must, of necessity, involve behaviour and rule enforcers. . . . The notion of a "real" crime rate, independent of social reaction—a simple measure of changes in criminal behaviour—is just as absurd as that of an epiphenomenal crime rate merely created by reactors. . . . The differential rates of crime between different social groups cannot be merely the result of different deployment of police resources nor merely differences in behaviour: they must—whatever the precise weighting between them—involve the two factors. The reductio ad absurdum of an either-or analysis is that all people behave similarly and the police act differentially between them, or that criminality varies and the police act totally similarly to every group. Either ideal scenario would be so extraordinary as to be untenable. (Young 1987, p. 339)

Conclusions

This chapter has focussed on what, for much of the history of criminology, has been the singularly most important datum of interest in developing theories of crime—i.e., the police-produced "crime statistic." But, as we have seen, rather than being a straightforward index of crime, criminal-justice-system records of crime have been the subject of much controversy. In describing the major dimensions of this debate, we have outlined four general species of interpretation, although it is important to stress, in conclusion, that there are many different inflections and nuances within each of these.

A *prima facie* or *positivist* interpretation views crime as a distinct entity, identifiable in terms of the behaviour of an offender, with the crime statistic being an index—albeit with some imperfection—of the amount and distribution of crime in society. With "criminal behaviour" situated in the person, the task of research throughout much of the history of criminology has been one of identifying and scrutinizing those persons in order to understand why and how they do what they do.

A *constructionist* or *institutionalist* perspective, in contrast, views "crime" and "criminal behaviour" as highly negotiable constructs, perceives the imposition of criminal labels to be more selective and unequally distributed than *prima facie* interpretations would admit, and hence interprets crime statistics as the product of organizational and individual imperatives, which at best only obliquely reflect the "actual" distribution of crime. With "criminal behaviour" seen as a negotiated or imposed designation, the task of research becomes one of describing the "recipe" rules underlying this negotiation/interaction process. Accordingly, it is the purveyors of justice—the police, the courts—who warrant scrutiny, because their daily activity defines where the line demarcating "criminal behaviour" is drawn, and hence how criminality is distributed in social and physical space.

Structural perspectives have viewed the day-to-day negotiation of criminal labels as a relatively trivial manifestation of a much broader issue, i.e., the political construction of the definition of crime itself. Why historically has the "street" thief been subject to criminal sanction while the "suite" thief faces civil action? Why does the individual serial murderer face a criminal trial while the corporate decision maker, whose decisions may also result directly in the deaths of third parties, faces civil prosecution and enjoys limited liability? Why have police agencies historically ignored corporate crime? The crime statistic is of interest only insofar as the definition of "who the 'real' criminals are" tells us something about who is in control, and is able to write the rules by which the rest of us live. With "criminal behaviour" situated in those who have the power to define it, the research task becomes one of unearthing the social structures that consolidate, shape, and execute that power.

An *integrationist* approach suggests that crime rates must be understood in terms of all of the above factors.

Contained within these perspectives are three different images of the way that official crime statistics are "biased." It is important to note here that much of the purpose of the institutionalist perspective on official crime statistics, as first elaborated by such authors as Kitsuse and Cicourel (1963), Black (1970), and Ditton (1979), is designed to problematize the notion that official crime data are biased in a statistical sense. They reject this view because it implies that there is a real "dark figure" of crime; their purpose is to provide a theoretical perspective that makes the "dark figure" nonsensical. Having noted this, however, it is appropriate to summarize the debate over official statistics in terms of different images of bias, since the word has a much broader use than its statistical meaning.[18] The purpose of this discussion of bias is not to suggest that there is a "true" amount of crime, but that sometimes it is helpful to acknowledge that "crime" can be an act knowingly engaged in by an "offender" and thought of as such, regardless of the actual social reaction to it or recording of it.

Ideological bias refers to the process through which some activities but not others are classified as crimes. *Instrumental bias* refers to the technical sources of error flowing from differences in the way information about crime is recorded and processed. *Essential* bias refers to the systematic effects of socially differentiated structures of meaning on the signification of behaviour as delinquent, criminal, or deviant (so that some persons or groups are more likely than others to have their behaviour considered criminal, *not* because of differences in behaviour, but because of their particular social status). The crucial difference between essential and instrumental bias is that essential bias arises from the way behaviour is interpreted as being delinquent or criminal, while instrumental bias arises from differences in the way this information is subsequently recorded.

Two subcategories of essential bias can be distinguished (although they are clearly interrelated): *organizational bias* arises from the institutional and organizational imperatives of people who produce crime statistics—most importantly, the police (but also other "gatekeepers," such as store detectives and school personnel)—in terms of both formal legal and administrative requirements; and *discretionary bias* arises in the context of police occupational culture and refers to the informal rules police (and other gatekeepers) use to apply the criminal law.

The conceptual lesson to be learned through an understanding of these various kinds of bias is that the explanation of who is caught and who is prosecuted is often as important in the explanation of crime rates as are the conditions or circumstances generating certain kinds of rule-breaking behaviour.

Discussion Questions

1. In what ways are criminal-justice system records of crime influenced by the activities and objectives of the persons and organizations constructing them? Do such statistics represent an "unbiased" sample of the overall amount of "crime"?

2. Are the problems of interpreting criminal-justice system records of crime simply a reflection of imperfections in the ways that we count "crime" or are they theoretical in nature? Does the distinction often made in social science between theory and observation make sense?

3. What kinds of evidence might one adduce to suggest that criminal-justice system records of crime cannot be explained solely in terms of the activities of the persons producing them?

Notes

1. Parts of this paper are adapted from Lowman (1982). Thanks to Paul Brantingham and Brian MacLean for bringing various items to our attention.

2. There is an important attrition in the number of incidences as one moves from the activities and occurrences that could potentially be defined as crimes, through to the number that are reported to the police, to the number subsequently recorded by the police as crimes, to the number in which an offender is identified, to the number in which a person is found guilty. A great deal of debate has focussed on which of these is the most appropriate level of statistics to use (see, particularly, Sellin, 1951), since it would seem that as one moves through this "funnel" the influence of the decisions of record keepers becomes cumulatively greater, because more and more cases are filtered out at each stage (cf. Brantingham & Brantingham, 1984, pp. 89–90).

3. But according to the report that subsequently led to the establishment of the Canadian Centre for Justice Statistics in 1981, the Uniform Crime Reporting Survey left much to be desired in terms of what it did *not* do (as the authors of the report lamented: "We can trace a hog from farm to market, but we cannot trace an individual through the criminal justice system"). A new Uniform Crime Reporting System is about to be adopted that will be incident-based (rather than aggregated), as is the case with the current system (which has remained virtually unchanged since 1962) so that there is a separate record for each criminal incident. The purpose of an incident-based reporting system is that it will facilitate much more detailed analysis of crime data and will make that information much more consistent and accurate than it is currently (Grainger, 1990). The new system is being designed in such a way that it will be directly comparable to the old one.

4. A crime report is "unfounded" or "no-crimed" if police decide that an incident originally defined as a crime should not have been defined thus. English studies reveal considerable disparities in rates of no-criming in different police jurisdictions (cf. Bottomley & Pease, 1986; McCabe & Sutcliffe, 1978).

5. For a critique of this argument, see Walker (1981).

6. For one of the most comprehensive discussions of uniform crime reports, self-report studies, and victimization surveys, and how to interpret them, see O'Brien (1985).

7. It should be noted that, since the enactment of the Young Offenders Act, the term "delinquency" is not used in Canadian law.

8. A good indication of the problem of interpreting self-report studies comes with the realization that the findings published by Short and Nye (1957) are contradicted by their own research results appearing one year later (1958). Downes (1966) argues that the later findings confirm the class distribution of delinquency contained in official statistics.

9. The willingness of a juvenile to respond to self-report delinquency surveys may be related to his or her degree of involvement in delinquency.

10. The results of this survey have been published in a series of bulletins published by the Programs Branch of the Solicitor General Canada.

11. The Canadian Urban Victimization Survey in 1982 involved a total of approximately 70 000 residents in seven cities (a replication study involving 10 000 residents was conducted in Edmonton in 1985), and in 1988, questions about criminal victimization were included in Statistics Canada's *Third General Social Survey* (Sacco and Johnson, 1990); this survey involved a total of 9870 residents in all ten provinces.

12. In 1982, 1984, and 1988.

13. Crime survey and UCR burglary rates in England reveal similar inconsistencies through the 1970s and suggest that increasing burglary rates evident in official police statistics may well reflect changes in crime-recording practices (Bottomley & Pease, 1986, pp. 22–23).

14. While it is not possible to create these kinds of comparison from British crime-survey data, it has been possible in the case of residential burglary from a "General Household Survey" conducted intermittently from 1972 to 1988. Again this shows considerable difference in the trends revealed by Uniform Crime Reports (which, from 1979 to 1984, rose sharply) and survey figures, which have remained reasonably stable, apart from 1985 when there was a sharp rise (Mayhew, Elliott, & Dowds, 1989, p. 21).

15. Although local crime surveys may turn out to be much more helpful in this respect.

16. Also see Bottomley and Pease (1986) for a detailed discussion of these issues.

17. It should also be noted that, while Mawby did not set out to study temporal crime rate trends in Sheffield, the author of another study that did reached a very different conclusion about the importance of police practices. Pepinsky (1987), examining crime rate changes in Sheffield between 1974 and 1982, suggested that changes in recording techniques and other police practices had a profound influence on crime rate changes over time.

18. For example, the *Living Webster Encyclopedic Dictionary* defines "bias" the following way: "inclination to one side. That which causes the mind to incline toward a particular object or course; inclination; bent; prejudice . . .; the quantity or direction of statistical variation from true value."

References

Beng-Huat Chua. (1977). Delineating a Marxist interest in ethno-methodology. *American Sociologist, 12,* 24–32.

Biderman, A.D., & Reiss, A.J. (1967). On exploring the dark figure of crime. *Annals,* American Academy of Political and Social Science, *374,* 1–15.

Black, D.J. (1970). The production of crime rates. *American Sociological Review, 35,* 733–47.

Bottomley, A.K., & Coleman, C.A. (1976). Criminal statistics: The police role in the discovery and detection of crime. *International Journal of Criminology and Penology, 4,* 33–58.

Bottomley, A.K., & Coleman, C.A. (1981). *Understanding crime rates: Police and public roles in the production of official statistics*. Westmead, Farnborough, Hants.: Saxon House.

Bottomley, A.K., & Pease, K. (1986). *Crime and punishment: Interpreting the data*. Milton Keynes, UK: Open University Press.

Bottoms, A.E., & Xanthos, P. (1981). Housing policy and crime in the British public sector. In P.J. Brantingham & P.L. Brantingham (Eds.), *Environmental Criminology* (pp. 203–25). Beverly Hills: Sage.

Box, S. (1971). *Deviance, reality and society*. New York: Holt Rinehart & Winston [rprt. 1981].

Brantingham, P.J., & Brantingham, P.L. (1984). *Patterns in crime*. New York: Macmillan.

Briar, I., & Piliavin, S. (1964). Police encounters with juveniles. *American Journal of Sociology, 70*, 206–14.

Brown, R.M., & Rankin, M. (1990). Persuasion, penalties and prosecution: The treatment of repeat offenders under British Columbia's occupational health and safety and pollution control legislation. In M. Friedland (Ed.), *Securing compliance: Seven case studies*. Toronto: University of Toronto Press.

Carr-Hill, R.A., & Stern, N.H. (1979). *Crime, the police and criminal statistics*. London: Academic Press.

Chan, J.B.L., & Ericson, R.V. (1981). *Decarceration and the economy of penal reform*. Toronto: Centre of Criminology, University of Toronto.

Cicourel, A.V. (1968). *The social organization of juvenile justice*. New York: Wiley [reprt. 1976].

Clelland, D., & Carter, T.J. (1980). The new myth of class and crime. *Criminology, 18*, 319–36.

Collins, H. (1984). *Marxism and law*. New York: Oxford University Press.

Ditton, J. (1979). *Controlology: Beyond the new criminology*. London: Macmillan.

Downes, D. (1966). *The delinquent solution*. London: Collier-Macmillan.

Elliott, D.S., & Ageton, S.S. (1980). Reconciling race and class difference in self-reported and official estimates of delinquency. *American Sociological Review, 45*, 95–110.

Ellis, D. (1987). *The wrong stuff: An introduction to the sociological study of deviance*. Don Mills, ON: Collier-Macmillan.

Ericson, R.V. (1981). *Making crime: A study of police detective work*. Toronto: Butterworths.

Ericson, R.V. (1982). *Reproducing order: A study of police patrol work*. Toronto: University of Toronto Press.

Farrington, D.P., & Dowds, E.A. (1985). Disentangling criminal behaviour and police reaction. In D.P. Farrington & J. Gunn (Eds.), *Reactions to crime: The public, the police, courts and prisons* (pp. 41–72). Chichester: Wiley.

Ferdinand, T.N. (1967). The criminal patterns of Boston since 1849. *American Journal of Sociology, 73*, 84–99.

Freund, P., & Abrams, M. (1976). Ethnomethodology and Marxism: Their use for critical theorizing. *Theory and Society, 3*, 377–93.

Gill, O. (1977). *Luke Street*. London: Macmillan.

Goff, C., & Reasons, C.E. (1978). *Corporate crime in Canada: An analysis of the anti-combines legislation*. Englewood Cliffs, NJ: Prentice-Hall.

Gold, M. (1966). Undetected delinquent behaviour. *Journal of Research in Crime and Delinquency, 13*, 27–46.

Gove, W.R., Hughes, M., & Geerken, M. (1985). Are uniform crime reports a valid indicator of the index crimes? An affirmative answer with minor qualifications. *Criminology, 23* (3), 451–501.

Grainger, R.N. (1990). The revised uniform crime reporting survey. Mimeo: Canadian Centre for Justice Statistics.

Greenwood, P.W., Chaiken, J.M., & Petersilia, J. (1977). *The criminal investigation process*. Lexington, MA: D.C. Heath.

Harries, K.D. (1980). *Crime and the environment*. Springfield, IL: Charles C. Thomos.

Hills, S.L. (1987). *Corporate violence: Injury and death for profit*. Tokowa, NJ: Rowman & Littlefield.

Hindess, B. (1973). *The use of official statistics in sociology: A critique of positivism and ethnomethodology*. London: Macmillan.

Jones, T., MacLean, B., & Young, J. (1986). *The Islington crime survey: Crime, victimization and policing in inner-city London*. Aldershot: Gower.

Kinsey, R., Lea, J., & Young, J. (1986). *Losing the fight against crime*. Oxford: Basil Blackwell.

Kitsuse, J.I., & Cicourel, A.V. (1963). A note on the uses of official statistics. *Social Problems, 11*, 131–39.

Lea, J., & Young, J. (1984). *What is to be done about law and order?* Harmondsworth: Penguin (in Association with the Socialist Society).

Lemert, E.M. (1967). *Human deviance, social problems and social control*. Englewood Cliffs, NJ: Prentice-Hall [rprt. 1972].

Lowman, J. (1982). Crime, criminal justice policy and the urban environment. In D.T. Herbert & R.J. Johnston (Eds.), *Geography and the urban environment*, Vol. 5 (pp. 307–41). Chichester: Wiley.

Lowman, J. (1991). "Police Practices and Crime Rates". In D.T. Herbert, D.J. Evans, & N.R. Fyfe (Eds.), *Crime and policing: New spatial perspectives*. London: Routledge.

MacLean, B. (1986). State expenditures on Canadian criminal justice. In B. Maclean, *The political economy of crime: Readings for a critical criminology* (pp. 106–133). Scarborough, ON: Prentice-Hall.

MacLean, B. (1989a). *The Islington crime survey 1985: A cross sectional study of crime and policing in the London borough of Islington*. Ph.D. Diss., University of London, London, UK.

MacLean, B. (1989b). In partial defense of Left Realism: Some theoretical and methodological concerns of the local crime survey. Paper presented at the Bristol Criminology Conference, Bristol Polytechnic, July 17–21.

Matza, D. (1964). *Delinquency and drift*. New York: Wiley.

Matza, D. (1969). *Becoming deviant*. Englewood Cliffs, NJ: Prentice-Hall.

Mawby, R.I. (1979). *Policing the city*. Westmead, Farnborough, Hants.: Saxon House.

Mawby, R.I. (1981). Police practices and crime rates. In P.J. Brantingham & P.L. Brantingham (Eds.), *Environmental criminology* (pp. 135–46). Beverly Hills: Sage.

Mawby, R.I. (1989). Policing and the criminal area. In D.J. Evans & D.T. Herbert (Eds.), *The geography of crime* (pp. 260–81). London: Routledge.

Mayhew, P., Elliott, D., & Dowds, L. (1989). *The 1988 British crime survey*. A Home Office Research and Planning Unit Report. London: Her Majesty's Stationery Office.

McCabe, S., & Sutcliffe, F. (1978). *Defining crime: A study of police decisions*. Oxford: Basil Blackwell.

McCleary, R., Neinstedt, B.C., & Erven, J.M. (1982). Uniform Crime Reports as organizational outcomes: Three time series experiments. *Social Problems, 29*(4), 361–72.

McDonald, L. (1989). Crime and punishment in Canada: A statistical test of the conventional wisdom. *The Canadian Review of Sociology and Anthropology, 6*(4), 212–36.

Miles, I., & Irvine, J. (1979). The critique of official statistics. In J. Irvine, I. Miles, & J. Evans (Eds.), *Demystifying social statistics* (pp. 113–29). London: Pluto Press.

Monahan, J., Novaco, R., & Geis, G. (1979). Corporate violence: Research strategies for community psychology. In D. Adelson & T. Sorbin (Eds.), *Challenges for the criminal justice system*. New

York: Human Sciences Press.

Nelson, J.F. (1979). Implications of the ecological study of crime: A research note. In W.H. Parsonage (Ed.), *Perspectives on victimology* (pp. 21–28). Beverly Hills: Sage.

O'Brien, R.M. (1985). *Crime and victimization data*. New York: Sage.

Pepinsky, H.E. (1987). Explaining police recorded crime trends in Sheffield. *Contemporary Crises, 11*(1), 59–73.

Quetelet, M.A. (1842). *A treatise on man and the development of his faculties*. Edinburgh: William & Robert Chambers.

Reiss, A.J., & Bordua, D.J. (1967). Environment and organization: A perspective on the police. In D.J. Bordua (Ed.), *The police: Six sociological essays* (pp. 25–55). New York: Wiley.

Robison, Sophie. (1937). *Can delinquency be measured?* New York: Columbia University Press.

Sacks, H. (1972). Notes on police assessment of moral character. In D. Sudnow (Ed.), *Studies in social interaction* (pp. 280–93). New York: Free Press.

Sacco, V.F., & Johnson, H. (1990). *Patterns of criminal victimization in Canada*. Ottawa: Statistics Canada. Catalogue 11-612E. No. 2.

Sellin, T. (1951). The significance of records on crime. *The Law Quarterly Review, 67*, 489–504.

Shaw, C.R., & McKay, H.D. (1931). *Social factors in juvenile delinquency: A study of the community, the family and the gang in relation to delinquent behaviour*. Washington, DC: U.S. Government Printing Office.

Short, J.F., & Nye, F.I. (1957). Reported behaviour as a criterion of deviant behaviour. *Social Problems, 15*, 207–13.

Short, J.F., & Nye, F.I. (1958). Extent of unrecorded juvenile delinquency: Tentative conclusions. *Journal of Criminal Law, Criminology and Police Science, 49*(4), 296–302.

Skogan, W.G. (1976). *Sample surveys of the victims of crime*. Cambridge, MA: Ballinger.

Skogan, W.G. (1981). *Issues in the measurement of victimization*. Washington: U.S. Government Printing Office.

Sparks, R.F. (1976). Crimes and victims in London. In W.G. Skogan (Ed.), *Sample surveys of the victims of crime* (pp. 43–71). Cambridge, MA: Ballinger.

Sparks, R.F. (1982). *Research on victims of crime: Accomplishments, issues and new directions*. Rockville, MD: U.S. Department of Health & Social Services.

Sparks, R.F., Genn, H.G., & Dodd, D.J. (1977). *Surveying victims: A study of the measurement of criminal victimizations, perceptions of crime and attitudes to criminal justice*. London: Wiley.

Taylor, I., Walton, P., & Young, J. (1973). *The new criminology: For a social theory of deviance*. London: Routledge & Kegan Paul.

Tittle, C.W., Villemez, W.J., & Smith, D.A. (1978). The myth of social class and criminality. *American Sociological Review, 43*, 643–56.

Turk, A.T. (1969). *Criminality and legal order*. Chicago: Rand McNally.

Turk, A.T. (1979). Analyzing official deviance for nonpartisan conflict analyses in criminology. *Criminology, 16*(4), 459–76.

U.S. Department of Justice. (1988). *Sourcebook*. Washington, DC: Bureau of Justice Statistics.

U.S. Department of Justice. (1989). Households touched by crime, 1988. Bureau of Justice Statistics Bulletin. Washington, DC: Bureau of Justice Statistics.

The Vancouver Sun. (1990, May 2). Government hiding worst offenders, p. A15.

Van Dijk, J.J.M., Mayhew, P., & Killias, M. (1990). *Experience of crime across the world*. Deventer: Kluwer Law and Taxation Publishers.

Walker, M.A. (1981). Review of: "Crime, the police and criminal statistics." *British Journal of Criminology, 21*, 88–89.

Werthman, C., & Piliavin, B. (1967). Gang members and the police. In D.J. Bordua (Ed.), *The police: Six sociological essays* (pp. 56–98). New York: John Wiley & Sons.

Wilkins, L.T. (1964). *Social deviance*. London: Tavistock.

Young, J. (1975). Working class criminology. In I. Taylor, P. Walton, & J. Young (Eds.), *Critical criminology* (pp. 63–94). London: Routledge & Kegan Paul.

Young, J. (1987). The tasks facing a realist criminology. *Contemporary crises, 11*(4), 337–56.

Paul J. Brantingham

14 Patterns in Canadian Crime

Crime is a generic term that covers a wide variety of very different behaviours that violate a *penal law*. It includes the unlawful taking of human life, trespass in order to steal, unwanted sexual contact, driving an automobile while intoxicated, selling a company share on the basis of falsified information, smuggling wine through customs without paying duty, practising medicine or law without a licence, parking in a fire lane, polluting a salmon stream, and a wide array of other formally prohibited activities.

Canadian offences are defined through more than 40 000 different federal and provincial statutes and municipal by-laws. The vast majority of these penal offences are found in provincial or municipal enactments carrying very minor penalties. Only those offences defined by federal law can technically be called "crimes," although all penal offences share some common procedural characteristics and impose direct punishments upon convicted violators.

The character and quantity of crime that a society knows about and must address vary in time and space. Laws change. People's behaviour changes. Social conditions, sensibilities, and concerns change. As a consequence, the patterns and problems of crime change.

One way to understand contemporary crime problems is to compare the crime problems found in different places and societies. The Canadian crime situation can be compared with the situation found in other countries such as the United States or the Soviet Union. The crime situations found in different parts of Canada can be compared with one another: the homicide rates in Nova Scotia, Ontario, and the Northwest Territories can be compared; the robbery rates in Montreal and Vancouver can be compared; the theft rates in the Maritimes and the Prairies can be compared. This comparison of situation from place to place allows us to assess variation in the crime problem in relation to variation in other things that might reasonably be related to the type and quantity of crime: employment conditions, the distribution of wealth, the mix of different cultures, the quantity of goods to steal, the volume of alcoholic beverages consumed, the number of high-school dropouts, and so forth. Patterns in covariation may well point to causes of criminal behaviour or methods of crime prevention.

Another important way to understand contemporary crime problems is to examine the historical evolution of those patterns. Variations in the amount and type of crime over a period of 50 or 100 years may relate to variations in social or economic or cultural conditions in a way that,

again, points to causes of criminal behaviour or ways to prevent crimes from occurring.

This chapter describes contemporary Canadian crime patterns, then examines them in space and time.

Canadian Crime in the 1980s

Crimes Known to the Police

Although the vast majority of all penal laws are found in provincial and municipal legislation, the vast majority of all known (nontraffic) offences are violations of the feder-

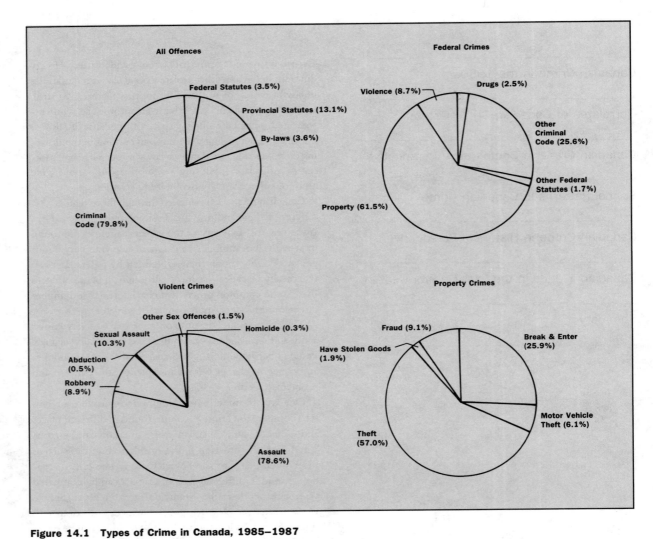

Figure 14.1 Types of Crime in Canada, 1985–1987

Source: Calculated from Canadian Centre for Justice Statistics (1987, 1988), *Canadian Crime Statistics, 1985–1987*. Ottawa: Ministry of Supply & Services Canada.

al **Criminal Code** and other federal statutes such as the **Narcotic Control Act** and the **Income Tax Act**. In both 1976 and 1986, offences under federal legislation, particularly the Criminal Code, accounted for about 80 percent of all offences known to the police, while provincial offences accounted for 15 percent, and municipal offences for less than 5 percent.

Canadians primarily commit *property* crime, not crimes of violence. Various common crimes against property account for the great majority of all known offences: in the mid-1980s, just three property-offence categories—**theft, break-and-enter**, and willful damage to property—accounted for almost two-thirds of Criminal Code offences and more than half of *all* offences known to the police in Canada (see Figure 14.1).

Violent crimes account for a relatively small proportion of the crimes known to the police or discoverable through victim surveys. In 1986, assaults—the most common crime of violence—accounted for only about 5 percent of all known offences; **robbery** and **sexual assault** each accounted for less than 1 percent of known offences; and homicides accounted for only about 2 out of every 10 000 known offences.

Crimes related to the sale and use of *drugs* are somewhat more frequent than crimes of violence. Various liquor-related offences, such as driving while intoxicated and public drunkenness, together accounted for about 9 percent of all known offences in 1986, while Narcotic Control Act offences accounted for another 2 percent.

Other *victimless* offences are relatively rare in police statistics. Prostitution offences such as **soliciting**, keeping a **bawdy-house**, and **living on the avails of prostitution** together accounted for only about 0.03 percent of all offences known to the police in 1986. Various **gambling** and betting-act offences accounted for about 0.05 percent.

Various types of **white-collar crime** are also relatively uncommon. **Fraud**, the most frequently reported of white-collar offences, accounted for about 4.5 percent of all known offences in 1986. Fewer frauds than assaults were reported to police. Other white-collar offences—violations of the Canada Shipping Act, Bankruptcy Act, Excise Act, or of the various provincial securities acts—together accounted for about 0.4 percent of all offences known to the police.

Table 14.1 sets out rates for all offences recorded by Canadian police in the years 1976 and 1986. Changes in

Table 14.1 Crime Known to Canadian Police, 1976 and 1986

Crime	1976		1986	
	Actual Offences	Rate	Actual Offences	Rate
Total	2 184 048	9498.9	2 858 205	11271.4
Criminal Code	1 628 018	7124.1	2 277 749	8982.3
Property	1 062 952	4623.0	1 448 550	5712.4
Criminal Code Other	418 030	1818.1	598 462	2360.0
Provincial	367 482	1598.3	381 354	1503.9
Violent	136 930	595.5	204 917	808.1
Municipal	64 178	279.1	102 600	404.6
Federal Statutes	50 497	219.6	40 251	158.7
Drugs	63 873	277.8	56 251	221.8
Specific Offences				
Theft over & under	603 043	2622.8	773 257	3049.4
Break & Enter	268 332	1167.0	365 140	1439.9
Willful Damage	236 725	1029.6	327.644	1292.1
Liquor Acts (Provincial)	305 209	1327.4	259 238	1022.3
Assault	104 914	456.3	155 775	614.3
Fraud	86 264	375.2	130 559	514.9
Motor Vehicle Theft	87 627	381.1	85 585	337.5
Narcotic Control Act	59 695	259.6	54 019	213.0
Cannabis	57 275	249.1	41 514	163.7
Cocaine	NA	NA	6 729	26.5
Heroin	NA	NA	914	3.6
Opiate-like Drugs	2 420	10.5	NA	NA
FDA Drugs	4 178	18.2	NA	NA

Table 14.1   (Continued)

Disturbing the Peace	41 921	182.3	50 755	200.2
Bail Violation	25 547	111.1	38 317	151.1
Possession Stolen Goods	17 686	76.9	25 985	102.5
Robbery	20 050	87.2	23 268	91.8
Sexual Assault	8 217	35.7	20 530	81.0
Sexual Assault Other	NA	NA	19 191	75.7
With Weapon	NA	NA	910	3.6
Aggravated	NA	NA	429	1.7
Rape	1 828	8.0	NA	NA
Indecent	6 389	27.8	NA	NA
Indecent/Female	5 273	22.9	NA	NA
Indecent/Male	1 116	4.9	NA	NA
Offensive Weapons	13 512	58.8	17 022	67.1
Indecent Acts	8 537	37.1	11 187	44.1
Trespass at Night	9 274	40.3	9 868	38.9
Canada Shipping Act	1 709	7.4	9 687	38.2
Immigration Act	NA	NA	8 680	34.2
Arson	7 206	31.3	7 550	29.8
Prostitution	2 841	12.4	7 426	29.3
Obstructing Peace Officer	3 317	19.2	6.845	27.0
Prisoner U.A.L.	2.136	9.3	4 159	16.4
Escape Custody	2 177	9.5	3 785	14.9
Sex Offences (non-assault)	2 394	10.4	3 003	11.8
Customs Act	5 663	24.6	2 720	10.7
Counterfeiting	2 845	12.4	2 044	8.1
Gaming & Betting Act	3 753	16.3	1 372	5.4
Public Morals	1 126	4.9	954	3.8
Abduction	NA	NA	892	3.5
Attempted Murder	692	3.0	880	3.5
Bankruptcy Act	396	1.7	684	2.7
Kidnapping	510	2.2	580	2.3
Homicide	663	2.9	569	2.2

Source: Statistics Canada (1987) *Canadian crime statistics 1986*; Statistics Canada (1977), *Crime and traffic enforcement statistics 1976*.

the legal definitions of some offences and formally acknowledged changes in recording or reporting practices with respect to some offences that occurred over this period are signalled by "NA," indicating that those data are "not available" for those offences for that year.

Several patterns are apparent in Table 14.1. Over the decade between the mid-1970s and the mid-1980s, rates for many of the property crimes known to the police rose substantially. Theft rates increased 16 percent. Breaking-and-entering rates increased 23 percent. Willful damage (i.e., **vandalism**) rates increased 25 percent. Fraud rates increased 37 percent.

The trends for violent crimes against the person are much less clear. **Homicide** rates declined slightly, while assault rates jumped 35 percent. Robbery and **kidnapping** rates remained nearly steady, varying by less than 5 percent in the decade.

Rates for a few offences declined appreciably. Motor-vehicle thefts known to the police declined almost 12 percent. Customs Act violations declined by more than half.

The actual variation in these crime rates over time, of course, followed a much more complicated course than the simple trend statements presented here. The patterns in these variations over time are discussed later in the chapter.

Changes in the amount of criminal behaviour is not the only factor that explains fluctuations in rates of reported crime. Some changes are thought to be produced by differences in law-enforcement practices; others are known to be produced by changes in the law; and some may be produced by changes in public willingness to report offences to the police.

One area where changed police emphasis seems to have altered the apparent crime pattern in detail, though not in general thrust, is in drugs offences. The police data indicate a shift toward hard-drug abuse that may reflect behavioural changes among Canadians, but is almost certainly a partial product of police attention to the problem of hard drugs. The Canadian drug-abuse pattern is dominated by the relatively "soft" recreational drugs, alcohol and cannabis. In both 1976 and 1986, police recorded more than four times as many offences against provincial liquor acts as all other drugs offences combined. Cannabis accounted for almost 90 percent of the known *illegal-drug* offences in 1976; but, after a decade of **criminal-justice system** emphasis on detecting and prosecuting cocaine and heroin dealers, cannabis offences had dropped to about 70 percent of known illegal-drugs offences in 1986. The total rate of illegal-drugs offences dropped over the period.

An example of the impact of changes in the law on police statistics can be seen in the area of **sex offences**, discussed in Chapter 9. Criminal laws controlling consumption of various *illegal services* and, consequently, police statistics based on the enforcement of those laws, also show a tendency to fluctuate with social attention over fairly short periods of time. As was seen in Chapter 4, prostitution offence rates have been affected by such factors. Gambling offences dropped by two-thirds between 1976 and 1986, while the federal and provincial governments greatly expanded their offerings of legalized, state-controlled lotteries and casinos (see Chapter 6).

Victimization Surveying in Canada

The dominant character of property crime in Canada is also reflected in the more limited set of crimes probed through the Canadian Urban Victimization Survey (CUVS). In a survey conducted by the Ministry of the Solicitor General,

in early 1982, 61 000 residents in Vancouver, Edmonton, Winnipeg, Toronto, Montreal, Halifax-Dartmouth, and St. John's were contacted by telephone and asked whether they had been victims of a variety of personal and household crimes during 1981 (Solicitor General Canada, 1983).

Four *personal* crimes were surveyed: assault, robbery, sexual assault, and personal theft. CUVS estimated that there were more than 700 000 such incidents representing a rate of 129 per 1000 persons over age 16. About half of these offences were for personal theft. Four *household* offences were also surveyed: break-and-enter; household theft, motor-vehicle theft, and vandalism. It was estimated that there were almost 900 000 such incidents, representing a rate of 369 per 1000 households (see Table 14.2).

The 1981 rates of victimization estimated for the seven cities through the CUVS were significantly higher than the rates derived from crimes reported to the police during 1981. Household break-and-enters, for instance, were estimated to have occurred at a rate of 4570 per 100 000 persons aged sixteen or older in the seven cities, compared with a national police-statistics rate of 1436 per 100 000 population for all types of break-and-enters. Robberies were estimated to have occurred at a rate of 993 per 100 000 population aged sixteen or older, compared with a national police statistics rate of 108 per 100 000 population. The police rates are calculated from total population, but even allowing for the differences in population bases,

Table 14.2 Canadian Urban Victimization Survey, 1981: Estimated Incidents and Rates per 1000 Persons/Household.

Type of Incident	Personal Offences Estimated Incidents	Rate per 1000 Persons
All Personal Incidents	702200	141
All Violent Incidents	352300	70
Assault	285700	57
Personal Theft	349900	70
Robbery	49400	10
Sexual Assault	17200	3.5

Type of Incident	Household Offences Estimated Incidents	Rate per 1000 Households
All Household Incidents	898400	369
Break & Enter	227400	94
Household Theft	417300	172
Motor Vehicle Theft	40600	17
Vandalism	213100	88

Source: Solicitor General Canada (1983), *Victims of crime: Canadian Urban Victimization Survey*, Bulletin 1 (p.3). Ottawa: Ministry Secretariat.

it is clear many many offences are not reported to the police (Solicitor General Canada, 1984a).

The difference between volumes of property crime and violent crime observed in the police statistics is reflected in the victimization data despite the relative emphasis in the CUVS set on violent victimization. Even the CUVS decision to exclude high-volume property offences, such as commercial theft, commercial break-and-enter, cheque fraud, and credit-card fraud, from its inquiries does not change our best estimate that Canadian crime is primarily a problem of property loss and damage. (For more information on the CUVS, see Solicitor General Canada, 1984b, 1985a, 1985b, 1986a, 1986b, 1987, 1988a, and 1988b.)

Correlates of Canadian Crime Rates

In searching for explanations of crime, criminologists look for similar patterns of variation in the demographic, spatial, and temporal distributions of crime and *other* aspects of life that might reasonably be thought to have some causal con-

nection. Although a pattern of similar variation, say, between unemployment rates and theft rates, would not *prove* that changes in unemployment *cause* changes in theft, similarity of variation would suggest that it would be worthwhile to look at the relationship in greater depth to test for a causal connection. At the same time, a total lack of similarity in the two patterns of variation would suggest that researchers should look elsewhere for explanations of changes in theft rates.

Demographic Correlates of Crime

There are a few consistent demographic correlates of both self-reported criminality and official crime statistics. They seem to be consistent both geographically and historically. Similar relationships are seen in medieval England and present-day Canada, and in contemporary Australia, India, and France as well.

Age
Crime and criminal behaviour are properties of youth. Most

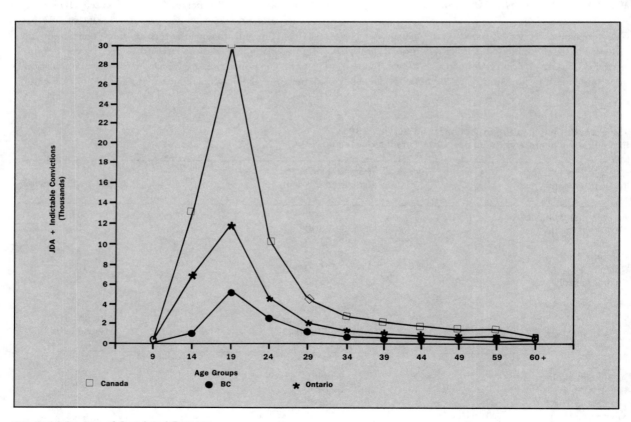

Figure 14.2   Age of Convicted Persons
Canada 1970

Source: Data from Statistics Canada (1971), *Statistics of criminal and other offences 1970*, cat. 85–201.

offenders, whether identified by the criminal-justice system or through self-report surveys, are young. Although there are a few offenders who begin to commit frequent serious offences when they are very young, and continue to commit offences at high rates throughout their lives, most criminal offenders commit their offences as adolescents or as young adults. This pattern appears to be consistent across nations and across offences. It is true of robbers in Quebec (Gabor et al., 1987); of murderers (Munford, et al., 1976) and white-collar offenders in the United States (Hirschi & Gottfredson, 1987); of violent offenders in Sweden (Wikstrom, 1985, p. 77); and of all types of offenders in Uganda (Clinard & Abbott, 1973, p. 95).

The same observation may be made about the *victims* of crime. The highest victimization rates are found among adolescents and young adults: victimization rates generally decline quite sharply after age 24 in both Canada and the United States (Solicitor General Canada, 1983, p. 6; U.S. Department of Justice, 1988b, pp. 26–27). Victims of violent offences in Sweden also show similar age distributions (Wikstrom, 1985, p. 77).

Canadian offending appears, in the aggregate, to rise through the teenage years to a peak at age nineteen, then drop off rapidly through the twenties to a long, low-volume tail through all age groups. This is shown in Figure 14.2, which charts the ages of persons convicted of indictable offences or held delinquent under the provisions of the **Juvenile Delinquents Act** in 1970. Canadian victimizations follow a nearly identical distribution by age (Solicitor General Canada, 1983, p. 6).

Sex

Crime is primarily a male activity. The overwhelming majority of persons charged for offences in Canada are male (see Figure 14.3). Of all persons charged with committing **homicide** in Canada in 1985, 89 percent were male; 94 percent of those charged with robbery were male; 96 percent of those charged with break-and-enter were male; and, 88 percent of those charged with drug offences were male. Shoplifting was the crime with the highest proportion of females, yet 59 percent of those charged were male.

This pattern is replicated virtually everywhere and at all times. It was true in medieval England: nine male offenders were known for every female offender (Brantingham & Brantingham, 1984, p. 167). It was true in Uganda in the late 1960s, when Clinard and Abbott found that 96 percent of all persons arrested for penal code offences were male (1973, p. 94). It was true in the Untied States in the mid-1980s, when 89 percent of persons arrested for violent offences and 78 percent of persons arrested for property offences were male (U.S. Department of Justice, 1988b, p. 41). It was true in Sweden in the mid-1980s, when 98

percent of violent offenders and 91 percent of victims of violent offences were male (Wikstrom, 1985, p. 77).

Race

Race is an extremely difficult concept. It represents, at best, a very crude look into complex issues of cultural, social, and biological differentiations in modern, complex societies. In Canada, the criminal-justice system makes distinctions between persons of *Native Indian* origin (lumping together persons of Haida, Dene, Inuit, Iroquois, and other indigenous cultures as if they were homogeneous) and persons of *Other* origin (lumping together persons of English, French, Lebanese, Sikh, Japanese, Chinese, Jamaican, and other nonindigenous heritage as if they were homogeneous). In the United States, the categories *Black, White,* and *Other* are used in the criminal-justice system, producing similar false impressions of homogeneity (see Figure 14.4).

In Canada, "Native Indians" constituted about 2 percent of the total population according to the 1981 Census; they made up 17 percent of the population of persons held in custody following conviction for crime in the 1986–87 fiscal year. There is substantial dispute about whether this eightfold overrepresentation of "Native Indians" in Canadian prisons and jails is a product of differences in criminal behaviour or a product of differences in criminal-justice system treatment of "Native Indian" and "other" Canadians. Recent governmental inquiries in Nova Scotia and Saskatchewan found evidence of systematic criminal-justice bias against Native Indians in those provinces (see Chapter 12).

In the United States, "Black" persons made up about 12 percent of the population in the 1980 Census, but constituted almost 25 percent of persons arrested. In 1983, "Blacks" constituted 48 percent of persons arrested for violent offences, 33 percent of persons arrested for property offences, 47 percent of state-prison inmates and 33 percent of federal-prison inmates (U.S. Department of Justice, 1988b, p. 41).

"Black" persons also had higher victimization rates than did American residents classified as "White" or "Other" in the mid-1980s. For instance, "Blacks" suffered nearly triple the robbery victimization rate and nearly double the rape rate suffered by "Whites" in 1984 and 1985, although assault victimization rates were similar. "Black" households suffered higher burglary, larceny, and motor-vehicle-theft rates than did "White" households during the same period (U.S. Department of Justice, 1988b, p. 27).

Class, Occupation, and Employment Status

One of the most heated continuing debates in the field of **criminology** centres on the correlation of measures of

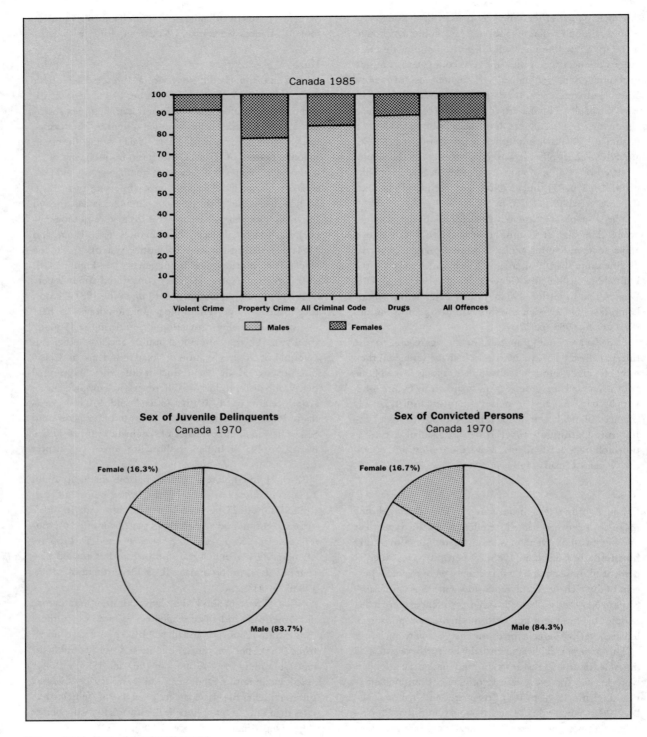

Figure 14.3   Sex of Adults Charged

Canada 1985

Source: Data from Statistics Canada (1986), *Canadian criminal statistics 1985*, cat. 85–205; Statistics Canada (1971), *Statistics of criminal and other offences 1970*, cat. 85–201.

social class, of income, and of employment status with offence and victimization rates. The arguments often seem driven by ideological disputes about what the situation *ought* to be, rather than by data on what the situation actually is. The dispute is theoretically important, because many of the major theories purporting to explain **criminality** make specific assumptions about the relationship between social class and criminal activity (as discussed in Chapter 10).

Class

Social class is difficult to define, but seems to involve a complex of group characteristics that include occupation, education, income level, access to political power, and group

cultural concerns. Much criminological theory is grounded on the assumption that persons of different social class have different propensities to commit criminal offences; other streams of theory are explicitly grounded on the assumption that propensity to commit criminal offences is not related to social class and that any apparent differences in the offence rates of persons of different social class are produced by biases in the criminal-justice system or biases on the part of researchers. Whether persons of different social class have differential propensities to commit offences or to be criminally victimized is clearly of great consequence to our understanding of crime.

The most extensive examination of this issue was con-

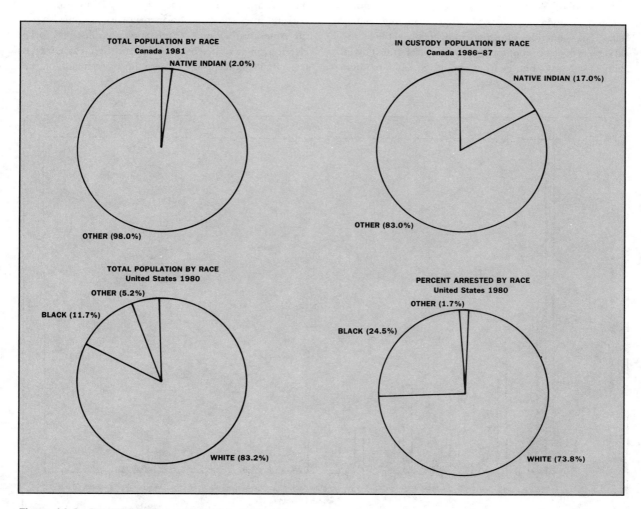

Figure 14.4   Total Population and Total in Custody by Race, Canada and the United States

Source: Data from Census of Canada (1981); Statistics Canada (1989), *Adult correctional services in Canada 1986–1987*, cat. 85–211, p. 56; Bureau of Justice Statistics (1988), *Report to the nation on crime and justice*, 2nd. ed. Washington, DC: Department of Justice.

ducted through the National Youth Survey project in the United States. This project gathered information on self-reported criminal and delinquent activity among a large, representative sample of American adolescents for 1976 through 1980. It found consistent class differences in both the **prevalence** and **incidence** of criminal and delinquent behaviour: middle-class youths had lower rates of criminal and delinquent behaviour than did working-class and lower-class youths. Class differences were stronger for males than for females. Class differences were much stronger for serious criminal offences than for less serious offences or for acts of general-status delinquency (Elliott & Huizinga, 1983).

The National Youth Survey findings are echoed in other longitudinal studies conducted in England and the United States. The Cambridge University study followed the criminal careers of a cohort of lower-class boys from the Tower Hamlets area of London from about age eight to their middle twenties. It found that, among this cohort, the boys of the lowest social standing had much more frequent and serious histories of criminal offending, whether measured by official criminal-justice-system records or self-reports of criminal and delinquent behaviour (West, 1982, pp. 166–67). The University of Pennsylvania longitudinal study of delinquency in a Philadelphia birth cohort found strong differences in the delinquency rates of juveniles of different classes: persons of lower socio-economic status had much more serious offence records that did persons judged to be of higher socio-economic status (Wolfgang, Figlio, & Sellin, 1972).

Dispute about the relationship of people's social class to their criminal-offending and criminal-victimization rates remains intense. Some scholars maintain, in concert with the American National Youth Survey results, that social class is strongly related to offending and victimization rates (e.g., Braithwaite, 1981). Other scholars maintain, on the

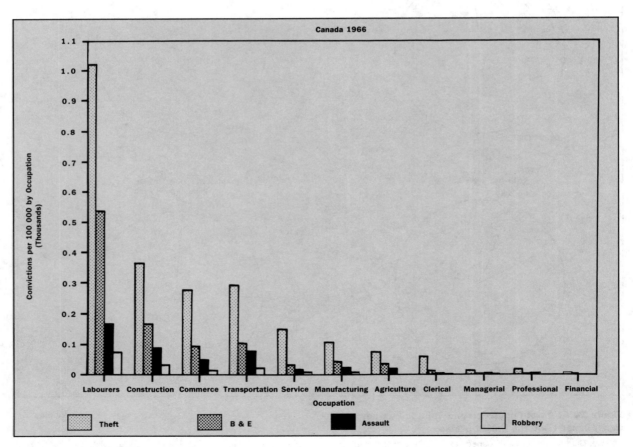

Figure 14.5   Conviction Rates by Occupation
Canada 1966

Source: Data from L. Tepperman (1977), *Crime control: The urge toward authority* (p. 183). Toronto: McGraw-Hill Ryerson.

basis of smaller studies, that there is no relationship between social class and propensity for criminal offending or victimization (e.g., Tittle & Villemez, 1977; Hindelang, Hirschi, & Weis, 1981).

At present, those arguing that social class does relate to offending and victimization rates appear to have the stronger evidence on their side. This evidence seems to establish, as a *prima facie* working hypothesis, the proposition that rates of criminal offending and criminal victimization will be higher among persons of lower social class and lower among persons of higher social class.

Occupation

Criminal offending and victimization rates appear to be higher among some occupational groups than others. In Canada, unskilled labourers have long had the highest conviction rates, whereas persons in clerical, managerial, professional, and financial occupations have long had the lowest conviction rates. Figure 14.5, derived from data presented by Tepperman (1977, p. 183), shows conviction rates per 100 000 persons working as unskilled labourers and for persons working in the construction trades, in commerce, in transportation, in service industries, in manufacturing, in agriculture, in clerical positions, in managerial positions, in professional occupations, and in financial occupations for the crimes of theft, breaking-and-entering, assault, and robbery for the year 1966. Clear occupational concentrations are apparent: unskilled labourers had much higher conviction rates for all of these offences than did skilled blue-collar and commercial workers; blue-collar workers in turn had much higher conviction rates for these offences than did white-collar and professional workers.

Poverty and Wealth

Crime is often reported to be related to poverty. When politicians or newspaper editorials speak about "the root causes of crime," they usually mean poverty. Historically, this relationship makes sense. In the economies of the past, large numbers of people lived at the bare subsistence level. When crops failed or the economy faltered, many were forced to turn to crime in order to survive. Crime varied directly with the price of foodstuffs: when prices were high, crime rates were high; when prices were low, crime rates were low as well. People stole the necessities of life—food and clothing. This relationship began to change, however, with the advance of the Industrial Revolution in the eighteenth century. By the mid-nineteenth century, crime rates developed a reversed relationship with economic conditions in Britain: crime rates went up when the economy was strong; crime rates declined when the economy faltered. This pattern also gradually appeared in the United States, in other leading European countries, and in Canada.

In Canada, crime rates rose rapidly to a peak during the boom years of the late 1970s and early 1980s, then declined during the recession of the mid-1980s and rebounded again during the economic expansion of the late 1980s.

Multivariate Analysis

Cross-sectional analysis of the correlations of the crime rates of each province and territory with measures of employment and relative wealth, alcohol consumption, and number of automobiles per capita for the year 1986 is instructive, as we see in Table 14.3. Economic conditions appear to be less important correlates of provincial crime rates than do leisure and mobility measures.

In 1986, violent-, property- and drug-offence rates, as well as total offence rates, were correlated with percent unemployed, and the ratio of rich families to poor families (those with incomes above $45 000 per annum compared to those with incomes below $10 000 per annum), but in different ways. Violent-, property-, and drug-offence rates were all correlated *negatively* with percent unemployed, but positively with the ratio of rich-to-poor families. Crime rates were high in provinces with low unemployment rates, and low in provinces with high unemployment rates. Provinces that had a relatively large number of rich families compared to the number of poor families had high crime rates.

This pattern might be explained in two different, but complementary, ways. One model would draw on notions of *relative deprivation*, arguing that, in the modern social welfare state, crime is associated with the number of persons experiencing relative deprivation rather than the absolute economic deprivation experienced in the past. Crimes go up when the number of rich people is greater, because the relatively few poor people left feel particularly deprived in their poverty when they compare themselves to the well-off.

The second explanatory model draws on modern **opportunity theory** and particularly on Professor Marcus Felson's concept of *guardianship* (Cohen & Felson, 1979). In this approach, as unemployment rises, and as more families become poorer, more people stay at home and exercise closer personal guardianship over their possessions. As unemployment declines and there are fewer poor families, there are more goods to steal and fewer people stay home to exercise personal guardianship over their possessions. This creates many more opportunities for property crime.

The complications associated with crime patterns are revealed a bit more when provincial crime rates are correlated with per-capita alcoholic-beverage consumption and motor-vehicle ownership. Violent-crime rates, property-crime rates, and, to a lesser extent, drug-offence rates were positively correlated with per-capita alcohol consumption

Table 14.3 Correlations Between Four Social Indicators of Each Province and Crime Rates

	Violent Crime Rate	Property Crime Rate	Drug Offence Rate	Total Offence Rate
Unemployment Rate	−0.41	−0.62	−0.26	−0.58
Rich Family/Poor Family Ratio	0.31	0.31	0.30	0.33
Alcohol Sales Per Capita	0.46	0.35	0.23	0.09
Motor Vehicles Per Capita	0.78	0.76	0.85	0.91

Source: Calculated from data in Centre for Justice Statistics (1987, 1988), *Canadian crime statistics 1985–1987*. Ottawa: Ministry of Supply and Services; Statistics Canada (1989), *Canada yearbook 1988*.

in 1986. The correlations between crime rates and per-capita motor-vehicle ownership were even stronger, ranging from +0.78 for violent offences to +0.91 for total offence rates.

Canadian Crime in Comparative Perspective

Does Canada have more or less crime than other countries? The question is an important one because it tells us something very important about the character of our society and it also helps us to gauge how our criminal-justice system is working.

The same question can be raised about the distribution of crime within Canada. Do some provinces or some cities have more or less crime than others? If some do, then we can seek to discover differences between provinces or cities with higher or lower crime rates that may tell us how to go about reducing crime everywhere.

International Patterns

There are, at present, only a few sources of information about the amount of crime experienced in many different countries at a given time. The United Nations collects statistical data on homicides in member states as part of its vital-statistics program. The United Nations also periodically sponsors surveys of crimes officially known in member states and has occasionally sponsored some other forms of criminological survey. The International Criminal Police Organization, commonly known as *Interpol* and headquartered in Paris, conducts bi-annual surveys of crimes known to its member states.

Data from both organizations have limitations. The U.N. homicide data, collected by the World Health Organization, are derived from medical records and are not directly cross-checked against criminal-justice data. The U.N. crime surveys use very crude categories and rely on voluntary participation. In the U.N. survey conducted in 1983, covering the period of 1975 to 1980, only 50 of 154 member states participated.

The Interpol data depend on the underlying data voluntarily collected and reported by official criminal-justice agencies in member states. Information is collected on the numbers and rates of offences known to police and the number of known offenders for eight different categories of offences, with some additional detail in some categories: murder; sex offences; serious assaults; thefts; fraud; counterfeit-currency offences; drug offences; and the total number of offences contained in National Crime Statistics of each reporting member state.

Some patterns do emerge from the international data on crime. First, as Table 14.4 makes clear, when the developed countries of Europe, North America, and the South Pacific are compared, some consistent groupings by order of magnitude of offence rates position Canada part way between the United States and Europe for many offences. Canada, Australia, and New Zealand as a group (CANZ) have reported homicide rates substantially below American homicide rates, but above European rates throughout the 1980s. This pattern holds true for the offences of rape and robbery as well. In contrast, the CANZ group have reported burglary and auto-theft rates much more like the American rates. In fact, the 1984 Interpol data show the CANZ group reporting higher levels of burglary and auto theft than the United States. (For more information on Australia, see Mukherjee, 1981.)

Second, when both the individual developed, industrialized countries and the individual underdeveloped countries that report to Interpol are considered, it becomes apparent that underdeveloped countries generally report higher rates of violent crimes against the person but relatively low property crime rates; for developed countries, the pattern is reversed.

Canada's murder rate of 2.66 per 100 000 population ranked 36th out of 80 nations reporting to Interpol in 1984,

Table 14.4   Summary Data on International Crime Rates

Crime and Data Series	Number of Crimes per 100 000 Population		
	United States	Europe[a]	Canada, Australia, and New Zealand[a]
Homicide (excluding attempts)			
WHO 1980	10.5	1.4	1.5
UN 1980	10.1	1.3	—
Interpol 1980	10.0	1.8	2.3
Interpol 1984	7.9	1.5	2.2[b]
Rape			
UN 1980	36.0	5.0	—
Interpol 1980	36.0	4.2	10.5
Interpol 1984	35.7	5.4	14.1[c]
Robbery			
UN 1980	240.9	25.4	—
Interpol 1980	244.0	38.4	56.4
Interpol 1984	205.4	49.1	63.8
Burglary			
Interpol 1980	1669.0	893.1	1498.4
Interpol 1984	1263.7	1055.3	1806.0
Theft			
UN 1980	5262.2	2086.8	—
Auto Theft			
Interpol 1980	495.0	233.8	418.0[d]
Interpol 1984	437.1	221.8	444.8[d]

[a]Rates represent averages for reporting countries; Interpol data for 1980 and 1984 are not directly comparable since identical sets of countries did not report for both years.
[b]Does not include Australia.
[c]Does not include Canada.
[d]Does not include New Zealand.

Sources: World Health Organization, *World health statistics annual*, vols. 1982–86; Interpol, *International crime statistics*, vols. 1979–80, 1981–82, 1983–84; United Nations, Second United Nations Crime Survey, U.S. Census Bureau, *Statistical abstract of the United States, 1987*.

and was well below the average reported murder rate of 4.74. The Philippines reported the highest murder rate, at 42.51 per 100 000, followed by Lesotho, Zimbabwe, Lebanon, Thailand, Angola, Venezuela, the Bahamas, the Dominican Republic, and Tanzania. The United States, which is very unusual among developed countries, ranked 12th in reported murder rates at 7.91 per 100 000 population.

A map of world murder rates for the year 1984 is presented in Figure 14.6. The map uses Interpol murder data supplemented by the most recent available U.N. homicide statistics when Interpol data are not available. Missing from the map are countries that do not participate in either the Interpol or the U.N. criminal-statistics programs: the Soviet Union and a number of its client states such as Poland, the German Democratic Republic (East Germany), South Yemen, Mongolia, and Cuba; a number of Islamic states such as Iraq, Iran, and Pakistan; the Asian giants China and India; and a pot-pourri of African and Latin American nations.

In contrast, Canada's breaking-and-entering rate of 1420.6 ranked 12th out of 61 nations reporting to Interpol about this crime in 1984, more than double the average reported rate of 617.9. The Netherlands ranked first for this offence at 2328.7 per 100 000 population, almost four times the average rate, followed by Denmark, Scotland, the

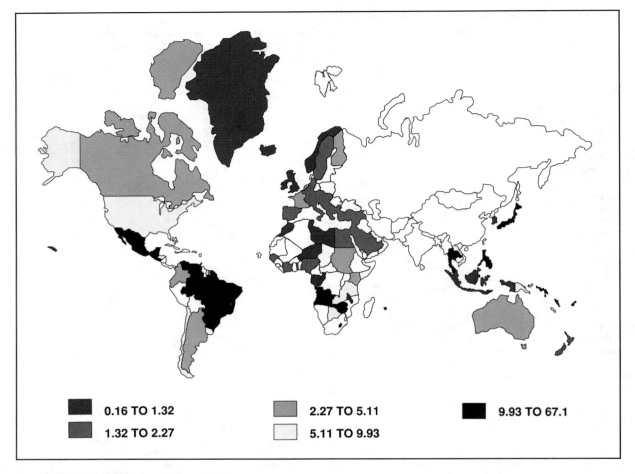

Figure 14.6 World Murder Patterns 1984
Rate/100 000 population

Source: Data from Interpol (1985), *International criminal police statistics 1983–1984*. Paris: International Criminal Police Organization; World Health Organization (1985), *World health statistics 1983–1984*. New York: United Nations.

Bahamas, Bermuda, Australia, Sweden, and the Cayman Islands. The United States ranked 15th.

This pattern of high levels of violent crime in the underdeveloped nations and high levels of property crime in the economically advanced nations has been consistently reflected in both Interpol statistics and U.N. data for more than three decades (Brantingham & Brantingham, 1984, pp. 251–260; Krohn, 1976; Wolf, 1971). Table 14.5 presents 1984 data for five offences for 35 selected Interpol member states.

Third, the absence of much reported crime data from the Soviet Bloc and other socialist countries poses a real problem for some sorts of comparative analyses. Socialist states have long publicly maintained, as a matter of ideology,

that their crime rates are much lower than those found in capitalist states, while refusing to publish systematic statistics on crimes known to police, on criminal convictions, or on the size or activities of their criminal-justice establishments. They have also been reluctant to participate in U.N. crime surveys. Poland and Yugoslavia were the only socialist states that responded with usable data to the U.N. crime survey in the 1970s (Brantingham & Brantingham, 1984, pp. 257–58).

The U.N. survey found that the two participating Eastern European states reported the lowest overall crime rates of any regional grouping, with homicide rates a third that of Western Europe, assault rates that were half those reported in Western Europe, and theft rates that were less than a tenth those reported in Western Europe. The relative mix of crimes reported in Eastern Europe was strikingly similar to that reported by the Caribbean region, with theft and assault together making up about 90 percent of all known offences (Brantingham & Brantingham, 1984, pp. 252–55).

Western scholars have, over the past quarter-century, painstakingly pieced together a picture of crime in the Soviet Union that suggests the long-maintained official picture is inaccurate. In 1967, it is thought, the Soviets convicted about 1064 persons per 100 000 population for serious crimes (Shelley, 1981, p. 109). In comparison, the criminal conviction rate in Canada in 1967 was 546 per 100 000 population, about half the apparent Soviet level. The Canadian indictable-conviction rate for persons aged

Table 14.5   Interpol Data on Crime Rates in 35 Selected Countries, 1984

	Number of crimes per 100 000 population					
	Murder					
Country	Actual	Including attempts	Rape	Robbery	Burglary	Auto theft
Australia	—	3.4	13.8	83.6	1754.3	584.7
Austria	1.3	2.4	5.3	29.8	805.8	16.9
Belgium	—	3.3	5.6	50.0	—	140.6
Canada	2.7	6.3	—	92.8	1420.6	304.9
Chile	5.8	6.3	10.6	36.4	—	7.6
Colombia	—	2.5	4.4	32.8	—	14.2
Denmark	1.2	5.8	7.7	35.6	2230.2	469.5
Ecuador	—	4.5	5.9	22.8	—	7.8
Egypt	1.0	1.5	—	.4	—	3.3
England and Wales	1.1[a]	1.4[a]	2.7[a]	44.6[a]	1,639.7[a]	656.6[a]
Finland	2.3	5.6	6.5	33.7	772.6	171.7
France	—	4.6	5.2	105.6	809.8	483.4
Germany (FRG)	1.5	4.5	9.7	45.8	1554.1	118.0
Greece	1.0	1.8	.9	2.3	72.8	—
Hungary	1.9	3.7	6.1	15.5	211.0	4.0
Indonesia	—	.9	1.2	5.1	38.4	4.9
Ireland	.8	1.1	2.0	5.4	1056.8	29.7
Italy	2.1[a]	5.3[a]	1.8[a]	35.7[a]	—	276.3
Japan	.8	1.5	1.6	1.8	231.2	29.4
Luxembourg	—	5.3	2.8	40.8	509.8	109.3
Monaco	—	—	—	43.2	500.0	176.3
Netherlands	1.2	—	7.2	52.9	2328.7	155.9
New Zealand	1.7	2.5	14.4	14.9	2243.1	—
Nigeria	1.5[a]	1.7[a]	—	—	—	—
Northern Ireland	4.0[a]	19.8[a]	5.0[a]	119.3[a]	1360.7[a]	106.2[a]
Norway	—	.9[a]	4.2[a]	—	—	273.1[a]
Philippines	—	42.5	2.6	33.0	—	2.0
Portugal	3.0	4.6	2.0	21.6	99.7	61.3
Scotland	—	1.4	4.4	86.9	2178.6	632.7
Spain	—	2.2	3.6	147.3	1069.9	278.2
Sweden	1.4	5.7	11.9	44.1	1708.8	460.0
Switzerland	1.1	2.2	5.8	24.2	276.8	—[b]
Thailand	—	16.6	5.3	10.0	8.7	2.0
United States	7.9	—	35.7	205.4	1263.7	437.1
Venezuela	—	9.9	17.4	161.0	—	85.9

— Not available.
[a] 1983 data
[b] Auto theft in Switzerland omitted because it includes bicycles.

Source: Interpol, *International crime statistics*, vols. 1983–84. Paris: Interpol.

sixteen years and older was 573 per 100 000 population. The juvenile-delinquency conviction rate for persons aged seven through fifteen years was 458 per 100 000 (Leacy, 1983).

The Soviets imprisoned a much larger proportion of their convicts during the 1970s than did countries in Western Europe or North America. Juviler (1976, p.106) estimated that, in the mid-1970s, Soviet prisons held between 400 and 600 prisoners per 100 000 population. In comparison, he estimated that the United States had about 180 prisoners per 100 000 population; and that Sweden had about 45 prisoners per 100 000 population in the mid-1970s. Canada had 123 adult prisoners per 100 000 population aged sixteen years or older in 1975 (Leacy, 1983).

More recent scholarship suggests that these differences between Soviet and Western conviction and imprisoned population rates are a function of the different types and volumes of crime experienced (Los, 1988). The process of *Glasnost* seems to offer support for these scholarly speculations about Soviet crime levels. Early in 1989, the Soviet Interior Minister spoke in *Pravda* about high levels of robbery and other street crime, pervasive problems of official and police corruption, and a large number of "mafias"— criminal syndicates—that control a wide range of products and services in the Soviet Union. He said that officially known crime rose by 16.9 percent in the Soviet Union in 1988. He also said, "We can boldly assert that the crime rate in the country is considerably higher than is fixed by the statistics" (*Ottawa Citizen*, 1989).

Canadian Crime in International Context

Canada belongs to several different but important groupings of nations: the Organization for Economic Cooperation and Development; the British Commonwealth; the Francophone Summit; and what might be termed the Arctic powers, that is, the group of nations with a territorial or jurisdictional presence above the Arctic Circle. Canada's crime pattern can be considered with respect to each.

Crime in the OECD
Perhaps the most relevant grouping of nations against which to compare Canadian crime rates is the group of economically advanced nations belonging to the Organization for Economic Cooperation and Development. The OECD is a group of 24 major industrialized Western Bloc countries (Yugoslavia is a 25th associate member).

Among OECD states reporting to Interpol in 1984, Canada ranked eighth in both its reported murder rate and its reported breaking-and-entering rate. The United States had the highest reported murder rate among OECD members, at 7.91 per 100 000 population. This was almost three times Canada's murder rate in 1984, almost twice that of France, and almost eight times the murder rate reported by England and Wales, which ranked 20th, tied with Switzerland, among OECD members.

The Netherlands had the highest reported rate for breaking-and-entering among OECD members in 1984, at 2329 offences per 100 000 population. This was 50 percent higher than Canada's breaking-and-entering rate, almost double the American rate, and almost triple the French rate.

The patterns of violent and property crimes experienced by the group of nations with the most advanced economies clearly differ by offence type. Luxembourg and Portugal, for instance, reported very high murder rates but very low breaking-and-entering rates. The Netherlands and England and Wales reported very low murder rates, but very high breaking-and-entering rates. Only Australia was among the top five ranked nations for both offences. Japan and Greece were striking for reporting very low rates for both offences.

Crime in the British Commonwealth
A second major grouping of nations in which Canada is a major force is the British Commonwealth. Canada was the first of the major self-governing dominions in the old British Empire and continues to play a major role in Commonwealth affairs. Canada hosted the 1987 Commonwealth summit in Vancouver. In 1984, Canada's murder rate ranked 19th and Canada's breaking-and-entering rate ranked 8th among Commonwealth nations reporting to Interpol.

The generally observed pattern of high violent-crime rates in underdeveloped countries and high property-crime rates in developed countries holds for the murder rates and breaking-and-entering rates reported to Interpol by Commonwealth nations. The very large proportion of underdeveloped nations belonging to the Commonwealth has the effect of giving the Commonwealth an average murder rate that is more than double the average murder rate among OECD nations, while the Commonwealth's average break-and-enter rate is only about half that of the OECD.

Crime in the Francophonie
Another major bloc of nations in which Canada is an important member is the bloc of French-speaking nations sometimes called the *Francophonie*, and generally organized through membership in the *Agence de Coopération Culturelle et Technique* (ACCT). Canada hosted the francophone summit in Quebec City in 1987.

Among the limited number of ACCT members that reported to Interpol in 1984, Canada had the highest break-

and-enter rate but a moderate murder rate. Canada's break-and-enter rate was almost twice as high as that of France, which ranked second, and almost three times as high as that of Luxembourg, which ranked fourth.

Canada's murder rate was a sixth that of Lebanon, a third that of Rwanda and half that of Luxembourg. France and Belgium also reported murder rates substantially above Canada's.

Spatial Patterns in Canadian Crime

Crime High in the West and North

The distribution of crime across the provinces and territories of Canada has some striking and persistent patterns. Crime rates have always been highest in the far west, in British Columbia and the Yukon. They have generally been lowest in the far-eastern provinces, in Quebec and the Maritimes. Crime rates in Ontario and the prairie provinces vary: sometimes they are high like those of British Columbia; sometimes they fall near the Canadian average. Since the 1950s, the Northwest Territories have also generally exhibited very high crime rates.

Crime Patterns across North America

Although Canada generally enjoys lower aggregate crime rates than the United States, the geographic distribution of known crimes across the provinces and states of the two countries presents more complex patterns than the aggregate comparison might suggest. Some Canadian jurisdictions have very high rates for some types of crime and rank with the worst of American states. Some American states have very low rates for some types of crime and rank with the very best of the Canadian provinces. The 1986 comparisons that follow are limited to two violent crimes—homicide and robbery—and three property crimes—burglary, theft, and motor-vehicle theft—principally because the rather primitive national police statistics gathered in the United States do not permit examination of many interesting and important crimes about which data have long been available in Canada.

Homicide Patterns

Canada generally has much lower homicide rates than the United States. Ten of the twelve Canadian jurisdictions fall into the bottom two quintiles when the states and provinces

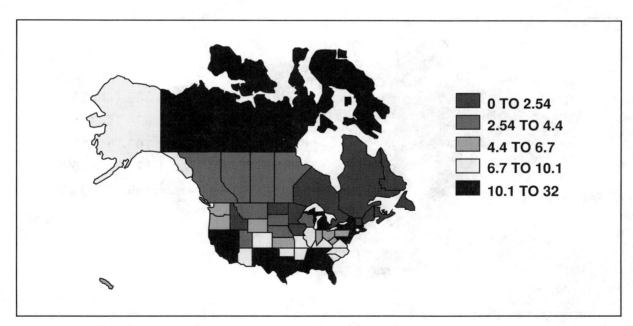

Figure 14.7   North American Homicide Patterns 1986
Rate/100 000 population

Source: Data from Statistics Canada (1987), *Canadian crime statistics 1986*, cat. 85–205; Federal Bureau of Investigation (1987), *Crime in the United States 1986*. Washington, DC: Department of Justice.

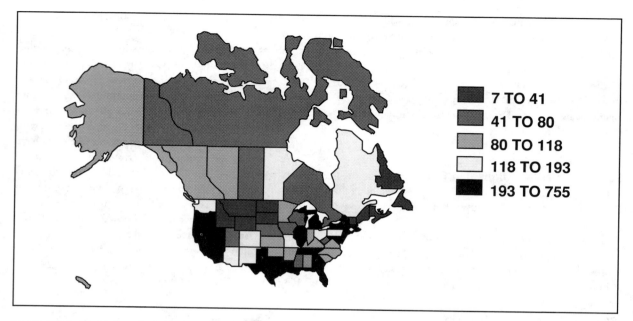

Figure 14.8   North American Robbery Patterns 1986
Rate/100 000 population

Source: Data from Statistics Canada (1987), *Canadian crime statistics 1986*, cat. 85–205; Federal Bureau of Investigation (1987), *Crime in the United States 1986*. Washington, DC: Department of Justice.

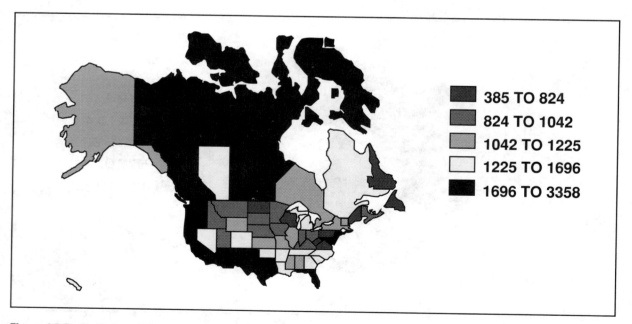

Figure 14.9   North American Burglary Patterns 1986
Rate/100 000 population

Source: Data from Statistics Canada (1987), *Canadian crime statistics 1986*, cat. 85–205; Federal Bureau of Investigation (1987), *Crime in the United States 1986*. Washington, DC: Department of Justice.

are ranked by homicide rate (see Figure 14.7). Many of the states with the lowest homicide rates are contiguous to Canada. The adjacent and related regions of the Maritimes and New England show very low homicide rates, as do the Canadian and American prairies. The general Canadian trend of lowest rates in the eastern parts of the country and higher rates in the West and in the North is clearly visible.

Canada's northern frontier territories, the Yukon and the Northwest Territories, exhibit very high rates of homicide. Indeed, they fall into the highest quintile of North American jurisdictions and form a northern murder belt to complement the long observed southern murder belt that stretches across the United States from Florida to California.

Robbery Patterns

Canadian robbery levels are much lower than those experienced in the United States, but there are some high-rate provinces and cities (see Figure 14.8). The highest-ranked provinces in 1986 were Quebec and Manitoba, which fell into the second-highest quintile of North American jurisdictions along with Pennsylvania and Ohio, New Mexico, Arizona, and Colorado. Criminologists have spent much effort in recent years trying to discover why Montreal is among the highest robbery rate cities on the continent (Gabor et al., 1987).

Burglary Patterns

During the 1980s, Canada generally reported higher break-and-enter rates than did the United States. This offence is generally known by the ancient and colourful common-law term "burglary" in the United States, although the full range of modern breaking offences are included within the definition.

The higher Canadian breaking-and-entering rates are reflected in the continental crime map. Five Canadian jurisdictions fall into the top quintile of all North American jurisdictions. They are all in the western and northern parts of the country. The high-rate American states are in the west and south. The Maritime provinces reported the lowest breaking-and-entering rates among Canadian jurisdictions in 1986 (see Figure 14.9).

Theft Patterns

The continental theft pattern was dominated by the western and northern jurisdictions in 1986. The highest quintile included a contiguous grouping composed of Alaska, the Yukon, the Northwest Territories, British Columbia, Alberta, Saskatchewan, Manitoba, Washington, Oregon, and Hawaii. Arizona, Utah and Texas were also in the quintile of highest-rate states, while California, Nevada, New Mexico, Colorado, Wyoming, and Montana were in the

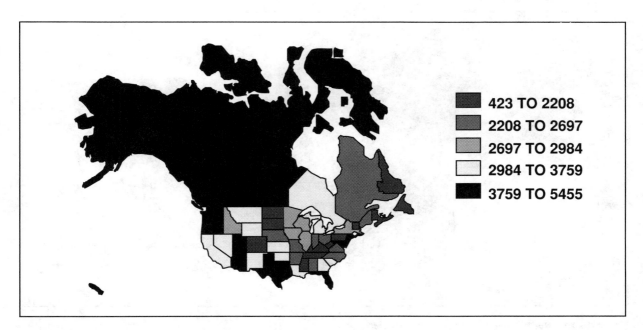

Figure 14.10   North American Theft Patterns 1986
Rate/100 000 population

Source: Data from Statistics Canada (1987), *Canadian crime statistics 1986*, cat. 85–205; Federal Bureau of Investigation (1987), *Crime in the United States 1986*. Washington, DC: Department of Justice.

second-highest quintile. Low theft rates were reported in the Maritime provinces and in a diverse sprinkling of states (see Figure 14.10).

Motor-Vehicle–Theft Patterns

It is harder to discern a pattern for motor-vehicle thefts than for the other crimes examined in this section. The high-rate jurisdictions included Alaska and the Northwest Territories; California, Texas, and Florida; Michigan, Illinois, and New York. The Maritime provinces reported relatively low motor-vehicle–theft rates, but New England reported relatively high rates. The Yukon, British Columbia, Manitoba, and Quebec were in the second-highest quintile of jurisdictions, but Ontario and New Brunswick were in the second-lowest quintile (see Figure 14.11).

Paired Jurisdiction Comparisons

A comparison between some contiguous or otherwise connected Canadian and American jurisdictions might prove useful. Four pairs of jurisdictions sweep across the continent: the province of New Brunswick, in Maritime Canada, and the contiguous state of Maine, in New England; the province of Ontario and the state of Michi-

gan in the continent's industrial heartland; the province of British Columbia and the state of Washington in the Pacific northwest; and the Yukon Territory and the state of Alaska in the Arctic (see Table 14.6).

New Brunswick and Maine had similar levels of homicide, robbery, burglary, and theft in 1986. Maine's reported motor-vehicle–theft rate was twice that of New Brunswick. New Brunswick had about 60 percent of Maine's population, but a higher proportion lived in urban areas. Maine had a higher per-capita income, but a much lower divorce rate. Maine's unemployment rate was 5.3 percent, compared to New Brunswick's rate of 13.2 percent. The two provincial economies were very similar, keyed to fishing, farming, forestry.

Ontario and Michigan had nearly identical populations in 1986. About 80 percent of the population in each jurisdiction lived in urban areas. Michigan had an unemployment rate of 8.8 percent, compared with Ontario's 6.1 percent. Both jurisdictions were keyed to the heavy industry surrounding automobile production. Yet the two jurisdictions had strikingly different violent-crime rates in 1986. Michigan's homicide rate was seven and a half times higher than Ontario's. Michigan's robbery rate was more

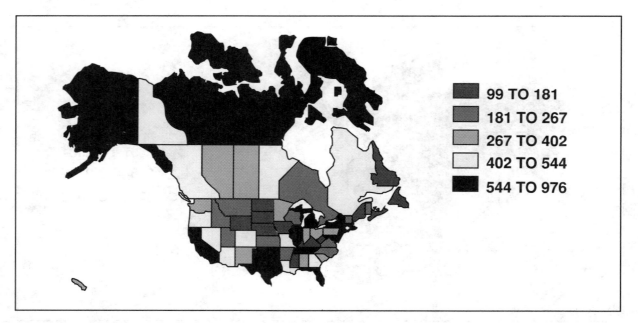

▨	99 TO 181
▨	181 TO 267
▨	267 TO 402
☐	402 TO 544
■	544 TO 976

Figure 14.11   North American Motor Vehicle Theft Patterns 1986
Rate/100 000 population

Source: Data from Statistics Canada (1987), *Canadian crime statistics 1986*, cat. 85–205; Federal Bureau of Investigation (1987), *Crime in the United States 1986*. Washington, DC: Department of Justice.

Table 14.6   Paired Jurisdiction Crime Comparisons, 1986

Jurisdiction	Rate/100 000 Population				
	Homicide	Robbery	Burglary	Theft	Motor Vehicle Theft
New Brunswick	1.7	26	947	2101	315
Maine	2.0	28	803	2347	164
Ontario	1.5	59	1128	3140	515
Michigan	11.3	601	1509	3378	800
British Columbia	3.0	110	2168	5454	480
Washington	5.0	135	1861	4267	315
Yukon	13.0	52	2074	5352	1174
Alaska	8.6	88	1162	3910	604

Source: Data from Statistics Canada (1987), *Canadian crime statistics, 1986*, Cat. 85–205; Federal Bureau of Investigation (1987), *Crime in the United States 1986*. Washington, DC: Department of Justice.

than ten times higher. But property crime rates were more similar. Michigan's burglary and motor-vehicle–theft rates were only one and a half times Ontario's. The theft rates reported in the two jurisdictions were most similar.

British Columbia and Washington have similar populations and similar economies keyed to forestry, fishing, farming, and shipping. Washington has a high-tech edge, with Boeing aircraft. British Columbia is a major finance and entertainment centre. British Columbia had higher unemployment in 1986, at 12 percent, compared to Washington's 6.1 percent. Similar proportions of the two jurisdictions' populations lived in urban areas and were exposed to similar levels of police per capita. Washington had higher levels of violent crime; British Columbia had higher levels of property crime.

A recent comparison of crime in the cities of Vancouver, British Columbia, and Seattle, Washington, during the years 1985–86 reinforces the patterns seen at the province/state level (Sloan et al., 1988). During that period, the two cities were nearly identical in total population count; had nearly identical median household incomes; and had nearly identical proportions of low-income households. The two cities had similar rates of robbery, burglary, and assaults and homicides not involving firearms. Seattle's firearm assault rate was eight times higher than Vancouver's. Seattle's firearm homicide rate was almost five times Vancouver's, enough to make Seattle's overall homicide rate almost twice as high as Vancouver's.

The researchers concluded that this substantial difference in dangerous violent-crime rates could best be attributed to differences in gun control, particularly handgun control:

Canada has a very strong national gun-control program; the United States leaves gun control to the states, and Washington has a relatively weak gun-control program in comparison with British Columbia's.

The National Rifle Association, an American lobby group committed to free availability of firearms, argued that gun availability could not explain these observed differences in the two cities' violent-crime rates, and pointed to ethnic differences as an alternative explanation (MacQueen, 1989). It is true that Vancouver has a much higher proportion of residents of Asian ancestry, while Seattle has a much higher proportion of residents of black and Hispanic ancestry, but such racialist explanations for the differences in firearm-related crime rates in the two cities seem self-serving, far-fetched, and mean-spirited. The more direct explanation—that ready access to handguns leads to more violence in which handguns are used—fits the data better.

Yukon and Alaska make up the northwesterly part of North America. Their histories are interwoven by the Klondike gold rush, by the Yukon River, and by the Inuit of the Arctic. Alaska had 21 times the Yukon's population, but both had very low population densities, scattered over vast stretches of mountain, boreal forest, and arctic plain. The Yukon had almost twice Alaska's homicide rate in 1986, and reported substantially higher property-crime rates.

The most striking contrasts in this brief comparison of paired Canadian and American jurisdictions are found in the industrial heartland and the Arctic. In the heartland, American crime rates are far higher; in the Arctic, Canadian crime rates are higher. The Seattle/Vancouver comparison suggests that differences in policy toward known direct criminogenic devices and situations, such as handgun availability, may contribute directly to crime differences in similar Canadian and American jurisdictions. Further analyses of the social and economic situations in these jurisdictions, in conjunction with analyses of direct situational contributors to criminal events such as alcohol consumption, handgun availability, and physical settings, might lead to a better understanding of the sources of crime.

Interurban Crime Patterns

Some of the geographic patterns in crime observed in the preceding sections are reinforced, and made somewhat clearer, when the focus of analysis is shifted from provinces to cities. Some new patterns also emerge when the focus of study is resolved at this finer level.

Ontario and Quebec dominate the listing of the 25 largest urban police jurisdictions in Canada presented in the first block in Table 14.7. In fact, Quebec had 36 percent of all police jurisdictions with at least 10 000 population in 1987, and Ontario had 24 percent. The four Maritime provinces together had only 7.5 percent of such jurisdictions. The four western provinces together had 32 percent

of these jurisdictions in 1987: 2 percent in Manitoba; 4 percent in Saskatchewan; 7 percent in Alberta; 19 percent in British Columbia. No police jurisdiction in the Yukon or the Northwest Territories had 10 000 population in 1987.

The municipalities with the highest crime rates are not, however, generally the largest Canadian cities: rank-order listings of Canadian police jurisdictions by reported crime rates are dominated by smaller-sized cities in the west. In 1987, no city east of Ontario was among the 25 with the highest rates for total Criminal Code offences, for total violent offences, or for total property offences. No city in Ontario or the Maritimes fell into the top 25 ranked by illegal-drug offence rates.

Of the 25 largest police jurisdictions in 1987, only Vancouver was also among the 25 cities with the highest reported rates for Criminal Code offences, for violent crimes, for property crimes, and for illegal-drugs offences. Only one other of the 25 largest jurisdictions, Burnaby, which is adjacent to Vancouver, appeared among the top jurisdictions for two offence categories. Only for property-offence rates did other large cities also appear among the top 25 by crime rate, and they were all western cities: Burnaby, Edmonton, Saskatoon, Vancouver, and Regina.

Table 14.7   25 Top-Ranked Canadian Jurisdictions

Urban Population, 1987		Criminal Code Rates, 1987		
Municipality	Total Population	Municipality		Rate/100 000 Population
Toronto	2 192 700	Prince Albert	S	26 832
Montreal	1 720 000	Thompson	M	24 932
Calgary	647 300	Williams Lake	BC	24 641
Winnipeg	611 300	Fort St. John	BC	23 420
Edmonton	576 200	North Battleford	S	23 401
Peel Regional	562 500	St. Thomas	O	23 263
Vancouver	437 100	Langley	BC	22 852
Hamilton-Wentworth Regional	423 400	Vernon	BC	22 441
Niagara Regional	370 100	New Westminster	BC	21 723
York Regional	350 500	Terrace	BC	21 710
Waterloo Regional	329 400	Wallaceburg	O	20 561
Durham Regional	326 200	Victoria	BC	20 540
Ottawa	300 800	Nanaimo	BC	19 970
Laval	284 200	Prince Rupert	BC	19 658
Halton Regional	271 400	Dawson Creek	BC	19 217
London	269 100	Campbell River	BC	19 068
Windson	193 100	Wetaskiwin	A	19 673
Surrey	191 100	Port Alberni	BC	18 544
Saskatoon	175 900	Brandon	M	18 003
Regina	173 200	Vancouver	BC	17 472
Quebec	164 600	Red Deer	A	17 451
St. John's	159 800	Prince George	BC	17 345
Sudbury Regional	152 500	Cranbrook	BC	17 162
Burnaby	146 200	Penticton	BC	16 695
Longueuil	125 400	Burnaby	BC	16 352

Table 14.7 **(Continued)**

Violent Crime Rates, 1987			Property Crime Rates, 1987		
Municipality		Rate/100 000 Population	Municipality		Rate/100 000 Population
Thomson	M	3761	Mission District	BC	21 362
Campbell River	BC	2829	North Battleford	S	15 482
Prince Rupert	BC	2784	Vernon	BC	14 647
Wallaceburg	O	2526	Langley	BC	14 396
Williams Lake	BC	2485	Williams Lake	BC	14 106
Terrace	BC	2308	New Westminster	BC	13 805
Squamish	BC	2283	Victoria	BC	13 485
New Westminster	BC	2255	Fort St. John	BC	12 832
Dawson Creek	BC	2254	Brandon	M	12 581
Port Alberni	BC	2137	Prince Albert	S	12 288
Langley	BC	1911	Red Deer	A	11 966
Fort St. John	BC	1893	Nanaimo	BC	11 851
Fort McMurray	A	1810	Dawson Creek	BC	11 613
Victoria	BC	1779	Vancouver	BC	11 603
North Battleford	S	1775	Burnaby	BC	11 209
St. Thomas	O	1730	Terrace	BC	10 990
Woodstock	O	1696	Wetaskiwin	A	10 980
Esquimalt	BC	1662	Edmonton	A	10 887
Prince Albert	S	1636	Saskatoon	S	10 791
Selkirk	M	1630	Kelowna	BC	10 654
Lindsay	O	1613	Prince George	BC	10 462
Chilliwack	BC	1613	Regina	S	10 438
Prince George	BC	1602	Kingston	O	10 378
Vanier	O	1592	Port Alberni	BC	10 104
Vancouver	BC	1564	Thompson	M	10 054

Source: data from Statistics Canada (1988), *Canadian crime statistics 1987*, cat.
85–205.

The dominance of this crime-rate league table by cities in British Columbia is particularly striking. For Criminal Code offence rates, 17 (68 percent) of the 25 police jurisdictions with the highest rates were in British Columbia in 1987. For crimes of violence and property crimes, 15 (60 percent) of the 25 police jurisdictions with the highest reported rates were in British Columbia. For illegal-drugs offences, 19 (84 percent) of the 25 police jurisdictions with the highest reported offence rates were in British Columbia.

For all of the offence categories considered in this section, more than 90 percent of the cities ranked in the top 25 by reported crime rate were in the four western provinces. Moreover, the limited information we have about victimization rates in Canadian cities supports this pattern of western dominance (Solicitor General Canada, 1984a).

For a further understanding of Canadian crime patterns, we turn next to consideration of crime in historical perspective.

Canadian Crime in Historical Perspective

Long-term crime trends in England, the United States, and Canada can be studied through examination of criminal-conviction records going back almost 800 years, to the high medieval period (see Figure 14.12). While criminal-conviction data are a step farther removed from criminal events than police data, they have been shown by a number of scholars to correlate quite strongly with data on crimes known to police and are thought to provide a reasonable index to broad trends in the quantity of crime experienced by a particular society (Archer & Gartner, 1984; Brantingham & Brantingham, 1984).

Three very broad patterns are apparent in the long-term crime trends of England, the United States, and Canada. The first is a long-term reduction in the overall level of violent crimes and a rise in the volume of property crime. The criminal homicide rate in England, for instance, has steadily dropped from a known rate of 28 per 100 000

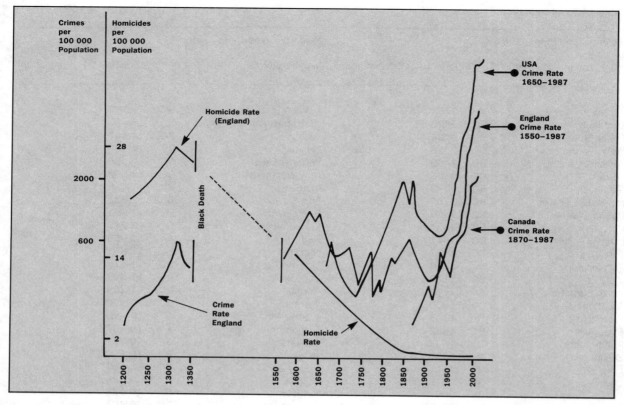

**Figure 14.12 Estimated Long-Term Crime Trends
Canada, England, United States, 1200–1987**

Source: Estimated from data in P. Brantingham and P.
Brantingham (1984), *Patterns in crime* (pp. 161–194). Toronto:
Collier Macmillan.

population in the early fourteenth century to a rate of around 1 per 100 000 population over the past 100 years or so. The second broad pattern is apparent in the repeating tidal waves of crime that seem to have rolled across the crime records of all three countries at intervals of perhaps 50 to 100 years. The third broad pattern in crime over time is the sustained and massive growth in known crime rates that has occurred in all three countries (and, indeed, most of the rest of the world) over the past half-century or so. The total known crime rates of the 1980s represent historical peaks of unprecedented height.

Canada

The Canadian historical record of trends in crime is much shorter than either the English or the American equivalent. Systematic information on crime is available only from

the period following Confederation in 1867, and realistically only since the 1880s (see Figure 14.13). The Canadian trend is somewhat different from the English and American trends over the last century or so. Canada experienced generally rising crime throughout the latter half of the nineteenth century, whereas England and the United States both experienced sustained declines. Canada also experienced much sharper fluctuations in its crime trend during World War I and during the Great Depression than did either England or the United States. Since the early 1950s, Canadian crime trends have closely resembled the English and American trends.

Two different time series must be used to examine the long-term trends. Criminal-convictions data are available for the period from the 1880s to the early 1970s. They show a generally rising trend over the entire period, with peaks in 1914 and 1939, just before the onset of the two world wars. Conviction rates fell during both world wars, as many young men went into military service. Conviction rates were relatively steady in the early 1930s, during the grimmest part of the Great Depression. They show a sharp rise during the later 1960s and early 1970s. Criminal-convictions data have not been available in Canada since the early 1970s.

Since 1962, the Uniform Crime Reporting program of Statistics Canada has collected data on persons charged by the police. This data series overlaps with the older conviction data and shows similar trends during the overlap period. The overall trend in persons charged in the last quarter-century has been a sharp rise, with rates per 100 000 population more than doubling between 1962 and 1982. This rising trend peaked in 1982, and declined during the deep economic recession of the early and mid-1980s.

A more detailed analysis of the Canadian crime record over time suggests some rather hopeful elements within the apparent general rise in crime levels. The *quality* of Canadian crime has become less dangerous and more tolerable as the quantity has increased enormously. In 1886, one crime in five was a violent crime against the person, such as murder, assault, or rape; more than half of all known crimes were crimes against property, without violence, such as theft and fraud. By 1936, crimes against the person had declined, and accounted for only one in eight known crimes, whereas violent crimes against property, such as robbery and breaking-and-entering, had increased to make up a similar proportion of known crimes. After World War II, violent crimes against the person continued their relative decline, whereas violent crimes against property continued a rapid relative increase. In 1986, violent crimes against the person had declined to one crime in twelve, while violent crimes against property had come to account to almost one in five. Malicious crimes against property, various forms of vandalism and malicious destruction, rose substantially, and accounted for one crime in seven (see Table 14.8).

This shift from crimes against the person to various forms

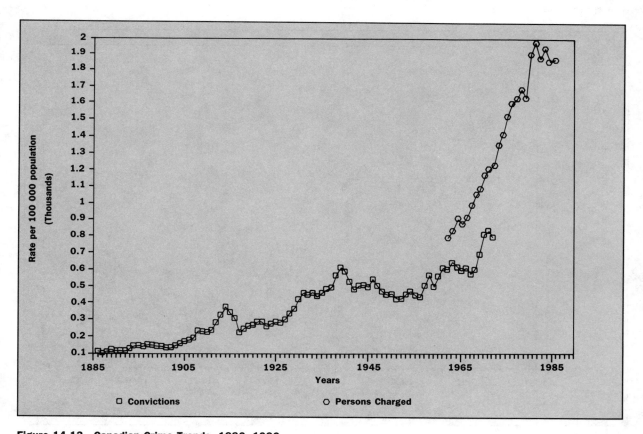

Figure 14.13 Canadian Crime Trends, 1886–1986

Source: Data from Statistics Canada (1983), *Historical statistics of Canada*, 2nd ed.; *Canadian Crime Statistics 1962–1986*, cat. 85–205.

Table 14.8 Canadian Crime Mix

	1886	1936	1986
Class I			
Crimes against The Person	20.90%	12.40%	8.00%
Class II			
Crimes against Property with Violence	7.60%	13.40%	17.33%
Class III			
Crimes against Property without Violence	58.80%	47.30%	45.26%
Class IV			
Malicious Crimes against Property	1.50%	1.40%	14.95%
Class V			
Counterfeiting	1.20%	3.00%	0.01%
Class VI			
Other Offences	10.00%	22.60%	14.32%

*May not add to 100% due to rounding
For 1886, convictions for indictable offences.
For 1936, convictions for indictable offences.
For 1986, actual offences known to police.

Source: Minister of Agriculture (1887), *Criminal statistics for the year 1886*. Ottawa: Maclean, Roger & Co.; Dominion Bureau of Statistics (1937), *Statistics of criminal and other offences 1936*. Ottawa: King's Printer; Statistics Canada (1987), *Canadian crime statistics 1986*.

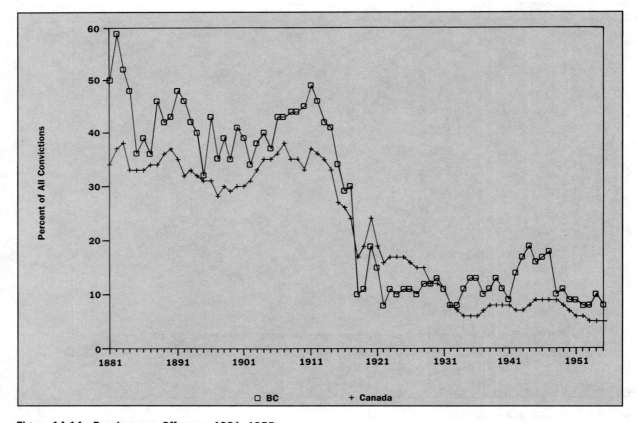

Figure 14.14 Drunkenness Offences, 1881–1955

Source: Data from R.E. Popham and W. Schmidt (1958),
Statistics of alcohol use and alcoholism in Canada 1871–1956
(pp. 37–38, 52–53). Toronto: University of Toronto Press.

of crime against property marks a major improvement in the quality of the crime problem: most of the growth in crime experienced in Canada over the past century has been directed at property, not at people. While high property-crime rates are not desirable, crimes against property are more tolerable than crimes against the person, because the harm done in the course of a residential break-in or a convenience-store hold-up or the slashing of an automobile tire can be repaired in ways that the harm done when someone is killed or injured cannot.

Another long-term Canadian crime trend is the reduction in the burden public drunkenness places on the criminal-justice system generally. In the period before World War I, drunkenness offences typically accounted for a third of all convictions in Canada each year. In British Columbia, drunkenness offences were even more prevalent, accounting for more than half of all convictions in the early 1880s and for more than 40 percent of all convictions in the decade before the outbreak of World War I. Canada introduced national prohibition during the war, but most provinces opted to keep prohibition in place until the early 1920s. The effect of prohibition was dramatic:

drunkenness offences dropped from a third of all convictions in 1912 to about 10 percent of all convictions in 1922, and remained at the lower level into the mid-1950s (see Figure 14.14).

Whether this change in the relative volume of convictions should be attributed to changes in the actual amount of public drunkenness or should be attributed to changed criminal-justice-system priorities in the face of a new wave of property offences is not known. Some alcohol abusers may have shifted to other illegal drugs, and some may have taken the pledge. Perhaps the advent of the popular automobile shifted public drunkenness to the more dangerous arena of drunken driving, though provincial liquor act offences have long-term trends quite comparable to those shown for public drunkenness.

More modern data on drug-abuse offences begin in 1962, with the initiation of the modern Canadian Uniform Crime Reports. Data on provincial liquor-act offences known to the police date from 1972. They show a steady, if slow, rise in the rate of illegal-drugs offences over the full quarter-century 1962 through 1987. Liquor-act offences rose from 1972 until 1981, then declined through the rest of the 1980s.

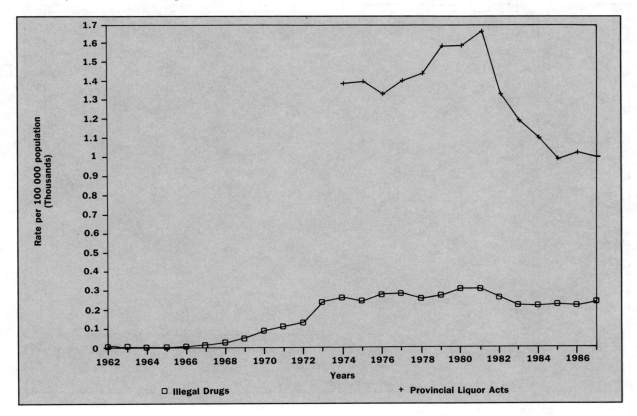

Figure 14.15   Canadian Rates for Drug & Alcohol Offences, 1962–1987

Source: Data from Statistics Canada, *Canadian crime statistics 1962–1987*, cat. 85–205.

In 1987, liquor-act offences comprised about 9 percent of all offences known to the police, a level commensurate with their general level in the convictions data following the major reductions that occurred during prohibition (see Figure 14.15; for further discussion on the topic, see Chapter 5).

Canadian Trends in the Last Quarter-Century

Crimes known to the police in Canada have risen steadily since the Uniform Crime Reporting system was established in 1962. Violent-crime rates per 100 000 population were four times higher in 1987 than they were in 1962. Moreover, the rise was steady, with only a single short reduction trend in the mid-1970s. When this category of offences is disaggregated, the general pattern is modified somewhat. Homicide rates rose sharply during the first part of this period, more than doubling from about 1.3 per

100 000 population in the mid-1960s to about 3.1 per 100 000 in 1975, then declining to fluctuate around 2.5 homicides per 100 000 population throughout the 1980s. Robbery rates quadrupled, climbing in a series of steep increases, each of which was followed by a short decline, to a 1982 peak of about 100 robberies per 100 000 population (see Figure 14.16).

Property-crime rates tripled over the quarter-century from 1962 to 1987, but the rise was more sinuous than for violent crime. Property crime rates experienced short-lived declines followed by sharp rises in the mid-1960s, in the early 1970s, and in the mid-1970s. Property-crime rates peaked in 1982, then declined for three years, before commencing another rise in the late 1980s. When disaggregated by offence, similar trend lines are visible for theft, for breaking-and-entering, and for fraud (see Figure 14.17).

Canadian prostitution and gambling offence rates, which are strongly influenced by changes in social fashion and law-enforcement attention, exhibit trends very different from

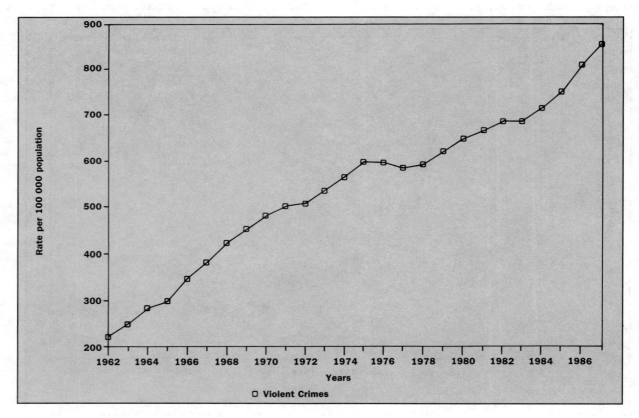

Figure 14.16 Canadian Violent Crime Rates, 1962–1987

Source: Data from Statistics Canada, *Canadian crime statistics 1962–1987*, cat. 85–205.

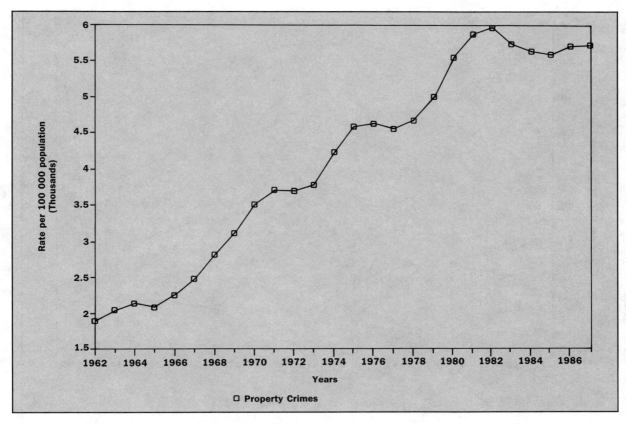

Figure 14.17   Canadian Property Crimes Rates, 1962–1987

Source: Data from Statistics Canada, *Canadian crime statistics 1962–1987*, cat. 85–205.

those for violent offences and property crimes over the quarter-century since the establishment of the Uniform Crime Reports. Rates for both of these socially sensitive offences fluctuated around a mild downward trend, suggesting declining law-enforcement attention to them (see Figure 14.18). The prostitution-offence rates changed radically in the late 1980s, as a new, and much more conservative, government gave the problem of prostitution more attention, amending the Criminal Code to make it easier for the Crown to establish a case of law violation in court. Prostitution offences known to the police increased by a factor of *six* in the first year following proclamation of the amended sections of the Criminal Code and by a factor of more than *eight* in the two years following 1985. Such massive vertical movements in offence rates are characteristic of changes in the law or changes in criminal-justice-system behaviour and ordinarily should not be taken to signal massive changes in the incidence of the underlying conduct (see chapters 4 and 6).

Summary

This chapter has presented data on the patterns and trends of crime in Canada and has related Canadian crime patterns to those of other relevant countries. Overall, Canada, like other industrially developed nations has relatively high property-crime rates, but relatively low rates of violent crime. This appears to be true whether crime is measured in terms of crimes known to the police or crimes discovered through victim surveys.

In more direct comparison, Canada has relatively less violent crime than the United States or France, but has more violent crime than England and Wales. Canada has, in recent years, had higher rates of breaking-and-entering than either France or the United States, but has had lower breaking-and-entering rates than England and Wales.

Canada can be considered in terms of several different blocs of countries to which it belongs: the Organization for Economic Cooperation and Development, the British

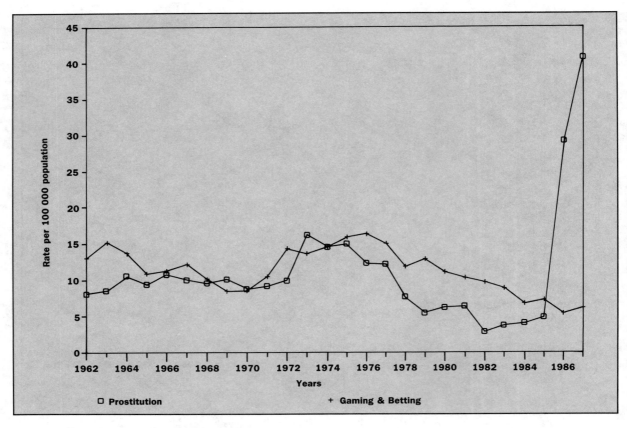

Figure 14.18   Canadian Prostitution and Gambling Rates, 1962–1987

Source: Data from Statistics Canada, *Canadian crime statistics 1962–1987*, cat. 85–205.

Commonwealth, the *Francophonie*, and the group of nations with jurisdiction in the Arctic. Among OECD nations, Canada has relatively high crime rates. Among the nations of the British Commonwealth and the *Francophonie*, Canada has relatively high property-crime rates, but relatively low violent-crime rates. Among the Arctic powers, Canada has high crime rates.

Within Canada, crime rates are generally highest in the western provinces and territories, and have been for a very long time. Viewed in the broader perspective of all Canadian and American jurisdictions, patterns are more complex. While Canada generally has lower homicide rates than the United States, the Yukon and Northwest Territories report some of the highest homicide rates on the continent. While Canada generally has low robbery rates, Quebec and Manitoba report relatively high rates, even by American standards. The western Canadian provinces and territories have very high breaking-and-entering (burglary) and theft rates, in concert with the western American states.

The western dominance of Canadian crime rates is made even clearer when crimes rates for individual cities are considered. Unlike the pattern commonly claimed in other countries, crime in Canada is not generally highest in the largest cities, but rather is highest in smaller cities in the west.

When crime trends are considered over fairly long periods of time, some striking patterns emerge. Crime rates can be traced through judicial records in England from the thirteenth century, in the United States from the seventeenth century, in Canada from soon after Confederation. Over the long term, crime seems to have come in great waves of about 100 years' duration. Both England and the United States experienced major peaks in the mid-nineteenth century followed by long declines that lasted until sometime around 1920. Since then crime has generally risen in both countries.

Canadian crime trends have generally risen since Confederation, with sharp subpeaks just before World War I and during the Great Depression of the early 1930s. The relative mixture of crime has changed quite substantially since Confederation: crimes of violence against the person have become much less important in relative volume than they used to be; crimes of violence against property, such as breaking-and-entering and vandalism, have become relatively much more important in relative volume than they were soon after Confederation. One of the interesting effects of prohibition in Canada was a major reduction in the relative importance of drunkenness in comparison to other kinds of offences. Prior to prohibition, drunkenness accounted for a third to a half of all convictions in Canada; after the repeal of prohibition, drunkenness offences declined to less than a tenth of all convictions. Rates for most types of offences have risen substantially in the past 25 years or so: in 1987 violent-offence rates were four times higher than in 1962; property-offences rates were about three times higher.

There are some clear correlates of crime in Canada. Crime is principally committed by youthful offenders.

Crime is principally committed by males. Native Indians are disproportionately imprisoned in Canada, just as blacks are disproportionately victimized and disproportionately arrested as offenders in the United States. Studies from the United States and from Britain indicate that crimes are disproportionately committed by persons of lower social status; Canadian data are unclear. Historically, Canadians in lower-status occupations have had much higher conviction rates than have persons in higher-status occupations.

Provincial crime rates are not correlated with poverty rates. Provincial crime rates are *negatively* correlated with unemployment rates. Provincial crime rates are mildly correlated with the ratio of rich families to poor families, a measure of relative deprivation, and with litres of alcoholic beverages sold per capita. Provincial crime rates are strongly correlated with the number of motor vehicles per capita.

Discussion Questions

1. What types of crimes do Canadians primarily engage in?

2. Describe the impact the relationship noted between various demographic variables, such as age, race, class, and sex, has upon the patterns of crime in Canada.

3. How does Canada compare with other countries, or even within its own borders, on the incidence of various forms of crime, such as homicide or property crime?

References

Archer, D., & Gartner, R. (1984). *Violence and crime in cross-national perspective.* New Haven: Yale University Press.

Braithwaite, J. (1981). The myth of social class and crime revisited. *American Sociological Review, 46,* 36–57.

Brantingham, P., & Brantingham, P.L. (1984). *Patterns in crime.* New York: Macmillan.

Clinard, M.B., and Abbott, D.J. (1973). *Crime in developing countries: A comparative perspective.* New York: Wiley.

Cohen, L., & Felson, M. (1979). Social change and crime rates: A routine activity approach. *American Sociological Review, 44,* 588–608.

Elliot, D.S., & Huizinga, D. (1983). Social class and delinquent behavior in a national youth panel. *Criminology, 21,* 149–77.

Gabor, T., Baril, M., Cusson, M., Elie, D., LeBlanc, M., &

Normandeau, A. (1987). *Armed robbery: Cops, robbers and victims.* Springfield, IL: Charles. C. Thomas.

Hindelang, M., Hirschi, T., & Weis, J. (1981). *Measuring delinquency.* Beverly Hills: Sage.

Hirschi, T., & Gottfredson., M. (1987). Causes of white collar crime. *Criminology, 25,* 949–74.

Juviler, P.D. (1967). *Revolutionary law and order: Politics and social change in the USSR.* New York: Free Press.

Krohn, M.D. (1976). Inequality, unemployment and crime: A cross-national analysis. *Sociological Quarterly, 17,* 303–13.

Leacy, F.H. (Ed.). (1983). *Historical statistics of Canada* (2nd ed.). Ottawa: Supply & Services Canada.

Los, M. (1988). *Communist ideology, law and crime: A comparative review of the USSR and Poland.* London: Macmillan.

MacQueen, K. (1989, February 18). Guns: Vancouver, Seattle—so similar except for shooting deaths. *Ottawa Citizen*, p. B6.

Mukherjee, S.E. (1981). *Crime trends in twentieth-century Australia.* Sydney: Allen & Unwin.

Munford, R.S., Kaser, R.S., Feldman, R.A., & Stivers, R.R. (1976). Homicide trends in Atlanta. *Criminology, 14,* 213–32.

Ottawa Citizen (1989, January 20) U.S.S.R. comes clean about crime, p. A16.

Shelley, L.I. (1981). *Crime and modernization: The impact of industrialization on crime.* Carbondale, IL: Southern Illinois University Press.

Sloan, J.H., Kellerman, A.L., Reay, D.T., Ferris, J.A., Koepsell, T., Rivara, F.P., Rice, C., Gray, L., & Logerfo, J. (1988). Handgun regulations, crime, assaults, and homicide. *New England Journal of Medicine, 319,* 1256.

Solicitor General Canada (1983). *Victims of crime: Canadian Urban Victimization Survey,* Bulletin No. 1. Ottawa: Ministry Secretariat.

Solicitor General Canada (1984a). *Reported and unreported crimes: Canadian Urban Victimization Survey,* Bulletin No. 2. Ottawa: Ministry Secretariat.

Solicitor General Canada (1984b). *Crime prevention: Awareness and practice, Canadian Urban Victimization Survey,* Bulletin No. 3. Ottawa: Ministry Secretariat.

Solicitor General Canada (1985a). *Female victims of Crime: Canadian Urban Victimization Survey,* Bulletin No. 4. Ottawa: Ministry Secretariat.

Solicitor General Canada (1985b). *Cost of crime to victims: Canadian Urban Victimization Survey,* Bulletin No. 5. Ottawa: Ministry Secretariat.

Solicitor General Canada (1986a). *Criminal victimization of elderly Canadians: Canadian Urban Victimization Survey,* Bulletin No. 6. Ottawa: Ministry Secretariat.

Solicitor General Canada (1986b). *Household property crimes: Canadian Urban Victimization Survey,* Bulletin No. 7. Ottawa: Ministry Secretariat.

Solicitor General Canada (1987). *Patterns in violent crime: Canadian Urban Victimization Survey,* Bulletin No. 8. Ottawa: Ministry Secretariat.

Solicitor General Canada (1988a). *Patterns in property crime: Canadian Urban Victimization Survey,* Bulletin No. 9. Ottawa: Ministry Secretariat.

Solicitor General Canada (1988b). *Multiple victimization: Canadian Urban Victimization Survey,* Bulletin No. 10. Ottawa: Ministry Secretariat.

Tepperman, L. (1977). *Crime control: The urge toward authority.* Toronto: McGraw-Hill Ryerson.

Thompson, E.P. (1976). *Whigs and hunters.* New York: Pantheon.

Tittle, C.R., & Villemez, W.J. (1977). Social class and criminality. *Social Forces, 56,* 474–502.

U.S. Department of Justice (1988a). *Bureau of Justice Statistics special report: International crime rates.* Washington, DC: Bureau of Justice Statistics. [NCJ-110776].

U.S. Department of Justice (1988b). *Report to the nation on crime and justice* (2nd ed.). Washington, DC: Bureau of Justice Statistics, [NCJ-105506].

West, D.J. (1982). *Delinquency: Its roots, careers and prospects.* London: Heinemann Educational.

Wikstrom, P. (1985). *Everyday violence in contemporary Sweden: Situational and ecological aspects.* Stockholm: National Council for Crime Prevention.

Wolf, P. (1971). Crime and development: An international comparison of crime rates. *Scandinavian Studies in Criminology, 3,* 107–20.

Wolfgang, M., Figlio, R.M., & Sellin, T. (1972). *Delinquency in a birth cohort.* Chicago: University of Chicago Press.

The Emerging Focus of Criminology

In the first three chapters of Part VI, we come to consider those acts that have only relatively recently become focussed on as categories of crime. Criminal actions are discussed with reference to the intended goals of the offender rather than to the offender himself or herself. These goals appear to be politically and economically driven and, for the most part, committed by the "elite" of society. Thus, we speak of crimes by the elite in discussing lawyer fraud, corporate criminality, and even terrorism (since it has been shown that terrorists are often socially elite). These crimes take on macro-level dimensions, whether reflected in the context of the crime, as in the wider dimensions of corporate crime, or in the actual status of the individual, as in professional crime, or in the geographic boundaries, as in political crime such as terrorism.

Overall, it has been suggested that these criminal acts should be viewed as far more serious than the "street level" crimes that criminologist have more traditionally studied. Gilbert Geis (1984) has expounded upon the devastation to society's morals and morale as a result of this different form of criminality. Not only is the citizen's trust in government and business organizations likely to be undermined, but actual physical destruction to the environment can result, as regulatory rules are ignored or intentionally flouted.

Chapter 15 begins the investigation of the less conventional focus of criminality of professionals with a consideration of white-collar crime and the effectiveness (or lack of same) of self-regulatory agencies created within various professional associations. Under the veil of self-regulation, the illicit practices of professionals can go undetected and unpunished by society. Moreover, professionals are often in positions of trust, which can facilitate criminal behaviour, such as embezzlement.

We next examine an area of crime that is also on the periphery of "mainstream" criminality, that is, corporate crime. In Chapter 16, it becomes clear that corporate criminality is insidious. It raises issues surrounding individual and corporate rights. It produces difficulties in normal criminal-justice processing, which is structured for dealing with individual criminals rather than with big business. It is hard to hold a corporate entity responsible for dangerous working conditions, for example, when the individual workers themselves are often blamed for accidents.

Chapter 17 focuses on political crime, particularly as it is expressed in terrorist acts. Historical and contemporary examples of acts of terrorism are set in the context of international and Canadian politics. In this area, as perhaps no other, Canadian law-enforcement officials must be attuned to international events in their investigation of such incidents as the Air India bombing. We also see that the government can use the criminal sanction against those groups and individuals who actually or apparently threaten its existence.

Chapter 18 appropriately concludes the text with the thought-provoking idea that crime is ubiquitous in society; crime, whether it is corporate, sexual, or petty, occurs everywhere and is committed by most everyone. Thus, the process of categorizing criminals, of creating typologies of offenders and offences in order to facilitate the study of them, is deceptive and ultimately rather misleading. The world is not made up of mutually exclusive categories of "criminals" and "noncriminals." Criminal involvement is a matter of degree; the term "criminal" can be applied to a broad spectrum of individuals ranging from career criminals to ordinary people who occasionally respond to temptation. In the end, Chapter 18 argues for a more general theory of human behaviour rather than a specific theory of crime to aid us in understanding the deviance within society.

Reference

Geis, G. (1984). White-collar and corporate crime. In R. Meier (Ed.), *Major forms of crime* (pp. 137–66). Beverly Hills, CA: Sage.

15 Controlling Crimes among the Professional Elite

Joan Brockman

As we have noted previously in this volume, criminologists have tended to focus their study on the more "traditional" types of criminal activity, such as break-and-enter, robbery, and homicide. One major attribute of individuals who are convicted of these types of **crime** is that they are often from the more disadvantaged sectors of Canadian society, a view confirmed by noting the low levels of education and job skills of offenders confined in Canadian correctional institutions.

Since roughly the 1940s, there has been an increased emphasis on the criminal activity of individuals who command power in Canadian society. While their crimes are often far less visible to the Canadian public than are the actions of an individual who robs the local Seven-11 convenience store, there is an increasing recognition that their crimes can do harm not only to individuals, but to the larger society as well. This chapter focusses on one group of these individuals, the "professional elite."

The professional elite[1] are individuals in society who have a privileged economic, social, and/or political status and are members of a recognized profession.[2] This group includes physicians, dentists, lawyers, university professors, accountants, teachers, stockbrokers, and members of the clergy. While individuals in these professions may become involved in the more "traditional" types of crime, our focus in this chapter is on the criminal activity that is related to their privileged status.

The Professional: In a Position of Trust

Elite crime is often characterized by someone in a position of trust taking advantage of that relationship to victimize another. For example, in the late 1980s, there was a spate of revelations of physical and sexual abuse suffered by children at the hands of teachers and clergymen. Members of the professional elite, because of their training or expertise, are often in positions of trust or authority in our society. There is some additional expectation that these individuals, because of their occupational positions, can be trusted. They have positions that bestow upon them a distinct advantage when it comes to committing crimes. Their occupation provides the opportunity for crime. Dentists, doctors, and teachers have greater opportunity to assault children sexually and escape detection than do individuals who lurk around playgrounds and schoolyards. While we expect and trust the former group to conform to certain standards of behaviour, we are suspicious of the latter group. Similarly, lawyers, financial planners, and stockbrokers are given access to financial and personal opportunities for crime provided to them by their occupational positions.

Crimes and Misconduct among the Professional Elite

Prosecution or Self-Regulation?

The excerpts in Box 15.1 illustrate a wide variety of behaviour, ranging from criminal activity (**fraud, embezzlement, sexual assault**) that was processed by the criminal-justice system to professional misconduct that was dealt with by administrative tribunals and self-regulating organizations. It is, at times, difficult to tell which system has dealt with the wayward professional. In the incidents discussed, the financial planner was dealt with by the criminal-justice system, the manager by the Vancouver Stock Exchange, and the two officials of a VSE company by the British Columbia Securities Commission. The dentist was dealt with by the **criminal-justice system**, the doc-

---

Box 15.1 News Reports of Elite Crime

There was no apparent reason not to trust Diane Lisle. The 38-year-old financial planner was dynamic, seemed compassionate and had the right credentials. . . . When the first complaint about her potential involvement in stock fraud surfaced in May 1986, she sidestepped queries from the Ontario Securities Commission. When another complaint came in, an OSC investigator tracked Lisle's activities and summoned the police. Her instincts were right: Lisle had bilked 29 clients of $309,000, driven in part by an expensive cocaine habit. Arrested for fraud in June 1987, she was later convicted and sentenced to an eighteen month prison term that began last February. (Melnbardis, 1989, p. 29)

A provincially appointed committee will soon urge the Alberta government to clamp down on financial planners, forcing them to apply for licences, meet minimum educational standards and adopt a code of ethics. (*Globe and Mail*, 1988a)

The branch manager of Canarim Investment Corporation's Kelowna office has been fined $40,000 and suspended three months for unduly affecting the share value of a Vancouver Stock Exchange company. The VSE said in a release Wednesday that Leonard Fiessel has also been disqualified from serving as branch manager for nine months, made subject to one year of strict supervision and assessed $4,000 in investigative costs. His wife, Colleen Fiessel, who worked as a broker at the same office, was suspended for one month, fined $10,000, assessed $900 investigative costs, and made subject to one year of strict supervision. (*Vancouver Sun*, 1989)

For the first time in B.C. history two officials of a Vancouver Stock Exchange company have been found guilty of illegal insider trading. (Hamilton, 1989)

The Ontario Securities Commission added a new spin to the market's moves: 21 pages of allegations, outlining gross misconduct by three of the most revered people in Canada's stock-trading fraternity. . . . For the past two years, the OSC has spent about $1 million investigating the trio—and dozens of other traders. Although their net caught only three fish, the inquiry exposed a seamy side in the securities industry. . . . Fraud charges are possible and the entire case could end up in the Supreme Court. (Stackhouse, 1989)

The Toronto Stock Exchange has fined Osler Inc. $4 million in the interest of protecting the public, but promised not to collect in the interest of practicality. (Westell, 1989)

Caught by a client, and protected from discovery, a dishonest lawyer went on to steal another million dollars. Should this have happened? Can it be stopped in the future? disturbing questions for the law society. (Lockhart, 1985, p. 10)

Mr. Kopyto was found guilty of professional misconduct by the [discipline committee of the Law Society of Upper Canada] on July 24, after admitting he knowingly over-

Box 15.1 *(Continued)*

billed the Legal Aid plan for 2,000 hours of work between 1984 and 1986. His actions included billing the plan for 25 hours of work on one day in December of 1986, and charging about 700 phone calls he never made. (Nagler, 1989)

A Toronto lawyer who has admitted counselling refugee claimants to make false statements at immigration hearings will testify for the Law Society of Upper Canada against the lawyer who hired her. (Haliechuk, 1989)

Shock and horror hit the Manitoba legal community after charges of ticket fixing were laid against judges, lawyers, magistrates and court workers in January. (Cox, 1988)

About 90 Manitoba doctors will be able to keep personal computers they were given for testing a new drug, the Manitoba College of Physicians and Surgeons has ruled. But assistant registrar Ken Brown says the college has issued guidelines to remind the province's 2,000 physicians that they should not accept excessive benefits from drug companies. The Ontario College of Physicians and Surgeons warned its members last winter that they could face charges of professional misconduct for accepting the computers. (*Globe and Mail*, 1989b)

The dentist who pleaded guilty Thursday to 17 counts of indecent and sexual assault has a history of being investigated by the B.C. College of Dental Surgeons for sexually molesting young patients. . . . However, he was allowed to continue in his practice after he admitted his guilt and promised to seek psychiatric help. (Bellett & Shaw, 1989)

A Prince George doctor has been suspended from practice for a year and fined a total of $10,000 after being found guilty of infamous conduct while attending a female patient. (*Vancouver Sun*, 1987)

Former Newfoundland lieutenant-governor Gordon Winter was appointed yesterday by the province's Roman Catholic Church to lead a five-member inquiry into sexual abuse of children by priests or other members of the church community. . . . In the past two years, 13 priests, former priests or members of the Roman Catholic order of teachers in Newfoundland have been charged with offences including sexual assault or gross indecency involving altar boys or former residents of . . . a home for aban-

doned or abused boys in St. John's. (*Globe and Mail*, 1989a, p. A1)

Rev. James Lockland Archibald, 64, an ordained minister in the full gospel church known as Gates of Praise, was convicted Friday on eight of nine counts of sexual assault. All the assaults occurred during private spiritual counselling sessions . . . when Archibald was purporting to cast out demons from the women. (Needham, 1989)

An inquiry into sex cases on the Sunshine Coast has urged the four provincial ministries involved with the protection of children to present a united front in the battle against sex abuse in B.C.'s schools. (Margoshes, 1986)

Twenty-one people were injured when 20 cars parked on the roof of the store at Station Square in Burnaby on April 23 crashed to the floor below . . . [The engineers] are charged under the *Engineers Act* with incompetence, negligence and misconduct. If found guilty they could face penalties ranging from reprimand to expulsion from the profession. (Moya, 1988)

A recent survey of psychiatrists throughout the United States indicated that six percent admitted to having had sexual relations with their patients. In fact, the medical and psychological professions have enacted ethical rules that expressly ban a professional from having sexual relations with a client or a patient under any circumstances. Consent is not a defence to the professional who violates this rule. . . . Ethical rules should eliminate any possible rationalization that may be used by a divorce lawyer when wanting to have sex with a client. Divorce clients need to be protected from sexually aggressive lawyers just as lawyers need to have clear advance warning that such acts are unethical. (Dubin, 1988)

The chairman of the Canadian Track and Field Association agreed to tip Ben Johnson's coach if the federally funded agency decided to institute random drug testing before the Seoul Olympics, a federal inquiry was told today. (*Vancouver Sun*, 1989, p. A1).

The Canadian Track and Field Association scrambled to reinstate a banned athlete when he threatened to expose Ben Johnson's steroid use, the Dubin inquiry heard yesterday. (Hynes, 1989, p. A1)

tor by the College of Physicians and Surgeons. Sometimes these individuals are dealt with by more than one system of social control.

One of the means of social control common to the professions is self-regulation. Members of professions belong to organizations that are expected to exercise control over and prevent crimes and other misconduct from occurring through the screening and testing of applicants, the creation of codes of ethics, and the monitoring of members. Should these preventative measures fail, the organization is expected to investigate, adjudicate, and penalize the member. The degree to which these organizations are backed by the state varies from one occupational group to another. However, all are expected, through some form of self-regulation, to "take care of" anyone who breaches the law or ethical rules.

These two structural features, a societal-induced aura of trustworthiness and self-regulation, allow the elite access to opportunities they would not otherwise have and provide alternatives to the **criminal law** when it comes to investigating and enforcing standards of conduct. But trustworthiness and self-regulation are not unique to the professional elite. An element of trust enters many encounters, and a type of self-regulation exists in less formal organizations (the family, or a class of schoolchildren). The difference is perhaps one of degree rather than kind.

Should the government use the criminal law to achieve social control, or should it use alternative governing instruments? An examination of how the professions are controlled uncovers the various methods of social control and their boundaries. It draws one's attention to those institutions and social structures that facilitate and disguise crimes of the elite. It raises questions regarding the nature and source of law, and alternatives to the use of criminal law as a means of social control.

The first part of this chapter will discuss why it is that we think of crimes of the professional elite as worthy of study. The next part will outline the various methods available to the government and private organizations to control and discipline professionals, not only for criminal acts but for a wide range of misconduct. We shall see that self-regulation is a means not only of social control, but of economic control. The final part of this chapter will examine what effect self-regulation can have on the provision of services to society and how it creates opportunities for crime and the exercise of personal power.

The Study of Crime among the Professional Elite

This power, to regulate how the profession is practised . . . gives rise to . . . "inconspicuous produc-

tion", the desire to do little work (or work calling for relatively little skill) for high fees. (Lieberman, 1978, p. 95)

The self-governing profession is the bulwark of our social system and institutions. Remove the self-governing profession and you dismember society. (Stephenson, 1977, p. 1)

It is fitting that the word "*profess*" and its derivatives are Janus-faced. As the quotations cited above illustrate, views of the role of the professions in society have been mixed. While originally "profess" connoted altruistic intentions, there have been periods in history when it was used pejoratively.[3] Some early writers held out the altruistic values of the professions as an alternative model to the acquisitive values of those in business,[4] but the business community in early Canada was less impressed.

In 1667, Jean Baptiste Colbert, the Minister of New France (the region settled by the French from 1534 to 1763, now covering parts of Canada and the United States), passed an ordinance that prohibited lawyers from practising law in New France (Eccles, 1965, p. 154; Francis, Jones, & Smith, 1988, p. 86). When Indendant Jacques de Meulles arrived in New France in 1682, he commented, "Never was anything so fittingly done as to ensure that there would be no lawyers or attorneys here" (quoted in Eccles, 1964, p. 33).

By the 1890s, the professions in Canada were under attack by business interests. The training of individuals in the liberal professions (lawyers, teachers, doctors, and clergymen) was viewed as the "educating of rich men's children . . . for which the country has no possible use" by the "taxing of manufacturers and their employees" (Bliss, 1974, p. 118). In 1891, the *Canadian Manufacturer* was of the view that

a good machinist, capable to grind a value seat or fit a key is worth a regiment of professional lawyers; and a miller who knows how to convert wheat into flour, or a farmer who knows how to cultivate wheat is worth more than all the incipient sawbones turned out of the medical colleges, and licensed to kill or cure, as the fates may determine. (quoted in Bliss, 1974, p. 117)

Those professionals who became politicians were seen as "failures in their overcrowded professions—the sediment of the learned professions" (Bliss, 1974, p. 125). In the French-Canadian business community, the "dominance of the liberal professions" was used to explain "the lack of French-Canadian business prowess" (1974, p. 118).

In 1935, Laski wrote about "the decline of the professions," critical that they were becoming more like business, as reflected in the corporate lawyer who is not, of course, the crude type who breaks the law. He is the more elegant type of hireling who devotes all his skill and learning to finding ways round the law of which, to the public detriment, his clients can take advantage. He see to it that the law is bent to the service of those who control the financial power of society. (1935, pp. 677–78)[5]

Talcott Parsons (1939, p. 458) also questioned a historical distinction between the professional man as "altruistically serving the interests of others regardless of his own" and the businessman as "egoistically pursuing his own self-interest regardless of the interests of others."

Further evidence that the professions were losing their status as altruistic is found in Edwin H. Sutherland's work. In 1939, speaking to a joint meeting of the American Sociological Association and the American Economic Society, he introduced the concept of **white-collar crime** to draw attention to the fact that crime was not unique to the lower class.[6] Individuals from the upper, white-collar class were equally capable of engaging in criminal behaviour and did so, even though they were often dealt with outside the criminal-justice system (Sutherland, 1940, pp. 7–8).

Sutherland was of the view that crime was a social construct, a phenomenon created by society rather than by reference to any inherent characteristics of the individual, and that the enforcement of criminal law was biased. The upper class played a major role in defining and enforcing criminal law, and the social control of crime favoured the more powerful over the less powerful (1940, pp. 8–9). White-collar crime was committed by powerful business and professional men against those less powerful; however, they enjoyed "relative immunity" because of their position vis-à-vis that of their victims. The medieval "benefit of clergy," where clerics were immune from prosecution for most crimes, had become the "benefit of business or profession." Members of the lower class, whose crimes were frequently against the rich and powerful, never fared as well (1940, p. 9).

The research that Sutherland carried out following his speech was on crimes committed by businessmen (1983); however, he had listed crimes engaged in by the medical profession, which he used as an example "because it [was] probably less criminalistic than some other professions" (1940, p. 3). He also referred to lawyers as the "inventive geniuses" of some white-collar crime (1940, p. 11). His observations about the nature of crime applied to the behaviour of those in business as well as the professions.

Numerous academics, since Sutherland, have tried to define the elusive concept of white-collar crime, which, as Hirschi and Gottfredson (1987) note, hangs like a "spectre" over criminology. It has been defined in terms of the offender's position in the social structure (high social status, respect, occupation), his or her relationship to the victim (trust, power), the means used (deception, fraud, concealment, nonphysical), and the objects sought (money, property). Some have suggested that the term be abandoned (Hirschi & Gottfredson, 1989; Horoszowski, 1980; Pepinsky, 1974); others that it be replaced with a more appropriate category, such as economic, occupational, corporate, or organizational crime (see Albanese, 1987; Clinard & Yeager, 1980; Ermann & Lundman, 1983; Frank & Lombness, 1988). However, Coleman suggests that "white-collar crime" is "too useful a conceptual tool to be thrown on the intellectual scrap heap" (1985, p. 4).

It is obvious that academics view the professions as a group worthy of study. Is there any other reason to distinguish between crimes of the professional elite and crimes of the "ordinary"? Do deviant or criminal members of a profession form a special class of criminal? What does a teacher, dentist, or religious leader who sexually assaults children have in common with a lawyer, financial planner, or doctor who benefits financially from fraud perpetrated upon clients or the public purse? Or with the administration of banned drugs in competitive sport? How do all of these crimes or criminals differ from "ordinary" crimes and criminals? Hirschi and Gottfredson (1987, 1989) have argued that there is no need to distinguish so-called white-collar from the other types when it comes to explanations of crime. A single theory can accommodate all crime. (This issue is addressed in Chapter 10.)

It is important to remember that the concept of white-collar crime was introduced to draw attention to the fact that educated and powerful people commit crimes. The commission of crimes is not confined to the uneducated who live in poverty and low economic circumstances. The concept draws attention to the following additional facts:

1. We have set up other means, in addition to the criminal law, to deal with crimes of the professional elite such that the perpetrators may be punished more lightly by our systems of social control than are "ordinary" criminals.

2. These structural features that are set up to control **deviance** are criminogenic in the sense that they facilitate the commission of crime against the members of society.

A study of the professional elite also shifts the focus of criminological inquiry from the etiology (study of explanations) of criminal behaviour to the etiology of criminal law and other forms of regulation often used instead of, or in conjunction with, the criminal law. The next section of this chapter outlines the numerous avenues available to the government to influence or control behaviour.

Methods of State Control over the Misconduct of Professionals

Regulation, through the use of criminal law, is only one of many governing instruments used by the state to exercise control over its citizens and other social and economic entities. The governing instruments listed in Box 15.2 give some indication as to the scope of social control exercised by the state (see, for example, Arthurs, 1986; Doern,

1979). The Law Reform Commission of Canada, in 1977, following the work of Packer (1968), expressed a concern about the "overkill" by the criminal law and the need to limit its use in today's society. It is through an examination of alternative means of governing that we are better able to understand the nature and the role of criminal law. Specifically, we will examine the use of legislative and delegated regulation as a method available to the government for influencing or controlling behaviour.

Box 15.2 Governing Instruments

1. *Exhortation or Persuasion*: The government can promote or encourage certain behaviour through speeches, advertising, or other noncoercive educative or propaganda-type means; for example, "use condoms," or "cigarettes kill" and "see your doctor about birth-control methods."[1]

2. *Providing Information to the Public*: This instrument is related to, and sometimes indistinguishable from, persuasion. In 1988, in response to the publicity over bank fees, the federal government announced that "consumer and corporate affairs would be issuing a regular comparison of fees between institutions" (Drohan, 1988). The government hoped to influence the banks indirectly by supplying the consumer with up-to-date information.

3. *Setting an Example*: If a government hired individuals who were not members of the appropriate occupational association, for example, psychologists not registered as members of the British Columbia Psychological Association, industry and the public might be convinced to do likewise, thereby reducing the overall power of the professional association and perhaps the quality of service provided.

4. *Negotiation*: Public-service contracts and native land claims can be negotiated rather than imposed or litigated. Recent negotiations between the federal Department of Consumer and Corporate Affairs and real-estate boards across Canada to eliminate the imposition of minimum fees were seen as an alternative to criminal prosecutions under the Competition Act (Willis & Melnbardis, 1988; Melnbardis, 1988).

5. *Mediation*: The Minister of State for Finance, in his statement with regard to publishing bank fees, also stated that a "senior federal official would mediate consumer complaints that could not be resolved with individual banks or trust companies" (Drohan, 1988). A late report indicated that the Superintendent of Financial Institutions would fulfil this role (Horvitch, 1988).

6. *Expenditure*: The government can give grants to those individuals or groups who are promoting what they want to see promoted. Tax breaks or tax expenditures are used as incentives to get individuals or corporations to behave in certain ways. The government can give a $1 million tax break (deduction) to a company to modernize its plant or it can give the company a $1 million grant.[2]

7. *Government Procurement*: Federal government procurement is a $10 billion a year industry (Bagnall, 1988, p. 37). Government contracts are sometimes awarded on the basis of political rather than substantive merit. The "privatization" of government services has resulted in the politicalization of some public services. That is, while public servants are ideally hired on nonpolitical grounds, government contracts are often viewed as fair game for political patronage.[3]

8. *Taxation*: Tax on alcohol, gas, and tobacco can be viewed as a form of penalty that can be avoided by not buying the products. The penalty is imposed without a charge being laid, without a court hearing, and without a sentence being imposed. Taxation is a very efficient penalty from the government's point of view. The federal government could make it an offence to smoke cigarettes or make it so expensive (through an oppressive tax on smoking, smoking flights, restaurants that allow smoking, or the use of a smoking room in a public building) that most people would voluntarily quit smoking. Rather than prohibit cigarette advertising, the government could impose an additional 500 percent tax on all tobacco advertising. Taxation would not eliminate the use of cigarettes and advertising, but it would likely reduce it. In this respect, taxation might have a similar or more powerful effect than the criminal law, which has not eliminated the use of other drugs (see Chapter 5). The use of a tax or surcharge is often raised and considered as a means of controlling the amount of pollution a company is allowed to discharge into the air or a river (see Chapter 6).[4]

Box 15.2 (Continued)

9. *Direct Ownership*: The government can control or alter behaviour by direct ownership of an industry or service in part or in its entirety through nationalization or by providing services through government employees. Legal and medical services, to those unable to afford them, could be provided by government-employed lawyers and doctors rather than a fee-for-service system.

10. *Regulation*: Finally, the government can make rules backed by sanctions from the state in the form of fines, imprisonment, and other penalties for breaches of rules.

[1] The double message in the last suggestion not only advocates birth control but also the notion that a doctor is the person who can tell the recipient about birth control. What type of information the government decides to disseminate is often influenced by those who are in a position to lobby government officials and politicians. For example, there was concern from antismoking groups that the federal government was being excessively influenced by the tobacco industry's lobbyists when it came to regulations regarding the type of information which was required on the outside of cigarette packages.

[2] The financial effect of a tax deduction is the same as a

government grant; however, deductions are preferred by recipients because the public generally perceives them in a more positive light. Not having to pay tax is viewed as less of a government handout than a grant. It is also less visible (see McQuaig, 1987). The two, however, have the same effect—less money in the government coffers.

[3] The patronage approach has been increasingly called into question both by the public and by the courts (Arrowsmith, 1988). Michael Bliss is of the view that "some day it will be recognized as unethical for the MP to try to interfere in rational decision-making by soliciting favours for his riding" (1988). He uses the CF-18 contract as an example of a government "Shor[ing] up political support in Quebec" rather than "reward[ing] excellence in Manitoba" (1988).

[4] Given these uses of taxation, some authors view tax as a form of regulation, that is, as a means of controlling behaviour by the imposition of penalties. For example, Doern (1979, p.13) considers taxation to be a form of regulation because it "is essentially the extraction, through regulation, by the state of private incomes and/or wealth." However, others maintain that there is a difference between trying to decrease behaviour by prohibiting it through the criminal law or by increasing the cost of engaging in it.

Governing by Legislative Regulation

The term "regulation" has been defined and redefined; it is used in this chapter to mean rules set by the state, either directly (through legislation) or indirectly (through delegating rule-making authority to government personnel, administrative agencies, or self-regulatory bodies), backed by state sanctions or remedies. The regulations may be enforced by private individuals, or by state agents (peace officers or other civil servants) through the judicial system (courts) or other adjudicative bodies (e.g., Securities Commission). And, as with most rules, they may be used only as a means of persuasion or threat by those seeking compliance from others or they may lie dormant, in effect, unenforced and thereby neutralized.

Criminal Law.   Direct regulation by the state through legislation can take a number of forms. At the one extreme is the criminal law, found in the Criminal Code and various other federal statutes. Provincially created offences, while not criminal law in the technical sense, are also enforced through the criminal-justice system (see Chapter 2). The state not only creates the rules, but also has state agents (peace officers, prosecutors, and other civil servants) who investigate and prosecute breaches of the rules before an independent and impartial court that adjudicates the issue

of guilt and imposes a penalty on those found guilty. While the criminal-justice system is open for use by private individuals who wish to launch a prosecution, it is seldom used by them. Penalties imposed through the criminal-justice system are not limited to punitive measures such as imprisonment, fines, and **probation**, but also include compensatory and restorative orders.

Civil Law.   Another means of regulating behaviour is for the state to impose certain duties or standards of care on people and then to allow anyone who has been harmed by someone who has not met the standard of care to act as **plaintiff** in a civil action and to seek damages through the courts against the **defendant** for the wrongful behaviour, which is usually referred to as a **tort**. Doctors are expected to meet certain standards of care. The surgeon who amputates the wrong leg can be sued by the victim. The plaintiff can sue the defendant for specific, general, and punitive **damages** in a civil action. *Specific damages* are amounts that are ascertainable (e.g., the amount of money required to fix a bridge that has collapsed). *General damages* are those for which an amount is not ascertainable but the courts are prepared to compensate the victim for his or her loss (money for an arm or a leg, or for general pain and suffering). The court can also award *punitive damages* to the plaintiff, as a form of punishment to the defendant.

When it comes to professional or occupational competence, **civil liability** is viewed as a means of maintaining such competence. The theory behind civil liability is that, if persons engaged in an occupation can be sued for not maintaining standards expected from their occupation, they are more likely to strive to meet expected standards to avoid liability and embarrassment. However, whether this is the case, that is, whether civil liability enhances competence, is a hotly debated issue among the professions and academics. For example, some would argue that good doctors will be good doctors whether or not they are threatened with lawsuits, and bad doctors will not be deterred by the possibility of civil liability. Others argue that civil liability is an effective deterrent (see, for example, Prichard, 1978; Belobaba, 1978).

Crime Versus Tort.   Generally speaking, crimes can be dealt with by civil proceedings, in addition to, or instead of, criminal proceedings. The difference is not so much in the behaviour but how the victim or the state decides to react to the behaviour. Owners of a food store, as plaintiffs, can sue a person (defendant) who steals a loaf of bread from their store. The thief can also be charged with **theft** under the Criminal Code. Similarly, the owners of the store can sue their accountant, stockbroker, or lawyer who steals $5000 from them. This thief can also be charged under the Code.

The dual approach also applies to damage to property and personal injury. The owners of the store can sue the person who throws a rock through their store's window and intentionally or negligently hits one of their employees. In addition, the rock thrower could face criminal charges (destruction of property and causing bodily harm). If the store's roof caves in and injures its employees, the engineers who designed the store could be sued for damages. The engineers might also face criminal charges for the collapse if their actions fell within the definition of **criminal negligence**. In addition, the engineers could face disciplinary action from their self-regulatory organization (discussed in more detail later).

While crimes may be torts and torts may be crimes, differences can arise in the use of these two means of social control. Having recovered damages from the accountant, stockbroker, engineer, or insurance company, the owners of the store may not want to proceed with the expense and time commitment of a criminal prosecution. Reluctant victims may result in no prosecution by the state. An interesting question arises: if the store owners could recover their loaf of bread or have their window fixed, would they be satisfied or would they still want the state to proceed with criminal charges against the "loaf lifter"

and the rock thrower? Why does the $5000 fraud sometimes remain the property of the two parties (civil) while the loaf of bread becomes so important that it requires the state to intervene and deal with the offender (criminal)?

While, in some cases, there is a **common-law** right (see Chapter 2) to sue civilly for damages resulting from the commission of an offence, in other instances there are *statutes* that spell out that a person suffering damages for criminal behaviour may sue the wrongdoer for damages. For example, the Competition Act states that "any person who has suffered loss or damage as a result of [an offence committed under the act, for conspiracy to lessen competition, resale-price maintenance, misleading advertising, etc.] may sue for . . . an amount equal to the loss of damage" plus costs incurred for investigating the matter and suing the person. In the United States, a person who has suffered a loss through anticompetitive behaviour can sue for treble damages.

Breach of Contract.   One might also say that the state regulates conduct by providing remedies for breaches of contracts. The conditions under which a contract can be enforced are set out either in legislation or by the courts through the development of the common law. The fact that the state sets up courts to enforce contracts can be seen as a form of government intervention.[7]

Governing by Delegated Regulation

Regulation by the federal and provincial governments is not limited to legislation passed by the Parliament of Canada or provincial legislatures. Governments would grind to a halt if they were limited to this form of regulation and did not delegate tasks to individuals or agencies. Legislative and other government functions can be delegated, formally (by legislative authority) or by a range of informal means, to a variety of government officials and other semipublic and private groups. Rules made by persons or bodies acting under formal state authority are referred to as **subordinate legislation**. A major difference between legislation and subordinate legislation is that the form can be amended or repealed only by an act of the legislative body that enacted it, whereas the latter can be altered so long as it is within the ambit of power delegated to the person or body. Here, we will outline the range of recipients of powers delegated by governments, the powers that are delegated, and some of the problems that attend delegated authority.

Cabinet.   Federal government functions can be legislatively delegated to the governor in council, which in effect is the federal cabinet. Similarly, provincial functions can be delegated to the lieutenant-governor in council (the provincial cabinet). For example, the **Narcotic Control Act** (s.20) provides that the governor in council may make regulations "requiring physicians, dentists, veterinarians, pharmacists and other person who deal in narcotics . . . to keep records and make returns." The Barbers Act of British Columbia (s.21) allows the lieutenant-governor in council to make "proper arrangement for the administration and enforcement of [the] Act" if it is satisfied that the Barbers' Association of British Columbia has not done so. In fact, much of the work done by "the cabinet" is performed by cabinet committees and the minister responsible for the particular area of concern takes primary responsibility (see Jones & de Villars, 1985, p. 67).

Government Ministers.   Government functions can be delegated to government ministers or departmental officials. For example, by-laws made by the Society of Notaries Public of British Columbia have no force until approved by the Attorney General of British Columbia. The Minister of Health appoints an examining board in order to determine who may register under the Naturopaths Act of British Columbia. The Superintendent of Brokers in British Columbia is delegated the task of granting or refusing registration of persons who want to trade in securities.

Independent Administrative Agencies.   Boards, commissions, or tribunals, also referred to as **independent administrative agencies** (IAAs), are delegated authority. Most are appointed by governments and are partly or completely detached from the government and the department or minister who might oversee other aspects of the IAAs' work. Historically, the use of these agencies developed in Canada prior to what might be viewed as the "professionalization" of the civil service in 1918. Prior to 1918, federal civil servants were often appointed not for their expertise but because of their political affiliation (Law Reform Commission of Canada, 1980, p. 22). In 1918, the Borden government introduced legislation that established a civil service commission with the power to set standards and job qualifications and to hire civil servants (1980, p. 25). Prior to this, one of the means used to depoliticize some government rule making and adjudication was to set up tribunals that functioned independently of government departments. For example, the Railway Committee of the Privy Council, the first nondepartmental regulatory body, was set up prior to Confederation in 1851 under the Railway Act. However, it was still a political body as it was composed of cabinet ministers (Schultz, 1979, p. 18).[8]

Nongovernment boards were seen as a means of introducing expertise and a sense of impartiality to decision making (Law Reform Commission of Canada, 1980, p. 35). Specialized boards were often better able than the courts to deal effectively and efficiently with issues. Boards relieved ministers of work that was sometimes politically sensitive (1980, p. 35). According to Arthurs (1985, p. 197), "ad-

ministrative law emerged in response to a series of judgments that the norms, institutions, and procedures of the formal legal system were unsuitable for the performance of particular social tasks."

To the extent that governments staff these tribunals on the basis of political patronage rather than expertise, the original goal behind establishing these tribunals is defeated. However, the flaw in the justifications given for establishing IAAs is that there is an assumption that experts can arrive at "right" decisions in situations where they are, in fact, making political decisions. The effect either is to cloak the political decision with a veil of expertise or to impart a sense of cynicism about the process to those who see through the veil.[9] There is also a debate over how independent independent administrative tribunals ought to be in a democratic country.

Whatever their merits, IAAs are widely used in governments. Some professions and occupational groups are governed by IAAs and other government officials on some aspects of their work or qualifications. For example, various provincial securities commissions across Canada regulate the activities of stockbrokers.

Municipalities.   Governing powers are also delegated by the provinces to municipalities and cities to run their local affairs through elected representatives. These bodies are often given licensing authority over various businesses and occupations within their jurisdiction. For example, escort services, electrical contractors, and taxicab drivers are required to hold a business licence in order to operate in cities across Canada.

Crown Corporations.   Both federal and provincial governments create Crown corporations through legislative enactments to carry out economic and other government activities. These corporations will, in turn, have authority over individuals they hire from the various occupational groups.

Private Groups.   Private groups, and to some extent semipublic groups (for example, banks, hospitals, and corporations), are often viewed as being excluded from the umbrella of what we think of as governmental regulation. However, it is legislation and other governmental policy that allow many of these institutions to prosper as they do and to exercise economic and social control over citizens. It may be necessary to include their rules and policies under the concept of delegated regulation.[10] To the extent that private groups benefit from state restrictions or largesse, they can be viewed as the beneficiaries of delegated power (McDonald, 1985, p. 89).

Self-Regulatory Organizations.   Finally, authority can be delegated to semipublic organizations that are self-regulating. **Self-regulatory organizations** (SROs) are not uniform beasts. They take a variety of forms, depending on their mandate or authority, their relationship to the government, the tasks they carry out (advisory, legislative, investigatory, adjudicative), and what issues they are concerned with (social, economic, etc.).

In relationship to government, two general categories of SROs are representative more of two ends of a continuum than of two distinct types of organizations. At the one end of the continuum are SROs that are created by statute, delegated certain powers, and backed by state sanctions or remedies. They are sometimes referred to as "mixed" or "hybrid" SROs because they mix private and public social control. They are also referred to as state-backed SROs. They act as agents of the government, and in many respects they are very similar to IAAs.

At the other end of the continuum is the pure or voluntary SRO, an organization that decides to regulate itself in circumstances where there is no government involvement. The government is not involved in setting up, maintaining, or backing the organization with state sanctions or remedies; however, there is usually legislation that facilitates the structuring of the organization. These organizations can range from being informal and loosely organized to being highly organized, and they usually establish rules or codes of ethics for their members.[11]

The Canadian Sociology and Anthropology Association (CSAA) is an example of a pure SRO. It is a voluntary organization set up under the Canada Corporations Act. Adherence to the association's Professional Code of Ethics is required under the organization's by-laws. The association's Code of Professional Ethics (1986) states, for example, that "the researcher should not falsify or distort his or her findings or omit data which might significantly alter the conclusions." The rest of the code sets out the procedure to be followed if there is a complaint against a member; the emphasis is on resolving disputes by mutual agreement. Possible sanctions include revocation of membership, and public notice thereof.

While this SRO is "pure" in its formal arrangement with the government, that is, the government is not involved in setting it up or backing the enforcement of its rules, the state could easily become involved in backing it in an informal way. If the government, for example, decided that it would not hire sociologists and anthropologists as employees or to carry out government research unless the applicants were in good standing with the CSAA, the nature of the relationship between the organization and the government becomes less clear. The nature of government practice or patronage can change what is structurally a pure SRO into what is, in effect, a state-backed organization.

The Canadian Track and Field Association, which controls who can compete in international sporting events, has by-laws and policies with regard to the control and use of drugs in international sports. To the extent that this organization is allowed to regulate itself, it takes on many of the characteristics of other professional organizations. Churches have similar power over their ministers. Many of these groups have been left to "take care of their own" when it comes to what would otherwise be considered criminal behaviour. However, the Dubin Inquiry, sparked by the revelation that sprinter Ben Johnson was using steroids prior to the 1988 Olympic Games, and the judicial inquiry ordered by the government of Newfoundland into allegations of sexual abuse against Roman Catholic clergy, may expose some of the problems that exist within organizations that are allowed to deal internally and quietly with matters that might otherwise be the subject of criminal investigation.

Many of the state-backed SROs in Canada today started out as pure SROs, and many of the pure SROs today favour a move to state-backed status. Financial planners see themselves on the verge of achieving state-backed status. In June 1988, the chairman of the Canadian Association of Financial Planners (which is a voluntary association with more than 1000 members) stated that "we have covered ethics, we've covered education, experience.... We have the registered financial planner exam, the designation.... All that is needed now is government recognition of the CAFP as the professional self-regulating body for all financial planners" (Lee, 1988).

The Acupuncture Association of British Columbia has recently lobbied the provincial government to pass legislation to allow it to regulate its members. Part of the concern is that some members are being harassed by the RCMP for practising medicine without a licence (Mullens, 1989). Interprofessional rivalry is a motivating factor behind many occupations that lobby for self-regulating status.

Another motivating factor for an occupation or industry to organize and regulate itself is the threat of government regulation (Levin, 1967; Usprich, 1975) or desire for improvement of professional status and better public relations. A reason to organize a voluntary organization, which later lobbies for state-backed status, is to have a system in place so that, if the government becomes concerned about regulating a particular occupation or industry, the organization can more readily convince the government to allow the group to regulate itself within the confines of a state-backed model (Usprich, 1975, p. 7).

SROs, whether pure or state-backed, sometimes have to compete or co-operate with government departments or IAAs in regulating their own members. Some groups that are granted self-regulating powers by statute are still supervised by a government department and, in some cases, a government agency or tribunal. For example, the Vancouver Stock Exchange, which is set up under statute and delegated powers to supervise its members (a state-backed SRO), is also subject to supervision by the British Columbia Securities Commission (an IAA). Some members of the Exchange may also be members of the Investment Dealers Association of Canada, which is a hybrid of a pure SRO and a state-backed SRO. The IAA was not set up by any governments, but it is recognized and delegated authority by some provincial securities legislation.

The powers that these governmental, quasi-public, and somewhat private agencies and organizations are delegated are often as varied as the agencies and organizations themselves, as illustrated in Box 15.3. IAAs and SROs are often delegated the tasks of making rules, investigating breaches, prosecuting rule breakers and adjudicating on their guilt or innocence, and imposing penalties. Except for recourse by appeal to the courts or to the legislatures, in many respects these organizations form "enclaves" or mini-governments within society and face a number of criticisms.

The Issue of Delegated Authority

There are many reasons for a government to delegate tasks. As was noted earlier, the government would grind to a halt if it did not delegate work to government officials or agen-

cies. The same argument is made for delegating work to SROs: it is efficient; there is more flexibility in changing and enforcing the rules; and those with knowledge of the subject matter are in charge of the social-control scheme. Some of the professions present further arguments in favour of self-regulation and against government regulation. Many professions contend that they alone have the knowledge and capacity to weed out incompetent, unethical, and fraudulent members, and thereby are better able to protect the "public interest." Through enforcing rules of conduct and ethics, the professions claim to exercise their authority over a greater variety of behaviour than government regulation can and are therefore offering greater protection to the public. Some professions provide reasons that they view as unique to the services they provide to the public. For example, the legal profession claims a need to be "independent from the pressures of partisan politics" (Williams, 1979, p. 347) in order to provide citizens with representation free from interference by government.

Notwithstanding these goals, delegated authority raises a number of issues, whether the authority is delegated to SROs or IAAs. Accountability is a major issue. When government tasks are delegated to other government officials or private individuals or groups, to whom are these

---

Box 15.3 Powers Delegated by Governments

1. *Law- or Rule-Making Powers*: Provincial securities commissions (IAAs) and law societies (SROs) across Canada are delegated certain rule-making powers in order to regulate stockbrokers and lawyers, respectively.

2. *Advisory Powers*: In some cases the power delegated to the body may simply be to make recommendations to the government. If a government is interested in maintaining close reins on its powers, it can delegate the task of making recommendations to the cabinet or government, which then makes the decision. While such powers are sometimes delegated, there may be little practical difference between these recommendations and the lobbying of government officials by some groups to bring about changes.

3. *Supervisory Powers*: These powers can be delegated. Security commissions (IAAs) often supervise or oversee the activities of stock exchanges (SROs).

4. *Conciliatory Tasks*: Governments can also delegate conciliatory tasks to bodies like a human rights tribunal (Ratushny, 1987, p. 2).

5. *Investigatory Functions*: These can be delegated to boards of individuals on a regular or *ad hoc* basis. For example, William Code was appointed under the Business Corporations Act of Alberta to investigate the collapses of two subsidiaries of Principal Group Inc. (Constantineau, 1987; Smith, 1988). Investigations and inquiries usually result in recommendations to governments.

6. *Prosecution*: The Benchers of the Law Society of British Columbia (a SRO) have been delegated the task of prosecuting those who engage in the unauthorized practice of law.

7. *Adjudicative Functions*: The Workers Compensation Board (an IAA) decides whether a worker's injury is one covered by compensation under the act and regulations. The parole board (an IAA) decides whether an inmate will be released on parole.

8. *Determination of Eligibility Requirements and Standards*: Some occupations are delegated the authority to control entrance or eligibility requirements for a profession and to set continuing standards of competence.

people accountable? Legislation that delegates authority can be repealed; so, in one sense, they are all accountable to the legislature. The chain of authority or accountability for government officials is traced to the cabinet or a minister or a government linked official who is ultimately responsible to the legislature. Government departments are controlled through the concept of ministerial responsibility. If a department steps out of line, the minister responsible for that department will have to answer to Parliament or to the legislative assembly for the conduct of departmental officials.

All government and nongovernment bodies with delegated state powers are accountable to the legislature, because the legislation that granted them powers can always be repealed or amended. However, some IAAs have achieved a certain amount of political independence. Their powers appear to be less in the nature of a delegation and more in the nature of an "investiture of power" (Law Reform Commission of Canada, 1980, p. 12). They operate in many ways as a miniature government (Schultz, 1979, p. 19). Historically, they have been described as "structured heretics" (Hodgetts, 1973, p. 138) and as a "a headless fourth branch of the government, a haphazard deposit of irresponsible agencies and uncoordinated powers" (quoted in Janisch, 1979, p. 58). While IAAs are statutory creatures, subject to legislative changes or dissolution, many have achieved widespread public support, such that they have become permanent institutional forces. The Canadian Radio-television and Telecommunications Commission (CRTC) is an example of an IAA that is undergoing a struggle to maintain independence from what some consider to be political meddling. Andre Bureau, the former chairman of the CRTC, commented: "We believe that you either accept the commission as a regulatory, quasi-judicial body, or if you really want to have larger participation [by government] in the decisions, then let's face it, you abolish the commission" (Bruce, 1988, p. 52).

Members of some SROs try to de-emphasize or ignore the fact that their powers of self-government and their exclusive right to practise behind a state-created and state-enforced monopoly are statutory in origin and subject to legislative interference. For example, Bette Stephenson (1977, p. 5) linked the "precious right of self-government" to ancient English common law in her talk, as the minister of labour, to the Ontario Association of Architects. Mary Southin, QC, upon resigning as a Bencher of the Law Society of British Columbia, wrote that "the public interest is not enhanced by the interference of the state in any profession; I believe that the public would be better off if there were more occupations with the right of self-government" (1980, p. 465). The British Columbia Psychological Association was more humble in a notice it placed in the *Vancouver Sun* (1988; see Box 15.4) to inform the public that amendments to the legislation that allowed nonregistered individuals working in schools to use the title "psychologist" might result in the employment by schools of individuals who "may *not* meet the minimum standards established for the profession."

Efforts to improve the accountability of SROs has resulted in an erosion of the differences between IAAs and SROs. Members of IAAs are appointed by governments. Members of state-backed SROs are generally elected by members of the organization; however, there has been a move to include more government-appointed members to the governing boards of SROs. The greater the percentage of state-appointed governors, the more the state-backed SRO resembles an IAA. It can work the other way: an IAA can take on the characteristics of state-backed SROs to the extent that the government appoints to the IAA individuals who are from the group they are supposed to govern. For example, a government-appointed agency (IAA) to oversee the regulation of a profession might be, in practice, similar to a SRO if the appointees to the IAA were all members of the profession. Some argue that the move to a mixed board will have the effect of improving accountability. However, Benham and Benham (1988, p. 45) suggest that perhaps "*lack* of membership in the profession" be a prerequisite for sitting on professional boards.

Lay representation has been suggested as another means of improving the accountability of such boards. However, there is some debate as to who these public representatives ought to represent and how they should be appointed. Olley (1978, p. 86) suggests that lay representatives ought to come from public-interest groups and be required to report to them in order to bring them back to the purpose of their being representatives. Otherwise, they lose perspective and become swallowed up in the ideology of the profession. Tupper (1980, p. 467), in presenting an argument to his legal colleagues for lay benchers on the governing board of lawyers in British Columbia, wrote, "Whilst laymen will open some windows, if they are welcomed into our midst as equals they will inevitably tend to emphathise [sic] and sympathise with the lawyers' point of view, at least so long as it is sensibly advanced." In 1988, the Attorney General of British Columbia appointed two lay benchers to the governing body of the Law Society of British Columbia. These "lay" benchers are actually government appointees. Lay representation varies from one law society to another, and there are still societies that do not have lay representatives or government-appointed members.

The use of lay persons, according to those who are critical of the concept of self-regulation, amounts to patchwork. Self-regulation, especially among the professions who have the power to make and enforce rules against their own members, has fundamental flaws that cannot be fixed with

Box 15.4 British Columbia Psychological Association Disclaimer about School Psychologists

British Columbia
Psychological Association

This notice is to inform the B.C. public that individuals designated by school boards as psychologists, but who are *not* Registered psychologists, may not meet the minimum standards established for the profession in B.C.

WHO IS A REGISTERED PSYCHOLOGIST?

In 1977 the B.C. Legislature enacted the *Psychologists Act*, enabling the B.C. Psychological Association to register professionals who have completed the Association's educational and procedural requirements and to designate them Registered Psychologists. The B.C. standards for registration are representative of the maturity of the field of psychology in this province. They put in place a mandatory Code of Ethics and regulate the practice of those registered to ensure the quality of psychological services offered to the public.

In 1987, the provincial government—over objections by the Association—created an exemption to the *Psychologists Act* allowing school boards to employ individuals who are not registered and to designate them as "psychologists".

The B.C. Psychological Association recognizes the authority of the government to exempt groups and to allow them use of the title "Psychologist". The Association believes, however, that it has a duty to inform the public of such actions. It does not believe exemptions to be in the best interests of the people of B.C. nor—in this case—the children of the province.

If you or your child use the services of a psychologist and want to know if he or she is registered, ask. If the answer is "NO", be aware that the person is not obliged to act in accordance with the ethical code of the B.C. Psychological Association and may not meet its standards for registration.

---

minor concessions to the public. The American Bar Association Special Committee on Evaluation of Disciplinary Enforcement (the Clark Committee) reached some condemning conclusions on the legal profession in the United States. The discipline of lawyers was "scandalous" and "practically nonexistent in many jurisdictions." There was "unofficial immunity from disciplinary action" for some lawyers who were "professionally and socially well acquainted" (1970, pp. 1,3).[12] While the disciplinary systems in the United States and Canada are quite different,[13] the problems with self-regulation are similar. Self-regulation, in, for example, the legal profession, requires that lawyers discipline lawyers who may, in turn, at some future date be in a position to discipline them. As Coleman states, SROs "have generally shown great leniency toward the offenses of their fellows—perhaps on the assumption that they might someday be on the other side of a consumer complaint" (1985, p. 153). An organization cannot serve both its members and the best interests of the public; self-regulation puts it in a position of a conflict of interest.

Another major complaint against SROs is that they "deflect criminal complaints away from the justice system and thus . . . protect members from prosecution" (Coleman, 1985, p. 153). This allegation is often directed at the professions; however, it is more difficult to find evidence to sup-

port or refute it. It is only recently that disciplinary hearings have been opened to the public and that some agencies have published summaries of the cases with which they deal. They have, however, received little attention from researchers, and it is difficult to draw conclusions from the reported information (Brockman & McEwen, 1990).

In order for SROs to fulfil their disciplinary functions, it is argued that they must be delegated the power to determine who will be admitted to their particular profession and to expel members who violate the rules of the professional body. In order to protect the public from those who are unqualified to deliver the specialized services, the SRO should have a state-imposed monopoly on the services that they provide to the public. That is, a person who is not a member of the SRO should not be allowed to deliver the services designated as those provided by the particular profession. This arrangement between an SRO and the government has the effect of creating a structure in which the SRO is in a position of exercising not only social control over its members, but also economic control. In addition, the state-backed monopoly allows members of the SRO to violate some of our laws against anticompetitive behaviour. Next, we will examine some of the economic crimes that can arise out of a system designed or put forth as a system of social control.

The Exercise of Economic Power and Economic Crimes

The fact that those with social, economic, and political power play a major role in defining crime is not novel to criminologists. And, there is growing support for the proposition that some industrial "accidents," pharmaceutical "errors," and manufacturing "defects" should be treated as **culpable homicide** (see Chapter 6). In the area of economic crimes, consumers are being taxed[14] at exorbitant rates by prices fixed through illegal agreements or by those who have managed to find or put themselves in a position of a monopoly.

Many professions are in the position of being allowed to enforce an artificial "monopoly" on their work through legislated authority and the courts. These professions do not form a true monopoly in which members are the only ones capable of or willing to perform their work. Nonmembers are prohibited from doing so by legislation that is backed by a criminal **sanction**, a **civil injunction**, or both.[15] For example, the unauthorized practice of law in British Columbia is an offence punishable by a fine of up to $2000 or six months' imprisonment, or both. The professions not only escape some aspects of the criminal law, but also use it as a tool to prevent others from providing "their" services to the public.

Below, we will briefly examine the rationale behind our competition laws and the means whereby some professions manage to escape these laws through a state-enforced monopoly and other anticompetitive behaviour, such as price-fixing and advertising restrictions.

Rationale for Competition Laws

According to one member of the business community, "there are often circumstances which seriously interfere with [a businessman's] ability to [earn a living]. . . . The greatest of these is competition" (quoted in Bliss, 1974, p. 33). Adam Smith, a political economist writing in the 1700s, similarly recognized the anticompetitive spirit of businessmen when he observed that "people of the same trade seldom meet together, even for merriment and diversion, but the conversation ends in a conspiracy against the public, or in some contrivance to raise prices" (quoted in Ostry, 1978, p. 17). All profit-minded people strive for market power, that is, the power to set prices and control the volume of production so as to make profits in excess of what would be expected in a competitive economy. The purpose of competition or antitrust laws is to ensure that the public is not gouged by inflated prices. Other benefits of competition (that is, keeping market power out of the hands of private individuals and groups) include the following: improved performance, reduction in inefficiencies,

lower cost to the consumer, and encouragement of new methods and products (see, for example, Dunlop, McQueen, & Trebilcock, 1987; Gorecki & Stanbury, 1984; Ostry, 1978).[16] The higher prices that emerge in noncompetitive economies often result in the product or service being priced out of the hands of those with lower incomes.

Despite these arguments in favour of competition, arguments are presented in favour of allowing some of the professions to have a monopoly on the services they provide and to engage in anticompetitive activities, including price-fixing and restrictions on advertising. It is argued that "a competitive unregulated market will not provide the correct amount of information in order for consumers as a whole to make the correct choice among providers of the service" (Waverman, 1979, p. 382). A regulated market is viewed as a necessary means to set minimum standards and protect the consumer from incompetence and fraud. All three of these behaviours—monopolies, price-fixing, and restrictions on advertising—are increasingly coming under attack.

State-Backed Monopolies

Until June 1986 it was an indictable offence, punishable by two years' imprisonment, for anyone to form a monopoly in Canada. The legislation suffered from underenforcement, and the criminal law was viewed as an inappropriate tool to deal with monopolies (see, for example, Dunlop, McQueen, & Trebilcock, 1987; and Stanbury, 1978). Anticompetitive activities engaged in by monopolies are now dealt with by the Director of Investigation and Research who can apply to the Competition Tribunal for an order prohibiting an abuse of a dominant position under the federal Competition Act.

The economic power of the professions is enhanced by a state-imposed monopoly on the services provided by some professions. Once the government decides to allow a profession to regulate itself, a number of models exist in terms of the degree of closure it allows a profession to exercise. "Closure" refers to the process whereby organizations "regulate market conditions in their favour, in face of actual or potential competition from the outside" (Saks, 1983, p. 5).

The most restrictive system of closure is one in which a person cannot carry out specified activities unless the person is licensed or has a practice certificate, which is usually distributed by a governing body. This system can be referred to as closed, an exclusive right to practice or **licensure**. The system restricts entry into an occupation to those who meet certain requirements and prohibits anyone else from engaging in the activities set aside for the occupation. The effect is a state-imposed monopoly on work done by the occupation. Licensure is enforced through legislation that allows an occupational organization to obtain injunctions against violators, to prosecute them, or both. For example, it is an offence for a person to engage in the practice of law in any province unless that person is a member of the provincial law society or falls within an exception. Law societies can also obtain injunctions restraining persons who are about to violate this prohibition. Legislation governing hairdressers, barbers, physiotherapists, and massage practitioners in some provinces makes it an offence to engage in the services of these professions without being a member of the respective associations.[17]

A less restrictive system is one that reserves a title for a particular occupation or profession. This system is often called **certification** or the "reserved title" system. Certification is not a prerequisite to engaging in the activities of an occupation; it restricts the use of the title reserved for the occupation. Anyone can carry out the activities of the occupation so long as that person does not use the reserved title. Agrologists,[18] naturopaths, and psychologists fall under this system in British Columbia. The legislation usually makes it an offence to use the title reserved for the occupation. In some occupations, an injunction is the only recourse.[19]

Most professions favour the licensure system, in which a professional organization can either prosecute or obtain an injunction against an outsider who engages in services reserved for the profession. The advantage of the licensure system is that the services will not be provided unless by a member of the regulated body. The assumption is that this type of system is needed on order to fully protect the public from incompetent and fraudulent entrepreneurs. Other pro-licensure arguments include: higher quality, reduced uncertainty, technological innovation, standardization, and improved manpower planning (Jenkins, 1986, pp. 38–45).

A number of authors have pointed out that the call for licensure "invariably comes not from the consumers it is to protect but from the trades and professions themselves" (Ostry, 1978, p. 21; see also Hamowy, 1984). A major review of the professions was undertaken by the Office des professions du Québec in 1976 because of growing demand by occupations with a certification system to change to a licensure system (1976, p. 11). The source of the concern and demand leads to suspicion concerning the interest being represented.

Arguments against licensure include the same types of arguments made in favour of competition and parallel those made *for* certification. Licensure is viewed as assuming a dubious relationship between qualifications at one point and performance at a later point. It is criticized for being a rigid, arbitrary, and "very crude quality signal" (Trebilcock & Reiter, 1982, pp. 67–68). Jenkins suggests that licen-

sure can *reduce* quality "by potential labour shortages and time pressures, lack of competition (which can directly reduce care and effort), and general erosion of various other *posterior* guarantees of quality" (1986, p. 45). Licensure can result in consumers substituting cheaper means, performing the service themselves, or doing without the service when faced with fees beyond their means. It also facilitates other anticompetitive activities such as **price-fixing** and restrictions on advertising (discussed later).

The advantage of certification over the licensure system is that members of the public are free to choose, when employing services, between a person who is a member of an association and regulated by his or her own kind and a person who is not a member and whose services probably cost less. However, there is a concern with the quality of the services provided by a nonregulated occupation.

Exclusive licensure eliminates competition and forces consumers who are unable to afford the services to turn to a completely unregulated black market or adopt a do-it-yourself approach. However, exclusive licensure is not its only form. Many services are provided by more than one profession. Notaries in British Columbia have managed to gain powers not achieved by their counterparts in other provinces. They **convey** real estate, draft wills that fall within specified classes, and draw up affidavits. In other provinces, these activities are exclusively reserved for lawyers. Real-estate brokers in Arizona prepare conveyancing documents (Rhode, 1981, p. 3). Chartered accountants, tax consultants, financial advisers, and lawyers give advice on tax matters. The work of accountants is presently shared between a number of independent professional groups with expertise in accounting (see Jenkins, 1986). There are Chartered Accountants, Certified General Accountants, and Registered Industrial Accountants in some provinces.

Almost all professions work in an environment in which their economic territory is being challenged by other professions working on the fringe or periphery of the licensed activities. Dominant professional groups (those with legislative authority to have members of other professions prosecuted for providing services in their licensed field) are sometimes the aggressor in territorial wars. Lawyers are moving into the area of family mediation, which was at one time the territory of social workers and family counsellors. Doctors have, over the years, not only invaded the territory once dominated by midwives, but also managed to exclude midwives from what was once their profession through a licensure system backed by state prosecutions (Burtch, 1988). Midwives can, in many provinces, be prosecuted for practising their profession. Acupuncturists have been investigated by the RCMP for practising medicine without a licence (Mullens, 1989).

The nature of the disputes and the means used to resolve them seem to vary on the basis of political and economic power. The dominant profession will often negotiate with a powerful intruder as to how best to "divvy up" various services between the professions; less powerful intruders are prosecuted. So, while law societies are prepared to prosecute paralegals who intrude in their territory (*Lawyers Weekly*, 1988, p. 18), they are more likely to negotiate with Chartered Accountants who duplicate their services. The Law Society of British Columbia has been carrying on a continuing dialogue with the Institute of Chartered Accountants "in an effort to reach a consensus on what the parameters are as between lawyer and accountant in the field of tax advice" (1987, p. 18). It reached an agreement with notaries in 1955 with regard to the services notaries would provide and the numbers of them allowed to practise at any one time (White, 1980). Law societies and associations continually "study" the role of paralegals and "their effect on the legal system" (Gogolek, 1988b). Rhode suggests that interprofessional understandings or agreements on which group delivers which service violate the competition laws in the United States (1981, p. 44). Their status in Canada has not been determined.

Another threat to licensure is the increasing number of self-help groups and the do-it-yourself manuals that suggest that professional services do not require the time and expense of those licensed to carry out the services. While often talked about in the context of "other" public legal-education programs (Kane & Myers, 1982), they may have different effects. Self-help groups often try to limit members of the professions to the roles of "referral, consultant and information-provider" (Clarke & Bayers, 1988), whereas public legal-education programs may result in members of the public realizing "that not all legal problems can be solved by the individual himself or herself" (Kane & Myers, 1982, p. 446). Public legal education is not only a means of disseminating information but also the ideology of legalism, that is "the structuring of all possible human relations into the form of claims and counterclaims under established rules" (Shklar, 1986, p. 10). Education, depending on who disseminates it, may actually expand or create the need for the professions.

The alternative to exclusive licensure is not necessarily unregulated services. The advantages of multigroup certification or licensure include interprofessional competition and increased inefficiency and innovation. Some professions already work in multigroup competitive environments; however, they find this an undesirable position to be in and strive to reduce or eliminate competition through agreements that run contrary to the intent of competition laws. Exclusive licensure completely eliminates competition between professions, and its existence should be carefully scrutinized.

Price-Fixing

Exclusive licensure not only controls or eliminates interprofessional competition, but also facilitates the control of intraprofessional competition through the use of fixed or suggested fee schedules and prohibitions or limitations on advertising. The professions have historically found themselves in a privileged position with regard to the competition laws in Canada. Up until 1976, the professions were not subject to the federal competition legislation. Early immunity from competition laws allowed the professions to set and enforce schedules that would otherwise have been illegal.

Amendments in 1976, designed to include the professions, have yet to receive a conclusive interpretation from the Supreme Court of Canada (see Stanbury, 1983). The professions have argued that they should be exempt from federal competition laws on the basis that they fall under provincial jurisdiction and are regulated by provincial statutes. It is probably within the jurisdiction of the province to set fees for professional services; however, the issue is whether the provinces can delegate this authority to a non-government agency such as a law society or a real-estate board. One author has suggested that the government appointees to these boards might bring them under the umbrella of provincial powers and exempt the board from the competition laws (Waverman, 1979, p. 383). The issue has yet to be finally resolved.

An agreement to prevent, or lessen, competition "unduly" is an indictable offence punishable by five years' imprisonment, a $10 million fine, or both. Agreements to fix prices and prohibitions on advertising can fall under this section of the Competition Act. However, the requirement of "unduly" provides a loophole through which business and occupational groups can escape. This restriction, which does not appear in competition laws in the United States, has been criticized for years as inappropriate. Trades and professions are provided a further loophole, in the Competition Act, in that price-fixing is not an offence if the agreement "relates only to a service and to standards of competence and integrity that are reasonably necessary for the protection of the public."

Recent investigations by the federal Department of Consumer and Corporate Affairs into minimum-fee schedules published and sometimes enforced by professional bodies have resulted in negotiated settlements rather than a test of the constitutional issue through the laying of criminal charges under the Competition Act (Gogolek, 1998a; Willis & Melnbardis, 1988; Melnbardis, 1988). For example, in

1985, the Waterloo Law Association, faced with lawyers not charging the suggested fee for real-estate transactions, "which hampered the efforts of others to charge the suggested fees" (Makin, 1988), advised its members that it was a breach of professional standards to charge less than the suggested fee and that any members doing so would be boycotted by other members (Makin, 1988). The Kent County Law Association in Ontario passed a by-law requiring that its members sign an agreement to use a fee schedule when conducting real-estate transactions. Penalties for not complying included fines and suspensions (Gogolek, 1988a). Real-estate boards investigated by the competition bureau were found to have fixed prices backed by such sanctions as not allowing individuals to list in the Multiple Listing Service unless they charged a fixed minimum (*Globe and Mail*, 1988b).

How these events were dealt with by the parties and by the media are of significance in our understanding of the nature of criminal law and its enforcement. Price-fixing or preventing or lessening competition unduly are criminal offences. The federal competition bureau did not pursue criminal charges against the law associations or the real-estate boards. Instead, they reached an agreement with the organizations involved, which was ratified by the Federal Court of Canada. That is, the Federal Court of Canada, upon application by the federal Department of Justice, issued a **prohibition order** under the Competition Act, prohibiting the organizations from engaging in the anticompetitive behaviour discussed above.[20] Thus, the Federal Court prohibited the organizations from committing criminal offences.

This approach would seem quite unusual, perhaps even outrageous, if used against individuals who engage in, for example, theft. A prohibition order, prohibiting someone who has allegedly committed theft from committing theft, would not be viewed as a major victory. The nature of the criminal offence of price-fixing (together with its loopholes) and the time, effort, and expense of prosecuting an organization that is prepared to use all of its resources to defend itself, often results in a decision to "settle" administratively or civilly that which would otherwise be dealt with as a criminal offence. One is entitled to be presumed innocent until proven guilty; therefore, the organizations are entitled to such a presumption. However, "the major victory for consumers" claimed by the federal competition bureau (Kohut, 1988) appears somewhat premature.

The other interesting aspect of these cases is the approach taken by the media. In reporting the investigation against the real-estate boards, the *Financial Times of Canada*, in its "Review of Events Dec. 19 to Dec. 25" (1988), announced that fixed real-estate commissions "became illegal under a Federal Court ruling." The *Globe and Mail* (1988b) ran one headline: "Investigation revealed real estate boards flirting with prosecution" and an article on the same page talked about a "major victory for consumers in a court's blessing of a strict new code" (Kohut, 1988). Price-fixing did not become illegal under the Federal Court ruling. There was nothing new about the code that prohibited price-fixing. The power that the news media have over our image of deviance is discussed by Ericson, Baranek, and Chan (1987). The professions and other elites get to negotiate the definition of what is to be considered a crime in pursuing greater profits; other "criminals" are not granted such a luxury, even if they are pursuing the necessities of life.

Advertising Restrictions

The self-imposed prohibition on advertising by the professions has recently been eroded. A committee of the Canadian Bar Association (Ontario) examined the arguments for and against advertising and concluded that lawyers ought to be allowed to advertise but that the Law Society should "regulate advertising to protect the public and to preserve the integrity and stature of the profession" (1985, p. 37). The committee saw little support for the arguments against advertising. Studies had shown that advertising improves the image of lawyers (not diminishes it), does not have adverse effects on the administration of justice, does not increase the cost of legal services (but rather decreases the cost and stimulates demand), and enhances quality (rather than adversely affecting it). The committee was also of the view that the "courts would ultimately protect lawyer advertising" (1985, p. 34) but that some restrictions were appropriate to avoid misleading or confusing advertising.

To summarize, the professions are often in a position not only to have their work excluded from the competition laws of Canada, but also to use the force of the state to enforce their monopoly by prosecuting competitors for "unauthorized practice." Agreements between professions to carve up services to the public have not been challenged in Canada, as they have been in the United States. The prohibitions in Canada on price-fixing and advertising are sufficiently vague to allow many occupational groups to escape conviction. These exemptions and provisos in Canadian competition laws probably reflect the power that the professions have in keeping the government out of their highly prized territory.

Here, we have examined only the power exercised by professional organizations in the area of competition laws. Individual members of professional bodies have power to define their client's or patient's problems and prescribe solutions (see, for example, Frankel, 1988). The professions are in a position not only to assist their client or patient but to assist the state in its task of social control. As social problems become legalized and medicalized, the power of the professions over individuals is increased and this power itself becomes a social problem (see Chapter 8).

The granting of self-regulatory powers to occupational groups often leads to expectations that these groups will regulate behaviour beyond the activities normally carried out by the occupation. Governing bodies will discipline dentists and lawyers for inappropriate or criminal sexual activities with patients and clients. Little is known about the actual effect that such self-regulating activity has on detection and enforcement of the criminal law.

Conclusion

This chapter examined one small aspect of white-collar crime, the means by which we as a society have allowed some occupational groups to control the behaviour of their members. As was seen, self-regulation is only one of many means of social control that governments have at their disposal. It is a form of delegated regulation designed to control a wider variety of behaviour than the criminal law but, in many cases, SROs will also deal with what is considered criminal behaviour. Along with this overlap comes a concern that the very existence of a SRO will result in criminals being deflected away from the criminal-justice system. Do SROs deflect criminals away from the criminal-justice system or do they provide additional means for detecting and dealing with criminal behaviour? Little research has been conducted into the actual effect that SROs have on the criminal-justice system.

The study of SROs also illustrates that the way we react to behaviour has more to do with whether the behaviour is considered criminal than with the actual behaviour itself. The range of social mechanisms available to deal with those who belong to occupational organizations blurs the lines between what is seen as a crime and what is seen as a civil or an administrative wrong. However, "common" crimes could be viewed in the same manner. The store owner could sue the "loaf lifter" for the cost of the loaf of bread. The "loaf lifter" could belong to a SRO (e.g., a family) that would take responsibility for disciplining and preventing the crime, tort, or unethical behaviour.

Members of professional organizations have the additional advantage of an aura of trust, which is often necessary in order to conduct their work. We trust doctors and dentists with our bodies, lawyers and stockbrokers with our money, ministers and social workers with our personal problems. This trust is often generalized. There is (or perhaps was) an expectation that members of the clergy can also be trusted not to take advantage of children who are left alone in their presence.

In order to fulfil their function of controlling the behaviour of their members, many SROs have a state-imposed monopoly on the services they provide to the public. This enables the SRO to impose restrictions on its members that have negative economic consequences to the consumer. An exclusive right to provide services, licensure, is not required in order to provide effective self-regulation. Multi-group licensure with interprofessional competition would likely provide the consumer with the most cost-efficient service.

The use of self-regulation is coming under closer scrutiny by the media and members of the public. It does, however, provide us with another model by which to compare the various means of social control in our society.

Discussion Questions

1. What can be learned about "traditional" types of crime by studying white-collar crime or crimes of the elite?

2. Use examples to describe how "theft" can be dealt with by criminal law, civil law, and administrative law.

3. SROs are supposed to protect the "public interest" and represent the interests of their members. Are these two goals compatible? Why or why not?

4. Would the public interest be better served by replacing SROs with IAAs or changing the nature of SROs? What types of concerns would we have to keep in mind in order to better protect the public interest?

Notes

1. The term "elite" is borrowed from elite theory where it is used to refer to the ruling or governing elite, such as corporate officials, political leaders, and military personnel, and not to self-regulating professions, such as doctors, lawyers, and engineers—the subject matter of this chapter. The concept was first introduced by the Classical elite theorists (Gaetano Mosca, Vilfredo Pareto, and Robert Michels) to illustrate the inevitability of elites and their necessity for societal stability and to destroy the credibility of Marxist alternatives (Burton & Higley, 1987). It has since lost some of its anti-Marxist flavour (Stone, 1987) and has been imported into the study of white-collar crime (see, for example, Coleman, 1985). It is used here as another catchword to draw attention to the fact that some groups in society have amassed not only sufficient economic and political power to control entry to their group and discipline of their members, but also the right to engage in certain economic activities and to prevent nonmembers from so doing at the risk of prosecution.

2. There is no clear definition of "profession." Various descriptions have been used to distinguish the "traditional" ("old," "real," "learned," "liberal") professions from the "new" ("quasi," "para," "mimic," "semi") professions and from other occupations ("crafts," "trades," "labour"). There has also been a great deal of attention focussed on the professionalization of other occupations and the deprofessionalization of the professions in general. Scales, continua, and inventories have been developed in order to determine where any occupation stands at any given time in history. Lists of traits and attributes have been created, modified, analyzed, and reanalyzed (see, for example, Larouche, 1987; Ritti, Ference, & Goldner, 1974; Rothman, 1984; Usprich, 1975). Roth suggests that the efforts of sociologists to distinguish the professions from other occupations "has decoyed students of occupations into becoming apologists for professionalism ideology" (1974, p. 6) and the "dupe of established professions (helping them justify their dominant position and its payoffs)" (1974, p. 17).

During the 1960s, in Quebec, an increasing number of occupations were demanding the same social status as "established" professions (Issalys, 1978, pp. 588–89). The legislative response was to increase the number of laws and regulations. A commission appointed by the Quebec government recommended, in 1970, that a single *professional code* regulate all professions (Issalys, 1978, pp. 592–93). Many of the recommendations were implemented on 1973.

In 1976, the research staff at the Office des professions du Québec set out to determine whether there was any consensus in North America on the concept of profession. After a comprehensive review of the literature, they concluded that Howard Becker's definition of a profession as an occupation that has been "fortunate enough to obtain and keep the title of profession" was most realistic (1976, p. 29). Other authors have given similar definitions: "a symbolic label for a desired status" (Elliott, 1972, p. 3, paraphrasing Hughes, 1958, p. 44). Evidence of the desirability of the status was seen by the research staff at the Office des professions du Québec whose research was stimulated by the growing pressure on the office to recognize an increasing number of professional corporations (1976, p. 11).

3. Prior to the sixteenth century, "profession" and "profess" were used to describe high-status occupations (the clergy, law, and medicine) and to imply positive intentions, "to dedicate oneself to a good end" (Freidson, 1986, pp. 21–22). By the sixteenth century, the words were also used to describe any occupation and to imply negative intentions like insincerity, for example, "he professes to know nothing about it" (Freidson, 1986, pp. 21–22).

4. Tawney suggested that industry might be better organized as a profession in order to emphasize public *duties* (as did the professions) rather than the *right* to monetary gain (1921, p. 89). Some saw business moving in the direction of professionalization (Brandeis, 1914) or examined it as a possible model for labour to follow (Webb & Webb, 1917). While these academics recognized that there were some "blacklegs" in every profession (Tawney, 1921, p. 90), the professions were generally viewed as altruistic, serving the public good in an unselfish manner, in contrast with the greed and acquisitive nature of business.

5. Speaking of the legal profession, Laski continued, "having been made a dependency of the business empire, it has had to adapt its habits to the standards of its protector . . . with its independence there has gone also any profound social consciousness it may once have professed" (1935, p. 679). The solution to these problems, according to Laski, was to make members of the professions public servants who worked for a fixed salary rather than "plying for hire" (1935, p. 682).

6. Sutherland was not the first to draw attention to this fact. Horoszowski (1980) gives examples of some of the earlier works of muckrakers and sociologists from whom Sutherland had borrowed ideas.

7. The government allows some trades and professions to bypass the more formal means of enforcing a contract. To illustrate, the usual means of enforcing the payment of a contract (for example, payment for yard work completed by a gardener) is for the aggrieved gardener (plaintiff) to sue the owner of the yard (defendant) in court for nonpayment. The gardener would have to prove the existence and nature of the contract, its performance (that is, that the yard work was carried out according to what was agreed upon), and that payment was not made by the owner. If the gardener won the lawsuit (i.e., obtained a court judgment that ordered the owner to pay the gardener), the court judgment could then be enforced. Lawyers who are not paid for their services by their clients do not have to sue their clients in court to obtain a judgment; rather, they need only have their bills reviewed or taxed by a taxing officer and filed in court in order to obtain an enforceable judgment. This procedure is much more informal, and much less costly than enforcing the payment of a bill through the courts.

8. There were numerous complaints about the committee, and

S.J. McLean was appointed to make recommendations for improving the system (Baggaley, 1981, pp. 76–77). He objected to the existing committee because of its "members'" lack of technical training, the dual political and administrative function of the committee; the lack of tenure; and its inability to move around the country" (Baggaley, 1981, p. 77). He was of the view "that if regulation was taken out of the hands of politicians and given to a specialized commission staffed by well-qualified professionals, the public interest would be served" (1981, p. 78). In 1903, the Board of Railway Commissioners was created (Schultz, 1979, p. 18; Baggaley, 1981, p. 79).

9. This effect is not limited to the work of IAAs. The slogan "law is politics" from the Critical Legal Studies movement illustrates that some are of the view that judges also make political decisions, disguised as neutral and impartial (see, for example, Hutchinson & Monahan, 1987; Kairys, 1982).

10. The adoption of the Charter in Canada has led to efforts to distinguish "state action" from private action. In the United States, where this effort has gone on for years, the courts and the scholars have concluded that the area is a "conceptual disaster" and that the problem is impossible to resolve (Gibson, 1983, p. 507). Part of this conceptual problem stems from the size of and the powers exercised by some corporations, which is often facilitated by governmental action or policy. Sutherland (1983, p. xvi) was of the view that a society within which large corporations existed "would be similar to socialism except that the public have no voice in industry."

11. There are also organizations created to carry out other activities such as lobbying and making money (legally or illegally); however, this chapter is concerned with occupational organizations that have as one of their chief functions the regulation of their members for the stated benefit of the group or society as a whole.

12. The Clark Committee was of the view that the "overdecentralized structure" (American Bar Association, 1970, p. 25) that existed in many districts meant that local trial judges were required to discipline lawyers with whom they socialized.

13. The courts in the United States have the inherent power to discipline lawyers, and legislation that interferes with this power is struck down in some states as an interference with the inherent *and* constitutional powers of the courts. There are some states in which the power to discipline lawyers is delegated to the Bar by either the courts or the legislators. In Canada, provincial legislation delegates the power to discipline lawyers to the lawyers, and disciplined lawyers can appeal such decisions to the courts.

14. The excessive price charged by the producers of goods and services through price-fixing and other anticompetitive activity is similar to taxation. The tax, however, is imposed by private industry rather than by government.

15. A civil injunction is an order by the court prohibiting someone from engaging in certain behaviour. Such injunctions are used for a wide variety of purposes, from prohibiting individuals from engaging in work reserved for particular professions to preventing individuals from picketing or occupying certain locations.

16. The economic theory behind competition laws is explained by Scherer (1980) and is beyond the scope of this chapter.

17. There are exceptions. For example, the Hairdressers Act in British Columbia applies only to "municipalities of a population of 750 persons or more and in the territory within 16 km of the boundaries of those municipalities" (s. 2). Control over prosecutions of unlicensed persons who engage in licensed occupations varies from one occupation to another. The Law Society of British Columbia has authority to prosecute those who engage in the unauthorized practice of law. Other statutes do not specify who has authority to prosecute, so the power is generally with the attorney general of the province; however, private prosecutions can be instituted in some cases. Committees have suggested that the control of prosecution to enforce a licensure system ought to be with the attorney general so that it is "administered in a disinterested way, informed exclusively by considerations of the public interest" (Trebilcock & Reiter, 1982, p. 81).

18. Agrologists teach, advise, and experiment in the production of agricultural plants and the raising and protection of farm animals.

19. Recently, the government of British Columbia moved from the use of penalties to the use of injunctions to enforce the reserve title or certification system for new professions. Amendments to the Society Act, effective April 15, 1986, allow a group of 50 individuals of an occupation or profession who are interested in representing the interests of their group to apply to register as a society. The effect of registration is that no person other than a member has the right to use the occupational or professional designation. The society can apply for injunctive relief if a person contravenes this provision but a contravention is not an offence.

20. There are some provisions of the prohibition order that may assist in preventing future offences. For example, the law associations have to notify the combines branch of any meeting over the next five years at which fees are likely to be discussed (Makin, 1988).

References

Albanese, Jay S. (1987). *Organizational offenders: Understanding corporate crime* (2nd ed.). Niagara Falls, NY: Apocalypse.

American Bar Association. (1970). *Problems and recommendations in disciplinary enforcement*. American Bar Association.

Arrowsmith, S. (1988). *Government procurement and judicial review*. Toronto: Carswell.

Arthurs, H.W. (1985). *Without the law: Administrative justice and legal pluralism in nineteenth-century England*. Toronto: University of Toronto Press.

Baggaley, C.D. (1981). *The emergence of the regulatory state in Canada 1867–1939*, Technical Report No. 15. Ottawa: Economic Council of Canada.

Bagnall J. (1988, March 28). Procurement game draws more players. *The Financial Post*, pp. 37, 38.

Belobaba, E.P. (1978). *Civil liability as a professional competence incentive*, Working Paper No. 9. Ontario: Professional Organizations Committee.

Bellett, G., & Shaw, G. (1989, April 8). Sex assault complaints marked dentist's career. *Vancouver Sun*, p. A1.

Benham, L., & Benham, A. (1978). Prospects for increasing competition in the professions. In P. Slayton & M.J. Trebilcock (Eds.), *The professions and public policy* (pp. 41–45). Toronto: University of Toronto Press.

Bliss, M. (1974). *A living profit.* Toronto: McClelland & Stewart.

Bliss, M. (1988, September 5). Taking the pork barrel from the politicians' soiled hands. *Financial Times of Canada*, p. 50.

Brandeis, L.D. (1914). *Business: A profession.* New York: Augustus M. Kelley &rprt. 1971é.

Brockman, J., & McEwen, C. (1990). Self regulation in the legal profession: Funnel in, funnel out or funnel away? *Canadian Journal of Law and Society, 5*, in press.

Bruce, A. (1988, February 13). Interview with Andre Bureau. Encounter: The outgoing head of the CRTC warns of the dangers of political meddling. *Financial Times of Canada*, p. 52.

Burtch, B.E. (1988). Promoting midwifery, prosecuting midwives: The state and the midwifery movement in Canada. In S. Bolaria & H.D. Dickinson (Eds.), *Sociology of health care in Canada* (pp. 313–27). Toronto: Harcourt Brace Jovanovich.

Burton, M.G., & Higley, J. (1987). Invitation to elite theory: The basic contentions reconsidered. In G.W. Domhoff & T.R. Dye (Eds.), *Power elites and organizations* (pp. 219–38). Newbury, CA: Sage.

Canadian Bar Association (Ontario). (1985). *Report of the committee on advertising by lawyers.* Canadian Bar Association, private publication.

Canadian Sociology and Anthropology Association. (1986). *Code of Professional Ethics.*

Clarke, M., and Bayers, L. (1988). How self-helpers can reach professionals. *Initiative: The Self-Help Newsletter, 4*(4), 1, 6.

Clinard, M.B., & Yeager, P.C. (1980). *Corporate crime.* New York: Free Press.

Coleman, J.W. (1985). *The criminal elite: The sociology of white collar crime.* New York: St. Martin's.

Constantineau, B. (1987, December 18). Investors staggered by inquiry testimony. *The Vancouver Sun*, pp. A1, A9.

Cox, Bob (1988, February). Ticket-fixing affair shakes Manitoba bar. *National*, p. 3.

Dewees, D.N., Mathewson, G.F., & Trebilcock, M.J. (1983). Policy alternatives in quality regulation. In D.N. Dewees (Ed.), *The regulation of quality* (pp. 27-51). Toronto: Butterworths.

Doern, B.G. (1979). *Rationalizing the regulatory decision-making process: The prospects for reform*, Working Paper No. 2. Ottawa: Economic Council of Canada.

Dorhan, M. (1988, July 4). Reform of bank charges gets lukewarm reception. *Financial Post*, p. 12.

Dubin, L. (1988, February). Sex with clients: A fatal attraction for lawyers. *National*, p. 25.

Dunlop, B., McQueen, D., & Trebilcock, M. (1987). *Canadian competition policy: A legal and economic analysis.* Toronto: Canada Law Book.

Eccles, W.J. (1964). *Canada under Louis XIV 1663–1701.* The Canadian Centenary Series. Toronto: McClelland & Stewart.

Eccles, W.J. (1965). *The government of New France.* Booklet No. 18. Ottawa: The Canadian Historical Association.

Elliott, P. (1972). *The sociology of the professions.* London: Macmillan.

Ericson, R.V., Baranek, P.M., & Chan, J.B.L. (1987). *Visualizing deviance: A study of news organization.* Toronto: University of Toronto Press.

Ermann, D.M., & Lundman, R.J. (1983). *Corporate deviance.* New York: Holt, Rinehart & Winston.

Financial Times of Canada (1988, December 26). Review of events Dec. 19 to Dec. 25, p. 3.

Francis, R.D., Jones, R., & Smith, D.B. (1988). *Orgins—Canadian history to Confederation.* Toronto: Holt, Rinehart & Winston.

Frank, N., & Lombness, M. (1988) *Controlling corporate illegality.* Cincinnati: Anderson.

Frankel, B.G. (1988). Patient-physician relationships: changing modes of interaction. In S. Bolaria & H.D. Dickinson (Eds.), *Sociology of health care in Canada* (pp. 104–14). Toronto: Harcourt Brace Jovanovich.

Freidson, E. (1986). *Professional powers: A study of the institutionalization of formal knowledge.* Chicago: University of Chicago Press.

Gibson, D. (1983). Distinguishing the governors from the governed: The meaning of "government" under section 32(1) of the Charter. *Manitoba Law Journal, 13*, 505–22.

Globe and Mail. (1988a, November 4). New rules recommended for Alberta planners, p. B12.

Globe and Mail.(1988b, December 21). Investigation revealed real estate boards flirting with prosecution, p. B8.

Globe and Mail. (1989a, April 24). Church launches own probe into cases of sexual abuse, pp. A1-2.

Globe and Mail. (1989b, August 25). 90 Manitoba doctors to keep free computers, p. A3.

Gogolek,V. (1988a, February). Fee schedules get groups in trouble. *National*, p. 7.

Gogolek,V. (1988b, September). Council approves $30,000 budget for paralegals study. *National*, p. 3.

Gorecki, P.K., & Stanbury, W.T. (1984). *The Objectives of Canadian competition policy, 1883-1983.* Montreal: Institute for Research on Public Policy.

Haliechuk, R. (1989, May 12). Ont. lawyer escapes disbarment by agreeing to testify. *Lawyers Weekly*, p. 7.

Hamilton, G. (1989, June 20). Two officials found guilty of insider trading. *Vancouver Sun*, p. C5.

Hamowy, R. (1984). *Canadian medicine: A study in restricted entry.* Vancouver: Fraser Institute.

Hirschi, T., & Gottfredson, M. (1987). Causes of white-collar crime. *Criminology, 25*, 949–74.

Hirschi, T., & Gottfredson, M. (1989). The significance of white-collar crime for a general theory of crime. *Criminology, 27*, 359–72.

Hodgetts, J.E. (1973). *The Canadian public service: A physiology of government, 1867–1970.* Toronto: University of Toronto Press.

Horoszowski, P. (1980). *Economic special opportunity conduct and crimes.* Lexington, MA: Lexington.

Horvitch, S. (1988, September 19). Businesses get break under new banking regulations. *Financial Post*, p. 17.

Hughes, E.C. (1958). *Men and their work.* Toronto: Collier-Macmillan.

Hutchinson, A.C., & Monahan, P. (Eds.). (1987). *The rule of law: Ideal or ideology.* Toronto: Carswell.

Hynes, M. (1989, April 27). Track officials knew of drug use, suspended athlete tells Dubin. *Globe and Mail*, pp. A1–2.

Issalys, P. (1978). The professions tribunal and the control of ethical conduct among professionals. *McGill Law Journal, 24*, 588–625.

Janisch, H.N. (1979). Policy making in regulation: Towards a new definition of the status of independent regulatory agencies in Canada. *Osgoode Hall Law Journal, 17*, 46–106.

Jenkins, A.W. (1986). *The accounting profession in Alberta: An economic analysis of licensure and self-regulatory reforms, and a counter-proposal.* Vancouver: Fraser Institute.

Jones, D.P., & de Villars, A.S. (1985). *Priniciples of administrative law.* Toronto: Carswell.

Kairys, D. (Ed.). (1982). *The politics of law: A progressive critique.* New York: Pantheon.

Kane, G., & Myers, E.R. (1982). The role of self-help in the provision of legal services. In R.G. Evans & M.J. Trebilcock (Eds.),

Lawyers and the consumer interest (pp. 439–59). Toronto: Butterworths.

Kohut, J. (1988, December 21). Court order on realtors' fees big win for competition watchdog. *Globe and Mail*, p. B8.

Larouche, R. (1987). *La sociologie des professions*. Collection Etudes 7. Quebec: Office des professions du Québec.

Laski, H.J. (1935, June–November). The decline of the professions. *Harper's Monthly Magazine*, pp. 676–85.

Law Reform Commission of Canada. (1980). *Independent administrative agencies*. Working Paper No. 25. Ottawa.

Law Society of British Columbia. (1987). Ontario law society stacks up convictions of paralegals. *Annual Report. The Lawyers Weekly* (1988, April 29), p. 18.

Lee, J. (1988, June 6). Financial planning industry taking steps to police itself. *Vancouver Sun*, p. C1.

Levin, H.J. (1967). The limits of self-regulation. *Columbia Law Review*, *67*, 603–44.

Lieberman, J.K. (1978). Some reflections on self-regulation. In P. Slayton & M.J. Trebilcock (Eds.), *The professions and public policy* (pp. 89–97). Toronto: University of Toronto Press.

Lockhart, K. (1985). The Scherer affair. *Canadian Lawyer*, *9*(3), 10–14.

Makin, K. (1988, January 29). Law associations knuckle under in fee schedule fight. *Lawyers Weekly*, p. 2.

Margoshes, D. (1986, August 21). Sex case inquiry urged united front. *Vancouver Sun*, p. A8.

McDonald, R.A. (1985). Understanding regulation by regulation. In I. Bernier & A. Lajoie (Eds.), *Regulations, Crown corporations and administrative tribunals*. Toronto: University of Toronto Press.

McQuaig, L. (1987) *Behind closed doors: How the rich won control of Canada's tax system and ended up richer*. Markham: Viking.

Melnbardis, C. (1989, April 10). Hanging on to your money in the financial planners' jungle. *Financial Times of Canada*, pp. 29–30.

Melnbardis, R. (1988, August 29). Deal splits real estate industry. *Financial Post*, p. 3.

Moya, M. (1988, December 14). Engineer says store beam solid enough. *Vancouver Sun*, p. A14.

Mullens, A. (1989, June 30). Group urges bill to control practice. *Vancouver Sun*, p. A11.

Nagler, J. (1989, August 12). Overbilling an error, Kopyto tells tribunal. *Globe and Mail*, p. A8.

Needham, P. (1989, April 22). Demon-chasing minister, 64, convicted of 8 sex assaults. *Vancouver Sun*, p. A3.

Office des professions du Québec. (1976). *The evolution of professionalism in Quebec*. Quebec: Office des professions du Québec.

Olley, R.E. (1978). The future of self-regulation: A consumer economist's viewpoint. In P. Slayton & M.J. Trebilcock (Eds.), *The professions and public policy* (pp. 77–88). Toronto: University of Toronto Press.

Ostry, S. (1978). Competition policy and the self-regulating professions. In P. Slayton & M.J. Trebilcock (Eds.), *The professions and public policy* (pp. 17–29). Toronto: University of Toronto Press.

Packer, H.L. (1968). *The limits of the criminal sanction*. Stanford: Stanford University Press.

Parsons, T. (1939). The professions and social structure. *Social Forces*, *17*, 457–67.

Pepinsky, H.E. (1974). From white collar crime to exploitation: Redefinition of a field. *Journal of Criminal Law and Criminology*, *65*, 225–33.

Prichard, J.R.S. (1978). Professional civil liability and continuing competence. In P. Slayton & M.J. Trebilcock (Eds.), *The professions and public policy* (pp. 303–20). Toronto: University of Toronto Press.

Ratushny, E. (1987). What are administrative tribunals? The pursuit of uniformity in diversity. *Canadian Public Administration*, *30*, 1–13.

Rhode, D.L. (1981). Policing the professional monopoly: A constitutional and empirical analysis of unauthorized practice. *Stanford Law Review*, *34*, 1–112.

Ritti, R., Ference, T.P., & Goldner, F.H. (1974). Professions and their plausibility: Priests, work and belief systems. *Sociology of Work and Occupations*, *1*.

Roth, J.A. (1974). Professionalism: The sociologist's decoy. *Sociology of Work and Occupations*, *1*, 6–23.

Rothman, R.A. (1984). Deprofessionalization: The case of law in America. *Work and Occupations*, *11*, 183–206.

Saks, M. (1983). Removing the blinkers? A critique of recent contributions to the sociology of the professions. *Sociological Review*, *31*, 1–21.

Scherer, F.M. (1980). *Industrial market structure and economic performance* (2nd ed.). Boston: Houghton Mifflin.

Schultz, R.J. (1979). *Federalism and the regulatory process*. Montreal: Institute for Research on Public Policy.

Shklar, J. (1986). *Legalism: Law, morals, and political trials* (2nd ed.). Cambridge: Harvard University Press.

Simon, D.R., & Eitzen, D.S. (1986). *Elite deviance* (2nd ed.). Boston: Allyn & Bacon.

Smith, W. (1988, March 21). A matter of Principal. *Financial Times of Canada*, pp. 18, 20.

Southin, M.F. (1980). Letter to the editor. *Advocate*, *38*, 464–66.

Stackhouse, J. (1989, March 6). Is that all there is? *Financial Times of Canada*, p. 15.

Stanbury, W.T. (1978). Monopoly, monopolization and joint monopolization: Policy development and Bill C-13. In J.W. Rowley & W.T. Stanbury (Eds.), *Competition policy in Canada: Stage II, Bill C-13* (pp. 133–75). Montreal: Institute for Research on Public Policy.

Stanbury, W.T. (1983). Provincial regulation and federal competition policy: The *Jabour* case. *Windsor Yearbook of Access to Justice*, *3*, 291–347.

Stephenson, B. (1977). The self-governing professions. *The Law Society of Upper Canada Gazette*, *11*, 1–7.

Stone, C.N. (1987). Elite distemper versus the promise of democracy. In G.W. Domhoff & T.R. Dye (Eds.), *Power elites and organizations* (pp. 239–65). Newbury, CA: Sage.

Sutherland, E.H. (1940). White-collar criminality. *American Sociological Review*, *5*, 1–12.

Sutherland, E.H. (1983). *White collar crime: The uncut version* (with an introduction by Gilbert Geis and Colin Goff). New Haven: Yale University Press.

Tawney, R.H. (1921). *The acquisitive society*. London: Victor Gollancz.

Trebilcock, M.J. & Reiter, B.J. (1982). Licensure in law. In R.G. Evans & M.J. Trebilcock (Eds.), *Lawyers and the consumer interest* (pp. 65–103). Toronto: Butterworths.

Tuohy, C.J. (1976). Private government, property, and professionalism. *Canadian Journal of Political Science*, *9*, 668–81.

Tupper, D. (1980). Letter to the editor. *Advocate*, *38*, 464–68.

Usprich, S.J. (1975). *The theory and practice of self-regulation*. Ottawa: Privacy & Computer Task Force.

Vancouver Sun. (1987, November 16). Doctor suspended, fined $10,000, p. A6.

Vancouver Sun. (1988, May 7). British Columbia psychological association. p. B5.

Vancouver Sun. (1989, March 7). Test tipoff pledge alleged by Francis, p. A1.

Vancouver Sun. (1989, March 23). $40,000 fine levied for vse share tampering, p. D10.

Waverman, L. (1979). The new competition policy and regulated industry in Canada, In J.S. Prichard, W.T. Stanbury, & T.A. Wilson (Eds.), *Canadian competition policy: Essays in law and economics* (pp. 375–91). Toronto: Butterworths.

Webb, S. & Webb, B. (1917, April 21). Special supplement on professional associations. *New Statesman, 211,* 1–48.

Westell, D. (1989, August 30). TSE won't collect $4 million Osler fine. *Globe and Mail,* p. B1.

White, K. (1980, October 14). Lawyers haunted by old agreement. *Vancouver Sun,* p. D2.

Williams, B. (1979). Abuse of power by professional self-governing bodies. In *Lectures of the Law Society of Upper Canada* (pp. 345–66). Toronto.

Willis, A., & Melnbardis, R. (1988, August 5). Real estate boards accept standards. *Financial Post,* p. 3.

Robert M. Gordon and

Ian T. Coneybeer[1]

16 Corporate Crime

The Categories of Corporate Criminality

Crimes against Employees and the Issues and Problems in the Field of Corporate Criminality

Corporate Crime in Canada: Future Research

The criminal, illegal, and otherwise questionable activities of business corporations in Canada have a long, fascinating, but underexplored history. As Naylor (1973) has pointed out, the sources of some of the great Canadian fortunes, and the origins of some well-known Canadian businesses and banks, can be traced to such activities as the nefarious commodity and currency dealings of British army contractors in New France, the system of extortion and human and environmental exploitation known as the fur trade, the processing of goods and the laundering of currency acquired through piracy in Nova Scotia and on the Great Lakes, and the practice of seizing and hoarding land and blocking settlement.

The economic history of Canada is filled with examples of corporate wrongdoing, including the exploitation of human and natural resources; pollution of the environment; conspiracies and scandals involving politicians and corporate interests; the formation of illegal monopolies and price-fixing cartels; and the erosion of economic sovereignty through the systematic domination of manufacturing and resource-extraction industries by foreign corporate interests (i.e., the theft of the nation's wealth) (see, e.g., Naylor, 1975; Clement, 1977; Snider, 1988).

Despite both this rich history and the burgeoning international body of research and literature addressing the nature, scope, and impact of corporate **criminality** (see, e.g., Clinard & Yeager, 1980; Geis, 1982; Ermann & Lundman, 1982; Wickman & Dailey, 1982; Simon & Eitzen, 1986), the phenomenon has occupied a low position on the Canadian criminological agenda (Casey, 1985). Indeed, very little had been accomplished by Canadian criminologists up until the late 1970s when Professors Goff and Reasons published their landmark analysis of Canadian anticombines legislation *Corporate Crime in Canada* (1978).

The authors traced the origins and evolution of federal legislation ostensibly aimed at preserving a competitive, free-enterprise system, identified the nature and scope of officially recorded corporate criminality in the period between the early 1950s and the early 1970s, and analyzed critically the federal government's dismal enforcement record.

The results were enlightening, and the text has stimulated a small but growing body of research aimed at describing, analyzing, and explaining Canadian corporate criminality. Studies have included examinations of the links between corporate deviance and profitability (Glasbeek, 1984; Henry, 1986); analyses of the nature and impact of crimes against consumers and employees (Reasons, Ross, & Paterson, 1981; Goff & Reasons, 1986); a review of the content and enforcement of municipal, provincial, and federal laws that protect consumers and the labour force (West & Snider, 1985; Snider, 1988); and a further study of the origins of anticombines legislation (Smandych, 1985).

Canadian research and analysis in the area of corporate crime is, therefore, in its infancy. However, the findings so far are generally consistent with those presented in the international literature, and it is possible to draw a number of general conclusions about corporate criminality in Canada:

1. Corporate criminality is widespread and may be categorized in five ways: crimes against the economy; crimes against the environment; crimes against consumers; crimes against humanity; and crimes against employees.

2. Corporate crime results in considerable material loss or damage and physical injury. It affects both the property and the physical persons of large numbers of Canadians, and the aggregate impact is greater than traditional, predatory street crime. While street crime attracts considerable public and state attention and condemnation, the same is not true of corporate crime. Corporate victimization of, for example, consumers is frequently diffuse, indirect, and of a low-visibility nature; consequently, there is little public awareness of, and concern regarding, harmful illegal actions. In addition, activities are masked by an ideological screen that explains and excuses corporate transgressions as the unfortunate but unavoidable by-product of a commonly beneficial economic system.

3. Despite the considerable social, economic, environmental, and individual harm caused by corporate crime, inappropriate behaviour is rarely defined and regulated through the medium of the **criminal law**, and violators are usually dealt with outside the **criminal-justice system**. Improper activities are defined in separate legislation and handled by special government departments and bodies in a "regulatory" and mediatory, rather than "punitive" manner. The system of regulation and mediation may include government schemes for the protection, compensation, and appeasement of victims.

4. Laws prohibiting forms of corporate behaviour are vaguely worded, weakly enforced, and impose penalties that fail to deter illegal actions, even though the latter frequently result from rational, cost/benefit analyses and might, therefore, be prevented by the likelihood of a strict, punitive response. The state provides only limited resources for the purposes of investigation and prosecution, and this reflects the purely symbolic nature of legislation and enforcement.

5. Laws governing corporate behaviour are constructed by the state in conjunction with corporate interests, and the latter influence the process of identifying and defining inappropriate conduct, specifying the procedures for investigation and prosecution, and determining the kinds of punishments or other **dispositions** that may be applied to offenders.

6. While some forms of corporate activity that result in social, economic, environmental, and individual harm may be defined as illegal, other equally damaging activities are not. There is a gap between official, state expressions of illegality and public sentiment, but there exists a set of universal human values—a higher morality—that transcends state and corporate perceptions and statements of improper conduct. Corporate activities may be quite legal but offend universal human values, fundamental human rights, and basic conceptions of justice, and the term "crime" is, therefore, used in a moral, rather than strictly legal, sense.

7. The causes of corporate criminality are three-dimensional and involve a complex interplay between individual, organizational, and structural factors. Illegal/immoral actions are planned and executed by individuals within and on behalf of their organization, in order to achieve both personal and corporate goals. Corporate goals are determined by the structure and logic of the prevailing economy and, within a capitalist economic system, are generally characterized by one primary consideration: profit maximization.

8. Criminological investigations of corporate transgressions are impeded by a variety of methodological problems; notably, limited research funding, access to data, and the complexities of corporate ownership.

As these general conclusions suggest, the field is characterized by a number of complex issues and problems, and the following constitutes only a brief and introductory examination of the phenomenon of corporate crime. Our chapter begins with a review of the five categories or types of corporate criminality and one of these—crimes against employees—is selected as a medium through which to briefly explore the general conclusions and some of the issues and problems. The discussion concludes with some comments on the possible future direction of Canadian criminological research and analysis in this area.

The Categories of Corporate Criminality

Corporate criminality has been conceptualized, categorized, and analyzed in different ways, and the field of inquiry is characterized by an often confusing array of terms; for example, the phenomenon is variously described as **white-collar crime**, suite crime, commercial crime, elite deviance, crimes of the powerful, upperworld crime, economic crime, organizational crime, and corporate crime. Generally, however, the illegal, criminal, and immoral actions of corporations can be categorized in five main ways: crimes against the economy; crimes against the environment; crimes against humanity; crimes against consumers; and crimes against employees.

In each instance, the category describes the type of person or physical entity upon which the corporate behaviour has a negative impact, and the categories involve a certain degree of overlap. For example, where a crime against the environment (e.g., water pollution) involves the destruction or waste of resources (e.g., fish), it might also constitute a crime against the economy. It is not possible, therefore, to always draw clear distinctions between the categories of crime, and the intention is merely to provide a typology that brings some order to the field and thereby aids analysis and understanding. The word *crime* is employed to characterize the behaviour but, in some instances, the irresponsible and damaging actions of corporations do not attract a formal designation as "criminal"; the word is used, therefore, in a nonlegal sense.

Crimes against the Economy

The term "crimes against the economy" encompasses corporate actions that contravene federal and provincial statutes designed to express, implement, and buttress state economic policies and strategies. These policies and strategies shift in accordance with national and international economic developments, and the types of conduct to be prohibited or regulated will change accordingly. Economic crimes in-

clude: breaches of national and international patent law (i.e., legislation established to protect innovative ideas and inventions, and prevent product piracy); violations of the rules and regulations governing the stock market and designed to prevent unfair and destabilizing practices (e.g., market manipulations aimed at enhancing the value of shares); and breaches of statutes aimed at protecting competition. The best-known example of this type of legislation is the federal **Competition Act**: a statute (formerly, the Combines Investigation Act) which is ostensibly aimed at preserving a competitive, free-enterprise, capitalist, economic system by, among other matters, regulating the extent to which economic power becomes concentrated in the hands of large, national, multinational, or transnational corporations.

The statute makes provision for the "general regulation of trade and commerce in respect of conspiracies, trade practices and mergers affecting competition" (s.18), and the official purpose is

> to maintain and encourage competition in Canada in order to promote the efficiency and adaptability of the Canadian economy, in order to expand opportunities for Canadian participation in world markets while at the same time recognizing the role of foreign competition in Canada, in order to ensure that small and medium-sized enterprises have an equitable opportunity to participate in the Canadian economy and in order to provide consumers with competitive prices and product choices. (s.19)

The extent to which the statute will accomplish these objectives (i.e., regulate the "merger mania" associated with the growth of monopoly capitalism), the corporate interests that have influenced its content, and the links with the "free-trade" issue, are the subjects of a debate that cannot be examined here.[2] For our purposes, it is sufficient to note that the statute both amends and preserves some provisions of the former Combines Investigation Act, and that it does so in accordance with new, state economic policies. The act either prohibits various forms of business activity or requires that these be subjected to review by a competition tribunal that may either approve or prohibit the behaviour. The activities include: (1) conspiracies, combines, and agreements that limit production and trade, increase prices, or restrict competition; (2) restrictive trade practices such as "refusal to deal" (e.g., refusing to supply products to another business) and "abuse of a dominant position" (e.g., an "anticompetitive act" involving the use of fighting brands introduced temporarily and selectively to discipline or eliminate a competitor); and (3) corporate mergers that prevent or lessen competition. Violations of the various provisions of the Competition Act and the decisions of the competition tribunal (e.g., **prohibition**

orders) attract penalties and constitute crimes against the economy.

Crimes against the Environment

The term "crimes against the environment" encompasses corporate actions that result in a general or specific pollution of land, air, and water; the contamination of both human beings and the sources of human nutrition; the depletion or destruction of species of fauna, flora, and marine and aerial life; or the wanton destruction and waste of valuable resources. Pollution, depletion, and destruction may be the consequences of the actions of an individual corporation (e.g., the discharge of toxic-waste substances into a river system), the outcome of an accumulation of industries in one particular area (e.g., acid rain), or the collective effect of global industrial activity (e.g., the global warming trend known as the "greenhouse effect" and the erosion of the ozone layer). Regardless, the impact upon the human and natural environment is immense and the consequences of 200 years of industrial growth and uncontrolled pollution and destruction are now appearing. As David Suzuki has recently pointed out,[3]

> In 30 years, all the curves indicate that there will be no wilderness left on the planet . . . it will all have been destroyed or put into tiny little parks. . . . In ten years, there will be no coastal rain forest left in British Columbia. . . . In 150 years, 50 percent of all plant and animal species will be extinct, and in 200 years, 80 percent will be extinct.
>
> Our problem today is that we live with one of the most pernicious and dangerous notions going . . . every politician, every businessman, every economist will say, "We must have growth" . . . it is the demand for growth and the steady increase in consumption that is destroying this planet, and yet we demand we have more.

The issue of crimes against the environment points, therefore, to an interesting contradiction. Pollution, the destruction of species, and the rapid consumption of non-renewable resources are the by-products of corporate activity within an economy dominated by the logic of profit maximization and the associated principle of endless consumption. Growth is seen as essential but results in both the steady destruction of the environment which sustains the life necessary for consumption (economic growth ceases when there are no humans left to purchase commodities), and the rapid depletion of the resources necessary for production.

In order to resolve this contradiction, in the interests of continued economic growth and profit maximization, the state must take action to control the activities of corporations. In addition, there is little doubt that governments are under mounting pressure to address the issue of environmental damage and that they cannot hope to retain legitimacy if they fail to respond to, in particular, the arguments and evidence presented by individual environmentalists such as David Suzuki, and independent bodies such as Greenpeace. Just as human- and civil-rights issues became a major concern during the 1960s and 1970s, and resulted in significant and lasting social reforms, so environmental protection and environmental rights will likely become major social and economic issues during the 1990s and into the next century.

There are already signs of a shift in policy at the federal and provincial levels, the objective being to ensure "environmentally sustainable economic growth." The Law Reform Commission of Canada has recommended a formal "criminalization" of actions that damage the environment and proposed that provision be made for "crimes against the environment" in the **Criminal Code** (Law Reform Commission, 1985). At the provincial level, there are some signs that governments are willing to prosecute blatant offenders and that the courts are prepared to hand down stiff sentences. For example, in 1986, the president of a Toronto company was sentenced to one year in prison for defying a court order halting the dumping of dangerous wastes into the city sewer system: the first time a corporate polluter had been jailed in Canada (Reasons, 1987). The extent to which this punitive response was merely a symbolic act remains to be seen. As Emond (1984) has pointed out, the thrust of most provincial legislation in this area is to regulate and legalize, rather than to prohibit, industrial pollution, and this may be a product of the difficulties faced by the state in introducing statutes that interfere with economic growth and short-term profitability (see also Rankin & Finkle, 1983).

As many analysts have noted (see, e.g., Ruggeri, 1981; Swaijen, 1981; Caputo, 1989), the nation's environmental-protection strategy is incoherent, uncertain; expressed through a complex body of statutes, regulations, policies and principles; and implemented by a confusing variety of regulatory bodies that lack the resources necessary to enforce laws. This may change as the public demand for the prohibition of environmental pollution and destruction mounts. In the interim, corporations will likely continue to dump their wastes in oceans and rivers, discharge pollutants into the atmosphere, and engage in other forms of environmental damage (see Box 16.1). Indisputably wrong, such behaviour is a prime example of corporate wrongdoing that should perhaps be defined as "criminal."

Box 16.1 Pollution and Crime

In January 1989, Inco Ltd. was fined $80 000 for releasing two tonnes of sulphur trioxide into the atmosphere, from the Copper Cliff refinery in Ontario. The incident occurred in August 1987. The contaminant combined with water vapour to form a cloud of sulphuric-acid mist one kilometre long and half a kilometre wide. This drifted over residential and summer resort areas and descended on a Girl Guide camp and a Ukrainian children's camp. Those caught in the mist experienced coughing, choking, vomiting, and burning eyes and noses, and 150 people were treated in hospital. The release was due, in part, to the failure of three safety systems, one of which had been deliberately by-passed during an earlier, routine plant shutdown. Other warning equipment failed to operate. In addition to paying the fine, Inco publicly apologized for the incident.

In February 1989, researchers announced that nursing mothers in northern Quebec had dangerously high levels of toxic polychlorinated biphenyls (PCBs) in their breast milk. The mothers were inadvertently contaminating their infants. The levels of PCBs were higher than those recorded anywhere else in the world and were the result of the consumption of fish and fat from marine life: foods in which PCBs tend to concentrate. The toxins descended with the rain and snow and probably came from industrial areas in the south.

In March 1989, a secret report compiled by Environment Canada was leaked to the press. This report indicated that 83 of the 149 pulpmills in Canada were dumping toxic chemicals (i.e., organochlorines, including the poison dioxin) into waterways at a rate and level higher than national pollution standards allowed. Fish and other marine life were being contaminated. The worst offenders were pulpmills in British Columbia and Quebec. The report indicated that the pulp-and-paper industry was choosing not to invest in pollution control.

In March 1989, an Environment Canada study of pollution in Vancouver harbour was released. High levels of lead, chromium, and petroleum hydrocarbons were found on the seabed, and bottom-feeding fish (notably sole) were found to have precancerous liver lesions or tumours. The pollution appeared to originate with the chemical works and petroleum refineries along the shoreline.

As these examples demonstrate, the pollution created by the activities of corporations can result in serious harm to not only the natural environment but also human beings. The harm may be immediate and direct, as in the cloud of sulphuric acid released from the Inco refinery. The harm may be long-term and indirect and involve the contamination of water that then affects one source of human food (e.g., fish), and consequently, the people who eat it.

While pollution can cause severe physical harm to humans, it is not treated in the same way as other physically damaging acts. It is not, for example, viewed and dealt with as a criminal assault. It is not defined as a "crime" in the Criminal Code, although there is growing public sentiment that it should be, particularly where the pollution is willful or reckless. Yet, if an individual entered a Girl Guide summer camp and began to spray people with a sulphuric-acid solution, or if an individual poisoned food in, for example, a supermarket, the full weight of the criminal law and the criminal-justice system would be brought to bear on the offender. Fines, public apologies, and assurances that the behaviour would not be repeated would not be deemed sufficient.

Where corporations are responsible for direct assaults on, or the slow poisoning of, human beings, their actions are defined and dealt with differently. A vast array of federal and provincial "anti-pollution" legislation exists and penalties may be imposed upon corporations that fail to comply with pollution "standards." The objective, however, is not to stop pollution but merely to contain it within "acceptable" boundaries. Corporations are granted permits to pollute: they are allowed to deliberately contaminate the environment and will only be restrained if they exceed the "safety" limits prescribed by government departments.

The validity of these "safe limits" has been challenged by environmentalists who point to, for example, the failure to account for the long-term, cumulative effects of continuous pollution. In addition, there is evidence that the permit system is ineffective. For example, two recent studies of the enforcement of the waste-management permit system in British Columbia have demonstrated that companies are persistently exceeding allowable pollution limits but are rarely prosecuted for doing so. The average fine imposed for a violation of the provision of provincial waste management legislation is $565. Once a permit has been issued, corporations are free to contaminate the environment without fear of prosecution. Even if prosecution does occur, the penalties are minor. Indeed, it is cheaper to pollute and pay the fines than it is to install pollution control equipment. The harm caused to both the environment and human beings does not appear to enter the corporate cost/benefit analysis.

Crimes against Consumers

Crimes against consumers include **price-fixing**, price-gouging, deceptive and misleading advertising, and the production and marketing of defective or dangerous products. Activities such as price-fixing (i.e., agreements among "competitors" to keep the price of a product artificially high in order to maximize profit), price-gouging (e.g., using contrived or real shortages of raw materials such as sugar, coffee, and oil to increase the price of products), and misleading advertising, each results in some form of material loss. The impact upon *individual* consumers may be minimal since, for example, a price-fixing cartel in the petroleum industry may cost a consumer only a fraction of a cent per litre at the gas pump. However, the *aggregate* impact will be massive and can result in enormous profits for the corporations involved. Defective or dangerous products (e.g., inadequately tested drugs, poorly designed automobiles, faulty aircraft parts, and adulterated foodstuffs such as canned tuna) can cause physical harm and will often become evident at the individual and aggregate levels as a result of deaths, foetal deformities, injuries, and sickness.

Consumers are protected by legislation governing business activities and, at the federal level, the provisions of statutes such as the Competition Act, the **Food and Drug Act**, and the Hazardous Products Act prohibit misleading advertising and packaging and the sale of unfit, harmful, or dangerous foods, drugs, cosmetics, and other products. The provinces have also introduced consumer-protection legislation governing such matters as the licensing and regulation of some businesses (e.g., those dealing in securities); the form and use of agreements to purchase goods; the disclosure of the full cost of borrowing money to buy a product (e.g., a new automobile); and advertising practices (West & Snider, 1985).

An impressive array of federal and provincial legislation is, therefore, in existence, and corporations that violate the provisions of the statutes face both fines and the payment of redress to victims. In some instances, individual employees can be imprisoned. However, as Goff and Reasons (1978, 1986), West and Snider (1985) and Snider (1988) have shown, enforcement is minimal, the penalties imposed are usually weak and ineffective, and the primary target of government agencies appears to be small- or medium-sized businesses, rather than the large corporations.

Crimes against Humanity

The term "crimes against humanity" encompasses a range of corporate activity that is quite legal (indeed, it may be encouraged by the state) but that violates universal human values, that is, a "higher morality." In other words, corporate activities may be legal because they are not deemed *mala prohibita* (wrongs that are recognized and prohibited by the law) but, nevertheless, be deemed immoral or *mala in se*: acts that are wrong in themselves but not recognized as such in law. To use a well-known example: during the early 1940s, the German chemical manufacturing company I.G. Farben used slave labour from concentration camps to construct factories for the production of synthetic oil and rubber. The prisoners were, literally, worked to death or reduced to the point of death. Along with other "useless" prisoners, the spent labourers were then placed in gas chambers where they were killed with Zyklon B, a substance manufactured by a company that was partly owned by I.G. Farben. The bodies then became a resource—hair for mattresses, fat for soap (Borkin, 1978). An exceptional case, perhaps, but one that conveys the main point: the activity was perfectly legal according to the laws in force in Germany at the time (it was not *mala prohibita*), but violated an overriding set of universal human values, or "higher morality," which, regardless of the content of laws, views enslavement and genocide as wrong (*mala in se*).

A major problem arises, however, in regard to classifying less outrageous and more contemporary forms of corporate activity as "crimes against humanity." It can be argued that the "warfare industry"—the multibillion-dollar business of manufacturing and selling equipment and weapons for the waging of war—is a crime against humanity since it results in death and destruction. But is this a fair and reasonable categorization? Similarly, are corporate involvement in the destabilization of the political and economic system of a foreign nation (e.g., Chile) or the deliberate underdevelopment of Third World countries in order to ensure a continuous supply of cheap raw materials and labour, to be classified as "crimes"?

It will be evident that the activities of many corporations could be classified as "crimes against humanity" but that the process of designation involves a value-laden interpretation of the tenets of a "higher morality." However, the corporate practices of both dumping unsafe products and irresponsibly marketing products in Third World countries have attracted widespread condemnation and provide a clear, contemporary example of corporate practices that are legal but, arguably, wrong. Corporate dumping involves the export and sale of products that have been declared unsafe in a corporation's home country. Examples of unsafe products that have been dumped by American corporations include the Dalkon Shield; a contraceptive substance known as Depo-Provera; various medicinal preparations; pesticides; and baby pacifiers and teething rings (Simon & Eitzen, 1986). The best-known example of irresponsible marketing involved the sale of baby formula to the inhabitants of poverty-stricken nations. The sale of baby formula by at least one company—Nestlé—was alleged to have caused the death of 10 000 babies per year because their parents were mixing formula with impure water. Millions of cases of infant starvation and diarrhea also allegedly occurred because parents who were unable to afford supplies of formula were diluting the product (Simon & Eitzen, 1986). This particular practice ceased as a result of an international boycott of the offending corporations, organized by the Interfaith Center on Corporate Responsibility: a body that justified its actions by reference to a "higher morality."

It is of interest to note that, in 1983, eight bishops of the Social Affairs Commission of the Canadian Conference of Catholic Bishops released a statement—"Ethical Reflections on the Economic Crisis"—criticizing the national economic situation. Their concerns were "inspired by the gospel message of Jesus Christ" and cited "two fundamental gospel principles": the "preferential option for the poor, the afflicted, and the oppressed" and "the special value and dignity of human work in God's plan for Creation" (Block, 1983, p. 68). In the bishops' view, Canadian economic policies violated these principles. No attempt was made to explicitly define the state and corporate activities that had produced the economic situation as a "crime against humanity," but this was an implicit component of the message. The management of the economy had not involved the violation of formal laws but it had offended a "higher morality."

Finally, we turn to our fifth category of corporate criminality and the subject of a more detailed analysis: "crimes against employees."

Crimes against Employees and the Issues and Problems in the Field of Corporate Criminality

Crimes against employees fall into three main groups: actions that result in material loss; actions that result in physical harm; and actions that interfere with the legitimate organization of labour (i.e., unions). Material loss can occur where employers effectively steal from their workers by violating provincial legislation or employer/employee agreements governing working conditions and the payment of the minimum wage. Violations of working conditions involve practices such as requiring that an employee work excessive hours; refusing to pay for overtime; refusing pregnancy leave; arbitrary dismissal; discrimination; and unreasonably withholding vacation pay, termination pay, or outstanding wages (West & Snider, 1985). Physical harm may result from violations of occupational health-and-safety legislation, rules, or standards. Corporate interference with

Photo 16.1   Farm workers continue to be denied protection from pesticide-related hazards, including field applications of pesticides, during which workers are sprayed, and exposed to the kind of inadequate and unregulated container dump site shown above.
Canadian Farmworkers' Union.

the organization of labour may occur where deliberate efforts are made to obstruct union participation and related activities. Arguably, a fourth type of "crime" also exists where employees are directed to engage in other categories of corporate wrongdoing; for example, dumping toxic waste into a river thereby causing environmental pollution. Sexual and other forms of harassment might constitute a fifth type of "crime." Each of these areas deserves a thorough explication but, for want of space, the focus of this discussion will be upon crimes that result in physical harm to employees.

Corporate activities that result in illnesses, diseases, injuries, and death can be divided into two categories: pollution in the working environment and operating practices that create workplace hazards that endanger employees. The nature, scope, and impact of workplace pollution have been the subjects of a recent report by the Law Reform Commission of Canada (1986), and this document provides an excellent review of the issues and problems in the area.

Workplace pollution is caused by physical and chemical agents that have an immediate or long-term impact upon the health of employees. The inhalation of toxic gases (e.g., hydrogen cyanide or nitrogen) and exposure to poisonous substances (e.g., lead) are examples of pollution that have an immediate impact and result in either death or sickness. Pollutants that have a long-term impact include:
   —silica particles, the inhalation of which causes a respiratory disease known as silicosis;
   —asbestos fibres, the inhalation of which causes a respiratory disease known as asbestosis;

—coal dust, the inhalation of which causes a respiratory condition known as "black lung."

The list of physical and chemical pollutants to which employees may be exposed is enormous, varied, and growing as researchers isolate the causes of work-related illnesses, diseases, and death. In addition to silicosis and other respiratory diseases, pollutants have been shown to cause (or are believed, with high levels of probability, to cause) cancers, sterility, birth defects, damage to the brain and nervous system, and many other ailments (Law Reform Commission of Canada, 1986).

Employees, particularly in the manufacturing, construction, and resource-extraction industries, may be killed or injured as a result of unsafe working conditions (Reasons, Ross & Paterson, 1981). Examples include:

—unguarded, improperly maintained, or malfunctioning machinery in manufacturing industries;

—mine and quarry explosions, cave-ins, and fires;

—logging operations involving the improper felling of trees and handling of logs, and overloading equipment and cables;

—construction-site incidents caused by, for example, the

collapse of scaffolding and cranes, falling equipment and materials, equipment malfunctions and overloading, design faults, and trench cave-ins (i.e., inadequate shoring-up or roping-off);

—oil-drilling incidents caused by improper or inadequate rig maintenance, the best-known example being the Piper Alpha rig disaster in the North Sea.

Both workplace pollution and unsafe working conditions result in considerable physical harm to employees. As the Law Reform Commission points out: "In 1982, there were 854 fatal on-the-job accidents in Canada, and more than half a million cases of disabling accidents or work-related illnesses. Between 1972 and 1981, more than 10,000 Canadians died from injuries received on the job . . ." (1986, p.5).

The risk of being killed at work is greatest in the primary industries, particularly in forestry and mining. In British Columbia, for example, forestry is the most hazardous industry and 144 loggers have been killed since 1984 (see Farrow, 1988).

Nationally, the fatality rate in forestry in 1982 was 119.7 deaths per 100 000 employees, while the fatality rate in mining, quarrying, and oil wells was 83.6 per 100 000 (Law Reform Commission of Canada, 1986). Estimates of the rates of sickness, disease, and injury cannot be determined accurately because of underreporting (injuries may be concealed by employers in order to protect their workers' compensation assessments) and, in the case of ailments caused by some forms of pollution, because of the long period of time between exposure and the appearance of a disease or sickness (Law Reform Commission of Canada, 1986). In addition, 15 to 20 percent of the Canadian labour force is not covered by Workers' Compensation and, therefore, is not represented in official data (Tataryn, 1979). Nevertheless, estimates of the rate of sickness, injury, and death have been made, together with comparisons with the rate of injury and death caused by traditional, predatory street crime.

Reasons, for example, argues that, on average, every working day, an employee is killed every two hours, and an injury occurs every six seconds. In his view,

occupational death remains the third leading cause of death in Canada, following heart disease and cancer, and twice as common as motor vehicle death. You are 18 times more likely to die from work than from criminal murder, and 28 times more likely to meet violence from work than from criminal assault. (1987, p.7)

Photo 16.2   The unregulated disposal of pesticide containers exposes farm workers, many of whom cannot speak English, to unnecessary dangers: the child farm worker above is drinking water from a pesticide container.

Canadian Farmworkers' Union (Craig Conde-Berghold).

Reasons, Ross, and Paterson (1981) point out that, while Criminal Code assaults in 1979 numbered 103 391, work-related assaults totalled approximately 1 296 121. Forty-six percent of these workplace assaults were categorized as "dis-

Photo 16.3   The deaths of four men working on the Bentall Tower in Vancouver in 1981 sparked the formation of the B.C. Health and Safety Council.

The Vancouver Province (Peter Hulbert).

abling.'' Boal (1985) points out that, in 1982, the actions of impaired drivers in British Columbia resulted in 6221 injuries. There is widespread acceptance of this behaviour as a "crime," and therefore it is worthy of considerable state attention. In the same year, there were 67 655 work-related injuries and 176 confirmed fatalities, in British Columbia alone, and at least twice this number die each year from unacknowledged diseases originating in the workplace.

The Law Reform Commission of Canada (1986) estimates that approximately 135 000 employees in Ontario are directly or indirectly exposed to ten different types of hazardous workplace pollutants including cadmium, chlorine, formaldehyde, and nickel. Many other hazards (e.g., asbestos and silica particles) exist but the number of workers affected is unknown. It is estimated that 200 000 to 500 000 workers throughout Canada are needlessly exposed to radioactive materials and chemical pollutants each year (Casey, 1985).

In the United States, it has been estimated that 100 000 workers die and 390 000 are disabled each year as a result of occupational disease, and that five times as many people die each year from work-related disease and injury as are murdered by all street criminals (Simon & Eitzen, 1986). American researchers have predicted 5000 deaths per year, for the next 30 to 35 years, as a result of exposure to asbestos fibres (Henry, 1986). As Goff and Reasons (1978) suggest, corporate deviance may not only cost the public purse more money than street crime, it also appears to be responsible for more extensive physical harm as a consequence of "accidents," diseases, and death. In short, corporate crimes may cause greater destruction, loss, and physical harm than all the activities that fall within the purview of the criminal-justice system.

The various statistics and associated projections are helpful in understanding the nature, scope, and impact of unsafe working conditions, and the extent to which these conditions result in greater harm than do traditional, predatory street crimes. However, the data are open to dispute, and a valid and reliable picture of "violence" in the workplace has yet to be fully developed. Nevertheless, three general conclusions can be drawn:

1. Workplace pollutants and unsafe working conditions result in alarming rates of death, injury, disease, and sickness. Vast numbers of employees are exposed to hazards without knowing the risks involved and without being aware that they are affected.

2. In addition to the human toll, unsafe working conditions have an adverse impact upon productivity; for example, in 1986, more than 1.9 million workdays were lost as a result of workplace injuries and diseases in British Columbia alone.[4]

3. Unsafe working conditions are more costly in human and economic terms than is traditional, predatory street crime, and employees are more likely to be victims of "assault" in the workplace than on the streets. Violence in the workplace is frequently caused by the callous, negligent, and often illegal practices of employers but the behaviour is not defined and treated as "crime" (see Box 16.2).

Deaths and injuries in the workplace are often attributed to either the carelessness or the incompetence of workers, or unavoidable accidents (West & Snider, 1985; Snider,

1988), and there is little doubt that this is sometimes the case. However, deaths, injuries, disease, and sickness also arise from the practices of employers; particularly, a failure to minimize risks in the workplace by, for example, properly maintaining or guarding machinery, or, as the following cases demonstrate, protecting employees from the dangerous and known effects of pollutants.

In 1982, a millwright employed at the MacMillan-Bloedel Alpulp operation in Port Alberni, British Columbia, died, seventeen days before his retirement, while repairing a leak in a pipe. Although the Canadian Paperworkers Union had protested the work conditions eighteen months prior to the worker's death, the individual was exposed to 45 times the "allowable" limits of methyl mercaptan, 320 times the "safe" limit of hydrogen-sulphide gas, and an undetermined amount of dimethyl-sulphide gas. When an inquest was held, it was discovered that workers were left to rely upon their olfactory senses or a portable gas sniffer that no one was sure was properly calibrated or even worked at all. Only days earlier, another millwright had been told at a company safety meeting that leaking methyl-mercaptan gas was not harmful, although it could cause nausea. This worker had also worked on the leaking pipe and stated that his personal limit for working near the gas

---

Box 16.2   A Crime against the Environment, Employees, and Humanity: The Sysco Case

Since the mid-1980s, the Sydney Steel Corporation of Sydney, Nova Scotia, has been associated with one of the most dangerous chemical dump sites in Canada. The corporation began to manufacture steel in the early 1900s and, for more than 80 years, engaged in the practice of depositing waste in "tar ponds" in the area surrounding the plant. The site, which is close to the downtown Sydney area and encompasses part of an inlet known as Muggah Creek, contains 700 000 tonnes of black, toxic material, including cancer-causing polynuclear aromatic hydrocarbons and twenty other dangerous substances.

In spring 1988, the major source of the pollutants—a battery of obsolete, open-hearth coke ovens—was permanently closed for economic reasons. Prior to this closure, Sysco coke-oven workers had been regularly exposed to a toxic combination of contaminants, including 66 types of polynuclear aromatic hydrocarbons, 7 types of gases, 4 types of polynuclear aza-heterocyclic compounds, and 2 types of aromatic amines.

After considerable pressure was exerted by environmentalists and steel workers in the mid 1980s, a $34 million clean-up operation was arranged by federal and provincial

environmental-protection agencies. However, little appears to have been accomplished and, once the operation begins, it seems likely that some contamination may be overlooked. Despite the fact that the coking operations occurred at a point above the Sydney municipality water tables, the benzol-saturated soil has not been slated for clean-up. Similarly, the sediment on the bottom of Sydney harbour, which contains polychlorinated biphenyls (PCBs), polynuclear aromatic hydrocarbons, and benzopyrene, has not been deemed worthy of attention. While the Nova Scotia environmental-protection authorities discounted the possibility of PCB concentration in the tar ponds, the Steelworkers Union contended that enormous quantities of the transformer coolant had, for generations, been indiscriminately dumped on the site. The local lobster fishery was closed in the early 1980s because of pollution caused by tar-pond leakage.

The predominantly working-class community in the vicinity of the Sysco plant and its dump site has been affected by a higher-than-average cancer rate. An unpublished report, issued by the director of the federal Bureau of Chemical Hazards in August 1985, indicated that coke-oven

Box 16.2 (Continued)

pollution could be expected to result in increases of morbidity and mortality in the coke-plant workers and probably in the residents of Sydney.

Two Environment Canada reports, both classified as "restricted" and intended only for internal circulation, revealed that the coke- and steel-making operations violated the provisions of the federal Clean Air Act. The emissions were between 2800 and 6000 percent higher than "allowable" standards. Workers had been advised that paper masks provided adequate protection from pollution, while residents in the neighbourhoods surrounding the Sysco plant were told to consume greater quantities of broccoli in order to counter the high incidence of cancer.

The closure of the coke ovens resulted in the layoff of 125 employees (some with 40 years' service), with no severance pay, workers' compensation benefits, or pensions for the widows of deceased coke workers. An investigation organized and funded by fired employees resulted in the formation, in 1987, of Coke Oven Workers United for Justice. This organization found that, of 103 worker deaths over a 25-year period, 64 died of cancer: a frequency almost six times the national average. Despite these and other findings, Sysco refuses to recognize that workers were exposed

to pollutants, and denies that the work site was hazardous. For example, when one eighteen-year veteran of the coke ovens, with a 41 percent loss of lung function, applied for compensation, Sysco's superintendent of personnel services advised the Nova Scotia Workers' Compensation Board that the corporation was not aware of the claimant being exposed to a hazardous working environment.

The willingness of workers to tolerate the dangerous working conditions may seem puzzling but can be easily explained: there was little, if any, choice. In an area historically high in unemployment, workers dared not complain about working conditions because the fear of being without a job, when there was no hope of obtaining another, outweighed any risk to health. In addition, Sysco continually reassured workers that they had no cause for concern. Industrial blackmail kept coke-oven workers quiet for decades. With the ovens closed and the jobs gone, the blackmail is no longer effective.

In the view of the Steelworkers Union, the behaviour of Sysco warrants criminal prosecution. This, however, seems extremely unlikely despite the evidence of the serious physical harm caused to the environment, employees, and the people living and working in the city of Sydney.

was when his mouth went numb. When the dead millwright was admitted for autopsy, the chemical odour was so overpowering that the door of the autopsy room had to be left open for ventilation.[5]

In October 1986, employees of Stelco—an Ontario-based steel manufacturer—underwent blood tests for polychlorinated bi-phenyl (PCB) contamination, after a plant electrician was found to have three times the "safe" level of contamination. PCBs have been linked to cancers of the skin, liver, and digestive system, as well as birth defects and neurological damage. Some 800 workers in Stelco's electrical division were regularly exposed to PCBs during the servicing of transformers, and cases of cancer have been discovered among these workers. In addition, PCB coolant was being poured on the ground outside the plant's transformer compound and, on occasion, sprayed on company parking lots to control dust during the summer months.[6]

Despite the availability of information concerning the dangers associated with asbestos, every ferry acquired by or constructed for the B.C. Ferry Corporation between 1961 and 1975 contained extensive quantities of the material. As a result of union agitation and a report by an indepen-

dent company, a decision was made to remove the asbestos. A contractor, hired to complete the work, threatened to lay off workers if the company was required to comply with safety regulations during the abatement operation.[7]

During the construction of the Four Seasons Hotel in the Pacific Centre in Vancouver, crews were applying a spray while other workers were required to remain in the vicinity. The spraying occurred in underground areas, and workers could see particulate matter in the air every day. Repeated inquiries were made of the employer and the Workers' Compensation Board, but a satisfactory explanation was never forthcoming. Workers were simply told the job site was "safe". Two years later, the painter-foreman stated that representatives of both the employer and the Workers' Compensation Board had told him to "keep his mouth shut" about the asbestos in the spray.[8]

In November 1987, it was discovered that employees at the McDonnell-Douglas plant in Toronto had been exposed to the carcinogenic chemical Alodine. The chemical manufacturer had warned the corporation of the danger but the chemical was stored in vast, open vats at various locations around the plant. Employees were told that the substance might cause ulceration of mucous membranes, but many of those who handled the chemical developed serious skin and respiratory ailments.[9]

The Farmworkers Union has discovered that, at one of the largest farms in the Fraser Valley in British Columbia, workers are being required to undertake between ten and twelve hours of continuous pesticide application, every day, without protective apparel. The clothing of workers becomes soaked, and the union reports at least one case of an individual who is suffering from permanent neurological impairment, which manifests itself as a sense of intoxication, nausea, blurred vision, and the "shakes." In 1982, another worker was caught in a pesticide-spray drift—a common occurrence—and, within two months, died from organophosphate insecticide poisoning.[10]

As these examples demonstrate, the responsibility for deaths, injuries, diseases, and sickness cannot always be laid at the door of the workforce. It is not valid simply to "blame

Photo 16.4   One construction worker was killed and four were injured at Vancouver's Fisherman's Wharf in 1977 when a hammerhead crane collapsed during construction of a high-rise building. A subsequent investigation revealed that the crane had not been recently inspected, and crew workers had not been given proper training.

Vancouver Sun (Glen Baglo).

the victims." Physical harm can be prevented but there is ample evidence of a routine failure to protect employees. Indeed, many corporations and employers seem more concerned with the protection of machinery and equipment than their labour force. For example, when new I.B.M. computer systems are installed in pulpmills, they require a controlled environment that is airconditioned and free of dust, corrosion, and vibration. Companies expend large sums of money to create "safe" environments for machines, but fail to extend the same concern to human resources.[11]

Two interlocking questions arise: Why do preventable deaths, injuries, diseases and sickness occur? Why is it that corporate wrongdoing in this area is not defined and dealt, with as "crime"? An answer to the first question can be secured by examining a general, three-dimensional, explanatory model that may be used to explain all forms of corporate "crime." An answer to the second question requires an examination of the relationship among corporate interests, the prevailing economic system, and the body that constructs and enforces legislation: the state.

The Causes of Corporate Crime

The body of Canadian and international literature addressing the phenomenon of corporate "crime" suggests that an explanation lies within three interlocking areas: the behaviour of individuals; the nature and imperatives of the organizations (i.e., corporations) within which individuals work; and the structure and imperatives of the economic system within which corporations operate (see e.g., Snider, 1988, and Figure 16.1). We shall briefly examine each of these areas and demonstrate how, in combination, they provide a comprehensive explanation of corporate actions that cause physical harm to employees. In so doing, the utility of the model for explaining other categories of corporate criminality (e.g., crimes against the environment) should become evident.

The individual level is of importance in understanding corporate criminality since it is people—owners, executives, managers, and supervisors—who implement (and sometimes plan) corporate wrongdoing. The question is: Why do they do it? Can the motivation for the behaviour be reduced to "need" (i.e., material gain to meet personal requirements or commitments), "greed" (i.e., material gain to satisfy particular personal goals), and "opportunity" (i.e., the availability of chances to satisfy need and greed)? These factors may be relevant and cannot be entirely discounted but they do not explain entirely the behaviour of those who, often deliberately, endanger the lives of others. In this regard, the famous American criminologist and pioneer of studies of "white-collar crime," Edwin Sutherland, utilized his general theory of "**differential association**" to explain the behaviour of errant business people, and this includes some persuasive and empirically verified propositions. Of particular importance is Sutherland's claim that individuals within corporations carry out illegal or improper actions as a consequence of learning (through association with others) both the ways of actually committing an act (i.e., the techniques involved) and the rationalizations necessary to override or "neutralize" moral constraints on behaviour (e.g., that it is improper to break the law, or put others at risk) (Sutherland, 1949).

Sutherland's theory may be used to explain the actions of the individuals who commit "crimes" against employees. Those responsible for exposing employees to hazards learn (from other managers or supervisors) not only the tactics necessary to persuade workers to carry out dangerous tasks, but also the ways of justifying such behaviour. Managers or supervisors might, for example, learn how to rationalize their actions by persuading themselves that, while workers are endangered, they receive high wages and are, therefore, well compensated for taking unavoidable risks. Alternatively, an employer might mobilize the notion of "choice," that is, the idealistic conception that any worker is always free to leave and seek employment in another industry if he or she does not wish to be exposed to hazards. As the Law Reform Commission of Canada suggests, these are common but ill-founded rationalizations for endangering the lives of workers (Law Reform Commission, 1986).

The extent to which Sutherland's theory is applicable in the context of Canadian corporate crime has yet to be determined. Consequently, issues such as the process of learning both the techniques and the rationalizations necessary to carry out, for example, crimes against employees, and the anatomy of these rationalizations, remain unexplored. However, the theory is compelling and may help to explain the actions of individuals. At the same time, the theory has limitations; for example, it is concerned more with explaining *how* improper actions can be carried out than with *why* they are committed in the first place. To understand the latter, it is necessary to shift to the next sphere of analysis: the nature and imperatives of organizations.

As Goff and Reasons (1986) and Snider (1988) point out, a full understanding of corporate crime requires an analysis of the behaviour of individuals within the context of an organization. Improper actions may be planned and carried out in order to achieve personal goals but these are usually linked to the body that can satisfy these objectives: the organization (e.g., a corporation) that employs the individual. The corporation is the source of material and psychological rewards (e.g., a higher salary and promotion) for those who comply with or facilitate organizational objec-

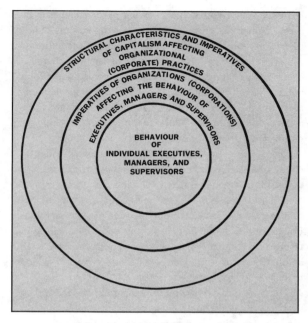

Figure 16.1 Corporate Crime: A General Explanatory Model

tives and, while the latter may be perfectly legitimate, the means by which they are accomplished may not. Ambitious employees may engage in illegal or improper behaviour in order to be rewarded, and it is in this sense that the organization is the cause of transgressions by individuals.

A corporation may, therefore, place direct and indirect pressure on an executive, manager, or supervisor to "cut corners" and take risks in order to achieve organizational goals (e.g., increased productivity, or the timely completion of a contract) for which he or she may be rewarded (Tataryn, 1979). The owners of, or senior personnel within, an organization may also direct that certain actions take place and threaten subordinate managers or supervisors with dismissal if they fail to comply. Senior personnel may conceal the illegal or improper nature of practices from subordinates, or they may be the direct or indirect source of the rationalizations necessary to facilitate, for example, violations of occupational health-and-safety legislation, rules, or standards. A corporation may encourage a manager or supervisor by assuring the individual that deaths and injuries are a regrettable but unavoidable feature of working in an inherently dangerous industry, or indirectly allow the individual to transfer responsibility to the organization (e.g., "It is the fault of the system" or "Higher-ups told me to do it"). The permutations are vast, largely unexplored in the Canadian context, and, in some industries, complicated by subcontracting practices that, as the following example demonstrates, obscure organizational boundaries and distribute responsibility in favour of large corporations.

In 1987, approximately 70 percent of the fatalities in the forest industry occurred in nonunion operations. These operations constitute less than 20 percent of the entire industry and a disproportionate share of fatalities therefore occurs in this setting. Large companies involved in the forest industry in British Columbia "contract out" to smaller operators and the latter are under considerable pressure to increase production. A failure to do so could result in a contract not being renewed.

Often, experienced fallers will refuse to work under the conditions specified by some unscrupulous contractors, with the result that younger, less experienced workers are employed. In some cases, "fellers" with *no* experience are given a chainsaw and directed to cut trees, with predictable results. For example, in one case, a worker was killed felling his first tree. In another case, a worker lasted less than two hours before being struck and killed by a "widow-maker" (a loose branch dislodged from the tree-top).

The large forest companies are apparently aware of these practices and consequent fatalities but, by contracting out, they are not held to be directly responsible. At the same time, the corporations benefit from the high levels of productivity achieved at the expense of workers. It is the contractor who is blamed and, where an "unacceptable" number of fatalities or injuries occurs, the larger corporations can simply refuse any further contracts, hire another contractor, and thereby allow the cycle to begin again.[12]

The organizational dimension (e.g., both the pressures placed upon executives, managers, and supervisors, and the way in which an industry is organized) is, therefore, an important component in the explanatory model. However, the activities of corporations (i.e., their owners and senior personnel), in turn, require explanation. In this regard, it is necessary to shift to the final sphere of analysis: the structure and imperatives of the economic system within which corporations operate.

Capitalism is an economic system with a number of interlocking, structural characteristics and imperatives:

—private ownership of the means whereby things are produced, for example, the manufacturing and resource-extraction industries, the financing of business activity, and agriculture;

—appropriation of the profits created by labour and technology, by private owners, for the purpose of private accumulation of wealth or reinvestment;

—a labour system whereby those who do not own the means of production, but work for the people who do, are paid wages according to the value of their work, as determined by private owners often in conjunction with labour organizations;

—flexibility and durability. Capitalism has passed through several periods of change (i.e., the mercantile and industrial periods) and is currently entering the "monopoly" phase. The system has flourished despite challenges, problems, and major crises;

—profit maximization as the primary motivating factor and, therefore, one of the major "forces" of production;

—a strain toward consolidation, amalgamation, and monopolization, in order to maximize profit. This is particularly evident in the current phase of capitalism (monopoly capitalism) and is reflected in the constant process of corporate "takeovers" and mergers;

—perpetual growth, expansion, and technological improvement in order to maintain or increase production, consumption, and profitability. This involves a constant hunt for, and stimulation of, the consumers of products (e.g., identifying and developing new markets for goods), and a constant search for both cheap raw materials and ways of reducing labour costs;

—a belief in the virtues of competition, free-enterprise, and limited direct state intervention in the routine operations of the economy. State involvement is restricted to activities that produce and reproduce the social, economic, political, and ideological conditions necessary for capitalism to continue by, for example, assisting with the resolution of the contradictions that characterize capitalism;

—structural contradictions that create problems and periodic crises and that, consequently, require constant attention and management. For example, while the concentration of industry (e.g., the creation of a monopoly) maximizes profitability, it also results in a concentration of labour and thereby increases the power of labour to secure a larger share of profits. Technological developments may increase productivity and therefore profitability; however, they may displace the labour force who consume goods and thereby result in a crisis of overproduction (too many products chasing a reduced number of consumers). Perpetual growth is necessary to maintain or increase profit, but this may result in the rapid consumption and loss of the finite, nonrenewable resources upon which production is based. In short, capitalism contains the seeds of its own destruction.

The foregoing is, by no means, a comprehensive and detailed description of the economic system known as capitalism. However, it should provide a picture of the larger context within which corporations operate and, therefore, the structural factors that might account for corporate crime. In the case of, for example, "crimes" against the environment, the imperative of profit maximization and the associated systemic characteristics (i.e., perpetual growth, expansion, consumption, production, and competition) create organizational pressures that are passed down to, and account for the behaviour of, executives, managers, and supervisors. Corporations find it cheaper to dump poisonous wastes into rivers or oceans, or allow toxic emissions, than to pay for the processing or safe storage of wastes, or the installation of emission scrubbers that prevent atmospheric pollution: measures that affect profitability (Tataryn, 1979).

Profit maximization and other characteristics and imperatives also have a bearing upon the issue of "crimes" against employees, and Carson's (1982) analysis of the process (and human cost) of extracting oil from the North Sea provides a good example of their impact. In the late 1970s and early 1980s, Britain was facing severe economic difficulties that were affecting the general rate of profit and that could have been eased by the availability of North Sea oil. The resource had to be tapped quickly, and the process of drilling, extraction, and production was occurring while the construction of rigs and equipment was still taking place. For companies such as British Petroleum and Shell Oil, the rapid retrieval of oil (a profitable activity given the so-called global energy crisis) took precedence over all other considerations and, in Carson's view, the labour force was consequently placed at risk. The "political economy of speed" reduced the lives of workers to one variable in a corporate cost/benefit calculation and accounted for the Piper Alpha rig disaster in which 160 workers were killed. Considerable pressure had been placed upon the rig crew to increase production, the workers had no time to undertake proper maintenance, and, in the view of the platform superintendent, the rig was a "time bomb" that eventually exploded (Carson, 1982). House's (1986) analysis of the 1982 Ocean Ranger disaster in the Hibernia oil fields off Newfoundland suggests that similar factors were at work, and that the political economy of speed and the concomitant social organization of the oil-rig workplace have a significant impact upon the frequency and severity of injuries in the industry.

Given the limited enforcement that takes place and the weak punishments that are imposed, the costs of engaging in illegal behaviour may be outweighed by the benefits (Barnett, 1981). As Henry (1986) points out, a failure to provide a clean and safe work environment may result in low fines and it is more profitable to violate than comply with legislation and regulations. Some Canadian examples help to further illustrate the importance of profit maximization in understanding both the willingness to expose employees to harm, and the reluctance to either remove dangers or protect workers once the risks are known.

There is considerable evidence that dioxin—a chemical used to defoliate trees during the Vietnam war—causes cancer and genetic damage. Despite the dangers, the pulp-and-paper industry in British Columbia has done little to eliminate dioxins that occur as a result of the chemical kraft pulping process. While one company is preparing to spend

$200 million in order to upgrade and improve productivity (and, therefore, the profitability) of a pulpmill, it is not prepared to also expend a considerably smaller amount ($5 million to $10 million) in order to prevent potential harm to its employees: an expenditure that would not directly increase corporate profits.[13]

Despite the harm caused to both workers and the environment, pesticides are used extensively in Canadian agriculture in order to increase productivity and, therefore, profitability. This benefits growers and, equally importantly, the companies that manufacture the chemicals: it has been estimated that annual pesticide sales in Canada are worth $250 million. Little effort is made to minimize the harm caused to workers by providing protective clothing and equipment since this expenditure would not necessarily improve productivity.[14]

In spring 1987, two workers were killed and three injured on a Toronto high-rise construction site. A personnel elevator that could have been carrying up to 35 workers rocketed from the ground floor, at a speed of 100 k.p.h., and smashed into barricades on the 44th floor. The cause of the incident was identified as a broken gear shaft in the elevator hoisting mechanism. When the shaft broke, the braking mechanism failed to operate, and the counterweight fell more than 40 floors, dragging the elevator upwards. The elevator had a history of breakdowns and malfunctions, including excessive vibration, stopping at the wrong floor, and stopping altogether for no apparent reason. Each time, there had been long delays in obtaining approval for service and repair. Commenting on deaths on construction sites generally, one Ontario Ministry of Labour safety officer stated that only two priorities existed on sites: the first, to finish the current project; the second, to start another one.[15]

Numerous, similar examples can be provided for many other Canadian industries where the imperative of profit maximization—an impelling and structural characteristic of capitalism—affects organizational practices and, therefore, the behaviour of individuals. At the same time, however, there are limits to corporate wrongdoing, particularly in the context of crimes against employees. A corporation cannot be concerned solely with, for example, profit maximization if the associated practices result in death, injuries, and sicknesses that either drastically deplete or reduce the productive capacity (i.e., profitability) of its skilled workforce. Corporate activities may result in a problem or crisis of legitimacy, that is, a company may experience widespread public condemnation and a boycott of its products. An errant company may encounter stiff union opposition in the form of strikes, which stop production. The state may investigate, prosecute, and penalize a corporation for breaches of occupational health-and-safety legislation, regulations or standards. In other words, while a structural imperative such as profit maximization may be an important variable in *explaining* corporate transgressions, this does not imply that, in the absence of an alternative economic system, such practices are inevitable and the problems irresolvable. For example, if all the companies in an industry were required to comply with standardized, international, environmental protection or worker-safety measures, a company's "competitive edge"—one source of increased sales, and hence, profitability—might not be eroded.

One of the limitations affecting corporate practices—the possibility of state intervention—raises a question that has a bearing upon the entire field of corporate criminality: why is it that many forms of corporate behaviour that result in extensive material loss and serious physical injury are not formally defined and treated as crimes? Why is it, for example, that the deliberate or negligent actions of corporations that result in the death, injury, or sickness of employees are not investigated and prosecuted as murder, manslaughter, criminal negligence, or assault—crimes that attract severe punishments capable of deterring corporate wrongdoing? The answer can be found in the relationship among the entity that defines and deals with crime (the state), the dominant economic system (capitalism), and the corporate interests that flourish within that system (see, e.g., Snider, 1988).

Corporate Criminality and the State

In the case of "crimes" against employees, both the state and business interests go to considerable lengths to shift the blame to the victims of corporate practices. Where this fails, efforts are made to ensure that corporate wrongdoing is defined as a regrettable but unavoidable by-product of a commonly beneficial economic system, which is best dealt with through one component of the welfare state—workers' compensation schemes—rather than the criminal-justice system. A fine example of state and corporate efforts at shifting the blame has recently appeared in British Columbia, a province where there is growing concern over the numbers of fatalities and injuries in the forest industry.

In spring 1988, a short video documentary, *Every Twelve Seconds*, was aired on commercial television in British Columbia. The video was produced by the Disabled Forestry Workers of British Columbia and funded by corporations and government departments: MacMillan-Bloedel, Noranda, the Council of Forest Industries, the Secretary of State, the Workers' Compensation Board of British Columbia, and Employment and Immigration Canada. While the workers and unions involved in the production intended the message to be "Beware, working is hazardous to your health," the outcome was entirely different. The

producers quickly found that securing much-needed support and funding from the Workers' Compensation Board would be impossible unless assurances were given that neither the forest companies nor the board would be portrayed in an unfavourable light. As a result, the video, and its promotional pamphlet, emphasize the "unpredictability of nature," the "imperfection of technology," and "simple human error." At no time is a reference made to the organizational or structural factors that account for violence in the workplace, or the responsibility of forest companies to ensure safer working conditions (e.g., better equipment and proper training for inexperienced workers). The blame is shifted, in the main, to "mother nature" and "dumb workers." In short, the program is an example of a bipartite (state and capital) effort to neutralize existing, and prevent any further, criticism of the forest industry. It helps to ensure that corporate wrongdoing remains either concealed or defined as a regrettable but unavoidable consequence of economic activity, rather than criminal behaviour.

Corporate attempts to attribute violence in the workplace to worker error or accident are not, however, always successful, and the government is empowered to intervene. The provinces have enacted legislation (and compiled associated regulations) governing occupational health and safety, and created workers' compensation systems, which specify and "police" standards, and impose penalties.[16] This is not to say that corporate wrongdoing is consequently defined and treated as "criminal"; instead, it is viewed as an issue for the "welfare state" and dealt with through a system of regulation, mediation, and compensation.

On the one hand, this approach may be viewed as providing better protection for workers; just and speedy compensation for death, injury, or sickness; and an effective way of resolving conflicts between companies and workers, thereby ensuring better capital/labour relations and industrial peace. On the other hand, critics of the system point to a number of deficiencies: the inadequate nature of occupational health-and-safety legislation and regulations; an insufficient number of fully trained and experienced inspectors to enforce regulations; ineffective penalties for wrongdoing that fail to deter corporations; the process of exempting work sites from health-and-safety standards; the length of time involved in securing compensation and the often inadequate amounts awarded to victims; the difficulties involved in gaining access to information held by workers' compensation boards; and the apparently close ties between boards and corporate interests (see, e.g., Paterson, 1985; Livesay, 1988; Law Reform Commission, 1986; Reasons, Ross, & Paterson, 1981). In short, the "welfarization," rather than "criminalization," of corporate practices may have been based upon a laudable vision of justice and fairness for workers; however, in practice, this approach may benefit corporate, rather than labour, interests.

Studies of the origins of both workers' compensation schemes and occupational health-and-safety legislation challenge the claim that they were a product of state and corporate benevolence. The legislation (e.g., Factory Acts) and schemes first appeared in the late nineteenth and early twentieth centuries: a time when there was growing labour unrest as a consequence of deaths and injuries in the workplace; an increasing organization of labour; and clear signs of international revolutionary activity. The "wounded soldiers of industry," and their unions, were creating a number of problems for the state and capital and, where civil litigation was pursued by casualties, the courts began to exhibit a greater tendency to both rule in favour of labour and award substantial damages. As Gough (1979) points out, action was taken to address the situation and, in most capitalist nations, the victims of industrial accidents became the first to receive social-security benefits. More importantly, both the state and capital recognized the value of a system of insurance and compensation that would distribute and minimize the costs of death and injury, avoid stigmatizing criminal prosecution and costly civil litigation, allow the state to administer the scheme and assume the task of caring for disabled workers and their families, and, equally importantly, appease labour. The latter abandoned their right to sue employers (a costly, cumbersome, and unpredictable process) but secured guaranteed, no-fault stipends to be paid in the event of workplace injury.

Workers' compensation was one solution to the growing problem of maintaining order in an increasingly militant and unionized workforce, and it may be argued that the various schemes that emerged also enhanced the legitimacy of both the state and capitalism. Labour was controlled through an ostensibly benign set of actions, and there was no disruption to the process of reproducing the social, economic, and ideological conditions necessary for capitalism to continue. The interests of the capitalist class were well served, rather than threatened, by both legislation governing working conditions and workers' compensation schemes (Gough, 1979; Casey, 1985).

Both the role of the contemporary workers' compensation system and the practices of this component of the welfare state can be better understood in the light of this brief historical sketch. From the outset, occupational health-and-safety laws and regulations, and compensation schemes, primarily served corporate interests, and this continues to be the case.

1. Cases of corporate violence against employees that cannot be screened as accidents or worker error are defined as a problem for the welfare, rather than criminal-justice, apparatus of the state and, as a consequence, offending companies are not subjected to criminal prosecution.

2. State-administered compensation schemes channel and resolve disputes and generally appease labour, thereby removing one possible source of capital/labour conflict that could lead to industrial unrest, lost production, and diminished profits.

3. Companies can avoid expensive civil litigation and the payment of damages (both of which affect profitability) by paying insurance premiums, the cost of which can be routinely built into the price of products and, therefore, passed on to consumers.

4. Occupational health-and-safety regulations apply equally to all competing companies within an industry but they are inadequate and weakly enforced. Penalties are minimal and do not seriously affect profitability. This allows flexibility in the interpretation and application of standards and periodic, deliberate transgressions that may be necessary in order to ensure continued productivity/profitability.

5. The system of legislation and compensation is generally viewed as an example of benevolent state and corporate action, and this helps to legitimate and preserve the popularity of both the state and capitalism.

At the same time, however, workers continue to be exposed to risks, sometimes with the knowledge and even the assistance of workers' compensation boards, and often as a result of board inaction. For example, repeated variances (modification or exemption) for engineering inspection of concrete forms prior to any pouring of concrete are granted to the construction industry by the Workers' Compensation Board in British Columbia: an action that is seen as indicative of the board's willingness to accommodate an employer so that production is not disrupted.[17]

In 1989, board regulations specified that workers in high lead-hazard areas were entitled to the time necessary to take a protective shower at the end of a shift. Workers employed at the Cominco lead-zinc smelter in Trail, British Columbia, were denied this entitlement by the company since it would mean a production slow-down, but the board refused to take action.[18]

The use of the chemical wood preservative 2-cyanothiomethylithio benzothiazole (TCMTB) in British Columbia pulpmills became a cause for concern in early 1988. Employees at one mill had suffered sicknesses, ranging from severe, uncontrollable epistaxis to nausea, sore throats, and sinus problems, after being exposed to the chemical. Information was requested about the "safe levels" of exposure (the measurement of which is viewed with skepticism [Law Reform Commission, 1986]) but it was several months before the Workers' Compensation Board considered undertaking a study.[19]

The strategy used by the state to define and manage violence in the workplace surfaces in other areas of corporate criminality. Crimes against the economy, consumers, and the environment are, in the main, defined in federal and provincial legislation, which is separate from the criminal or quasi-criminal law, despite material loss, harm, and injury far in excess of that caused by traditional, predatory street crime. The "crimes" are viewed as problems best dealt with through regulation and mediation, and more appropriately managed by government agencies and administrative bodies that lie outside the criminal-justice system (e.g., the "Competition Tribunal").

The question is: why have the federal and provincial levels of the state responded to corporate criminality in this manner? The answer lies with the nature and role of the state in capitalist societies. The state constructs laws and undertakes investigations and prosecutions but also plays a key role in protecting and advancing the interests of capitalism (Glasbeek, 1984; Reasons, Ross, & Paterson, 1981). This is not to suggest that the federal and provincial governments are merely the faithful servants, or "instruments," of a particular social class—the corporate elite—that dictates policy in the area of, for example, corporate "crime." Close ties exist between senior levels of government and business corporations (Clement, 1975, 1977; Olsen, 1980), but this does not mean that the state acts at the behest of one social class, factions within that class, or individual capitalists. It is evident that the state has some independence (i.e., autonomy), but that this autonomy is, nevertheless, relative to the requirements of capitalism as a whole. The state plays a particular "managerial" role within the structure of capitalism and has the relative autonomy to exercise and attempt to synchronize three potentially contradictory "cardinal functions": order maintenance, legitimation, and reproducing the conditions necessary for capitalist economic activity to continue (see, e.g., Ratner, McMullan, & Burtch, 1987).

As Canadian political economists and sociologists have demonstrated, problems and crises of, for example, order maintenance and legitimation periodically arise, and the process of exercising and attempting to synchronize all three cardinal functions can account for a wide variety of state practices and policies (see, e.g., Panitch, 1979; Ratner & McMullan, 1987). The construction of anticombines legislation is no exception (Smandych, 1985), and this "structuralist" theory may explain the state's response to the different categories of corporate wrongdoing.

The "order maintenance" function of the state involves the use of various components of the state apparatus (e.g., the legal system, the criminal-justice system, and the wel-

fare system) in an attempt to ensure peace and harmony in society, in the interests of capitalism as a whole. This task may extend to maintaining "order" in the economy where conflicts between different and competing capitalist factions may threaten the common capitalist endeavour. To this end, the state is empowered to "discipline" particular corporations or even an entire industry. For example, governments may intervene in conflicts between corporations involved in resource extraction and those involved in secondary manufacture, or act to prevent one industry (e.g., pulp and paper) from polluting and destroying the natural resources essential to another (e.g., fishing and canning).

In fulfilling this "managerial" role, however, the state must take account of the need to preserve legitimacy (i.e., popular support) and ensure that there is no disruption to capitalist economic activity as a whole. Laws can be introduced and enforced to deal with a problem but, in so doing, the state must avoid the use of harsh and repressive measures that might attract the criticism of capitalist interests. Conversely, the state cannot hope to retain legitimacy if serious corporate wrongdoing is exposed but ignored and, where the actions of a corporation or corporations threaten the legitimacy of both the state and capitalism as a whole, disciplinary action may follow. For example, the state may control the practices of corporations that, driven by the imperative of profit maximization, raise the ire or threaten the health of the public by polluting the environment. At the same time, however, state practices aimed at maintaining order and preserving legitimacy are constrained by the third "cardinal function": producing and reproducing the conditions necessary for capitalist economic activity to continue. Governments cannot tackle a problem of order maintenance or legitimation by introducing repressive measures that might deter all forms of capitalist endeavour and thereby disrupt the general process of production, consumption, and the accumulation of profits.

The state must, therefore, perform a complex, managerial "balancing act" in regard to its cardinal functions within the structure of capitalism. If a problem or crisis emerges in regard to, for example, legitimation, the state's response is conditioned by the need to ensure that order is maintained and that the general conditions necessary for capitalist economic activity are preserved. The state has the autonomy to deal with these problems or crises by using disciplinary or other measures, and is not necessarily influenced by particular capitalists or capitalist factions. The autonomy of the state, however, is not absolute: it is an autonomy that is relative to the common interests and requirements of capitalism as a whole.

So, how might this "structuralist" theory of the nature and role of the capitalist state explain government strategies and policies in the area of corporate criminality? In particular, how might it explain the failure to define and deal with corporate wrongdoing as "crime"? How does the theory help us to understand the state's apparent reluctance to utilize the full weight of the resources available to fulfil its order-maintenance function (i.e., the criminal law and the criminal-justice system)?

Arguably, the answers lie with the state's role in ensuring legitimation and reproducing the conditions necessary for capitalism to continue (see, e.g., Barnett, 1981). The use of strong, repressive measures to combat corporate wrongdoing could result in a legitimation problem for capitalism. The appearance of the captains of industry in the docks of criminal courts might well discredit corporations and awaken widespread public doubt about the propriety of the prevailing economic and social system. Similarly, there would almost certainly be a disruption to capitalist economic activity as corporations were impelled to abandon, for example, the imperative of relentless profit maximization. This might be replaced by, for example, the imperatives of environmental and worker protection, which, while laudable, might well conflict with the general, structural characteristics and other features of capitalism. Indeed, they would probably have an adverse impact upon production, growth, international competitiveness and investment, and hence the nation's economy. This, in turn, might create a legitimation crisis for the state as economic stagnation emerged and unemployment became widesread.

The state's role in exercising and, equally importantly, attempting to synchronize its cardinal functions may, therefore, explain its strategies and policies in the area of corporate criminality. It may explain the adoption and use of a regulatory and disciplinary system for dealing with corporate wrongdoing that is separate from the disciplinary system designed to deal with traditional, predatory street crime: the criminal law and the criminal-justice system. However, before this account can be accepted as valid it must be subjected to further and substantial empirical examination.

The discussion of the phenomenon of crimes against employees was offered as a way of exploring some of the key issues and problems in the entire field of corporate criminality. That task is now completed. It is customary to close a discussion of corporate criminality with a review of the tactics used to control the behaviour, and to make recommendations for reform. We intend to deviate from that tradition by concluding with a brief examination of the areas where research should be conducted by Canadian criminologists. In our view, "control talk" is largely meaningless without a clear picture of the nature, scope, impact, and causes of corporate criminality, as well as the relationship among the state, the economy, and corporate interests. We are also deviating from another tradition: a call for *more*

research. This implies that a substantial body of research already exists, and such is not the case in Canada. While some areas of corporate wrongdoing have been separately researched and analyzed (e.g., competition law and policy, environmental pollution, and employee health and safety), the studies have not been undertaken within the context of criminological inquiry. Links have not been forged between the different forms of corporate activity and, as a consequence, a broader picture of the nature, scope, and impact of corporate crime in Canada has not been developed. Our suggestion is that the phenomenon be shifted to a more prominent position on the criminological agenda and that work commence without delay.

Corporate Crime in Canada: Future Research

There is little doubt that Canadian criminologists have been unduly preoccupied with traditional, predatory street crime. This is hardly surprising since the body that, in the main, funds criminological research in Canada (i.e., the state) is also preoccupied with the topic. Consequently, Canadian criminology suffers from a surfeit of studies designed to unlock the secrets of strategies such as crime prevention through environmental design and seemingly inexplicable transgressions such as breaking-and-entering, vandalism, theft, youth crime, and robbery. All of this is, of course, important but, arguably, less so when compared with the scope and impact of corporate wrongdoing.

Criminologists who seek to explore corporate criminality will, however, encounter some difficulties (see, e.g., Casey, 1985; West & Snider, 1985; Snider, 1988). Research funds may not be available from state and corporate sources unless the topic happens to one that may assist the former in resolving a growing legitimation problem (e.g., crimes against the environment). The information available from official data sources is sparse, and a researcher may wish to seek access to more detailed state and corporate records. While co-operation might be forthcoming from government departments, corporate assistance is unlikely. A researcher could turn to interviews with "whistle-blowers," anonymous informants working within corporations, corporate employees who have been convicted of wrongdoing, workers and their unions, or independent "watchdog" agencies that have been accumulating information on corporate activity, and this might produce valuable data. The process of unravelling the complexities of corporate ownership may pose some difficulties but, as Clement (1975, 1977) has demonstrated, this is not insurmountable. Generally, then, various methodological problems exist but an enthusiastic and tenacious researcher should be able to accomplish his or her goals.

The field of corporate criminality is vast, and there is

no shortage of topics to be studied. Canadian political economists have already provided a framework for historical studies of corporate criminality (see, e.g., Naylor, 1975), and work in this area could yield important empirical and theoretical insights. There is a pressing need for studies in the largely untapped areas of corporate criminality; notably, crimes against the economy (e.g., patent violation, product piracy, and anticompetitive actions). Forms of corporate wrongdoing that have already been subjected to some examination (e.g., crimes against consumers, the environment, and employees) need intensive and rigorous examination. In each case, empirical studies should be theoretically informed, and a researcher may choose to focus upon either a testing of the three interlocking components of the general causal model set out in this discussion, or the theories that might account for the state's response to corporate crime (e.g., the structuralist theory). Whatever the empirical or theoretical focus, the results will make an important contribution to Canadian criminology.

Discussion Questions

1. What have criminologists generally concluded about the nature, scope, and impact of corporate "crimes"?

2. What are the main categories of corporate crime? Assess the extent to which you have been, are, and are likely to be a victim of corporate wrongdoing.

3. Why is corporate "crime" not perceived, defined, and dealt with in the same manner as is predatory street crime? Why is there now a trend toward a criminalization of corporate actions that cause harm to the environment?

Notes

1. The authors gratefully acknowledge the assistance provided by Raj Santini, Pauline Davidson, Bruce Elphinstone of the B.C. Federation of Labour; Don McPherson of the United Steelworkers of America, Local 1064; and the workers and union personnel who shared their experiences, insights, and information.

2. See, Parliamentary *Hansard* (House of Commons Debates): April 7–10, May 27, and June 2–5, 1986.

3. On *Newscience*: CHEK 6 Television, Victoria, B.C., October 30, 1987.

4. Data supplied by the Workers' Compensation Board of British Columbia.

5. Case reported in *Alberni Valley Times*, March 15–17, 1983.

6. Case reported in *Toronto Star*, October 18, 1986; *Vancouver Sun*, October 20, 1986; and *Globe and Mail*, December 12, 1986.

7. Bennie et al. (1987); interview with Mr. B. Redlin, Canadian Union of Public Employees, Burnaby, B.C., April 26, 1988.

8. Interview with Mr. W.C. Denault, Director, B.C. Construction Health and Safety Council, Burnaby, B.C., April 22, 1988.

9. Case reported in *Toronto Star*, November 20, 21, & 27, and December 23, 1987; *Globe and Mail*, November 20, 21, & 27, and December 7, 1987.

10. Interview with Mr. S. Boal and Mr. M. Fleming, Canadian Farmworkers Union, Burnaby, B.C., May 5, 1988.

11. Interview with Mr. B. Payne, Canadian Paperworkers Union, Vancouver, B.C., April 25, 1988.

12. Interview with Mr. B. Patterson, Safety Director, International Woodworkers of America/Canada, Local 1-71 (Logging), Vancouver, B.C., May 6, 1988.

13. Payne interview. Some pulpmills have started to reduce the level of dioxin and other toxic discharges, since this interview. This has occurred primarily in response to public concern over environmental pollution and the closure of fisheries.

14. Boal and Fleming interview.

15. Incident reported in *Globe and Mail*, May 21, 1987; *Sunday Star*, August 30, 1987; *Calgary Herald*, August 30 and September 1, 1987; *Toronto Star*, August 31, 1987.

16. See, e.g., Workers Compensation Act, Revised Statutes of British Columbia, 1979, chapter 437 (as amended), and the Health

and Safety Regulations made pursuant to the Act.

17. Denault interview.

18. See British Columbia *Hansard* (Debates of the Legislative

Assembly), May 15, 1980.

19. See British Columbia *Hansard* (Debates of the Legislative Assembly), March 21, April 21, and April 28, 1988.

References

Barnett, H.C. (1981). Corporate capitalism, corporate crime. *Crime and Delinquency, 27*, 5–23.

Bennie, R., Oram, T., Brewin, J., & Brewin - Marley, J. (1987). *Report on asbestos and the B.C. ferries: Years of neglect, years of pain.* Victoria: B.C. Ferry and Marine Workers Union.

Block, W. (1983) *On economics and the Canadian bishops.* Vancouver: Fraser Institute.

Boal, S. (1985). *Presentation to the B.C. Federation of Labour's inquiry into the Workers' Compensation Board.* Burnaby: Canadian Farmworkers Union.

Borkin, J. (1978). *The crime and punishment of I.G. Farben.* New York: Free Press.

Caputo, T. (1989). Political economy, law and environmental protection. In T. Caputo, M. Kennedy, C.E. Reasons, and A. Brannigan (Eds.), *Law and society: A critical perspective* (pp. 161–206). Toronto: HBJ.

Carson, W.G. (1982). *The other price of Britain's oil: Safety and control in the North Sea.* Oxford: Martin Robertson.

Casey, J. (1985). Corporate crime and the state. In T. Fleming (Ed.), *The new criminologies in Canada* (pp. 100–111). Toronto: Oxford University Press.

Clement, W. (1975). The *Canadian corporate elite: An analysis of economic power.* Toronto: McClelland & Stewart.

Clement, W. (1977). *Continental corporate power: Economic linkages between Canada and the United States.* Toronto: McClelland & Stewart.

Clinard, M.B., & Yeager, P.C. (1980). *Corporate crime.* New York; Free Press.

Emond, D.P. (1984). Co-operation in nature: A new foundation for environmental law. *Osgood Hall Law Journal, 22*, 323–48.

Ermann, M.D., & Lundman, R.J. (1982). *Corporate deviance.* New York: Holt, Rinehart & Winston.

Farrow, M. (1988, August 27). Chopper forestry rules found lax. *Vancouver Sun,* p. A12.

Geis, G. (1982). *On white collar crime.* Toronto: D.C. Heath.

Glasbeek, H.J. (1984). Why corporate deviance is not treated as a crime—the need to make "profits" a dirty word. *Osgood Hall Law Journal, 22*, 393–439.

Goff, C.H., & Reasons, C.E. (1978). *Corporate crime in Canada: A critical analysis of anti-combines legislation.* Scarborough: Prentice-Hall.

Goff, C.H., & Reasons, C.E. (1986). Organizational crimes against employees, consumers, and the public. In B. Maclean (Ed.), *The political economy of crime* (pp. 204–31). Scarborough: Prentice-Hall.

Gough, I. (1979). *The political economy of the welfare state.* New York: Macmillan.

Henry, F. (1986). Crime—a profitable approach. In B. Maclean (Ed.), *The political economy of crime.* Scarborough: Prentice-Hall.

House, J.D. (1986). Working offshore: The other price of Newfoundland's oil. In K.L.P. Lundy & B. Warme (Eds.), *Work in the Canadian context.* Toronto: Butterworths.

Law Reform Commission of Canada. (1985). *Crimes against the environment.* Working Paper No. 44. Ottawa: Law Reform Commission of Canada.

Law Reform Commission of Canada. (1986). *Workplace pollution.* Working Paper No. 53. Ottawa: Law Reform Commission of Canada.

Livesay, B. (1988). Dying for a living. *This Magazine, 21*(7), 22–26.

Naylor, T. (1973). The history of domestic and foreign capital in Canada. In R. Laxer (Ed.), *(Canada) Ltd.: The political economy of dependency* (pp. 42–56). Toronto: McClelland & Stewart.

Naylor, T. (1975). *The history of Canadian business, 1867–1914,* 2 vols. Toronto: James Lorimer.

Olsen, D. (1980). *The state elite.* Toronto: McClelland & Stewart.

Panitch, L. (Ed.). (1979). *The Canadian state: Political economy and political power.* Toronto: University of Toronto Press.

Paterson, C. (1985). W.C.B. deficiencies. *The Facts* 7(1).

Rankin, M., & Finkle, P. (1983). The enforcement of environmental law: Taking the environment seriously. *University of B.C. Law Review 17*(1), 35–57.

Ratner, R.S., McMullan J., & Burch, B. (1987). The problem of relative autonomy and criminal justice in the Canadian state. In R.S. Ratner & J. McMullan (Eds.), *State control: Criminal justice politics in Canada* (pp. 85–125). Vancouver: University of British Columbia Press.

Ratner, R.S., & McMullan, J. (Eds.). (1987). *State control: Criminal justice politics in Canada.* Vancouver: University of British Columbia Press.

Reasons, C.E., Ross, L.L., & Paterson, C. (1981). *Assault on the worker: Occupational health and safety in Canada.* Toronto: Butterworths.

Reasons, C.E. (1987). Workplace terrorism. *The Facts, 9*(3), 6–11.

Ruggeri, G.C. (1981). *The Canadian economy: Problems and policies* (2nd ed.). Toronto: Gage.

Simon, D.R., & Eitzen, D.S. (1986). Elite deviance (2nd ed.). Boston: Allyn & Bacon.

Smandych, R. (1985). Re-examining the origins of Canadian anti-combines legislation, 1890–1910. In Fleming, T. (Ed.), *The new criminologies in Canada* (pp.87–99). Toronto: Oxford University Press.

Snider, L. (1988). Commercial crime. In V.F. Sacco (Ed.), *Deviance, conformity and control in Canadian society.* pp. 231–83. Scarborough: Prentice-Hall.

Sutherland, E. (1949). *White collar crime.* New York: Holt Rinehart & Winston.

Swaijen, J. (Ed.). (1981). *Environmental rights in Canada.* Toronto: Butterworths.

Tataryn, L. (1979). *Dying for a living.* Toronto: Deneau & Greenberg.

West, W.G., & Snider, D.L. (1985). A critical perspective on law in the Canadian state: Delinquency and corporate crime. In T. Fleming (Ed.), *The new criminologies in Canada* (pp. 138–69). Toronto: Oxford University Press.

Wickman, P., & Dailey, T. (Eds.). (1982). *White-collar and economic crime.* Lexington, MA: D.C. Heath.

17 Contemporary Political Crime: National and International Terrorism

Raymond R. Corrado

Demarcation of Politically Motivated Crime

Theoretical Perspectives

Historical Overview of Political Terrorism in Canada

Conclusion

An important question is posed when one is trying to understand politically motivated **crime** in Canada. For most Canadians, "political" crime is not likely to be a familiar concept, while for theorists who adopt the **conflict approach** to **criminology**, it is critical in understanding **deviance** in Canada, especially criminal deviance. Why does the public generally ignore this concept that is so central to explanations of major political controversies such as government corruption and terrorism? The government of Prime Minister Brian Mulroney, for example, suffered through numerous scandals involving cabinet ministers who were accused of financial conflict of interest and criminal offences. With regard to antistate terrorism, the most violent criminal act in Canadian history took place in 1985 when an Air India jumbo jet with 329 passengers was blown out of the sky above Ireland by a bomb allegedly planted by Sikh political extremists living in Canada.

For conflict theorists, it comes as no surprise that most Canadians, while angry with both such incidents of corruption and terrorism, shy away from describing them as political crimes. We have been introduced to conflict theories in several earlier chapters. Theorists such as Austin Turk (1982) claim that the power and authority of governments depend, in part, on their ability to define deviant social phenomena as political crimes. Politicians such as Brian Mulroney, for example, can avoid complete political embarrassment, and recover from a negative media image, if they successfully can project the message that *individual greed* rather than flawed government structures and policies are to blame for corruption. Similarly, if acts of terrorism can be portrayed by governments as *criminal*, then the political grievances underlying these acts will be downplayed or missed by the public.

Three general points emerge from this brief description

of the public's view of political crime versus the conflict theorists' view. First, there is no consensus concerning the definition of the concept of political crime and, therefore, little agreement over which acts constitute political crime. Second, these conceptual disagreements result invariably in theoretical disagreements about why political crimes occur. While these discussions preclude any simple depiction of political crime in Canada, it is still possible to begin to examine it through (1) a discussion of how the concept is used; (2) a review of the salient theoretical perspectives; and (3) historical and contemporary case studies. The third and final point is that political terrorism represents one of the most serious and controversial political crimes. In the last 30 years, political terrorism has exhibited several phases involving the Sons of Freedom (from the Doukhobor ethnic group—see Chapter 12), the Front de libération du Québec (FLQ), government or state terrorism and the Khalistani nationalists (from the Sikh ethnic group).

This chapter will briefly discuss the topic area of politically motivated crime in Canada; it will thus focus on that category of crime traditionally labelled "political crime," although it will be argued at the conclusion that any crime might be so defined if an imputation of political motivation can be attached to it. Illustrated by events in the Canadian setting, various perspectives on the theories of political crime will be described. The last section of the chapter will focus upon antistate and state terrorist trends as examples for the theoretical perspectives previously presented.

Demarcation of Politically Motivated Crime

Lombroso (1918) and Proal (1898) defined political crime broadly as any unlawful attack on societal structures and traditions. Proal introduced explicit political dimensions by referring to crimes committed by government officials and politicians seeking political advantage and expediency. Yet, Proal expanded the scope beyond corruption and explicit political crimes such as treason to include ordinary crime such as robbery and homicide in which a political advantage or opportunity was involved.

Political crime is, in fact, a concept of relatively recent origin since Ingram (1979) claims the term was first used in the late eighteenth century during the tumultuous period of the French revolution. There is no doubt, however, that the phenomenon now labelled as political crime has existed ever since governments began. The central elements to any definition of political crime are two seemingly opposite situations: illegal use of political power by the *state*, or a threatening act *against* the legitimacy of the state. As we shall see, such acts differ from more conventional crime in intent and motivation.

Intent of Political Criminals

The distinction between ordinary and extraordinary crime has been a central issue in conceptualizing political crime. Ordinary crime occurs when the intent of the act is not to defy the legitimacy of laws but rather to achieve a personal, i.e., nonpolitical gain. In contrast, Merton (1968) maintains that those individuals who challenge the legitimacy of social norms openly and not for personal advantage are nonconformists, not criminals. Merton stipulated five criteria for identifying the differences in intent that would distinguish the nonconformer from the aberrant or ordinary criminal. The political criminal, first, engages in public dissent; second, violates norms and laws because they are illegitimate; third, seeks to remove the illegitimate laws and norms; fourth, is recognized by conforming citizens as motivated by nonpersonal or nonmaterial values; and, fifth, is motivated by a higher morality that transcends particular societal norms (Clinard & Quinney, 1973).

The relevance of these criteria is illustrated in the trial of the Squamish Five in New Westminster, British Columbia, in 1983. The five individuals involved had bombed a Litton Industries plant in Toronto, a Hydro power station on Vancouver Island, and a Red Hot Video outlet in Vancouver, and, in addition, were conspiring to rob a Brinks armoured truck and bomb a Canadian Armed Forces base in Alberta. The media characterized them as terrorists. However, during the trial, the five accused denied both that they were criminals and the legitimacy of their criminal trials. They engaged in violence not for personal gain, but for their moral commitment to save the environment, to prevent nuclear war, and to stop the exploitation of women and children.

Similarly, Khalastani nationalists deny they were violating Canadian criminal laws when they formed political organizations in the immigrant Sikh communities that seek the violent overthrow of the government of India. The assassination attempt on a visiting Punjabi cabinet minister on Vancouver Island was explained as a political act designed to counter the routine violence by the Indian army and police against Sikhs in India. These examples illustrate the difficulty of trying to apply Merton's criteria. Criminal intent, in particular, is not easily established since the alleged perpetrators vary considerably in their responses about their stated motives. For the Squamish Five, it was to their advantage to claim that they were moralists, because they were attempting to convince the jury at their trial that they were not ordinary criminals but politically conscious activists.

The question of intent is also important because many legal codes provide for separate correctional status and treatment for political prisoners. In Northern Ireland, for example, inmates who are members of the Irish Republican

Army (IRA) are officially designated as political prisoners and, consequently, wear personal clothing, congregate in separate units, and are allowed similar privileges denied other inmates. Intent is also a consideration in sentencing as in the recent trial of Colonel Oliver North in Washington, D.C. North was charged with a wide range of offences, including selling weapons to the Iranians and funnelling the profits to the Nicaraguan Contras to fund their guerrilla war. He denied being a criminal, even though he broke the law, because he was acting in an official capacity as a member of the President's National Security Council. North claimed he was following orders from the office of the president and, in addition, that he was motivated by his commitment to democracy and anticommunism in Central America.

These examples not only demonstrate Merton's five criteria but they also illustrate the considerable importance of the concept of intent for decisions in the **criminal-justice system**, from sentencing to **parole** and even **pardon**. The trial judge in the Squamish Five case meted out particularly harsh sentences because he asserted that politically motivated violence was a sinister threat that must be punished and deterred. However, when one of the Squamish Five renounced political violence in principle, it became a positive factor in an early paroled-release decision. Finally, it is not uncommon for governments to grant pardons for political inmates after a certain period of time has elapsed in order to acknowledge changes in historical circumstances, i.e., the political threat no longer exists and a pardon is seen as a political healing tactic.

Nature of the Consequences

Another conceptualization of political crime focusses on the amount of harm inflicted on society. In reviewing this perspective, Lauderdale (1980, p. 6) concludes that the proponents of the conflict perspective argue "that certain acts are inherently criminal [apolitical] or deviant [political] depending on the magnitude of the harm they cause; the 'real' crimes (exploitations, sexism, racism, imperialism, the profit motive, consumer fraud) are objectively defined by their harmful consequences."

In effect, politicians and government officials are seen as engaging in political crimes when their policies directly and indirectly result in the death and suffering of thousands of innocent people through poverty, neglect, and foreign policies. Chomsky and Herman (1979), for example, insist that U.S. foreign policy since World War II has caused the death of millions of Third World people at the hands of U.S.–sponsored, right-wing dictatorships and civil wars, such as in Vietnam and El Salvador. Chambliss (1976), as well, holds politicians and their corporate-elite financiers responsible for the grossly inequitable distribution of wealth, power, and justice in the United States, which, in turn, is connected to the poverty, ill-health, and violence in urban, racially segregated ghettoes.

Conceptualizing political crime primarily in terms of the degree of harmful consequences creates a fundamental operational problem of trying to assess causal linkages between the intention of a policy and an actual harmful outcome. Could the U.S. invasion of Panama, where dozens of civilians were either killed or injured, be categorized as political crime? Similarly, in Canada, was the **War Measures Act** invoked in October 1970 by civil libertarian Prime Minister Pierre Trudeau to deal with the terrorist kidnapping of two officials in Montreal, a political crime because many innocent Canadians were arrested and detained without normal **due process** rights? For Trudeau and most Canadians at that time, such a designation would be preposterous because the policy intention was to prevent the violent overthrow of a provincial government and the secession of Quebec. That hundreds of French Canadians were adversely affected does not constitute a political crime, but rather an unfortunate outcome of a necessary emergency policy.

Governments as Political Criminals

Another issue in conceptualizing political crime is whether to include crimes committed by governments. Many of the examples discussed above involve *representatives* of the state or the political system and government as political criminals. Conflict theorists, such as William Chambliss (1976) and Charles Reasons (1973) contend that governments are overwhelmingly the most serious or dangerous political criminals. However, Austin Turk (1982) maintains that the illegal behaviour of governments or their representatives should not be considered as political crime. Accordingly, he contends that this concept should be restricted to challenges or threats *to* the authorities who have power. Turk's intent is to avoid confusing political crimes with political policing and conventional politics. He argues that legal and illegal means used by authorities to maintain the *status quo* authority structure are inevitable, as are political crime or challenges to this *status quo*. Conflict over power is inherent in all social relationships as social order and societal structures emerge. Maintaining this key distinction allows analysts greater insight into the complex, and often subtle, relationships between those with power and those seeking it.

The relationship between political process and concepts of crime focusses attention on the inherent relativity of criminal definitions, as Lauderdale (1980, p. 37) asserts, "latent structure of politicality which makes possible the redefinition of the [deviant] action as conventional." A deviant act at a particular time, be it political or not, can be redefined informally and/or formally as nondeviant. Unions, for example, were considered subversive in many Western countries, yet today they are legitimate institutions with considerable political power. The Winnipeg General Strike is an illustration of how a divisive and threatening deviant incident involving political violence can, in the space of a single federal election, result in the redefinition of political crime manifested by the official recognition of the economic and political role of unions (see Box 17.1).

Despite the problems associated with conceptualizing and defining political crime, there is little doubt that it exists in Canada and throughout the world. Before describing some of the major incidents of political crime in Canada, we will review the dominant theoretical perspectives.

Theoretical Perspectives

Even excluding "ordinary crimes," the range of behaviours subject to categorization as political crime is considerable. This variation poses several theoretical problems. Foremost among these is whether the differences among the types of political crime is so great that it precludes a single or unitary theory. *Terrorism*, for example, is an enormously complex and diverse phenomenon that has been the focus of extensive theoretical accounts. At the same time, *corruption* also covers a diversity of activities, and there are competing explanations. Terrorism and corruption, while sharing common definitional elements of political crime, are fundamentally different. Corruption usually involves criminal acts that do not intend to change the political process but rather to utilize it for political and economic advantage. Antistate terrorism, in contrast, is often based

Box 17.1 The Winnipeg General Strike, 1919

The use of the Royal North-West Mounted Police (RNWMP) to break up a labour demonstration by force and to arrest labour leaders is one example of what Torrance (1988) calls "public violence." When members of the RNWMP charged the crowd on horseback, 2 men were killed and 30 injured. Furthermore, criminal laws were amended to broaden the definition of sedition, and seven labour leaders were eventually convicted of trying to overthrow the state. Soon after, the legitimacy of unions was recognized.

The Winnipeg General Strike began on May 1, 1919, when the building and metal trade workers went out on strike for higher wages. Members of the local labour council voted overwhelmingly to support this action with a general strike and, on May 15, 30 000 private-industry and public-sector workers walked out. Essential services, such as milk delivery and law enforcement, were permitted to continue by the Strike Committee, but the overall result was a paralysis of the city. This situation continued for 42 days.

To understand the reaction to this situation, we must consider the temper of the times. Only one month before the strike, discontented with the conservative, eastern wing of the trade-union movement, western members had organized into One Big Union (OBU). Their platform was somewhat radical, calling for the control of industry by the workers. Despite the rhetoric, however, the demands of the OBU would today seem reasonable, such as the five-day work week. It has also been contended that the call for radical reforms was an effort ultimately to achieve more

modest gains (Young, 1969).

Nevertheless, such talk alarmed many Canadians, especially coming so soon after the Russian Revolution of 1917. The fear of "Bolshevism" was also fuelled by suspicion of the flood of new immigrants, and the wave of sympathy strikes across the country was thought to be evidence of a Russian plot. These fears were encouraged by the press. The labour movement was relatively new in Canada and viewed with suspicion by many "as an unwarranted interference with the free action of the market and as a deliberate affront to the rights of private property" (Young, 1969, p. 12).

In Winnipeg, the Citizen's Committee of 1000 was formed, made up of influential businessmen. As a group, they were against any management concessions that might end the strike. In Ottawa, Prime Minister Borden viewed the strike as an attempt to replace the Canadian government with one patterned after the Soviet system. The RNWMP had infiltrated the union movement, but intelligence information sent to Ottawa was often misinterpreted and the government came to believe that a Bolshevik revolution was being planned and that the radicals were heavily armed (Horrall, 1980). This belief prompted federal action. The Immigration Act was amended to permit the deportation of undesirable immigrants, even if they were British-born, a move clearly aimed at the labour leaders. Furthermore, the Criminal Code provisions regarding sedition were also broadened by the passage of section 98 that prohibited "unlawful associations." On June 17, eight leaders had been

Box 17.1 (Continued)

jailed, charged with **seditious conspiracy.** Four days later, the Mounted Police charged a crowd of demonstrators and took over the streets. The strikers decided to return to work on June 25.

There were several legacies of the Winnipeg General strike. Horrall (1980) asserts that the strike prompted the creation of the RCMP as a national, federal police force in 1920. The sedition provisions in the Criminal Code were amended to increase the penalty from two to twenty years

and to repeal the "saving clause" that permitted a defence of good faith if it could be proved that the criticism of the state was constructive and that only legal measures were advocated. These provisions were repealed in 1930, as was section 98 (in 1936), but until then they were frequently used to harass and prosecute communists. Such attempts to criminalize legitimate political dissent have been more common in Canadian history than is popularly thought (Torrance, 1988).

The Royal North-West Mounted Police after charging through the crowds in Winnipeg, June 21, 1919.
Provincial Archives of Manitoba, Winnipeg Strike Collection no. 29.

on either the radical restructuring of existing society or the creation of a new nation-state. Another key distinguishing feature is the violence often associated with terrorism, which rarely emerges with corruption. Thus, certain types of corruption and terrorism have very little in common except they both involve the political process, and even this commonality is conceptually strained. It is far beyond the scope of this chapter to attempt even a cursory review of all the theories of terrorism and corruption. It is possible,

though, to focus on certain political crimes such as terrorism to illustrate the main theoretical explanations of political crime. Other forms of political crime such as crimes among the elite (Chapter 15) and corporate crime (Chapter 16) are discussed elsewhere in the book.

One obvious explanation for political crime is that it provides a personal or group advantage. Individuals make a rational choice, according to cost/benefit criteria, to commit such a crime. This simplistic hypothesis is intuitively appealing, partly because political criminals, in comparison to popular images of at least some ordinary criminals, appear to be particularly calculating.

A contrasting image of political criminals is based, in part, on the need both to utilize political processes and to plan a long-term agenda. Clearly, authorities who engage in political crime are, by definition, part of the governing political structures and, therefore, are often fulfilling a preconceived plan. Similarly, political criminals who challenge the authorities or government belong to organizations whose actions also are planned and co-ordinated to some degree. In effect, most political criminals belong to organizations, whereas, excluding those involved in organized crime and certain forms of **white-collar crimes**, ordinary criminals act alone or, at the most, belong to loosely affiliated groups.

Simply because individuals who commit political crime often belong to an organization does not necessarily preclude the applicability of some of the above-noted factors generally associated with ordinary crime. It is possible, for example, that individuals who join terrorists groups, whether state or antistate, do so because they are opportunistic, mentally disordered, or belong to violent subcultures. However, the limited research to date on the motivation of state terrorists and antistate terrorists (Corrado, 1987) does not provide much support for the psychopathological perspective. Ideology, rational choice, and frustration perspectives received the most empirical support (Wardlaw, 1982).

Individual-Level Perspective

Individuals commit political crimes; therefore, it is reasonable to begin at this level of analysis to try and understand why an individual would engage in this type of activity. Political crimes can be committed by individuals acting alone; however, that is unusual. When it does occur, it typically involves a single, often tragic incident. Denis Lortie, a Canadian solider stationed near Ottawa, for example, maintained initially that he went to the provincial legislative assembly in Quebec city to kill Parti Québécois legislators who he claimed were ruining Quebec with their policies. He sprayed offices and the main legislative chamber with an automatic rifle, killing three people and wounding thirteen. He then proceeded to hold hostages for several hours before surrendering. Lortie's initial position was that he committed a political crime, but, at his trial, he maintained that he was not guilty by reason of insanity. The jury rejected the **insanity defence** and found Lortie guilty of murder.

The motives behind "political crime" can consist of narrow concerns such as revenge for a particular wrongdoing or broad, revolutionary goals. Even among individuals with severe mental disorders, it is possible that political motives can play a role. In cases of extreme psychotic disorders, such as the various forms of schizophrenia, an assessment of political motivation is difficult because it is usually impossible to disentangle such motives within the context of mental delusions and hallucinations.

However, neurotic disorders and even a prior history of psychotic disorder do not necessarily negate political motivation. Louis Riel, for example, feared that his political motives for engaging in the bloody North West Rebellion of 1885, which resulted in the death of 140 rebels and 38 soldiers, would be denied or dismissed by the Canadian government and public if his psychiatric history, involving several institutional commitments, was portrayed as the cause of his political crimes (Berger, 1981; Torrance, 1988; see also Chapter 8). Similarly, there is a continuing debate among historians whether the genocidal atrocities instigated by politicians such as Adolf Hitler and Josef Stalin were motivated either by ideology or by psychotic disorders. Both these leaders, it has been alleged, were suffering from schizophrenic paranoia while they were in power. And their irrational fears of certain social groups, such as Jews for Hitler and the senior officer corps for Stalin, resulted in the respective genocide policies toward these groups. In effect, the argument is that both Hitler and Stalin employed ideology to obscure their psychotic motives for implementing objectively inexplicable atrocities. In the absence of clinical evidence, there is no way of substantiating these historical conjectures about the motivations of Hitler and Stalin. There is little doubt, however, that they committed political crimes since their victims were arrested and killed without any pretense of legal procedure and to further their respective totalitarian visions and/or psychotic delusions.

Organizational or Middle-Level Perspective

Individual motivations are shaped not only by the long-term socialization process, but also by the social context of group interactions. Social organizations such as the family, peer group, unions, and the university provide the opportunities for individuals to act in concert and regularly. Formal organizations institutionalize behaviour and make it predictable.

A good example of the type of influence these group or institutional infractions have can be seen with the RCMP, here in Canada. The RCMP did engage in illegal acts in the 1970s while pursuing information on the FLQ. The officers who committed the criminal acts maintained they were following orders and that, in essence, the illegal means were justified by the need to protect the national security of Canada from political terrorists. Throughout testimony given in the hearings held by the federal Macdonald Commission to investigate RCMP "wrongdoings," it was evident that the organizational structure of the security division of the RCMP was a critically important factor in explaining why police officers committed crimes. The difficulty RCMP officers traditionally had in distinguishing legitimate political opposition from genuine political threats to national security was attributed to their lack of appropriate training and university education as well as the ingrained or virtually automatic response to a rigid command hierarchy. In effect, the Macdonald Commission (1981) concluded that, to avoid future political crimes by national security police, it was necessary to form a new civilian organization. The Canadian Security Intelligence Service (CSIS) was created in 1984, ideally to recruit and train individuals in a nonparamilitary organizational context. The assumption behind the creation of CSIS is that organizational culture (i.e., values, attitudes, beliefs, roles, and expected functions) is critical in preventing further illegal behaviour.

The importance of organizational factors is further evident in the emergence of social movements, which, depending on the threat they posed to governments and other authority institutions such as schools and businesses, have often been identified with political crimes. Universities, for example, historically have been connected with antistate terrorists such as the FLQ, while union movements have also been labelled subversive. Though less institutionalized than universities or unions, the Peace movement, environmental groups, civil rights organizations, or any social movement that challenges government policies are routinely considered by the authorities as potential spawning-grounds for political crimes. Both the Squamish Five activities and the "terrorist" act of sinking Icelandic whaling ships can be viewed as emerging from the larger Peace and environmental movements. Organizations, therefore, provide an essential ingredient for political crime—the conspiratorial context—whether by or against governments. Planning logistical resources, emotional support, and recruitment—all are facilitated by group structures.

Conflict theorists assert that certain social movements are so threatening to authorities that the latter often attempt to sway public opinion by labelling the former as criminal groups, or worse, as subversives under the control of foreign governments, usually the Soviet Union. Leftist student organizations and even the Parti Québécois were subjected to illegal acts by the RCMP in the 1970s because of the concern that the communist Cuban government was secretly providing funding for these organizations. Both Turk (1982) and Lauderdale (1980) maintain that a wide range of protest groups are monitored by the authorities, particularly the police and security agents, to assess any

potential threat. They further argue that labelling of groups as politically subversive or criminal is a function of power politics among competing elite groups and political parties. During the first two decades of the twentieth century, for example, unions were labelled as politically dangerous, communist-controlled organizations by Conservative governments in Canada. However, they became legitimate when the Liberal Party championed their legal rights during the 1920 national election. Once in power, the Liberal government reversed the previous official policy by recognizing the political and economic interest and functions of unions.

There is little doubt then that group dynamics are related to political crime. The relationship is complex, because a broad range of phenomena are subsumed under the concept of group dynamics. The FLQ, for example, consisted of cells of as few as three individuals each, while mass social movements such as civil rights and government agencies can involve thousands of members. The degree of organizational structure and the amount of economic and political power also can vary tremendously among groups involved in political crime. There is, therefore, no theory or theoretical perspective that explains all the relationships between group dynamics and political crime. Most authors concentrate upon one specific group, such as police or antistate terrorists. There is a voluminous literature in this area.

Lauderdale (1980), however, has attempted to develop an encompassing theoretical perspective that can generalize beyond specific group dynamics to explain how deviance can be transformed definitionally to political crime. Where conflict situations between groups and authorities create a high degree of fear in the latter group, the political process will be utilized to define the threatening group as political deviants or criminals. The dimensions of the character and relations of parties in conflict shown in Table 17.1 is illustrative of the tremendous complexity of this topic. However, there is theoretical consensus that most political crime cannot be understood without examining economic, political, and social processes, and specific group-organizational dynamics.

Societal-Level Perspective

There is little doubt that cultural and societal factors also contribute to explaining political crime. Individuals are exposed to distinctive cultural values that can motivate them to commit political crimes. It is equally evident that society-wide phenomena such as industrialization; urbanization; capitalist, socialist, or mixed economic systems; and democracy structure how people routinely interact. The individual decision to join a group or even act alone might

Table 17.1 Conflict Situations: Dimensions of the Character and Relations of Parties in Conflict

Resulting Popular Definition of the Conflict Situation	Size and Organization Feared	Relative Power of the Party Feared	Degree to Which Opposing Party Feels Fearful or Threatened
Deviance, "crime," etc.	Individuals or small, loosely organized groups	Almost none	Very high
Civil uprising or disorder	Small, loosely organized minority	Relatively low	Very high
Social movement	Sizable, organized minority	Relatively low	Mild
Civil war	Large, well-organized minority	Relatively high or almost equal	Very high
Mainstream party politics in the United States	Large, organized minority	About equal	Mild

Source: Pat Lauderdale (1980), *A political analysis of deviance* (p.8). Minneapolis: University of Minnesota Press (as adapted from John Lofland [1969], *Deviance and identity* (p.8). Englewood Cliffs, NJ: Prentice-Hall).

occur because of a particular culture, historical period, economic system, political system, or some combination of these factors. In other words, without the presence of one of these societal factors, a political crime might not have taken place. Similarly, the types of groups available for individuals to join are determined by societal factors. Multiple political parties, for example, are not found in totalitarian societies such as Nazi Germany.

Another example is the FLQ and the changing societal context of Quebec and Canada during the 1960s and 1970s. The success of the Parti Québécois in being elected to form the government of Quebec in 1976 and the transformation of Quebec to an urban and secular society and to a service economy may explain the total absence of political terrorism since there are many easily accessible organizations for individuals to join in contemporary Quebec that allow them to actualize their evolving cultural values. As well, the Parti Québécois government and its Liberal government successor have passed legislation ensuring the primacy of the French language, thereby diffusing a potentially explosive political issue. The combination of sweeping changes in Quebec society as a whole and the diminution of tense political issues appears to have created an unfavourable context for political terrorism.

This situation contrasts sharply with the societal context of the 1960s and early 1970s when Quebec was in transition from a rural, conservative, and Catholic-dominated society to an urban, cosmopolitan, and secular one. Political terrorism reached its zenith in this transition phase (see Box 17.2), and then steadily declined as Quebec's advanced industrial economy emerged. Economic relative depriva-

tion no longer appears to be a divisive concern of the majority of French Canadians who previously resented the disproportionate economic advantage English Canadians enjoyed both in Quebec and in English Canada. Quebec's standard of living is now comparable to the other two prosperous provinces, Ontario and British Columbia, and while provincial taxes are the highest in the country, Quebec is considered the most progressive in providing social-welfare and other services to its citizens. In effect, the wealth and opportunity provided by Quebec's advanced industrial economy has enhanced the standard of living in the province. This, along with the legal entrenchment of the primacy of the French language, has removed some, if not most, of the motivation for individuals to join political terrorist organizations.

Societal and cultural factors undoubtedly affect political crime. Judy Torrance (1988), in an analysis of this relationship in her book *Public Violence in Canada*, concluded that Canadian culture promoted the myth that Canada historically shunned violence (in contrast to another former British colony, the United States). She maintains that various forms of public violence, such as terrorism and riots, while not as infrequent as the "peaceful Kingdom of Canada" myth suggests, are not as common as in other Western countries. Torrance contends that public violence is lower also because, historically, most Canadians have supported the severe government response to violent political crime against the state, such as the hanging of Louis Riel and the use of the RNWMP to suppress the Winnipeg General Strike. Finally, Torrance argues that factors at the societal and cultural levels interact with group and individual levels to best explain political crime in the form of public violence. We now turn to an examination of three competing theoretical perspectives about the relationship between the Canadian political system and political crime.

Political Process and Political Crime

A conceptual problem endemic to the study of political crime is that, in the final analysis, governments themselves define what behaviours are "criminal," because they have the ability to make law.

But it should be evident now that it is difficult to define political crime simply in terms of illegality. It is nevertheless clear that political process is crucial in determining both what is an illegal act as well as the public image of political crime. There are three general theoretical perspectives that link political process and political crime in Canada—liberal-democratic, pluralist-democratic, and capitalist-democratic (see Corrado, 1987). Each perspective purports to explain how and why deviant political acts become categorized or labelled "political crime."

Liberal-Democratic Perspective on Political Process: Consensus

According to the liberal-democratic perspective, the majority of the Canadian electorate are ultimately responsible for the criminal law because they elect the Members of Parliament who have the power to amend the **Criminal Code** to create a law that defines political crime. Such reform is ideally undertaken by politicians with due consideration for the views of Canadians. The various criminal-justice agencies, beginning with the police, then impartially administer the law to identify and process **alleged** political criminals and then to punish those convicted. In effect, the liberal-democratic perspective describes a straightforward relationship, with the majority of voting Canadians deciding what is political crime and what should be done about it. Laws are created, amended, or repealed as public sentiments change. This perspective shares much with the **consensus approach** presented in the Introduction.

Trudeau adhered to this theoretical perspective in explaining his government's response to the October Crisis. He argued that there were no conspiratorial political mo-

---

Box 17.2 The FLQ Crisis, October 1970

The Front de libération du Québec (FLQ) was a small group of extremists on the fringe of the separatist movement in the 1960s who used violence as a means of achieving social change. This distinguished them from the other separatist parties of the day, such as the Rassemblement pour l'indépendance nationale (RIN), which ran candidates in provincial elections and used other nonviolent tactics. The FLQ disbanded shortly after most of its members were incarcerated or exiled in the aftermath of the "October Crisis" of 1970.

The FLQ undertook the first of 200 bombings in 1963. These incidents ranged from mail bombs sent to individuals to the bombing of the Montreal Stock Exchange, where 27 people were injured. Government buildings were a common target. To finance their efforts, they engaged in robberies, of money and armaments, and during one such incident, two people were killed (one innocent being shot by police).

The most noted and intellectual member was Pierre Vallières, the author of *Nègres Blancs d'Amérique* (White Niggers of America). But its membership was never very large. In 1969, it split into two cells of about twelve each. One group kidnapped James Cross, the British trade commissioner, from his Westmount home, on October 5, 1970. They demanded the release of FLQ members from jail and the broadcast of their nationalist manifesto. The latter was accomplished, but a second kidnapping took place on October 10, when Pierre Laporte, the Quebec Minister of Labour, was abducted.

The response of the federal government to these incidents remains controversial, even to this day. At the request of the Quebec provincial government, members of the armed forces were called in, on October 15. The next day, the federal government declared that a state of "apprehended insurrection" existed, allowing them to use the emergency provisions of the War Measures Act (see Chapter 1). Being a member of the FLQ was immediately outlawed and normal due process rights were suspended to permit law-enforcement officers broader investigative powers. In effect, Canada became a police state. More than 450 persons were detained without charge, many of whom were associated with law-abiding separatist groups.

Two days later, the body of Pierre Laporte was discovered in the trunk of a car. He had been strangled with a religious medallion, apparently while trying to escape. James Cross remained in captivity until the police

Box 17.2 (Continued)

discovered his whereabouts, in early December. After negotiation, five of his captors were permitted to fly to Cuba in exchange for Cross's safe release. The members of the cell that kidnapped Laporte were arrested a month later. Paul Rose and Francis Simard were eventually convicted of murder and sentenced to life imprisonment. Several others, including Rose's brother Jacques, were convicted of lesser offences.

In retrospect, many feel that the imposition of the War Measures Act was too extreme a response under the circumstances. Indeed, it has been the only occasion on which the War Measures Act has been used for an internal, domestic crisis. The freedom given police led to abuses, in that people not remotely associated with the FLQ were detained or harassed, as far away as Vancouver. But the move, made by the very popular Pierre Trudeau, was supported by the vast majority of the public at the time.

Controversy also surrounds the events in the year that followed the October Crisis. The RCMP security division attempted to monitor the activities of the Parti Québécois and other political groups. These activities, euphemistically labelled "wrongdoings," included bugging, opening mail, break-ins, theft, and the burning of a barn (see Sawatsky, 1980). The 1981 report of the Macdonald Commission was critical of the inability of the RCMP to distinguish between threats to national security and the legitimate political opposition central to democratic systems. The recommendations led ultimately to the creation of the civilian Canadian Security Intelligence Service (CSIS).

A corporal in the Canadian Armed Forces stands near a Quebec provincial flag flying at half mast for Pierre Laporte.

Canadian Forces Photographic Unit, no. VL 70-155-7.

---

tives behind the imposition of the War Measures Act or the subsequent RCMP antiterrorist policies. Instead, he claimed he was earnestly implementing legitimate policies that all but a small minority of Canadians supported. For Trudeau, it became necessary to take extreme measures since the FLQ promised to escalate terrorist violence by assassinating government leaders if imprisoned FLQ members were not released. Along with most Canadians, Trudeau believed this terrorist threat constituted an "apprehended insurrection" or an attempt by a tiny minority of fanatics violently to impose their political values.

The Pluralist-Democratic Perspective on Political Process: Interest-Group Competition

The pluralist-democratic perspective depicts a more com-

plicated picture of the relationship between political process and political crime. Political power is shared between the electorate, on the one hand, and political elites, on the other. On a daily basis, it is the competition and co-operation of political elites that determines government policies. Business and union leaders, senior civil servants, political-party fundraisers, Members of Parliament, cabinet members, premiers, and the prime minister belong to various competing interest groups that both share and compete for political power to distribute advantages or rewards. Lucrative government contracts to private businesses, favourable tax legislation, appointments to powerful administrative bodies, international trade agreements, and cabinet positions are among the rewards and opportunities that elites compete for on a routine basis.

The competition is structured by "informal rules of the game," which are often hidden from the public and of which they are ignorant, because the elites want to avoid the appearance of corruption. The awarding of contracts, for example, has traditionally gone to businesses that are financial supporters of the political party in power, even though the public often assumes that government contracts are subject to competitive bidding. The government of Prime Minister Brian Mulroney attempted to challenge the media image that portrayed some of its cabinet members and key Progressive Conservative political-party leaders as corrupt. Many of those caught in scandals claim they are simply engaging in traditional politics, because the Liberal government and party members engage in the same practices when they are in power.

According to proponents of the pluralist perspective, the competing elites are aware that their ability to control the daily political process requires the placation of the public. In effect, elites must either give the majority enough of what it expects or deceive the public so that it believes the political process is under its ultimate control. With regard to corruption, for example, the elites will attempt to change the political process to prevent its occurring too frequently because widespread and persistent corruption can foster radical changes that are extremely disadvantageous for most of the elites. The other option is to change the appearance of the political process so that the public is likely to be unaware of the "unjust" or unfair advantages claimed by the elites. Taxes, for example, are so complicated to most Canadians that the elites are able to manipulate them and often avoid paying their own share.

Under the pluralist political process, elites attempt to control both the legal definition and the popular or media image of the political crime. Political terrorism is especially threatening because it has the potential to undermine or change the basic pluralist political process. Ideological, antistate terrorists, by definition, seek to substitute an entirely new political system, whereas ethnic nationalist terrorists seek to partition the geographical boundaries of a country. In either scenario, the dominant elites will lose all or some of their control of the political process. The Squamish Five, for example, could have been seen as particularly threatening, had they not been portrayed as careless and naive idealists. In other words, the protection of the environment and the prevention of both sexual exploitation and an escalation of the arms race—ideals central to their motives—are positions supported by most Canadians. However, the media portrayal of the Squamish Five focussed considerably more on individual traits than these types of values. In effect, the political message of the Squamish Five was suppressed because the elites were virtually united in their attempt to convince the public that no crisis existed and that these five individuals were dangerous terrorists.

In Canada, elites disagree, to some extent, about limiting public expressions of the extremist, anti-Semitic views of individuals such as Ernst Zundel from Toronto and Jim Keegstra from Alberta. Both have had celebrated criminal trials over their right to print and teach their conspiratorial theory about Nazi Germany and the alleged "holocaust" or killing of six million Jews in concentration camps. They vehemently asserted that the holocaust did not take place and that an international Zionist (pro-Israeli Jews) conspiracy has fabricated and perpetuated the holocaust myth. The dominant or controlling elites eventually chose to criminalize public expressions of ethnic and racial defamation by amending the Criminal Code, but for many years no action was taken to pass the necessary laws (see Chapter 1). One of the reasons cited for this inaction was the threat to free speech that such a law might constitute. The civil libertarian elite objects to the limitation of the freedom to express political opinions of any ideological persuasion, and they hope and expect that the Supreme Court of Canada eventually will declare this limitation contrary to the freedom of speech provision in the **Canadian Charter of Rights and Freedoms**.

The dilemma for the elites is exacerbated by the feared linkage between anti-Semitic public statements and right-wing ideological terrorism. In Alberta, for example, two individuals were charged with a conspiracy to assassinate a leading Jewish businessman in Edmonton. The two charged were associated with fascist terrorist organizations based across the U.S. border in the state of Idaho. Members of a variety of white supremacist and anti-Semitic terrorist organizations such as the Aryan Brotherhood have been arrested and convicted of numerous assaults, bank robberies, and murders. One of the most notorious cases involved the machine gun killing of the controversial and acerbic Denver radio talk-show host, and Jew, Alan Berg. His accused assassins were members of the Bruder Schweigen (New Order). Another notorious group was the Aryan Nation, whose leader, Robert Matthews, was trapped in a log cabin on Whidbey Island in Washington State near the British Columbia border. Federal Bureau of Investigation (FBI) officials and other law enforcement officers had engaged in an enormous manhunt that led to Matthews being cornered and killed. These right-wing terrorist groups are considered as major threats in certain midwestern and western states. Many members have been arrested, and they have formed powerful prison gangs in the California, Texas, and Illinois state prison systems.

In Canada, the concern is that this evolutionary pattern

not develop with similar murderous results. "Skin-head" gangs in Toronto also are related to the right-wing extremist reaction to the recent major influx of visible minorities from the Indian subcontinent, Asia, and the Caribbean. It is this immigration trend that has the elites worried about the escalation of fascist terrorism, i.e., those who believe violence is appropriate to maintain the dominant states and population majority of white Anglo-Saxon Protestants (WASPs).

For elites to maintain control of the political process, they have historically had not only to absorb new elites, but also to deal with violent ethnic and ideological challenges to the traditional political system. For most conflict theorists, therefore, the key to understanding the pluralist political process is the competition among elites for control of the political institutions, such as Parliament, that officially define political crime; the agencies, such as police, that enforce the elite definitions of this crime; and the media, which is so critical in reinforcing the elite desired image of the "only way" of dealing with political crime. As mentioned above, competition among elites varies according to the type of political crime and the degree to which it threatens specific elite interests *vis-à-vis* the entire political process. Since political terrorism can constitute the latter threat, substantial consensus is not uncommon among elites when a sustained and particularly violent terrorist group exists. Again, this scenario was evident in Canada during the October Crisis of 1970. However, such a consensus can dissipate if the threat is unfounded. Torrance (1988) maintains that, since the inception of Canada, governments have nearly always succeeded in obtaining sufficient elite co-operation and public support to deal severely with political rebellions and terrorism.

The Capitalist-Democratic Perspective on Political Process: Elite Control

The third view of the relationship between the political process and political crime centres on the capitalist system. The political process is seen as being directed by the elite who, through ownership of economic enterprises, control the economic structures of Canada. The electorate, other interest groups, and political parties exercise limited influence on the political process because the capitalist, or corporate elite, have ultimate power through their elaborate connections to the key institutions of political power. These connections include political party financing, personal ties, mutual employment exchanges and appointments to powerful administrative bodies, both federally and provincially.

Wallace Clement (1977) has traced this maze of connections and exchange of economic advantage for political power in Canada and concludes that the capitalist elite's fundamental objective is to ensure that the politicians pass laws that maintain the conditions necessary for accumulation of private profit. Clement (1977) acknowledges that, in a capitalist democracy, it is necessary that the majority of the electorate perceive that their interests are satisfied. Therefore, the capitalist elite willingly moderate the inequalities of the capitalism system with the welfare state. Unemployment and health insurance and universal access to education and social welfare services are all part of the welfare net that is supposed to maintain a minimum standard of living. In return, the capitalist elite benefit from the political stability and the healthy and educated work force needed to produce profits in the advanced industrial economy. When problems such as a recession arise, solutions are sought that satisfy workers sufficiently without threatening the dominant economic and political position of the capitalist elite.

From this perspective, therefore, political crime is legally defined and responded to by the criminal-justice system in a manner that is desired by the capitalist elite. This may change over time. During the Winnipeg General Strike of 1919, for example, the capitalist elite labelled union leaders political criminals and used the criminal-justice system to control, punish, and deter. Yet, by the 1960s, unions had become fundamentally integrated and accepted in both the economic and political process. For the capitalist elite, co-operative unions could assist capital accumulation if their wage and related job demands did not interfere significantly with business competitiveness and profits. Unions were beneficial if they increased worker organization and morale and a company's public image. Nonetheless, the capitalist elite, when suffering profit losses during the major recessions of the post–World War II period, used the political process to limit and even reduce union power. The United Kingdom, under the government of Prime Minister Margaret Thatcher, is a classic illustration of the capitalist-elite backlash against unions. Virtually overnight, laws were enacted to destroy the considerable accumulated political and economic power of unions. Faced with prolonged strikes by coal miners, the government responded with aggressive police attacks and media manipulation to break the striking unions. Legislation also was passed that stripped the union leadership of much of their financial and organizational power. The prime minister was generally successful in convincing the British electorate that radical, political criminal elements, i.e., communists and subversives, were destroying the British economy and directly threatening British parliamentary democracy. The antiunion legislation was followed with legislation that sharply reduced taxes on corporations and the wealthy, and privatized many long-standing state corporations.

Where necessary then, the capitalist elite will direct the political process to utilize the political-criminal label against groups and organizations that are perceived as constituting a threat to stability and order. Terrorism is one of the ultimate threats and it is usually dealt with severely in response. For the capitalist elite, antistate terrorist groups committed to leftist ideologies, such as communism and anarchism, are considered particularly dangerous because they are seen to be connected to an international anticapitalist conspiracy directed by revolutionary countries such as the Soviet Union and Cuba. This type of antistate terrorism is even more individually threatening because members of the capitalist elite have been popular targets for kidnapping and/or assassination. The terrorist Italian Red Brigades and the West German Red Army Faction, for example, have assassinated several leading industrialists in their respective countries. The military and police have also been victims of these antistate terrorists. Generals and other officers are considered symbols of capitalist oppression because it is the military and the police that are employed by the capitalist elite to violently intimidate and control the working class.

In Canada, the FLQ and, to a lesser extent, the Squamish Five followed the pattern of attacking the capitalist elite. During the October Crisis of 1970, the FLQ cells that had kidnapped James Cross and Pierre Laporte demanded that the media broadcast communiqués that described their Marxist ideological critique of Canadian society. The Squamish Five viewed the military/industrial complex as a primary target, bombing a Lytton Industry plant in Toronto that produced parts for the Cruise missile. They had also planned to bomb an Armed Forces base in Alberta.

Ethnic nationalism as a goal of terrorists is seen to be as dangerous as acts fuelled by ideology because both the stability and the geographical integrity of the capitalist economy are threatened. The FLQ's goal of an independent Quebec would jeopardize the enormous capitalist wealth invested in that province since not only would a populous and resource-rich market be splintered from the Canadian market, but also the capitalist industries in Quebec would be nationalized according to the FLQ's Marxist ideology.

The Khalistani terrorists, as well, threaten the capitalist elite because they can create an unfavourable investment image in Canada for international capital, and they particularly jeopardize the growing trade with India, whose domestic market potential for Canadian business is enormous.

In summary, the three competing perspectives about the relationship between the Canadian political process and political crime remain contentious primarily because there are insufficient data to assess their validity. Each perspective can be applied to a specific historical event identified as a political crime and provide some critical insights (Corrado, 1987). No one perspective, however, appears theoretically dominant.

Historical Overview of Political Terrorism in Canada

In Canada, one of the most recent little-understood political crimes was the 1985 bombing of Air India Flight 182. No single incident in Canadian history has caused so many deaths, yet no one has been charged with, let alone convicted of, this heinous crime that killed so many innocent Indo-Canadians. There is not doubt that a bomb exploded aboard the plane, but who had planted it and why remain at issue despite an enormous and expensive RCMP and CSIS investigation. The most obvious explanation for this political crime is found in the development of the Khalistani political terrorist movement in India and the historical response of various Indian governments to it.

Before examining this Sikh case (see Box 17.4), it is important to review briefly the historical context of political terrorism in Canada. It can be maintained that political crime has been a persistent part of Canadian history. Political corruption and the ensuing scandals date back to the government of Sir John A. Macdonald (see Box 17.3) and have continued through to today. Violent political crime

---

Box 17.3 The Ten Worst Political Scandals in Canadian History

1. **The Pacific Scandal, 1872**
Through Sir Hugh Allan, American contractors contributed heavily to the Tory election fund in 1872 in return for a controlling interest in Canada's proposed Pacific railway. When Sir John A. Macdonald balked at their demands, they tried blackmail and, finally, with a lot of help from the Liberals, brought the facts to light. Even the hardened

political consciences of the time were shocked, and the "Pacific Scandal" drove Macdonald from office for all his claims that "these hands are clean."

2. **The Beauharnois Scandal, 1930**
Whoever won the hydro power rights to the Beauharnois section of the St. Lawrence River would have made the

Box 17.3 *(Continued)*

deal of the century. A House of Commons committee found that the successful syndicate had been remarkably generous to the sanctimonious but tight-fisted William Lyon Mackenzie King and two top Liberals. As graft goes, the amounts paid to King were trifling, but they were enough to send him and the Liberals, in King's words, into "the valley of humiliation."

3.   The Manitoba Legislature Scandal, 1915

For most of a year, Manitoba voters followed the details of how the price of their new Legislature had doubled, with the proceeds going to a shabby network of contractors, officials, and Conservative fundraisers. The Tories were swept from office and the premier, Sir Rodmond Roblin, and three ministers faced trial. Others escaped by fleeing to the United States. The chief contractor, Thomas Kelly, went to jail, but the politicians had their charges dropped because of ill health.

4.   The Langevin–McGreevy Scandals, 1891

J. Israel Tarte, the Conservative organizer in Quebec, kept all his secrets in a little black bag. When he opened it, the revelations of kickbacks, payoffs, and fraud sent Thomas McGreevy, the Tories' Quebec fundraiser, to jail. It took all the efforts of a weakened Conservative government to save eminent Sir Hector Langevin, Minister of Public Works, from the same fate. For the Tories, leaderless after the death of Sir John A. Macdonald, the scandal could well have been fatal.

5.   The Baie de Chaleur Scandal, 1891

If the Tories were saved, it was because the same black bag contained enough scandal to destroy the Nationalist regime of Quebec's premier, Honoré Mercier. Payoffs for a contract to build a railway to Baie de Chaleur helped pay Mercier's expenses on a lavish trip to Paris and Rome. Mercier's personal ruin helped the career of another Quebec liberal, Wilfrid Laurier.

6.   The Brownlee Scandal, 1934

The Chief Justice of Alberta did not believe the claim of pretty Vivian MacMillan that her boss, Premier John Brownlee, had had a three-year affair with her. The people of drought-stricken, puritanical Alberta preferred to believe Miss MacMillan. What they really wanted was vengeance against a bankrupt, ineffective government. Within a year, they had William (Bible Bill) Aberhart and Social Credit.

7.   The Squires Scandal, 1932

It did not take much of a scandal to destroy a government during the Depression. Major Peter Cashin's claim that Newfoundland premier Sir Richard Squires had falsified cabinet minutes to conceal illegal payments to himself and cabinet cronies was enough to send the hungry, desperate people of St. John's on a rampage of destruction through the House of Assembly. Squires barely escaped with his life. A British cruiser hurried to St. John's, and Newfoundland's bankrupt government surrendered the island's Dominion status to a British-appointed commission.

8.   The Rivard Scandal, 1964

An assistant to the Liberal Minister of Citizenship and Immigration offered a $20 000 bribe to a Montreal lawyer to get bail for Lucien Rivard, a narcotics smuggler. There was also a promise of money for Liberal-party funds. The prime minister, Lester Pearson, claimed that his Minister of Justice, Guy Favreau, had told him nothing of the affair. It did not help that Rivard later escaped with amazing ease from his Montreal prison. It was even less helpful that most of those contaminated were French-Canadian Liberals. Those who raised the scandal were accused of anti-French bias.

9.   The Northern Ontario Natural Gas Scandal, 1958

Three Ontario Tory cabinet ministers, a mayor of Sudbury (later a federally appointed judge), and several other favoured people were allowed to buy Northern Ontario Natural Gas (NON) stock before public sales began. They just happened to be the people who had most influence over where the natural-gas line would run. But times were good, and Ontario voters were loyal to their belief that scandals happen only elsewhere in Canada.

10.   The Soldier Vote Scandal, 1917

As part of their efforts to win victory for the pro-conscription Union government in the wartime election of 1917, organizers persuaded military voters to switch their ballots to ridings where the Unionist candidates needed help. This disgraceful proceeding enraged the Liberals and led them to cry corruption . . . and all of these switched ballots were disallowed by election officials.

Source: Jeremy Brown & David Ondaatje (1978), *The first original unexpurgated authentic Canadian book of lists* (pp. 384–86). Scarborough: Macmillan.

in the form of rebellions and riots has occurred periodically and with sufficient regularity for Torrance (1988) to assert that the image of Canada as a "peaceable kingdom" is a myth. Yet political terrorism has not been as common as these other forms of political crime.

Political terrorism has occurred in Canada primarily during the post–World War II period of the 1960s and early 1970s, and the mid-1980s (see Table 17.2). The first political-terrorist incidents can be traced to the Sons of Freedom who were religious and cultural fundamentalists belonging to the Doukhobor ethnic group. Violent clashes occurred among factions with the Doukhobor community over cultural assimilation and leadership issues and the first recorded incident took place in 1924 when an explosion in a railway car killed a Doukhobor leader and eight other passengers. The Sons of Freedom were associated with a major outbreak of terrorism between 1958 and 1962 in the Kootenay area in the southeastern interior region of British Columbia. Three Doukhobors were killed and more than a hundred bombings and burnings took place. One estimate of the total number of Doukhobor terrorist acts was over a thousand (Torrance, 1988). Since 1962, when most of the terrorists were arrested and imprisoned, there have been only a few isolated incidents of violence, apparently associated with leadership squabbles (see also Chapter 12).

Table 17.2 Frequency of Events of Domestic Political Terrorism, by Year

Year	Quebec Separatists[1]	Sons of Freedom[2]	Other Groups[3]	Total[4]	Percent
1960		6		6	1.5
1961		39	2	41	9.9
1962		34		34	8.2
1963	22	1	2	25	6.0
1964	6	2	3	11	2.7
1965	8	1	6	15	3.6
1966	3		2	5	1.2
1967	3		4	7	1.7
1968	38		13	51	12.3
1969	34		16	40	9.6
1970	30	6	6	42	10.1
1971	19	2	15	36	8.7
1972	2	3	2	7	1.7
1973		4	1	5	1.2
1974			3	3	0.7
1975		3		3	0.7
1976		2		2	0.5
1977		1	3	4	1.0
1978		4	1	5	1.2
1979		4	1	5	1.2
1980	1	4	6	11	2.7
1981		7	18	25	6.0
1982		3	7	10	2.4
1983			15	15	3.6
1984		2	1	3	0.7
1985		2	1	3	0.7
Total	166	130	128	414	100.0

[1]Based on events that were either claimed by the organization or reliably attributed to them.

[2]Based on events that were either claimed by the organization or reliably attributed to them.

[3]Based on events that were either claimed by the organization or reliably attributed to them minus total number of actions.

[4]Based on claimed, reliably attributed, and inferred actions.

Source: Jeffrey Ian Ross (1988), Attributes of domestic political terrorism in Canada, 1960–1985 (p.220). *Terrorism, 11.*

The other major period of antistate terrorism took place between 1963 and 1970 and involved the FLQ. Approximately 170 violent acts, including eight deaths, occurred during this period. As discussed above, the FLQ terrorism was responded to by a series of state terrorist incidents, none of which resulted in fatalities. More recently the Squamish Five were briefly involved in terrorist activity, but this too ceased with their arrest and imprisonment.

The form of international terrorism represented by the Air India incident (see Box 17.4) appears to be perplexing to the Canadian government and confusing to the Cana-dian public. There appears to be no political outrage among the Canadian electorate that would galvanize the elites to take the extraordinary counterterrorist tactics that were involved in the far less violent incidents of the October Crisis of 1970. The outrage appears confined to the Indo-Canadian community, many of whom feel that racism toward their culture mitigates any official dramatic response. In effect, had the 329 victims of the Air India flight been Caucasian Canadians, the government and other elites, along with the vast majority of the public, most likely would insist on extraordinary counterterrorist measures.

Box 17.4 Sikh Nationalism and the International Political Process

There is insufficient space in this chapter to review the complex history of Sikh nationalism in India, yet this history is the key to explaining why this movement is the cause of the most violent terrorist act in Canadian history—the bombing of the Air India Flight 182. This flight, which originated in Toronto, crashed into the North Atlantic off the coast of Ireland, killing all passengers on board on June 23, 1985. A large majority were Indo-Canadians.

Sikh nationalists want the Indian government to allow for the creation of an autonomous Sikh state in the Punjab area of northern India. Khalistani nationalists take the extreme stance that an independent nation-state of Khalistan must be established in the entire northwestern region that traditionally has been dominated by Sikhs. The situation is complicated by the fact that this region includes areas where the Indian government encouraged Hindu immigration and population growth, along with Hindu economic and political domination. Both moderate and extremist Sikh nationalists fear the gradual demise of the Sikh religion and its related culture. Religious fundamentalists are more immediately concerned with maintaining the strict adherence to dress and other religious rituals that so clearly distinguish them from other major Indo religions, such as the Hindu and Moslem.

With only approximately 13 million Sikhs (living primarily in the Punjab region of India and also in the Pakistani-controlled sections of Kashmir), Sikh nationalists fear the enormous Hindu and Moslem populations, which together will soon approach one billion. With such a small population base, Sikhs are in a politically vulnerable position in India's national parliamentary system. It is the national Parliament that ultimately decides the geographic configuration of states, economic policies, and access to interstate economic resources, such as irrigation water.

Former prime minister Indira Gandhi and her Congress party were in control of the Indian government when a series of decisions and events took place in India that precipitated Sikh political terrorism in Canada. Prior to these political events, there had been a dramatic increase in immigration to Canada from India that began in earnest in the early 1970s. Within a decade, substantial Sikh and Hindu communities existed in major Canadian metropolitan areas, particularly Vancouver. These immigrants rapidly integrated into the economic system and developed viable ethnic community organizations.

For the Sikhs, their temples, or *gurdwaras*, became the focal point for maintaining ethnic solidarity. During the initial phase, the *gurdwaras* elected politically moderate individuals. The more extreme organizations that developed were the International Sikh Youth Federation (ISYF) and the Balbar Khala (Tigers of the Faith). The ISYF co-ordinated branches in Canada and maintained ties with branches in Great Britain and India in order to promote the sacred homeland of Khalistan. Its members completely deny any involvement with terrorism, and, instead, argue vehemently that the Indian government has an unofficial policy of barbaric state terrorism against Sikhs in India and illegal spying and infiltration of the Sikh communities in Canada. The Balbar Khala claim their goal is to protect the Sikh faith and create Khalistan. Their leader, Talwinder S. Parmar, who lives in Vancouver, is considered a living martyr. He too denies any involvement in terrorist activity in Canada, but his group allegedly has been linked to random bombings, beatings, and assassinations, primarily in India (Mulgrew, 1988). Supporters of these radical organizations have been accused of using violence and intimidation to take control of certain Sikh temples in Canada. This control allows the radicals access to the financing necessary to carry out their clandestine activities, as well as monitor their political opposition in the Sikh

Box 17.4 *(Continued)*

communities. In addition, the radicals can now more directly attempt to influence the media image in Canada concerning the Khalistani cause, which they claim is grossly distorted by Indian government propaganda.

It is within the context of the Sikh community that events in India further radicalized the Khalistani movement in Canada. In response to the demand of the moderate Sikh political party, the Akali Dal, Prime Minister Indira Gandhi attempted to introduce political compromise in the Punjab by creating three new states. Sikhs constituted the majority in the Punjab Suba; Hindus became the majority in the state of Haryana. However, additional issues arose that set the stage for the emergence of the radical nationalist and fundamentalist leader, Sant Jarnail Singh Bindranwale. These issues focussed on the desire of Sikhs for further delegation of political power to the Punjab Suba, particularly control over economic policy. An outstanding issue involved the India Water Agreement, which Sikhs feared would divert too much water from their state to the neighbouring Haryana state. The Punjab Suba has India's most productive agricultural economy, and many Sikhs already resented what they believed was the unfair redistribution of economic wealth to less successful states. The federal government refused to alter its traditional control of agricultural policies and, consequently, political polarization continued in spite of the creation of the new Sikh-dominated state.

The extremist Bindranwale opposed the Akali Dal's moderate political strategy of electoral politics and argued that violence was the only solution. With the increase in terrorist incidents in the Punjab, the Indian government claimed that Bindranwale was being supported by both an international terrorist movement, including extremists in Canada, and the Pakistani military government (India's arch-enemy). To escape Indian security police, Bindranwale and his other key leaders took refuge in the Sikhs' most holy shrine, the Golden Temple in Amritsar. According to the Indian government, Bindranwale had turned this temple into an armed fortress and used it to direct the escalating terrorism, including the assassination of moderate Sikh politicians and attacks against police officials and Hindus. More than 300 people were killed in a four-month period in 1984 (*Time*, June 18, 1984).

Operation Blue Star was set in motion in June 1984 by Gandhi and her senior army officers. She was well aware than an assault on the holy shrine would be considered a sacrilegious invasion to Sikhs and would result in brutal acts of revenge against the invaders. The Indian army encountered considerable armed resistance in its initial attack on the Gold Temple, and this led to more forceful and indiscriminate attacks, resulting in the death not only of Bindranwale but also of innocent pilgrims. The army also was accused of torturing those who surrendered.

As expected, many Sikhs, including political moderates in India and abroad, were outraged with Gandhi. Radicals vowed revenge against the Indian government, and it came four months later when two Sikh members of Indira Gandhi's personal security force shot her to death in her housing compound. Riots erupted immediately in the northern and central states, and thousands of Sikhs were viciously murdered in the streets by Hindus. This indiscriminate violence further infuriated radical Sikhs who again vowed not only to continue to assassinate other leaders involved with Operation Blue Star, but also to use terrorism to attack the Indian economy.

It was within this bitter and vengeful context originating in India that the radical or extremist element in the Sikh community in Canada resorted to terrorism. In fall 1985, more radical elements in the Sikh community began to seize control of the *gurdwaras* in B.C. Moderate temple leaders were intimidated through vicious beatings, which scared away many of the voters. Criminal trials have taken place against those who committed the assaults. Nonetheless, a majority of the temples in the populous Greater Vancouver area of B.C. are now in the control of pro-Khalistani executives, primarily members of the International Sikh Youth Federation (Dornan, 1989).

The escalating campaign of terrorism reached its zenith on June 23, 1985, when Air India Flight 182 exploded off the coast of Ireland. Another explosion took place the same day at the airport in Narita, Japan, while luggage was being transferred from a Canadian Pacific flight from Vancouver to an Air India plane.

The World Sikh Organization immediately issued denials of any Sikh involvement with the bombings and asserted that the Indian government was behind the two terrorist incidents: "This is only the latest attack in the continuing campaign of defamation of the Sikhs by attempting to brand them as terrorists in the eyes of the western world" (Reuters, June 24, 1985). While no one has been charged directly with the bombings, two Sikh Vancouver Island residents were prime suspects. One of the suspects moved

Box 17.4 *(Continued)*

to England, and recently the Canadian government has sought his extradition so he can stand trial here for charges related to the two bombings.

Sikh extremists also were accused of plotting to assassinate Indira Gandhi's successor, her son Rajiv Gandhi, while he was on a state visit to England. Two Sikhs suspected of involvement with the Air India bombings were arrested in the United States after having attended a privately run mercenary and special-weapons training facility in Alabama. They were accused of plotting another assassination attempt against the new prime minister. Other Sikh extremists were accused of attending a similar private school in Surrey, B.C. Finally, on September 25, 1986, Malkiat Singh Sidhu, a minister from the Punjab region, was shot several times while travelling alone in his car during a private visit in British Columbia. Those who committed the assassination were arrested and convicted. Crown Counsel claimed the motive was political revenge for Sidhu's public support for Gandhi and that those who committed the terrorist act were members of the ISYF. The defence lawyer denied the terrorist affiliations.

Conclusion

This chapter examined politically motivated criminality primarily as it is expressed in national and international terrorism. Regardless of which theoretical perspective is employed to explain the phenomenon, it is clear that it must ultimately account for a complex interaction of motives, organizational dynamics, cultural values, and institutional economic structures. Moreover, it could be argued that any crime can be labelled "political" if it can be shown to be motivated by a desire to foster specific power interests. Thus, murder, arson, drugs, kidnapping, each may be overlain with the imputation of being a political crime, if it is deemed to be bound to the organization and interests of a political cause. And, in this sense, there is nothing particularly unique about politically motivated crime that might lead to the creation of theories about the causation of crime different from the ones we have already discussed in this text. The question of pressing interest to criminologists, however, is *who* defines the crime as politically motivated; who has the power to make such an imputation "stick"; and, finally, who has the power to mobilize a sanctioning response from the state in relation to it?

Terrorism, as the most violent form of politically motivated crime, has been descriptively profiled in this chapter because of its relatively recent emergence as a crime feared not only in Canada, but worldwide. Relative to our discussion of theories earlier in the text, it would seem difficult for "individual" theorists to suggest ways to "treat" terrorists; however, it appears that no one sociological theory offers adequate direction for dealing with the range of terrorist criminality in evidence today. But, with further research and study, it is hoped we can come to understand its causal context better in order to more effectively curb its occurrence.

Discussion Questions

1. What are the central elements to any definition of political crime? How do these elements interact in reality?

2. Describe forms of political criminality that would "fit" into each of the three levels of perspectives identified in the chapter: individual, organization, and societal.

3. How would a conflict theorist respond to the following statement: governments themselves define that behaviours are "criminal"—because they have the ability to make laws.

4. Taking the FLQ crisis as your example, describe how the liberal-democratic perspective would differ from the pluralist-democratic perspective and the capitalist-democratic perspective in explaining what occurred.

References

Berger, T. (1981). *Fragile freedoms* . Toronto: Clark, Irwin.

Chambliss, W. (1976). Functional and conflict theories of crime: The heritage of Emile Durkheim and Karl Marx. In W. Chambliss & M. Mankoff (Eds.), *Who's law? What order? A conflict approach to criminology* (pp. 1–28). New York: Wiley.

Chomsky, N., & Herman, E.S. (1979). *The political economy of human rights*, Vol. 1 & 2. Nottingham: Spokesman.

Clement, W. (1977). The corporate elite, the capitalist class, and the Canadian state. In L. Panitch (Ed.), *The Canadian state: Political economy and political power* (pp. 225–48). Toronto: University of Toronto Press.

Clinard, M.B., & Quinney, R. (1973). *Criminal behaviour systems: A typology*. New York: Holt, Rinehart & Winston.

Corrado, R.R. (1987). Political crime in Canada. In R. Linden (Ed.), *Criminology: A Canadian perspective* (pp. 295–319). Toronto: Holt, Rinehart & Winston.

Crelinsten, R.D. (1985). *Limits to criminal justice in the control of insurgent political violence: A case study of the October Crisis of 1970*. Unpublished doctoral dissertation, University of Montreal.

Crelinsten, R.D. (1987). Power and meaning: Terrorism as a struggle over access to the communication structure. In P. Wilkinson and A.M. Steward (eds.), *Research on terrorism* (pp. 419–50). Great Britain: Aberdeen.

Dornan, W. (1989). *A policy analysis of current legislation in Canada dealing with terrorism. A case study: Sikh extremism*. Incomplete Master of Arts (Criminology) thesis, Simon Fraser University, Burnaby, BC.

Horrall, S.W. (1980). The Royal North-West Mounted Police and labour unrest in Western Canada, 1919. *Canadian Historical Review, 61,* 169–90.

Ingram, B.L. (1979). *Political crime in Europe*. Berkeley: University of California Press.

Lauderdale, P. (1980). *A political analysis of deviance*. Minneapolis: University of Minnesota Press.

Lofland, J. (1969). *Deviance and identity*. Englewood Cliffs, NJ: Prentice-Hall.

Lombroso, C. (1918). *Crime: Its causes and remedies*. Boston: Little, Brown.

McDonald, D.C. (1981). *Commission of inquiry concerning activities of the Royal Canadian Mounted Police*. Ottawa: Minister of Supply & Services.

Merton, R.K. (1968). *Social theory and social structure*. New York: Free Press.

Mulgrew, I. (1988). *Unholy terror: The Sikhs and international terrorism*. Toronto: Key Porter.

Proal, L. (1898). *Political crime*. Montclair, NJ: Patterson Smith &rpt 1973é.

Rasch, W. (1979). Psychological dimensions of political terrorism in the Federal Republic of Germany. *International Journal of Law and Psychiatry, 2,* 79–85.

Reasons, C. (1973). The politicization of crime, the criminal, and the criminologist. *Journal of Criminal Law and Criminology, 64,* 471–77.

Ross, J.I. (1988). Attributes of domestic political terrorism in Canada, 1960-1985." *Terrorism, 11,* 213–33.

Sawatsky, J. (1980). *Men in the shadows: The R.C.M.P. Security Service*. Toronto: Doubleday.

Schafer, S. (1974). *The political criminal*. New York: Free Press, Macmillan.

Schmid, A., & de Graaf, J. (1982). *Violence as communication: Insurgent terrorism and the Western news media*. Beverly Hills: Sage.

Schmid, A., & Jongman, A.J. (1988). *Political terrorism*. New York: Transaction Books.

Torrance, J.M. (1988). *Public violence in Canada*. Montreal & Kingston: McGill-Queen's University Press.

Turk, A.T. (1982). *Political criminality: The defiance and defense of authority*. Beverly Hills: Sage.

Wardlaw, G. (1982). *Political terrorism: Theory, tactics and counter measures*. Cambridge: Cambridge University Press.

Weschler, L. (1989, Apr. 3; Apr. 10). A reporter at large (Uruguay). *New Yorker*, pp. 43–85; 85–108.

Young, W.D. (1969). *Democracy and discontent: Progressivism, socialism and Social Credit in the Canadian West*. Toronto: McGraw-Hill Ryerson.

Thomas Gabor

18 Crime by the Public

A-T-O [Corporation] is pleased to sponsor *The Figgie Report on Fear of Crime* because as Americans, and as members of the international business community, we believe that there are few greater threats to our freedom than crime and the fear of crime. Approximately 1% of the population is terrorizing the other 99%. If the public and our corporate leaders do not join together to draft solutions to their common problems, the law-abiding citizens will continue to be held hostage. (A-T-O, 1980, Preface)

The imagery is powerful: 1 percent terrorizing 99 percent. The idea that criminals and law-abiding citizens can easily be distinguished permeated criminological thinking of the nineteenth and early twentieth centuries. Moreover, many criminological theories of that time attempted to explain why members of the lower classes seemed to be disproportionately represented in offender populations, assuming some moral or social defect to be the cause. Today, the stereotype of the violent, predatory criminal is perpetuated by the media, politicians, and corporations, such as the one that sponsored the *Figgie Report*. Yet, as we have seen in Chapter 16, corporate crime represents a potentially greater threat to our collective well-being than does street crime. How members of many professions have greater opportunities to victimize us yet may avoid criminal prosecution is the topic of Chapter 15, and crime by those with political power has been discussed in Chapter 17. Clearly, to focus upon muggers, shoplifters, prostitutes, and bank robbers to the exclusion of embezzlers, polluters, price-fixers, and crooked politicians would be to miss a significant portion of criminal behaviour. We also have to extend our theoretical analyses to explain crimes among high-status individuals.

As discussed in Chapter 7, recent years have seen a radical shift away from criminological research that focusses upon the offender and toward a critical perspective of the process of law creation and enforcement. The traditional **consensus approach** to crime and law (see Introduction) first came under attack after World War II when Edwin Sutherland recognized **criminality** among white-collar workers and when surveys of nonoffender populations revealed that ordinary citizens engage in law breaking. It is upon this last topic, crime by the general public, that this chapter focusses. Towels that are taken from hotel rooms, expense accounts that are padded, videotapes that are copied, postage stamps that are reused—these are some of the crimes of the public. Moreover, your neighbours, co-workers, teachers, and fellow students, on the surface respectable and apparently law-abiding, may be engaging in undetected crime of a more serious nature; for example, spousal abuse. Certainly, some of society's leading citizens have recently been the subject of sensational trials that have revealed sexual improprieties, fraud, and political corruption. We begin with a discussion of the source of criminal **stereotypes** that focus our attention on street crime to the exclusion of public crime.

Criminal Stereotypes

Few social issues have been marked by more distortion than that of crime. The topics of **crime** and criminals have been subject to relentless stereotyping. The impressions of criminals the public is fed, and largely subscribes to, is of sinister people who are clearly discernible, by their characteristics, from the rest of society. The actions of this "fringe" element of society are seen as being qualitatively different from what law-abiding people are capable of committing. Criminals are often thought to be vicious characters, inclined toward the commission of heinous acts inconceivable to the rest of us. The presence of prisons attests to the belief, enshrined in policy, that a small fraction of Canadians cannot live by the rules to which everyone else adheres and must consequently be segregated or quarantined. The view that the world can be divided into good and evil or the dangerous and endangered is a popular one, perpetuated by the media, politicians, corporations, and even by criminologists.

The Media as Perpetuators of Criminal Stereotypes

The media tend to focus on sensationalistic violent crimes, such as particularly brutal killings, sadistic rapes, and elaborately planned robberies, because such incidents invite more viewers and readers. Politicians, for their part, often play on public fears of violent crime in order to gain the sympathy of the electorate—a useful ploy at election time. Big business, of course, would prefer that the public attend to street crime rather than misleading advertisements, corporate violations of the health and safety of employees, the marketing of dangerous products, and environmental dumping. As for criminologists, they, too, from the nineteenth century to the present, have contributed in large numbers to the belief that there are clear differences between criminals and the rest of society. Lombroso went as far as to suggest that some criminals possessed physical signs or "stigmata" of inferiority (see Chapter 7). Even today, many criminologists persist in research aiming to demonstrate that fundamental differences can be found in the biological or psychological makeup of criminals and the rest of society.

Actually, as this chapter will show, criminal involvement is a matter of degree. Those committing crimes or engaging in other antisocial acts range from career criminals who violate the law habitually to ordinary people who occasionally respond to temptation or stressful circumstances. Although the former group fills the prisons and probably accounts for a disproportionate amount of conventional violent or property crime, people normally considered to be law-abiding commit a nontrivial proportion of the following infractions: homicide, assault (often of a spouse), sexual assault, petty theft (such as stealing on the job and shoplifting), vandalism, insurance fraud, income-tax violations, and embezzlement. This list contains just a few of the offences often committed by people who have no criminal records and who are considered to be respectable citizens.

The Proportion of People Committing Crimes

Before exploring the range of crimes committed by the general public, let us turn to the proportion of people involved in lawbreaking. If a significant proportion of Canadians are found to engage in criminal violations, the idea that crime is the exclusive domain of a small group of antisocial recidivists will be in question. Unfortunately, our only source of information on this topic is limited to statistics collected by criminal-justice agencies and data from isolated self-report studies. Even with the limitations of these sources, we can see that a significant proportion of the general population has probably engaged in criminal behaviour and a surprisingly large group will be arrested at some point in their lives.

Official Statistics as a Measure of Prevalence of Criminality

The files of Correctional Services of Canada tell us that almost two million Canadians have a criminal record (Correctional Services of Canada, 1982). However, given the problems with official statistics as indicators of crime, discussed in Chapter 13, we can consider this number to be far below the true figure of criminal involvement. Even so, about 8 percent of all Canadians have been processed by the justice system. This official figure would be greater if males were only considered—in the neighbourhood of 12 or 13 percent. The proportion of those with a criminal record would be higher still if those not yet old enough to be liable for criminal prosecution (i.e., those under twelve years of age) were excluded under our calculations. Moreover, there is some evidence that people born in the last few decades have been more criminally active than have previous birth cohorts (Wolfgang & Tracy, 1982; Gabor, 1983). Thus, if we consider only males born after 1950 who are also old enough to be subject to criminal prosecution, the **prevalence** rates of criminality may well be in the vicinity of 20 to 25 percent. The data simply do not exist to make more than a very crude estimation.

These figures are not surprising in light of estimates arrived at in the United States and England. Christiansen (1967), on behalf of the President's Crime Commission in the 1960s, estimated that 50 percent of American males and 12 percent of females would be arrested for a non–traffic-related offence in their lifetime. A recalculation using Christiansen's methods and more current data found the respective probabilities of arrest over a lifespan to be 60 percent for males and 16 percent for females (Belkin, Blumstein, & Glass, 1973). Still more recent research has found that one in every four American males from a large city can be expected to be arrested for an index offence (serious violent or property crime) during his lifetime (Blumstein & Graddy, 1981-82). Even more striking is the finding that for nonwhites living in America's large urban centres, the lifetime probability of being arrested for an index offence is over 50 percent.

Since America's crime problem is more serious than that of most countries, we might be justifiably cautious about generalizing such findings to Canada. Research in England, a country with crime rates more closely resembling those of Canada, indicates that there, too, a large proportion of the population contributes to crime. Farrington (1981), on the basis of 1977 data, has estimated that an English male has a 44 percent chance in his lifetime of being *convicted* for a nontraffic offence. No comparable national estimates of a systematic nature have been undertaken in Canada.

Self-Report Surveys as a Measure of Prevalence of Criminality

Arrest-based and, especially, conviction-based data provide conservative estimates of actual criminal involvement as many wrongdoers never come in contact with the **criminal-justice system**. One way of getting around this problem and of trying to tap criminal involvement directly is through the self-report procedure. Average people are asked, anonymously or with confidentiality ensured, whether they have ever participated in offences specified by an investigator. The self-report methodology is, of course, vulnerable to problems of recall, interpretation, and deliberate attempts to mislead on the part of respondents (see Brantingham & Brantingham, 1984). Nevertheless, this technique was used extensively in the 1960s and 1970s in support of **labelling-theory** and **conflict-approach** contentions that only the criminal behaviour of disadvantaged groups is officially recognized by the criminal-justice system. In more recent years, a controversy has arisen regarding the ability of self-report techniques to address key theoretical concerns (e.g., is crime more prevalent in the lower classes, among males, etc.) but, despite the methodological problems, the evidence gained using this technique is astonishing.

The studies, as a whole, show that most, if not virtually all, people break the law at one time or another. One of the earliest studies was a survey conducted in New York City in which almost 1700 adults were asked to provide information about their involvement in relation to 49 offences listed in a questionnaire (Wallerstein & Wyle, 1947). The subjects were selected so as to include only those people who did *not* have a criminal record. Ninety-nine percent of the respondents admitted to committing at least one of the 49 offences listed. The average number of different offences committed in adulthood was 18 for the men and 11 for the female subjects. Table 18.1 provides a sample of the offences in the questionnaire and the proportion of males and females admitting to each of them.

Similar findings have characterized all subsequent self-report surveys. For example, Short and Nye (1958) administered a questionnaire to students in three western and three midwestern American high schools. They found delinquency to be both "extensive and variable" among these students. More than half the boys in both regions admitted to committing the following acts at least once: driving a car without a permit, truancy, fighting, petty theft, and unlawful drinking. A sizable proportion also admitted to living recklessly, destroying property, and physically bullying others.

Gold (1970), in interviews with a representative sample

Table 18.1 Admission of Criminal Conduct, Wallerstein and Wyle (1947)

Offence	Percent of Respondents Admitting to Offence	
	Men (N = 1020)	Women (N = 678)
Malicious Mischief	84	81
Disorderly Conduct	85	76
Assault	49	5
Auto Misdemeanors	61	39
Indecency	77	74
Gambling	74	54
Larceny	89	83
Auto Theft	26	8
Burglary	17	4
Robbery	11	1
Concealed Weapons	35	3
Falsification and Fraud	46	34
Tax Evasion	57	40

Source: J.S. Wallerstein & C.J. Wyle (1947), Our law-abiding lawbreakers (pp. 107–12). *Probation, 25* (April).

of teenagers in Flint, Michigan, found that 83 percent confessed to having committed at least a few delinquent acts. His conclusion (1970, p. 4) was emphatic:

> Studies of delinquent behavior itself, such as the Flint study, will, I believe, promote considerable change in our whole concept of juvenile delinquency. Most important, the idea of "the delinquent" should disappear altogether. For if social science demonstrates empirically that almost everyone sometimes breaks the law, but there are wide differences in how frequently and seriously individuals do so, delinquency should then be recognized as a matter of degree.

In Canada, Vaz (1965) interviewed middle-class high-school boys to tap their involvement in illicit behaviour. More than half of those fifteen to nineteen years of age admitted to driving without a licence, petty theft, fighting, gambling, and destroying or damaging property. Other Canadian studies include Leblanc (1971) and Linden and Filmore (1980) (see West, 1984).

The Dishonesty of "Law-Abiding" Citizens

Now that we have begun to establish that criminal behaviour is widespread, rather than confined to a marginal group of people called "criminals," let us turn to the diverse forms of illegality that ordinary people participate in. The most common crimes are those involving dishonesty. Dishonesty has been defined as lying, cheating, or stealing (Nettler, 1982). If a generalized trait of "honesty" existed, a case could be made for placing people into "honest" and "dishonest" categories. In other words, if people were either entirely honest or entirely dishonest, without being affected by the situations they encounter, a simple dichotomous classification would suffice. People do not behave, however, with complete consistency across situations, as found by psychologists Hartshorne and May (1928). After giving school children a variety of opportunities to cheat, they found that their behaviour tended to be particularly sensitive to the settings in which opportunities to deceive were present (whether in the home, school, Sunday school, etc.). They concluded that honesty and dishonesty do not derive from an overriding predisposition to behave in one way or the other; instead, behaviour was felt to be specific to the situation at hand.

The debate about whether behaviour is primarily guided by personality traits or situational contingencies is still very much alive in the field of psychology, and it will not be resolved here. Undoubtedly, both positions have merit and their respective applicability varies from case to case. A person strongly disposed to honesty may show substantial behavioural consistency across situations and may resist temptation in the most trying circumstances. At the same time, in a very oppressive situation in which the risks of censure are profound, people may show remarkable uniformity in their behaviour. Thus the strength of personalities may override situations in some cases, and situations that allow for little behavioural flexibility may override individual differences in others (Mischel, 1971).

Hartshorne and May's study showed that people rarely fit into an extreme category of being completely honest or dishonest. Only about 10 percent of their subjects were either honest or dishonest every time a chance to deceive was presented to them. Most of the children cheated between 20 and 70 percent of the time. Thus, although there were differences in the degree to which they were dishonest, most were honest some of the time and dishonest at other times. This finding suggests that some situational factors must be eliciting deceit in some cases and suppressing it in others. This would seem to argue against the possibility of finding a unicausal theory of crime, especially one that centres on individual defects.

A variety of experimental techniques have been used to gauge the public's honesty. Riis (1941a, 1941b, 1941c) reported on three studies, conducted on behalf of *Reader's Digest*, to test the honesty of garages, as well as radio-repair and watch-repair shops. Men and women, posing as couples, brought in cars, radios, and watches that were not working properly but had merely been "jimmied." They found that 63 percent of the garages, 64 percent of the radio-repair shops, and 49 percent of the watch-repair shops made charges for repairs that were unnecessary.

Feldman (1968) has conducted a series of cross-cultural experiments in which he tested the respective honesty of the French, Greeks, and Americans. In one such experiment, investigators entered pastry shops, made a purchase, and then pretended to unwittingly overpay the cashier. The test of honesty was whether the cashier informed the investigator of the overpayment. The investigators were drawn from among both compatriots and foreigners. The study revealed that, in Paris, 54 percent of the clerks kept the money from both compatriots and foreigners. In Athens, the overpayment was not returned to either the compatriot or the foreigner about 50 percent of the time. In Boston, interestingly, the money was kept 38 percent of the time from the compatriot and 27 percent of the time from the foreigner.

The "lost letter" technique has been used in another set of experiments to determine the return rate of letters that are left in public places and appear to be lost. Merritt and Fowler (1948) dropped self-addressed envelopes and postcards on the streets of a number of American cities. Some envelopes contained letters and others appeared to contain a 50-cent piece. Seventy-two percent of the postcards and 85 percent of the letters were mailed, whereas only 54 percent of the envelopes containing a coin were mailed. Furthermore some of the envelopes with a coin that were returned had been tampered with. In another study of this type conducted in London, England, Farrington and Knight (1979) dropped letters containing no cash, one-pound notes, and five-pound notes on the street. Ninety-four percent of the letters with no cash, 72 percent of those containing one pound, and 58 percent of those containing five pounds were returned. Both of these, as well as other studies, suggest that increasing the value of an item makes a dishonest response more likely.

A study of vandalism by Zimbardo (1973) conducted in New York City is particularly telling about the honesty and destructiveness of the public. A car was left on the street as though it had been abandoned. Hidden cameras recorded what ensued. Unexpectedly, the vandalism was initiated by a white, middle-class family, rather than teenagers. This family stripped the car of its most valuable components. An adult male then took its best tires. Finally, after the car had little else of value, passers-by broke the windows and pounded the metal, leaving only a worthless hulk.

Many other field experiments probing the public's honesty have been conducted and, with few exceptions, they tend to show that ordinary people are only too willing to succumb to temptation when opportunities to make a quick monetary gain present themselves. Apparently, the striking findings from other countries also apply to Canada (see Box 18.1).

Box 18.1 Ottawa Field Experiments on Honesty

Gabor et al. (1986) undertook a study to test the honesty of cashiers in Ottawa convenience stores. A total of 125 stores were included in the sample; some were part of larger chains, others were owner-operated. Two of the investigators were males (one being Caucasian, the other East Indian), and the other a female.

In each test situation, an investigator entered a store and purchased a local newspaper. The newspaper, costing 30 cents at the time, was paid for, in each case, with a single Canadian dollar bill. The investigator then pretended to forget the change and proceeded toward the door at a pace slow enough to give the cashier enough time to inform him or her of the apparent mistake. The test of dishonesty was whether the cashier stopped the investigator prior to his or her departure from the store in order to return the overpayment. The investigators, in each instance, recorded the sex and estimated the age of the cashier.

The change was not returned to the "customer" in a total of 20 (16 percent) cases. Cashiers under the age of 25 failed to return the change almost twice as often as those over 25 years of age. This difference was almost completely accounted for by the behaviour of the younger females who

Box 18.1 *(Continued)*

were two and a half times as likely to keep the change as were women over 25. As a whole, no difference was found in the behaviour of the male and female cashiers. Also, the nature of the store (whether a chain store or family business) did not appear to have a bearing on the cashiers' behaviour. As for the likelihood of victimization, the race of the investigators was not found to be important but, interestingly, the male investigators were more than twice as likely to be victimized than was the female.

In one of every six stores, therefore, cashiers appeared to act dishonestly. The argument that what appeared to be dishonesty was really an honest mistake can be ruled out, for the most part, because the transaction was very straightforward, and the stores were only entered at times when the cashiers were not busy. Given just one opportunity, one out of six ordinary people acted dishonestly. Although this figure is not astronomical, it is significant, and other research indicates it probably would have been greater if a larger sum of money was at stake. One cashier made this point succinctly, saying, "Seventy cents isn't worth keeping."

The "lost letter" technique was used in a second field experiment directed by Gabor and Barker (1989). A total of 112 stamped, self-addressed letters were planted securely under the windshield wipers of cars witnessed arriving and parking in various shopping-centre parking lots throughout Ottawa. The sex and age of the drivers were noted, and the envelopes were coded so that, if they were returned, the investigators would be aware of the characteristics of the people returning them. The letters were accompanied by a note containing the message "found near your car," suggesting that the letters had been picked up from the ground by a passer-by. The letters were semi-sealed: half the letters contained an old Canadian penny along with a "formal" letter stating the coin was appraised at $150, and the other half contained only a personal "thank you" note.

Three-quarters of the letters were mailed, although, in some cases, drivers were observed tearing open the envelopes. Those containing coins were slightly less likely to be returned. Males were less likely to return the letters than were females, and young subjects, overall, were substantially less likely than were older subjects to mail the letters. As in the other Ottawa study, young females behaved the least honestly and/or responsibly. Males of both age groups were in between these two extremes.

A recent poll conducted at Concordia University in Montreal shows that fraudulent behaviour is not confined to persons having little education (*Ottawa Citizen*, 1986a). A total of 552 students were asked whether they had plagiarized, used the same term paper in two or more classes, or used an old exam to prepare for a test without obtaining the instructor's permission within the previous six months. Forty percent admitted to one or more of these forms of academic fraud. Younger students were more likely to cheat than were their older counterparts, and females were less likely to cheat than were males.

One indication of the pervasiveness of dishonesty in society comes from the growing use by businesses of honesty and psychological tests in the screening of potential employees. In the United States, each year, about two million employees and job applicants are given polygraph or lie-detector tests by actual or potential employers (*Newsweek*, 1986a). The goal is to identify those capable of, or actually engaging in, theft on the job. Questionnaires, too, have become popular means of gauging what people have done in the past or are doing presently, as well as their attitudes toward stealing from an employer. Drug testing has become widespread as drug abuse costs companies billions of dollars in medical costs, absenteeism, loss of productivity, accidents, and theft (the means by which addicted workers can finance their habits).

The boom in the private-security industry in recent years is another indication of the fears of businesses, public institutions, and individuals. Private-security personnel outnumber police officers by a ratio of two or three to one (Shaikun, 1987). In addition to the growing number of personnel employed by the private-security sector, a great deal more is being spent by companies and individuals on security systems, armoured vehicles, fences, and so on.

The Crimes Committed by "Respectable" People

In this section, some of the crimes committed by "respectable" people are discussed. The coverage of each offence category is by no means exhaustive. The intention is to provide some representative examples within each category.

Theft

One of the most common crimes committed by people without a criminal record is that of shoplifting. It is difficult to determine with precision the extent of losses attributable to this offence because most cases go undetected, and losses in inventory also could result from employee theft, damage, or poor inventory control. One Canadian estimate put the value of merchandise lost due to customer theft at over $300 million per year (Hiew, 1981).

A classic study of shoplifting by Mary Owen Cameron (1964) indicated that most of those prosecuted had no prior criminal record (about 80 percent). Recent studies, in which investigators follow customers around a store, reveal that participation in shoplifting is widespread. Investigations in New York, Philadelphia, and Boston department stores indicate that between one in twenty to one in twelve customers shoplift (Buckle & Farrington, 1984). The largest single group is teenagers. College students, too, are well represented. One study found that almost 40 percent admitted to shoplifting at least once (El-Dirghami, 1974).

Employee theft is a problem of monumental proportions. White-collar employees routinely take office supplies home,

make personal long-distance phone calls from the office, and mail personal letters through their workplace. Blue-collar workers often pilfer tools and industrial materials. There have even been reports of workers, on occasion, stealing automobile parts one-by-one until they had enough to assemble an entire car (Gibbons, 1983).

The hotel industry is particularly susceptible to theft by both staff and customers. Employees take such things as furniture, television sets, dishes, laundry, liquor, and meat. One security officer interviewed in a Canadian study indicated that a bartender at his hotel had furnished his entire apartment with the property of his employer (Irini & Prus, 1982). Hotel and restaurant staff often feel entitled to certain "perks" such as complete meals at their employer's expense. They may, for example, in collusion with a cook or "food checker," order extra meals without having to account for them and eat these following their shift. More systematic pilferage also takes place among employees, where stolen goods are bartered or even resold. These networks are called "hidden economies," and are discussed later in the chapter.

Hotel guests, too, are renowned for the amount of "souvenirs" they take with them annually. Towels and ashtrays are only the "tip of the iceberg" of what guests take with them (see Box 18.2).

Box 18.2 The Irresistible Lure of Hotel Linen Lifting

I was bad once, admitted Susan, standing in the lobby of the Château Laurier hotel.

"I was staying at a hotel in Philadelphia and I don't know how many people were there, but it was a madhouse—I don't know how many hours I waited in line."

To get even, Susan took the fluffy comforter off her bed, stuffed the thing in her duffel bag on check-out day, and went home. Guilt free.

"It looked great on my bed," she said. "I figured they owed it to me."

No, she said she didn't think she'd take anything from the Château before heading home to Toronto.

As long as hotels and motels continue to stock their rooms with tempting items like bathrobes, towels, pillows, silverware or anything else that isn't nailed down, guests will help themselves.

Hotel managers, on one hand, say the theft of hotel property is a serious issue. They insist that guests ultimately foot the bill through higher hotel rates.

But on the other hand, like sports fisherman bull-shooting their buddies about the one that got away, they love to swap stories about strange thefts.

Edward Macies, manager of Macies Ottawan Motor Inn for the past 28 years, stopped by the front desk one day, then did a double-take when he noticed that a six-foot artificial tree was gone.

Hume Rogers, manager of the Beacon Arms, is still puzzled when he considers the handywork required 18 months ago when someone walked off with a TV set. It was still bolted to a hefty metal stand.

Westin Hotel executive assistant manager Michel Géday chuckles when describing how two rather efficient chaps walked off with a massive $2000 vase and artificial flower arrangement from the lobby in the middle of the night.

The new vase in the Westin lobby has an electronic trip-wire attached to the base which, if disturbed, triggers an alarm at the front desk.

And Château Laurier bellman Jean Claude Côté who's been close to the action for 40 years, says he'll never forget the time he and another bellman went to pick up the bags from several rooms used by a tour group from Mexico.

"All the beds were stripped, so we told the assistant manager who told the tour guide what happened. They

Box 18.2 *(Continued)*

took all the luggage and opened it by the front door of the hotel," said Côté. "I remember it like yesterday. Sheets and bedspreads all over the place."

Still, these are the more bizarre cases. Nothing like the hum-drum, but constant theft of towels and other trinkets.

Hot items these days are tea-strainers and demi-tasse spoons. But it's towels that are the timeless favorite.

Phil, a frequent hotel user, says without doubt the Sheraton Regina has the best towels for the taking.

"The quality of towels has dropped significantly in the past few years. Most of them are rougher than sandpaper," said Phil, who travels the country regularly on government business. "But those ones in Regina are the Cadillac of towels. They're super thick—you can hardly close your suitcase with two of them in there."

Even the Westin's Géday concedes he likes to take the little packages of toothpaste that sit in that tempting $9 basket of toiletries by the bathroom sink. They might come in handy in the future.

Actually, hotel managers expect guests to use some or all of those items like mini-shampoos, hand lotion or shower caps. But some guests like the look of those cute little baskets so much, they take the whole lot for their own bathroom, basket included.

Château general manager Peter Howard figures the more goodies you put in the room, the more chances people will walk off with them.

"I would assume most people who take things say to themselves, 'Hey, I like this, I've paid for my room so I'll just help myself.'"

Susan Tomshyshyn, director of housekeeping at the Westin, deals head-on with the terrible towel trauma every day.

She budgets $3200 every three months to replace missing or soiled towels. That's 400 bath towels, 700 face cloths, 175 hand towels and two or three terry bath robes.

Some hotels, such as the Lord Elgin, have switched from monogrammed to plain towels to try to foil the souvenir hunters. TV sets and some paintings are usually bolted down or attached to an alarm system.

Source: Greg Barr (1988, May 14), *Ottawa Citizen*, p.3.

Fraud

Official statistics will indicate that fraud involving cheques and credit cards is among the most common types committed in Canada, but we do not have a good picture of the incidence of embezzlement, where people typically violate positions of trust by converting the funds of their employer to their own use. The financial losses stemming from embezzlement and other offences involving fraudulent practices may exceed those accruing from conventional crimes such as robbery (Bureau of Justice Statistics, 1987). Embezzlers are usually seen and see themselves as law-abiding citizens and, when imprisoned, feel little affinity with other inmates. Typically, even their spouses and closest friends are in the dark about their activities, as was the case with Brian Molony, who embezzled millions of dollars to finance his gambling addiction (see Chapter 6).

Perhaps the most common form of fraud practised by the population at large is that of income-tax evasion. In the English House of Commons, the Chairman of the Board of Inland Revenue estimated that one in eight people fail to declare £1000 income and one in four do not declare £500. Furthermore, two thirds of the respondents in a survey thought that most people would conceal a small amount of their income if they thought they could get away with it (Deane, 1981).

Members of the public try to cash in on their own misfortune when they make exaggerated insurance claims following fires, break-ins, or accidents. In the aftermath of the severe tornado that struck Edmonton during the summer of 1987, the Alberta Minister of Public Safety contemplated filing fraud charges against victims making outrageous damage claims (*Ottawa Citizen,* 1987b). One family of four, for example, claimed $198 000 in losses. Their claim, covering 46 pages and 1300 items, included 74 bath towels, 48 hand towels, 48 face towels, a cream and sugar set valued at $620, and a cup and saucer set worth $320.

While not a *criminal* offence, academic fraud is widespread, as indicated by the poll of Concordia University students mentioned above. Plagiarism is a daily part of academic life, and student responses to accusations are all too often less than apologetic. Writing on the subject, Skom (1986) says that the arrogance of plagiarists knows no bounds. The writer expects that any day now a student will approach her and complain: "What do you mean giving me a *B* on this paper? This is an old family term paper—it got my uncle an *A* at Rutgers."

Academic fraud, of course, is not confined to students. Books and published articles frequently do not give sufficient credit to the sources from which they have been drawn. The outright fabrication of results in research is not uncommon; indeed, a long list of eminent scholars have been accused of such conduct (*Newsweek*, 1987a). One of the best-known examples is that of Sir Cyril Burt, the British psychologist whose falsified twin data served as the basis for much of the thinking on the impact of heredity on IQ scores in the early twentieth century.

Another example of fraud among professionals can be found in the medical field. Misbehaviour by physicians, whether it involves fraud, malpractice, or unethical conduct, rarely receives public attention because it is handled quietly by the disciplinary arms of a province's College of Physicians and Surgeons (*Ottawa Citizen*, 1988a; see also Chapter 15). It has been estimated that between $300 million and $400 million worth of services are fraudulently claimed annually by medical practitioners from Canada's various medical plans (Wilson, Lincoln, & Chappell, 1986).

Physicians can defraud or abuse these Medicare schemes in a number of ways (Wilson, Lincoln, & Chappell, 1986). They can examine patients superficially in order to process as many as possible and, hence, maximize their earnings. In one case, a British Columbia ophthalmologist billed for more than 100 examinations of native Canadians he claimed to have done in less than an hour. Doctors in some provinces can also claim twice the normal rate for extended consultations. This policy is abused by those who offer extended consultations when they are not needed or by others who charge extra when only a standard consultation was given. Surgeons can claim that their therapeutic intervention was more involved or major than was actually the case. Other scams include recommending needless consultations, charging for services never performed, giving "kickbacks" to other doctors for referring patients and worst of all, performing unnecessary treatments and operations.

Hidden Economies

Hidden economies involve a variety of illegal activities, engaged in by ordinary working people, to gain desired goods and services. Although some of these activities include stealing from an employer or the state, they differ from pilfering in general in the sense that the stealing is carried on by a large number of people—it is therefore not considered deviant in that milieu—and/or the goods stolen are not appropriated for personal use but are used to barter for other goods, to gain recognition from others, or to be sold for cash. The extent of the activity varies greatly from one country to the next. Usually, however, it complements a person's lawful work activities and is on a small scale, thereby distinguishing it from the criminal activity of, for example, a professional fence.

Stuart Henry (1978) has described how hidden-economy activity frequently takes place in England. A typical case is that of collusion between a truck driver and an individual working in a warehouse. The warehouse employee may be required to load 100 television sets on the truck and, instead, loads 104 and subsequently "fixes" the books or reports the merchandise as lost. The truck driver can either pay the warehouse employee a sum of money or offer him cheap goods from another warehouse. The driver then can sell the sets for a nominal amount to friends and family. Such networks not only make desired goods more accessible to people with modest incomes; they also give workers a sense of belonging in a social network. The cost of nonparticipation sometimes may be ostracism. Furthermore, hidden-economy trading gives people with dull, routine jobs a greater feeling of control over their work environment.

Hidden-economy activity can also result from the disenchantment of workers with a political or economic system, and the scarcity of valued goods. Where meat is scarce, for example, butchers may hoard it and sell only to friends or those willing to pay inflated prices. Under wartime conditions or where the butcher is a state employee, the behaviour is clearly illegal. In the Soviet Union, Poland, and other Eastern European socialist countries, stealing public property or circumventing official channels to do business has been routine. Crimes against "socialist" property have been among the largest categories of prosecuted offences (Los, 1988).

In some cases, entire "parallel" economies have existed—economies that have considerably outproduced the official economy. About the Polish peasants, Los (1988, p. 212) writes:

In their attempts to achieve their goals, farmers use illegal means to purchase adequate quantities of fertilizers and pesticides, to construct necessary buildings and to secure needed tools and machines. As well, they must resort to illegal markets to sell their surplus produce in order to obtain funds to finance these investments. They perceive the state trade channels as uneconomical, not simply because of the low wholesale prices paid to farmers, but also because of the poor organization of transport and of state purchasing centres which mean that farmers must wait in endless lines while their products often deteriorate and thereby depreciate.

Violent Crimes

The extent to which the public participates in a variety of violent crimes would be surprising to many. Beginning with homicide, we quickly observe that most killings in Canada do not occur "gangland" style or in dark alleys, but in the context of a pre-existing relationship between offender and victim. In over a third of the cases, both parties are members of the same family (Reed, Bleszynski, & Gaucher, 1978). In only a small fraction of the cases are offenders and victims complete strangers. A significant proportion of people who kill do not have a criminal record or an antisocial lifestyle. It is for this reason that murderers, as a group, are considered among the best candidates for **parole**.

Sexual assault, too, is not merely confined to pathological offenders. According to the Canadian Advisory Council on the Status of Women (1985), one in every seventeen Canadian women is sexually assaulted, through forced sexual intercourse, at some point in her life, and one in five is sexually assaulted in other ways. Only one in every three cases involves total strangers and, in fact, one-sixth of the victims of forced intercourse are attacked by a friend. Some of the most common scenarios involve family members, boyfriends, and dates. An American survey found that 22 percent of female college students had been forced, at some point, into sexual intercourse on a first date (*Ottawa Citizen*, 1987c).

Much of society's violence takes place in the home. In many jurisdictions, a large proportion of calls to the police involve domestic disturbances. These disturbances not only account for many injuries stemming from assaults, but also are a leading cause of police killings and injuries (Martin, 1981). It has been estimated, on the basis of a representative sample of American families, that interspousal violence takes place in about 60 percent of all families (Straus, 1974).

Child physical abuse is a major component of family violence. It is such a serious problem that it has even been claimed that child abuse is the leading cause of death in infants between six months and one year of age (Ledger & Williams, 1980). In the province of Alberta, it has been estimated that purposeful physical abuse takes place in 10 percent of all families (Bagley, 1988).

The amount of violence exhibited by young people indicates the extent to which violence is embedded in our society. Research surveying Canadian teenagers indicates that between two and three out of five males are assaultive at some point (Vaz, 1965; Kupfer, 1966). The problem of violence among youths is even more pronounced in the United States. More than 125 000 school teachers are threatened with physical violence each month, and more than twice that number of students are assaulted (Brooks, 1985). The possession of firearms, including automatic weapons, is becoming more commonplace among the young. A survey of Baltimore high-schoolers revealed that 64 percent knew someone in school who had carried a handgun within the preceding six months (*Newsweek*, 1988a).

Substance Abuse

The nonmedical use of illicit drugs, underage drinking, and impaired driving are widespread in our society. In the United States, academics and the media alike have characterized the drug problem as "epidemic" and as warranting a full-scale war on the part of the military and law-enforcement agencies. According to a survey of a representative sample of American high-school students, 59 percent had used marijuana, 16 percent had used cocaine, 70 percent had consumed alcohol in the previous month, and 14 percent had used stimulants in the preceding month (MacDonald, 1984). Thirty percent of all college students will have tried cocaine by their senior year (*Newsweek*, 1986b). Americans spend between $15 billion and $20 billion a year on cocaine alone, and a great deal of violent crime, as well as gang wars, is attributed to competition in the drug trade (*Newsweek*, 1988b). Drug abuse is so pervasive that about a third of all major businesses and government operations in the United States have established drug-testing programs for their employees (*Newsweek*, 1987b).

Not only is the demand for drugs provided by people from all sectors of society, but their cultivation, production, and distribution are often undertaken by people who are not hardened criminals. Whether the crop is marijuana and opium in Thailand or coca leaves in Bolivia, farmers find that growing them can be far more profitable than growing others; in fact, such enterprises can be essential to their survival. Also, a number of governments have co-operated with those in the drug trade or have even engaged in **trafficking**, and law-enforcement personnel are not infrequently corrupted. Furthermore, at the street level, the burgeoning traffic in "crack," a smokeable version of cocaine, has provided lucrative employment, in the capacity of look-outs and couriers, for many inner-city teens and preteens.

Although the problem is not of the same magnitude as that of its neighbour to the south, Canada has not been immune from the problem of substance abuse. Many people have at least tried or occasionally use soft drugs, and there are many alcohol abusers. A good indicator of the latter is the extent of impaired driving, a form of conduct that, today, is in considerable disrepute. According to Ontario's Addiction Research Foundation (1988), males under 27 years of age are most likely to be killed or injured in an alcohol-related car crash. Some of their other findings are

Box 18.3 Facts about Impaired Driving

In 1986, 28,036 licence suspensions were registered for charges relating to drinking and driving. More than 30% of these suspensions were for second or subsequent offences.

More than 50% of drivers admit to driving after drinking at least once a month.

More than 14% admit to driving while impaired at least once a month.

Alcohol is estimated to be involved in approximately 50% of all traffic fatality crashes and 30% of all personal injury crashes.

Source: Addiction Research Foundation (1988), Ontario report (p.2), *The Journal, 2*(4).

---

contained in Box 18.3. A great deal of crime, public disorderliness, and domestic abuse is attributable, at least in part, to the consumption of alcohol and illicit drugs (see also Chapter 5).

Environmental Abuse

The sociologist Don Gibbons (1983) has used the term "environmental abuse" for actions ranging from the malicious destruction of property (**vandalism**) to the dumping of refuse on back roads by suburbanites. Vandalism can range from graffiti and petty property damage committed by minors to industrial sabotage undertaken by politically motivated individuals (Whittingham, 1981). Graffiti itself can vary from the inoffensive to the racist. The graffiti-ridden New York Subway system provides a good example of the environmental damage inflicted by amateur "artists."

Environmental abuse also can take the form of littering with anything from a candy wrapper to truckloads of personal or industrial waste. The latter is particularly serious where hazardous materials (such as toxic chemicals) have been dumped illegally in order to save the costs of proper disposal. One of the most celebrated cases of corporate dumping was of the Hooker Chemical Company, which buried thousands of tons of toxic chemicals near Niagara Falls, New York, eventually forcing the entire community of Love Canal to be evacuated. The rates of cancer, other illnesses, and chromosomal damage were well above national rates (Ermann & Lundman, 1982).

Another aspect of environmental abuse is poaching. By hunting more animals than a permit allows, the poacher threatens the delicate balance of wildlife. Poachers may also use a variety of illegal tactics to catch their prey. As Quig (1986, p. 1) writes:

They spear pickerel and jig sturgeon when they are

swollen with eggs and ready to spawn. They set snares to strangle moose and ruffled grouse. In speeding motorboats with guns blazing, they charge flocks of resting ducks—and if a great blue heron flies by, they kill it too. It doesn't matter that the big bird is a protected species . . . they can sell it for $200. It will end up on a mantlepiece. . . . They entice deer with ripe, juicy apples that are imbedded with fish hooks and anchored to trees with steel wire. Sometimes the deer is already dead when they make the rounds of their trapline. Often it is still struggling on the hook. . . . He [the poacher] kills any animal he can, any time he can, any way he can.

Such sordid scenes are not the work of only a handful of individuals. In Quebec alone, 10 000 people are convicted each year for poaching (Quig, 1986). For a more extensive discussion of crimes against the environment, see Chapter 16.

Vigilantism and Mob Activity

How does the public behave when law and order break down? Natural experiments have occurred during police strikes, electrical blackouts, and natural disasters. In 1970, during a police strike in Montreal, looting and break-ins took place throughout the city. Such pervasive antisocial behaviour and disorder do not always occur; they appear when the informal bonds that tie people to one another are weak and large numbers of people suddenly have access to goods they desire and to which they feel entitled.

In the New York City blackout of July 13 and 14, 1977, looting was extremely widespread, with losses amounting to tens of millions of dollars. A carnival atmosphere prevailed in which people in deprived neighbourhoods felt they had to steal something because so many of their neighbours were looting. As one looter said, "Everyone's got a little thievery, a little wrong in them. . . . It's nature. You're walking down the street and there's a store open, and there's TVs and stuff in there, and won't nothing happen to you if you go in and get it. You wouldn't go in and get one?" (quoted in Curvin & Porter, 1979, p. 10).

Sometimes the breakdown in law and order is not so clear-cut; people merely feel that crime is getting out of hand and the justice system can not deal adequately with it. The case of Bernhard Goetz, the New York vigilante who shot four menacing youths on the subway, is particularly noteworthy, not only because the event occurred but because he received support from many fellow New Yorkers.

As discussed in Chapter 1, the history of criminal justice in Canada is replete with many examples of the general public taking the law into their own hands in the face of nonexistent or ineffective law enforcement. Despite the reputation Canadians enjoy as being generally less violent than our southern neighbours, **vigilantism** was a feature of pioneer life we shared with Americans (Boisjoli, 1987). In addition, Torrance (1986) has documented many examples of violent reactions by the government against strikers, ethnic groups, and political dissenters.

To what extent is vigilantism present today? There is some evidence that individuals who doubt the ability of law-enforcement agencies to adequately protect them will act defensively, sometimes offensively. In December 1986, there were three shootings of robbers and burglars by shopkeepers in Quebec alone (Curran, 1986). Just a few months earlier that year, in Montreal, bus drivers were arming themselves with billy clubs, brass knuckles, and cans of mace following a string of shootings, assaults, and robberies of drivers (*Ottawa Citizen*, 1986b). Many of these altercations occurred when passengers refused to pay the fare, apparently the case for one-quarter of all passengers (*Ottawa Citizen*, 1986c). However, there are few modern examples of groups of people acting in concert in an extralegal way against criminal groups.

Technological Crimes

A whole series of crimes have developed as a result of technological advances. One of the best known is that of computer hackers or those who illegally penetrate the computer systems of private corporations or public institutions by gaining access to their security codes. The term "hacker" tends to conjure up images of young computer whizzes, obsessed with their personal computers, who playfully try to penetrate various computer systems and are a mere nuisance when they succeed. In reality, there are many forms of computer crime and criminals, as well as different motives for this type of activity. The volume of these crimes is greatly in excess of that known by law-enforcement agencies, as companies and other organizations that have been penetrated try to hush up incidents in order to conceal their vulnerability.

Indeed, there are computer hackers, many of whom are males in their late teens and early twenties, who try to gain access to systems for the sheer thrill of it. There are those, however, who have infiltrated military computers and have compromised national security (Elmer-De Witt, 1988). The fear is that, before long, critical hospital computer information on drug dosages or crucial elements of financial systems will be tampered with. The widespread threat of computer viruses has prompted defensive strategies (sometimes called vaccines) on the part of computer users, from multinational corporations to individual owners of personal computers.

Employees with access to company computers constitute a major source of computer-related sabotage (Makin, 1987). Disgruntled employees have used "logic bombs" to knock out entire computer systems. Employees can alter computer-access codes and blackmail their employers into paying them a large sum of money in return for revealing the new code. A bank employee can embezzle small amounts of money from thousands of bank accounts. Other forms of illegality include the unlawful use of another's computer account and stealing information from a rival company. Most computer criminals have no criminal record, have good social standing, and are well educated and, hence, tend to be treated leniently by the courts (Makin, 1987).

Another form of technological crime is the pirating of videos and music (Pauley, Friday, & Foote, 1987). Video pirating is said to cost Hollywood more than one billion dollars a year. The pirates range from small-time operators to well-organized syndicates that copy movies and sell or rent the tapes, often at discount prices. Sometimes films are copied by movie-industry personnel even before they are shown in theatres. It has been estimated that 15 percent of all movie videos in American stores have been pirated.

Offences by Criminal-Justice Personnel

Illegal activities are not confined to the civilian population. Police, judges, and other personnel within the criminal-justice system often are engaged in questionable, if not blatantly illegal, conduct. Such personnel can commit traditional crimes; be involved in extortion and corruption; commit acts of brutality; and otherwise violate the rights of suspected offenders. Two recent cases occurring in Canada illustrate the extent of the problem.

The Edmonton police department was rocked by scandals in 1987–88 (*Maclean's*, 1988). Ten officers had been charged with criminal offences over an eighteen-month period. The offences included attempted murder, assault, theft, fraud, and drug trafficking. In one highly publicized case, which merely culminated in the resignation of an officer, an Edmonton prostitute alleged the officer had handcuffed and raped her, as well as bought cocaine for her.

In January 1988, a major scandal surfaced in Winnipeg as eleven persons, including a provincial court judge, two magistrates, a Crown attorney, and two other lawyers, were charged (Edmonds, 1988). The chief provincial court judge was also removed from his position. The charges were laid as a result of the accusation that the defendants had been involved in a conspiracy to fix traffic tickets in return for payoffs.

The number of people involved in both the Edmonton and Winnipeg scandals suggest that the criminality of police, lawyers, and judges often is not the result of a few "rotten apples" but the existence of conduct norms that are favourable to misbehaviour. Ellwyn Stoddard (1968) has written about the informal code that fosters police deviance, or "blue-coat" crime. He found that criminal activity, on the part of the police, was widespread in most major departments. Some of the activities police officers engage in are listed in Box 18.4.

Stoddard's informant, an ex–police officer, emphasized the pressure placed on new recruits to go along with illegal practices. Officers who are overly honest are regarded with suspicion as they may disclose illicit activities. As the informant says:

> take a man that has just joined the department, has good intentions and is basically honest, . . . these aren't degrees. It's all either black or white. And the illegal activity I know shocks a lot of these young men . . . because it was the thing to do. It's a way to be accepted by the other people. It's a terrible thing the way one policeman will talk about another. Say an old timer will have a new man working with him and he'll tell you, "You've got to watch him, because he's honest!" (Stoddard, 1968, p. 208)

Those who refuse to abide by the "code" may be subject to ostracism and harassment.

Crimes by Society's Leaders

Among the most harmful crimes to society are those committed by people held in high esteem by the public, whether these are political, corporate, or religious leaders, or merely celebrities. The misbehaviour of such individuals is highly visible, and because they serve as role models to many, their fall from grace leads to a general disillusionment with society's values and laws. When the rich and powerful lie, cheat, and steal, those at the other end of the social ladder can hardly be expected to maintain high ethical standards.

Box 18.4 Varieties of Police Misconduct

Mooching:	Receiving free coffee, cigarettes, meals, liquor, groceries, etc., as compensation for being underpaid or for future acts of favouritism.
Chiselling:	Demanding free admission to entertainment, price discounts, etc.
Favouritism:	Using licence tabs, window stickers, or courtesy cards to gain immunity from traffic arrest for self, family, or friends.
Prejudice:	Giving differential treatment to minorities and others who have little political influence and, hence, cannot cause trouble for the officer.
Shopping:	Picking up small items such as candy bars and cigarettes when a store is accidentally unlocked after business hours.
Extortion:	Demanding payments for traffic violations in lieu of issuing tickets.
Bribery:	Accepting cash or gifts of greater value than in mooching and, in return, not providing evidence against an accused person(s).
Shakedown:	Taking items (having greater value than in shopping) while investigating a burglary.
Perjury:	Lying to provide an alibi for a fellow officer who has been caught for unlawful activity.
Premeditated Theft:	Undertaking a planned burglary or theft that cannot be explained as a "spur of the moment" act.

In Canada, the Mulroney government has been involved in an unprecedented number of scandals. Patronage has been a hallmark of his government, as many major federal appointments went to political supporters and relatives of cabinet members. When John Crosbie was Justice minister, the law firms employing two of his sons were appointed legal agents of the federal government (Howard, 1987). External Affairs minister Joe Clark's brother was lawyer for the Calgary Olympics. An advertising company headed by Finance minister Michael Wilson's brother-in-law was awarded a contract with the Finance department. Several cabinet members tried to amass large personal fortunes through their influential positions. Also, Progressive Conservative Party campaign money apparently has been used to help finance Brian and Mila Mulroney's extravagant lifestyle (Hoy, 1987).

Business, in the 1980s, has certainly lived up to the adage "There's a sucker born every minute." Ivan Boesky, the Wall Street financier, was involved in the "Super Bowl" of scandals as he illegally earned tens of millions of dollars after receiving "insider" tips about corporations that were about to be taken over (Samuelson, 1986). Speaking to graduating students at the University of California, Boesky said: "Greed is all right, by the way. I want you to know that. I think greed is healthy. You can be greedy and still feel good about yourself" (Newsweek, 1986c). A classic example of extreme greed was furnished by Leona Helmsley, the New York billionairess who was convicted in 1989 of tax violations after trying to pass off millions of dollars in personal purchases as business expenses (Kinsley, 1988).

Corporate misbehaviour in relation to both employees and consumers is legendary (Sherrill, 1987). There is the case of the Ford Motor Company, which poured millions of Pintos off its assembly lines although Ford executives knew the gas tanks were defective and could rupture after a rear-end collision, burning passengers alive. For decades, the Johns-Manville Corporation, producer of asbestos products, failed to inform its workers that inhaling asbestos can be lethal—about 10 000 persons die each year of asbestos-related cancer. There is A.H. Robins, manufacturer of the Dalkon Shield, an intrauterine contraceptive device. Despite the fact that women using the device were dying, miscarrying, becoming sterile, and suffering from internal injuries on a large scale, the company for years tried to cover up its dangers and did not recall the device for several years after they ceased production.

Virtually all of Canada's leading corporations, at one time or another, break the law, and most are repeat offenders (Goff & Reasons, 1978). A poll of Chicago-area business executives revealed that 73 percent felt that practices in their own industry were unethical (Ottawa Citizen, 1987d). Furthermore, more than one-fifth of the executives said they would bribe a public official if this would help them achieve their business goals.

Religious leaders, in recent years, also have taken a considerable fall from the pedestals on which they have stood. Jim Bakker, former televangelist, was sentenced in 1989 to 45 years after being convicted of defrauding his viewers. Together with his wife, Tammy Faye, he had amassed a large personal fortune: they had a combined salary of over $1.6 million, four homes, a Mercedes-Benz and a Rolls-Royce, and Tammy had a wardrobe that few could equal (Newsweek, 1987c). Although their lavish lifestyle, stormy marriage, and her drug habit brought controversy, what finally did them in was the revelation that he had an affair with a church secretary and paid for her silence out of church funds. The Bakkers are not alone in their moral failures; it is the discrepancy between their message and their deeds that demoralizes those who have held them in high esteem.

Innumerable cases of sexual indiscretions and even assaultive behaviour have surfaced in the media in the last few years on the part of "respectable" citizens. The perpetrators have included politicians, preachers, teachers, and even psychologists. One highly publicized case involved another popular televangelist, Jimmy Swaggart, who reached more than ten million people in North America and many others in 145 countries. By day, he heaped unrelenting scorn upon the sinners; at night, he cruised seedy motel strips, wearing disguises, and paid prostitutes to perform pornographic acts for him (Evenson, 1988).

In the late 1980s, the revelations about child sexual and physical abuse by clergymen in Canada were coming so fast that few could keep count (e.g., Maclean's, 1989). There have also been several highly publicized cases of sexual assault or other abuse on the part of teachers, such as the case against Robert Noyes discussed in Chapter 8. Serious accusations were made against a psychologist who both worked in a clinic and taught psychology in university. In another high-profile case in Ontario, the former head of a Big Brothers and Big Sisters organization was charged with sexually assaulting a young girl over a three-year period (Ottawa Citizen, 1988b). Chapter 15 discusses the climate that facilitates unscrutinized and unpunished criminal activity among the professional elite.

Rationalizing Criminality

When criminal or other socially harmful conduct is committed by people who do not see themselves as criminal, certain mental processes must be activated to reconcile their behaviour with their self-image. These processes often take the form of rationalizations or explanations that excuse the transgression and thereby leave perpetrators' views of themselves intact.

Two sociologists, Gresham Sykes and David Matza (1957), have coined the term "neutralization techniques" to refer to the methods they theorize are used by delinquents to help them cope with the guilt induced by, or free themselves from recriminations arising from, their illicit behaviour. They can deny personal responsibility for their behaviour by claiming that their delinquency was an inevitable outcome of their disadvantaged background. They can also claim that nobody is being hurt by their conduct ("They're so rich they can afford it"), the victim had it coming, they did it for the group, or because "all of society is corrupt."

Psychiatrist Samuel Yochelson and clinical psychologist Stanton Samenow took the argument farther by contending that the persistent use of rationalizations is the hallmark of the criminal personality (Yochelson & Samenow, 1976). It signals, according to them, a disturbance in the way criminals think.

When we examine the misbehaviour of people not ordinarily considered criminal, we find that the use of excuses and justifications is not confined to hard-core criminals. Rationalizations can serve to protect oneself from one's own conscience or the accusations of others. Consider some explanations drivers have given police officers for speeding violations. They have ranged from the plausible ("I never saw the sign") to the outrageous: "I never realized I had so much power with my new shoes on"; "I left my stove on and I'm rushing home to turn it off"; "I heard that my daughter's boyfriend is at my home"; "I'm late for my wedding" (Armstrong 1986, p.29).

Guests pilfering goods from hotels often regard them as souvenirs to which they are entitled after paying for their rooms. Employees can justify stealing on the job as revenge for mistreatment or being underpaid. Drug peddlers and users can maintain that the use of illicit substances hurts only the user and, furthermore, that alcohol and other dangerous substances are not illegal. Business people can claim that false advertising and dishonest sales techniques are proper business practices. Computer hackers can say they were just playing around and meant no harm. One man explained hidden-economy trading this way:

People today feel that they are being got at from all sides, particularly by commerce. From morning to night they are being bombarded with advertising slogans and high-pressure salesmanship. They get forced into buying things they don't want at prices they can't afford. Then when they get home, they find the goods are faulty anyway. They take their cars to garages and find the work charged for hasn't been

done. They find the milkman starts delivering a kind of milk they haven't asked for just because he gets a bigger profit for it. Those things are happening to them all the time and it seems like they have no redress. So they get resentful and try to get their own back by stealing a little here and cheating a little there. Everyone does it so why shouldn't they? (quoted in Henry, 1978, p. 49)

This type of explanation suggests that much criminality by ordinary people is not rationalized by *ad hoc* or after-the-fact explanations. Many people develop a view of the world as highly competitive and exploitative. Such a view then allows them to see opportunities to behave dishonestly in the context of a "survivalist" mentality. They have to take advantage of opportunities to stay even with others; if they fail to take advantage, others will do so. Thus, views, conducive to dishonesty may take shape before specific opportunities arise.

Aside from justifying behaviour on the basis that "everyone does it," people use various mechanisms to minimize or downplay the seriousness or repugnance of their actions. The contract killer is often referred to as a "hit man." Prostitutes frequently refer to themselves as "working girls" and their customers as "clients" or "dates." Armed robbers may be referred to as "heavies," and their crimes as "hits," "scores," heists," or "jobs."

This type of terminology is popular among those who are engaged in crime on a full-time basis. Although a criminal argot may have evolved for a number of reasons, one key function it serves is to "soften" a criminal act, thereby making it more palatable to its perpetrators. By calling themselves "working girls" and their customers "clients," prostitutes make their activities appear more mundane or routine and sound more as though they are conducting a business than engaging in activity that is deviant and disreputable. By sharing a dialect, full-time practitioners of crime can promote the mutual delusion that their activities are those of a legitimate profession.

The use of euphemisms also facilitates the misbehaviour of ordinary citizens. In hidden-economy trading, people tend to use terms such as "cheap" goods or "bargains" rather than "stolen" goods to make transactions more acceptable morally. As one of Henry's (1978, p. 57) informants stated:

If somebody came along and said to me, "This is stolen goods. Do you want it?" I wouldn't want to know. No thanks. I wouldn't take it. But if they said "It's off the back of a lorry [truck]," I wouldn't mind. I don't think I'd like to know if they were stolen. I'd like to kid myself it was alright. I wouldn't like to know it was pinched. I wouldn't like it right out. It might enter the back of my mind but provided they didn't tell me straight to my face I would try to avoid the issue. I'd say "I'd like it very much."

Thus, in the hidden economy, goods are presented in an ambiguous way so that recipients are protected legally as well as from their own consciences. The ambiguous presentation leaves room for the possibility that the goods were not, in fact, stolen but were truly bargains, lost, or damaged.

Another means of minimizing behaviour is to point to behaviour that is more serious or offensive. Professional burglars will say that their activities are respectable because they involve finesse rather than violence, as is the case in armed robbery. Armed robbers, however, might criticize burglars for the use of stealth rather than the honest confrontation of victims. Both burglars and robbers may be highly contemptuous of child molesters. Even in the criminal underworld, therefore, it is common for offenders to have some code of ethics and to draw the line at certain types of criminality. The feeling that the behaviour of others is more reprehensible makes them more comfortable with their own conduct.

Members of the general public also share this strategy when breaking the law. Looting in many American race riots, for example, was selective. It was considered acceptable to loot a large business owned by people outside the ghetto, but taboo to burn and loot an establishment owned and operated by a local ghetto dweller (Quarantelli & Dynes, 1975). Hidden-economy traders echo this philosophy of selective victimization:

> It's important who we pick from. If we pick from our friends we deserve to get done. We certainly don't deserve to have any friends. If we pick from a big supermarket we're doing nothing wrong. It's a crime to steal from your brothers and sisters; it's a public service to help each other pick from millionaire companies. (quoted in Henry, 1978, p. 53)

Rationalizations, whether they involve wholesale justifications for criminal activity or merely minimize its seriousness, facilitate criminal conduct; they also explain it to the extent that they are based on accurate perceptions of society.

Conclusion

This chapter has dealt with the misconception that society can be divided into two camps: criminals and noncriminals. The evidence shows that almost all people commit illegal acts at some point and, in fact, a large proportion of the public (especially males) is in contact with the police during their lifespan. Yet, most traditional criminological

theories assume that criminals can be distinguished from law-abiding citizens because of biological defects, personality disorders, or inappropriate socialization, as discussed in chapters 7 and 10. It is only in recent years that theorists have addressed the issue of public crime by trying to explain why members of the disadvantaged classes are disproportionately represented in criminal-justice populations. As we saw in Chapter 10, the labelling and **Marxist** approaches purport to explain this. Societal reaction and labelling theorists point to the biases that characterize criminal-justice decisionmaking. From arrest to sentencing, it is contended, those in middle-income and upper-income groups are treated more leniently and are more likely to be subject only to extrajudicial measures. In fact, the Canadian criminal-justice system is able to accommodate only about 25 000 people at any one time, about one one-thousandth of the population. Therefore, only a fraction of all law violators *can* be prosecuted. Most have to be screened out. Marxist criminologists go one step farther and place this dynamic within a larger framework of the class struggle endemic to capitalist society.

However, as we've seen in chapters 7 and 10, criminologists have been unsuccessful in finding a unitary explanation for the cause of crime. Likewise, no one explanation can be advanced for the diverse array of crimes committed by ordinary people. However, the knowledge that most people break the law or otherwise behave in unscrupulous ways from time to time carries different implications from the idea that only a small fraction of the population does so. Given the pervasiveness of crime in our society, perhaps we need a more general theory of human behaviour rather than a specific theory of crime. In fact, given the pervasiveness of dishonesty, we need to understand the normality of crime and exploitative behaviour.

It can be argued that cultural values that promote dishonesty are pervasive in North American society. Individual rights and interests often take precedence over those of the community. The pursuit of material success is pre-eminent, yet how one arrives at one's fortune or who is exploited on the way is less relevant. The fortunes of many business tycoons have been made through unscrupulous means (Krisberg, 1975). Because of the competitiveness of our society, people are taught that, to be successful, they must be aggressive, whether they are in an electronics firm or on a hockey rink. Indeed, dishonesty is a taken-for-granted component of everyday business practices. Misrepresentations in advertising and deceptive sales techniques are commonplace. Many of us admire a particularly clever operator or business scam. There are other aspects of the predominant North American culture that are especially conducive to norm-violating behaviour (Barron, 1981). Although these may be more evident in the United States, their presence is felt in Canada as well.

As Robert Merton argued, there are great inequities in our society in terms of wealth and opportunities. At the same time, unlike the case in traditional societies, the have-nots are not socialized to accept their inferior status. Everybody therefore aspires to achieve a measure of success, and those failing to do so often become restless and frustrated. Finding their opportunities to achieve their goals blocked, some may resort to illicit means. Our cultural emphasis on the individual rather than on the collective and the fact that young males are socialized to be aggressive are other cultural contributors to crime.

It should not be surprising that criminal involvement is so widespread when our culture contains so many criminogenic characteristics. Each generation assimilates these cultural elements through observing role models—parents, peers, celebrities, and society's leaders. The last-mentioned are profoundly influential because misbehaviour on their part has what adherents of **social-learning theory** call a "disinhibiting effect" on the rest of society. People feel that if society's leaders are dishonest and break the law, it is all right for everyone to do so. At the same time, the public becomes demoralized as they have no standards to aspire to with the ascendance of an "anything goes" ideology.

Highly visible incidents of political corruption and elite crime can shake a society at its foundations and lead people to believe that no ethical standards of conduct remain. In such a state of suspended morality or normlessness, society becomes a battlefield where the only inhibiting factor is the fear of punishment, and this fear is often neutralized by the low certainty of punishment for most crimes. The rationalizations of hidden-economy traders, discussed above, attest to the idea that people feel they must cheat and steal when the opportunity arises to keep up with everyone else. Such trading not only yields material rewards but also gives participants with little social power a sense of control in their dull, routine, and poorly paying jobs (Henry, 1978).

Yet, to say that cheating and stealing are ingrained in our culture and that all of us are potential, it not actual, criminals, does not explain why some people are more honest and committed to our laws than others; nor does it explain why people are honest some of the time and dishonest at other times. Traditional criminological theories have tended to focus on *antecedent* factors that predispose some people to criminality (e.g., personality traits or social conditions). There are apparently strong correlations between some of these factors and crime. For example, people who are impulsive, have low self-esteem, and are less intelligent are more likely to exhibit dishonesty than are those with the opposite characteristics (Nettler, 1982).

Aside from these *antecedent* factors, **situational contingencies** are important. A greater emphasis has been given recently in the behavioural sciences to the situational determinants of conduct. According to a situationist model, people are not viewed as being "programmed" in their formative years to behave in a set way. Their behaviour is seen as fluid and dynamic. Although they may carry with them predispositions to act in a certain way, the circumstances they encounter will also affect the way they act. This is why a person may be honest, conforming, and nonviolent in one context and behave very differently in another. We often talk of the person who is passive at work and then comes home and "kicks the dog." Research into the situational contingencies that affect criminal behaviour has yielded some of the following conclusions:

1. Dishonesty is more likely when an object is valuable than when it is of low value (Gabor & Barker, 1987).
2. People are more likely to cheat and steal when opportunities are more readily available and when the likelihood of punishment is low (Nettler, 1982).
3. Cheating is more likely to occur when it is the means to an important goal and when other opportunities to reach that goal are limited (Nettler, 1982).
4. Victims' characteristics affected the likelihood of dishonesty. People find victims who are impersonal (e.g., large business) or remote easier to victimize than those with whom they have a face-to-face confrontation (Smigel & Ross, 1970). Those who are disliked, have lower social status, or are male are more likely to be victimized than are those who are liked, have high social status, and are female (Quarantelli & Dynes, 1975; Gabor et al., 1986; Bickman, 1971).

The fact that situational factors have been found to affect the inclinations of people to be dishonest or to commit other socially undesirable acts attests to the absurdity of placing people into discrete categories such as "honest" and "dishonest," or "criminal" and "noncriminal." It also makes absurd the search for a "cause" of crime. Although some people may be more disposed to dishonesty and criminality, such inclinations are not explainable merely by differences in personality. According to some schools of thought, crime is normal behaviour as people strive to pursue their own interests, some of which inevitably clash with the interests of the community at large. The pursuit of self-interest can be promoted by cultural conditions that stress individualism, success, status, competition, and aggression.

These criminogenic cultural conditions are said to characterize North American society. In such a context, therefore, much crime can be seen as part of a normal assimilation of the predominant cultural values. The number of scandals among political leaders and general criminality of the public indicate that crime is embedded in our society.

Crime and immorality beget more of the same as people model themselves on those around them and feel less inhibited because the number of people violating society's laws appear to justify further transgressions.

People also misbehave because they are exposed to situational stresses and temptations that are not curbed by the fear of punishment, as the likelihood of repercussion for most crimes is very remote. The other major form of restraint on behaviour is internal, that is, one's conscience may prompt one to refrain from antisocial acts. The pervasiveness of illegality in society, as well as injustices, makes it all too easy for people to rationalize their conduct in ways that are remarkably similar to the "neutralization techniques" employed by highly active offenders. The fact that many people feel immune from prosecution, by virtue of their status or the type of transgressions they engage in, only reinforces the belief that what they have done is not really "criminal."

The forms of behaviour that seem socially excusable, because they are committed by many "respectable" people and are rarely punished, range from the petty to the very serious. On one end of the continuum are petty thefts and public-order offences; on the other are serious offences against the person (domestic and sexual assaults, child abuse, etc.), violations of trust (fraud and embezzlement), and corporate crimes that endanger people and the environment. Many of the most serious infractions of the respectable have been treated as being of only secondary importance by both legal personnel and academics. The most visible crimes (murder, robbery, rape, assault, burglary, and theft) of low-status individuals have served as the primary focus of criminologists and the criminal-justice system. Social power and stereotypes have served as important guides for our responses to crime.

A number of implications stem from the recognition that most people are transgressors and that there are many socially harmful acts other than those that have traditionally received the attention of most criminologists. Research and theorizing ought to, perhaps, be directed toward understanding the different levels of criminal participation, rather than at establishing differences between catch-all groupings such as "criminals" and "noncriminals." More careful analyses should be done of nontraditional crimes and their impact to enable a more realistic appraisal of the harms they engender relative to the traditional concerns of murder, robbery, and so on. Further study should be done of the cultural and other factors that lead most people to break society's rules. Intervention strategies may need to be more innovative than the traditional approaches of incarceration, probation, and fines, as the prevention of hidden-economy trading, for example, will necessitate different measures from those needed to deal with armed robbery.

A multitude of other implications, for both research and policy, flow from the recognition that criminality is widespread and multifaceted. This recognition alone justifies our interest as we may all be more hesitant to glibly apply the destructive label "criminal." Moral behaviour entails taking personal responsibility for one's actions rather than attributing social problems to others through simplistic stereotypes.

Discussion Questions

1. Does this chapter support a "typology" approach to explaining criminality; that is, does the author suggest we can explain criminal behaviour by determining who are criminal types? Why or why not?

2. If there is no criminal type, how do we set about to prevent crime or rehabilitate criminals—individuals who are apparently like ourselves?

3. What is the lesson to be derived from the Ottawa field experiments on honesty?

References

Addiction Research Foundation. (1988). Ontario report. *The Journal, 2*(4), 2.

Armstrong S. (1986, September 21). A funny thing happened on the way to the... *The Sunday Herald*, p. 29.

A-T-O Inc. (1980). *The Figgie report part II: The corporate response to fear of crime*. Research and Forecasts.

Bagley, C. (1988). Child abuse and neglect. In G. Charles & P. Gabor (Eds.), *Issues in child and youth care practice in Alberta* (pp. 52–72). Lethbridge: Lethbridge Community College

Barron, M.L. (1981). The criminogenic society: Social values and deviance. In A.S. Blumberg & J. Douglas (Eds.), *Current perspectives on criminal behavior: Essays on criminology* (pp. 136–52). New York: Knopf.

Belkin, J., Blumstein, A., & Glass, W. (1973). Recidivism as a feedback process: An analytical model and empirical validation. *Journal of Criminal Justice, 1*, 7–26.

Bickman L. (1971). The effect of social status on the honesty of others. *Journal of Social Psychology. 85*, 87–92.

Blumstein, A., & Graddy, E. (1981–82). Prevalence and recidivism in index arrests: A feedback model. *Law and Society Review, 16*(2), 265–90.

Boisjoli, R. (1987). *Vigilantism in Canada*. Unpublished master's thesis, University of Ottawa, Ottawa.

Brantingham, P.J., & Brantingham, P.L. (1984). *Patterns in crime*. New York: Macmillan.

Brooks, D. (1985, December 13). Order in the classroom: Forget the fire—just keep teaching. *National Review*, pp.24–29.

Buckle, A., & Farrington, D.P. (1984). An observational study of shoplifting. *British Journal of Criminology, 24*(1), 36–41.

Bureau of Justice Statistics (1987, September). *Special report: Federal offenses and offenders: White collar crime*. Washington, DC: U.S. Department of Justice.

Cameron, M.O. (1964). *The booster and the snitch: Departmental store shoplifting*. New York: Free Press.

Canadian Advisory Council on the Status of Women. (1985, February). *Sexual assault*. Ottawa.

Christiansen, R. (1967). Projected percentage of U.S. population with criminal arrest and conviction records. In President's Commission on Law Enforcement and Administration of Justice, *Task Force Report: Science and Technology*. Washington, DC: U.S. Government Printing Office.

Chock. C.H. Prevention of shoplifting: A community action approach. *Canadian Journal of Criminology, 23*(1), 57–68.

Correctional Services of Canada. (1982). *Basic facts about corrections in Canada*. Ottawa: Ministry of Supply & Services.

Curran, P. (1986, December 11). Third shopkeeper shoots intruder. *The Gazette*, pp. A1, A7.

Curvin, R., & Porter, B. (1979). *Blackout looting*. New York: Gardner.

Deane, K.D. (1981). Tax evasion, criminality, and sentencing the tax offender. *British Journal of Criminology, 21*(1), 47–57.

Edmonds, S. (1988, January 16). Manitoba judges, magistrates charged: 11 accused of conspiracy in traffic-ticket fixing scam. *Ottawa Citizen*, p. 1A.

El-Dirghami A. (1974). Shoplifting among students. *Journal of Retailing, 50*(3), 33–42.

Elmer-De Witt, P. (1988, May 2). A bold raid on computer security. *Time*, p. 56.

Ermann, M.D., & Lundman, R.J. (1982). *Corporate deviance*. New York: Holt, Rinehart & Winston.

Evenson, B. (1988, February 27). "I have sinned": A righteous preacher sunk by his dark side. *Ottawa Citizen*, p. B1.

Farrington, D.P. (1981). The prevalence of convictions. *British Journal of Criminology, 21*(2), 173–75.

Farrington, D.P., & Knight, B.J. (1979). Two non-reactive field experiments on stealing from a "lost" letter. *British Journal of Social and Clinical Psychology, 18*, 277–84.

Gabor, T. (1983). *The dangerous criminal and incapacitation policies*. Ph.D. diss., Department of Sociology, Ohio State University, Columbus, OH.

Gabor, T., & Barker, T.G. (1989). Probing the public's honesty: A field experiment using the "lost letter" technique. *Deviant Behaviour, 10*;387–99.

Gabor, T., Strean, J., Singh, G., & Varis, D. (1986). Public deviance: An experimental study. *Canadian Journal of Criminology, 28*(1), 17–29.

Gibbons, D.C. (1983). Mundane crime. *Journal of Crime and Delinquency, 29*(2), 213–27.

Goff, C.H., & Reasons, C.E. (1978). *Corporate crime in Canada*. London: Prentice-Hall.

Gold, M. (1970). *Delinquent behavior in an American city*. Belmont, CA: Brooks.

Hartshorn, H., & May, M.A. (1928). *Studies in deceit*. New York: Macmillan.

Henry, S. (1978). *The hidden economy: The context and control of borderline crime*. Oxford: Martin Robertson.

Howard, R. (1987, December 3). Stevens inquiry to spawn new rules for ministers: Mulroney package expected in weeks. *Globe and Mail*, p. A14.

Hoy, C. (1987). *Friends in high places: Politics and patronage in the Mulroney government*. Toronto: Key Porter.

Irini, S., & Prus, R. (1982). Doing security work: Keeping order in the hotel setting. *Canadian Journal of Criminology, 24*(1), 61–82.

Kinsley, M. (1988, May 23). The superrich are different. *Time*, p. 78.

Krisberg, B. (1975). *Crime and privilege: Toward a new criminology*. Englewood Cliffs, NJ: Prentice-Hall.

Kupfer, G. (1966). *Middle class delinquency in a Canadian city*. Ph.D. diss., Department of Sociology, University of Washington, Washington, DC.

Leblanc M. (1971). La réaction sociale à la délinquance juvénile: Une analyse stigmatique. *Acta Criminologica, 4*, 131–91.

Ledger, K., & Williams, D. (1980). *Parents at risk*. Victoria, BC: Queen Alexandra Hospital.

Linden, R., & Filmore, C. (1980). A comparative study of delinquent involvement. In R.A. Silverman & J.J. Tevan (Eds.), *Crime in Canadian Society* (pp. 154–70). Toronto: Butterworths.

Los, M. (1988). *Communist ideology. Law and crime: A comparative view of the USSR and Poland*. London: Macmillan.

MacDonald, D.I. (1984). *Drugs, drinking and adolescents*. Chicago: Year Book Medical Publishers.

Maclean's. (1980, May 9). Police-force scandals, p. 28.

Maclean's (1989, July 17). Sins of the flesh. pp. 10–12.

Makin, K. (1987, November 3). Computer systems hit by "logic bombs:. *Globe and Mail*, p. A1.

Martin, D. (1981). *Battered wives*. San Francisco, CA: Volcano.

Merritt, C.B., & Fowler, R.G. (1948). The pecuniary honesty of the public at large. *Journal of Abnormal and Social Psychology, 43*, 90–93.

Mischel, W. (1971). *Introduction to personality*. New York: Holt, Rinehart & Winston.

Nettler, G. (1982). *Lying, cheating, stealing*. Cincinnati, OH: Anderson.

Newsweek. (1986a, May 5). Can you pass the job test (validity or honesty tests)?, pp. 46–52.

Newsweek. (1986b, August 11). Trying to say "no": The drug crisis, pp. 14–21.

Newsweek. (1986c, December 1). True greed, p. 48.

Newsweek. (1987a, February 2). Tempests in a test tube, p. 64.

Newsweek. (1987b, September 14). Drug abuse: Testing, testing, p. 4.

Newsweek. (1987c, May 11). Fresh out of miracles: Evangelists Jim and Tammy Faye Bakker lose their TV ministry over the sex-and-money scandal, pp. 70–72.

Newsweek. (1988a, January 11) Kids: Deadly force, p. 18.

Newsweek. (1988b, March 14). Losing the war?: The drug crisis, pp. 16–18.

Ottawa Citizen. (1986a, August 25). 40% of students cheat, poll finds, p. A5.

Ottawa Citizen. (1986b, August 26). Montreal bus drivers arming themselves, p. A5.

Ottawa Citizen. (1986c, August 27). Cool it, Montreal transit bosses tell drivers, p. A18.

Ottawa Citizen. (1987b, October 16). Edmonton tornado victims may face fraud charges for outrageous damage claims, p. A3.

Ottawa Citizen. (1987c, May 16). Male students forced into sex, p. A19.

Ottawa Citizen. (1987d). 20% of Chicago executives would bribe official: Poll, p.27.

Ottawa Citizen. (1988a, January 9). Medical profession reluctant to open hearings to public, p. B5.

Ottawa Citizen. (1988b, April 28). 3 more charged in assaults, p.5.

Pauly, D., Friday, C., & Foote, J. (1987, July 27). A scourge of video pirates. *Newsweek*, pp. 40–41.

Quarantelli, E.L., & Dynes, R.R. (1975). Organizations as victims in American mass racial disturbances: a re-examination. In I. Drapkin & E. Viano (Eds.), *Victimology: A new focus* (pp.178–202) Lexington, MA: D.C. Heath.

Quig, J. (1986, October 11). Setting traps for people who hunt dirty: Poachers insult laws of nature and sneer at laws of man. *The Gazette*, pp. A1, A4.

Reed, P., Bleszynski, T., & Gaucher, R. (1978). Homicide in Canada: A statistical synopsis. In M.A. Beyer Gammon (Ed.), *Violence in Canada* (pp.178–200). Toronto: Methuen.

Riis, R.W. (1941a). The radio repair man will gyp you if you don't watch out. *The Reader's Digest, 39*, 6–13.

Riis, R.W. (1941b). The auto repair man will gyp you if you don't watch out. *The Reader's Digest, 39*, 1–6.

Riis, R.W. (1941c). The watch repair man will gyp you if you don't watch out. *The Reader's Digest, 39*, 10–12.

Samuelson, R.J. (1986, December 1). The Super Bowl of scandal. *Newsweek*, p. 64.

Shaikun, P. (1987, June 28). Private security nabs more business amid growing fears. *St. Petersburg Times*, pp. 1–I, 4–I.

Sherrill, R. (1987, March/April). Murder Inc.—What happens to corporate criminals? *Utne Reader*, pp. 48–56.

Short, J.F., & Nye, F.I. (1958). Extent of unrecorded juvenile delinquency, tentative conclusions. *Journal of Criminal Law, Criminology, and Police Science, 49*, 296–302.

Skom, E. (1986). Plagiarism: Quite a rather bad little crime. *AAHE Journal*.

Smigel, E.O., & Ross, H.L. (1970). *Crimes against bureaucracy*. New York: Van Norstrand Reinhold.

Stoddard, E.R. (1968). The informal "code" of police deviancy: A group approach to "blue-coat crime." *Journal of Criminal Law, Criminology, and Police Science, 59*(2), 201–13.

Straus, M.A. (1974). Leveling, civility, and violence in the family. *Journal of Marriage and the Family, 36*(February), 13–30.

Sykes, G.M., & Matza, D. (1957). Techniques of neutralization: A theory of delinquency. *American Sociological Review, 22*, 667–70.

Torrance, J.M. (1986). *Public violence in Canada, 1867–1982*. Toronto: University of Toronto Press.

Vaz, E.W. (1965). Delinquency among middle-class boys. *Canadian Review of Sociology and Anthropology, 2*, 514–15.

Wallerstein, J.S., & Wyle, C.J. (1947). Our law-abiding lawbreakers. *Probation, 25* (April), 107–12.

West, W.G. (1984) *Young offenders and the state: A Canadian perspective on delinquency*. Toronto: Butterworths.

Whittingham, M.D. (1981). Vandalism—the urge to damage and destroy. *Canadian Journal of Criminology, 23*(1), 69–73.

Wilson, P.R., Lincoln, R., & Chappell, D. (1986). Physician fraud and abuse in Canada: A preliminary examination. *Canadian Journal of Criminology, 28*(2), 129–46.

Wolfgang, M.E., & Tracy, P.E. (1982). The 1945 and 1958 birth cohorts: A comparison of the prevalence, incidence, and severity of delinquent behavior. Paper presented at a conference on public danger, dangerous offenders, and the criminal justice system, sponsored by the National Institute of Justice at Harvard University.

Yochelson, S., & Samenow, S.E. (1976). *The criminal personality, Vol. I*. New York: Jason Aronson.

Zimbardo, P.G. (1976). A field experiment in autoshaping. In C. Ward (Ed.), *Vandalism*. London: Architectural Press.

Glossary

The authors acknowledge that a generic glossary cannot possibly capture all of the varied but valid meanings reflected in a text representing many interdisciplinary perspectives. However, we hope the following will be of assistance to those readers who may be unfamiliar with the terms highlighted in the text.

Absolute liability. A category of **criminal offence** in which no **mens rea** is required and no defence of due diligence is available.

Actions. Legal proceedings, both civil and criminal, in which one party (the **plaintiff** or the Crown) prosecutes or sues another.

Actus reus (Lat.: the guilty act). A generic component for the physical compound of criminal responsibility; one of the two essential ingredients of a crime. See also **mens rea**.

Advisory review board. Under section 619 of the **Criminal Code**, a panel of three to five members (two licensed psychiatrists and one lawyer, at minimum) assesses the status of all **Warrant of the Lieutenant-Governor** cases six months after initial confinement, and once per year thereafter.

Aggravating factors. Those factors that make the **crime** more serious, such as premeditation.

Allegation. A statement of the issue that must be proved.

Alleged. See **Allegation**.

Anomie. A sense of alienation from prevailing social values; the opposite of social solidarity, such that confusion or lack of values becomes more prevalent.

Atavism. Resemblance to remote ancestors rather than parents; reversion to an earlier type.

Attempted murder. As stipulated in section 239 of the **Criminal Code**: "every one who attempts by any means to commit murder is guilty of an indictable offence and liable to imprisonment for life."

Automatism. Four categories of unconscious actions performed while in a state of automatism exist in law: (1) automatism resulting from the voluntary ingestion of intoxicants; (2) automatism caused by an apparently normal state such as sleepwalking or hypnosis ; (3) automatism caused by an external event; (4) automatism caused by a "disease of the mind." Category (2) is judged to be sane automatism; category (4) is judged to be insane automatism.

Base rate. The **incidence** of a given phenomenon in a given population.

Bawdy-house. A place "kept occupied, or resorted to by one or more persons for the purpose of prostitution or acts of indecency" (**Criminal Code**, subsection 210 [1]). Those convicted of "keeping a common bawdy-house" face up to two years' imprisonment.

Behaviour modification. The use of learning techniques as a means of changing human behaviour, improving the ability of the subject to adapt, and alleviating the subject's symptoms. Techniques include: operant conditioning, biofeedback, modelling, and aversive conditioning.

Beyond a reasonable doubt. The basis on which the Crown must establish **criminal responsibility**; construed as "moral certainty," i.e., less than absolute certainty, but more than certainty based on the balance of probabilities (the proof necessary in civil actions).

Binding precedents. Precedents under the **common law** system that apply to a case under review and affect the court's decision on that case.

Biological determinism. A belief that the causes of an individual's behaviour lie within the realm of genetic influence.

Blameworthiness. See **Criminal responsibility.**

Break-and-enter. In common law, "the breaking and entering of the dwelling house of another, in the night time, with the intent to commit a felony therein whether or not the felony is committed." The **Criminal Code** broadens this definition to include other than "dwelling houses" and daytime commissions.

British North America Act, 1867, 30–31 Vict., c. 3 (UK). An act of the British parliament providing for Confederation. As part of the patriation of the constitution in 1982, it was renamed the **Constitution Act**, 1867. It is one of many constitutional instruments still valid in Canada. One of the most noteworthy parts is the section that outlines the distribution of power between the federal and provincial governments.

Calculus of felicity. A pseudo-mathematical formula developed by Jeremy Bentham to calculate the value of a behaviour in terms of its goodness and badness.

Canadian Charter of Rights and Freedoms. Part I of the Constitution Act, 1982, being Schedule B of the Canada Act 1982 (U.K.), 1982, c. 11. Enacted on April 17, 1982, this is the only charter of rights entrenched in the Canadian Constitution. Its object is to protect the citizen against the state and to protect minorities against parliamentary majorities.

Capital cases. Cases involving criminal **offences** punishable by death. See also **Capital punishment**.

Capital punishment. Punishment of death for **criminal offences** in **capital cases**. Abolished in Canada in 1976.

Certification Process. The means by which an individual is assessed to be in need of clinical institutionalization for mental disturbance.

Chivalry-paternalism thesis. An argument, put forward initially by Otto Pollak, that the female offender is treated more leniently than her male equivalent because of the inclination of male lawmakers and enforcers to be chivalrous and protective or paternalistic toward women.

Civil injunction. An order by the court prohibiting someone from engaging in certain behaviour.

Civil law. The branch of law that pertains to **suits** other than criminal ones. In Canada, "civil law" is usually a reference to Quebec law.

Civil liability. Liability related to actions seeking private remedies or the enforcement of personal rights. Compare **Criminal liability**.

"Classical" conditioning. A process by which a response comes to be elicited by a stimulus object, or situation other than that to which is the natural or normal response.

Classical School. A theoretical perspective which is based upon the assumption that individuals have complete freedom in the natural state. Society, in its governing, should maximize the greatest happiness for the greatest good; goods are maximized through rewards and evils are minimized through punishment.

Cognitive-development theory. A theory developed by Jean Piaget to explain how the child gradually evolves complex thinking.

Collective conscience. One of the "collective representations" posited by Emile Durkheim, according to whom a healthy social order is characterized by a general value consensus. When the collective conscience weakens, crime increases.

Common law. The English law tradition in which legal rules and principles are set by the courts of the land rather than being laid down by a legislative body.

Communicating for the purpose of prostitution. Section 213 of the **Criminal Code**, enacted in 1985, to replace soliciting (section 195.1). It is an offence punishable on summary conviction.

Commutation. The change to a lesser penalty from a greater one, or to a shorter term. The governor general in council has the power of clemency (or **pardon**) as stipulated in sections 749 and 750 of the **Criminal Code**. Such powers are commonly used in capital cases to commute the sentence of death to one of life imprisonment.

Competency. See **Fitness to stand trial.**

Competition Act. S.C. 1986, c. C-91 (formerly the Combines Investigation Act), proclaimed in force June 19, 1986. The formal purpose is "to maintain and encourage competition in Canada in order to promote the efficiency and adaptability of the Canadian economy, in order to expand opportunities for Canadian participation in world markets while at the same time recognizing the role of foreign competition in Canada, in order to ensure that small- and medium-sized enterprises have an equitable opportunity to participate in the Canadian economy and in order to provide consumers with competitive prices and product choices" (s. 19).

Compulsion defence. See **Duress defence.**

Conflict approach. A perspective among criminologists that sees criminal law as formulated and applied by the more economically powerful groups in society to maintain their control and to protect their interests. Compare **Consensus approach**.

Conflict crimes. Crimes characterized by a high degree of public debate and a lack of societal consensus as to their seriousness. Such crimes include alcohol and drug offences; "right-to-life" offences, such as abortion and euthanasia; public-order offences, such as mischief and **vagrancy**; and the political crimes of terrorism and treason. Compare **Consensus crimes**.

Consensus approach. A perspective among criminologists that sees **criminal law** as reflecting consensus and shared values. Compare **Conflict approach**.

Consensus crimes. The term used by John Hagan to describe crimes which are characterized by a high degree of public agreement regarding the seriousness of the behaviour and the needed response to it.

Constitution Act, 1867 (U.K.), 30 & 31 Vict. c. 3. (originally, the **British North America Act**). The statute, enacted on March 29, 1867, by the British Parliament, provided for the confederation of the Province of Canada (Ontario and Quebec), Nova Scotia, and New Brunswick into a federal state. The act does not contain the entire constitution. See **British North America Act**.

Constructive malice. Where the intent to commit a criminal act (typically murder) is inferred from the state of mind for a lesser criminal act or from certain actions.

Constructive murder. See **constructive malice.**

Contempt of court. An act or omission that obstructs or interferes with the orderly administration of justice or undermines the dignity or respect for the authority of the court. Contempt of court may be either statutory (or criminal) or civil.

Contrological perspective. An approach within the social-constructionist interpretation of crime statistics that asserts that crime rates are independent of "criminal" behaviour, to the extent that they are exclusively the product of control activity, and are accurate as indicators of control, but not actual crime.

Convey. In the law of real property, to transfer property, or title to it, from one person to another.

Court-martial. A court for the trial of a member of Her Majesty's Forces for having committed a service offence, as defined in the National Defence Act.

Crime. Any act that has been legally prohibited by the state such that, if done, it renders the actor liable to punishment or treatment or both. In Canada, the term **crime** is reserved for actions in violation of federal laws such as the **Criminal Code,** the **Income Tax Act**, the Customs Act or the **Narcotic Control Act**. Similar violations of provincial or municipal by-laws that render the actor subject to punishment are penal offences in Canada. Compare **Deviance**.

Crime policy. A form or process of organized society which attempts to effect compromise between basic social values which are in tension (e.g, liberty, security).

Criminal Code, R.S.C., 1985, c. C-46. A federal statute, first enacted in 1892, that embodies the **criminal law** of Canada, but is not the sole repository of such law.

Criminal courts. An assembly of judges or other persons acting as tribunals whose purpose is to adjudicate legal cases in which a crime has been alleged to have occurred.

Criminal-justice system. Refers to the complex group of connected components in society whose function it is to process individuals and associations alleged to have broken the criminal law (e.g, police and courts).

Criminal law. Law which is applicable when an action is taken that has been deemed criminal.

Criminal liability. Responsibility for criminal acts; the legal components thereof.

Criminal libel. In a printed or permanent form, defamation, and in a spoken form, slander, that exposes a person to public scorn, hatred, contempt, or ridicule; includes seditious libel under s.59(2); blasphemous libel, 296; and defamatory libel, 298-301, 304. Redress for a defamed individual is typically sought through the **civil laws** for each province.

Criminal negligence. Failure to exercise the care that the law sets as a minimum; defined in Section 219 of the Criminal Code.
219. (1) Everyone is criminally negligent who
    (a)   in doing anything, or
    (b)   in omitting to do anything that it is his duty to do, shows wanton or reckless disregard for the lives or safety of other persons
    (2)   For the purpose of this section, "duty" means a duty imposed by law.

Criminal offence. An act or omission punished under the **criminal law.**

Criminal responsibility. The principle that people must not be held accountable for wrongdoing unless they are of sound mind at the time of committing such wrongdoing; those failing to meet a minimum standard of mental capacity must be found not guilty.

Criminality. The propensity of a particular person to commit a crime in a given set of circumstances. A person with a high degree of criminality will commit offences in many circumstances. A person with low degree of criminality will commit offences only in rare and special circumstances.

Criminally insane. Refers to the state of natural imbecility or disease of the mind, which renders a person incapable of appreciating the nature and gravity of an act or omission or of knowing that an act or omission is wrong.

Criminology. An interdisciplinary field of study which utilizes the perspective of sociology, psychology, law, political science, geography and anthropology to examine a wide range of issues related to crime and the criminal-justice system.

Critical psychiatry. A critique of psychiatry that is concerned with the relationship between mental health professionals and the wider politicoeconomic, patriarchial, ideological and social order.

Cruel and unusual punishment. Section 12 of the **Canadian Charter of Rights and Freedoms** provides that everyone "has the right not to be subjected to any cruel and unusual treatment or punishment."

Culpable homicide. Murder, manslaughter, or infanticide; committed when a person causes the death of another person by means of an unlawful act, by **criminal negligence,** by causing that person to do anything that results in his or her death, or by willfully frightening that person (a child or a sick person).

Damages. Money awarded by the court to compensate for injury done to the person, property, or rights of another. In addition to compensatory damages, a civil court can order punitive damages.

Dangerous-offender legislation. Part XXIV of the **Criminal Code**, passed by Parliament in 1976. Permits the Crown, following a person's conviction for either a **sexual assault** or a violent offence (other than murder or treason) punishable by a term of ten years or more to apply for a hearing to determine whether the offender should be held indefinitely in prison.

Dangerous sexual offender. See **Dangerous-offender legislation.**

Dangerousness. An individual's potential for violent conduct, usually against others but also, in certain contexts, against himself or herself.

De minimis (Lat.: from *de minimis non curat lex*—the law does not concern itself with trifles). That which is *de minimis* is not of sufficient importance to be dealt with judicially.

Death. In law, defined as an event inexorably linked with heartbeat and circulation.

Death penalty. See **Capital punishment.**

Decriminalization. The process of systematically making activities or behaviour formerly criminalized less so, e.g., no longer considering simple possession of marijuana an indictable offence.

Defendant. In criminal proceedings, the accused; in civil proceedings, the person responding to the claim of the **plaintiff**.

Deinstitutionalization. The process of releasing institutionalized individuals, whether criminal or mentally disturbed persons; assigning them to the community rather than to continue confining them.

Deviance. A category of behaviour that includes a wide range of behaviours that depart from social norms or accepted ways of acting in a society but that are not necessarily against the law. See also **Secondary deviance**. Compare **Crime**.

Due process. A course of formal (legal) proceedings carried out on a regular basis and according to established rules and principles; fundamental fairness and justice in the state's treatment of its citizens.

Duress defence. Section 17 of the **Criminal Code**, which refers to "duress" as "compulsion," defines it as: "threats of immediate death or grievous bodily harm from a person who is present when the offence is committed." The defence of duress applies when the person against whom the threats are made is not a party to a conspiracy or is not involved in committing rape, arson, murder, or robbery.

Embezzlement. There is no crime in the **Criminal Code** known as "embezzlement." At common law and common understanding, theft of property entrusted to the actor in a fudiciary capacity by conversion of the funds held to the actor's personal use. A bank clerk is thought to embezzle when stealing money from the till and preparing false account books in order to hide the theft. In Canada, included under the law of **theft**.

Extortion. According to section 346 of the **Criminal Code**, the inducing of a person to do anything by the use of threats, accusations, menaces, or violence, without reasonable justification.

Extra-chromosome theory. A biological argument put forward to explain an inherited criminality. If an individual possesses one more Y chromosome than normal, it was felt that he/she would become an aggressive antisocial deviant.

False positive. A statistical error which occurs when something is said to exist when in fact it does not, i.e., a type I error.

Familial ideology. The pervasive belief that the nuclear family, organized around a heterosexual marriage relationship and the sexual division of labour, is the natural and inevitable form of family.

Fault. See **Criminal responsibility**.

Felony-murder rule. Where death occurs during the course of certain other serious crimes, that death is categorized as murder.

Fine-option programs. A type of community correctional program which allows for the offender to pay a fine instead of receiving a term of incarceration.

First-degree murder. According to subsection 231 (4) of the **Criminal Code**, an unlawful killing that is planned and deliberate; the killing of a police officer, prison employee, or other person employed for the preservation and maintenance of the public peace, while he or she was acting in the course of duty.

Fitness to stand trial. A defendant can be deemed unfit, according to subsection 615 (1) of the **Criminal Code**, only if "on account of insanity" he or she is not "capable of conducting his [or her] defence."

Food and Drug Act. A statute governing the manufacturing or sale of food, drugs, cosmetics, and therapeutic devices in Canada.

Forensic psychiatry. A branch of psychiatry concerned with legal issues, hearings, and trials, including insanity pleas, commitment procedures, theories and laws dealing with **criminal responsibility, competency**, and the legal definition of insanity.

Forensic psychology. The branch of psychology concerned with the application of psychological principles and techniques in situations involving the law, such as the evaluation of testimony, guilt detection, and diagnosis and therapy in correctional facilities.

Fraud. Intentional deception resulting in injury to another.

Frontier justice. The form of "rough" justice ascribed to early settlers. An informal means of sanctioning in the community which has no inherent due process safeguards.

Functional-equivalence thesis. A theory of **criminality** based on the assumption that men and women are equally likely to be deviant, but that they engage in sex-specific forms of **deviance**, relative to their respective natures.

Fundamental justice. A right entrenched in the **Canadian Charter of Rights and Freedoms** (s. 7): Everyone has the right to life, liberty, and security of the person and the right not to be deprived thereof except in accordance with the principle of fundamental justice.

Gambling. An activity in which participants engage to transfer money or something of value among themselves contingent upon the uncertain outcome of some future event.

Gaming. Participation in "games" that entail a combination of skill and chance. May or may not involve **gambling**.

Good Samaritan. A doctrine in law that preserves from **liability** or harm a person who helps another in distress, or in imminent danger (for example, a doctor attending to an accident victim on the street), providing no intentional malice or negligence occurred.

Habeas corpus. (Lat.: you have the body). A procedure for obtaining a judicial determination of the legality of an individual's custody.

Hazardous Products Act. An act prohibiting the advertising, sale, and importation of hazardous products into Canada.

High hit. An accurate prediction of a future event, attribute, or state of affairs, for example, the dangerousness of psychiatric patients and criminals.

High treason. An offence punishable by life imprisonment, defined in section 46 of the **Criminal Code** as: (a) killing or harming or attempting to kill Her Majesty; (b) levying war against Canada, or so preparing; or (c) assisting an enemy at war Canada, or with any armed forces engaged in hostilities with Canadian armed forces.

Homicide. A person commits homicide when, directly or indirectly, he or she, by any means, causes the death of a human being.

Hybrid offence. See **Mixed offence.**

Incidence. The rate at which members of a group under study acquire a particular attribute within a given time frame.

Income Tax Conscientious Interpretation Act. An act respecting the interpretation of Canada's international conventions relating to income tax and the Acts implementing those conventions.

Independent administrative agencies. Board, commission or tribunals that are created by governments and delegated governing authority over specific matters.

Index offence. One of the offences included in the categories of serious violent and property offences of the Uniform Crime Reporting System of the U.S. Federal Bureau of Investigation (e.g. homicide, rape, aggravated assault, robbery, burglary, theft, auto theft, arson). The total number of crimes in each is used as an index of crime in the United States.

Indictable offence. An offence considered more serious than a summary conviction and that carries a more severe penalty. Compare **Summary-conviction offence.**

Infanticide. According to section 233 of the **Criminal Code**: "A female person commits infanticide when by a wilful act or omission she causes the death of her newly-born child, if at the time of the act or omission she is not fully recovered from the effects of giving birth to the child and by reason thereof or of the effect of lactation consequent on the birth of the child her mind is then disturbed."

Insane automatism. See **Automatism.**

Insanity defence. According to section 16 of the **Criminal Code**, a person is insane who is "in a state of natural imbecility or has disease of the mind to an extent that renders him [or her] incapable of appreciating the nature and quality of an act or omission or of knowing" that it is wrong.

Integrationist interpretation. A type of crime-statistic interpretation that views crime rates as being influenced by a variety of forces, the relative importance of which must be decided empirically.

Intoxication defence. The reduction of criminal liability for some offences in which a person is voluntarily intoxicated by drugs or alcohol.

Juvenile Delinquents Act, R.S.C. 1970, c. J-3. A federal statute originally passed in 1908, the JDA created the criminal offence of deliquency that encompassed violations of federal, provincial, and municipal laws and provincially defined **status offences.** It encouraged juvenile courts to adopt a paternal approach. Replaced by the **Young Offenders Act**, 1984.

Kidnapping. The unlawful taking and carrying away of a person against his or her will (**Criminal Code**, s. 279).

Labelling theory. A perspective that holds that crime and deviance are socially constructed.

Law-as-ideology thesis. The argument that lawmakers

and administrators are not overtly lenient or discriminatory towards certain categories of offenders, yet they help reproduce class, gender, and social/ethnic inequalities indirectly because they are influenced by stereotypical assumptions and beliefs about social reality.

Learning theory. Based upon the idea that an individual's behaviour is formed and influenced by environmental factors and experience.

Left Idealism. A theoretical approach that dramatizes the gap between law as an ideal, and as a political practice. For left idealists, this gap cannot be closed, and political efforts should be directed toward revolution, not mere reforms to an inherently unjust capitalist system.

Left Realism. Meant to address a "vacuum" in left-wing thinking, Lea and Young and others developed an approach that takes crime seriously, as a problem faced by the working class. It does not deny the seriousness of crimes, or the impact of corporate crime, but seeks to measure the nature of "victimization" and of capitalist reactions.

Left Reformism. See **Left Idealism.** While recognizing the gap between legal ideas and legal practices, left realists see possibilities for political democracy and more equitable economic arrangements.

Liability. Legal responsibility.

Licensure. A system in which a person cannot carry out specific occupational activities unless the person is licensed by a governing body.

Liquor Control Act, S.O. 1927. The Ontario version of the statutes passed in each province that provided for government regulation of the sale and consumption of alcoholic beverages after the repeal of prohibition.

Lynch mob. An *ad hoc* group formed to execute an accused, usually by hanging, without his or her having had a fair trial. Named for Charles Lynch (1736-1796), a Virginia justice of the peace, who presided over an extralegal court to punish lawlessness during the American Revolution.

Mala in se (Lat.: wrong in themselves). Acts that are perceived as so inherently evil as to constitute a violation of "natural law." Compare *Mala prohibita*.

Mala prohibita (Lat.: wrong because prohibited). Acts considered criminal because they violate a criminal statute. Compare *Mala in se*.

"Man in the house" rule. The stipulation in all provincial welfare legislation (except Ontario's) that a woman who lives with a man is ineligible for welfare benefits because it is assumed he must be supporting her.

Manslaughter. Culpable homicide that is not **murder** or **infanticide;** committed in the heat of passion caused by sudden provocation.

Marxist theory. A perspective that proposes that the historical development of capitalism is directly correlated to the historical development of criminal law.

McNaughtan Rule. The principle of **criminal responsibility** that holds that an accused is not legally liable for his or her act if it can be proved that the accused did not know what he or she was doing, could not distinguish right from wrong, or was otherwise insanely deluded.

Medical model. Framework for explaining mental illness in which such illness is seen as a disease, a tangible pathology of the brain, that is not qualitatively different from physical disorders in other parts of the human body.

Mens rea (Lat.: from *actus non facit reum, nisi mens est rea*—the act does not make a person guilty unless the mind [or intentions] be guilty). The mental intent to commit an act; one of the two essential ingredients of a **crime.** See also *Actus reus*.

Mental disorder. A mental condition that causes distress or disability to the person. Defined by the American Psychiatric Association as an illness with psychologic or behavioural manifestations and/or impairment as a result of social, psychologic, genetic, physical/chemical, or biologic disturbance.

Mistake of fact defence. In a case where a person commits a criminal act due to a mistaken belief as to the facts of the situation, that error will absolve him or her from from criminal liability.

Mitigating factors. Those factors that reduce the **defendant's** culpability, such as efforts to aid the victim; often discussed in context of the sentencing process.

Mixed offence. An offence for which the prosecutor may choose, based on the circumstances of the case, to proceed summarily or by indictment.

Modelling. Aspect of **social-learning theory** identified by Albert Bandura. It occurs as a result of observing others' behaviour being rewarded, in real life or through media coverage.

Moral-development theory. A theory based upon the idea that individuals develop visual reasoning in rather discrete stages. Lawrence Kohlberg advanced this notion of the existence of six stages of moral development.

Murder. See **Culpable homicide.**

Narcotic Control Act, R.S.C., 1985, c-N-1. A federal law prohibiting the importation, sale, possession, or use of a variety of non-prescription drugs such as opiates, cocaine, and cannabis.

National Defence Act, R.S.C. 1985, c. N-4. A federal statute that governs the Canadian Armed Forces and the Department of National Defence. Among other things, it establishes the **Court Martial** Appeal Court, which hears appeals from decisions of service tribunals. Although capital punishment was abolished in 1976, the National Defence Act provides for the death sentence for cowardice, desertion, unlawful surrender, and spying for the enemy.

Nature/nurture debate. A continuing controversy about what constitutes the ultimate causality for behaviour—genetic or learned factors.

Necessity defence. The defence that the accused had no other alternative but to commit the offence in order to prevent a greater harm.

Neoclassical School. The "transitional" philosophy that emerged after the classical school fell into disrepute. It placed more emphasis upon intervening circumstance as cause in man's behaviour.

Pardon. The governor-in-council may grant a free or conditional pardon. If the former is granted, the accused is thereafter deemed to never have committed the offence; the latter imposes some conditions on the pardon and is usually granted on compassionate grounds.

Parens patriae (Lat.: parent of the country). Originally, the duty of the English sovereign to protect his or her subjects; now used to support the power of U.S. courts to deal with the civil offence of juvenile delinquency.

Parole. The conditional release from imprisonment or other confinement after part of the sentence has been served. Compare **Probation.**

Penal law. A law enacted to preserve the public order that defines an offence against the public and inflicts a penalty for its violation. Compare **Civil law,** which is remedial rather than penal.

Perjury. Section 136 of the **Criminal Code** defines the act of perjury as false testimony by a witness in a judicial proceeding, with the intent to mislead, knowing that the evidence is false.

Physical-blow automatism. See **Automatism.**

Plaintiff. The one who brings the **suit** or action; a **defendant** who brings a counterclaim will be considered a plaintiff in regard to it.

Plea bargain. In Canada, an informal practice whereby the accused can use his or her right to plead not guilty thereby demanding a full trial to bargain with the crown for a variety of benefits that most typically include withdrawal of charges, reduction of charges, and lower sentencing.

Positive School. A theoretical perspective that is based upon the assumption that an individual's behaviour is determined by forces beyond his or her control.

Positivism. See **Positive School.**

Positivist approach. See **Positive School.**

Power-control theory. An empirically-based approach to the ways in which the presence (or absence) of power and control may affect patterns of crime and delinquency.

Precedent. Under the **common law** system, the previous decisions of the courts that relate to a current case and on which a decision in that case will be based. See also **Binding precedents.**

Prejudice. An aversive or hostile attitude toward an individual because he or she belongs to a particular group and is assumed to share the objectionable qualities ascribed to that group. Often called stereotyping.

Premenstrual-syndrome theory. A biogenetic theory of female criminality that posits that women commit **criminal offences** during periods of hormone imbalance. Also called premenstrual-tension theory.

Presumption of innocence. Subsection 11(d) of the **Canadian Charter of Rights and Freedoms** provides that anyone charged with an offence has the right "to be presumed innocent until proven guilty according to law in a fair and public hearing by an independent and impartial tribunal."

Prevalence. The proportion of members of a group under study who have acquired a particular attribute within a given time frame.

Prima facie (Lat.: at first view). Apparently, on the face of it, true and, in the absence of any contradictory evidence, sufficient to prevail in court.

Prima facie interpretation. A type of crime-statistic interpretation in which crime statistics are seen as a fairly accurate index of **crime**, and crime is conceived of as a discrete behaviour.

Prisons and Reformatories Act, R.S.C., 1985, c. P-20. A statute establishing procedures for offender processing and release from Canadian penal institutions.

Private law. Law that regulates those areas in which private disputes arise; one of the basic components of positive law.

Probation. As a sentence of the court, the conditional release of a convicted person into the community, usually under the supervision of a probation officer.

Provocation defence. Section 232 of the **Criminal Code** provides that murder may be reduced to manslaughter, if the person is killed in the heat of passion caused by sudden provocation.

Psychiatric remand. See **Warrant of Remand**.

Psychometry. The science or process of measuring abilities and personality through psychological tests and statistics.

Psychopathy. A broad term for any psychological disorder or mental disease, usually of an unspecified nature.

Public law. Law that involves the public interest; one of the basic components of positive law.

Public policy. A result of an activity or exercise of government undertaken to achieve governmental and societal ends.

Public-welfare offence. An offence, usually one of strict or absolute liability, which entails broad public harm, e.g., pollution.

Quasi offence. An offence found in provincial law which can be prosecuted in criminal court and be penalized by fines and imprisonment.

Ratio decidendi (Lat.: the basis of a decision). A phrase often used in opposition to *obiter dictum* (a decision made by a judge on a point that is not directly relevant to the particular case under review).

Realist interpretation. See *Prima facie* **interpretation**.

Reasonable doubt. See **Beyond a reasonable doubt**.

Reasonable person. The hypothetical personification of the legal standard of intelligence and care expected of the population at large.

Recidivism. The committing of a further offence by a convicted offender upon his or her completion of sentence or **pardon**.

Regulatory offence. See **public-welfare offence**.

Residual deviants. In **labelling theory**, the mentally ill, i.e., those whose behaviour breaks **residual rules**, not through **criminality** or obvious wrongdoing, but by disrupting our unstated standards of normalcy.

Residual rules. In **labelling theory**, the cultural laws (unwritten or unspoken) that govern our collective sense of normality.

Result equality. A perspective on mental illness that was spearheaded by writers like Thomas Szasz and R.D. Laing, and that adopts a libertarian critique of psychiatric powers.

Robbery. According to section 343 of the **Criminal Code**, "everyone commits robbery who (a) steals, and for the purpose of extorting whatever is stolen or to prevent or to overcome resistance to the stealing, uses violence or threats of violence to a person or property; (b) steals from any person and, at the time he [or she] steals or immediately before or immediately thereafter, wounds, beats, strikes or uses any personal violence to that person; (c) assaults any person with intent to steal from him [or her]; or (d) steals from any person while armed with an offensive weapon or imitation thereof."

Role theory. Conceived in the 1940s, this theory is used in explaining the result emerging from the fact that the sons and daughters receive different socialization to prepare them for future roles in the nuclear-family unit. Boys, who will become breadwinners, learn to be assertive, tough, and risk-taking; girls, who will become caregivers and housekeepers, learn to be passive, dependent, and cautious.

Sanction. A consequence or punishment for violation of accepted norms of social conduct. May be remedial or penal.

Sane automatism. See **Automatism**.

Search and seizure. A police practice whereby premises are searched and property is seized that may be pertinent in the investigation and prosecution of a **crime**. Section 8 of the **Canadian Charter of Rights and Freedoms** guarantees everyone security against "unreasonable search or seizure."

Second-degree murder. All **murder** that does not come within the definition of **first-degree murder** (**Criminal Code**, s. 231 [7]).

Secondary deviance. Originates in a redefinition of self-image following social reaction from others, including criminal-justice officials. See also **Deviance**.

Secondary injury. The exacerbation of the original victimization of a person resulting from contact with the **criminal-justice system**.

Sedition. According to sections 34 to 37 of the **Criminal Code**, it is an **indictable offence** to speak seditious words, i.e., words expressing the intention to raise disaffection and discontent among Her Majesty's subjects or to promote public disorder.

Seditious conspiracy. An agreement between two or more persons to carry out a seditious intention.

Self-defence defence. A defence which permits individuals to defend themselves, their property and persons under their care without incurring criminal liability.

Self-regulatory organizations. A semi-public organization that is delegated authority over its members and specified matters.

Sexual assault. A new offence defined in Bill C-127, proclaimed in 1983, to replace the offences of rape and indecent assault.

Slander. The defamatory spoken word. The distinction between slander and libel is becoming increasingly blurred. See **Criminal libel**.

Social Darwinism. A theory based upon the theory of evolution, formulated by Darwin, which emphasizes the principle of natural selection in social groupings.

Social-control theory. A theory that posits that an individual's bonds to conventional society—family, school, work, community, friendships, and church affiliation—are crucial to whether or not that individual engages in criminal or delinquent behaviour. Also called bond theory.

Social-learning theory. A theory which explains the learning process as one informed by social influence; the elements of an influence relationship are important.

Sociobiological approach. A way of studying the biological bases of social behaviour, employing evolution as the basic explanatory tool.

Somatotyping. Categorizing temperament or behavioural characteristics according to body type or physique.

Stare decisis (Lat.: to stand by that which was decided). The rule by which **common law** courts follow prior decisions or **precedents**.

Stereotypes. Commonly accepted but erroneous beliefs; the primary focus of **labelling theory**.

Strict liability. A category of **criminal offence** in which the Crown need not prove ***mens rea*** but for which the defence of due diligence is available. Includes **public-welfare offences**.

Structural interpretation. A type of crime-statistic interpretation in which crime statistics are seen as telling us more about power structures and ideological forces than about the social distribution of misconduct.

Subcultural theory. A theory that posits that children learn to become delinquent through contact with delinquent subcultures, especially the delinquent gang.

Subordinate legislation. Rules made by persons or bodies acting under authority from a government.

Subpoena (Lat.: under penalty). A writ issued under the authority of a court that compels a witness to appear at a judicial proceeding or be found in **contempt of court**.

Suit. A legal proceeding to obtain a remedy. Properly used in reference to civil **actions**.

Summary-conviction offences. Minor offences for which the penalty is restricted to a maximum of six months in jail, a $2000 fine, or both, unless otherwise provided by law (**Criminal Code** S.787).

Taxonomy. A system of classifying items according to their ordered relationships.

Temporary-absence provision. Temporary release of inmates from secure institutions for specific purposes (home leave, employment, education, emergency medical treatment, etc), legislated in the **Prisons and Reformatories Act**.

Theft. The act of acquiring without consent, by someone without title, another's property with intent to deprive (**Criminal Code**, s. 322).

Tort. A civil wrong, other than a breach of contract, which the law will redress by an award of **damages**. See **Tort law**.

Tort law. A branch of **civil law** dealing with violations that do not arise out of contracts but result in damage or injury to another.

Two-year rule. Jurisdictional ruling whereby offenders sentenced to two years or more come under federal jurisdiction and those sentenced to two years less a day, or less, come under provincial jurisdiction.

Ultra vires (Lat.: beyond, outside of, in excess of powers). A term used in constitutional law. If either the Parliament of Canada or a provincial legislature enacts a law which goes beyond its constitutionally-defined jurisdiction (See **British North America Act**), the courts can declare the law *ultra vires*, and, therefore, invalid.

Vagrancy. Two offences under the **Criminal Code** (subsections 179 [1] [a] and [b]: supporting oneself in whole or in part by gaming or crime, having no lawful profession or calling; and—having been convicted of certain specified offences—being found loitering in or near a school yard, playground, public park, or bathing area.

Vandalism. A common term for the malicious destruction of property. Technically this conduct constitutes the offence of mischief under section 430 of the **Criminal Code**.

Vigilantism. The formation of volunteer groups to maintain order or to suppress and punish law breakers summarily, when **due process** seems inadequate in a community without state-appointed law enforcement agents, or where community sentiment is not being considered in law enforcement priorities.

War Measures Act. A 1914 statute conferring emergency powers on the federal cabinet, allowing it to govern by decree when it perceives "war, invasion or insurrection, real or apprehended." This was repealed July 21, 1988. We now have the Emergencies Act.

Warrant of Remand. The statutory authority within the **Criminal Code** (ss. 537, 615, 681, 803) suspending a trial pending the submission of a psychiatric report.

Warrant of the Lieutenant-Governor. A certificate that permits the indeterminate confinement of insane **defendants** at the lieutenant-governor's "pleasure," that is, until the provincial cabinet decides otherwise.

White-collar crime. Illegal acts committed through nonphysical means for the purpose of obtaining financial or personal gain; a form of criminality attributed to relatively high-status persons.

Women's liberation thesis. An explanation of **crime**, put forward by Frieda Adler, that attributes increases in amounts and types of female **criminality** to women's increasing equality with men as a result of the women's liberation movement.

Writ of assistance. The writ was available in Canadian law in certain instances to enable its holder to conduct a warrantless search of a dwelling house, but was found to be unconstitutional in 1984 as it contravened section 8 of the **Canadian Charter of Rights and Freedoms**.

Young Offenders Act, R.S.C. 1985, c. Y-1. A federal statute that replaced the **Juvenile Delinquents Act** in 1984. Mandated a change from a paternal orientation to a rights and responsibilities model, closer to the **due process** of the adult court system. Several aspects of the act remain controversial, including the raising of the age of criminal responsibility from seven to twelve and the upper limit on sentence length.

Zero-order correlation. A test of statistical relationship between sets of interval data variables using Pearson's product moment correlation. No potentially intervening variables are statistically controlled in a zero-order correlation.

Name Index

Subject Index

To the owner of this book:

We are interested in your reaction to *Canadian Criminology: Perspectives on Crime and Criminality*, Margaret A. Jackson and Curt T. Griffiths, eds.

1. What was your reason for using this book?

    ____ university course   ____ continuing education course

    ____ college course   ____ personal interest

                                    ____ other (specify)

2. In which school are you enrolled?_____

3.   Approximately how much of the book did you use?

       ____ 1/4   ____ 1/2   ____ 3/4   ____ all

4. What is the best aspect of the book?

5. Have you any suggestions for impovement?

6. Is there anything that should be added?

                         Fold here

**Business
Reply Mail**

No Postage Stamp
Necessary if Mailed
in Canada

43652

POSTAGE WILL BE PAID BY

SHEILA MALLOCH
Acquisitions Editor
College Editorial Department
HARCOURT BRACE JOVANOVICH,
   CANADA
55 HORNER AVENUE
TORONTO, ONTARIO
M8Z 9Z9

Tape shut